T0180501

Lecture Notes in Artificial Intelligence   12415

Subseries of Lecture Notes in Computer Science

More information about this series at http://www.springer.com/series/1244

Leszek Rutkowski · Rafał Scherer ·
Marcin Korytkowski · Witold Pedrycz ·
Ryszard Tadeusiewicz · Jacek M. Zurada (Eds.)

Artificial Intelligence and Soft Computing

19th International Conference, ICAISC 2020
Zakopane, Poland, October 12–14, 2020
Proceedings, Part I

 Springer

Editors
Leszek Rutkowski (iD)
Częstochowa University of Technology
Częstochowa, Poland

Marcin Korytkowski
Częstochowa University of Technology
Częstochowa, Poland

Ryszard Tadeusiewicz
AGH University of Science and Technology
Kraków, Poland

Rafał Scherer
Częstochowa University of Technology
Częstochowa, Poland

Witold Pedrycz
Electrical and Computer Engineering
University of Alberta
Edmonton, AB, Canada

Jacek M. Zurada
Electrical and Computer Engineering
University of Louisville
Louisville, KY, USA

ISSN 0302-9743   ISSN 1611-3349   (electronic)
Lecture Notes in Artificial Intelligence
ISBN 978-3-030-61400-3   ISBN 978-3-030-61401-0   (eBook)
https://doi.org/10.1007/978-3-030-61401-0

LNCS Sublibrary: SL7 – Artificial Intelligence

This Springer imprint is published by the registered company Springer Nature Switzerland AG
The registered company address is: Gewerbestrasse 11, 6330 Cham, Switzerland

Preface

This volume constitutes the proceedings of the 19th International Conference on Artificial Intelligence and Soft Computing (ICAISC 2020), held in Zakopane, Poland, during October 12–14, 2020. The conference was held virtually due to the COVID-19 pandemic and was organized by the Polish Neural Network Society in cooperation with the University of Social Sciences in Łódź, the Department of Intelligent Computer Systems at the Częstochowa University of Technology, and the IEEE Computational Intelligence Society, Poland Chapter. Previous conferences took place in Kule (1994), Szczyrk (1996), Kule (1997), and Zakopane (1999, 2000, 2002, 2004, 2006, 2008, 2010, 2012, 2013, 2014, 2015, 2016, 2017, 2018, and 2019) and attracted a large number of papers and internationally recognized speakers: Lotfi A. Zadeh, Hojjat Adeli, Rafal Angryk, Igor Aizenberg, Cesare Alippi, Shun-ichi Amari, Daniel Amit, Plamen Angelov, Albert Bifet, Piero P. Bonissone, Jim Bezdek, Zdzisław Bubnicki, Andrzej Cichocki, Swagatam Das, Ewa Dudek-Dyduch, Włodzisław Duch, Adel S. Elmaghraby, Pablo A. Estévez, João Gama, Erol Gelenbe, Jerzy Grzymala-Busse, Martin Hagan, Yoichi Hayashi, Akira Hirose, Kaoru Hirota, Adrian Horzyk, Eyke Hüllermeier, Hisao Ishibuchi, Er Meng Joo, Janusz Kacprzyk, Jim Keller, Laszlo T. Koczy, Tomasz Kopacz, Jacek Koronacki, Zdzisław Kowalczuk, Adam Krzyzak, Rudolf Kruse, James Tin-Yau Kwok, Soo-Young Lee, Derong Liu, Robert Marks, Ujjwal Maulik, Zbigniew Michalewicz, Evangelia Micheli-Tzanakou, Kaisa Miettinen, Krystian Mikołajczyk, Henning Müller, Ngoc Thanh Nguyen, Andrzej Obuchowicz, Erkki Oja, Witold Pedrycz, Marios M. Polycarpou, José C. Príncipe, Jagath C. Rajapakse, Šarunas Raudys, Enrique Ruspini, Jörg Siekmann, Andrzej Skowron, Roman Słowiński, Igor Spiridonov, Boris Stilman, Ponnuthurai Nagaratnam Suganthan, Ryszard Tadeusiewicz, Ah-Hwee Tan, Dacheng Tao, Shiro Usui, Thomas Villmann, Fei-Yue Wang, Jun Wang, Bogdan M. Wilamowski, Ronald Y. Yager, Xin Yao, Syozo Yasui, Gary Yen, Ivan Zelinka, and Jacek Zurada. The aim of this conference is to build a bridge between traditional artificial intelligence techniques and so-called soft computing techniques. It was pointed out by Lotfi A. Zadeh that "soft computing (SC) is a coalition of methodologies which are oriented toward the conception and design of information/intelligent systems. The principal members of the coalition are: fuzzy logic (FL), neurocomputing (NC), evolutionary computing (EC), probabilistic computing (PC), chaotic computing (CC), and machine learning (ML). The constituent methodologies of SC are, for the most part, complementary and synergistic rather than competitive." These proceedings present both traditional artificial intelligence methods and SC techniques. Our goal is to bring together scientists representing both areas of research. This volume is divided into six parts:

- Neural Networks and Their Applications
- Fuzzy Systems and Their Applications
- Evolutionary Algorithms and Their Applications
- Pattern Classification

- Bioinformatics, Biometrics and Medical Applications
- Artificial Intelligence in Modeling and Simulation

The conference attracted a total of 265 submissions from 32 countries, and after the review process, 112 papers were accepted for publication.

I would like to thank our participants, invited speakers, and reviewers of the papers for their scientific and personal contribution to the conference. The following reviewers were very helpful in reviewing the papers:

M. Baczyński	P. Klęsk	G. Papa
Z. Boger	J. Kluska	A. Parkes
R. Burduk	A. Kołakowska	A. Paszyńska
C. Castro	M. Korytkowski	Y. Pei
P. Ciskowski	L. Kotulski	V. Piuri
M. Clerc	Z. Kowalczuk	Ł. Rauch
J. Cytowski	M. Kretowska	S. Rovetta
L. Diosan	E. Kucharska	A. Rusiecki
A. Dockhorn	P. Kudová	A. Sashima
P. Głomb	J. Kulikowski	R. Scherer
Z. Gomółka	J. Kwiecień	M. Sepesy Maucec
G. Gosztolya	M. Ławryńczuk	D. Słota
D. Grabowski	A. Marszałek	B. Starosta
C. Grosan	F. Masulli	N. Tsapanos
J. Grzymala-Busse	R. Matuk Herrera	M. Vajgl
F. Hermann	J. Mazurkiewicz	E. Volna
J. Ishikawa	J. Michalkiewicz	R. Vorobel
D. Jakóbczak	M. Morzy	J. Wąs
E. Jamro	H. Nakamoto	E. Weitschek
M. Jirina	G. Nalepa	J. Yeomans
A. Kasperski	A. Owczarek	A. Zamuda
E. Kerre	E. Ozcan	Q. Zhao
H. Kim	W. Palacz	

Finally, I thank my co-workers Łukasz Bartczuk, Piotr Dziwiński, Marcin Gabryel, Marcin Korytkowski, and Rafał Scherer, for their enormous efforts in making the conference a very successful event. Moreover, I would like to acknowledge the work of Marcin Korytkowski who was responsible for the Internet submission system.

October 2020   Leszek Rutkowski

Organization

ICAISC 2020 was organized by the Polish Neural Network Society in cooperation with the University of Social Sciences in Łódź and Department of Intelligent Computer Systems at Częstochowa University of Technology.

ICAISC Chairpersons

General Chair

Leszek Rutkowski, Poland

Area Chairs

Fuzzy Systems

Witold Pedrycz, Canada

Evolutionary Algorithms

Zbigniew Michalewicz, Australia

Neural Networks

Jinde Cao, China

Computer Vision

Dacheng Tao, Australia

Machine Learning

Nikhil R. Pal, India

Artificial Intelligence with Applications

Janusz Kacprzyk, Poland

International Liaison

Jacek Żurada, USA

ICAISC Program Committee

Shiro Usui, Japan
Deliang Wang, USA
Jun Wang, Hong Kong
Lipo Wang, Singapore
Paul Werbos, USA
Bernard Widrow, USA
Kay C. Wiese, Canada

Bogdan M. Wilamowski, USA
Donald C. Wunsch, USA
Ronald R. Yager, USA
Xin-She Yang, UK
Gary Yen, USA
Sławomir Zadrożny, Poland
Jacek Zurada, USA

ICAISC Organizing Committee

Rafał Scherer, Poland
Łukasz Bartczuk, Poland
Piotr Dziwiński, Poland
Marcin Gabryel (Finance Chair), Poland
Rafał Grycuk, Poland
Marcin Korytkowski (Databases and Internet Submissions), Poland

Contents – Part I

Neural Networks and Their Applications

A Synergy of Freezing and Dropout - A New Learning Strategy
of Convolutional Networks.   3
    Michał Banach and Ewa Skubalska-Rafajłowicz

A New Algorithm with a Line Search for Feedforward Neural
Networks Training   15
    Jarosław Bilski, Bartosz Kowalczyk, and Jacek M. Żurada

Fast Conjugate Gradient Algorithm for Feedforward Neural Networks.   27
    Jarosław Bilski and Jacek Smoląg

Comparison of Text Classification Methods for Government Documents   39
    Konrad A. Ciecierski and Mariusz Kamola

DeepCloud: An Investigation of Geostationary Satellite Imagery Frame
Interpolation for Improved Temporal Resolution   50
    Luigi Freitas Cruz, Priscila Tiemi Maeda Saito,
    and Pedro Henrique Bugatti

Are Direct Links Necessary in Random Vector Functional Link Networks
for Regression?.   60
    Grzegorz Dudek

Artificial Intelligent Methods for the Location of Vortex Points   71
    Ewa Frączek and Bartosz Idźkowski

Optimal Fog Services Placement in SDN IoT Network Using Random
Neural Networks and Cognitive Network Map   77
    Piotr Fröhlich and Erol Gelenbe

Building Best Predictive Models Using ML and DL Approaches
to Categorize Fashion Clothes.   90
    Said Gadri and Erich Neuhold

Method of Real Time Calculation of Learning Rate Value to Improve
Convergence of Neural Network Training 103
    Anton I. Glushchenko, Vladislav A. Petrov,
    and Konstantin A. Lastochkin

Application of an Improved Focal Loss in Vehicle Detection 114
    Xuanlin He, Jie Yang, and Nikola Kasabov

Concept Drift Detection Using Autoencoders in Data Streams Processing. . . .   124
  Maciej Jaworski, Leszek Rutkowski, and Plamen Angelov

Explainable AI for Inspecting Adversarial Attacks on Deep
Neural Networks.   134
  Zuzanna Klawikowska, Agnieszka Mikołajczyk, and Michał Grochowski

On the Similarity Between Neural Network and Evolutionary Algorithm   147
  Lumír Kojecký and Ivan Zelinka

3D Convolutional Neural Networks for Ultrasound-Based Silent
Speech Interfaces   159
  László Tóth and Amin Honarmandi Shandiz

Deep Recurrent Modelling of Stationary Bitcoin Price Formation Using
the Order Flow.   170
  Ye-Sheen Lim and Denise Gorse

6D Pose Estimation of Texture-Less Objects on RGB Images
Using CNNs.   180
  Vladyslav Lopatin and Bogdan Kwolek

Application of Neural Networks and Graphical Representations for Musical
Genre Classification   193
  Mateusz Modrzejewski, Jakub Szachewicz, and Przemysław Rokita

Deep Learning with Data Augmentation for Fruit Counting   203
  Pornntiwa Pawara, Alina Boshchenko, Lambert R. B. Schomaker,
  and Marco A. Wiering

Approximation of Fractional Order Dynamic Systems Using Elman, GRU
and LSTM Neural Networks.   215
  Bartosz Puchalski and Tomasz A. Rutkowski

A Layer-Wise Information Reinforcement Approach to Improve Learning
in Deep Belief Networks   231
  Mateus Roder, Leandro A. Passos, Luiz Carlos Felix Ribeiro,
  Clayton Pereira, and João Paulo Papa

Intestinal Parasites Classification Using Deep Belief Networks   242
  Mateus Roder, Leandro A. Passos, Luiz Carlos Felix Ribeiro,
  Barbara Caroline Benato, Alexandre Xavier Falcão,
  and João Paulo Papa

Speaker Recognition Using SincNet and X-Vector Fusion   252
  Mayank Tripathi, Divyanshu Singh, and Seba Susan

Multiobjective Evolution for Convolutional Neural Network
Architecture Search   261
  Petra Vidnerová, Štěpán Procházka, and Roman Neruda

Neural Network Subgraphs Correlation with Trained Model Accuracy   271
  Izajasz Wrosz

Weighted Feature Selection Method for Improving Decisions in Milling
Process Diagnosis   280
  Roman Zajdel, Maciej Kusy, Jacek Kluska, and Tomasz Zabinski

Generative Modeling in Application to Point Cloud Completion   292
  Maciej Zamorski, Maciej Zięba, and Jerzy Świątek

Fuzzy Systems and Their Applications

A Numerical Solution of Fully Fuzzy Distribution Problem   305
  Ludmila Dymova

Nonlinear Fuzzy Modelling of Dynamic Objects with Fuzzy Hybrid Particle
Swarm Optimization and Genetic Algorithm.   315
  Łukasz Bartczuk, Piotr Dziwiński, and Piotr Goetzen

Application of Time Series Analysis and Forecasting Methods
for Enterprise Decision-Management   326
  Anton Romanov, Nadezhda Yarushkina, and Aleksey Filippov

Face Recognition with Explanation by Fuzzy Rules
and Linguistic Description   338
  Danuta Rutkowska, Damian Kurach, and Elisabeth Rakus-Andersson

Redefinition of Intuitionistic Fuzzy TOPSIS Method in the Framework
of Evidence Theory   351
  Pavel Sevastjanov

Evolutionary Algorithms and Their Applications

On the Performance and Complexity of Crossover in Differential
Evolution Algorithm   363
  Petr Bujok

Obstacle Avoidance for Drones Based on the Self-Organizing
Migrating Algorithm   376
  Quoc Bao Diep, Thanh Cong Truong, and Ivan Zelinka

An Empirical Evaluation of Global Fitness Surrogate Models
in Evolutionary Computation   387
   Leonardo Ramos Emmendorfer

Automatic Story Generation Based on Graph Model Using Godot Engine . . .   397
   Iwona Grabska-Gradzińska, Leszek Nowak, and Ewa Grabska

Cascade PID Controller Optimization Using Bison Algorithm.   406
   Anezka Kazikova, Krystian Łapa, Michal Pluhacek, and Roman Senkerik

Optimization of the Values of Classifiers Parameters – Is it Still Worthwhile
to Deal with it?.   417
   Daniel Kostrzewa, Konrad Karczewski, and Robert Brzeski

A Population-Based Method with Selection of a Search Operator   429
   *Krystian Łapa, Krzysztof Cpałka, Tacjana Niksa-Rynkiewicz,
   and Lipo Wang*

A Markov Process Approach to Redundancy in Genetic Algorithms   445
   Wojciech Rafajłowicz

Fuzzy Control of Exploration and Exploitation Trade-Off with On-Line
Convergence Rate Estimation in Evolutionary Algorithms   454
   Adam Slowik

An Improved Local Search Genetic Algorithm with Multi-crossover
for Job Shop Scheduling Problem   464
   *Monique Simplicio Viana, Orides Morandin Junior,
   and Rodrigo Colnago Contreras*

Signature Partitioning Using Selected Population-Based Algorithms   480
   *Marcin Zalasiński, Krzysztof Cpałka, Tacjana Niksa-Rynkiewicz,
   and Yoichi Hayashi*

Pattern Classification

Breast Cancer Classification from Histopathological Images Using Transfer
Learning and Deep Neural Networks.   491
   Abdulrahman Aloyayri and Adam Krzyżak

Visualization of Membership Distribution in Strings Using Heat Maps   503
   Łukasz Culer and Olgierd Unold

Random Projection in the Presence of Concept Drift
in Supervised Environments   514
   Moritz Heusinger and Frank-Michael Schleif

Brazilian Lyrics-Based Music Genre Classification Using
a BLSTM Network 525
  Raul de Araújo Lima, Rômulo César Costa de Sousa, Hélio Lopes,
  and Simone Diniz Junqueira Barbosa

Machine Learning for Web Intrusion Detection: A Comparative Analysis
of Feature Selection Methods mRMR and PFI 535
  Thiago José Lucas, Carlos Alexandre Carvalho Tojeiro,
  Rafael Gonçalves Pires, Kelton Augusto Pontara da Costa,
  and João Paulo Papa

A Mathematical Model for Optimum Error-Reject Trade-Off for Learning
of Secure Classification Models in the Presence of Label Noise
During Training 547
  Seyedfakhredin Musavishavazi, Mehrdad Mohannazadeh Bakhtiari,
  and Thomas Villmann

Grid-Based Approach to Determining Parameters
of the DBSCAN Algorithm 555
  Artur Starczewski and Andrzej Cader

Particle Classification Based on Movement Behavior in IPSO
Stochastic Model. 566
  Krzysztof Wójcik, Tomasz Kulpa, and Krzysztof Trojanowski

Combination of Active and Random Labeling Strategy in the
Non-stationary Data Stream Classification 576
  Paweł Zyblewski, Paweł Ksieniewicz, and Michał Woźniak

Bioinformatics, Biometrics and Medical Applications

The Utilization of Different Classifiers to Perform Drug Repositioning
in Inclusion Body Myositis Supports the Concept of Biological Invariance. . . 589
  Óscar Álvarez-Machancoses, Enrique deAndrés-Galiana,
  Juan Luis Fernández-Martínez, and Andrzej Kloczkowski

Predicting Coronary Artery Calcium Score from Retinal Fundus
Photographs Using Convolutional Neural Networks. 599
  Sooah Cho, Su Jeong Song, Joonseok Lee, JiEun Song, Min Soo Kim,
  Minyoung Lee, and JoonHo Lee

Mesh Geometric Parameters for Modeling Signal Transmission
in the Presynaptic Bouton 613
  Maciej Gierdziewicz

Instance Segmentation of Densely Packed Cells Using a Hybrid Model
of U-Net and Mask R-CNN   626
   Tomasz Konopczyński, Ron Heiman, Piotr Woźnicki, Paweł Gniewek,
   Marie-Cécilia Duvernoy, Oskar Hallatschek, and Jürgen Hesser

Blue-White Veil Classification in Dermoscopy Images of the Skin Lesions
Using Convolutional Neural Networks   636
   Piotr Milczarski and Łukasz Wąs

Automatic Generation of Parallel Cache-Efficient Code Implementing
Zuker's RNA Folding   646
   Marek Palkowski, Wlodzimierz Bielecki, and Mateusz Gruzewski

Artificial Intelligence in Modeling and Simulation

Semantic Classifier Approach to Document Classification   657
   Piotr Borkowski, Krzysztof Ciesielski, and Mieczysław A. Kłopotek

A Parallel and Distributed Topological Approach to 3D IC Optimal Layout
Design   668
   Katarzyna Grzesiak-Kopeć and Maciej Ogorzałek

From Victim to Survivor: A Multilayered Adaptive Mental Network Model
of a Bully Victim   679
   Fakhra Jabeen, Charlotte Gerritsen, and Jan Treur

Faster Convention Emergence by Avoiding Local Conventions
in Reinforcement Social Learning   690
   Muzi Liu, Ho-fung Leung, and Jianye Hao

Empirical Mode Decomposition Based Data Augmentation for Time Series
Prediction Using NARX Network   702
   Olusola Oluwakemi Abayomi-Alli, Tatjana Sidekerskienė, Robertas
   Damaševičius, Jakub Siłka, and Dawid Połap

Ensemble Forecasting of Monthly Electricity Demand Using Pattern
Similarity-Based Methods   712
   Paweł Pełka and Grzegorz Dudek

Author Index   725

Contents – Part II

Computer Vision, Image and Speech Analysis

A New Approach to Detection of Abrupt Changes
in Black-and-White Images   3
   Tomasz Gałkowski and Adam Krzyżak

Active Region-Based Full-Disc Solar Image Hashing.   19
   Rafał Grycuk, Kelton Costa, and Rafał Scherer

Inferring Colors in Paintings of M.F. Husain by Using Cluster Analysis   31
   Shailendra Gurjar and Usha Ananthakumar

Data Augmentation Using Principal Component Resampling for Image
Recognition by Deep Learning   39
   Olusola Oluwakemi Abayomi-Alli, Robertas Damaševičius,
   Michał Wieczorek, and Marcin Woźniak

Multi-agent Architecture for Internet of Medical Things.   49
   Dawid Połap, Gautam Srivastava, and Marcin Woźniak

Automatic Visual Quality Assessment of Biscuits Using
Machine Learning   59
   Mardlla de Sousa Silva, Luigi Freitas Cruz, Pedro Henrique Bugatti,
   and Priscila Tiemi Maeda Saito

Classifying Image Series with a Reoccurring Concept Drift Using
a Markov Chain Predictor as a Feedback   71
   Magda Skoczeń, Wojciech Rafajłowicz, and Ewaryst Rafajłowicz

Explainable Cluster-Based Rules Generation for Image Retrieval
and Classification   85
   Paweł Staszewski, Maciej Jaworski, Leszek Rutkowski,
   and Dacheng Tao

SURF Algorithm with Convolutional Neural Network as Face Recognition
Technique   95
   Alicja Winnicka, Karolina Kęsik, Dawid Połap, and Marcin Woźniak

Grouping Handwritten Letter Strokes Using a Fuzzy Decision Tree.   103
   Michał Wróbel, Janusz T. Starczewski, and Christian Napoli

Data Mining

A Density-Based Prototype Selection Approach 117
  Joel Luís Carbonera and Mara Abel

FlexTrustRank: A New Approach to Link Spam Combating. 130
  Dariusz Czerski, Paweł Łoziński, Mieczysław Alojzy Kłopotek,
  Bartłomiej Starosta, and Marcin Sydow

A Comparative Analysis of Similarity Measures in Memory-Based
Collaborative Filtering. 140
  Mara Renata Deac-Petruşel

Constructing Interpretable Decision Trees Using Parallel Coordinates 152
  Vladimir Estivill-Castro, Eugene Gilmore, and René Hexel

A Framework for e-Recruitment Recommender Systems 165
  Mauricio Noris Freire and Leandro Nunes de Castro

The Influence of Feature Selection on Job Clustering for an E-recruitment
Recommender System 176
  Joel J. S. Junior, Fabricio G. Vilasbôas, and Leandro N. de Castro

n-ary Isolation Forest: An Experimental Comparative Analysis 188
  Paweł Karczmarek, Adam Kiersztyn, and Witold Pedrycz

In-The-Limit Clustering Axioms 199
  Mieczysław A. Kłopotek and Robert A. Kłopotek

Hybrid Features for Twitter Sentiment Analysis 210
  Sergiu Limboi and Laura Dioşan

Computer Based Stylometric Analysis of Texts in Ukrainian Language 220
  Anton Mazurko and Tomasz Walkowiak

Newsminer: Enriched Multidimensional Corpus
for Text-Based Applications 231
  Sahudy Montenegro González, Tiemi C. Sakata,
  and Rodrigo Ramos Nogueira

Detecting Causalities in Production Environments Using Time Lag
Identification with Cross-Correlation in Production State Time Series 243
  Dirk Saller, Bora I. Kumova, and Christoph Hennebold

Identification of Delays in AMUSE Algorithm for Blind Signal Separation
of Financial Data 253
  Ryszard Szupiluk and Paweł Rubach

Various Problems of Artificial Intelligence

MOEA-RS: A Content-Based Recommendation System Supported
by a Multi-objective Evolutionary Algorithm   265
    Matheus Santos Almeida and André Britto

A Study of Bi-space Search for Solving the One-Dimensional
Bin Packing Problem.   277
    Derrick Beckedahl and Nelishia Pillay

Explaining Machine Learning Models of Emotion Using the BIRAFFE
Dataset   290
    Szymon Bobek, Magdalena M. Tragarz, Maciej Szelążek,
    and Grzegorz J. Nalepa

Pre-training Polish Transformer-Based Language Models at Scale   301
    Sławomir Dadas, Michał Perełkiewicz, and Rafał Poświata

On a Streaming Approach for Training Denoising Auto-encoders   315
    Piotr Duda and Lipo Wang

Methods of Searching for Similar Device Fingerprints Using Changes
in Unstable Parameters   325
    Marcin Gabryel and Krzysztof Przybyszewski

Gradient Boosting and Deep Learning Models Approach to Forecasting
Promotions Efficiency in FMCG Retail   336
    Joanna Henzel and Marek Sikora

A Fuzzy Multi-Agent Problem in a Conceptual and Operational Depiction. . .   346
    Krystian Jobczyk and Antoni Ligęza

Generating Descriptions in Polish Language for BPMN Business
Process Models.   357
    Krzysztof Kluza, Maciej Znamirowski, Piotr Wiśniewski, Paweł Jemioło,
    and Antoni Ligęza

Machine Learning Application in Energy Consumption Calculation
and Assessment in Food Processing Industry   369
    Piotr Milczarski, Bartosz Zieliński, Zofia Stawska, Artur Hłobaż,
    Paweł Maślanka, and Piotr Kosiński

Job Offer Analysis Using Convolutional and Recurrent Convolutional
Networks.   380
    Jakub Nowak, Kamila Milkowska, Magdalena Scherer,
    Arkadiusz Talun, and Marcin Korytkowski

Team Up! Cohesive Text Summarization Scoring Sentence Coalitions   388
Inez Okulska

New Surrogate Approaches Applied to Meta-Heuristic Algorithms   400
Joel A. Oliveira, Matheus Santos Almeida, Reneilson Y. C. Santos,
Rene Pereira de Gusmão, and André Britto

A Novel Explainable Recommender for Investment Managers   412
Tomasz Rutkowski, Radosław Nielek, Danuta Rutkowska,
and Leszek Rutkowski

Is Chaotic Randomization Advantageous for Higher Dimensional
Optimization Problems?   423
Roman Senkerik, Adam Viktorin, Tomas Kadavy, Michal Pluhacek,
and Ivan Zelinka

FastText and XGBoost Content-Based Classification for Employment Web
Scraping   435
Arkadiusz Talun, Pawel Drozda, Leszek Bukowski, and Rafał Scherer

Supervised Classification Methods for Fake News Identification   445
Thanh Cong Truong, Quoc Bao Diep, Ivan Zelinka, and Roman Senkerik

Visual Hybrid Recommendation Systems Based
on the Content-Based Filtering   455
Piotr Woldan, Piotr Duda, and Yoichi Hayashi

Short-Term Traffic Flow Prediction Based on the Intelligent Parameter
Adjustment K-Nearest Neighbor Algorithm   466
Xuan Zhao, Ruixuan Bi, Ran Yang, Yue Chu, Jianhua Guo, Wei Huang,
and Jinde Cao

Agent Systems, Robotics and Control

Some Technical Challenges in Designing an Artificial Moral Agent   481
Jarek Gryz

Hierarchical Intelligent-Geometric Control Architecture for Unmanned
Aerial Vehicles Operating in Uncertain Environments   492
Mikhail Khachumov

Challenging Human Supremacy: Evaluating Monte Carlo Tree Search
and Deep Learning for the Trick Taking Card Game Jass   505
Joel Niklaus, Michele Alberti, Rolf Ingold, Markus Stolze,
and Thomas Koller

How Motivated Are You? A Mental Network Model for Dynamic Goal
Driven Emotion Regulation   518
    Nimat Ullah and Jan Treur

Author Index   531

Neural Networks and Their Applications

A Synergy of Freezing and Dropout - A New Learning Strategy of Convolutional Networks

Michał Banach[ID] and Ewa Skubalska-Rafajłowicz[(✉)][ID]

Faculty of Electronics, Department of Computer Engineering,
Wrocław University of Science and Technology, Wrocław, Poland
ewa.rafajlowicz@pwr.edu.pl

Abstract. In this work, we explore training efficiency and generalization results on testing sets of a new learning strategy applied to convolutional neural networks. The proposed strategy is to limit the modification of the weights of the networks entering a randomly selected set of neurons (activation function). Randomizing a fragment of the network whose parameters are modified is carried out in parallel with the selection of a mini-batch based on which a stochastic gradient is determined. The strategy of combining dropout with random freezing allows for better generalization while shortening the duration of training in individual epochs. An interesting phenomenon is the widening of the generalization gap while reducing the error on the test set. Computational experiments were carried out on CNN networks with about 1–2 M trainable parameters and CIFAR-10 and CIFAR-100 benchmark data sets.

Keywords: Deep learning · Image classification · Convolutional neural nets · Stochastic gradient · Randomized training · Dropout

1 Introduction

Convolutional neural networks (CNN) are feed-forward artificial neural networks widely used models for image and video recognition [8, 22–24]. CNN's are specific multilayer perceptrons where the individual neurons in the convolutional layers are tiled in such a way that they respond to overlapping regions in the visual field. The convolutional layers are supposed to supersede image preprocessing and feature extraction in contrast to [3, 6, 33, 36]. Developing and improvements in computer hardware allow us to design new more sophisticated CNN-based architectures such as Residual Networks (ResNets) [11, 13], Dense Convolutional Network (DenseNet) [15] among many others.

Stochastic Gradient Descent (SGD) [4, 25, 31, 38] and its variants are usually used for training deep networks. In our experiments, we have applied the SGD training algorithm with Nesterov momentum [10, 27, 31] and as an alternative to the Adam method [20].

© Springer Nature Switzerland AG 2020
L. Rutkowski et al. (Eds.): ICAISC 2020, LNAI 12415, pp. 3–14, 2020.
https://doi.org/10.1007/978-3-030-61401-0_1

In addition to the random selection of a batch, also other randomization based techniques, such as dropout, allow us to increase the practical usability of deep networks, including convolutional networks.

Recently, a random choice of variables or blocks of variables has been explored in large optimization problems with an additive structure. From the optimization point of view, our approach is even more randomized than in the randomized block-coordinate descent methods [28,30] since we use randomly selected sets of variables. We propose to use blocks of variables (network weights) with a random structure but the same size treated as an additional hyper-parameter. Change at every iteration only some of the decision variables is applied in many optimization (and other numerical) methods starting from the coordinate descent (Gauss-Seidel) strategy or the alternating direction method of multipliers [5]. However, these methods are based on the fixed partition of optimized variables.

In this paper, we propose a randomized freezing methodology applied to CNN's. In this approach, only a randomly chosen subset of neurons along with their connections, i.e., in-going weights, is adjusted in every training iteration, i.e., many times during the epoch. The rest of the network's weights remains temporarily unchanged. We will say that the weights not chosen for updating are temporarily frozen. Randomizing a fragment of the network whose parameters are modified is carried out in parallel with the random selection of a mini-batch, based on which a stochastic gradient is determined.

In our training experiments performed on CNNs, it occurred that the proposed randomized freezing works visibly better in combination with the dropout regularization method [37].

Dropout [9,10,14,37], is now a very popular method of deep neural networks regularization which introduces temporal randomization into the structure of the network's layers.

We do not analyze the behavior of CNN's with loss functions other than the cross-entropy applied to softmax activation of the output of the network [10,17], as this is a typical approach in classification problems.

It should be emphasized that it is not our goal to achieve state-of-the-art results across competitive benchmarks such as CIFAR-10 or CIFAR-100 but rather to research the impact of randomized updating of a small subset of the network's parameters on improving the generalization accuracy. Thus, we do not use weight decay or data augmentation [22,26,41], normalization approaches, e.g., batch normalization [16,32,39] and layer normalization [2], which have also achieved empirical success. It turned out that applying only frozen weights during the CNN learning process does not give good results, however, it improves the efficiency of fast learning algorithms such as Adam [20] in conjunction with dropout.

Our experiments show that a very important role in achieving good learning effects of deep networks is introducing random disturbances during the training process and slowing down the whole procedure in order to explore even shallow local extremes.

The main message of this paper is that a training strategy combining dropout with random freezing of neurons creates a synergy effect providing better classification results on test data sets.

Observed enlargement of a generalization gap, i.e., the difference between the training and the testing accuracy, is an interesting phenomenon. It definitely shows that the strategy of training proposed in the paper is a good method of large-scale optimization.

The deep CNN networks used in experimental research are drastically over-parameterized and they can easily memorize training data or even fit random labels to the data [40, 42]. Learning on concatenated training and testing sets can easily provide network models that memorize both of them [29]. Thus checking various deep network structures for their generalization capabilities seems to be a kind of random search for a structure that best defines the features that characterize objects from both the training and test sets.

The paper is organized as follows. In the next section, we provide a concise description of the training strategy with random freezing of neurons' weights. In Sect. 3 we present numerical results to support the observation that in many cases combining dropout with random neuron freezing results in a better generalization on testing sets. Finally, some comments, conclusions, and open questions are summarized. The network models' architectures are described in the Appendix.

2   Random Freezing as a Learning Strategy

The training strategy proposed in the paper is a new variant of randomized optimization [28, 30].

A random weight's freezing was previously proposed by one of the authors as a method of training shallow (with only one hidden layer) regression networks [34]. The approach consisted in that in every epoch of training only the random part of the neural network (a randomly chosen set of neurons and its connections) is updated. It was shown experimentally that over-parametrized neural network models can be learned efficiently using the small-batch stochastic gradient (SGD) method without overfitting symptoms.

In the present paper, a randomly chosen subset of neurons along with their in-going connections is adjusted in every training iteration, i.e., many times during the epoch. As a method of optimizations a small-batch SGD method and its more efficient modifications, such as Adam, are used.

Let $W = \{w_1, \ldots, w_N\}$ stand for the set of CNN trainable weights and $\gamma \in (0, 1)$ is a freezing parameter. In contrast to the dropout [37], each neuron and its in-going weights are temporarily frozen (but not removed) with a probability γ independently of other neurons. As a consequence, we obtain the set of temporarily frozen network weights $F \subset W$. Let $V = W - F$ be a set of non-frozen weights.

The general scheme for updating the weights is as follows:

$$w_i^{k+1} = w_i^k - \frac{\alpha_k}{|B_k|} \sum_{j \in B_k} \frac{\partial f_j(W)}{\partial w_i}\Big|_{W=W^k}, \ w_i \in V, \tag{1}$$

where α_k is the current value of the learning parameter (step size), B_k is the batch sampled from the data set and $f_j(W)$ is a loss function for data point $j \in \{1, \ldots, D\}$. W^k is the set of weights values at k-th iteration. D denotes the size of the training set.

In the case of dropout, both chosen procedures, freezing and dropout, are performed independently. So, both frozen and non-frozen parameters can be temporarily removed and not all weights left by the dropout procedure will be updated in the actual iteration.

3   Experiments

In our experimental studies we have restricted to two very popular data sets: CIFAR-10 and CIFAR-100.

Table 1. Test and train classification accuracy CIFAR-10 using Adam and SGD. $\star$) Number epoch of training (without early-stopping)

Data set	Network A	Method	Train acc. %	Test acc. %	Epochs$\star$
CIFAR-10	Without dropout	Adam	98.91	74.0	100
CIFAR-10	With dropout	Adam	88.80	81.99	100
CIFAR-10	Without dropout	Adam with freezing 85%	99.98	72.04	100
CIFAR-10	with dropout	Adam with freezing 85%	99.99	84.21	800
CIFAR-10	Without dropout	SGD	100.0	72.35	25
CIFAR-10	Without dropout	SGD with freezing 85%	100.0	69.23	100
CIFAR-10	With dropout	SGD	95.74	84.00	500
CIFAR-10	With dropout	SGD with freezing 85%	99.85	83.52	1500

The CIFAR datasets consist of colored natural scene images, with 32×32 pixels. CIFAR-10 consists of images drawn from 10 and CIFAR-100 from 100 classes. The train and test sets contain 50,000 and 10,000 images respectively [21].

The images are not preprocessed, as done for example in [37]. The implementation of CNN was performed using Tensorflow and Keras [7]. For the CIFAR-10 data set we used a convolutional network consisting of 8 layers (Network A): 4 convolutional layers with ReLU activation functions ($f(x) = max\{0, x\}$), and two max pooling layers, followed by a single fully connected hidden layer with 512 neurons with ReLU activation functions, and finally a softmax layer with 10 neurons.

For the CIFAR-100 data set, we used the same convolutional network structure consisting of 8 layers but ending with a softmax layer with 100 neurons. Additionally, some experiments were conducted on a similar convolutional network (Network B) consisting of 12 layers. The network's structures, including position and parameters of the dropout layers when dropout was used, can be found in the Appendix.

Table 2. Test and train classification accuracy CIFAR-100 using Adam and SGD. ⋆) SGD training has been stopped and it is not known what values were obtained in the saturation phase.

Data set	Network A or B	Method	Train acc. %	Test acc. %	Epochs
CIFAR-100	A without dropout	SGD	99.97	35.57	100
CIFAR-100	A with dropout	SGD	64.90	52.70	300
CIFAR-100	A without dropout	Adam	96.68	38.22	100
CIFAR-100	A with dropout	Adam	48.62	45.01	300
CIFAR-100	A with dropout	Adam with freezing 85%	92.24	54.78	800
CIFAR-100	B without dropout	Adam	89.48	32.38	150
CIFAR-100	B with dropout	Adam	19.0	23.32	100
CIFAR-100	B without dropout	SGD	99.70	35.76	150
CIFAR-100	B with dropout	SGD	70.06	57.05	1500 ⋆
CIFAR-100	B with dropout	Adam with freezing 95%	96.25	56.3	1000
CIFAR-100	B with dropout	SGD with freezing 95%	49.07	42.19	1000 ⋆

In every case, convolutional layers are formed with $(3,3)$ kernels and with steps of the convolution along both axes of the input tensors, i.e., stride $(1,1)$. All experiments were initialized from different uniformly distributed random points, i.e., using He uniform weight initializer [12]. The training was performed using Adam [20] with learning rate of 0.001, $\beta_1 = 0.9$, $\beta_2 = 0.999$ and stochastic gradient method SGD with learning rate 0.01, learning rate decay 0.000001 and Nesterov momentum 0.9. Both methods are employed in a mini-batch gradients regime with a batch size of 32 samples to minimize the cross-entropy loss (applied to softmax activation of the output of the network) [10]. Dropout and freezing hyper-parameters were selected using rough effect checking. The computations were performed on a 2× Intel Xeon Silver 4114 CPU at 2.20 GHz with an NVIDIA TITAN RTX GPU.

We conducted many training/testing experiments, of which the most significant results were included in the tables: Table 1 (CIFAR-10) and Table 2 (CIFAR-100). These tables show the maximum accuracy values obtained for training and testing with different optimization regimes. Training time is shown in the "epochs" column. The training was performed until the saturation phase was reached in the learning process.

It should be emphasized that the learning processes we received are characterized by very little variability. In the case of the dropout-freezing strategy combined with Adam, we repeated the experiments 5 times from different (uniformly distributed randomly) starting points obtaining an average of 83.96% with a standard deviation of 0.16% (see Table 1 where the obtained maximum value 84.21% is given).

Figures 1, 2, 3, 4 and 5 show the exact learning process in selected regimes. The best results for both benchmarks (CIFAR-10 and CIFAR-100) were obtained either for SGD with dropout or for Adam with dropout and freezing.

The use of freezing with the dropout strategy requires an increase in the number of epochs to the saturation phase. However, one should pay attention to the fact that at the same time the number of parameter modifications estimated as $(1 - \gamma)E$, where E denotes the number of epochs, decreases. Especially in the case of the larger problem (CIFAR-100), this difference becomes significant.

It should be noted that except in the case of using the Adam optimization method without dropout (both on CIFAR-10, as well CIFAR-100 task), no signs of overfitting were observed involving a systematic decrease in accuracy obtained on the test set. In other cases, the accuracy of the test set slowly increased, after which slightly oscillated around the level of convergence.

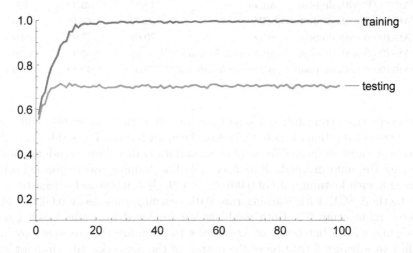

Fig. 1. Results of 100 epochs of the training on CIFAR-10 using Adam with freezing $\gamma = 0.85$). Network A without dropout.

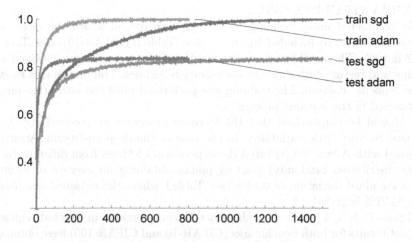

Fig. 2. Results of training and testing model A on CIFAR-10 using Adam (800 epochs) and SGD (1500 epochs) with dropout and freezing of 85% of neurons.

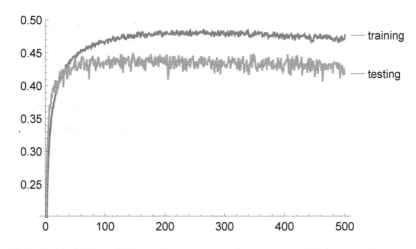

Fig. 3. Results of 500 epochs of the training on CIFAR-100 using Adam method on network A with dropout.

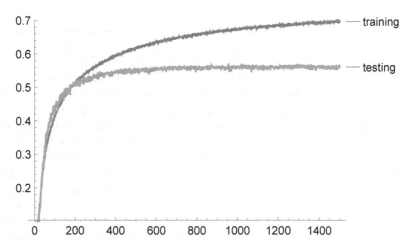

Fig. 4. Results of training on CIFAR-100 data set using SGD with dropout (network B).

4   Discussion and Conclusions

In this paper, we present a new training strategy of convolutional neural networks combining dropout with random freezing of neurons. The proposed approach creates a synergy effect providing better classification results on CIFAR test data sets in the case of the Adam optimization procedure. Additionally, the number of needed weights updates is visibly smaller in comparison to the methods which do not use freezing.

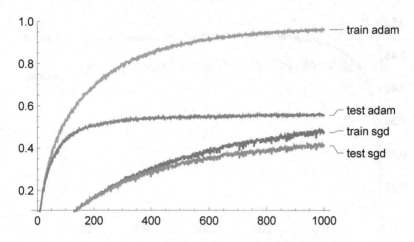

Fig. 5. Results of 1000 epochs of the training on CIFAR-100 using Adam and SGD with dropout and freezing ($\gamma = 0.95$) - network B.

The proposed strategy of combining dropout with freezing slows down the learning process but additionally not only improves the learning effects, but also improves the results of testing for CIFAR benchmarks. This is associated with the creation of a large generalization gap, which, however, in our case does not indicate overfitting. Similar effects have been observed and described in the paper [19] about completely different aspects of deep network training.

Many papers formulate the observation that deep network models can assign perfectly arbitrary labels to the training set and simultaneously they can generalize well on real testing sets [35,40,41]. In many cases, increasing the model size could help in decreasing the generalization error [29]. In our opinion, checking the generalization capabilities of different deep network structures is a kind of random search for a structure that best defines the features that characterize objects from both the training and test sets. But it is still an open question how to evaluate deep network models, especially in the case of image classification, when cross-validation or other approaches are too costly [1,18].

Acknowledgments. This research was supported by scientific grant at the Faculty of Electronics, Wrocław University of Science and Technology.

Appendix

Network A (structure of CNN used for evaluation on CIFAR-10 and CIFAR-100 datasets):

```
model = models.Sequential()
model.add(layers.Conv2D(32, (3, 3), activation='relu',
    input_shape=(32, 32, 3)))
model.add(layers.Conv2D(32, (3, 3), activation='relu'))
```

```
model.add(layers.MaxPooling2D(pool_size=(2, 2)))
model.add(layers.Dropout(0.3))
model.add(layers.Conv2D(64, (3, 3), activation='relu'))
model.add(layers.Conv2D(64, (3, 3), activation='relu'))
model.add(layers.MaxPooling2D(pool_size=(2, 2)))
model.add(layers.Dropout(0.4))
model.add(layers.Flatten())
model.add(layers.Dense(512, activation='relu'))
model.add(layers.Dropout(0.5))
model.add(layers.Dense(number_of_classes, activation='softmax'))
```

Number of trainable parameters: 0.89 M (for CIFAR-10) and 0.94 M (for CIFAR-100).

Network B (the larger structure of CNN used for evaluation on CIFAR-100):

```
model = models.Sequential()
model.add(layers.Conv2D(32, (3, 3), activation='relu',
    input_shape=(32, 32, 3)))
model.add(layers.Conv2D(32, (3, 3), activation='relu'))
model.add(layers.MaxPooling2D(pool_size=(2, 2)))
model.add(layers.Dropout(0.3))
model.add(layers.Conv2D(64, (3, 3), activation='relu'))
model.add(layers.Conv2D(64, (3, 3), activation='relu'))
model.add(layers.MaxPooling2D(pool_size=(2, 2)))
model.add(layers.Dropout(0.4))
model.add(layers.Conv2D(128, (3, 3), padding="same",
                                        activation='relu'))
model.add(layers.Conv2D(128, (3, 3), padding="same",
                                        activation='relu'))
model.add(layers.MaxPooling2D(padding="same",pool_size=(2, 2)))
model.add(layers.Dropout(0.4))
model.add(layers.Flatten())
model.add(layers.Dense(1024, activation='relu'))
model.add(layers.Dropout(0.5))
model.add(layers.Dense(512, activation='relu'))
model.add(layers.Dropout(0.5))
model.add(layers.Dense(100, activation='softmax'))
```

Number of trainable parameters: 2.043 M.

References

1. Anguita, D., Ghelardoni, L., Ghio, A., Ridella, S.: A survey of old and new results for the test error estimation of a classifier. J. Artif. Intell. Soft Comput. Res. **3**(4), 229–242 (2013)
2. Ba, J.L., Kiros, J.R., and Hinton, G.E.: Layer normalization. arXiv preprint arXiv:1607.06450 (2016)
3. Bologna, G., Hayashi, Y.: Characterization of symbolic rules embedded in deep DIMLP networks: a challenge to transparency of deep learning. J. Artif. Intell. Soft Comput. Res. **7**(4), 265–286 (2017)

4. Bottou, L.: Online learning and stochastic approximations. On-Line Learn. Neural Netw. **17**(9), 142 (1998)
5. Boyd, S., Parikh, N., Chu, E., Peleato, B., Eckstein, J.: Distributed optimization and statistical learning via the alternating direction method of multipliers. Found. Trends Mach. Learn. **3**(1), 1–122 (2011)
6. Chang, O., Constante, P., Gordon, A., Singana, M.: A novel deep neural network that uses space-time features for tracking and recognizing a moving object. J. Artif. Intell. Soft Comput. Res. **7**(2), 125–136 (2017)
7. Ketkar, N.: Deep Learning with Python. Apress, Berkeley (2017). https://doi.org/10.1007/978-1-4842-2766-4_14
8. Chu, J.L., Krzyżak, A.: The recognition of partially occluded objects with support vector machines. convolutional neural networks and deep belief networks. J. Artif. Intell. Soft Comput. Res. **4**(1), 5–19 (2014)
9. Dahl, G.E., Sainath, T.N., Hinton, G.E. : Improving deep neural networks for LVCSR using rectified linear units and dropout. In: IEEE International Conference on Acoustic Speech and Signal Processing (ICASSP 2013), Vancouver (2013)
10. Goodfellow, I.J., Bengio, Y., Courville, A.: Deep Learning. MIT Press, Cambridge (2017)
11. He, K., Zhang, X., Ren, S., Sun, J.: Deep residual learning for image recognition. In: Proceedings of the IEEE Conference on Computer Vision and Pattern Recognition, pp. 770–778 (2016)
12. He, K., Zhang, X., Ren, S., Sun, J.: Delving deep into rectifiers: surpassing human-level performance on ImageNet classification, arXiv:1502.01852v1 (2015)
13. He, K., Zhang, X., Ren, S., Sun, J.: Identity mappings in deep residual networks. In: Leibe, B., Matas, J., Sebe, N., Welling, M. (eds.) ECCV 2016. LNCS, vol. 9908, pp. 630–645. Springer, Cham (2016). https://doi.org/10.1007/978-3-319-46493-0_38
14. Hinton, G.E., Srivastava, N., Krizhevsky, A., Sutskever, I., Salakhutdinov, R.R.: Improving neural networks by preventing co-adaptation of feature detectors (2012). http://arxiv.org/abs/1207.0580
15. Huang, G., Liu, Z., Pleiss, G., Van Der Maaten, L., Weinberger, K.: Convolutional networks with dense connectivity. IEEE Trans. Pattern Anal. Mach. Intell. (early access) (2019). https://doi.org/10.1109/TPAMI.2019.2918284
16. Ioffe, S., Szegedy, C.: Batch normalization: accelerating deep network training by reducing internal covariate shift. In: International Conference on Machine Learning, pp. 448–456 (2015)
17. Janocha, K., Czarnecki, W.: On loss functions for deep neural networks in classification, arXiv:1702.05659v1 (2017)
18. Kamimura, K.: Supposed maximum mutual information for improving generalization and interpretation of multi-layered neural networks. J. Artif. Intell. Soft Comput. Res. **9**(2), 123–147 (2019)
19. Keskar, N.S., Mudigere, D., Nocedal, J., Smelyanskiy, M., Tang, P.P.: On large-batch training for deep learning: generalization gap and sharp minima. In: ICLR 2017, arXiv:1609.04836v2 (2017)
20. Kingma, D.P., Ba, J.: Adam: a method for stochastic optimization. arXiv preprint arXiv:1412.6980 (2014)
21. Krizhevsky, A., Hinton, G.: Learning multiple layers of features from tiny images, Technical report (2009)
22. Krizhevsky, A., Sutskever, I., Hinton, G.: Imagenet classification with deep convolutional neural networks. In: Advances in Neural Information Processing Systems, pp. 1097–1105 (2012)

23. LeCun, Y., et al.: Backpropagation applied to handwritten zip code recognition. Neural Comput. **1**(4), 541–551 (1989)
24. LeCun, Y., Bengio, Y.: Convolutional networks for images, speech, and time-series. In: Arbib, M.A., (ed.) The Handbook of Brain Theory and Neural Networks. MIT Press (1995)
25. LeCun, Y., Bengio, Y., Hinton, G.: Deep learning (Review). Nature **521**, 436–444 (2015)
26. Lim, S., Kim, I., Kim, T., Kim, C., Kim, S.: Fast autoAugment, arXiv:1905.00397v2 (2019)
27. Nesterov, Y.: A method of solving a convex program-ming problem with convergence rate $O(1/\sqrt{(k)})$. Sov. Math. Dokl. **27**, 372–376 (1983)
28. Nesterov, Y.: Efficiency of coordinate descent methods on huge-scale optimization problems. SIAM J. Optim. **22**(2), 341–362 (2010)
29. Neyshabur, B., Li, Z., Bhojanapalli, S., LeCun, Y., Srebro, N.: Towards understanding the role of over-parametrization in generalization of neural networks, arXiv:1805.12076v1 (2018)
30. Richtárik, P., Takác, M.: Iteration complexity of randomized block-coordinate descent methods for minimizing a composite function. Math. Program. Ser. A **144**(1–2), 1–38 (2011)
31. Ruder, S.: An overview of gradient descent optimization algorithms, arXiv:1609.04747v2 (2017)
32. Santurkar, S., Tsipras, D., Ilyas, A., Madry, A.: How does batch normalization help optimization? In: Advances in Neural Information Processing Systems, p. 31 (2018)
33. Sari, C.T., Gunduz-Demir, C.: Unsupervised feature extraction via deep learning for histopathological classification of colon tissue images. IEEE Trans. Med. Imaging **38**(5), 1139–1149 (2019)
34. Skubalska-Rafajłowicz, E.: Training neural networks by optimizing random subspaces of the weight space. In: Rutkowski, L., Korytkowski, M., Scherer, R., Tadeusiewicz, R., Zadeh, L.A., Zurada, J.M. (eds.) ICAISC 2016. LNCS (LNAI), vol. 9692, pp. 148–157. Springer, Cham (2016). https://doi.org/10.1007/978-3-319-39378-0_14
35. Smith, S.L., Le, Q.V.: A Bayesian perspective on generalization and stochastic gradient descent, arXiv:1710.06451v3 (2018)
36. Souza, G., Santos, D., Pires, R., Marana, A., Papa, J.: Deep features extraction for robust fingerprint spoofing attack detection. J. Artif. Intell. Soft Comput. Res. **9**(1), 41–49 (2019)
37. Srivastava, N., Hinton, G., Krizhevsky, A., Sutskever, I., Salakhutdinov, R.: Dropout: a simple way to prevent neural networks from overfitting. J. Mach. Learn. Res. **15**, 1929–1958 (2014)
38. Sutskever, I., Martens, J., Dahl, G., Hinton, G.: On the importance of initialization and momentum in deep learning. In: Proceedings of the 30th International Conference on Machine Learning, Atlanta, Georgia, USA (2013)
39. Wu, S., et al.: $L1$ -norm batch normalization for efficient training of deep neural networks. IEEE Trans. Neural Netw. Learn. Syst. **30**(7), 2043–2051 (2019)
40. Zhang, C., Bengio, S., Hardt,, Recht, B., Vinyals, O.: Understanding deep learning requires rethinking generalization. In: International Conference on Learning Representations, arXiv:1611.03530v2 (2017)

41. Zhang, H., Cisse, M., Dauphin, Y. N., Lopez-Paz, D.: Mixup: beyond empirical risk minimization. In: ILCR 2018, arXiv:1710.09412v2 (2018)
42. Zhou, P., Feng, J.: Understanding generalization and optimization performance of deep CNNs. In: Proceedings of the 35th International Conference on Machine Learning, Stockholm, Sweden, PMLR 80 (2018). arXiv preprint arXiv:1805.10767

A New Algorithm with a Line Search for Feedforward Neural Networks Training

Jarosław Bilski[1]([⊠])(iD), Bartosz Kowalczyk[1](iD), and Jacek M. Żurada[2](iD)

[1] Department of Computational Intelligence, Częstochowa University of Technology, Al. Armii Krajowej 36, 42-200 Częstochowa, Poland
{jaroslaw.bilski,bartosz.kowalczyk}@pcz.pl
[2] Department Electrical and Computer Engineering, University of Louisville, Louisville, KY 40292, USA
jacek.zurada@louisville.edu

Abstract. A new algorithm for feedforward neural networks training is presented. Its core is based on the Givens rotations and QR decomposition (GQR) with an application of a line search method. Similar algorithms based on the QR decomposition utilize a runtime fixed size of the training step. In some situations that might result in inaccurate weight corrections in a given step. The proposed algorithm solves this issue by finding the exact spot of the optimal solution. The performance of the proposed algorithm has been tested on several benchmarks and various networks.

Keywords: Feedforward neural networks · QR decomposition · Givens rotation · Supervised training · Line search

1 Introduction

In the modern world artificial intelligence is a very important branch of science researched by numerous authors [1–8]. Its areas of application are continuously finding new use in, e.g.. speech recognition, image processing, patterns classification, finance, medicine, safety, entertainment, and many more [9–18]. The branch of artificial neural networks which is being researched by many authors is of special interest [19–23]. One of the biggest challenges in neural networks is the training process. Most of the popular algorithms such as [24–27] originate from the backpropagation method [28]. This everlasting trend of increasing computational power of processing devices opens an opportunity for a continuous development of more powerful training algorithms.

In this paper, a new algorithm for feedforward networks training is presented. It combines advantages of the modified GQR algorithm [29] and the line search

This work has been supported by the Polish National Science Center under Grant 2017/27/B/ST6/02852 and the program of the Polish Minister of Science and Higher Education under the name "Regional Initiative of Excellence" in the years 2019–2022 project number 020/RID/2018/19, the amount of financing PLN 12,000,000.00.

© Springer Nature Switzerland AG 2020
L. Rutkowski et al. (Eds.): ICAISC 2020, LNAI 12415, pp. 15–26, 2020.
https://doi.org/10.1007/978-3-030-61401-0_2

method [30], which is a well known algebraic operation for finding the function minimum. An epoch variant of the GQR algorithm [31] uses a predefined value of the training step, which is constant across all epochs. It might result in inaccurate weight corrections due to missing the optimal solutions. Utilizing the line search method helps to reduce this problem by finding the exact minimum of the error function before applying the weight update. This results in a shorter convergence time comparing to the epoch variant of the GQR algorithm which is described in the Experiment section of this article.

2 Epoch Variant of the GQR Algorithm

2.1 Rotation Basics

The Givens rotation is a commonly used algebraic method for orthogonal transformations of class $\mathbf{x} \rightarrow \mathbf{y} = \mathbf{G}\mathbf{x}$. It is obtained by a dedicated rotation matrix $\mathbf{G}_{pq}$ of the following structure

$$
\mathbf{G}_{pq} = \begin{bmatrix} 1 & & & \cdots & & & 0 \\ & \ddots & & & & & \\ & & c & \cdots & s & & \\ & \vdots & \vdots & \ddots & \vdots & \vdots & \\ & & -s & \cdots & c & & \\ & & & & & \ddots & \\ 0 & & & \cdots & & & 1 \end{bmatrix} \begin{matrix} \\ \\ p \\ \\ q \\ \\ \\ \end{matrix}
$$

$$ p q $$

(1)

where

$$c^2 + s^2 = 1 \tag{2}$$

$$g_{pp} = g_{qq} = c = \frac{a_p}{\rho} \tag{3}$$

$$g_{pq} = -g_{qp} = s = \frac{a_q}{\rho} \tag{4}$$

$$\rho = \pm\sqrt{a_p^2 + a_q^2} \tag{5}$$

This implies that $\mathbf{G}_{pq}^T \mathbf{G}_{pq} = \mathbf{I}$, which proves that $\mathbf{G}_{pq}$ is an orthogonal matrix.

2.2 QR Decomposition

The QR decomposition is a universal method for orthogonal transformations. As an iterative algorithm, it can be realized by the Givens rotations. Let $\mathbf{A} \in \mathbb{R}^{m,n}$, the main goal of the QR decomposition is to transform matrix $\mathbf{A}$ into the product of matrices $\mathbf{Q}$ and $\mathbf{R}$ in the following way

$$\mathbf{A} = \mathbf{Q}\mathbf{R} \tag{6}$$

$\mathbf{Q}$ is an orthogonal matrix (with properties $\mathbf{Q}^T\mathbf{Q} = \mathbf{I}$ and $\mathbf{Q}^T = \mathbf{Q}^{-1}$) and $\mathbf{R}$ is an upper triangle matrix. The decomposition process utilizes Eqs. (1)–(5) in the way that a_q is always substituted by 0

$$\bar{a}_q = -sa_p + ca_q = 0 \qquad (7)$$

This opens a possibility for calculating a sequence of rotations to eliminate the elements under the diagonal of the k-th column as shown in the following equation

$$\mathbf{G}_k = \mathbf{G}_{k,k+1}\ldots\mathbf{G}_{k,m-1}\mathbf{G}_{km} \quad \text{for } (k = 1,\ldots, m-1) \qquad (8)$$

The desired form of matrix $\mathbf{R} \in \mathbb{R}^{m,n}$ is obtained after $m-1$ iterations of the algorithm, which can be summarized as follows

$$\mathbf{R} = \mathbf{G}_{m-1}\ldots\mathbf{G}_1\mathbf{A}_1 = \mathbf{G}_{m-1,m}\ldots\mathbf{G}_{23}\ldots\mathbf{G}_{2m}\mathbf{G}_{12}\ldots\mathbf{G}_{1m}\mathbf{A}_1 = \mathbf{Q}^T\mathbf{A} \qquad (9)$$

2.3 A Training Algorithm

The proposed algorithm performs a supervised training with an epoch update for feedforward neural networks. The criterion function $J(n)$ is given by the following equation

$$\begin{aligned}
J(n) &= \sum_{t=1}^{n} \lambda^{n-t} \sum_{p=1}^{np} \sum_{j=1}^{N_L} \varepsilon_j^{(L)2} \\
&= \sum_{t=1}^{n} \lambda^{n-t} \sum_{p=1}^{np} \sum_{j=1}^{N_L} \left[d_j^{(L)}(t) - f\left(\mathbf{x}^{(L)T}(t)\,\mathbf{w}_j^{(L)}(n)\right) \right]^2 \qquad (10) \\
&= \sum_{p=1}^{np} \sum_{t=1}^{n} \lambda^{n-t} \sum_{j=1}^{N_L} \varepsilon_{jp}^{(L)2} = \sum_{p=1}^{np} J_p(n)
\end{aligned}$$

where np stands for the total number of samples utilized in the training set, N_L stands for the total number of output neurons, and n is the index of consecutive epoch. The QR decomposition process based on the Givens rotations is going to be used in order to find the correct direction for minimizing the value of (10). Let us calculate the partial derivative for the i-th neuron of the l-th layer as

$$\begin{aligned}
\frac{\partial J(n)}{\partial \mathbf{w}_i^{(l)}(n)} &= \sum_{p=1}^{np} \sum_{t=1}^{n} \lambda^{n-t} \sum_{j=1}^{N_L} \frac{\partial \varepsilon_{jp}^{(L)}(t)}{\partial \mathbf{w}_i^{(l)}(n)} \varepsilon_{jp}^{(L)}(t) \\
&= \sum_{p=1}^{np} \sum_{t=1}^{n} \lambda^{n-t} \sum_{j=1}^{N_L} \frac{\partial y_{jp}^{(L)}(t)}{\partial \mathbf{w}_i^{(l)}(n)} \varepsilon_{jp}^{(L)}(t) = \mathbf{0}
\end{aligned} \qquad (11)$$

In order to solve the composite derivative from (10), the chain rule is used

$$
\sum_{p=1}^{np}\sum_{t=1}^{n}\lambda^{n-t}\sum_{j=1}^{N_L}\frac{\partial y_{jp}^{(L)}(t)}{\partial s_{jp}^{(L)}(t)}\sum_{k=1}^{N_{L-1}}\frac{\partial s_{jp}^{(L)}(t)}{\partial y_{kp}^{(L-1)}(t)}\frac{\partial y_{kp}^{(L-1)}(t)}{\partial \mathbf{w}_i^{(l)}(n)}\varepsilon_{jp}^{(L)}(t)
$$

$$
=\sum_{p=1}^{np}\sum_{t=1}^{n}\lambda^{n-t}\sum_{k=1}^{N_{L-1}}\frac{\partial y_{kp}^{(L-1)}(t)}{\partial \mathbf{w}_i^{(l)}(n)}\sum_{j=1}^{N_L}\frac{\partial y_{jp}^{(L)}(t)}{\partial s_{jp}^{(L)}(t)}w_{jk}^{(L)}\varepsilon_{jp}^{(L)}(t)
$$

$$
=\sum_{p=1}^{np}\sum_{t=1}^{n}\lambda^{n-t}\sum_{k=1}^{N_{L-1}}\frac{\partial y_{kp}^{(L-1)}(t)}{\partial \mathbf{w}_i^{(l)}(n)}\varepsilon_{kp}^{(L-1)}(t) \tag{12}
$$

$$
=\sum_{p=1}^{np}\sum_{t=1}^{n}\lambda^{n-t}\sum_{h=1}^{N_l}\frac{\partial y_{hp}^{(l)}(t)}{\partial \mathbf{w}_i^{(l)}(n)}\varepsilon_{hp}^{(l)}(t)=\mathbf{0}
$$

where $\varepsilon_{hp}^{(l)}(t)$ stands for the nonlinear error of the h-th neuron of the l-th layer in the p-th sample during the t-th epoch and denotes

$$
\varepsilon_{hp}^{(l)}(t)=\sum_{j=1}^{N_{l+1}}\frac{\partial y_{jp}^{(l+1)}(t)}{\partial s_{jp}^{(l+1)}(t)}w_{jh}^{(l+1)}(n)\varepsilon_{jp}^{(l+1)}(t) \tag{13}
$$

Taking (13) into account, let us perform the final transformations of (12) and make it equal to 0

$$
\sum_{p=1}^{np}\sum_{t=1}^{n}\lambda^{n-t}\sum_{h=1}^{N_l}\frac{\partial y_{hp}^{(l)}(t)}{\partial \mathbf{w}_i^{(l)}(n)}\varepsilon_{hp}^{(l)}(t)
$$

$$
=\sum_{p=1}^{np}\sum_{t=1}^{n}\lambda^{n-t}\sum_{h=1}^{N_l}\frac{\partial y_{hp}^{(l)}(t)}{\partial s_{hp}^{(l)}(n)}\frac{\partial s_{hp}^{(l)}(t)}{\partial \mathbf{w}_i^{(l)}(n)}\varepsilon_{hp}^{(l)}(t)
$$

$$
=\sum_{p=1}^{np}\sum_{t=1}^{n}\lambda^{n-t}\frac{\partial y_{ip}^{(l)}(t)}{\partial s_{ip}^{(l)}(n)}\mathbf{y}_p^{(l-1)T}(t)\varepsilon_{hp}^{(l)}(t) \tag{14}
$$

$$
=\sum_{p=1}^{np}\sum_{t=1}^{n}\lambda^{n-t}\frac{\partial y_{ip}^{(l)}(t)}{\partial s_{ip}^{(l)}(n)}\mathbf{y}_p^{(l-1)T}(t)\left[d_{ip}^{(l)}(t)-y_{ip}^{(l)}(t)\right]=\mathbf{0}
$$

Since the presented algorithm can be used with any differentiable activation function, the result of the transformation (14) is linearized by

$$
f\left(b_{ip}^{(l)}(t)\right)\approx f\left(s_{ip}^{(l)}(t)\right)+f'\left(s_{ip}^{(l)}(t)\right)\left(b_{ip}^{(l)}(t)-s_{hp}^{(l)}(t)\right), \tag{15}
$$

which reveals the entry point to the QR decomposition process formulated as follows

$$
\sum_{p=1}^{np}\sum_{t=1}^{n}\lambda^{n-t}f'^2\left(s_{ip}^{(l)}(t)\right)\left[b_{ip}^{(l)}(t)-\mathbf{x}_p^{(l)T}(t)\mathbf{w}_i^{(l)}(n)\right]\mathbf{x}_p^{(l)T}(t)=\mathbf{0} \tag{16}
$$

Before obtaining the weight update formula, let us recall the QR decomposition definition given by (6). This equation needs to be solved for each neuron in order to find suitable weight corrections. In the first step, combine (6) and (16), which results in the following

$$\mathbf{A}_i^{(l)}(n)\,\mathbf{w}_i^{(l)}(n) = \mathbf{h}_i^{(l)}(n) \tag{17}$$

where

$$\mathbf{A}_i^{(l)}(n) = \sum_{p=1}^{np}\sum_{t=1}^{n}\lambda^{n-t}\mathbf{z}_{ip}^{(l)}(t)\,\mathbf{z}_{ip}^{(l)T}(t) \tag{18}$$

$$\mathbf{h}_i^{(l)}(n) = \sum_{p=1}^{np}\sum_{t=1}^{n}\lambda^{n-t}f'\left(s_{ip}^{(l)}(t)\right)b_{ip}^{(l)}(t)\,\mathbf{z}_{ip}^{(l)}(t) \tag{19}$$

in order to improve the readability, let

$$\mathbf{z}_{ip}^{(l)}(t) = f'\left(s_{ip}^{(l)}(t)\right)\mathbf{x}_p^{(l)}(t) \tag{20}$$

while the expected value is calculated differently in the output layer $l = L$ than in all hidden neurons

$$b_{ip}^{(l)}(n) = \begin{cases} f^{-1}\left(d_{ip}^{(l)}(n)\right) & \text{for } l = L \\ s_{ip}^{(l)}(n) + e_{ip}^{(l)}(n) & \text{for } l = 1\ldots L-1 \end{cases} \tag{21}$$

The errors of the hidden neurons are calculated based on the backpropagation scheme

$$e_{ip}^{(k)}(n) = \sum_{p=1}^{np}\sum_{j=1}^{N_{k+1}}f'\left(s_{ip}^{(k)}(n)\right)w_{ji}^{(k+1)}(n)\,e_{jp}^{(k+1)}(n) \text{ for } k = 1\ldots L-1 \tag{22}$$

As the result of the QR decomposition, the orthogonal $\mathbf{Q}^T$ matrix is implicitly obtained by

$$\mathbf{Q}_i^{(l)T}(n)\,\mathbf{A}_i^{(l)}(n)\,\mathbf{w}_i^{(l)}(n) = \mathbf{Q}_i^{(l)T}(n)\,\mathbf{h}_i^{(l)}(n) \tag{23}$$

In practical applications, the $\mathbf{Q}^T$ matrix is not stored because the rotations are being done *in situ* in the transformed matrix, which at the end results in the upper triangle matrix $\mathbf{R}_i^{(l)}$ in the following way

$$\mathbf{R}_i^{(l)}(n)\,\mathbf{w}_i^{(l)}(n) = \mathbf{Q}_i^{(l)T}(n)\,\mathbf{h}_i^{(l)}(n) \tag{24}$$

Note that vector $\mathbf{h}_i^{(l)}(n)$ is rotated alongside matrix $\mathbf{A}_i^{(l)}(n)$ during its transformation in the QR decomposition process. In order to obtain weight updates, Eq. (24) needs to be left sided multiplied by $\mathbf{R}_i^{(l)-1}(n)$

$$\hat{\mathbf{w}}_i^{(l)}(n) = \mathbf{R}_i^{(l)-1}(n)\,\mathbf{Q}_i^{(l)T}(n)\,\mathbf{h}_i^{(l)}(n) \tag{25}$$

Since $\mathbf{R}_i^{(l)}(n)$ is an upper triangle matrix, Eq. (25) can be solved easily, which results in the weight update vector in the following way

$$\mathbf{w}_i^{(l)}(n) = (1-\eta)\,\mathbf{w}_i^{(l)}(n-1) + \eta\hat{\mathbf{w}}_i^{(l)}(n) \tag{26}$$

3   Line Search

In the classic GQR algorithm, the size of weight update η is a training time constant. Its value has a huge impact on the training stability and convergence, but it is selected experimentally. If its value is inappropriate, the training might be ineffective or fail completely. The line search method can be used in order to dynamically adjust the step size. Its main goal is to find the minimum of a single variable function in a determined direction:

$$\psi\left(\alpha\right) = J\left(\mathbf{w}\left(n\right) + \alpha\mathbf{d}\left(n\right)\right) \tag{27}$$

where α is a current step size, J is an error measure given by (10), $\mathbf{w}\left(n\right)$ is the network's weights vector and $\mathbf{d}\left(n\right)$ is the training direction calculated by

$$\mathbf{d}\left(n\right) = \sum_{p=1}^{np} \hat{\mathbf{w}}_p\left(n\right) - \mathbf{w}\left(n\right) \tag{28}$$

The line search algorithm utilizes the slopes of $\psi\left(\alpha\right)$ function given by

$$s = \mathbf{d}^T\left(n\right) \cdot \nabla\mathbf{J}\left(\mathbf{w}\left(n\right) + \alpha\mathbf{d}\left(n\right)\right) \tag{29}$$

The gradient $\nabla\mathbf{J}$ is calculated in the following way

$$
\begin{aligned}
\frac{\partial J\left(n\right)}{\partial w_{ij}^{(l)}} &= \nabla J_{ij}^{(l)}\left(n\right) = \sum_{p=1}^{np} \nabla J_{ijp}^{(l)} = \sum_{p=1}^{np} \frac{\partial J_p\left(n\right)}{\partial w_{ij}^{(l)}\left(n\right)} \\
&= \sum_{p=1}^{np} \frac{\partial J_p\left(n\right)}{\partial s_{ip}^{(l)}\left(n\right)} \frac{\partial s_{ip}^{(l)}\left(n\right)}{\partial w_{ij}^{(l)}\left(n\right)} = \sum_{p=1}^{np} \frac{\partial J_p\left(n\right)}{\partial s_{ip}^{(l)}\left(n\right)} x_{jp}^{(l)}
\end{aligned} \tag{30}
$$

In order to simplify further calculations, let us define

$$\delta_{ip}^{(l)}\left(n\right) \triangleq -\frac{\partial J_p\left(n\right)}{\partial s_{ip}^{(l)}\left(n\right)} \tag{31}$$

Then, Eq. (30) takes its final form for calculating the gradient of the j-th weight of the i-th neuron

$$\nabla J_{ij}^{(l)}\left(n\right) = \sum_{p=1}^{np} \frac{\partial J_p\left(n\right)}{\partial w_{ij}^{(l)}\left(n\right)} = -\sum_{p=1}^{np} \delta_{ip}^{(l)} x_{jp}^{(l)} \tag{32}$$

Since the discussed algorithm performs supervised training, the value of $\delta_{ip}^{(l)}$ needs to be calculated differently in the output layer than in the hidden layers. The derivation of $\delta_{ip}^{(l)}$ in the output layer where $l = L$ is as follows

$$\delta_{ip}^{(L)}(n) = -\frac{\partial \sum_{t=1}^{n} \lambda^{n-t} \sum_{j=1}^{N_L} \varepsilon_{jp}^{(L)2}(n)}{\partial s_{ip}^{(L)}(n)} = -\frac{\partial \sum_{t=1}^{n} \lambda^{n-t} \varepsilon_{ip}^{(L)2}(n)}{\partial s_{ip}^{(L)}(n)}$$

$$= -\sum_{t=1}^{n} \lambda^{n-t} \frac{\partial \varepsilon_{ip}^{(L)2}(n)}{\partial s_{ip}^{(L)}(n)} = 2 \sum_{t=1}^{n} \lambda^{n-t} \varepsilon_{ip}^{(L)}(n) f'\left(s_{ip}^{(L)}(n)\right) \tag{33}$$

$$= 2 \sum_{t=1}^{n-1} \lambda^{n-1-t} \varepsilon_{ip}^{(L)}(n-1) f'\left(s_{ip}^{(L)}(n-1)\right) + \varepsilon_{ip}^{(L)}(n) f'\left(s_{ip}^{(L)}(n)\right)$$

$$= \varepsilon_{ip}^{(L)}(n) f'\left(s_{ip}^{(L)}(n)\right) + \delta_{ip}^{(L)}(n-1)$$

For $\delta_{ip}^{(l)}$ of the hidden neurons, where $l = (1, 2, \ldots, L-1)$, it is required to calculate all preceding $\delta_{ip}^{(l+1)}$ first. It is necessary due to the error backpropagation phase of the algorithm and can be depicted as follows

$$\delta_{ip}^{(l)} = -\frac{\partial J_p(n)}{\partial s_{ip}^{(l)}(n)} = -\sum_{m=1}^{N_{l+1}} \frac{\partial J_p(n)}{\partial s_{mp}^{(l+1)}(n)} \frac{\partial s_{mp}^{(l+1)}(n)}{\partial s_{ip}^{(l)}(n)}$$

$$= \sum_{m=1}^{N_{l+1}} \delta_{mp}^{(l+1)}(n) \frac{\partial s_{mp}^{(l+1)}(n)}{\partial s_{ip}^{(l)}(n)} \tag{34}$$

$$= \sum_{m=1}^{N_{l+1}} \delta_{mp}^{(l+1)}(n) w_{mi}^{(l+1)}(n) f'\left(s_{ip}^{(l)}(n)\right)$$

$$= f'\left(s_{ip}^{(l)}(n)\right) \sum_{m=1}^{N_{l+1}} \delta_{mp}^{(l+1)}(n) w_{mi}^{(l+1)}(n)$$

4   Experiment

The goal of the experiment is to analyse the performance of the proposed algorithm. It contains several approximation benchmarks performed on various networks. Each benchmark assumes a common set of predefined parameters and has been retried 100 times in order to gather valuable statistics. In each trial, the network is restarted to its initial state and weights are randomly selected in the range of $[-0.5, 0.5]$ excluding 0. The training succeeds if the average value of the error measure given by (10) is below the certain threshold defined by the benchmark. The training is assumed to have failed once the epoch count reaches the limit of 1000 epochs. All hidden neurons have used a hyperbolic tangent as an activation function while the output neurons have used a linear function.

4.1   The Logistic Function Approximation

The logistic function benchmark is utilizing the following formula

$$y = f(x) = 4x(1-x) \qquad x \in [0, 1] \tag{35}$$

The training set contains 11 samples. The target error has been set to 0.001. The results of the training are presented in Table 1. In this benchmark, the proposed modification has achieved very good results in both the success ratio and the average epoch count.

Table 1. Results of the logistic function training

Network	EGQR+LS		EGQR	
	SR [%]	Epochs	SR [%]	Epochs
FCC-4	86	78.74	82	100.9
FCC-5	95	65	81	85.69
FCC-6	93	52.02	71	85.15
FCC-7	98	46.4	54	59.26
MLP-5-1	88	70.56	98	57.91
MLP-10-1	99	36.64	88	40.75
MLP-15-1	98	31.01	98	46.2
FCMLP-5-1	99	54.21	73	23.7
FCMLP-10-1	98	33.05	100	90.44
FCMLP-15-1	100	29.96	83	48.95

4.2   The Composite Function Approximation

The composite function benchmark is utilizing the following formula

$$f(x) = \sin x \cdot \log x \quad x \in [0.1, 4] \tag{36}$$

The training set contains 40 samples. The target error has been set to 0.001. The results of the training are presented in Table 2. While both algorithms maintain a high success ratio, it is worth noting that the proposed modification has a much better average epoch convergence time.

Table 2. Results of the $\sin x \cdot \log x$ function training

Network	EGQR+LS		EGQR	
	SR [%]	Epochs	SR [%]	Epochs
FCC-4	91	14.84	89	32.26
FCC-5	99	9.76	82	27.21
FCC-6	97	6.42	90	21.47
FCC-7	100	5.85	94	16.19
MLP-5-1	96	46.09	98	25.03
MLP-10-1	98	12.74	91	10.56
MLP-15-1	98	11.52	96	16.01
FCMLP-5-1	82	11.01	83	6.94
FCMLP-10-1	97	5.52	100	43.66
FCMLP-15-1	97	4.45	98	26.22

4.3   The Hang Function Approximation

The Hang function benchmark is utilizing the following formula

$$y = f(x_1, x_2) = \left(1 + x_1^{-2} + \sqrt{x_2^{-3}}\right)^2 \qquad x_1, x_2 \in [1, 5] \tag{37}$$

The training set contains 50 samples. The target error has been set to 0.001. The results of the training are presented in Table 3. The proposed modification improves the success ratio for bigger networks comparing to the epoch variant of the GQR algorithm.

Table 3. Results of the Hang function training

Network	EGQR+LS		EGQR	
	SR [%]	Epochs	SR [%]	Epochs
FCC-8	68	208.01	73	124.66
FCC-10	78	145.24	90	118.48
FCC-12	90	135.5	89	92.6
FCC-14	98	83.96	80	68.66
FCC-16	98	66.36	70	53.26
FCC-18	99	51.4	91	59.68

4.4   The Sinc Function Approximation

The Sinc function benchmark is utilizing the following formula

$$y = f(x_1, x_2) = \begin{cases} 1 & \text{for } x_1 = x_2 = 0 \\ \frac{\sin x_2}{x_2} & \text{for } x_1 = 0 \wedge x_2 \neq 0 \\ \frac{\sin x_1}{x_1} & \text{for } x_2 = 0 \wedge x_1 \neq 0 \\ \frac{\sin x_1}{x_1} \frac{\sin x_2}{x_2} & \text{for other cases} \end{cases} \tag{38}$$

The training set contains 121 samples. The target error has been set to 0.005. The results of the training are presented in Table 4. While both algorithms maintain a high success ratio, it is worth noting that the proposed modification performs slightly better in terms of an average epoch convergence time.

Table 4. Results of the Sinc function training

Network	EGQR+LS		EGQR	
	SR [%]	Epochs	SR [%]	Epochs
FCC-8	100	18.33	99	17.94
FCC-10	100	10.36	98	10.45
FCC-12	100	6.78	100	7.85
FCC-14	100	5.62	100	6.91
FCC-16	100	4.76	100	6.32
FCC-18	100	4.13	100	5.5

5   Conclusions

The paper covers a full mathematical derivation of the epoch variant of the GQR algorithm used together with the line search method. It is used to find the best size for the training step in order to speed up the algorithm's convergence process. Based on the provided benchmarks, the proposed algorithm improves the success rate and the average epoch count in most cases comparing to the epoch variant of the GQR algorithm. The results might differ based on the provided internal parameters of the line search algorithm. In the future, an additional effort will be made to tune the internal parameters of the line search algorithm to obtain even better results. As a future perspective, a parallel variant of the proposed modification will be attempted as presented in [32,33]. Moreover, the algorithm can be adjusted to several industrial problems [34–36].

References

1. Gabryel, M., Damaševičius, R., Przybyszewski, K.: Application of the bag-of-words algorithm in classification the quality of sales leads. In: Rutkowski, L., et al. (eds.) ICAISC 2018. LNCS (LNAI), vol. 10841, pp. 615–622. Springer, Cham (2018). https://doi.org/10.1007/978-3-319-91253-0_57
2. Gabryel, M., Damaševičius, R.: The image classification with different types of image features. In: Rutkowski, L., Korytkowski, M., Scherer, R., Tadeusiewicz, R., Zadeh, L.A., Zurada, J.M. (eds.) ICAISC 2017. LNCS (LNAI), vol. 10245, pp. 497–506. Springer, Cham (2017). https://doi.org/10.1007/978-3-319-59063-9_44
3. Starczewski, A., Cader, A.: Determining the EPS parameter of the DBSCAN algorithm. In: Rutkowski, L., Scherer, R., Korytkowski, M., Pedrycz, W., Tadeusiewicz, R., Zurada, J.M. (eds.) ICAISC 2019. LNCS (LNAI), vol. 11509, pp. 420–430. Springer, Cham (2019). https://doi.org/10.1007/978-3-030-20915-5_38
4. Koren, O., Hallin, C.A., Perel, N., Bendet, D.: Decision-making enhancement in a big data environment: application of the k-means algorithm to mixed data. J. Artif. Intell. Soft Comput. Res. **9**(4), 293–302 (2019)
5. Albawi, S., Mohammed, T.A., Al-Zawi, S.: Understanding of a convolutional neural network. In: 2017 International Conference on Engineering and Technology (ICET), pp. 1–6 (2017)

6. Taqi, A.M., Awad, A., Al-Azzo, F., Milanova, M.: The impact of multi-optimizers and data augmentation on tensorFlow convolutional neural network performance. In: 2018 IEEE Conference on Multimedia Information Processing and Retrieval (MIPR), pp. 140–145, April 2018
7. Rutkowski, T., Romanowski, J., Woldan, P., Staszewski, P., Nielek, R., Rutkowski, L.: A content-based recommendation system using neuro-fuzzy approach. In: 2018 IEEE International Conference on Fuzzy Systems (FUZZ-IEEE), pp. 1–8 (2018)
8. Rutkowski, T., Łapa, K., Nowicki, R., Nielek, R., Grzanek, K.: On explainable recommender systems based on fuzzy rule generation techniques. In: Rutkowski, L., Scherer, R., Korytkowski, M., Pedrycz, W., Tadeusiewicz, R., Zurada, J.M. (eds.) ICAISC 2019. LNCS (LNAI), vol. 11508, pp. 358–372. Springer, Cham (2019). https://doi.org/10.1007/978-3-030-20912-4_34
9. Nobukawa, S., Nishimura, H., Yamanishi, T.: Pattern classification by spiking neural networks combining self-organized and reward-related spike-timing-dependent plasticity. J. Artif. Intell. Soft Comput. Res. 9(4), 283–291 (2019)
10. Wang, X., Guo, Y., Wang, Y., Jinhua, Yu.: Automatic breast tumor detection in ABVS images based on convolutional neural network and superpixel patterns. Neural Comput. Appl. 31(4), 1069–1081 (2019)
11. Mohamed Shakeel, P., Tobely, T.E.E.E., Al-Feel, H., Manogaran, G., Baskar, S.: Neural network based brain tumor detection using wireless infrared imaging sensor. IEEE Access 7, 5577–5588 (2019)
12. Cai, X., Qian, Y., Bai, Q., Liu, W.: Exploration on the financing risks of enterprise supply chain using back propagation neural network. J. Comput. Appl. Math. 367, 112457 (2020)
13. Moghaddam, A.H., Moghaddam, M.H., Esfandyari, M.: Stock market index prediction using artificial neural network. J. Econ. Financ. Adm. Sci. 21(41), 89–93 (2016)
14. Qi, S., Jin, K., Li, B., Qian, Y.: The exploration of internet finance by using neural network. J. Comput. Appl. Math. 369, 112630 (2020)
15. de Souza, G.B., da Silva Santos, D.F., Pires, R.G., Marananil, A.N., Papa, J.P.: Deep features extraction for robust fingerprint spoofing attack detection. J. Artif. Intell. Soft Comput. Res. 9(1), 41–49 (2019)
16. Yurii, K., Liudmila, G.: Application of artificial neural networks in vehicles' design self-diagnostic systems for safety reasons. In: Transportation Research Procedia, 20:283–287: 12th International Conference "Organization and Traffic Safety Management in large cities" SPbOTSIC-2016, 28–30 September 2016. St, Petersburg, Russia (2017)
17. Lam, M.W.Y.: One-match-ahead forecasting in two-team sports with stacked Bayesian regressions. J. Artif. Intell. Soft Comput. Res. 8(3), 159–171 (2018)
18. Mou, Y., Kun, X.: The media inequality: comparing the initial human-human and human-AI social interactions. Comput. Hum. Behav. 72, 432–440 (2017)
19. Shewalkar, A., Nyavanandi, D., Ludwig, S.A.: Performance evaluation of deep neural networks applied to speech recognition: RNN, LSTM and GRU. J. Artif. Intell. Soft Comput. Res. 9(4), 235–245 (2019)
20. Costa, M., Oliveira, D., Pinto, S., Tavares, A.: Detecting driver's fatigue, distraction and activity using a non-intrusive AI-based monitoring system. J. Artif. Intell. Soft Comput. Res. 9(4), 247–266 (2019)
21. Abbas, M., Javaid, M., Liu, J.-B., Teh, W.C., Cao, J.: Topological properties of four-layered neural networks. J. Artif. Intell. Soft Comput. Res. 9(2), 111–122 (2019)

22. Kamimura, R.: Supposed maximum mutual information for improving generalization and interpretation of multi-layered neural networks. J. Artif. Intell. Soft Comput. Res. **9**(2), 123–147 (2019)

23. Liu, J.-B., Zhao, J., Wang, S., Javaid, M., Cao, J.: On the topological properties of the certain neural networks. J. Artif. Intell. Soft Comput. Res. **8**(4), 257–268 (2018)

24. Fahlman, S.E.: An empirical study of learning speed in back-propagation networks, Technical report (1988)

25. Riedmiller, M., Braun, H.: A direct adaptive method for faster backpropagation learning: the RPROP algorithm. In: IEEE International Conference on Neural Networks, vol. 1, pp. 586–591, March 1993

26. Sutskever, I., Martens, J., Dahl, G., Hinton, G.: On the importance of initialization and momentum in deep learning. In: Proceedings of the 30th International Conference on International Conference on Machine Learning, ICML 2013, vol. 28, pp. III-1139–III-1147. JMLR.org (2013)

27. Hagan, M.T., Menhaj, M.B.: Training feedforward networks with the Marquardt algorithm. IEEE Trans. Neural Netw. **5**, 989–993 (1994)

28. Werbos, J.: Beyond regression: new tools for prediction and analysis in the behavioral sciences. Harvard University (1974)

29. Bilski, J., Kowalczyk, B., Żurada, J.M.: Application of the givens rotations in the neural network learning algorithm. In: Rutkowski, L., Korytkowski, M., Scherer, R., Tadeusiewicz, R., Zadeh, L.A., Zurada, J.M. (eds.) ICAISC 2016. LNCS (LNAI), vol. 9692, pp. 46–56. Springer, Cham (2016). https://doi.org/10.1007/978-3-319-39378-0_5

30. Charalambous, C.: Conjugate gradient algorithm for efficient training of artificial neural networks. IEE Proc. G Circuits Devices Syst. **139**(3), 301–310 (1992)

31. Bilski, J., Kowalczyk, B., Żurada, J.M.: Application of the givens rotations in the neural network learning algorithm. In: Rutkowski, L., Korytkowski, M., Scherer, R., Tadeusiewicz, R., Zadeh, L.A., Zurada, J.M. (eds.) ICAISC 2016. LNCS (LNAI), vol. 9692, pp. 46–56. Springer, Cham (2016). https://doi.org/10.1007/978-3-319-39378-0_5

32. Bilski, J., Kowalczyk, B., Żurada, J.M.: Parallel implementation of the givens rotations in the neural network learning algorithm. In: Rutkowski, L., Korytkowski, M., Scherer, R., Tadeusiewicz, R., Zadeh, L.A., Zurada, J.M. (eds.) ICAISC 2017. LNCS (LNAI), vol. 10245, pp. 14–24. Springer, Cham (2017). https://doi.org/10.1007/978-3-319-59063-9_2

33. Bilski, J., Kowalczyk, B., Grzanek, K.: The parallel modification to the Levenberg-Marquardt algorithm. In: Rutkowski, L., Scherer, R., Korytkowski, M., Pedrycz, W., Tadeusiewicz, R., Zurada, J.M. (eds.) ICAISC 2018. LNCS (LNAI), vol. 10841, pp. 15–24. Springer, Cham (2018). https://doi.org/10.1007/978-3-319-91253-0_2

34. Rafajłowicz, E., Rafajłowicz, W.: Iterative learning in optimal control of linear dynamic processes. Int. J. Control **91**(7), 1522–1540 (2018)

35. Rafajłowicz, E., Rafajłowicz, W.: Iterative learning in repetitive optimal control of linear dynamic processes. In: Rutkowski, L., Korytkowski, M., Scherer, R., Tadeusiewicz, R., Zadeh, L.A., Zurada, J.M. (eds.) ICAISC 2016. LNCS (LNAI), vol. 9692, pp. 705–717. Springer, Cham (2016). https://doi.org/10.1007/978-3-319-39378-0_60

36. Jurewicz, P., Rafajłowicz, W., Reiner, J., Rafajłowicz, E.: Simulations for tuning a laser power control system of the cladding process. In: Saeed, K., Homenda, W. (eds.) CISIM 2016. LNCS, vol. 9842, pp. 218–229. Springer, Cham (2016). https://doi.org/10.1007/978-3-319-45378-1_20

Fast Conjugate Gradient Algorithm for Feedforward Neural Networks

Jarosław Bilski$^{(\boxtimes)}$ⓘ and Jacek Smoląg ⓘ

Department of Computer Engineering, Częstochowa University of Technology,
al. Armii Krajowej 36, 42-200 Częstochowa, Poland
{Jaroslaw.Bilski,Jacek.Smolag}@pcz.pl

Abstract. The conjugate gradient (CG) algorithm is a method for learning neural networks. The highest computational load in this method is directional minimization. In this paper a new modification of the conjugate gradient algorithm is presented. The proposed solution speeds up the directional minimization, which result in a significant reduction of the calculation time. This modification of the CG algorithm was tested on selected examples. The performance of our method and the classic CG method was compared.

Keywords: Feedforward neural network · Neural network learning algorithm · Conjugate gradient algorithm · Parallel computation

1 Introduction

Artificial intelligence is a very important and interesting field of science and industry studied by many authors e.g. [1–12]. Feedforward neural networks (FNN) are very popular in many applications. They can be applied in many areas, e.g.: approximation, classification, prediction, pattern recognition, or signal processing [13–17]. They have been investigated by many researchers, e.g. [18–23]. There are also a number of works on neural networks application [24, 25] and parallel processing in neural networks [26–33]. The most important issue is the training of feedforward neural networks. In order to train FNNs, gradient methods are often used, see e.g. [34–37]. The conjugate gradient (CG) algorithm is an important learning method [38–44]. The conjugate gradient algorithm is based on directional minimization for each epoch of the learning process. Most commonly the neural networks learning algorithms are simulated on a serial computer. Generally, learning algorithms require high computational load. Contemporary computers have many cores, which is used in the presented method.

This paper presents a new modification of the conjugate gradient learning algorithm based on accelerating directional minimization which uses multiple

This work has been supported by the Polish National Science Center under Grant 2017/27/B/ST6/02852 and the program of the Polish Minister of Sciencea and higher Education under the name "Regional Initiative of Excellence" in the years 2019–2022 project number 020/RID/2018/19, the amount of financing PLN 12,000,000.00.

© Springer Nature Switzerland AG 2020
L. Rutkowski et al. (Eds.): ICAISC 2020, LNAI 12415, pp. 27–38, 2020.
https://doi.org/10.1007/978-3-030-61401-0_3

cores. The proposed solution executes two minimization steps simultaneously. The two second steps are realized at the same time when the first step is being calculated. Then, depending on the result of the first step, the suitable second step is chosen. This is achieved by using multi-threaded calculations. As a result, the calculation time is significantly reduced. The efficiency of this newly proposed method is very promising and is shown in the results part of the paper.

2 Background

In this paper the CG algorithm is used for FNNs. FNNs can have various structures. Each feedforward neural network has an input, an output and neurons between them. Three structures of FNNs are used in this paper. The first is the multilayer perceptron (MLP). This network is built from a few layers, and each layer from a number of neurons. The input of the network is connected to the first layer. The first layer outputs work as inputs to the second layer, and so on. The last layer outputs are the FNN outputs. This layer is called the output layer. All other layers are called hidden layers. The next FNN structure is the fully connected multilayer perceptron (FCMLP). This type of network bases on the classic MLP, but each layer is connected to the network inputs and outputs of all the previous layers. The last considered structure is the fully connected cascade network (FCC). This network is similar to the FCMLP network, but each layer contains only one neuron.

The FNN has L layers, N_l neurons in each $l - th$ layer and N_L outputs. Therefore, the input vector contains N_0 input values. The recall phase of the FNN is represented by the formulas

$$s_i^{(l)} = \sum_{j=0}^{N_{l-1}} w_{ij}^{(l)} x_i^{(l)}$$
$$y_i^{(l)}(t) = f(s_i^{(l)}(t)) \tag{1}$$

The CG algorithm [41] is used to train FNNs. We minimize the following target criterion

$$J(t) = \frac{1}{2} \sum_{i=1}^{N_L} \varepsilon_i^{(L)^2}(t) = \frac{1}{2} \sum_{i=1}^{N_L} \left(y_i^{(L)}(t) - d_i^{(L)}(t) \right)^2 \tag{2}$$

where $\varepsilon_i^{(L)}$ is defined as

$$\varepsilon_i^{(L)}(t) = y_i^{(L)}(t) - d_i^{(L)}(t) \tag{3}$$

and $d_i^{(L)}(t)$ is the $i - th$ desired output. The errors $\varepsilon_i^{(l)}$ in the hidden layers are calculated as follows

$$\varepsilon_i^{(l)}(t) \triangleq \sum_{m=1}^{N_{l+1}} \delta_i^{(l+1)}(t) w_{mi}^{(l+1)}(t) \tag{4}$$

$$\delta_i^{(l)}(t) = \varepsilon_i^{(l)}(t) f'\left(s_i^{(l)}(t)\right) \tag{5}$$

The gradient vector for each weight is determined by

$$\nabla w_{ij}^{(l)}(t) = \delta_i^{(l)} x_j^{(l)} \tag{6}$$

The CG algorithm is based on the first three elements of the Taylor series expansion of the goal function (2). This requires the knowledge of the gradient vector and the Hessian matrix. The CG algorithm can find the search direction and step length without knowledge of the Hessian matrix. Instead, it uses the directional minimization in a chosen direction. The CG algorithm treats the weights of the entire network as a single vector and their derivatives as gradient vector $\mathbf{g}$. The steps of the CG algorithm are shown below.

1. Randomize the initial weight vector values.
2. Calculate the weight gradient (6) and set initial direction $\mathbf{p}_1$ of minimization

$$\mathbf{p}_1 = -\mathbf{g}_1 \tag{7}$$

3. Minimize in the chosen direction

$$\mathbf{w}_{t+1} = \mathbf{w}_t + \alpha^* \mathbf{p}_t \tag{8}$$

where α^* is the factor which minimizes vector $\mathbf{w}_t$ in direction $\mathbf{p}_t$.
4. Calculate the new values of the weights.
5. Calculate the new values of the gradient.
6. Calculate the new direction vector for minimization

$$\mathbf{p}_{t+1} = -\mathbf{g}_{t+1} + \beta_t \mathbf{p}_t \tag{9}$$

where β_t is given by (10), (11) or (12).
7. If the network has not been learned, return to step 3.

There are a few different methods to calculate β_t.

– Hestenes-Stiefel

$$\beta_t = \frac{\mathbf{g}_{t+1}^T(\mathbf{g}_{t+1} - \mathbf{g}_t)}{\mathbf{p}_t^T(\mathbf{g}_{t+1} - \mathbf{g}_t)} \tag{10}$$

– Polak-Ribiere

$$\beta_t = \frac{\mathbf{g}_{t+1}^T(\mathbf{g}_{t+1} - \mathbf{g}_t)}{\mathbf{g}_t^T \mathbf{g}_t} \tag{11}$$

– Fletc.her-Reeves [40]

$$\beta_t = \frac{\mathbf{g}_{t+1}^T \mathbf{g}_{t+1}}{\mathbf{g}_t^T \mathbf{g}_t} \tag{12}$$

In this paper, the Fletcher and Reeves method of calculating β_t is used.

3 Improvement of the Directional Minimization

The classic CG algorithm uses a directional minimization (a line search) based on cubic interpolation [38] to find the minimum of the function:

$$\psi(\alpha) = \phi(\mathbf{w}_t + \alpha\mathbf{p}_t) \tag{13}$$

where

$$\phi(\mathbf{w}_t) = \frac{1}{2} \sum_{p=1}^{np} \sum_{o=1}^{no} \varepsilon_{op}^2 \tag{14}$$

and np is the number of samples and no is the number of network outputs. Sample function $\psi(\alpha)$ is presented in Fig. 1. The main goal is to find small enough interval AB containing a minimum of (13). There are a few possibilities to search next point T:

a) If the function value in point B (see B_1 and B_7 in Fig. 1) is smaller than in point A and the slope in point B is negative, then the next point T is beyond point B see Fig. 2 a). The step is multiplied by factor $scale > 1$.

b) If the function value in point B (see B_5 and B_6 in Fig. 1) is greater or equal than in point A and the slope in point B is negative, then the next point T is between points A and B, see Fig. 2 b). The step is divided by $scale > 1$.

c) If the slope in point B (see B_3 and B_4 in Fig. 1) is positive, then the next point T is between points A and B, see Fig. 2 c). The step is computed as the minimum of the cubic function, see [40].

d) If distance between A and B is short enough, than in this case as the minimum the lower value from points A and B is accepted.

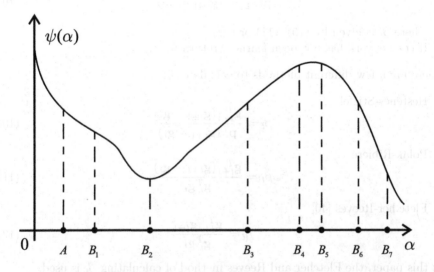

Fig. 1. Sample illustration for directional minimization.

a)

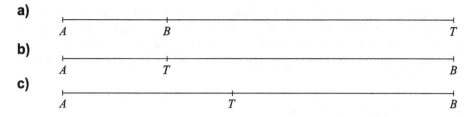

Fig. 2. Classic search of the next point.

a)

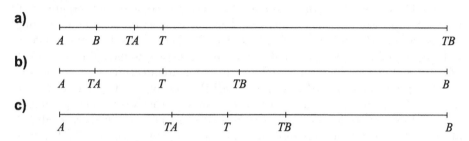

Fig. 3. New method of searching for the next points with the use of two steps.

In this paper a new approach to searching for the directional minimization is proposed. The new method takes two steps of directional minimization at the same time: the first - classic (identical with the classic CG algorithm) and the second - predicting the next points. For this purpose the fast CG (FCG) algorithm computes two additional alternative points TA and TB, see Fig. 3. These points are possible variants of the next step and are computed parallelly on another processor's cores. After completing the first classic step, in the second step, the next point is only selected from TA and TB, as its calculations are made during the first step. For this reason, the computation of TA and TB points do not need extra time and the real learning time is significantly shortened.

Each case of searching for TA and TB points in Fig. 3 has a corresponding case in Fig. 2. The procedure for determining the points in the second step corresponds to the following variants:

a) If the function value in point T (see Fig. 3) is smaller than in point B and the slope in point T is negative, then the next point TB is selected (it is beyond point T and its step is multiplied by factor $scale > 1$), otherwise point TA which is between points B and T is selected.

b) If the function value in point T is greater or equal than in point A and the slope in point T is negative, then the next point TA between points A and T is selected and its step is divided by factor $scale > 1$, otherwise point TB is selected.

c) If the slope in point T is positive, then the next point TA is selected, otherwise point TB is selected.

Points TA in variant a), TB in variant b), TA and TB in variant c) are away from point T by the desired percentage of the stretch $T - B$, $T - B$, $T - A$ and $T - B$, respectively. It should be noted that the points in the second step are determined differently than the points in the first step, but the search interval is significantly smaller.

4   Experimental Results

The paper compares the classic conjugate gradients algorithm with the method proposed by the authors. All the simulations were carried out on a computer with i9-7900X processor and 64 GiB memory. Three problems were selected for testing the algorithms: the logistic function, the HANG function and the circle problem. Individual problems were simulated for various networks including the MLP, FCMLP and FCC with selected architectures. Ten architectures were considered for each problem: three MLPs, three FCMLPs and four FCCs. The results of individual simulations are presented in the tables. In each case, 100 experiments were performed with a maximum of 1000 epochs and at a specified error rate. In all cases, the weights are set random values in the range $[-0.5 - 0.5]$. The first column of each table shows network architectures with a statement numbers of inputs, the number of hidden neurons and the number of outputs for the MLP and FCMLP networks or with number of neurons for the FCC network. The next columns present the success ratio (SR), the average number of epochs and the average time for the classic CG and the FCG algorithms. The last column gives the acceleration (A) of the FCG algorithm relative to the classic CG algorithm.

4.1   The Logistic Function

The logistic function used in this point is given by the equation:

$$f(x) = 4x(1 - x) \quad x \in [0, 1]. \tag{15}$$

The training set has 11 samples from the range of $x \in [0, 1]$. The target error is 0.002. All simulation results are presented in Table 1. It should be noted that the success ratio and the number of epochs are similar in both algorithms, but the time for the FCG algorithm is significantly shorter. The average acceleration is 37.41%. A sample graph for the MLP 1-7-1 network is depicted in Fig. 4.

4.2   The HANG 2D Function

The HANG two-dimensional function is given by equation:

$$f(x_1, x_2) = \left(1 + x_1^{-2} + \sqrt{x_2^{-3}}\right)^2 \quad x_1, x_2 \in [1, 5]. \tag{16}$$

The training set consists of 50 samples from the range of $x_1 \in (1, 5)$ and $x_2 \in (1, 5)$. The target error is 0.009. All simulation results are presented in Table 2. The success ratio and the number of epochs are similar in both algorithms, but the time for the FCG algorithm is significantly shorter. The average acceleration is 37.60%. A sample graph for the FCMLP 2-8-8-1 network is presented in Fig. 5.

Table 1. Training results for the logistic function.

	Classic CG			Fast CG			
Network	SR [%]	Epochs	T [ms]	SR [%]	Epochs	T [ms]	A [%]
MLP 3-1	99.4	40.15	1.23	99.4	39.93	0.75	38.99
MLP 5-1	100	41.49	1.93	99.9	41.66	1.19	38.40
MLP 7-1	100	44.85	2.79	100	44.54	1.69	39.56
FCMLP 3-1	99.6	37.22	1.16	99.9	37.55	0.72	37.95
FCMLP 5-1	100	39.84	1.86	100	39.62	1.14	38.74
FCMLP 7-1	100	43.16	2.68	100	43.91	1.67	37.64
FCC 2	90.5	38.84	0.83	90.6	39.85	0.55	33.63
FCC 3	98.9	38.15	1.50	98.7	38.64	0.91	39.45
FCC 4	99.1	44.46	1.97	99.5	45.95	1.34	32.06
FCC 5	98.6	53.16	3.54	98.9	56.40	2.20	37.72

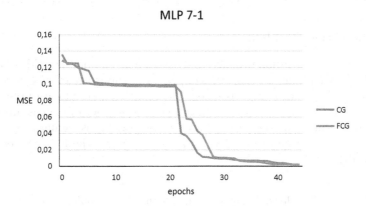

Fig. 4. Exemplary training process of the logistic function using the MLP 7-1 network.

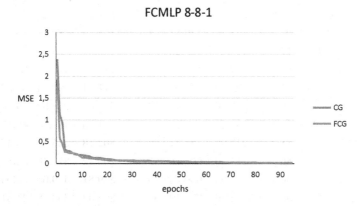

Fig. 5. Exemplary training process of the HANG function using the FCMLP 8-8-1 network.

Table 2. Training results for the HANG 2D function.

	Classic CG			Fast CG			
Network	SR [%]	Epochs	T [ms]	SR [%]	Epochs	T [ms]	A [%]
MLP 4-4-1	64	170.27	49.55	70	213.43	36.37	26.59
MLP 6-6-1	92	156.76	74.85	91	156.75	44.49	40.55
MLP 8-8-1	99	126.14	85.69	96	132.08	53.02	38.12
FCMLP 4-4-1	92	95.77	35.25	92	101.49	22.54	36.05
FCMLP 6-6-1	100	49.82	36.78	100	97.80	23.68	35.62
FCMLP 8-8-1	100	96.78	76.72	100	96.25	46.34	39.60
FCC 12	97	114.53	73.26	95	113.52	44.32	39.51
FCC 14	100	112.88	90.47	100	109.36	53.20	41.20
FCC 16	100	101.46	101.96	100	110.25	65.82	35.45
FCC 18	100	93.82	112.34	100	88.19	63.63	43.36

4.3   The Circle Problem

The circle is a classification problem that says if a given point is inside or outside the circle. The training set has 100 samples from the range of $x_1 \in [-5, 5]$ and $x_2 \in [-5, 5]$. The target error is 0.009. All simulation results are presented in Table 3. As previously, the success ratio and the number of epochs are similar in both algorithms, but the time for the FCG algorithm is significantly shorter. The average acceleration is 39.31%. A sample graph for the FCC 18 network is shown in Fig. 6.

Table 3. Training results for the circle problem.

	Classic CG			Fast CG			
Network	SR [%]	Epochs	T [ms]	SR [%]	Epochs	T [ms]	A [%]
MLP 3-3-1	67	194.76	139.81	67	194.72	88.88	36.43
MLP 4-4-1	77	179.77	128.26	80	145.09	63.99	50.11
MLP 5-5-1	86	183.17	195.72	79	183.63	117.98	39.72
FCMLP 3-3-1	81	190.84	143.64	81	217.91	90.04	37.32
FCMLP 4-4-1	66	560.56	477.15	57	543.61	288.88	39.46
FCMLP 5-5-1	86	234.02	279.92	85	231.45	161.87	42.17
FCC 12	88	277.90	528.41	82	302.18	335.70	36.47
FCC 14	86	255.20	607.78	87	265.12	371.46	38.88
FCC 16	86	239.93	650.12	95	259.81	449.05	30.93
FCC 18	96	224.96	777.12	96	215.34	453.78	41.61

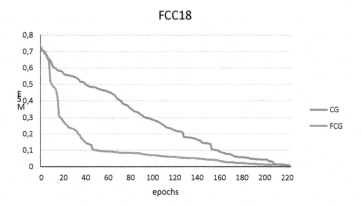

Fig. 6. Exemplary training process of the circle problem using the FCC 18 network.

5 Conclusion

In this paper a new fast modification of Conjugate Gradient algorithm is presented. Our modification is based on performing two learning steps simultaneously. This results in accelerating the learning process. The experiments shows that the fast modification of the CG algorithm significantly decreases the neural network's learning time (almost 40%). The acceleration is independent of the problem because it is obtained in the directional minimization process.

In our future work we plan to extend our algorithm to deal with temporal dynamics and to implement our algorithm to solve several industrial problems, see e.g. [45–47].

References

1. Wang, Z., Cao, J., Cai, Z., Rutkowski, L.: Anti-synchronization in fixed time for discontinuous reaction-diffusion neural networks with time-varying coefficients and time delay. IEEE Trans. Cybern. **50**(6), 2758–2769 (2020). https://doi.org/10.1109/TCYB.2019.2913200
2. Duda, P., Rutkowski, L., Jaworski, M., Rutkowska, D.: On the Parzen Kernel-based probability density function learning procedures over time-varying streaming data with applications to pattern classification. IEEE Trans. Cybern. **50**(4), 1683–1696 (2020). https://doi.org/10.1109/TCYB.2018.2877611
3. Lin, L., Cao, J., Rutkowski, L.: Robust event-triggered control invariance of probabilistic Boolean control networks. IEEE Trans. Neural Netw. Learn. Syst. **31**(3), 1060–1065 (2020). https://doi.org/10.1109/TNNLS.2019.2917753
4. Liu, Y., Zheng, Y., Lu, J., Cao, J., Rutkowski, L.: Constrained quaternion-variable convex optimization: a quaternion-valued recurrent neural network approach. IEEE Trans. Neural Netw. Learn. Syst. **31**(3), 1022–1035 (2020). https://doi.org/10.1109/TNNLS.2019.2916597

5. Gabryel, M., Przybyszewski, K.: The dynamically modified BoW algorithm used in assessing clicks in online ads. In: Rutkowski, L., Scherer, R., Korytkowski, M., Pedrycz, W., Tadeusiewicz, R., Zurada, J.M. (eds.) ICAISC 2019. LNCS (LNAI), vol. 11509, pp. 350–360. Springer, Cham (2019). https://doi.org/10.1007/978-3-030-20915-5_32

6. Gabryel, M.: The bag-of-words method with different types of image features and dictionary analysis. J. Univ. Comput. Sci. **24**(4), 357–371 (2018)

7. Starczewski, A.: A new validity index for crisp clusters. Pattern Anal. Appl. **20**, 687–700 (2017)

8. Łapa, K., Cpałka, K., Wang, L.: New method for design of fuzzy systems for nonlinear modelling using different criteria of interpretability. In: Rutkowski, L., Korytkowski, M., Scherer, R., Tadeusiewicz, R., Zadeh, L.A., Zurada, J.M. (eds.) ICAISC 2014. LNCS (LNAI), vol. 8467, pp. 217–232. Springer, Cham (2014). https://doi.org/10.1007/978-3-319-07173-2_20

9. Zalasiński, M., Cpałka, K., Er, M.J.: New method for dynamic signature verification using hybrid partitioning. In: Rutkowski, L., Korytkowski, M., Scherer, R., Tadeusiewicz, R., Zadeh, L.A., Zurada, J.M. (eds.) ICAISC 2014. LNCS (LNAI), vol. 8468, pp. 216–230. Springer, Cham (2014). https://doi.org/10.1007/978-3-319-07176-3_20

10. Szczypta, J., Przybył, A., Cpałka, K.: Some aspects of evolutionary designing optimal controllers. In: Rutkowski, L., Korytkowski, M., Scherer, R., Tadeusiewicz, R., Zadeh, L.A., Zurada, J.M. (eds.) ICAISC 2013. LNCS (LNAI), vol. 7895, pp. 91–100. Springer, Heidelberg (2013). https://doi.org/10.1007/978-3-642-38610-7_9

11. Rutkowski, T., Romanowski, J., Woldan, P., Staszewski, P., Nielek, R., Rutkowski, L.: A content-based recommendation system using neuro-fuzzy approach. In: 2018 IEEE International Conference on Fuzzy Systems (FUZZ-IEEE), pp. 1–8 (2018)

12. Rutkowski, T., Łapa, K., Nowicki, R., Nielek, R., Grzanek, K.: On explainable recommender systems based on fuzzy rule generation techniques. In: Rutkowski, L., Scherer, R., Korytkowski, M., Pedrycz, W., Tadeusiewicz, R., Zurada, J.M. (eds.) ICAISC 2019. LNCS (LNAI), vol. 11508, pp. 358–372. Springer, Cham (2019). https://doi.org/10.1007/978-3-030-20912-4_34

13. Rutkowski, L.: Computational Intelligence. Methods and Techniques. Springer, Heidelberg (2008). https://doi.org/10.1007/978-3-540-76288-1

14. Liao, J., Liu, T., Liu, M., Wang, J., Wang, Y., Sun, H.: Multi-context integrated deep neural network model for next location prediction. IEEE Access **6**, 21980–21990 (2018)

15. Akdeniz, E., Egrioglu, E., Bas, E., Yolcu, U.: An ARMA type pi-sigma artificial neural network for nonlinear time series forecasting. J. Artif. Intell. Soft Comput. Res. **8**(2), 121–132 (2017)

16. Nobukawa, S., Nishimura, H., Yamanishi, T.: Pattern classification by spiking neural networks combining self-organized and reward-related spike-timing-dependent plasticity. J. Artif. Intell. Soft Comput. Res. **9**(4), 283–291 (2019)

17. de Souza, G.B., da Silva Santos, D.F., Pires, R.G., Marananil, A.N., Papa, J.P.: Deep features extraction for robust fingerprint spoofing attack detection. J. Artif. Intell. Soft Comput. Res. **9**(1), 41–49 (2019)

18. Bilski, J.: The UD RLS algorithm for training the feedforward neural networks. Int. J. Appl. Math. Comput. Sci. **15**(1), 101–109 (2005)

19. Rumelhart D.E., Hinton G.E., Williams R.J.: Learning internal representations by error propagation. In: Rumelhart, E., McCelland, J., (eds.) Parallel Distributed Processing, vol. 1, chap. 8. The MIT Press, Cambridge (1986)

20. Wilamowski, B.M., Yo, H.: Neural network learning without backpropagation. IEEE Trans. Neural Netw. **21**(11), 1793–1803 (2010)

21. Bilski, J., Kowalczyk, B., Marchlewska, A., Zurada, J.M.: Local Levenberg-Marquardt algorithm for learning feedforwad neural networks. J. Artif. Intell. Soft Comput. Res. **10**(4), 299–316 (2020). https://doi.org/10.2478/jaiscr-2020-0020

22. Żurada, J.: Introduction to Artificial Neural Systems. West Publishing Co., Eagan (1992)

23. Liu, J.-B., Zhao, J., Wang, S., Javaid, M., Cao, J.: On the topological properties of the certain neural networks. J. Artif. Intell. Soft Comput. Res. **8**(4), 257–268 (2018)

24. Shewalkar, A., Nyavanandi, D., Ludwig, S., A.: Performance evaluation of deep neural networks applied to speech recognition: RNN, LSTM AND GRU. J. Artif. Intell. Soft Comput. Res. **9**(4), 235–245 (2019)

25. Ludwig, S.A.: Applying a neural network ensemble to intrusion detection. J. Artif. Intell. Soft Comput. Res. **9**(3), 177–188 (2019)

26. Bilski, J., Litwiński, S., Smolag, J.: Parallel realisation of QR algorithm for neural networks learning. In: Rutkowski, L., Siekmann, J.H., Tadeusiewicz, R., Zadeh, L.A. (eds.) ICAISC 2004. LNCS (LNAI), vol. 3070, pp. 158–165. Springer, Heidelberg (2004). https://doi.org/10.1007/978-3-540-24844-6_19

27. Bilski, J., Smolag, J.: Parallel realisation of the recurrent RTRN neural network learning. In: Rutkowski, L., Tadeusiewicz, R., Zadeh, L.A., Zurada, J.M. (eds.) ICAISC 2008. LNCS (LNAI), vol. 5097, pp. 11–16. Springer, Heidelberg (2008). https://doi.org/10.1007/978-3-540-69731-2_2

28. Bilski, J., Smolag, J.: Parallel realisation of the recurrent Elman neural network learning. In: Rutkowski, L., Scherer, R., Tadeusiewicz, R., Zadeh, L.A., Zurada, J.M. (eds.) ICAISC 2010. LNCS (LNAI), vol. 6114, pp. 19–25. Springer, Heidelberg (2010). https://doi.org/10.1007/978-3-642-13232-2_3

29. Bilski, J., Smolag, J.: Parallel realisation of the recurrent multi layer perceptron learning. In: Rutkowski, L., Korytkowski, M., Scherer, R., Tadeusiewicz, R., Zadeh, L.A., Zurada, J.M. (eds.) ICAISC 2012. LNCS (LNAI), vol. 7267, pp. 12–20. Springer, Heidelberg (2012). https://doi.org/10.1007/978-3-642-29347-4_2

30. Bilski, J., Smolag, J.: Parallel realisation of the recurrent multi layer perceptron learning. In: Rutkowski, L., Korytkowski, M., Scherer, R., Tadeusiewicz, R., Zadeh, L.A., Zurada, J.M. (eds.) ICAISC 2012. LNCS (LNAI), vol. 7267, pp. 12–20. Springer, Heidelberg (2012). https://doi.org/10.1007/978-3-642-29347-4_2

31. Bilski, J., Wilamowski, B.M.: Parallel Levenberg-Marquardt algorithm without error backpropagation. In: Rutkowski, L., Korytkowski, M., Scherer, R., Tadeusiewicz, R., Zadeh, L.A., Zurada, J.M. (eds.) ICAISC 2017. LNCS (LNAI), vol. 10245, pp. 25–39. Springer, Cham (2017). https://doi.org/10.1007/978-3-319-59063-9_3

32. Smolag, J., Bilski, J.: A systolic array for fast learning of neural networks. In: Tenne, Y., Goh, C.K., (eds.) Proceedings of V Conference on Neural Networks and Soft Computing, Zakopane, pp. 754–758 (2000)

33. Smolag, J., Rutkowski, L., Bilski, J.: Systolic array for neural networks. In: Proceedings of IV Conference on Neural Networks and Their Applications, Zakopane, pp. 487–497 (1999)

34. Fahlman S.: Faster learning variations on backpropagation: an empirical study. In: Proceedings of Connectionist Models Summer School, Los Atos (1988)

35. Hagan, M.T., Menhaj, M.B.: Training feedforward networks with the Marquardt algorithm. IEEE Trans. Neural Netw. **5**(6), 989–993 (1994)

36. Riedmiller, M., Braun, H.: A direct method for faster backpropagation learning: the RPROP algorithm. In: IEEE International Conference on Neural Networks, San Francisco (1993)
37. Werbos, J.: Backpropagation through time: what it does and how to do it. In: Proceedings of the IEEE, vol. 78, p. 10 (1990)
38. Charalambous, C.: Conjugate gradient algorithm for efficient training of artificial neural networks. IEE Proc. G Circuits Devices Syst. **139**(3), 301–310 (1992)
39. Fletcher, R., Powell, M.J.D.: A rapidly convergent descent method for minimization. Comput. J. **6**, 163–168 (1963)
40. Fletcher, R., Reeves, C.M.: Function minimization by conjugate gradients. Comput. J. **7**, 149–154 (1964)
41. Nocedal, J., Wright, S.J.: Conjugate Gradient Methods in Numerical Optimization, pp. 497–528. Springer, New York (2006)
42. Polak, E.: Computational Methods in Optimization: A Unified Approach. Academic Press, New York (1971)
43. Navi, N.M.F., Ransing, M.R., Ransing, R.S.: An improved learning algorithm based on the conjugate gradient method for back propagation neural networks. Int. J. Comput. Inf. Eng. **2**(8), 2770–2774 (2008)
44. Jin, X.-B., Zhang, X.-Y., Huang, K., Geng, G.-G.: Stochastic conjugate gradient algorithm with variance reduction. IEEE Trans. Neural Netw. Learn. Syst. **30**(5), 1360–1369 (2019)
45. Rafajłowicz, E., Rafajłowicz, W.: Iterative learning in optimal control of linear dynamic processes. Int. J. Control **91**(7), 1522–1540 (2018)
46. Rafajłowicz, E., Rafajłowicz, W.: Iterative learning in repetitive optimal control of linear dynamic processes. In: Rutkowski, L., Korytkowski, M., Scherer, R., Tadeusiewicz, R., Zadeh, L.A., Zurada, J.M. (eds.) ICAISC 2016. LNCS (LNAI), vol. 9692, pp. 705–717. Springer, Cham (2016). https://doi.org/10.1007/978-3-319-39378-0_60
47. Jurewicz, P., Rafajłowicz, W., Reiner, J., Rafajłowicz, E.: Simulations for tuning a laser power control system of the cladding process. In: Saeed, K., Homenda, W. (eds.) CISIM 2016. LNCS, vol. 9842, pp. 218–229. Springer, Cham (2016). https://doi.org/10.1007/978-3-319-45378-1_20

Comparison of Text Classification Methods for Government Documents

Konrad A. Ciecierski$^{(\boxtimes)}$ and Mariusz Kamola

Research and Academic Computer Network, Warsaw, Poland
{konrad.ciecierski,mariusz.kamola}@nask.pl

Abstract. Classification of documents is a task which is rapidly gaining popularity in machine learning application. I can be used for such tasks as detection of spam, detection of phishing attempts or for detection of fake messages. One of the areas where document classification is of growing importance is automatic assessment of civic, legal and government documents. Using automated classification, a governmental institution might scan all its incoming correspondence, and automatically assign it to the proper departments. In this paper results of various classification approaches to classification of official documents are presented. Presented results are based upon classification of two sets of document: first, where given class of documents is derived from their common origin; and second, where class is determined by the common destination of the documents.

Keywords: Document classification · Machine learning · LSTM · Document summary

Introduction

The goal of this paper is to compare results of document classification obtained using different machine learning approaches used for two selected sets of government official documents. For testing purposes two sets of documents were chosen.

First set of documents consists of Parliamentary Interpellations. Those interpellations can be freely downloaded from https://www.sejm.gov.pl/Sejm7.nsf/interpelacje.xsp. In this dataset, documents are grouped according to the government institution/office they are addressed to. All documents in each class share the same destination, e.g. Minister of Finance.

Second corpus is obtained from Polish Journal of Laws (Dziennik Ustaw). Data from Polish Journal of Laws can be freely obtained from WWW site http://www.dziennikustaw.gov.pl. In this dataset documents are grouped according to the government institution that created them. In other words, all documents in a given class share the same government institution that is their source, e.g. Ministry of Agriculture.

The problem of text classification is long known in machine learning. There are various approaches and algorithm devised for this purpose. Classifiers focus

© Springer Nature Switzerland AG 2020
L. Rutkowski et al. (Eds.): ICAISC 2020, LNAI 12415, pp. 39–49, 2020.
https://doi.org/10.1007/978-3-030-61401-0_4

on words present in text or also on order of this words. Methods basing on statistics of occurrence, like for example TF-IDF, treat the text as a bag of words. Others like (Long Short-Term Memory) LSTM [5] or (Bidirectional Encoder Representations from Transformers) BERT [4] based, focus more on the word order in the text [1].

Statistical text classification models, termed here the classical ones, are known to support well documents of varying length [7]. This is why we tried them with the interpellation dataset as is. Naturally, the classical models can handle fixed length document excerpts in particular. We used this option in case of Journal of Laws dataset, using 150-word passages, either from the very beginning or from the middle of a document. This was done to provide similar training conditions as for neural network model, explained below, to make fairer performance comparisons of the two approaches (model contest not being the aim of this study, though).

In LSTM [5] based approach, classified were snippets of documents that were 150 words long and with class sizes ranging from 5,000 to 50,000 snippets each. In training of each model, all of the classes were of the same size. After the classifier for the snippets was trained, whole documents were classified. At this stage, from each document, a set of snippets was taken, classified, and the final class of the whole document derived from result of classification of all snippets. In this way, for each document, one obtains not only class that fits it the most, but also suggestions of other less fitting but potentially good classes.

1   Materials and Methods

The research was carried out on two datasets and generally with two modeling approaches. They get presented, respectively, in the following sections.

1.1   Document Corpora

The requirement that document classification methodology should be capable to deal with official correspondence of various kinds, heavily constrained our choice of training sets. Finally we decided to acquire and use two of them, i.e., inter-pellations and law acts. Both concern most civic activities, showing considerable diversity in size and style, and therefore are a good substitute of the to-be real input data.

These two sets, termed by computational linguists *corpora*, are set of documents, D_i, where a document, after some basic preprocessing, is a sequence of *text tokens*

$$D_i = (T_{ij}), \quad T_{ij} \in V \tag{1}$$

from a vocabulary V, i.e., a set of all tokens from the whole corpus. We take plain words as text tokens throughout this study, however, other approaches exist, i.e. using n-character substrings (a.k.a. n-grams).

Interpellations. This corpus contains nearly 166,000 interpellations made by Polish member of parliament (MP) in years 2011–2015. The corpus is publicly available online; it has been downloaded with custom script that used HTML parser [13]. Interpellation metadata are: MP's name, release date and the addressee. Average interpellation length is 320 words. The addressees include Polish ministries as well as the office of Prime Minister. We consider interpellation addressee to be the target for a classification models. Quite naturally, classes turned out heavily imbalanced in this corpus; however there are 14 classes accounting for almost all data and with at least 1,000 interpellations in each class. Therefore we decided to form a balanced training set of 14,000 documents from these classes, with class identifiers as follows: **Ministry of Administration and Digital Affairs, Ministry of Health, Ministry of Labour and Social Policy, Prime Minister, Ministry of Transport, Construction and Marine Economy, Ministry of Finance, Ministry of National Education, Ministry of Justice, Ministry of Environment, Ministry of Internal Affairs, Ministry of Economy, Ministry of Agriculture and Rural Development, Ministry of Foreign Affairs, Ministry of State Treasury.** The interpellations, although composed by MPs' offices, really differ in style; from professional and concise, to amateur and emotional. Probably, such diversity is intentional because their real addressees are not only top-level national institutions but also MPs' electorate in their constituencies. This is exactly why we consider them as valuable and adequate approximation of the popular correspondence addressed to administration at different levels and by diversity of people and institutions.

Polish Journal of Laws. This corpus contains legal acts created by polish government in years between 2012 and 2018. It contains 12,449 files in 83 categories. Due to the frequent changes in the structure of the polish government, many of those categories contain very small amounts of documents. For set of counts of documents in classes, the 75TH percentile is only 145 while the 90TH percentile is 470. Set of twelve most numerous classes is as follows: **Marshal of Polish Parliament, Ministry of Agriculture and Rural Development, Ministry of Defense, Ministry of Economy and Finance, Ministry of Environment, Ministry of Finance, Ministry of Health, Ministry of Internal Affairs, Ministry of Internal Affairs and Administration, Ministry of Justice, Prime Minister, The Cabinet.**

Lengths of documents in this dataset are characterized by following measures:

$$\mu = 5,664.19 \quad \sigma^2 = 398,617,920 \quad Q_1 = 487 \quad Q_2 = 1,293 \quad Q3 = 4,262$$

What is immediately noticeable is the huge variance in length of legal acts. Some acts are just dozens of word long while others have over hundred of pages.

1.2 Classification Approaches

Text classification models can be divided into two broad types: white-box and black-box ones. The earlier allow easy explanation of reasons that caused a text to be classified in a particular way, but often perform inferior to black-box ones. The latter offer unprecedented accuracy if much of time-invariant data is available. Their major drawback, despite current efforts, is opacity. We investigated models of both types for available data; their details are presented below.

White-Box Models. As the classification models of our interest require to represent a document as fixed length vector of digits instead of variable length sequence of tokens, we need to perform adequate conversions. They are common for all models considered, but they can be done in many ways. The common idea is to represent a document as a vector $\mathbf{w}$ of size equal to $|V|$. Each element w_k from $\mathbf{w}$ corresponds to a vocabulary word and contains some measure of this word appearance in the document. The considered measures are:

- binary count of w_k appearance in D_i—w_i is set to one if the corresponding word appears in the document at least once;
- integer count of w_k appearance in D_i—w_i is set to the count of word appearances in the document;
- tf-idf index for w_i—proportional to the count of word appearances in the document, and inversely proportional to frequency of documents containing that word in the corpus [11];

Apart from the above, classical vectorization schemes, we developed and tested the mean of embeddings for a set of words in a document. With such approach, we get document vector representation equal the size of embedding used. Specifically nkjp+wiki-forms-all-100-skipg-hs was adopted for this purpose [12], available from http://dsmodels.nlp.ipipan.waw.pl/.

Prior to vectorization, all documents underwent a standard tokenization procedure, i.e. word extraction and lowercase conversion, punctuation and stopwords (most frequent words) removal. Moreover, in case of inflective languages, like Polish, many forms of the same word appear in V as unrelated entries. To address this unnecessary vocabulary swell, we performed word sense disambiguation, as an option. We used an online tool, WoSeDon [8], which brought all words in text to their basic form. Most probable word senses were chosen by this tool in case of homonymy.

Once vectorized, a document was classified independently by two cornerstone methods: Naive Bayes (NB) and Logistic Regression (LR) [7,11]. Naive Bayes is a generative method, i.e. it tries to reconstruct the model that will *generate* observed samples with highest probability, whereas LR's goal is to identify features (elements of $\mathbf{w}$) that distinguish the classes most. In other words, LR tries do *describe* efficiently differences between classes in terms of selected document features.

Despite conceptual differences, both methods compute similarity scores for each target class, for a given document. And both methods allow easy inspection of document features responsible for such a score. Therefore, they can provide useful information about reasons for classification success or failure.

Black-Box Models. Black-box models are based upon the deep recurrent neural networks [6]. Here one classifies the snippets of text taken from documents. In approach presented in this paper snippets of 150 continuous words were used. During training, the network was learning to classify each of the snippets to the class of the file the snippet was taken from. Textual information prior to being fed into the neural network, has to be transformed into the numerical format. For this, computed embeddings for Polish Language were used. For conversion of textual data in case of neural network based approach, the **nkjp+wiki-forms-all-300-skipg-ns** embedding [12] from http://dsmodels.nlp.ipipan.waw.pl/ was used [9]. This embedding was created from the National Corpus of Polish Language and polish Wikipedia [3] using skipgrams [9]. It maps words and their forms to the $\mathbb{R}^{300}$ space. In this manner a snippet that is 150 words long is mapped to a tensor S of size $(150, 300)$ i.e. $S \in \mathbb{R}^{150,300}$.

Architecture of the network used for training is shown in Fig. 1. The batch is containing n snippets, where each snippet has 150 words. Now, as each word is mapped to $\mathbb{R}^{300}$ space, the size of the input batch is $(n, 150, 300)$.

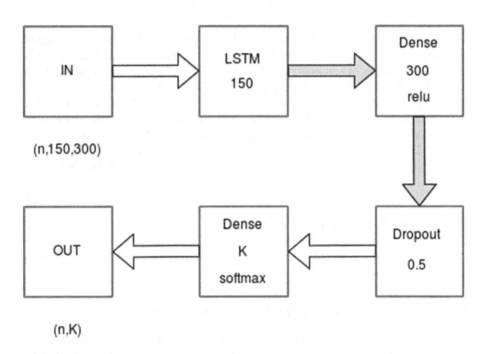

Fig. 1. Network architecture

The input fed into the network is passed to the LSTM recurrent layer [5] with internal data representation of size 150. While size of the internal representation of the LSTM layer equals here the snippet size, it is not a requirement, and those sizes may differ. Out of the last element of the LSTM layer one obtains tensor of size $(n, 150)$ which after batch normalization – represented by grey arrow – is passed to a dense layer. This layer has 300 output neurons with relu [10] activation function. Output from dense layer having size $(n, 300)$ is then put through another batch normalization and through the dropout layer. The dropout layer with probability 50% zeroes any cell of the tensor that passes through it. Finally, after dropout regularization layer [14], the final dense layer has as many output neurons as there are classes in the dataset. Those neurons by means of the softmax [2] activation function yields the id of the class for each snippet in the input. Training has been done using classes of equal size. In various approaches this size varied from 5000 to 50 000 distinct snippets.

After the classifier has been trained, it can be used for classification of whole documents. From given document that is to be classified into one on n classes, the pool of $k \leq 100$ snippets is gathered. Assuming that file has m words and the length of the snippet is sl, then step between beginning offsets of consecutive gathered snippets is given as

$$step = max(5, \lfloor \frac{m - sl}{100 - 1} \rfloor)$$

The goal is to gather a 100 snippets for the classification pool. In case of small files, the pool might be smaller to maintain the distance of minimum 5 words between beginnings of consecutive snippets. Snippets in pool are classified, with cnt_j being the count of snippets classified to class j and $\sum_{j=1}^{n} cnt_j = k$. Counts are sorted in reversed order, so that $cnt_{s_1} \geq cnt_{s_2} \geq \cdots \geq cnt_{s_n}$. Class with index s_1 is then denoted as $C1$ and is returned as best fitting class for the document. Additionally returned are also classes with indexes s_2 and s_3 as alternative best choices, Those classes are identified as $C2$ and $C3$ respectively. With classes returned are also likelihoods $\frac{cnt_{s_1}}{k}$, $\frac{cnt_{s_2}}{k}$ and $\frac{cnt_{s_3}}{k}$. of given document belonging to each of returned classes.

2   Evaluation and Interpretation

Models presented in Subsect. 1.2 have been tested for classification of data described in Subsect. 1.1. Detailed numerical results are provided below.

2.1   Naive Bayes and Logistic Regression Results

Model training and classification experiments were performed in each case on a input data set with equal number of samples in each class. Those input data were split at random into training, development and test sets of predefined sizes. The development set was used to examine impact of model parameters, and the test set was used for final evaluation of model performance. As the input data were always balanced across document classess, there was no need to resort to more complex performance measures than classification accuracy, i.e. the ratio of correctly classified documents to the total number of test documents.

Table 1. Classification accuracy for NB model (upright typeface) and for LR model (italics), for interpellation corpus and different combinations of text preprocessing and vectorization methods.

	Vectorization			
	Binary	Sum	tf-idf	Embedding
Raw text	0.724	0.761		
	0.812	*0.819*	*0.822*	*0.636*
Disambiguated text	0.706	0.750		
	0.806	*0.814*	*0.823*	*0.619*

Table 2. Keywords with biggest positive (+) and negative (−) impact on document classification to selected classes, LR model for disambiguated texts of interpellations, with tf-idf vectorization. English translation in italics, with UK counterparts for acronyms of Polish institutions.

class	keywords
1	+zabytek +żołnierz +uczelnia +sportowy +narodowy +dziedzictwo +sport +kultura +wojskowy +pani
	+monument +soldier +university +sports +national +heritage +sport +culture +military +Mrs.
2	+pielęgniarka +lekarz +leczniczy +nfz +leczenie +pacjent +medyczny +szpital +lek +zdrowie
	+nurse +doctor +therapeutic +NHS +therapy +patient +medical +hospital +medicine +health
3	+zus +rodzina +dziecko +świadczenie +emerytura +osoba +pracodawca +emerytalny +społeczny +praca
	+NI +family +child +benefit +pension +person +employer +retirement +social +labour
4	+łączyć +rad +skw +sąużba -2013 -ministerstwo +prezes +rząd -minister +premier
	+connect +radium +MI5 +service -2013 -ministry +president +government -minister +PM

Results for interpellation classification are provided in Table 1, with different typeface for NB and LR models. NB model was run only with binary and summation vectorization methods as it is not customary to combine it with the other ones [7]. It turns out that, in line with common opinion, LR performs considerably better in sense of classification accuracy. Embedding based vectorization is the only exception, consistently inferior to other approaches.

White-box models make it possible to have an insight on their operation; Table 2 presents words that influence classification most, in the case of best configuration (LR for disambiguated text with tf-idf vectorization). Most of the keywords are reasonably related to the class, especially in case of the Minister of

Health (line 2) and Minister of Labour and Social Policy (line 3). Texts addressed to PM (line 4) are general, so it is rather more effective to indicate the keywords that should *not* appear in a document to consider it to belong to this class. Words *ministry* and *minister* are certainly of this type.

All the other words observed in Table 2 reveal weaknesses of the processing scheme and the model. First, disambiguation process may go wrong, cf. *radium* keyword in line 4, which is a homonym in Polish and actually should be identified as *council*. Next, *2013* (line 4) is an artefact of statistical or organizational nature: either there were unusually few interpellations to PM in year 2013 or ministries were undergoing some rearrangements that year. Anyhow, year numbers should not be considered important by the classification models. Likewise, keywords for texts addressed to Minister of Administration and Digital Affairs (line 1) appear affect many topics that do not match any of the document classes, and have gone to class 1. This class is therefore a sort of a sink, a class of last resort if no better match can be found. This situation, having a sink class is an intended one. Without such approach, the number of classes selected from the corpus would have to be approximately twice as big which would result in the definitely inferior performance.

Table 3. Classification accuracy for LR model, for Polish Journal of Laws corpus, for different pieces of Laws used as model input (row-wise), and for different assumed class cardinalities used in classifications (column-wise). Binary vectorization on original text was applied.

Sample content	Cardinality of samples in classes		
	300	400	500
(T_{ij}), $j \in< 1, 150 >$	A: 0.994	C: 0.984	E: 1.000
(T_{ij}), $j \in< 201, 350 >$	B: 0.971	D: 0.975	F: 0.988

Table 3 provides classification accuracies when fixed-length passages from Journal of Laws documents were used for training. Note that the assumed number of training samples for each class (300, 400 and 500) implied that the number of classes were different in each configuration. This is because there were not enough documents with length of 150 and 350 (cf. lines 1 and 2, respectively) to satisfy cardinality constraint. An so, there were 11 classes in configuration A, 8 in configuration B&C, 6 in D and only 5 in E&F.

The model performs very well and shows predictable loss of accuracy in configurations with higher number of target classes. Also, operating on non-initial document words (line 2) results in performance drop. This is natural as well because the initial words usually contain the issuer name.

2.2   Results Obtained Using LSTM Network

Neural network model described in Subsect. 1.2 have been tested for classification of data described in Subsect. 1.1. For each dataset, four classifiers were trained, with class size being 5000, 10000, 25000 and 50000 unique snippets. Assuming that desired class size is nc then for each class c, snippets for training, validation and test were gathered in following way.

1. Set of files FS from class c is split into three disjoint sets: FS_{TR}, FS_{VL}, FS_{TS} in proportions 80:10:10
2. Count of training, validating and testing snippets is obtained as follows:
   $nc_{train} = \lfloor 0.8 * nc \rfloor$, $nc_{validate} = \lfloor 0.5 * (nc - nc_{train}) \rfloor$,
   $nc_{test} = nc - nc_{train} - nc_{validate}$
3. nc_{train} unique training snippets are randomly gathered from FS_{TR}
4. $nc_{validate}$ unique validating snippets are randomly gathered from FS_{VL}
5. nc_{test} unique test snippets are randomly gathered from FS_{TS}

For uniqueness, each snippet is identified by the ordered pair $(file\_id, offset)$. $file\_id$ is the unique identifier of each file and $offset$ is the position from which snippet has been taken from file.

Accuracy of classification done for test documents from interpellation corpus is shown in Table 4. Looking only at the class of the 1st choice one can see that the results are relatively good. They range from accuracy of 0.737 when class size is small i.e. 5,000, to above 0.8 for classes with 25,000 or more snippets.

Table 4. Classification accuracy for LSTM based model, for interpellation corpus.

True class equals	Number of snippets in class			
	5 000	10 000	25 000	50 000
$C1$	0,737	0,787	0,802	0,805
$C1$ or $C2$	0,830	0,885	0,890	0,901
$C1$ or $C2$ or $C3$	0,870	0,912	0,914	0,922

The quality of classification increases with increase of class size. Already with class size 25 000, for over 90% of test documents, their true class is among the two best classes returned by the classifier.

Accuracy of classification done for test documents from Polish Journal of Laws corpus is shown in Table 5. One can see that when taking into account only the class of the 1st choice – i.e. class obtained for majority of snippets taken from given document – the results are very good. They range from accuracy of 0.87 when class size is 5,000, to 0.92 for classes with 25,000 snippets.

One can observe that quality of classification increases with increase of class size up to 25 000 snippets per class. After this point no further increase in accuracy is observed. When one is to take into account also classes returned as 2nd or even 3rd choice, the quality is even better. With class size 50 000, for 98% of test documents, their true class is among the two best classes returned by the classifier.

Table 5. Classification accuracy for LSTM based model, for Polish Journal of Laws corpus.

True class equals	Number of snippets in class			
	5 000	10 000	25 000	50 000
$C1$	0,871	0,901	0,921	0,920
$C1$ or $C2$	0,958	0,978	0,978	0,978
$C1$ or $C2$ or $C3$	0,979	0,985	0,986	0,990

3   Conclusions

While for the black-box i.e. neural network based models, there is no explanation why given class has been chosen for given document, one does obtain not only the class deemed best fitting but also other classes that might be of alternative choice. This gives essential boost because as in the case of Journal of Laws corpus the true class equals $C1$ for 92% of test documents, it equals $C1$ or $C2$ for 98% of test documents. In case of interpellation corpus, this increase in accuracy is from 81% to 90%.

Interpretation of increase in accuracy when class $C2$ is also considered.

For most of the documents, the likelihood of the $C1$ class is clearly the biggest one and decision about classification is clear. It is also correct one for 92% of documents from the Journal of Laws corpus and 81% of documents from the interpellation corpus. In some cases, the document deals with matters that are subject of concern for two ministries. For example the Ministry of Finance and Ministry of Health are clearly both applicable when document deals with financing of public health system. For such documents, one finds that likelihood of $C1$ and $C2$ is similar and usually around 0.4. Those documents are responsible for increase in accuracy when not only $C1$ class but also $C2$ class is considered.

In conclusion, results obtained using Logistic Regression are better then those obtained using LSTM network, 0.823 to 0.805 for interpellation corpus, and 0.988 to 0.920 for Journal of Laws. Above has been confirmed using Wilcoxon signed-rank test [15] with p-value below 0.05.

While one may of course compare results provided by both approaches, it is important to pinpoint differences in methodologies. White-box models when used with word embeddings, i.e. representation of text solely used by the black-box models, provide results much inferior to those obtained from LSTM networks.

Neural network based classification uses ensembles of classification results obtained for snippets taken throughout the document. The white-box model (see Table 3) looks only at first 150 words taken from the document or at 150 words taken starting with 201ST word. This is especially important distinction as in Journal o Laws corpus, the name of the institution is given in plain form in the heading of the document. Logistic Regression focuses here more on key words present in the heading of document while neural network makes its decision basing upon context of the whole document. The number of classes used for classifications shown in Table 3 is also not constant, while black-box model always uses all twelve classes.

LSTM comprehensive nature of operation is exactly the reason we do not look at studied models as competitors but as complements. LSTM model is designed to carry out main classification task. Complementary role of white-box models is to provide hints about reasons for false classification results, related to document content. Those detected so far are: person names, sex-related forms of titles and adjectives, and year numbers. These artefacts have nothing to do with the matter of a document and should be removed or normalized in preprocessing phase for LSTM operation. It may result in apparent accuracy drop, but also it would make the model more robust in longer term, which is usually a concern for neural network model creators.

References

1. Aggarwal, C.C., Zhai, C.: A survey of text classification algorithms. In: Aggarwal, C.C., Zhai, C. (eds.) Mining Text Data, pp. 163–222. Springer, Boston (2012). https://doi.org/10.1007/978-1-4614-3223-4_6
2. Bishop, C.M.: Pattern Recognition and Machine Learning. Information Science and Statistics. Springer, New York (2006)
3. Denoyer, L., Gallinari, P.: The wikipedia XML corpus. In: Fuhr, N., Lalmas, M., Trotman, A. (eds.) INEX 2006. LNCS, vol. 4518, pp. 12–19. Springer, Heidelberg (2007). https://doi.org/10.1007/978-3-540-73888-6_2
4. Devlin, J., Chang, M.W., Lee, K., Toutanova, K.: BERT: pre-training of deep bidirectional transformers for language understanding. arXiv preprint arXiv:1810.04805 (2018)
5. Gers, F.A., Schmidhuber, J., Cummins, F.: Learning to forget: Continual prediction with LSTM (1999)
6. Goodfellow, I., Bengio, Y., Courville, A.: Deep Learning. MIT Press, Cambridge (2016)
7. Jurafsky, D., Martin, J.H.: Speech and Language Processing, 2nd edn. Prentice-Hall Inc, Upper Saddle River (2009)
8. Kędzia, P., Piasecki, M., Orlińska, M.: WoSeDon (2016). http://hdl.handle.net/11321/290. CLARIN-PL digital repository
9. Levy, O., Goldberg, Y.: Dependency-based word embeddings. In: Proceedings of the 52nd Annual Meeting of the Association for Computational Linguistics (Short Papers), vol. 2, pp. 302–308 (2014)
10. Nair, V., Hinton, G.E.: Rectified linear units improve restricted boltzmann machines. In: Proceedings of the 27th International Conference on Machine Learning (ICML 2010), pp. 807–814 (2010)
11. Pedregosa, F., et al.: Scikit-learn: machine learning in python. J. Mach. Learn. Res. **12**, 2825–2830 (2011)
12. Rehurek, R., Sojka, P.: Software framework for topic modelling with large corpora. In: Proceedings of the LREC 2010 Workshop on New Challenges for NLP Frameworks. CiteSeer (2010)
13. Richardson, L.: Beautiful soup documentation (2007)
14. Srivastava, N., Hinton, G., Krizhevsky, A., Sutskever, I., Salakhutdinov, R.: Dropout: a simple way to prevent neural networks from overfitting. J. Mach. Learn. Res. **15**(1), 1929–1958 (2014)
15. Wilcoxon, F., Katti, S., Wilcox, R.A.: Critical values and probability levels for the wilcoxon rank sum test and the wilcoxon signed rank test. Selected Tables in Mathematical Statistics, vol. 1, pp. 171–259 (1970)

DeepCloud: An Investigation of Geostationary Satellite Imagery Frame Interpolation for Improved Temporal Resolution

Luigi Freitas Cruz[1]([⊠]) [iD], Priscila Tiemi Maeda Saito[1,2] [iD],
and Pedro Henrique Bugatti[1] [iD]

[1] Department of Computing, Federal University of Technology - Paraná, Cornélio Procópio, Brazil
[2] Institute of Computing, University of Campinas, Campinas, Brazil
luigicruz@alunos.utfpr.edu.br, {psaito,pbugatti}@utfpr.edu.br

Abstract. Satellite imagery is a crucial product for today's weather forecasts. Worldwide, billions of dollars are invested annually on state-of-the-art satellites to produce imagery with better resolution and more spectral channels. This paper proposes a deep-learning methodology to enhance the temporal resolution of multi-spectral weather products from already deployed geostationary spacecraft (GOES or Himawari). Our method can dramatically improve the smoothness of an animation made with a series of pictures from an area of interest (Hurricanes, Tropical Storms, or Polar Jet Streams or Cold Fronts) while maintaining a good level of detail. To do so, we applied the transfer learning technique to fine-tune an already published frame interpolation neural network with real satellite weather imagery. By doing so, our technique can synthesize an intermediate frame of two adjacent frames scanned at the standard image interval. We also investigated the effects of using multiple combinations of spectral channels (e.g. Visible, True-Color, and Infrared) to test and train this network. The proposed temporal improvement can be helpful for weather forecasters to recognize atmospheric trends faster and more precisely. Moreover, our method does not require space hardware modifications thus being a safe and cost-effective solution.

Keywords: Deep learning · Weather · Satellites · Frame interpolation · Hurricanes

1 Introduction

Satellite imagery generated by weather satellites is one of the most crucial tools used by meteorologists. These images help the forecaster to accurately identify

This research has been supported by grants from CNPq (grants #431668/2016-7, #422811/2016-5), CAPES, Araucária Foundation, SETI and UTFPR.

atmospheric trends. The data generated by spacecraft are also fed into meteorological models that run daily on supercomputers to predict atmospheric interactions before they happen. Particularly in the last decade, weather models are becoming more and more accurate. All of these methods are decisive to predict natural disasters in advance to prevent loss of life.

Since investments in spacecraft are often expensive, our method aims to contribute with improved temporal resolution imagery generated by current satellites without expensive hardware modifications. This method can also be deployed at locations with limited data bandwidth available (e.g. islands or sub-developed countries).

In this investigation, we propose a methodology, called DeepCloud, based on the Depth-Aware Video Frame Interpolation (DAIN) model proposed by [1] to interpolate and consequently increase the temporal resolution of weather imagery generated by geostationary satellites. We also compared interpolation accuracies produced by models trained with three different spectral channels: Visible (Red), True-Color (RGB), and Infrared (Low-Level Water Vapor). To streamline the data collection and processing, we used imagery from a single source, the Geostationary Operational Environmental Satellite. These spacecraft are operated by the United States government agency called National Oceanic and Atmospheric Administration (NOAA).

This paper is structured as follows. In Sect. 2, we introduce the concepts necessary to understand our methodology. In Sect. 3, we present our methodology with a description of the dataset used for training and the approach used by our experiments. Data obtained from the experimental evaluation are discussed in Sect. 4. Finally, our conclusions are presented in Sect. 5.

2 Background

The first purpose-built geostationary orbit weather satellite called GOES-1 was launched by NASA in 1975. Since its introduction, the data collected by this new category of satellites has become an essential tool for weather forecasts. It provides near real-time imagery of one-third of the Earth's surface from a relatively fixed point constantly [5].

The main type of data collected by a weather satellite is photographic imagery. This data is organized in multi-spectral bands ranging from visible light to infrared. Each of these bands is tuned for a range of desirable features, for example, CO_2 on upper-infrared, and Snow/Ice on near-infrared [3]. Given its operational importance, the spacecraft imager has received sizable improvements since the first generation. These modifications are improved temporal/spatial resolution, increased number of spectral bands, and decrease of time between scans.

The current generation of geostationary orbit satellites developed by Lockheed Martin in a contract for NOAA cost in total $11.4 billion US dollars for the entire series [7]. These two satellites are equipped with the Advanced Baseline Imager capable of producing a full-disk image of one-third of the planet every

10 min while providing 16 spectral bands. This sensor can also be programmed manually to improve the temporal resolution to up to 30 s for a limited number of regional weather events [4].

3   Proposed Methodology

In this paper, we propose a methodology, called DeepCloud, based on the Depth-Aware Video Frame Interpolation (DAIN) model proposed by [1] to interpolate and consequently increase the temporal resolution of weather imagery generated by geostationary satellites.

Our proposed methodology (DeepCloud) increases the temporal resolution of weather images obtained from geostationary satellites. We modified the frame interpolation model DAIN to be used with multi-spectral geostationary satellite imagery. To do so, we interpolated three consecutive image samples (i.e. triplets) modifying the input of the Depth-Aware Video Frame Interpolation Network (DAIN) [1] that is a state-of-the-art method. We chose DAIN because this network obtained interpolations with better temporal coherence in high-frequency areas by cross-referencing the data of multiple sub-networks within the model: Depth Estimation, Context Extraction, Kernel Estimation, and Flow Estimation.

This network was originally built to generate a smoother video by increasing the temporal resolution with inter-frame interpolation. As the input in the training process, the network receives the first and last frame of the triplet and compares the predicted middle-ground with the inner frame of the triplet.

To generate the increased temporal resolution animation, the trained model receives an array of consecutive frames with equivalent intervals. After this, the model takes a pair of frames and infer the middle-frame. This can be done repeatedly until exhaustion.

To accomplish our goal with this network, we applied a fine-tuning to the original pre-trained model to improve accuracy with our geostationary satellite weather imagery samples. This is a crucial step because the network was originally trained to be used with day-to-day videos from the internet and not with satellite imagery.

The performance of each fine-tuned model was measured by running interpolation tests against each spectral channel set of triplets. The original DAIN model was also tested as a baseline. Figure 1 illustrates the steps of our proposed methodology.

3.1   Dataset Description

The dataset for this experiment is constituted of a set of three consecutive image samples also called triplets. Each sample is a cropped rectangle from a full-disk image featuring one-third of the Earth's surface collected from geostationary orbit by the GOES-16 spacecraft (Fig. 2). This state-of-the-art satellite generates

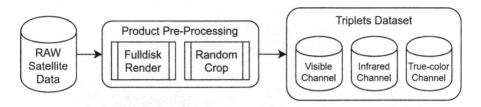

Fig. 1. An illustration of the dataset pre-processing pipeline. In the pre-processing block, the full-disk render and random crop products are represented by Figs. 2 and 3, respectively.

one full-disk image every 10 min. Therefore, each triplet represents a three-frame animation of 30 min.

The full-disk images produced by this satellite are also available in different light spectral ranges (Fig. 3). To take advantage of this fact, we created three different sets of triplets, each one with a different spectral range: Visible (Red), True-Color (RGB), and Infrared (Low-Level Water Vapor). The position and time of each triplet are coherent between all sets with the only difference being the spectral channel of each.

A free open-source Python tool called SatPy [6] was used to download and process the brute satellite data previously downloaded from the internet. The dataset pre-processing pipeline is further explained in Fig. 1. The final dataset is composed of six days worth of samples collected from random dates along with the 2019 summer in the northern hemisphere. We used 80% of the data for training and the rest for validation.

3.2 Implementation Details

The DAIN model was built and trained to be used with RGB images. A sizable amount of refactoring would be necessary to adapt the network to work with grayscale satellite imagery. The sub-networks employed would also need to be modified and retrained. This process would take multiple weeks of computing time given the size and complexity of the DAIN model with both PWCNet [8] and MegaDepth [2] sub-networks.

Hence, as an alternative method, we converted the grayscale pictures into a three-channel image fully compatible with the existing model. By picking this method, a single network can be used to process both grayscale and color products. Therefore, the interpolation workflow is greatly simplified reducing the computing time necessary for training.

We used two types of channel conversions. The primary (RRR) method copies the original grayscale image into the RGB channels. The secondary (RXX) method copies the original channel into the first layer and leaves the rest black. To evaluate the efficiency of each method, we processed each set of triplets with both aforementioned conversion techniques.

Fig. 2. Red channel full-disk product before being cropped into smaller rectangles. Produced by GOES-16 spacecraft with the Advanced Baseline Imager on september 16, 2019. The Hurricane Dorian is visible near the coast of Florida, USA.

3.3 Scenarios

As a pre-requisite to initiate the training process with the datasets mentioned in the last subsection, we downloaded the provided checkpoint that was trained until exhaustion with the Vimeo90k dataset [9]. This dataset consists of 89,800 animations compiled from videos containing a myriad of environments. This served as a starting point for the fine-tuning with the weather data.

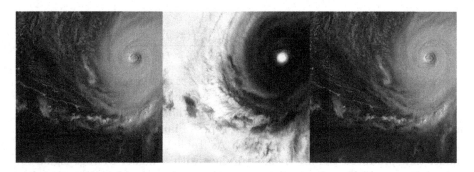

Fig. 3. An illustration of visual differences between spectral channels. The three images were collected at the same place and time. Visible (left), infrared (center), and true-color (right).

The script to train this model was provided by the authors of the original paper [1]. This code was configured with the initial checkpoint previously downloaded. The initial learning rate was set to $lr = 1e-05$. A checkpoint was created automatically every time the validation accuracy decreased.

After completion, three different checkpoints were generated. Each of those trained with only one dataset containing a single light spectrum. As a result, we can infer how the light spectrum channel can change the interpolation accuracy while being used with different channels than originally trained.

We used a batch size of one image with the sample size being hard-coded by the DAIN model at 256 by 256 pixels. All networks were trained until exhaustion with the automatic learning rate optimizer that decreases the value when the validation loss starts to increase after four epochs. The hardware used to compute the networks for this experiment was an Nvidia GTX 1070 Ti graphics processing unit. The entire training process took approximately 96 h to complete.

4   Results and Discussion

To evaluate our proposed methodology under different conditions and against the state-of-the-art method we used the signal-to-noise ratio (SNR) metric. It compares the level of the desired signal (e.g. ground-truth images) to the level of background noise (obtained interpolated images). Thus, it characterizes the image quality generated by an interpolation method, since it shows the relationship between the real image and the estimated one (i.e. indicates how strong the noise corrupted the original image). As a rule of thumb, the higher the SNR the better the method. SNR is formally defined by Eq. 1.

$$SNR = \frac{\sum_{x=0}^{M-1} \sum_{y=0}^{N-1} \hat{f}(x,y)^2}{\sum_{x=0}^{M-1} \sum_{y=0}^{N-1} [f(x,y) - \hat{f}(x,y)]^2} \tag{1}$$

where M and N are the number of pixels in axes x and y, respectively; f is the original image (ground-truth); and $\hat{f}$ comprises the interpolated image.

In Table 1, we compared our proposed methodology against the DAIN method. To do so, we used three different types of input: visible image, infrared image, and true-color image (see Fig. 3). As Table 1 illustrates, the fine-tuned model that produced the interpolated frames with a higher average signal-to-noise ratio was the True-Color. This model was fine-tuned with the set of triplets constituted of true-color weather images. The performance was also higher than the DAIN method (baseline literature) on two occasions. Furthermore, the True-Color model had the best signal-to-noise ratio (SNR) average between all tests.

These results also indicate that no single channel fine-tuned model performed the best. This happened even when they were fed with the same channel that they were trained with. This indicates that our method of training a colored RGB network with grayscale images is sub-optimal.

Table 1. Average signal-to-noise ratio obtained by each combination of model and test dataset. The model that produced the best SNR for each test is highlighted in bold.

Models	Fine-tuned models – interpolation			
	Our visible	Our infrared	Our true-color	DAIN
Visible	29.08	28.74	**29.12**	**29.12**
Infrared	34.01	33.79	**34.02**	33.99
True-Color	27.08	26.48	**27.17**	26.94

The Violin Plot (Fig. 4) illustrates the normalized Interpolation Error. This is another form of measuring the frame interpolation performance of each trained model. Here, we can notice a similar pattern presented by the signal-to-noise ratio corroborating our findings. The probability density provided by this plot also shows that the True-Color model presented one of the lowest probability variances among the tested models.

We also correlated the accuracy of both grayscale conversion methods. As mentioned in Sect. 3, every test-set was duplicated and processed by a different method. As shown in Fig. 5, the RXX technique yielded the best result. The average signal-to-noise ratio was up to 4.5 dB higher and the Interpolation Error was 3.26 less than the RRR method.

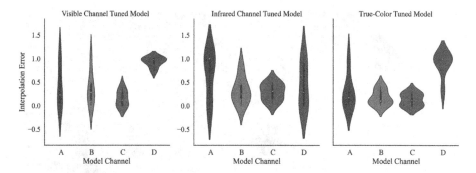

Fig. 4. A set of Violin plots showing the interpolation error distribution between the four models: baseline (A), visible (B), true-color (C), and infrared (D).

By visually inspecting the RRR interpolated frames, as shown in Fig. 6, we can notice a brightness overshooting on high contrast areas when a fast transition happens. We think this is some kind of constructive interference generated by the lack of color nuances introduced by copying the same layer three times to fill all color channels. This ghosting was non-existent on RXX frames, corroborating their better efficiency discussed above.

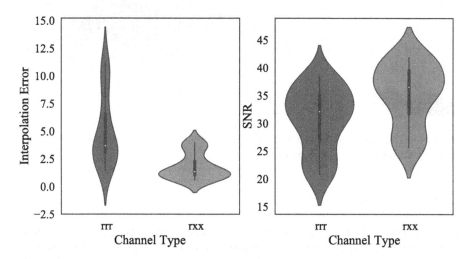

Fig. 5. Violin plot representing the interpolation error (left) and the signal-to-noise ratio (right) of both grayscale representation methods.

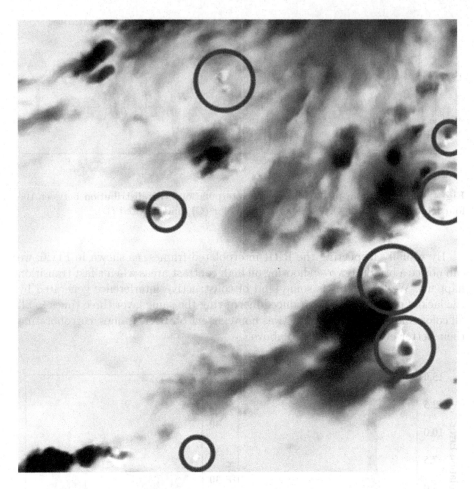

Fig. 6. Overshooting artifacts (highlighted with blue circles) supposedly created by the RRR grayscale conversion method.

5   Conclusions

In this paper, we successfully modified a frame interpolation model DAIN to be used with multi-spectral geostationary satellite imagery instead of internet videos as it was originally built for. To do so, we fine-tuned a pre-trained neural network with satellite imagery. This technique has produced acceptable results and important insights for future research.

We also documented the limitations of a method to train a colored network using converted grayscale pictures. Unveiled the most suitable technique to convert a grayscale image to be used with a model that only accepts pictures with colored images with three spectral channels.

As future work, we intend to fine-tune the MegaDepth depth estimation sub-network with real satellite imagery. By doing this, we expect a sizable improvement of the overall network performance.

References

1. Bao, W., Lai, W.S., Ma, C., Zhang, X., Gao, Z., Yang, M.H.: Depth-aware video frame interpolation. In: IEEE Conference on Computer Vision and Pattern Recognition (2019)
2. Li, Z., Snavely, N.: MegaDepth: learning single-view depth prediction from internet photos. In: Computer Vision and Pattern Recognition (2018)
3. NASA/NOAA: ABI bands table. https://www.goes-r.gov/spacesegment/ABI-tech-summary.html
4. NASA/NOAA: Instruments: advanced baseline imager (ABI). https://www.goes-r.gov/spacesegment/abi.html
5. NASA/NOAA: The road to modern weather satellites: NOAA and NASA celebrate 60 years of America in space|NOAA national environmental satellite, data, and information service (NESDIS). https://www.nesdis.noaa.gov/content/road-modern-weather-satellites-noaa-and-nasa-celebrate-60-years-america-space
6. Raspaud, M., et al.: Software pytroll/satpy: version 0.19.1 (2020). https://doi.org/10.5281/zenodo.3604355
7. SpaceNews Editor: NOAA tells congress GOES R cost nearly double previous estimate (2004). https://spacenews.com/noaa-tells-congress-goes-r-cost-nearly-double-previous-estimate/
8. Sun, D., Yang, X., Liu, M.Y., Kautz, J.: PWC-Net: CNNs for optical flow using pyramid, warping, and cost volume. In: Computer Vision and Pattern Recognition (2018)
9. Xue, T., Chen, B., Wu, J., Wei, D., Freeman, W.T.: Video enhancement with task-oriented flow. Int. J. Comput. Vision 127(8), 1106–1125 (2019)

Are Direct Links Necessary in Random Vector Functional Link Networks for Regression?

Grzegorz Dudek$^{(\boxtimes)}$ ⓘ

Electrical Engineering Faculty, Czestochowa University of Technology,
Czestochowa, Poland
dudek@el.pcz.czest.pl

Abstract. A random vector functional link network (RVFL) is widely used as a universal approximator for classification and regression problems. The big advantage of RVFL is fast training without backpropagation. This is because the weights and biases of hidden nodes are selected randomly and stay untrained. Recently, alternative architectures with randomized learning are developed which differ from RVFL in that they have no direct links and a bias term in the output layer. In this study, we investigate the effect of direct links and output node bias on the regression performance of RVFL. For generating random parameters of hidden nodes we use the classical method and two new methods recently proposed in the literature. We test the RVFL performance on several function approximation problems with target functions of different nature: nonlinear, nonlinear with strong fluctuations, nonlinear with linear component and linear. Surprisingly, we found that the direct links and output node bias do not play an important role in improving RVFL accuracy for typical nonlinear regression problems.

Keywords: Random vector functional link network · Neural networks with random hidden nodes · Randomized learning algorithms

1 Introduction

A random vector functional link network (RVFL) is a type of feedforward neural network (FNN) with a single hidden layer and direct links between input and output layers. Unlike typical FNN, in RVFL the weights and biases of the hidden nodes are selected randomly and stay fixed. The only parameters which are learned are weights and biases of the output layer. Due to randomization in RVFL we can avoid complicated and time-consuming gradient descent methods for solving the optimization problem which is non-convex in typical FNNs. It is commonly known that the gradient learning methods have many drawbacks such as sensitivity to initial values of parameters, convergence to local minima,

Supported by Grant 2017/27/B/ST6/01804 from the National Science Centre, Poland.

L. Rutkowski et al. (Eds.): ICAISC 2020, LNAI 12415, pp. 60–70, 2020.
https://doi.org/10.1007/978-3-030-61401-0_6

vanishing/exploding gradients in deep neural structures, and usually additional hyperparameters to tune. In RVFL the resulting optimization problem becomes convex and the output weights can be determined analytically by using a simple standard linear least-squares method [1].

RVFL is extensively used for classification and regression problems due to its adaptive nature and universal approximation property. Many simulation studies reported in the literature show the high performance of the randomized models which is compared to fully adaptable ones. Randomization which is cheaper than optimization ensures faster training and simpler implementation.

RVFL is not the only FNN solution with randomization. Alternative approaches such as [2] and many other new solutions do not have direct links between the input and output layers [3]. The effect of direct links as well as a bias in the output layer on the RVFL performance in classification tasks was investigated in [4]. The basic conclusion of that work was that the direct link plays an important performance enhancing role in RVFL, while the bias term in the output neuron had no significant effect. In this work, we investigate the effect of direct links and output node bias on the regression performance of RVFL. For generating random parameters of hidden nodes we use the classical method and two new methods recently proposed in the literature. We test the RVFL performance on several function approximation problems with target functions of different nature: nonlinear, nonlinear with strong fluctuations, nonlinear with linear component and linear.

The remainder of this paper is structured as follows. In Sect. 2, we briefly present RVFL learning algorithm and the decomposition of the function built by RVFL. In Sect. 3, we describe three methods of generating weights and biases of hidden nodes. Section 4 reports the simulation study and compares results for different RVFL configurations, different methods of random parameters generation, and different regression problems. Finally, Sect. 5 concludes the work.

2   Random Vector Functional Link Network

RVFL was proposed by Pao and Takefuji [5]. It was proven in [6] that RVFL is a universal approximator for a continuous function on a bounded finite dimensional set with a closed-form solution. RVFL can be regarded as a single hidden layer FNN built with a specific randomized algorithm. The RVFL architecture is shown in Fig. 1. Note that in addition to a hidden layer transforming inputs nonlinearly, RVFL also has direct links connecting an input layer with output nodes. The weights and biases of hidden nodes, $a_{i,j}, b_i$, respectively, are randomly assigned and fixed during the training phase. The output weights, β_i, are analytically evaluated using a linear least-square method. This results in a flat-net architecture for which only weights β_i must be learned. The learning problem, which is non-convex for the full learning of all parameters, becomes convex in RVFL. So, the time-consuming gradient-based learning algorithms are not needed, which makes the learning process much easier to implement and extremely rapid.

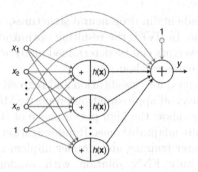

Fig. 1. RVFL architecture (random links in blue, direct links and output node bias in green). (Color figure online)

The learning algorithm of RVFL is as follows. One output is considered, m hidden nodes and n inputs. The training set is $\Phi = \{(\mathbf{x}_l, y_l) | \mathbf{x}_l \in \mathbb{R}^n, y_l \in \mathbb{R}, l = 1, 2, ..., N\}$ and the activation function of hidden nodes is $h(\mathbf{x})$, which is nonlinear piecewise continuous function, e.g. a sigmoid:

$$h(\mathbf{x}) = \frac{1}{1 + \exp\left(-\left(\mathbf{a}^T \mathbf{x} + b\right)\right)} \tag{1}$$

1. Randomly generate hidden node parameters: weights $\mathbf{a}_i = \left[a_{i,1}, a_{i,2}, ..., a_{i,n}\right]^T$ and biases b_i for all nodes, $i = 1, 2, ..., m$, according to any continuous sampling distribution.
2. Calculate the hidden layer output matrix $\mathbf{H}$:

$$\mathbf{H} = \begin{bmatrix} \mathbf{h}(\mathbf{x}_1) \\ \vdots \\ \mathbf{h}(\mathbf{x}_N) \end{bmatrix} = \begin{bmatrix} h_1(\mathbf{x}_1) \cdots h_m(\mathbf{x}_1) \\ \vdots \quad \vdots \quad \vdots \\ h_1(\mathbf{x}_N) \cdots h_m(\mathbf{x}_N) \end{bmatrix} \tag{2}$$

where $h_i(\mathbf{x})$ is an activation function of the i-th node.

The i-th column of $\mathbf{H}$ is the i-th hidden node output vector with respect to inputs $\mathbf{x}_1, \mathbf{x}_2, ..., \mathbf{x}_N$. Hidden nodes map nonlinearly inputs from n-dimensional input space to m-dimensional space. The output matrix $\mathbf{H}$ remains unchanged because parameters of hidden nodes, $\mathbf{a}_i$ and b_i, are fixed.
3. Calculate the output weights:

$$\boldsymbol{\beta} = [\mathbf{1}\,\mathbf{X}\,\mathbf{H}]^+ \mathbf{Y} \tag{3}$$

where $\boldsymbol{\beta} = [\beta_0, \beta_1, ..., \beta_{n+m}]^T$ is a vector of output weights, $\mathbf{1}$ is an $N \times 1$ one vector corresponding to an output node bias, $\mathbf{X}$ is a $N \times n$ input matrix, $\mathbf{Y} = [y_1, y_2, ..., y_N]^T$ is a vector of target outputs, and $[.]^+$ is the Moore-Penrose generalized inverse of matrix $[.]$.

The above equation for β results from the following criterion for minimizing the approximation error:

$$\min \| [\mathbf{1}\ \mathbf{X}\ \mathbf{H}]\beta - \mathbf{Y} \| \tag{4}$$

A function expressed by RVFL is a linear combination of inputs x_i and activation functions $h_i(\mathbf{x})$:

$$f(\mathbf{x}) = \sum_{i=1}^{n} \beta_i x_i + \sum_{i=1}^{m} \beta_{n+i} h_i(\mathbf{x}) + \beta_0 \tag{5}$$

Note that the first component in (5) is linear and represents a hyperplane, the second component expresses a nonlinear function and the last component is a bias. These three components of function $f(\mathbf{x})$ are depicted in Fig. 2. The nonlinear component is a linear combination of hidden node activation functions $h_i(\mathbf{x})$ (sigmoids in our case) which are also shown in this figure.

A natural question that arises is: are all these three components of function $f(\mathbf{x})$ necessary for an approximation of the target function? Is only a nonlinear component not enough? In the experimental part of this work, we try to answer these questions.

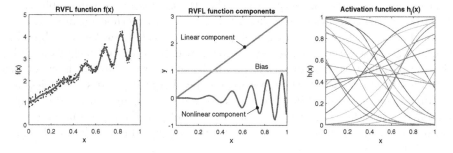

Fig. 2. An example of RVFL function $f(\mathbf{x})$ (left panel), its decomposition (middle panel) and sigmoids of hidden nodes constructing a nonlinear component (right panel).

3   Generating Weights and Biases of Hidden Nodes

The key issue in FNN randomized learning is finding a way of generating the random hidden node parameters to obtain a good projection space [7]. The standard approach is to generate both weights and biases randomly with a fixed interval from any continuous sampling distribution. The symmetric interval ensures a universal approximation property for the functions which meet Lipschitz condition [8]. The appropriate selection of this interval is a problem that has not been solved as yet and is considered to be one of the major research challenges in the area of FNN randomized learning [9,10]. In many cases the interval is selected as $[-1, 1]$ without any justification, regardless of the problem solved, data distribution, and activation functions type. In practical applications, the optimization of this interval is recommended for better model performance [11], [3,8].

In the experimental part of this work, we use three methods of generating random parameters. One of them is a standard approach, where both weights and biases of hidden nodes are generated uniformly from interval $[-u, u]$. A bound of this symmetrical interval, u, is adjusted to the target function (TF). This method of generating random parameters is denoted as Gs. Note that in the right panel of Fig. 2 the sigmoids are randomly evenly distributed in the input interval which is a correct solution. Unfortunately, the Gs method does not ensure such even distribution (see [7]).

Another method (denoted as Gu in this work) was proposed in [12]. Due to different functions of the hidden node parameters, i.e. weights express slopes of the sigmoids and biases express their shifts, they should be generated separately, not both from the same interval. According to Gu method, first, the weights $a_{i,j}$ are selected randomly from $U(-u, u)$ and then biases are determined as follows:

$$b_i = -\mathbf{a}_i^T \mathbf{x}_i^* \tag{6}$$

where $\mathbf{x}_i^*$ is one of the training point selected randomly (see [12] for other variants).

Determining biases from (6) ensures that the hidden nodes will be placed in accordance with the input data density [13]. The Gu method ensures that all sigmoids have their steepest fragments, which are most useful for modeling TF fluctuations, inside the input hypercube as shown in the right panel of Fig. 2. In this way, Gu improves a drawback of Gs which can generate sigmoids having their saturated fragments inside the input hypercube. These fragments are useless for building a nonlinear fitted function. Moreover, in Gs, it is difficult to adjust both parameters, weights and biases, when they are selected from the same interval. Gu selects weights first and then calculates biases depending on the weights and data distribution.

The third method of generating random parameters of hidden nodes ensures sigmoids with uniformly distributed slope angles [12,14]. This method is denoted as $G\alpha$ in this work. In many cases $G\alpha$ gives better performance of the model than Gu, especially for highly nonlinear TFs (see [12] for comparison of Gs, Gu and $G\alpha$). In the first step, $G\alpha$ generates slope angles of sigmoids $|\alpha_{i,j}| \sim U(\alpha_{min}, \alpha_{max})$, where $\alpha_{min} \in (0°, 90°)$ and $\alpha_{max} \in (\alpha_{min}, 90°)$. The bound angles, α_{min} and α_{max}, are tuned to the TF. For highly nonlinear TFs, with strong fluctuations, only α_{min} can be adjusted, keeping $\alpha_{max} = 90°$. The weights are calculated on the basis of the angles from:

$$a_{i,j} = 4 \tan \alpha_{i,j} \tag{7}$$

$G\alpha$ ensures random slopes between α_{min} and α_{max} for the multidimensional sigmoids in each of n directions. The biases of the hidden nodes are calculated from (6) to set the sigmoids inside the input hypercube depending on data density.

4   Experiments and Results

In this section, to asses the impact of the direct links and bias in the output node on RVFL performance we consider the following RVFL configurations:

+dl+b – RVFL with direct links and output node bias,
+dl−b – RVFL with direct links and without output node bias,
−dl+b – RVFL without direct links and with output node bias,
−dl−b – RVFL without direct links and output node bias.

We use sigmoids as activation functions. The hidden node weights and biases are generated using three methods described in Sect. 3:

Gs – the standard approach of generating both weights and biases from $U(-u, u)$,
Gu – generating weights from $U(-u, u)$ and biases according to (6),
Gα – generating slope angles of sigmoids $|\alpha_{i,j}| \sim U(\alpha_{min}, \alpha_{max})$, then calculating weights from (7), and biases from (6).

The parameters of these methods as well as the number of hidden nodes m were selected in grid search for each RVFL variant and TF from the sets: $m = \{1, 2, ..., 10, 20, ..., 100, 200, ..., 1000\}$, $u = \{1, 2, ..., 10, 20, 50, 100\}$ for 2-dimensional data or $u = \{0.1, 0.2, ..., 1, 2, ..., 5\}$ for 5 and 10-dimensional data, $\alpha_{min} = \{0, 15, ..., 75\}$, and $\alpha_{max} = \{\alpha_{min} + 15, \alpha_{min} + 30, ..., 90\}$.

We test RVFL performance over several regression problems using TFs defined as:

$$g(\mathbf{x}) = \exp\left(-\sum_{j=1}^{n}(x_j - 0.5)^2\right) \tag{8}$$

$$g(\mathbf{x}) = \alpha \sum_{j=1}^{n} \sin\left(20 \cdot \exp x_j\right) \cdot x_j^2 + \delta \cdot 3 \sum_{j=1}^{n} x_j \tag{9}$$

where α and δ are 0/1 variables.

Function (8) is a simple nonlinear function shown in the left panel of Fig. 3. The first component of function (9) is a highly nonlinear function shown in the middle panel of Fig. 3. The second component is a hyperplane. The TF can be composed of these both components if $\alpha = 1$ and $\delta = 1$ or of only one component if $\alpha = 0$ or $\delta = 0$. The TF with both components is shown in the right panel of Fig. 3. To asses the RVFL regression performance on TFs of different character four types of TFs were used:

NL – nonlinear (8),
NLF – nonlinear with strong fluctuations, (9) with $\alpha = 1$ and $\delta = 0$,
NLF+L – nonlinear with fluctuations and a linear component, (9) with $\alpha = 1$ and $\delta = 1$,
L – linear, (9) with $\alpha = 0$ and $\delta = 1$.

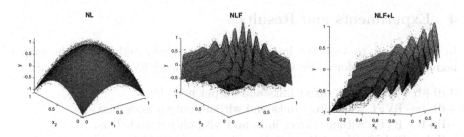

Fig. 3. Target functions and training points for $n = 2$.

The experiments were carried out for $n = 2$ and $N = 5000$, $n = 5$ and $N = 20000$, and $n = 10$ and $N = 50000$. As an accuracy measure, we used root mean squares error (RMSE). In each case, RFVL networks were trained 100 times and the final errors were calculated as the averages over 100 trials.

Tables 1, 2, 3 and 4 show RMSE for different TFs and RVFL variants. To confirm the significance of error differences between RVFL without direct links and output node bias (configuration –dl–b) and other RVFL configurations we used a two-sided Wilcoxon signed-rank test. We performed the tests separately for Gs, Gu and Gα. The null hypothesis was as follows: $d = RMSE_{-dl-b} - RMSE_v$, where v is $+dl + b, +dl - b$ or $-dl + b$, respectively, comes from a distribution with zero median. It was assumed that p-value below 5% indicates a rejection of the null hypothesis. The cases of the null hypothesis rejection are underlined in the tables (i.e. the cases +dl+b, +dl–b or –dl+b for which the error was significantly lower than for –dl–b).

Table 1. RMSE for NL.

RVFL variant		$n = 2$	$n = 5$	$n = 10$
Gs	+dl+b	7.50E−03 ± 9.39E−04	0.0121 ± 5.29E−04	0.0236 ± 4.72E−04
	+dl–b	7.41E−03 ± 9.21E−04	0.0121 ± 5.33E−04	0.0236 ± 4.70E−04
	–dl+b	7.30E−03 ± 9.42E−04	0.0121 ± 5.28E−04	0.0237 ± 4.46E−04
	–dl–b	7.20E−03 ± 9.11E−04	0.0121 ± 5.22E−04	0.0237 ± 4.44E−04
Gu	+dl+b	7.45E−03 ± 9.07E−04	0.0128 ± 5.05E−04	<u>0.0227</u> ± 4.10E−04
	+dl–b	7.38E−03 ± 9.14E−04	0.0128 ± 5.13E−04	0.0229 ± 4.21E−04
	–dl+b	7.28E−03 ± 9.75E−04	0.0128 ± 5.16E−04	<u>0.0227</u> ± 4.07E−04
	–dl–b	7.20E−03 ± 9.95E−04	0.0128 ± 5.15E−04	0.0230 ± 4.23E−04
Gα	+dl+b	7.47E−03 ± 9.39E−04	0.0130 ± 5.05E−04	0.0217 ± 4.11E−04
	+dl–b	7.39E−03 ± 9.31E−04	0.0130 ± 5.10E−04	0.0219 ± 4.20E−04
	–dl+b	7.27E−03 ± 9.53E−04	0.0129 ± 4.92E−04	0.0217 ± 4.06E−04
	–dl–b	7.16E−03 ± 9.87E−04	0.0130 ± 4.98E−04	0.0219 ± 4.20E−04

Table 2. RMSE for NLF.

RVFL variant		$n = 2$	$n = 5$	$n = 10$
Gs	+dl+b	0.0414 ± 0.0055	0.2268 ± 0.0122	0.2203 ± 0.0098
	+dl−b	0.0414 ± 0.0055	0.2268 ± 0.0122	0.2203 ± 0.0098
	−dl+b	0.0415 ± 0.0056	0.2268 ± 0.0122	0.2203 ± 0.0098
	−dl−b	0.0415 ± 0.0056	0.2268 ± 0.0122	0.2203 ± 0.0098
Gu	+dl+b	0.0378 ± 0.0028	0.2268 ± 0.0121	0.2203 ± 0.0098
	+dl−b	0.0378 ± 0.0028	0.2268 ± 0.0121	0.2203 ± 0.0098
	−dl+b	0.0379 ± 0.0027	0.2268 ± 0.0121	0.2203 ± 0.0098
	−dl−b	0.0379 ± 0.0027	0.2268 ± 0.0121	0.2203 ± 0.0098
Gα	+dl+b	0.0335 ± 0.0021	0.1702 ± 0.0111	0.2026 ± 0.0099
	+dl−b	0.0335 ± 0.0021	0.1702 ± 0.0111	0.2026 ± 0.0099
	−dl+b	0.0336 ± 0.0022	0.1704 ± 0.0111	0.2030 ± 0.0099
	−dl−b	0.0336 ± 0.0022	0.1704 ± 0.0111	0.2030 ± 0.0099

Table 3. RMSE for NLF+L.

RVFL variant		$n = 2$	$n = 5$	$n = 10$
Gs	+dl+b	0.0375 ± 0.0044	0.0887 ± 0.0030	0.0802 ± 0.0030
	+dl−b	0.0375 ± 0.0044	0.0887 ± 0.0030	0.0802 ± 0.0030
	−dl+b	0.0374 ± 0.0043	0.0888 ± 0.0030	0.0803 ± 0.0030
	−dl−b	0.0374 ± 0.0043	0.0888 ± 0.0030	0.0803 ± 0.0030
Gu	+dl+b	0.0351 ± 0.0019	0.0887 ± 0.0030	0.0802 ± 0.0030
	+dl−b	0.0351 ± 0.0019	0.0887 ± 0.0030	0.0802 ± 0.0030
	−dl+b	0.0351 ± 0.0019	0.0888 ± 0.0030	0.0802 ± 0.0030
	−dl−b	0.0351 ± 0.0019	0.0888 ± 0.0030	0.0802 ± 0.0030
Gα	+dl+b	0.0307 ± 0.0018	0.0706 ± 0.0033	$\underline{0.0750} \pm 0.0028$
	+dl−b	0.0307 ± 0.0018	0.0706 ± 0.0033	$\underline{0.0754} \pm 0.0028$
	−dl+b	0.0308 ± 0.0018	0.0707 ± 0.0033	0.0762 ± 0.0028
	−dl−b	0.0308 ± 0.0018	0.0707 ± 0.0033	0.0763 ± 0.0028

From Tables 1–3 can be seen that for nonlinear functions all RVFL configurations (+dl+b, +dl−b, −dl+b and −dl−b) produce very similar results. Even in the case of NLF+L where TF contains a significant linear component. Only in four cases out of 81, the errors were slightly lower than for corresponding −dl−b configurations. These cases are: Gu +dl+b for NL, Gu −dl+b for NL, Gα +dl+b for NLF+L, and Gα +dl−b for NLF+L. Note that for 2-dimensional NL, −dl−b configurations gave lower errors than other configurations for each method of generating random parameters.

The optimal numbers of hidden nodes (averaged over 100 trials in each case) are shown in Table 5. Note that for NL there is no difference in the optimal

Table 4. RMSE for L.

RVFL variant		$n = 2$	$n = 5$	$n = 10$
Gs	+dl+b	2.61E−03 ± 1.10E−03	1.89E−03 ± 5.40E−04	1.52E−03 ± 3.80E−04
	+dl−b	2.62E−03 ± 1.09E−03	1.89E−03 ± 5.40E−04	1.70E−03 ± 4.10E−04
	−dl+b	3.97E−03 ± 9.87E−04	1.98E−03 ± 5.20E−04	2.20E−03 ± 4.30E−04
	−dl−b	4.08E−03 ± 9.63E−04	1.99E−03 ± 5.20E−04	2.33E−03 ± 3.46E−04
Gu	+dl+b	2.61E−03 ± 1.10E−03	1.89E−03 ± 5.40E−04	1.52E−03 ± 3.80E−04
	+dl−b	2.72E−03 ± 1.05E−03	1.89E−03 ± 5.40E−04	1.70E−03 ± 4.10E−04
	−dl+b	3.38E−03 ± 9.94E−04	1.93E−03 ± 5.26E−04	2.02E−03 ± 4.45E−04
	−dl−b	3.78E−03 ± 1.04E−03	1.93E−03 ± 5.32E−04	2.26E−03 ± 3.77E−04
Gα	+dl+b	2.61E−03 ± 1.10E−03	1.89E−03 ± 5.39E−04	1.72E−03 ± 4.14E−04
	+dl−b	2.73E−03 ± 1.07E−03	2.53E−03 ± 5.27E−04	3.94E−03 ± 4.25E−04
	−dl+b	3.51E−03 ± 1.05E−03	4.87E−03 ± 6.33E−04	6.69E−03 ± 3.76E−04
	−dl−b	3.78E−03 ± 9.96E−04	4.96E−03 ± 6.20E−04	6.73E−03 ± 3.94E−04

number of nodes between RVFL configurations. Differences appear for multidimensional TFs with fluctuations, NLF and NLF+L, when random parameters are generated using Gs or Gu. In these cases, the configurations with direct links (+dl) need less hidden nodes than those without direct links (−dl). This is maybe because the hyperplane introduced by the direct links is useful for modeling the linear parts of the TFs (see the linear TF regions near the corner $\mathbf{x} = (0, 0, ..., 0)$ in the middle and right panels of Fig. 3). We can see from Table 5 that for multidimensional TFs with fluctuations Gα needs more nodes than Gs and Gu. But it was observed that also with a small number of nodes, Gα still outperformed Gs and Gu in accuracy. Adding nodes led to decreasing in error for Gα, while for Gs and Gu increasing in error was observed at the same time [12]. This can be related to overfitting caused by the steeper nodes generated by Gs and Gu then by Gα, where the node slope angles are distributed uniformly. This phenomenon needs to be explored in detail on other TFs.

Table 4 shows the results for linear TF. This TF can be modeled with only direct links and bias. So, the hidden layer is unnecessary. Note that the optimal number of hidden nodes for the +dl+b configurations is around one (see Table 5) which is the minimum value of m in our tests. The results for configurations without direct links (−dl) for L are usually much worse than those with direct links. Only for variants Gs and Gu at $n = 5$ the errors were at a similar level for all network configurations. In the −dl configurations the linear TF is modeled with sigmoids and overfitting is a real threat when training data is noisy as in our case. Using only direct links and bias prevents overfitting for linear TFs. But it should be noted that for linear TFs we do not need to use NNs. Simple linear regression is a better choice. Moreover, linear TFs are rare in practice.

Note that for highly nonlinear TFs such as NLF and NLF+L, Gα ensures much more accurate fitting than other methods of generating random parameters (see Tables 2 and 3). For low dimensional TFs with fluctuations, Gu was more

Table 5. Optimal numbers of hidden nodes.

n		NL			NLF			NLF+L			L		
		2	5	10	2	5	10	2	5	10	2	5	10
Gs	+dl+b	20	200	987	849	41	48	804	15	23	1.35	1.07	1.10
	+dl−b	20	200	988	849	41	51	809	17	25	1.62	1.04	1.19
	−dl+b	20	200	983	852	49	61	801	24	39	5.18	5.98	15.59
	−dl−b	20	200	982	852	50	62	800	25	40	6.62	7.07	20.80
Gu	+dl+b	19	232	963	638	44	53	476	17	26	1.14	1.08	1.17
	+dl−b	20	233	968	637	45	54	472	19	25	1.70	1.05	1.02
	−dl+b	20	228	968	641	51	58	483	26	34	4.12	5.58	13.50
	−dl−b	20	226	973	639	53	60	480	28	36	5.81	6.63	19.90
Gα	+dl+b	20	199	898	395	941	940	314	927	929	1.02	1.10	1.06
	+dl−b	20	200	901	395	941	940	315	930	930	1.63	5.21	25.87
	−dl+b	20	200	898	391	940	941	314	927	940	4.33	27.00	83.20
	−dl−b	20	200	901	391	940	941	314	929	940	5.69	30.00	82.90

accurate than Gs. This is because, for low n, Gs generates many sigmoids that are saturated in the input hypercube and thus they are useless for modeling fluctuations. This phenomenon decreases with n (see [12]).

5 Conclusion

In this work, we investigate whether direct links and an output node bias are necessary in RVFL for regression problems. RVFL can be decomposed into a linear component represented by the direct links, a nonlinear component represented by the hidden nodes and a bias term. The experimental study showed that nonlinear target functions can be modeled with only nonlinear component. The fitting errors with and without direct links and bias in these cases were at a similar level. The linear component and bias term, if needed, can be replaced by hidden nodes. The direct links seem to be useful for modeling the target functions with linear regions. In our simulations modeling of such functions, NLF and NLF+L, required less hidden nodes when direct links were also used. This issue requires further research with target functions of different nature.

In our study, we used three methods of generating random parameters of hidden nodes. The most sophisticated method proposed recently in the literature, Gα, was the most accurate especially for highly nonlinear target functions.

References

1. Principe, J., Chen, B.: Universal approximation with convex optimization: Gimmick or reality? IEEE Comput. Intell. Mag. **10**, 68–77 (2015)

2. Schmidt, W.F., Kraaijveld, M.A., Duin, R.P.W.: Feedforward neural networks with random weights. In: Proceedings of 11th IAPR International Conference Pattern Recognition Methodology and Systems, vol. II, pp. 1–4 (1992)

3. Wang, D., Li, M.: Stochastic configuration networks: Fundamentals and algorithms. IEEE Trans. Cybern. **47**(10), 3466–3479 (2017)

4. Zhang, L., Suganthan, P.N.: A comprehensive evaluation of random vector functional link networks. Inf. Sci. **367–368**, 1094–1105 (2016)

5. Pao, Y.H., Takefuji, Y.: Functional-link net computing: Theory, system architecture, and functionalities. IEEE Comput. **25**(5), 76–79 (1992)

6. Igelnik, B., Pao, Y.H.: Stochastic choice of basis functions in adaptive function approximation and the functional-link net. IEEE Trans. Neural Netw. **6**(6), 1320–1329 (1995)

7. Dudek, G.: Generating random weights and biases in feedforward neural networks with random hidden nodes. Inf. Sci. **481**, 33–56 (2019)

8. Husmeier, D.: Random vector functional link (RVFL) networks. In: Neural Networks for Conditional Probability Estimation: Forecasting Beyond Point Predictions, chapter 6. Springer, London (1999)

9. Zhang, L., Suganthan, P.N.: A survey of randomized algorithms for training neural networks. Inf. Sci. **364–365**, 146–155 (2016)

10. Cao, W., Wang, X., Ming, Z., Gao, J.: A review on neural networks with random weights. Neurocomputing **275**, 278–287 (2018)

11. Pao, Y.H., Park, G., Sobajic, D.: Learning and generalization characteristics of the random vector functional-link net. Neurocomputing **6**(2), 163–180 (1994)

12. Dudek, G.: Generating random parameters in feedforward neural networks with random hidden nodes: Drawbacks of the standard method and how to improve it (2019). ArXiv:1908.05864

13. Tyukin, I., Prokhorov, D.: Feasibility of random basis function approximators for modeling and control. In: Proceedings of IEEE International Symposium on Intelligent Control, pp. 1391–1396 (2009)

14. Dudek, G.: Improving randomized learning of feedforward neural networks by appropriate generation of random parameters. In: Rojas, I., Joya, G., Catala, A. (eds.) IWANN 2019. LNCS, vol. 11506, pp. 517–530. Springer, Cham (2019). https://doi.org/10.1007/978-3-030-20521-8_43

Artificial Intelligent Methods for the Location of Vortex Points

Ewa Frączek[1]([envelope]) [iD] and Bartosz Idźkowski[2] [iD]

[1] Department of Telecommunications and Teleinformatics, Wroclaw University
of Science and Technology, Wroclaw, Poland
ewa.fraczek@pwr.edu.pl
[2] Astronomical Observatory, University of Warsaw, Warsaw, Poland
bidzkowski@astrouw.edu.pl

Abstract. The ability to precisely determine the position of the optical vortex is necessary to increase the accuracy of existing measurement methods using these singularities as markers. In this manuscript we will show that the method of deep learning of neural networks gives these possibilities.

Keywords: Optical vortices · Deep neuron network · Location of vortex points

1 Introduction

The optical vortex is an object with an interesting physical properties [1]. At the central point of the optical vortex, the intensity of the wave equals zero and the phase is undetermined. These properties have been exploited in various fields of classical and quantum optics, for example: optical metrology [2–4], microscopy [5–7], photon entanglement [8], optical communication [9] and in the detection of rotating black holes [10]. Such singularities carry non-Gaussian light beams. One such beam, a Laguerre-Gauss (LG) beam, is described by a helical shape of the wavefront and also by an annular intensity distribution [11]. Light beams carrying the optical vortex were used for microscopy where such vortex acts as a marker. In the analysis of results being obtained, numerical methods should be used in order to precisely locate and track the marker. This publication will present a vortex point location method based on an artificial neural network (ANN). Earlier, work was undertaken to locate the network of optical vortices arranged in a regular pattern using a neural network [12, 13]. Deep neural networks have also been used to classify numerically-generated, noisy Laguerre-Gauss modes of up to 100 quanta of orbital angular momentum [14]. This work will show vortex localization method based on a single vortex wave phase.

© Springer Nature Switzerland AG 2020
L. Rutkowski et al. (Eds.): ICAISC 2020, LNAI 12415, pp. 71–77, 2020.
https://doi.org/10.1007/978-3-030-61401-0_7

2 Localized Object

The Laguerre-Gaussian beam was used for generation. The complex amplitude of the LG beam can be expressed by the equation [11]:

$$
LG(r, \varphi, z) = E_0 \frac{w_0}{w} \left(\frac{r}{w(z)^2} \right)^{|m|} \exp\left(\frac{-r^2}{w(z)^2} \right) \exp\left[-i\left(m\varphi + \frac{k \cdot r^2}{2R(z)} + kz + \Phi_G \right) \right],
\tag{1}
$$

where r is a radial coordinate of the center axis of the beam, z is the axial distance from the beam's focus (or "waist"), E_0 is the electric field amplitude, k is the wave number, φ stands for an azimuth angle, m is a natural number denoting a topological charge of an optical vortex (the topological charge can either be negative or positive), w describes transversal beam dimension, w_0 is the waist radius, R is a radius of curvature of a wavefront and Φ_G is the Gouy phase.

The LG beams are characterized by the intensity distribution which takes the shape of a doughnut. In the intensity pattern one can observe the dark area (vortex core) surrounded by the bright ring. Figure 1 shows the amplitude distribution obtained from Eq. 1.

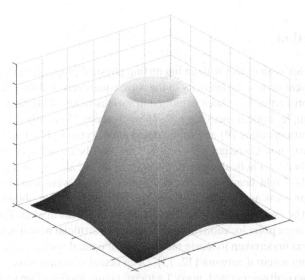

Fig. 1. The Laguerre-Gaussian beam amplitude distribution.

Figure 2 shows the phase distribution of the vortex beam. In the central point of the beam there is a singularity – a point at which the phase is undetermined. This point is marked with an arrow.

In Fig. 2 the phase jump of 2π is visible together with the point where the jump has its beginning. This unique feature, of low amplitude and fast changing phase, makes the beam sensitive to any phase or amplitude perturbations. Such objects have already been

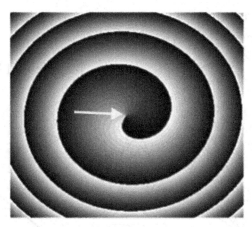

Fig. 2. The LG beam phase distribution. Grayscale: white for the phase value π, black - the phase is $-\pi$. The arrow indicates the point of the optical vortex. (Color figure online)

used in the construction of the optical vortex scanning microscope (OVSM) [7, 15]. The results obtained with the help of the OVSM were affected by the accuracy of the location determination of the vortex points.

Distribution of wave intensities generated in experiments were recorded by cameras. The accuracy of the location determination of the vortex points depends on the size of the pixels. In the methods of scanning objects using vortex beams, a small phase distribution area is being analyzed in the reconstruction. The small area makes it difficult to locate the vortex points based on the surroundings. In this paper, we show that this inconvenience can be overcome by using the artificial neural networks to locate the singular points.

The phase maps are obtained in experiments by the technique of interferogram detection with a characteristic fork pattern. From the light intensity distributions, phase maps are being calculated using the Fourier transform. This procedure allows to eliminate most of the noise that is visible in the intensity distributions. Phase distributions have a well-recognizable edge. Reducing the size of the analysis to the beginning of the spiral, eliminates the numerous phase disturbances that occur in experiments - known as edge buckling - the wavy of the spiral.

3   Artificial Neural Network

The work uses an feedforward artificial neural network technique with a several hidden layers. The hidden layers had the hyperbolic tangent activation function, the output layer was characterized by a linear activation function. In general, each neuron applies a nonlinear transformation on its weighted and biased input, then applies an activation function before the feed-forward process to the next layer of neurons. A learning algorithm is then used to back-propagate error, which results in the network's ability to learn. The tested networks had 400 input neurons for 20×20 pixel phase maps. Hidden layers were varying from 1 to 3. All tested networks had two output neurons corresponding to the x and y coordinates of the localized optical vortex. The diagram of the tested networks is shown in Fig. 3.

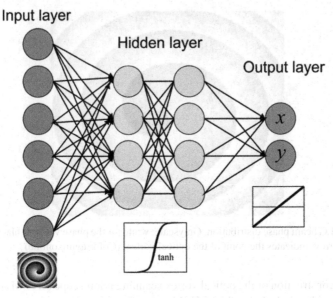

Fig. 3. Schematic of a sample deep neural network that has two hidden layers.

The image that is being analyzed is a cutout fragment. For analysis, a small 20 by 20 pixels format is taken into account. For this reason, convolution-type networks were not considered when choosing the neural network. The purpose of this work was to use a relatively simple structure of a neural network that does not require high computing power. In the future, a mathematical curve describing the phase jump is planned. One of the features that will be used for this will be the position of the beginning of the spiral.

3.1 Preparation of the Input Data

For teaching and testing purposes the artificial neural network, a simulation of interferograms recorded with a 3.5 μm CCD camera was made. Several thousand amplitude distributions with different parameters were generated, e.g. such as the density of the spiral phase jump for an optical vortex with a positive topological charge. The helical wave front rotation and various positions of the vortex point relative to the center of the phase map were also simulated. Figure 4 shows examples of such phase maps included in the training set.

Learning samples included Laguerre-Gauss mods with topological charge 1 and Bessel-Gauss mods. With separate tests made on sets containing these two types of modes, no difference was observed in the location accuracy of the optical vortices. These results are due to the fact that small areas were being cut out for the analysis.

3.2 Results

All learned artificial neural networks had an input layer with 400 neurons and an output layer with 2 neurons. Tests started using an artificial neural network with one hidden layer. Next, networks with two and three hidden layers were checked.

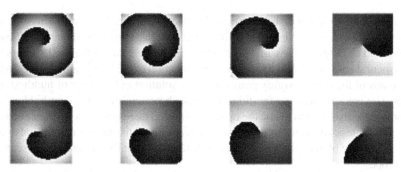

Fig. 4. Sample phase maps for different densities of the spiral phase jump and rotational phase orientation of the phase jump.

A neural network which number of hidden layers is greater than 1 is referred to as a deep neural network. Applying such configuration for deep learning has significantly reduced the learning time of the neural network and improved the location accuracy.

The table below presents selected results of the location of the optical vortex points depending on the number of neurons in the hidden layer. The notation 30 20 means that there were 30 neurons in the first hidden layer and 20 neurons in the second layer. The notation 20 22 18 means three hidden layers, with 18 neurons in the third layer. BVP means Best Validation Performance.

The results presented in Table 1 were obtained for a set of samples in which the position of the vortex relative to the center of the phase map was not more than 2.5 pixels. The initial location of the vortex point determination in the center of the considered area is possible by using the methods of finding the edges in the pictures. Without the initial vortex setting in the center of the area, the tested neural networks give about 40 times worse location results.

Table 1. Table of results of the location of the optical vortex points depending on the number of hidden layers and neurons.

Hidden layer	BVP [pix]	The number of epoch	Hidden layer	BVP [pix]	The number of epoch
16 10	0.041	15	20 10 18	0.023	12
16 12	0.019	23	20 18 10	0.011	13
16 14	0.026	11	20 20 4	0.020	19
20 14	0.030	19	20 20 10	0.0064	14
20 20	0.039	14	20 20 14	0.011	13
30 20	0.0035	8	20 20 18	0.014	14
36 20	0.011	8	20 22 18	0.011	17

Among the population of the deep neural networks examined, the most often obtained results were for a network composed of 400 input neurons, two hidden layers of 30 and 20 neurons, and an output layer with two neurons. From the results obtained, we conclude that the neural networks allow determining the location of the vortex points based on the phase maps of the optical vortex points with a resolution of the order of hundredths of a pixel. The methods used so far did not give such possibilities. The one-hidden-layer networks were also used to locate the optical vortices. The results obtained were an order of magnitude less accurate. In this case, the learning of the neural network also took much longer. We plan to extend our present research to test the optical vortex scanning microscope.

4   Conclusions

In this paper we have demonstrated the ability of deep neural networks to effectively locate the optical vortices. We show that such deep learning techniques are able to improve the accuracy of the measurements. We hope that these results can stimulate the use of deep learning techniques, experiments with classical and quantum optics, as well as various communication protocols or control of broadcasting directions.

Acknowledgement. We acknowledge support of this work by the Wroclaw University of Science and Technology statutory fund no. 8201003902/K34W04D03.

References

1. Nye, J.F., Berry, M.V.: Dislocations in wave trains. Proc. R. Soc. Lond. A **336**, 165–190 (1974)
2. Frączek, E., Frączek, W., Masajada, J.: The new method of topological charge determination of optical vortices in the interference field of the optical vortex interferometer. Optik **117**(9), 423–425 (2006)
3. Wang, W., et al.: Optical vortex metrology for nanometric speckle displacement measurement. Opt. Exp. **14**, 120–127 (2006)
4. Frączek, W., Mroczka, J.: Optical vortices as phase markers to wave-front deformation measurement. Metrol. Meas. Syst. **15**(4), 433–440 (2008)
5. Jesacher, A., Fürhapter, S., Bernet, S., Ritsch-Marte, M.: Shadow effects in spiral phase contrast microscopy. Phys. Rev. Lett. **94**, 233902 (2005)
6. Bouchal, P., Štrbková, L., Dostál, Z., Bouchal, Z.: Vortex topographic microscopy for full-field reference-free imaging and testing Opt. Express **25**, 21428–21443 (2017)
7. Popiołek-Masajada, A., Masajada, J., Lamperska, W.: Phase recovery with the optical vortex microscope. Meas. Sci. Technol. **30**, 105202 (2019)
8. Fickler, R., et al.: Quantum entanglement of high angular momenta. Science **338**, 640–643 (2012)
9. Krenn, M., et al.: Twisted light transmission over 143 kilometers. PNAS **113**(48), 13648–13653 (2016)
10. Tamburini, F., Thidé, B., Molina-Terriza, G., Anzolin, G.: Twisting of light around rotating black holes. Nat. Phys. **7**, 195–197 (2011)

11. Gbur, G.: Singular optics. In: The Optics Encyclopedia, pp. 1–23. Wiley (2015). https://doi.org/10.1002/9783527600441.oe1011, ISBN 9783527600441

12. Frączek, W., Guszkowski, T.: Optical vortices localization with artificial neural network. In: Slovakia, L.J., Müllerová, J., Senderáková, D., Jurečka, S. (eds.) 17th Slovak-Czech-Polish Optical Conference on Wave and Quantum Aspects of Contemporary Optics, SPIE, Bellingham, Wash, vol. 2010, pp. 77460C-1–77460C-7 (2010)

13. Guszkowski, T., Frączek, E.: Sieć neuronowa lokalizująca wiry optyczne rozmieszczone w regularnej strukturze. Pomiary Automatyka Kontrola **56**(9), 1074–1076 (2010)

14. Sanjaya, L.: at all: On the use of deep neural networks in optical communications. Appl. Opt. **57**(15), 4180–4190 (2018)

15. Popiołek-Masajada, A., Masajada, J., Szatkowski, M.: Internal scanning method as unique imaging method of optical vortex scanning microscope. Opt. Lasers Eng. **105**, 201–208 (2018)

Optimal Fog Services Placement in SDN IoT Network Using Random Neural Networks and Cognitive Network Map

Piotr Fröhlich$^{(\boxtimes)}$ and Erol Gelenbe

Institute of Theoretical and Applied Informatics, Polish Academy of Sciences,
Gliwice, Poland
pfrohlich@iitis.pl, e.gelenbe@imperial.ac.uk

Abstract. Due to a massive increase in the number of IoT devices and the number of cloud-based services a crucial task arises of optimally placing (both topologically and resource-wise) services in the network so that no of the clients will be victimized and all of them will receive the best possible time of response. Also - there must be a balance not to instantiate a service on every possible machine - which would take too many resources. The task which must be solved is an optimization of parameters such as QoS between service and client, equality of clients and usage of resources. Using the SDN - which is designed to answer some of the problems posed in this section such as QoS and knowledge about the topology of the whole network and newly connected clients - is a gateway to better-adapted service management. Machine learning provides less stiff rules to follow and more intelligent behavior of the manager.

Keywords: Random Neural Network · Reinforcement Learning · Artificial Intelligence · IoT · SDN · Fog Computing · Cloud Computing

1 Introduction

Currently, a lot of online services are based on cloud or fog management - by certain calculations *82%* of the workload will reside within the cloud by 2020 [17]. It poses a serious problem of the management of used resources and the location on which such service should be optimally placed. This problem seems to be more and more serious, especially when the number of *IoT* devices is growing rapidly (as much as 5.8 Billion *IoT* endpoints [12] by 2020) and consequently - the number of queries to servers supporting these devices is growing. It gets more and more crucial for operators and providers to be able to deploy services in the best possible place. Users expect efficient service, which means low response time

This research has been supported by the EC H2020-IOT-2016-2017 (H2020-IOT-2017) Program under Grant Agreement 780139 for the SerIoT Research and Innovation Action.

© Springer Nature Switzerland AG 2020
L. Rutkowski et al. (Eds.): ICAISC 2020, LNAI 12415, pp. 78–89, 2020.
https://doi.org/10.1007/978-3-030-61401-0_8

and fair service, i.e. similar service time regardless of the customer's location. On the other hand, for the infrastructure operator, it is important to optimize the use of computing and network resources - to maximize the number of supported users (which is associated with the number of launched services) and minimize the consumed energy. The sage of *SDN* [4] gives this solution a lot of information that is otherwise impossible or hard to obtain in regular networks. The fact that *SDN* is used speeds up the setup of the required application. What's more *SDN* is often used in Cloud and Fog networks [13,14]. Also Cognitive Network Map which is fed by Cognitive Packets [8,10] with information about the current state of the network (e.g. *QoS*-wise) and stores it within the controller. The whole network is constantly monitored with the use of real, cognitive packets using real interfaces to travel through. It provides the Cognitive Network Map (*CNM*) with actual measurements of *QoS* parameters.

Today's development of information processing technology allows the use of one of the many heuristic methods of solving optimization problems. Artificial intelligence systems [11,16] are particularly promising. In this paper, we decided to test the usefulness of Random Neural Networks [6,7] for tasks related to supporting the work of a distributed system operator of Fog-for-*IoT* type systems.

Using the *RNN* based algorithm with the *RL* algorithm [9] for constantly deciding on optimal placement of a given service provides end-user with stable *QoS* parameters and provider with close to optimal resource consumption. The work is based on the work carried out within the framework of the SerIoT project [2,5], which includes the use of the Fog subsystem for the installation of services for *IoT* equipment. The choice of *RNN* network was also motivated by the use of the type neural networks in this project[15].

In the following section all submodules and algorithms will be described. Then the actual solution will be presented, followed by a description of testbed and experiments. Everything will be concluded in the last section with an emphasis on possible improvements.

2   Description of Used Algorithms and Submodules

2.1   Description of Random Neural Network

The topology of the neural network used in the decision process is a fully recurrent equivalent of the topology of the real network (see Fig. 1). For every service that can be deployed such a network is created. Neuron(s) with a potential

$$P \in (P_{MAX} - TR, P_{MAX}) \tag{1}$$

where P_{MAX} is a maximal potential in the whole neural network and

$$TR = 1 - (CPU_{USED}/CPU_{MAX}) \tag{2}$$

are considered winning neurons. On every forwarder which corresponds to a winning neuron a service is then instantiated - the process of spawning a service is

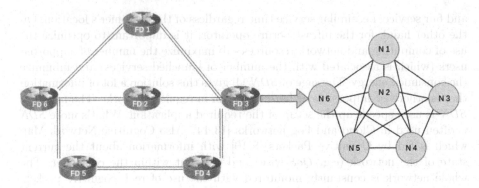

Fig. 1. The topology of the real network and the Random Neural Network corresponding to it.

described in Subsect. 2.3. Once a decision of a neuron takes place it is constantly scored based on that decision - reward, R, which a single neuron receives can be described in the equation below. Every part of this equation is explained in respective subsections. α, β, γ are parameters that represent the importance of a given part of the equation.

$$G(service) = \alpha * S(service) + \beta * \sum_{i=0}^{i=C} D(p_i) + \gamma * W(service) \qquad (3)$$

$$R = \frac{1}{G} \qquad (4)$$

Function S(Service). This function is a standard deviation estimator(s) calculated for every client connected to a given service at a given time. This part of the goal function corresponds to the equality of clients. The higher the value the bigger the punishment.

$$s = \sqrt{\frac{\sum_{i=0}^{i=N}(p_i - \bar{p})^2}{N-1}} \qquad (5)$$

Function Corresponding to the β Parameter. This function is an averaged QoS parameter of every client connected to a given service. QoS parameters are taken from the *Cognitive Network Map* which is described in Subsect. 2.2. This part of the goal function corresponds with the overall QoS score of the placement of a given service. Note that C is a number of clients connected to a given service.

Function W(Service). This function returns the workload of a given service. The higher the workload of a single service the higher is the need for instantiating another service.

As was stated the task of Random Neural Network is to minimize goal function using the Reinforcement Learning algorithm. Firstly the learning algorithm will update a given value:

$$T_l = \delta * T_{l-1} + (1 - \delta) * R_l, 0 < \delta < 1 \tag{6}$$

where δ is a responsiveness parameter describing how important historical values of rewards are. Setting it to a very high value will prevent the neural network from taking hasty decisions. The R_l is calculated as described in (1) so every time the *CNM* is updated, new reward R_l will be calculated and neurons' weights will be recalculated as described below. As stated in the [3] *RNN*'s learning algorithm works rewarding neurons that were able to produce better reward value, R_l, than the history-aware value T_l calculated in (6). Then all positive weights leading towards that neuron are increased and negative weights leading from that neuron to the others are also increased. The *Reinforcement Learning* algorithm is described in [3,9] (7–12).

$$If \quad R_l >= T_{l-1} \quad then \quad for \quad j \neq k \tag{7}$$

$$\forall i \neq k, \quad W_{ik}^+ \leftarrow W_{ik}^+ + R_l, \quad W_{ij}^- \leftarrow W_{ij}^- + R_l \tag{8}$$

$$If \quad R_l < T_{l-1} \quad then \quad for \quad j \neq k \tag{9}$$

$$\forall i \neq k, \quad W_{ik}^- \leftarrow W_{ik}^- + R_l, \quad W_{ij}^+ \leftarrow W_{ij}^+ + R_l \tag{10}$$

After the normalization of weights, preventing weights from constantly increasing or decreasing, te reevaluation of the potential q_i takes place as follows:

$$q_i = \frac{\sum_{j=1}^{j=N} q_i * W_{ji}^+}{r_i + \sum_{j=1}^{j=N} q_i * W_{ji}^-} \tag{11}$$

and r_i is known as 'total firing rate' [3]:

$$r_i = \sum_{j=1}^{j=N} [W_{ij}^+ + W_{ij}^-] \tag{12}$$

2.2 Description of Cognitive Network Map and Cognitive Packets

Cognitive Packets mechanism provides a way to gather information regarding the physical status of the network. Every flow set by the controller in forwarders is being monitored with a certain frequency, f, by sending a Cognitive Packet through the given flow. All forwarders then add required information stored within themselves such as delay, packet loss, etc. Those packets are being sent to monitor every flow status.

Assume network such as described in Fig. 2. For every flow installed by a controller - e.g. flow leading from the client connected to the *FD 1* to the client connected to the *FD 4*. Once every defined frequency f a packet is sent via this

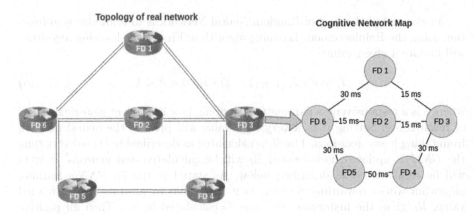

Fig. 2. The topology of the real network and the Cognitive Network Map for delay measurements only.

flow to monitor its state. Then, after receiving the data, it's sent to the controller for further processing. Using data collected by Cognitive Packets (*CP*) [8,10] which are collected from real interfaces of a real network the Cognitive Network Map (Fig. 2) is created. To avoid being dependable on Cognitive Packets alone in providing data to the Random Neural Network a data aggregator is introduced to store necessary data.

In the described approach data provided by *CP* is averaged using the time frame of *T*. In time t all packets which arrived in an interval $(t-T, t)$ are taken into account in creating the *CNM*, thus giving a solution an insight into the history. When Cognitive Packets are not reaching the controller (let's say on flow assumed previously) in a given time interval $(t-T, t)$ links which are in the assumed flow begin to deteriorate at the given rate *R* - Fig.3.

2.3   Description of the Service Placement Algorithm

The service placement algorithm can be divided into two stages - the setup stage and the online stage. They will be covered in respective sections. The algorithm is working under two assumptions - firstly it starts its work with the stable *CNM* map. Secondly that controller knows every client connected to the network at any given moment. Using indications of the *RNN* which returns a number of maximally excited neurons corresponding with a machine on which a service can be instantiated. Working under the assumption that *CNM* is stable (meaning links are being monitored and *CNM* is an equivalent of the real network state) the first stage of the algorithm can take place.

Setup Stage of the Algorithm. After creating the *RNN* for a given service as described in Subsect. 2.1 algorithm proceeds with deciding on initial placement and number of services. Simulation is run, based on *CNM* data - every possible

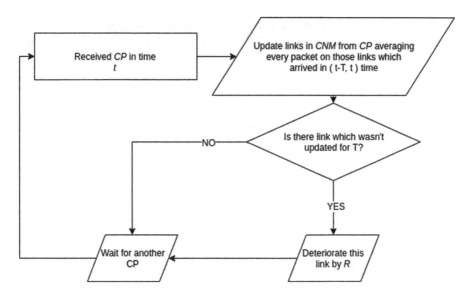

Fig. 3. Diagram showing the *CNM* creation algorithm.

neuron is considered a winner and punished or awarded for it I number of times. After this phase, there are $S = \{s_0, s_1, ..., s_n\}$, N active services running in the network.

2.4 Online Stage of the Algorithm

After the setup stage of the algorithm there are N running services and C connected clients. Every time the *CNM* is updated the RNN is also updated. If there are differences between sets $S_{t-1} = \{s_0, s_1, ..., s_n\}$, and $S_t = \{s_0, s_1, ..., s_m\}$ - winning services and winning neurons had changed, then all services:

$$S_{on} = S_t/S_{t-1} \tag{13}$$

$$S_{off} = S_{t-1}/S_t \tag{14}$$

are queued for starting and stopping. After Δ time, where Δ is proportional to δ that is the number of decisions of the *RNN* with the same tendency, all of S_{on} services will be started and all of S_{off} will be stopped.

3   Description of Implementation, Requirements and Limitations

The use of the *SDN* made it possible to develop an application in a high-level language. As a controller *ONOS* [1] - an open-source solution - was used. It provided a base for installing flow rules, routing, topology and host information.

The controller is responsible for making changes in services placement - transparent for every client, store the *CNM* and *RNNs*. The whole *RNN* plugin is run as a thread inside of the controller.

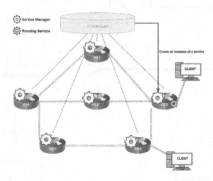

Fig. 4. Real topology used to deploy the presented solution.

Services must also be run on machines available for the service spawning - to know when and what service should be run. Therefore an independent, management network (Fig. 4, dotted line) must be provided between machines running services and the controller. Those machines are marked as Service Manager (blue cog) and are in fact a REST interface daemons needed for communication between the controller and spawners of new services. Assume that a service must be instantiated on *FD 3*.

A REST request is sent to the *Service Manager* on that device which then instantiates a real service. From the client's point of view moving of the service is not visible due to masking flow rules installed by the controller. A client must only know an IP address and a port on which service *S* will be available all the time (regardless of placement) - rest is taken care of by the controller and the service manager. Regarding the requirements - a mentioned earlier management network directly connecting machines for spawning services and the controller is required. The *SDN* based switches are required - in this implementation both hardware *SDN* switches and *Open V Switch* based machines were used.

Since one of the assumptions made for the service placement algorithm is that the controller knows every connected host at all times - multiple clients connected to a router with the single IP address will be treated as one client (and will influence the balance of the algorithm). The network must also support Cognitive Packets - have nodes or clients running Cognitive Packets Managers all the time.

4   Description of Testbeds and Experiments

4.1   Description of Testbeds

Testbeds used to conduct experiments can be divided into two groups - virtualized and real. For virtualized testbed setup a *mininet* environment was used. It provided required insight into large networks that are hard to create in the real world and it was easier to use as a performance testing tool. From now on it'll be referenced as the virtual testbed. The second testbed consists of real devices. Both *Switch 1* and *Switch 2* are providing both links in the abstract topology and the management network.

Machines marked with red colour are configured as *SDN* switches, *ARM*-based raspberry pi 3B+ devices. Those devices are running *OpenVSwitch* in version *2.3.0*. Other machines are (despite mentioned *switches 1* and *2*) regular desktop *PC*'s with *Ubuntu 18.04 LTS* running on them. Machine marked as *SerCon* is a machine on which the controller runs. In Fig. 5 there is an abstract topology used during experiments conducted on real devices. This testbed will be referenced as the real testbed from now on.

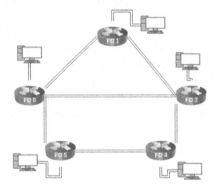

Fig. 5. Abstract topology used during experiments.

Several experiments were done to confirm that the solution is behaving correctly. To measure that every host connected to the network is treated equally a standard deviation of time of processing a request of every client was measured. Average processing time for all clients has been also measured as well as the average resource consumption. Described experiments were conducted both on the virtual and the real testbed.

4.2   Description of Experiments

In experiments a network consisting of N nodes was created and C clients were randomly connected to those nodes. After T time a network state was captured and stored. Using the information in the CNM the solution based on the RNN was able to provide optimal or suboptimal placements of services. Those experiments were run in the virtual testbed due to the ease of creating networks. Since packets using this virtual testbed are not transported by the real medium another set of experiments was needed. On the real testbed, a real value of time of the response, variation and resource consumption was measured. Note that all experiments conducted on real testbed were real services running on real machines. What's more - all traffic was transported via real medium - what's caused white noise.

5   Results

All experiments described in the previous section were conducted as described. Using both the *real* and the *virtual* testbed helped determine that this solution provides the network with optimal or suboptimal placements of services based on parameters such as the *QoS*, the *equality* of clients and *resource* usage. It also provided an insight into larger networks as well as real networks with real transportation media (carrying and implying a lot of white noise). All charts (Figs. 6, 7, 8) are charts taken from the real testbed from experiments carried out on the topology from Fig. 5 with $C = 10$ and every forwarder ready to start a service at any time. The used service was a simple *TCP* based server which took N parameters and returned M parameters for the client. Both N and M were randomized but both of them were proportional to the *time of response*

Next experiments were conducted on the virtual testbed (Figs. 9, 10) with the use of bigger networks. Note that this isn't simulation - this is a virtualized solution with real systems, interfaces and services running in one environment

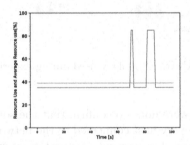

Fig. 6. Plot of use of percentage of used resourced against time.

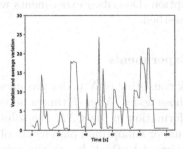

Fig. 7. The plot of the variation of the response time of every client against time. The orange line shows average variation through the whole experiment. (Color figure online)

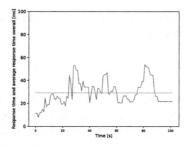

Fig. 8. The plot of the averaged response time for every client against time. The orange line shows average response time through the whole experiments (Color figure online)

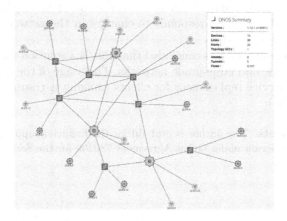

Fig. 9. The diagram showing the result of the algorithm. The red cog is a client, the violet cog is a running service. (Color figure online)

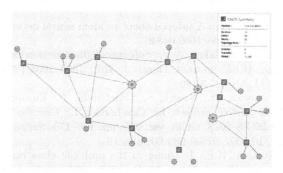

Fig. 10. The diagram showing the result of the algorithm. The red cog is a client, the violet cog is a running service. (Color figure online)

(without the influence of the medium of transportation). All experiments were run for *100* [s], on topologies sized [*5, 10, 15*] forwarders. Placement of the clients was randomized but clipped to a maximum of *2* connected hosts to one forwarder. The number of clients is equal to the number of forwarders to assure a stable condition of the network.

6   Conclusion

The result of experiments that the *Random Neural Network* is a suitable solution for the service placement in the network. It provides means for optimization of required parameters and as a result best possible services for clients. Using the *CNM* provided the *RNN* with a stable source of data on the state of the network - as a result the service placement algorithm is also aware of a deterioration of the link quality, new clients and their location, etc. Combining decisions provided from the *RNN* and the data from the *CNM* resulted in a self-aware service placement algorithm that corresponds to changes in the network providing an optimal placement of services.

What's more, experiments concluded that this is a solution that can be used both in small-grade and large-grade networks. The usage of the *SDN* provides a way to mask a service replacement for clients (making it transparent to clients at any given time).

Acknowledgements. The author is grateful for the financial support of the H2020-IOT-2016-2017 Program under Grant Agreement 780139 for the SerIoT Research and Innovation Action.

References

1. Home page of onosproject - open source SDN controller (2020). https://onosproject.org. Accessed 13 Mar 2020
2. Home page of SerIoT project (2020). https://seriot-project.eu. Accessed 13 Mar 2020
3. Basterrech, S., Rubino, G.: A tutorial about random neural networks in supervised learning (2016). ArXiv abs/1609.04846
4. Bera, S., Misra, S., Vasilakos, A.V.: Software-defined networking for internet of things: A survey. IEEE Internet Things J. **4**(6), 1994–2008 (2017). https://doi.org/10.1109/JIOT.2017.2746186
5. Domańska, J., Nowak, M., Nowak, S., Czachórski, T.: European cybersecurity research and the SerIoT project. In: Czachórski, T., Gelenbe, E., Grochla, K., Lent, R. (eds.) ISCIS 2018. CCIS, vol. 935, pp. 166–173. Springer, Cham (2018). https://doi.org/10.1007/978-3-030-00840-6_19
6. Gelenbe, E., Hussain, K.F.: Learning in the multiple class random neural network. IEEE Trans. Neural Netw. **13**(6), 1257–1267 (2002). https://doi.org/10.1109/TNN.2002.804228
7. Gelenbe, E., Koubi, V., Pekergin, F.: Dynamical random neural network approach to the traveling salesman problem. In: Proceedings of IEEE Systems Man and Cybernetics Conference - SMC, vol. 2, pp. 630–635 (1993). https://doi.org/10.1109/ICSMC.1993.384945
8. Gelenbe, E., Xu, Z., Seref, E.: Cognitive packet networks. In: Proceedings 11th International Conference on Tools with Artificial Intelligence, pp. 47–54 (1999). https://doi.org/10.1109/TAI.1999.809765

9. Gelenbe, E.: Learning in the recurrent random neural network. Neural Comput. **5**, 154–164 (1993). https://doi.org/10.1162/neco.1993.5.1.154

10. Gelenbe, E.: Cognitive Packet Patent (2020). https://patents.google.com/patent/US6804201B1/en. Accessed 20 Nov 2019

11. Gupta, L., Samaka, M., Jain, R., Erbad, A., Bhamare, D., Metz, C.: Colap: A predictive framework for service function chain placement in a multi-cloud environment. In: 2017 IEEE 7th Annual Computing and Communication Workshop and Conference (CCWC), pp. 1–9 (2017). https://doi.org/10.1109/CCWC.2017.7868377

12. Inc., G.: IoT endpoint number (2020). https://www.gartner.com/en/newsroom/press-releases/2019-08-29-gartner-says-5-8-billion-enterprise-and-automotive-io. Accessed 20 Nov 2019

13. Levin, A., Barabash, K., Ben-Itzhak, Y., Guenender, S., Schour, L.: Networking architecture for seamless cloud interoperability. In: 2015 IEEE 8th International Conference on Cloud Computing, pp. 1021–1024 (2015). https://doi.org/10.1109/CLOUD.2015.141

14. Mambretti, J., Chen, J., Yeh, F.: Next generation clouds, the chameleon cloud testbed, and software defined networking (SDN). In: 2015 International Conference on Cloud Computing Research and Innovation (ICCCRI), pp. 73–79 (2015). https://doi.org/10.1109/ICCCRI.2015.10

15. Nowak, M., Nowak, S., Domańska, J.: Cognitive routing for improvement of iot security (2019). https://doi.org/10.13140/RG.2.2.28667.36648

16. Ooi, B.Y., Chan, H.Y., Cheah, Y.N.: Dynamic service placement and replication framework to enhance service availability using team formation algorithm. J. Syst. Softw. **85**(9), 2048–2062 (2012). https://doi.org/10.1016/j.jss.2012.02.010. Selected Papers from the 2011 Joint Working IEEE/IFIP Conference on Software Architecture (WICSA 2011)

17. Radoslav Ch., T.: Cloud Computing Statistics 2020 (2020). https://techjury.net/stats-about/cloud-computing/#gref. Accessed 20 Nov 2019

Building Best Predictive Models Using ML and DL Approaches to Categorize Fashion Clothes

Said Gadri[1(✉)] and Erich Neuhold[2]

[1] Department of Computer Science, Faculty of Mathematics and Informatics,
University Mohamed Boudiaf of Msila, 28000 M'sila, Algeria
said.kadri@univ-msila.dz
[2] Department of Computer Science, University of Vienna, Vienna, Austria
erich.neuhold@univie.ac.at

Abstract. Today Deep learning approach DL becomes the new tendency of machine learning approach ML which is used since it gives much more sophisticated pattern recognition and image classification than classic machine learning approach. Among the most used methods in DL, CNNs are for a special interest. In this work, we have developed an automatic classifier that permits to classify a large number of fashion clothing articles based on ML and DL approaches. Initially, we proceeded to the classification task using many ML algorithms, then we proposed a new CNN model composed of many convolutional layers, one maxpooling layer, and one full connected layer. Finally, we established a comparison between different algorithms. As programming tools, we have used Python, Tensoflow, and Keras which are the most used in the field.

Keywords: Machine learning · Deep learning · Pattern recognition · Neural networks · Convolutional Neural Networks

1 Introduction

The machine Learning area is based on a set of methods that allow a machine to learn meaningful features (patterns) from data without the interaction of the human. So, the performance of these methods depends on human knowledge. In the last years, many IA tasks like object recognition are based essentially on Machine Learning approaches ML which gave a high performance. The Mckinsey Global Institute asserts that ML discipline will be the guide of the next big wave of innovation [1, 2, 3]. Currently, we are able to use larger datasets to learn more powerful models, and better techniques to avoid overfitting and under-fitting. Many algorithms have been developed in this area of research, including logistic regression, k-nearest neighbors, naïve Bayes, decision trees, support vector machine, artificial neural networks, etc. Researches on Artificial Neural Networks ANN can be considered as the oldest discipline in ML and AI that dates back to McCarthy in 1943, but these researches were quickly interrupted for a long time due to their high requirements in term hardware, software and running time. Many years later,

© Springer Nature Switzerland AG 2020
L. Rutkowski et al. (Eds.): ICAISC 2020, LNAI 12415, pp. 90–102, 2020.
https://doi.org/10.1007/978-3-030-61401-0_9

they were revived in parallel with the apparition of new sub-field called deep learning DL. The DL approach greatly simplifies the feature engineering process especially in some vital areas such as medical imaging analysis. Among the DL methods, CNNs are of special interest. When exploiting local connectivity patterns efficiently which is the case of those used in the ImageNET competition [4]. There are many works that try to apply CNNs on image analysis [5, 6] using a variety of methods like the rectified linear unit [7] and deep residual learning [8]. In the present paper, we have used CNN model as well as some ML algorithms to categorize fashion clothes. The paper is organized as follows: Sect. 1 is a short introduction presenting the area of our work and its advantages and benefits. Section 2 presents the background of our research field. In the third section, we described our proposed model. The fourth section exposes the experimental part of our work. In Sect. 5, we illustrated the obtained results when applying the proposed model. In Sect. 6, we discussed the results obtained in the previous section. In the last section, we summarized the realized work and suggested some perspectives for future researches.

2 Deep Learning Background

Deep Learning DL becomes one of the most popular sub-field of IA and ML, especially in speech recognition, computer vision, and some other interesting topics. Its success is motivated by three factors: the increased amount of available data, the improvement and the lowest cost of hardware and software [9–13], the increased chip processing abilities (e.g., GPU units) [14]. DL is based essentially on the use of ANNs with two layers or many hidden layers. The convolutional neural network CNN is a specialized feedforward neural network that was developed to process multidimensional data, such as images. Its origins refer to the neo-cognition proposed by Fukushima in 1980 [15]. The first model of CNN was proposed by LeCUN et al. [16] in 1998 and used in the field of character recognition. Furthermore, many other alternative ANN architectures have been developed later, including recurrent neural networks RNNs, autoencoders, and stochastic networks [17–19]. Deep learning also refers to an efficient solution to the problem of input data representation which is a critical phase in ML especially for complex problems such as image and speech recognition [20]. DNNs are favorable to learn high-level feature representations of inputs through their multiple hidden layers. The first DNNs had appeared in 1960s, but abandoned, after that for a long time in favor of ML approach, due to its high requirements in term of difficulties in training and inadequate performance [21]. In 1986, RumelHart et al. [22] proposed the back-propagation method to update efficiently neural network weights using the gradient of the loss function through multiple layers. Despite the promising results given by DNNs in the late of 1980s [23] and 1990s [24], they were abandoned in practice and research due to many problems. In 2006, researches in DL were revived especially when some new methods for sensibility initializing DNN weights have been developed by researchers [25, 26]. It is the case of deep belief networks DBNs which proved their efficiency in image and speech tasks in 2009 and 2012 [11]. In 2012, Krizhevsky et al., [17] proposed a deep CNN for the large-scale visual recognition challenge (LSVRC) [27] reducing the error rate from the previous year's 26% down to just 16%. This CNN has been implemented on multiple graphics processing units GPUs for the first time, this new technique has allowed the training of large datasets and increase significantly the speed of processing and the research productivity. Furthermore, the use of a new activation function RELU (Rectified Linear Unit) has ended the problem of gradient and allowed faster training of data. The dropout technique is also used as a regularization method to decrease over-fitting in large networks with many layers. All these interesting improvements and the increasing internet in DL let the leading technical companies to increase the research efforts, producing many other advances in the field. Many DL frameworks abstract-ing have tensor computation [12–15] and GPU compatibility libraries [16] have been developed and made available to researchers through an open-source software [28] and cloud services [29, 30]. On the other hand, many companies have met the challenges of big data when exploring large amounts of data to predict value decisions [30]. The concept of big data refers to data that exceeds the capability of standard data storage and data processing systems [31]. This large volume of data requires also high-performance hardware and very efficient analysis tools. Some other ML challenges appeared with big data including high dimensionality, distributed infrastructures, real-time requirements, feature engineering. Najafabadi et al. [32] discuss the use of DL to solve big data chal-lenges, the capacity of DNNs to extract meaningful features from large sets of unlabeled data is extremely important as it is commonly encountered in big data analytics. The automatic extraction of features from unstructured and heterogeneous data, e.g., image text, audio is a very useful and difficult task. But this task becomes easy with the use of DL methods. Other tasks including semantic indexing and hashing [33, 34] also become possible with these high-level features, furthermore, DL is also used to classify and organize fast-moving data [32]. In general, high capacity DNNs are suitable for learning from the large datasets issued of big data sources. As a conclusion, we can say that DL is currently growing faster than over before.

3 The Proposed Approach

In the present work, we have developed an automatic classifier that permits to classify a large number of fashion clothes into ten (10) given classes based on two approaches: the classic ML approach and the DL approach. Initially, we have proceeded the classification task using many ML algorithms including LR, KNN, CART, NB, and SVM. Then we proposed a CNN model composed of many convolutional layers, one MaxPooling layer, and one fully connected layer. Finally, we established a comparison between the different algorithms. As programming tools, we have used Python, Tensorflow, and Keras which are the most used in this field. Figure 1 summarizes the classification task based on the two approaches, while Fig. 2 presents a detailed diagram of the proposed CNN model to improve the performance of the classification task.

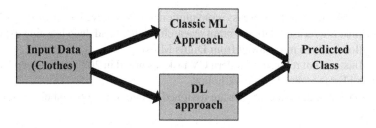

Fig. 1. Clothes classification process

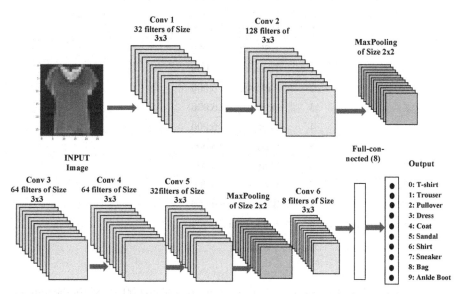

Fig. 2. The architecture of the proposed CNN model

4   Experimental Work

4.1   Used Dataset

In our experiments, we have used the Fashion Mnist dataset which is the replacing of the classic Digits Mnist dataset containing a large set of handwritten digits. We note that members of AI, ML, and data science community prefer working on Digits Mnist dataset and use it as a benchmark to validate their algorithms. Furthermore, Digits mnist is often the first dataset used by researchers in the field of ML as the golden rule for them is "if doesn't work on Mnist, it won't work at all". Fashion Mnist Dataset is the best evolution of Digits Mnist dataset. It contains 70.000 grayscale images distributed on 10 categories. Each image represents an individual article of clothing at low resolution (28 × 28 pixels). Our dataset can be divided into two subsets: the training subset containing 60.000 images to build and train the classification model, and the test subset containing 10.000 images to evaluate the performance of this model. Fashion Mnist Dataset is often privileged by researchers for many reasons:

- The Digits Mnist dataset is too easy: convolutional nets achieve 99,7% on digits Mnist.
- Digits Mnist is overused: Google brain research scientist and deep learning expert Ian GoodFellow calls to move away from Digits Mnist.
- Digits Mnist cannot represent modern CV tasks as noted in 2017 by the deep learning expert and keras author François Chollet.
- In Fashion Mnist dataset, samples are assigned to one of ten (10) labels as described on Table 1:

Table 1. Labels assigned to each occurrence in F-Mnist Dataset

Label	Description	Nb.Examples
0	T-Shirt/Top	6.000
1	Trouser	6.000
2	Pullover	6.000
3	Dress	6.000
4	Coat	6.000
5	Sandal	6.000
6	Shirt	6.000
7	Sneaker	6.000
8	Bag	6.000
9	Ankle boot	6.000

The Fashion Mnist dataset takes the form of an array of 60.000×785 for the training set and 10.000×785 for the test set. Where the first dimension expresses the number of examples or clothing images, the second dimension expresses the number of attributes. So, each row in the array represents the image of a clothing article as it is explained in Table 1, column 0 represents the image label, columns 1,…,784 are the pixels composing each article image. For example, row 50 represents sneaker, 100 is a T-shirt, 800 a dress, etc. (Figs. 3 and 4).

Fig. 3. Row 50: Grayscale image representing a Sneaker

Fig. 4. Row 100: Grayscale image representing a T-Shirt

4.2 Programming Tools

Python: Python is currently one of the most popular languages for scientific applications. It has a high-level interactive nature and a rich collection of scientific libraries which lets it a good choice for algorithmic development and exploratory data analysis. It is increasingly used in academic establishments and also in industry. It contains a famous module called scikit-learn tool integrating a large number of ML algorithms for supervised and unsupervised problems such as decision trees, logistic regression, Naïve Bayes, KNN, ANN, etc. this package of algorithms allows to simplify ML to non-spcialists working on a general purpose.

Tensorflow: TensorFlow is a multipurpose open-source library for numerical computation using data flow graphs. It offers APIs for beginners and experts to develop for desktop, mobile, web, and cloud. TensorFlow can be used from many programming languages such as Python, C++, Java, Scala, R and Runs on a variety of platforms including: Unix, Windows, iOS, Android. We note also that Tensorflow can be run on single machines (CPU, GPU, TPU) or distributed machines of many 100s of GPU cards.

Keras: Keras is the official high-level API of TensorFlow which is characterized by many important characteristics: Minimalist, highly modular neural networks library written in Python, Capable of running on top of either TensorFlow or Theano, Large adoption in the industry and research community, Easy production of models, Supports both convolutional networks and recurrent networks and combinations of the two, Supports arbitrary connectivity schemes (including multi-input and multi-output training), Runs seamlessly on CPU and GPU.

4.3 Evaluation

To validate the different ML algorithms, and obtain the best model, we have used the cross-validation method consisting in splitting our dataset into 10 parts, train on 9 and test on 1 and repeat for all combinations of train/test splits. For the CNN model, we have used two parameters which are: loss value and accuracy metric.

1. *Accuracy metric:* This is a ratio of the number of correctly predicted instances divided by the total number of instances in the dataset multiplied by 100 to give a percentage (e.g., 90% accurate).
2. *Loss value:* used to optimize an ML algorithm or DL model. It must be calculated on training and validation datasets. Its simple interpretation is based on how well the ML algorithm or the DL built model is doing in these two datasets. It gives the sum of errors made for each example in the training or validation set.
3. *Precision:* It is the number of real correct positive results divided by the total number of positive results predicted by the classifier.
4. *Recall:* It is the number of real correct positive results divided by the number of all relevant samples in the dataset (all samples that should have been identified as positive).

5. ***F1-Score:*** is the Harmonic Mean between precision and recall. The range for F1-Score is [0, 1]. It tells you how precise your classifier is (how many instances it classifies correctly), as well as how robust it is.
6. ***Confusion Matrix:*** The Confusion matrix is one of the most intuitive and easiest metrics used for finding the correctness and accuracy of the model. It is used for the classification problem where the output can be of two or more types of classes and gives the correctness for each class.

5 Illustration of Obtained Results

To build the best predictive model and achieve a higher accuracy rate, we have performed two tasks:

1. Building a classification model using many classic ML algorithms, including logistic Regression LR, K-nearest Neighbors KNN, Decision Tree (CART variant), Support Vector Machine SVM. For this purpose, we used scikit-learn library of python containing the most known learning algorithms.
2. Designing a CNN (Convolutional Neural Network) model composed of many layers as it was explained in Sect. 3, Fig. 2. Here more details about its architecture:

   - A first convolutional layer Conv1 constituted of 32 filters of size (3 × 3).
   - A second convolutional layer Conv2 constituted of 128 filters of size (3 × 3).
   - A dropout layer to avoid overfitting.
   - A MaxPooling MaxPool of size (2 × 2) allowing to reduce dimensions (weigh, high) of images issued of the previous layer after applying the different filters of Conv3.
   - A third convolutional layer Conv3 constituted of 64 filters of size (3 × 3).
   - A fourth convolutional layer Conv3 constituted of 64 filters of size (3 × 3).
   - A fifth convolutional layer Conv3 constituted of 32 filters of size (3 × 3).
   - A dropout layer to avoid overfitting.
   - A MaxPooling MaxPool of size (2 × 2) allowing to reduce dimensions
   - A sixth convolutional layer Conv3 constituted of 8 filters of size (3 × 3).
   - A full connected layer FC allowing to transform the output of the previous layer into a mono-dimensional vector (size: 8).
   - An output layer represented by a reduced mono-dimensional vector having as size the number of classes (10).
   - For all the previous layers a Relu activation function and a softmax function are used to normalize values obtained in each layer (Table 2).

Table 2. Description of the proposed CNN model

Layer type	Output shape	Nb. parameters
Conv_Layer 1 (Conv2D)	(None, 26, 26, 32)	320
Conv_Layer 2 (Conv2D)	(None, 24, 24, 64)	36992
Droput_Layer 1 (Dropout)	(None, 24, 24, 128)	0
Max_pooling Layer 1 (MaxPooling2)	(None, 12, 12, 128)	0
Conv_Layer 3 (Conv2D)	(None, 10, 10, 64)	73792
Conv_Layer 4 (Conv2D)	(None, 8, 8, 64)	36928
Conv_Layer 5 (Conv2D)	(None, 6, 6, 32)	18464
Droput_Layer 2 (Dropout)	(None, 6, 6, 32)	0
Max_pooling Layer 2 (MaxPooling2)	(None, 3, 3, 32)	0
Conv_Layer 6 (Conv2D)	(None, 1, 1, 8)	2312
Flatten_Layer (Flatten)	(None, 7744)	0
Dense_Layer (Dense)	(None, 10)	90
Total parameters		168,898
Trainable parameters		168,898

Table 3 below summarizes the obtained results when applying ML algorithms.

Table 3. Accuracy after applying different ML algorithms

Algorithm	Accuracy
LR	84,95%
KNN (K = 5, Metric = minkowski)	85,31%
CART	79,26%
SVM	84,92%

Tables 4, 5 below summarize the obtained results after applying the CNN model.

Table 4. Loss value and accuracy value obtained when applying the proposed model

	Loss value	Accuracy value
Training set	0,2845	91,17%
Test set	0,2922	90.23%

Table 5. Performance report for CNN model

Class	Precision	Recall	F1-score
0	0.92	0.78	0.84
1	0.99	0.98	0.99
2	0.94	0.78	0.85
3	0.96	0.88	0.92
4	0.78	0.93	0.85
5	0.96	0.98	0.97
6	0.67	0.82	0.74
7	0.97	0.92	0.94
8	0.98	0.98	0.98
9	0.94	0.97	0.95
Micro Avg	0.90	0.90	0.90
Macro Avg	0.91	0.90	0.90
Weighed Avg	0.91	0.90	0.90

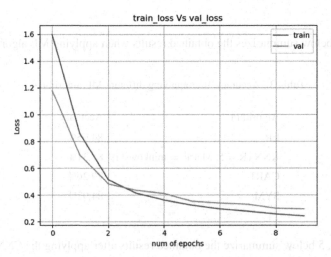

Fig. 5. Training loss vs Validation loss of the CNN model

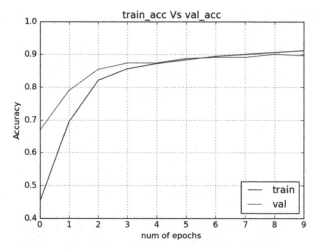

Fig. 6. Training accuracy vs Validation accuracy of the CNN model

6 Discussion

Table 3 summarizes the obtained results when applying the different ML algorithms including LR, KNN, CART, SVM. We observe that LR, KNN, and SVM give a high classification accuracy (>80%), while CART gives a low accuracy (<80%) compared to the previous algorithms. We note also, that the similarity metric used with the KNN algorithm is Minkowski similarity. Table 4 presents the obtained results when applying the proposed CNN model on the training set and the test set. Two performance measures are considered in this case, the loss value which calculates the sum of errors after training the model, and the accuracy value which gives the rate of correctness. It is clear that the loss value is very low against the accuracy which is very high and depends on the size of the used set. It is the reason for which the accuracy of the training set is higher than the accuracy of test set. Table 5 gives a complete performance report for the CNN model trained for nb-epochs = 10 and batch-size = 256. It contains the achieved rates for; precision, recall, F1-score related to each class (clothing article). All values are high compared with those obtained for the classic ML approach. In the same way, Fig. 5 shows the evaluation of training loss and validation loss over time and in function of the number of epochs. It begins very high for the training set and ends very low because of the large number of samples, but its variation for the validation set is not very quick and appears relatively stable. Similarly, Fig. 6 plots the evolution of training accuracy and validation accuracy in function of the number of epochs. Contrary to the loss value, the accuracy starts very low and ends very high. This property is clearer with the training set because of its large size. As a conclusion, the proposed CNN model gives the best accuracy compared with ML algorithms.

7 Comparison Between ML and CNN Approaches

In this section, we try to establish a comparison between different algorithms, ML algorithms, and the CNN model. The result of this comparison appears in Table 6.

Table 6. Comparison between the ML approach and the DL Approach

Algorithm	Accuracy
LR	84,95%
KNN (K = 5, Metric = minkowski)	85,31%
CART	79,26%
SVM	84,92%
CNN (nb-epochs = 8, batch-size = 256)	90,23%

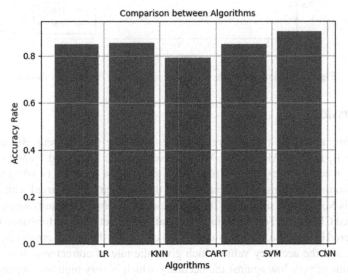

Fig. 7. Comparison between different Algorithms

According to Table 6 and Fig. 7, The comparison favors the CNN model over ML algorithms in term of accuracy rate, i.e., it gives the best performance of the classification task.

8 Conclusion and Future Suggestions

During the last years, object recognition is based essentially on the ML approach that gives high performance. A few years later, some important progress on the ML area has been made especially with the apparition of a new subfield called deep learning. It is mainly based on the use of many neural networks of simple interconnected units in order to extract meaningful patterns from a large amount of data to solve some complex problem such as medical image classification, fraud detection, character recognition, etc. currently, we are able to use larger datasets to learn powerful models, and better techniques to avoid overfitting and underfitting. Until our days, the obtained results in this area of research are very surprising in different domains. We talk about very high values of accuracy which often exceed the threshold of 90%. For example, the accuracy rate on the digits set is over 97%. In the present paper, we have performed a task of clothing article classification on the Fashion mnist dataset. We have used in the first stage many ML algorithms including LR, KNN, CART, SVM. We obtained good results of accuracy, especially for LR, KNN, and SVM. In the second stage, we have built a CNN model to perform the same task of classification. The achieved performance is very surprising. We concluded our work by establishing a large comparison between different algorithms. The result of this comparison was in favor of DL approach through the CNN model we have built. As a perspective of this promising work, we propose to improve these results by improving the architecture of the proposed CNN model by changing some model parameters such as the number of filters, the number of convolution and maxpooling layers, the size of each filter, the number of training epochs and the size of data batches. Another suggestion seems important, is to combine CNN with recurrent networks Resnets.

References

1. Hinton, G.E., Osindero, S., Teh, Y.-W.: A fast learning algorithm for deep belief nets. Neural Computation **18**, 1527–1554 (2006)
2. Bengio, Y., Lamblin, P., Popovici, D., Larochelle, H.: Greedy layer-wise training of deep networks. In: NIPS'2006 (2007)
3. Ranzato, M., Poultney, C., Chopra, S., LeCun, Y.: Efficient learning of sparse representations with an energy-based model. In: NIPS'06 (2007)
4. Jarrett, K., Kavukcuoglu, K., Ranzato, M.A., LeCun, Y.: What is the best multi-stage architecture for object recognition? In: International Conference on Computer Vision, pp. 2146–2153. IEEE (2009)
5. Krizhevsky, A.: Convolutional deep belief networks on cifar-10. Unpublished manuscript (2010)
6. LeCun, Y., et al.: Handwritten digit recognition with a back-propagation network. In: Advances in Neural Information Processing Systems (1990)
7. LeCun, Y., Huang, F.J., Bottou, L.: Learning methods for generic object recognition with invariance to pose and lighting. In: Computer Vision and Pattern Recognition, 2004. CVPR 2004. Proceedings of the 2004 IEEE Computer Society Conference, vol. 2, pp. II–97. IEEE (2004)
8. Lee, H., Grosse, R., Ranganath, R., Ng, A.Y.: Convolutional deep belief networks for scalable unsupervised learning of hierarchical representations. In: Proceedings of the 26th Annual International Conference on Machine Learning, pp. 609–616. ACM (2009)
9. Pinto, N., Doukhan, D., DiCarlo, J.J., Cox, D.D.: A high-throughput screening approach to discovering good forms of biologically inspired visual representation. PLoS Comput. Biol. **5**(11), e1000579 (2009)
10. Turaga, S.C., et al.: Convolutional networks can learn to generate affinity graphs for image segmentation. Neural Comput. **22**(2), 511–538 (2010)
11. Abadi, B., et al.: TensorFlow: large-scale machine learning on heterogeneous systems (2015). http://tensorflow.org/. Accessed 1 Nov 2018
12. Theano Development Team. Theano: a Python framework for fast computation of mathematical expressions (2016). arXiv e-prints arXiv:1605.02688
13. Chollet, F., et al.: Keras (2015). https://keras.io. Accessed 1 Nov 2018

14. Paszke, A., et al.: Automatic differentiation in pytorch. In: NIPS-W (2017)
15. Chetlur, S., et al.: cudnn: Efficient primitives for deep learning (2014)
16. Krizhevsky, A., Sutskever, I., Hinton, G.E.: Imagenet classification with deep convolutional neural networks. In: Neural Information Processing systems, p. 25 (2012)
17. Fukushima, K.: Neocognitron: a self-organizing neural network model for a mechanism of pattern recognition unaffected by shift in position. Biol. Cybern. **36**(4), 193–202 (1980)
18. LeCun, Y., Bottou, L., Bengio, Y., Haffner, P.: Gradient-based learning applied to document recognition. Proc. IEEE **86**(11), 2278–2324 (1998)
19. Witten, I.H., Frank, E., Hall, M.A., Pal, C.J.: Data mining, Fourth Edition: Practical Machine Learning Tools and Techniques, 4th edn. Morgan Kaufmann Publishers Inc., San Francisco (2016)
20. Goodfellow, I., Bengio, Y., Courville, A.: Deep Learning. The MIT Press, Cambridge (2016)
21. Wang, X., Zhao, Y., Pourpanah, F.: Recent advances in deep learning. Int. J. Mach. Learn. Cybernet. **11**(4), 747–750 (2020). https://doi.org/10.1007/s13042-020-01096-5
22. LeCun, Y., Bengio, Y., Hinton, G.: Deep Learning. Nature **521**, 436 (2015)
23. Schmidhuber, J.: Deep learning in neural networks: an overview. Neural Net. **61**, 85–117 (2015)
24. Rumelhart, D.E., Hinton, G.E., Williams, R.J.: Learning representations by back-propagating errors. Nature **323**, 533 (1986)
25. LeCun, Y., et al.: Backpropagation applied to handwritten zip code recognition. Neural Comput. **1**(4), 541–551 (1989)
26. Hinton, G.E., Osindero, S., Teh, Y.-W.: A fast learning algorithm for deep belief nets. Neural Comput. **18**(7), 1527–1554 (2006). https://doi.org/10.1162/neco.2006.18.7.1527
27. Bengio, Y., Lamblin, P., Popovici, D., Larochelle, H.: Greedy layer-wise training of deep networks. In: Proceedings of the 19th International Conference on Neural Information Processing Systems, NIPS'06, pp. 153–160. MIT Press, Cambridge (2016)
28. Russakovsky, O., et al.: ImageNet large scale visual recognition challenge. Int. J. Comput. Vision **115**(3), 211–252 (2015). https://doi.org/10.1007/s11263-015-0816-y
29. Kumar, M.: An incorporation of artificial intelligence capabilities in cloud computing. Int. J. Eng. Comput. Sci. (2016). https://doi.org/10.18535/ijecs/v5i11.63
30. Saiyeda, A., Mir, M.A.: Cloud computing for deep learning analytics: a survey of current trends and challenges. Int. J. Adv. Res. Comput. Sci. **8**(2), 68–72 (2017)
31. Dumbill, E.: What is big data?: an introduction to the big data landscape (2012). http://radar.oreilly.com/2012/01/what-is-big-data.html
32. Najafabadi, M.M., Villanustre, F., Khoshgoftaar, T.M., Seliya, N., Wald, R., Muharemagic, E.: Deep learning applications and challenges in big data analytics. J. Big Data **2**(1), 1–21 (2015). https://doi.org/10.1186/s40537-014-0007-7
33. Hinton, G., Salakhutdinov, R.: Discovering binary codes for documents by learning deep generative models. Top Cogn. Sci. **3**(1), 74–91 (2011)
34. Salakhutdinov, R., Hinton, G.: Semantic hashing. Int. J. Approx. Reason. **50**(7), 969–978 (2009)

Method of Real Time Calculation of Learning Rate Value to Improve Convergence of Neural Network Training

Anton I. Glushchenko$^{(\boxtimes)}$ ⓘ, Vladislav A. Petrov ⓘ,
and Konstantin A. Lastochkin ⓘ

A.A. Ugarov Stary Oskol Technological Institute (Branch) NUST "MISIS",
Stary Oskol, Russia
glushchenko@ieee.org

Abstract. The scope of this research is a problem of correct initialization and further correction of a neural network learning rate. It is one of the main hyperparameters, which helps to increase a convergence rate of a training process. There are known techniques of time-based decay, step decay and exponential decay, in which the learning rate is initialized manually and then corrected downwards proportionally to some value. In contrast, in this paper, it is proposed to focus on an excitation level of a regressor - an output amplitude of a previous network layer. The formulas, which are based on the recursive least squares method, are derived to calculate the learning rate for each network layer, and their convergence is proved. Using them, the initial learning rate can be chosen arbitrarily, and not only can such rate decrease, but also it is able to increase when the value of the regressor has become lower. Experiments are conducted for a task of image recognition using multilayer networks and the MNIST database. For networks of different structures, the proposed method allows reducing the number of training epochs significantly in comparison with the backpropagation method with a constant learning rate.

Keywords: Neural network · Backpropagation · Learning rate · Recursive least squares · Convergence rate

1 Introduction

Nowadays neural networks are very popular to solve various applied tasks related to computer vision, prediction, text processing, generation of new content, etc. [1]. Every year the number of research papers, which are devoted to the development of new structures and types of neural networks that would meet the increasing requirements of practical applicability, is growing. Such networks, which have

This research was supported by Russian Foundation for Basic Research. Grant No 18-47-310003-r a.

L. Rutkowski et al. (Eds.): ICAISC 2020, LNAI 12415, pp. 103–113, 2020.
https://doi.org/10.1007/978-3-030-61401-0_10

become widely applicable in recent years, include convolutional, LSTM, GRU, GAN ones, as well as variable auto-encoders [2]. Analyzing them and the history of their development, it can be concluded that today the vector of the neural network development is aimed at the layer number increase, development of new special layers and search for the most effective way to combine them. Even nowadays such approaches allow obtaining efficiency, which is impossible for multilayer perceptrons in terms of accuracy [3].

As the structure of neural networks becomes more complex, and the amount of training data increases, the time, which is spent on a training process, inevitably increases too. Sometimes one epoch of training of a modern deep neural network, using even a powerful PC, takes several hours or even days. This prevents a developer from operative correction of the neural network hyperparameters. That is why it takes weeks or months to obtain a solution of a required accuracy [4]. Therefore, an improvement of the convergence rate of neural network training is actual.

Nowadays a widely used approach of neural network training is the method of error backpropagation [5], as well as its modern modifications - Stochastic Gradient Descent, AdaGrad, RMSProp, AdaDelta, Adam and others [6]. Their core algorithm is based on the calculation of a matrix of first derivatives of an objective function with respect to adjustable parameters. So it has relatively low performance. The above-mentioned modifications, in general, do not help to increase it. They are used to reduce memory consumption, cope with overfitting and unbalanced training sets.

Second-order optimization methods have a higher convergence rate. They include the Levenberg-Marquardt algorithm [7], the BFGS algorithm and its modification with limited memory use [8]. They are quasi-Newtonian. Using second-order methods, the number of training epochs is lower than for first-order ones, but the duration of each epoch increases significantly. This is caused by the high complexity of the second-order methods implementation. Besides, considering an arbitrary deep neural network, the problem of approximation of a matrix of the objective function second-order derivatives, in general, is not trivial and in some cases cannot be solved at all.

Considering the backpropagation method (and its known modifications), the values of layers learning rate are hyperparameters, which are chosen before the start of the training process. Such rate values may not be optimal for the current layer input. This results in an excessively long training process. There are approaches, in which the learning rate is decreased over time proportionally to some criterion (time-based decay, step decay and exponential decay [6,9,10]). In such a case, results still depend on the manual selection of the initial learning rate value, which may be wrong. In order to overcome this shortcoming, in this study, it is proposed to use the recursive least squares method [11] to obtain the equations to adjust the neural network parameters. Such equations will allow calculating the learning rate for each layer at each training step on the basis of the current value of the considered layer input excitation (amplitude of its input signal). This online calculation of the learning rate value will allow increasing the convergence rate of the network training process.

2   Derivation of Learning Rate Adjustment Formulas

2.1   Neural Network Training Based on Recursive Least Squares

A neural network structure with one hidden layer (Fig. 1) is considered to simplify the representation of formulas to be derived. Its input-output relation is represented as (1). Here φ and σ are activation functions, W^1 and W^2 are weights matrices of a hidden and an output layers, which dimensions are $N_2 \times (N_1 + 1)$ and $N_3 \times (N_2 + 1)$ respectively, z is an input vector, b^1 and b^2 are scalars equaled to one, Θ^1 and Θ^2 are vectors of biases.

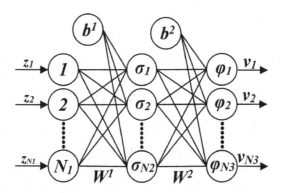

Fig. 1. Neural network structure.

$$u_k = \varphi \left(W^2 \sigma \left(W^1 \bar{z} \right) \right) \tag{1}$$

The matrices W^1 and W^2, the vector z and the hidden layer output vector σ are defined as (2). The numbers of neurons in all layers (N_1, N_2 and N_3) are chosen as a result of the network structural synthesis (this is not the scope of this research).

$$\bar{z} = \begin{bmatrix} b^1 \ z_1 \ z_2 \cdots z_{N1} \end{bmatrix}^T = \begin{bmatrix} b^1 \ z \end{bmatrix}^T; \quad \sigma \left(W^1 \bar{z} \right) = \begin{bmatrix} b^2 \ \sigma_1 \ \sigma_2 \cdots \sigma_{N2} \end{bmatrix}^T$$

$$W^1 = \begin{bmatrix} \theta_1^1 & \cdots & \theta_{N2}^1 \\ w_{1,1}^1 & \cdots & w_{1,N2}^1 \\ \vdots & \ddots & \vdots \\ w_{N1,1}^1 & \cdots & w_{N1,N2}^1 \end{bmatrix}^T; W^2 = \begin{bmatrix} \theta_1^2 & \cdots & \theta_{N3}^2 \\ w_{1,1}^2 & \cdots & w_{1,N3}^2 \\ \vdots & \ddots & \vdots \\ w_{N2,1}^2 & \cdots & w_{N2,N3}^2 \end{bmatrix}^T \tag{2}$$

Let a notion of an ideal continuous function $f(z) \in \Omega \subset R^{N1}$ be introduced, which is a solution of the problem, for which the neural network is developed.

Using the fundamental results of [12] and considering (1), there exist such ideal parameters W^1, W^2 in a subset Ω of R^{N1} that (3) becomes true. ε is an approximation error.

$$f(z) = \varphi\left(W^2\sigma\left(W^1\bar{z}\right)\right) + \varepsilon \tag{3}$$

Let a notion of a neural network with current parameters (4), tuned during training, be introduced. An error between ideal and real network outputs is (5).

$$\hat{u}_k = \varphi\left(\hat{W}^2\sigma\left(\hat{W}^1\bar{z}\right)\right) \tag{4}$$

$$e = \varphi\left(W^2\sigma\left(W^1\bar{z}\right)\right) - \varphi\left(\hat{W}^2\sigma\left(\hat{W}^1\bar{z}\right)\right) + \varepsilon \tag{5}$$

A training objective criterion is (6). Its minimum will be achieved when its gradients with respect to the network adjustable parameters become zero (7).

$$Q\left(\hat{W}^1, \hat{W}^2\right) = \frac{1}{2}e^T e \tag{6}$$

$$
\begin{aligned}
\nabla_{\hat{W}^1} Q\left(\hat{W}^1, \hat{W}^2\right) &= -\sigma'\left(\hat{W}^1\bar{z}\right)\left(\hat{W}^2\right)^T \varphi'\left(\hat{W}^2\sigma\left(\hat{W}^1\bar{z}\right)\right) e\bar{z}^T \\
&= -e_1\bar{z}^T = 0 \\
\nabla_{\hat{W}^2} Q\left(\hat{W}^1, \hat{W}^2\right) &= -\varphi'\left(\hat{W}^2\sigma\left(\hat{W}^1\bar{z}\right)\right) e\sigma^T\left(\hat{W}^1\bar{z}\right) \\
&= -e_2\sigma^T\left(\hat{W}^1\bar{z}\right) = 0
\end{aligned}
\tag{7}
$$

Here e_1 and e_2 are vectors of errors of the hidden and output layers. As the training of the neural network is made with the help of the recursive least squares method, then (6) is reformulated separately for the hidden and output layers as (8). Here λ_1 and λ_2 are forgetting factors, t is a current moment of time, $\tau \in [0; t]$.

$$
\begin{aligned}
Q_1\left(\hat{W}^1\right) &= \frac{1}{2}\int_0^t \exp\left(-\lambda_1(t-\tau)\right) e_1^T e_1 d\tau, \\
Q_2\left(\hat{W}^2\right) &= \frac{1}{2}\int_0^t \exp\left(-\lambda_2(t-\tau)\right) e_2^T e_2 d\tau
\end{aligned}
\tag{8}
$$

In this case, errors of each layer, taking into account their dependence on time, can be written as (9) using ideal parameters of each layer and current value of its regressor ($\bar{z}(\tau)$ - for the hidden layer, $\sigma\left(\hat{W}^1\bar{z}\right)$ - for the output layer). The network weights depend on t in (9), but not on τ, as they are not changed during the period of time from zero to t (for in instance, in the course of a certain batch).

$$
\begin{aligned}
e_1 &= W^1\bar{z} - \hat{W}^1\bar{z} = y_1(\tau) - \hat{W}^1(t)\bar{z}(\tau) \\
e_2 &= W^2\sigma\left(\hat{W}^1\bar{z}\right) - \hat{W}^2\sigma\left(\hat{W}^1\bar{z}\right) = y_2(\tau) - \hat{W}^2(t)\hat{\sigma}(\tau)
\end{aligned}
\tag{9}
$$

The minimum of (8) will be achieved when their gradients with respect to the adjustable parameters of the network become zeros (10).

$$
\nabla_{\hat{W}^1} Q_1^T = -\int_0^t \exp\left(-\lambda_1 \left(t - \tau\right)\right) \bar{z}\left(\tau\right) \left[y_1\left(\tau\right) - \hat{W}^1\left(t\right)\bar{z}\left(\tau\right)\right]^T d\tau = 0
$$
$$
\nabla_{\hat{W}^2} Q_2^T = -\int_0^t \exp\left(-\lambda_2 \left(t - \tau\right)\right) \hat{\sigma}\left(\tau\right) \left[y_2\left(\tau\right) - \hat{W}^2\left(t\right)\hat{\sigma}\left(\tau\right)\right]^T d\tau = 0
$$

(10)

Using the properties of a sum of integrals, brackets are expanded in (10). Then a term, which includes the ideal parameters, is moved to the right part of (11). To make the Eq. (11) narrower, $\exp\left(-\lambda_1 \left(t - \tau\right)\right)$ is denoted as exp1, $\exp\left(-\lambda_2 \left(t - \tau\right)\right)$ - as exp2. Estimations of the hidden and output layers parameters, obtained with the help of the recursive least squares method, are (12).

$$
\int_0^t \text{exp1} \cdot \bar{z}\left(\tau\right)\bar{z}^T\left(\tau\right)\left(\hat{W}^1\left(t\right)\right)^T d\tau = \int_0^t \text{exp1} \cdot \bar{z}\left(\tau\right)y_1^T\left(\tau\right)d\tau
$$
$$
\int_0^t \text{exp2} \cdot \hat{\sigma}\left(\tau\right)\hat{\sigma}^T\left(\tau\right)\left(\hat{W}^2\left(t\right)\right)^T d\tau = \int_0^t \text{exp2} \cdot \hat{\sigma}\left(\tau\right)y_2^T\left(\tau\right)d\tau
$$

(11)

$$
\left(\hat{W}^1\left(t\right)\right)^T = P_1\left(t\right)\int_0^t \exp\left(-\lambda_1 \left(t - \tau\right)\right)\bar{z}\left(\tau\right)y_1^T\left(\tau\right)d\tau
$$
$$
P_1\left(t\right) = \left[\int_0^t \exp\left(-\lambda_1 \left(t - \tau\right)\right)\bar{z}\left(\tau\right)\bar{z}^T\left(\tau\right)d\tau\right]^{-1}
$$
$$
\left(\hat{W}^2\left(t\right)\right)^T = P_2\left(t\right)\int_0^t \exp\left(-\lambda_2 \left(t - \tau\right)\right)\hat{\sigma}\left(\tau\right)y_2^T\left(\tau\right)d\tau
$$
$$
P_2\left(t\right) = \left[\int_0^t \exp\left(-\lambda_2 \left(t - \tau\right)\right)\hat{\sigma}\left(\tau\right)\hat{\sigma}^T\left(\tau\right)d\tau\right]^{-1}
$$

(12)

Here $P_1(t)$ and $P_2(t)$ are the learning rate values of the hidden and output layers. The derivatives of $P_1^{-1}(t)$ and $P_2^{-1}(t)$ (13) are found with the help of the fundamental theorem of calculus. The derivatives of the learning rates of the neural network training (15) are found with respect to (12) and (14).

$$
\frac{dP_1^{-1}(t)}{dt} = \bar{z}\left(t\right)\bar{z}^T\left(t\right) - \lambda_1 \int_0^t \exp\left(-\lambda_1 \left(t - \tau\right)\right)\bar{z}\left(\tau\right)\bar{z}^T\left(\tau\right)d\tau
$$
$$
\frac{dP_2^{-1}(t)}{dt} = \hat{\sigma}\left(t\right)\hat{\sigma}^T\left(t\right) - \lambda_2 \int_0^t \exp\left(-\lambda_2 \left(t - \tau\right)\right)\hat{\sigma}\left(\tau\right)\hat{\sigma}^T\left(\tau\right)d\tau
$$

(13)

$$
\frac{dI}{dt} = \frac{d}{dt}\left[P\left(t\right)P^{-1}\left(t\right)\right] = \frac{dP\left(t\right)}{dt}P^{-1}\left(t\right) + \frac{dP^{-1}\left(t\right)}{dt}P\left(t\right) = 0
$$

(14)

$$
\frac{dP_1(t)}{dt} = -P_1\left(t\right)\frac{dP_1^{-1}(t)}{dt}P_1\left(t\right) = \lambda_1 P_1\left(t\right) - P_1\left(t\right)\bar{z}\left(t\right)\bar{z}^T\left(t\right)P_1\left(t\right)
$$
$$
\frac{dP_2(t)}{dt} = -P_2\left(t\right)\frac{dP_2^{-1}(t)}{dt}P_2\left(t\right) = \lambda_2 P_2\left(t\right) - P_2\left(t\right)\hat{\sigma}\left(t\right)\hat{\sigma}^T\left(t\right)P_2\left(t\right)
$$

(15)

The equations of the network parameters adjustment (16) and (17) are found by taking derivative of their least-squares estimations (12) with respect to time.

$$
\begin{aligned}
\left(\dot{\hat{W}}^{1}(t)\right)^{T} &= \tfrac{d}{dt}\left[P_{1}(t)\right]\int_{0}^{t}\exp\left(-\lambda_{1}(t-\tau)\right)\bar{z}(\tau)\,y_{1}^{T}(\tau)\,d\tau \\
&\quad + P_{1}(t)\tfrac{d}{dt}\int_{0}^{t}\exp\left(-\lambda_{1}(t-\tau)\right)\bar{z}(\tau)\,y_{1}^{T}(\tau)\,d\tau \\
&= \left(\lambda_{1}-P_{1}(t)\,\bar{z}(t)\,\bar{z}^{T}(t)\right)\left(\hat{W}^{1}(t)\right)^{T}-\lambda_{1}\left(\hat{W}^{1}(t)\right)^{T} \\
&\quad + P_{1}(t)\,\bar{z}(t)\,y_{1}^{T}(t)=P_{1}(t)\,\bar{z}(t)\left(y_{1}(t)-\hat{W}^{1}(t)\,\bar{z}(t)\right)^{T}=P_{1}(t)\,\bar{z}(t)\,e_{1}^{T}
\end{aligned}
\tag{16}
$$

$$
\begin{aligned}
\left(\dot{\hat{W}}^{2}(t)\right)^{T} &= \tfrac{d}{dt}\left[P_{2}(t)\right]\int_{0}^{t}\exp\left(-\lambda_{2}(t-\tau)\right)\hat{\sigma}(\tau)\,y_{2}^{T}(\tau)\,d\tau \\
&\quad + P_{2}(t)\tfrac{d}{dt}\int_{0}^{t}\exp\left(-\lambda_{2}(t-\tau)\right)\hat{\sigma}(\tau)\,y_{2}^{T}(\tau)\,d\tau \\
&= \left(\lambda_{2}-P_{2}(t)\,\hat{\sigma}(t)\,\hat{\sigma}^{T}(t)\right)\left(\hat{W}^{2}(t)\right)^{T}-\lambda_{2}\left(\hat{W}^{2}(t)\right)^{T} \\
&\quad + P_{2}(t)\,\hat{\sigma}(t)\,y_{2}^{T}(t)=P_{2}(t)\,\hat{\sigma}(t)\left(y_{2}(t)-\hat{W}^{2}(t)\,\hat{\sigma}(t)\right)^{T}=P_{2}(t)\,\hat{\sigma}(t)\,e_{2}^{T}
\end{aligned}
\tag{17}
$$

Taking into account e_{1} and e_{2} definition from (7), formulas (16) and (17) are written as (18). The derived equations of neural network parameters adjustment differ from the conventional formulas of the backpropagation method because Eqs. (15) of the learning rate tuning are used. Having $P_{1}(t)=\eta^{1}=const$ and $P_{2}(t)=\eta^{2}=const$, the formulas coincide with the classical ones of the above mentioned method. The variable learning rate is to improve the convergence of the objective criterion (6) to its minimum. In the next section, the obtained training algorithm convergence is studied.

$$
\begin{aligned}
\left(\dot{\hat{W}}^{1}(t)\right)^{T} &= P_{1}(t)\,\bar{z}(t)\,e_{1}^{T}=P_{1}(t)\,\bar{z}e^{T}\varphi'\left(\hat{W}^{2}\sigma\left(\hat{W}^{1}\bar{z}\right)\right)\left(\hat{W}^{2}\right)^{T}\sigma' \\
\left(\dot{\hat{W}}^{2}(t)\right)^{T} &= P_{2}(t)\,\hat{\sigma}(t)\,e_{2}^{T}=P_{2}(t)\,\sigma\left(\hat{W}^{1}\bar{z}\right)e^{T}\varphi'\left(\hat{W}^{2}\sigma\left(\hat{W}^{1}\bar{z}\right)\right)
\end{aligned}
\tag{18}
$$

2.2   Parametric Convergence

Now the parametric convergence of neural network parameters to ideal values with the help of algorithm (15)–(18) will be proved. Doing this and considering (9), let the difference between ideal and current neural network parameters (19) be introduced.

$$
\begin{aligned}
e_{1} &= W^{1}\bar{z}-\hat{W}^{1}\bar{z}=\tilde{W}^{1}\bar{z} \\
e_{2} &= W^{2}\sigma\left(\hat{W}^{1}\bar{z}\right)-\hat{W}^{2}\sigma\left(\hat{W}^{1}\bar{z}\right)=\tilde{W}^{2}\sigma\left(\hat{W}^{1}\bar{z}\right)
\end{aligned}
\tag{19}
$$

Since the ideal parameters do not change over time, the Eqs. (16) and (17) with consideration of (19) can be presented as (20). Considering (13), Eqs. (20) are written as (21). Hence, the solutions of Eqs. (21) are (22).

$$P_1^{-1}(t)\left(\dot{\tilde{W}}^1(t)\right)^T = -\bar{z}(t)\,\bar{z}^T(t)\left(\tilde{W}^1\right)^T,$$
$$P_2^{-1}(t)\left(\dot{\tilde{W}}^2(t)\right)^T = -\hat{\sigma}(t)\,\hat{\sigma}^T(t)\left(\tilde{W}^2\right)^T \tag{20}$$

$$\frac{d}{dt}\left[P_1^{-1}(t)\left(\tilde{W}^1\right)^T\right] = -\lambda_1 P_1^{-1}(t)\left(\tilde{W}^1\right)^T,$$
$$\frac{d}{dt}\left[P_2^{-1}(t)\left(\tilde{W}^2\right)^T\right] = -\lambda_2 P_2^{-1}(t)\left(\tilde{W}^2\right)^T \tag{21}$$

$$\left(\tilde{W}^1(t)\right)^T = \exp\left(-\lambda_1 t\right) P_1^{-1}(0)\,P_1(t)\left(\tilde{W}^1(0)\right)^T$$
$$\left(\tilde{W}^2(t)\right)^T = \exp\left(-\lambda_2 t\right) P_2^{-1}(0)\,P_2(t)\left(\tilde{W}^2(0)\right)^T \tag{22}$$

Having analyzed solutions (23) of the differential equations (13), it becomes clear that, if the hidden and output neural network layers regressors meet the conditions of permanent excitation (24), $P_1(t)$ and $P_2(t)$ are limited from above, and the parametric errors (22) converge to zero with the rates λ_1 and λ_2. $\alpha_1 > 0$ and $\alpha_2 > 0$ in (24).

$$P_1^{-1}(t) = P_1^{-1}(0)\exp\left(-\lambda_1 t\right) + \int_0^t \exp\left(-\lambda_1(t-\tau)\right)\bar{z}(\tau)\,\bar{z}^T(\tau)\,d\tau$$
$$P_2^{-1}(t) = P_2^{-1}(0)\exp\left(-\lambda_2 t\right) + \int_0^t \exp\left(-\lambda_2(t-\tau)\right)\hat{\sigma}(\tau)\,\hat{\sigma}^T(\tau)\,d\tau \tag{23}$$

$$\int_t^{t+T} \bar{z}(\tau)\,\bar{z}^T(\tau)\,d\tau \geq \alpha_1 I_1, \qquad \int_t^{t+T} \hat{\sigma}(\tau)\,\hat{\sigma}^T(\tau)\,d\tau \geq \alpha_2 I_2 \tag{24}$$

2.3   Iterative Form of Derived Formulas

It is necessary to transform obtained training formulas into an iterative form for their successful practical application. As for the Eqs. (18), which coincide with the error backpropagation method, their recurrence implementation (25) is known quite for a long time. Such implementation of (15) is written as (26).

$$\left(\hat{W}_{n+1}^1\right)^T = \left(\hat{W}_n^1\right)^T + P_{1n}\bar{z}_n e_n^T \varphi'\left(\hat{W}_n^2 \sigma\left(\hat{W}_n^1 \bar{z}_n\right)\right)\left(\hat{W}_n^2\right)^T \sigma'\left(\hat{W}_n^1 \bar{z}_n\right)$$
$$\left(\hat{W}_{n+1}^2\right)^T = \left(\hat{W}_n^2\right)^T + P_{2n}\sigma\left(\hat{W}_n^1 \bar{z}_n\right) e_n^T \varphi'\left(\hat{W}_n^2 \sigma\left(\hat{W}_n^1 \bar{z}_n\right)\right) \tag{25}$$

$$P_{1n+1} = P_{1n} + \lambda_1 P_{1n} - P_{1n}\bar{z}_n \bar{z}_n^T P_{1n}, \qquad P_{2n+1} = P_{2n} + \lambda_2 P_{2n} - P_{2n}\hat{\sigma}_n \hat{\sigma}_n^T P_{2n} \tag{26}$$

Here n is the current iteration, $n+1$ is the next iteration of the adjustment. The main condition to get to the minimum of (6) and (8) is that the learning rate (26) is kept positive at each iteration of the training algorithm (25). This needs to be met for (26). So (27) is obtained to keep positive values of (26).

$$\|P_{1n}\| < \frac{1+\lambda_1}{\|\bar{z}_n \bar{z}_n^T\|}, \qquad \|P_{2n}\| < \frac{1+\lambda_2}{\|\hat{\sigma}_n \hat{\sigma}_n^T\|} \tag{27}$$

Conditions (27) may not be met in course of the neural network training due to: incorrect choice of the initial learning rate (too high or low for the current input of a layer), insufficient excitation of regressors $\bar{z}_n$ and $\hat{\sigma}_n$. Considering the most common case, when the same value of learning rate is used for all elements in a certain weights matrix, a descent of objective criteria (6) and (8) to their minima at iteration $(n+1)$ can be ensured with the help of (28) in case (27) are false.

$$P_{1n} = 0.99 \frac{1+\lambda_1}{\|\bar{z}_n \bar{z}_n^T\|} I_1, \quad P_{2n} = 0.99 \frac{1+\lambda_2}{\|\hat{\sigma}_n \hat{\sigma}_n^T\|} I_2 \tag{28}$$

As an alternative to formulas (28), it is also possible to use the normalized law of the learning rate adjustment (29) (derived from the matrix inversion lemma). In such case criteria (27) turns into (30), which are always fulfilled.

$$
\begin{aligned}
P_{1n+1} &= \frac{P_{1n} + \lambda_1 P_{1n} - P_{1n} \bar{z}_n \bar{z}_n^T P_{1n} \left(1 + 2\bar{z}_n P_{1n} \bar{z}_n^T\right)^{-1}}{1 + \bar{z}_n P_{1n} \bar{z}_n^T} \\
P_{2n+1} &= \frac{P_{2n} + \lambda_2 P_{2n} - P_{2n} \hat{\sigma}_n \hat{\sigma}_n^T P_{2n} \left(1 + 2\hat{\sigma}_n P_{1n} \hat{\sigma}_n^T\right)^{-1}}{1 + \hat{\sigma}_n P_{1n} \hat{\sigma}_n^T}
\end{aligned}
\tag{29}
$$

$$\|P_{1n}\| > \frac{-(1+\lambda_1)}{(1+2\lambda_1)\|\bar{z}_n \bar{z}_n^T\|}; \|P_{2n}\| > \frac{-(1+\lambda_2)}{(1+2\lambda_2)\|\hat{\sigma}_n \hat{\sigma}_n^T\|} \tag{30}$$

3   Conducted Experiments

The aim of the experiments was to compare the convergence rate of the conventional backpropagation method with a constant learning rate with the proposed approach. A handwritten digits recognition task (MNIST database) was chosen for experiments. MNIST contained 60000 images in a train set and 10000 – in a test one. The training process was always started from the same randomly selected weights. The batch size was 1000 images. To avoid overfitting, the training was stopped if the accuracy on the test set had been less than the one on the training set for two epochs in a row.

A neural network was used, which contained one hidden layer (Fig. 1) with 784 input neurons, 10 output neurons (sigmoid activation function) and 80 hidden neurons (sigmoid activation function). The learning rate of its hidden and output layers was set as $\eta^1 = \eta^2 = 1$ for the formulas of the error backpropagation method. Equations (25), (26), (29) used the same values as the initial ones: $P_1(0) = P_2(0) = 1$. $\lambda_1 = 4000$, $\lambda_2 = 20$. All experiments (Fig. 2) were conducted for three methods: 1) backpropagation – BackProp, 2) formulas (25)–(28) – RLS, 3) formulas (25) and (29) – RLS1. Figure 2A shows the curves of network accuracy on training (solid lines) and test (dashed lines) sets, Fig. 2B shows the same curves using the expanded scale.

As it can be seen from Fig. 2A and Table 1, obtained training formulas with variable learning rate provided faster convergence to the maximum accuracy comparing to the backpropagation method with the constant learning rate.

Considering data in Table 1, it is clear that the proposed approaches of learning rate calculation allowed reducing training time comparing to the backpropagation with constant learning rate. Figure 3 shows the curves of the learning rate of the hidden and output layers obtained at each batch of the training process.

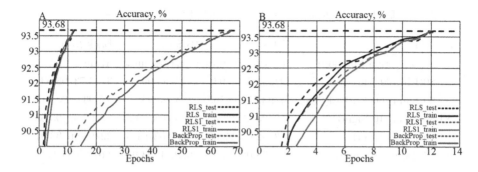

Fig. 2. Results of training of neural network 784-80(sigmoid)-10(sigmoid).

Table 1. Performance indexes of training methods – network structure 784-80-10.

Indexes	RLS	RLS1	BackProp
Epochs/Accuracy test/Accuracy Train	12/93.66/93.59	12/93.68/93.61	67/93.67/93.53
Average time per epoch, seconds	7.908	7.179	7.845
Training time, seconds	102.8	93.329	525.635

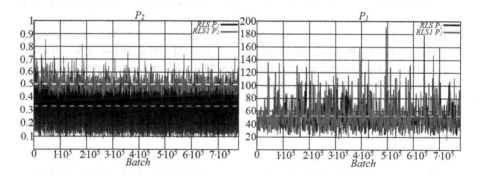

Fig. 3. Learning rate values for RLS and RLS1 methods (dashed lines – average value).

Similar results were obtained from various positive initial values of the learning rate. In general, RLS and RLS1 achieved the same accuracy. Experiments, conducted with networks of other structures (Table 2), also proved the correctness of obtained formulas. Thus, the experiments showed the main advantages of the derived formulas of neural network training (RLS and RLS1) in comparison with the backpropagation method with the constant learning rate: 1) initial learning rate can be chosen randomly; 2) training time was sufficiently reduced, i.e. convergence rate was improved.

Table 2. Performance indexes of tested training methods.

Structure	RLS	RLS1	BackProp
Layer (activation function)	Epochs/Accuracy test/Accuracy Train		
784-80(Elu)-60(Elu)-10(Elu)	2/93.94/93.93	2/94/93.96	3/93.73/93.63
784-80(Sigm)-60(Elu)-10(Sigm)	4/93.77/93.765	3/94/93.95	47/93.9/93.81
784-80(Sigm)-10(Sigm)	12/93.66/93.59	12/93.68/93.61	67/93.67/93.53
784-80(Elu)-10(Elu)	13/92.64/92.02	16/92.03/91.8	32/93.96/93.91
784-80(Tanh)-10(Tanh)	26/93.08/92.97	26/93.1/93.08	110/93.34/93.3

4 Conclusion

The developed method of neural network training with variable learning rate can be used both independently to increase the convergence rate of the training process and together with a group of adaptive optimization algorithms (Adagrad, Adadelta, RMSProp, Adam, quickProp). The fact is that all these algorithms use some initial learning rate for each layer of the neural network, which is then normalized for each neuron of this layer. Formulas for the neural network rate adjustment, developed in this research, will allow updating this base rate dynamically for the neural network layer. This should lead to the improvement of neural network efficiency in terms of accuracy. Further research scopes are to: 1) combine the developed formulas with Adagrad and Adam algorithms, 2) apply obtained formulas to convolutional neural networks.

References

1. Chollet, F.: Deep Learning with Python. Manning Publications, New York (2018)
2. Goodfellow, I., Bengio Y., Courville A.: Deep Learning. MIT Press, Cambridge (2016)
3. He, K., et al.: Delving deep into rectifiers: surpassing human-level performance on imagenet classification. In: IEEE Proceedings of International Conference on Computer Vision (ICCV), Santiago, pp. 1026–1034 (2015)
4. Wu, B. et al.: FBNet: hardware-aware efficient convnet design via differentiable neural architecture search. In: Proceedings of 2019 IEEE/CVF Conference on Computer Vision and Pattern Recognition (CVPR), Long Beach, CA, USA, pp. 10726–10734 (2019)
5. Omatu, S., Khalid, M.B., Yusof, R.: Neuro-Control and Its Applications. Springer, London (1996)
6. Kingma, D.P., Ba, J.: Adam: a method for stochastic optimization. In: Proceedings of 3rd International Conference on Learning Representations, San Diego, USA, pp. 1–15 (2015)
7. Yu, H., Wilamowski, B.M.: Levenberg-Marquardt training. Ind. Electron. Handbook **5**(12), 12.1–12.16 (2011)
8. Rafati, J., Marica, R.F.: Quasi-Newton optimization methods for deep learning applications. Deep Learn. Appl. **1098**, 9–38 (2020)

9. Sanjeev, A., Zhiyuan, L., Kaifeng, L.: Theoretical analysis of auto rate-tuning by batch normalization. In: Proceedings of International Conference on Learning Representations, New Orleans (2019)
10. An, W., et al.: Exponential decay sine wave learning rate for fast deep neural network training. In: Proceedings of Visual Communications and Image Processing, pp. 1–4 (2017)
11. Monson, H.H.: Statistical Digital Signal Processing and Modeling. Wiley, Chichester (1996)
12. Funahashi, K.I.: On the approximate realization of continuous mappings by neural networks. Neural Networks **2**, 183–192 (1989)

Application of an Improved Focal Loss in Vehicle Detection

Xuanlin He[1], Jie Yang[1(✉)], and Nikola Kasabov[2]

[1] Institute of Image Processing and Pattern Recognition,
Shanghai Jiao Tong University, Shanghai, China
`jieyang@sjtu.edu.cn`
[2] Auckland University of Technology, Auckland, New Zealand

Abstract. Object detection is an important and fundamental task in computer vision. Recently, the emergence of deep neural network has made considerable progress in object detection. Deep neural network object detectors can be grouped in two broad categories: the two-stage detector and the one-stage detector. One-stage detectors are faster than two-stage detectors. However, they suffer from a severe foreground-backg-round class imbalance during training that causes a low accuracy performance. RetinaNet is a one-stage detector with a novel loss function named Focal Loss which can reduce the class imbalance effect. Thereby RetinaNet outperforms all the two-stage and one-stage detectors in term of accuracy. The main idea of focal loss is to add a modulating factor to rectify the cross-entropy loss, which down-weights the loss of easy examples during training and thus focuses on the hard examples. However, cross-entropy loss only focuses on the loss of the ground-truth classes and thus it can't gain the loss feedback from the false classes. Thereby cross-entropy loss does not achieve the best convergence. In this paper, we proposed a new loss function named Dual Cross-Entropy Focal Loss, which improves on the focal loss. Dual cross-entropy focal loss adds a modulating factor to rectify the dual cross-entropy loss towards focusing on the hard samples. Dual cross-entropy loss is an improved variant of cross-entropy loss, which gains the loss feedback from both the ground-truth classes and the false classes. We changed the loss function of RetinaNet from focal loss to our dual cross-entropy focal loss and performed some experiments on a small vehicle dataset. The experimental results show that our new loss function improves the vehicle detection performance.

Keywords: Focal loss · Class imbalance · Cross-entropy loss · RetinaNet · Vehicle detection · Object detection · Deep neural network

1 Introduction

Object detection is one of the most fundamental tasks in computer vision, which has received considerable attention for several decades. The emergence of deep

This research was partly supported by NSFC, China (No:61876107,U1803261).

© Springer Nature Switzerland AG 2020
L. Rutkowski et al. (Eds.): ICAISC 2020, LNAI 12415, pp. 114–123, 2020.
https://doi.org/10.1007/978-3-030-61401-0_11

convolutional neural networks, including CNNs [1–3], has provided a significant improvement in object detection [4–6]. The CNN-based object detection methods are mainly divided into two categories: the two-stage method and the one-stage method.

The R-CNN-like two-stage detectors generate the object candidate regions in the first stage and then classify each candidate region as one of the foreground classes or as background in the second stage. Generation of the object candidate regions in the first stage greatly improves the detection accuracy; however it reduces the detection speed. The representatives of the two-stage method are the region proposal based detectors, such as RCNN [7], Fast RCNN [8], Faster RCNN [9] and RFCN [10].

The one-stage detectors skip the process of generating the oject candidate regions. In order to cover the space of possible image boxes, the one-stage detectors use a dense set of fixed sampling grids, such as multiple 'anchors' [9], at each spatial position, and thus they must process a much larger set of regions sampled across an image. As compared to the two-stage detectors, the one-stage detectors improve the detection speed but reduce the detection accuracy. The representatives of the one-stage method are YOLO [11], YOLO9000 [12], YOLOv3 [13], SSD [14] and DSSD [15].

In the two-stage method, the positive and negative samples are relatively balanced (e.g., 1:3). Because in the first stage, a large set (e.g., 1–2) of object candidate regions are selected and most of the background regions (the negative samples) are discarded. In the one-stage method, the positive and negative samples are extremely unbalanced (e.g., 1:1000). Because a dense sampling of regions (e.g., 100 k) which cover various locations, scales, and aspect ratios need to be classified, and the majority of the regions are background regions (the negative samples). Each sampled region can be treated as an training sample. In the one-stage detector, when the convolutional neural network trains the large set of sampled regions, the majority of the loss function consists of the easily classified negatives (background exam-ples) and they dominate the gradient. Thus, extreme foreground-background class imbalance during training is one of the main reasons that causes the two-stage detectors perform more accurate than one-stage detectors.

RetinaNet [16] is a one-stage detector that has a superior performance for dense sampling of object locations in an input image. The network structure of RetinaNet draws on a variety of recent ideas, such as the concept of anchor in RPN [9], the feature pyramids in SSD [14] and FPN [17]. However, Lin et al. [16] emphasized, "We emphasize that our simple detector achieves top results not based on innovations in network design but due to our novel loss." Lin et al. [16] proposed a new loss function named Focal Loss to address the extreme class imbalance. They greatly reduced the weight of easy negatives in the loss function by adding a modulating factor to the standard cross-entropy loss. As a one-stage detector, "RetinaNet is able to match the speed of previous one-stage detectors while surpas-sing the accuracy of all existing state-of-the-art two-stage detectors" [16].

Focal loss is based on the cross-entropy loss. However, cross-entropy loss only focuses on the loss of the ground-truth classes and thus it can't gain the loss feed-back from the false classes. Li et al. [20] proposed an improved variant of cross-entropy loss named Dual Cross-Entropy Loss to gain the loss feedback from both the ground-truth classes and the false classes. In this paper, we combined the idea of focal loss [16] to focus more on hard examples with dual cross-entropy loss and proposed a new loss function named Dual Cross-Entropy Focal Loss. We substituted the loss of RetinaNet [16] with our proposed dual cross-entropy focal loss and applied it to a small vehicle dataset. The experimental results show that our new loss function improves the vehicle detection performance.

2   Related Work

In this section, we will introduce cross-entropy loss and focal loss first. We will analyse why focal loss can reduce the class imbalance effect. Then we will point out the shortage of the cross-entropy loss and introduce the dual cross-entropy loss. We will analyse the advantages of the dual cross-entropy loss compared with the cross-entropy loss. Finally, we will integrate the dual cross-entropy loss and focal loss to create a new loss function named Dual Cross-Entropy Focal Loss.

2.1   Cross-Entropy Loss and Focal Loss

Suppose that $D = \{(x_1, \mathbf{Y}_1), ..., (x_k, \mathbf{Y}_k), ..., (x_M, \mathbf{Y}_M)\}$ is a training dataset of M samples. We assume that all the samples have C categories: background and $C-1$ types of objects. $\mathbf{Y}_k$ is the ground-truth label of the kth $(k \in \{1, 2, ..., M\})$ sample x_k and $\mathbf{Y}_k$ is a C-dimensional one-hot vector. Only one component in $\mathbf{Y}_k$ is 1, and the other components are equal to zero. $y_k^{(i)}$ denotes the ith $(i \in \{1, 2, ..., C\})$ component of the vector $\mathbf{Y}_k$, then $y_k^{(i)}$ is defined as follows:

$$y_k^{(i)} = \begin{cases} 1 & \text{if } x_k \text{ belongs to the } ith\,(i \in \{1, 2, ..., C\}) \text{ class} \\ 0 & \text{if } x_k \text{ does not belong to the } ith\,(i \in \{1, 2, ..., C\}) \text{ class} \end{cases} \tag{1}$$

$\mathbf{P}_k$ is the probability distribution of the kth $(k \in \{1, 2, ..., M\})$ sample x_k predicted by the detector and $\mathbf{P}_k$ is also a C-dimensional vector. $p_k^{(i)}$ denotes the ith $(i \in \{1, 2, ..., C\})$ component of the vector $\mathbf{P}_k$. $p_k^{(i)}$ is the probability that the detector predicts the sample x_k belonging to the ith $(i \in \{1, 2, ..., C\})$ class.

Because of the softmax function, we have $\forall k\,(k \in \{1, 2, ..., M\})$, $\sum_{i=1}^{C} p_k^{(i)} = 1$.

For the sake of brevity, we use t_k $(t_k \in \{1, 2, ..., C\})$ to represent the ground-truth class of the kth $(k \in \{1, 2, ..., M\})$ sample x_k, and then the cross-entropy loss of the sample x_k is defined as follows:

$$CE\,(x_k, \mathbf{Y}_k) = -\mathbf{Y}_k^T \cdot \log(\mathbf{P}_k) = -\log\left(p_k^{(t_k)}\right) \tag{2}$$

The total cross-entropy loss of M samples is defined as follows:

$$L_{CE} = \sum_{k=1}^{M} CE\left(x_k, \mathbf{Y}_k\right) = -\sum_{k=1}^{M}\left(\mathbf{Y}_k^T \cdot \log\left(\mathbf{P}_k\right)\right) = -\sum_{k=1}^{M} \log\left(p_k^{(t_k)}\right) \quad (3)$$

According to Eq. (3), the cross-entropy loss of each training sample is accumulated by an equal weight. It means that, the easy examples $(p_k^{(t_k)} \gg 0.5)$ and the hard examples have the same weight. Even easy examples have a loss with non-trivial magnitude. Most of the training examples of the one-stage detectors are easy negatives. Lin [16] said, "When summed over a large number of easy examples, these small loss values can overwhelm the rare class." Therefore, easy negatives generally lead to degenerate models.

Focal loss [16] multiplies the cross-entropy loss of the sample x_k by a modulating factor $\left(1-p_k^{(t_k)}\right)^{\gamma}$. $\gamma \geqslant 0$ is a constant variable that is suggested to be $\gamma = 2$ in [16]. The focal loss of the sample x_k is defined as follows:

$$\begin{aligned}
FL\left(x_k, \mathbf{Y}_k\right) &= \left(1-p_k^{(t_k)}\right)^{\gamma} \cdot CE\left(x_k, \mathbf{Y}_k\right) \\
&= -\left(1-p_k^{(t_k)}\right)^{\gamma} \cdot \mathbf{Y}_k^T \cdot \log\left(\mathbf{P}_k\right) \qquad (4) \\
&= -\left(1-p_k^{(t_k)}\right)^{\gamma} \cdot \log\left(p_k^{(t_k)}\right)
\end{aligned}$$

The total focal loss of M samples is defined as follows:

$$\begin{aligned}
L_{FL} &= \sum_{k=1}^{M} FL\left(x_k, \mathbf{Y}_k\right) \\
&= -\sum_{k=1}^{M}\left(\left(1-p_k^{(t_k)}\right)^{\gamma} \cdot \mathbf{Y}_k^T \cdot \log\left(\mathbf{P}_k\right)\right) \qquad (5) \\
&= -\sum_{k=1}^{M}\left(1-p_k^{(t_k)}\right)^{\gamma} \cdot \log\left(p_k^{(t_k)}\right)
\end{aligned}$$

$\gamma \geqslant 0$. When $\gamma = 0$, the focal loss is equivalent to the cross-entropy loss. When an example is easy to classify and $p_k^{(t_k)}$ is near 1, the modulating factor $\left(1-p_k^{(t_k)}\right)^{\gamma}$ is near 0 and the loss is down-weighted. When an example is hard to classify and $p_k^{(t_k)}$ is small, the modulating factor $\left(1-p_k^{(t_k)}\right)^{\gamma}$ is near 1 and the loss is unaffected. Indeed, focal loss significantly down-weights the loss of the easy examples, and thus focuses on the hard examples. Therefore, focal loss can reduce the class imbalance effect.

2.2 Dual Cross-Entropy Loss

More recently, dual cross-entropy loss [20] is proposed to apply for the vehicle image classification, in which the accuracy of the model improves.

During training, the cross-entropy loss (Eq. (2)) only focuses on increasing the probability that a sample is classified to its corresponding ground-truth class. Although due to the effect of the softmax function, the probability that a sample is classified to a class other than its ground-truth class correspondingly reduces. The cross-entropy loss does not achieve the best convergence because it can't gain the loss feedback from the false classes.

The dual cross-entropy loss not only increases the probability that a sample is correctly classified but also decreases the probability that a sample is classified to a class other than its ground-truth class. The dual cross-entropy loss of the sample x_k is defined as follows:

$$
\begin{aligned}
DCE\left(x_k, \mathbf{Y}_k\right) &= CE\left(x_k, \mathbf{Y}_k\right) + \beta \cdot Reg\left(x_k, \mathbf{Y}_k\right) \\
&= -\mathbf{Y}_k^T \cdot \log\left(\mathbf{P}_k\right) + \beta \cdot \left(1 - \mathbf{Y}_k^T\right) \cdot \log\left(\alpha + \mathbf{P}_k\right) \\
&= -\log\left(p_k^{(t_k)}\right) + \beta \cdot \sum_{\substack{i=1 \\ i \neq t_k}}^{C} \log\left(\alpha + p_k^{(i)}\right)
\end{aligned}
\tag{6}
$$

The total dual cross-entropy loss of M samples is defined as follows:

$$
\begin{aligned}
L_{DCE} &= L_{CE} + \beta \cdot L_R \\
&= \sum_{k=1}^{M} CE\left(x_k, \mathbf{Y}_k\right) + \beta \cdot \sum_{k=1}^{M} Reg\left(x_k, \mathbf{Y}_k\right) \\
&= -\sum_{k=1}^{M} \left(\mathbf{Y}_k^T \cdot \log\left(\mathbf{P}_k\right)\right) + \beta \cdot \sum_{k=1}^{M} \left(\left(1 - \mathbf{Y}_k^T\right) \cdot \log\left(\alpha + \mathbf{P}_k\right)\right) \\
&= -\sum_{k=1}^{M} \left(\log\left(p_k^{(t_k)}\right)\right) + \beta \cdot \sum_{k=1}^{M} \sum_{\substack{i=1 \\ i \neq t_k}}^{C} \log\left(\alpha + p_k^{(i)}\right)
\end{aligned}
\tag{7}
$$

L_{CE} is the cross-entropy loss in Eq. (3) and L_R is a regularization term. $\alpha > 0, \beta \geqslant 0$. When $\beta = 0$, the dual cross-entropy loss has a same value as the cross-entropy loss. We set the $\alpha = 1$ and $\beta = 10$ as suggested in [20]. While training, L_{CE} is increasing the probability that a sample is correctly classified($p_k^{(t_k)}$), and L_R is decreasing the probability that a sample is classified to another class (rather than its ground-truth).

Li et al. [20] summarized the advantages of the dual cross-entropy loss compared with the cross-entropy loss as follows:

First, dual cross-entropy loss can accelerate the optimization of the neural network.

Second, dual cross-entropy loss works better on small-sample datasets and per-forms well on large-sample datasets.

Third, dual cross-entropy loss can ensure the network or model has a more stable performance compared to the cross-entropy loss.

2.3 Dual Cross-Entropy Focal Los

We take the idea of focusing more on hard examples from focal loss and add a modulating factor to the dual cross-entropy loss to down-weights the loss of the easy examples. We named the new loss Dual Cross-Entropy Focal Loss. We define the dual cross-entropy focal loss of the sample x_k as follows:

$$DCFL\left(x_k, \mathbf{Y}_k\right) = -\left(1-p_k^{(t_k)}\right)^{\gamma_1} \cdot \log\left(p_k^{(t_k)}\right)$$

$$+\beta \cdot \sum_{\substack{i=1 \\ i \neq t_k}}^{C} \left(\left(p_k^{(i)}\right)^{\gamma_2} \cdot \log\left(\alpha + p_k^{(i)}\right)\right) \tag{8}$$

$\gamma_1 \geqslant 0, \gamma_2 \geqslant 0$. When $\gamma_1 = \gamma_2 = 0$, the dual cross-entropy focal loss is the same as the dual cross-entropy loss in Eq. (6). The dual cross-entropy focal loss consists of two parts. The first part is $-\left(1 - p_k^{(t_k)}\right)^{\gamma_1} \cdot \log\left(p_k^{(t_k)}\right)$, which is the same as the focal loss in Eq. (4). This part increases the probability that a sample is assigned to its ground-truth class $(p_k^{(t_k)})$, and focuses on the hard examples whose $p_k^{(t_k)}$ is small. The second part is $\left(p_k^{(i)}\right)^{\gamma_2} \cdot \log\left(\alpha + p_k^{(i)}\right)$, which decreases the probability that a sample is classified to a class other than its ground-truth class. The second part also focuses on the hard examples. Because some of the probabilities that a hard example is classified to a class other than its ground-truth class are large. For example, for a hard example, if $p_k^{(i)}$ ($i \in \{1, 2, ..., C\}$, $i \neq t_k$) is large, the loss can focus on decreasing $p_k^{(i)}$. Dual cross-entropy focal loss gains the loss feedback from both the ground-truth classes and the false classes through the two parts and focuses on the hard examples.

The total dual cross-entropy focal loss of M samples is defined as follows:

$$L_{DCFL} = \sum_{k=1}^{M} DCFL\left(x_k, \mathbf{Y}_k\right)$$

$$= -\sum_{k=1}^{M} \left(\left(1-p_k^{(t_k)}\right)^{\gamma_1} \cdot \log\left(p_k^{(t_k)}\right)\right)$$

$$+\beta \cdot \sum_{k=1}^{M} \sum_{\substack{i=1 \\ i \neq t_k}}^{C} \left(\left(p_k^{(i)}\right)^{\gamma_2} \cdot \log\left(\alpha + p_k^{(i)}\right)\right) \tag{9}$$

3   Experimental Results

3.1   UA-DETRAC Dataset

We verified the dual cross-entropy focal loss on an open vehicle dataset named UA-DETRAC. UA-DETRAC is a real-world multi-object detection dataset that consists of 10 h of videos. The videos are captured at 24 different locations in Beijing and Tianjin, China. The resolution of each picture is 960 × 540 pixels. There are more than 140 thousand frames in the UA-DETRAC dataset, and 8250 vehicles have been manually annotated, with a total of 1.21 million labeled bounding boxes of objects. In Fig. 1, we have shown some examples of the dataset. Our GPU resources are limited, to save experimental time, we only selected 2000 pictures from UA-DETRAC to create our dataset. We divided the obtained dataset into three parts. The training set consists of 1200 pictures. The validation set consists of 400 pictures. The test set consists of 400 pictures.

Fig. 1. Examples in the dataset

3.2   Comparison of Focal Loss and Dual Cross-Entropy Focal Loss on Our Dataset

For the experiments and performance evaluation, we trained the same RetinaNet [16] model by minimizing the focal loss or our dual cross-entropy focal loss on the same training set for 100 epochs. In our work, we set focal loss (Eq. (5)) as $\gamma = 2$ as suggested in [16]. Dual cross-entropy focal loss (Eq. (8)) was set to $\gamma_1 = \gamma_2 = 2, \alpha = 1, \beta = 10$ as suggested in [20]. The cited reference [16] provides the structural details and description of RetinaNet. We saved the trained models after each epoch, and finally, we tested each saved model on the same test set. The mAP50 index ($IoU = 0.5$) on the same test set for the saved models trained by minimizing two loss functions after each epoch is shown in Fig. 2.

We trained the same RetinaNet model by minimizing the focal loss or our dual cross-entropy focal loss on the same training set 10 times respectively. In each training epoch, the performance of the model was monitored on the validation dataset, and the model that had the best performance was saved. Finally, we tested all the saved models that trained by minimizing two loss functions on the same test set and calculated the mean and standard deviation of the 10 mAP50 indexes. As shown in Table 1, dual cross-entropy focal loss improves the mAP50 index by 1.6% and has a smaller standard deviation.

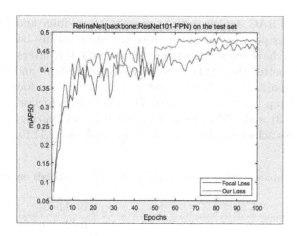

Fig. 2. Curves of the mAP50 index obtained by the RetinaNet network trained by minimizing the focal loss and our dual cross-entropy focal loss on the same dataset

Table 1. The means and standard deviations of the 10 mAP50 indexes obtained by the RetinaNet network trained by minimizing the focal loss and our loss on the same dataset

Loss function	Mean	Std
Focal Loss	0.471	0.018
Dual Cross-Entropy Focal Loss	0.487	0.013

3.3 Comparison to Traditional Object Detecters on Our Dataset

We evaluated three different one-stage detectors on the bounding box detection task on our dataset. SSD [14] and RetinaNet [16] used depth 101 ResNet [4] as their backbone network. YOLOv3 [13] used the 53 depth Darknet [13] as its backbone network. Redmon et al. [13] said that Darknet-53 has equal accuracy to ResNet-101. The ResNet-101 and Darknet-53 were pre-trained on the ImageNet dataset. In order to match the default input image size of the detectors, we resized the image. The input images for SSD were resized into 512×512 dimension. The input images for YOLOv3 were resized into 608×608 dimension. The shorter side of the input images for RetinaNet was resized into 608 dimension. For the data augmentation, horizontal flipping was only used. The corresponding cited references provide the structural details and description of the three detectors..

We trained SSD and YOLOv3 on the same training set for 100 epochs. For SSD and YOLOv3, we monitored the performance of its network on the same validation set. For SSD and YOLOv3, the model which had the best performance was saved and then used to predict the test data. We used the performance of RetinaNet in Table 1 and we get Table 2.

The UA-DETRAC dataset mainly consists of medium and small objects. SSD [14] performs poor on the small objects. This is mainly because the small objects may not have even information at the very top layers. YOLOv3 [13] performs much better than SSD, especially on the medium and small objects. As shown in Table 2, RetinaNet trained by minimizing the focal loss achieves a 1.5 point AP gap (47.1 vs. 45.6) with YOLOv3 and achieves a 9.8 point AP gap (47.1 vs. 37.3) with SSD. RetinaNet trained by minimizing our dual cross-entropy focal loss achieves a 1.6 point AP gap (48.7 vs. 47.1) further.

Table 2. Comparison of traditional object detection methods on our dataset

Methods	Backbone	mAP50
SSD [14]	ResNet101-SSD	0.373
YOLOv3 [13]	Darknet-53	0.456
RetinaNet [16] + Focal Loss	ResNet101-FPN	0.471
RetinaNet [16] + Dual Cross-Entropy Focal Loss	ResNet101-FPN	0.487

4   Conclusions

In this paper, we integrated the dual cross-entropy loss and focal loss to create a new loss function named Dual Cross-Entropy Focal Loss. As compared to the focal loss, our proposed loss considers loss on both the ground-truth classes and the false classes by adding a regularization term which places a constraint on the probability that the example belongs to a false class. Figure 2 shows that our new loss can accelerate the convergence of the network and improve the detection accuracy. Table 2 shows that RetinaNet [16] trained by minimizing our new loss achieves best accuracy on our dataset compared to the baselines.

References

1. Krizhevsky, A., Sutskever, I., Hinton, G.E.: ImageNet classification with deep convolutional neural networks. In: Advances in Neural Information Processing Systems, pp. 1097–1105 (2012)
2. Simonyan, K., Zisserman, A.: Very deep convolutional networks for large-scale image recognition. arXiv preprint arXiv:1409.1556 (2014)
3. Zhou, B., Lapedriza, A., Xiao, J., Torralba, A., Oliva, A.: Learning deep features for scene recognition using places database. In: Advances in Neural Information Processing Systems, pp. 487–495 (2014)
4. He, K., Zhang, X., Ren, S., Sun, J.: Deep residual learning for image recognition. In: Proceedings of the IEEE Conference on Computer Vision and Pattern Recognition, pp. 770–778 (2016)
5. LeCun, Y., et al.: Backpropagation applied to handwritten zip code recognition. Neural Comput. 1(4), 541–551 (1989)

6. Szegedy, C., et al.: Going deeper with convolutions. In: Proceedings of the IEEE Conference on Computer Vision and Pattern Recognition, pp. 1–9 (2015)

7. Girshick, R.B., Donahue, J., Darrell, T., Malik, J.: Rich feature hierarchies for accurate object detection and semantic segmentation. In: Proceedings of the IEEE Conference on Computer Vision and Pattern Recognition, pp. 580–587 (2014)

8. Girshick, R.B.: Fast R-CNN. In: Proceedings of the IEEE International Conference on Computer Vision, pp. 1440–1448 (2015)

9. Ren, S., He, K., Girshick, R., Sun, J.: Faster R-CNN: towards real-time object detection with region proposal networks. In: Advances in Neural Information Processing Systems, pp. 91–99 (2015)

10. Dai, J., Li, Y., He, K., Sun, J.: R-FCN: Object detection via region-based fully convolutional networks. In: Advances in Neural Information Processing Systems, pp. 379–387 (2016)

11. Redmon, J., Divvala, S., Girshick, R., Farhadi, A.: You only look once: unified, real-time object detection. In: Proceedings of the IEEE Conference on Computer Vision and Pattern Recognition, pp. 779–788 (2016)

12. Redmon, J., Farhadi, A.: YOLO9000: better, faster, stronger. In: Proceedings of the IEEE Conference on Computer Vision and Pattern Recognition, pp. 7263–7271 (2017)

13. Redmon, J., Farhadi, A.: YOLOv3: an incremental improvement. arXiv preprint arXiv: 1804.02767 (2018)

14. Liu, W.: SSD: single shot multibox detector. In: Leibe, B., Matas, J., Sebe, N., Welling, M. (eds.) ECCV 2016. LNCS, vol. 9905, pp. 21–37. Springer, Cham (2016). https://doi.org/10.1007/978-3-319-46448-0_2

15. Fu, C.-Y., Liu, W., Ranga, A., Tyagi, A., Berg, A.C.: DSSD: deconvolutional single shot detector. arXiv preprint arXiv:1701.06659 (2016)

16. Lin, T.-Y., Goyal, P., Girshick, R., He, K., Dollar, P.: Focal loss for dense object detection. In: Proceedings of the IEEE International Conference on Computer Vision, pp. 2980–2988 (2017)

17. Lin, T.-Y., Dollar, P., Girshick, R., He, K., Hariharan, B., Belongie, S.: Feature pyramid networks for object detection. In: Proceedings of the IEEE Conference on Computer Vision and Pattern Recognition, pp. 2117–2125 (2017)

18. Huang, J., et al.: Speed/accuracy trade-offs for modern convolutional object detectors. In: Proceedings of the IEEE Conference on Computer Vision and Pattern Recognition, pp. 7310–7321 (2017)

19. Shrivastava, A., Sukthankar, R., Malik, J., Gupta, A.: Beyond skip connections: top-down modulation for object detection. arXiv preprint arXiv:1612.06851 (2016)

20. Li, X., Yu, L., Chang, D., Ma, Z., Cao, J.: Dual cross-entropy loss for small-sample fine-grained vehicle classification. IEEE Trans. Veh. Technol. **68**(5), 4204–4212 (2019)

Concept Drift Detection Using Autoencoders in Data Streams Processing

Maciej Jaworski[1]([✉]) [iD], Leszek Rutkowski[1,2] [iD], and Plamen Angelov[3] [iD]

[1] Department of Computational Intelligence, Czestochowa University of Technology, Czestochowa, Poland
{maciej.jaworski,leszek.rutkowski}@pcz.pl
[2] Information Technology Institute, University of Social Sciences, Łódź, Poland
[3] Department of Computing and Communications, Lancaster University, Lancaster, UK
p.angelov@lancaster.ac.uk

Abstract. In this paper, the problem of concept drift detection in data stream mining algorithms is considered. The autoencoder is proposed to be applied as a drift detector. The autoencoders are neural networks that are learned how to reconstruct input data. As a side effect, they are able to learn compact nonlinear codes, which summarize the most important features of input data. We suspect that the properly learned autoencoder on one part of the data stream can then be used to monitor possible changes in the following stream parts. The changes are analyzed by monitoring variations of the autoencoder cost function. Two cost functions are applied in this paper: the cross-entropy and the reconstruction error. Preliminary experimental results show that the proposed autoencoder-based detector is able to handle different types of concept drift, e.g. the sudden or the gradual.

Keywords: Autoencoder · Data stream mining · Concept drift detection

1 Introduction

In recent years, the topics connected with data stream mining attracted much attention of machine learning researchers [1,6,9–17,24,27–34,37,38]. In data streams it is quite common that the underlying data distribution can change over time. It is known in the literature as the 'concept drift' [40,41]. Another characteristics of the streaming data is their potentially infinite size and high rates of arriving at the system. Therefore, proper data stream mining algorithms should be resource-aware [8,15].

The data stream can be defined as a sequence of data elements

$$S = (x_0, x_1, x_2, \dots).\qquad(1)$$

L. Rutkowski et al. (Eds.): ICAISC 2020, LNAI 12415, pp. 124–133, 2020.
https://doi.org/10.1007/978-3-030-61401-0_12

In this paper the case of unsupervised learning is considered, which means that there are no classes assigned to data elements. Hence, the data stream element s_n is a D-dimensional vector defined as follows

$$x_n = \left[x_n^1, \dots, x_n^D\right].\qquad(2)$$

The data stream mining algorithm should be able to react to possible changes in data distribution [16,20,41]. The concept drift handling can be realized in two ways, i.e. passively or actively. In the passive approach, a concept drift reaction mechanism is incorporated in the data stream mining algorithm itself. It can bed done by applying the sliding window techniques [7] or ensemble methods [28,29]. In the active approach, there is an external drift detector functioning in parallel to the main algorithm. Based on the information from the detector the algorithm can make a decision about rebuilding the model. Many active drift detectors focus on monitoring the current accuracy of the model. If it decreases, then it means that the model becomes invalid and needs to be modified. En examples of such methods are the Drift Detection Method (DDM) [18] and the Early Drift Detection Method (EDDM) [3]. Other active drift detection methods rely on statistical tests. They look for possible changes in parameters of data probability density functions. Among others, the Welch's, the Kolmogorov-Smirnov's [27], or the Page-Hinkley's tests are often used [19].

In this paper, we present an active concept drift detection approach based on autoencoders. This approach is similar to the one presented in [23], in which the Restricted Boltzmann Machine (RBM) [39] was applied as a drift detector. This idea was further extended with resource-awareness strategies to deal with fast data streams [26] or to deal with missing values [25]. Autoencoders are important neural network models often used in the field of deep learning [21]. They are used, for example, in greedy-pretraining methods of learning deep neural networks [4,5]. Similarly to RBMs, the properly learned autoencoder contains in its middle layer the information about the data probability distribution. It can be then used to check whether the data from another part of the data stream belong to the same distribution as the part on which the autoencoder was trained. This can be checked, for example, by measuring the reconstruction error or the cross-entropy of new data.

The rest of the paper is organized as follows. In Sect. 2 autoencoders are presented in more detail. In Sect. 3 methods for concept drift detection using autoencoders are proposed. In Sect. 4 the results obtained in numerical simulations are demonstrated. Sect. 5 concludes the paper and indicates possible future research directions.

2   Autoencoders

The autoencoder is a kind of feed-forward neural network, which is learned to reconstruct input data [22]. There are many types of autoencoders [21], like the denoising autoencoder [2], the sparse autoencoder [35] or the contractive autoencoder [36]. Generally, the autoencoder is composed of two parts: the encoder and the decoder. The aim of the encoder is to transform input data in a nonlinear way, extracting the most important features of the data. The decoder is learned to reconstruct the output of the encoder back to the input data as close as possible. In this paper, we consider autoencoders consisting of $L + 1$ layers. Let $y_j^{(l)}(x_n)$ denote the value of the j-th neuron in the l-th layer obtained for input data x_n. Then, the values of neurons in the l-th layer can be computed using the following formula

$$y_j^{(l)}(x_n) = \sigma \left(\sum_{i=1}^{N_{l-1}} w_{ij}^{(l)} y_i^{(l-1)}(x_n) + b_j^{(l)} \right), \quad l = 1, \ldots, L, \qquad (3)$$

where $w_{ij}^{(l)}$ are weights of synapses between the $(l-1)$-th and the l-th layers, $b_j^{(l)}$ are the biases, and N_l is the size of the l-th layer. Function $\sigma(z)$ is an activation function. Many different types of activation functions can be applied in autoencoder. In this paper, we apply the most common one, i.e. the sigmoid function defined below

$$\sigma(z) = \frac{1}{1 + \exp(-z)}. \qquad (4)$$

The 0-th layer is the input layer, i.e. $y_j^{(0)}(x_n) = x_n^j$. The size of the output layer is equal to the input layer size, i.e. $N_L = N_0 = D$. If we do not apply any sparsity constraints while learning the autoencoder, the middle layer should be of the smallest size, i.e.

$$D = N_0 > N_1 > \cdots > N_{\frac{L}{2}} < \cdots < N_{L-1} < N_L = D \qquad (5)$$

The autoencoder is trained as a usual feedforward neural network by minimizing a cost function. Let $C(x_n)$ be the cost function obtained for the x_n data element. Then, for example, a weight $w_{ij}^{(l)}$ would be updated in each step using the following formula

$$w_{ij}^{(l)} := w_{ij}^{(l)} - \eta \frac{\partial C(x_n)}{\partial w_{ij}^{(l)}}, \qquad (6)$$

where η is the learning rate. Analogous formula applies for biases.

In practice, the learning is often performed on minibatches of data instead of single data elements. Let us assume that the minibatch M_t consists of B subsequent data

$$M_t = (x_{tB}, \ldots, x_{(t+1)B-1}). \qquad (7)$$

Then, the neural network parameters are obtained using the arithmetic average of gradients obtained for all data from the minibatch

$$w_{ij}^{(l)} := w_{ij}^{(l)} - \eta \frac{1}{B} \sum_{m=tB}^{t(B+1)-1} \frac{\partial C(x_m)}{\partial w_{ij}^{(l)}}. \qquad (8)$$

Many different types of cost functions can be used. In this paper, we consider two of them. The cross-entropy:

$$C_{CE}(x_n) = -\sum_{j=1}^{D} \left[x_n^j \log_2 \left(y_j^{(L)}(x_n) \right) + \left(1 - x_n^j \right) \log_2 \left(1 - y_j^{(L)}(x) \right) \right], \quad (9)$$

and the reconstruction error:

$$C_{RE}(x_n) = \sqrt{\sum_{j=1}^{D} \left(x_n^j - y_j^{(L)}(x_n) \right)^2}. \quad (10)$$

The monitoring of cost function values can be used to detect potential drifts in data distribution. The detection procedure is described in the next section.

3   Concept Drift Detection with the Autoencoder

We suspect that the autoencoder properly trained on one part of the data stream can be applied to monitor possible changes in data distribution in the following parts. For any cost function C (given by (9) or (10), the average value of this cost function for minibatch M_t of size B is given by

$$C(M_t) = \frac{1}{B} \sum_{x_m \in M_t} C(x_m) \quad (11)$$

Apart from the cost function itself, we want to investigate also the trend $Q(C, t)$ of cost function C for subsequent minibatches. To ensure that the trend is computed only on the basis of the most recent data, we apply additionally the forgetting mechanism, as it was done in [23]. The trend at time t is given by the following formula

$$Q(C, t) = \frac{\overline{n}_t \overline{TC}_t - \overline{T}_t \overline{C}_t}{\overline{n}_t \overline{T^2}_t - \left(\overline{T}_t \right)^2}. \quad (12)$$

In standard regression procedure, the terms in formula (12) are given simply by appropriate arithmetic averages. In our case, because of the forgetting mechanism applied, the arithmetic averages are replaced by the following recurrent formulas

$$\overline{TC}_t = \lambda \overline{TC}_{t-1} + t * C(M_t), \ \overline{TC}_0 = 0, \quad (13)$$

$$\overline{T}_t = \lambda \overline{T}_{t-1} + t, \ \overline{T}_0 = 0, \quad (14)$$

$$\overline{C}_t = \lambda \overline{C}_{t-1} + C(M_t), \ \overline{C}_0 = 0, \quad (15)$$

$$\overline{T^2}_t = \lambda \overline{T^2}_{t-1} + t^2, \ \overline{T^2}_0 = 0, \quad (16)$$

$$\overline{n}_t = \lambda \overline{n}_{t-1} + 1, \ \overline{n}_0 = 0, \quad (17)$$

where λ is a forgetting factor and it takes values lower than 1. The trend of the cost function should be close to 0 as long as there is no concept drift in the data stream. After the drift occurs, then $Q(C, t)$ is suspected to increase to some positive value. Since we consider two cost functions in this paper, there are two trends analyzed as well, i.e. $Q(C_{CE}, t)$ and $Q(C_{RE}, t)$.

4   Experimental Results

In this section, we present preliminary simulation results of experiments conducted on simple synthetic datasets with concept drift[1]. The dataset was generated in the same manner as it was done in [23], i.e. based on synthetic Boltzmann machines with randomly chosen parameters. At the beginning, we applied two Boltzmann machines, which then were used to generate to datasets with static probability distributions

$$S_1 = (x_{1,1}, x_{1,2}, x_{1,3} \ldots), \tag{18}$$
$$S_2 = (x_{2,1}, x_{2,2}, x_{2,3}, \ldots). \tag{19}$$

The dimensionality of the data in both sets is $D = 20$. The datasets S_1 and S_2 were used to generate two datasets with concept drifts. The dataset with sudden concept drift is denoted as $S_s = (x_{s,1}, x_{s,2}, \ldots)$, where $x_{s,n}$ is taken from S_1 if $n < 500000$ and from S_2 if $n \geq 500000$. The dataset with gradual concept drift is denoted as $S_g = (x_{g,1}, x_{g,2}, \ldots)$, where $x_{g,n}$ is from S_1 if $n < 500000$ and from S_2 if $n \geq 600000$. In the interval $[500000; 600000)$ the data element $x_{g,n}$ is drawn from S_1 with probability $\frac{600000 - n}{100000}$ and from S_2 with probability $\frac{n - 500000}{100000}$. Hence, the two datasets S_s and S_g are constructed in such a way, that the concept drift occurs at after processing 500000 data elements.

In the experiments, we used the simple 3-layered autoencoder ($L = 3$). The sizes of the 0-th and the 2-nd layer are equal to $N_0 = N_2 = D = 20$, to match the dimensionality of the data. The middle layer is chosen to be of size $N_1 = 15$. The learning rate and minibatches sizes are set to $\eta = 0.05$ and $B = 20$, respectively. In each experiment, the autoencoder is trained only for the first 400000 data elements. Then, it is turned to the monitoring mode (no learning is performed, only the values of the cost functions are analyzed). The forgetting factor λ for trend measures was set to 0.998.

4.1   Sudden Concept Drift Detection

The first experiment was conducted on the S_s dataset, with the sudden drift. The results obtained for the cross-entropy loss function are presented in Fig. 1. As can be seen, the value of the cross-entropy decreases while the autoencoder learns until the 400000-th data element. Then it monitors the incoming data. Since the distribution of data does not change until the 500000-th element, the

---

[1] All the experiments were conducted using our own software implemented in C/C++ and it can be found at www.iisi.pcz.pl/~mjaworski.

cross-entropy values fluctuate around some fixed level. Then the sudden drift occurs and the cross-entropy suddenly achieves higher values. It is more clearly visible in Fig. 1(b), where the trend of cross-entropy values is presented. The peak at $n = 500000$ matches the occurrence of the sudden drift.

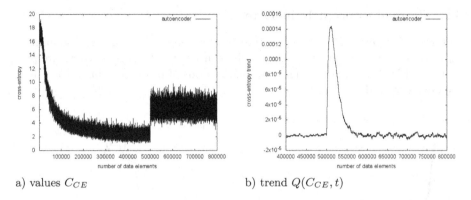

a) values C_{CE} b) trend $Q(C_{CE}, t)$

Fig. 1. Cross-entropy values and trend as a function of the number of processed data elements, for dataset S_s with sudden concept drift.

In the case of the reconstruction error, the results can be additionally compared with the drift detector based on the RBM, presented in [23]. We applied the same parameters as for the autoencoder. The RBM was learned using the Contrastive Divergence (CD-k) method with $K = 1$. The results are shown in Fig. 2.

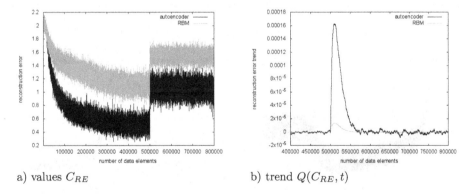

a) values C_{RE} b) trend $Q(C_{RE}, t)$

Fig. 2. Reconstruction error values and time as a function of the number of processed data elements, for data set S_s with sudden concept drift.

It seems that the autoencoder wins with the RBM approach in both considered aspects. In Fig. 2(a) we can observe that the values of the reconstruction error are lower for the autoencoder. It might be important if we wanted to use the network simultaneously for other purposes, besides the concept drift detection. In Fig. 2(b) it is visible that the signal peak of sudden change detection is significantly higher for the autoencoder.

4.2   Gradual Concept Drift Detection

In the next experiment, analogous simulations were carried out for the dataset S_g with gradual concept drift. The results concerning the cross-entropy are presented in Fig. 3, whereas in Fig. 4 the comparisons of reconstruction error values are demonstrated.

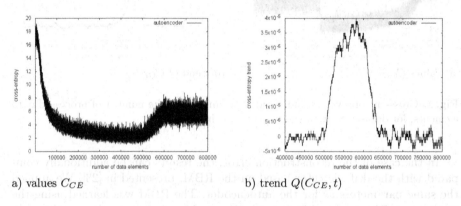

a) values C_{CE} b) trend $Q(C_{CE}, t)$

Fig. 3. Cross-entropy values and trend as a function of the number of processed data elements, for dataset S_g with gradual concept drift.

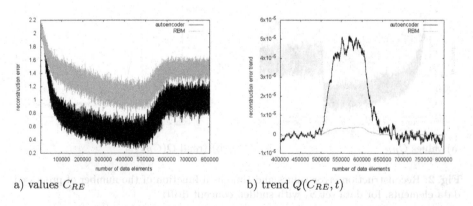

a) values C_{RE} b) trend $Q(C_{RE}, t)$

Fig. 4. Reconstruction error values and trend as a function of the number of processed data elements, for data set S_g with gradual concept drift.

In this experiment, the values of cost functions raise smoothly whilst the gradual drift takes place between the 500000-th and the 600000-th data elements. Figure 4 confirms the superiority of the autoencoder over the RBM-based approach also in the case of gradual drift.

5   Conclusions and Future Work

In this paper, the autoencoder was proposed as a drift detector in time-changing data streams. First, the neural network learns the model on the beginning part of the stream. Then it is used to monitor possible changes in the following parts. The variations of the cost function values are analyzed. If he changes turn out to be large, it means that the concept drift occurred, and it can be a signal for the data stream mining algorithm to rebuild the current model. Two cost functions were applied in this paper, i.e. the cross-entropy and the reconstruction error. The preliminary results obtained in experiments carried out on simple synthetic datasets confirmed that the autoencoder can be successfully used as a concept drift detector. It was demonstrated that it is capable of handling both sudden and gradual concept drifts. In future research, we plan to extend the proposed method to make it more resource-aware for fast-changing data streams and to make it able to deal with missing values.

Acknowledgments. This work was supported by the Polish National Science Centre under grant no. 2017/27/B/ST6/02852.

References

1. Aggarwal, C.: Data Streams: Models and Algorithms. Springer, New York (2007)
2. Alain, G., Bengio, Y.: What regularized auto-encoders learn from the data-generating distribution. J. Mach. Learn. Res. **15**(1), 3563–3593 (2014)
3. Baena-García, M., del Campo-Ávila, J., Fidalgo, R., Bifet, A., Gavalda, R., Morales-Bueno, R.: Early drift detection method. In: Fourth International Workshop on Knowledge Discovery from Data Streams, vol. 6, pp. 77–86 (2006)
4. Bengio, Y.: Learning deep architectures for AI. Found. Trends Mach. Learn. **2**(1), 1–127 (2009)
5. Bengio, Y., Lamblin, P., Popovici, D., Larochelle, H.: Greedy layer-wise training of deep networks. In: Proceedings of the 19th International Conference on Neural Information Processing Systems. NIPS 2006, pp. 153–160. MIT Press, Cambridge, MA, USA (2006)
6. Bifet, A.: Adaptive Stream Mining: Pattern Learning and Mining from Evolving Data Streams. Frontiers in Artificial Intelligence and Applications. IOS Press, Amsterdam, Berlin (2010)
7. Bifet, A., Gavaldá, R.: Learning from time-changing data with adaptive windowing, pp. 443–448 (2007)
8. Bilski, J., Kowalczyk, B., Grzanek, K.: The parallel modification to the Levenberg-Marquardt algorithm. In: Rutkowski, L., Scherer, R., Korytkowski, M., Pedrycz, W., Tadeusiewicz, R., Zurada, J.M. (eds.) Artificial Intelligence and Soft Computing, pp. 15–24. Springer, Cham (2018)

9. Domingos, P., Hulten, G.: Mining high-speed data streams. In: Proceedings of the 6th ACM SIGKDD International Conference on Knowledge Discovery and Data Mining, pp. 71–80 (2000)
10. Duda, P., Rutkowski, L., Jaworski, M., Rutkowska, D.: On the Parzen Kernel-based probability density function learning procedures over time-varying streaming data with applications to pattern classification. IEEE Trans. Cybern. **50**(4), 1683–1696 (2020)
11. Duda, P., Jaworski, M., Cader, A., Wang, L.: On training deep neural networks using a streaming approach. J. Artif. Intell. Soft Comput. Res. **10**(1), 15–26 (2020)
12. Duda, P., Jaworski, M., Rutkowski, L.: Convergent time-varying regression models for data streams: tracking concept drift by the recursive Parzen-based generalized regression neural networks. Int. J. Neural Syst. **28**(02), 1750048 (2018)
13. Duda, P., Jaworski, M., Rutkowski, L.: Knowledge discovery in data streams with the orthogonal series-based generalized regression neural networks. Inf. Sci. **460–461**, 497–518 (2018)
14. Dyer, K.B., Capo, R., Polikar, R.: COMPOSE: a semisupervised learning framework for initially labeled nonstationary streaming data. IEEE Trans. Neural Netw. Learn. Syst. **25**(1), 12–26 (2014)
15. Gaber, M., Zaslavsky, A., Krishnaswamy, S.: Mining data streams: a review. Sigmod Rec. **34**(2), 18–26 (2005)
16. Gałkowski, T., Krzyżak, A., Filutowicz, Z.: A new approach to detection of changes in multidimensional patterns. J. Artif. Intell. Soft Comput. Res. 10(2), 125–136 (2020). https://doi.org/10.2478/jaiscr-2020-0009
17. Gama, J.: A survey on learning from data streams: current and future trends. Prog. Artif. Intell. **1**(1), 45–55 (2012)
18. Gama, J., Medas, P., Castillo, G., Rodrigues, P.: Learning with drift detection. In: Bazzan, A.L.C., Labidi, S. (eds.) SBIA 2004. LNCS (LNAI), vol. 3171, pp. 286–295. Springer, Heidelberg (2004). https://doi.org/10.1007/978-3-540-28645-5_29
19. Gama, J., Sebastião, R., Rodrigues, P.P.: Issues in evaluation of stream learning algorithms. In: Proceedings of the 15th ACM SIGKDD International Conference on Knowledge Discovery and Data Mining. KDD 2009, pp. 329–338. ACM, New York (2009)
20. Gomes, J., Gaber, M., Sousa, P., Menasalvas, E.: Mining recurring concepts in a dynamic feature space. IEEE Trans. Neural Netw. Learn. Syst. **25**(1), 95–110 (2014)
21. Goodfellow, I., Bengio, Y., Courville, A.: Deep Learning. MIT Press (2016). http://www.deeplearningbook.org
22. Hinton, G.E., Zemel, R.S.: Autoencoders, minimum description length and Helmholtz free energy. In: Proceedings of the 6th International Conference on Neural Information Processing Systems. NIPS 1993, pp. 3–10. Morgan Kaufmann Publishers Inc., San Francisco, CA, USA (1993)
23. Jaworski, M., Duda, P., Rutkowski, L.: On applying the restricted Boltzmann machine to active concept drift detection. In: Proceedings of the 2017 IEEE Symposium Series on Computational Intelligence Honolulu, USA, pp. 3512–3519 (2017)
24. Jaworski, M., Duda, P., Rutkowski, L.: New splitting criteria for decision trees in stationary data streams. IEEE Trans. Neural Netw. Learn. Syst. **29**(6), 2516–2529 (2018)
25. Jaworski, M., Duda, P., Rutkowska, D., Rutkowski, L.: On handling missing values in data stream mining algorithms based on the restricted Boltzmann machine. In: Gedeon, T., Wong, K.W., Lee, M. (eds.) ICONIP 2019. CCIS, vol. 1143, pp. 347–354. Springer, Cham (2019). https://doi.org/10.1007/978-3-030-36802-9_37

26. Jaworski, M., Rutkowski, L., Duda, P., Cader, A.: Resource-aware data stream mining using the restricted Boltzmann machine. In: Rutkowski, L., Scherer, R., Korytkowski, M., Pedrycz, W., Tadeusiewicz, R., Zurada, J.M. (eds.) ICAISC 2019. LNCS (LNAI), vol. 11509, pp. 384–396. Springer, Cham (2019). https://doi.org/10.1007/978-3-030-20915-5_35

27. Lemaire, V., Salperwyck, C., Bondu, A.: A survey on supervised classification on data streams. In: Zimányi, E., Kutsche, R.-D. (eds.) eBISS 2014. LNBIP, vol. 205, pp. 88–125. Springer, Cham (2015). https://doi.org/10.1007/978-3-319-17551-5_4

28. Ludwig, S.A.: Applying a neural network ensemble to intrusion detection. J. Artif. Intelli. Soft Comput. Res. **9**(3), 177–188 (2019)

29. Pietruczuk, L., Rutkowski, L., Jaworski, M., Duda, P.: How to adjust an ensemble size in stream data mining? Inf. Sci. **381**(C), 46–54 (2017)

30. Rafajłowicz, E., Rafajłowicz, W.: Testing (non-) linearity of distributed-parameter systems from a video sequence. Asian J. Control **12**(2), 146–158 (2010)

31. Rafajłowicz, E., Rafajłowicz, W.: Iterative learning in repetitive optimal control of linear dynamic processes. In: Rutkowski, L., Korytkowski, M., Scherer, R., Tadeusiewicz, R., Zadeh, L.A., Zurada, J.M. (eds.) ICAISC 2016. LNCS (LNAI), vol. 9692, pp. 705–717. Springer, Cham (2016). https://doi.org/10.1007/978-3-319-39378-0_60

32. Rafajłowicz, E., Rafajłowicz, W.: Iterative learning in optimal control of linear dynamic processes. Int. J. Control **91**(7), 1522–1540 (2018)

33. Rafajłowicz, E., Wnuk, M., Rafajłowicz, W.: Local detection of defects from image sequences. Int. J. Appl. Math. Comput. Sci. **18**(4), 581–592 (2008)

34. Ramírez-Gallego, S., Krawczyk, B., García, S., Woźniak, M., Herrera, F.: A survey on data preprocessing for data stream mining: current status and future directions. Neurocomputing **239**, 39–57 (2017)

35. Ranzato, M., Poultney, C., Chopra, S., LeCun, Y.: Efficient learning of sparse representations with an energy-based model. In: Proceedings of the 19th International Conference on Neural Information Processing Systems. NIPS 2006, pp. 1137–1144. MIT Press, Cambridge (2006)

36. Rifai, S., Vincent, P., Muller, X., Glorot, X., Bengio, Y.: Contractive auto-encoders: explicit invariance during feature extraction. In: Proceedings of the 28th International Conference on Machine Learning. ICML 2001, pp. 833–840. Omnipress, Madison (2011)

37. Rutkowski, L., Jaworski, M., Pietruczuk, L., Duda, P.: A new method for data stream mining based on the misclassification error. IEEE Trans. Neural Netw. Learn. Syst. **26**(5), 1048–1059 (2015)

38. Rutkowski, L., Pietruczuk, L., Duda, P., Jaworski, M.: Decision trees for mining data streams based on the McDiarmid's bound. IEEE Trans. Knowl. Data Eng. **25**(6), 1272–1279 (2013)

39. Smolensky, P.: Parallel distributed processing: explorations in the microstructure of cognition. In: Information Processing in Dynamical Systems: Foundations of Harmony Theory, vol. 1, pp. 194–281. MIT Press, Cambridge (1986)

40. Tsymbal, A.: The problem of concept drift: definitions and related work. Technical report. TCD-CS-2004-15. Computer Science Department, Trinity College Dublin, Ireland (2004)

41. Zliobaite, I., Bifet, A., Pfahringer, B., Holmes, G.: Active learning with drifting streaming data. IEEE Trans. Neural Netw. Learn. Syst. **25**(1), 27–39 (2014)

Explainable AI for Inspecting Adversarial Attacks on Deep Neural Networks

Zuzanna Klawikowska, Agnieszka Mikołajczyk⬤, and Michał Grochowski[✉]⬤

Gdańsk University of Technology, Gabriela Narutowicza 11/12, 80-233 Gdańsk, Poland
zklawikowska97@gmail.com,
{agnieszka.mikolajczyk,michal.grochowski}@pg.edu.pl

Abstract. Deep Neural Networks (DNN) are state of the art algorithms for image classification. Although significant achievements and perspectives, deep neural networks and accompanying learning algorithms have some important challenges to tackle. However, it appears that it is relatively easy to attack and fool with well-designed input samples called adversarial examples. Adversarial perturbations are unnoticeable for humans. Such attacks are a severe threat to the development of these systems in critical applications, such as medical or military systems. Hence, it is necessary to develop methods of counteracting these attacks. These methods are called defense strategies and aim at increasing the neural model's robustness against adversarial attacks. In this paper, we reviewed the recent findings in adversarial attacks and defense strategies. We also analyzed the effects of attacks and defense strategies applied, using the local and global analyzing methods from the family of explainable artificial intelligence.

Keywords: Deep neural networks · Explainable artificial intelligence · Adversarial attacks · Convolutional neural networks

1 Introduction

These days deep learning is the fastest-growing field in the field of image analysis and classification. Deep Neural Networks (DNN) are considered state of the art algorithms for image classification, [1, 2]. Despite great achievements and perspectives, deep neural networks and accompanying learning algorithms have some crucial challenges to tackle [3, 4]. DNNs are data-hungry [5, 6], it is challenging to select the optimal network structure [7, 8], and to understand neural networks reasoning process [9]. Another essential concern is the subject of attacks on neural networks. Regarding image classification, neural model designing is based on learning a given structure from data and then analyzing the input-output relation, on the pixel-level. This makes it relatively easy to cause such a system to perform incorrectly by changing these values so that these changes are not noticeable to the system user. Such fragile black-box deep neural network models are used to solve very sensitive and critical tasks. Modification of the input pixel that causes system malfunction is called an adversarial attack. The adversarial attack is

L. Rutkowski et al. (Eds.): ICAISC 2020, LNAI 12415, pp. 134–146, 2020.
https://doi.org/10.1007/978-3-030-61401-0_14

carefully selected and is a severe threat to the development of these systems in critical-safety applications, such as medicine, military, and even urban scene recognition used in autonomous vehicles. To ensure the safety of this technology and make it widely usable, it is necessary to develop methods of detecting, understanding, and counteracting these attacks.

To address those challenges, we employ the methods of Explainable Artificial Intelligence (XAI) which have a wide range of tools that can be used to tackle mentioned problems, in particular in detecting and identifying the types of attacks. Knowing the kind of attack, we can more easily counteract it. Following [10] we review and explain the recent findings in adversarial attacks, including white-box and black-box attacks, targeted and non-targeted attacks as well as one-time and iterative attacks. In the case study, we test the white-box Fast Gradient Sign Method (FGSM) and black box One-pixel attack.

We applied XAI local and global explanations methods to analyze the attacks. The local analysis aims to explain a single prediction of a model, e.g. one input image. In contrast, the global one tries to explain how the whole model works in general, i.e. it shows how a particular machine learning model analyzes a given set of data. In the paper, we have shown how selected attacks affect the process of classification of individual images, and how this process looks globally, i.e. we try to conduct a qualitative analysis of the features of data sets that are more and less vulnerable to attacks. We use Layer-wise Relevance Propagation (LRP) method for the local analysis and XAI signatures supported by Uniform Manifold Approximation and Projection (UMAP) for a global one. Finally, we describe the most popular methods that aim at increasing neural model's robustness against adversarial attacks. We implement an Adversarial retraining approach to investigate the DNN robustifying process.

2   Adversarial Attacks and Defenses

Most often, the adversarial attacks are targeted against AI-based computer vision systems. Those systems are mainly based on deep neural models trained on raw data, which capture the input-output relations, on the pixel-level. It turns out that it is relatively easy to fool such systems to perform incorrectly, just by carefully modifying those pixels in a way that these changes are not visible to the unaided eye of the average system user. One of the reasons is that even if the network classifies input data correctly, it does not understand its meaning in the same way as a human. Therefore, classification is not always made based on the relevant premises. A common situation is when the network has correctly classified a given input but based on inappropriate premises. Such model behavior cannot be regarded as correct. Szegedy et al. [11] showed that an unnoticeable change of pixels in the input image can completely change the label assigned to it earlier. The modified images have been called adversarial examples, and the process that aims to mislead the neural network has been called an adversarial attack. In [12], it was demonstrated that the system could recognize with 99.99% accuracy objects in the input image. Other examples of adversarial attacks are also widely reported, e.g. failing to acknowledge the STOP sign by traffic sign recognition system [13], failing to recognize pedestrians by the scene segmentation system [14], changing medical diagnosis [15].

2.1 Adversarial Attacks

Following [10], we present taxonomy related to adversarial attacks. In terms of the attacker's knowledge of the system, attacks might be divided into a white-box and a black-box. In terms of the aim of the attack on targeted and untargeted.

Adversary's Knowledge

White-Box Attacks. In this type of attack, attackers know all elements related to a system, i.e. training set, model's architecture, hyper-parameters, number of layers, activations, and model weights. One of the methods is FGSM (Fast Gradient Sign Method) [10]. The idea is to modify the input e.g. image, in such a way that added perturbation is consistent with the gradient sign obtained in the process of backpropagation. In the most common case of images, the generated perturbation might look similar to a color noise. The magnitude of the perturbation can be weighted by the gain factor. When it is small, the change in the output image is not noticeable. As it increases, the change is more and more visible. Therefore, during the generation, an iterative approach is adopted to allow for a gradual increase in perturbation until the label of a class recognized by the model changes. The effect of the one-time version of the FGSM algorithm is shown in Fig. 1. In this type of attack, the number of modified pixels is limited only to the image size.

Black-Box Attacks. On the contrary to white-box attacks, here attackers have no knowledge about attacked neural networks, except the outputs of the neural model. An example of such an attack is the so-called one-pixel attack [10]. It consists of changing one pixel of an input image to obtain another DNN prediction. The generation of adversarial examples is realized by solving a constrained optimization problem. The task is to find the optimal perturbation, namely to change just one pixel, causing a change of class by DNN. In this method, the differential evolution algorithm is used. It consists of comparing successive, generated children (in the form of pixels) with corresponding parents in each iteration, to check if the value of the class activation function has been increased. The effect of the one-pixel attack algorithm is shown in Fig. 1.

Adversarial Specificity

Targeted Attacks. These involve confusing the neural network by changing the input image in such a way that the input image is assigned a specific, defined class [10]. This type of attack is usually used in the problem of multi-class classification, and it aims to ensure that all attacked input images are classified as one class. In the case of a two-class classification task, a targeted attack becomes a non-targeted attack.

Non-targeted Attacks. The goal of undirected attacks is to change the input in such a way that the predicted class also changes [10]. A real-world example of a non-targeted attack is placing the sticker on a road STOP that will make an autonomous car recognize it as another sign. The generation of adverse examples for this type of attack usually takes place twofold. The first one consists of a series of targeted attacks and then selecting the least modified image. The second consists in minimizing the probability of obtaining the correct label.

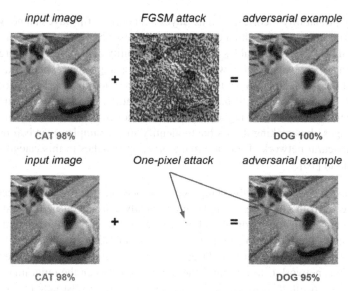

Fig. 1. Illustration of the FGSM and one-pixel attacks.

Attack Frequency. One-time attacks take a single trial to generate adversarial examples [10]. On the contrary, *Iterative attacks* take multiple trials to produce optimal adversarial examples. The latter have higher efficiency, but due to the large computation effort, they can rarely be used in real-time applications.

Adversarial Falsification. This category distinguishes attacks between False positives and False-negatives. The former generate hostile examples that are misclassified as positive ones, while the latter generates adverse examples that are misclassified as negative ones (Type I and Type II errors, respectively).

2.2   Countermeasures for Adversarial Attacks

Quick emergence of attacks, begun a new category of methods appear: *adversarial defense strategies.* These strategies can be divided into two categories: *reactive* and *proactive.* Reactive defenses focus on the detection of adversarial examples after the deep neural network has already been built, while the proactive strategies aim to increase the resistance (robustness) of the network to attacks by proper design of the training process or model's architecture.

Reactive. Reactive methods are used to defend an already trained neural network. One of the main methods is to prepare an additional model to check if an attack modified the input image. The second approach uses denoising autoencoder acting as a dedicated filter that removes adversarial perturbations from the input.

Adversarial Detecting. In this method, an auxiliary binary classifier is designed to recognize whether the input image is an adversarial example. This model uses the solutions provided by probability theories, such as Bayes's theorem [16]. Bayesian networks use a set of neural networks, in which each network is described by a parameter vector w (weights and bias). This set enables finding the probability density for the entire weights space, instead of choosing a set of weights describing a single neural network. The final output from the Bayesian network is obtained by calculating the average of the outputs from all the created networks. It has been proven that the uncertainty obtained by the Bayesian network classifier is higher in the case of adverse examples than in the case of clean images, thus making it possible to identify such examples even before they are fed into the neural network. There are many other approaches in this category, details can be found in [10].

Input Reconstruction. The method employs an autoencoder acting as a dedicated filter, to eliminate from the adverse example, intentionally introduced perturbations. After such input image transformation, it no longer significantly affects the prediction of the network. One of the tools allowing to recreate a perturbation-free image is Denoising autoencoder or its improved version - Deep Contractive Autoencoder [17]. The objective function of this network is to minimize the difference between the input image and the target one. As a result of learning, its outputs become the reconstructed version of the input. Because the middle layer has fewer neurons than the input and output layers, hence the latent representation is smaller, the network learns the most important features of the image so that the output image is as close as possible to the input image. Because of that AE is often used for dimensionality or noise reduction. In this case, it ensures that the network through training will learn the input features that are not related to perturbations, so that the original input image will be correctly restored.

Proactive. Proactive strategies involve training the neural network to increase its robustness against adverse attacks. The main defense strategy is to train the network using adversarial examples to increase its robustness. Another approach is network distillation which consists of creating several neural networks and transferring knowledge between them so that the final network becomes less sensitive to small changes in the image.

Adversarial (Re)training. The method is relatively simple yet effective. It is based on complementing the training set with adverse examples, and then, retraining the network. Network retraining consists in transferring the weights of the previously trained network and starting the training with such initial weights. By adding a set with adverse input to the training set, the network is forced to recognize also adverse examples as belonging to the correct class [18]. The robustness of the network against a given type of attack depends on whether it was included in the training stage.

Knowledge Distillation. Knowledge distillation [19] method was developed to reduce the size of the network by transferring knowledge from so-called teacher (larger) network to a student (smaller) one while maintaining its accuracy. In application to defense against adverse examples, this method aims to reduce the sensitivity of the network to small input perturbations.

Probability obtained at the output of a teacher network by using the softmax function becomes the soft-labels for the inputs of a student network. The method takes advantage of the fact that the knowledge acquired by the deep neural network during training is contained not only in the weights and thresholds but also in the probability vectors generated by the network. The teacher network uses the vector of similar probabilities as a set of new labels for images from the original set. In this vector, the information about the similarity between the classes is stored. The student network is trained on an original training set, but with labels generated by the teacher network. The student network achieves a similar predictive efficiency as the original model but provides lower calculation costs. By training the network on labels with coded similarities between the classes, it prevents overtraining. This also results in a better generalization of the network around the training points, hence the network becomes more robust to small image disturbances.

For the descriptions of other approaches to counteract the attacks, like: Classifier robustifying, Network verification, Ensembling defenses we refer the readers to [10]. Unfortunately, all defense strategies make the network robust only to a certain extent and to specific types of attacks. Additionally, these strategies do not work on new attacks. Moreover, it is unknown what type of attack will be used against a given neural network, making it extremely difficult to choose the right strategy [20].

3 XAI Methods of Inspecting Adversarial Attacks

Explainable Artificial Intelligence is a field of artificial intelligence that focuses on research and development of tools that allow the user to understand the decisions made by complex black-box ML models. With such tools, the user can better understand the premises underlying the model's decisions by trusting their credibility and accepting them. In case when XAI analyses indicate that the inference process is not in line with reality, the AI system can be improved, which contributes to the development of these models. In addition, recent papers report that XAI allows the detection and elimination of data biases that affect model performance [9]. Understanding how different attacks affect the model allows one to choose the right ways to increase its robustness. XAI methods can be divided into local and global explanations. Local analysis tries to explain a single prediction of a model, while the global approach shows the global model behavior. In this paper, we applied XAI methods to the analysis of the attacks and their influence on the neural model's predictions.

3.1 Local Explanations

There are several approaches realizing the idea of local explanations SHAP [21], LRP [22], LIME [23], Anchors [24]. In the paper, we decided to apply a method that allows generating visual explanation in the form of attention maps. In case of problems related to image analysis, the attention map visualizes how important each pixel in the input image is for the final DNN prediction. There is a wide range of approaches under this type of analysis e.g. Gradient SmoothGrad [25], DeConvNet [26], Guided Backpropagation [27], Input*Gradient [28]. After initial testing, for further analysis, we employed the Layer-wise Relevance Propagation method (LRP), more precisely its variant LRP present A flat. The LRP explains a neural network decision by decomposing the output of the model (prediction) at the pixel-level. The goal is to find the relevance scores of each input image pixels to a corresponding prediction, positive or negative. Those relevance sores might be visualized in the form of heatmaps. Simplifying the matter, heat maps indicate the pixels (areas) of the input image that affect the corresponding output value of the model most and least. A detailed description of the method can be found e.g. in [29]. The effect of employing this method to analysis of Convolution DNN model applied to image classification problem is shown in Fig. 2. In the upper row, one can find original images, and in the lower row the corresponding heatmaps. The red color indicates the pixels that most strongly correspond to the model output, while the blue color indicates the pixels that have the least influence on the model output. Such a visual analysis enables the end-user, or the developer of the model/system, to verify its correctness.

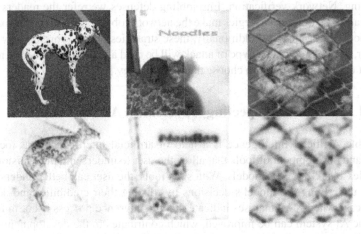

Fig. 2. Examples of attention maps (lower) generated by LRP present A flat.

In the case of the first image, we do not doubt that the model relies on rational premises when it generates the decision (dog's shape). In the next case, the situation is not so obvious anymore. The model takes into account the cat, but it focuses mostly on the text placed on the picture. Such behavior of the model, despite its correct classification, makes the trustworthiness of the model questionable. Analyzing the heatmaps of the third image, we can clearly see that the network pays attention only to the bars behind which the dog is placed. The reason for this obviously incorrect reasoning of the model is the fact that in the database used to learn the model [30], in the pictures with bars, there were mostly dogs, which suggested to the network that as there are bars in the picture, therefore the result of classification should be a 'dog'.

3.2 Global Explanations

XAI tools from the family of Global analyzers, are used for analyzing both ML models and datasets. Most of them are semi-supervised ones. They enable to analyze the ML models decisions learned from the large datasets, as well as to find the bias in the dataset.

One of the most important method of global explanations is Spectral Relevance Analysis (SpRAy) [31]. It takes advantage of the results of local analysis, namely the LRP attention maps, to extract knowledge about the overall behavior of the analyzed model, in the form of clusters representing data-driven model features, from the global perspective. Authors of [9] proposed improved version of SpRAy, in which they employ both original images and heatmaps for analysis, which has significantly improved the method's efficiency in the problem of identifying the data bias. In this paper, as a global analyzer we exploit another effective method based on XAI signatures [32]. We approached the problem with LRP signatures instead of SHAP ones and applied the LRP on the last layer instead of the penultimate layer. Next, we reduced its dimensionality with algorithm Uniform Manifold Approximation and Projection [33]. UMAP is a manifold learning technique for dimension reduction of large-scale multidimensional data. It utilizes mathematical foundations related to Laplacian eigenmaps and Riemannian geometry.

4 Case Study

4.1 Case Study Description

Our research aimed to analyze the influence of two representative types of attacks, i.e. FGSM and one-pixel attack on the performance of the attacked deep, convolutional neural network. For this purpose, we took advantage of local and global tools from the XAI family. We analyzed whether, normally unnoticed by the naked eye, the attack can be detected using appropriate XAI tools. In the case of individual images, a local analysis approach using heatmaps, namely the LRP present A flat method, was used for this purpose. To demonstrate the impact of these attacks convincingly and to be able to conclude, a database containing well-known figures, namely cats and dogs, was used. Figure 3 contains exemplary images, original and attacked. The upper row contains the input images that are given to the input of the neural network, while the lower row depicts the corresponding heatmaps, generated by LRP method. As mentioned, red color indicates the pixels that most strongly correspond to the model output, while the blue one shows the pixels that have the least influence on the model output. Figure 3 illustrate the effect of FGSM and one-pixel attacks onto the network. In both cases, it appears that the effectiveness of the prediction has decreased significantly after attack. Despite the previous proper classification of the image ('cat'), after the attack, the network classified the image incorrectly ('dog'), with high accuracy. Before the attack, the heatmap indicating the significance of the input image pixels appeared as in Fig. 3a. After the FGSM attack, the colors of the map, and thus the pixel significance, have practically reversed (Fig. 3b). This is due to the nature of this method, a white-box method, i.e. it uses the full knowledge of the network and dataset to change the prediction. In case of one pixel attack (Fig. 3d), it is clearly visible that the network is focusing its attention on this single, adverse pixel, which unfortunately results in a change of classification result. Similar results and effects were achieved for the whole analyzed dataset (see Table 1). This clearly proves how fragile deep models are these days, and that much attention needs to be paid to proper learning, improving the generalization abilities and robustness of these models, as well as to cybersecurity issues, especially for critical applications.

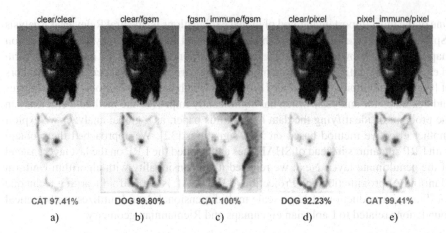

Fig. 3. FGSM and one-pixel attacks effect visualization. The arrows indicate the adverse pixel.

This problem can be partially remedied by the defense methods against attacks, described in Sect. 2.B. In this paper, the Adversarial retraining approach was used. For this purpose, a new training set was supplemented with successfully attacked with FGSM images. The extended training set was then used for retraining the 'FGSM_immune' model. Then it was checked whether the previously generated, extended testing set containing adversarial examples still affects the predictions. Using different testing images, it was then verified how many images can be attacked for 'clear' and 'FGSM_immune' models. The same procedure was applied to the one-pixel attack ('One-pixel_immune model'). The averaged results for the entire dataset were gathered in Table 1. The effects of the applied approach can also be observed in Fig. 3. In the case of both FGSM (Fig. 3c) and One-pixel attacks (Fig. 3e), the network proved to be robust against them. In the case of One-pixel attack, the attention map looks similar to the one from before the attack (adverse pixel was ignored). The attention map for FGSM type attack looks a little different. Noises on the map are caused by their appearance in the training set utilized during retraining. Despite different heatmaps, the classification result is correct. The differences in effects observed on heatmaps caused by different attacks can be used to detect and identify the types of attacks and to select the appropriate defensive strategy. The analysis of other images allows concluding that the described effects are representative. The results for the whole analyzed dataset are gathered in Table 1. It can be seen that such an approach has turned out to be successful in this case.

Table 1. Effectiveness of prediction depending on model and validation set type.

Model name/dataset	Clear	Clear	Clear	FGSM immune	One-pixel immune
Testing set	clear_test	clear + fgsm_test	clear + OP_test	clear + fgsm_test	clear + OP_test
Accuracy [%]	85.80	58.37	64.62	84.15	86.09

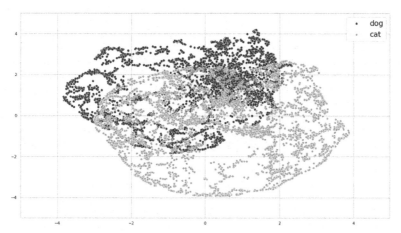

Fig. 4. Global UMAP visualization of local LRP signatures for examples of 'cat' and 'dog' images.

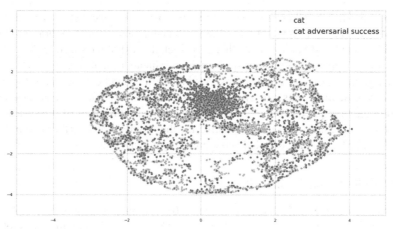

Fig. 5. Global UMAP visualization of local LRP signatures for examples and adversarial examples of 'cat' images – FGSM type of attack.

We have also attempted to analyze how the considered attacks affect the analyzed datasets globally, whether there are any specific patterns related to the type of attack and the dataset. Analyzed original and perturbed by FGSM and one-pixel attacks datasets were explored by taking advantage of the local explanation approach – LRP generating the attention maps, becoming the XAI signatures, and UMAP dimensionality reducer. To visualize the datasets before and after the attack was executed, we project these onto 2d space, via UMAP. The results for the FGSM type of attack are illustrated in Figs. 4, 5 and 6. Figure 4 shows the placement of images belonging to the class 'dogs' and 'cats', before the attack. Taking into account the correction for the fact that this is a projection of a multidimensional space into just 2 dimensions, please notice that some of the images belonging to both classes have a small topological distance from each other. Intuitively,

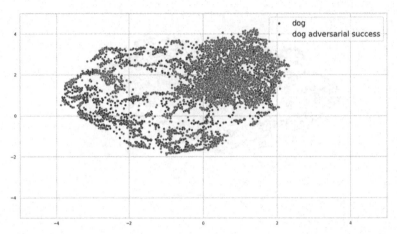

Fig. 6. Global UMAP visualization of local LRP signatures for examples and adversarial examples of 'dog' images – FGSM type of attack.

it can be expected that those images will be the easiest to effectively attack. Figure 5 shows which images from the class of 'dogs' changed their class affiliation into 'cats', as a result of the FGSM attack. Note that as predicted, most of the successfully attacked images are grouped in the first quarter of the coordinate system, which is where both classes have the most common features. A similar effect can be observed in Fig. 6, for the class representing 'cats'. In this case, most of the effectively attacked images are located in the first quarter of the coordinate system, near the center of the system. The aforementioned results are only qualitative for the moment, and further much deeper research is needed to draw detailed and convincing conclusions.

4.2 Implementation Details

During the research Kaggle dataset was used [30]. The images resolution is 112×112 px,. The training dataset ('clear'- before the attack) consists of 8000 images (4000 cats and dogs); original testing set - 'clear_test': 2000 images (1000 cats and dogs); new (extended) training dataset for defense against FGSM –'clear + FGSM': 6078 cats 5878 dogs; new testing dataset-'clear + FGSM_test': 1408 cats 1532 dogs; new (extended) training dataset for defense against one-pixel attack –'clear + OP': 5178 cats 5454 dogs; new testing dataset–'clear + OP_test': 1244 cats 1416 dogs.

CNN model: VGG16, with binary crossentropy loos function. SGD optimizer with: lr = 0.001, decay = 1e-6, was used during the training. Software libraries used: LRP attention maps [34]; FGSM [35]; one-pixel attack [36]; UMAP [33].

5 Summary and Concluding Remarks

In this paper, we reviewed the recent findings in adversarial attacks and defense strategies. We also analyzed the effects of the attacks and the defense strategies applied, using recent

XAI local and global approaches. We proposed to take advantage of the LRP attention maps and UMAP methods.

The results shown are preliminary, can be used for exploring the effects of adverse attacks, and allow to draw qualitative conclusions, only. However, undertaken analyses have confirmed that deep models are still fragile and are often not robust to well-prepared, intentional input perturbation.

Conducted research show that much attention needs to be paid to proper learning, improving the generalization and robustness of deep models, as well as to cybersecurity issues, especially for critical applications. It has also been demonstrated how valuable for process analysis XAI tools can be.

References

1. Goodfellow, I., Bengio, Y., Courville, A.: Deep Learning. MIT Press, Cambridge (2016). ISBN: 0262035618
2. Krizhevsky, A., Sutskever, I., Hinton, G.: ImageNet classification with deep convolutional neural networks. In: Neural Information Processing Systems, vol. 25, pp. 1097–1105 (2012)
3. Kukačka, J., Golkov, V., Cremers, D.: Regularization for Deep Learning: a Taxonomy (2017). arXiv:1710.10686
4. Grochowski, M., Kwasigroch, A., Mikołajczyk, A.: Selected technical issues of deep neural networks for image classification purposes. Bull. Pol. Acad. Sci. Tech. Sci. **67**(2) (2019)
5. Mikołajczyk, A., Grochowski, M.: Data augmentation for improving deep learning in image classification problem. In: International Interdisciplinary PhD Workshop (IIPhDW), pp. 117–122 (2018)
6. Mikołajczyk, A., Grochowski, M.: Style transfer-based image synthesis as an efficient regularization technique in deep learning. In: 24th International Methods and Models in Automation and Robotics (MMAR), pp. 42–47 (2019)
7. Elsken, T., Metzen, J.H., Hutter, F.: Neural Architecture Search: A Survey (2019). arXiv: 1808.05377
8. Kwasigroch, A., Grochowski, M., Mikołajczyk, A.: Neural architecture search for skin lesion classification. IEEE Access **8**, 9061–9071 (2020)
9. Mikołajczyk, A., Grochowski, M., Kwasigroch, A.: Towards explainable classifiers using the counterfactual approach - global explanations for discovering bias in data. J. Artif. Intell. Soft Comput. Res. (in press)
10. Yuan, X., He, P., Li, X., Zhu, Q.: Adversarial examples: attacks and defenses for deep learning. IEEE Trans. Neural Netw. Learn. Syst. **30**, 2805–2824 (2019)
11. Szegedy, C., Zaremba, W., Sutskever, I., Bruna, J., Erhan, D., Goodfellow, I., Fergus, R.: Intriguing properties of neural networks. In: 2nd International Conference on Learning Representations (2014)
12. Nguyen, A., Clune, J., Yosinski, J.: Deep neural networks are easily fooled: high confidence predictions. In: 2015 IEEE Conference on Computer Vision and Pattern Recognition (CVPR), pp. 427–436 (2015)
13. Eykholt, K., et al.: Robust physical-world attacks on deep learning visual classification. In: 2018 IEEE/CVF Conference on Computer Vision and Pattern Recognition, Salt Lake City, UT, pp. 1625–1634 (2018)
14. Cisse, M., Adi, Y., Keshet, J., Neverova, N.: Houdini: Fooling Deep Structured Prediction Models (2017). arXiv:1707.05373
15. Finlayson, S.G., Chung, H.W., Beam, A., Kohane I.S.: Adversarial attacks against medical deep learning systems (2018). arXiv:1804.05296

16. Feinman, R., Curtin, R., Gardner, A., Shintre, S.: Detecting Adversarial Samples from Artifacts (2017). arXiv:1703.00410
17. Rigazio, L., Gu, S.: Towards Deep Neural Network Architectures Robust to Adversarial Examples (2014). arXiv:1412.5068
18. Xu, H., et al.: Adversarial Attacks and Defenses in Images, Graphs and Text: A Review (2019). arXiv:1909.08072
19. Papernot, N., McDaniel, P., Wu, X., Swami, A., Jha, S.: Distillation as a defense to adversarial perturbations against deep neural networks. In: IEEE Symposium on Security and Privacy, pp. 582–597 (2016)
20. Goodfellow, I., McDaniel, P., Papernot, N.: Making machine learning robust against adversarial inputs. Commun. ACM Assoc. Comput. Mach. **61**, 56–66 (2018)
21. Fidel, G., Bitton R., Shabtai, A.: When Explainability Meets Adversarial Learning: Detecting Adversarial Examples using SHAP Signatures (2019). arXiv:1909.03418
22. Binder, A., Samek, W., Montavon, G., Lapuschkin, S., Müller, K.R.: Analyzing and validating neural networks predictions. In: ICML'16 Workshop on Visualization for Deep Learning (2016)
23. Ribeiro, M.T., Singh, S., Guestrin, C.: "Why Should I Trust You?": Explaining the Predictions of Any Classifier (2016). arXiv:1602.04938
24. Ribeiro, M.T., Singh, S., Guestrin, C.: Anchors: high-precision model-agnostic explanations. In: 32nd AAAI Conference on Artificial Intelligence (2018)
25. Smilkov, D., Thorat, N., Kim, B., Wattenberg, M., Viégas, F.: SmoothGrad: removing noise by adding noise (2017). arXiv:1706.03825
26. Zeiler, M.D., Fergus, R.: Visualizing and understanding convolutional networks. In: Fleet, D., Pajdla, T., Schiele, B., Tuytelaars, T. (eds.) ECCV 2014. LNCS, vol. 8689, pp. 818–833. Springer, Cham (2014). https://doi.org/10.1007/978-3-319-10590-1_53
27. Moeys, D.P., et al.: Steering a predator robot using a mixed frame/event-driven convolutional neural network. In: Second International Conference on Event-based Control, Communication and Signal Processing (EBCCSP), Krakow, pp. 1–8 (2016)
28. Ancona, M., Ceolini, E., Gross, M., Öztireli, C.: A unified view of gradient-based attribution methods for Deep Neural Networks. In: NIPS 2017-Workshop on Interpreting, Explaining and Visualizing Deep Learning, ETH, Zurich (2017)
29. Binder, A., Montavon, G., Lapuschkin, S., Müller, K.-R., Samek, W.: Layer-wise relevance propagation for neural networks with local renormalization layers. In: Villa, A.E.P., Masulli, P., Pons Rivero, A.J. (eds.) ICANN 2016. LNCS, vol. 9887, pp. 63–71. Springer, Cham (2016). https://doi.org/10.1007/978-3-319-44781-0_8
30. Kaggle: Dogs & Cats Images (2020). https://kaggle.com/chetankv/dogs-cats-images
31. Lapuschkin, S., Wäldchen, S., Binder, A., Montavon, G., Samek, W., Müller, K.R.: Unmasking clever hans predictors and assessing what machines really learn. Nat. Commun. **10**(1), 1096 (2019)
32. Fidel, G., Bitton, R., Shabtai, A.: When Explainability Meets Adversarial Learning: Detecting Adversarial Examples using SHAP Signatures (2019). arXiv:1909.03418
33. McInnes, L.: Umap (2020). https://github.com/lmcinnes/umap
34. Alber, M.: Innvestigate (2020). https://github.com/albermax/innvestigate
35. FGSM-Keras, GitHub. https://github.com/soumyac1999/FGSM-Keras
36. GitHub. https://github.com/Hyperparticle/one-pixel-attack-keras

On the Similarity Between Neural Network and Evolutionary Algorithm

Lumír Kojecký[(✉)] and Ivan Zelinka

Department of Computer Science, FEECS, VŠB - Technical University of Ostrava,
17. listopadu 15, 708 33 Ostrava - Poruba, Czechia
{lumir.kojecky,ivan.zelinka}@vsb.cz

Abstract. Artificial neural networks, evolutionary algorithms (and swarm intelligence) are common algorithms belonging to well known soft-computing algorithms. Both classes of algorithms have their history, principles and represent two different biological areas, converted to computer technology. Despite fact that scientists already exhibited that both systems exhibit almost the same behavior dynamics (chaotic regimes etc.), researchers still take both classes of algorithms as two different classes. We show in this paper, that there are some similarities, that can help to understand evolutionary algorithms as neural networks and vice versa.

Keywords: Artificial neural network · Evolutionary algorithms · Swarm intelligence

1 Introduction

Currently, there are many approaches how to synthesize a neural network structure, using constructive, destructive, or evolutionary approaches [9], like ANN synthesis by means of analytic programming, evolutionary algorithm, and network growth model [7]. In fact, a graph with an arbitrary structure can be considered as a neural network. Besides the structure synthesis, there are also many approaches to how to train a neural network, including backpropagation [5], deep learning [4], or training by means of an evolutionary algorithm [6].

This paper will propose a new model of neural network and the algorithm of its training. The model unifies the structure of a neural network and an evolutionary algorithm as well as the process of the network training and searching the global optimum by the evolutionary algorithm. Although evolutionary/swarm and neural-based algorithms are two different kinds of algorithms that are distinct in their nature (swarm-based algorithms mimic natural systems like bees colony, ant colony, a flock of birds, vs. neural systems like a brain), they have common attributes of its dynamics. Both are based on parallelism, both process information, store information, exhibit universal behavior like chaos [1,3], intermittence and more. This paper will demonstrate a close relationship between different kinds of systems with the aim that from an internal point of view they are the same.

© Springer Nature Switzerland AG 2020
L. Rutkowski et al. (Eds.): ICAISC 2020, LNAI 12415, pp. 147–158, 2020.
https://doi.org/10.1007/978-3-030-61401-0_15

For our experiments described here, specific hardware and algorithms have been used. All important information about algorithms used in our experiments is mentioned and referred here. This paper presents an initial study and proposal of an algorithm that combines neural and evolutionary structures and processes. Since this is an initial study, to keep this paper concise, readable and to follow the formal paper requirements, experiments showing the comparison in real-life problems were excluded and will be presented in further studies.

2   Neural Network Model as an Evolutionary Algorithm

For further simplicity, clarity, and easier imagination, let us consider a classic feedforward neural network having a standard set of neurons, neural synapses, and designated inputs and outputs. In the following terminology, a neuron in the neural network will be unified with an individual in the evolutionary algorithm with the following common attributes:

- Weighted inputs, output, and an activation function.
- A position in an n-dimensional space (vector) and a fitness function.

This model, therefore, allows being treated as a classic neural network as well as an evolutionary algorithm. The values of all synaptic weights $w_{i,j}$ are here calculated as Euclidean distance between the neurons i and j, as is defined in Eq. (1). In many cases, for correct network response, it is necessary to have also negative weight values. Since the equation to calculate Euclidean distance can return only non-negative numbers, another mechanism is incorporated into the synaptic weight value calculation – signum function. This allows returning any value of a synaptic weight. The mechanism is for a better understanding visualized in Fig. 1.

$$w_{i,j} = \prod_{d=1}^{dim} sgn\left(x_{d,N_i} - x_{d,N_j}\right) \cdot \sqrt{\sum_{d=1}^{dim} \left(x_{d,N_i} - x_{d,N_j}\right)^2} \qquad (1)$$

where dim = The dimensionality of the EA/ANN search space

$sgn(x)$ = Signum function (returning 1 at $x = 0$)

x_{d,N_x} = A d-th coordinate of the dim-dimensional neuron's position

Like a classic individual in an evolutionary algorithm, also the neuron's basic attribute is a position – a point in n-dimensional space (vector). Simply structured neural networks will get along with low-dimensional search space. However, with the increasing complexity of the neural network structure (i.e. multiple fully interconnected layers), it is also necessary to increase the dimensionality of the search space. Otherwise, it would be impossible to adjust the positions of the neurons and synaptic weights, respectively, for the correct network response.

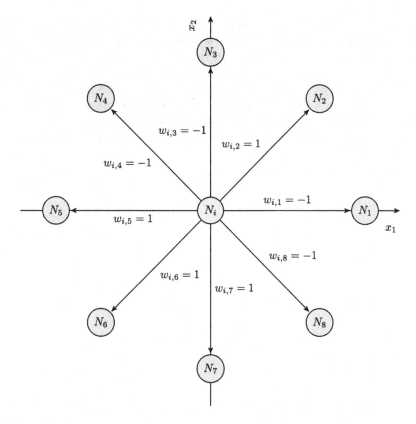

Fig. 1. Visualization of mechanism for weight value calculation, where $dim = 2$.

Increasing dimensionality of the search space provides a possibility of movement of a neuron in other coordinates, while the current can be fixed, thus adjustment of particular weights independently on the others.

Based on the description above, the network consists of n dim-dimensional vectors (where n means the number of neurons in the network). The next part of the proposed algorithm is to search for the position of each neuron/individual so that each weight will be correctly set up and the neural network will correctly respond to a given training set. The search can be performed by means of an arbitrary evolutionary algorithm, where each neuron's position is considered as one individual. For experiment purposes, All-To-Random version of the SOMA algorithm was used [10,11].

The only difference between commonly used evolutionary algorithms and the proposed algorithm is the calculation of fitness of an individual. Since a single neuron in a neural network cannot be evaluated separately and the global network error is evaluated instead,only the network output (global network error) is considered as each individual's fitness in this algorithm. In commonly used evolutionary algorithms, where every individual is independent of each other, the population would most likely converge to a single point (global optimum). In the proposed algorithm, this would result in a network with all zero weights and thus incorrect network response. Unlikely in the commonly used evolutionary algorithms, individuals in the proposed algorithm depend on each other and act as a team – improvement of one individual means improvement of the whole team. In the end, there is a diverse population of individuals, network with nonzero weights and thus most probably correct network response. A sample neural network using weight value calculation by the proposed model is constructed and visualized in Fig. 2.

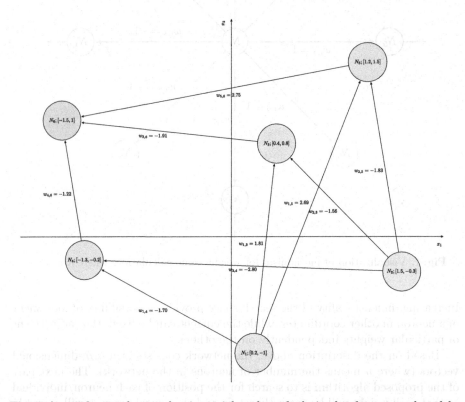

Fig. 2. A sample neural network using weight value calculation by the proposed model. The green nodes represent the network input, while the red node represents the network output. (Color figure online)

3   Mathematical Model of the Neural Network/Evolutionary Algorithm

The model described and implemented above is also possible to describe by mathematical equations. Equation (2) describes the general calculation of global network error for feedforward ANN, which is a simplified version of the equation proposed in [5]. This equation simply returns the exact difference between actual and expected output values of the output neurons for all training set entries.

$$NetworkError = \sum_{i=1}^{t} \sum_{j=1}^{n} \left| (O_{N_j} - T_j)_i \right| \tag{2}$$

where $t =$ The number of training set entries

$n =$ The number of the output neurons

$O_{N_j} =$ The actual output value of j-th output neuron

$T_j =$ The output value of j-th output neuron required by the training set

Output value for the input neurons is calculated also simply as the activation function of the input – as in Eq. (3).

$$O_{N_{Input}} = f(Input) \tag{3}$$

where $f(x) =$ The activation function of a neuron

Output value for the non-input neurons, given by Eq. (4), is, in fact, recursive equation, also based on standard signal feedforward (i.e. $O_{N_x} = f\left(\sum_{i=1}^{n} O_{N_i} \cdot w_{i,x}\right)$, where $w_{i,x}$ means the value of the synaptic weight from a neuron i to the neuron x). Equation (4), however, considers $w_{i,x}$ calculated as Euclidean distance between neuron i and neuron x, as was proposed in Sect. 2. The value is based on the neurons' coordinates and therefore we can express the complete equation as follows:

$$O_{N_x} = f\left(\sum_{i=1}^{n} O_{N_i} \cdot \prod_{j=1}^{dim} sgn\left(x_{j,N_i} - x_{j,N_x}\right) \cdot \sqrt{\sum_{j=1}^{dim} \left(x_{j,N_i} - x_{j,N_x}\right)^2} \right) \tag{4}$$

where $f(x) =$ The activation function of a neuron

$n =$ The number of inputs of neuron N_x

$dim =$ The dimensionality of the EA/ANN search space

$sgn(x) =$ Signum function (returning 1 at $x = 0$)

$x_{j,N_i} =$ A j-th coordinate of the dim-dimensional neuron's position

3.1   Model of a Sample Network

Let us consider a very simple network as an example – the network should be as simple as possible to ease the following manual steps. The sample network consists of two input and one output node. Based on the explanation in Sect. 2, each neuron can have only one coordinate, therefore $dim = 1$. Based on Eq. (3) and Eq. (4), we can assemble Eq. (5), which expresses the whole network output with substituted inputs and neurons' coordinates.

$$O_{N_3} = f\left(f\left(I_1\right) \cdot sgn\left(x_{1,N_1} - x_{1,N_3}\right) \cdot \sqrt{\left(x_{1,N_1} - x_{1,N_3}\right)^2} + \right.$$
$$\left. + f\left(I_2\right) \cdot sgn\left(x_{1,N_2} - x_{1,N_3}\right) \cdot \sqrt{\left(x_{1,N_2} - x_{1,N_3}\right)^2} \right) \tag{5}$$

where $I_1 =$ Input from the training set for the first input neuron

$I_2 =$ Input from the training set for the second input neuron

As can be seen from Eq. (5), for correct network output, it is necessary to properly set coordinates of N_1, N_2 and N_3. Since this network is so simple, it is also possible to keep one of the neurons at a fixed position. Let us keep neuron N_3 fixed at position $x_{1,N_3} = 0$. This step will simplify the equation by reducing one variable as in Eq. (6).

$$O_{N_3} = f\left(f\left(I_1\right) \cdot sgn\left(x_{1,N_1}\right) \cdot \sqrt{\left(x_{1,N_1}\right)^2} + \right.$$
$$\left. + f\left(I_2\right) \cdot sgn\left(x_{1,N_2}\right) \cdot \sqrt{\left(x_{1,N_2}\right)^2} \right) \tag{6}$$

Function f can be now substituted with concrete activation function (i.e. hyperbolic tangent) as in Eq. (7).

$$O_{N_3} = \tanh\left(\tanh\left(I_1\right) \cdot sgn\left(x_{1,N_1}\right) \cdot \sqrt{\left(x_{1,N_1}\right)^2} + \right.$$
$$\left. + \tanh\left(I_2\right) \cdot sgn\left(x_{1,N_2}\right) \cdot \sqrt{\left(x_{1,N_2}\right)^2} \right) \tag{7}$$

Finally, in Eq. (8) there is, for simplicity and clarity, x_{1,N_1} renamed to x and x_{1,N_2} renamed to y. This equation can be considered as the real network output based on inputs.

$$O_{N_3} = \tanh\left(\tanh\left(I_1\right) \cdot sgn\left(x\right) \cdot \sqrt{x^2} + \tanh\left(I_2\right) \cdot sgn\left(y\right) \cdot \sqrt{y^2} \right) \tag{8}$$

3.2   A Sample Training Set

Since the sample network is very simple, also the training set must be very simple. In the Table 1 there are four entries for the sample network to learn. Using the approach proposed in Sect. 2, the final network error was 0.087294394.

Table 1. A sample training set.

Input (I_1)	Input (I_2)	Expected output
0	0	0.0
0	1	0.1
1	0	0.2
1	1	0.3

3.3   Applying the Model to the Training Set

At this time, the mathematical model of the network and also training set for the network are both set up. If we substitute each of four training entries (inputs) from Table 1 to Eq. (8), we will obtain totally four equations:

1. $I_1 = 0, I_2 = 0 : O_{N_3} = \tanh(0)$
2. $I_1 = 0, I_2 = 1 : O_{N_3} = \tanh\left(\tanh(1) \cdot sgn(y) \cdot \sqrt{y^2}\right)$
3. $I_1 = 1, I_2 = 0 : O_{N_3} = \tanh\left(\tanh(1) \cdot sgn(x) \cdot \sqrt{x^2}\right)$
4. $I_1 = 1, I_2 = 1 :$

$$O_{N_3} = \tanh\left(\tanh(1) \cdot sgn(x) \cdot \sqrt{x^2} + \tanh(1) \cdot sgn(y) \cdot \sqrt{y^2}\right)$$

These 4 equations represent the complete behavior of the sample network in terms of output to the input. Considering Eq. (2), the sum of the following four function results will result in the global network error:

1. $\left|\tanh(0) - 0.0\right|$
2. $\left|\tanh\left(\tanh(1) \cdot sgn(y) \cdot \sqrt{y^2}\right) - 0.1\right|$
3. $\left|\tanh\left(\tanh(1) \cdot sgn(x) \cdot \sqrt{x^2}\right) - 0.2\right|$
4. $\left|\tanh\left(\tanh(1) \cdot sgn(x) \cdot \sqrt{x^2} + \tanh(1) \cdot sgn(y) \cdot \sqrt{y^2}\right) - 0.3\right|$

Based on these functions, we have to find positions x and y so that each function above will provide a minimal result (ideally 0) and also the global network error will be minimal. In this sample, training the network means searching for vector (x, y) to minimize the global network error. Generally, the network training means searching for $(n \cdot dim)$-dimensional vector as an optimal solution (where n means the number of neurons in the network).

The vector can be obtained by means of the approach proposed in Sect. 2 by means of an arbitrary evolutionary algorithm (i.e. SOMA), or even by means of calculation. For simplicity, for each training entry in the training set let us tolerate maximal error 0.005. This allows us to compose the following four inequations:

1. $|\tanh(0) - 0.0| \leq 0.005$
2. $\left|\tanh\left(\tanh(1) \cdot sgn(y) \cdot \sqrt{y^2}\right) - 0.1\right| \leq 0.005$
3. $\left|\tanh\left(\tanh(1) \cdot sgn(x) \cdot \sqrt{x^2}\right) - 0.2\right| \leq 0.005$
4. $\left|\tanh\left(\tanh(1) \cdot sgn(x) \cdot \sqrt{x^2} + \tanh(1) \cdot sgn(y) \cdot \sqrt{y^2}\right) - 0.3\right| \leq 0.005$

Each inequation above can be solved separately now. The results below were calculated by Wolfram engine [8] for each inequation:

1. $x \in \mathbb{R}, y \in \mathbb{R}$
2. $x \in \mathbb{R}, 0.125116 \leq y \leq 0.138379$
3. $0.259363 \leq x \leq 0.273041, y \in \mathbb{R}$
4. Union of the following intervals:
   (a) $x < 0, 0.399207 - x \leq y \leq 0.413637 - x$
   (b) $0.399207 \leq x \leq 0.413637, y = 0$
   (c) $0 < x < 0.399207, 0.399207 - x \leq y \leq 0.413637 - x$
   (d) $x \approx 0.399207, 0 < y \leq 0.0144291$
   (e) $0.399207 < x < 0.413637, 0 < y \leq 0.413637 - x$

The calculated results represent independent solutions for each inequation. As was written above, we are searching for vector (x, y) to minimize the global network error. Therefore (x, y) must be at the intersection of the calculated four intervals. Let us choose $(x, y) = (0.265, 0.135)$ as a solution and check whether the numbers belong to all the intervals:

1. $\mathbf{0.265} \in \mathbb{R}, \mathbf{0.135} \in \mathbb{R}$
2. $\mathbf{0.265} \in \mathbb{R}, 0.125116 \leq \mathbf{0.135} \leq 0.138379$
3. $0.259363 \leq \mathbf{0.265} \leq 0.273041, \mathbf{0.135} \in \mathbb{R}$
4. The 4. (c) interval was selected:
   $0 < \mathbf{0.265} < 0.399207$
   $0.399207 - x \leq y \leq 0.413637 - x \rightarrow 0.134207 \leq \mathbf{0.135} \leq 0.418637$

Since $(0.265, 0.135)$ belongs to all the intervals, we can consider it as the equations' solution, which means this is also the final configuration for our sample neural network, which is able to respond properly to each entry in the training set. Substitution of $(x, y) = (0.265, 0.135)$ to the Eq. (8) resulted in global network error 0.007777365. Compared to the error 0.087294394 mentioned in Sect. 3.2, this is an improvement in terms of an order of magnitude smaller error.

4 On the Equivalence Between Neural Networks and Evolutionary Algorithms

In this section, possible similarity/equivalence between neural networks and evolutionary algorithms is discussed.

4.1   Multi-objective Optimization

The method of calculation of (x, y), which was proposed in Sect. 3.3 — searching a number or interval, that belongs to an intersection of all inequations' result intervals — can be in fact considered as searching a feasible decision space in multi-objective optimization process [2]. Generally, the proposed method and also a neural network training itself can be considered as multi-objective optimization:

- Neural network structure and training set can be considered as a number of inequations – objective functions
- Searching an interval belonging to an intersection of all inequations' result intervals can be considered as searching a feasible decision space of the objective functions
- In the end, there is a configuration of a trained neural network that can be considered as a solution that defines the best trade-off between the objective functions

4.2   Parallel Implementation Approach

In case of bigger and more complex networks, it would be beneficial to implement the algorithm in a parallel environment. According to the standard approach — to evaluate each individual separately — for each individual it would be necessary to adjust its position, recalculate all input and output synapse weight values and evaluate the global network error. This would not be beneficial because the fitness function is relatively cheap (if the training set is not huge) and therefore the impact of the parallelization would be minimal due to a communication cost. Above all, this approach to parallelization of the algorithm does not make much sense – as is written in Sect. 2, individuals in the proposed algorithm depend on each other and act as a team.

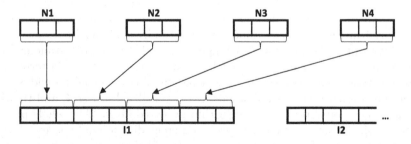

Fig. 3. Joining all n dim-dimensional vectors into one super-individual.

Evolutionary algorithm - Population of individuals (D = 12)

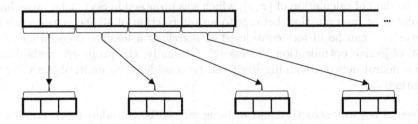

Neural network - Population of neurons (D = 3)

Fig. 4. Dividing the super-individual into n dim-dimensional vectors.

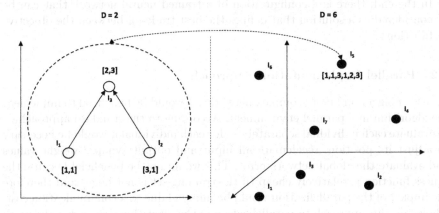

Fig. 5. Example of the conversion between different dimensional spaces. On the left, there is a neural network, on the right, there is an evolutionary algorithm.

However, as is mentioned in Sect. 3.3, we search for $(n \cdot dim)$-dimensional vector as optimal solution. Therefore it is possible to join all n dim-dimensional vectors (individuals) from the original population into one super-individual, as is visualized in Fig. 3. At this time, the super-individual can be a member of a population of regular evolutionary algorithm and treated in a standard way – independently and mainly in parallel. As the opposite process, in terms of a fitness function calculation, can be considered dividing the super-individual into n dim-dimensional vectors (individuals), as is visualized in Fig. 4, and treating them as a new population in the algorithm proposed above. The whole process can be considered as conversion between different dimensional spaces — dim-dimensional in case of a neural network and $(n \cdot dim)$-dimensional in case of an evolutionary algorithm — as is visualized in Fig. 5.

5   Conclusion

This paper basically describes a concept of transformation of an artificial neural network training to multi-objective optimization and vice versa as follows:

- **Artificial Neural Networks** – there are neurons, synapses, inputs, outputs, and a training set. The network training is performed in fact by adjusting weight values – minimizing the global network error.
- **Evolutionary Algorithms** – there are individuals in the population traversing through n-dimensional space, searching for the best trade-off between the objective functions. The search is performed in fact by vector operations (crossover, mutation) between the individuals.
- **In the middle** – there is the proposed model and algorithm, which unifies neuron and individual, neural network and population, global network error and objective functions, and neural network training and multi-objective optimization. The model shows that one system is included in the other and transformation between the two systems is feasible through the model. Therefore, we can consider these two systems as equivalent.

Acknowledgment. The following grants are acknowledged for the financial support provided for this research: Grant of SGS No. 2020/78, VSB-Technical University of Ostrava.

References

1. Das, S., Goswami, D., Chatterjee, S., Mukherjee, S.: Stability and chaos analysis of a novel swarm dynamics with applications to multi-agent systems. Eng. Appl. Artif. Intell. **30**, 189–198 (2014)
2. Deb, K.: Multi-objective Optimization Using Evolutionary Algorithms, vol. 16. John Wiley & Sons, Hoboken (2001)
3. Garliauskas, A.: Neural network chaos analysis. Nonlinear Anal. Model. Control **3**, 43–57 (1998)
4. Glorot, X., Bengio, Y.: Understanding the difficulty of training deep feedforward neural networks. In: Proceedings of the Thirteenth International Conference on Artificial Intelligence and Statistics, pp. 249–256 (2010)
5. Hecht-Nielsen, R.: Theory of the backpropagation neural network. In: Neural Networks for Perception, pp. 65–93. Elsevier (1992)
6. Ilonen, J., Kamarainen, J.K., Lampinen, J.: Differential evolution training algorithm for feed-forward neural networks. Neural Process. Lett. **17**(1), 93–105 (2003)
7. Kojecký, L., Zelinka, I.: Evolutionary design and training of artificial neural networks. In: Rutkowski, L., Scherer, R., Korytkowski, M., Pedrycz, W., Tadeusiewicz, R., Zurada, J.M. (eds.) ICAISC 2018. LNCS (LNAI), vol. 10841, pp. 427–437. Springer, Cham (2018). https://doi.org/10.1007/978-3-319-91253-0_40
8. Wolfram, S.: Wolfram—Alpha (2009). http://www.wolframalpha.com

9. Yao, X.: Evolving artificial neural networks. Proc. IEEE **87**(9), 1423–1447 (1999)
10. Zelinka, I.: SOMA-self-organizing migrating algorithm. In: Onwubolu, G.C., Babu, B.V. (eds.) New Optimization Techniques in Engineering. SCI, vol. 141, pp. 167–217. Springer, Heidelberg (2004). https://doi.org/10.1007/978-3-540-39930-8_7
11. Zelinka, I.: SOMA—self-organizing migrating algorithm. In: Davendra, D., Zelinka, I. (eds.) Self-Organizing Migrating Algorithm. SCI, vol. 626, pp. 3–49. Springer, Cham (2016). https://doi.org/10.1007/978-3-319-28161-2_1

3D Convolutional Neural Networks for Ultrasound-Based Silent Speech Interfaces

László Tóth[(✉)] and Amin Honarmandi Shandiz

Institute of Informatics, University of Szeged, Szeged, Hungary
{tothl,shandiz}@inf.u-szeged.hu

Abstract. Silent speech interfaces (SSI) aim to reconstruct the speech signal from a recording of the articulatory movement, such as an ultrasound video of the tongue. Currently, deep neural networks are the most successful technology for this task. The efficient solution requires methods that do not simply process single images, but are able to extract the tongue movement information from a sequence of video frames. One option for this is to apply recurrent neural structures such as the long short-term memory network (LSTM) in combination with 2D convolutional neural networks (CNNs). Here, we experiment with another approach that extends the CNN to perform 3D convolution, where the extra dimension corresponds to time. In particular, we apply the spatial and temporal convolutions in a decomposed form, which proved very successful recently in video action recognition. We find experimentally that our 3D network outperforms the CNN+LSTM model, indicating that 3D CNNs may be a feasible alternative to CNN+LSTM networks in SSI systems.

Keywords: Silent speech interface · Convolutional neural network · 3D convolution · Ultrasound video

1 Introduction

During the last couple of years, there has been an increasing interest in articulatory-to-acoustic conversion, which seeks to reproduce the speech signal from a recording of the articulatory organs, giving the technological background for creating "Silent Speech Interfaces" (SSI) [6,28]. These interfaces allow us to record the soundless articulatory movement, and then automatically generate speech from the movement information, while the subject is actually not producing any sound. Such an SSI system could be very useful for the speaking impaired who are able to move their articulators, but have lost their ability to produce any sound (e.g. due to a laryngectomy or some injury of the vocal chords). It could also be applied in human-computer interaction in situations where regular speech is not feasible (e.g. extremely noisy environments or military applications). Several solutions exist for the recording of the articulatory

© Springer Nature Switzerland AG 2020
L. Rutkowski et al. (Eds.): ICAISC 2020, LNAI 12415, pp. 159–169, 2020.
https://doi.org/10.1007/978-3-030-61401-0_16

movements, the simplest approach being a lip video [1,8]. But one may also apply electromagnetic articulography (EMA, [18,19]), ultrasound tongue imaging (UTI, [5,10,16,20]) or permanent magnetic articulography (PMA, [9]). Surface Electromiography (sEMG, [14,15,24]) is also an option, while some authors use a combination of the above methods [6]. Here we are going to work with ultrasound tongue videos.

To convert the movement recordings into speech, the conventional approach is to apply a two-step procedure of 'recognition-and-synthesis' [28]. In this case, the biosignal is first converted into text by a properly adjusted speech recognition system. The text is then converted into speech using text-to-speech synthesis [7, 13,31]. The drawbacks of this approach are the relatively large delay between the input and the output, and that the errors made by the speech recognizer will inevitably appear as errors in the TTS output. Also, all information related to speech prosody is lost, while certain prosodic components such as energy and pitch can be reasonably well estimated from the articulatory signal [10].

Current SSI systems prefer the 'direct synthesis' principle, where speech is generated directly from the articulatory data, without any intermediate step. Moreover, as recently the Deep Neural Network (DNN) technology have become dominant in practically all areas of speech technology, such as speech recognition [11], speech synthesis [22] and language modeling [33], most recent studies have attempted to solve the articulatory-to-acoustic conversion problem by using deep learning, regardless of the recording technique applied [5,9,10,14,16,20,25]. In this paper, we also apply deep neural networks to convert the ultrasound video of the tongue movement to speech. Although some early studies used simple fully connected neural networks [5,16], as we are working with images, it seems more reasonable to apply convolutional neural networks (CNN), which are currently very popular and successful in image recognition [21]. Thus, many recent studies on SSI systems use CNNs [14,20,25].

Our input here is a video, that is, not just one still image, but a sequence of images. This sequence carries extra information about the time trajectory of the tongue movement, which might be exploited by processing several neighboring video frames at the same time. There are several options to create a network structure for processing a time sequences. For such data, usually recurrent neural networks such as the long short-term memory network (LSTM) are applied, typically stacking it on top of a 2D CNN that seeks to process the individual frames [9,19,23,25]. Alternatively, one may experiment with extending the 2D CNN structure to 3D, by adding time as an extra dimension [17,20,32]. Here, we follow the latter approach, and we investigate the applicability of a special 3D CNN model called the (2+1)D CNN [30] for ultrasound-based direct speech synthesis, and compare the results with those of a CNN+LSTM model. We find that our 3D CNN model achieves a lower error rate, while it is smaller, and its training is faster. We conclude that for ultrasound video-based SSI systems, 3D CNNs are definitely a feasible alternative to recurrent neural models.

The paper is structured as follows. Section 2 gives a technological overview of the CNNs we are going to apply. In Sect. 3 we describe the data acquisition and processing steps for the ultrasound videos and the speech signal. Section 4 presents our experimental set-up. We present the experimental results and discuss them in Sect. 5, and the paper is closed with the conclusions in Sect. 6.

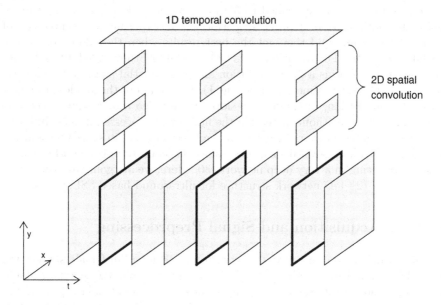

Fig. 1. Illustration of how the (2+1)D CNN operates. The video frames (at the bottom) are first processed by layers that perform 2D spatial convolution, then their outputs are combined by 1D temporal convolution. The model is allowed to skip video frames by changing the stride parameter of the temporal convolution.

2   Convolutional Neural Networks for Video Processing

Ever since the invention of 'Alexnet', CNNs have remained the leading technology in the recognition of still images [21]. These standard CNNs apply the convolution along the two spatial axes, that is, in two dimensions (2D). However, there are several tasks where the input is a video, and handling the video as a sequence (instead of simply processing separate frames) is vital for obtaining good recognition results. The best example is human gait recognition, but we can talk about action recognition in general [17,36,37]. In these cases, the sequence of video frames forms a three-dimensional data array, with the temporal axis being the third dimension in addition to the two spatial dimensions (cf. Fig. 1).

For the processing of sequences, recurrent neural structures such as the LSTM are the most powerful tool [12]. However, the training of these networks is known to be slow and problematic, which led to the invention of simplified models, such as the gated recurrent unit (GRU) [3] or the quasi-recurrent neural network [2]. Alternatively, several convolutional network structures have been proposed that handle time sequences without recurrent connections. In speech recognition, time-delay neural networks (TDNNs) have proved very successful [26,29], but we can also mention the feedforward sequential memory network [34]. As regards video processing, several modified CNN structures have been proposed to handle the temporal sequence of video frames [17,36,37]. Unfortunately, the standard 2D convolution may be extended to 3D in many possible ways, giving a lot of choices for optimization. Tran et al. performed an experimental comparison of several 3D variants, and they got the best results when they decomposed the spatial and temporal convolution steps [30]. The model they called '(2+1)D convolution' first performs a 2D convolution along the spatial axes, and then a 1D convolution along the time axis (see Fig. 1). By changing the stride parameter of the 1D convolution, the model can skip several video frames, thus covering a wider time context without increasing the number of processed frames. Interestingly, a very similar network structure proved very efficient in speech recognition as well [29]. Stacking several such processing blocks on top of each other is also possible, resulting in a very deep network [30]. Here, we are going to experiment with a similar (2+1)D network structure for ultrasound-based SSI systems.

3   Data Acquisition and Signal Preprocessing

The ultrasound recordings were collected from a Hungarian female subject (42 years old, with normal speaking abilities) while she was reading sentences aloud. Her tongue movement was recorded in a midsagittal orientation – placing the ultrasonic imaging probe under the jaw – using a "Micro" ultrasound system by Articulate Instruments Ltd. The transducer was fixed using a stabilization headset. The 2–4 MHz/64 element 20 mm radius convex ultrasound transducer produced 82 images per second. The speech signal was recorded in parallel with an Audio-Technica ATR 3350 omnidirectional condenser microphone placed at a distance of 20 cm from the lips. The ultrasound and the audio signals were synchronized using the software tool provided with the equipment. Altogether 438 sentences (approximately half an hour) were recorded from the subject, which was divided into train, development and test sets in a 310-41-87 ratio. We should add that the same dataset was used in several earlier studies [5,10].

The ultrasound probe records 946 samples along each of its 64 scan lines. The recorded data can be converted to conventional ultrasound images using the software tools provided. However, due to its irregular shape, this image is harder to process by computers, while it contains no extra information compared to the original scan data. Hence, we worked with the original 964 × 64 data items, which were downsampled to 128 × 64 pixels. Figure 2 shows an example of the data samples arranged as a rectangular image, and the standard ultrasound-style display generated from it. The intensity range of the data was min-max normalized to the [−1, 1] interval before feeding it to the network.

The speech signal was recorded with a sampling rate of 11025 Hz, and then processed by a vocoder from the SPTK toolkit (http://sp-tk.sourceforge.net). The vocoder represented the speech signals by 12 Mel-Generalized Cepstral Coefficients (MGCC) converted to a Line Spectral Pair representation (LSP), with

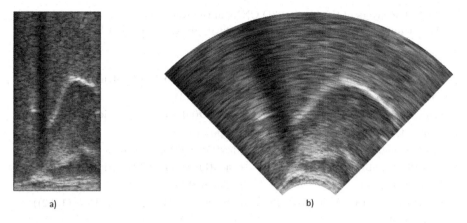

Fig. 2. Example of displaying the ultrasound recordings as a) a rectangular image of raw data samples b) an anatomically correct image, obtained by interpolation.

the signal's gain being the 13th parameter. These 13 coefficients served as the training targets in the DNN modeling experiments, as the speech signal can be reasonably well reconstructed from these parameters. Although perfect reconstruction would require the estimation of the pitch (F0 parameter) as well, in this study we ignored this component during the experiments. To facilitate training, each of the 13 targets were standardized to zero mean and unit variance.

4   Experimental Set-Up

We implemented our deep neural networks in Keras, using a Tensorflow backend [4]. We created three different models: a simple fully connected network (FCN), a convolutional network that processes one frame of video (2D CNN), and a convolutional network that can process several subsequent video frames as input (3D CNN). To keep them comparable with respect to parameter count, all three models had approximately 3.3 million tunable parameters. Training was performed using the stochatic gradient descent method (SGD) with a batch size of 100. The training objective function was the mean squared error (MSE).

Fully Connected Network (FCN): The simplest possible DNN type is a network with fully connected layers. To be comparable with an earlier study [5], our FCN model consisted of 5 fully connected hidden layers, with an output layer of 13 neurons for the 13 training targets. The input of the network consisted of one video frame ($128 \times 64 = 8192$ pixels). Each hidden layers had 350 neurons, so the model was about 4 times smaller compared to the FCN described in [5]. Apart from the linear output layer, all layers applied the swish activation function [27], and were followed by a dropout layer with the dropout rate set to 0.2.

Convolutional Network (2D CNN): Similar to the FCN, the input to this network consisted of only one frame of data. The network performed spatial convolution on the input image via its four convolutional layers below the uppermost

Table 1. The layers of the 2D and 3D CNNs in the Keras implementation, along with their most important parameters. The differences are highlighted in bold.

2D CNN	3D CNN
Conv2D(30, (13,13), strides = (2,2))	Conv**3D**(30, (**5**,13,13), strides = (**s**, 2,2))
Dropout(0.2)	Dropout(0.2)
Conv2D(60, (13,13), strides = (2,2))	Conv**3D**(60, (**1**,13,13), strides = (**1**,2,2))
Dropout(0.2)	Dropout(0.2)
MaxPooling2D(pool_size = (2,2))	MaxPooling**3D**(pool_size = (**1**,2,2))
Conv2D(90, (13,13), strides = (2,1))	Conv**3D**(90, (**1**,13,13), strides = (**1**,2,1))
Dropout(0.2)	Dropout(0.2)
Conv2D(120, (13,13), strides = (2,2))	Conv**3D**(**85**, (**1**,13,13), strides = (**1**,2,2))
Dropout(0.2)	Dropout(0.2)
MaxPooling2D(pool_size = (2,2))	MaxPooling**3D**(pool_size = (**1**,2,2))
Flatten()	Flatten()
Dense(500)	Dense(500)
Dropout(0.2)	Dropout(0.2)
Dense(13, activation = 'linear')	Dense(13, activation = 'linear')

fully connected layer. The actual network configuration is shown in Table 1. The optimal network meta-parameters were found experimentally, and all hidden layers applied the swish activation function [27].

3D Convolutional Network (3D CNN): To enable the processing of video frames sequences, we changed the 2D convolution to 3D convolution in our CNN. This network processed 5 frames of video that were s frames apart, where s is the stride parameter of the convolution along the time axis. Following the concept of (2+1)D convolution described in Sect. 2, the five frames were first processed only spatially, and then got combined along the time axis just below the uppermost dense layer. Table 1 shows the actual network configuration. The modifications compared to the 2D CNN are shown in bold. We note that the number of filters in the uppermost convolutional layer was decreased in order to keep the number of parameters in the same range as that for the 2D CNN.

There are several options for evaluating the performance of our networks. In the simplest case, we can compare their performance by simple objective metrics, such as the value of the target function optimized during training (the MSE function in our case). Unfortunately, these metrics do not perfectly correlate with the users' subjective sense of quality of the synthesized speech. Hence, many authors apply subjective listening tests such as the MUSHRA method [25]. This kind of evaluation is tedious, as it requires averaging the scores of a lot of human subjects. As an interesting shortcut, Kimura et al. applied a set of commercial speech recognizers to substitute the human listeners in the listening tests [20]. In this paper, we will simply apply objective measures, namely the mean squared error (MSE) and the (mean) R^2 score, which are simple and popular methods for evaluating the performance of neural networks on regression tasks.

5   Results and Discussion

As for the 3D CNN, we found that the value of the stride parameter s has a significant impact on the error rate attained. The size of the input time context covered by the network can be calculated as $w = 4 \cdot s + 1$. For example, for $s = 6$ the distance between the first and the last time frames was $w = 25$, meaning that the network input should consist of a sequence of 25 video frames. According to the 82 fps sampling rate, this corresponds to video chunks of about 300 ms.

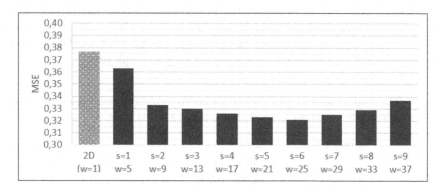

Fig. 3. MSE rates of the 3D CNN on the development set for various s stride values. For comparison, the MSE attained by the 2D CNN is also shown (leftmost column).

Figure 3 shows the MSE obtained on the development set with the 3D CNN network for various s values. As a base of comparison, the MSE attained by the 2D CNN that processes a single frame is also shown. It can be clearly seen that extending the actual frame with its context can significantly reduce the error rate. Including 2-2 immediate neighbors is already effective $(s = 1)$, but the largest gain was achieved when setting s to a value between 3 and 8.

Table 2 summarizes the best results for the three network configurations, both for the development and test sets. Along with the MSE values, now the correlation-based R^2 scores are also shown. The 2D CNN network was superior to the fully connected network, but the 3D CNN clearly outperformed it, reducing the MSE on the test set by about 21% in a relative sense. The R^2 score increased by 14% absolute.

The two bottom rows of Table 2 compare our results with two earlier studies. The authors of [5] applied a fully connected network on the same data set. They obtained slightly better results than those given by our FCN, presumably due to the fact that their network had about 4 times as many parameters. More interestingly, they attempted to include more neighboring frames in the processing, simply by concatenating the corresponding image data. Feature selection was applied to alleviate the problems caused by the large size of the images (~8000 pixel per image), These simple methods failed to significantly reduce the error rate. Our current experiments show that the frames should be placed farther apart ($3 \leq s \leq 8$) for optimal performance. Moreover, instead of reducing the input size by feature selection, it seems to be more efficient to send the frames through several neural layers, with a relatively narrow 'bottleneck' layer on top.

Moliner and Csapó combined the 2D CNN with an LSTM, this way processing video chunks of 32 frames [25]. As we explained in Sect. 2, this is the most viable and competitive alternative to our approach. Unfortunately, their study reports no MSE scores, but they provided us with their code. We retrained their (uni-directional) LSTM with some minimal and unavoidable modifications, e.g. adjusting the input and output layer sizes (they used different training targets and a slightly different input resampling). Their model had five times a many tunable parameters than our models, and its training also took much longer. While it clearly outperformed both the FCN and the 2D CNN models, it could not compete with our 3D CNN, in spite of its larger complexity.

Table 2. The results obtained with the various network configurations. For comparison, two results from the literature are also shown in the bottom rows.

Network type	Dev		Test	
	MSE	Mean R^2	MSE	Mean R^2
FCN	0.408	0.599	0.400	0.598
2D CNN	0.377	0.630	0.366	0.633
3D CNN (s = 6)	0.321	0.684	0.315	0.683
FCN [5]	0.384	0.619	n/a	n/a
CNN + LSTM [25]	0.345	0.653	0.336	0.661

6   Conclusions

Here, we implemented a 3D CNN for ultrasound-based articulation-to-acoustic conversion, where the CNN applied separate spatial and temporal components, motivated by the (2+1)D CNN of Tran et al. [30]. The model was compared with a CNN+LSTM architecture that was recently proposed for the same task. We found that the 3D CNN performed slightly better, while it was smaller and faster to train. Though asserting the superiority of the 3D CNN would require more thorough comparisons, we can safely conclude that 3D CNNs are viable competitive alternatives to CNN+LSTMs for the task of building SSI systems based on ultrasound videos of the tongue movement. In the future, we plan to investigate more sophisticated network types such as the ConvLSTM network that directly integrates the advantages of the convolutional and LSTM units [35].

Acknowledgements. This study was supported by the National Research, Development and Innovation Office of Hungary through project FK 124584 and by the AI National Excellence Program (grant 2018-1.2.1-NKP-2018-00008) and by grant TUDFO/47138-1/2019-ITM of the Ministry of Innovation and Technology. László Tóth was supported by the UNKP 19-4 National Excellence Programme of the Ministry of Innovation and Technology, and by the János Bolyai Research Scholarship of the Hungarian Academy of Science. The GPU card used for the computations was donated by the NVIDIA Corporation. We thank the MTA-ELTE Lendület Lingual Articulation Research Group for providing the ultrasound recordings.

References

1. Akbari, H., Arora, H., Cao, L., Mesgarani, N.: Lip2AudSpec: speech reconstruction from silent lip movements video. In: Proceedings of ICASSP, pp. 2516–2520 (2018)
2. Bradbury, J., Merity, S., Xiong, C., Socher, R.: Quasi-recurrent neural networks. In: Proceedings of ICLR (2017)
3. Cho, K., et al: Learning phrase representations using RNN encoder-decoder for statistical machine translation. In: Proceedings of EMNLP, pp. 1724–1734 (2014)
4. Chollet, F., et al.: Keras (2015). https://github.com/fchollet/keras
5. Csapó, T.G., Grósz, T., Gosztolya, G., Tóth, L., Markó, A.: DNN-based ultrasound-to-speech conversion for a silent speech interface. In: Proceedings of Interspeech, pp. 3672–3676 (2017)
6. Denby, B., Schultz, T., Honda, K., Hueber, T., Gilbert, J.M., Brumberg, J.S.: Silent speech interfaces. Speech Commun. **52**(4), 270–287 (2010)
7. Denby, B., et al: Towards a practical silent speech interface based on vocal tract imaging. In: Proceedings of ISSP, pp. 89–94 (2011)
8. Ephrat, A., Peleg, S.: Vid2speech: speech reconstruction from silent video. In: Proceedings of ICASSP, pp. 5095–5099 (2017)
9. Gonzalez, J.A., et al.: Direct speech reconstruction from articulatory sensor data by machine learning. IEEE/ACM Trans. Audio Speech Lang. Process. **25**(12), 2362–2374 (2017)
10. Grósz, T., Gosztolya, G., Tóth, L., Csapó, T.G., Markó, A.: F0 estimation for DNN-based ultrasound silent speech interfaces. In: Proceedings of ICASSP, pp. 291–295 (2018)
11. Hinton, G., et al.: Deep neural networks for acoustic modeling in speech recognition: The shared views of four research groups. IEEE Signal Process. Mag. **29**(6), 82–97 (2012)
12. Hochreiter, S., Schmidhuber, J.: Long short-term memory. Neural Comput. **9**(8), 1735–1780 (1997)
13. Hueber, T., Benaroya, E.L., Chollet, G., Dreyfus, G., Stone, M.: Development of a silent speech interface driven by ultrasound and optical images of the tongue and lips. Speech Commun. **52**(4), 288–300 (2010)
14. Janke, M., Diener, L.: EMG-to-speech: direct generation of speech from facial electromyographic signals. IEEE/ACM Trans. Audio Speech Lang. Process. **25**(12), 2375–2385 (2017)
15. Janke, M., Wand, M., Nakamura, K., Schultz, T.: Further investigations on EMG-to-speech conversion. In: Proceedings of ICASSP, pp. 365–368 (2012)
16. Jaumard-Hakoun, A., Xu, K., Leboullenger, C., Roussel-Ragot, P., Denby, B.: An articulatory-based singing voice synthesis using tongue and lips imaging. In: Proceedings of Interspeech, pp. 1467–1471 (2016)

17. Ji, S., Xu, W., Yang, M., Yu, K.: 3D convolutional neural networks for human action recognition. IEEE Trans. Pattern Anal. Mach. Intell. **35**(1), 221–231 (2013)
18. Kim, M., Cao, B., Mau, T., Wang, J.: Multiview representation learning via deep CCA for silent speech recognition. In: Proceedings of Interspeech, pp. 2769–2773 (2017)
19. Kim, M., Cao, B., Mau, T., Wang, J.: Speaker-independent silent speech recognition from flesh-point articulatory movements using an LSTM neural network. IEEE/ACM Trans. ASLP **25**(12), 2323–2336 (2017)
20. Kimura, N., Kono, M., Rekimoto, J.: SottoVoce: an ultrasound imaging-based silent speech interaction using deep neural networks. In: Proceedings of CHI Conference on Human Factors in Computing Systems (2019)
21. Krizhevsky, A., Sutskever, I., Hinton, G.: Imagenet classification with deep convolutional neural networks. In: Advances in Neural Information Processing Systems 25, pp. 1097–1105 (2012)
22. Ling, Z.H., et al.: Deep learning for acoustic modeling in parametric speech generation. IEEE Signal Process. Mag. **32**(3), 35–52 (2015)
23. Liu, Z.C., Ling, Z.H., Dai, L.R.: Articulatory-to-acoustic conversion using BLSTM-RNNs with augmented input representation. Speech Commun. **99**(2017), 161–172 (2018)
24. Maier-Hein, L., Metze, F., Schultz, T., Waibel, A.: Session independent non-audible speech recognition using surface electromyography. In: Proceedings of ASRU, pp. 331–336 (2005)
25. Moliner, E., Csapó, T.: Ultrasound-based silent speech interface using convolutional and recurrent neural networks. Acta Acust. United Acust. **105**, 587–590 (2019)
26. Peddinti, V., Povey, D., Khudanpur, S.: A time delay neural network architecture for efficient modeling of long temporal contexts. In: Proceedings of Interspeech, pp. 3214–3218 (2015)
27. Ramachandran, P., Zoph, B., Le, Q.V.: Swish: a self-gated activation function. ArXiv e-prints 1710.05941 (2017)
28. Schultz, T., Wand, M., Hueber, T., Krusienski, D.J., Herff, C., Brumberg, J.S.: Biosignal-based spoken communication: a survey. IEEE/ACM Trans. ASLP **25**(12), 2257–2271 (2017)
29. Tóth, L.: Combining time-and frequency-domain convolution in convolutional neural network-based phone recognition. In: Proceedings of ICASSP, pp. 190–194 (2014)
30. Tran, D., Wang, H., Torresani, L., Ray, J., LeCun, Y., Paluri, M.: A closer look at spatiotemporal convolutions for action recognition. In: Proceedings of CVPR (2018)
31. Wang, J., Samal, A., Green, J.: Preliminary test of a real-time, interactive silent speech interface based on electromagnetic articulograph. In: Proceedings of SLPAT, pp. 38–45 (2014)
32. Wu, C., Chen, S., Sheng, G., Roussel, P., Denby, B.: Predicting tongue motion in unlabeled ultrasound video using 3D convolutional neural networks. In: Proceedings of ICASSP, pp. 5764–5768 (2018)
33. Young, T., Hazarika, D., Poria, S., Cambria, E.: Recent trends in deep learning based natural language processing. IEEE Comput. Intell. Mag. **13**(3), 55–75 (2018)
34. Zhang, S., Lei, M., Yan, Z., Dai, L.: Deep-FSMN for large vocabulary continuous speech recognition. In: Proceedings of ICASSP (2018)

35. Zhao, C., Zhang, J., Wu, C., Wang, H., Xu, K.: Predicting tongue motion in unlabeled ultrasound video using convolutional LSTM neural networks. In: Proceedings of ICASSP, pp. 5926–5930 (2019)
36. Zhao, S., Liu, Y., Han, Y., Hong, R., Hu, Q., Tian, Q.: Pooling the convolutional layers in deep convnets for video action recognition. IEEE Trans. Circuits Syst. Video Technol. **28**(8), 1839–1849 (2018)
37. Zhao, Y., Xiong, Y., Lin, D.: Trajectory convolution for action recognition. In: Advances in Neural Information Processing Systems 31, pp. 2204–2215 (2018)

Deep Recurrent Modelling of Stationary Bitcoin Price Formation Using the Order Flow

Ye-Sheen Lim[✉] and Denise Gorse

University College London - Computer Science, Gower Street,
London WC1E 6BT, UK
yesheenlim@gmail.com

Abstract. In this paper we propose a deep recurrent model based on the order flow for the stationary modelling of the high-frequency directional prices movements. The order flow is the microsecond stream of orders arriving at the exchange, driving the formation of prices seen on the price chart of a stock or currency. To test the stationarity of our proposed model we train our model on data before the 2017 Bitcoin bubble period and test our model during and after the bubble. We show that without any retraining, the proposed model is temporally stable even as Bitcoin trading shifts into an extremely volatile "bubble trouble" period. The significance of the result is shown by benchmarking against existing state-of-the-art models in the literature for modelling price formation using deep learning.

1 Introduction

The aim of this paper is to investigate the stationary modelling of price formation using deep learning approaches. *Price formation* is an important area in the study of market microstructure, concerning the process by which asset prices form. When modelling price formation in practice, one of the biggest concerns is the *stationarity* of the model. Stationarity is the ability of a model to maintain prediction performance not just out-of-sample, but across a range of periods where the underlying process that generates the data undergoes drastic changes. The financial market is subject to chaotic shift in regimes, and, as a consequence a model that is trained and tested in a particular period is not guaranteed to perform as well if some unobservable underlying process of the financial market causes a drastic shift in the statistical properties of the data. Also, the stationary of price formation modelling is of much interest to financial academia as it is tied closely to the study of the financial markets as a complex dynamical system.

In this paper, we propose a deep recurrent model for modelling the price formation of Bitcoin using the *order flow*. The work is novel in that we are the first to employ an order flow based deep learning model for the modelling of price formation. The order flow is the microsecond timestamped sequence of events arriving at an exchange. Each event is an order placed by a market participant;

L. Rutkowski et al. (Eds.): ICAISC 2020, LNAI 12415, pp. 170–179, 2020.
https://doi.org/10.1007/978-3-030-61401-0_17

therefore, order flow is the main endogenous driver of the eventual rise and fall of prices we see on Google Finance charts, for instance. We formulate the *price formation* modelling problem as the forecasting of *high-frequency directional price movements*, as is common in quantitative finance literature [1,2]. Bitcoin data is used in our experiment due to the ease of obtaining the high-frequency form of such data as opposed to equivalent data for other financial assets. Also, we are able to obtain Bitcoin data covering periods before and after an extremely volatile bubble period, which is crucial for allowing us to study the stationarity of the models. We train our proposed order flow model on this data and show that our model is able to display the very desirable property of stationarity. We in addition implement state-of-the-art deep learning models from price formation modelling literature, and benchmark our proposed model against them to show the significance of the results.

The paper is organised as follows. In Sect. 2, we begin by providing a background to the financial concepts touched upon in this paper. In Sect. 3, we present an overview of related work in the existing literature. Our proposed method and the benchmarks will be presented in Sect. 4. Sections 5 and 6 cover the data acquisition, experimental setup and results. Finally we conclude with a discussion in Sect. 7.

2   Financial Background

Most, if not all, modern electronic stock or currency exchanges are driven by *limit order books* (LOBs). The electronic LOB is a platform that aggregates the quantities market participants desire to buy or sell at different prices. Most trading activities revolve around the lowest sell and highest buy prices. Readers are directed to [4] for a comprehensive introduction to LOBs.

Any exchange that uses a LOB is order-driven, such that any trader can submit *limit orders* (LO) to buy or sell a quantity of an asset at a specific limit price. If the order cannot be satisfied (at the specified limit price or better) on arrival to an exchange, then the LO is added to the LOB to be matched against subsequent orders arriving at the exchange. LOs in the LOB can also be cancelled at any time using a cancellation order (CO). Traders can also submit a *market order* (MO), which has no limit price and is always immediately executed at the best price in the LOB. The sequential stream of order book events is called the *order flow*.

Although there are many useful measures that can be computed from LOBs and order book events, of interest to this paper are the *mid-price, best bid, best ask* and the *relative price*. The *best bid* and *best ask* are the highest buying and lowest selling prices in the LOB respectively. The *mid-price* is the mean of the best ask and best bid, essentially the mid-point between the highest buying and lowest selling prices in the LOB. The *relative price* is the number of *ticks* between any two prices, where a *tick* is the lowest price increment or decrement allowed by the exchange.

3   Related Work

Theory-driven modelling of high-frequency (HF) price movements is an extensively researched topic. These approaches usually apply well defined stochastic models, chosen based on empirical analysis and market theories, for modelling HF price movements as a function of different measures of the LOB and order book events. Selected works in this area include [1,2,10]. The advantage of these approaches is their ability to simultaneously produce probabilistic forecasts of high-frequency price movements and confidently explain the predictions using the well-defined theory-driven models. However, major drawbacks include reliance on parametric models, intractability of the models and the lack of generalisation power of the models.

Data-driven modelling of HF price movements is a relatively recent area of research, especially so in the area of deep learning due to the difficulty of obtaining enough data to train a deep learning model. State-of-the-art models in the literature are based on taking dynamic snapshots of the limit order book to model price movements [9,11], where a snapshot of the limit order book (LOB) is the price and quantity of a given number of highest bid and lowest ask prices, at a given point in time. It has been shown that these LOB snapshot models can be augmented with market order arrival sequences to improve performance [3]. Among these existing work, only [3] performed an analysis on the stationarity of the model. We will later show that while these benchmark models are powerful, our proposed order flow model outperforms them and also exhibits stronger stationarity in the forecasting of Bitcoin during the bubble period.

4   Methods

Let us denote the directional price movement at time $T+1$ as $y_i \in \{0,1\}$, where $y_i = 0$ indicates a downward price movement and $y_i = 1$ indicates an upward price movement. In our proposed order flow based approach, we want to model the probability distribution of y_i conditioned on a sequence of irregularly spaced order flow events $\mathbf{x}_i$ of length T:

$$p(y_i|\mathbf{x}_{i,1}, \mathbf{x}_{i,2}, \mathbf{x}_{i,3}, \dots \mathbf{x}_{i,T}) \tag{1}$$

where $\mathbf{x}_{i,t}$ is an order event (e.g. market order, limit order, cancellation order). Each event $\mathbf{x}_{i,t}$ can be described as the tuple $\mathbf{x}_{i,t} = \{x\}_{i,t}^{(j)}$, where:

- $x_{i,t}^{(1)} \in \mathbb{N}$ is the number of milliseconds between the arrival of $\mathbf{x}_{i,t-1}$ and $\mathbf{x}_{i,t}$
- $x_{i,t}^{(2)} \in \mathbb{N}$ is the hour of the arrival of $\mathbf{x}_{i,t}$ according its timestamp
- $x_{i,t}^{(3)} \in \mathbb{R}^{+}$ is the size of the order $\mathbf{x}_{i,t}$
- $x_{i,t}^{(4)} \in \{1,2,3\}$ is the categorical variable for $\mathbf{x}_{i,t}$ being a limit order, market order or cancellation order
- $x_{i,t}^{(5)} \in \{1,2\}$ is the categorical variable for $\mathbf{x}_{i,t}$ being a buy or sell order

- $x_{i,t}^{(6)} \in \mathbb{N}^+$ is the relative price of the order $x_{i,t}$ divided by the tick (if $x_{i,t}^{(5)} = 1$ then the price is relative to the highest buy price in the LOB, and if $x_{i,t}^{(5)} = 2$ then it is relative to the lowest sell price)

We compute the probability distribution of Eq. 1 using a softmax function as follows:

$$P(y_i = j \mid \mathbf{h}_{i,T}^L, \mathbf{W}_j^D) = \frac{e^{z_j^D(\mathbf{h}_{i,T}^L, \mathbf{W}_j^D)}}{\sum_{k=0}^{K-1} e^{z_k^D(\mathbf{h}_{i,T}^L, \mathbf{W}_k^D)}} , \qquad (2)$$

where $j \in \{0, 1\}$, $\mathbf{h}_{i,T}^L$ is some learnt L-layer deep representation of order flow, and z_k^D is the output layer of a D-layer fully-connected neural network. The representation $\mathbf{h}_{i,T}^L$ is the output of a deep L-layer recurrent neural network taken at the end of a length T order flow:

$$\mathbf{h}_{i,T}^l = \begin{cases} h(\mathbf{h}_{i,T}^{l-1}, \mathbf{h}_{i,T-1}^l, \Theta^l) & \text{if } 1 < l \le L \\ h(\mathbf{x}_{i,T}, \mathbf{h}_{i,T-1}^l, \Theta^l) & \text{if } l = 1 \end{cases} , \qquad (3)$$

where $h(.)$ is a function implementing a recurrent neural network with long short-term memory (LSTM) cells, Θ^l are LSTM parameters to be fitted, and $\mathbf{x}_{i,T}$ will be soon addressed. Since LSTM cells are commonly implemented RNN components in the literature, we will not discuss their architecture here and direct readers instead to [5].

For each order $x_{i,t}$ all non-ordinal categorical covariates are embedded into a multidimensional continuous space before feeding into the inputs of the RNNs. The embeddings can be described as follows:

$$e(q_{i,t}) = g\left(\mathbf{U}_q^{\mathsf{T}} o(q_{i,t}) + \mathbf{b}_q\right) \qquad (4)$$

where $o(.)$ is a function mapping the categorical features to one-hot vectors, $g(.)$ is some non-linear activation function, and $\mathbf{U}_q$ and $\mathbf{b}_q$ are parameters to be fitted.

Then, the parameters of the model $\mathbf{W}_k^d$ and Θ^l, as well as the weights and bias terms in the embedding layers for all covariates, can be fitted using any variant of the stochastic gradient descent optimisation algorithms by minimising the negative log-likelihood:

$$\mathcal{L}(\mathbf{y}) = -\frac{1}{N} \sum_{i=1}^{N} \sum_{j=0}^{K-1} \mathbb{I}_{y_i=j} \, log \, p(j) \qquad (5)$$

where $\mathbb{I}$ is the identity function that is equal to one if $y_i = j$ and is zero otherwise, K is the number of classes, and N is the size of our dataset.

The performance of the model will be evaluated using the Matthews correlation coefficient (MCC) [8]. We choose this metric as it has a very intuitive interpretation, it handles imbalanced classes naturally. For binary classification, the metric lies in the range $(-1, 1)$ where 1 indicates a perfect classifier, -1 indicates a completely wrong classifier and 0 means the classifier is doing no better than making random predictions (making this measure very useful in the context of quantitative trading). As it summarises the confusion matrix into one balanced and intuitively interpretable measure, it allows us to perform concise and extensive comparisons without needing to delve into the relative contributions of different elements of the confusion matrix.

We benchmark the performance of our order flow model against two state-of-the-art models found in the literature applying deep learning to high-frequency price modelling. These models can be described as follows:

- **Benchmark 1** [3] models the probability distribution of y_i as in Eq. 1, but each element $\mathbf{x}_{i,t}$ in the irregularly spaced sequence $\mathbf{x}_i$ is defined as follows:

$$x_{i,t} = (b_{i,t}^1, b_{i,t}^2, \ldots b_{i,t}^S, s_{i,t}^1, s_{i,t}^2, \ldots s_{i,t}^S, \alpha_{i,t}^b, \alpha_{i,t}^s) \ , \tag{6}$$

where $b_{i,t}^j = (\pi_{i,t}^j, \omega_{i,t}^j)$ is the tuple of price π and volume ω at the j'th highest buy price, $s_{i,t}^j = (\phi_{i,t}^j, \kappa_{i,t}^j)$ is the tuple of price ϕ and volume κ at the j'th lowest sell price, and S is the number of highest buy or lowest sell prices we are considering in the snapshot. The market order (MO) rate on the buy side of the LOB, $\alpha_{i,t}^b$, is computed by dividing the number of buy MOs in the period between $t = 0$ and T by the total number of orders that make up the volume in the highest bid price. The MO rate on the sell side of the LOB, $\alpha_{i,t}^s$, is computed similarly.
- **Benchmark 2** [9,11] models the probability distribution of y_i as in Eq. 1, but each element $\mathbf{x}_{i,t}$ in the irregularly spaced sequence $\mathbf{x}_i$ is here defined similarly to Benchmark 1 but without the MO rates:

$$x_{i,t} = (b_{i,t}^1, b_{i,t}^2, \ldots b_{i,t}^S, s_{i,t}^1, s_{i,t}^2, \ldots s_{i,t}^S) \ , \tag{7}$$

For both these benchmark models, the probability distributions of y_i are computed using softmax functions that take as inputs deep representations of $\mathbf{x}_i$ learnt from recurrent neural networks.

5   Experimental Set-Up

The dataset for the experiments was obtained from Coinbase, a digital currency exchange. Through a websocket feed provided by the exchange, we log the real-time message stream containing trades and orders data in the form of order flow for BTC-USD, BTC-EUR and BTC-GBP from 4 Nov 2017 to 29 Jan 2018. Since these are raw JSON messages, the dataset for training the model cannot be obtained directly from the messages. To build the datasets, we had to reconstruct the limit order book by sequentially processing the JSON messages.

During the order book reconstruction, we build the dataset in real-time using the following method. Before we begin building the dataset, we have to "warm up" the order book using messages from 4 Nov 2017–5 Nov 2017. This needs to be done because we are starting from an empty book that needs to be sufficiently populated for us to extract sensible data. Now we begin tracking the mid-price.

If the mid-price moves after an order $x_{i,T+1}$ arrives, then the mid-price is stored as the target variable class $y_i \in \{0, 1\}$, for downward or upward mid-price movements respectively. We ignore any events that do not move the price on arrival since we are only interested in modelling price formation (predicting up or down price movements). After a mid-price change is registered, we look back into the order flow and the limit order book to obtain the measures needed to build the datasets for our proposed model and for the benchmark models.

Each dataset is then split into training, validation and test sets by dates to avoid any look-ahead bias. About 1.1 million datapoints between 6 Nov 2017 and 16 Nov 2017 are taken as the training set. Cross-validation and early-stopping checks are performed on a set taken from between 17 Nov 2017 to 20 Nov 2017 containing about 0.55 million datapoints. The rest is kept strictly for testing and is never seen by the model aside from the final testing phase, giving us about 7.3 million test points in total.

We set up the order flow and benchmark models as described in Sect. 4. Then we fit the parameters of individual models using the Adam optimisation algorithm with dropout on all non-recurrent connections. Cross-validation is performed with Bayesian hyperparameter tuning to find the number of recurrent layers, the LSTM state size, the number of dense layer in the output, the size of each output dense layers, and the embedding dimensions. Embedding is not used for the benchmark models since they do not contain categorical variables. We then make predictions on the test sets. The results are then grouped by date and we compute the Matthews correlation coefficient (MCC) for each date.

6   Results

6.1   Comparison of Model Performances

Let us evaluate the relative performance of the various models, with results presented in Figs. 1a–c. Figure 1a shows the MCC over each day for models trained and tested on the BTC-USD dataset. Note that the abbreviation *OrderFlow* refers to our proposed model, while *Bench1* and *Bench2* refer to Benchmark 1 and Benchmark 2 respectively. We first note in addition that in all the figures of Fig. 1 we can see that *Bench1* (which augments the model with market order rates) outperforms *Bench2* (which only models the price movements on the LOB snapshot) throughout the whole test period. However, we observe that throughout the test period, the order flow model outperforms those of both benchmark models. Although not presented, we also performed paired Student t-tests on the null hypothesis that there is no difference between the test results of the order flow model and that of benchmark models individually. In each test, the null hypothesis is rejected with very high confidence intervals. Similarly, Fig. 1b and Fig. 1c show the test performance for models trained and tested on BTC-EUR and BTC-GBP, respectively. We are again able to visually verify that models trained on order flow outperform the benchmark models, and once again paired Student t-tests reject with high confidence the null hypotheses that *OrderFlow* test results are no different from the benchmark models *Bench1* and *Bench2*.

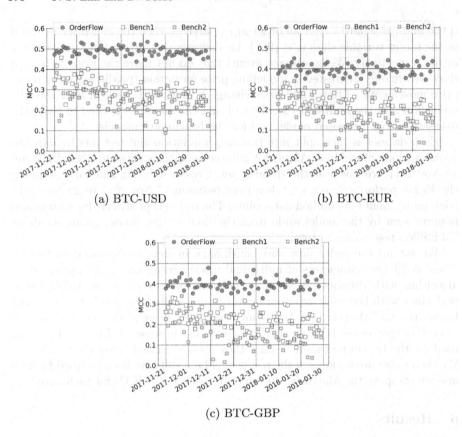

(a) BTC-USD

(b) BTC-EUR

(c) BTC-GBP

Fig. 1. MCC plots for models trained and tested on BTC-USD, BTC-EUR and BTC-GBP respectively

6.2   Analysis of Model Stationarity

The range of dates in our test period covers the climax of the Bitcoin bubble where the price of Bitcoin rapidly peaks to an all-time-high and subsequently bursts [6]. We can see in Fig. 2 that compared to the training and validation period, our test period for BTC-USD (and in fact for BTC-EUR and BTC-GBP also) corresponds to a shift in regime characterised by more volatile price changes and much higher trading activity. With this test period, we can evaluate the stationarity of our proposed order flow model and the benchmark model.

From Figs. 1a and 1b, we can in all cases (BTC-USD, BTC-EUR, BTC-GBP) visually observe that while the performance of *Bench2* degrades less quickly than *Bench1*, the model trained on order flow is the only one to display substantial stationarity. This implies that the representation learnt from the order flow is transferable from a non-volatile to an extremely volatile period, suggesting that the learnt representation encodes some sort of temporally universal information about Bitcoin price movements. On the other hand, we can visually observe that

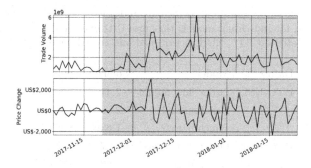

Fig. 2. Plot of: i) volume of trading activity (Trade Volume), ii) BTC-USD 1-day lagged difference prices (Price Change), the shaded area being our test period 21 Nov 2017–29 Jan 2018

the benchmark models struggle to maintain performance in the volatile period. To scientifically evaluate and statistically compare the stationarity of the order flow model and the benchmark models, we fit a linear regression model on the test results of each model. This will then allow us to compare the rate at which the performance of each model degrades over time.

Specifically, we fit a simple linear regression on the MCC over the test period dates. Table 1 shows the corresponding slope coefficients and p-values for each model trained and tested on a particular currency pair. Although the model trained on order flow has negative slope coefficients for all datasets, implying some degradation in performance over time, the p-values reveal that the coefficient is not statistically significant. However, for the benchmark models we can very confidently reject the null hypotheses that the slopes are zero, meaning that we can use the negative coefficients as strong evidence for performance degradation over time.

7   Analysis of Model Universality

Although we set out primarily to study stationarity in our model, it is in addition possible to show that the representations learnt from the order flow exhibit a hint of the very valuable property of universality [9], the ability to learn market structures which to some degree generalise across asset classes.

Table 2 shows the drop in performance on the out of sample test set, when training on one currency pair and testing on the others, is considerably less when using the order flow model than the benchmark models, demonstrating the above-mentioned hint of universality. This innate ability to generalise is most evident when training on BTC-USD and least when training on BTC-GBP. This is likely due to the different volumes traded: the trading volumes of BTC-USD, BTC-EUR, and BTC-GBP between the start of the training period (6 Nov 2017) and the end of the test period (29 Jan 2018) are, respectively, $151.6e9$, $20.7e9$, and $1.5e9$ – when an asset is heavily traded there are more activities at the order

Table 1. The table shows the slope coefficients and p-value of MCC regressed on dates in the test period for individual models that are: i) trained and tested on BTC-USD, ii) trained and tested on BTC-EUR, iii) trained and tested on BTC-GBP.

Dataset	Model	Coeff	p-value
BTC-USD	Order flow model	$-2.41e^{-4}$	$5.87e^{-2}$
	Benchmark 1	$-2.76e^{-3}$	$1.27e^{-13}$
	Benchmark 2	$-1.63e^{-3}$	$8.27e^{-4}$
BTC-EUR	Order flow model	$-5.67e^{-5}$	$7.50e^{-1}$
	Benchmark 1	$-2.02e^{-3}$	$1.27e^{-8}$
	Benchmark 2	$-2.01e^{-3}$	$1.19e^{-5}$
BTC-GBP	Order flow model	$-4.01e^{-4}$	$1.68e^{-1}$
	Benchmark 1	$-2.36e^{-3}$	$1.29e^{-11}$
	Benchmark 2	$-1.35e^{-3}$	$4.22e^{-5}$

book level, resulting in a richer order flow and hence a richer dataset that helps to avoid overfitting.

Table 2. For each model (leftmost column), the presentation tabulates the mean percentage drop (%) in test MCC between training and testing on the same currency pair, and training on a given currency pair and testing on the other currency pairs.

Trained	BTC-USD		BTC-EUR		BTC-GBP	
Tested	BTC-EUR	BTC-GBP	BTC-USD	BTC-GBP	BTC-USD	BTC-EUR
Order flow	9.299	20.306	19.606	17.387	28.816	32.232
Benchmark 1	59.857	71.749	74.368	80.000	67.157	67.642
Benchmark 2	91.017	81.869	99.619	84.049	80.432	70.483

8   Discussion

We have presented a model for the prediction of the directional price movements of Bitcoin using the order flow (which is the raw market data). We showed that the model is able to partially achieve a temporally universal representation (the very valuable property of stationarity) of the price formation process such that even when the statistical behaviour of the market changes dramatically (here, after the bursting of the Bitcoin bubble), the model remains relatively unaffected. We also show that the stationarity performance of our proposed order flow model is substantially better than benchmark deep models obtained from the existing literature. A secondary analysis of the results also hints at a universality property of our proposed model, and this too is benchmarked against the same deep models from the existing literature, to the benefit of our order flow model.

For future work, since our predictions give encouragingly high MCC values, it will be of interest to apply black-box feature explainers such as Shapley Additive Explanations [7] to address the interpretation issue of these data-driven models and understand exactly what it is that drives price formation across BTC-USD, BTC-EUR and BTC-GBP, and (in future work) other cryptocurrency pairs. This would provide a data-driven view of the market microstructural behavior of cryptocurrencies. Also of interest is what we can learn about the cryptocurrency market microstructure from analysis of the embeddings of categorical features of the order flow.

References

1. Bacry, E., Muzy, J.F.: Hawkes model for price and trades high-frequency dynamics. Quant. Finan. **14**(7), 1147–1166 (2014)
2. Cont, R., Stoikov, S., Talreja, R.: A stochastic model for order book dynamics. Oper. Res. **58**(3), 549–563 (2010)
3. Dixon, M.: Sequence classification of the limit order book using recurrent neural networks. J. Comput. Sci. **24**, 277–286 (2018)
4. Gould, M.D., Porter, M.A., Williams, S., McDonald, M., Fenn, D.J., Howison, S.D.: Limit order books. Quant. Finan. **13**(11), 1709–1742 (2013)
5. Hochreiter, S., Schmidhuber, J.: Long short-term memory. Neural Comput. **9**(8), 1735–1780 (1997)
6. Kreuser, J.L., Sornette, D.: Bitcoin bubble trouble. Forthcoming in Wilmott Magazine, pp. 18–24 (2018)
7. Lundberg, S.M., Lee, S.I.: A unified approach to interpreting model predictions. In: Guyon, I., et al. (eds.) Advances in Neural Information Processing Systems 30, pp. 4765–4774. Curran Associates, Inc. (2017). http://papers.nips.cc/paper/7062-a-unified-approach-to-interpreting-model-predictions.pdf
8. Powers, D.M.W.: Evaluation: from precision, recall and F-measure to ROC., informedness & markedness correlation. J. Mach. Learn. Technol. **2**(1), 37–63 (2011)
9. Sirignano, J., Cont, R.: Universal features of price formation in financial markets: perspectives from deep learning. Quant. Finance 1–11 (2019)
10. Toke, I.M.: An introduction to hawkes processes with applications to finance. Lect. Notes Ecole Centrale Paris BNP Paribas Chair Quant. Finance **193** (2011)
11. Tsantekidis, A., Passalis, N., Tefas, A., Kanniainen, J., Gabbouj, M., Iosifidis, A.: Using deep learning to detect price change indications in financial markets. In: 2017 25th European Signal Processing Conference (EUSIPCO), pp. 2511–2515. IEEE (2017)

6D Pose Estimation of Texture-Less Objects on RGB Images Using CNNs

Vladyslav Lopatin and Bogdan Kwolek[✉]

AGH University of Science and Technology, 30 Mickiewicza, 30-059 Krakow, Poland
bkw@agh.edu.pl
http://home.agh.edu.pl/~bkw/contact.html

Abstract. In this paper, we present a convolutional neural network-based approach to 6D pose estimation on RGB images segmented in advance. We designed and trained two neural networks to achieve reliable 6D object pose estimation on such images. The first neural network detects fiducial points of objects, which are then fed to a PnP algorithm responsible for pose estimation. The second one is an rotation regression network delivering at the output the quaternion. The neural networks were trained on our datasets containing both real images as well as photo-realistic images, which have been rendered on the basis of our 3D models. The performance of neural networks for object segmentation and 6D pose estimation was evaluated using both real and synthesized images. Experimental results demonstrate a high potential of our approach to pose estimation of texture-less objects observed by RGB camera and mounted on arm of the Franka-Emika robot.

Keywords: 6D object pose estimation · Convolutional neural networks · Robotics

1 Introduction

Estimating the 6-DoF pose (3D rotations + 3D translations) of an object in relation to the camera is not an easy task. The problem is challenging due to the variety of objects in the real world, which have varying 3D shape and the appearances in captured images. Detecting objects and their 6D poses on sequences of RGB images is an important task for many robotic applications, particularly where not only efficient and flexible object inspection is needed, but also grasping or manipulation abilities are required. Considerable research efforts over the last decade were made to address the 6D pose estimation problem from computer vision community [1,2], robotics community [3] and augmented reality [4]. In virtual reality applications, 6D pose of the object is required for interaction with it as well as for initialization of the tracking. In augmented reality applications the pose of several objects has to be efficiently estimated while the user interacts with them.

Conventional methods match feature points detected on 2D images and the corresponding 3D models to estimate object 6D poses. The pose estimation is

© Springer Nature Switzerland AG 2020
L. Rutkowski et al. (Eds.): ICAISC 2020, LNAI 12415, pp. 180–192, 2020.
https://doi.org/10.1007/978-3-030-61401-0_18

done on the basis of 2D-3D correspondences between such local features and a Perspective-n-Point (PnP) algorithm [5], often in a RANSAC [5] framework for outlier rejection. However, feature matching is usually not robust for poorly textured objects, leading to poor pose estimates. Hinterstoisser et al. [3,6] introduced holistic template-based methods capable of coping with recovering the 6D pose of texture-less objects in cluttered scenes. Such template-based approaches compare an input image with a set of template images of the object to determine its 3D pose. An approach presented in [7] is based on learning so-called object coordinates. However, methods based on learning the regressing of image pixels to 3D object coordinates in order to establish the 2D-3D correspondences for estimation of 6D pose cannot handle symmetric objects well.

One of the areas where computer vision has made vast progress is image classification, image segmentation and object detection [8]. Detection is a crucial part of estimating object's 6D pose and therefore a remarkable work has been devoted to this problem. Recent 6D pose estimation methods, particularly for dealing with poorly textured objects rely on feature learning. In a method proposed in [9] a large Euclidean distance between descriptors reflects different category attributes and distances between descriptors corresponding to two poses are bigger when the poses are dissimilar, whereas they smaller if the poses are similar. A first attempt to employ a convolutional neural network (CNN) for direct regression of 6DoF object poses was PoseCNN [10]. It decouples the pose estimation into estimating the translation and rotation in end-to-end framework. It utilizes features determined by convolutional layers of the VGG16 network and then three different branches. Two convolutional branches carry out a semantic segmentation and 2D center voting for handling occlusions. The third branch comprises a RoI pooling and a fully-connected architecture responsible for regressing each RoI to a quaternion. In general, CNN-based approaches to estimation of 6D pose of objects rely either on regressing the 6D object pose from the image directly [10] or on predicting 2D key-point locations in the image [11], from which the 6D object pose can be determined by the PnP algorithm.

Most of the approaches to 6D pose recovery on the basis of RGB images has focused on accuracies as well as processing times. The majority of currently available methods to 6D pose estimation ignore temporal information and provide only a single hypothesis for object pose [12]. Recently, in order to give robots greater spatial perception so they can manipulate objects and navigate through space, a Rao-Blackwellized Particle Filter (PoseRBPF) [12] for object pose estimation has been proposed. There are several publicly available datasets for benchmarking the performance of algorithms for 6D object pose estimation, including OccludedLinemod [1], YCB-Video [10]. Having on regard a need to prepare a 3D model of particular object quickly in order to perform object grasping, with fast adoption to novel set of objects, in this paper we discuss our approach to collecting data with ground-truth for object segmentation as well as 6D object pose estimation. We investigate the problem of 6-DOF object pose estimation on RGB images, where the object of interest is rigid and texture-less. The object is segmented from the background using an U-Net convolutional neural network.

We show that a relatively small training dataset permits achieving object seg-
mentations that can be further utilized by convolutional neural networks. We
designed and trained two neural networks to achieve reliable 6D object pose
estimation on RGB images. The first neural network detects fiducial points on
the object of interest, which are then fed to the PnP algorithm responsible for
6D pose estimation. The second one is a rotation regression network delivering
at the output the quaternion. The neural networks were trained on our datasets
containing both real images and synthesized images, which were created using
3D models of the objects and rendering techniques. The performance of the algorithms was evaluated using both real and synthesized objects. In order to keep
necessary human intervention minimal, we employed an automated turntable
setup to prepare the 3D object model as well as to determine the ground-truth
poses.

2   Neural Network for Object Segmentation

The objects of interest were segmented using an U-Net neural network [13]. The
architecture of the employed neural network is depicted on Fig. 1. The neural
network has been trained on RGB images of size 320×240. It has been trained
on synthetic images with delineated objects as well images with pixel-level annotations of real objects. In order to reduce the training time, as well as to prevent
overfitting and to increase performance of the U-Net we added Batch Normalization (BN) [14] after each Conv2D, see Fig. 1. A data augmentation has been
utilized during the training of the U-Net.

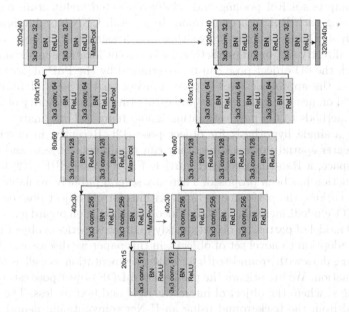

Fig. 1. Architecture of U-Net used for objects segmentation.

The pixel-wise cross-entropy has been used as the loss function in training of the neural network:

$$\mathcal{L}_{\text{CE}} = -\frac{1}{N}\sum_{i=1}^{N}[y_i \log(\hat{y}_i) + (1 - y_i)\log(1 - \hat{y}_i)] \tag{1}$$

where N is number of training samples, y is true value and $\hat{y}$ denotes the predicted value. It has been selected for training the U-Net due to its nice differentiable properties and easy optimization by the backpropagation algorithm.

3   6D Object Pose Estimation

At the beginning of this Section we describe our network for detection of fiducial points and estimating their 2D positions as well as outline the PnP algorithm. Afterwards, we present neural network for regression of the object rotation.

3.1   6D Object Pose Estimation Using Fiducial Points and PnP

In the first approach the 6D pose of each object is estimated using a convolutional neural network, which delivers 2D locations of eight fiducial points of the object. The 2D locations of such points are then fed to a PnP algorithm, which delivers the 6D pose of the object. Figure 2 depicts the architecture of the neural network. For every object we rendered 720 synthetic images of size 640×480 with ground-truth data as well as manually segmented and annotated 144 real images. The neural networks have been trained on scaled RGB images of size 128×128, see Fig. 2, in 512 epochs with batch size set to 48. The loss function was mean absolute error (MAE). The ground-truth data on synthesized images was determined on the basis of 3D positions of the fiducial points on the model, which were projected onto 2D images using the model of calibrated camera. It is worth noting that even if a point is hidden then it is still projected onto 2D image. This means that the number of the projected fiducial points on every image is equal to eight.

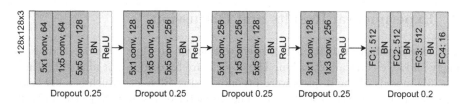

Fig. 2. Architecture of convolutional neural network for estimation of 2D positions of fiducial points.

In general formulation of 3D-to-2D transformation the aim is to find T_k that minimizes the reprojection error:

$$\arg\min_{T_k} \sum_i ||p_k^i - \hat{p}_{k-1}^i||^2 \tag{2}$$

where $\hat{p}^i_{k-1}$ is the reprojection of the 3D point X^i_{k-1} into the image I_k with the transformation T_k. This problem is known as Perspective from n Points (PnP) and it basically determines the extrinsic camera parameters according to 3D-to-2D correspondences. This means that the PnP estimates the pose of calibrated camera given a set of n 3D points in the world and their corresponding 2D projections. There are many solutions to this problem [4]. In our approach we employed EPnP [15] from OpenCV library [16].

3.2 Neural Network for Object Rotation Regression

For each object we trained a separate neural network delivering at the output the quaternion representing the rotation of the object of interest. Figure 3 illustrates the architecture of convolutional neural network for regression of the object rotation. The neural networks have been trained on scaled RGB images of size 128×128 in 512 epochs with batch size set to 48. Each neural network has been trained and evaluated on 720 rendered images and 144 real images. The ground-truth data for synthesized images was determined using Python scripts. The loss function was mean squared error (MSE).

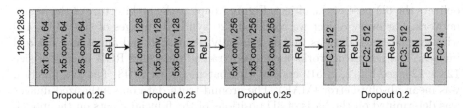

Fig. 3. Architecture of convolutional neural network for estimation of object rotation, which is expressed by the quaternion.

4   Experimental Results and Discussion

The experimental evaluation has been conducted on three objects: a duck, a piggy and an electrical extension. The objects are texture-less or almost texture-less. 3D models of the objects were prepared using Blender, which is a 3D computer graphics software toolset [17]. The diameter of the first object is 117 mm and the 3D model consists 140148 vertices, the diameter of the second object is 116 mm and 3D model contains 132620 vertices, whereas the diameter of the third object is equal to 103 mm and its 3D model consists of 216233 vertices. The models have been designed using 2.81 software version. The training and test images were rendered using Python scripts. Figure 4 depicts real objects and corresponding rendered images, which were obtained on the basis of our 3D models. As we can observe, our 3D models permit photo-realistic rendering of the objects in the requested poses.

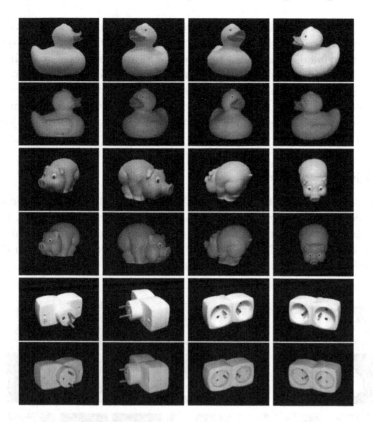

Fig. 4. Real and synthesized objects. Odd rows contain images of real objects, whereas even rows contain images with rendered objects

The camera has been calibrated using the OpenCV library [16]. The ground truths of the object poses have been determined using measurements provided by a turnable device. Each object has been observed from four different camera views, see Fig. 5. The objects were rotated in range $0° \ldots 360°$. During object rotation, every ten degrees an image has been acquired with corresponding rotation angle. This means that for each object the number of images acquired in such a way is equal to 144.

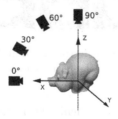

Fig. 5. Experiments setup.

In order to prepare the segmentation model the objects were rotated and observed by the camera from different views. For each considered object 150 images with manual delineations were prepared and then used to train neural networks for object segmentation. The models trained in such a way were then used to segment the considered objects from the background. Afterwards, a dataset consisting of RGB images with the corresponding ground truth data has been prepared for the evaluation of the neural networks for 6D object pose estimation and tracking.

4.1   Object Segmentation

A single U-Net neural network discussed in Subsect. 2 has been trained to segment the considered object using the set of manually segmented images. Figure 6 depicts example RGB images with corresponding binary masks, which were obtained on the basis of U-Net outputs. The depicted images are from the test subset and were not included in the training subset.

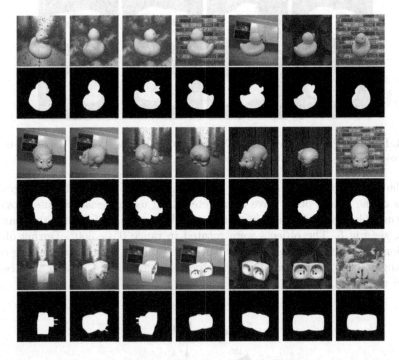

Fig. 6. Segmentation of the objects. Odd rows contain RGB images, whereas even rows contain binary masks determined on the basis of U-Net outputs.

Table 1 presents the Dice scores achieved on the test subset of the dataset. The Dice similarity coefficient for two sets A and B can be expressed in the following manner:

$$dice(A, B) = \frac{2 * |intersection(A, B)|}{(|A| + |B|)} \tag{3}$$

where $|A|$ and $|B|$ stand for the cardinal of the set A and B, respectively. The Dice score can also be expressed in terms of true positives (TP), false positives (FP) and false negatives (FN) as follows:

$$dice(A, B) = \frac{2 * TP}{2 * TP + FP + FN} \tag{4}$$

The test subset contains thirty images for each object. As we can observe in Table 1, better segmentation results were achieved for U-Net trained separately for each of the considered objects. Having on regard a better applicability of a single U-Net for segmentation of all three objects, in the following subsections we present the experimental results achieved on the basis of the single U-Net.

Table 1. Dice scores on the test sub-dataset.

	Duck	Piggy	Extension
U-Net for each object	0.9864	0.9877	0.9639
Single U-Net for all objects	0.9831	0.9742	0.9541

4.2 Evaluation Metric for 6D Pose Estimation

We evaluated the quality of 6-DoF object pose estimation using ADD score [3]. ADD is defined as average Euclidean distance between model vertices transformed using the estimated pose and the ground truth pose. This means that it expresses the average distance between the 3D points transformed using the estimated pose and those obtained with the ground-truth one. It is defined as follows:

$$ADD = \mathrm{avg}_{x \in M} ||(Rx + t) - (\hat{R}x + \hat{t})||_2 \tag{5}$$

where M is a set of 3D object model points, t and R are the translation and rotation of a ground truth transformation, respectively, whereas $\hat{t}$ and $\hat{R}$ correspond to those of the estimated transformation. We determined also the rotation error on the basis of the following formula:

$$err_{\mathrm{rot}} = \arccos((Tr(\hat{R}R^{-1}) - 1)/2) \tag{6}$$

where Tr stands for matrix trace, $\hat{R}$ and R denote rotation matrixes corresponding to ground-truth and estimated poses, respectively.

4.3 Experimental Evaluation

Table 2 presents experimental results that were obtained by our neural network and the PnP algorithm in estimation of 6D pose of duck, piggy and extension in single RGB images. The neural network has been trained on only synthesized images and it has been evaluated on real images. The 6D object pose estimate is considered valid if the ADD is smaller than ten percent of object's diameter. The experiments were conducted on RGB images of size 128 × 128. As we can observe, the neural networks trained on synthesized images only and evaluated on real ones are capable of achieving satisfactory results.

Table 3 presents ADD scores achieved by neural network for fiducial points detection and their 2D positions estimation with PnP algorithm, where the neural network has been trained on both synthesized and real images. As we can observe, the neural networks trained on both synthesized and real images, and evaluated on real ones achieve better results in comparison to neural networks trained on synthesized images only, c.f. results in Table 2.

Table 2. ADD scores [%] achieved by our neural networks for fiducial point detection and the PnP. Neural networks were trained on synthesized images and tested on real images.

Camera view	Object		
	Duck	Piggy	Extension
0°	79	80	76
	ADD < 1.4 cm	ADD < 1.1 cm	ADD < 1.3 cm
30°	82	82	77
	ADD < 1.2 cm	ADD < 1.2 cm	ADD < 1.3 cm
60°	78	78	79
	ADD < 1.4 cm	ADD < 1.1 cm	ADD < 1.2 cm
90°	82	83	78
	ADD < 1.2 cm	ADD < 1.3 cm	ADD < 1.3 cm

Table 3. ADD scores [%] achieved by neural network for fiducial point detection and the PnP. Neural networks were trained both on synthesized and real images, and tested on real images.

Camera view	Object		
	Duck	Piggy	Extension
0°	90	90	87
	ADD < 1.0 cm	ADD < 0.9 cm	ADD < 1.0 cm
30°	88	90	88
	ADD < 1.1 cm	ADD < 1.0 cm	ADD < 1.0 cm
60°	90	89	88
	ADD < 1.0 cm	ADD < 1.1 cm	ADD < 1.0 cm
90°	90	89	86
	ADD < 1.0 cm	ADD < 1.0 cm	ADD < 1.1 cm

Figure 7 depicts rotation errors vs. rotation angles, which were calculated on the basis of (6). As we can observe, the maximum rotation errors are below three degrees. Although best results were achieved for the duck, the errors for the electrical extension are not considerably bigger.

Table 4 presents results that were achieved by neural network regressing the object rotation. To calculate the ADD scores given rotations estimated by the neural network we used 3D positions that were determined by the PnP. As we can observe, this approach achieves comparable results with results obtained on the basis of fiduacial points and the PnP estimating the 6D object pose, c.f. results in Table 2. We also calculated the 3D object positions by projecting the 3D model onto image and then matching the rendered object with the segmented object. The 3D object positions have been estimated using a simple PSO [2]. The quaternions were converted to Euler angles and the 3D object positions were calculated by matching the segmented objects and projected 3D model (simplified) onto image plane on the basis of the camera model. Initial evaluations showed that improvements of ADD scores are not statistically significant.

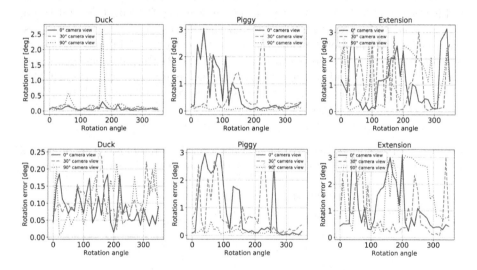

Fig. 7. Rotation errors vs. rotation angle: neural network estimating 2D location of fiducial points and PnP algorithm (upper row), neural network regressing the object rotation that is expressed by the quaternion (bottom row).

Table 5 presents ADD scores that were achieved by the second approach using neural network trained both on synthesized and real images. Comparing the results shown in discussed table and results in Table 3, we can observe that the discussed approach allows achieving better ADD scores.

Table 4. ADD scores [%] achieved by our neural network for rotation regression. Neural networks were trained on synthesized images and tested on real images.

Camera view	Object		
	Duck	Piggy	Extension
0°	85	82	81
	ADD < 1.0 cm	ADD < 1.1 cm	ADD < 1.2 cm
30°	81	81	79
	ADD < 1.2 cm	ADD < 1.1 cm	ADD < 1.3 cm
60°	78	84	79
	ADD < 1.2 cm	ADD < 0.9 cm	ADD < 1.2 cm
90°	79	84	80
	ADD < 1.2 cm	ADD < 1.3 cm	ADD < 1.3 cm

The complete system for 6D pose estimation has been implemented in Python and Keras framework. The system runs on an ordinary PC with CPU/GPU. On PC equipped with i5-8300H CPU 2.30 GHz the segmentation time is about 0.3 s, whereas running-times of the neural network detecting fiducial points and neural network regressing the object rotation are about 0.03 s. Initial experiments conducted with Franka-Emika robot, which has been equipped with Xtion RGB-D sensor, see Fig. 8, demonstrated usefulness of the proposed approach to estimation of 6D pose of the objects.

Table 5. ADD scores [%] achieved by neural networks for rotation regression. Neural networks were trained on both synthesized and real images, and tested on real images.

Camera view	Object		
	Duck	Piggy	Extension
0°	89	89	85
	ADD < 0.8 cm	ADD < 1.0 cm	ADD < 1.0 cm
30°	91	89	81
	ADD < 0.9 cm	ADD < 1.1 cm	ADD < 1.3 cm
60°	89	92	83
	ADD < 0.9 cm	ADD < 0.9 cm	ADD < 1.1 cm
90°	90	88	84
	ADD < 0.8 cm	ADD < 1.1 cm	ADD < 1.1 cm

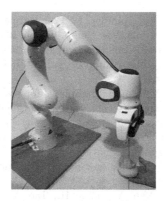

Fig. 8. 6D Pose estimation and tracking using Franka-Emika robot equipped with an Xtion RGB-D sensor.

5   Conclusions

We have presented and compared two different convolutional neural networks for 6D object pose estimation on RGB images. The objects have been segmented using U-Net neural network. The first neural network detects eight fiducial points on the objects, which are then fed to a PnP algorithm responsible for 6D pose estimation. The second one is a pose regression network delivering at the output the quaternion. They were compared in terms of ADDs and rotation errors on sequences of RGB images. We have presented the segmentation results obtained by the U-Net. We conducted also experiments consisting in pose estimation on the basis of images acquired by an RGB camera mounted on the Franka-Emika robot. The experimental results demonstrated usefulness and potential of the proposed approach.

Acknowledgment. This work was supported by Polish National Science Center (NCN) under a research grant 2017/27/B/ST6/01743.

References

1. Brachmann, E., Krull, A., Michel, F., Gumhold, S., Shotton, J., Rother, C.: Learning 6D Object pose estimation using 3D object coordinates. In: Fleet, D., Pajdla, T., Schiele, B., Tuytelaars, T. (eds.) ECCV 2014, Part II. LNCS, vol. 8690, pp. 536–551. Springer, Cham (2014). https://doi.org/10.1007/978-3-319-10605-2_35
2. Majcher, M., Kwolek, B.: 3D model-based 6D object pose tracking on RGB images using particle filtering and heuristic optimization. In: VISAPP, INSTICC (2020)
3. Hinterstoisser, S., et al.: Model based training, detection and pose estimation of texture-less 3D objects in heavily cluttered scenes. In: Lee, K.M., Matsushita, Y., Rehg, J.M., Hu, Z. (eds.) ACCV 2012, Part I. LNCS, vol. 7724, pp. 548–562. Springer, Heidelberg (2013). https://doi.org/10.1007/978-3-642-37331-2_42

4. Marchand, E., Uchiyama, H., Spindler, F.: Pose estimation for augmented reality: a hands-on survey. IEEE Trans. Vis. Comp. Graph. **22**(12), 2633–2651 (2016)
5. Fischler, M.A., Bolles, R.C.: Random sample consensus: a paradigm for model fitting with applications to image analysis and automated cartography. Commun. ACM **24**(6), 381–395 (1981)
6. Hinterstoisser, S., et al.: Multimodal templates for real-time detection of texture-less objects in heavily cluttered scenes. In: International Conference on Computer Vision, pp. 858–865 (2011)
7. Brachmann, E., Michel, F., Krull, A., Yang, M., Gumhold, S., Rother, C.: Uncertainty-driven 6D pose estimation of objects and scenes from a single RGB image. In: IEEE Conference on Computer Vision and Pattern Recognition (CVPR), pp. 3364–3372 (2016)
8. Pouyanfar, S., Sadiq, S., Yan, Y., Tian, H., Tao, Y., Reyes, M.P., Shyu, M.L., Chen, S.C., Iyengar, S.S.: A survey on deep learning: algorithms, techniques, and applications. ACM Comput. Surv. **51**(5), 92:1–92:36 (2018)
9. Wohlhart, P., Lepetit, V.: Learning descriptors for object recognition and 3D pose estimation. In: Conference on Computer Vision and Pattern Recognition, pp. 1–10 (2015)
10. Xiang, Y., Schmidt, T., Narayanan, V., Fox, D.: PoseCNN: a convolutional neural network for 6D object pose estimation in cluttered scenes. In: Robotics: Science and Systems XIV (RSS) (2018)
11. Rad, M., Lepetit, V.: BB8: a scalable, accurate, robust to partial occlusion method for predicting the 3D poses of challenging objects without using depth. In: IEEE International Conference on Computer Vision, ICCV, pp. 3848–3856 (2017)
12. Deng, X., Mousavian, A., Xiang, Y., Xia, F., Bretl, T., Fox, D.: PoseRBPF: a Rao-Blackwellized particle filter for 6D object pose tracking. In: Robotics: Science and Systems (RSS) (2019)
13. Ronneberger, O., Fischer, P., Brox, T.: U-Net: convolutional networks for biomedical image segmentation. In: Navab, N., Hornegger, J., Wells, W.M., Frangi, A.F. (eds.) MICCAI 2015, Part III. LNCS, vol. 9351, pp. 234–241. Springer, Cham (2015). https://doi.org/10.1007/978-3-319-24574-4_28
14. Ioffe, S., Szegedy, C.: Batch normalization: accelerating deep network training by reducing internal covariate shift. In: ICML, vol. 37, pp. 448–456 (2015)
15. Lepetit, V., Moreno-Noguer, F., Fua, P.: EPnP: an accurate O(n) solution to the PnP problem. Int. J. Comput. Vis. **81**(2), 155–166 (2009)
16. Bradski, G., Kaehler, A.: Learning OpenCV: Computer Vision in C++ with the OpenCV Library, 2nd edn. O'Reilly Media, Inc., Sebastopol (2013)
17. Blender Online Community: Blender - a 3D modelling and rendering package. Blender Foundation, Stichting Blender Foundation, Amsterdam (2020)

Application of Neural Networks and Graphical Representations for Musical Genre Classification

Mateusz Modrzejewski[(✉)], Jakub Szachewicz, and Przemysław Rokita

Division of Computer Graphics, Institute of Computer Science, The Faculty of
Electronics and Information Technology, Warsaw University of Technology,
Nowowiejska 15/19, 00-665 Warsaw, Poland
{M.Modrzejewski,P.Rokita}@ii.pw.edu.pl, jszachew@mion.elka.pw.edu.pl

Abstract. In this paper we have presented a method for musical genre
classification using neural networks. We have used two algorithms (CNN
and PRCNN) and two graphical representations: chromograms and spectrograms. We have used a large dataset of music divided into eight genres,
with certain overlapping musical features. Key, style-defining elements
and the overall character of specific genres are represented in our proposed visual representation and recognized by the networks. We show
that the networks have learned to distinguish between genres upon features observable by a human listener and compare the metrics for the
network models. Results of the conducted experiments are described and
discussed, along with our conclusions and comparison with similar solutions.

Keywords: AI · Artificial intelligence · Neural networks · Music ·
Classification

1 Introduction

The issue of classification has been an incredibly important part of artificial
intelligence almost since its beginnings: all in all, a system that could be considered intelligent should have some degree of cognition relative to human skills.
Music is a vital part of our civilization - it is also form of art and communication
that is present in all human cultures. Popular music, as we know it today, can
be broken down into several genres. Some of them have emerged somewhat as a
response to the cultural and social events happening throughout history, some
be considered as defining statements of entire subsequent generations.

Labels given to music, such as genre, mood or similarity to other artists,
play a huge role not only in our understanding of music, but also in the music
business. Streaming service providers offer themed playlists and having a song
on a trending Spotify playlist means today as much, as a number one single on
the radio used to mean. On the other hand, the number of subgenres and musical

© Springer Nature Switzerland AG 2020
L. Rutkowski et al. (Eds.): ICAISC 2020, LNAI 12415, pp. 193–202, 2020.
https://doi.org/10.1007/978-3-030-61401-0_19

ideas present in the overall pool is constantly rising and does not seem to have limits other than the artists' creativity.

Music genre recognition is the base of most of music information retrieval algorithms [1]. Some significant work in the field has been done, including solutions spanning from GMM and K-NN algorithms, SVMs to deep learning models and so on. However, the issue is far from solved and many of the reference solutions have a limitation of available data and lack of actual musical analysis of the features of the genres.

We propose a broader approach, utilizing a bigger dataset and graphical representations in order to classify music. Parts of our human, intuitive understanding of musical genre can be accurately represented using latent image formats, which capture various aspects of modern musical recordings: the tempo, rhythmic and harmonic structure, variety of arrangement and production values.

2   Previous Work

Each of the authors of this paper possesses a certain degree of musical training and/or musical performance experience and we feel that too little effort in MGR (musical genre recognition) is being put into the qualitative analysis of the studied musical content. While much effort has been put into the improvement of proposed MGR solutions, many of them seem to be algorithmic fine-tunings over somewhat unrealistic scenarios with little analysis of musical context. The extensive survey by Sturm [2] cites over 450 previous works in the field of music genre recognition and yet still describes the problem as relevant and difficult for machines. The survey states 58% of the works use non-disclosed, private data out of which over 75% using private data exclusively, thus preventing from further reflection. Works like [3–5] and [6] propose various approaches like classic classification algorithms and time-delay neural networks. The metrics of existing approaches vary as does the discussion over contingency and confusion (for instance [4] is one of the few works to provide specific information about misclassified songs). [7] implicitly states that improving accuracy and other figures of merit is not enough to address the problem of music recognition itself and further work has to be put both in the algorithmis development, as well as defining and rethinking the core of the issue.

3   Datasets

3.1   Dataset and Genre Selection

One of the datasets most frequently used for genre classification in music is the GTZAN dataset (as referenced in [8–11] and many others) by G. Tzanetakis [9]. The set contains 1000 songs samples, 30 s each (16 bit audio in .wav format). It's divided into 10 basic music genres, 100 examples per genre. Taking into account the huge diversity found in music, we have decided upon basing our experiments upon a much bigger dataset. As a sidenote, although accuracies over 90% have been obtained using the GTZAN dataset [12], even the GTZAN author himself does not recommend using it for further experiments with genre classification [13]. We have used the FMA (Free Music Archive) [14] dataset which contains a massive library of songs. The music is not only labelled by genre, but is also described by rich metadata. Some information about the subgenre is also available. The FMA provides access to four sets of songs, as shown in Table 1:

Table 1. FMA sub datasets

Name	Number of songs	Sample length	Number of genres	Size of dataset
FMA small	8000	30 s	8	7,2 GiB
FMA medium	25000	30 s	16	22 GiB
FMA large	106574	30 s	161	93 GiB
FMA full	106574	Full length	161	879 GiB

We have decided upon the medium FMA subset and 8 genres. Our selection of genres is based upon a number of musical features, like overall rhythm structure, song structure, tempo clarity and stability (or lack thereof) and production variety. The selected genres, sample count per genre and a short description of commonly observable features of the genre is shown in Table 2:

Table 2. Number of samples per genre

Genre	Count	Interesting and distinguishable genre features
Classical	447	Rich harmony and arrangements; unstable tempo; abrupt dynamic changes; overall very high musical complexity
Electronic	3851	Very stable tempo; distinguishable rhythm - loud; driving bass drum quarter notes; high presence of bass in the mix of the song; very regular song structure
Folk	1131	High variety of music labelled as folk; rich arrangements with instruments unlikely to be found in other genres of music; complex vocal performances; unique rhythm structures
Hip-hop	1922	Steady tempo (considerably slower than in other genres); very rhythmic structure; overall quite low dynamic variance
Jazz	286	High tempo variance, pulse generally described by quarter notes played by double bass and ride cymbal; high rhythmic and harmonic complexity; presence of ballads (dramatically different than faster tunes; much more ambient in overall character); oftentimes live recordings
Pop	646	Steady tempo; repetitive harmonic structure; presence of repetitive, "catchy" melodies (*riffs*, *hooks*); rich and highly polished production values
Punk	1392	Overall high volume and tempo; mosts recordings consist of drums; electric and bass guitars and vocals; dense rhythmic structure with low overall musical complexity
Rock	2380	Steady rhythm in a wide spectrum of tempos; rich arrangements; regular song structures
Σ	12055	

4   Data Processing

4.1   Chromograms

When creating chromograms, we take into consideration the chroma vector which describes the amount of energy carried by each of the notes (C, C#, D, D#, E , F, F#, G, G#, A, A#, B). According to [15], notes an octave apart are seen as similar, therefore the chroma vector allows us to find similarities between songs that have not been previously heard. [16] states that the human ear perceives notes an octave apart in a very similar way. Although the flattening of the octaves may be considered somewhat a cognitive limitation, here our attempt is to capture particular features of the music for recognition purposes. A very interesting feature is that the chromogram closely resembles the sheet notation of the music it was created from [17] - we therefore expect to draw some conclusions about whether visual qualities of sheet music may be relevant to the problem of genre recognition.

For each of the 12055 samples, a 300×300 pixel image has been created. Sample chromograms created for the purpose of training our networks are shown on Fig. 1. The shown samples are, left to right, top to bottom: electronic, rock, classical, folk, jazz, hip-hop, pop, punk.

We can observe more black pixels in chromograms of "calmer" genres, while the more dynamic ones contain much more yellow and bright pink. This corresponds to the frequency of notes changing and variance of notes.

4.2   Spectrograms

Spectrograms are heatmap-like visualisations of signal variations over time that. We have obtained 12055 300×300 pixel spectrograms in .PNG format. Although spectrograms have much less similarity to the sheet music notation than chromograms, they also determine how many low, high and mid frequencies are there in the recording. This allows us to easily describe the dynamics of the tune [18]. Sample spectrograms that we have obtained are shown in Fig. 2 in the same order as previously, that is, left to right, top to bottom: electronic, rock, classical, folk, jazz, hip-hop, pop, punk.

5   Method

We have used two networks: a modified reference CNN model used for solving the CIFAR-10 problem (subject of [19–24], among others) and a modified PRCNN [25] based on recurrent and convolutional networks. The PRCNN processes data in convolutional and recurrent networks in a parallel fashion with separation of the blocks.

The convolutional block of our PRCNN consists of five covolutional layers (16, 32, 64, 64, 64 filters) with $MaxPooling2D$ and $(3, 1)$ kernel. It's worth noting that in the context of music analysis, the $MaxPooling2D$ layer is responsible for

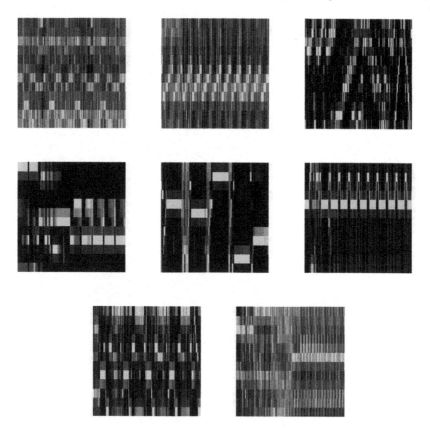

Fig. 1. Sample chromograms

choosing the most prominent features, like the amplitude. The recurrent block has a *MaxPooling2D* layer followed by a gated recurrent unit. We have used *RMSProp* as our optimization algorithm.

All experiments were conducted using the training images that we have created from our dataset. The networks were trained using Keras and NVidia GeForce GTX 960 M with CUDA architecture. The training time for the networks was c.a. 20 h.

6   Results

6.1   Training and Testing Results

Upon training, we have obtained 4 models of neural networks (chromogram PRCNN, spectrogram PRCNN, chromogram CNN, spectrogram CNN). Figure 3 shows the loss plots for both networks using both input data formats.

The following tables show precision and recall metrics for the network models. Also provided are confusion matrices in Fig. 4.

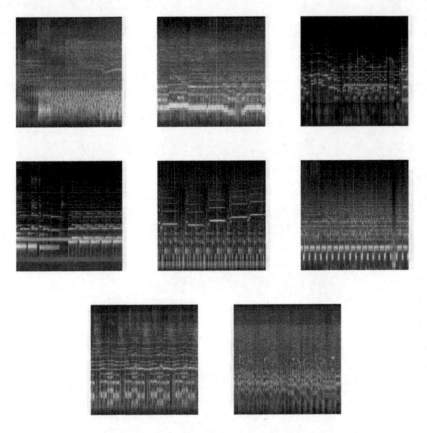

Fig. 2. Sample spectrograms for all considered genres

6.2 Result Summary

Upon analysis of our results, we have found that all models produced good results for classical and electronic music. In musical terms, we can attribute this to how well-defined are the genres in terms of purely musical qualities. An electronic track will have a steady kick drum pattern most of the times, while classical music will have a highly varied, "fluent" rhythmic structure. Both of these phenomenons are clearly visible in the chromograms and spectrograms (Table 3).

An interesting phenomenon occurs in the jazz genre - we have obtained much better precision than recall. This means that if the network chose jazz, it was usually right, but also it missed a lot of the jazz samples. Another interesting situation occurs also with the PRCNN for rock music. The recall is greater than the precision, which means that the network worked properly when classifying rock, but also it oftentimes classified non-rock samples as rock (Table 4).

Chromograms seem to blur the lines between the louder genres such as punk and rock. The PRCNN with spectrograms has achieved very good results for

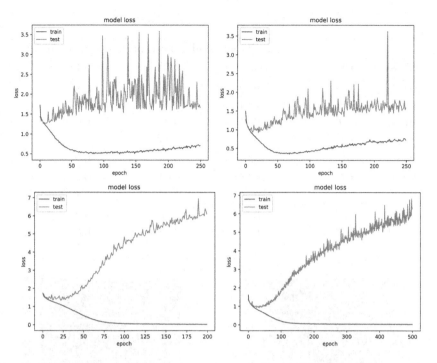

Fig. 3. Loss plots for the CNN (top) and PRCNN (bottom) using chromograms (left) and spectrograms (right)

Table 3. Precision and recall for the CNN

	Chrom. precision	Chrom. recall	Spect. precision	Spect. recall
Classical	0.66	0.87	0.90	0.54
Electronic	0.65	0.80	0.71	0.79
Folk	0.57	0.72	0.55	0.68
Hip-hop	0.80	0.49	0.65	0.66
Jazz	0.80	0.07	0.83	0.10
Pop	0.17	0.05	0.35	0.09
Punk	0.44	0.38	0.46	0.19
Rock	0.51	0.58	0.50	0.69
Avg	0.57	0.49	0.62	0.47
Weighed	0.60	0.60	0.60	0.61

these genres, but here also a closer musical analysis is needed: the musical samples indeed sound quite similar. The similarity can also be clearly seen on the spectrograms. Punk music has also evolved directly from the roots of rock music, hence explaining the difficulties the networks have faced.

Table 4. Precision and recall for the PRCNN

	Chrom. precision	Chrom. recall	Spect. precision	Spect. recall
Classical	0.45	0.73	0.79	0.78
Electronic	0.63	0.63	0.80	0.74
Folk	0.47	0.61	0.47	0.84
Hip-hop	0.66	0.45	0.87	0.51
Jazz	0.22	0.03	0.25	0.01
Pop	0.18	0.02	0.18	0.06
Punk	0.35	0.25	0.64	0.14
Rock	0.39	0.60	0.48	0.87
Avg	0.42	0.41	0.56	0.50
Weighed	0.50	0.50	0.65	0.62

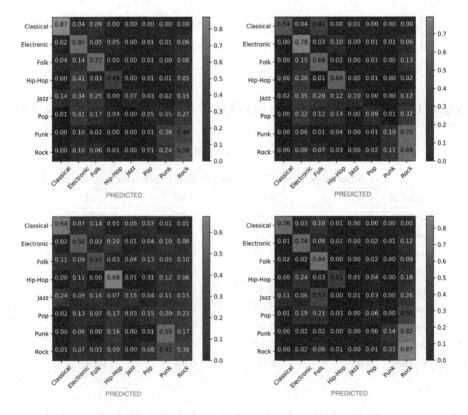

Fig. 4. Confusion matrices for the CNN (top) and PRCNN (bottom) using chromograms (left) and spectrograms (right)

Hip-hop was oftentimes classified as electronic music, which can be attributed to the fact that many of the samples contained only the beat and no vocals. Pop music was often mistaken as electronic music or rock, which is very interesting when we realize that modern pop music is based on both of these genres, making the classifying process much less obvious.

Interestingly enough, jazz was also often classified as electronic music. This may be attributed to the *walking bass line*, a way for the double bass to play in a jazz ensemble. The bass plays steady quarter notes with little to none rhythmic variation while improvising over the harmony of the tune - when translated to a graphical format, this might have been interpreted as the bass drum pulse from electronic music. This is also true when considering how the music would look like when written down into sheet music, as the quarter note pulse in both cases would be represented by very similar symbols evenly spread across the paper.

7   Conclusions and Further Work

In this paper we have proposed a method for music classification according to genre using a graphical representation. In our approach we have chosen popular genres of music with awareness of their distinct musical features. In comparison with existing approaches (like [26–28]...), we have conducted our experiments on a much larger, better described and more demanding dataset and have obtained satisfying classification results within interesting genres of music. We have been able to successfully train our networks to distinguish the most common musical genres with mistakes arising when the chosen set of musical differences could not have been clearly represented within the proposed graphical formats. We have also provided a musical explanation of our results.

The obtained results allow us to conclude that the issue of musical genre classification is a matter not only of algorithmic efforts, but also a very inspiring problem in terms of our understanding of musical labels: as new genres emerge and musicians continue to influence each other, many musical and stylistic boundaries get blurred. In our future works we wish to further our research in music information retrieval by applying other network architectures to classification by subgenre and overall style of similar artists.

References

1. Tzanetakis, G., Cook, P.: Musical genre classification of audio signals. IEEE Trans. Speech Audio Process. **10**, 293–302 (2002)
2. Sturm, B.L.: A survey of evaluation in music genre recognition. In: Nürnberger, A., Stober, S., Larsen, B., Detyniecki, M. (eds.) AMR 2012. LNCS, vol. 8382, pp. 29–66. Springer, Cham (2014). https://doi.org/10.1007/978-3-319-12093-5_2
3. Dixon, S., Gouyon, F., Widmer, G.: Towards characterisation of music via rhythmic patterns. In: ISMIR (2004)
4. Lee, J.-W., Park, S.-B., Kim, S.-K.: Music genre classification using a time-delay neural network. In: Wang, J., Yi, Z., Zurada, J.M., Lu, B.-L., Yin, H. (eds.) ISNN 2006. LNCS, vol. 3972, pp. 178–187. Springer, Heidelberg (2006). https://doi.org/10.1007/11760023_27

5. Zhouyu, F., Guojun, L., Ting, K., Zhang, D.: A survey of audio-based music classification and annotation. IEEE Trans. Multimedia **13**(2), 303–319 (2011)
6. Bergstra, J., Mandel, M., Eck, D.: Scalable genre and tag prediction with spectral covariance. In: Proceedings of the 11th International Society for Music Information Retrieval Conference, Utrecht, The Netherlands, 9–13 August 2010, pp. 507–512 (2010)
7. Sturm, B.L.: Classification accuracy is not enough. J. Intell. Inf. Syst. **41**(3), 371–406 (2013). https://doi.org/10.1007/s10844-013-0250-y
8. Jones, D.W.M.: Genre-detectrion with Deep Neural Networks (2019). arXiv preprint
9. Sturm, B.L.: An analysis of the GTZAN music genre dataset (2012)
10. Archit Rathore, M.D.: Music Genre Classification (2012). arXiv preprint
11. Peeters, G., Marchand, U., Fresnel. Q.: GTZAN-Rhythm: extending the GTZAN test-set with beat, downbeat and swing annotations. hal-01252607 (2015)
12. Guaus, E.: Audio content processing for automatic music genre classification: descriptors, databases, and classifiers. PhD thesis, University Pompeu Fabra, Barcelona, Spain (2009)
13. Sturm. B.L.: The gtzan dataset: its contents, its faults, their effects on evaluation, and its future use (2013). arXiv preprint arXiv:1306.1461
14. Free Music Archive. https://freemusicarchive.org
15. Ellis, D.: Chroma feature analysis and synthesis. Columbia University (2007)
16. Muller, M.: Chroma toolbox: MATLAB implementations for extracting variants of chroma-based audio features (2011)
17. Schuller, B., Weninger, F.: Music information retrieval: an inspirational guide to transfer from related disciplines (2012)
18. Costa, Y., de Oliveira, L.S., Silla, C.: An evaluation of convolutional neural networks for music classification using spectrograms. Appl. Soft Comput. **52**, 28–38 (2017)
19. Krizhevsky, A.: Convolutional Deep Belief Networks on CIFAR-10 (2010)
20. Warde-Farley, D., Goodfellow, I.J.: Maxout networks (2013)
21. Zagoruyko, S.: Wide Residual Networks (2016)
22. Zoph, B.: Neural Architecture Search with Reinforcement Learnings (2017)
23. Grahams, B.: Fractional Max-Pooling (2015)
24. Liu, Z., Huang, G.: Densely Connected Convolutional Networks (2018)
25. Feng, L., Liu, S., Yao, J.: Music genre classification with paralleling recurrent convolutional neural network (2017)
26. Ghosal, D., Kolekar, M.: Music genre recognition using deep neural networks and transfer learning. In: Interspeech, pp. 2087–2091 (2018)
27. Panagakis, Y., Kotropoulos, C., Arce, G.: Music genre classification via sparse representations of auditory temporal modulations. In: European Signal Processing Conference (2009)
28. Panagakis, Y., Kotropoulos, C.: Music genre classification via topology preserving non-negative tensor factorization and sparse representations, pp. 249–252 (2010)

Deep Learning with Data Augmentation for Fruit Counting

Pornntiwa Pawara[1]([✉])[iD], Alina Boshchenko[2][iD], Lambert R.B. Schomaker[1][iD], and Marco A. Wiering[1][iD]

[1] Bernoulli Institute for Mathematics, Computer Science and Artificial Intelligence, University of Groningen, 9747 AG Groningen, The Netherlands
{p.pawara,l.r.b.schomaker,m.a.wiering}@rug.nl
[2] Faculty of Mathematics and Mechanics, Saint Petersburg State University, Saint Petersburg, Russia
alina_boshenko@mail.ru

Abstract. Counting the number of fruits in an image is important for orchard management, but is complex due to different challenging problems such as overlapping fruits and the difficulty to create large labeled datasets. In this paper, we propose the use of a data-augmentation technique that creates novel images by adding a number of manually cropped fruits to original images. This helps to increase the size of a dataset with new images containing more fruits and guarantees correct label information. Furthermore, two different approaches for fruit counting are compared: a holistic regression-based approach, and a detection-based approach. The regression-based approach has the advantage that it only needs as target value the number of fruits in an image compared to the detection-based approach where bounding boxes need to be specified. We combine both approaches with different deep convolutional neural network architectures and object-detection methods. We also introduce a new dataset of 1500 images named the Five-Tropical-Fruits dataset and perform experiments to evaluate the usefulness of augmenting the dataset for the different fruit-counting approaches. The results show that the regression-based approaches profit a lot from the data-augmentation method, whereas the detection-based approaches are not aided by data augmentation. Although one detection-based approach finally still works best, this comes with the cost of much more labeling effort.

Keywords: Computer vision · Fruit counting · Deep learning · Regression · Object detection

1 Introduction

Estimating the number of fruits in orchards is an important task for farming management. Computer vision techniques and convolutional neural networks (CNNs) [13,24] have been used for the fruit-counting task and achieved very good performances [9,17,22]. Researchers have worked on two different approaches of counting: regression-based counting [2,14,25] and detection-based counting [14,19].

© Springer Nature Switzerland AG 2020
L. Rutkowski et al. (Eds.): ICAISC 2020, LNAI 12415, pp. 203–214, 2020.
https://doi.org/10.1007/978-3-030-61401-0_20

Despite obtaining high accuracies using deep learning for object counting tasks [12,18,30], fruit counting in images is still challenging due to several reasons [17,22], including high variances in illumination, overlapping fruits, fruit occluded by other parts of the tree, different sizes of fruits, and different degrees of ripeness of fruits leading to high variances in colors. In addition to these obstacles, there are few datasets with images of fruits, especially for the fruit-counting task, because making an annotation for the dataset can be very time consuming [5].

It has been shown that increasing the number of images in the training set by using data-augmentation techniques helps to improve the performance of training CNNs [21,27]. Data-augmentation methods can be based on different approaches, and generally modify the image properties [3,20], such as changing color or contrast, horizontal/vertical flipping, using rotation, scaling, and translation, or synthesizing data [22,28]. Several researchers successfully used generative adversarial networks (GANs) [1,8] or random elastic morphing [4] for data augmentation. The augmentation approach described in [5] combines real and synthetic images by adding collages from real objects to the images.

Contributions of this Paper. To address the challenges discussed before, we extend previous research in several ways: (1) We introduce a new fruit dataset, namely the Five-Tropic-Fruits (FTF) dataset[1], which can be used for classification, detection, and counting. (2) We propose a fruit data-augmentation (FDA) technique which is useful to increase the number of images and the number of fruits in the images and apply FDA on the training set of the FTF dataset. FDA is helpful to add as many fruits as we want to the training images and can compute exact label information (total number of fruits or bounding boxes). (3) We compare two fruit-counting approaches (regression-based counting, and detection-based counting) on the original and the augmented training set of FTF and evaluate and compare the performances of two CNN architectures. For regression-based counting, the CNN architectures ResNet50 [10], and Inception-V3 [26] are used. For detection-based counting, two object-detection architectures, Faster R-CNN [23] and SSD-MobileNet [11], are trained for performing fruit detection and subsequently fruit counting.

The rest of the paper is organized as follows. Section 2 covers details of the proposed approach of our research. Section 3 discusses results of the experiments and Sect. 4 draws conclusions and describes possible future work.

2 Proposed Approach

2.1 Overall Pipeline

Figure 1 illustrates the overall fruit-counting pipeline. The proposed approach starts with dataset pre-processing, consisting of data collection and data annotation (Subsect. 2.2). Then we perform FDA on the original training set (Subsection 2.3) resulting in an augmented set. The original and the augmented training

---

[1] The dataset has been made publicly available and can be accessed at https://www.ai.rug.nl/~p.pawara/.

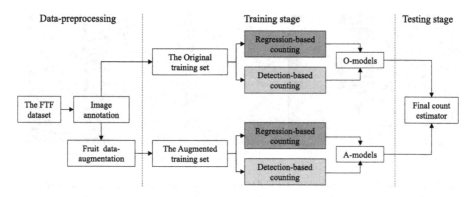

Fig. 1. System pipeline

images are used as inputs for the training stage of two fruit-counting approaches (Subsect. 2.4): regression-based counting and detection-based counting. Each of the counting approaches CNNs are trained on the original training set (yielding the O-models), and the augmented training set (resulting in the A-models). Finally, we evaluate and compare the performances of the O-models and the A-models in the testing stage. The details of each stage are explained in the following subsections.

2.2 Dataset

Data Collection. The Five-Tropic-Fruits (FTF) dataset contains 5 classes of fruit images: apple, custard apple, lemon, pear, and persimmon. All images have been collected from internet. Each image contains only one type of fruit and can consist of up to 15 fruits. The images can be either an indoor or outdoor scene and can cover various objects and backgrounds. The fruits in the images may be occluded and have different levels of overlapping. Some fruits can also be truncated around the border of the images. For each class we collected 300 images and the dataset is split into a training set of 80% and a test set of 20%.

Image Annotations. We compare two counting approaches: regression-based counting and detection-based counting. These two approaches require different formats of ground truths, which we will explain in more details in Subsect. 2.4. For both approaches, we start by manually annotating each image using LabelImg [29]. Each fruit will be labeled and counted as one fruit even if it is occluded or truncated. Locations (bounding boxes) of fruits in the images and the total counts and class names are kept in XML files. Figure 2 shows some example images from the FTF dataset, their bounding-box annotations and the ground truths (total counts) for the regression-based counting task.

{2,0,0,0,0}   {0,6,0,0,0}   {0,0,6,0,0}   {0,0,0,2,0}   {0,0,0,0,9}

Fig. 2. Example images from the FTF dataset. Some images show that some fruits are occluded or truncated. The first row shows example images from the classes: apple, custard apple, lemon, pear, and persimmon, respectively. The second and the third row show the bounding boxes and the labels (total counts) of the images used for the detection-based and regression-based counting approach, respectively.

2.3   Fruit Data Augmentation (FDA)

In this subsection, we present the fruit data-augmentation method used for the counting task. The objective of FDA is to increase the number of fruits in the training images and the total number of images in the training set. The steps of FDA are:

1. **Create fruit masks:** We manually created 20 object masks of each fruit in a Portable Bit Map (PBM) format with a white object and black background.
2. **Select background images:** Background images are selected from the training set of the FTF dataset. Only images with a number between 1 and 8 fruits will be used as the background images.
3. **Augment the fruit masks:** We extracted the masks and perform the following augmentation methods on the masks:
   - **Rotation:** The mask objects are rotated with random angles in $[-30°, 30°]$.
   - **Scaling:** The mask objects are relatively big compared to the background images. So we rescaled the mask images to smaller sizes with a random factor in $[0.4, 0.6]$.
4. **Add fruit masks to the background images:** While placing the masks on the background images, the following cases are considered:
   - **Number of objects to be added:** The specified task is to count up to 15 fruits. As we selected background images that can already contain up to 8 fruits, we set a maximum number of objects to be placed in the background images to 7. Therefore the fruits added are of the same class and their total amount is randomly chosen between 1 and 7.
   - **Occlusion and truncation:** There are two cases of occlusion: the occlusion between the masks, and the occlusion between the masks and the existing fruits in the background images. Both occlusion factors are set to a maximum Intersection-over-Union (IoU) score of 0.5 which means

each object can be overlapped up to 50%. A truncation factor is set to 0.1 to ensure that at least 90% of the masks will be placed on the background images. The positions of the existing fruits in the background images can be retrieved from the corresponding XML file of the image.

– **Blending mode:** Our preliminary experiments showed that adding objects on background images with Gaussian smoothing can reduce boundary artifacts and give better performance. Hence, we place the objects on background images using Gaussian Blurring with a Gaussian kernel size set to [5,5] for which the standard deviation of the kernel is set to 2.

Figure 3 shows the overall process of FDA. We used FDA to add around 13,100 images to the original training set of 1200 images.

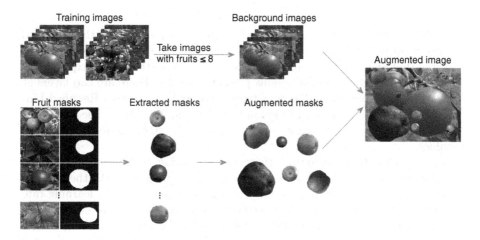

Fig. 3. The fruit data-augmentation (FDA) process. The flowchart shows an example of its working on the apple class. In the example, 6 apples were added to the background (original) image.

2.4 Deep Learning for Fruit Counting

In this subsection, we explain the deep learning architectures for the regression-based and the detection-based counting approaches.

Regression-Based Counting. There are two stages for regression-based counting: the training and testing stage.

1. **Training stage:** In our work, two state-of-the-art deep learning architectures (ResNet50 [10], and Inception-V3 [26]) are trained on the original and the augmented training set of the FTF dataset. Both CNN models are trained with two training schemes by using randomly initialized networks (scratch) or

networks that were trained on ImageNet (pre-trained). In the usual regression task, a single value is used as a target value. For example, an image with 5 apples is assigned the target value 5. For the proposed regression-based counting task, we predict both the total count and the class of the possible fruits in an image. Hence, instead of using a single value, we construct a target vector with $n = 5$ values. We obtain the ground truth during the training process from the XML files described in Subsect. 2.2, and compute the target output using the number of fruits and class. For example {5,0,0,0,0} means an image contains 5 apples, while {0,0,0,0,13} means an image contains 13 persimmons. The deep learning architectures are trained by optimizing the mean absolute error (MAE) loss function using stochastic gradient descent (SGD) with momentum. The MAE loss function L_{MAE} for a single training example is defined as:

$$L_{MAE} = \frac{1}{n} \sum_{i=1}^{n} |y_i - \hat{y}_i| \tag{1}$$

Given n classes, y_i is the target value for a given class i, and $\hat{y}_i$ is the predicted value estimated by the network (for example, {2, 0, 3, 0, 0} if the network predicted that an image has 2 apples and 3 lemons). Note that in the experiments we do not round off the continuous predicted values. There are two layers at the end of the networks. The first fully-connected layer uses a Rectified Linear Unit (ReLU) activation function with 1024 hidden units. The final layer uses linear activation functions and n output units to compute the predicted values.

For regression-based counting, there are 8 training configurations (2 CNN architectures × 2 (pre-trained or scratch) × 2 training sets). All the configurations use the same hyper-parameters values (momentum 0.9, learning rate 0.0001, batch size 64, and 1,000 epochs), which were selected after some preliminary experiments. The models trained with the original training images are called the O-models, whereas the models trained with the augmented training images are called the A-models.

2. **Evaluation metrics for counting (testing stage):** We evaluate the performance of the CNN models by comparing the mean absolute value (MAE) obtained from the models trained on the original set (the O-models) and the models trained on the augmented set (the A-models). As our tasks consider both counting and classification, we report three loss values for different purposes; MAE for counting and classification purposes (MAE$_{CC}$), MAE for the count-only purpose (MAE$_{CO}$), and MAE for evaluating misclassifications (MAE$_{MC}$). Each of these three loss functions is explained below.

MAE$_{CC}$: Given n classes and m test instances, MAE$_{CC}$ for counting and classification is calculated as:

$$MAE_{CC} = \frac{1}{n \cdot m} \sum_{i=1}^{n} \sum_{k=1}^{m} |y_i^k - \hat{y}_i^k| \tag{2}$$

where y_i^k is the number of fruits in the k-th test image of class i and 0 otherwise, and $\hat{y}_i^k$ denotes the predicted values for the corresponding image.

MAE$_{CO}$: We also want to evaluate the models by only considering the number of fruits of the correct class (without considering the other wrongly detected fruits). MAE$_{CO}$ is calculated as:

$$MAE_{CO} = \frac{1}{m} \sum_{k=1}^{m} |y_c^k - \hat{y}_c^k| \tag{3}$$

where c is the class of the k-th image in the test set.

MAE$_{MC}$: To evaluate the performance of the model when considering only misclassified fruits, MAE$_{MC}$ is calculated as:

$$MAE_{MC} = \frac{1}{(n-1) \cdot m} \sum_{\substack{i=1, \\ i \neq c}}^{n} \sum_{k=1}^{m} |y_i^k - \hat{y}_i^k| \tag{4}$$

Table 1 shows some examples of possible image content, the corresponding target and predicted counts and the values for the three loss functions.

Table 1. Examples of the target and predicted outputs and the values of the three loss functions for a single example in the testing stage.

Images	Count and classification			Count only			Misclassification		
	target	predicted	MAE$_{CC}$	target	predicted	MAE$_{CO}$	target	predicted	MAE$_{MC}$
5 apples	{5,0,0,0,0}	{0,0,0,5,0}	2.00	{5}	{0}	5.00	{0,0,0,0}	{0,0,5,0}	1.25
8 lemons	{0,0,8,0,0}	{0,4,2,0,0}	2.00	{8}	{2}	6.00	{0,0,0,0}	{0,4,0,0}	1.00
7 pears	{0,0,0,7,0}	{0,3,6,0,0}	3.20	{7}	{0}	7.00	{0,0,0,0}	{0,3,6,0}	2.25

Detection-Based Counting: Similar to regression-based counting, there are two stages for detection-based counting: the training and the testing stage. We train two CNN object-detection architectures: Faster R-CNN [23], and SSD-MobileNet [11] for performing fruit detection and apply the CNN models to detect and count the fruits on the test images.

Faster R-CNN is a state-of-the-art object-detection architecture, which was developed based on the Region-based Convolutional Neural Network (R-CNN) [7] and Fast R-CNN [6]. It consists of two networks: (1) a region proposal network (RPN) for generating region proposals or regions of interest (ROI), and (2) a convolutional network for classifying the regions of the image into objects and refining the bounding box corresponding to each proposal. We used the pre-trained network for the MS-COCO [15] dataset to fine-tune Faster R-CNN for detection-based counting.

While Faster R-CNN uses a region proposal network to classify objects, Single Shot Multibox Detector (SSD) [16] uses VGG-16 as a backbone network to extract feature maps of different resolutions and applies convolution filters to detect objects. Each cell of the higher feature maps uses a larger area of the image for detecting large objects whereas the smaller feature maps can be used for detecting smaller objects. SSD-MobileNet [11] is an adaptive version of the original SSD architecture using the MobileNet network leading to a light-weight model and has been shown to achieve a similar detection accuracy as VGG-16. For the detection-based counting task, we used fine-tuning on the network trained on the MS-COCO dataset to train SSD-MobileNet.

We train the CNN models of Faster R-CNN and SSD-MobileNet using either the original or augmented training set of the FTF dataset. Then we evaluate the models on the test set. For each test image, the models predict the bounding boxes of the detected fruits and the confidence of each detected box. We count the number of detected fruits (using a confidence threshold of 0.6) and evaluate the performances of the detection-based counting models by using the same three loss functions used for the regression-based counting approach.

3   Results

We train CNNs for regression-based counting and detection-based counting on the original and the augmented training set of the FTF dataset. Then we compare the performance between the models trained on the original set (the O-models) and the models trained on the augmented set (the A-models) by testing the models on the test images. This section reports the results of the regression-based counting and the detection-based counting approaches.

3.1   Regression-Based Counting Results

Table 2 shows the performance of the O-models and the A-models for regression-based counting obtained from training ResNet50 and Inception-V3 with both scratch and fine-tuned models.

The MAE_{CC} values indicate that all A-models perform significantly better than the O-models with a 15%–31% improvement (e.g., 0.26 vs 0.38). Scratch ResNet50 and fine-tuned ResNet50 profit most from training on the augmented set with an improvement of 29% and 31%, respectively. The highest performance (the lowest average testing error) was achieved by the A-model trained by fine-tuning ResNet50 with $MAE_{CC} = 0.26$.

When considering MAE_{CO}, all A-models also obtain significantly better performances than the O-models. Scratch ResNet50 profits the most from training on the augmented images with a 38% improvement (3.1 to 1.93). The best performing model is the A-model+ResNet50 fine-tuned with $MAE_{CO} = 1.07$.

For MAE_{MC}, which considers the misclassification predictions, the fine-tuned versions of both deep learning architectures profit a lot from training on the augmented set with a loss improvement of 67%. For the scratch versions, the A-models perform similarly to the O-models.

Figure 4 shows some example images from the test set, the ground truths, and the predicted labels obtained from training Fine-tuned-ResNet50 on the original and the augmented training set of the FTF dataset.

Table 2. Performance of different CNNs (average loss and standard deviation) for regression-based counting on the test set. All models were trained on the original and the augmented training set of the FTF dataset using five-fold cross validation. The bold numbers indicate significant differences between the loss values obtained by the two models (p < 0.05).

CNNs	MAE_{CC}		MAE_{CO}		MAE_{MC}	
	O-models	A-models	O-models	A-models	O-models	A-models
Resnet50-Scratch	0.72 ± 0.04	**0.51 ± 0.02**	3.10 ± 0.29	**1.93 ± 0.07**	0.12 ± 0.04	0.15 ± 0.01
Resnet50-Fine-tuned	0.38 ± 0.03	**0.26 ± 0.02**	1.28 ± 0.11	**1.07 ± 0.09**	0.15 ± 0.01	**0.05 ± 0.01**
Inception-V3-Scratch	0.60 ± 0.03	**0.51 ± 0.02**	2.40 ± 0.21	**1.91 ± 0.10**	0.15 ± 0.03	0.16 ± 0.01
Inception-V3-Fine-tuned	0.34 ± 0.03	**0.27 ± 0.03**	1.35 ± 0.11	**1.12 ± 0.10**	0.09 ± 0.01	**0.03 ± 0.02**

	(a)	(b)	(c)
[G]	{0,0,0,11,0}	{0,0,0,0,9}	{0,1,0,0,0}
[O]	{0,0,0,**6**,0}	{0,0,0,0,9}	{0,1,0,0,1}
[A]	{0,0,0,11,0}	{0,0,0,0,**10**}	{0,1,0,0,1}

Fig. 4. Examples of test images, ground truths and predicted outputs obtained from regression-based counting using the Fine-tuned-ResNet50 architecture. (a) the A-model performs better, (b) the O-model performs better, and (c) Misclassified prediction. The [G], [O], and [A] symbols denote the ground truths, predicted labels from the O-model, and predicted labels from the A-model, respectively. The bold numbers in the predicted labels show wrong predicted values.

There are some wrong counts and misclassified images due to different reasons: extensive shading effects, extra objects in the images, a high similarity between fruits and leaves, the occlusion or truncation of some fruits, the similarity among different fruits and possible dissimilarity within the same fruit (i.e., green and ripe fruits or round and oval shapes of pears), which can confuse the CNN models.

3.2 Detection-Based Counting Results

In this subsection, we report the performances of the O-models and the A-models for the detection-based counting approach obtained from training Faster R-CNN and SSD-MobileNet. Table 3 shows the detection-based counting results.

Table 3. Performances of different detection models (average loss and standard deviation) for the detection-based counting methods on the test set. All models were trained on the original and the augmented training set of the FTF dataset using five-fold cross validation. Note that there are no significant differences between the results of the O-models and the A-models ($p < 0.05$).

Object Detection	MAE_{CC}		MAE_{CO}		MAE_{MC}	
	O-models	A-models	O-models	A-models	O-models	A-models
Faster R-CNN	0.22 ± 0.03	0.21 ± 0.03	0.62 ± 0.11	0.67 ± 0.13	0.12 ± 0.02	0.10 ± 0.02
SSD-MobileNet	0.34 ± 0.07	0.35 ± 0.06	1.38 ± 0.34	1.35 ± 0.26	0.08 ± 0.02	0.10 ± 0.02

For all loss functions, there are no significant differences between the A-models and the O-models. This shows that the fruit data-augmentation method is not useful when training the object-detection algorithms Faster R-CNN and SSD. The reason is that no new fruits (objects) with different appearances are introduced in the images, except for slight differences in scale and rotation. Therefore, the detection algorithm can either locate a specific instance of a fruit or not. The FDA method can therefore only be helpful to make more challenging images with more occlusion, but this does not seem to aid counting performance.

We can also observe that Faster R-CNN performs much better than SSD with MobileNet. This may be because MobileNet is a light-weight CNN, but another reason could be that for this dataset, Faster R-CNN is more accurate.

When we compare the results of the detection-based counting approaches to the regression-based counting approaches, we observe that the results of the Faster R-CNN counting approach are better than the results of the regression-based counting approaches. The only exception to this is that the loss function of the misclassified fruits is lower for the regression-based counting methods when fine-tuned models are used with the augmented dataset. On the other hand, SSD-MobileNet is significantly outperformed by the regression-based approaches when the CNNs are fine-tuned on the augmented dataset.

4   Conclusion

In this paper we researched the usefulness of performing data augmentation for counting fruits. The proposed method adds segmented objects (fruits) to existing images and has as advantage that novel labels (counts or bounding boxes) are exactly computed. We also created a novel dataset consisting of images consisting of between 1 and 15 fruits of five different fruit types. For the counting task, we compared two widely different approaches: a holistic regression-based approach and a detection-based approach. For both approaches we used different convolutional neural networks or object-detection algorithms.

The results show that the fruit data-augmentation method is very helpful for the regression-based approaches. These methods directly predict the total count based on the entire image and profit from the new images which both look different and have higher total counts (which makes the problem more difficult).

The performances of the detection-based algorithms did not improve by using the data-augmentation method. This can be explained because no new differently looking fruits are added and therefore locally no new variances are introduced.

Although the best detection-based counting approach (Faster R-CNN) outperforms the regression-based approaches, it requires a human to manually draw bounding boxes around each fruit in the training set. This is much more time-intensive than only labeling an image with the total count. Furthermore, SSD-MobileNet was outperformed by the regression-based counting approaches when data augmentation was used together with pre-trained CNNs.

In future work, we are planning to work on plant-disease detection and will study different data-augmentation methods to deal with the limited amount of training images for diseased plants.

References

1. Antoniou, A., Storkey, A., Edwards, H.: Data augmentation generative adversarial networks (2017). arXiv preprint arXiv:1711.04340
2. Arteta, C., Lempitsky, V., Zisserman, A.: Counting in the wild. In: Leibe, B., Matas, J., Sebe, N., Welling, M. (eds.) ECCV 2016. LNCS, vol. 9911, pp. 483–498. Springer, Cham (2016). https://doi.org/10.1007/978-3-319-46478-7_30
3. Brahimi, M., Arsenovic, M., Laraba, S., Sladojevic, S., Boukhalfa, K., Moussaoui, A.: Deep learning for plant diseases: detection and saliency map visualisation. In: Zhou, J., Chen, F. (eds.) Human and Machine Learning. HIS, pp. 93–117. Springer, Cham (2018). https://doi.org/10.1007/978-3-319-90403-0_6
4. Bulacu, M., Brink, A., van der Zant, T., Schomaker, L.: Recognition of handwritten numerical fields in a large single-writer historical collection. In: 10th International Conference on Document Analysis and Recognition, pp. 808–812. IEEE (2009)
5. Dwibedi, D., Misra, I., Hebert, M.: Cut, paste and learn: surprisingly easy synthesis for instance detection. In: The IEEE International Conference on Computer Vision (ICCV), pp. 1301–1310 (2017)
6. Girshick, R.: Fast R-CNN. In: Proceedings of the IEEE International Conference on Computer Vision, pp. 1440–1448 (2015)
7. Girshick, R., Donahue, J., Darrell, T., Malik, J.: Region-based convolutional networks for accurate object detection and segmentation. IEEE Trans. Pattern Anal. Mach. Intell. **38**(1), 142–158 (2015)
8. Goodfellow, I., et al.: Generative adversarial nets. In: Advances in Neural Information Processing Systems, pp. 2672–2680 (2014)
9. Häni, N., Roy, P., Isler, V.: A comparative study of fruit detection and counting methods for yield mapping in apple orchards. J. Field Rob. **37**, 263–282 (2019)
10. He, K., Zhang, X., Ren, S., Sun, J.: Deep residual learning for image recognition. In: Proceedings of the IEEE Conference on Computer Vision and Pattern Recognition, pp. 770–778 (2016)
11. Howard, A.G., et al.: MobileNets: efficient convolutional neural networks for mobile vision applications (2017). arXiv preprint arXiv:1704.04861
12. Koirala, A., Walsh, K., Wang, Z., McCarthy, C.: Deep learning for real-time fruit detection and orchard fruit load estimation: Benchmarking of 'MangoYOLO'. Precis. Agric. **20**, 1–29 (2019)
13. LeCun, Y., Bengio, Y., Hinton, G.: Deep learning. Nature **521**(7553), 436 (2015)

14. Lempitsky, V., Zisserman, A.: Learning to count objects in images. In: Advances in Neural Information Processing Systems, pp. 1324–1332 (2010)
15. Lin, T.Y., et al.: Microsoft COCO: Common Objects in Context. In: Fleet, D., Pajdla, T., Schiele, B., Tuytelaars, T. (eds.) ECCV 2014. LNCS, vol. 8693, pp. 740–755. Springer, Cham (2014). https://doi.org/10.1007/978-3-319-10602-1_48
16. Liu, W., et al.: SSD: single shot multibox detector. In: Leibe, B., Matas, J., Sebe, N., Welling, M. (eds.) ECCV 2016. LNCS, vol. 9905, pp. 21–37. Springer, Cham (2016). https://doi.org/10.1007/978-3-319-46448-0_2
17. Liu, X., et al.: Robust fruit counting: combining deep learning, tracking, and structure from motion. In: 2018 IEEE/RSJ International Conference on Intelligent Robots and Systems (IROS), pp. 1045–1052. IEEE (2018)
18. Oñoro-Rubio, D., López-Sastre, R.J.: Towards perspective-free object counting with deep learning. In: Leibe, B., Matas, J., Sebe, N., Welling, M. (eds.) ECCV 2016. LNCS, vol. 9911, pp. 615–629. Springer, Cham (2016). https://doi.org/10.1007/978-3-319-46478-7_38
19. Paul Cohen, J., Boucher, G., Glastonbury, C.A., Lo, H.Z., Bengio, Y.: Countception: counting by fully convolutional redundant counting. In: Proceedings of the IEEE International Conference on Computer Vision, pp. 18–26 (2017)
20. Pawara, P., Okafor, E., Schomaker, L., Wiering, M.: Data augmentation for plant classification. In: Blanc-Talon, J., Penne, R., Philips, W., Popescu, D., Scheunders, P. (eds.) ACIVS 2017. LNCS, vol. 10617, pp. 615–626. Springer, Cham (2017). https://doi.org/10.1007/978-3-319-70353-4_52
21. Perez, L., Wang, J.: The effectiveness of data augmentation in image classification using deep learning (2017). arXiv preprint arXiv:1712.04621
22. Rahnemoonfar, M., Sheppard, C.: Deep count: fruit counting based on deep simulated learning. Sensors **17**(4), 905 (2017)
23. Ren, S., He, K., Girshick, R., Sun, J.: Faster R-CNN: towards real-time object detection with region proposal networks. In: Advances in Neural Information Processing Systems, pp. 91–99 (2015)
24. Schmidhuber, J.: Deep learning in neural networks: an overview. Neural Netw. **61**, 85–117 (2015)
25. Stahl, T., Pintea, S.L., van Gemert, J.C.: Divide and count: generic object counting by image divisions. IEEE Trans. Image Process. **28**(2), 1035–1044 (2018)
26. Szegedy, C., Vanhoucke, V., Ioffe, S., Shlens, J., Wojna, Z.: Rethinking the inception architecture for computer vision. In: Proceedings of the IEEE Conference on Computer Vision and Pattern Recognition, pp. 2818–2826 (2016)
27. Taylor, L., Nitschke, G.: Improving deep learning using generic data augmentation (2017). arXiv preprint arXiv:1708.06020
28. Tremblay, J., et al.: Training deep networks with synthetic data: Bridging the reality gap by domain randomization. In: Proceedings of the IEEE Conference on Computer Vision and Pattern Recognition Workshops, pp. 969–977 (2018)
29. Tzutalin: LabelImg homepage. https://github.com/tzutalin/labelImg
30. Zhang, C., Li, H., Wang, X., Yang, X.: Cross-scene crowd counting via deep convolutional neural networks. In: Proceedings of the IEEE Conference on Computer Vision and Pattern Recognition, pp. 833–841 (2015)

Approximation of Fractional Order Dynamic Systems Using Elman, GRU and LSTM Neural Networks

Bartosz Puchalski$^{(\boxtimes)}$ [iD] and Tomasz A. Rutkowski [iD]

Faculty of Electrical and Control Engineering, Gdańsk University of Technology,
G. Narutowicza Street 11/12, 80-233 Gdańsk, Poland
{bartosz.puchalski,tomasz.adam.rutkowski}@pg.edu.pl
http://pg.edu.pl/en

Abstract. In the paper, authors explore the possibility of using the recurrent neural networks (RNN) - Elman, GRU and LSTM - for an approximation of the solution of the fractional-orders differential equations. The RNN network parameters are estimated via optimisation with the second order L-BFGS algorithm. It is done based on data from four systems: simple first and second fractional order LTI systems, a system of fractional-order point kinetics and heat exchange in the nuclear reactor core and complex nonlinear system. The obtained result shows that the studied RNNs are very promising as approximators of the fractional-order systems. On the other hand, these approximations may be easily implemented in real digital control platforms.

Keywords: Neural networks · Recurrent neural networks · Fractional order systems · Nonlinear systems · Mathematical modelling

1 Introduction

The methods of the Fractional Order Calculus (FOC) involving, non-integer derivatives and integrals, have been known since XVII century but only in recent years have their technical applications been extensively reported in numerous fields of science and engineering [13]. Also, in the field of control systems, FOC has found its application that is mainly used for fractional-order modelling of complex system dynamics and the fractional-order control strategies synthesis. Literature studies demonstrate that the dynamics of many complex systems taking part in the field of control theory can be described more accurately with the differential equations of non-integer order. The fractional-order control strategies, with appropriate tuning and design methodologies, may achieve better control quality in various control systems (e.g. fractional-order PID controllers [17,19]).

The fractional-order dynamic systems are characterised by infinite memory, or in other words, they are of infinite dimensions. Consequently, the mathematical models of such systems in the Laplace or $\mathcal{Z}$ domain are characterised by

© Springer Nature Switzerland AG 2020
L. Rutkowski et al. (Eds.): ICAISC 2020, LNAI 12415, pp. 215–230, 2020.
https://doi.org/10.1007/978-3-030-61401-0_21

an irrational order and the discrete models by an infinite memory of processed samples. While the synthesis of systems based on fractional order operators is not particularly problematic, the implementation of such systems on digital control platforms (e.g. FPGA, DSP, PLC) is a demanding task. In the latter case, techniques that allow for the approximation of fractional systems are needed. Such approximation techniques most often lead to the identification of appropriate dynamic systems, which will be described by integer-order models or will use finite memory resources. The most popular and widely used approximations of fractional order systems include: continued fraction-based approximations, Oustaloup filters, frequency response fitting approach and many other [19].

Each of the mentioned approximation methods has its own cons and pros. Generally, they allow for an approximation of non-integer order operators with the use of structures of classical digital, mostly linear and sometimes nonlinear, filters. Especially in the case of approximation, the long memory length is needed what may cause problems during the real time implementation on the real digital control platforms. Moreover, resulting polynomials: (i) may be ill-conditioned (coefficients with very large values), which may lead to the computational instability and overflow errors on the digital platform, (ii) may contain internal instability related to the inappropriate location of polynomials zeros and poles, and additionally, (iii) the same approximation cannot be used if there are changes in the value of fractional-order of differentiation or integration operator, or characteristic system parameters in the time/frequency domain - the approximation procedure must be carried out again.

To more or less overcome these problems various authors propose in literature the use of Artificial Neural Networks to approximate the fractional-order operators or linear and nonlinear fractional-order systems [9,18,20]. Typically, various authors in their works use the feed-forward multi-layer perceptron structure of the ANN, to model fractional-order dynamic systems. In literature, the analysis of dynamics and stability of the fractional-order neural network with the structure of recurrent Hopfield network may be found [10].

In this paper, the authors explore the possibility of using some recent structures of recurrent neural networks (RNN), with dynamic memory, as a more natural substitute for the approximation of evolving process states according to various mathematical models of the dynamic systems which may be described by ordinary, and especially by the fractional-orders differential equations sets. Those RNN structures are: (i) Elman recurrent neural network [4], (ii) networks consisting of GRU cells [3], (iii) and networks consisting of LSTM cells [8].

The proposed RNN structures are verified based on a series of numerical experiments with fractional-order systems models in the form of: (i) a simple linear fractional first-order LTI system, (ii) a simple linear fractional secondorder LTI system, (iii) nonlinear fractional-order physical system of point kinetics and heat exchange in the nuclear reactor core [5,14], (iv) and a complex nonlinear system [19].

The paper is organised as follows. In Sect. 2 the considered problem is described. In Sect. 3 the methodology used in the paper is presented. Section 4 presents the results of numerical simulations. Finally, Sect. 5 concludes the paper.

2 Problem Statement

The recurrent neural networks are known for their excellent approximation properties. Following [7, 12] it's worthwhile to quote here the universal approximation theorem:

Theorem 1. *Any nonlinear dynamic system may be approximated by a recurrent neural network to any desired degree of accuracy and with no restrictions imposed on the compactness of the state space, provided that the network is equipped with an adequate number of hidden neurons.*

The quoted theorem about the universal approximation of systems using recurrent neural networks is the foundation on which the research presented in the paper is based. In the context of the usability of the above mentioned theorem, the following problems should be kept in mind:

1. selection of appropriate recursive network architecture i.e. selection of adequate number of neurons in the hidden layer and selection of cell type of hidden neurons,
2. selection of appropriate network parameters i.e. weights and biases,
3. selection of an appropriate optimisation algorithm to obtain satisfactory quality indicators that measure the deviation between the training/validation data and the output of a given recursive network.

Referring to the first problem, selecting an appropriate network architecture is a complex task. The research was limited only to increasing the number of neurons/cells in one hidden network layer. It was assumed that networks will consist of 1 to 5 cells/neurons in the hidden layer respectively. During this research, the performance of Elman-type networks (Elman RNN), networks consisting of GRU cells and networks consisting of LSTM cells was compared.

With regard to the second problem, the choice of network parameters was made using optimisation techniques. It should be noted here, that on the basis of the universal approximation theorem, it can be concluded that such a recurrent neural network exists, which will be able to approximate with satisfactory accuracy the dynamic system of a fractional order. Also, it should be important to note that there is no certainty of finding the appropriate set of network parameters that will allow for satisfactory approximation.

The last of the problems mentioned above concerns the optimisation algorithm that is used to select network parameters. In the research, the L-BFGS algorithm [11] was used, which belongs to the family of 2nd order quasi-Newton methods. This method has been chosen because it is characterised by the fact that during one optimisation step, an immediate jump to the local minimum is possible and also there is a built-in mechanism for selecting the optimiser step size. Additionally, the L-BFGS algorithm is less memory demanding in comparison to the standard BFGS algorithm. It was also noted that Hessian information processed by the algorithm significantly accelerates the optimisation process so that multiple optimiser runs were not an issue.

2.1   Recurrent Neural Network Architectures Used in the Research

As mentioned earlier in Sect. 2, in this study three recursive neural network architectures were used. These architectures are described below in a compact form [1]:

Elman RNN

$$h_t = \tanh(W_{ih}x_t + b_{ih} + W_{hh}h_{(t-1)} + b_{hh}) \tag{1}$$

where h_t is the hidden state at time t, x_t is the input at time t and $h_{(t-1)}$ is the hidden state at time $t-1$ or the initial hidden state at time 0, W_{ih} is the learnable input-hidden weights matrix, W_{hh} is the learnable hidden-hidden weights matrix, b_{ih} is the learnable input-hidden bias and b_{hh} is the learnable hidden-hidden bias. As the authors of the PyTorch library state, that the second bias vector is included for NVIDIA CUDA® Deep Neural Network library compatibility.

GRU

$$
\begin{aligned}
r_t &= \sigma(W_{ir}x_t + b_{ir} + W_{hr}h_{(t-1)} + b_{hr}) \\
z_t &= \sigma(W_{iz}x_t + b_{iz} + W_{hz}h_{(t-1)} + b_{hz}) \\
n_t &= \tanh(W_{in}x_t + b_{in} + r_t * (W_{hh}h_{(h-1)} + b_{hn})) \\
h_t &= (1 - z_t) * n_t + z_t * h_{(t-1)}
\end{aligned}
\tag{2}
$$

where r_t, z_t, n_t are the reset, update and new gates, respectively, σ is the sigmoid function, $*$ is the Hadamard product, W_{ir}, W_{iz}, W_{in} are learnable input-reset, input-update and input-new weights matrices, W_{hr}, W_{hz} are hidden-reset and hidden-update weights matrices, b_{ir}, b_{iz}, b_{in} are lernable input-reset, input-update and input-new biases, b_{hr}, b_{hz}, b_{hn} are learnable hidden-reset, hidden-update, and hidden-new biases.

LSTM

$$
\begin{aligned}
i_t &= \sigma(W_{ii}x_t + b_{ii} + W_{hi}h_{(t-1)} + b_{hi}) \\
f_t &= \sigma(W_{if}x_t + b_{if} + W_{hf}h_{(t-1)} + b_{hf}) \\
g_t &= \tanh(W_{ig}x_t + b_{ig} + W_{hg}h_{(t-1)} + b_{hg}) \\
o_t &= \sigma(W_{io}x_t + b_{io} + W_{ho}h_{(t-1)} + b_{ho}) \\
c_t &= f_t * c_{(t-1)} + i_t * g_t \\
h_t &= o_t * \tanh(c_t)
\end{aligned}
\tag{3}
$$

where c_t is the cell state at time t, i_t, f_t, g_t, o_t are input, forget, cell and output gates respectively, W_{ii}, W_{if}, W_{ig}, W_{io}, are learnable input-input, input-forget, input-cell and input-output weights matrices, W_{hi}, W_{hf}, W_{hg}, W_{ho} are learnable hidden-input, hidden-forget, hidden-cell and hidden-output weights matrices, b_{hi}, b_{hf}, b_{hg}, b_{ho} are learnable hidden-input, hidden-forget, hidden-cell, hidden-output biases.

Hidden state in each analysed neural network was subjected to linear transformation in order to obtain a single network output. The first network used in the presented study, i.e. Elman RNN is a classic recurrent neural network. In fact, it was used as background for more advanced architectures that use gated units. In general, gated neural networks, such as GRU and LSTM networks are based on the idea of creating paths through time that have derivatives that neither vanish nor explode [6]. This is achieved by allowing connection weights to change at each time step. Such a mechanism, together with the network's ability to learn when the self-decision about clearing the state should be taken, allows to accumulate information over long periods of time [6]. These properties match closely with the problem of approximation of dynamic systems of fractional order discussed in the article and therefore it was decided to use gated networks such as GRU and LSTM networks for this purpose.

3 Research Method

3.1 Fractional Order Dynamic Systems Models

In order to examine the approximation performance of fractional systems by recurrent neural networks, four mathematical models involving fractional operators were used. The first model is a fractional first order LTI system (FFOS). This model is described by the following fractional order differential equation

$$\tau \mathscr{D}^{\alpha_1} x(t) + x(t) = k_1 u(t) \tag{4}$$

where $\tau = 1,5$ is exponential decay time constant, $\alpha_1 = 0,8$ is fractional order of differential operator $\mathscr{D}$ ($\mathscr{D}^\alpha = \frac{d^\alpha}{dt^\alpha}$, $\alpha \epsilon R, \alpha > 0$), $k_1 = 0,8$ is the forcing function gain, $u(t)$ is the forcing function and $x(t)$ is a function of time.

The second model is a fractional second order LTI system (FSOS) of an oscillatory character described by the following system of fractional commensurate order differential equations

$$\begin{cases} \mathscr{D}^{\alpha_2} x_1(t) &= x_2(t) \\ \mathscr{D}^{\alpha_2} x_2(t) &= -\omega_n^2 x_1(t) - 2\zeta\omega_n x_2(t) + k_2\omega_n^2 u(t) \end{cases} \tag{5}$$

where $\alpha_2 = 1,2$ parameter is used as the base order of the system, $\omega_n = 2$ is natural frequency of the system and $\zeta = 0,707$ is the damping ratio of the system. The initial conditions for LTI models were set to 0. In order to obtain responses to the above mentioned models, the definition of Grunwald-Letnikov fractional order operator was used.

The third system used in the study is a nonlinear nuclear reactor model in which point-neutron kinetics is described by a system of fractional-order differential equations, based on one group of delayed-neutron precursor nuclei (6–7). In the later part of the article this model is referred to as Nuclear Reactor model. The fractional model retains the main dynamic characteristics of the neutron motion in which the relaxation time associated with a rapid variation in the neutron flux contains a fractional order, acting as an exponent of the relaxation time, to obtain the better representation of a nuclear reactor dynamics with anomalous diffusion (the diffusion processes do not follow the Fick's diffusion law) [14]. The kinetic model is presented as follows

$$
\mathscr{D}^{1+\kappa}n(t) + \frac{1}{\tau^{\kappa}}\mathscr{D}^{1}n(t) + \left(\frac{1}{l} + \frac{1-\beta}{\Lambda}\right)\mathscr{D}^{\kappa}n(t)
$$
$$
+ \frac{1}{\tau^{\kappa}}\left(\frac{\beta - \rho(t)}{\Lambda}\right)n(t) = \lambda\mathscr{D}^{\kappa}c(t) + \frac{\lambda}{\tau^{\kappa}}c(t), \tag{6}
$$

$$
\mathscr{D}^{1}c(t) + \lambda c(t) = \frac{\beta}{\Lambda}n(t), \tag{7}
$$

where τ is the relaxation time, κ is the anomalous diffusion order $(0 < \kappa \leq 1)$, n is the neutron density, c is the concentration of the neutron delayed precursor, l is the mean prompt-neutron lifetime, Λ is the neutron generation time, β is the fraction of delayed neutrons, λ is the decay constant and ρ is the reactivity. The initial conditions for equations (6–7) are specified as follows $n(0) = n_0$, $c(0) = c_0$.

The Nuclear Reactor model also contains equations describing the thermal-hydraulic relations and the reactivity feedback from fuel and coolant temperature, which are described by means of integer-order differential equations and algebraic equations based on the classic Newton law of cooling [15, 16]

$$
\mathscr{D}^{1}T_F(t) = \frac{1}{m_F c_{pF}}\left(f_F P_{th}(t) - Ah(T_F(t) - T_C(t))\right), \tag{8}
$$

$$
\mathscr{D}^{1}T_C(t) = \frac{1}{m_C c_{pC}}((1 - f_F)P_{th}(t) + Ah(T_F(t) - T_C(t)) +
$$
$$
- 2W_C c_{pC}(T_C(t) - T_{Cin}))), \tag{9}
$$

where m_F is the mass of the fuel, c_{pF} is the specific heat capacity of the fuel, T_F is the fuel temperature, f_F is the fraction of the total power generated in the fuel, P_{th} is the nominal reactor thermal power, A is the effective heat transfer area, h is the average overall heat transfer coefficient, T_C is the average coolant temperature, m_C is the mass of the coolant, c_{pC} is the specific heat capacity of the coolant, W_C is the coolant mass flow rate within the core, T_{Cout} is the coolant outlet temperature, and T_{Cin} is the coolant inlet temperature.

While the reactivity feedback balance related to the main internal mechanisms (fuel and coolant temperature effects) and external mechanisms (control rod bank movements) is represented by the following algebraic equation [15, 16].

$$
\rho(t) = \rho_{ext} + \alpha_F(T_F(t) - T_{F,0}) + \alpha_C(T_C(t) - T_{C,0}), \tag{10}
$$

where ρ_{ext} is the deviation of the external reactivity from the initial (critical) value, α_F is the fuel reactivity coefficient, $T_{F,0}$ is the initial condition for the fuel temperature, α_C is the coolant reactivity coefficient, $T_{C,0}$ is the initial condition for the average coolant temperature. Parameters used in this research for the fractional nuclear reactor model are presented in Table 1. The nuclear model equations were discretised using the Diethelms approach and the trapezoidal method.

Table 1. Parameters of the fractional nuclear reactor model

τ	κ	β	λ	Λ	l	c_{pF}	c_{pC}
$1.2559 \cdot 10^{-4}$	0.99	0.007	0.0810958	0.002	0.00024	247.02	5819.65
f_F	A	P_{th}	h	W_C	T_{Cin}	α_F	α_C
0.974	5564.89	$3436 \cdot 10^6$	1135.65	19851.92	281.94	$-1.98 \cdot 10^{-5}$	$-3.6 \cdot 10^{-5}$
m_F	m_C	$T_{F,0}$	$T_{C,0}$	n_0	c_0		
101032.71	11196.20	826.3684	296.8149	1.0	102.667		

The last but no less important model used in the study was a non-linear system of fractional order described by the following equation

$$y(t) = \frac{3}{4}\left[5\sin(10t) - \frac{3\mathscr{D}^{0.9}y(t)}{3 + 0.2\mathscr{D}^{0.8}y(t) + 0.9\mathscr{D}^{0.2}y(t)} - \left|2\mathscr{D}^{0.7}y(t)\right|^{1.5}\right] \quad (11)$$

This model was taken from [19] as an example of a system that is characterised by dynamics of fractional order and a strongly non-linear structure of the mathematical model. In terms of sophistication, this model is the most complex, and it is expected to be the most difficult to approximate by neural networks used in the research. In the later part of the article, this model is referred to as a Nonlinear model.

3.2 Data

In order to generate the training and validation data, Amplitude Modulated Pseudo Random Binary Sequence (APRBS) was introduced as the input for each examined dynamic system. For all systems except Nonlinear model the APRBS consisted of 600 samples, minimum hold time was 10 samples and maximum hold time was 100 samples. For Nonlinear model the APRBS consisted of 3000 samples, minimum hold time was 50 samples and maximum hold time was 400 samples.

For Fractional LTI systems the amplitude was within a range of $[-1, 1]$, for the Nuclear Reactor system the amplitude was within a range of $[-0.005, 0.005]$, and for Nonlinear system the amplitude was within a range of $[-3, 3]$ (Figs. 1, 2, 3 and 4). In order to check the ability of investigated networks to generalise, a study was carried out based on two test signals, the sinusoidal signal and the saw tooth signal respectively (Figs. 1, 2, 3 and 4).

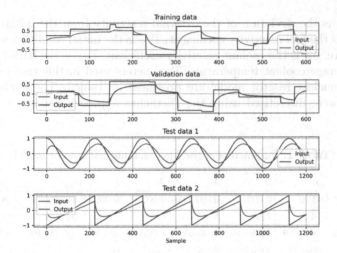

Fig. 1. Data generated on the basis of the FFOS model.

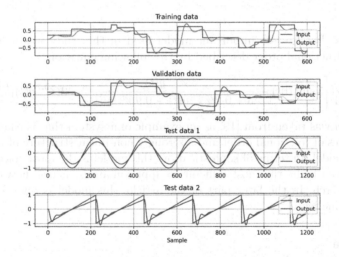

Fig. 2. Data generated on the basis of the FSOS model.

3.3   Software Environment and Optimisation

The research presented in the paper was conducted using Python [2] environment in version 3.8.2 and PyTorch [1] library in version 1.4. The optimisation was performed using the L-BFGS algorithm, which is part of the PyTorch library.

In order to maintain consistency of computations between optimisation of different neural networks, the following common optimisation conditions have been defined: (i) update history size of the L-BFGS algorithm was set to 100, (ii) maximum number of iterations per optimisation step of the L-BFGS algorithm was set to 10, (iii) line search conditions of the L-BFGS algorithm were set to

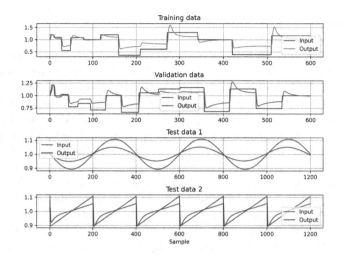

Fig. 3. Data generated on the basis of the Nuclear Reactor model. For presentation purposes, the input data has been scaled to output data level.

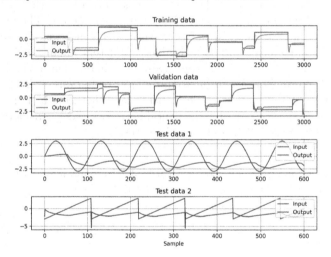

Fig. 4. Data generated on the basis of the Nonlinear model.

`strong_wolfe`, (iv) number of training epochs was set to 30, (v) number of optimiser runs for a specific neural network was set to 50, (vi) the initial neural network parameters are randomly selected from uniform distribution $\mathcal{U}\left(-\sqrt{k}, \sqrt{k}\right)$ where $k = \frac{1}{\text{hidden size}}$, (vii) the loss function has been set as `MSELoss`. Other properties of the optimisation package included in the PyTorch library were left as `defaults`.

4   Results

In this section, tables with mean and minimum loss functions values are presented (Tables 2, 3, 4, 5, 6, 7, 8, 9, 10, 11, 12 and 13). The abbreviations in the column names of the tables are as follows: HU - hidden units, Train - training data, Val - validation data, P.no. - number of parameters. The mean values were arranged for the training, validation and test data depending on the number of neurons/units in the hidden layer of each neural network. The last row in each table contains the minimum value of the loss function for each data set. In this row, the hidden column contains information about the number of neurons/units in the hidden layer for which the minimum value of the loss function was obtained. Tables 2–4, 5–7, 8–10 and 11–13 contain results for FFOS, FSOS, Nuclear Reactor and Nonlinear dynamic systems respectively.

This section also contains exemplary plots (Figs. 5, 6, 7 and 8) which contain outputs from the considered dynamic systems (System) and outputs from the considered neural networks (Net). The plots contain only the results from neural networks, which were characterised by the lowest value of the loss function for the second testing data set. For each data set, the best network was the GRU network with 4 units in the hidden layer and 89 learnable parameters. The exception to this was a network approximating a Nonlinear model, which was characterised by 2 units in the hidden layer and 33 learnable parameters. As in previous cases, it was also a GRU network. Tables 2, 3 and 4 also contain information on the number of all learnable parameters according to the number of neurons in the hidden layer, which are similar for other tables. The last figure in this section (Fig. 9) presents exemplary residual error plots for the neural networks under consideration. This figure is based on Figs. 5, 6, 7 and 8 labelled 'Test data 2'.

Table 2. Mean and minimal Loss of Elman RNN for FFOS data

HU	Train.	Val.	Test1	Test2	P.no.
1	3.25e−03	6.89e−03	6.14e−03	6.52e−03	6
2	7.33e−04	1.45e−03	1.88e−03	1.18e−03	13
3	3.11e−04	8.02e−04	8.55e−04	5.82e−04	22
4	2.68e−04	8.03e−04	1.24e−03	5.94e−04	33
5	2.50e−04	8.26e−04	1.20e−03	5.38e−04	46
3,3,4,3	7.25e−05	3.06e−04	2.86e−04	1.76e−04	

Table 3. Mean and minimal Loss of GRU nets for FFOS data

HU	Train.	Val.	Test1	Test2	P.no.
1	5.00e−04	2.11e−03	3.29e−03	1.25e−03	14
2	6.05e−05	1.32e−04	2.06e−04	2.34e−04	33
3	2.35e−05	1.29e−04	2.06e−04	1.53e−04	58
4	1.07e−05	1.30e−04	2.56e−04	1.65e−04	89
5	6.11e−06	9.90e−05	1.92e−04	1.53e−04	126
5,4,2,4	9.92e−07	2.22e−05	9.26e−06	1.88e−05	

Table 4. Mean and minimal Loss of LSTM nets for FFOS data

HU	Train.	Val.	Test1	Test2	P.no.
1	5.71e−04	3.19e−03	3.65e+04	5.25e+00	18
2	1.64e−04	5.62e−04	6.66e−04	5.40e−04	43
3	8.85e−05	4.56e−04	8.58e−04	1.47e−01	76
4	6.55e−05	4.23e−04	6.68e−04	5.54e−04	117
5	4.58e−05	8.80e−04	2.99e−03	1.40e−02	166
4,5,2,4	1.73e−06	1.04e−04	6.27e−05	6.86e−05	

Table 5. Mean and minimal Loss of Elman RNN for FSOS data

HU	Train.	Val.	Test1	Test2
1	1.92e−02	1.72e−02	6.83e−03	3.04e−02
2	5.02e−03	4.38e−03	2.50e−02	2.92e−02
3	1.27e−03	1.51e−03	1.63e−03	3.35e−03
4	6.30e−04	7.62e−04	9.79e−04	1.92e−03
5	3.97e−04	4.31e−04	4.02e−04	2.13e−03
4,5,2,3	7.54e−05	1.01e−04	4.97e−05	1.95e−04

Table 6. Mean and minimal Loss of GRU nets for FSOS data

HU	Train.	Val.	Test1	Test2
1	1.40e−02	1.73e+04	3.73e+04	2.29e+00
2	5.19e−04	4.42e−03	2.80e−03	3.20e−03
3	2.04e−04	2.70e−04	4.75e−04	1.82e−03
4	3.60e−05	7.90e−05	2.37e−04	5.05e−04
5	2.93e−05	8.51e−05	5.55e−04	1.48e−03
4,5,5,4	3.20e−06	4.60e−06	2.56e−06	3.25e−05

Table 7. Mean and minimal Loss of LSTM nets for FSOS data

HU	Train.	Val.	Test1	Test2
1	1.04e−02	4.66e−02	4.70e−02	1.34e−01
2	1.76e−03	3.31e−02	9.16e−03	1.28e−02
3	2.70e−04	1.04e−03	1.98e−03	2.21e−02
4	6.48e−05	7.32e−04	2.42e−03	5.13e−03
5	5.05e−05	1.07e−04	4.78e−04	2.70e−03
5,4,2,3	3.30e−05	7.21e−05	2.34e−05	9.12e−05

Table 8. Mean and minimal Loss of Elman RNN for Reactor data

HU	Train.	Val.	Test1	Test2
1	1.95e−02	6.75e−03	1.51e−03	1.67e−03
2	7.08e−03	2.84e−03	9.73e−04	1.06e−03
3	6.61e−03	7.00e−03	7.42e−03	3.27e−02
4	4.65e−03	1.69e−03	4.90e−04	5.44e−04
5	4.81e−03	2.88e−03	2.03e−03	2.04e−03
3,4,5,3	9.34e−04	3.62e−04	2.08e−05	4.95e−05

Table 9. Mean and minimal Loss of GRU nets for Reactor data

HU	Train.	Val.	Test1	Test2
1	9.87e−03	3.29e−03	7.53e−04	8.35e−04
2	6.77e−03	2.23e−03	5.83e−04	6.32e−04
3	5.38e−03	1.74e−03	5.49e−04	5.76e−04
4	4.75e−03	1.48e−03	4.50e−04	4.73e−04
5	3.89e−03	1.28e−03	4.69e−04	4.94e−04
3,3,2,4	4.18e−04	1.36e−04	4.73e−06	2.23e−05

Table 10. Mean and minimal Loss of LSTM nets for Reactor data

HU	Train.	Val.	Test1	Test2
1	1.75e−02	6.01e−03	1.31e−03	1.44e−03
2	6.26e−03	2.23e−03	6.02e−04	6.82e−04
3	5.26e−03	1.81e−03	5.78e−04	6.19e−04
4	6.26e−03	2.09e−03	6.24e−04	6.74e−04
5	4.50e−03	1.52e−03	5.51e−04	5.87e−04
5,5,3,3	6.32e−04	1.96e−04	7.29e−06	3.93e−05

Table 11. Mean and minimal Loss of Elman RNN for Nonlinear model data

HU	Train.	Val.	Test1	Test2
1	1.09e−01	1.21e−01	3.75e+00	3.20e+00
2	6.40e−02	4.02e+00	3.16e+00	2.56e+00
3	5.22e−02	7.33e−01	2.92e+00	3.83e+00
4	4.71e−02	5.47e−01	2.07e+00	3.47e+00
5	4.00e−02	4.56e−01	2.14e+00	2.96e+00
4,2,3,5	8.73e−03	3.26e−02	6.17e−01	7.31e−01

Table 12. Mean and minimal Loss of GRU nets for Nonlinear model data

Hidden	Train.	Val.	Test1	Test2
1	6.90e−02	1.84e+00	3.21e+01	1.37e+01
2	1.43e−02	9.23e−01	2.87e+00	5.98e+00
3	1.00e−02	3.62e−01	3.60e+00	5.06e+00
4	4.85e−03	2.03e−01	4.70e+00	5.75e+00
5	3.54e−02	2.76e−01	6.11e+00	7.51e+00
5,4,2,2	5.86e−04	1.56e−02	2.57e−01	3.91e−01

Table 13. Mean and minimal Loss of LSTM nets for Nonlinear model data

Hidden	Train.	Val.	Test1	Test2
1	5.63e−02	5.36e+04	2.68e+04	9.36e+03
2	3.14e−02	1.24e+00	3.26e+00	4.43e+00
3	1.69e−02	6.75e−01	4.20e+00	4.74e+00
4	1.25e−02	3.11e−01	3.10e+00	3.75e+00
5	1.11e−02	6.24e−01	5.22e+00	5.87e+00
3,2,3,2	1.12e−03	3.31e−02	1.95e−01	4.31e−01

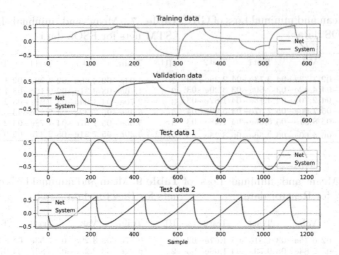

Fig. 5. The best approximation for the FFOS Testing2 data @ GRU net with 4 hidden units.

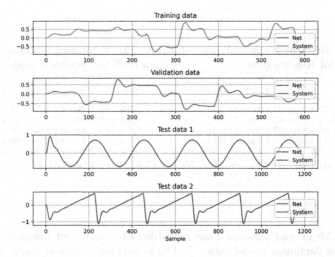

Fig. 6. The best approximation for the FSOS Testing2 data @ GRU net with 4 hidden units.

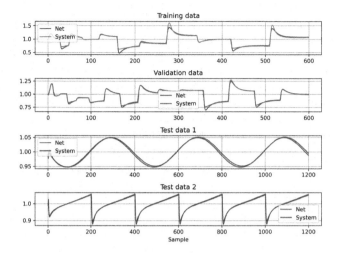

Fig. 7. The best approximation for the nuclear reactor Testing2 data @ GRU net with 4 hidden units.

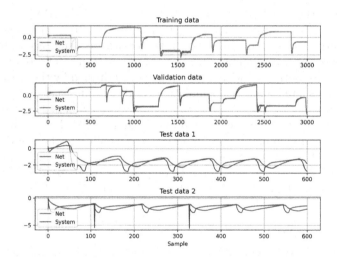

Fig. 8. The best approximation for the Nonlinear model Testing2 data @ GRU net with 2 hidden units.

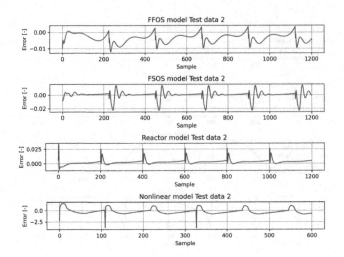

Fig. 9. Residual error plot for the best fitted networks based on Test2 data

5   Conclusions

In this paper, the capabilities of recurrent neural networks (RNN) were examined as the fractional-order dynamic systems approximators. Their effectiveness in that approach was validated based on the linear, first and second fractional-order systems and two nonlinear fractional-order systems. The RNN networks parameters were optimised with the least squares criterion by the L-BFGS algorithm. The presented numerical simulation results, in most cases, showed satisfactory approximation performance and reliability of examined recurrent artificial neural networks structures: Elman, GRU and LSTM. Especially the GRU network showed its potential in its practical applicability in the real digital control platform. The advantages are high accuracy with a relatively small network structure and a relatively low number of parameters to be determined. The presented methodology with additional extensions may be used to cover approximations of fractional-order operators occurring in the control algorithms which are planned for implementation in the digital control platforms such as FPGA, DSP or PLC controllers.

During the study, a typical phenomenon associated with neural network over fitting was observed. The more complicated the neural network is, the lower the average loss for training data is observed. This relationship is visible for each neural net structure involved and for each dynamic system studied. In the case of conducted research, the phenomenon of over fitting is reflected especially in the loss function values for two approximated models, i.e. a nuclear reactor model and a complex non-linear model.

In the case of recurrent neural networks, this problem can be addressed by focusing on the analysis of signals processed by neural network structures and, in particular, on the analysis of the effectiveness of the utilisation and impact of historical samples of processed signals stored within the network on the network output. A second element that can reduce the over fitting problem in this type of networks would be to develop training signals that allow to recognise both the dynamics of the fractional order and the nonlinearities present in the dynamic system under consideration. The problems mentioned here represent a very interesting extension of the research presented in the article, which the authors would like to focus on in the future.

The second open research path related to the presented work focuses on the problem of modification of existing structures and, in general, the development of new recursive structures. These will be able to approximate objects with fractional dynamics to a suitable degree. The authors also plan to address this direction of research in the future.

References

1. http://pytorch.org/, 05 April 2020
2. http://www.python.org/, 05 April 2020
3. Cho, K., et al.: Learning phrase representations using RNN encoder-decoder for statistical machine translation. arXiv preprint arXiv:1406.1078 (2014)
4. Elman, J.L.: Finding structure in time. Cogn. Sci. **14**(2), 179–211 (1990)
5. Espinosa-Paredes, G., Polo-Labarrios, M.A., Espinosa-Martínez, E.G., del Valle-Gallegos, E.: Fractional neutron point kinetics equations for nuclear reactor dynamics. Ann. Nucl. Energy **38**(2), 307–330 (2011)
6. Goodfellow, I., Bengio, Y., Courville, A.: Deep Learning. MIT Press, Cambridge (2016)
7. Haykin, S.S., et al.: Neural Networks and Learning Machines. Prentice Hall, New York (2009)
8. Hochreiter, S., Schmidhuber, J.: Long short-term memory. Neural Comput. **9**(8), 1735–1780 (1997)
9. Jafarian, A., Mokhtarpour, M., Baleanu, D.: Artificial neural network approach for a class of fractional ordinary differential equation. Neural Comput. Appl. **28**(4), 765–773 (2016). https://doi.org/10.1007/s00521-015-2104-8
10. Kaslik, E., Rădulescu, I.R.: Dynamics of complex-valued fractional-order neural networks. Neural Netw. **89**, 39–49 (2017)
11. Liu, D.C., Nocedal, J.: On the limited memory BFGS method for large scale optimization. Math. Program. **45**(1–3), 503–528 (1989). https://doi.org/10.1007/BF01589116
12. Lo, J.: Dynamical system identification by recurrent multilayer perceptron. In: Proceedings of the 1993 World Congress on Neural Networks (1993)
13. Machado, J.T., Kiryakova, V., Mainardi, F.: Recent history of fractional calculus. Commun. Nonlinear Sci. Numer. Simul. **16**(3), 1140–1153 (2011)
14. Nowak, T.K., Duzinkiewicz, K., Piotrowski, R.: Fractional neutron point kinetics equations for nuclear reactor dynamics - numerical solution investigations. Ann. Nucl. Energy **73**, 317–329 (2014)
15. Puchalski, B., Rutkowski, T.A., Duzinkiewicz, K.: Multi-nodal PWR reactor model - methodology proposition for power distribution coefficients calculation. In: 2016 21st International Conference on Methods and Models in Automation and Robotics (MMAR), pp. 385–390, August 2016. https://doi.org/10.1109/MMAR.2016.7575166

16. Puchalski, B., Rutkowski, T.A., Duzinkiewicz, K.: Nodal models of pressurized water reactor core for control purposes - a comparison study. Nucl. Eng. Des. **322**, 444–463 (2017)

17. Puchalski, B., Rutkowski, T.A., Duzinkiewicz, K.: Fuzzy multi-regional fractional PID controller for pressurized water nuclear reactor. ISA Trans. (2020). https://doi.org/10.1016/j.isatra.2020.04.003, http://www.sciencedirect.com/science/article/pii/S0019057820301567

18. Vyawahare, V.A., Espinosa-Paredes, G., Datkhile, G., Kadam, P.: Artificial neural network approximations of linear fractional neutron models. Ann. Nucl. Energy **113**, 75–88 (2018)

19. Xue, D.: Fractional-Order Control Systems: Fundamentals and Numerical Implementations, vol. 1. Walter de Gruyter GmbH & Co KG, Berlin (2017)

20. Zúñiga-Aguilar, C.J., Coronel-Escamilla, A., Gómez-Aguilar, J.F., Alvarado-Martínez, V.M., Romero-Ugalde, H.M.: New numerical approximation for solving fractional delay differential equations of variable order using artificial neural networks. Eur. Phys. J. Plus **133**(2), 1–16 (2018). https://doi.org/10.1140/epjp/i2018-11917-0

A Layer-Wise Information Reinforcement Approach to Improve Learning in Deep Belief Networks

Mateus Roder$^{(\boxtimes)}$ (iD), Leandro A. Passos (iD), Luiz Carlos Felix Ribeiro (iD),
Clayton Pereira (iD), and João Paulo Papa (iD)

São Paulo State University - UNESP, Bauru, Brazil
{mateus.roder,leandro.passos,luiz.felix,clayton.pereira,
joao.papa}@unesp.br
https://www.fc.unesp.br/

Abstract. With the advent of deep learning, the number of works proposing new methods or improving existent ones has grown exponentially in the last years. In this scenario, "very deep" models were emerging, once they were expected to extract more intrinsic and abstract features while supporting a better performance. However, such models suffer from the gradient vanishing problem, i.e., backpropagation values become too close to zero in their shallower layers, ultimately causing learning to stagnate. Such an issue was overcome in the context of convolution neural networks by creating "shortcut connections" between layers, in a so-called deep residual learning framework. Nonetheless, a very popular deep learning technique called Deep Belief Network still suffers from gradient vanishing when dealing with discriminative tasks. Therefore, this paper proposes the Residual Deep Belief Network, which considers the information reinforcement layer-by-layer to improve the feature extraction and knowledge retaining, that support better discriminative performance. Experiments conducted over three public datasets demonstrate its robustness concerning the task of binary image classification.

Keywords: Deep Belief Networks · Residual networks · Restricted Boltzmann Machines

1 Introduction

Machine learning-based approaches have been massively studied and applied to daily tasks in the last decades, mostly due to the remarkable accomplishments achieved by deep learning models. Despite the success attained by these techniques, they still suffer from a well-known drawback regarding the backpropagation-based learning procedure: the vanishing gradient. This kind of problem becomes more prominent on deeper models since the gradient vanishes and is not propagated adequately to former layers, thus, preventing a proper parameter update.

© Springer Nature Switzerland AG 2020
L. Rutkowski et al. (Eds.): ICAISC 2020, LNAI 12415, pp. 231–241, 2020.
https://doi.org/10.1007/978-3-030-61401-0_22

To tackle such an issue, He et al. [4] proposed the ResNet, a framework where the layers learn residual functions concerning the layer inputs, instead of learning unreferenced functions. In short, the idea is mapping a set of stacked layers to a residual map, which comprises a combination of the set input and output and then mapping it back to the desired underlying mapping.

The model achieved fast popularity, being applied in a wide range of applications, such as traffic surveillance [7], medicine [8,12], and action recognition [2], to cite a few. Moreover, many works proposed different approaches using the idea of residual functions. Lin et al. [11], for instance, proposed the RetinaNet, a pyramidal-shaped network that employs residual stages to deal with one-shot small object detection over unbalanced datasets. Meanwhile, Szegedy et al. [17] proposed the Inception-ResNet for object recognition. Later, Santos et al. [16] proposed the Cascade Residual Convolutional Neural Network for video segmentation.

In the context of deep neural networks, there exist another class of methods that are composed of Restricted Boltzmann Machines (RBMs) [6], a stochastic approach represented by a bipartite graph whose training is given by the minimization of the energy between a visible and a latent layer. Among these methods, Deep Belief Networks (DBNs) [5] and Deep Boltzmann Machines [13,15] achieved a considerable popularity in the last years due the satisfactory results over a wide variety of applications [3,14,18].

However, as far as we are concerned, no work addressed the concept of reinforcing the feature extraction over those models in a layer-by-layer fashion. Therefore, the main contributions of this paper are twofold: (i) to propose the Residual Deep Belief Network (Res-DBN), a novel approach that combines each layer input and output to reinforce the information conveyed through it, and (ii) to support the literature concerning both DBNs and residual-based models.

The remainder of this paper is presented as follows: Sect. 2 introduces the main concepts regarding RBMs and DBNs, while Sect. 3 proposes the Residual Deep Belief Network. Further, Sect. 4 describes the methodology and datasets employed in this work. Finally, Sects. 5 and 6 provide the experimental results and conclusions, respectively.

2   Theoretical Background

This section introduces a brief theoretical background regarding Restricted Boltzmann Machines and Deep Belief Networks.

2.1   Restricted Boltzmann Machines

Restricted Boltzmann Machine stands for a stochastic physics-inspired computational model capable of learning data distribution intrinsic patterns. The process is represented as a bipartite graph where the data composes a visible input-like layer v, and a latent n-dimensional vector h, composed of a set of hidden neurons whose the model tries to map such inputs onto. The model's training procedure dwells on the minimization of the system's energy, given as follows:

$$E(\boldsymbol{v}, \boldsymbol{h}) = -\sum_{i=1}^{m} b_i v_i - \sum_{j=1}^{n} c_j h_j - \sum_{i=1}^{m}\sum_{j=1}^{n} w_{ij} v_i h_j, \tag{1}$$

where m and n stand for the dimensions of the visible and hidden layers, respectively, while b and c denote their respective bias vectors, further, $\mathbf{W}$ corresponds to the weight matrix connecting both layers, in which w_{ij} stands for the connection between visible unit i and the j hidden one. Notice the model is restricted, thus implying no connection is allowed among the same layer neurons.

Ideally, the model was supposed to be solved by computing the joint probability of the visible and hidden neurons in an analytic fashion. However, such an approach is intractable since it requires the partition function calculation, i.e., computing every possible configuration of the system. Therefore, Hinton proposed the Contrastive Divergence (CD) [6], an alternative method to estimate the conditional probabilities of the visible and hidden neurons using Gibbs sampling over a Monte Carlo Markov Chain (MCMC). Hence, the probabilities of both input and hidden units are computed as follows:

$$p(h_j = 1 | \boldsymbol{v}) = \sigma \left(c_j + \sum_{i=1}^{m} w_{ij} v_i \right), \tag{2}$$

and

$$p(v_i = 1 | \boldsymbol{h}) = \sigma \left(b_i + \sum_{j=1}^{n} w_{ij} h_j \right), \tag{3}$$

where σ stands for the logistic-sigmoid function.

2.2 Deep Belief Networks

Conceptually, Deep Belief Networks are graph-based generative models composed of a visible and a set of hidden layers connected by weight matrices, with no connection between neurons in the same layer. In practice, the model comprises a set of stacked RBMs whose hidden layers greedily feeds the subsequent RBM visible layer. Finally, a softmax layer is attached at the top of the model, and the weights are fine-tuned using backpropagation for classification purposes. Figure 1 depicts the model. Notice that $\mathbf{W}^{(l)}$, $l \in [1, L]$, stands for the weight matrix at layer l, where L denotes the number of hidden layers. Moreover, $\boldsymbol{v}$ stands for the visible layer, as well as $\boldsymbol{h}^{(l)}$ represents the lth hidden layer.

3 Information Reinforcement in DBNs

In this section, we present the proposed approach concerning the residual reinforcement layer-by-layer in Deep Belief Networks, from now on called Res-DBN. Since such a network is a hybrid model between sigmoid belief networks and binary RBMs [5], it is important to highlight some "tricks" to make use of the information provided layer-by-layer.

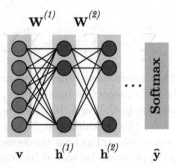

Fig. 1. DBN architecture with two hidden layers for classification purposes.

As aforementioned, DBNs can be viewed as hybrid networks that model the data's prior distribution in a layer-by-layer fashion to improve the lower bound from model distribution. Such a fact motivated us to make use of the information learned in each stack of RBM for reinforcement since the greedy-layer pre-training uses the activation of latent binary variables as the input of the next visible layer. Generally speaking, such activation is defined by Eq. 2, and its pre-activation vector, $a^{(l)}$, as follows:

$$a_j^{(l)} = c_j^{(l)} + \sum_{i=1}^{m} w_{ij}^{(l)} x_i^{(l-1)}, \tag{4}$$

where, $c_j^{(l)}$ stands for the bias from hidden layer l, m is the number of units present on the previous layer, $w_{ij}^{(l)}$ represents the weight matrix for layer l, and $x_i^{(l-1)}$ stands for the input data from layer $l-1$, where $x_i^0 = v_i$.

Therefore, it is possible to use the "reinforcement pre-activation" vector, denoted as $\hat{a}^{(l)}$, from layer l, $\forall\, l > 1$. Since the standard RBM output of post-activation (provided by Eq. 2) is in $[0, 1]$ interval, it is necessary to limit the reinforcement term of the proposed approach as follows:

$$\hat{a}^{(l)} = \frac{\delta(a^{(l-1)})}{max\{\delta(a_j^{(l-1)})\}}, \tag{5}$$

where, δ stands for the Rectifier[1] function, while max returns the maximum value from the δ output vector for normalization purposes. Then, the new input data and the information aggregation for layer l is defined by adding the values obtained from Eq. 5 to the post-activation, i.e., applying $\sigma(a^{(l-1)})$, as follows:

$$x_i^{(l-1)} = \sigma(a_j^{(l-1)}) + \hat{a}_j^{(l)}, \tag{6}$$

where $x_i^{(l-1)}$ stands for the new input data to layer l, $\forall\, l > 1$, and its normalized and vectorized form can be obtained as follows:

---

[1] $\delta(z) = max(0, z)$.

$$\boldsymbol{x}^{(l-1)} = \frac{\boldsymbol{x}^{(l-1)}}{max\{x_i^{(l-1)}\}}. \qquad (7)$$

It is important to highlight that, in Eq. 5, we only use the positive pre-activations to retrieve and propagate the signal that is meaningful for neurons excitation, i.e., values greater than 0, which generates a probability of more than 50% after applying sigmoid activation.

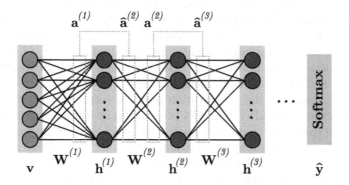

Fig. 2. Res-DBN architecture with 3 hidden layers.

The Fig. 2 depicts the Res-DBN architecture, with hidden layers connected by the weights $\mathbf{W}^{(l)}$. The dashed connections stand for the reinforcement approach, with the information aggregation occuring as covered by the Eqs. 4 to 7, from a generic hidden layer to the next one ($\boldsymbol{h}^{(1)} \rightarrow \boldsymbol{h}^{(2)}$, for instance).

4 Methodology

In this section, we present details regarding the datasets employed in our experiments, as well as the experimental setup applied for this paper.

4.1 Datasets

Three well-known image datasets were employed throughout the experiments:

- MNIST[2] [10]: set of 28×28 binary images of handwritten digits (0–9), i.e., 10 classes. The original version contains a training set with 60, 000 images from digits '0'–'9', as well as a test set with 10, 000 images.
- Fashion-MNIST[3] [20]: set of 28×28 binary images of clothing objects. The original version contains a training set with 60, 000 images from 10 distinct objects (t-shirt, trouser, pullover, dress, coat, sandal, shirt, sneaker, bag, and ankle boot), and a test set with 10, 000 images.

---

[2] http://yann.lecun.com/exdb/mnist.
[3] https://github.com/zalandoresearch/fashion-mnist.

- Kuzushiji-MNIST[4] [1]: set of 28×28 binary images of hiragana characters. The original version contains a training set with $60,000$ images from 10 previously selected hiragana characters, and a test set with $10,000$ images.

4.2 Experimental Setup

Concerning the experiments, we employed the concepts mentioned in Sect. 3, considering two main phases: (i) the DBN pre-training and (ii) the discriminative fine-tuning. Regarding the former, it is important to highlight that the information reinforcement is performed during the greedy layer-wise process, in which the hidden layers ($l = 1, 2, \ldots, L$) receive the positive "residual" information. Such a process takes into account a mini-batch of size 128, a learning rate of 0.1, 50 epochs for the bottommost RBM convergence, and 25 epochs for the intermediate and top layers convergence.[5]

Moreover, regarding the classification phase, a softmax layer was attached at the top of the model after the DBN pre-training, performing the fine-tuning process for 20 epochs through backpropagation using the well-known ADAM [9] optimizer. The process employed a learning rate of 10^{-3} for all layers. Furthermore, it was performed 15 independent executions for each model to provide statistical analysis. To assess the robustness of the proposed approach, we employed seven different DBN architectures changing the number of hidden neurons and layers, as denoted in Table 1.

Table 1. Different setups, where i stands for the number of neurons on the input layer.

Model	Res-DBN	DBN
(a)	i:500:500:10	i:500:500:10
(b)	i:500:500:500:10	i:500:500:500:10
(c)	i:500:500:500:500:10	i:500:500:500:500:10
(d)	i:1000:1000:10	i:1000:1000:10
(e)	i:1000:1000:1000:10	i:1000:1000:1000:10
(f)	i:1000:1000:1000:1000:10	i:1000:1000:1000:1000:10
(g)	i:2000:2000:2000:2000:10	i:2000:2000:2000:2000:10

5 Experiments

In this Section, we present the experimental results concerning seven distinct DBN architectures, i.e., (a), (b), (c), (d), (e), (f) and (g), over the aforementioned datasets. Table 2 provides the average accuracies and standard deviations

---

[4] https://github.com/rois-codh/kmnist.
[5] Such a value is half of the initial one to evaluate Res-DBN earlier convergence.

for each configuration on 15 trials, where the proposed approach is compared against the standard DBN formulation in each dataset for each configuration. Further, results in bold represent the best values according to the statistical Wilcoxon signed-rank test [19] with significance $p \leq 0.05$ concerning each model configuration. On the other hand, underlined values represent the best results overall models regarding each dataset, without a statistical difference, i.e., results similar to the best one achieved.

Table 2. Experimental results on different datasets.

Experiment	MNIST		Fashion MNIST		Kuzushiji MNIST	
	Res-DBN	DBN	Res-DBN	DBN	Res-DBN	DBN
(a)	**97.39 ± 0.08**	97.23 ± 0.09	81.13 ± 0.33	**81.52 ± 0.27**	**86.49 ± 0.18**	84.78 ± 0.29
(b)	**97.61 ± 0.07**	97.44 ± 0.11	81.49 ± 0.50	81.41 ± 0.57	**87.75 ± 0.20**	85.81 ± 0.18
(c)	97.59 ± 0.10	97.57 ± 0.09	81.66 ± 0.33	81.51 ± 0.60	**88.21 ± 0.18**	86.97 ± 0.30
(d)	**97.66 ± 0.10**	97.40 ± 0.10	81.55 ± 0.35	81.15 ± 0.64	**87.67 ± 0.19**	86.24 ± 0.21
(e)	**97.85 ± 0.06**	97.48 ± 0.12	**82.05 ± 0.48**	81.59 ± 0.51	**88.95 ± 0.16**	87.57 ± 0.20
(f)	<u>97.80 ± 0.37</u>	97.68 ± 0.29	82.16 ± 0.50	82.19 ± 0.46	**89.63 ± 0.23**	88.81 ± 0.40
(g)	**97.88 ± 0.19**	97.51 ± 0.30	<u>82.73 ± 0.53</u>	82.63 ± 0.36	<u>89.45 ± 0.78</u>	88.70 ± 0.60

Regarding the original MNIST dataset, the preeminence of the proposed model over the standard version of the RBM is evident, since the best results were obtained exclusively by Res-DBN and, from these, five out of seven scenarios presented statistical significance. Such a behavior is stressed in the Kuzushiji MNIST dataset, where the best results were obtained solely by the Res-DBN over every possible configuration. The results' similarity between these datasets is somehow expected since both are composed of handwritten digits or letters.

The Fashion MNIST dataset presents the single experimental scenario, i.e., model (a), where the proposed model was outperformed by the traditional DBN, although by a small margin. In all other cases Res-DBN presented results superior or equal to the traditional formulation, which favors the Res-DBN use over the DBNs.

Finally, one can observe the best results overall were obtained using a more complex model, i.e., with a higher number of layers and neurons, as denoted by the underlined values. Additionally, the proposed model outperformed or at least is equivalent, to the standard DBN in virtually all scenarios, except one concerning the Fashion-MNIST dataset.

5.1 Training Evaluation

Figures 3, 4, and 5 depict the models' learning curves over the test sets regarding MNIST, Fashion MNIST, and Kuzushiji MNIST, respectively. In Fig. 3, one can observe that Res-DBN(e) converged faster than the remaining approaches, obtained reasonably good results after seven iterations. At the end of the process,

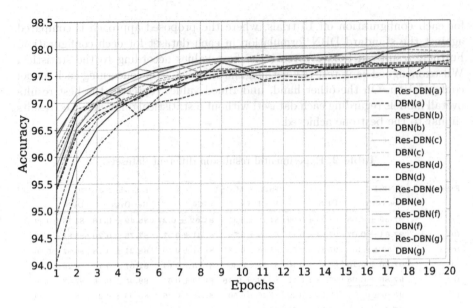

Fig. 3. Accuracy on MNIST test set.

Res-DBN(f) and (g) boosted and outperformed Res-DBN(e), as well as any of standard DBN approaches, depicted as dashed lines.

Regarding Fashion MNIST, it can be observed in Fig. 4 that Res-DBN(e) was once again the fastest technique to converge, obtaining acceptable results after five iterations. However, after iteration number five, all models seem to overfit, explaining the performance decrease observed over the testing samples. Finally, after 14 iterations, the results start increasing once again, being Res-DBN(g) the most accurate technique after 20 iterations.

Finally, the Kuzushiji learning curve, depicted in Fig. 5, displays a behavior silimiar to the MNIST dataset. Moreover, it shows that Res-DBN provided better results than its traditional variant in all cases right from the beginning of the training. In some cases with a margin greater than 2%, showing a promising improvement.

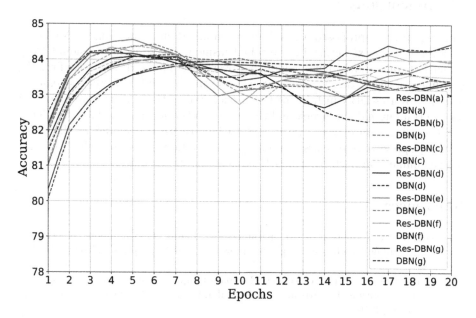

Fig. 4. Accuracy on Fashion MNIST test set.

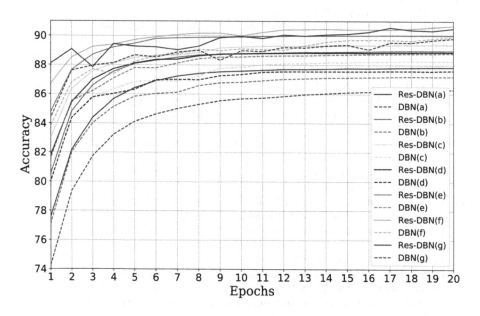

Fig. 5. Accuracy on Kuzushiji MNIST test set.

6　Conclusions

In this paper, we proposed a novel approach based on reinforcing DBN's layer-by-layer feature extraction in a residual fashion, the so-called Residual Deep Belief Network. Experiments conducted over three public datasets confirm the sturdiness of the model. Moreover, it is important to highlight faster convergence achieved by Res-DBN in front of DBN, once half of the epochs were employed for pre-training hidden layers, and the results outperformed the latter model.

Regarding future work, we intend to investigate the model in the video domain, applying it to classification and recognition tasks, as well as to propose a similar approach regarding Deep Boltzmann Machines.

References

1. Clanuwat, T., Bober-Irizar, M., Kitamoto, A., Lamb, A., Yamamoto, K., Ha, D.: Deep learning for classical Japanese literature. arXiv preprint arXiv:1812.01718 (2018)
2. Feichtenhofer, C., Pinz, A., Wildes, R.: Spatiotemporal residual networks for video action recognition. In: Advances in Neural Information Processing Systems, pp. 3468–3476 (2016)
3. Hassan, M.M., Alam, M.G.R., Uddin, M.Z., Huda, S., Almogren, A., Fortino, G.: Human emotion recognition using deep belief network architecture. Inf. Fusion **51**, 10–18 (2019)
4. He, K., Zhang, X., Ren, S., Sun, J.: Deep residual learning for image recognition. In: IEEE CVPR, pp. 770–778 (2016)
5. Hinton, G.E., Osindero, S., Teh, Y.W.: A fast learning algorithm for deep belief nets. Neural Comput. **18**(7), 1527–1554 (2006)
6. Hinton, G.: Training products of experts by minimizing contrastive divergence. Neural Comput. **14**(8), 1771–1800 (2002)
7. Jung, H., Choi, M.K., Jung, J., Lee, J.H., Kwon, S., Young Jung, W.: ResNet-based vehicle classification and localization in traffic surveillance systems. In: Proceedings of the IEEE Conference on Computer Vision and Pattern Recognition Workshops, pp. 61–67 (2017)
8. Khojasteh, P.: Exudate detection in fundus images using deeply-learnable features. Comput. Biol. Med. **104**, 62–69 (2019)
9. Kingma, D.P., Ba, J.: Adam: a method for stochastic optimization. arXiv preprint arXiv:1412.6980 (2014)
10. LeCun, Y., Bottou, L., Bengio, Y., Haffner, P.: Gradient-based learning applied to document recognition. Proc. IEEE **86**(11), 2278–2324 (1998)
11. Lin, T.Y., Goyal, P., Girshick, R., He, K., Dollár, P.: Focal loss for dense object detection. In: Proceedings of the IEEE International Conference on Computer Vision, pp. 2980–2988 (2017)
12. Passos, L.A., et al.: Parkinson disease identification using residual networks and optimum-path forest. In: 2018 IEEE 12th International Symposium on Applied Computational Intelligence and Informatics (SACI), pp. 000325–000330. IEEE (2018)
13. Passos, L.A., Papa, J.P.: A metaheuristic-driven approach to fine-tune deep Boltzmann machines. Appl. Soft Comput. 105717 (2019)

14. Pereira, C.R., Passos, L.A., Lopes, R.R., Weber, S.A.T., Hook, C., Papa, J.P.: Parkinson's disease identification using restricted Boltzmann machines. In: Felsberg, M., Heyden, A., Krüger, N. (eds.) CAIP 2017. LNCS, vol. 10425, pp. 70–80. Springer, Cham (2017). https://doi.org/10.1007/978-3-319-64698-5_7

15. Salakhutdinov, R., Hinton, G.E.: Deep Boltzmann machines. In: AISTATS, vol. 1, p. 3 (2009)

16. Santos, D.F., Pires, R.G., Colombo, D., Papa, J.P.: Video segmentation learning using cascade residual convolutional neural network. In: 2019 32nd SIBGRAPI Conference on Graphics, Patterns and Images (SIBGRAPI), pp. 1–7. IEEE (2019)

17. Szegedy, C., Ioffe, S., Vanhoucke, V., Alemi, A.A.: Inception-v4, inception-ResNet and the impact of residual connections on learning. In: Thirty-First AAAI Conference on Artificial Intelligence (2017)

18. Wang, J., Wang, K., Wang, Y., Huang, Z., Xue, R.: Deep boltzmann machine based condition prediction for smart manufacturing. J. Ambient Intell. Humaniz. Comput. **10**(3), 851–861 (2019). https://doi.org/10.1007/s12652-018-0794-3

19. Wilcoxon, F.: Individual comparisons by ranking methods. Biom. Bull. **1**(6), 80–83 (1945)

20. Xiao, H., Rasul, K., Vollgraf, R.: Fashion-MNIST: a novel image dataset for benchmarking machine learning algorithms. arXiv preprint arXiv:1708.07747 (2017)

Intestinal Parasites Classification Using Deep Belief Networks

Mateus Roder[1](✉)(iD), Leandro A. Passos[1](iD), Luiz Carlos Felix Ribeiro[1](iD),
Barbara Caroline Benato[2](iD), Alexandre Xavier Falcão[2](iD),
and João Paulo Papa[1](iD)

[1] School of Sciences, São Paulo State University, Bauru, Brazil
{mateus.roder,leandro.passos,joao.papa}@unesp.br
[2] Institute of Computing, University of Campinas, Campinas, Brazil
barbara.benato@students.ic.unicamp.br, afalcao@unicamp.br

Abstract. Currently, approximately 4 billion people are infected by intestinal parasites worldwide. Diseases caused by such infections constitute a public health problem in most tropical countries, leading to physical and mental disorders, and even death to children and immunodeficient individuals. Although subjected to high error rates, human visual inspection is still in charge of the vast majority of clinical diagnoses. In the past years, some works addressed intelligent computer-aided intestinal parasites classification, but they usually suffer from misclassification due to similarities between parasites and fecal impurities. In this paper, we introduce Deep Belief Networks to the context of automatic intestinal parasites classification. Experiments conducted over three datasets composed of eggs, larvae, and protozoa provided promising results, even considering unbalanced classes and also fecal impurities.

Keywords: Intestinal parasites · Deep Belief Networks · Restricted Boltzmann Machines · Data augmentation

1 Introduction

Estimates reveal that around 4 billion people in the world are infected with some intestinal parasite [21]. The human intestinal parasitism is a public health problem, especially in tropical countries [9], in which such infections can lead children and immunodeficient adults to death. The detection and diagnosis of human intestinal parasitosis depend on the visual analysis of optical microscopy images obtained from fecal samples mostly. However, the manual analysis of those images is time-consuming and error-prone. In order to circumvent this problem, Suzuki et al. [19] proposed a fully automated enteroparasitosis diagnosis system via image analysis, which addressed the 15 most common species of protozoa and helminths in Brazil. The proposed approach is composed of three main steps: (i) image segmentation, (ii) object delineation, and its further (iii) classification.

© Springer Nature Switzerland AG 2020
L. Rutkowski et al. (Eds.): ICAISC 2020, LNAI 12415, pp. 242–251, 2020.
https://doi.org/10.1007/978-3-030-61401-0_23

Previous works have also investigated protozoa and helminth parasites classification. Suzuki et al. [20], for instance, introduced the Optimum Path Forest [10,11] classifier for such a task, with results that outperformed Support Vector Machines and Artificial Neural Networks. Later on, Peixinho et al. [14] explored Convolutional Neural Networks (CNNs) in this context. Further, Peixinho et al. [13] proposed generating synthetic samples to increase the number of images for under-represented classes by adding points onto a 2D projection space. Furthermore, Benato et al. [1] investigated an approach to cope with the lack of supervised data by interactively propagating labels to reduce the user effort in data annotation. Finally, Castelo et al. [3] used bag of visual words to extract key points from superpixel-segmented images and further build a visual dictionary to automatic classify intestinal parasites.

Apart from the techniques mentioned earlier, Restricted Boltzmann Machines (RBMs) [17] obtained notorious attention due to their promising results in a wide variety of tasks such as data reconstruction [12], exudate identification in retinal images [7], and collaborative filtering [16], to cite a few. Moreover, RBMs can be used as the building block for more complex and deep models such as Deep Belief Networks (DBNs) [6] and Deep Boltzmann Machines (DBMs) [15].

However, as far as we are concerned, no work has employed RBM-based models in the task of intestinal parasite classification to date. Therefore, the main contributions of this work are threefold: (i) to propose an effective method for parasite classification using RBMs and DBNs; (ii) to evaluate the ability of Restricted Boltzmann Machines ability for data augmentation; and (iii) to foster the scientific literature concerning both RBM-based applications and intestinal parasites identification.

The remainder of this paper is organized as follows: Sect. 2 introduces the theoretical background concerning RBMs and DBNs, while Sects. 3 and 4 present the methodology and the experimental results, respectively. Finally, Sect. 5 states conclusions and future works.

2   Theoretical Background

In this section, we provide a brief description of the main concepts regarding RBM and DBN formulations, as well as their discriminative variant to deal with classification problems.

2.1   Restricted Boltzmann Machines

Restricted Boltzmann Machines stand for energy-based neural networks that can learn the probability distribution over a set of input vectors. Such models are named after the Boltzmann distribution, a measurement that uses the system's energy to obtain the probability of a given state. Energy-based models are inspired by physics since they assign a scalar energy value for each variable configuration, thus learning by adjusting their parameters to minimize the energy of the system. Moreover, they are modeled as a bipartite graph, i.e., there are no connections between units from the same layer. Such a technique assumes binary-valued nodes, although there are extensions to real- and even complex-valued inputs [8,18].

Given an initial configuration (v, h), the energy of the system can be computed as follows:

$$E(v, h) = -\sum_{i=1}^{m} b_i v_i - \sum_{j=1}^{n} c_j h_j - \sum_{i=1}^{m} \sum_{j=1}^{n} W_{ij} v_i h_j, \tag{1}$$

where $v \in \Re^m$ and $h \in \Re^n$ stand for the visible and hidden layers, respectively, and $b \in \Re^m$ and $c \in \Re^n$ denote their bias vectors. Additionally, $W_{m \times n}$ corresponds to the weight matrix concerning the connections between layers v and h.

The learning procedure aims at finding W, a, and b in such a way Eq. 1 is minimized. However, calculating the joint probability of the model is intractable since it requires computing every possible initial configuration. Moreover, one can estimate the conditional probabilities using alternated iterations over a Monte Carlo Markov Chain (MCMC) approach, where the probabilities of both input and hidden units can be computed as follows:

$$p(h_j = 1|v) = \sigma \left(c_j + \sum_{i=1}^{m} W_{ij} v_i \right), \tag{2}$$

and

$$p(v_i = 1|h) = \sigma \left(b_i + \sum_{j=1}^{n} W_{ij} h_j \right), \tag{3}$$

where σ stands for the logistic-sigmoid function. Since the visible and hidden units are conditionally independent, one can train the network using the MCMC algorithm with Gibbs sampling through Contrastive Divergence (CD) [5].

2.2 Deep Belief Networks

Restricted Boltzmann Machines can also be employed to compose more complex models. They are commonly used as building blocks to generate the so-called Deep Belief Networks [6], which are composed of a visible and a set of L hidden layers. In this model, each layer is connected to the next through a weight matrix $W^{(l)}$, $l \in [1, L]$. In short, DBNs consider each set of two subsequent layers as an RBM trained in a greedy fashion, where the hidden layer of the bottommost RBM feeds the next RBM's visible layer. For classification purposes, a Softmax layer is appended to the model. Afterwards, the model is fine-tuned using the backpropagation algorithm, as depicted in Fig. 1. Notice that $\mathbf{h}^{(l)}$ stand for the l-th hidden layer.

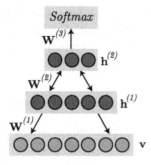

Fig. 1. DBN architecture with two hidden layers for classification purposes.

3 Methodology

In this section, we introduce the dataset employed in this work, as well as the technical details concerning the experimental setup.

3.1 Dataset

The experiments consider datasets from human intestinal parasites divided into three groups: (i) **Helminth eggs** (i.e., Eggs) with $12,691$ images, (ii) **Helminth larvae** (i.e., Larvae) with $1,598$ images, and (iii) **Protozoan cysts** (i.e., Protozoa) with $37,372$ images. Notice that all datasets contain fecal impurities, which is a diverse class that looks alike to some parasites. Each dataset comprises the following categories and their respective label in parenthesis:

- **Helminth eggs**: *H.nana* (1), *H.diminuta* (2), *Ancilostomideo* (3), *E.vermicularis* (4), *A.lumbricoides* (5), *T.trichiura* (6), *S.mansoni* (7), *Taenia* (8), and impurities (9).
- **Helminth larvae**: larvae (1) and impurities (2); and
- **Protozoan cysts**: *E.coli* (1), *E.histolytica* (2), *E.nana* (3), *Giardia* (4), *I.butschlii* (5), *B.hominis* (6), and impurities (7).

These are the most common species of human intestinal parasites in Brazil, and they are also responsible for public health problems in most tropical countries [19]. Notice that all datasets are unbalanced with considerably more impurity samples. The objects of interest were first segmented from the background, converted to grayscale, and further resized to 50×50 pixels. Table 2(a) presents the distribution of samples per class.

3.2 Data Augmentation

In this paper, we proposed two different synthetic data generation approaches to overcome the class imbalance problem: (i) an Autoencoder (AE) and (ii) an additional RBM for image reconstruction purposes. In all cases, the models were trained with examples of the class to be oversampled only. Further, to allow a fair comparison, both the RBM and the AE contain similar architectures. Table 1 presents the hyperparameters employed while training the models for data augmentation.

Table 1. Hyper-parameter setting up.

Model	Hyper-parameter	Search interval	Best value
AE	η	$[10^{-5}, 10^{-2}]$	10^{-3}
	p_{drop}	$[0, 0.4]$	0.2
	Hidden dim	$\{250, 500, 2000\}$	500
	Batch size	$\{16, 32, 128\}$	32
RBM	η	$[10^{-5}, 10^{-2}]$	10^{-4}
	Hidden dim	$\{500, 2000\}$	500
	Batch size	$\{4, 8, 16\}$	8

Regarding the synthetic data generation, our policy is to oversample the minority classes in which the sum of total samples generated, for all classes, does not overpass approximately 50% of the majority class (impurities). Table 2(b) presents the augmentation results.

Table 2. Class frequency regarding the (a) original and (b) augmented datasets. The values in parenthesis stand for the number of samples generated artificially.

(a) Original				(b) Augmented			
Class	# samples			Class	# samples		
	Eggs	Larvae	Protozoa		Eggs	Larvae	Protozoa
1	500	246	868	1	1,000 (500)	738 (492)	868
2	83	1,352	659	2	415 (332)	1,352	1,977 (1,318)
3	286	–	1,783	3	572 (286)	–	1,783
4	103	–	1,931	4	412 (309)	–	1,931
5	835	–	3,297	5	835	–	3,297
6	435	–	309	6	870 (435)	–	1,236 (927)
7	254	–	28,525	7	2,508 (2,254)	–	28,525
8	379	–	–	8	379	–	–
9	9,816	–	–	9	9,816	–	–
Total	12,691	1,598	37,372	Total	14,807 (2,116)	2,090 (492)	39,619 (2,245)

3.3 Experimental Setup

Three different models were considered in this paper: one RBM with 500 hidden neurons and two DBNs, i.e., the first with two hidden layers (DBN-2) containing

500 neurons each, and the other comprising three hidden layers (DBN-3) with 2,000 neurons in the first two levels and 500 neurons in the uppermost layer[1]. All models were trained for 100 epochs considering each RBM stack with a learning rate $\eta = 10^{-5}$ and mini-batches of 64 samples. Further, the networks were fine-tuned for an additional 100 epochs with mini-batches of size 128.

3.4 Evaluation Procedure

Since we have unbalanced datasets, the standard accuracy (ACC) may not be suitable to evaluate the proposed models since it favors classifiers biased towards the most common classes. To address such an issue, we considered the Balanced Accuracy score (BAC) [2] implemented in sklearn[2]. Additionally, the Cohen's kappa coefficient [4] is employed to assess the degree of agreement between the classifier and the ground truth labels. Such a value lies in the interval $[-1, 1]$, where the lower and upper boundaries represent a complete disagreement and an agreement, respectively. Finally, we employed the Wilcoxon signed-rank test [22] with significance of 5% to evaluate the statistical similarity among the best results.

4   Experimental Results

In this section, we present the experimental results concerning automatic human parasites classification.

4.1   Classification Results

Table 3 presents the mean results, concerning the standard accuracy, the balanced accuracy, and the Kappa value with respect to the Larvae dataset. Results are presented over the RBM, DBN-2, and DBN-3 techniques using three distinct configurations, i.e., the original dataset and its augmented versions using RBM (Aug-RBM) and AE (Aug-AE). Moreover, the best ones regarding Wilcoxon test are in bold.

The results confirm the robustness of the proposed approaches since all models with RBM Augmentor achieved more than 94% of BAC. One can highlight the DBN-2 results using the Aug-RBM with 95% and 0.901 of mean accuracy and Kappa values, respectively. Such results provide good shreds of evidence towards the relevance of data augmentation with respect to the baseline, once Aug-RBM supported an improvement of around 5.6% concerning the standard accuracy, 17.3% regarding BAC, and 38% considering the Kappa value. Although Aug-AE provided some improvements, RBM figures as the most accurate approach for such a task.

Table 4 presents the results regarding the Eggs dataset. In this scenario, DBN-3 obtained the best results concerning the ACC and Kappa values, while

---

[1] In case of acceptance, we shall provide the link to the source-code.
[2] Available at https://scikit-learn.org.

Table 3. Effectiveness over Larvae dataset using the proposed approaches.

	RBM			DBN-2			DBN-3		
	Aug-RBM	Aug-AE	Baseline	Aug-RBM	Aug-AE	Baseline	Aug-RBM	Aug-AE	Baseline
ACC	94.03±0.30	77.03±1.85	90.14±0.14	**95.05±0.34**	90.66±0.87	90.53±0.23	94.85±0.33	92.15±0.65	89.61±1.26
BAC	94.07±0.28	69.71±2.95	80.19±0.38	**95.09±0.33**	90.63±0.75	81.24±0.41	**94.87±0.34**	91.40±0.79	80.99±2.29
Kappa	0.880±0.005	0.445±0.053	0.637±0.006	**0.901±0.007**	0.804±0.018	0.653±0.007	**0.897±0.007**	0.832±0.014	0.630±0.041

the standard RBM performed better over the BAC measure. This behavior is surprising since both Kappa and BAC were proposed to cope with unbalanced data evaluation, thus expecting to behave similarly to the other models.

Table 4. Effectiveness over Eggs dataset using the proposed approaches.

	RBM			DBN-2			DBN-3		
	Aug-RBM	Aug-AE	Baseline	Aug-RBM	Aug-AE	Baseline	Aug-RBM	Aug-AE	Baseline
ACC	93.54±0.37	84.25±1.13	90.30±0.052	94.03±0.19	92.13±0.99	91.91±0.45	**94.41±0.32**	94.01±0.19	93.08±0.31
BAC	**92.09±0.68**	67.15±2.54	79.94±0.55	90.98±0.77	88.36±1.77	78.34±1.33	91.06±0.62	90.39±0.30	78.67±1.75
Kappa	0.884±0.006	0.685±0.025	0.769±0.009	0.891±0.004	0.857±0.015	0.794±0.009	**0.897±0.006**	0.890±0.003	0.820±0.009

The behavior observed in the Protozoa dataset, presented in Table 5, highlights an interesting scenario. One of the best ACC (87.51%) and Kappa (0.736) results were achieved with the simplest model, i.e., an RBM using Aug-RBM. Such behavior points out that, for such a dataset, we can compress the input data into a small latent space, thus extracting useful and representative features with only 500 units, while the performance is still remarkable even with unbalanced classes. Moreover, concerning BAC values, one can observe that DBN-2 and DBN-3 with data augmentation by Restricted Boltzmann Machines, as well as DBN-3 using AE for synthetic data generation, obtained similar results.

Table 5. Effectiveness over Protozoa dataset using the proposed approaches.

	RBM			DBN-2			DBN-3		
	Aug-RBM	Aug-AE	Baseline	Aug-RBM	Aug-AE	Baseline	Aug-RBM	Aug-AE	Baseline
ACC	**87.51±0.14**	75.85±0.13	86.21±0.30	86.97±0.31	87.01±0.22	85.97±0.50	85.97±0.59	**87.29±0.37**	84.73±0.94
BAC	77.84±0.82	43.85±0.84	63.77±1.15	**78.84±1.22**	73.83±0.74	62.97±2.88	**77.66±1.88**	**77.87±1.58**	60.55±2.85
Kappa	**0.736±0.004**	0.368±0.009	0.662±0.006	**0.731±0.007**	0.710±0.005	0.659±0.012	0.711±0.010	0.724±0.009	0.615±0.023

4.2 Training Analysis

Regarding the training analysis, we considered the datasets aumented with RBMs only since these models outperformed the ones using Autoencoders. Figure 2 depicts the evolution of the Kappa values over the testing set during training. One can notice that: (i) data augmentation provided a considerable improvement in the results, (ii) training with data augmentation led to more stable results (Figs. 2a and 2b), and (iii) differently from the other two datasets, techniques over Protozoa kept learning up to 80 epochs (Fig. 2c). Such behavior is somehow expected since Protozoa dataset poses a more challenging scenario. The stable results provided by data augmentation may allow us to apply some criteria for convergence analysis during training, such as early stop.

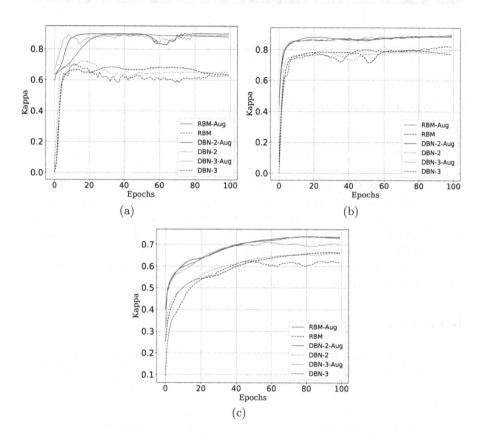

Fig. 2. Average Kappa values over the testing set concerning (a) Larvae, (b) Eggs, and (c) Protozoa datasets.

4.3   Data Augmentation Analysis

Figure 3 shows some synthetic data generated by RBMs using 500 hidden neurons. One can observe that RBMs were able to generate useful samples, which corroborates the aforementioned results, i.e., such a process improved the parasites classification. Besides, the less accurate results concern the ones related to the Larvae dataset since we have a small subset of samples and their shape change considerably among the parasites.

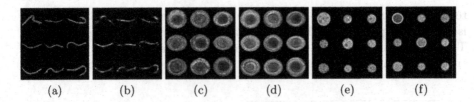

(a)   (b)   (c)   (d)   (e)   (f)

Fig. 3. Data augmentation analysis: (a) real and (b) synthetic Larvae samples, (c) real and (d) synthetic Eggs samples, and (e) real and (f) synthetic Protozoa samples.

5   Conclusions and Future Works

This paper dealt with the problem of human intestinal parasites classification through RBM and DBN approaches. Experiments conducted over three distinct scenarios composed of Larvae, Eggs, and Protozoa, which are also partially surrounded by fecal impurities, confirmed the robustness of the models for classification purposes. Additionally, the performance of RBMs was also compared against Autoencoders for data augmentation since the datasets are highly unbalanced. Regarding future works, we intend to analyze the behavior of the models over a broader spectrum using colored images, as well as employing other RBM-based models, such as the Infinite RBMs (iRBMs) and the DBMs, to the task of human intestinal parasites classification.

References

1. Benato, B.C., Telea, A.C., Falcão, A.X.: Semi-supervised learning with interactive label propagation guided by feature space projections. In: 2018 31st SIBGRAPI Conference on Graphics, Patterns and Images (SIBGRAPI), pp. 392–399. IEEE (2018)
2. Brodersen, K.H., Ong, C.S., Stephan, K.E., Buhmann, J.M.: The balanced accuracy and its posterior distribution. In: Proceedings of the 2010 20th International Conference on Pattern Recognition, ICPR 2010, pp. 3121–3124. IEEE Computer Society, Washington (2010). https://doi.org/10.1109/ICPR.2010.764
3. Castelo-Fernández, C., Falcão, A.X.: Learning visual dictionaries from class-specific superpixel segmentation. In: Vento, M., Percannella, G. (eds.) CAIP 2019. LNCS, vol. 11678, pp. 171–182. Springer, Cham (2019). https://doi.org/10.1007/978-3-030-29888-3_14
4. Fleiss, J.L., Cohen, J.: The equivalence of weighted kappa and the intraclass correlation coefficient as measures of reliability. Educ. Psychol. Measur. **33**(3), 613–619 (1973)
5. Hinton, G.E.: Training products of experts by minimizing contrastive divergence. Neural Comput. **14**(8), 1771–1800 (2002)
6. Hinton, G.E., Osindero, S., Teh, Y.W.: A fast learning algorithm for deep belief nets. Neural Comput. **18**(7), 1527–1554 (2006)
7. Khojasteh, P., et al.: Exudate detection in fundus images using deeply-learnable features. Comput. Biol. Med. **104**, 62–69 (2019)

8. Nakashika, T., Takaki, S., Yamagishi, J.: Complex-valued restricted Boltzmann machine for direct learning of frequency spectra. In: Interspeech, pp. 4021–4025 (2017)
9. World Health Organization: Working to overcome the global impact of neglected tropical diseases. First WHO report on neglected tropical diseases (2010)
10. Papa, J.P., Falcão, A.X., Albuquerque, V.H.C., Tavares, J.M.R.S.: Efficient supervised optimum-path forest classification for large datasets. Pattern Recogn. **45**(1), 512–520 (2012)
11. Papa, J.P., Falcão, A.X., Suzuki, C.T.N.: Supervised pattern classification based on optimum-path forest. Int. J. Imaging Syst. Technol. **19**(2), 120–131 (2009)
12. Passos, L.A., Santana, M.C., Moreira, T., Papa, J.P.: κ-entropy based restricted Boltzmann machines. In: The 2019 International Joint Conference on Neural Networks (IJCNN), pp. 1–8. IEEE (2019)
13. Peixinho, A.Z., Benato, B.C., Nonato, L.G., Falcão, A.X.: Delaunay triangulation data augmentation guided by visual analytics for deep learning. In: 2018 31st SIBGRAPI Conference on Graphics, Patterns and Images (SIBGRAPI), pp. 384–391. IEEE (2018)
14. Peixinho, A.Z., Martins, S.B., Vargas, J.E., Falcão, A.X., Gomes, J.F., Suzuki, C.T.N.: Diagnosis of human intestinal parasites by deep learning. In: Computational Vision and Medical Image Processing V: Proceedings of the 5th Eccomas Thematic Conference (VipIMAGE) (2015). https://doi.org/10.1201/b19241
15. Salakhutdinov, R., Hinton, G.E.: Deep Boltzmann machines. In: AISTATS, vol. 1, p. 3 (2009)
16. Salakhutdinov, R., Mnih, A., Hinton, G.: Restricted Boltzmann machines for collaborative filtering. In: Proceedings of the 24th International Conference on Machine Learning, pp. 791–798. ACM (2007)
17. Smolensky, P.: Information processing in dynamical systems: foundations of harmony theory. In: Rumelhart, D.E., McClelland, J.L. (eds.) Parallel Distributed Processing: Explorations in the Microstructure of Cognition, vol. 1, pp. 194–281. MIT Press, Cambridge (1986)
18. Srivastava, N., Salakhutdinov, R.R.: Multimodal learning with deep Boltzmann machines. In: Pereira, F., Burges, C.J.C., Bottou, L., Weinberger, K.Q. (eds.) Advances in Neural Information Processing Systems, vol. 25, pp. 2222–2230. Curran Associates, Inc. (2012)
19. Suzuki, C.T.N., Gomes, J.F., Falcão, A.X., Papa, J.P., Hoshino-Shimizu, S.: Automatic segmentation and classification of human intestinal parasites from microscopy images. IEEE Trans. Biomed. Eng. **60**(3), 803–812 (2013). https://doi.org/10.1109/TBME.2012.2187204
20. Suzuki, C.T.N., Gomes, J.F., Falcão, A.X., Shimizu, S.H., Papa, J.P.: Automated diagnosis of human intestinal parasites using optical microscopy images. In: 2013 IEEE 10th International Symposium on Biomedical Imaging, pp. 460–463, April 2013. https://doi.org/10.1109/ISBI.2013.6556511
21. World Health Organization, The Pan American Health Organization: French-Speaking Caribbean: Towards World Health Assembly Resolution 54.19, May 2007
22. Wilcoxon, F.: Individual comparisons by ranking methods. Biom. Bull. **1**(6), 80–83 (1945)

Speaker Recognition Using SincNet and X-Vector Fusion

Mayank Tripathi, Divyanshu Singh, and Seba Susan$^{(\boxtimes)}$ (iD)

Department of Information Technology, Delhi Technological University,
Delhi 110042, India
mayank_bt2k16@dtu.ac.in, divyanshu_bt2k16@dtu.ac.in, seba_406@yahoo.in

Abstract. In this paper we propose an innovative approach to perform speaker recognition by fusing two recently introduced deep neural networks (DNNs) namely - SincNet and X-Vector. The idea behind using SincNet filters on the raw speech waveform is to extract more distinguishing frequency-related features in the initial convolution layers of the CNN architecture. X-Vectors are used to take advantage of the fact that this embedding is an efficient method to churn out fixed dimension features from variable length speech utterances, something which is challenging in plain CNN techniques, making it efficient both in terms of speed and accuracy. Our approach uses the best of both worlds by combining X- vector in the later layers while using SincNet filters in the initial layers of our deep model. This approach allows the network to learn better embedding and converge quicker. Previous works use either X-Vector or SincNet Filters or some modifications, however we introduce a novel fusion architecture wherein we have combined both the techniques to gather more information about the speech signal hence, giving us better results. Our method focuses on the VoxCeleb1 dataset for speaker recognition, and we have used it for both training and testing purposes.

Keywords: Speaker recognition · Deep neural networks · SincNet · X-vector · VoxCeleb1 · Fusion model

1 Introduction

Speaker Recognition and Automatic Speech Recognition (ASR) are two of the actively researched and interesting fields in the computer science domain. Speaker recognition has applications in various fields such as biometric authentication, forensics, security and speech recognition, which has contributed to steady interest in this discipline [1]. The conventional method of speaker identification involves classification of features extracted from speech such as the Mel Frequency Cepstral Coefficients (MFCC) [19].

With the advent of i-vectors [4], speaker verification has become faster and more efficient as compared to the preceding model based on the higher dimensional Gaussian Mixture Model (GMM) supervectors. The i-vectors are low

© Springer Nature Switzerland AG 2020
L. Rutkowski et al. (Eds.): ICAISC 2020, LNAI 12415, pp. 252–260, 2020.
https://doi.org/10.1007/978-3-030-61401-0_24

dimensional vectors that are rich in information and represent distinguishing features of the speaker. i-vectors are used to generate a verification score between the embedding of two speakers. This score gives us information about whether both belong to the same speaker or different speakers. Previous experiments have shown that i-vectors perform better with Probabilistic Linear Discriminant Analysis (PLDA) [7]. Work has also been carried out in the field of training the i-vectors using different techniques in order to get better embedding, therefore, better results [5,12].

Currently, researchers are moving towards Deep Neural Network (DNN) to obtain speaker embedding. DNN can be directly optimized to distinguish between speakers. DNN showed promising results in comparison to statistical measures such as i-vectors [6,17]. X-vectors are seen as an improvement over the i-vector system (which is also a fixed-dimension vector system) because they are more robust and have yielded better results [18]. X-vector extraction methodology employs a Time-Delayed Neural Network (TDNN) to learn features from the variable-length audio samples and converts them to fixed dimension vectors. This architecture can broadly be broken down in their order of occurrence into three units, namely, frame-level layers, statistics pooling layer and the segment level layers. X- vectors can then be used with classifiers of any kind to carry out recognition tasks.

SincNet [14] is a deep neural network that has embedded band pass filters for extracting features from the audio sample. The features are then fed into DNN based classifiers. We have used SincNet filters and not fed the audio waveform directly into the DNN based classifiers as the latter technique poses problems like high convergence time and less appealing results. The SincNet filters are actually band pass filters which are derived from parameterized sinc functions. This gives us a compact and an efficient way to get a filter bank that can be customized and specifically tuned for a given application.

Our novel architecture combines the goodness of both the methodologies - SincNet and X-Vector, by extracting features using both the techniques and feeding them to fully connected dense layers which acts as a classifier. The organization of this paper is as follows: the related works are described in Sect. 2, the proposed fusion architecture is presented in Sect. 3, the experimental setup and the results are discussed in Sects. 4 and 5 respectively, and the final conclusions are drawn in Sect. 6.

2   Related Works

The i-vectors [4] feature extraction method has proved to be state of the art for quite some time now for the speaker recognition tasks. Techniques like the Probabilistic Linear Discriminant Analysis (PLDA) and Gauss-PLDA [3,7] are fed with the extracted features and based upon which they carry out classification. Despite being a state of the art technique, we can still improve the performance in terms of accuracy.

With the advent of various deep learning techniques in multiple domains for feature extraction, work has also been carried out to extract features from audio signals using deep learning architectures [9]. These architectures can range from using deep learning just for feature extraction to using neural networks as classifiers as well. The deep learning methods give better results when compared to older techniques based on feature engineering [20].

The most commonly used deep learning method for feature extraction is the one based on the Convolution Neural Network (CNN) architecture [17]. The CNN has been a preferred choice for researchers as it has given good quality results in tasks such as image recognition. Initially the CNN was fed with spectrogram in order to extract features from the audio signals [2,13,15,17,22]. Despite the fact that, spectrogram-based CNN methods were giving good results there were again many drawbacks of using this method [21]. Firstly, the spectrogram is the temporal representation of data unlike images which are spatio-temporal representations. Secondly, a frame in spectrogram can be a result of superposition of multiple waves and not just a single wave which means that a single result can be obtained using different waves super-positioned in different manner. Also, even though spectrograms retain more information than standard hand-crafted features, their design still requires careful tuning of some hyper-parameters, such as the duration, overlap, and typology of the frame window.

The above drawbacks also inspired researchers to directly input raw waveforms into CNN [8] so that no information is lost. This was a good methodology to follow but it results in slower convergence since it processes the complete frequency band of the audio signal.

SincNet [14] and X-vector [18] are amongst the most recent deep learning methods for speech signal classification. Both of them have proved to be more robust than methods which have preceded them.

3   Proposed Fusion Model

We propose a novel fusion of SincNet [14] and X-Vector [18] embedding which will enable us to take the temporal features into account, which is quite important for any audio based recognition task since the signal at any point at time t in an audio signal is affected by points preceding and succeeding it.

3.1   X-Vector Embedding

We have used a pre-trained X-vector system which was trained on the Vox-Celeb1 [11] dataset. The pre-trained x-vector system is available in the kaldi toolkit which is available for public use [16]. Table 1 shows the architecture of the x-vector feature extractor system which has been trained on the VoxCeleb1 dataset. X-vector extraction methodology employs a Time-Delayed Neural Network (TDNN) to learn features from the variable-length audio samples and converts them to fixed dimension vectors. This architecture can broadly be broken down in their order of occurrence into three units, namely, frame-level layers, statistics pooling layer and the segment level layers. X- vectors can then be used with classifiers of any kind to carry out recognition tasks.

Table 1. X-vector DNN architecture [18]

Layer	Layer context	Table context	Input × Output
frame 1	[t-2, t+2]	5	120 × 512
frame 2	{t-2, t, t+2}	9	1536 × 512
frame 3	{t-3, t, t+3}	15	1536 × 512
frame 4	{t}	15	512 × 512
frame 5	{t}	15	512 × 1500
stats pooling	[0, T)	T	1500T × 3000
segment 6	{0}	T	3000 × 512
segment 7	{0}	T	512 × 512
softmax	{0}	T	512 × N

3.2 SincNet Architecture

The SincNet architecture implements various band pass filters in its initial layers, that learns from raw audio signals. The SincNet filters are implemented using a set of mathematical operations which are stated below [14].

The function $h[.]$ is the Finite Impulse Response (FIR) filter used as a convolution filter.

$$y[n] = x[n] * h[n] = \sum_{l=0}^{L-1} x[l] * h[n - l] \tag{1}$$

$g[.]$ is a predefined function that depends on a few learnable parameters θ.

$$y[n] = x[n] * g[n, \theta] \tag{2}$$

$rect(.)$ is the rectangular function in the magnitude frequency domain and f_1 and f_2 are cut-off frequencies.

$$G[f, f_1, f_2] = rect\left(\frac{f}{2f_2}\right) - rect\left(\frac{f}{2f_1}\right) \tag{3}$$

Here, the $sinc$ function is defined as $sinc(x) = \sin(x) / x$

$$g[n, f_1, f_2] = 2f_2 sinc(2\pi f_2 n) - 2f_1 sinc(2\pi f_1 n) \tag{4}$$

We have to ensure that $f_1 \geq 0$ and $f_2 \geq f_1$, therefore, the previous equation is actually fed with the following parameters:

$$f_1^{abs} = |f1| \tag{5}$$

$$f_2^{abs} = f1 + |f2 - f1| \tag{6}$$

Windowing is performed by multiplying the function with a window function w.

$$g_w[n, f_1, f_2] = g[n, f_1, f_2] * w[n] \tag{7}$$

The windowing function w is a hamming window which is given by Eq. 8.

$$w[n] = 0.54 - 0.46 * cos\left(\frac{2\pi n}{L}\right) \tag{8}$$

Once the filters are applied on the raw audio, we get features. These features can now be fed into any classifier. The vanilla SincNet architecture can be seen in Fig. 1. It takes raw audio signals as input, applies SincNet filters and then feeds it into a CNN model which is used as a classifier.

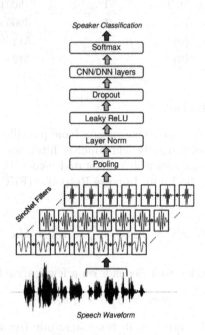

Fig. 1. This is the SincNet architecture. The image has been taken from the original paper [14].

3.3   Fusion Model

Our proposed fusion model fuses the pre-trained X-Vector with features extracted from the trained SincNet model. The concatenated features are fed to a fully connected dense layer. This is followed by two more fully connected dense layers as shown in Fig. 2. The idea behind using SincNet filters on the raw waveform is to extract more distinguishing features in the initial convolution layers of the CNN architecture. X-Vectors are used to take advantage of the fact that this embedding is an efficient method to churn out fixed dimension features variable length speech utterances, something which is challenging in plain CNN techniques, making it efficient both in terms of speed and accuracy.

4   Experimental Setup

4.1   Dataset

We have carried out our experiments on the publicly available dataset Vox-Celeb1 [11]. VoxCeleb is an audio-visual dataset consisting of short clips of human speech, extracted from interview videos uploaded to YouTube. We have used the raw audio files for our experiments. The VoxCeleb1 dataset consists of videos from 1,251 celebrity speakers. Altogether, there are 1,251 speakers and about 21k recordings.

Table 2. VoxCeleb1 dataset distribution [11].

	Dev	Test
Number of speakers	1,251	1,251
Number of videos	21,245	1,251
Number of utterances	145,265	8,251

4.2   Model Architecture

In order to carry out comparative results we have experimented with the original SincNet architecture and our proposed architecture. The original SincNet architecture uses SincNet filters for feature extraction whereas our architecture makes use of both SincNet and X-Vector. The classifier used in all the cases consists of several fully connected layers (DNN classifier) with softmax layer as the output layer. The models can be categorized as:

1. SincNet based feature extractor and DNN classifier.
2. X-Vector embedding and DNN classifier.
3. X-Vector and SincNet based feature extractor and DNN classifier *(Proposed)*.

Our proposed fusion model fuses the pre-trained X-Vector with features extracted from the trained SincNet model. The concatenated features are fed to a fully connected dense layers as shown in Fig. 2. The output obtained after convolution step is flattened and fed into the Dense Layer which is further concatenated with X-vector Embedding. The X-vector combined with the Dense layer constitutes fully connected layer 1 (FC1) which is further connected to FC2 and FC3. All the dense layers use Leaky ReLU as activation. The softmax layer is used as the output layer.

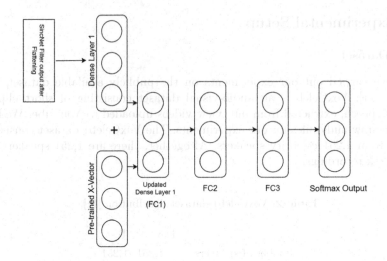

Fig. 2. The proposed fusion model.

5   Experimental Results

The experiments were carried out in Python 3 on a Nvidia *GeForce GTX 1080 Ti* GPU equipped with 16GB of memory. The software implementation of our code is made available online on GitHub [10]. The tests were carried out on the VoxCeleb1 dataset and the results are summarised in Table 3. We calculated the Equal Error Rate (EER) for all the experiments and lower the value the of EER, the better is our model. The results were in alignment with our expectations which means that our system performed the best out of all the architectures tested.

We have an EER score 8.2 for pure SincNet based architecture, an EER score of 5.8 for the X-vector based architecture, and the best EER score of 3.56 using our SincNet and X-vector embedding based architecture. Our architecture proposed a framework which resulted in the EER score of 3.56 which was an improvement over the previous best EER score of 4.16 using X-vector over SITW core [18]. Figure 3 shows a comparison of EER score of various architectures as the number of epochs increases. The proposed fusion model exhibits a consistently low EER over all epochs.

Table 3. Experimental results

Architecture used	Training dataset	EER (on test data)
SincNet	VoxCeleb1	8.2
X-Vector	VoxCeleb1	5.8
Proposed	**VoxCeleb1**	**3.56**

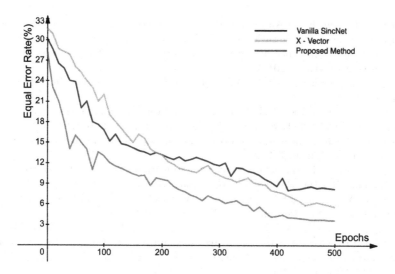

Fig. 3. Comparison of EER score of various architectures over epochs.

6   Conclusions

In this paper we propose a novel fusion model involving two successful deep architectures for speaker recognition:- SincNet and X-Vector. The features extracted from the two sources are fused by concatenation and learnt using fully connected dense layers. We achieved an increase in the EER score from current state of the art by 14.5% on the VoxCeleb1 Dataset. It also showed quite a significant improvement over using vanilla SincNet which resulted in an EER score of 8.2. Further improvement over this architecture can be carried out by combining the VoxCeleb2 dataset along with VoxCeleb1 dataset and using noise removal techniques prior to feeding into the network.

References

1. Beigi, H.: Speaker Recognition. Springer, Boston (2011)
2. Chung, J.S., Nagrani, A., Zisserman, A.: Voxceleb2: deep speaker recognition. arXiv preprint arXiv:1806.05622 (2018)
3. Cumani, S., Plchot, O., Laface, P.: Probabilistic linear discriminant analysis of i-vector posterior distributions. In: 2013 IEEE International Conference on Acoustics, Speech and Signal Processing, pp. 7644–7648. IEEE (2013)
4. Dehak, N., Kenny, P.J., Dehak, R., Dumouchel, P., Ouellet, P.: Front-end factor analysis for speaker verification. IEEE Trans. Audio Speech Lang. Process. **19**(4), 788–798 (2010)
5. Ghalehjegh, S.H., Rose, R.C.: Deep bottleneck features for i-vector based text-independent speaker verification. In: 2015 IEEE Workshop on Automatic Speech Recognition and Understanding (ASRU), pp. 555–560. IEEE (2015)

6. Huang, H., Sim, K.C.: An investigation of augmenting speaker representations to improve speaker normalisation for DNN-based speech recognition. In: 2015 IEEE International Conference on Acoustics, Speech and Signal Processing (ICASSP), pp. 4610–4613. IEEE (2015)
7. Kenny, P.: Bayesian speaker verification with heavy-tailed priors. In: Odyssey, vol. 14 (2010)
8. Lee, J., Kim, T., Park, J., Nam, J.: Raw waveform-based audio classification using sample-level CNN architectures. arXiv preprint arXiv:1712.00866 (2017)
9. Li, C., et al.: Deep speaker: an end-to-end neural speaker embedding system. arXiv preprint arXiv:1705.02304 (2017)
10. Mayank Tripathi, D.: Icaisc-speaker-identification-system. https://github.com/mayank408/ICAISC-Speaker-Identification-System
11. Nagrani, A., Chung, J.S., Zisserman, A.: Voxceleb: a large-scale speaker identification dataset. arXiv preprint arXiv:1706.08612 (2017)
12. Novotný, O., Plchot, O., Glembek, O., Burget, L., Matějka, P.: Discriminatively re-trained i-vector extractor for speaker recognition. In: ICASSP 2019–2019 IEEE International Conference on Acoustics, Speech and Signal Processing (ICASSP), pp. 6031–6035. IEEE (2019)
13. Palaz, D., Collobert, R., et al.: Analysis of CNN-based speech recognition system using raw speech as input. Technical report, Idiap (2015)
14. Ravanelli, M., Bengio, Y.: Speaker recognition from raw waveform with sincnet. In: 2018 IEEE Spoken Language Technology Workshop (SLT), pp. 1021–1028. IEEE (2018)
15. Sainath, T.N., Weiss, R.J., Senior, A., Wilson, K.W., Vinyals, O.: Learning the speech front-end with raw waveform CLDNNS. In: Sixteenth Annual Conference of the International Speech Communication Association (2015)
16. Snyder, D., Garcia-Romero, D., Povey, D.: Voxceleb models. http://kaldi-asr.org/models/m7. Accessed 30 November 2019
17. Snyder, D., Garcia-Romero, D., Povey, D., Khudanpur, S.: Deep neural network embeddings for text-independent speaker verification. In: Interspeech, pp. 999–1003 (2017)
18. Snyder, D., Garcia-Romero, D., Sell, G., Povey, D., Khudanpur, S.: X-vectors: robust DNN embeddings for speaker recognition. In: 2018 IEEE International Conference on Acoustics, Speech and Signal Processing (ICASSP), pp. 5329–5333. IEEE (2018)
19. Susan, S., Sharma, S.: A fuzzy nearest neighbor classifier for speaker identification. In: 2012 Fourth International Conference on Computational Intelligence and Communication Networks, pp. 842–845. IEEE (2012)
20. Variani, E., Lei, X., McDermott, E., Moreno, I.L., Gonzalez-Dominguez, J.: Deep neural networks for small footprint text-dependent speaker verification. In: 2014 IEEE International Conference on Acoustics, Speech and Signal Processing (ICASSP), pp. 4052–4056. IEEE (2014)
21. Wyse, L.: Audio spectrogram representations for processing with convolutional neural networks. arXiv preprint arXiv:1706.09559 (2017)
22. Zhang, C., Koishida, K., Hansen, J.H.: Text-independent speaker verification based on triplet convolutional neural network embeddings. IEEE/ACM Trans. Audio Speech Lang. Process. (TASLP) 26(9), 1633–1644 (2018)

Multiobjective Evolution for Convolutional Neural Network Architecture Search

Petra Vidnerová$^{(\boxtimes)}$ ⓘ, Štěpán Procházka, and Roman Neruda ⓘ

Institute of Computer Science, The Czech Academy of Sciences,
Pod Vodárenskou věží 2, 182 07 Prague 8, Czech Republic
{petra,proste,roman}@cs.cas.cz

Abstract. The choice of an architecture is crucial for the performance of the neural network, and thus automatic methods for architecture search have been proposed to provide a data-dependent solution to this problem. In this paper, we deal with an automatic neural architecture search for convolutional neural networks. We propose a novel approach for architecture selection based on multi-objective evolutionary optimisation. Our algorithm optimises not only the performance of the network, but it controls also the size of the network, in terms of the number of network parameters. The proposed algorithm is evaluated on experiments, including MNIST and fashionMNIST classification problems. Our approach outperforms both the considered baseline architectures and the standard genetic algorithm.

Keywords: Multi-objective evolution · Neural architecture search · Convolutional neural networks

1 Introduction

In the last decade, we witness the boom of deep learning. Neural networks are successfully applied in a wide variety of domains, including image recognition, natural language processing, and others [8,11]. There is a variety of efficient learning algorithms to use, however the performance of the model depends always also on the choice of the right architecture. The choice of architecture is still done manually, requires expert knowledge and time-demanding trial and error approach.

In recent years, the need for automation of neural architecture search (NAS) is getting more and more apparent. As the accessibility of efficient hardware resources improved significantly, many automatic approaches for the setup of hyper-parameters of learning models appeared. Many machine learning software

This work was partially supported by the Czech Grant Agency grant 18-23827S and the long-term strategic development financing of the Institute of Computer Science RVO 67985807.

L. Rutkowski et al. (Eds.): ICAISC 2020, LNAI 12415, pp. 261–270, 2020.
https://doi.org/10.1007/978-3-030-61401-0_25

tools offer automatic search for various hyper-parameters, typically based on grid search techniques. These simple techniques are however applicable on simple hyper-parameters – as real numbers (such as learning rates, dropout rates, etc.) or categorical values from some choice set (such as the type of activation function). The whole architecture, however, is a structured information and has to be searched for as an entire entity. It is hardly possible to use grid search or similar exhaustive technique for NAS.

In this paper, we evaluate the possibility of application of multiobjective evolutionary algorithms on NAS. We restrict the problem to feed-forward convolutional neural networks. This is not the first application of evolutionary algorithms to NAS, the most known is a work [14] that we mention in the next section. In our previous work [16–18] we already tried to apply evolutionary algorithms to simple feed-forward neural networks. However, these works suffered from the huge computational requirements of the approach. The time requirements stem from the necessity to learn and evaluate many candidate networks during the search and also from the fact that the candidate solutions tend to grow uncontrollably. The resulting networks typically had a good performance but the needlessly huge number of parameters. Therefore, we decided to employ the multi-objective optimisation approach, and optimise not only the performance of the network but also its size (number of learnable parameters). In many applications the need for reasonably small models is inherent. This paper shows how the use of multiobjective optimisation may help to tackle this problem.

The paper is organised as follows. The next section revises the related work, including available tools for hyper-parameter search and works directly focused on NAS. Section 3 briefly defines convolutional neural networks. Section 4 explains the proposed algorithm. Section 5 describes the results of our experiments. And finally, Sect. 6 contains conclusion.

2   Related Work

Recently, several tools for automatic neural model selection have appeared. The first of them, AutoKeras [10], is a software library for automated machine learning. It provides functions for automatic architecture and hyper-parameters search. The optimisation process is based on Bayesian optimisation. From our experience with this software, it works well but often produces quite complicated architectures.

The second tool, that deserves to mention, is Talos [2]. It provides a semiautomatic approach to hyper-parameters search for Keras models (Keras [4] is a generally known Python library for neural network implementation, this year it became part of Tensorflow [9]). It enables a user to automatically search for listed hyper-parameters in user-provided ranges, but does not include architecture search. It is based on grid search.

Those two tools appeared quite recently. However, hyper-optimisation frameworks exist a little bit longer. The library hyperopt [3] is even from 2013. It is a Python library that enables distributed hyper-parameter optimisation. Although it is again designed for hyper-parameters only (not architectures), due to the possibility of conditional hyper-parameters, it enables a user to tune also the architecture (however only in a very limited way, such as tune a number of layers).

Last but not least is the hyperas [1] that is a wrapper around the hyperopt library, designed directly for Keras.

The works focused directly on NAS are summarised in a survey [7]. They classify the NAS approaches based on search space, search strategy, and performance estimation strategy. The search space means what types of architectures are allowed. Often human bias is introduced. In our case, the search space is limited to convolutional neural networks. The search strategy represents the particular optimisation algorithm, works vary from random search to evolutionary techniques, Bayesian optimisation, or reinforcement learning. The performance estimation strategy is the way how to set up the objective of the optimisation. The simplest way is to learn on training data and use the performance on validation data.

The most famous evolutionary approaches to NAS for deep neural network come from Miikkulainen [14]. His approaches are built on the well established NEAT algorithm [15]. While the use of multi-objective optimisation for NAS is quite natural, it is not generally used. One of the exceptions is the paper [6] that uses multiobjective Lamarckian evolution for NAS.

Our approach differs from existing approaches in several points:

- the search space – we were inspired by implementation of feedforward neural networks in Keras and designed the algorithm directly for Keras. So, as in the Keras Sequential model, the network is a list of layers, we consider only networks that can be defined as a list of layers (each layer always fully interconnected with the following layer). Moreover, in this paper only convolutional networks are considered.
- the search strategy – we use multiobjective evolution that optimises concurrently both the performance of the network and the network size. The state-of-the-art NSGA-II algorithm [5] was chosen for this purpose.
- the performance estimation strategy – since the split for training and validation data always introduces a bias, we use cross-validation to evaluate network performance.

3   Convolutional Neural Networks

As deep neural networks (DNN) we generally understand neural networks with more (typically many) hidden layers. Convolutional neural networks (CNN) represent an important subset of DNN containing one or more convolutional layers.

The typical architecture of a CNN is depicted at Fig. 1. The front part of the network is responsible for feature extraction and besides convolutional layers it contains pooling layers (typically max-pooling) that perform downsampling. The top layers of the network perform the classification itself and are often fully connected dense layers. In this paper, we work with such a network architecture.

Further details about the DNN and CNN concepts can be found, e.g. in the book [8].

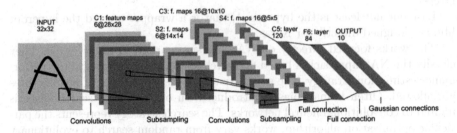

Fig. 1. Convolutional neural network [12].

4 Multi-objective Evolution for Convolutional Neural Networks

We defined the problem of NAS as not only to find the architecture with good performance, but also with a reasonable size. Therefore we decided to use a multiobjective optimisation, and to optimise both the network performance and the network size given by the number of network parameters. To this end, we chose the NSGA II [5] algorithm, considered to be the state of the art of the field, to perform the multiobjective optimisation.

4.1 NSGA II Algorithm

The abbreviation NSGA stands for non-dominated sorting genetic algorithm, the number II stands for the second (improved) variant of the algorithm.

Multi-objective optimization problems consider optimisation problems with more objectives, where the objectives may be conflicting, in the sense that if one objective increases the other decreases. Such problems have no unique solution but a set of solutions.

Our case of NAS can be formalized as follows:

$$max f(x) \text{ and } min \ g(x),$$

where $f(x)$ is a network accuracy (in case of classification) and $g(x)$ is a network size, x stands for a particular architecture.

A solution x is said to dominate the other solution x' if

1. x is no worse than x' for all objectives
2. x is strictly better than x' in at least one objective

Among the set of feasible solutions P, the *non-dominated set of solutions P* is such a set that contains all solutions that are not dominated by any other member of P. The non-dominated set of the entire search space is called the *Pareto-optimal set*. The goal of multiobjective optimisation is to find the Pareto-optimal set.

NSGA II is an evolutionary algorithm for multiobjective optimisation. It's main characteristics are

- it uses elitism (elites of the population are preserved to the future generation)
- it uses an explicit diversity preserving mechanism
- it favours the non-dominated solutions

The algorithm produces new generations from parents and offspring population by

1. a non-dominated sorting of all individuals and labelling them by fronts (they are sorted by an ascending level of non-domination)
2. filling the new generation according to front-ranking
   - if the whole front does not fit into the new population, it performs Crowding-sort (crowding distance is related to the density of solutions around each solution), less dense solutions are preferred
3. creating new offspring by crossover and mutation operators, and by crowded tournament selection (selection based on front ranking and crowding distance if ranking equals)

The detailed description of the algorithm is out of the scope of this paper and can be found in the paper [5].

4.2   Coding of Individuals

The feasible solutions of our problem are the possible architectures of CNNs. Therefore the individuals should code the corresponding architectures.

Our proposal for encoding closely follows the architecture description and implementation in the Keras [4] model *Sequential*. The model implemented as *Sequential* is built layer by layer. Similarly, the individual consists of blocks representing individual layers.

The individual representing a CNN can be presented as follows:

$$I \qquad\qquad\qquad = (I_1, I_2), \tag{1}$$
$$I_1 \quad = ([type, params]_1, \ldots, [type, params]_{H1}) \tag{2}$$
$$I_2 = ([size, dropout, act]_1, \ldots, [size, dropout, act]_{H2}) \tag{3}$$

where I_1 and I_2 are the convolutional and dense part, respectively, $H1$, $H2$ is the number of layers in convolutional and dense part, respectively. The blocks in convolutional part encode $type \in \{\texttt{convolutional}, \texttt{max-pooling}\}$ type of layer and *params* other parameters of the layer (for convolutional layer it is number of filters, size of the filter, and activation function; for a max-pooling layer it is the size of the pool only). The blocks in the dense part code dense layers, so they consist of *size* the number of neurons, *drop* the dropout rate (zero value represents no dropout), *act* activation function.

The output layer is not the part of an individual and is fixed, for classification the softmax layer is used.

4.3   Genetic Operators

We have to define *mutation* and *crossover* operators for our individuals.

In our implementation, the majority of work is done by mutations. Each time an individual is mutated, one of the following mutation operators is randomly chosen (each of mutation operators has its probability):

- mutateLayer - introduces random changes to one randomly selected layer.
- addLayer - one randomly generated block is inserted at random position. If it is inserted to the first part of the individual, it is either a convolutional layer or a max-pooling layer; otherwise it is a dense layer.
- delLayer - one randomly selected block is deleted.

When *mutateLayer* is performed, again one of the available operators is chosen.

For dense layers they are:

- changeLayerSize - the number of neurons is changed. The Gaussian mutation is used, the final number is rounded (since size has to be an integer).
- changeDropOut - the dropout rate is changed using the Gaussian mutation.
- changeActivation - the activation function is changed, randomly chosen from the list of available activations.

For max-pooling layers:

- changePoolSize - the size of pooling is changed.

For convolutional layers:

- changeNumberOfFilters - the number of filters is changed. The Gaussian mutation is used, the final number is rounded.
- changeFilterSize - the size of the filter is changed.
- changeActivation - the activation function is changed, randomly chosen from the list of available activations.

The crossover operator is implemented as the one-point crossover, where the crossing point is determined at random, but on the border of a block only. Thus, only the whole layers are interchanged between individuals. In addition, the two parts of the individual are crossed over separately, so if parents are $I = (I_1, I_2)$ and $J = (J_1, J_2)$ we run $crossover(I_1, J_1)$ and $crossover(I_2, J_2)$.

4.4 Fitness Function

The fitness function should reflect the performance of the network. By the performance, it is generally understood the generalization ability of the network. Therefore the commonly used approach is to evaluate the performance measure (such as accuracy) on the validation set. From our experience, the bias introduced by the random split to training and validation sets is too high. Therefore we prefer to use cross-validation despite its high time requirements.

The fitness function is two-valued. The first value is the network accuracy evaluated by a k-fold cross-validation. The second value is the network size.

5 Experiments

For experimental evaluation we have selected two classification tasks – MNIST [13] and fashionMNIST datasets [20]. Both datasets contain 70 000 images 28×28 pixel each. 60 000 are used for training, 10 000 for testing. MNIST contains images of handwritten digits, fashionMNIST contains greyscale images of fashion objects.

Both datasets are quite small, but this was necessary for performing proper experimental evaluation. Since all algorithms (evolutionary, learning) include random factor, the evaluations have to be repeated several times.

We call our implementation nsga-keras and it is publicly available [19].

It was run five times on each task. The architecture from Pareto front with the best cross-validation accuracy was chosen as the result (i.e. it is typically the largest from the solutions). The corresponding network was trained on the whole training set and evaluated on the test set. This final training and evaluation were done ten times and average values were obtained.

In addition, the classical genetic algorithm - with the same individual coding, crossover and mutation operators, but only a single value fitness function, was run five times on both tasks. The resulting architecture was evaluated in the same way as for multiobjective algorithm.

Also, we have for each task one baseline solution, that is the fixed architecture that is taken from Keras examples.

The Table 1 contains the overview of accuracies of resulting networks for a baseline solution, a solution produced by classical genetic algorithm (GA-CNN) and a solution found by NSGA-II algorithm (NSGA-CNN). The average values of the five runs are taken.

The Table 2 lists the sizes of the resulting networks. Letter K stands for thousand, i.e. 77K stands for 77 000 learnable parameters.

The Fig. 2 shows the flow of the fitness functions during the evolution. We can see that the number of generations needed to converge is not too high.

Regarding the setup of evolution, the population with 30 individuals was used, networks were trained for 20 epochs (during cross-validation in fitness evaluation), categorical cross-entropy was used as a loss function, and the algorithm was run for 150 generations (while even the lower number would be sufficient).

Table 1. Lists accuracies of networks found by classical genetic algorithm (GA-CNN), NSGA-II algorithm (NSGA-CNN), and a baseline solution. In the case of genetic algorithms average values, standard deviations and minimal a maximal values over five runs are listed.

Task	baseline	GA-CNN				NSGA-CNN			
		avg	std	min	max	avg	std	min	max
MNIST	98.97	99.19	0.26	98.75	99.38	99.36	0.02	99.33	99.39
Fashion-MNIST	91.64	93.13	0.20	92.87	93.43	92.67	0.42	91.95	93.07

Table 2. Lists sizes of networks found by classical genetic algorithm (GA-CNN), NSGA-II algorithm (NSGA-CNN), and a baseline solution. In case of genetic algorithms average values, standard deviations and minimal a maximal values over five runs are listed.

Task	baseline	GA-CNN				NSGA-CNN			
		avg	std	min	max	avg	std	min	max
MNIST	600K	690K	399K	277K	1345K	77K	48K	28K	168K
Fashion-MNIST	356K	769K	339K	500K	1228K	418K	311K	64K	876K

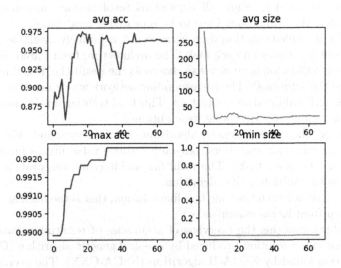

Fig. 2. Example of one run of nsga-keras. On the left, average and maximal accuracy. On the right, average and minimal network size.

We also tried to use a lower number of epochs to save time, but it did not work well.

The experiments were run on GPUs GeForce GTX 1080 Ti. To save the time, the whole population was evaluated at once (on a single card) and also the cross-validation parts were evaluated in parallel. This optimisation was not possible for classical genetic algorithm, where larger architectures evolved and therefore it was no more possible to squeeze the whole population to the memory of one card, and so the fitness evaluation was done in two batches. The time required for the evaluation of one generation was on average 52.24 min for NSGA-II and 178.61 min for classical GA on MNIST.

From the tables we can see the evolutionary approaches outperform the baseline solution and that our proposed multiobjective approach produces a smaller solution with competitive performance.

6   Conclusion

In the paper we proposed a novel approach of neural architecture search for convolutional networks. The algorithm is based on multi-objective evolution utilizing the well known NSGA-II algorithm. The performance of the network and network size are optimised simultaneously, so it produces competitive networks of reasonable size. The benefits from size optimisation are two-fold, first it prevents the candidate solutions to bloat and slow down the evolution, second the smaller solutions learn faster and are suitable for devices with limited memory.

We confirmed the applicability of both evolutionary and multi-objective evolutionary approaches to NAS. The proposed approach is implemented and is publicly available, it is possible to run it both on GPUs and CPUs.

Since we understand that our experimental evaluations are quite limited, which is caused by the high time requirements of the experiments, our future work includes more experimental evaluations (including more data sets). Then, we plan to explore other multi-objective evolutionary algorithms, including NSGA-III.

So far the algorithm is limited to CNNs, but can be easily modified to work for any feedforward neural network. Extension to general networks, including recurrent or modular architectures, is another challenge for future research.

References

1. Keras + Hyperopt: A very simple wrapper for convenient hyperparameter optimization. http://maxpumperla.com/hyperas/
2. Autonomio talos [computer software] (2019). http://github.com/autonomio/talos
3. Bergstra, J., Yamins, D., Cox, D.D.: Making a science of model search: hyperparameter optimization in hundreds of dimensions for vision architectures. In: Proceedings of the 30th International Conference on Machine Learning (ICML 2013) (2013)
4. Chollet, F.: Keras (2015). https://github.com/fchollet/keras
5. Deb, K., Pratap, A., Agarwal, S., Meyarivan, T.: A fast and elitist multiobjective genetic algorithm: NSGA-II. IEEE Trans. Evol. Comput. **6**(2), 182–197 (2002). https://doi.org/10.1109/4235.996017
6. Elsken, T., Metzen, J.H., Hutter, F.: Efficient multi-objective neural architecture search via Lamarckian evolution. In: International Conference on Learning Representations (2019). https://openreview.net/forum?id=ByME42AqK7

7. Elsken, T., Metzen, J.H., Hutter, F.: Neural architecture search: a survey. J. Mach. Learn. Res. **20**(55), 1–21 (2019). http://jmlr.org/papers/v20/18-598.html

8. Goodfellow, I., Bengio, Y., Courville, A.: Deep Learning. MIT Press, Cambridge (2016). http://www.deeplearningbook.org

9. Goodfellow, I., et al.: TensorFlow: large-scale machine learning on heterogeneous systems (2015). Software available from tensorflow.org. https://www.tensorflow.org/

10. Jin, H., Song, Q., Hu, X.: Auto-keras: an efficient neural architecture search system. In: Proceedings of the 25th ACM SIGKDD International Conference on Knowledge Discovery & Data Mining, pp. 1946–1956. ACM (2019)

11. Lecun, Y., Bengio, Y., Hinton, G.: Deep learning. Nature **521**(7553), 436–444 (2015). https://doi.org/10.1038/nature14539

12. Lecun, Y., Bottou, L., Bengio, Y., Haffner, P.: Gradient-based learning applied to document recognition. Proc. IEEE **86**(11), 2278–2324 (1998). https://doi.org/10.1109/5.726791

13. LeCun, Y., Cortes, C.: The MNIST database of handwritten digits (2012). http://research.microsoft.com/apps/pubs/default.aspx?id=204699

14. Miikkulainen, R., et al.: Evolving deep neural networks. CoRR abs/1703.00548 (2017). http://arxiv.org/abs/1703.00548

15. Stanley, K.O., Miikkulainen, R.: Evolving neural networks through augmenting topologies. Evol. Comput. **10**(2), 99–127 (2002). http://nn.cs.utexas.edu/?stanley:ec02

16. Vidnerová, P., Neruda, R.: Evolution strategies for deep neural network models design. In: Proceedings ITAT 2017: Information Technologies - Applications and Theory. Aachen & Charleston: Technical University & CreateSpace Independent Publishing Platform, 2017 - (Hlaváčová, J.), CEUR Workshop Proceedings, V-1885, pp. 159–166 (2017)

17. Vidnerova, P., Neruda, R.: Evolving keras architectures for sensor data analysis. In: 2017 Federated Conference on Computer Science and Information Systems (FedCSIS), pp. 109–112, September 2017. https://doi.org/10.15439/2017F241

18. Vidnerová, P., Neruda, R.: Asynchronous evolution of convolutional networks. In: Proceedings ITAT 2018 (2018)

19. Vidnerová, P., Procházka, Š.: NSGA-keras: neural architecture search for keras sequential models. https://github.com/PetraVidnerova/nsga-keras

20. Xiao, H., Rasul, K., Vollgraf, R.: Fashion-MNIST: a novel image dataset for benchmarking machine learning algorithms (2017)

Neural Network Subgraphs Correlation with Trained Model Accuracy

Izajasz Wrosz[1,2($\boxtimes$)] (iD)

[1] Faculty of Electronics, Telecommunications and Informatics,
Gdańsk University of Technology, Gdańsk, Poland
`izajasz.wrosz@pg.edu.pl`
[2] Intel, Gdansk, Poland

Abstract. Neural Architecture Search (NAS) is a computationally demanding process of finding optimal neural network architecture for a given task. Conceptually, NAS comprises applying a search strategy on a predefined search space accompanied by a performance evaluation method. The design of search space alone is expected to substantially impact NAS efficiency. We consider neural networks as graphs and find a correlation between the presence of subgraphs and the network's final test accuracy by analyzing a dataset of convolutional neural networks trained for image recognition. We also consider a subgraph based network distance measure and suggest opportunities for improved NAS algorithms that could benefit from our observations.

Keywords: Neural networks · Neural architecture search · NAS · Graph matching · Graph distance metric

1 Introduction

Neural Architecture Search (NAS) is a process of finding optimal neural network architecture for a task [4,20]. NAS looks for an optimal number of layers in the network, selection of layer operations (e.g., convolution, max pooling), and connections between the layers. NAS can be seen as a subset of AutoML, a wider task considering also hyperparameter optimization, meta-learning as well as the construction of automated end-to-end learning systems [7]. There are three main aspects of the neural architecture optimization problem: search space design, the search strategy, and a method of neural network fitness evaluation. All three determine the efficiency of the NAS process.

Search space defines the set of neural architectures to be considered during the search process. Although unbounded search spaces are also considered [6, 17], significant interest has been made to stack architectures of repeated small neural nets, dubbed cells, or blocks [24]. In the cell-based approach, the general structure of the network, e.g., number of cells, connections between them is fixed and network variability, hence richness of the search space, is provided through the variability of relatively small cells. The cell approach allows to reduce the

© Springer Nature Switzerland AG 2020
L. Rutkowski et al. (Eds.): ICAISC 2020, LNAI 12415, pp. 271–279, 2020.
https://doi.org/10.1007/978-3-030-61401-0_26

search space and incorporates prior knowledge obtained during hand designing of networks with repeated motifs [19].

The search strategy is expected to explore the set of considered networks and find optimal architecture according to neural network fitness metric while making as few queries as possible, reducing the time and amount of compute resources needed for optimization task. Random Search (recommended as the baseline for strategy comparison [11,12], Reinforcement Learning, Bayesian Optimization, and Evolutionary Methods are examples of search strategies used in NAS. In Reinforcement Learning, selecting new neural architecture is seen as agent's action, while trained network fitness estimate provides the reward. In Evolutionary Methods, in each step at least one neural network is selected from the population. By applying mutations, defined as changing the number of layers, their type or connections, off-springs are generated. The network evaluation method is used to determine which off-springs should be included in the population. Bayesian Optimization methods are adapted to discrete and relatively high dimensional spaces, through the application of kernel functions [9,14] and efficient tree-based models [8].

Since the breakthrough results of Zoph and Le [24], much effort has been devoted to NAS leading to discoveries of novel neural network architectures with superior accuracy in image recognition and natural language processing benchmarks, but also revealed important shortcomings of the method such as significant compute power requirements, difficulties in results reproduction or assessment of the method efficiency [21].

A valuable step towards reproducible NAS research was creation of open databases containing results of large amount of trained neural networks [3,23]. In our work we analyze subgraph isomorphism and graph matching of neural network models in NAS-Bench-101 [23] and correlate the property of subgraph presence with test accuracy of trained networks. Additionally, we study the applicability of maximal common subgraph based distance metric [2] to finding neural architectures with similar performance.

2   Related Work

NAS-Bench-101 [23] is an open dataset of cell-based feedforward neural networks. It maps 423k unique convolutional architectures with their train time and performance metrics based on the CIFAR-10 [10] benchmark. All architectures in NAS-Bench-101 share the same overall structure. Each network starts with a convolutional stem, followed by a repeated pattern of stacked cells and a downsampling layer. The chain-like sequence ends with a global average polling and a dense softmax layer. See Fig. 1. The analyzed neural networks are generated through the variability in the small cells: directed acyclic graphs consisting of a maximum of 7 nodes (layers) and 9 edges. Each node is labeled with one of 5 allowed operations. Beyond the labels representing the cell's input and output, the permitted operations are 3x3 convolution, 1x1 convolution, and 3x3 maxpool. The convolutional layers use batch normalization and ReLU. The stem is composed of a single 3x3 convolution with 128 output channels.

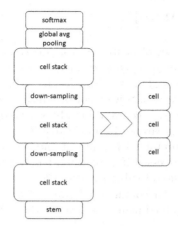

Fig. 1. The structure of the analyzed neural networks. The motif of a stack of 3 cells followed by a down-sampling layer is repeated 3 times. Each network starts with a convolutional stem and is finalized by a global average pooling layer followed by a softmax layer.

The first statistical insights into the NAS-Bench-101 data set were made by its authors who studied the distribution of neural network properties such as accuracy and train time over the whole search space. They also noticed the importance of network topology and node operation selection, analyzed the impact of swapping node operations, and correlated graph width and depth with training time and network accuracy. Our work is extending studies of Ying et al. by extensively analyzing subgraphs of the cell graphs. Authors of NAS-Bench-101 also analyzed data set locality employing graph edit distance and Random Walk Autocorrelation. In our work, we reproduce the locality results by randomly sampling pairs of graphs and analyze a different graph similarity measure based on maximal common subgraph size.

Radosovic et al. [15] performed a comprehensive analysis of network search (design) spaces, which they specify by providing general model family (e.g., a family of ResNet like architectures) and a set of parameters used to generate all considered neural network models. They developed a framework for comparing design spaces through distributions of network fitness parameters over the respective data sets. In our work, we use an analogical, distribution-based approach to compare distance metrics for neural networks. Our analysis of network subgraphs can be seen as a step towards a subgraph based parametrization of neural network search spaces.

A variety of network distance metrics were studied in the context of image recognition, network analysis, and general data mining [2]. In the context of neural architecture search, metrics derived from graph edit distance are often used for Bayesian Optimization based search strategies [9,14]. We analyze a different, subgraph based neural network distance metric in its application to NAS.

3   Our Work and Results

To verify if graph properties of neural networks correlate with the accuracy of
trained models we generated a data set of all connected, induced subgraphs
of the cell graphs defined in [23]. We also considered basic properties like graph
width, height, rank, but the results were not promising, except for the correlation
between graph width and test accuracy already observed in [23]. For each of the
subgraphs we calculated Spearman Rank Correlation [5,18] between categorical
property of a subgraph contained in the cell and test accuracy of the trained
neural network. We also assessed if a subgraph based distance measure between
neural networks could be used to identify those of similar accuracy and compared
applicability of the maximal common subgraph distance metric [2] with edit
distance metric [16] on trained neural networks from NAS-Bench-101.

3.1   Experimental Setup and Terminology

In this paper, we use the term *parent graph* when describing graph models of
neural network cells containing all nodes and edges of a subgraph. We also use
the term *model* when describing graph models of neural networks.

To obtain our results we implemented a set of python scripts and used the
interface library provided with NAS-Bench-101 [23] to access the data. We used
the implementation of graph invariant hash from [23]. For graph analysis we
used the NetworkX library [1]. We generated all induced subgraphs of the cells
by exhaustively iterating over all subsets of cells' vertices. If the selected subset constituted a connected graph we calculated the invariant hash [22], hence
recording in our data set only unique subgraphs. For every subgraph, we stored
a list of parent graph hashes and subgraph nodes according to a selected parent graph to induce subgraph connectivity. To ease further analysis, we also
generated mapping from parent graphs to their respective subgraphs. The computation of results presented in this paper took about 3 CPU weeks.

3.2   Subgraph Presence Correlation with Neural Network Accuracy

The NAS-Bench-101 data set contains 423,624 unique neural networks specified
by the cell building blocks [23]. As seen in Table 1, the number of cell subgraphs
grows very quickly with the number of nodes, yielding a total of 876,951. Almost
half of all subgraphs consist of 6 nodes, at the same time, subgraphs with up to
4 vertices amount for less than 5% of all examples. Since we analyze induced
subgraphs, the 7 node structures are isomorphic only with their originating cell
graphs, while smaller subgraphs are present in many neural network models.
Most of the network models have approx. 60 subgraphs. See Fig. 2.

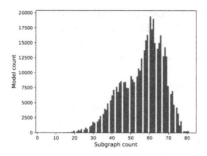

Fig. 2. The number of subgraphs histogram among neural network models. Most of the network models have app. 60 subgraphs. Relatively few network models have less then 30 or more than 75 subgraphs.

Table 1. Summary of subgraph sizes and the number of matching network models (parents). Almost half of all subgraphs consist of 6 nodes. On average, the 3 node subgraphs are contained in 28k different neural networks (6.77% of all models).

Size	Subgraph count	%	Mean Parents	%
1	5	0.001	386904	91.33
2	16	0.002	178452	42.13
3	168	0.02	28684	6.77
4	3290	0.38	1888	0.78
5	88447	10.09	59.8	0.05
6	425943	48.57	5.5	0.001
7	359082	40.95	1	0.0002
Total	876951	100		

We grouped the networks into categories of the same cardinality according to their accuracy. The number of categories was selected by observing an inflection point of the mean in-category variance of network accuracy as a function of the number of categories. For each subgraph, we calculated the fraction of those networks which contained the subgraph and belonged to specific category according to the accuracy. The per-category subgraph presence frequencies were used to calculate Spearman Rank Correlation with the per-category mean accuracy of neural networks.

For over 80% of 2, 3, and 4 node subgraphs, the Spearman Rank Correlation null hypothesis was rejected with a p-value below 0.05, which can be interpreted as evidence of a strong correlation between the frequency of subgraph presence in a group of neural networks and its mean test accuracy.

Table 2. The number of subgraphs with spearman rank correlation p-value less than 0.05 for different subgraph sizes. The correlation with network accuracy is observed for the majority of subgraphs with 2, 3, 4 nodes. The mean (absolute) correlation coefficient decreases as the subgraph size increases.

Subgraph size	Correlated count	%	Mean correlation coefficient
1	2	40.0	0.903
2	14	87.5	0.821
3	154	91.7	0.794
4	2742	83.3	0.694
5	34902	39.5	0.483
6	72676	17.1	0.373
7	0	0.00	Not applicable

Figures 3 and 4 show the accuracy of parent neural networks for randomly selected 3 and 4 node subgraphs for which the null hypothesis of the Spearman Rank Correlation test could be rejected. The box plots for larger subgraphs characterize higher variability of mean accuracy, potentially allowing efficient separation of neural networks.

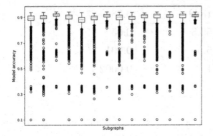

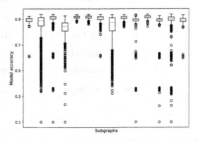

Fig. 3. Accuracy of neural networks containing three-node-subgraphs drawn from the set of subgraphs correlated with network accuracy

Fig. 4. Accuracy of neural networks containing four-node-subgraphs drawn from the set of subgraphs correlated with network accuracy

3.3 Subgraph Distance Measure

Observing evidence of subgraphs correlation with network accuracy, we studied the applicability of a subgraph based distance metric for graph models of neural networks. For 40k randomly sampled pairs of NAS-Bench-101 graphs, we calculated their similarity measure according to graph edit distance and the maximum common subgraph size in addition to recording the difference between their accuracy in the image recognition task. With graph edit distance as the number of elementary operations (add node, edge, etc.) that must be applied

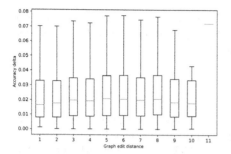 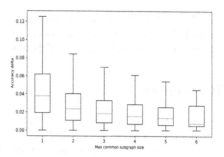

Fig. 5. Network accuracy delta for graph pairs separated by specific edit distance. Mean value correlation is observed locally until the distance of 6 edits is reached. Outlier points are not shown.

Fig. 6. Network accuracy delta for graph pairs with a specific maximal common subgraph size. Correlation is observed across all sampled pairs. Distribution of data points narrows with increasing maximal common subgraph size. Outlier points are not shown.

on one graph to obtain another one, as can be seen in Fig. 5, the mean difference of neural network accuracy grows monotonically with edit distance up to 6 edits. Beyond that point, graph edit metric seems to be not correlated with the accuracy difference of corresponding neural networks which is coherent with results of Random Walk Autocorrelation analysis in [23]. The size of the maximal common subgraph correlates with the difference in accuracy across all analyzed graphs. With increasing size of the maximal common subgraph, the distribution of network accuracy differences narrows as shown by box plots' whiskers in Fig. 6.

4   Conclusions

In the context of Neural Architecture Search, we analyzed subgraphs of neural network graph models in NAS-Bench-101 dataset and calculated Spearman Rank Correlation between subgraph presence and trained network accuracy. We showed that the majority of 2, 3, 4 node subgraphs correlate with neural network ability to learn the task of image recognition. We analyzed the applicability of maximal common subgraph based graph distance metric and observed long-range correlation with networks' difference in accuracy, compared to the relatively local applicability of graph edit distance. We suggest that the application of a subgraph based distance metric could result in improved efficiency of Bayesian Optimization based algorithms. Potentially, new Reinforcement Learning policies could be created by reconstructing neural network architecture graphs by sampling from a set of considered subgraphs [13].

Acknowledgments. The author would like to express heartfelt gratitude to prof. Dariusz Dereniowski, Faculty of Electronics, Telecommunications and Informatics, Gdańsk University of Technology, Poland, for multiple discussions and ideas which greatly supported the presented work. Utmost gratitude is directed towards Marek M Landowski from Intel, Data Platforms Group, for supporting the presented research and providing valuable feedback. The author has been partially supported under ministry subsidy for research for Gdansk University of Technology.

References

1. Aric, A., Hagberg, D.A.S., Swart, P.J.: Exploring network structure, dynamics, and function using networkx. In: Gäel Varoquaux, T.V., Millman, J. (eds.) Proceedings of the 7th Python in Science Conference (SciPy2008), 9–15, June 2019, Pasadena, California, USA, pp. 11–15 (2008)
2. Bunke, H., Shearer, K.: A graph distance metric based on the maximal common subgraph. Pattern Recognit. Lett. **19**(3–4), 255–259 (1998). https://doi.org/10.1016/S0167-8655(97)00179-7
3. Dong, X., Yang, Y.: Nas-bench-201: extending the scope of reproducible neural architecture search. CoRR abs/2001.00326 (2020). http://arxiv.org/abs/2001.00326
4. Elsken, T., Metzen, J.H., Hutter, F.: Neural architecture search: a survey. J. Mach. Learn. Res. **20**, 55:1–55:21 (2019)
5. Glasser, G.J., Winter, R.F.: Critical values of the coefficient of rank correlation for testing the hypothesis of independence. Biometrika **48**(3/4), 444–448 (1961)
6. Ha, H., Rana, S., Gupta, S., Nguyen, T., Tran-The, H., Venkatesh, S.: Bayesian optimization with unknown search space. In: Wallach, H., Larochelle, H., Beygelzimer, A., d'Alché-Buc, F., Fox, E., Garnett, R. (eds.) Advances in Neural Information Processing Systems, vol. 32, pp. 11795–11804. Curran Associates, Inc (2019)
7. Hutter, F., Kotthoff, L., Vanschoren, J. (eds.): Automated Machine Learning. TSSCML. Springer, Cham (2019). https://doi.org/10.1007/978-3-030-05318-5
8. Jin, H., Song, Q., Hu, X.: Auto-keras: an efficient neural architecture search system. In: Teredesai, A., Kumar, V., Li, Y., Rosales, R., Terzi, E., Karypis, G. (eds.) Proceedings of the 25th ACM SIGKDD International Conference on Knowledge Discovery And Data Mining, KDD 2019, Anchorage, AK, USA, 4–8, August 2019, pp. 1946–1956. ACM (2019). https://doi.org/10.1145/3292500.3330648
9. Kandasamy, K., Neiswanger, W., Schneider, J., Poczos, B., Xing, E.P.: Neural architecture search with bayesian optimisation and optimal transport. In: Bengio, S., Wallach, H., Larochelle, H., Grauman, K., Cesa-Bianchi, N., Garnett, R. (eds.) Advances in Neural Information Processing Systems, vol. 31, pp. 2016–2025. Curran Associates, Inc (2018)
10. Krizhevsky, A.: Learning multiple layers of features from tiny images. Technical report, Department of Computer Science, U. of Toronto (2009)
11. Li, L., Talwalkar, A.: Random search and reproducibility for neural architecture search. In: Globerson, A., Silva, R. (eds.) Proceedings of the Thirty-Fifth Conference on Uncertainty in Artificial Intelligence, UAI 2019, Tel Aviv, Israel, 22–25, July 2019, p. 129. AUAI Press (2019)
12. Lindauer, M., Hutter, F.: Best practices for scientific research on neural architecture search. CoRR abs/1909.02453 (2019). http://arxiv.org/abs/1909.02453
13. Nýdl, V.: Graph reconstruction from subgraphs. Discret. Math. **235**(1–3), 335–341 (2001). https://doi.org/10.1016/S0012-365X(00)00287-9

14. Oh, C., Tomczak, J.M., Gavves, E., Welling, M.: Combinatorial bayesian optimization using the graph cartesian product. In: Wallach, H.M., Larochelle, H., Beygelzimer, A., d'Alché-Buc, F., Fox, E.B., Garnett, R. (eds.) Advances in Neural Information Processing Systems 32: Annual Conference on Neural Information Processing Systems 2019, NeurIPS 2019, 8–14 December 2019, pp. 2910–2920. Canada, Vancouver, BC (2019)

15. Radosavovic, I., Johnson, J., Xie, S., Lo, W., Dollár, P.: On network design spaces for visual recognition. CoRR abs/1905.13214 (2019). http://arxiv.org/abs/1905.13214

16. Sanfeliu, A., Fu, K.: A distance measure between attributed relational graphs for pattern recognition. IEEE Trans. Syst. Man Cybern. **13**(3), 353–362 (1983). https://doi.org/10.1109/TSMC.1983.6313167

17. Shahriari, B., Bouchard-Côté, A., de Freitas, N.: Unbounded bayesian optimization via regularization. In: Gretton, A., Robert, C.C. (eds.) Proceedings of the 19th International Conference on Artificial Intelligence and Statistics, AISTATS 2016, Cadiz, Spain, 9–11, May 2016. JMLR Workshop and Conference Proceedings JMLR.org, vol. 51, pp. 1168–1176 (2016)

18. Spearman, C.: The proof and measurement of association between two things. Am. J. Psychol. **15**(1), 72–101 (1904)

19. Szegedy, C., Vanhoucke, V., Ioffe, S., Shlens, J., Wojna, Z.: Rethinking the inception architecture for computer vision. In: The IEEE Conference on Computer Vision and Pattern Recognition (CVPR), June 2016

20. Wistuba, M., Rawat, A., Pedapati, T.: A survey on neural architecture search. CoRR abs/1905.01392 (2019). http://arxiv.org/abs/1905.01392

21. Yang, A., Esperança, P.M., Carlucci, F.M.: NAS evaluation is frustratingly hard. In: 8th International Conference on Learning Representations, ICLR 2020, Addis Ababa, Ethiopia, 26–30, April 2020. OpenReview.net (2020)

22. Ying, C.: Enumerating unique computational graphs via an iterative graph invariant. CoRR abs/1902.06192 (2019). http://arxiv.org/abs/1902.06192

23. Ying, C., Klein, A., Christiansen, E., Real, E., Murphy, K., Hutter, F.: Nas-bench-101: towards reproducible neural architecture search. In: Chaudhuri, K., Salakhutdinov, R. (eds.) Proceedings of the 36th International Conference on Machine Learning, ICML 2019, 9–15 June 2019, Long Beach, California, USA. Proceedings of Machine Learning Research PMLR, vol. 97, pp. 7105–7114 (2019)

24. Zoph, B., Vasudevan, V., Shlens, J., Le, Q.V.: Learning transferable architectures for scalable image recognition. In: 2018 IEEE Conference on Computer Vision and Pattern Recognition, CVPR 2018, Salt Lake City, UT, USA, 18–22, June 2018, pp. 8697–8710. IEEE Computer Society (2018). https://doi.org/10.1109/CVPR.2018.00907

Weighted Feature Selection Method for Improving Decisions in Milling Process Diagnosis

Roman Zajdel[iD], Maciej Kusy[✉][iD], Jacek Kluska[iD], and Tomasz Zabinski[iD]

Faculty of Electrical and Computer Engineering, Rzeszow University of Technology,
al. Powstancow Warszawy 12, 35-959 Rzeszow, Poland
{rzajdel,mkusy,jacklu,tomz}@prz.edu.pl

Abstract. In this article, a new feature selection method is introduced. It is based on the weighted combined ranking score which fuses feature significance provided by three approaches: the Pearson's linear correlation coefficient, ReliefF and single decision tree. During the successive steps, we eliminate the least significant features using binary weights corresponding to individual features. The utilized data set is represented by 1709 records and 44 attributes determined based on the signals acquired in the milling process. The efficiency of the proposed method is tested on reduced and original data set by a multilayer perceptron classifier. The obtained results confirm the usefulness of the solution.

Keywords: Feature selection · Weights · Combined ranking · Multilayer perceptron · Milling process

1 Introduction

In machine learning, the process of choosing a subset of significant features is known as feature selection (FS). The application of FS results in lower data dimensionality with original attribute values preserved. The FOCUS algorithm [1], fast correlation based filter approach [12], ReliefF [5] or a decision tree [3] are commonly used FS methods.

FS is frequently applied in the milling processes. For example, in [4], a decision tree and a crosscorrelation method are utilized to establish features' subsets out of all available features from the data representing a wear of the face mill. The effect of FS application is tested by a neural network. A noticeable improvement of the network's classification capability is observed after performing FS. The work presented in [14] shows FS based on a modified Fisher's linear discriminant analysis applied to cutting force signals collected in the micro-milling process. The data set with significantly lower number of features is used as input for hidden Markov model in a classification problem. The proposed method improves performance of the considered model. The authors of [7] utilize a decision tree to select attributes out of all available features extracted from the signals provided

© Springer Nature Switzerland AG 2020
L. Rutkowski et al. (Eds.): ICAISC 2020, LNAI 12415, pp. 280–291, 2020.
https://doi.org/10.1007/978-3-030-61401-0_27

by a face milling tool during machining of a steel alloy. A K–star algorithm is then used as a classifier; after FS, its higher performance is observed.

It must be stressed that applying exclusively a single FS technique in a particular task may turn out to be insufficient. One method may suit to certain problem while the other will not be appropriate. Finding "sole best" solution for a given task is therefore difficult. Recent research has shown that it is worth to consider a combination of state-of-the-art FS methods to find a significant subset of attributes. In [6], an algorithm for combining multiple FS methods is proposed. It uses combinatorial fusion analysis paradigm. A rank-score function and its associated graph are adopted to measure the diversity of different feature selection methods. The paper [10] shows how an ensemble approach can be used for improving feature selection performance. A general framework is presented for creating several feature sets which are then combined into a single subset. The combination is based on the voting scheme. The algorithm introduced in [9] presents how to utilize an ensemble of FS methods to reject redundant set of attributes. The idea is based on feature "rankers" which provide the list of features ordered according to their importance. These features are then combined into a single ensemble list using a suitable aggregation function that assigns each feature some score based on the feature's position in the original lists ranking.

Taking the validity and efficacy of aforementioned strategies into considera-tion, in this article, we present a new FS method, which by fusing the Pearson's linear correlation coefficient (PLCC), ReliefF and single decision tree (SDT) approaches, selects the most significant subset of attributes from the input sig-nals acquired in the milling process. The weighted combined ranking score is introduced which forms a criterion of choosing attributes which contribute to a performance improvement of the multilayer perceptron (MLP). MLP is tested on the data set with features generated by the introduced solution, PLCC, ReliefF, SDT and original set of attributes. The proposed approach provides the highest accuracy results.

The remainder of this paper is the following. Section 2 presents the structure of the platform used for data acquisition and the way the milling experiments are done. In Sect. 3, the extracted features from the input signals are highlighted. The MLP applied in the classification task and the utilized FS methods are outlined in Sect. 4 and 5, respectively. In Sect. 6, the proposed FS method is introduced. The obtained results are presented in Sect. 7 while Sect. 8 constitutes the summary of the study.

2   Machining Process and Data Representation

The process of data acquisition is conducted by means of a platform for rapid prototyping of intelligent diagnostic systems developed in [13].

2.1   Testbed

Milling experiments are conducted on Haas VM–3 CNC machining center, equipped with a set of sensors and a data acquisition system based on

Matlab/Simulink and TwinCAT 3 factory automation software. Signals from accelerometer (ACC, sensitivity 100 mV/g, bandwidth 10 kHz) and acoustic emission sensor (AE, sensitivity 53 mV/Pa) mounted on the lower bearing of the spindle and in the machine cabin respectively are used in this study. In the data acquisition system, Beckhoff Industrial Computer C6920 equipped with analog input modules (EL3632) is used. Data collection is performed using Matlab/Simulink project running in External Mode. The sampling frequency is equal to 25 kHz. Data are stored in mat-files; each file (buffer) includes 16,000 samples collected simultaneously from ACC and AE sensors.

2.2   Milling Experiments

Eleven experiments are analyzed in this study. During each experiment, one circular milling trajectory is performed at the edge of one Inconel 625 disc (diameter: 100 mm, thickness: 8 mm). The machining process is realized with the use of one four-teeth milling cutter. Seven and four experiments are done using sharp and blunt cutters, respectively. After each experiment, the quality of obtained surface roughness is measured using profilometer. For sharp cutters it is approximately 0.5 μm, and 1 μm for blunt cutters. Finally, 1085 files (buffers) are collected for experiments done with sharp cutters and 624 files (buffers) for blunt cutters.

3   Features Extracted from the Input Signals

As a result of processing the signals collected by the ACC and AE sensors in the time domain, 1709 records of two classes (sharp or blunt cutters) are obtained. Each record consists of 44 attributes. The features 1–22 and 23–44 are determined for the ACC and AE signal, respectively. The list of features in the format: name, formula, indices: ACC-feature-index, AE-feature-index, is as follows:

- Maximum, $\max = \max\limits_{i=1,\ldots,n} \{x_i\}$, indices: 1, 23;
- Minimum, $\min = \min\limits_{i=1,\ldots,n} \{x_i\}$, indices: 2, 24;
- Peak to peak, $P = \max - \min$, indices: 3, 25;
- Median, "middle" value in the sample, indices: 4, 26;
- Maximum of the absolute value, $\max_a = \max\limits_{i=1,\ldots,n} \{|x_i|\}$, indices: 5, 27;
- Mean, $\mu = \frac{1}{n}\sum_{i=1}^{n} x_i$, indices: 6, 28;
- Mean of the absolute value, $\mu_a = \frac{1}{n}\sum_{i=1}^{n} |x_i|$, indices: 7, 29;
- Variance, $\sigma^2 = \frac{1}{n}\sum_{i=1}^{n} (x_i - \mu)^2$, indices: 8, 30;
- Root mean square, $RMS = (\frac{1}{n}\sum_{i=1}^{n} x_i^2)^{1/2}$, indices: 9, 31;
- Standard deviation, σ, indices: 10, 32;
- Energy, $E = \sum_{i=1}^{n} x_i^2$, indices: 11, 33;
- Energy of the centered signal, $E_c = \sum_{i=1}^{n} (x_i - \mu)^2$, indices: 12, 34;
- Kurtosis, $K = m_4/\sigma^4$, indices: 13, 35;
- Skewness, $S = m_3/\sigma^3$, indices: 14, 36;

- k-th order moment, $m_k = \frac{1}{n} \sum_{i=1}^{n} (x_i - \mu)^k$ for $k = 5, \ldots, 10$, indices: 15–20, 37–42;
- Shannon entropy, $I = -\sum_{i=1}^{n} x_i^2 \log_2 x_i^2$, indices: 21, 43;
- Signal rate, $S = P/\mu$, indices: 22, 44.

4   Multilayer Perceptron

MLP [11] is one or two hidden layer feedforward neural network with neurons activated by some assumed transfer function. Constraining the architecture of the MLP to a single hidden layer, the o-th network output signal for the unknown test record $\mathbf{x} = [x_1, \ldots, x_I]$ is computed as follows:

$$
y_o = f \left(\sum_{h=1}^{H} w_{oh}^{(2)} z_h + b_o^{(2)} \right), \tag{1}
$$

where H is the number of hidden neurons; $w_{oh}^{(2)}$ and $b_o^{(2)}$ are the output layer weight and bias, respectively while z_h is the h-th hidden neuron output signal defined as:

$$
z_h = g \left(\sum_{i=1}^{I} w_{hi}^{(1)} x_i + b_h^{(1)} \right), \tag{2}
$$

where $w_{hi}^{(1)}$ and $b_h^{(1)}$ are the hidden layer weight and bias, respectively and x_i is the i-th feature of $\mathbf{x}$; f and g denote activation functions. In this work, there is a single neuron in the MLP's output layer, therefore $y_o = y$ and $t_{lo} = t_l$.

5   Feature Selection

In this section, we outline three FS methods which are applied to feature subset selection among all 44 available attributes described in Sect. 3. The significance of the features established by considered methods is also discussed.

5.1   Pearson's Linear Correlation Coefficient

For the i-th feature of the available input–output pair $(\mathbf{x}_l, t_l)$, PLCC is defined as follows [2]:

$$
r_i = \frac{\sum_{l=1}^{L} (x_{li} - \overline{x}_i)(t_l - \overline{t})}{\left(\sum_{l=1}^{L} (x_{li} - \overline{x}_i)^2 \sum_{l=1}^{L} (t_l - \overline{t})^2 \right)^{\frac{1}{2}}}, \tag{3}
$$

where $\overline{x}_i = \frac{1}{L} \sum_{l=1}^{L} x_{li}$ is the mean over the i-th feature, and $\overline{t} = \frac{1}{L} \sum_{l=1}^{L} t_l$ is the mean over the class outputs of all $\mathbf{x}_l$ records. It is known that $r_i = \pm 1$ if $\mathbf{x}_l$ and t_l are linearly dependent and 0 if they are uncorrelated. Furthermore, the values of r_i are independent of outputs coding. The ranking of feature significance can be determined based on decreasing values of $|r_i|$.

5.2   ReliefF Algorithm

ReliefF [5] determines the set of weights which represent the relevance of input features. The algorithm finds K nearest neighbors for the record $\mathbf{x}_l$ among the data of the same class (nearest hits) and the data from the remaining classes (nearest misses). The feature weights are calculated as follows:

$$
w_i^{\text{new}} = w_i^{\text{old}} - \frac{1}{L \cdot K} \left(\sum_{k=1}^{K} \Delta(x_{li}, h_{ki})^2 - \sum_{j=1,\, j \neq c}^{J} \frac{P(j)}{1 - P(c)} \sum_{k=1}^{K} \Delta \left(x_{li}, m_{ki}^{(j)} \right)^2 \right),
$$
(4)

where h_{ki} is the i-th feature of the k-th nearest hit; $m_{ki}^{(j)}$ denotes the i-th feature of the k-th nearest miss found in the j-th class; $P(j)$ and $P(c)$ are the occurrence probabilities of class j and c, respectively; Δ computes the difference between the i-th feature of two vectors: $\Delta = \{0, 1\}$ and $\Delta \in [0, 1]$ for discrete and continuous attributes, respectively. The greater weight value, the higher relevance of a feature.

5.3   Single Decision Tree

SDT consists of one root, a number of branches, nodes and leaves. At each decision node in the tree, one can select the most useful feature for classification using appropriate estimation criteria based on entropy and information gain. Information gain $G(S, F)$ of a feature F relative to a set S measures how well a feature F separates the training examples according to their target classification:

$$
G(S, F) = E(S) - \sum_{k \in V_F} (|S_k| / |S|) E(S_k),
$$
(5)

where V_F contains all possible values for attribute F, and $S_k = \{x \in S \mid F(x) = k\}$. The entropy $E(S) = -\sum_{i=1}^{c} p_i \log_2 p_i$, where c is the number of classes ($c = 2$), p_i is the proportion of S belonging to the class i. The features in the nodes of SDT appear in descending order of importance, from the root to the leaves. The only features that contribute to the classification appear in the tree and others do not. Some nodes might be removed from the tree by using the pruning procedure. Features, which have less discriminating capability, can be consciously discarded by deciding on the threshold. This concept is made use of for selecting 'the best' features.

5.4   Generated Importance of the Features

Table 1 shows the indices of the features defined in Sect. 3 ranked by PLCC, ReliefF and SDT in terms of their decreasing importance. As delineated, there are only 19 features specified by SDT since the grown tree selected only 19 features as nodes rejecting remaining 25 attributes. The first row of the table indicates that all three selection methods provide different feature as the most significant, i.e.: m_6 for the accelerometer and μ_a for both the accelerometer and the microfon.

Table 1. The indices of features positioned in terms of their significance obtained by PLCC (**P**), ReliefF (**R**) and SDT (**T**); the rank column N presents the established order from the most to least important attribute.

N	**P**	**R**	**T**	N	**P**	**R**
1	15	7	29	20	20	38
2	14	14	7	21	3	36
3	17	29	8	22	5	15
4	19	35	15	23	33	39
5	29	28	13	24	30	43
6	10	32	17	25	34	21
7	9	31	32	26	36	37
8	8	25	23	27	22	22
9	12	24	5	28	37	11
10	11	27	31	29	39	12
11	7	13	6	30	38	8
12	31	23	28	31	6	9
13	32	26	25	32	28	10
14	16	34	20	33	41	16
15	1	30	33	34	44	44
16	27	33	1	35	40	17
17	18	42	18	36	42	3
18	23	40	2	37	2	18
19	25	41	24	38	26	19
				39	43	2
				40	13	5
				41	24	1
				42	21	20
				43	4	6
				44	35	4

6   Proposed Method

The goal of this paper is to present a new approach which finds the most relevant subset of features in the data set under investigation. Three different FS methods are used for this purpose, where each one determines different outcome in terms of the ranking of features's significance, as shown in Table 1. We propose a fusion of these methods to find a suboptimal subset of features as the result. The weighted combined ranking score criterion is introduced which allows us to exclude the outcome of the method providing the lowest classification accuracy.

The performance is evaluated with the use of the classification accuracy computed as follows:

$$Acc = \frac{1}{L} \sum_{l=1}^{L} \delta \left[y(\mathbf{x}_l) = t_l \right], \tag{6}$$

where $y(\mathbf{x}_l)$ is the MLP's output calculated for $\mathbf{x}_l$. In (6), $\delta\,[\cdot]=1$ when $y(\mathbf{x}_l)=t_l$ and 0, otherwise. Acc is determined using a 10–fold cross validation procedure.

Three following definitions are required to elect a feature as important.

Definition 1. *Let: (i) $\mathbf{P}$, $\mathbf{R}$ and $\mathbf{T}$ denote the sets of features' indices ordered according to the criterion of significance determined by PLCC, ReliefF and SDT methods, respectively; (ii) Acc_i^s, where $s = \{\mathbf{P}, \mathbf{R}, \mathbf{T}\}$ and $i = 1, \ldots,$ $\min\{|\mathbf{P}|, |\mathbf{R}|, |\mathbf{T}|\}$, denote the accuracy determined for i initial elements of $\mathbf{P}$, $\mathbf{R}$ and $\mathbf{T}$. Then the vector $\mathbf{w}^s$ composed of elements:*

$$w_i^s = \begin{cases} 0 & \text{if } Acc_i^s = \min\left\{Acc_i^\mathbf{P}, Acc_i^\mathbf{R}, Acc_i^\mathbf{T}\right\} \\ 1 & \text{otherwise} \end{cases} \tag{7}$$

defines the weights of features provided by particular FS methods.

It is worth to observe that the use of the weights defined according to (7) will result in omitting these features which contribute to the lowest accuracy. Also note, that not all the features may be included as tree nodes by SDT; therefore, it is assumed that $|\mathbf{P}| = |\mathbf{R}| > |\mathbf{T}|$, where $|\cdot|$ is the set's cardinality.

Definition 2. *Let: (i) $\mathbf{P}_j$, $\mathbf{R}_j$ and $\mathbf{T}_j$ stand for the subsets of the first j elements of $\mathbf{P}$, $\mathbf{R}$ and $\mathbf{T}$, respectively; (ii) $\mathbf{w}^{\mathbf{P}_j}$, $\mathbf{w}^{\mathbf{R}_j}$ and $\mathbf{w}^{\mathbf{T}_j}$ stand for the first j weights determined for $\mathbf{P}$, $\mathbf{R}$ and $\mathbf{T}$ according to (7), respectively. Then the set of common features' indices is defined as follows:*

$$\mathbf{C}_j = \left[\left(\mathbf{w}^{\mathbf{P}_j} \odot \mathbf{P}_j \cup \mathbf{w}^{\mathbf{R}_j} \odot \mathbf{R}_j\right) \cap \mathbf{T}\right] \cup \mathbf{w}^{\mathbf{T}_j} \odot \mathbf{T}_j, \tag{8}$$

where $j = 1, \ldots, |\mathbf{T}|$ and $\odot$ denotes the element-wise multiplication operator.

Some commentary is worth adding here. Taking (7) into consideration, the expressions $\mathbf{w}^{\mathbf{P}_j} \odot \mathbf{P}_j$, $\mathbf{w}^{\mathbf{R}_j} \odot \mathbf{R}_j$ and $\mathbf{w}^{\mathbf{T}_j} \odot \mathbf{T}_j$ provide the possibility of omitting these features which are responsible for the lowest value of the accuracy in PLCC, ReliefF and SDT methods, respectively. Once they are discovered, the computation of $\left(\mathbf{w}^{\mathbf{P}_j} \odot \mathbf{P}_j \cup \mathbf{w}^{\mathbf{R}_j} \odot \mathbf{R}_j\right) \cap \mathbf{T}$ enables us to select the most significant attributes from $\mathbf{P}_j$ and $\mathbf{R}_j$ which occur in $\mathbf{T}$. Such features, along with the ones in $\mathbf{w}^{\mathbf{T}_j} \odot \mathbf{T}_j$, establish the set of common features' indices $\mathbf{C}_j$.

Definition 3. *Given the set of common features' indices $\mathbf{C}_j$ defined in (8). Let: (i) C_{jk} stand for some feature that is the k-th element of $\mathbf{C}_j$; (ii) $\mathbf{X}\{C_{jk}\}$ indicate some natural number, which directly corresponds to the index of C_{jk} in $\mathbf{X}$ where $\mathbf{X}$ is any of predefined sets of features' indices. A combined ranking score which is determined for the feature C_{jk} selected in $\mathbf{P}_j$, $\mathbf{R}_j$ and $\mathbf{T}_j$ simultaneously is defined as follows:*

$$R_{C_{jk}} = \sum_{s=1}^{3} w_k^s \left(|\mathbf{T}| - \mathbf{X}_s\{C_{jk}\} + 1\right) \tag{9}$$

for $\mathbf{X}_s\{C_{jk}\} \leqslant |\mathbf{T}|$. In (9), $\mathbf{X}_1 = \mathbf{P}$, $\mathbf{X}_2 = \mathbf{R}$, $\mathbf{X}_3 = \mathbf{T}$ and $k = 1, \ldots, |\mathbf{C}_j|$. For any $\mathbf{X}_s\{C_{jk}\} > |\mathbf{T}|$, the s-th summand is not considered in computing $R_{C_{jk}}$. Adding 1 ensures assignment of the score from the set $\{1, \ldots, |\mathbf{T}|\}$ for each s.

To clarify the idea behind the proposed method, it is good to elaborate an example. Let us consider $j = 4$ first feature indices provided in Table 1 by each FS method: $\mathbf{P}_4 = [15, 14, 17, 19]$, $\mathbf{R}_4 = [7, 14, 29, 35]$ and $\mathbf{T}_4 = [29, 7, 8, 15]$. Table 2 presents the accuracy Acc_i^s for $i = 1, \ldots, 4$ and $s = \{\mathbf{P}_4, \mathbf{R}_4, \mathbf{T}_4\}$.

Table 2. The accuracy determined for $j = 4$ initial elements of $\mathbf{P}$, $\mathbf{R}$ and $\mathbf{T}$.

Accuracy	$i = 1$	$i = 2$	$i = 3$	$i = 4$
$Acc_i^{\mathbf{P}_4}$	65.02	66.06	66.16	66.71
$Acc_i^{\mathbf{R}_4}$	70.34	70.71	83.55	83.63
$Acc_i^{\mathbf{T}_4}$	74.18	83.87	84.63	85.39

Since for $i = 1, \ldots, 4$, particular $Acc_i^{\mathbf{P}_4}$ values are the lowest in contrast to the corresponding $Acc_i^{\mathbf{R}_4}$ and $Acc_i^{\mathbf{T}_4}$, the weight vectors are as follows: $\mathbf{w}^{\mathbf{P}_4} = [0, 0, 0, 0]$, $\mathbf{w}^{\mathbf{R}_4} = [1, 1, 1, 1]$ and $\mathbf{w}^{\mathbf{T}_4} = [1, 1, 1, 1]$. Applying the element-wise multiplication operator, we obtain: $\mathbf{w}^{\mathbf{P}_4} \odot \mathbf{P}_4 = [0, 0, 0, 0]$, $\mathbf{w}^{\mathbf{R}_4} \odot \mathbf{R}_4 = [7, 14, 29, 35]$ and $\mathbf{w}^{\mathbf{T}_4} \odot \mathbf{T}_4 = [29, 7, 8, 15]$. Therefore, $\mathbf{C}_4 = [7, 14, 29, 35] \cap \mathbf{T} \cup [29, 7, 8, 15] = [7, 29, 8, 15]$. Now, it is necessary to determine the ranking of $\mathbf{C}_4$ elements. For $k = 1$, $C_{41} = 7$; therefore, $\mathbf{P}\{7\} = 11$, $\mathbf{R}\{7\} = 1$ and $\mathbf{T}\{7\} = 2$. Thus, the combined ranking score for the feature 7 chosen in $\mathbf{P}_4$, $\mathbf{R}_4$, and $\mathbf{T}_4$ is equal to $R_7 = 0(19 - 11 + 1) + 1(19 - 1 + 1) + 1(19 - 2 + 1) = 37$. After similar calculations, $R_{29} = 36$, $R_8 = 17$ and $R_{15} = 16$. Thus, the first four indices of common features ranked in terms of the importance are represented by the set: $\boldsymbol{\Gamma}_4 = [7, 29, 8, 15]$.

The upper part of Table 3 shows the combined ranking sets for the indices of particular common features in $\boldsymbol{\Gamma}_j$. As indicated in the table, $\boldsymbol{\Gamma}_j$ are not included for $j = \{2, 10, 12, 13, 16, 19\}$. This results from the fact that in these cases, $\boldsymbol{\Gamma}_j = \boldsymbol{\Gamma}_{j-1}$ holds.

Table 3. The upper part: the combined ranking sets for the indices of particular common features' stored in $\mathbf{C}_j$. The lower part: the maximal values of accuracy (in %) achieved by MLP for the attributes included in the first N elements of $\boldsymbol{\Gamma}_j$.

		$\boldsymbol{\Gamma}_1$	$\boldsymbol{\Gamma}_3$	$\boldsymbol{\Gamma}_4$	$\boldsymbol{\Gamma}_5$	$\boldsymbol{\Gamma}_6$	$\boldsymbol{\Gamma}_7$	$\boldsymbol{\Gamma}_8$	$\boldsymbol{\Gamma}_9$	$\boldsymbol{\Gamma}_{11}$	$\boldsymbol{\Gamma}_{14}$	$\boldsymbol{\Gamma}_{15}$	$\boldsymbol{\Gamma}_{17}$	$\boldsymbol{\Gamma}_{18}$
	1	7	7	7	7	7	7	7	7	15	15	15	15	15
	2	29	29	29	29	29	29	29	29	29	29	29	29	29
	3		8	8	13	32	32	32	32	17	17	17	17	17
	4			15	28	13	13	13	13	8	8	8	8	8
	5				8	28	28	28	28	7	7	7	7	7
	6				15	8	31	31	31	32	32	32	32	32
	7					15	8	23	23	31	31	31	31	31
	8					17	15	25	25	13	13	13	13	13
Indices	9						17	8	8	23	23	23	23	23
	10							15	15	5	5	5	5	5
	11							17	17	6	6	1	1	1
	12							24	25		25	6	6	6
	13							5	28		28	25	25	25
	14								24		20	28	28	28
	15										24	20	18	18
	16											33	20	20
	17											24	33	33
	18												24	2
	19													24

Acc	83.72	83.92	84.67	88.66	88.64	**89.51**	88.38	84.20	87.84	87.92	88.23	**89.16**	87.99
	±1.28	±1.97	±0.85	±0.39	±0.58	**±0.72**	±0.20	±2.76	±2.20	±0.68	±1.43	**±0.20**	±0.72
N	2	3	4	5	8	**8**	10	13	10	14	8	**8**	15

7   Results

This section presents the performance of MLP in the classification of the data from the milling process. We consider the input records with: (i) the number of attributes reduced by the considered FS methods, (ii) the features selected with the use of the proposed method, and (iii) 44 original attributes. MLP is tuned with the number of neurons H in (1) from 1 to 20 with the step 1; the network activated by sigmoidal and linear transfer functions is trained by Levenberg-Marquardt algorithm [8].

Given the features ordered from the most to least significant according to PLCC, ReliffF and SDT (Table 1), the MLP is firstly applied in the classification task of the records with single, most relevant feature. Next, individual less meaningful feature is included to the input space and data classification is conducted again. The procedure is repeated until MLP is presented with all attributes (44 for PLCC, ReliefF and 19 for SDT).

For the proposed method, the set of attributes is chosen using (8). For partic-ular value of j, the number of features is incremented from 1 to $|\Gamma_j|$ in the order determined by the ranking score (9). Exemplary performance results attained by MLP for $H = 6$ are shown in Fig. 1. Each plot in this figure represents Acc for the attributes from the set Γ_j (see Table 3) and consists of $|\Gamma_j|$ points. The number features from the set Γ_j, for which the maximal accuracy is achieved, is denoted by N. The maximal accuracy values for each Γ_j are included in the bottom part of Table 3. As shown, the highest $Acc = 89.51\%$ is obtained for $j = 7$ at $N = 8$, i.e.: when 8 first features from Γ_7 are presented to MLP.

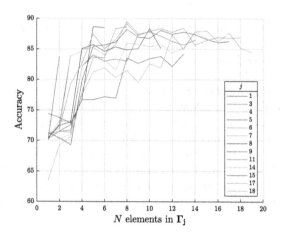

Fig. 1. The values of the accuracy (in %) for the MLP composed of $H = 6$ hidden neurons for the data with attributes from the set Γ_j.

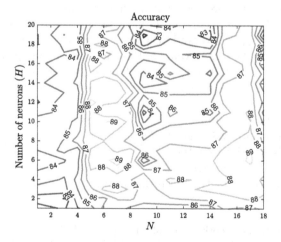

Fig. 2. MLP's accuracy values (in %) as the function of the first N elements of Γ_j and the number of neurons (H) used to build the network.

Table 4. First three columns: the highest Acc (in %) for MLP determined on the data set with the number of attributes reduced to N according to three FS methods; next column: the highest accuracy achieved on Γ_j; last column: the accuracy of original data set.

PLCC		ReliefF		SDT		Proposed method		All features	
Acc	N	Acc	N	Acc	N	Acc	N	Acc	N
88.13 ±1.66	15	87.98 ±1.44	31	88.51 ±1.43	7	89.51 ±0.72	8	87.07 ±1.59	44

Table 4 presents the highest accuracy results achieved by MLP in the classification of the considered data set with features reduced by PLCC, ReliefF, SDT and the proposed method, and when no attribute selection occurs. It can be noted that the values of Acc obtained by all four feature selection methods are higher for smaller number of attributes than Acc for the entire data set. Furthermore, the new method allows us to determine the highest accuracy among all reduction approaches. The number of features for which the maximal Acc is attained by the proposed method is 2–4 lower the one of PLCC and ReliefF.

Figure 2 illustrates the influence of the number of neurons (H) and the first N elements of Γ_j on the MLP's accuracy. One observes that the value of Acc exceeding 89% occurs three times, i.e., for: $H = 6$ at Γ_7 and Γ_{17}, and for $H = 10$ at Γ_7. One can also discover the trend of reaching higher accuracies for Γ_7 when $H = 3, \ldots, 18$.

8   Conclusions

In this study, a new feature selection method was proposed. Its main concept relied on comparing the accuracy of the MLP on the data set with features reduced by the PLCC, ReliefF and SDT approaches and discarding those, which were responsible for the lowest value of this indicator among primary FS methods. Based on the weighted combined ranking score, the attributes selected by two most efficient methods were used to create the final set of features. The idea was applied to real data set represented by 44 parameters computed from 1709 signals acquired in the milling process. The presented results confirmed that adopted approach improved the MLP's accuracy in comparison to the results achieved by this classifier on the data set where features were generated by PLCC, ReliefF, SDT and original set of attributes. Such a solution might have a nature of an universal method of fusing primary FS methods in order to find optimal set of features.

Acknowledgment. This work is partially financed by Polish Ministry of Science and Higher Education under the program "Regional Initiative of Excellence" in 2019–2022, project number 027/RID/2018/19, funding amount 11 999 900 PLN and the funds granted to the Department of Electronics Fundamentals, Rzeszow University of Technology, within the subsidy for maintaining research potential (UPB).

References

1. Almuallim, H., Dietterich, T.: Learning with many irrelevant features. In: The Ninth National Conference on Artificial Intelligence, pp. 547–552 (1991)
2. Benesty J., Chen J., Huang Y., Cohen I.: Pearson correlation coefficient. In: Noise Reduction in Speech Processing. STSP, vol. 2, pp. 1–4. Springer, Heidelberg (2009). https://doi.org/10.1007/978-3-642-00296-0_5
3. Cardie, C.: Using decision trees to improve case-based learning. In: The 10th International Conference on Machine Learning, pp. 25–32 (1993)
4. Goebel, K., Yan, W.: Feature selection for tool wear diagnosis using soft computing techniques. In: The ASME International Mechanical Engineering Congress and Exhibition, pp. 5–10 (2000)
5. Kononenko, I.: Estimating attributes: analysis and extensions of RELIEF. In: Bergadano, F., De Raedt, L. (eds.) ECML 1994. LNCS, vol. 784, pp. 171–182. Springer, Heidelberg (1994). https://doi.org/10.1007/3-540-57868-4_57
6. Li, Y., Hsu, D.F., Chung, S.M.: Combination of multiple feature selection methods for text categorization by using combinatorial fusion analysis and rank-score characteristic. Int. J. Artif. Intell. Tools **22**(02), 1350001 (2013)
7. Madhusudana, C., Kumar, H., Narendranath, S.: Condition monitoring of face milling tool using k-star algorithm and histogram features of vibration signal. Eng. Sci. Technol. Int. J. **19**(3), 1543–1551 (2016)
8. Marquardt, D.W.: An algorithm for least-squares estimation of nonlinear parameters. J. Soc. Ind. Appl. Math. **11**(2), 431–441 (1963)
9. Pes, B.: Ensemble feature selection for high-dimensional data: a stability analysis across multiple domains. Neural Comput. Appl. **32**(10), 5951–5973 (2019). https://doi.org/10.1007/s00521-019-04082-3
10. Rokach, L., Chizi, B., Maimon, O.: Feature selection by combining multiple methods. In: Advances in Web Intelligence and Data Mining, pp. 295–304 (2006)
11. Rumelhart, D.E., Hinton, G.E., Williams, R.J.: Learning internal representations by error propagation. In: Rumelhart, D.E., McClelland, J.L. (eds.) Parallel Distributed Processing, Chap. 8, pp. 318–362. MIT Press (1986)
12. Yu, L., Liu, H.: Feature selection for high-dimensional data: a fast correlation-based filter solution. In: The 20th International Conference on Machine Learning, pp. 547–552 (2003)
13. Zabinski, T., Maczka, T., Kluska, J.: Industrial platform for rapid prototyping of intelligent diagnostic systems. In: Mitkowski, W., Kacprzyk, J., Oprzedkiewicz, K., Skruch, P. (eds.) Trends in Advanced Intelligent Control, Optimization and Automation, pp. 712–721. Springer, Cham (2017). https://doi.org/10.1007/978-3-319-60699-6_69
14. Zhu, K., Hong, G., Wong, Y.: A comparative study of feature selection for hidden Markov model-based micro-milling tool wear monitoring. Mach. Sci. Technol. **12**(3), 348–369 (2008)

Generative Modeling in Application to Point Cloud Completion

Maciej Zamorski[1,2(✉)], Maciej Zięba[1,2], and Jerzy Świątek[1]

[1] Wrocław University of Science and Technology, Wrocław, Poland
maciej.zamorski@pwr.edu.pl
[2] Tooploox, Wrocław, Poland

Abstract. The three-dimensional data representations have found numerous applications, most notably in SLAM and autonomous driving, where the most widely used type of data is a point cloud. In contrast to the image data, point clouds are unstructured objects, represented as sets of points in three- or six-dimensional (if the colors of surroundings are captured as well) space. Each of the point clouds can have a variable number of points, that in turn, are in $\mathbb{R}^3$ space. All those factors dramatically increase the complexity of the data. The PointNet model offers an easy way to process point cloud data and can perform classification and segmentation tasks, based on raw point clouds. However, in literature, PointNet is usually trained on the complete data that captures the shape features from every side of the object. In real-world applications, the collected data may be moved, occluded, and noisy. In this work, we focus on training generative models on partial data in order to predict how the point clouds may have looked as complete objects. Such completed point clouds may then later be used in other downstream tasks.

Keywords: Generative models · Point clouds · Input reconstruction

1 Introduction

The rise of the deep learning methods offered the possibilities unmatched by the previous approaches. They revolutionized processing the images, natural text, and even videos. The particular advancement that allowed a big-scale analysis of vision data was introducing deep architectures [10] called convolutional neural networks (CNNs) that utilized the convolutional filters as the network layers.

Unlike the previous approaches, which mainly used feed-forward networks with data flattened to 1-dimensional vectors, convolutional filters enabled to consider spatial information, producing more essential features about patterns in the data. Thanks to that, CNNs can be used in discriminative tasks (such as object detection, recognition or segmentation) and generative modeling, usually as part of a bigger model, e.g., VAE [9] or GAN [5,24]) However, while usage of convolutional filters allowed to achieve state-of-the-art performance in tasks, they by design require data to be highly structured, e.g., consistent size of a pixel grid of the dataset images.

© Springer Nature Switzerland AG 2020
L. Rutkowski et al. (Eds.): ICAISC 2020, LNAI 12415, pp. 292–302, 2020.
https://doi.org/10.1007/978-3-030-61401-0_28

Extending those approaches to 3D space, particularly unstructured point clouds, is not trivial. First, point clouds offer no grid, which makes the use of the filters to be impossible. Second, continuous representation of points in 3D space can vary in density between different parts of the point cloud, which makes the voxelization of data lose meaningful information about the input shape. Another difficulty in processing point clouds, also due to lack of a grid, is the point cloud invariance to permutation. Having a point cloud P containing N points there exists $N!$ (assuming no duplicated points) ways to represent a single cloud.

To overcome those difficulties, the PointNet [14] was introduced. PointNet processes 3d shapes with no regard for the order of points in the point cloud. Practically, it means that for two identical point clouds (except for the order of points), the model will return the same feature vector. It is achieved by processing each point separately and performing the feature-wise aggregation using a permutation-invariant function.

One of the key areas for the point cloud data utilization is an environment mapping with LIDAR devices. LIDAR mapping provides point cloud maps that are irregular in size and density of points. Moreover, the scanned environment can be partially incomplete, due to objects that are potentially moving and that are able to cover other objects. During training, PointNet learns to obtain point cloud feature embeddings, regardless of point cloud size, that are able to represent different 3D shape types [14] accurately. However, the training procedure is usually done using only complete 360° models. Those learned representations can be used to reconstruct the incomplete point cloud shapes using deep generative models, such as Autoencoders, Variational Autoencoders [9], and Adversarial Autoencoders [11].

In this work, we present a training procedure for generative models based on PointNet for point cloud shape completion. First, we propose an extension of the standard PointNet model, dubbed "Double PointNet". Next, we analyze the completion quality using the baseline Autoencoder model and the competing results from the regularized models. We show that the usage of Double PointNet leads to better shape completions, comparing to the standard encoder. For the evaluation purposes, we use two classes from the ShapeNet dataset and compare the results quantitatively and qualitatively.

This work is organized as follows. Section 2 gives a brief overview of the machine learning methods for the 3D shape completion tasks. Section 3 introduces the generative models based on PointNet that we evaluate in this work. Experiments and the conclusions are discussed in Sect. 4. The Sect. 5 provides a summary of the article.

2   Related Works

To reduce the complexity resulting from a continuously-valued point space, the initial works often used voxel data, that presented 3D shapes as a volumetric grids [3,12,22] or a collection of 2D images taken from the different angles of the 3D object [8,18].

However, converting the point cloud data to voxel requires prior knowledge about the bounds of possible point locations, as well as manually selecting the density of the volumetric grid. In order to benefit from fine details of point cloud shapes the PointNet [14] was introduced, along with its hierarchical extension PointNet++ [15]. The idea behind them is to obtain features about each point composing the cloud separately, followed by aggregating the resulting encoding matrix feature-wise resulting in a representation vector that captures information about the whole shape. This idea inspired many deep learning techniques, especially in the area of graph neural networks [6,20,21]. PointNet's architecture, due to being well-suited for learning representations, is also often used as an encoder part of deep generative models [1,25].

Recently, novel approaches utilizing normalizing flows are being used. In terms of learning the data manifold of point clouds, they offer tractable computation of a sample likelihood as a clear metric of the model's generalization quality. In PointFlow [23], authors present a continuous normalizing flow approach to constructing point clouds by rearranging points sampled from a simple prior. On the other hand, in CIF [17], authors propose a meta-learning setting using conditional flows.

A traditional approach to shape completion treated it as an optimization problem [13,16]. After an introduction of large 3D shape datasets, such as ShapeNet [2], it became possible to train the deep models directly on shapes. More recent approaches were based on a voxel inputs [4,7,22]. One of the recent works for point cloud input is TopNet [19], employing a multi-stage architecture to decoding shapes.

3 Method

In this section, we describe the deep learning framework that was used for the processing of the point cloud data. First, we define the point cloud completion task, and we state the importance of using the models that take the raw points as an input to the network, in contrast to simplified representations, e.g., voxels. Following that, we describe in detail the architectures of PointNet and PointNet extended and their usage as a way to encode data with application to a point cloud completion task on a ShapeNet dataset.

3.1 Point Cloud Completion Task

One of the possible tasks on the image data is an image completion. Given the image split in two, the task consists of producing the output by generating one of the splits, while getting the second one as an input. We can define a similar task in the space of the 3d point cloud data.

Let's assume a set of point clouds, denoted as $\mathcal{S} = \{S_1, S_2, \ldots, S_n\}$. Each point cloud S_k, is made of points $s_{k,1}, s_{k,2}, \ldots, s_{k,l} \in \mathbb{R}^3$. For each point cloud $S_k \in \mathcal{S}$ we perform a split into two equinumerous subsets $S_{k,1}, S_{k,2}$, s.t. $S_{k,1} \cap$

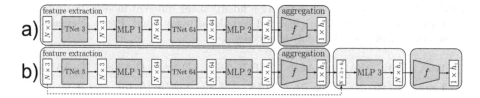

Fig. 1. A PointNet architecture that consists of two parts: 1) feature extraction that encodes each point separately to a feature vector of length h_z, 2) aggregation function, combining features feature-wise across all points to obtain shape representation. Two architectures are presented: a) base version of PointNet, b) "Double" PointNet, with an additional network calculating global features based on a point location and intermediate shape representation. The TNet K refers to learnable affine transforms in K dimensions introduced in [14]. The MLP M networks architecture is described in a Sect. 3.2.

$S_{k,2} = \emptyset \wedge S_{k,1} \cup S_{k,2} = S$. Assuming model $M : \mathbb{R}^{1024 \times 3} \rightarrow \mathbb{R}^{1024 \times 3}$ with parameters θ, we want to arrive at solution θ^*, s.t. $M_{\theta^*}(S_{k,1}) = M_{\theta^*}(S_{k,2}) = S_{k,1} \cup S_{k,2} = S_k$.

3.2   PointNet Architecture

In this work we use 3 popular generative models: Autoencoders, Variational Autoencoders [9] and Adversarial Autoencoders [11]. Each of those models consists of at least two parts: 1) encoder $E : \mathcal{X} \rightarrow \mathbf{z}$, transforming a sample $X \in \mathcal{X}$ from the data space into an encoding $z \in \mathbf{z}$ in the feature space, and 2) generator $G : \mathbf{z} \rightarrow \mathcal{X}$. Additionally, VAE adds the KL-divergence regularization term to make the distribution of the posterior follow the normal distribution. In AAEs, the regularization is done with an additional discriminator $D : \mathbf{z} \rightarrow [0,1]$, judging whether an encoding sample $z \in \mathbf{z}$ comes from the specified prior or not. The goal of the discriminator is to assign high confidence values to the samples from the prior distribution and low confidence values to the samples obtained by an encoder. Conversely, one of the objectives of the encoder is to produce such samples, that they will receive high confidence scores from the discriminator. The discriminator approach used in AAEs offers far more flexibility than KL divergence from VAEs. The only thing required to regularize to given probability distribution is the ability to obtain samples from that distribution. On the other hand, regularization in VAE requires KL divergence between posterior and prior distributions to be expressed in the closed-form.

For the encoder part, we use the PointNet model, introduced in [14]. The architecture schema of the PointNet is presented in the Fig. 1. One of the main ideas of PointNet is performing feature extraction point-wise, without taking the whole shape into consideration until the very end. By implementing multilayer perceptrons (MLPs) as a 1-dimensional convolution, the model becomes invariant to the number of points N in the input. The characteristic block of the architecture of PointNet is a smaller subnet called TNet. By outputting the 3×3

Table 1. Comparison of a reconstruction fidelity using different models, measured as the EMD distance between original and completed point cloud. Prefix D symbolizes architectures using Double PointNet encoder.

Class	AE	VAE	AAE-N	AAE-B	D-AE	D-VAE	D-AAE-N	D-AAE-B
Chair	64.99	216.22	68.79	72.58	56.29	122.59	64.76	70.69
Airplane	39.65	143.24	48.19	51.08	31.08	104.94	36.05	43.47

and 64×64 (for TNet3 and 64 respectively), TNets learn the affine transformations applied to the input (TNet3) and the point cloud with each point encoded into an intermediate 64-dimensional representation (TNet64). This is done to ensure the model's invariance to the scaling, shifting, and rotating of the input. The last step in the standard PointNet model is aggregating features obtained for each point into one vector for the whole shape. Function $f : \mathbb{R}^N - > \mathbb{R}$ is applied column-wise on the $N \times h_z$ feature matrix, resulting in the feature vector z. By choosing a permutation-invariant function f (such as $\max(\cdot)$), the Point-Net is able to return the same output, regardless of the order of the points in the input.

In the original approach, features extracted from each point are calculated without considering the whole shape. As a way of extending the feature extraction procedure, we also try two additional steps to the standard model. In this work, we call this extended approach "Double PointNet". After obtaining the output feature vector, it is then appended to each point vector, resulting in a matrix of size $N \times (3 + h_z)$. This matrix is then processed by an additional Multilayer Perceptron, and the resulting features are aggregated in the same manner as before.

For each generative model (AE, VAE, AAE-N, AAE-B) we construct two architectures — with a standard autoencoder presented in the Fig. 1a, and with Double PointNet (Fig. 1b). We add prefix "Double" to each model's name that uses Double PointNet as an encoder.

4   Experiment

The goal of the experiment is to evaluate the completion abilities of the autoencoding networks, based on different architectures with different approaches to F space regularization and whole-shape embedding. Using a standard Autoencoder (AE) architecture as a baseline, we have also checked Variational Autoencoders (VAE) [9], regularized with Kullback–Leibler divergence and Adversarial Autoencoders (AAE) [11] employing adversarial discriminator as a regularizer. Furthermore, two different priors were used for the AAE, resulting in two types of this architecture — AAE-N regularized with the standard normal distribution $\mathcal{N}(\mu = 0, \sigma^2 = 1)$ and AAE-B regularized with Beta distribution $\text{Beta}(\alpha = 0.01, \beta = 0.01)$. The goal of regularization with the Beta prior is to produce binary embeddings, since a Beta distribution with coefficients $\alpha, \beta \ll 1$

will result in most of the probability mass concentrated close to values 0 and 1. In practice, for implementation convenience, the binary values are often encoded as ±1. In this work we follow this convention, transforming the values sampled from a distribution $2 * \text{Beta}(\alpha = 0.01, \beta = 0.01) - 1$.

All the mentioned models have trained on a single class (airplane or chair) of the ShapeNet [2] dataset. We describe this dataset in Sect. 4.1.

4.1 Dataset

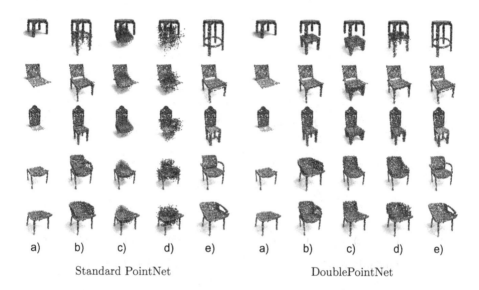

| a) | b) | c) | d) | e) | a) | b) | c) | d) | e) |

Standard PointNet   DoublePointNet

Fig. 2. Visualizations of the point clouds completions for 5 examples from the test set of the chair class. Columns represent: a) input, b) Autoencoder output, c) Variational Autoencoder output, d) Adversarial Autoencoder with Normal prior output, e) ground truth.

All experiments presented in this work we performed using the ShapeNet [2] dataset. It consists of over 50000 point clouds, each given as 2048 points in 3-dimensional space and belonging to 55 classes. The classes are heavily imbalanced, ranging from 65 to 23 thousand samples per class. Each point cloud is given pre-aligned to a vertical axis (usually denoted in Cartesian coordinates as axis "z"). Each of the models was trained only on a single class, which was either "airplane" or "chair". Class datasets were split into 85% train — 5% validation — 10% test parts.

To train models for solving the completion tasks, we split the 2048 points of each point cloud into the two disjoint, equinumerous subsets of size 1024. Split is performed by randomly choosing an axis (x, y, or z) and taking points with the biggest or the lowest 1024 values for this axis. This results in a total of 6 possible splits for a single point cloud.

4.2 Results

In this section, we present the results on the point cloud completion tasks achieved by the various generative models based on PointNet and Double Point-Net models. The experiments were conducted for a total of eight different architectures — Autoencoder (baseline), Variational Autoencoder, Adversarial Autoencoder - Normal, and Beta with either PointNet or Double PointNet as an encoder. All the models were trained with the length of the feature vector $h_z = 100$.

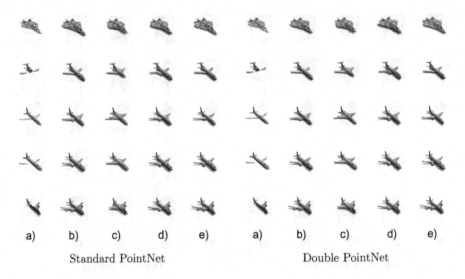

Standard PointNet   Double PointNet

Fig. 3. Visualizations of the point clouds completions for 5 examples from the test set of the airplane class. Columns represent: a) input, b) Autoencoder output, c) Variational Autoencoder output, d) Adversarial Autoencoder with Normal prior output, e) ground truth.

In Table 1 we present results of point cloud completion fidelity. Each of the eight architectures was trained on two shape classes from the ShapeNet dataset: airplane and chair. The evaluation was performed on the test splits of those classes. Each point cloud from the test split was further used to produce six test samples (3 possible dimensions for reconstructions times two halves). The essential observation is that the better completions achieved by models based on the Double PointNet encoder. This suggests that processing the points in the point cloud with regard to the complete shape of the cloud can lead to significant improvement in a generalization of the model to the unseen shapes. Moreover, by comparing the results for VAE and AAE-N models, it can be seen that VAE is unable to learn any meaningful completions, leading to the conclusion, that KL divergence-based regularization may be too strong of a constraint for the encoder. On the other hand, AAE-N and D-AAE-N do not seem to suffer from imposing

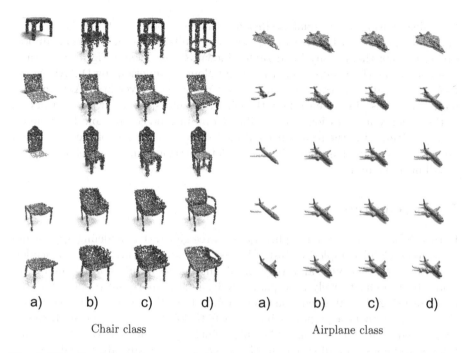

Fig. 4. Visualizations of the point clouds completions for 5 examples from the test set. Columns represent: a) input, b) Double Adversarial Autoencoder with Normal prior output, c) Double Adversarial Autoencoder with Beta prior output, d) ground truth.

a latent space regularization, having only a slight decrease in completion quality in comparison to the baseline. The important insight comes from comparing the results of (D-)AAEs regularized with Normal and Beta distributions. As the Beta-regularized models scored only slightly worse than Normal-regularized models, it shows that an efficient binarization of shape representations may be possible. This can have an added benefit of a possibility of creating a retrieval approach with the partial shapes database for efficient completing new shapes, which can result in a processing speed improvements, that are critical in real-time environments such as autonomous driving.

By comparing qualitative results on chair class for generative models using standard (Fig. 2a) and double PointNet (Fig. 2b), the difference in the shape completion can be seen. The case is similar for standard (Fig. 3a) and double (Fig. 3b) versions of models that were trained on an airplane class point clouds. The presented visual results show that the AAE/D-AAE models learned the point cloud completion task instead of underfitting (like in the case of VAE models) or landing early in the bad local minima. Moreover, the differences between AE- and AAE-models are minuscule and focused on the details.

As mentioned before, the goal of training AAE and D-AAE models lies in the ability to regularize the latent representation with any probability distribution that we have the possibility to sample from. By regularizing it with the

Beta distribution with equal coefficients that are close to 0, the latent variables are encouraged to have values near the limits of the distribution support range, making them easily binarizable. Shown in Fig. 4a and Fig. 4b are examples comparing the results of creating point cloud completions by D-AAE-N and D-AAE-B models. It can be seen that by using the Adversarial Autoencoder model, which is able to encode both point-wise and structure-wise information to the latent representation, it is possible to obtain good completions from binary vectors. Comparing the results from Table 1 show that the loss of the completion fidelity between models regularized with Beta distribution, compared to Normal distribution is minimal.

5   Conclusions

In this work, we present an application of three generative modeling approaches to a point cloud completion task. We test the architectures of Autoencoder, Variational Autoencoder, and Adversarial Autoencoder (with normal and binary prior) both quantitatively and qualitatively. Furthermore, we propose an approach of using the extended PointNet model, dubbed here as a "Double Point-Net" in order to process points based on both location and the overall shape. Experiments show that by using Double PointNet, we can achieve better results than by using a standard variation. Moreover, employing an Adversarial Autoencoder framework allow for an easy binarization of the latent codes of the inputs with minimal losses in completion quality.

References

1. Achlioptas, P., Diamanti, O., Mitliagkas, I., Guibas, L.: Learning representations and generative models for 3d point clouds. arXiv preprint arXiv:1707.02392 (2017)
2. Chang, A.X., et al.: Shapenet: an information-rich 3d model repository. arXiv preprint arXiv:1512.03012 (2015)
3. Çiçek, O., Abdulkadir, A., Lienkamp, S.S., Brox, T., Ronneberger, O.: 3D U-Net: learning dense volumetric segmentation from sparse annotation. In: Ourselin, S., Joskowicz, L., Sabuncu, M.R., Unal, G., Wells, W. (eds.) MICCAI 2016. LNCS, vol. 9901, pp. 424–432. Springer, Cham (2016). https://doi.org/10.1007/978-3-319-46723-8_49
4. Firman, M., Mac Aodha, O., Julier, S., Brostow, G.J.: Structured prediction of unobserved voxels from a single depth image. In: Proceedings of the IEEE Conference on Computer Vision and Pattern Recognition, pp. 5431–5440 (2016)
5. Goodfellow, I., et al.: Generative adversarial nets. In: Advances in Neural Information Processing Systems, pp. 2672–2680 (2014)
6. Hamilton, W., Ying, Z., Leskovec, J.: Inductive representation learning on large graphs. In: Advances in Neural Information Processing Systems, pp. 1024–1034 (2017)
7. Han, X., Li, Z., Huang, H., Kalogerakis, E., Yu, Y.: High-resolution shape completion using deep neural networks for global structure and local geometry inference. In: Proceedings of the IEEE International Conference on Computer Vision, pp. 85–93 (2017)

8. Kanezaki, A., Matsushita, Y., Nishida, Y.: Rotationnet: joint object categorization and pose estimation using multiviews from unsupervised viewpoints. In: Proceedings of the IEEE Conference on Computer Vision and Pattern Recognition, pp. 5010–5019 (2018)
9. Kingma, D.P., Welling, M.: Auto-encoding variational bayes. arXiv preprint arXiv:1312.6114 (2013)
10. Krizhevsky, A., Sutskever, I., Hinton, G.E.: Imagenet classification with deep convolutional neural networks. In: Advances in Neural Information Processing Systems, pp. 1097–1105 (2012)
11. Makhzani, A., Shlens, J., Jaitly, N., Goodfellow, I., Frey, B.: Adversarial autoencoders. arXiv preprint arXiv:1511.05644 (2015)
12. Maturana, D., Scherer, S.: Voxnet: a 3d convolutional neural network for real-time object recognition. In: 2015 IEEE/RSJ International Conference on Intelligent Robots and Systems (IROS), pp. 922–928. IEEE (2015)
13. Nealen, A., Igarashi, T., Sorkine, O., Alexa, M.: Laplacian mesh optimization. In: Proceedings of the 4th International Conference on Computer Graphics and Interactive Techniques in Australasia and Southeast Asia, pp. 381–389 (2006)
14. Qi, C.R., Su, H., Mo, K., Guibas, L.J.: Pointnet: deep learning on point sets for 3d classification and segmentation. In: Proceedings of the IEEE Conference on Computer Vision and Pattern Recognition, pp. 652–660 (2017)
15. Qi, C.R., Yi, L., Su, H., Guibas, L.J.: Pointnet++: deep hierarchical feature learning on point sets in a metric space. CoRR abs/1706.02413v1 (2017). http://arxiv.org/abs/1706.02413v1
16. Sorkine, O., Cohen-Or, D.: Least-squares meshes. In: Proceedings Shape Modeling Applications, 2004, pp. 191–199. IEEE (2004)
17. Stypułkowski, M., Zamorski, M., Zięba, M., Chorowski, J.: Conditional invertible flow for point cloud generation. arXiv preprint arXiv:1910.07344 (2019)
18. Su, H., Maji, S., Kalogerakis, E., Learned-Miller, E.: Multi-view convolutional neural networks for 3d shape recognition. In: Proceedings of the 2015 IEEE International Conference on Computer Vision (ICCV), pp. 945–953. ICCV '15, IEEE Computer Society, Washington, DC, USA (2015). https://doi.org/10.1109/ICCV.2015.114, http://dx.doi.org/10.1109/ICCV.2015.114
19. Tchapmi, L.P., Kosaraju, V., Rezatofighi, H., Reid, I., Savarese, S.: Topnet: structural point cloud decoder. In: The IEEE Conference on Computer Vision and Pattern Recognition (CVPR), June 2019
20. Wang, P.S., Liu, Y., Guo, Y.X., Sun, C.Y., Tong, X.: O-cnn: octree-based convolutional neural networks for 3d shape analysis. ACM Trans. Graph. (TOG) 36(4), 1–11 (2017)
21. Wang, Y., Sun, Y., Liu, Z., Sarma, S.E., Bronstein, M.M., Solomon, J.M.: Dynamic graph CNN for learning on point clouds. ACM Trans. Graph. (TOG) 38(5), 1–12 (2019)
22. Wu, Z., et al.: 3D shapenets: a deep representation for volumetric shapes. In: Proceedings of the IEEE Conference on Computer Vision and Pattern Recognition, pp. 1912–1920 (2015)

23. Yang, G., Huang, X., Hao, Z., Liu, M.Y., Belongie, S., Hariharan, B.: Pointflow: 3d point cloud generation with continuous normalizing flows. In: Proceedings of the IEEE International Conference on Computer Vision, pp. 4541–4550 (2019)

24. Zamorski, M., Zdobylak, A., Zięba, M., Świątek, J.: Generative adversarial networks: recent developments. In: Rutkowski, L., Scherer, R., Korytkowski, M., Pedrycz, W., Tadeusiewicz, R., Zurada, J.M. (eds.) ICAISC 2019. LNCS (LNAI), vol. 11508, pp. 248–258. Springer, Cham (2019). https://doi.org/10.1007/978-3-030-20912-4_24

25. Zamorski, M., et al.: Adversarial autoencoders for compact representations of 3d point clouds. Comput. Vis. Image Underst. **193**, 102921 (2020)

Fuzzy Systems and Their Applications

A Numerical Solution of Fully Fuzzy Distribution Problem

Ludmila Dymova[✉]

Department of Computer Science, Czestochowa University of Technology,
Dabrowskiego 73, 42-200 Czestochowa, Poland
dymova@icis.pcz.pl

Abstract. A new numerical approach to solution of the fuzzy distribution problem based on the direct fuzzy extension of the simplex method is developed. The fuzzy extension is based on fuzzy arithmetic rules and the method for fuzzy values comparison. In the framework of proposed approach, all parameters and variables may be fuzzy values without any additional restrictions, and the results are obtained in the fuzzy form. The α-cut representation of all fuzzy parameters and variables is used and any additional assumption regarding their form is not needed. The advantages of the proposed approach are illustrated with the use of case study, where the fuzzy solution of the fuzzy distribution problem is compared with that obtained using the Monte-Carlo method.

Keywords: Fuzzy extension · Simplex method · Fuzzy distribution problem

1 Introduction

The transportation and distribution problems have similar mathematical structures and are usually treated as particular cases of the general linear programming problem. In practice, we often meet different kinds of uncertainty when the parameters of these optimization problems are presented by intervals or fuzzy values. The fuzzy linear programming problem $FLPP$ is said to be a fully fuzzy linear programming ($FFLP$) problem if all parameters and decision variables are considered as fuzzy values.

There are many papers devoted to the approximate solution of FFLPP in the literature. Usually different restrictions on the shape of fuzzy parameters are used. Some or all the parameters are represented by unrestricted $L - R$ fuzzy numbers or unrestricted $L - R$ flat fuzzy numbers in [7,9]. In [10], the authors used the symmetric trapezoidal fuzzy numbers. The trapezoidal fuzzy numbers are used in [4,11]. The triangular fuzzy numbers are used in [6,12]. The method proposed in [5] is based on a new lexicographic ordering on triangular fuzzy numbers. In [14], the fully fuzzy multi-objective linear programming problem using nearest interval approximation of fuzzy number is transformed finally into the crisp linear programming problem.

© Springer Nature Switzerland AG 2020
L. Rutkowski et al. (Eds.): ICAISC 2020, LNAI 12415, pp. 305–314, 2020.
https://doi.org/10.1007/978-3-030-61401-0_29

Of course, it is hard to estimate all the possible negative consequences of above mentioned restrictions and simplifications. Therefore, more promising seem to be the approaches based on the α-cuts representation of fuzzy values because they are free of any restrictions on the shape of fuzzy values.

In [1], the solution of fully fuzzy reverse logistics network design ($FFRLND$) problem is presented. This paper proposes a new parametric method for solving mathematical programs with fuzzy decision variables. The proposed method is based on α-cuts. Unfortunately, the ranking function used for the fuzzy values comparison (FVC) based on the comparison of the expected values of triangular fuzzy numbers seems to be too simplified whereas FVC plays an important role in the solution of the considered problem. In [2], the detailed literature review of fuzzy transportation problem is presented. the authors proposed the direct approach to the solution of fully fuzzy transportation problems. The method is based on the α-cuts representation of fuzzy values and fuzzy decoding procedure based on constrained fuzzy arithmetic operation and a fuzzy ranking technique. In our opinion, the use of constrained fuzzy arithmetic and simplified fuzzy ranking technique makes it possible to avoid some known problems, but generates addition new ones.

Therefore, in the current paper we propose a new numerical approach to the solution of fully fuzzy distribution problem ($FFDP$) based on the direct fuzzy extension of the simplex method. This extension is based on the fuzzy arithmetic rules and the probabilistic method for fuzzy values comparison. The α-cut representation of all fuzzy parameters and variables is used and any additional assumption regarding their form is not needed. The implementation of this extension is made using object-oriented technique.

It is important that the numerical solution of $FFDP$ is obtained in the fuzzy form without any restrictions on the form of fuzzy parameters of the fuzzy task.

The reminder of the paper is set out as follows. Section 2 is devoted to the mathematical tools used for the fuzzy extension of simplex method. The selection of the method for fuzzy values comparison is carefully argued since it plays a pivotal role in the implementation of the fuzzy simplex method. In Sect. 3, the $FFDP$ is formulated. It is shown how the initial $FFDP$ is transformed to the canonical form $FLPP$. Section 4 presents the results obtained with the use of the developed method for illustrative example and their comparison with those obtained using the Monte-Carlo method. Conclusions are covered in Sect. 5.

2   Mathematical Tools

In the framework of the proposed approach to the fuzzy extension of the simplex method, all the steps of the developed algorithm are similar to those of the standard simplex method with only one difference: the usual arithmetical operations and operation of comparison are replaced by the corresponding operations on the fuzzy values. Obviously, the choice of appropriate operations on fuzzy values, especially the operation of fuzzy values comparison, plays a pivotal role in the development of the proposed method.

2.1 Applied Interval Analysis as the Basis of Fuzzy Arithmetic

The most frequently used approach to implementation of fuzzy arithmetic is based on the α-cuts presentation of fuzzy values [8].

So, if A is a fuzzy value, then $A = \bigcup_{\alpha} \alpha A_{\alpha}$, where αA_{α} is the fuzzy subset $: x \in U, \mu_A(x) \geq \alpha$, A_{α} is the support set of fuzzy subset αA_{α} and U is the universe of discourse. It was proved that if A and B are fuzzy values, then all the operations on them may be presented as operations on the set of crisp intervals corresponding to their α-cuts.

Here we will use the standard interval arithmetic rules. If $A = [a_1, a_2]$ and $B = [b_1, b_2]$ are crisp intervals then

$$A + B = [a_1 + b_1, a_2 + b_2], A - B = [a_1 - b_2, a_2 - b_1],$$

$$AB = [min(a_1b_1, a_2b_2, a_1b_2, a_2b_1), max(a_1b_1, a_2b_2, a_1b_2, a_2b_1)],$$

$$A/B = [a_1, a_2][1/b_2, 1/b_1], 0 \notin B.$$

As the natural consequence of the assumed basic concept, the method for fuzzy values comparison should be developed on the basis of crisp interval comparison.

2.2 Interval and Fuzzy Values Comparison

Theoretically, intervals can only be partially ordered and hence cannot be compared in ordinary sense. However, if intervals are used in applications, the comparison of them becomes necessary. There are different approaches to interval (and fuzzy values) comparison proposed in the literature. Here we will use the so-called probabilistic approach to the interval comparison (see review of the methods based on this approach in [13]). Two sets of expressions containing the separate interval equality relation were introduced in [13]. There are two different possible assumptions concerned with conditional probabilities in the framework of this method which provide two sets of interval relations referred to as "weak" and "strong" relations. We will use here only the "strong" relations (the probabilities of $B > A$, $B < A$ and $B = A$) as they are a particular case of the more general approach based on the Dempster-Shafer theory (see [13]).

For overlapping intervals (Fig. 1a):

$$P(B < A) = 0, P(B = A) = \frac{(a_2 - b_1)^2}{(a_2 - a_1)(b_2 - b_1)}, P(B > A) = 1 - P(B = A).$$

In the inclusion case (Fig. 1b):

$$P(B < A) = \frac{a_1 - b_1}{b_2 - b_1}, P(B = A) = \frac{a_2 - a_1}{b_2 - b_1}, P(B > A) = \frac{b_2 - a_1}{b_2 - b_1}.$$

Observe that in all cases $P(A < B) + P(A = B) + P(A > B) = 1$.

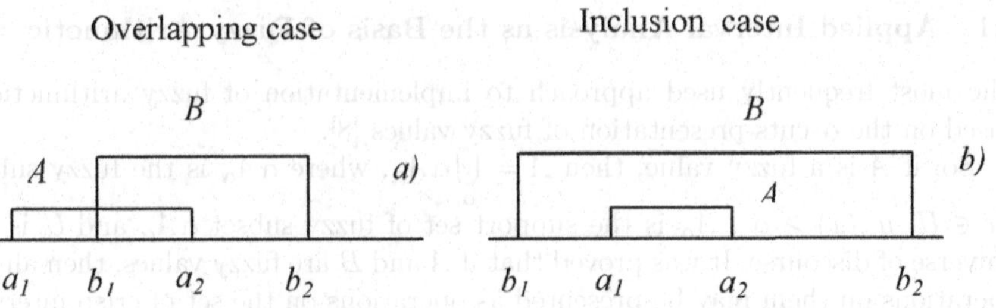

Overlapping case   Inclusion case

Fig. 1. The examples of interval relations

The set of fuzzy interval relations can be obtained using the above crisp interval relations and the α-cut representation of compared fuzzy values. Let $\hat{A}$ and $\hat{B}$ be fuzzy values on X with corresponding membership functions $\mu_A(x)$, $\mu_B(x)$: $X \to [0,1]$. We can represent $\hat{A}$ and $\hat{B}$ by the sets of α-cuts $\hat{A} = \bigcup_\alpha A_\alpha$, $\hat{B} = \bigcup_\alpha B_\alpha$, where $A_\alpha = \{x \in X : \mu_A(x) \geq \alpha\}$, $B_\alpha = \{x \in X : \mu_B(x) \geq \alpha\}$ are crisp intervals. Then all fuzzy values relations $\hat{A}$ rel $\hat{B}$, rel $\in \{<, =, >\}$ may be presented by the set of α-cut relations

$$\hat{A} \ rel \ \hat{B} = \bigcup_\alpha A_\alpha \ rel \ B_\alpha.$$

Since A_α and B_α are crisp intervals, the probability $P_\alpha(B_\alpha > A_\alpha)$ for each pair A_α and B_α can be calculated in the way described above. The set of the probabilities P_α, ($\alpha \in (0,1]$) may be treated as the support of fuzzy subset

$$P(\hat{B} > \hat{A}) = \left\{ \frac{\alpha}{P_\alpha(B_\alpha > A_\alpha)} \right\},$$

where the value of α denotes the grade of membership to the fuzzy value $P(\hat{B} > \hat{A})$. In this way, the fuzzy subset $P(\hat{B} = \hat{A})$ may also be easily obtained. In practice, the real value indices are sometimes needed for fuzzy values ordering. For this purpose, some characteristic numbers of fuzzy set could be used. But it seems more natural to use the defuzzification, which for a discrete set of α-cuts can be presented as follows:

$$\overline{P}(\hat{B} > \hat{A}) = \frac{\sum_\alpha \alpha \cdot P_\alpha(B_\alpha > A_\alpha)}{\sum_\alpha \alpha}.$$

The last expression indicates that the contribution of α-cut to the overall probability estimation is rising along with the rise in its number.

3   The Direct Fuzzy Extension of the Simplex Method

When dealing with the distribution problem, we not only minimize the transportation costs, but in addition we maximize the distributor's profits. Suppose the distributor deals with M wholesalers and N consumers. Let a_i, $i=1$ to M, be the maximal quantities of goods that can be proposed by wholesalers and b_i, $j=1$ to N, be the maximal good requirements of consumers. The fuzzy profit $\hat{z}_{ij}$ obtained as the result of delivering of a good unit from ith wholesaler to jth consumer can be calculated as $\hat{z}_{ij} = c_j - c_i - \hat{t}_{ij}$, where c_j is the price of selling, c_i is the price of buying, $\hat{t}_{ij}$ is the total fuzzy transportation cost of delivering of a good unit from ith wholesaler to jth consumer. In accordance with the signed contracts, a distributor must buy at least p_i good units at price of c_i monetary units for unit of good from each ith wholesaler and to sell at least q_j good units at price of c_j monetary units for unit of good to each jth consumer. These constraints p_i, q_j limit only the lower bounds for the possible optimal quantities of goods which can be bought and sold. Therefore, they can be negotiated and hereinafter we shall treat them as the fuzzy constraints denoted as $\hat{p}_i$, $\hat{q}_j$. Therefore, the problem is to find such optimal good quantities $\hat{x}_{ij}$ ($i=1,...,M;j=1,...,N$) delivered from ith wholesaler to jth consumer which maximize the distributor's total fuzzy profit $\hat{D}$ under fuzzy constraints:

$$\hat{D} = \sum_{i=1}^{M} \sum_{j=1}^{N} (\hat{z}_{ij} * \hat{x}_{ij}) \to \max, \tag{1}$$

$$\sum_{j=1}^{N} \hat{x}_{ij} \leq a_i \ (i = 1..M), \sum_{i=1}^{M} \hat{x}_{ij} \leq b_j \ (j = 1..N), \tag{2}$$

$$\sum_{j=1}^{N} \hat{x}_{ij} \geq \hat{p}_i \ (i = 1..M), \sum_{i=1}^{M} \hat{x}_{ij} \geq \hat{q}_j \ (j = 1..N). \tag{3}$$

In the above model, only the parameters a_i and b_j are real valued as they represent the maximal quantities of goods proposed by wholesalers and the maximal good requirements of consumers that in common practice usually can not be negotiated.

To transform the model (1)–(3) into its canonical form, we substitute the two-index representation of this model for the single-index one.

To illustrate this routine procedure, let us consider the case of $N=M=2$. Then introducing $\hat{x}_1 = \hat{x}_{11}$, $\hat{x}_2 = \hat{x}_{12}$, $\hat{x}_3 = \hat{x}_{21}$, $\hat{x}_4 = \hat{x}_{22}$ and $\hat{z}_1 = \hat{z}_{11}$, $\hat{z}_2 = \hat{z}_{12}$, $\hat{z}_3 = \hat{z}_{21}$, $\hat{z}_4 = \hat{z}_{22}$ we rewrite (7) as follows:

$$\hat{D} = \sum_{i=1}^{f} \hat{z}_i \hat{x}_i \to \max, \tag{4}$$

where in our case $f = M * N = 4$. Introducing the variable $\hat{g}_i$ ($i=1$ to $2N+2M$) such that
$g_1 = a_1$, $g_2 = a_2$, $g_3 = b_1$, $g_4 = b_2$, $\hat{g}_5 = \hat{p}_1$, $\hat{g}_6 = \hat{p}_2$, $\hat{g}_7 = \hat{q}_1$, $\hat{g}_8 = \hat{q}_2$ from (2) and (3) we get
$\hat{x}_1 + \hat{x}_2 \leq g_1$, $\hat{x}_3 + \hat{x}_4 \leq g_2$, $\hat{x}_1 + \hat{x}_3 \leq g_3$, $\hat{x}_2 + \hat{x}_4 \leq g_4$, $\hat{x}_1 + \hat{x}_2 \geq \hat{g}_5$, $\hat{x}_3 + \hat{x}_4 \geq \hat{g}_6$, $\hat{x}_1 + \hat{x}_3 \geq \hat{g}_7$, $\hat{x}_2 + \hat{x}_4 \geq \hat{g}_8$.

The simplex algorithm requires the linear programming problem to be in augmented form, so that the inequalities are replaced by equalities [3]. Therefore, the next step is the presentation of the above inequalities in the canonical form. Introducing the so-called slack variables $\hat{s}_i$, $i=1$ to r ($r = 2M+2N$), we transform these inequalities to the set of equalities in the canonical form:

$$\hat{x}_1 + \hat{x}_2 + \hat{s}_1 = g_1, \hat{x}_3 + \hat{x}_4 + \hat{s}_2 = g_2, \hat{x}_1 + \hat{x}_3 + \hat{s}_3 = g_3, \hat{x}_2 + \hat{x}_4 + \hat{s}_4 = g_4, \quad (5)$$

$$\hat{x}_1 + \hat{x}_2 - \hat{s}_5 = \hat{g}_5, \hat{x}_3 + \hat{x}_4 - \hat{s}_6 = \hat{g}_6, \hat{x}_1 + \hat{x}_3 - \hat{s}_7 = \hat{g}_7, \hat{x}_2 + \hat{x}_4 - \hat{s}_8 = \hat{g}_8. \quad (6)$$

Expressions (4), (5), (6) with the constraints $\hat{x}_i \geq 0$ ($i=1$ to $N \cdot M$), $\hat{s}_i \geq 0$ ($i=1$ to $2M+2N$) represent the canonical form of $FLPP$ for the considered example. Of course, the presented routine procedure of the transformation of the initial fuzzy distribution problem to the canonical form can be easily generalized, but corresponding general mathematical expressions are too cumbersome to be relevant in the scientific paper. Indeed, this transformation (in its non-fuzzy form) is presented in the textbooks. All the following steps of the developed approach are similar to those of standard simplex method with only one difference: usual arithmetical operations and the operation of comparison are replaced by the corresponding operations on fuzzy values.

Let us consider an illustrative example. We first solve the simplest distribution problem with $N=2$, $M=2$ and real valued parameters:
$z_{11}=3$, $z_{12}=5$, $z_{21}=6$, $z_{22}=4$, $a_1=20$, $a_2=30$, $b_1=25$, $b_2=25$, $p_1=20$, $p_2=25$, $q_1=20$, $q_2=25$.

Its solution (in the two-index form) is $x_{11}=0$, $x_{12}=20$, $x_{21}=25$, $x_{22}=5$ and for the total optimal profit we have obtained $D=270$.

The second step is the fuzzy extension of the above example such that all fuzzy parameters are centered around the corresponding real valued parameters of this distribution problem. To perform the fuzzy extension, we have used trapezoidal fuzzy values so that the real-valued parameters and fuzzy parameters were presented by real values and quadruples as follows:
$a_1=20$, $a_2=30$, $b_1=25$, $b_2=25$, $\hat{z}_{11}=[2,2.5,3.5,4]$, $\hat{z}_{12}=[4,4.5,5.5,6]$,
$\hat{z}_{21} =[5,5.5,6.5,6]$, $\hat{z}_{22}=[3,3.5,4.5,5]$, $\hat{p}_1 =[19,19.5,20.5,21]$, $\hat{p}_2 =[24,24.5,25.5,26]$,
$\hat{q}_1=[19,19.5,20.5,21]$, $\hat{q}_2=[24,24.5,25.5,26]$.

Using the developed algorithm for the direct fuzzy extension of the simplex method, the following results (in the two-index form) were obtained
$\hat{x}_{11}=[0,0,0,0]$, $\hat{x}_{12} =[10,14,26,30]$, $\hat{x}_{21} =[12,17,28,33]$, $\hat{x}_{22} =[2,3.5,6.5,8]$,
$\hat{D}=[220,240,300,320]$.

It is easy to see that these results are centered around those obtained using real valued version of the considered distribution problem. This may be treated as an evidence in favor of the method's correctness. On the other hand, we can see that the relative widths of the results $\hat{x}_{11}$, $\hat{x}_{12}$, $\hat{x}_{21}$, $\hat{x}_{22}$ are greater than those of the initial fuzzy parameters. This phenomenon is well known in interval analysis as the "access width effect" and will be analyzed in the next section on the base of comparison of the fuzzy solution with that obtained using Monte-Carlo method.

4 Numerical Studies

Obviously, our method will provide the results which will be different from those obtained using the methods proposed in the literature as our method is free of limitations of known methods, and only what we can say is that our results will be more reliable since they are obtained without limitations and restrictions of known methods.

Therefore, to perform the proposed method, we compare the results of $FFDP$ solution with those obtained from (1)–(3) when all the uncertain parameters are considered as normally distributed random values.

Using a proper method for transformation of these distributions to the fuzzy values we obtain the corresponding FDP problem with fuzzy parameters, the fuzzy solutions of which is comparable with that obtained using the Monte-Carlo method.

The standard Monte-Carlo procedure was used, i.e., for each set of randomly chosen real valued parameters the real valued solution of problem (1)–(3) was obtained. Finally, repeating such a procedure the results were presented in the form of probability density functions of optimal x_{ij} and D.

To make the results obtained using the fuzzy and probability approaches comparable, the special simple method for the transformation of probability density distributions into fuzzy values without drastic loss of useful information was used. This method makes it possible to achieve the comparability of uncertain initial data in the fuzzy and the random cases. For the sake of simplicity, we have used the simplest normally distributed probability density functions, exhaustively represented be their averages m and standard deviations σ. This method consist of two steps.

At the first step, using initial probability density function $f(x)$, the cumulative distribution function $F(x)$ is obtained as follows: $F(x) = \int\limits_{-\infty}^{x} f(x)dx$.

At the second step, the function $F(x)$ is used to obtain a trapezoidal fuzzy number. We ask the decision-makers (experts) for the four values $F(x_i)$, i=1 to 4, which define the mapping of $F(x)$ on X in such a way that they provide the bottom and upper α-cuts of the trapezoidal fuzzy number.

It is easy to see that an accuracy of the proposed transformation depends only on the expert's subjective opinion about suitability and correctness of chosen upper and button confidence intervals. Of course, this subjectivity is the source of additional uncertainty. Nevertheless, taking into account that the transformation of a probability density function into a fuzzy value leads inevitable to the loss of some information, we can expect that the choice of 30% and 90% confidence intervals will provide at least satisfactory results of transformation.

Let us consider the example of the distribution problem (1)–(3) with $N = 3$, $M = 3$. To compare the results of fuzzy programming with those obtained when using the Monte-Carlo method, all the uncertain parameters were previously represented by normally distributed probability density functions. As the parameters a_i and b_j are not negotiated they were presented by the real values $a_1 = 460$,

$a_2 = 460$, $a_3 = 610$, $b_1 = 410$, $b_2 = 510$, $b_3 = 610$. The other parameters were represented by normally distributed probability density functions with the following averages:
$p_1 = 440$, $p_2 = 440$, $p_3 = 590$, $q_1 = 390$, $q_2 = 490$, $q_3 = 590$, $z_{11} = 300$, $z_{12} = 480$, $z_{13} = 490$, $z_{21} = 400$, $z_{22} = 580$, $z_{23} = 290$, $z_{31} = 300$, $z_{32} = 380$, $z_{33} = 600$.

For simplicity, all the standard deviations σ were equal to 10. Using the described above method for the transformation of probability distribution function into a fuzzy value, the following trapezoidal fuzzy parameters of the problem (7)–(9) have been obtained:
$\hat{p}_1=[417,435,444,459]$, $\hat{p}_2=[417,435,444,459]$, $\hat{p}_3=[567,585,594,609]$,
$\hat{q}_1=[367,385,394,409]$, $\hat{q}_2=[467,485,494,509]$, $\hat{q}_3=[567,585,594,609]$,
$\hat{z}_{11}=[277,295,304,319]$, $\hat{z}_{12}=[457,475,484,499]$, $\hat{z}_{12}=[467,485,494,509]$,
$\hat{z}_{21}=[377,395,304,319]$, $\hat{z}_{22}=[561,579,588,603]$, $\hat{z}_{23}=[272,290,299,314]$,
$\hat{z}_{31}=[377,395,304,319]$, $\hat{z}_{32}=[561,579,588,603]$, $\hat{z}_{33}=[272,290,299,314]$.

One of the results we have obtained using the fuzzy optimization method and the Monte-Carlo method (usual linear programming with real valued, but random parameters) is presented in Fig. 2. All the probability density functions in our example were obtained using Monte-Carlo method with 1 000 000 random steps.

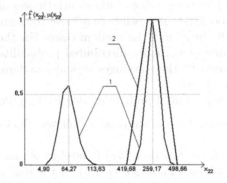

Fig. 2. The probability density function f -(1) and the fuzzy value μ -(2) for optimal x_{22}.

It is easy to see that the Monte-Carlo method sometimes provides two-extreme resulting probability density functions. Obviously, it is difficult to interpret these results, whereas when using the fuzzy optimization we have no such a problem since the results are always presented by trapezoidal fuzzy values. It is seen that the resulting fuzzy values are wider than the corresponding probability density functions. Partially, this is the consequence of the "access width effect", but on the other hand, using the fuzzy optimization we implicitly take into account the events which in the framework of Monte-Carlo method are treated as those with extremely low probability. The observed "access width effect" is not so drastic and it does not prevent to use the developed direct fuzzy extension of the simplex method for the solution of the fuzzy distribution problem.

Since in practice a decision maker deals with the real valued x_{ij}, the obtained fuzzy $\hat{x}_{ij}$ should be defizzified. On the other hand, it is known that in many cases a decision maker can not use the real valued results of optimization directly since in practice there may be many addition circumstances concerned with the problems of real business, which can not be completely formalized. In such cases, the fuzzy $\hat{x}_{ij}$ may be used directly when a decision maker chooses the real value x_{ij} in the supports of $\hat{x}_{ij}$. In these cases, a decision maker may control an extent to which his/her decision differs from the optimal one using the membership functions of $\hat{x}_{ij}$.

In is worth noting that the methods based on the real valued solution of fully fuzzy transportation or fully fuzzy distribution problems do not provide such a possibility.

5   Conclusion

A new approach to the direct fuzzy extension of the simplex method is developed. In the framework of the proposed approach all the parameters and variables may be fuzzy values without any additional restrictions and the results of optimization are obtained in the fuzzy form too. The method for the fuzzy extension is based on the fuzzy arithmetic rules and the method for fuzzy values comparison. Taking into account that the fuzzy values comparison plays a pivotal role in the fuzzy simplex method, the choice of the method for the fuzzy values comparison is thoroughly justified in the paper. The α-cut representation of all fuzzy parameters and variables is used. The developed approach is used to the solution of the fully fuzzy distribution problem. The advantages of the proposed approach are illustrated with the use of case study, where the fuzzy solution of the fuzzy distribution problem is compared with that obtained using the Monte-Carlo method (linear programming with real valued, but random parameters). It is shown the observed "access width effect" (increasing of the width of the resulting fuzzy solution) is not so drastic and does not prevent to use the developed direct fuzzy extension of the simplex method for the solution of the practical fuzzy distribution problems.

References

1. Baykasoglu, A., Subulan, K.: An analysis of fully fuzzy linear programming with fuzzy decision variables through logistics network design problem. Knowl. Based Syst. **90**, 165–184 (2015)
2. Baykasoğlu, A., Subulan, K.: A direct solution approach based on constrained fuzzy arithmetic and metaheuristic for fuzzy transportation problems. Soft Comput. **23**(5), 1667–1698 (2017). https://doi.org/10.1007/s00500-017-2890-2
3. Dantzig, G.B., Princeton, N.J.: Linear Programming and Extensions. Princeton University Press, New Jersey (1963)

4. Das, S.K., Mandal, T., Edalatpanah, S.A.: A mathematical model for solving fully fuzzy linear programming problem with trapezoidal fuzzy numbers. Appl. Intell. **46**(3), 509–519 (2017). https://doi.org/10.1007/s10489-017-0923-2

5. Ezzati, R., Khorram, E., Enayati, R.: A new algorithm to solve fully fuzzy linear programming problems using the MOLP problem. Appl. Math. Model. **39**, 3183–3193 (2015)

6. Hamadameen, A.O., Hassan, N.: A compromise solution for the fully fuzzy multi-objective linear programming problems. IEEE Access **6**, 43696–43710 (2018)

7. Hosseinzadeh, A., Edalatpanah, S.A.: A new approach for solving fully fuzzy linear programming by using the lexicography method. Adv. Fuzzy Syst. **2016**, 6 (2016)

8. Kaufmann, A., Gupta, M.: Introduction to Fuzzy Arithmetic-theory and Applications. Van Nostrand Reinhold, New York (1985)

9. Kaur, J., Kumar, A.: Mehar's method for solving fully fuzzy linear programming problems with L-R fuzzy parameters. Appl. Math. Model. **37**, 7142–7153 (2013)

10. Kheirfam, B., Verdegay, J.L.: The dual simplex method and sensitivity analysis for fuzzy linear programming with symmetric trapezoidal numbers. Fuzzy Optim. Decis. Making **12**, 171–189 (2013)

11. Nasseri, S.H., Saeidi, Z.: A new method for solving semi fully fuzzy linear programming problems. Int. J. Appl. Optim. Stud. **1**, 39–48 (2018)

12. Ozkoka, B.A., Albayrak, I., Kocken, H.G., Ahlatcioglu, M.: An approach for finding fuzzy optimal and approximate fuzzy optimal solution of fully fuzzy linear programming problems with mixed constraints. J. Intell. Fuzzy Syst. **31**, 623–632 (2016)

13. Sevastianov, P.: Numerical methods for interval and fuzzy number comparison based on the probabilistic approach and dempster-shafer theory. Inform. Sci. **177**, 4645–4661 (2007)

14. Sharma, U., Aggarwal, S.: Solving fully fuzzy multi-objective linear programming problem using nearest interval approximation of fuzzy number and interval programming. Int. J. Fuzzy Syst. **20**(2), 488–499 (2017). https://doi.org/10.1007/s40815-017-0336-8

Nonlinear Fuzzy Modelling of Dynamic Objects with Fuzzy Hybrid Particle Swarm Optimization and Genetic Algorithm

Łukasz Bartczuk[1]([✉]), Piotr Dziwiński[1], and Piotr Goetzen[2,3]

[1] Department of Computational Intelligence, Czestochowa University of Technology, Czestochowa, Poland
{lukasz.bartczuk,piotr.dziwinski}@pcz.pl
[2] Information Technology Institute University of Social Sciences, Łódź, Poland
[3] Clark University Worcester, Worcester, USA

Abstract. Algorithms based on populations are a very popular family of methods for solving optimization problems. One of the more frequently used representatives of this group is the Particle Swarm Optimization algorithm. The social learning mechanism used in the Particle Swarm Optimization algorithm allows this method to converge quickly. However, it can lead to catching the swarm in the local optimum. The solution to this issue may be the use of genetic operators whose random nature allows them to leave this point. The degree of use of these operators can be controlled using a neuro-fuzzy system. Such a mechanism exists in the FSHPSO-E algorithm presented in our previous paper. To test it, we used the set of benchmark functions widely adapted in the literature. The results proved effectiveness, efficiency, and scalability of this solution. In this paper, we show the effectiveness of this method in solving practical problems of optimization of fuzzy-neural systems used to model non-linear dynamic objects.

1 Introduction

Particle swarm algorithm is a well-known optimization method, introduced by Kennedy and Eberhart [9,31]. It has been successfully used to solve problems in various areas (see e.g. [1,2,4,6,18,23,30,34–37,39,40]). Like other population-based methods (see e.g. [12,16,17,22,24,27]) it processes not one, but the entire population of potential solutions. However in the PSO algorithm, the potential solution (the particle) is modified based on its current position, its historical best position, and the best position found so far by the swarm. These factors allow the PSO to converge quickly. On the other hand, they can also lead to a situation where the algorithm gets stuck in the local extreme. This situation may especially occur when seeking the optimal solution for multimodal and multidimensional problems. For this reason, interest in hybrid methods has increased in recent

© Springer Nature Switzerland AG 2020
L. Rutkowski et al. (Eds.): ICAISC 2020, LNAI 12415, pp. 315–325, 2020.
https://doi.org/10.1007/978-3-030-61401-0_30

years. They allow combining PSO mechanisms with other methods, e.g. genetic algorithm [12,17,38].

In paper [7] Dziwinski and Bartczuk proposed the HPSO-E hybrid method. It used mechanism from the PSO and genetic algorithms, while the impact of the latter on the process of searching for the optimal solution is determined by the influence factor. In the proposed algorithm, the influence factor is a fixed value and should be set before the algorithm is run. As shown in paper [7], this method allows for obtaining good accuracy for benchmarks problems. However, the simulations show that this value should not be a constant, but it should change depending on the current state of the PSO algorithm. When the number of better solutions found by PSO decreases, increasing the impact of genetic operators may direct the search process into new, perhaps more promising areas. From this reason, in paper [8] we extended this method by introducing a fuzzy system which is responsible for computing the current value of influence factor dynamically. We called this method Fuzzy Hybrid Particle Swarm Optimization and Genetic Algorithm (FSHPSO-E). In this paper, we show the usefulness of the FSHPSO-E method when optimizing the parameters of the fuzzy system used to model non-linear dynamic objects.

2   Fuzzy Hybrid Particle Swarm Optimization and Genetic Algorithm

In paper [8], Dziwiński and Bartczuk presented new hybrid optimization method which is based on PSO algorithm but, using mechanism from Genetic Algorithm also. The impact of genetic operators on the search process is determined by the influence factor p_e, which value is controlled by a fuzzy system. The fuzzy system determines the value Δp_e based on information about the current value of the p_e and normalized efficiency of genetic algorithm ΔEN_{GA}. Next Δp_e is used to modify the value of influence factor p_e:

$$p_e = p_e + \Delta p_e = p_e + FS(\Delta EN_{GA}, p_e) \tag{1}$$

We defined the normalized efficiency of the genetic algorithm as follows:

$$\Delta EN_{GA} = \frac{\Delta E'_{GA}}{\Delta E'_{GA} + \Delta E'_{PSO}} \tag{2}$$

where $\Delta E'_{GA}$ and $\Delta E'_{PSO}$ determine the efficiency of GA and PSO defined as the average improvement (decrease) of the fitness function during the last w_o iterations:

$$\Delta E'_{GA} = \frac{\sum\limits_{t'=t-w_o}^{t} E_{GA}(t')}{\sum\limits_{t'=t-w_o}^{t} |\mathbf{CH}(t')|} \tag{3}$$

$$\Delta E'_{PSO} = \frac{\sum\limits_{t'=t-w_o}^{t} E_{PSO}(t')}{\sum\limits_{t'=t-w_o}^{t} N} \tag{4}$$

where $|\mathbf{CH}(t')|$ is the size of a temporary population of solution created by the genetic operators in the iteration t'. $E_{GA}(t')$ and $E_{PSO}(t')$ mean the effectiveness of GA and PSO in the iteration t' and are defined as a total improvement (decrease) of the fitness of the best solution:

$$E_{GA}(t') = \sum_{j=1}^{|\mathbf{CH}(t)|} \begin{cases} f(\mathbf{g}(t')) - f(\mathbf{o}_j)) & \text{if } f(\mathbf{g}(t')) > f(\mathbf{o}_j) \\ 0 & \text{otherwise} \end{cases} \tag{5}$$

$$E_{PSO}(t') = \sum_{i=1}^{N} \begin{cases} f(\mathbf{g}(t')) - f(\mathbf{s}_i(t')) & \text{if } f.(\mathbf{g}(t')) > f(\mathbf{s}_i(t')) \\ 0 & \text{otherwise} \end{cases} \tag{6}$$

where $\mathbf{o}_j \in \mathbf{CH}(t')$ and $\mathbf{s}_i(t')$ mean the new elements obtained as the result of genetic operators and PSO modification, respectively. It should be noted that these values are affected only by solutions that improve the global best solution in the t' iteration. The efficiency of the PSO algorithm can be defined similarly:

$$\Delta EN_{PSO} = \frac{\Delta E'_{PSO}}{\Delta E'_{GA} + \Delta E'_{PSO}} \tag{7}$$

Since the ΔEN_{PSO} value complements the ΔEN_{GA} efficiency measure (i.e. $\Delta EN_{GA} = 1 - \Delta EN_{PSO}$), these values can be used interchangeably without affecting the accuracy and effectiveness of the algorithm.

The important element of the HPSO-E and FSHPSO-E methods is the merging strategy which is used to merge the temporary population with the PSO swarm $\mathbf{S}(t)$. It allows that particle $\mathbf{o}_i \in \mathbf{CH}(t)$ to replace its parent $\mathbf{x}_i$ from PSO swarm $\mathbf{S}(t)$ if and only if it is better (in the sense of fitness function) than $\mathbf{p}_i(t)$:

$$\mathbf{x}_i(t) = \begin{cases} \mathbf{o}_i & \text{if } f(\mathbf{o}_i) < f(\mathbf{p}_i(t)) \\ \mathbf{s}_i(t) & \text{otherwise,} \end{cases} \tag{8}$$

The purpose of this strategy is to minimize the influence of genetic operators on swarm's dynamic. The pseudocode of this method is presented as Algorithms 1 and 2, and its detailed description can be found in [8].

3   The Fuzzy System for Modelling Nonlinear Dynamic Objects

Let's consider the nonlinear state equation:

$$\frac{d\mathbf{x}}{dt} = f(\mathbf{x}, \mathbf{u}) = \mathbf{Ax} + \mathbf{Bu} + \eta g(\mathbf{x}, \mathbf{u}) \tag{9}$$

Algorithm 1. FSHPSO-E algorithm

$t \leftarrow 0$
for $i \leftarrow 1$ to N **do**
    Randomly initialize $\mathbf{s}_i(t)$ and $\mathbf{v}_i(t)$
    $\mathbf{p}_i(t) \leftarrow \mathbf{s}_i(t)$
    Evaluate $f(\mathbf{s}_i(t))$
Set $\mathbf{g}(t)$

while Term. cond. has not been met **do**

    for $i \leftarrow 1, N$ **do**
        Modify $\mathbf{v}_i(t+1)$
        Modify $\mathbf{s}_i(t+1)$
        Evaluate $f(\mathbf{s}_i(t))$
        Update $\mathbf{p}_i(t)$

    $\mathbf{CH}(t) \leftarrow \text{CreateTemp}(\mathbf{S}(t), p_e, p_m, p_c, T)$

    Combine $\mathbf{S}(t)$ with $\mathbf{CH}(t)$
    Update $\mathbf{p}_i(t)$ and $\mathbf{g}(t)$

    Compute $E_{GA}(t)$ and $E_{PSO}(t)$
    if $t \mod w_m = 0$ **then**
        Compute ΔE_{GA}
        $p_e \leftarrow p_e + \Delta p_e = p_e + FS(\Delta E_{GA}, p_e)$
    $t \leftarrow t + 1$
Select the best global solution $\mathbf{g}(t_{max})$

Algorithm 2. Create Temporary Population

---

function CreateTemp($\mathbf{S}(t), p_e, p_m, p_c, T$)
    Set $\mathbf{CH} = \emptyset$
    for $m \leftarrow 1, \lfloor p_e \cdot N \rfloor$ **do**
        if $(p_m > r(0,1))$ **then**
            $\mathbf{p}_i(t) \leftarrow \text{Tournament}(\mathbf{S}(t), T)$
            $\mathbf{o}_i \leftarrow Mutate(\mathbf{p}_i(t))$
            Evaluate $f(\mathbf{o}_i)$
            Insert $\mathbf{o}_i$ into $\mathbf{CH}$
        if $(p_c > r(0,1))$ **then**
            $(\mathbf{p}_{i1}(t), \mathbf{p}_{i2}(t)) \leftarrow \text{Tournament}(\mathbf{S}(t), T)$
            $(\mathbf{o}_{i1}, \mathbf{o}_{i2}) = Crossover(\mathbf{p}_{i1}, \mathbf{p}_{i2})$
            Evaluate $f(\mathbf{o}_{i1})$, $f(\mathbf{o}_{i2})$
            Insert $\mathbf{o}_{i1}$ and $\mathbf{o}_{i2}$ into $\mathbf{CH}$
    return $\mathbf{CH}$

---

where $\mathbf{A}$ is a system matrix (defining the system dynamics, i.e., the impact of the state variable on the state change), $\mathbf{B}$ is an input matrix (defining the impact of the system input on the state change), $g(\cdot)$ is a function which defines the nonlinearity of the system and η determines the impact of function $g(\cdot)$ on the entire object. If we assume that η is small and the system is weakly nonlinear, then the linear approximation about an equilibrium point will be useful in some strictly defined range. However, it should be noted that such a model is often unsuitable for many practical applications because of too low accuracy. This is especially true if the actual operating point goes beyond the defined boundaries.

In paper [3], another way of approximating the nonlinear system was proposed:

$$\frac{d\mathbf{x}}{dt} \approx (\mathbf{A} + \mathbf{P_A}(\mathbf{x}))\mathbf{x} + \mathbf{Bu} \tag{10}$$

where $\mathbf{P_A}(\mathbf{x})$ is a matrix of functions that compute the correction values in such a way that the error of the linear approximation is as small as possible.

Because it is difficult to determine the exact, analytical form of the $\mathbf{P_A}$ matrix elements, they can be approximate using the neuro-fuzzy system. Such a system can be described as a collection of N IF-THEN rules in form:

$$\mathcal{R}^k : \text{IF } x_1 \text{ IS } A_1^k \text{ AND } \dots \text{ AND } x_n \text{ IS } A_n^k$$
$$\text{THEN } y_1 \text{ IS } B_1^k \text{ AND } \dots \text{ AND } y_m \text{ IS } B_m^k \tag{11}$$

where $\mathbf{x} = [x_1, \dots, x_n] \in \mathbf{X} \subset \mathbf{R}^n; y = [y_1, \dots, y_m] \in \mathbf{Y} \subset \mathbf{R}^m$ are the vectors of input and output values, $A_1^k, \dots, A_n^k, B_1^k, B_m^k$ are fuzzy sets used in the k-th rule, $k = 1, \dots, N; i = 1, \dots, n; j = 1, \dots, m$. Let's assume that outputs fuzzy set is characterized by singleton membership functions, and we use the Center of Averages defuzzification method. Then the output value of such a system can be defined with the following equation:

$$\overline{y}_j = \frac{\sum\limits_{k=1}^{N} \overline{y}_j^k \cdot \mathop{T}\limits_{i=1}^{n} \left(\mu_{A_i^k}(x_i) \right)}{\sum\limits_{k=1}^{N} \mathop{T}\limits_{i=1}^{n} \left(\mu_{A_i^k}(x_i) \right)} \tag{12}$$

where $\mu_{A_i^k}(x_i)$ is a membership function that describes the A_i^k fuzzy set, and T is a T-norm operator.

There is a lot of different methods to tune the parameters of fuzzy systems (see, e.g. [5, 10, 20, 28, 29, 32, 33]). Some of them, like FSHPSO-E method, belongs to the group of population-based algorithms. In those methods, we have to encode the parameters of the neuro-fuzzy systems as $s_i(t)$ vectors. The size of these vectors depends on the number of fuzzy sets and the type of membership functions.

In this paper, we assume that input and output fuzzy sets are described by the Gaussian and singleton membership functions, respectively. Each Gaussian MF has two parameters mean $(\overline{x})$ and standard deviation (σ). Each singleton membership function has one parameter ($\bar{y}$). That allows to encode the parameters of the fuzzy system as a vector $\mathbf{s}_i$ in the following way:

$$
\mathbf{s}_i(t) = \begin{pmatrix} \bar{x}_1^1, \sigma_1^1, \ldots, \bar{x}_n^1, \sigma_n^1, \\ \ldots \\ \bar{x}_1^N, \sigma_1^N, \ldots, \bar{x}_n^N, \sigma_n^N, \\ \bar{y}_1^1, \ldots, \bar{y}_m^1, \\ \ldots \\ \bar{y}_1^N, \ldots, \bar{y}_m^N \end{pmatrix},
\tag{13}
$$

In population-based algorithms, the quality of each potential solution is determined by a fitness function, which in this case is defined as follows:

$$
f(\mathbf{s}_i) = \sqrt{\frac{\sum\limits_{h=1}^{H} \sum\limits_{j=1}^{m} (y_{h,j} - \hat{y}_{h,j})^2}{m \cdot (H-1)}}
\tag{14}
$$

where m is the number of output signals, H is the number of samples, $y_{h,j}$ is a value of the $j-th$ output signals in the h-th sample determined by model and $\hat{y}_{h,j}$ is a reference value of the j-th output signal in the h-th sample.

4   Experimental Results

To assess the usability and performance of the FSHPSO-E algorithm, we have used two modelling problems: (1) well-known harmonic oscillator and, (2) nonlinear electric circuit with a DC motor supplied by a solar generator [13].

The harmonic oscillator can be defined by the following formula:

$$
\frac{d^2x}{dt^2} + 2\zeta\frac{dx}{dt} + \omega^2 x = 0
\tag{15}
$$

where ζ, ω are oscillator parameters and $x(t)$ is a reference value of the modelled process as function of time. We used the following state variables $x_1(t) = dx(t)/dt$ and $x_2(t) = x(t)$. In such a case the system matrix $\mathbf{A}$ and the matrix of corrections coefficients $\mathbf{P_A}$ is described as follows:

$$
\mathbf{A} = \begin{bmatrix} 0 & \omega \\ -\omega & 0 \end{bmatrix} \qquad \mathbf{P_A} = \begin{bmatrix} 0 & p_{12}(\mathbf{x}) \\ p_{21}(\mathbf{x}) & 0 \end{bmatrix}
$$

To make this simple model nonlinear the parameter ω has been modified according to the following formula:

$$
\omega(x) = 2\pi - \frac{\pi}{(1+2x^6)}
\tag{16}
$$

In the second experiment the nonlinear electrical circuit with solar generator and DC drive system was modelled. In this case the following state variables were used: $x_1(k) = -\frac{I_s}{C}e^{-au(k)} - \frac{1}{C}i(k) + \frac{I_s+I_0}{C}$, $x_2(k) = \frac{1}{L}i(k) - \frac{R_m}{L}u(k) - \frac{K_x}{L}\Omega(k)$, $x_3(k) = \frac{K_x}{L}u(k) - \frac{K_r}{J}\Omega(k)$, where: $u(k)$ is the generator voltage, $i(k)$ is the rotor current, $\Omega(k)$ is DC motor rotational speed. The parameters of the circuit were chosen as in [13] and had values: $R_m = 12.045\,\Omega$, $L = 0.1\,\text{H}$, $C = 500\,\mu\text{F}$, $K_x = 0.5\,\text{Vs}$, $K_r = 0.1\,\text{Vs}^2$, $J = 10^{-3}\,\text{Ws}^3$, $I_0 = 2\,\text{A}$, $I_s = 1.28 \cdot 10^{-5}\,\text{A}$, $a = 0.54\,\text{V}^{-1}$. In this experiment we also assumed that the system matrix $\mathbf{A}$ and correction matrix $\mathbf{P_A}$ have values:

$$\mathbf{A} = \begin{bmatrix} -2163.86 & 2000.00 & 0.00 \\ 10.00 & -120.45 & -5.00 \\ 0.00 & 500.00 & -100.00 \end{bmatrix} \qquad \mathbf{P_A} = \begin{bmatrix} p_{11}(\mathbf{x}) & 0 & 0 \\ 0 & 0 & 0 \\ 0 & 0 & 0 \end{bmatrix}$$

In both experiments we assume the system matrix $\mathbf{A}$ is known, so the goal of the modelling was recreating the unknown coefficient of the correction matrix $\mathbf{P_A}$ in such a way that the model reproduces the reference data as accurately as possible.

In our simulations, the neuro-fuzzy systems (12) with Gaussian membership functions for inputs, singleton membership functions for output and algebraic t-norm were used. In the first problem, the fuzzy system contains three rules with two inputs and two outputs, and in the second problem, three rules with three inputs and one output.

The parameters of membership functions were determined by the following methods:

1. Genetic Algorithm
2. PSO with interia weight (GPSO) [31],
3. Fully informed PSO (FIPSO) [21],
4. Comprehensive learning PSO (CLPSO) [19],
5. A Hybrid PSO-GA algorithm (HPSO-GA) [11],
6. A Hybrid of GA and PSO (HGAPSO) [14],
7. A Hybrid PSO and GA (HPSO-E) [7].

During the simulations their parameters have been set at the values proposed in the corresponding articles and are presented in the Table 1.

It should be noted that in the FSHPSO-E method, the parameters of the fuzzy system used to determine the value of the influence factor should be optimized for the given problem. This can be a time-consuming task. From this reason, when carrying out the simulations described in this paper, we did not optimize the fuzzy system again. Instead, we used structures that were obtained during the experiments described in [8].

For Harmonic oscillator problem, we achieve the best results when the FSHPSO-E algorithm was controlled by the fuzzy system trained by the Ackley function:

$$F(x) = -20e^{-0.2\sqrt{\frac{1}{D}\sum_{i=1}^{D} x_i^2}} - e^{\frac{1}{D}\sum_{i=1}^{D}\cos(2\pi x_i)} + 20 + e, \qquad (17)$$

Table 1. The parameters of algorithms.

Algorithm	Parameters	Source
GA	p_c: 0.9, n_c: 4, p_m: 0.2, n_m: 1, T: 100	[12]
GPSO	w: 0.75, ψ_1: 1.5, ψ_2: 1.7	[31]
FIPSO	χ: 0.7298, ψ: 4.1	[21]
CLPSO	w_0: 0.9, w_1: 0.4, c: 1.49445, m: 7, T: 2	[19]
HPSO-GA	w: 0.828, ψ_1: 1.5, ψ_2: 1.5,	[11]
	p_c: 0.85, p_m: 0.02, γ: 10, β: 15, GA_{NumMax}: 20, GA_{NumMin}: 1,	
	GA_{PsMax}: 20, GA_{PsMin}: 10, $GA_{MaxIter}$: 20, $GA_{MinIter}$: 10	
HGAPSO	χ: 0.8, ψ_1: 1, ψ_2: 1, p_c: 0.8, p_m: 0.1, T: 2	[14]
HPSO-E	w: 0.76, ψ_1: 1.5, ψ_2: 1.75, p_e: 0.1,	[7]
	p_c: 0.3, n_c: 3, p_m: 0.9, n_m: 2, T: 9	
FSHPSO-E	w: 0.65, ψ_1: 1.5, ψ_2: 1.75,	[8]
	p_e: 0.5, p_c: 0.3, n_c: 3, p_m: 0.7, n_m: 2, T: 9	

and for nonlinear electrical circuit problem when it was controlled by the fuzzy system trained by the Step function:

$$F(x) = \sum_{i=1}^{D} (\lfloor x_i + 0.5 \rfloor)^2 \qquad (18)$$

To obtain reliable and comparable results, for all analysed algorithms, the maximum number of calls of the evaluation function (FEs) was set to 200,000, and in addition each simulation was repeated 30 times.

Figure 1 presents the average results obtained by each algorithm.

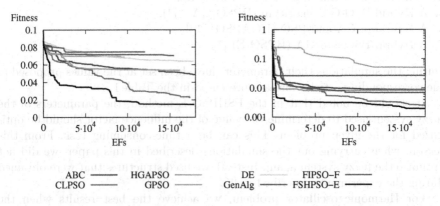

Fig. 1. The average performance of the algorithms for the harmonic oscillator problem (the left chart) and for nonlinear electrical circuit problem (the right chart)

The results show that the proposed method reach the best results for both analysed, real-world optimization problem. It should be noted that these results can be improved by increasing the FEs value and retraining the fuzzy system controlling the FSHPSO-E algorithm for a specific problem.

5 Conclusions

In this article, we briefly describe the FSHPSO-E algorithm and show its application to solve practical problems of optimization of neural-fuzzy systems used to model non-linear dynamic objects. The obtained results show the effectiveness of this algorithm as well as demonstrate its usefulness not only in solving the benchmarks, but also the real-world optimisation problems. In future work, we plan to apply our method for modelling various industrial processes, e.g. [15,25,26].

References

1. Abdel-Basset, M., Fakhry, A.E., El-Henawy, I., Qiu, T., Sangaiah, A.K.: Feature and intensity based medical image registration using particle swarm optimization. J. Med. Syst. **41**(12), 197 (2017)
2. Babu, T.S., Ram, J.P., Dragičević, T., Miyatake, M., Blaabjerg, F., Rajasekar, N.: Particle swarm optimization based solar pv array reconfiguration of the maximum power extraction under partial shading conditions. IEEE Trans. Sust. Energy **9**(1), 74–85 (2017)
3. Bartczuk, Ł., Przybył, A., Cpałka, K.: A new approach to nonlinear modelling of dynamic systems based on fuzzy rules. Int. J. Appl. Math. Comput. Sci. **26**(3), 603–621 (2016)
4. Benedetti, M., Azaro, R., Massa, A.: Memory enhanced PSO-based optimization approach for smart antennas control in complex interference scenarios. IEEE Trans. Ant. Prop. **56**(7), 1939–1947 (2008)
5. Cpałka, K., Łapa, K., Przybył, A., Zalasiński, M.: A new method for designing neuro-fuzzy systems for nonlinear modelling with interpretability aspects. Neurocomputing **135**, 203–217 (2014)
6. Delgarm, N., Sajadi, B., Kowsary, F., Delgarm, S.: Multi-objective optimization of the building energy performance: A simulation-based approach by means of particle swarm optimization (pso). Appl. Energy **170**, 293–303 (2016)
7. Dziwiński, P., Bartczuk, Ł., Goetzen, P.: A new hybrid particle swarm optimization and evolutionary algorithm. In: Rutkowski, L., Scherer, R., Korytkowski, M., Pedrycz, W., Tadeusiewicz, R., Zurada, J.M. (eds.) ICAISC 2019. LNCS (LNAI), vol. 11508, pp. 432–444. Springer, Cham (2019). https://doi.org/10.1007/978-3-030-20912-4_40
8. Dziwiński, P., Bartczuk, Ł.: A new hybrid particle swarm optimization and genetic algorithm method controlled by fuzzy logic. IEEE Trans. Fuzzy Syst. **28**, 1140–1154 (2019)
9. Eberhart, R., Kennedy, J.: A new optimizer using particle swarm theory. In: MHS'95. Proceedings of the Sixth International Symposium on Micro Machine and Human Science, pp. 39–43. IEEE (1995)
10. Ferdaus, M.M., Anavatti, S.G., Garratt, M.A., Pratama, M.: Development of c-means clustering based adaptive fuzzy controller for a flapping wing micro air vehicle. J. Artif. Intell. Soft Comput. Res. **9**(2), 99–109 (2019)

11. Garg, H.: A hybrid PSO-GA algorithm for constrained optimization problems. Appl. Math. Comput. **274**, 292–305 (2016)
12. Goldberg, D.E.: Genetic Algorithms. Pearson Education India (2006)
13. Jordan, A.J.: Linearization of non-linear state equation. Bull. Polish Acad. Sci. Tech. Sci. **54**(1), 63–73 (2006)
14. Juang, C.F.: A hybrid of genetic algorithm and particle swarm optimization for recurrent network design. IEEE Trans. Syst. Man Cybern. **34**(2), 997–1006 (2004)
15. Jurewicz, P., Rafajłowicz, W., Reiner, J., Rafajłowicz, E.: Simulations for tuning a laser power control system of the cladding process. In: Saeed, K., Homenda, W. (eds.) CISIM 2016. LNCS, vol. 9842, pp. 218–229. Springer, Cham (2016). https://doi.org/10.1007/978-3-319-45378-1_20
16. Ono, M.K.K., Hanada, Y., Kimura, M.: Enhancing island model genetic programming by controlling frequent trees. J. Artif. Intell. Soft Comput. Res. **9**(1), 51–65 (2019)
17. Kramer, O.: Genetic Algorithm Essentials. SCI, vol. 679. Springer, Cham (2017). https://doi.org/10.1007/978-3-319-52156-5
18. Krell, E., Sheta, A., Balasubramanian, A.P.R., King, S.A.: Collision-free autonomous robot navigation in unknown environments utilizing PSO for path planning. J. Artif. Intell. Soft Comput. Res. **9**(4), 267–282 (2019)
19. Liang, J.J., Qin, A.K., Suganthan, P.N., Baskar, S.: Comprehensive learning particle swarm optimizer for global optimization of multimodal functions. IEEE Trans. Evol. Comput. **10**(3), 281–295 (2006)
20. Malchiodi, D., Pedrycz, W.: Learning membership functions for fuzzy sets through modified support vector clustering. In: Masulli, F., Pasi, G., Yager, R. (eds.) WILF 2013. LNCS (LNAI), vol. 8256, pp. 52–59. Springer, Cham (2013). https://doi.org/10.1007/978-3-319-03200-9_6
21. Mendes, R., Kennedy, J., Neves, J.: The fully informed particle swarm: simpler, maybe better. IEEE Trans. Evol. Comput. **8**(3), 204–210 (2004)
22. Nasim, A., Burattini, L., Fateh, M.F., Zameer, A.: Solution of linear and non-linear boundary value problems using population-distributed parallel differential evolution. J. Artif. Intelli. Soft Comput. Res. **9**(3), 205–218 (2019)
23. Pare, S., Kumar, A., Bajaj, V., Singh, G.K.: A context sensitive multilevel thresholding using swarm based algorithms. IEEE/CAA J. Autom. Sinica **6**, 1471–1486 (2017)
24. Rafajłowicz, E., Rafajłowicz, W.: Fletcher's filter methodology as a soft selector in evolutionary algorithms for constrained optimization. In: Rutkowski, L., Korytkowski, M., Scherer, R., Tadeusiewicz, R., Zadeh, L.A., Zurada, J.M. (eds.) EC/SIDE -2012. LNCS, vol. 7269, pp. 333–341. Springer, Heidelberg (2012). https://doi.org/10.1007/978-3-642-29353-5_39
25. Rafajłowicz, E., Rafajłowicz, W.: Iterative learning in repetitive optimal control of linear dynamic processes. In: Rutkowski, L., Korytkowski, M., Scherer, R., Tadeusiewicz, R., Zadeh, L.A., Zurada, J.M. (eds.) ICAISC 2016. LNCS (LNAI), vol. 9692, pp. 705–717. Springer, Cham (2016). https://doi.org/10.1007/978-3-319-39378-0_60
26. Rafajłowicz, E., Rafajłowicz, W.: Iterative learning in optimal control of linear dynamic processes. Int. J. Control **91**(7), 1522–1540 (2018)
27. Rafajłowicz, W.: Method of handling constraints in differential evolution using fletcher's filter. In: Rutkowski, L., Korytkowski, M., Scherer, R., Tadeusiewicz, R., Zadeh, L.A., Zurada, J.M. (eds.) ICAISC 2013. LNCS (LNAI), vol. 7895, pp. 46–55. Springer, Heidelberg (2013). https://doi.org/10.1007/978-3-642-38610-7_5

28. Rutkowski, T., Łapa, K., Nielek, R.: On explainable fuzzy recommenders and their performance evaluation. Int. J. Appl. Math. Comput. Sci. **29**(3), 595–610 (2019)
29. Rutkowski, T., Łapa, K., Nowicki, R., Nielek, R., Grzanek, K.: On explainable recommender systems based on fuzzy rule generation techniques. In: Rutkowski, L., Scherer, R., Korytkowski, M., Pedrycz, W., Tadeusiewicz, R., Zurada, J.M. (eds.) ICAISC 2019. LNCS (LNAI), vol. 11508, pp. 358–372. Springer, Cham (2019). https://doi.org/10.1007/978-3-030-20912-4_34
30. Sadiqbatcha, S., Jafarzadeh, S., Ampatzidis, Y.: Particle swarm optimization for solving a class of type-1 and type-2 fuzzy nonlinear equations. J. Artif. Intell. Soft Comput. Res. **8**(2), 103–110 (2018)
31. Shi, Y., Eberhart, R.: A modified particle swarm optimizer. In: 1998 IEEE International Conference on Evolutionary Computer Proceedings, pp. 69–73. IEEE (1998)
32. Slowik, A., Cpałka, K., Łapa, K.: Multi-population nature-inspired algorithm (mnia) for the designing of interpretable fuzzy systems. IEEE Trans. Fuzzy Syst. **28**, 1125–1139 (2019)
33. Starczewski, J.T., Bartczuk, Ł., Dziwiński, P., Marvuglia, A.: Learning methods for type-2 FLS based on FCM. In: Rutkowski, L., Scherer, R., Tadeusiewicz, R., Zadeh, L.A., Zurada, J.M. (eds.) ICAISC 2010. LNCS (LNAI), vol. 6113, pp. 224–231. Springer, Heidelberg (2010). https://doi.org/10.1007/978-3-642-13208-7_29
34. Subbulakshmi, C.V., Deepa, S.N.: Medical dataset classification: a machine learning paradigm integrating particle swarm optimization with extreme learning machine classifier. Sci. World J. (2015)
35. Tambouratzis, G.: Using particle swarm optimization to accurately identify syntactic phrases in free text. J. Artif. Intell. Soft Comput. Res. **8**(1), 63–67 (2018)
36. Tambouratzis, G., Vassiliou, M.: Swarm algorithms for NLP - the case of limited training data. J. Artif. Intell. Soft Comput. Res. **9**(3), 219–234 (2019)
37. Wang, X.: Corporate financial warning model based on PSO and SVM. In: 2010 2nd International Conference on Information Engineering and Computer Science, pp. 1–5 (2010)
38. Wei, Y., et al.: Vehicle emission computation through microscopic traffic simulation calibrated using genetic algorithm. J. Artif. Intell. Soft Comput. Res. **9**(1), 67–80 (2019)
39. Zhang, F., Fan, W., Wu, X., Pedersen, G.F.: Performance testing of mimo device with the wireless cable method based on particle swarm optimization algorithm. In: 2018 International Workshop on Antenna Technology (iWAT), pp. 1–4. IEEE (2018)
40. Zhu, H., Wang, Y., Wang, K., Chen, Y.: Particle swarm optimization (PSO) for the constrained portfolio optimization problem. Exp. Syst. Appl. **38**(8), 10161–10169 (2011)

Application of Time Series Analysis and Forecasting Methods for Enterprise Decision-Management

Anton Romanov(✉) ⓘ, Nadezhda Yarushkina ⓘ, and Aleksey Filippov ⓘ

Ulyanovsk State Technical University, Street Severny Venets 32, 432027 Ulyanovsk,
Russian Federation
romanov73@gmail.com, {jng,al.filippov}@ulstu.ru
http://www.ulstu.ru/

Abstract. The management of a complex manufacturing enterprise requires great attention to all interrelated business processes. Such processes are characterized by a high level of complexity, and additionally, by massive volumes of aggregated information. The current approach of production management is based on using a standard industrial methodology adopted for various enterprises. The industrial methodology contains algorithms and coefficients, accumulated from the statistic of the whole industry. The principal disadvantage of this approach is a strong contrariety between real production indicators and indicators described in the methodology. Enterprise management tasks must be solved using new automation and intellectualization approaches to analysis and forecasting of production indicators. Information systems of the enterprise contain all the necessary information to evaluate the state of production. The production processes can easily be represented by a discrete time series that could be extracted from information systems. It is necessary to use time series that modeling with type 2 fuzzy sets to account for the fuzziness of the real world. Using the fuzzy approach allows creating models that can improve the quality of the decision-making. The fuzzy approach and ontology engineering methods are used in this research. The hybridization of these approaches allows analyze the data about production processes and makes linguistic summarization of the production state in the process of decision-making.

Keywords: Time series · Type-2 fuzzy sets · Production management · Ontology · Linguistic summarization

1 Introduction

The management of a complex manufacturing enterprise requires great attention to all interrelated business processes [1]. Such processes are characterized by a high level of complexity, and additionally, by massive volumes of aggregated information [2].

© Springer Nature Switzerland AG 2020
L. Rutkowski et al. (Eds.): ICAISC 2020, LNAI 12415, pp. 326–337, 2020.
https://doi.org/10.1007/978-3-030-61401-0_31

The production processes have unobvious relations, so the decision-maker does not always recognize or understand the correlation between them [3].

The current approach of production management is based on using a standard industrial methodology adopted for various enterprises. The industrial methodology contains algorithms and coefficients, accumulated from the statistic of the whole industry [4]. The principal disadvantage of this approach is a strong contrariety between real production indicators and indicators described in the methodology. The industrial methodology is inflexible and can't be operatively modified according to changes in the problem area. Therefore the development of the governance framework for data quality and traceability of information used in decision-making is needed [5]. Qualitative data management is critical in this context, but can also be very time-consuming for implementation.

Thus, the limitations of the industry methodology in the decision-making process are:

- the complexity of calculation of statistical coefficients based on production indicators analysis;
- the impossibility of dynamic adaptation of calculations into periods that shorter than the forecast horizon;
- the methodology does not provide adaptation to the specific production.

Enterprise management tasks must be solved using new automation and intellectualization approaches to analysis and forecasting of production indicators [6, 7].

To solve this problem the next tasks must be solved:

- definition of input data;
- creation of models that reflect the state of production processes;
- development of algorithms for linguistic summarization of the current state of the enterprise.

In the process of analyzing the industrial methodology was found that the production indicators (for example, staff time, staff performance, equipment performance and depreciation of equipment) are aggregated and averaged that decrease the accuracy of the decision-making. Information systems of the enterprise contain all the necessary information to evaluate the state of production. The production processes can easily be represented by a discrete time series that could be extracted from information systems. It is necessary to use time series that modeling with type 2 fuzzy sets to account for the fuzziness of the real world [8]. Using the fuzzy approach allows creating models that can improve the quality of the decision-making [9–11]. The fuzzy approach and ontology engineering methods are used in this research. The hybridization of these approaches allows analyze the data about production processes and makes linguistic summarization of the production state in the process of decision-making.

2   Types of Enterprise Time Series

The main point of the proposed approach is to find changes in the values of production processes indicators and react to these changes operatively. Time series models are used for tracking these changes. The industrial methodology for production management based on a set of statistical coefficients. But these coefficients not always can be given by an expert or calculated. Each of them can be extracted from the enterprise information systems.

The following types of time series were extracted from enterprise information systems:

- unit productivity dynamics as a sum of employees labor productivities;
- the number of equipment in units grouped by type and type of work;
- the number of employees grouped by type and type of work;
- area usage as a sum of equipment sizes;
- utilization of equipment as a planned load in the framework of the production program.

The number of points in the time series is in the range of 12–40 points because data were collected for the past period from a year to three years. Time series are discrete nature with a monthly average value at a point. Finding the seasonality, local and global tendencies of time series is critical for the quality of time series analysis.

Let see models for smoothing, extracting, and forecasting of production processes time series that proposed in this research.

3   Time Series Model Based on Type 2 Fuzzy Sets

Time series modeling based on type 2 fuzzy sets allows building the model that reflects the uncertainty of the choice of values of coefficients or indicators determined by an expert. An interval time series was chosen as the representation of the modeling object. In [12] is described the algorithm for constructing a model for interval time series.

The formal model of the interval time series can be represented as the following expression:

$$TS = \{ts_i\}, i \in N,$$

where $ts_i = [t_i, \tilde{A}_{t_i}]$ is an element of the time series at the moment of time t_i and a value in the form of a type 2 fuzzy set $\tilde{A}_{t_i}$. The universe of type 2 fuzzy sets is defined as $U = (\tilde{A}_1, \ldots, \tilde{A}_l), \tilde{A}_{t-i} \in U, l \in N$, for the entire time series, where l is the number of fuzzy sets in the universe. A set $\tilde{A}_{t_i}$ is a type 2 fuzzy set, therefore, a fuzzy set of type 1 is assigned to it as a value.

A triangular is used as the form of fuzzy sets due to the small computational complexity.

Type 2 fuzzy sets $\tilde{A}$ in the universum U can be defined using type 2 membership function. Type 2 fuzzy sets can be represented as:

$$\tilde{A} = ((x, u), \mu_{\tilde{A}}(x, u)) | \forall x \in U, \forall u \in J_x \subseteq [0, 1]$$

where $x \in U$ and $u \in J_x \subseteq [0, 1]$ in which $0 \leq \mu_{\tilde{A}}(x, u) \leq 1$. The main membership function is in the range from 0 to 1, so the appearance of the fuzzy set is expressed as:

$$\tilde{A} = \int_{x \in U} \int_{u \in J_x} \mu_{\tilde{A}}(x, u) / (x, u) J_x \subseteq [0, 1]$$

where the operator $\int \int$ denotes the union over all incoming x and u.

Time series modeling needs to define interval fuzzy sets and their shape. The Fig. 1 shows the appearance of the sets.

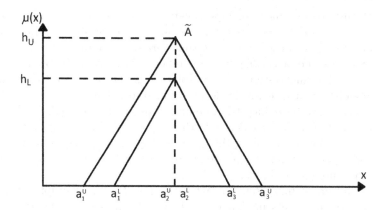

Fig. 1. The shape of the upper and lower membership functions

Triangular fuzzy sets are defined as follows:

$$\tilde{A}_i = (\tilde{A}_i^U, \tilde{A}_i^L) = ((a_{i1}^u, a_{i2}^u, a_{i3}^u, h(\tilde{A}_i^U)), (a_{i1}^l, a_{i2}^l, a_{i3}^l, h(\tilde{A}_i^l))).$$

where $\tilde{A}_i^U$ and $\tilde{A}_i^L$ is a triangular type 1 fuzzy sets, $a_{i1}^u, a_{i2}^u, a_{i3}^u, a_{i1}^l, a_{i2}^l, a_{i3}^l$, is reference points of type 2 interval fuzzy set $\tilde{A}_i$, h is the value of the membership function of the element a_i (for the upper and lower membership functions, respectively).

An operation of combining fuzzy sets of type 2 is required in the process of working with a rule base based on the values of a time series. The combining operation defined as follows:

$$\tilde{A}_1 \oplus \tilde{A}_2 = (\tilde{A}_1^U, \tilde{A}_1^L) \oplus (\tilde{A}_2^U, \tilde{A}_2^L)$$
$$= ((a_{11}^u + a_{21}^u, a_{12}^u + a_{22}^u, a_{13}^u + a_{23}^u;$$
$$min(h_1(\tilde{A}_1^U), h_1(\tilde{A}_2^U)\tilde{A}_1^U)), min(h_2(\tilde{A}_1^U), h_2(\tilde{A}_2^U)),);$$
$$(a_{11}^l + a_{21}^l, a_{12}^l + a_{22}^l, a_{13}^l + a_{23}^l;$$
$$min(h_1(\tilde{A}_1^L), h_1(\tilde{A}_2^L)), min(h_2(\tilde{A}_1^L), h_2(\tilde{A}_2^L)));$$

4 Algorithm for Smoothing and Forecasting of Time Series

The main principle of the proposed algorithm is closely related to the nature of the time series. Type 2 fuzzy sets are used for modeling in the process of smoothing and forecasting of time series because the time series has the interval nature [13].

The proposed algorithm can be represented as a sequence of the following steps:

Step 1. Determination of the universe of observations. $U = [U_{min}, U_{max}]$, where U_{min} and U_{max} are minimal and maximal values of a time series respectively.

Step 2. Definition of membership functions for a time series $M = \{\mu_1, ..., \mu_l\}, l << n$, where l is the number of membership functions of fuzzy sets, n is the length of a time series. The number of membership functions and, accordingly, the number of fuzzy sets is chosen relatively small. The motivation for this solution is the multi-level approach to modeling a time series. To decrease the dimension of the set of relations is necessary to reduce the number of fuzzy sets at each level. Obliviously, this approach decrease the approximation accuracy of a time series. However, creating the set of membership functions at the second and higher levels increase the approximation accuracy with an increase in the number of levels.

Step 3. Definition of fuzzy sets for a time series. The superscript defines the type of fuzzy sets in that case. $A^1 = \{A_1^1, ..., A_l^1\}, A^2 = \{A_1^2, ..., A_m^2\}$, where l is the number of type 1 fuzzy sets, m is the number of type 2 fuzzy sets.

Step 4. Fuzzification of a time series by type 1 sets. $\forall x_i \; \tilde{y}_i = Fuzzy(x_i)$

Step 5. Fuzzification a time series by type 2 sets.

Step 6. Creation of relations. The rules for the creation of relations are represented in the form of pairs of fuzzy sets in terms of antecedents and consequents, for example: $A_1^1 A_1^2 ... \longrightarrow A_2^1 A^2 1$.

Step 7. Forecasting for the first and second levels based on a set of rules. The forecast is calculated by the centroid method, first on type 1 fuzzy sets $A^1 = \{A_1^1, ..., A_l^1\}$, then on type 2 fuzzy sets.

Step 8. Evaluation of forecasting errors.

The prediction step should include trend analysis for the best results [14–16].

5   Experiments

5.1   Time Series Approximation

The experiment with the approximation method of a time series is needed for verification of the hypothesis that the approximation of the time series that used a time series model based on higher orders fuzzy sets have high accuracy when selected the optimal number and shape of fuzzy sets.

The formation of an approximate representation of a time series based on higher orders fuzzy sets consist of the creation of a set of fuzzy sets at each level.

Additionally, the universe of values will be determined for each level: for the whole time series at the first level, then for the intervals of values of each of the sets at the previous level.

The following parameters were determined in the experiment:

- Fuzzification of the time series by type 1 and type 2 fuzzy sets.
- The number of fuzzy sets of each type is 3.
- The shape of fuzzy sets is isosceles triangles.

The Fig. 2 shows the approximation result of the time series of the unit productivity dynamic (production coefficient). A small number of fuzzy sets at the first level allow get only a rough approximation of the time series. The usage of type 2 fuzzy sets for approximation improves the accuracy of the approximation result. 80% of the time series was used as experimental data, and 20% to assess the quality of the proposed methods. The accuracy of the approximation result is evaluated using the SMAPE criterion [17] (the lower, the better):

- for type 1 fuzzy sets the SMAPE is 5.06%.
- for type 2 fuzzy sets the SMAPE is 2.82%.

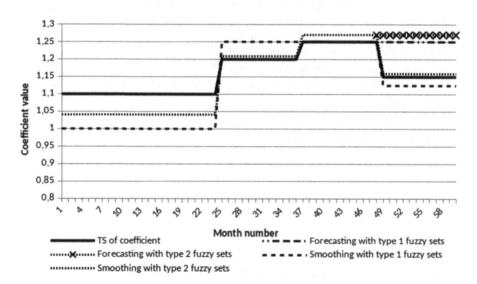

Fig. 2. Approximation and forecasting of the time series of the production coefficient

For the time series of the number of employees (employee count) (see Fig. 3) the SMAPE scores are:

- for type 1 fuzzy sets the SMAPE is 18.61%.
- for type 2 fuzzy sets the SMAPE is 9.66%.

Conclusions from the experiment with the approximation of the time series:

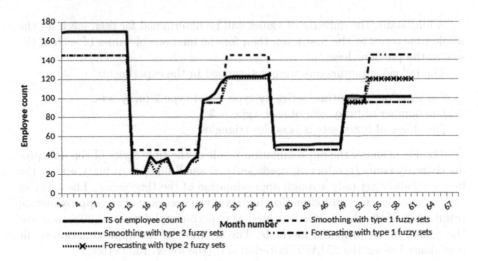

Fig. 3. Approximation and forecasting the time series of the number of employees

1. The accuracy of the approximation is depended on the number of fuzzy sets. The experiment has shown that the small number of fuzzy sets possible to achieve a high approximation accuracy.
2. The boundaries of the fuzzy sets is also important. The approximation result has a low accuracy at the initial segments for both time series presented in the experiment. The problem of choosing the boundaries of fuzzy sets intervals remains relevant.

5.2 Time Series Forecasting

The time series forecasting experiment is conducted using the "If-Then" rule base.

Rules are extracted from time series in the form of sequences of fuzzy sets acting as antecedents (number $>= 2$) and consequent values, which are also a fuzzy set. The formed rule base makes it possible to get a one-point forecast.

The conditions of the experiment:

– The forecast was made for the test interval that contains 10 points.
– The forecast was made based on both type 1 and type 2 fuzzy sets.

The forecasting of the time series of the production coefficient (see Fig. 2) is complicated by the fact that the testing interval contains the previously not presented values, and the rules do not have specific series behavior.

Forecasting result accuracy of the production coefficient is evaluated using the SMAPE criterion:

– for type 1 fuzzy sets the SMAPE is 7.69%.
– for type 2 fuzzy sets the SMAPE is 9.27%.

The Fig. 3 shows the forecasting result of the time series of the number of employees.

Forecasting result quality of the number of employees is evaluated by SMAPE:

- for type 1 fuzzy sets the SMAPE is 39.41%.
- for type 1 fuzzy sets the SMAPE is 27.91%.

The conclusions of the experiment with time series forecasting correlate with the conclusions of the experiment with approximation: the quality of modeling and forecasting of a time series depends on the number and boundaries of fuzzy sets.

5.3   Ontology-Oriented Linguistic Summarization of the Time Series Forecast Values

The subsystem for ontology-oriented linguistic summarization of the time series forecast values allows to decision-maker operatively react to changes in the situation at the factory. The basic input data of the subsystem is the production program. The result of the subsystem calculated based on the values of production indicators and their dynamics. The using of natural language in the process of summarization allows the decision-maker to understand the resulting summaries in an easy way [18]. The ontology [19,20] of the following structure is used to organize the rule base of the linguistic summarization subsystem:

$$O = \langle V, D, R, F \rangle, \tag{1}$$

where $V = \{v_1, v_2, \ldots, v_k\}$ is the set of indicators that determine a state of production (for example, the number of equipment, equipment productivity, number of employees, etc.);
$D = \{d_1, d_2, \ldots, d_i, \ldots, d_k\}$ is the set of indicator summarization variants. A d_i can be represented as the following expression:

$$d_i = \{\langle s_1, t_1 \rangle, \langle s_2, t_2 \rangle, \ldots \langle s_j, t_j \rangle, \ldots \langle s_l, t_l \rangle\},$$

where s_j is a characteristic of the indicator d_i value (for example, low, medium, high);
t_j is a linguistic representation of the indicator d_i state for a specific characteristic s_j;
R is the set of ontology ties that define the relationship between an indicator and its summarization variants;
F is the algorithmically defined interpretation function that allows to specify a subset $\hat{D} \in D$ of the summarization variants that correspond to the specified indicator values.

The $\mathcal{ALCHF(D)}$ extension of the description logic $\mathcal{ALC}$ [21–23] is used for the logical representation of the ontology O (Eq. 1) for the linguistic summarization of the time series forecast values. With using the description logic $\mathcal{ALCHF}(\mathcal{D})$ the ontology O can be represented as:

$$O = TBox \cup ABox,$$

where $TBox$ is the terminological box;
$ABox$ is the assertional box.

The TBox contains statements describing concept hierarchies and relations between them. The ABox contains axioms defined as a set of individuals and relations between individuals and concepts.

Terminological box $TBox$

$Values \sqsubseteq \top$

$Values \equiv \top \sqcap \exists hasValueEquipmentProductivity.Double \sqcap$

$\sqcap \exists hasValueEquipmentNumber.Double \sqcap$

$\sqcap \exists hasValueEmployeeNumber.Double \sqcap \exists hasResume.Resume$

$Resume \sqsubseteq \top$

$Values \sqsubseteq \neg Resume$

$Resume \equiv \top \sqcap \exists hasTextDescription.String$

$EquipmentNumber \sqsubseteq Resume$

$EquipmentNumberLow \sqsubseteq EquipmentNumber$

$EquipmentNumberMiddle \sqsubseteq EquipmentNumber$

$EquipmentNumberHigh \sqsubseteq EquipmentNumber$

$EquipmentProductivity \sqsubseteq Resume$

$EquipmentProductivityLow \sqsubseteq EquipmentProductivity$

$EquipmentProductivityMiddle \sqsubseteq EquipmentProductivity$

$EquipmentProductivityHigh \sqsubseteq EquipmentProductivity$

$EmployeeNumber \sqsubseteq Resume$

$EmployeeNumberLow \sqsubseteq EmployeeNumber$

$EmployeeNumberMiddle \sqsubseteq EmployeeNumber$

$EmployeeNumberHigh \sqsubseteq EmployeeNumber$

where $Values$ is the set of indicators V;
$Resume$ is the set of indicator summarization variants D;
$EquipmentNumber \sqsubseteq Resume, EquipmentNumberLow \sqsubseteq Equipment$ $Number$ is the summarization variant of the "number of equipment" indicator at low value of this indicator;
$hasValue*$ is the name of the role "the indicator has a value";
$hasResume$ is the name of the role "the indicator has a summarization variant";
$hasTextDescription$ is the name of the functional role "the summarization variant has a text description";

String is the concrete string domain;
Double is the concrete double domain.

Assertional box *ABox*

$currentValues: Values$

$(currentValues, valueEqP : Double) : hasValueEquipmentProductivity$

$(currentValues, valueEqN : Double) : hasValueEquipmentNumber$

$(currentValues, valueEmN : Double) : hasValueEmployeeNumber$

$equipmentNumberLow: EquipmentNumberLow$

$(equipmentNumberLow, valueEqNLowDescr : String) : hasTextDescription$

...

$employeeNumberHigh: EmployeeNumberHigh$

$(employeeNumberHigh, valueEmNHighDescr : String) : hasTextDescription$

Inference-Based Linguistic Summarization of the Time Series Forecast Values. The set of SWRL rules [24] is used to organize the inference-based linguistic summarization of the time series forecast values. Each SWRL rule allows assing the indicator to the specific summarization variant, for example:

hasValueEquipmentNumber(?ind, ?val) ^
swrlb:greaterThanOrEqual(?val, 200) ^
EquipmentNumberHigh(?res) −> hasResume(?ind, ?res)

hasValueEquipmentNumber(?ind, ?val) ^
swrlb:lessThan(?val, 200) ^ swrlb:greaterThanOrEqual(?val, 150) ^
EquipmentNumberMiddle(?res) −> hasResume(?ind, ?res)

hasValueEquipmentNumber(?ind, ?val) ^
swrlb:lessThan(?val, 150) ^
EquipmentNumberLow(?res) −> hasResume(?ind, ?res)

The following SQWRL query [25] is used to obtain results of the ontology-oriented linguistic summarization of the time series forecast values:

Values(?ind) ^ hasResume(?ind, ?res) ^
hasTextDescription(?res, ?descr) −> sqwrl:select(?res, ?descr)

For example, if the value of the "equipment number" indicator is 171, the result of the SQWRL query will be:

ResumeEquipmentNumberMiddle −>
    "Equipment number is middle so ... ."^^rdf:PlainLiteral

6   Conclusion

The approach to analysis and forecasting of time series of production indicators based on the type-2 fuzzy sets was proposed in this article. This approach helps to avoid the problems of usage of the industrial methodology for production management by adding more operativeness in decision-making.

Proposed methods of forecasting of type-2 time series improve the quality of management decisions, because they can to create a model of real production processes of the factory.

The ontology-oriented linguistic summarization of the time series forecast values allows to decision-maker operatively react to changes in the situation at the factory.

The SWRL rules used in the inference allow decision-maker to get into a deeper knowledge not only of the production processes but also to their interrelations.

These principles can help decision-makers improve the quality of the technological preparation of complex industries.

Acknowledgments. The reported study was funded by RFBR and the government of Ulyanovsk region according to the research projects: 18-47-732016, 18-47-730022, 18-47-730019, and 19-47-730005.

References

1. Meng, H., Fan, G.: Forecasting of gas supply in self-provided power plant of iron and steel enterprises based on time series. In: IOP Conference Series: Earth and Environmental Science, vol. 227, no. 4, p. 042008. IOP Publishing (2019)
2. Yu, Y., Hao, Q., Hao, P.: The research and application of enterprises' dynamic risk monitoring and assessment model based on related time series. In 2017 Chinese Automation Congress (CAC), pp. 7407–7410. IEEE (2017)
3. Ravikumar, K., Kumar, K., Thokala, N., Chandra, M.G.: Enterprise system response time prediction using non-stationary function approximations. In: Rojas, I., Joya, G., Catala, A. (eds.) IWANN 2019. LNCS, vol. 11506, pp. 74–87. Springer, Cham (2019). https://doi.org/10.1007/978-3-030-20521-8_7
4. Li, M.J., Tao, W.Q.: Review of methodologies and polices for evaluation of energy efficiency in high energy-consuming industry. Appl. Energy **187**, 203–215 (2017)
5. Isnaini, W., Sudiarso, A.: Demand forecasting in Small and Medium Enterprises (SMEs) ED Aluminium Yogyakarta using causal, time series, and combined causal-time series approaches. In: MATEC Web of Conferences, vol. 204, p. 01004. EDP Sciences (2018)
6. Alalwan, J.A., Thomas, M.A., Roland Weistroffer, H.: Decision support capabilities of enterprise content management systems: an empirical investigation. Decis. Support Syst. **68**, 39–48 (2014)
7. Tavares, P., Silva, J.A., Costa, P., Veiga, G., Moreira, A.P.: Flexible work cell simulator using digital twin methodology for highly complex systems in industry 4.0. In: Ollero, A., Sanfeliu, A., Montano, L., Lau, N., Cardeira, C. (eds.) ROBOT 2017. AISC, vol. 693, pp. 541–552. Springer, Cham (2018). https://doi.org/10.1007/978-3-319-70833-1_44

8. Zadeh, L.A.: Fuzzy logic. Computer **21**(4), 83–93 (1988)
9. Sarkar, M.: Ruggedness measures of medical time series using fuzzy-rough sets and fractals. Pattern Recogn. Lett. Arch. **27**, 447–454 (2006)
10. Hwang, J.R., Chen, S.M., Lee, C.H.: Handling forecasting problems using fuzzy time series. Fuzzy Sets Syst. **100**, 217–228 (1998)
11. Novak, V.: Mining information from time series in the form of sentences of natural language. Int. J. Approximate Reasoning **78**, 1119–1125 (2016)
12. Bajestani, N.S., Zare, A.: Forecasting TAIEX using improved type 2 fuzzy time series. Expert Syst. Appl. **38**–5, 5816–5821 (2011)
13. Mendel, J.M., John, R.I.B.: Type-2 fuzzy sets made simple. IEEE Trans. Fuzzy Syst. **10**(2), 117–127 (2002)
14. Herbst, G., Bocklish, S.F.: Online Recognition of fuzzy time series patterns. In: 2009 International Fuzzy Systems Association World Congress and 2009 European Society for Fuzzy (2009)
15. Kacprzyk, J., Wilbik, A. (2009). Using Fuzzy Linguistic summaries for the comparison of time series. In: 2009 International Fuzzy Systems Association World Congress and 2009 European Society for Fuzzy Logic (2009)
16. Pedrycz, W., Chen, S.M.: Time Series Analysis, Modeling and Applications: A Computational Intelligence Perspective (e-book Google) Intelligent Systems Reference Library, vol. 47, p. 404 (2013)
17. SMAPE criterion by Computational Intelligence in Forecasting (CIF). http:// irafm.osu.cz/cif/main.php
18. Castillo-Ortega, R., Marin, N., Sanchez, D., Tettamanzi, A.: Linguistic summarization of time series data using genetic algorithms. In: Proceedings of the 7th Conference of the European Society for Fuzzy Logic and Technology (EUSFLAT-11) (2011). https://doi.org/10.2991/eusflat.2011.145
19. Gruber, T.: Ontology. In: Liu, L., Ozsu, M.T. (eds.) Entry in the Encyclopedia of Database Systems. Springer, Boston (2009). https://doi.org/10.1007/978-0-387-39940-9_1318
20. Guarino, N., Musen, M.A.: Ten Years of Applied Ontology: Applied Ontology. **10**, 169–170 (2015). https://doi.org/10.3233/AO-150160
21. Baader, F., Calvanese, D., McGuinness, D., Nardi, D., Patel-Schneider, P.F.: The Description Logic Handbook: Theory, Implementation, and Applications. Cambridge University Press (2003)
22. Bonatti, P.A., Tettamanzi, A.G.B.: Some complexity results on fuzzy description logics. In: Di Gesú, V., Masulli, F., Petrosino, A. (eds.) WILF 2003. LNCS (LNAI), vol. 2955, pp. 19–24. Springer, Heidelberg (2006). https://doi.org/10.1007/10983652_3
23. Grosof, B., Horrocks, I., Volz, R., Decker, S.: Description logic programs: combining logic programs with description logics. In: Proceedings of WWW 2003, Budapest, Hungary, May 2003, pp. 48–57. ACM (2003)
24. SWRL: A Semantic Web Rule Language Combining OWL and RuleML. https:// www.w3.org/Submission/SWRL/
25. O'Connor, M.J., Das, A.: SQWRL: a query language for OWL: OWL: experiences and directions (OWLED). In: 6th International Workshop, Chantilly, VA (2009)

Face Recognition with Explanation
by Fuzzy Rules and Linguistic Description

Danuta Rutkowska[1]([✉]), Damian Kurach[2], and Elisabeth Rakus-Andersson[3]

[1] Information Technology Institute, University of Social Sciences,
90-113 Lodz, Poland
`drutkowska@san.edu.pl`
[2] Czestochowa University of Technology, 42-201 Czestochowa, Poland
[3] Department of Mathematics and Natural Sciences,
Blekinge Institute of Technology, 37179 Karlskrona, Sweden

Abstract. In this paper, a new approach to face recognition is proposed. The knowledge represented by fuzzy IF-THEN rules, with type-1 and type-2 fuzzy sets, are employed in order to generate the linguistic description of human faces in digital pictures. Then, an image recognition system can recognize and retrieve a picture (image of a face) or classify face images based on the linguistic description. Such a system is explainable – it can explain its decision based on the fuzzy rules.

Keywords: Face recognition and classification · Linguistic description · Fuzzy IF-THEN rules · Type-2 fuzzy sets · Explainable AI

1 Introduction

There are many publications concerning face recognition, including top biometric technologies, and projects realized by Google, Apple, Facebook, Amazon, Microsoft, in the field of Artificial Intelligence. A list of highly cited papers, journals and books, can be found on the Internet, e.g.: face-rec-org. However, as mentioned in [9], there is a need of linguistic description of the facial features, based on fuzzy approach to image recognition and retrieval [7]. This is still reasonable to study and apply despite the great success of the deep learning methods in image recognition (see e.g. [29]).

It seems obvious that faces - with regard to recognition or classification with explanation - should be considered using fuzzy sets. According to Lotfi Zadeh - who introduced fuzzy sets [32] and fuzzy logic [34] - it is not possible to determine precise borders between particular parts of a human face, such as the nose, cheek, etc. Thus, the regions of a face corresponding to the specific parts (e.g. nose, cheek) should be viewed as fuzzy areas of every face. An illustration of this concept is presented in [16,26]. This idea is also applied and developed by other authors, e.g. [8–12,14].

© Springer Nature Switzerland AG 2020
L. Rutkowski et al. (Eds.): ICAISC 2020, LNAI 12415, pp. 338–350, 2020.
https://doi.org/10.1007/978-3-030-61401-0_32

2 Face Description by Use of Fuzzy Sets

In [16] fuzzy sets with their membership functions for selected facial features of particular parts of a human face have been created and fuzzy IF-THEN rules formulated for a fuzzy classifier. Different features have been distinguished, including eye colors. In this paper, we focus our attention on two attributes: height and width, with regard to different parts of a face, as well as the face as a whole.

The regions corresponding to the specific parts of a face can be defined by membership functions of two arguments associated with the height and width attributes (see [16,26]). In this way, the face is partitioned by fuzzy granulation into particular fuzzy regions, like nose, eyes, cheeks, etc.

Let us imagine that a face, and its particular parts are detected and indicated by use of rectangle frames around them. These frames can be viewed as crisp values that characterize the face. Using the fuzzy approach, these crisp values (rectangular frames) are compared with fuzzy sets (defined by the membership functions of two arguments associated with the height and width attributes). The fuzzy sets correspond to linguistic values, such as: *long* and *narrow* nose.

Fuzzy IF-THEN rules that include linguistic variables, representing particular parts of a face, and the face as a whole, allow to infer a linguistic description of the face, e.g. in the following form: *This is a rectangle shape face, with wide and short forehead, big eyes, long and narrow nose, wide and thin mouth, etc.*

The problem is – how to define the membership functions? We can assume the Gaussian, triangular, or trapezoidal shapes of these functions but we do not know the exact values of the parameters, e.g. centers and widths of the Gaussian functions.

Usually, in fuzzy expert systems, the fuzzy IF-THEN rules are formulated based on expert knowledge. However, in many cases it is difficult to acquire such a domain knowledge. On the other hand, in the cases when a sufficient amount of data is available, the knowlegde represented by the rules can be gathered by a learning procedure, e.g. in a neuro-fuzzy system; see e.g. [25].

When a face is considered, with regard to the linguistic description, we can use the anthropological data and the statistical knowledge applied to the results of measurement of a large number of human faces. For example, the results concerning measurements of human heads can be found on the Internet: antropologia-fizyczna.pl.

In this paper, we propose to use the anthropological data in order to define membership functions of fuzzy sets refering to linguistic values of face attributes, first of all - the height and width of a face. The data of this kind, also with regard to other attributes, summarize the measurements of a large number of different human heads, conducted by anthropologists.

The table of average head dimensions based on data from Wikipedia Anthropometry pages, provided by Mark Steven Cohen [4], has served as a source of the average values of measurements of human heads. Values of the vertical distance from the bottom of the chin to the level of the top of the head, in inches, for 1st, 5th, 50th, 95th, 99th pecentiles, are presented in Table 1; different ones for men and women. The corresponding values in centimeters are given in the parentheses.

Figure 1 illustrates, only in a visual way, not precisely, membership functions (MFs) of fuzzy sets representing linguistic values of the height of men and women faces. The crisp values of centers of the triangular fuzzy sets and the crisp values corresponding to the extreme fuzzy sets refer to the values presented in Table 1. The membership functions of different shapes, e.g. Gaussian or trapezoidal, instead of triangular, can be applied but with the same center values (see [24]). Of course, the values in centimeters can be used. However, it is easier to choose the face of the height equal 10 in. as a base interval for further considerations.

Table 1. Average head sizes: height of faces

Percentiles	1st	5th	50th	95th	99th
Men	8.3 (21.082)	8.6 (21.844)	9.1 (23.114)	9.7 (24.638)	10.0 (25.4)
Women	7.8 (19.812)	8.0 (20.32)	8.6 (21.844)	9.1 (23.114)	9.4 (23.876)

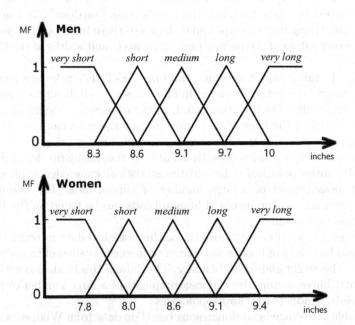

Fig. 1. Membership functions (MF) of fuzzy sets representing linguistic values of the height of men and women faces, respectively; crisp values of centers of the triangular fuzzy sets are indicated, as well as the crisp values corresponding to the extreme fuzzy sets (*very short, very long*).

Apart from the height of human faces, many other results of face measurements are presented in [4], in the form of tables – similar to Table 1. Among others, there are values of measurements of the head breadth (usually above and behind the ears) and the bitragion breadth (from the right tragion to the left). The former head breadth is wider because it includes ears while the latter one concerns the distance between the tragions, i.e. anthropometric points situated in the notch just above the tragus of each ear. The table with the lower values of the head breadth are more suitable when the shape of human faces is considered. Speaking more precisely, the proportion of the height of a face to the width of the face (breadth of the head) is analized in such a case. Therefore, these values are portrayed in Table 2; in inches, and approximate values in centimeters.

Analogously like for the height of faces, based on Table 2, type-1 and type-2 fuzzy sets can be created, with regard to linguistic values concerning the width of faces, e.g. *very narrow, narrow, medium wide, wide, very wide*.

Table 2. Average head sizes: width of faces

Percentiles	1st	5th	50th	95th	99th
Men	5.2 (13.1)	5.3 (13.5)	5.7 (14.5)	6.1 (15.5)	6.3 (15.9)
Women	4.9 (12.5)	5.0 (12.8)	5.2 (13.3)	5.6 (14.3)	5.9 (15.0)

In the situation when human faces are classified based on their height and/or width, separately within the groups of men and women faces, we can use the fuzzy sets presented in Fig. 1 for the height parameter (and analogous, for the width) in fuzzy inference rules. However, the problem of face classification or recognition can be considered without such a differentiation. This means that the fuzzy IF-THEN rules can also be formulated in more general forms, related to human faces, not distinguishing men and women groups.

It is worth noticing that combining both results shown in Table 1, for men and women, we transform the triangular MFs depicted in Fig. 1 into trapezoidal MFs – where membership values within intervals [8.0, 8.6], [8.6, 9.1], [9.1, 9.7] equal 1. These intervals correspond to 5th, 50th, and 95th percentile in the table.

In the next sections, we describe and apply fuzzy sets of type-2, in addition to the type-1 fuzzy sets, depicted in Fig. 1, and similar for other face attributes.

3 Face Description by Use of Type-2 Fuzzy Sets

Now, let us introduce type-2 fuzzy sets to the face description. The MFs of fuzzy sets representing linguistic values of the height of men and women faces, portrayed in Fig. 1, can be used in order to construct the Lower Membership Function (LMF) and Upper MF (UMF), respectively, with regard to the type-2 fuzzy sets (see e.g. [21,30,31,33,34]). Figure 2 shows the MF of type-2 fuzzy set with linguistic label *medium*, created based on the fuzzy sets (*medium*) for both cases (for men and women) sketched in Fig. 1. In the similar way, type-2 fuzzy sets corresponding to other linguistic labels (*short, long,* as well as *very short,* and *very long*) are defined; see Fig. 3.

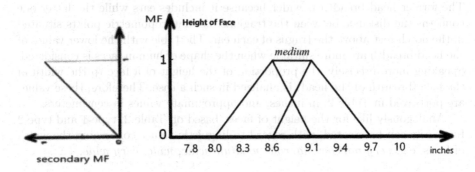

Fig. 2. Membership function (MF) of type-2 fuzzy set representing linguistic value *medium* of the height of human faces; created based on fuzzy sets *medium* of type-1, for both men and women cases shown in Fig. 1, with the secondary MF on the left.

It is easy to show (in Fig. 2) the Lower and Upper MFs, as well as the Footprint of Uncertainty (FOU) that is the area between the LMF and UMF. The FOU is the uncertainty of a type-2 MF represented by the region bounded by the LMF and UMF, where the LMF and UMF are subsets with minimum and maximum membership grades of the FOU, respectively. For details, see e.g. [17].

It should be noticing that the type-2 fuzzy sets, like the *medium* in Fig. 2, correspond to the trapezoidal type-1 fuzzy sets, mentioned in Sect. 2 with regard to the combination of results from Table 1, for men and women. Both the trapezoidal type-1 fuzzy sets and the type-2 fuzzy sets are constructed based the triangular MFs depicted in Fig. 1 and the intervals [8.0, 8.6], [8.6, 9.1], [9.1, 9.7]. However, the type-2 MFs carry more information concerning the intervals and the uncertainty included in the FOU.

As mentioned in Sect. 2, in the similar way, type-2 fuzzy sets can be defined for the width attribute of a face, with linguistic labels: *very narrow, narrow, medium wide, wide, very wide.* Moreover, the same approach can be applied to every part of a human face, such as nose, eyes, cheeks, viewed as fuzzy regions of the face.

Let us focus our attention on the example of type-2 fuzzy set *medium* depicted in Fig. 2. As a matter of fact, a type-2 fuzzy set should be considered in the 3D space where the third dimension is used in order to illustrate secondary MFs, while the primary MF is presented as in the example in Fig. 2.

Usually type-2 fuzzy sets are applied as interval type-2 case that is much simpler than the general type-2 fuzzy sets (see e.g. [27]). Both cases concern type-2 fuzzy sets that have grades of membership that are themselves fuzzy [5]. A type-2 membership grade can be any subset in [0, 1] that is the interval of the primary membership. The secondary MFs, which also take values in $[0, 1]$, define the possibilities for the primary membership; see also [17]. A type-1 fuzzy set is a special case of a type-2 fuzzy set – where its secondary MF is a subset of only one element (equal 1). In the case of interval type-2 fuzzy sets, the secondary MFs are either 0 or 1. In our approach, we use the general type-2 fuzzy sets, and employ the secondary MFs defined as presented on the left side in Fig. 2. This means that we prefer the highest value of the membership within an interval of membership values.

In our application, it is possible to define the secondary MFs in a different way, depending on the closeness of a value of the height (or width) of human faces to the men and women cases in Table 1 (or Table 2, respectively).

However, the type-2 fuzzy sets of the form presented in Fig. 2 allow to infer the decision indicated that e.g. the *medium* height is rather *medium* with regard to the men or women case. Such an inference can be done by the aggregation of the rules with the type-2 fuzzy sets.

For example, if an input value of the height of a face matches the type-2 fuzzy sets *medium* and *long* with certain degrees of membership (greater than zero) and does not match the type-2 fuzzy set *short* (membership grade equal 0), then the following decision is inferred: the height of the input face is *medium* with the meaning of the measure standard for men. Otherwise, if an input value of the face height matches the type-2 fuzzy sets *medium* and *short* with certain degrees of membership and does not match the type-2 fuzzy set *long*, then the inferred decision is: the height of the input face is *medium* with the meaning of the measure standard for women. This is seen in Fig. 3.

In the case when an input value of the height of a face matches the type-2 fuzzy sets *medium* with the degree of membership equal 1, then the inferred decision is: the height of the input face is *medium*, without any information concerning the belongingness to the group of men or women.

Figure 3 illustrates the type-2 fuzzy set *medium* (the same as in Fig. 2, enhanced by the yellow color), as well as others: *short, long, very short, very long*. Let us notice that interval $[8.6, 9.1]$ in Figs. 2 and 3 refers to 50th percentile in Table 1. Analogously, intervals $[8.0, 8.6]$, $[9.1, 9.7]$, and $[7.8, 8.3]$, $[9.4, 10]$ refer to 5th, 95th, and 1st, 99th percentiles, respectively. These intervals represent margines of uncertainty concerning the difference in measurements for men and women standards.

Similar illustration as in Fig. 3 can be presented for the values concerning the width attribute of a face, included in Table 2. Moreover, the analogous approach can be applied when membership functions with regard to particular parts of human faces, e.g. nose, mouth, eyes, ears, should be defined (see the next sections).

4   Face Shape Recognition and Classification

Values of measurements of the height and width of a human face can be used in order to recognize and/or classify the shape of the face. The ratio of the face

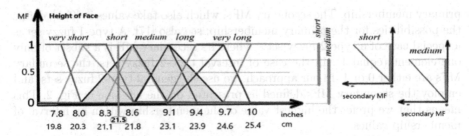

Fig. 3. Membership functions (MFs) of type-2 fuzzy sets, representing linguistic values *medium*, as well as *short*, *long*, and *very short*, *very long*, of the height of human faces; created based on fuzzy sets of type-1, for both men and women cases shown in Fig. 1; see also Fig. 2. An example of type-2 membership values for the height of a face 21.5 cm is also indicated.

width to the face height describes the proportional relationship between these two measurements of a head. Thus, this provides an information about the shape, e.g. narrow, rectangle or round head. Of course, in our approach we consider the shape in terms of the fuzzy concept.

There are several different shapes of a face distinguished in the literature, e.g. oblong, oval, round, rectangular, square, triangular, diamond, inverted triangle, heart; for details see [19]. It is obvious that for recognition the specific shapes, we need more measurements than only the height and width of a human face. We have to know values of the measurements in more parts of the face, for example the width under the nose and in the lines of the mouth and within the forehead. Some useful values can be found in [4], as well as in other sources, e.g. [13].

For simplicity, let us consider only two attributes, the height and width of a human face, and use the values from Tables 1 and 2. It is easy to calculate the ratio for 50 percentile, and the extreme proportion. In this way, we obtain the following values: 1.59, 1.65, 1.95, which can be applied as centers of type-1 fuzzy sets (triangular or Gaussian) that represent *wide*, *normal*, and *narrow* face, respectively.

Taking into account more measurements of human faces (see an example in Fig. 4), we can define appropriate fuzzy sets and formulate fuzzy IF-THEN rules in order to classify more sophisticated shapes of faces.

It should be mentioned that there are some computer programs that recognize shapes of human faces based on a photo. However, they do not use fuzzy rules that allow to explain the result with regard to grades of membership.

5   A Type-2 Fuzzy System for Face Classification with Linguistic Description

Analogously to the shapes of human faces, considered in Sect. 4, we can describe particular parts of a face by use of properly defined fuzzy sets, and formulate fuzzy IF-THEN rules in order to classify human faces. Then, we can construct a system for image recognition and face classification, where input images are digital pictures of human faces.

As mentioned earlier, in Sect. 2, it is convenient to choose the height of a face equal 10 in. as a base interval for our consideration. Then, we can assume *normal* proportion concerning the shape of a face, and analyze the size of particular parts of the face, such as mouth, nose, eyes, etc.

Analogously to our approach with regard to the height and width attributes of the whole face, we can analyze the parts of a face by use of these two features. At first, the particular parts, e.g. mouth, nose, eyes, should be detected on a face, then each of the rectangles (shown in Fig. 5) are treated in the same way by means of their height and width values.

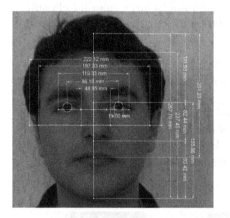

Fig. 4. Measurements of a face.

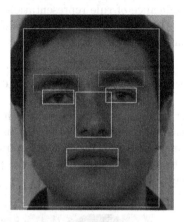

Fig. 5. Parts of a face.

Having data concerning measurements of the parts of human faces, we can define suitable fuzzy sets (type-1), and formulate fuzzy IF-THEN rules with conclusions refering to linguistic descriptions of the face attributes.

As presented in Table 1, there are different heights of human faces. Therefore, instead of type-1 fuzzy sets, we define type-2 fuzzy sets that take into account the uncertainty about values of the height of a face. In the same way, we can use anthropological measurements of parts of human faces.

Thus, fuzzy IF-THEN rules with type-2 fuzzy sets are employed in the system proposed in this paper, for face classification (including the particular parts of faces). These rules allow to produce the linguistic description of the classified faces. In this way, the system generates an explanation supported its decision.

It should be emphasized that the main goal is to recognize and classify faces (pictures of faces) with explanation. The system has to produce a linguistic description that explains the decision concerning recognized, retrieved, and classified pictures. Such an explanation is possible based on the knowledge represented by fuzzy IF-THEN rules. If attribute values of the input picture match the antecedent (IF part) of a rule, it is easy to explain the conclusion – included in THEN parts of the rule (or rules). It is also important that the decision is inferred by use of fuzzy logic, so grades of membership – with linguistic labels, such as *little, medium, much* – can be applied in the explanation.

The interpretability and explainability of a model or system is significant from the XAI (Explainable Artificial Intelligence) point of view; see [6]. Unlike many machine learning (ML) methods, including neural networks (see e.g. [35]) and deep learning (see e.g. [2]) that are data-driven and viewed as "black boxes" (with hidden knowledge), rule-based methods are knowledge-driven and hence they are interpretable and explainable. Therefore, some researchers try to extract knowledge (in the form of rules) from "black box models" like neural networks (see e.g. [28]), and also deep networks, e.g. [3]. Many authors emphasize the significance of rule representation, e.g. [18], and apply fuzzy rules for classification (e.g. [23]). Fuzzy rules are also employed by other reserchers in problems of image retrieval, e.g. [15].

6   Examples of Using Real Face Images

In this section, the fuzzy approach proposed in this paper is illustrated on examples of pictures of real faces. Let us consider our attention on three selected faces of man, shown in Fig. 6, and denoted as A, B, C. The white horizontal lines help us to notice the difference in the propotions concerning particular parts of the faces.

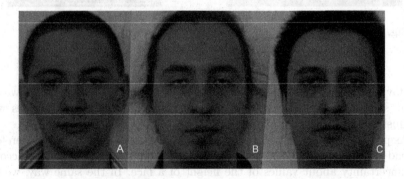

Fig. 6. Pictures of selected men faces.

In Fig. 6, the ratio of the length of the nose to the height of the face is the same for the persons in pictures A and B. However, the length of the nose of each of them is different but the height of the face of both persons differ proportionally. Comparing pictures B and C, the length of the nose of both persons is the same but the ratio of the length of the nose to the height of the face is different because the men differ in the height of their faces.

This example shows that – according to [20] – "words mean different things to different people, so there is uncertainty associated with words". In this case, words *short, medium, long*, with regard to the person's nose, have different meaning because of the incertainty depending on the height of the face. Therefore, additional membership grades are introduced to the primary membership functions in order to represent the uncertainty. Hence, type-2 fuzzy sets are considered and applied. The fuzzy sets (type-1) with linguistic labels *short, medium, long*, are defined by their primary and secondary membership functions, where the latter comprise membership grades of the former.

Let us also consider two pictures, presenting faces of a man and woman. Both are similar with regard to the height and width of the face: for the woman, the height 21.6 cm and the width equals 14.8 cm, while for the man, the height 21.4 cm and the width is 14.9 cm. Indeed, there is not much of a difference. Thus, the shape of both faces are also similar concerning the proportion expressed by the ratio that represents the relationship between the height and width of each of these faces. An example of type-2 membership values for the height of a face 21.5 cm is presented in Fig. 3.

In the example described above, according to fuzzy sets defined in Fig. 1, the height of the woman's face is *medium* and the width is *wide*, while the height of the man's face is *short* and the width is *medium*. As we see, also in this example "words mean different things to different people". In this case, the uncertainty that concerns the difference in the measurements for men and women is included in the type-2 fuzzy sets, as shown in Fig. 2.

It is worth emphasizing that the system can produce the linguistic description of input images of human faces without any information whether the pictures present male or female faces. Therefore, the type-2 fuzzy sets are employed in the rules. However, in the case when such an information is introduced to the system, the type-1 fuzzy sets can be sufficient, like those in Fig. 1, different for men and women.

Let us notice that the shape of a human face is determined, according to the approach described in Sect. 4, regardless of the information whether the face is masculine or feminine.

Based on the fuzzy sets of type-1 and type-2, applied in order to formulate fuzzy IF-THEN rules, it is possible to generate the linguistic description of a face, for example, in the following form: *This is small, round-shaped face, with long and narrow nose, small eyes, medium mouth, big ears, and wide forehead.*

7 Conclusions and Final Remarks

The main aim of this paper is to present a concept of a system that generates a linguistic description of a face portrayed in a digital picture (photo). Then, the system can retrieve a picture or classify pictures based on such a description.

The linguistic description is created by use of fuzzy IF-THEN rules that include fuzzy sets of type-1 and type-2. The fuzzy rules can be employed to provide an explanation of the system's decision concerning a face recognition, retrieval, and/or classification.

The measurements of human faces and their particular parts, as presented in Fig. 4, concern a picture of a face. Of course, the pictures (photos) can be taken from different distances. In order to determine real values of the face measurements, we use the unit 12 cm that is the iris diameter (of a human eye); see e.g. [1], and also [22]. In this way, we can obtain values of the measurements of a human face from its picture of any size.

Different uncertainties appear with regard to the face measurements, also concerning the iris unit. By use of type-2 fuzzy sets in the fuzzy IF-THEN rules, we can cope with the problem of measurement ucertainty.

A very important aspect of the approach proposed in this paper is the utilization of the knowledge comming from the anthropological data. Therefore, the system can infer decisions, and generate the linguistic description, based on a small collection of digital pictures of faces, without learning from examples of face images in large datasets.

References

1. Armstrong, R.A., Cubbidge, R.C.: The eye and vision: an overview. In: Preedy, V.R., Watson, R.R. (eds.) Handbook of Nutrition, Diet, and the Eye. Elsevier Inc. (2019)
2. Bengio, Y.: Learning deep architectures for AI. Found. Trends Mach. Learn. **2**(1), 1–127 (2009)
3. Bologna, G., Hayashi, Y.: Characterization of symbolic rules embedded in deep DIMLP networks: a challange to transparency of deep learning. J. Artif. Intelli. Soft Comput. Res. **7**(4), 265–286 (2017)
4. Cohen, M.S.: Table of average head dimensions based on data from Wikipedia Anthropometry pages. File:AvgHeadSizes.png. Wikipedia (2017). commons. wikimedia.org/wiki/File:AvgHeadSizes.png
5. Dubois, D., Prade, H.: Fuzzy Sets and Systems: Theory and Applications. Academic Press, New York (1980)
6. Gunning, D., Aha, D.: DARPA's explainable artificial intelligence (XAI) program. AI Mag. **40**(2), 44–58 (2019)
7. Iwamoto, H., Ralescu, A.: Towards a multimedia model-based image retrieval system using fuzzy logic. In: Proceedings SPIE 1827. Model-Based Vision, pp. 177–185 (1992)
8. Kaczmarek, P., Pedrycz, W., Reformat, M., Akhoundi, E.: A study of facial regions saliency: a fuzzy measure approach. Soft. Comput. **18**, 379–391 (2014)
9. Kaczmarek, P., Kiersztyn, A., Rutka, P., Pedrycz, W.: Linguistic descriptors in face recognition: a literature survey and the perspectives of future development. In: Proceedings SPA 2015 (Signal Processing: Algorithms, Architectures, Arrangements, and Applications), Poznań. Poland, pp. 98–103 (2015)
10. Kaczmarek, P., Pedrycz, W., Kiersztyn, A., Rutka, P.: A study in facial features saliency in face recognition: an analytic hierarchy process approach. Soft Comput. **21**, 7503–7517 (2016)
11. Karczmarek, P., Kiersztyn, A., Pedrycz, W., Dolecki, M.: Linguistic descriptors and analytic hierarchy process in face recognition realized by humans. In: Rutkowski, L., Korytkowski, M., Scherer, R., Tadeusiewicz, R., Zadeh, L.A., Zurada, J.M. (eds.) ICAISC 2016. LNCS (LNAI), vol. 9692, pp. 584–596. Springer, Cham (2016). https://doi.org/10.1007/978-3-319-39378-0_50

12. Karczmarek, P., Kiersztyn, A., Pedrycz, W.: An evaluation of fuzzy measure for face recognition. In: Rutkowski, L., Korytkowski, M., Scherer, R., Tadeusiewicz, R., Zadeh, L.A., Zurada, J.M. (eds.) ICAISC 2017. LNCS (LNAI), vol. 10245, pp. 668–676. Springer, Cham (2017). https://doi.org/10.1007/978-3-319-59063-9_60

13. Katsikitis, M. (ed.): The Human Face: Measurement and Meaning. Kluwer Academic Publisher (2003)

14. Kiersztyn, A., Kaczmarek, P., Dolecki, M., Pedrycz, W.: Linguistic descriptors and fuzzy sets in face recognition realized by humans. In: Proceedings 2016 IEEE International Conference on Fuzzy Systems (FUZZ), pp. 1120–1126 (2016)

15. Korytkowski, M., Senkerik, R., Scherer, M.M., Angryk, R.A., Kordos, M., Siwocha, A.: Efficient image retrieval by fuzzy rules from boosting and metaheuristic. J. Artif. Intell. Soft Comput. Res. **10**(1), 57–69 (2020)

16. Kurach, D., Rutkowska, D., Rakus-Andersson, E.: Face classification based on linguistic description of facial features. In: Rutkowski, L., Korytkowski, M., Scherer, R., Tadeusiewicz, R., Zadeh, L.A., Zurada, J.M. (eds.) ICAISC 2014. LNCS (LNAI), vol. 8468, pp. 155–166. Springer, Cham (2014). https://doi.org/10.1007/978-3-319-07176-3_14

17. Liang, Q., Mendel, J.M.: Interval type-2 fuzzy logic systems: theory and design. IEEE Trans. Fuzzy Syst. **8**(5), 535–550 (2000)

18. Liu, H., Gegov, A., Cocea, M.: Rule based networks: an efficient and interpretable representation of computational models. J. Artif. Intell. Soft Comput. Res. **7**(2), 111–123 (2017)

19. Medlej, J.: Human Anatomy Fundamentals. Design & Illustration. https://design.tutsplus.com

20. Mendel, J.M.: Computing with words, when words can mean different things to different people. Methods and applications. In: ICSS Symposium on Fuzzy Logic and Applications, International Congress on Computational Intelligence (1999)

21. Mendel, J.M.: Uncertain Rule-Based Fuzzy Logic Systems: Introduction and New Directions. Prentice-Hall, Upper-Saddle River (2001)

22. Milczarski, P., Kompanets, L., Kurach, D.: An approach to brain thinker type recognition based on facial asymmetry. In: Rutkowski, L., Scherer, R., Tadeusiewicz, R., Zadeh, L.A., Zurada, J.M. (eds.) ICAISC 2010. LNCS (LNAI), vol. 6113, pp. 643–650. Springer, Heidelberg (2010). https://doi.org/10.1007/978-3-642-13208-7_80

23. Riid, A., Preden, J.-S.: Design of fuzzy rule-based classifiers through granulation and consolidation. J. Artif. Intell. Soft Comput. Res. **7**(2), 137–147 (2017)

24. Rakus-Andersson, E.: The new approach to the construction of parametric membership functions for fuzzy sets with unequal supports. In: International Conference on Knowledge-Based and Intelligent Information & Engineering Systems. KES-2017 Procedia Computer Science, pp. 2057–2065 (2017)

25. Rutkowska, D.: Neuro-Fuzzy Architectures and Hybrid Learning. Springer, Heidelberg (2002). https://doi.org/10.1007/978-3-7908-1802-4

26. Rutkowska, D.: An expert system for human personality characteristics recognition. In: Rutkowski, L., Scherer, R., Tadeusiewicz, R., Zadeh, L.A., Zurada, J.M. (eds.) ICAISC 2010. LNCS (LNAI), vol. 6113, pp. 665–672. Springer, Heidelberg (2010). https://doi.org/10.1007/978-3-642-13208-7_83

27. Sadiqbatcha, S., Jafarzadeh, S., Ampatzidis, Y.: Particle swarm optimization for solving a class of type-1 and type-2 fuzzy nonlinear equations. J. Artif. Intell. Soft Comput. Res. **8**(2), 103–110 (2018)

28. Setiono, R.: Extracting rules from neural networks by prunning and hidden-unit splitting. Neural Comput. **9**, 205–225 (1997)

29. Singh, H.: Practical Machine Learning and Image Processing: For Facial Recognition, Object Detection, and Pattern Recognition Using Python. Apress (2019)
30. Starczewski, J.T.: A triangular type-2 fuzzy logic system. FUZZ-IEEE, pp. 1460–1467 (2006)
31. Starczewski, J., Rutkowski, L.: Connectionist structures of type 2 fuzzy inference systems. In: Wyrzykowski, R., Dongarra, J., Paprzycki, M., Waśniewski, J. (eds.) PPAM 2001. LNCS, vol. 2328, pp. 634–642. Springer, Heidelberg (2002). https://doi.org/10.1007/3-540-48086-2_70
32. Zadeh, L.A.: Fuzzy sets. Inf. Control **8**, 338–353 (1965)
33. Zadeh, L.A.: The concept of a linguistic variable and its application to approximate reasoning-1. Inf. Sci. **8**, 199–249 (1975)
34. Zadeh, L.A.: Fuzzy logic = computing with words. IEEE Trans. Fuzzy Syst. **4**, 103–111 (1996)
35. Zurada, J.M.: Introduction to Artificial Neural Systems. West Publishing Company (1992)

Redefinition of Intuitionistic Fuzzy TOPSIS Method in the Framework of Evidence Theory

Pavel Sevastjanov[✉]

Department of Computer Science, Czestochowa University of Technology,
Dabrowskiego 73, 42-200 Czestochowa, Poland
dymova@icis.pcz.pl

Abstract. A redefinition of technique for establishing order preference by similarity to the ideal solution ($TOPSIS$) in the intuitionistic fuzzy setting is proposed. Recently it was shown that the operation laws of classical intuitionistic fuzzy sets theory ($A - IFS$) have some drawbacks which may provide undesirable results in the solution of multiple criteria decision making problems. Therefore, in this paper we propose the redefinition of intuitionistic fuzzy $TOPSIS$ method in the framework of the Dempster-Shafer theory of evidence which is free of drawbacks and limitation of operations defined in the conventional $A - IFS$. An illustrative example is presented to show the features of the proposed approach.

Keywords: TOPSIS · Intuitionistic fuzzy sets · Dempster-Shafer theory

1 Introduction

Technique for Order Preference by Similarity to Ideal Solution ($TOPSIS$) developed by Hwang and Yoon [14] currently is very popular in the solution of multiple criteria ($MCDM$) problems. Intuitionistic fuzzy set proposed by Atanassov [1], abbreviated here as $A - IFS$ (the reasons for this are presented in [8]), is one of the possible generalizations of Fuzzy Sets Theory and currently is used mainly for solving $MCDM$ problems. Currently, the intuitionistic fuzzy extensions of $TOPSIS$ method (see for example [3,15,16,21]) are based on the classical approach to the arithmetical operation on $IFVs$ (see [18,20]) and the comparison rule [19]. Nevertheless, in [10] it is shown that classical operations on IFV have some undesirable properties and may provide counterintuitive results. In [10], it is shown that the operations on intuitionistic fuzzy values may be rewritten in terms of Dempster-Shafer theory (DST) and substituted with the operations on belief intervals. With the use of corresponding theorems, it was proved in [10] that a new set of operations is free of drawbacks of the classical operations on intuitionistic fuzzy values. When comparing methods used for $MCDM$, the methods which make it possible to take into account more available information or based on more correct operation laws are usually treated as the better ones.

© Springer Nature Switzerland AG 2020
L. Rutkowski et al. (Eds.): ICAISC 2020, LNAI 12415, pp. 351–360, 2020.
https://doi.org/10.1007/978-3-030-61401-0_33

The rest of paper is set out as follows: In Sect. 2, we recall some definitions needed for our analysis. Section 3 presents our approach to the generalisation of *TOPSIS* method in the intuitionistic fuzzy setting in the framework of evidence theory. A numerical example is presented in Sect. 4. Section 5 concludes with some remarks.

2 Preliminaries

2.1 The Basics of the *TOPSIS* Method

Suppose a *MCDM* problem is based on m alternatives A_1, A_2, ..., A_m and n local criteria C_1, C_2, ..., C_n. Each alternative is evaluated with respect to the n criteria. All the ratings are assigned to alternatives and presented in the decision matrix $D[x_{ij}]_{m \times n}$, where x_{ij} is the rating of alternative A_i with respect to the criterion C_j. Let $W = (w_1, w_2, ..., w_n)$ be the vector of local criteria weights satisfying $\sum_{j=1}^{n} w_j = 1$.

The *TOPSIS* method consists of the following steps [14]:

1. Normalize the decision matrix:

$$r_{ij} = \frac{x_{ij}}{\sqrt{\sum_{k=1}^{m} x_{kj}^2}}, \ i = 1, ..., m; \ j = 1, ..., n. \tag{1}$$

Multiply the columns of normalized decision matrix by the associated weights:

$$v_{ij} = w_j \times r_{ij}, \ i = 1, ..., m; \ j = 1, ..., n. \tag{2}$$

2. Determine the positive ideal and negative ideal solutions, respectively, as follows:

$$\begin{aligned} A^+ &= \{v_1^+, v_2^+, ..., v_n^+\} \\ &= \{(\max_i v_{ij} \, | j \in K_b) \, (\min_i v_{ij} \, | j \in K_c)\}, \end{aligned} \tag{3}$$

$$\begin{aligned} A^- &= \{v_1^-, v_2^-, ..., v_n^-\} \\ &= \{(\min_i v_{ij} \, | j \in K_b) \, (\max_i v_{ij} \, | j \in K_c)\}, \end{aligned} \tag{4}$$

where K_b is a set of benefit criteria and K_c is a set of cost criteria.

3. Obtain the distances of the existing alternatives from the positive ideal and negative ideal solutions: two Euclidean distances for each alternatives are, respectively, calculated as follows:

$$\begin{aligned} S_i^+ &= \sqrt{\sum_{j=1}^{n} (v_{ij} - v_j^+)^2}, \ i = 1, ..., m, \\ S_i^- &= \sqrt{\sum_{j=1}^{n} (v_{ij} - v_j^-)^2}, \ i = 1, ..., m. \end{aligned} \tag{5}$$

4. Calculate the relative closeness to the ideal alternatives:

$$RC_i = \frac{S_i^-}{S_i^+ + S_i^-}, \ i = 1, 2, ..., m, \ 0 \le RC_i \le 1. \tag{6}$$

5. Rank the alternatives according to their relative closeness to the ideal alternatives: the bigger is RC_i, the better is alternative A_i.

2.2 The Operations on Intuitionistic Fuzzy Values

Atanassov [1] defined A-IFS as follows.

Definition 1. Let $X = \{x_1, x_2, ..., x_n\}$ be a finite universal set. An intuitionistic fuzzy set A in X is an object having the following form: $A = \{< x_j, \mu_A(x_j), \nu_A(x_j) > | x_j \in X\}$, where the functions $\mu_A : X \to [0,1]$, $x_j \in X \to \mu_A(x_j) \in [0,1]$ and $\nu_A : X \to [0,1]$, $x_j \in X \to \nu_A(x_j) \in [0,1]$ define the degree of membership and degree of non-membership of the element $x_j \in X$ to the set $A \subseteq X$, respectively, and for every $x_j \in X$, $0 \le \mu_A(x_j) + \nu_A(x_j) \le 1$.

Following to Atanassov [1], we call $\pi_A(x_j) = 1 - \mu_A(x_j) - \nu_A(x_j)$ the intuitionistic index (or the hesitation degree) of the element x_j in the set A. Obviously, for every $x_j \in X$ we have $0 \le \pi_A(x_j) \le 1$.

The classical operations on intuitionistic fuzzy values ($IFVs$) were introduced in [2,7]. With the use of these operations, we can aggregate local criteria to solve $MCDM$ problems in the intuitionistic fuzzy setting.

Let $A_1, ..., A_n$ be $IFVs$ representing the values of local criteria and $w_1, ..., w_n$, $\sum_{i=1}^{n} w_i = 1$, be their real-valued weights. Then Intuitionistic Weighted Arithmetic Mean ($IWAM$) can be obtained as follows:

$$IWAM = w_1 A_1 \oplus w_2 A_2 \oplus ... \oplus w_n A_n = \left\langle 1 - \prod_{i=1}^{n}(1 - \mu_{A_i})^{w_i}, \prod_{i=1}^{n} \nu_{A_i}^{w_i} \right\rangle. \quad (7)$$

Since final scores of alternatives are presented by $IFVs$, e.g., by $IWAM$, to choose the best alternative we should compare $IFVs$. For this aim, Chen and Tan [4] proposed to use the so-called score function (or net membership) $S(x) = \mu(x) - \nu(x)$, where x is IFV. Hong and Choi [13] introduced the so-called accuracy function $H(x) = \mu(x) + \nu(x)$ and showed that the relation between functions S and H is similar to the relation between mean and variance in statistics. Xu [19] used the functions S and H to represent order relations between any pair of intuitionistic fuzzy values.

In [10], it is shown that classical operations on IFV and order relations have some undesirable properties and may provide counter-intuitive results in applications. Particularly, the aggregation operation (7) is not consistent with the aggregation operation on the ordinary fuzzy sets (Ordinary Weighted Arithmetic Mean) and is not monotone with respect to the ordering.

The explanations and convincing numerical examples are presented in [10].

Therefore, to avoid the above mentioned drawbacks and limitations of classical $A - IFS$ we will use the another approach to the interpretation of $A - IFS$.

2.3 Interpretation of A-IFS in the Framework of DST

The DST was developed by Dempster [5,6] and Shafer [17]. A DST belief structure has the associated mapping m, called basic assignment function, from subsets of X into a unit interval, $m : 2^X \to [0,1]$ such that $m(\emptyset) = 0$, $\sum_{A \subseteq X} m(A) = 1$ (A is a subset of X).

The measures of belief (Bel) and plausibility (Pl) associated with DST belief structure were introduced in [17] as follows:

$$Bel(B) = \sum_{\emptyset \neq A \subseteq B} m(A), Pl(B) = \sum_{A \cap B \neq \emptyset} m(A). \tag{8}$$

It is seen that $Bel(B) \leq Pl(B)$. An interval $[Bel(B), Pl(B)]$ is called the belief interval (BI).

In [9], it was shown that in the framework of DST the triplet $\mu_A(x)$, $\nu_A(x)$, $\pi_A(x)$ represents the correct basic assignment function and IFV $A(x) = \langle \mu_A(x), \nu_A(x) \rangle$ may be represented as follows:

$$A(x) = BI_A(x) = [Bel_A(x), Pl_A(x)] = [\mu_A(x), 1 - \nu_A(x)].$$

In this notation, $Bel(A)$ and $Pl(A)$ are the measures of belief and plausibility that $x_j \in X$ belongs to the set $A \subseteq X$. Therefore, the operations on the $IFVs$ A and B may be substituted by the corresponding operations on the belief intervals $BI(A)$ and $BI(B)$. The set of such operations based on non-probabilistic treatment of belief interval was proposed in [10]. This treatment is justified in [10] as follows.

Let $X = \{x_1, x_2, ..., x_n\}$ be a finite universal set. Assume A are subsets of X. It is known that in the framework of DST a subset A may be treated also as a question or proposition and X as a set of propositions or mutually exclusive hypotheses or answers. In this context, $Bel(A)$ and $Pl(A)$ are the measures of belief and plausibility that $x_j \in X$ belongs to the set $A \subseteq X$.

In a such context, a belief interval $BI(A) = [Bel(A), Pl(A)]$ may be treated as an interval enclosing a true power of statement (argument, proposition, hypothesis, ets) that $x_j \in X$ belongs to the set $A \subseteq X$. Obviously, the value of such a power lies in interval $[0, 1]$.

Therefore, a belief interval $BI(A) = [Bel(A), Pl(A)]$ as a whole may be treated as a not exact (interval valued) statement (argument, proposition, hypothesis, ets) that $x_j \in X$ belongs to the set $A \subseteq X$.

Basing on the above reasoning, we can say that if we pronounce this statement, we can obtain some result, e.g., as a reaction on this statement and if we repeat this statement twice, the result does not change.

Such a reasoning implies the following property of addition operator: $BI(A) = BI(A) + BI(A) + ... + BI(A)$. This is possible only if we define the addition $\oplus$ of belief intervals as follows: $BI(A) \oplus BI(A) = \left[\frac{Bel(A) + Bel(A)}{2}, \frac{Pl(A) + Pl(A)}{2} \right]$. So the addition of belief intervals is represented by their averaging.

Therefore, if we have n different statements represented by belief intervals $BI(A_i)$ then their sum $\oplus$ should be defined as follows [10]:

$$BI(A_1) \oplus BI(A_2) \oplus .... \oplus BI(A_n) = \left[\frac{1}{n} \sum_{i=1}^{n} Bel(A_i), \frac{1}{n} \sum_{i=1}^{n} Pl(A_i) \right]. \tag{9}$$

The other operations presented in [10] are the same as in usual interval arithmetic.

The operator of belief interval comparison was presented in [10] as follows:

$$if \ (Bel(A) + Pl(A)) > (Bel(B) + Pl(B)) \ then \ BI(B) < BI(A),$$
$$if \ (Bel(A) + Pl(A)) = (Bel(B) + Pl(B)) \ then \ BI(B) = BI(A). \tag{10}$$

Using corresponding theorems, it was proved in [10] that introduced set of operations on the belief intervals representing $IFVs$ is free of drawbacks and limitations of conventional $A - IFS$.

3 The Intuitionistic Fuzzy *TOPSIS* Method in the Framework of *DST*

It was proved in [12] in context of fuzzy $TOPSIS$ method that there is no need to use n-dimensional Euclidean or Hamming distances for obtaining S_i^+ and S_i^-, $i = 1, 2, ..., m$, as they can be calculated as follows:

$$S_i^+ = \sum_{j \in K_b} w_j(r_j^+ - r_{ij}) + \sum_{j \in K_c} w_j(r_{ij} - r_j^+),$$
$$S_i^- = \sum_{j \in K_b} w_j(r_{ij} - r_j^-) + \sum_{j \in K_c} w_j(r_j^- - r_{ij}), \ i = 1, ..., m. \tag{11}$$

As all the expressions

$$r_j^+ - r_{ij}, \ i = 1, 2, ..., m, \ j \in K_b,$$

$$r_{ij} - r_j^+, \ i = 1, 2, ..., m, \ j \in K_c,$$

$$r_{ij} - r_j^-, \ i = 1, 2, ..., m, \ j \in K_b,$$

$$r_j^- - r_{ij}, \ i = 1, 2, ..., m, \ j \in K_c$$

are non negative, they may be treated as some modified values of local criteria based on the initial ones. Therefore, expressions (11) may be considered as the modified weighted sum aggregations of modified local criteria.

Let us consider a $MCDM$ problem which is based on m alternatives A_1, A_2, ..., A_m and n local criteria C_1, C_2, ..., C_n. Each alternative is evaluated with respect to the n criteria. Let all ratings assigned to alternatives and are intuitionistic fuzzy (IF) values. Then the decision matrix may be presented as follows: $D\left[\langle \mu_{ij}, \nu_{ij} \rangle\right]_{m \times n}$, $i = 1, 2, ...m$, $j = 1, 2, ..., n$, where $\langle \mu_{ij}, \nu_{ij} \rangle$ is the IF-valued rating of alternative A_i with respect to the criterion C_j.

Let $W = \{\langle \mu_{wj}, \nu_{wj} \rangle\}$, $j = 1, 2, ..., n$, be the IF-valued vector of local criteria weights. Let us replace intuitionistic fuzzy values in the decision matrix and in the the vector of weights by corresponding belief intervals as follows:

$$BI_{ij} = [Bel_{ij}, Pl_{ij}], \ Bel_{ij} = \mu_{ij}, \ Pl_{ij} = 1 - \nu_{ij}, \ i = 1, 2, ...m, \ j = 1, 2, ..., n,$$
$$BI_{wj} = [Bel_{wj}, Pl_{wj}], \ Bel_{wj} = \mu_{wj}, \ Pl_{wj} = 1 - \nu_{wj}, \ j = 1, 2, ..., n.$$

Then using the rule of belief interval comparison (10), the positive ideal and negative ideal solutions can be obtained from the expressions

$$
\begin{aligned}
BI^+ &= \{[Bel_j^+, Pl_j^+]\} = \{\max_i \{[Bel_{ij}, Pl_{ij}]\} \mid j \in K_b, \\
&\quad \min_i \{[Bel_{ij}, Pl_{ij}]\} \mid j \in K_c\}, \\
BI^- &= \{[Bel_j^-, Pl_j^-]\} = \{\min_i \{[Bel_{ij}, Pl_{ij}]\} \mid j \in K_b, \\
&\quad \max_i \{[Bel_{ij}, Pl_{ij}]\} \mid j \in K_c\},
\end{aligned}
\tag{12}
$$

where K_b is a set of benefit criteria and K_c is a set of cost criteria.

Let us consider the weighted sum type of aggregation. Then the expressions for the calculation of the distances S_i^+ and S_i^-, $i = 1, 2, ..., m$ may be obtained as the belief interval extension of expressions (11) as follows:

$$
\begin{aligned}
S_i^+ &= \sum_{j \in K_b} \left([Bel_{wj}, Pl_{wj}] \otimes \left([Bel_j^+, Pl_j^+] - [Bel_{ij}, Pl_{ij}]\right)\right) + \\
&\quad \sum_{j \in K_c} \left([Bel_{wj}, Pl_{wj}] \otimes \left([Bel_{ij}, Pl_{ij}] - [Bel_j^-, Pl_j^-]\right)\right), \\
S_i^- &= \sum_{j \in K_b} \left([Bel_{wj}, Pl_{wj}] \otimes \left([Bel_{ij}, Pl_{ij}] - [Bel_j^-, Pl_j^-]\right)\right) + \\
&\quad \sum_{j \in K_c} \left([Bel_{wj}, Pl_{wj}] \otimes \left([Bel_j^-, Pl_j^-] - [Bel_{ij}, Pl_{ij}]\right)\right), \; i = 1, ..., m.
\end{aligned}
\tag{13}
$$

We can see that to use S_i^+ and S_i^- presented in (13) for the subsequent analysis, the distance between belief intervals and the rule for interval comparison should be defined.

Then following to [11], we will use directly the operation of interval subtraction to define the distance between intervals. This approach makes it possible to calculate also the possibility that one interval is greater/lesser that another.

For intervals $A = [a^L, a^U]$ and $B = [b^L, b^U]$, the result of subtraction is the interval $C = A - B = [c^L, c^U]$; $c^L = a^L - b^U$, $c^U = a^U - b^L$. Then, to get a measure of distance between intervals which additionally indicates which interval is greater/lesser, we will use the following value:

$$
\Delta_{A-B} = \frac{1}{2} \left((a^L - b^U) + (a^U - b^L)\right).
\tag{14}
$$

It is easy to see that the above expression (14) represents the distance between the centers of compared intervals A and B. It easy to prove that the result of subtraction of intervals with common centers is an interval centered around 0. In the framework of interval analysis, such intervals are treated as the interval 0.

Therefore, the value of Δ_{A-B} equal to 0 for A and B having a common center may be treated as a real-valued representation of interval zero.

A similar situation we can see in statistics. Let A and B be two samples of measurements with uniform probability distributions such that they have a common mean ($mean_A = mean_B$), but different variances ($\sigma_A > \sigma_B$). Then, using statistical methods, it is impossible to prove that the sample B is greater than the sample A or that the sample A is greater than the sample B.

Taking into account the above consideration we can say that interval comparison based on the assumption that intervals having a common centre are equal seems to be justified and reasonable. It is important that this assumption is in compliance with the rules for belief interval comparison (10).

Then based on the above consideration we can introduce the distances between belief intervals in (13). The centers of corresponding belief intervals may be calculated as follows:

$$p_j^+ = \frac{Bel_j^+ + Pl_j^+}{2}, \ p_j^- = \frac{Bel_j^- + Pl_j^-}{2}, \ l_{ij} = \frac{Bel_{ij} + Pl_{ij}}{2}, \tag{15}$$

$i = 1, 2, ..., m, \ j = 1, 2, ..., n$.
Therefore, the expressions (13) can be transformed as follows:

$$
\begin{aligned}
S_i^+ &= \sum_{j \in K_b} \left([Bel_{wj}, Pl_{wj}] \otimes (p_j^+ - l_{ij})\right) + \sum_{j \in K_c} \left([Bel_{wj}, Pl_{wj}] \otimes (l_{ij} - p_j^+)\right), \\
S_i^- &= \sum_{j \in K_b} \left([Bel_{wj}, Pl_{wj}] \otimes (l_{ij} - p_j^-)\right) + \sum_{j \in K_c} \left([Bel_{wj}, Pl_{wj}] \otimes (p_j^- - l_{ij})\right),
\end{aligned}
\tag{16}
$$

$i = 1, 2, ..., m$.
The expressions (16) produce belief intervals which should be compared. Therefore taking into account the rules for belief interval comparison (10), we can obtain from (16) the real-valued representations of S_i^+ and S_i^- as follows:

$$
\begin{aligned}
\overline{S}_i^+ &= \sum_{j \in K_b} \left(Bel_{wj} (p_j^+ - l_{ij}) + Pl_{wj} (p_j^+ - l_{ij})\right) + \\
&\quad \sum_{j \in K_c} \left(Bel_{wj} (l_{ij} - p_j^+) + Pl_{wj} (l_{ij} - p_j^+)\right), \\
\overline{S}_i^- &= \sum_{j \in K_b} \left(Bel_{wj} (l_{ij} - p_j^-) + Pl_{wj} (l_{ij} - p_j^-)\right) + \\
&\quad \sum_{j \in K_c} \left(Bel_{wj} (p_j^- - l_{ij}) + Pl_{wj} (p_j^- - l_{ij})\right).
\end{aligned}
\tag{17}
$$

$i = 1, 2, ..., m, \ j = 1, 2, ..., n$.
To facilitate the analysis and make it possible to compare results obtained with the use of other aggregation modes, the following intermediate normalization has been introduced:

$$
\begin{aligned}
T_i^+ &= \overline{S}_i^+ / \max \left\{ \max \left\{ \overline{S}_i^+ \right\}, \max \left\{ \overline{S}_i^- \right\} \right\}, \\
T_i^- &= \overline{S}_i^- / \max \left\{ \max \left\{ \overline{S}_i^+ \right\}, \max \left\{ \overline{S}_i^- \right\} \right\},
\end{aligned}
\tag{18}
$$

$i = 1, 2, ..., m$.
The final ratings of alternatives was calculated as follows:

$$R_i = \frac{T_i^-}{T_i^- + T_i^+}, \ i = 1, 2, ..., m. \tag{19}$$

4   Numerical Examples

To illustrate the results obtained with the use of proposed method we will use the example from [3] partially adapted for our purposes.

Suppose a company is desired to select the most appropriate supplier for one of important element in its manufacturing process. After pre-evaluation, five suppliers (alternatives A_1, A_2, A_3, A_4, A_5) have been remained for further evaluations. The following local criteria were used: C_1 (Product quality), C_2 (Relationship closeness), C_3 (Delivery performance) and C_4 (Price). Suppose that the ratings of alternatives with respect to the criteria and the weights of local criteria are presented by a decision maker in the form of IFVs. The corresponding decision matrix $D\left[\langle\mu_{ij},\nu_{ij}\rangle\right]_{m\times n}$, $i=1,2,...m$, $j=1,2,...,n$, where $\langle\mu_{ij},\nu_{ij}\rangle$ is the IF-valued rating of alternative A_i with respect to the criterion C_j is presented in Table 1.

The IF-valued vector of weights of local criteria is presented as follows:

$$W = (<0.861, 0.128>, <0.750, 0.200>, <0.680, 0.267>, <0.567, 0.371>).$$

Let us replace intuitionistic fuzzy values in the decision matrix and in the the vector of weights by corresponding belief intervals as follows:

$$BI_{ij} = [Bel_{ij}, Pl_{ij}], \ Bel_{ij} = \mu_{ij}, \ Pl_{ij} = 1 - \nu_{ij}, \ i = 1, 2, ...m, \ j = 1, 2, ..., n,$$
$$BI_{wj} = [Bel_{wj}, Pl_{wj}], \ Bel_{wj} = \mu_{wj}, \ Pl_{wj} = 1 - \nu_{wj}, \ j = 1, 2, ..., n.$$

Then the belief interval-valued vector of weights of local criteria is presented as follows:

$$W = ([0.861, 0.872], [0.750, 0.800], [0.680, 0.733], [0.567, 0.629]) \qquad (20)$$

The resulting belief interval-valued decision matrix is presented in Table 2.

Table 1. IF valued decision matrix

	C_1	C_2	C_3	C_4
A_1	$<0.728, 0.170>$	$<0.626, 0.272>$	$<0.780, 0.118>$	$<0.700.0.200>$
A_2	$<0.596, 0.302>$	$<0.605, 0.292>$	$<0.644, 0.256>$	$<0.578, 0.321>$
A_3	$<0.849, 0.100>$	$<0.780, 0.118>$	$<0.769, 0.170>$	$<0.769, 0.128>$
A_4	$<0.663, 0.236>$	$<0.538, 0.361>$	$<0.746, 0.151>$	$<0.644, 0.254>$
A_5	$<0.562, 0.337>$	$<0.462, 0.438>$	$<0.668, 0.231>$	$<0.526, 0.374>$

Then using the rule of belief interval comparison (10) and expressions (12) from the decision matrix presented in Table 2 we obtain the positive ideal and negative ideal solutions:

$$BI^+ = ([0.849, 0.900], [0.780, 0.882], [0.780, 0.882], [0.526, 0.626]),$$
$$BI^- = ([0.562, 0.663], [0.462, 0.562], [0.644, 0.744], [0.759, 0.872]). \qquad (21)$$

Table 2. Belief interval-valued decision matrix

	C_1	C_2	C_3	C_4
A_1	[0.728, 0.830]	[0.626, 0.728]	[0.780, 0.882]	[0.700.0.800]
A_2	[0.596, 0.698]	[0.605, 0.708]	[0.644, 0.774]	[0.578, 0.679]
A_3	[0.849, 0.900]	[0.780, 0.882]	[0.769, 0.830]	[0.769, 0.872]
A_4	[0.663, 0.764]	[0.538, 0.639]	[0.746, 0.849]	[0.644, 0.746]
A_5	[0.562, 0.663]	[0.462, 0.562]	[0.668, 0.769]	[0.526, 0.626]

Let us consider the weighted sum type of aggregation. Then using (17)–(19) from (19), (20) and Table 2 we obtain the final ratings of alternatives R_i presented in Table 3.

Table 3. The final ratings of alternatives

R_1	R_2	R_3	R_4	R_5
0.5284	0.3337	0.6965	0.3798	0.2139

From Table 3 we get the following ranking of alternatives:
$A_5 < A_2 < A_4 < A_1 < A_3$.

5   Conclusion

In this paper, we have developed a generalisation of $TOPSIS$ method in the intuitionistic fuzzy setting. Recently, it was shown that the operation on $IFVs$ defined in the classical intuitionistic fuzzy sets theory $(A - IFS)$ have some drawbacks which may produce controversial results in the solution of $MCDM)$ problems. Therefore we have used the redefinition of $A - IFS$ in the framework of the Dempster-Shafer theory of evidence (DST) which is free of drawbacks and limitation of operations defined in the conventional $A - IFS$. It is shown that the distances of the alternatives from the ideal solutions in the $TOPSIS$ method may be treated (in some sense) as modified weighted sums of local criteria. Finally, the intuitionistic fuzzy $TOPSIS$ method was redefined in the framework of DST using the transformation of initial intuitionistic fuzzy values into belief intervals. The numerical example is presented to show the features of the proposed approach.

References

1. Atanassov, K.T.: Intuitionistic fuzzy sets. Fuzzy Sets Syst. **20**, 87–96 (1986)
2. Atanassov, K.: New operations defined over the intuitionistic fuzzy sets. Fuzzy Sets Syst. **61**, 137–142 (1994)

3. Boran, F.E., Genc, S., Kurt, M., Akay, D.: A multi-criteria intuitionistic fuzzy group decision making for supplier selection with TOPSIS method. Expert Syst. Appl. **36**, 11363–11368 (2009)
4. Chen, S.M., Tan, J.M.: Handling multicriteria fuzzy decision-making problems based on vague set theory. Fuzzy Sets Syst. **67**, 163–172 (1994)
5. Dempster, A.P.: Upper and lower probabilities induced by a multi-valued mapping. Ann. Math. Stat. **38**, 325–339 (1967)
6. Dempster, A.P.: A generalization of Bayesian inference (with discussion). J. Roy. Stat. Soc., Series B. **30**(2), 208–247 (1968)
7. Dey, S.K., Biswas, R., Roy, A.R.: Some operations on intuitionistic fuzzy sets. Fuzzy Sets Syst. **114**, 477–484 (2000)
8. Dubois, D., Gottwald, S., Hajek, P., Kacprzyk, J., Prade, H.: Terminological difficulties in fuzzy set theory-the case of "Intuitionistic Fuzzy Sets". Fuzzy Sets Syst. **156**, 485–491 (2005)
9. Dymova, L., Sevastjanov, P.: An interpretation of intuitionistic fuzzy sets in terms of evidence theory. Decision making aspect. Knowl. Based Syst. **23**, 772–782 (2010)
10. Dymova, L., Sevastjanov, P.: The operations on intuitionistic fuzzy values in the framework of Dempster-Shafer theory. Knowl. Based Syst. **35**, 132–143 (2012)
11. Dymova, L., Sevastjanov, P., Tikhonenko, A.: A direct interval extension of TOPSIS method. Expert Syst. Appl. **40**, 4841–4847 (2013)
12. Dymova, L., Sevastjanov, P., Tikhonenko, A.: An approach to generalization of fuzzy TOPSIS method. Inf. Sci. **238**, 149–162 (2013)
13. Hong, D.H., Choi, C.-H.: Multicriteria fuzzy decision-making problems based on vague set theory. Fuzzy Sets Syst. **114**, 103–113 (2000)
14. Hwang, C.L., Yoon, K.: Multiple Attribute Decision Making Methods and Applications. Springer, Heidelberg (1981). https://doi.org/10.1007/978-3-642-48318-910. 1007/978-3-642-48318-9
15. Li, M., Jin, L., Wang, J.: A new MCDM method combining QFD with TOPSIS for knowledge management system selection from the user's perspective in intuitionistic fuzzy environment. Expert Syst. Appl. **36**, 11363–11368 (2009)
16. Lourenzutti, R., Krohling, A.: The Hellinger distance in multicriteria decision making: an illustration to the TOPSIS and TODIM methods. Expert Syst. Appl. **41**, 4414–4421 (2014)
17. Shafer, G.: A Mathematical Theory of Evidence. Princeton University Press, Princeton (1976)
18. Xu, Z.: Intuitionistic fuzzy aggregation operators. IEEE Trans. Fuzzy Syst. **15**, 1179–1183 (2007)
19. Xu, Z.: Intuitionistic preference relations and their application in group decision making. Inf. Sci. **177**, 2363–2379 (2007)
20. Xu, Z., Yager, R.: Some geometric aggregation operators based on intuitionistic fuzzy sets. Int. J. Gen.Syst. **35**(4), 417–433 (2006)
21. Xu, Z., Zhang, X.: Hesitant fuzzy multi-attribute decision making based on TOPSIS with incomplete weight information. Knowl. Based Syst. **52**, 53–64 (2013)

Evolutionary Algorithms and Their Applications

On the Performance and Complexity of Crossover in Differential Evolution Algorithm

Petr Bujok[(✉)] [iD]

University of Ostrava, 30. dubna 22, 70200 Ostrava, Czech Republic
petr.bujok@osu.cz

Abstract. In this study, the efficiency and complexity of four different crossover variants in Differential evolution (DE) algorithm are experimentally studied. Three well-known crossover variants with a newly designed crossover are applied in nine state-of-the-art and one standard DE algorithm. The results obtained from CEC 2011 real-world problems showed a significant difference between different DE variants and crossover types in performance and time complexity. Higher time complexity is for Eigen crossover, higher efficiency s for newly designed crossover.

Keywords: Differential evolution · Crossover · Time complexity · Real-world problems · Experimental study

1 Introduction

A problem of global optimisation is solved in many fields of production, development and economy. The main reason lies in an increasing amount of consumer goods and decreasing natural resources. Therefore, optimal setting of natural resources consumption is a natural necessity. The global optimisation problem is mentioned as follows. For the objective function $f : \Omega \rightarrow \mathbb{R}$, $\Omega \subseteq \mathbb{R}^D$, where D is the dimension of the problem, the global minimum is such a point $\boldsymbol{x}^*$, $\forall \boldsymbol{x} \in \Omega : f(\boldsymbol{x}^*) \leq f(\boldsymbol{x})$. A search space is usually bounded, $\Omega : [a_1, \ b_1] \times [a_2, \ b_2] \times \ldots \times [a_D, \ b_D], a_j < b_j, \ j = 1, \ 2, \ \ldots, \ D$.

A very popular group of stochastic optimisation methods inspired by nature is called Evolutionary Algorithms (EA). One of the most frequently used EA is the Differential Evolution (DE) algorithm. This paper is focused on an experimental analysis of crossover variants in the DE algorithm. An efficiency and estimation of time complexity of four different crossover variants in state-of-the-art DE variants are studied.

The rest of the paper is organised as follows. The basic idea of popular DE algorithm is in Sect. 2, and a brief description of the state-of-the-art DE variants is in Sect. 2.1. Well-known crossover variants and proposed design of a crossover are shown in Sect. 3. Details of experimental settings are depicted in Sect. 4. The results of the experimental analysis are discussed in Sect. 5 and conclusions are made in Sect. 6.

© Springer Nature Switzerland AG 2020
L. Rutkowski et al. (Eds.): ICAISC 2020, LNAI 12415, pp. 363–375, 2020.
https://doi.org/10.1007/978-3-030-61401-0_34

2   Differential Evolution Algorithm

The Differential Evolution (DE) algorithm was introduced by Storn and Price [13]. The main reason of popularity of DE is its simplicity, universality, and a small number of control parameters. DE uses three evolutionary operators - mutation, crossover, and selection. A mutation is controlled by a scale factor $F \in [0, 2]$, whereas a crossover is driven by crossover ratio $CR \in [0, 1]$. Although DE provides high efficiency in many optimisation problems, the DE performance is not very high in more complex tasks. It is caused by fixed settings of F, CR parameters because one setting is efficient only in part of optimisation problems. This situation results in an adaptation mechanism of the control parameters in the DE algorithm. There exist a lot of adaptive DE variants, but only some of them were selected as state-of-the-art optimisers.

In this experimental study, nine various adaptive DE variants are used to study the influence of a crossover. Beside adaptive DE variants, the classic DE algorithm with fixed control parameters values [13] is also included in the comparison. A mutation strategy $randrl/1$ is applied along with a binomial crossover. The reason for the mutation is based on the success in experimental study [6]. Both control parameters of DE are set to the same values $F = CR = 0.8$. These values are selected for higher exploration and a preference for new individuals.

2.1   Adaptive Variants of Differential Evolution

Nine state-of-the-art DE variants used in the experiments are briefly described chronologically in the following text. Details are available in the original papers.

In 2006, Brest et al. introduced a simple and efficient adaptive DE variant called jDE [1]. The jDE algorithm employs a well-known strategy DE/rand/1/bin with self-adaptation of both control parameters F and CR. The values of F and CR are initialised randomly uniformly for each point in the population and they are randomly mutated with probabilities τ_1 (F) and τ_2 (CR). Values of CR are uniformly distributed in $[0, 1]$, and similarly values of F are uniformly distributed in $[F_l, F_u]$. The authors recommended to set the input parameters $F_l = 0.1$, $F_u = 0.9$, $\tau_1 = 0.1$, and $\tau_2 = 0.1$ [1].

In 2006, Zhang and Sanderson published a new adaptive DE variant called JADE [21]. The proposed JADE variant extends the original DE algorithm by three elements - current-to-$p$best mutation strategy, adaptive control of parameters F, CR, and optional archive A. In the archive, the good old solutions are stored to be used in reproduction. When the size of the archive exceeds the population size, randomly chosen points are deleted. The solutions from the archive are used in the mutation, where one point is selected from the union of population P and archive A. Moreover, the base point of the mutation is randomly chosen from $100p$ % best individuals with input parameter $p = 0.05$. The parameters of JADE - F, CR - are independently generated for each individual according to the Gaussian (CR) and Cauchy (F) distribution, based on the success in previous generations.

In 2009, Qin and Suganthan proposed Differential evolution with strategy adaptation (SaDE) [12]. Four different mutation strategies are used to produce new trial points, rand/1/bin, rand/2/bin, rand-to-best/2/bin, and current-to-rand/1. The mutation is selected according to the probability to be used, which is set to 1/4 for each strategy. The probabilities are updated based on their successes and failures in previous LP generations. The length of the learning period is set to the recommended value of $LP = 50$ in the experiments. The values of parameter F are generated randomly, independently for each trial vector from a Gaussian distribution with a mean of 0.5 and a standard deviation of 0.3. The values of CR are randomly generated from the Gaussian distribution with a mean CRm_k and a standard deviation of 0.1. Initial values of $CRm_k = 0.5$, $k = 1, 2, 3, 4$ are employed by all the strategies. Moreover, the parameter $CRmem_k$ is adapted based on the success in previous LP generations after each generation.

In 2011, Mallipeddi et al. introduced DE with an ensemble of parameters and mutation strategies (EPSDE) [11] (abbreviated 'EPS'). This algorithm uses pools of mutation strategies and control parameters settings. For each individual, a triplet of (*strategy*, F, CR) is selected randomly. If the triplet produces a new successful trial vector, the settings survive with the trial vector, and it is also stored in auxiliary memory. Conversely, the triplet is randomly re-initialised from the pools. The adaptation process is controlled by learning period LP, and the authors recommended to use $LP = N$.

In 2013, Tanabe and Fukunaga proposed a Success-History Based Parameter Adaptation for Differential Evolution (SHADE) [16] (abbreviated 'SHA'). This DE variant was the best performing algorithm of the CEC 2013 competition, and it was derived from the original JADE algorithm. The SHADE algorithm extends the original JADE in a history-based adaptation of the control parameters F and CR. SHADE employs circle memories to generate new values of F and CR. New values in the memories are computed as weighted arithmetic mean (CR) and as a weighted Lehmer mean (F). Moreover, the parameter p used for selecting the best point in mutation is randomly generated for each point of the population from uniform distribution $p_i = rand[2/N,\ 0.2]$.

In 2014, Tanabe and Fukunaga introduced a derived variant of SHADE with a linear reduction of the population size called L-SHADE [14] (abbreviated 'LSHA'). The main new enhancement of L-SHADE is that the population size in L-SHADE is linearly decreased. The reason is to set exploration in the early stages and exploitation in the later stages of the search. The control parameters F and CR are adapted according to the success in previous generations. An archive of outperformed good solutions is employed by the current-to-$p$best mutation. The L-SHADE algorithm was the winner of the CEC 2014 competition.

In 2015, Tang et al. proposed a DE algorithm with an individual-dependent mechanism [17]. The authors of IDE divided the search process into two stages, a more exploratory first stage, and a more exploitative second stage. The values of F and CR are dynamically set in accordance with the evaluation of the individuals. For better individuals, smaller values of F and CR are generated and vice versa, regarding its function values. The population is divided into two parts - better individuals (superior part) and worse individuals (inferior part), based on function values. This information is used in a new mutation strategy, where the superior parent individual current-to-rand mutation is performed. For the inferior parent individual, a variant of current-to-best is used. Moreover, the last individual in the mutation strategy is perturbed with low probability.

In 2016, Bujok et al. designed an enhanced variant of the original SHADE algorithm called SHADE4 [7] for the CEC 2016 competition. The SHADE4 variant differs from the original SHADE in the competition of four different strategies and settings (abbreviated 'SHA2' because it uses only two mutation strategies). The strategies are composed of two mutation variants and two types of crossover (current-to-$p$best and randrl/1 mutation, binomial and exponential crossover). These strategies compete to be used in the population reproduction process. The remaining settings of SHADE4 are adopted from the original SHADE algorithm.

In 2017, Brest et al. proposed an adaptive DE variant with fine-tuned parameter settings and a weighted mutation variant called jSO [2]. The jSO algorithm is an extended variant of the L-SHADE algorithm, and it was the second-best optimiser at the CEC 2017 competition. Main differences between the jSO algorithm and L-SHADE consist of a weighted mutation strategy and a modified adaptation of DE control parameters. The adaptation process of jSO control parameters is based on the current stage of the search process. A detailed description of the jSO algorithm is in the original paper [2]. Although jSO is a very efficient optimisation method, the authors of [3] increased the performance of jSO by competition of strategies.

3   Crossover in Differential Evolution

A crossover in a DE algorithm is employed to combine elements from a parent and mutated vectors into a trial vector. Three well-known crossover variants were proposed for the DE algorithm. The most used crossover variant is called *binomial* (abbreviated by index $_b$ in experiments). Here, each element of the trial vector is selected from the parent or mutated individuals independently of other elements (see Fig. 1), based on the value of CR. In the case of $CR = 0$, one randomly selected point from the mutated individual is used in the trial vector. Another well-known crossover variant in DE is the *exponential* one (abbreviated by symbol $_e$). It was employed in the first DE variant, and typically several contiguous elements from the mutated vector are used in the trial individual (Fig. 1). Some authors recommended to use binomial crossover when real-world problems are solved [15]. The reason is in related parameters of real-world problems in contiguous dimensions. Third crossover variant is different from previous ones because it employs transformation of vectors into Eigen coordinate system (denoted *Eigenvector* crossover and abbreviated by index $_E$) was proposed [18]. The main idea was to increase the performance in problems with highly correlated coordinates. A covariance matrix C from a portion of the population ($ps \in (0, 1)$) is decomposed into Eigenvectors and Eigenvalues. Eigenvectors are used to transform parent and mutated individuals to Eigen coordinate system. Then, a standard binomial crossover is applied, and a new trial point is transformed back to a standard coordinate system using the same Eigenvectors. The Eigenvector crossover is used over the whole population with the probability $pb \in (0, 1)$. Otherwise, a standard binomial crossover is applied.

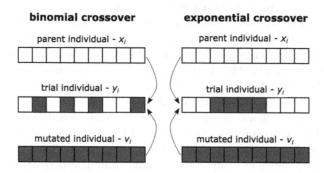

Fig. 1. Visualisation of difference between binomial and exponential crossover.

It is obvious that the main difference between binomial and exponential crossover variants is that elements are selected randomly independently (binomial) or continuously (exponential). In this paper, the exponential crossover with randomly ordered continuously selected coordinates is proposed. After combination, coordinates of the new trial vector are arranged to the original (right) order of coordinates. The main reason for this approach is that many real optimisation problems have contiguously ordered coordinates, and it could be a reason that exponential crossover outperforms a binomial crossover. A newly designed variant of exponential crossover with randomly ordered contiguous coordinates is denoted in experiments by symbol $_n$. The motivation for this experimental study was inspired by the following studies from a similar research area.

In 2011, Lin et al. analysed the performance of a binomial and exponential crossover in a simple DE [10]. Originally, the binomial crossover is non-consecutive, the authors analysed a consecutive binomial variant. Originally, the exponential crossover is consecutive, and the authors analysed a non-consecutive exponential variant. Four crossover variants along with two mutation variants are tested on several benchmark problems. The experimental results show a better performance of the exponential crossover if the problems are separable. For non-separable problems, the binomial crossover variants performed better.

In 2012, Weber and Neri proposed a continuous variant of a binomial crossover in simple DE [19]. The main idea was a higher speed of the DE algorithm using another crossover variant. A new variant of a binomial crossover, called contiguous, was proposed and compared with the original binomial crossover. In the experiment, test problems with various dimensionality are used. The results show that in the middle and high dimensionality, the contiguous crossover occasionally provides better results, and it decreases the time complexity of a simple DE algorithm.

In 2014, Tanabe and Fukunaga analysed the performance of crossover variants in DE in the CEC 2014 test problems [15]. The authors tested a binomial and exponential crossover used in one simple and three advanced DE variants. A shuffled exponential crossover was designed and compared with the original crossover variants. The results showed that a binomial crossover performed better than a shuffled exponential crossover, and the original exponential crossover performed worse than a shuffled exponential variant. The authors conclude that an exponential crossover generally performs better on synthetic (non-real) problems. In another study [5], the authors showed that an exponential crossover used in various advanced DE variants performed significantly better than a binomial crossover when solving real-world CEC 2011 problems.

In 2018, Zámečníková et al. studied rotationally-invariant settings of a crossover in DE algorithm [20]. The results of the experimental study obtained from rotated and non-rotated problems showed that the analysed settings are not significantly more efficient compared with non-rotated settings. Better results of adaptive DE based on covariance matrix learning (CoBiDE [18]) are achieved particularly by bi-modal settings of the mutation parameters.

In 2019, Bujok and Poláková analysed the efficiency of Eigenvector crossover used in a successful adaptive DE called jSO [4]. The proposed variants of the adaptive DE called jSOe differ in different settings of Eigenvector crossover and are applied to CEC 2017 test problems. The results showed that Eigenvector crossover could increase the efficiency of fine-tuned jSO significantly. The efficiency of jSOe is higher if the original setting of $ps = 0.5$ is used, and the proposed mechanism is used rarely (i.e. $pb = 0.1$).

In this paper, each of the three well-known crossover variants and one derived crossover variant is employed in ten various differential evolution algorithms, i.e. 40 different DE algorithms are compared. The motivation is to distinguish a more and less appropriate crossover over various state-of-the-art DE variants for a real application. Moreover, the estimation of the time complexity of the proposed algorithm is analysed.

4   Setting of the Experiment

All DE variants in the experimental study are applied to a suite of 22 real-world problems from the CEC 2011 [8]. The complexity of the tasks differs in the dimensionality of the search area ($D \in (1, 240)$). There are 12 constrained problems restricted by equality or inequality, nine boundary-constrained tasks, and one unconstrained problem. For each algorithm and optimisation problem, 25 independent runs were conducted. The search process of the algorithms is limited to a given number of function evaluations, $maxFES = 150000$. The best-achieved results of the algorithms are also stored when $maxFES = 50000$ and $maxFES = 100000$ is achieved. The best-achieved solution of the algorithm on the problem is represented by the individual with the minimal function value.

The jSO and L-SHADE algorithms use the mechanism of a linear population-size reduction with initial values $N_{init} = \text{round}(25 \times \log(D) \times \sqrt{D})$ (jSO), and $N_{init} = 18 \times D$ (L-SHADE). For problems with $D < 6$, the minimal initial population size is estimated from value $D = 6$. The population size of the remaining algorithms in is set to $N = 90$. The control parameters of a simple DE variant are set to $F = 0.8$, and $CR = 0.8$. All parameters of adaptive DE algorithms are set to values recommended by the authors in the referred papers.

5   Results

In this study, nine state-of-the-art DE variants and one standard DE are used. In each algorithm, each of four different crossover variants is used independently to show its efficiency. The results of 40 different DE algorithms on 25 real-world problems are analysed from two points of view. At first, the efficiency of the algorithms is compared to find better performing and worse performing DE variants and crossover types. Afterwards, the estimated time complexity of the compared optimisers is presented to show time demands to achieve the results of the real tasks.

5.1   Crossover Efficiency in DE

Regarding the amount of the results (ten algorithms, four crossover variants and 22 problems), the detailed basic characteristics of the algorithms are not printed. The best way to present these results is to apply the Friedman non-parametric test, which provides an overview of the efficiency of the algorithms. The test is applied to medians of minimal function values at three stages of the search ($FES = 50000, 100000, 150000$). Details of the Friedman test are available in [9]. The test provides mean ranks of the methods over all 22 problems, where a lower mean rank denotes a better performing algorithm and vice versa. Naturally, a worse performing algorithm could achieve better results in some real problem, compared with a better performing method. The results regarding all 40 algorithms are in Table 1, which is divided into four parts. The algorithms in columns are ordered from the most efficient to the worst performing, based on the mean rank values in the final stage (row denoted $FES = 150000$). The least mean ranks in each stage are printed bold and underlined, the second position is in bold, and the third position is underlined.

It is not surprising that the first eight positions are for variants of efficient jSO and L-SHADE. It means that no crossover variant significantly decreases the efficiency of those algorithms. Further positions are not clearly ordered, variants of SHADE, SHADE2, and EPSDE are followed by JADE, IDE, and SaDE. Variants of jDE and standard DE take worse positions in the comparison. A very interesting is the order of the algorithms in the first and second stage, where SHADE and SHADE2 variants are the best performing. Studying the order of the crossover variants for each DE (Table 1), the newly designed crossover is the best performing in five cases (L-SHADE, SHADE, EPSDE, IDE, SHADE2), the

Table 1. Results of the Friedman test of all DE variants and four crossover types.

FES	jSO_b	jSO_E	jSO_e	jSO_n	$LSHA_n$	$LSHA_e$	$LSHA_b$	$LSHA_E$	SHA_n	$SHA2_n$
50000	25.1	24.0	27.0	25.8	29.1	28.2	29.0	26.0	**8.5**	10.3
100000	19.0	15.7	20.9	19.6	25.8	25.7	27.0	25.3	10.7	12.2
150000	**8.3**	**8.3**	8.6	8.7	12.4	13.4	13.9	14.2	15.1	15.6
Time	1264	1417	1291	1306	1568	1480	1584	1745	80	51
FES	EPS_n	$SHA2_e$	$SHA2_b$	EPS_e	SHA_e	$JADE_b$	IDE_n	$SaDE_b$	$SaDE_n$	IDE_b
50000	14.8	10.9	10.5	15.1	**10.0**	11.0	20.0	15.4	15.1	18.2
100000	13.5	12.1	12.1	14.9	**11.5**	14.5	18.3	16.3	17.0	18.7
150000	15.7	15.8	15.9	16.3	16.5	19.0	20.1	20.2	20.5	20.7
Time	68	46	37	60	73	47	111	77	73	129
FES	EPS_b	IDE_e	$JADE_E$	EPS_E	SHA_E	SHA_b	IDE_E	$SHA2_E$	$SaDE_E$	jDE_b
50000	17.3	19.9	19.3	19.9	15.5	20.5	17.2	17.7	20.9	21.4
100000	18.8	17.6	20.3	22.6	19.7	21.9	18.5	20.4	21.7	22.3
150000	20.7	21.5	22.7	23.0	23.2	23.4	23.8	24.1	24.8	24.9
Time	59	92	75	80	77	56	174	50	87	54
FES	$JADE_e$	jDE_E	$JADE_n$	jDE_n	jDE_e	DE_e	$SaDE_e$	DE_n	DE_E	DE_b
50000	19.9	21.2	21.8	24.4	23.0	24.7	27.4	25.7	33.0	35.4
100000	21.5	24.1	23.4	24.9	24.5	26.9	27.8	28.3	31.0	33.2
150000	25.0	25.8	26.9	27.6	27.8	30.3	30.5	30.8	31.3	32.6
Time	**33**	77	**34**	65	59	59	66	65	78	54

binomial crossover is the most powerful in four algorithms (jSO, JADE, SaDE, jDE), and the exponential crossover is the most efficient in one algorithm (simple DE).

A comparison of 40 algorithms is not unambiguous, because four crossover variants influence the efficiency of various DE differently. Therefore, the Friedman test was applied to each DE separately to show the efficiency of each crossover variant. For better insight, the mean ranks of four crossover variants for each DE independently are presented in Fig. 2 and 3. The binomial crossover achieves the best results in JADE and jDE, and the worst performance in standard DE and L-SHADE. The exponential crossover is efficient in standard DE, and it performs worse in IDE, jDE, jSO, and SaDE. The Eigenvector crossover performs better in jSO and L-SHADE, and worse in EPSDE, SaDE, and SHADE. Finally, the newly proposed randomly ordered exponential crossover performs better in EPSDE, SaDE, SHADE2, and SHADE, whereas it is not efficient in IDE, JADE, and jDE variants. Regarding the final stage, the new variant of exponential crossover performs better than the original one in seven (EPSDE, IDE, jDE, L-SHADE, SaDE, SHADE2, and SHADE) and worse in two (JADE and jSO) algorithms.

5.2   Crossover Time Complexity in DE

The time complexity of the compared DE variants is estimated on the problem with the highest dimensionality ($D = 240$). At first, the current CPU performance is estimated by standardised iterative operations. Then, each algorithm is applied to a given problem in five independent runs to achieve accurate results.

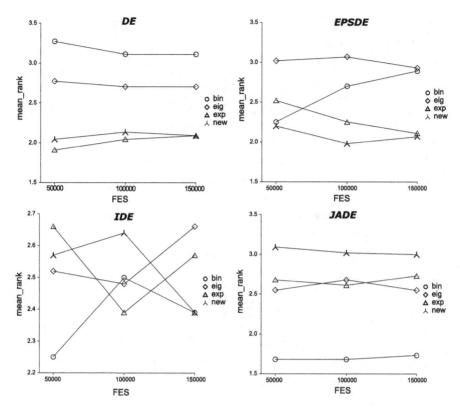

Fig. 2. Efficiency of four crossover variants in the DE, EPSDE, IDE and JADE algorithms.

The average estimated time complexity of each compared DE variant is presented in Fig. 4. The same results, in a numerical representation, are available in Table 1 (row 'time'). In the legend of the plot, the average time complexity of each DE variant regarding four crossover types is presented in brackets.

The most complex methods regarding the time are L-SHADE and jSO. The reason consists of very big initialised populations of these methods. The least complex method is JADE with an exponential crossover, followed by JADE with the newly proposed crossover. Regarding all crossover variants, SHADE2 is the least complex method on average (46 s per run). When considering both efficiency and complexity, SHADE, SHADE2, and EPSDE provide a good compromise on how to solve real-world problems in an acceptable time.

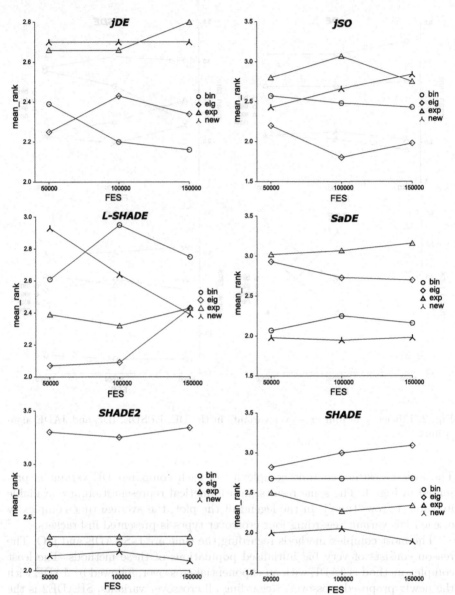

Fig. 3. Efficiency of four crossover variants in the jDE, jSO, L-SHADE, SaDE, SHADE2, and SHADE algorithms.

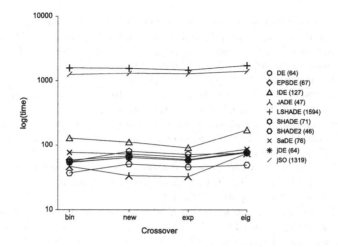

Fig. 4. Estimated time complexity of four crossover variants in ten DE algorithms.

6   Conclusion

Efficiency and complexity of four crossover types in Differential algorithm are experimentally analysed. At the first part of this study, the overall performance of each crossover variant in each DE variant regarding all real-world problems was assessed. As supposed, each crossover variant performs better in some DE variants. The best performing and the most complex are jSO and L-SHADE variants. The worst results are provided by standard DE and adaptive jDE. The newly designed crossover is the best performing in five cases, the binomial crossover is the most powerful in four algorithms, and the exponential crossover is the most efficient in one DE variant.

Regarding the complexity, the least time demands are required by SHADE2 and JADE algorithms. When combining efficiency and complexity, SHADE2 provides acceptable performance in a short time. Moreover, the least complex crossover is the binomial one in six algorithms and the exponential one in four DE variants. The Eigenvector crossover is the most complex approach in eight DE variants. The newly proposed exponential crossover with randomly ordered coordinates performs better than the original exponential crossover in seven, and worse in two DE variants.

References

1. Brest, J., Greiner, S., Boškovič, B., Mernik, M., Žumer, V.: Self-adapting control parameters in differential evolution: a comparative study on numerical benchmark problems. IEEE Trans. Evol. Comput. **10**, 646–657 (2006)
2. Brest, J., Maučec, M.S., Bošković, B.: Single objective real-parameter optimization: algorithm jSO. In: 2017 IEEE Congress on Evolutionary Computation (CEC), pp. 1311–1318 (2017)

3. Bujok, P.: Competition of strategies in jSO algorithm. In: Zamuda, A., Das, S., Suganthan, P.N., Panigrahi, B.K. (eds.) Swarm, Evolutionary, and Memetic Computing and Fuzzy and Neural Computing, pp. 113–121. Springer, Cham (2020). https://doi.org/10.1007/978-3-030-37838-7_11

4. Bujok, P., Poláková, R.: Eigenvector crossover in the efficient jSO algorithm. MENDEL 25(1), 65–72 (2019). https://doi.org/10.13164/mendel.2019.1.065

5. Bujok, P.: Tvrdík: Enhanced success-history based parameter adaptation for differential evolution and real-world optimization problems. In: Papa, G., Mernik, M. (eds.) BIOMA, pp. 159–171. Slovenia, Bioinspired Optimization Methods and their Applications, Bled (2016)

6. Bujok, P., Tvrdík, J.: A comparison of various strategies in differential evolution. In: Matoušek, R. (ed.) MENDEL, 17th International Conference on Soft Computing, pp. 48–55. Czech Republic, Brno (2011)

7. Bujok, P., Tvrdík, J., Poláková, R.: Evaluating the performance of shade with competing strategies on CEC 2014 single-parameter test suite. In: IEEE Congress on Evolutionary Computation (CEC), vol. 2016, pp. 5002–5009 (2016)

8. Das, S., Suganthan, P.N.: Problem definitions and evaluation criteria for CEC 2011 competition on testing evolutionary algorithms on real world optimization problems. Jadavpur University, India and Nanyang Technological University, Singapore, Technical report (2010)

9. Hollander, M., Wolfe, D.: Nonparametric Statistical Methods. Wiley Series in Probability and Statistics. Wiley (1999)

10. Lin, C., Qing, A., Feng, Q.: A comparative study of crossover in differential evolution. J. Heuristics 17, 675–703 (2011). https://doi.org/10.1007/s10732-010-9151-1

11. Mallipeddi, R., Suganthan, P.N., Pan, Q.K., Tasgetiren, M.F.: Differential evolution algorithm with ensemble of parameters and mutation strategies. Appl. Soft Comput. 11, 1679–1696 (2011)

12. Qin, A.K., Huang, V.L., Suganthan, P.N.: Differential evolution algorithm with strategy adaptation for global numerical optimization. IEEE Trans. Evol. Comput. 13, 398–417 (2009)

13. Storn, R., Price, K.V.: Differential evolution - a simple and efficient heuristic for global optimization over continuous spaces. J. Global Optim. 11, 341–359 (1997)

14. Tanabe, R., Fukunaga, A.S.: Improving the search performance of shade using linear population size reduction. In: IEEE Congress on Evolutionary Computation (CEC), vol. 2014, pp. 1658–1665 (2014)

15. Tanabe, R., Fukunaga, A.: Reevaluating exponential crossover in differential evolution. In: Bartz-Beielstein, T., Branke, J., Filipič, B., Smith, J. (eds.) PPSN 2014. LNCS, vol. 8672, pp. 201–210. Springer, Cham (2014). https://doi.org/10.1007/978-3-319-10762-2_20

16. Tanabe, R., Fukunaga, A.S.: Success-history based parameter adaptation for differential evolution. In: IEEE Congress on Evolutionary Computation (CEC), vol. 2013, pp. 71–78 (2013)

17. Tang, L., Dong, Y., Liu, J.: Differential evolution with an individual-dependent mechanism. IEEE Trans. Evol. Comput. 19(4), 560–574 (2015)

18. Wang, Y., Li, H.X., Huang, T., Li, L.: Differential evolution based on covariance matrix learning and bimodal distribution parameter setting. Appl. Soft Comput. 18, 232–247 (2014)

19. Weber, M., Neri, F.: Contiguous binomial crossover in differential evolution. In: Rutkowski, L., Korytkowski, M., Scherer, R., Tadeusiewicz, R., Zadeh, L.A., Zurada, J.M. (eds.) EC/SIDE -2012. LNCS, vol. 7269, pp. 145–153. Springer, Heidelberg (2012). https://doi.org/10.1007/978-3-642-29353-5_17
20. Zámečníková, H., Einšpiglová, D., Poláková, R., Bujok, P.: Is differential evolution rotationally invariant? Tatra Mountains Math. Publ. **72**(1), 155–165 (2018). https://doi.org/10.2478/tmmp-2018-0027
21. Zhang, J., Sanderson, A.C.: JADE: adaptive differential evolution with optional external archive. IEEE Trans. Evol. Comput. **13**, 945–958 (2009)

Obstacle Avoidance for Drones Based on the Self-Organizing Migrating Algorithm

Quoc Bao Diep$^{(\boxtimes)}$ ⓘ, Thanh Cong Truong ⓘ, and Ivan Zelinka ⓘ

Faculty of Electrical Engineering and Computer Science, Technical University
of Ostrava, 17. listopadu 15, Ostrava, Czech Republic
diepquocbao@gmail.com, {cong.thanh.truong.st,ivan.zelinka}@vsb.cz

Abstract. The paper proposes a method for the drone to catch the given target and avoid detected obstacles in its path based on the self-organizing migrating algorithm. In particular, a two-component fitness function is proposed based on the principle that the closer the target, the lower the fitness value, and the closer the obstacle, the higher the fitness value. Self-organizing migrating algorithm, a swarm intelligence algorithm, is used to predict the next positions that the drone will move to. These positions both satisfy the requirement to avoid obstacles and shorten the distance to the target. A map of two drones, two corresponding targets and four static obstacles was modeled on Matlab. The simulation results verify the correctness and effectiveness of the proposed method.

Keywords: Self-organizing migrating algorithm · Obstacle avoidance · Drone · Path planning

1 Introduction

Over the years, science and technology have been developing strongly, getting many outstanding achievements [5], especially in the field of artificial intelligence (AI) [7], where swarm intelligence optimization algorithm (SA) is an integral part [3], such as particle swarm optimization [6,11], artificial bee colony [10,14], and genetic algorithm [1,13]. Along with the general development of AI, the SA has made great leaps and bounds [9,16], and applied in many fields of science and technology such as [20], and [4,12]. One of the most important and common applications is path planning for autonomous robots on the ground, underwater and in the space.

The control of the unmanned aerial vehicles (UAVs) is often more complicated, requiring not only the speed of the algorithm, but also real-time accuracy. Many solutions have been proposed and successfully applied to path planning for UAVs such as sampling-based path planning for UAV collision avoidance [8], cooperative path planning with applications to target tracking and obstacle avoidance for multi-UAVs [17], and grid-based coverage path planning with minimum energy over irregular-shaped areas with UAVs [2].

© Springer Nature Switzerland AG 2020
L. Rutkowski et al. (Eds.): ICAISC 2020, LNAI 12415, pp. 376–386, 2020.
https://doi.org/10.1007/978-3-030-61401-0_35

The self-organizing migrating algorithm is swarm intelligence algorithm, based on competition - cooperation among individuals in the population to find an optimal solution to the given problem. It is applied to solve many complex problems in various fields such as games [21], virus [15], etc. However, the application of SOMA algorithm to plan the trajectory of the drone is unprecedented.

In this paper, we propose the application of the SOMA to generate the trajectory for the drone, avoid detected obstacles and catch the given target.

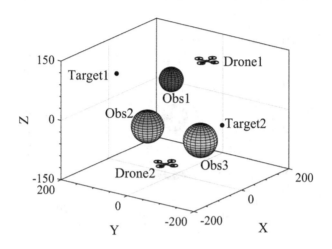

Fig. 1. The drones and obstacles model.

2   The Principle

The primary goal of the drone is to move toward and hit the given target without any collision with obstacles along the way. To accomplish this, the following assumptions are needed.

- *Obstacles*: Obstacles come in many different shapes and sizes in nature. However, within the framework of this study, we assume that the entire physical size of the obstacle is surrounded by a sphere of radius $r_{obstacle}$. These obstacles do not move in space and they will be detected and located by the sensors fitted on the drone.
- *Drone*: In this study, we assume that the drone is capable of freely moving through space, being able to fly from point A to point B near A without any problem, called the moving step $r_{movingstep}$. Depending on the size, structure, and controller, each drone has a different moving step. Besides, the drone is equipped with a sensor system to detect and identify obstacles within its operating range with radius r_{detect}. The target position is given before and provided to the drone.

The operating model of drones and obstacles is shown in Fig. 1.

Now, it is conceivable that the task of the algorithm is to find all B positions consecutively from start position A, forming a set of points that the drone will have to move through. The next B position must both shorten the distance of the drone to the target while avoiding collisions with obstacles. To formulate this idea, we propose an equation containing two components: the first component acts as a magnet to pull the drone towards the target and the second component pushes the drone away from the obstacles. This equation is proposed in Eq. 1.

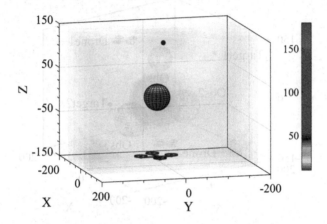

Fig. 2. The drone model in 4-dimensional space.

$$f_{value} = a_1 * e^{a_2 * dis_{tar}^{a_3}} + \sum_{n=0}^{n_{obs}} b_1 * e^{b_2 * dis_{obs}^{b_3}} \tag{1}$$

where:

- f_{value} : the fitness value,
- n_{obs} : the number of detected obstacles,
- dis_{tar} : the distance from the drone to the given target, in Eq. 2,
- dis_{obs} : the distance from the drone to each detected obstacle, in Eq. 3,
- a_x, b_x : the equilibrium coefficients ($x = 1, 2, 3.$).

$$dis_{tar} = \sqrt{(x_{target} - x_{drone})^2 + (y_{target} - y_{drone})^2 + (z_{target} - z_{drone})^2} \tag{2}$$

$$dis_{obs} = \sqrt{(x_{obs} - x_{drone})^2 + (y_{obs} - y_{drone})^2 + (z_{obs} - z_{drone})^2} \tag{3}$$

The problem of catching the target and avoiding obstacles for the drone has now become an optimization problem. Accordingly, generating the trajectory of the drone is to find the optimal solutions for Eq. 1.

Figure 2 depicts drone activity in 4-dimensional space. The color represents the fitness space. This space will change as the drone changes its position. Determining a set of points as mentioned will be executed by an algorithm named SOMA as presented in the next section.

3   Self-Organizing Migrating Algorithm

SOMA, proposed in the 2000 s [18, 19], is a swarm intelligence algorithm, inspired by the foraging activities of animals such as birds and fish. It works based on the interaction between individuals in the initial population to create new individuals as the optimal candidate solutions to the given problem.

In this problem, each individual represents a possible position of the drone. These individuals will first be randomly generated around the initial position of the drone, as in Eq. 4. They will then be evaluated based on the given fitness function 1. Next, these individuals will go into a loop called a migration loop.

$$P_{indi} = P_{actual} + rand_{-1 \to 1}\, r_{movingstep} \tag{4}$$

where:

- P_{indi}: the position of the ith individual,
- P_{actual}: the actual position of the drone,
- $r_{movingstep}$: the moving step of drone,
- $rand_{-1 \to 1}$: random number from -1 to 1.

At the beginning of each migration loop, an individual with the best fitness value is chosen to be the leader, the remaining individuals will be the travelling individuals that will move towards this leader. After each individual completes the move towards the leader, a number of new individuals will be created based on Eq. 5.

$$P_{os}^{new} = P_{current} + (P_{leader} - P_{current})\, n\, Step\, PRTVector_j \tag{5}$$

where:

- P_{os}^{new}: the offspring position in new migration loop,
- $P_{current}$: the offspring position in current migration loop,
- P_{leader} : the leader position in current migration loop,
- $PRTVector_j$: the perturbatively factor,
- $Step$: the step of each jump,
- n: the number of jumping step, from 1 to N_{jump}.

However, before an individual takes its jump, a $PRTVector_j$ parameter is created within two values of 0 or 1 to make the individual perturbatively move in the $N - k$ dimensional space that perpendicular to the original space instead of moving directly towards the leader. To implement it, a uniformly distributed random number is generated and compared with the given PRT threshold, if it is smaller than PRT then $PRTVector_j$ will get a value of 1, and vice versa, get a value of 0. Equation 6 describes this process.

$$if\ rand < PRT;\ \ PRTVector_j = 1;\ \ else,\ 0. \tag{6}$$

After each individual finishes the jumping, the best position on the traveling path of this individual is selected and compared to the original position. It will replace the initial if it is better, otherwise, it will be skipped.

This process is done for all individuals in the population, and after the last individual completes the migration process, a new migration loop begins. The best new individual is chosen to be the new leader and the movement is started again. The algorithm runs until it meets the given stop conditions, where it is the maximum number of migration loops.

Finally, the best individual of all is the predicted position for the drone.

4   Simulation Results

4.1   Experimental Settings

Table 1. The positions and radius of obstacles (in *meters*)

$Obstacle_i$	1	2	3	4
x_i	−30	10	50	−20
y_i	−10	90	−40	−140
z_i	100	−10	−70	0
r_i	40	30	50	20

Table 2. The initial position of drones and targets (in *meters*)

The object	Drone 1	Drone 2	Target 1	Target 2
x_i	110	60	−50	−100
y_i	−140	−50	140	−120
z_i	−130	130	90	−100

We implemented the operational experiment of drones using the self-organizing migrating algorithm in the Matlab environment, under the Windows 10 64-bit operating system.

Configuration parameters of the SOMA are listed below:

- The number of individuals in the population: $PopSize = 100$
- The number of jumps: $N_{jump} = 30$

- The PRT threshold: $PRT = 0.1$
- The granularity of each jump: $Step = 0.11$
- The maximum number of the migration loop: $MaxMig = 50$

Table 1 shows the positions of obstacles in the Cartesian coordinate system. The entire physical size of the obstacle is considered to be a sphere with radius $r_{obstacle}$. These obstacles do not move and are placed in positions that prevent the direct movement of the drones to the targets. Table 2 presents the starting position of the drones as well as the position of the respective targets.

In this simulation, we have assumed that the drones can move easily within a radius $r_{movingstep} = 1.5$ m without any difficulty. Sensors on drones are capable of detecting obstacles within a radius of 15m. The drones are provided with the location of the target as indicated above.

4.2 Results and Discussions

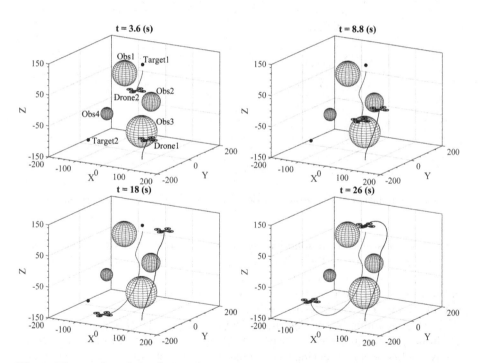

Fig. 3. The results of simulating the trajectories of drones and avoiding obstacles in their path in the form of 3D. (Color figure online)

Figure 3 shows the simulation results of the flighting trajectories of drones, where drone 1 will start from a given initial position and catch the target 1, and drone 2 will catch the target 2. For each drone, there are five obstacles, including four

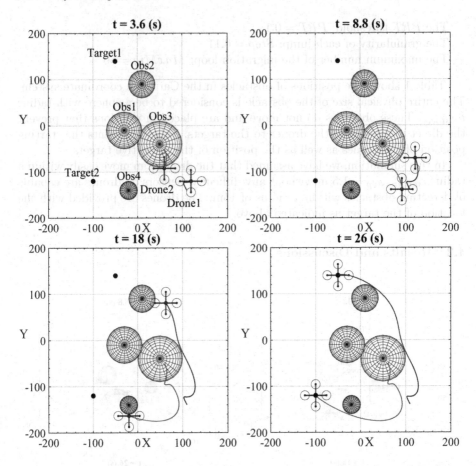

Fig. 4. Simulation of the drone's trajectory in X-Y view. (Color figure online)

given static obstacles in a spherical shape and the rest one is the other drone. The blue and red dotted lines represent the paths of drone 1 and 2, respectively. These figures were captured at 3.6^{th}, 8.8^{th}, 18th and 26th seconds. Figure 4, 5, and 6 present the trajectories of the drones at different views in more detail, X-Y, X-Z, and Y-Z view, respectively.

At the beginning of the algorithm, the position of the target is provided to the drone, and no obstacles are detected. Therefore, in the fitness function, there is only the first element, acting as a magnet to attract the drone to move towards the target. The predicted position that the drone will move to is created by the SOMA algorithm. This position satisfies both the requirement of the drone's limited step and the minimum distance to the target.

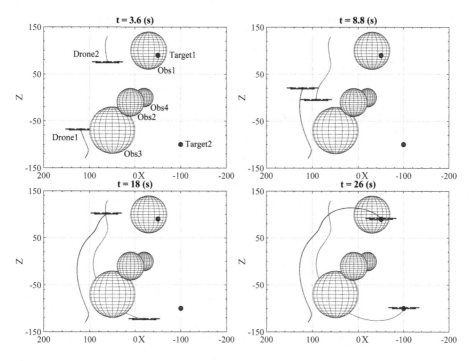

Fig. 5. Simulation of the drone's trajectory in X-Z view. (Color figure online)

At 3.6 s, drone 1 detected obstacle 3 and drone 2 detected obstacles 1 and 2. At this point, the second component in Eq. 1 appeared. This component makes the drone stay away from obstacles because if it moves closer to the obstacles, the value of the fitness function will increase. So the next predicted position provided by SOMA will both avoid obstacles and shorten the distance to the target.

The process continues as shown at the 8.8 and 18 s of Fig. 3 until the drones accomplished their purpose of catching targets at 26 s.

From these Figs. 3, 4, 5, and 6, it can be seen that the drone's paths change when obstacles were detected. Drone 1 and drone 2 have accomplished the goal of catching targets 1 and 2 without colliding with each other as well as hitting obstacles from 1 to 4. This fact proves the correctness and effectiveness of the proposed method.

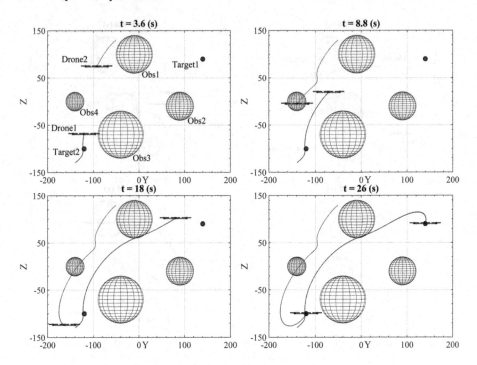

Fig. 6. Simulation of the drone's trajectory in Y-Z view. (Color figure online)

5   Conclusion

The paper completely addressed the problem of driving the drone to catch the given targets without colliding any obstacles and other drones. Besides, the SOMA, a population-based swarm intelligence algorithm, has been applied to create a set of points that constitute the trajectory of the drone. The paper also proposed a fitness function based on the principle of pull-push from the target-obstacle effect on the drone. The simulation results on Matlab have also proved the effectiveness and correctness of the method. However, the paper only deals with the case of static obstacles, non-moving targets and a limited number of drones, and not point out how to build the self-turning equilibrium coefficients as well as how to handle when the drone is trapped in an enclosed space including many obstacles around, a classic problem of the swarm algorithm. These issues will be addressed in the next paper.

Acknowledgment. The following grants are acknowledged for the financial support provided for this research: Grant of SGS No. SP2020/78, VSB-Technical University of Ostrava.

References

1. Arantes, M.S., Arantes, J.S., Toledo, C.F.M., Williams, B.C.: A hybrid multi-population genetic algorithm for UAV path planning. In: Proceedings of the Genetic and Evolutionary Computation Conference 2016, pp. 853–860 (2016)
2. Cabreira, T.M., Ferreira, P.R., Di Franco, C., Buttazzo, G.C.: Grid-based coverage path planning with minimum energy over irregular-shaped areas with UAVs. In: 2019 International Conference on Unmanned Aircraft Systems (ICUAS), pp. 758–767. IEEE (2019)
3. Del Ser, J., et al.: Bio-inspired computation: where we stand and what's next. Swarm Evol. Comput. **48**, 220–250 (2019)
4. Diep, Q.B., Zelinka, I.: The movement of swarm robots in an unknown complex environment. In: Zelinka, I., Brandstetter, P., Trong Dao, T., Hoang Duy, V., Kim, S.B. (eds.) AETA 2018. LNEE, vol. 554, pp. 949–959. Springer, Cham (2020). https://doi.org/10.1007/978-3-030-14907-9_92
5. Evenson, R., Ranis, G.: Science and Technology: Lessons for Development Policy. Routledge (2019)
6. Ghamry, K.A., Kamel, M.A., Zhang, Y.: Multiple UAVs in forest fire fighting mission using particle swarm optimization. In: 2017 International Conference on Unmanned Aircraft Systems (ICUAS), pp. 1404–1409. IEEE (2017)
7. Haenlein, M., Kaplan, A.: A brief history of artificial intelligence: on the past, present, and future of artificial intelligence. Calif. Manag. Rev. **61**(4), 5–14 (2019)
8. Lin, Y., Saripalli, S.: Sampling-based path planning for UAV collision avoidance. IEEE Trans. Intell. Transp. Syst. **18**(11), 3179–3192 (2017)
9. Mavrovouniotis, M., Li, C., Yang, S.: A survey of swarm intelligence for dynamic optimization: algorithms and applications. Swarm Evol. Comput. **33**, 1–17 (2017)
10. Pan, T.-S., Dao, T.-K., Pan, J.-S., Nguyen, T.-T.: An unmanned aerial vehicle optimal route planning based on compact artificial bee colony. Advances in Intelligent Information Hiding and Multimedia Signal Processing. SIST, vol. 64, pp. 361–369. Springer, Cham (2017). https://doi.org/10.1007/978-3-319-50212-0_43
11. Phung, M.D., Quach, C.H., Dinh, T.H., Ha, Q.: Enhanced discrete particle swarm optimization path planning for UAV vision-based surface inspection. Autom. Constr. **81**, 25–33 (2017)
12. Revay, L., Zelinka, I.: Swarm intelligence in virtual environment. J. Adv. Eng. Comput. **3**(2), 415–424 (2019)
13. Roberge, V., Tarbouchi, M., Labonté, G.: Fast genetic algorithm path planner for fixed-wing military UAV using GPU. IEEE Trans. Aerosp. Electron. Syst. **54**(5), 2105–2117 (2018)
14. Tian, G., Zhang, L., Bai, X., Wang, B.: Real-time dynamic track planning of multi-UAV formation based on improved artificial bee colony algorithm. In: 2018 37th Chinese Control Conference (CCC), pp. 10055–10060. IEEE (2018)
15. Truong, T.C., Zelinka, I., Senkerik, R.: Neural swarm virus. In: Zamuda, A., Das, S., Suganthan, P.N., Panigrahi, B.K. (eds.) SEMCCO/FANCCO - 2019. CCIS, vol. 1092, pp. 122–134. Springer, Cham (2020). https://doi.org/10.1007/978-3-030-37838-7_12
16. Wanka, R.: Swarm intelligence. IT Inf. Technol. **61**(4), 157–158 (2019)
17. Yao, P., Wang, H., Su, Z.: Cooperative path planning with applications to target tracking and obstacle avoidance for multi-UAVs. Aerosp. Sci. Technol. **54**, 10–22 (2016)

18. Zelinka, I.: SOMA—self-organizing migrating algorithm. In: New Optimization Techniques in Engineering, pp. 167–217. Springer, Heidelberg (2004). https://doi.org/10.1007/978-3-540-39930-8_7

19. Zelinka, I.: SOMA—self-organizing migrating algorithm. In: Davendra, D., Zelinka, I. (eds.) Self-Organizing Migrating Algorithm. SCI, vol. 626, pp. 3–49. Springer, Cham (2016). https://doi.org/10.1007/978-3-319-28161-2_1

20. Zelinka, I., Das, S., Sikora, L., Šenkeřík, R.: Swarm virus-next-generation virus and antivirus paradigm? Swarm Evol. Comput. **43**, 207–224 (2018)

21. Zelinka, I., Sikora, L.: StarCraft: brood war—strategy powered by the soma swarm algorithm. In: 2015 IEEE Conference on Computational Intelligence and Games (CIG), pp. 511–516. IEEE (2015)

An Empirical Evaluation of Global Fitness Surrogate Models in Evolutionary Computation

Leonardo Ramos Emmendorfer$^{(\boxtimes)}$ (ID)

Centro de Ciências Computacionais, Federal University of Rio Grande,
Rio Grande 96203-900, Brazil
`leonardoemmendorfer@furg.br`

Abstract. In evolutionary computation, the fitness of an individual corresponds to its evaluation as a candidate solution. Fitness surrogate models are intended to achieve a reduction in the number of real fitness computations in situations where these computations are expensive. This paper evaluates the effectiveness of three global fitness surrogates: a quadratic model, the inverse distance weighting (IDW) interpolation algorithm and a variant from the later (IDWR). The evaluation is performed using four benchmark functions form the optimization literature. The IDWR algorithm was able to achieve a significantly lower number of real fitness evaluations until convergence when compared to the alternative models for most of the functions considered.

Keywords: Fitness surrogate · Inverse distance weighting · Optimization

1 Introduction

In black-block optimization, the objective function cannot be described explicitly in closed form but it is known from evaluations in a finite number of points from the input domain. Surrogate models provide computationally efficient and accurate approximations for the overall behavior of a system at a smaller set of sample points. Those are widely adopted for the estimation of fitness surfaces in evolutionary computation [9], in order to reduce the number of actual, real fitness computations by replacing most of the real computations by fitness estimates. This approach is useful in applications where obtaining a single fitness value requires substantial computation time, which can take several days in some cases [6].

There is very little guidance in the literature about the choice of the model for approximation of computationally expensive functions. A model is either selected randomly or due to its popularity in the area with which the problem is associated [2]. The purpose of this paper is to provide an evaluation of three simple global models for fitness surrogate in evolutionary computation.

© Springer Nature Switzerland AG 2020
L. Rutkowski et al. (Eds.): ICAISC 2020, LNAI 12415, pp. 387–396, 2020.
https://doi.org/10.1007/978-3-030-61401-0_36

This work is organized as follows. Section 2 reviews the application of surrogate models for fitness estimation in evolutionary computation. Section 3 presents the methodology adopted for the evaluation performed. In Sect. 4 the results form the experiments are shown and discussed. Section 5 concludes the paper.

2   Fitness Surrogate Models in Evolutionary Computation

In evolutionary computation the fitness value of an individual can be computed using an explicit fitness function, a computational simulation, or an experiment. In practice, however, fitness evaluations may be computationally expensive or the experiments for fitness estimation are prohibitively costly [9]. Surrogates are used together with the real fitness function, as long as such a fitness function is able to prevent the evolutionary algorithm from being misled by a false optimum introduced by the surrogates [11].

Surrogates can be applied to almost all operations of evolutionary algorithms, such as population initialization, cross-over, mutation, local search and fitness evaluations [9]. Techniques for managing surrogates for fitness evaluations vary on how the circumstances and mechanisms which determine when the real fitness function will be actually applied or replaced by the surrogate. The surrogates can replace the real fitness function for entire generations, or just for some individuals in a generation [8]. Population-based approaches co-evolve different populations, each using its own surrogate for fitness evaluations [9]. Another taxonomy for fitness surrogate models is based on the scope of the model. Local models are built from local neighborhoods of a point in search space and are expected to be valid on that neighborhood while global models are expected to perform useful estimation over the whole search space.

The diverse methods for the adoption of fitness surrogates also differ on how individuals which had their fitness computed by an approximate model are selected for a real fitness computation. The most straightforward idea is to evaluate those individuals that potentially have a good surrogate fitness value [11], but other approaches also exist. For instance, individuals having a large degree of uncertainty in approximation can be good candidates for reevaluation, since this uncertainty might result from a smaller degree of exploration of the fitness landscape around these solutions and therefore may provide a good chance of finding better solutions [9].

Several other aspects can be considered in the adoption of fitness surrogates in evolutionary computation. The frequency of using the surrogates, for instance, can be increased or decreased depending on the model quality estimation [10]. For a broader review on the adoptions of surrogates in evolutionary computation, the reader is referred to [2,8–10].

3   Evaluation Methodology

In order to allow a comparison of alternative fitness surrogate models in evolutionary computation, one must specify the type of evolutionary algorithm to be used. In this evaluation, a simple evolutionary approach is adopted, as illustrated by Algorithm 1.

Input:
N: size of the main population
K: number of linear combinations generated for each pair of individuals in the population at each generation
$fitness(\mathbf{x})$: real fitness function of an individual $\mathbf{x}$
Output: The best individual $\mathbf{x}^*$
$P \leftarrow$ initial randomly generated main population $\{\mathbf{p_1}, \mathbf{p_2} \ldots \mathbf{p_N}\}$;
$F \leftarrow$ real $f_i = fitness(\mathbf{p_i})$ computed for each individual $\mathbf{p_i} \in P$
$(F = \{f_1, f_2 \ldots f_N\})$;
repeat
$\quad$ $r \leftarrow$ a randomly generated novel individual;
$\quad$ $Q \leftarrow$ linear combinations of individuals from $P \cup \{\mathbf{r}\}$;
$\quad$ $G \leftarrow$ estimate the fitness g_i of all individuals $\mathbf{q_i} \in Q$ as $g_i \leftarrow \mathcal{M}(q_i)$ where
$\quad$ $\mathcal{M}$ is the fitness estimation model adopted;
$\quad$ **repeat**
$\quad\quad$ Replace the individual in P which has the worse value in the
$\quad\quad$ corresponding position in F by the individual $q_{best} \in Q$ which has the
$\quad\quad$ best value in G, conditioned to the real evaluation of $fitness(\mathbf{q_{best}})$ be
$\quad\quad$ actually higher than $\min(F)$;
$\quad\quad$ Remove $\mathbf{q_{best}}$ and its estimated fitness from the respective sets Q, G
$\quad$ **until** $max(G) < min(F)$ *or the total of replaced individuals reaches* N;
until *no individuals are replaced in the population* P *in the last iteration*;
Return $\mathbf{x}^* \in P$: the individual with better fitness in the main population;

Algorithm 1. Fitness Surrogate Evolutionary Algorithm (FSEA)

Two populations are maintained during the evolutionary process: a main population P with N individuals, which are characterized by the real fitness computation for each individual and a greater, secondary population for which the fitness is only approximated by a model $\mathcal{M}$.

The parameters of the algorithm are the size of the main population (N), the number of linear combinations generated for each pair of individuals when creating a secondary population (K) and the function $fitness(\mathbf{x})$ which computes the fitness of an individual $\mathbf{x}$. From a randomly generated initial population P the algorithm obtains the real fitness of all the individuals. At each generation, the worst individuals in the main population P are replaced by the best individuals in the secondary population Q. A similar approach for selection and population update was already adopted in [5].

The secondary population Q is composed by linear combinations of all pairs of individuals from $P \cup \{\mathbf{r}\}$ where $\mathbf{r}$ is a randomly generated novel individual. The inclusion of the random individual r prevents the premature convergence of the algorithm. In our experiments the number of linear combinations for each pair $(\mathbf{p_a}, \mathbf{p_b})$, $\mathbf{p_a} \in P$, $\mathbf{p_b} \in P$ is set to $K = 4$ and the linear combinations which generate individuals $\mathbf{q_i} \in Q$ are restricted to the ad-hoc rule:

$$\{\mathbf{q}_{++}, \mathbf{q}_{--}, \mathbf{q}_{-+}, \mathbf{q}_{+-}\} = \frac{\pm \mathbf{p_a} \pm \mathbf{p_b}}{2} \tag{1}$$

The linear combinations generated form this rule include the mean $\frac{\mathbf{p_a} + \mathbf{p_b}}{2}$ and three others which represent a simple exploration of the search space. The fitness of all $\frac{KN(N+1)}{2}$ pairs from $P \cup \{\mathbf{r}\}$ are computed and the individuals with the best estimated fitness are candidates to replace the worst individuals in P. In order to actually be inserted in P, the real fitness of the best $\mathbf{q_i} \in Q$ must be computed and checked whether it is actually better than the worst individual in P. The procedure is repeated while the condition $\max(G) > \min(F)$ holds and the main population was not entirely replaced. The main loop finishes when no individuals were replaced in the population P during the previous iteration.

The FSEA algorithm, like other evolutionary approaches that rely on fitness surrogates, requires the specification of a fitness estimation model. In this work, three simple global models are compared. Since the evaluation is restricted to bidimensional functions, each individual is represented by a pair of coordinates. The quadratic model for the estimation of the fitness $\hat{f}_j$ of an individual at coordinates (x_1^j, x_2^j) is:

$$\hat{f}_j^{quadratic} = \alpha + \beta_{1,1} x_1^j + \beta_{2,1} x_2^j + \beta_{1,2} (x_1^j)^2 + \beta_{2,2} (x_2^j)^2 \tag{2}$$

where the coefficients α, $\beta_{1,1}$, $\beta_{2,1}$, $\beta_{1,2}$ and $\beta_{2,2}$ are obtained by least squares from the set individuals in the main population and their corresponding real fitness.

The other two models adopted here are both point interpolators. Point interpolation deals with data collectable at a point [13]. Inverse distance weighting (IDW) [17] is one of the most simple and widespread adopted [14]. The method does not require specific statistical assumptions, as the case for Kriging and other statistical interpolation methods.

The IDW interpolation for an individual at a set of coordinates (x_1^j, x_2^j) is computed as:

$$\hat{f}_j^{IDW} = \sum_{i=1}^{N} w_{i,j} f_i \tag{3}$$

where each f_i, $i = 1, \cdots, N$ is the real fitness of an individual at (x_1^i, x_2^i) in the main population. The weights $w_{i,j}$ for each pair (i, j) are given as:

$$w_{i,j} = \frac{d_{i,j}^{-\gamma}}{\sum_{k=1}^{N} d_{k,j}^{-\gamma}} \tag{4}$$

where $d_{i,j}$ is the Euclidean distance between the coordinates of the individual i in the main population and the coordinates of the individual j in the secondary population. γ means the power, which is a control parameter. In this work, IDW is restricted $\gamma = 2$, which is a default value widely adopted.

The maximum and minimum of the estimated values from IDW are limited to the extreme data points: $\min y_i \leq \hat{y}^{IDW} \leq \max y_i$. This is considered to be an important shortcoming because, to be useful, an interpolated surface should predict accurately certain important features of the original surface, such as the locations and magnitudes of maxima and minima even when they are not included as original sample points [13]. Therefore, we also included a novel variation from IDW which is reported to overcome those shortcomings. The Inverse Distance Weighted Regression (IDWR) [4] is derived from a simple weighted linear regression. The resulting expression for the estimation at a given location j is equivalent to IDW with an additional term:

$$\hat{f}^{IDWR} = \hat{f}_j^{IDW} + N \frac{\sum_{i=1}^{N} f_i - N\hat{f}_j^{IDW}}{N^2 - \sum_{i=1}^{N} d_{i,j}^{-2} \sum_{i=1}^{N} d_{i,j}^{2}} \tag{5}$$

where $d_{i,j}$ has the same definition as in (4).

IDWR algorithm is not limited to the extreme data points $\min y_i$ and $\max y_i$ and it was shown to be able to perform useful extrapolation from data [4] which is relevant for fitness estimation.

3.1 Benchmark Functions

Table 1 summarizes the definitions of the functions adopted. Figure 1 provides a perspective visualization of the topology of those functions.

Ackley [1] is a highly multimodal function widely to test the performance of evolutionary algorithms. Its global optimum is $y(0,0) = 0$. Himmelblau [7] is a non-linear, non-convex functions also adopted for testing optimization algorithms in general. Here in this work, the FSEA searches for the minimal value of Himmelblau. There are four local minima at $(3.0, 2.0)$, $(-2.805118, 3.131312)$, $(-3.779310, -3.283186)$ and $(3.584428, -1.848126)$, all corresponding to $y = 0$. Log Goldstein-Price is an adjusted version of the Goldstein-Price function [3] proposed by [16]. Both the original and the adjusted forms are useful for the evaluation of optimization algorithms since they have several local minima. The global minimum of the Log Goldstein-Price is $y(0, -1) = -3.1291$. The Sombrero function was also included in our evaluation since it was adopted as a benchmark for interpolation algorithms [18]. The global optimum is $y(0.5, 0.5) = 1$, which is a maximum.

4 Results

The success rate of FSEA, shown in Fig. 2, is computed as the number of runs where the correct optimum is found divided by the total number of runs (100). Quadratic interpolation achieved the best results for the Ackley function, as shown in Fig. 2(a). While IDW and IDWR obtained success rates below 0.1 for all population sizes, the quadratic interpolation led to success rates around 0.4 consistently. However, as population size grows, the differences between the quadratic model and the other two algorithms reduce, which might indicate that population sizes for both IDW and IDWR should be higher in this case. The type

Table 1. Functions of two real variables $(x_1, x_2) = \mathbf{x}$, adopted in empirical evaluation

Function	Expression	Interval for x_1 and x_2
Ackley	$y(\mathbf{x}) = -20e^{-0.2\sqrt{0.5(x^2+y^2)}} - e^{0.5(cos(2\pi x_1)+cos(2\pi x_2))} + e + 20$	$[-5, 5]$
Sombrero	$y(\mathbf{x}) = \begin{cases} \frac{\sin((16(x_1-0.5))^2+(16(x_2-0.5))^2)}{16(x_1-0.5))^2+(16(x_2-0.5))^2)} & \text{if } x_1 \neq 0.5 \text{ and } x_2 \neq 0.5; \\ 1 & \text{otherwise} \end{cases}$	$[0, 1]$
Himmelblau	$y(\mathbf{x}) = (x_1^2 + x_2 - 11)^2 + (x_1 + x_2^2 - 7)^2$	$[-5, 5]$
Log Goldstein-Price	$y(\mathbf{x}) = \frac{1}{2.427}(\log((1 + (x_1 + x_2 + 1)^2$ $\times(19 - 14x_1 + 3x_1^2 - 14x_2 + 6x_1x_2 + 3x_2^2))$ $\times(30 + (2x_1 - 3x_2)^2$ $\times(18 - 32x_1 + 12x_1^2 + 48x_2 - 36x_1x_2 + 27\bar{x}_2^2)))$ $-8.693)$	$[-2, 2]$

of model adopted by the latter two algorithms is more sensitive to the roughness represented by the Ackley function, since both interpolators are exact, in the sense that the interpolated surface must pass through the exact values of the sampled points. The quadratic interpolation achieved better robustness under the circumstance represented by the Ackley function.

The quadratic model also benefits from the topology of the Sombrero function. The quadratic model achieved the best success rate for all population sizes when compared to the other two models. The success rate with the quadratic model remains above 0.9, while IDW and IDWR achieved values around 0.7 and 0.8 respectively, for all population sizes. IDWR was also consistently better than IDW under this evaluation.

The IDW interpolation algorithm performs better for the Himmelblau function since it reaches the best success rates for all population sizes considered. The success rate of IDW remains around 0.4 while the other two models reached values below 0.12 independently from population size adopted. The function Log Goldstein-Price led to a similarly low performance for all models adopted. Success rates around 0.2 were obtained for all population sizes considered. IDWR was superior to IDW under this evaluation for all population sizes.

Table 2 shows the average and standard deviation of the number of real fitness evaluations until convergence computed from 100 runs of FSEA with different initial populations at each run. This evaluation is relevant since the aim of fitness surrogate models is to reduce the number of real fitness evaluations.

We performed Friedman rank-sum tests for the evaluation of the results from each population size and each function in order to check if the average number of fitness evaluations from the three models are actually different at $\alpha = 0.05$ significance level. If the test indicates a significant difference between the models, we performed pairwise Wilcoxon signed-rank tests between the models to verify if one of the models is superior to the other two at $\alpha = 0.05$ significance level. In that case, the value corresponding average and standard deviation of the number of fitness evaluations are shown in bold in Table 2.

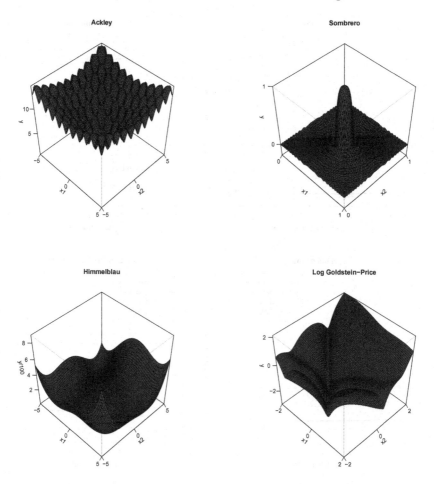

Fig. 1. Perspective visualization of the 4 functions adopted in the evaluation.

For the Ackley function, there is no superior model in terms of the number of fitness evaluations for all population sizes tested, except for $N = 20$ where IDWR is superior to the other two models. The models are also equivalent when the Sombrero function is considered.

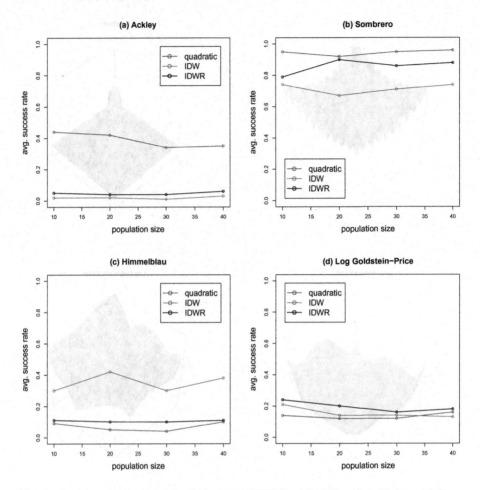

Fig. 2. Average success rate for 100 runs of FSEA with different initial populations at each run and varying population sizes. Four benchmark functions are optimized by FSEA: (a) Ackley (b) Sombrero (c) Himmelblau (d) Log Goldstein-Price. Three global models $\mathcal{M}$ are adopted for fitness estimation: quadratic, IDW and IDWR.

For the Himmelblau function, the IDWR interpolation algorithm is significantly superior to the alternative models for all population sizes considered. The same holds true for the Log Goldstein-Price function for all population sizes when $N = 20$ where the Friedman test actually indicates a statistically significant difference between the models (p-value $= 0.005$) and pairwise Wilcoxon signed-rank tests revealed that IDWR is, in fact, superior to IDW (p-value $= 0.042$) but failed to reveal any significant difference between IDWR and the quadratic model (p-value $= 0.775$).

Table 2. Average ± standard deviation of the number of real fitness evaluations until convergence computed from 100 runs of FSEA with varying initial populations. Three fitness estimation models are adopted and results are compared for four benchmark functions from the literature with varying population sizes.

Function	Model	Population Size			
		10	20	30	40
Ackley	quadratic	115.4 ± 65.9	127.5 ± 68.3	133.3 ± 81.0	126.9 ± 71.5
	IDW	154.1 ± 83.2	147.1 ± 65.3	158.0 ± 82.1	154.4 ± 77.8
	IDWR	113.1 ± 62.7	**112.4 ± 58.9**	119.8 ± 71.7	117.7 ± 74.8
Sombrero	quadratic	74.7 ± 33.6	75.4 ± 37.2	75.4 ± 32.8	74.7 ± 40.4
	IDW	86.8 ± 50.6	83.0 ± 47.7	82.3 ± 50.5	85.1 ± 57.6
	IDWR	80.8 ± 46.2	74.3 ± 49.8	80.6 ± 53.4	72.7 ± 35.3
Himmelblau	quadratic	150.0 ± 90.6	143.1 ± 78.2	152.0 ± 90.6	153.9 ± 90.6
	IDW	175.2 ± 84.9	162.7 ± 84.9	181.3 ± 84.9	182.4 ± 84.9
	IDWR	**122.2 ± 66.5**	**122.9± 66.5**	**120.9 ± 66.5**	**109.3 ± 66.5**
Log Goldstein-Price	quadratic	164.6 ± 91.9	154.3 ± 91.9	161.9 ± 91.9	160.0 ± 91.9
	IDW	134.0 ± 68.4	141.3 ± 68.4	134.2 ± 68.4	144.4 ± 68.4
	IDWR	**119.4 ± 74.8**	130.1 ± 74.8	**119.6 ± 74.8**	**116.6 ± 74.8**

5   Conclusions and Further Work

This paper evaluated three global models for the estimation of fitness in evolutionary computation. When the IDWR algorithm is adopted as the fitness estimation model $\mathcal{M}$ the evolutionary algorithm was able to achieve a significantly lower number of real fitness evaluations until convergence when compared to the adoption of both original IDW and a quadratic model for most of the functions considered. For two of the functions, the result is relatively independent from the population sizes, while for one of the functions the result is valid for a specific population size. IDWR achieved consistently better success rates when compared to IDW for all functions, except for the Himmelblau. This behavior, however, should be better explained in further works.

The success rates of the quadratic model are clearly superior for the Ackley function. This might be due to the fact that when higher frequencies are discarded, the Ackley function becomes easier to solve. The quadratic model is able to overcome the higher frequencies efficiently.

Many alternatives exist in the literature for the exploration of fitness surrogates. In this work, however, a simple evolutionary algorithm with a very low number of parameters called FSEA is proposed and adopted. This allowed a simplified parameter setting process, which revealed adequate for the purpose of this evaluation. However, further work should better explore the evolutionary approaches available in the literature. Further work should also adopt other models that are already useful as fitness surrogates in the literature such as Kriging [12, 15], splines and radial basis functions. Other benchmark optimization functions should also be included.

References

1. Ackley, D.: A connectionist machine for genetic hillclimbing. Ph.D. thesis (1987)
2. Chugh, T., Sindhya, K., Hakanen, J., Miettinen, K.: A survey on handling computationally expensive multiobjective optimization problems with evolutionary algorithms. Soft. Comput. **23**(9), 3137–3166 (2019)
3. Dixon, L.C.W., Szegö, G.P.: Towards global optimization, vol. 2, chap. In: The Global Optimization Problem: An Introduction. North-Holland, Amsterdan (1978)
4. Emmendorfer, L.R., Dimuro, G.: A novel formulation for inverse distance weighting from weighted linear regression (2020, submitted)
5. Emmendorfer, L.R., Pozo, A.T.R.: Effective linkage learning using low-order statistics and clustering. IEEE Trans. Evol. Comput. **13**(6), 1233–1246 (2009)
6. Gorissen, D., Couckuyt, I., Demeester, P., Dhaene, T., Crombecq, K.: A surrogate modeling and adaptive sampling toolbox for computer based design. J. Mach. Learn. Res. **11**, 2051–2055 (2010)
7. Himmelblau, D.: Applied Nonlinear Programming. McGraw-Hill (1972)
8. Jin, Y.: A comprehensive survey of fitness approximation in evolutionary computation. Soft. Comput. **9**(1), 3–12 (2005)
9. Jin, Y.: Surrogate-assisted evolutionary computation: recent advances and future challenges. Swarm Evol. Comput. **1**(2), 61–70 (2011)
10. Jin, Y., Hüsken, M., Sendhoff, B.: Quality measures for approximate models in evolutionary computation. In: GECCO Workshop on Adaptation, Learning and Approximation in Evolutionary Computation, pp. 170–173 (2003)
11. Jin, Y., Olhofer, M., Sendhoff, B.: On evolutionary optimization with approximate fitness functions. In: Proceedings of the 2nd Annual Conference on Genetic and Evolutionary Computation, pp. 786–793. Morgan Kaufmann Publishers Inc. (2000)
12. Krige, D.: A review of the development of geostatistics in south Africa. In: Guarascio, M., David, M., Huijbregts, C. (eds.) Advanced Geostatistics in the Mining Industry, pp. 279–293. Springer, Dordrecht (1976). https://doi.org/10.1007/978-94-010-1470-0_17
13. Lam, N.S.N.: Spatial interpolation methods: a review. Am. Cartographer **10**(2), 129–150 (1983)
14. Li, J., Heap, A.D.: A review of comparative studies of spatial interpolation methods in environmental sciences: performance and impact factors. Ecol. Inf. **6**(3–4), 228–241 (2011)
15. Matheron, G.: The theory of regionalised variables and its applications. Les Cahiers du Centre de Morphologie Mathématique **5**, 212 (1971)
16. Picheny, V., Wagner, T., Ginsbourger, D.: A benchmark of kriging-based infill criteria for noisy optimization. Struct. Multidiscip. Optim. **48**(3), 607–626 (2013)
17. Shepard, D.: A two-dimensional interpolation function for irregularly-spaced data. In: Proceedings of the 1968 ACM National Conference, pp. 517–524 (1968)
18. Zimmerman, D., Pavlik, C., Ruggles, A., Armstrong, M.P.: An experimental comparison of ordinary and universal kriging and inverse distance weighting. Math. Geol. **31**(4), 375–390 (1999)

Automatic Story Generation Based on Graph Model Using Godot Engine

Iwona Grabska-Gradzińska[1] ⓘ, Leszek Nowak[2](✉) ⓘ, and Ewa Grabska[3] ⓘ

[1] Department of Games Technology, Faculty of Physics, Astronomy and Applied Computer Science, Jagiellonian University, Krakow, Poland
iwona.grabska@uj.edu.pl
[2] Department of Information Technologies, Faculty of Physics, Astronomy and Applied Computer Science, Jagiellonian University, Krakow, Poland
leszek.nowak@uj.edu.pl
[3] Department of Design and Computer Graphics, Faculty of Physics, Astronomy and Applied Computer Science, Jagiellonian University, Krakow, Poland
ewa.grabska@uj.edu.pl

Abstract. This paper deals with storytelling aspects of computer games. A new approach to automatic story generation based on graph modelling is proposed. Godot Engine for visualization of output stories is used. In our research the plot is represented by a specific graph called the layered graph composed of story building blocks, namely layer of locations, layer of characters, layer of items, layer of narration and plot dependencies. An appropriate set of graph rules (productions) stored in JSON format is a generative tool for the building blocks. Graph rules are internal representation of actions which can be taken by the hero of the story. A sequence of the rules from start to end can describe the whole gameplay of one player or can be generated in automatic way as a possible gameplay. All such sequences of the rules create the space of all potential gameplays. Every rule corresponds to a certain animation made in Godot Engine. It allows to visualize every possible story, represented by sequence of rules, by seamless animation. Given a rule, animation is based on graphic assets corresponding to the rule nodes of the layered graph.

Keywords: Games design · Graph transformations · Procedural storytelling

1 Motivation

In game research graph-based model is often used to represent game structure, as it provides advantages in comparing and describing plots, plot elements and players behavior [1–4]. Having such graph-based model we can define plot design process and gameplay process as a sequence of the elementary plot elements (actions represented by graph rules), that can be recorded using one consistent formal structure. Such formal structure gives us possibility to use methods of Computer Aided Design (CAD) [5–7].

In our research it was necessary to define the way that the graph model is represented. The representation needed to allow:

© Springer Nature Switzerland AG 2020
L. Rutkowski et al. (Eds.): ICAISC 2020, LNAI 12415, pp. 397–405, 2020.
https://doi.org/10.1007/978-3-030-61401-0_37

- storywriters to easily create rules and plot twists;
- graph automatic processing;
- visualizing of graph rules in the form of animated gameplay.

The main goal of this paper is to propose the implementation of graph-based data structures composed of layered graphs and control diagrams. Use of such a structure in computer games is presented in [8]. Later the animated gameplay is generated based on the control diagram path going from start to end of the story.

Such an implementation creates a system, which allows to test the consistency of the game world and narrative elements and gives the option to automatically generate animations for every possible story path of final user. The game designers using the system have the options to evaluate the game and analyze the narration sequences, their length and utilized objects in the context of the story.

2 Methods

The implementation of the system requires practical usage of layered graphs as representation of game state, graph traversing methods for finding possible storytelling routes, and finally visualization of said story route in form of automatically generated animation using Godot Engine.

2.1 Layered Graphs

Layered graphs [9] in games research is a proven concept used in serious games, e.g. behavior analysis [10], or for solving typical game problems like finding shortest path [11].

Gameplay State Graph. In presented application graph is built of different types of vertices called "layers" and is representing current game state. This formal construction is especially useful in the process of embedding transformations of the applied productions [12]. The graph is defined also as hierarchical structure, which means that every node of the graph can be treated as a subgraph with nested nodes.

Defined vertex types correspond with different functions of elements in the game world. We categorize the vertices as follows (see Fig. 1a):

- layer of locations;
- layer of characters;
- layer of items;
- layer of plot dependencies.

Another peculiar feature of a gameplay layered graph is a subgraph that is essential for actions of players, called "sheaf subgraph" (see Fig. 1b). This formal structure allows to use different ways of creating the plot chains (formally represented by graph rule sequences).

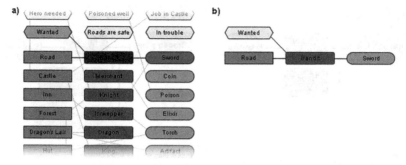

Fig. 1. a) Layered graph consist of vertices of four layers: Locations – green, Characters – yellow, Items – blue and Narration – gray. Selected in darker colors is a sheaf subgraph. b) Sheaf subgraph made of selected vertices. (Color figure online)

Formal definitions of the structure, based on [8], is presented below.

Let L be a set of labels and A be a set of attributes.

Definition 1. An attributed and labeled hierarchical graph over L and A is a system:

$$G = (V, E, source, target, child, label, attribute), \qquad (1)$$

where:

- V and E are finite disjoint sets of nodes and edges, respectively,
- $source : E \rightarrow V$ and $target : E \rightarrow V$ are edge source and edge target functions,
- $child : V \cup E \rightarrow 2^{V \cup E}$ is a child nesting function,
- $label : V \cup E \rightarrow L$ is a labelling function,
- $attribute : V \cup E \rightarrow 2^{A}$ is an attributing function.

Definition 2. Gameplay graph is a graph consisting of four layers, thus:

$$GameplayGraph = \{PLOT, CHARACTERS, LOCATIONS, ITEMS\}. \qquad (2)$$

where:

- *PLOT* is a layer consisting of narration information,
- *CHARACTERS* is a layer consisting of characters of the story,
- *LOCATIONS* is a layer consisting of all places used in the story,
- *ITEMS* is a layer consisting of all items belonging to the characters or placed in any location.

Graph Productions. Current Gameplay State Graph is continuously modified (process of graph rewriting) using the set of productions, extended to handle nodes with any label belonging to a specific layer. A production is a pair of layered subgraphs (left and right side of the production) with defined embedding transformation.

All productions that have identical left sides are grouped into a group called "actions". To these productions are assigned different probability of occurrence, that's why they

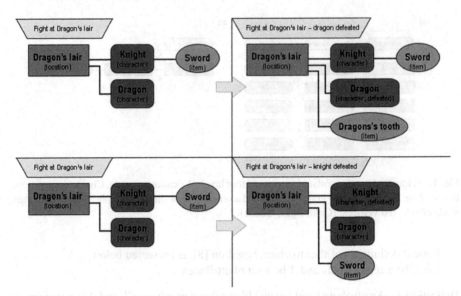

Fig. 2. Graphs of two productions that share the same initial condition (left side) but produce different outcomes (right side). The pair indicate that the story point "Dragon fight" can conclude in different outcomes depending on random factor.

represent uncertainty of the results of actions taken by character in the story. Example of this is presented in Fig. 2.

Control Diagram. Control diagram is a directed graph that contains nodes representing productions identifier. There are many ways to create this type of diagram. In this paper the main goal is not the representation the real gameplay of a specific user, but the automatic generation of as many stories as possible. A control diagram is created to recognize two productions as successive with the accuracy of sheaf subgraph existing both in the right-hand side of the previous production and in the left-hand side of the next production, without checking of Game State Graph.

2.2 From Graph to Story

A sequence of the productions from start to end can describe one of possible story arcs.

The list of production is representing a decision pool from which the player chose. Each location in the game world can have multiple matching productions. We consider a production as matching when every element of the left side has its representation in the game world. The productions are used one after the another. Therefore, the gameplay can be represented as a sequence of graph productions (see Fig. 3).

There can be multiple production with identical left side, those production are representing different actions that can be taken in given instance E.g. combat action can result in defeat, yielding or retreating of any participating characters. Thus, not every sequence of productions will represent a gameplay where all productions are used. In

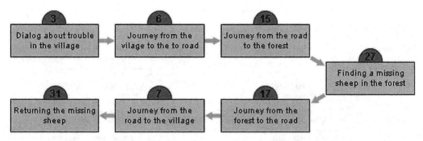

Fig. 3. Example sequence of productions, representing a short story of a character who helps to find missing sheep.

some cases the consequences of certain series of productions may result in the death of the main hero. In such a case the game ends in player failure.

In most of the games there is more than one way to complete the story. Therefore, more than one sequence of productions can represent a valid gameplay.

For this paper we decided to construct sequences of productions automatically. Starting with initial state of the world, subset of productions describe decision a player has chosen. For each given moment a set of productions is available, depending on complexity of the story. Form the available set of production one can be selected according to player characteristics. That way we can decide that we want to explore the world as a player prone to aggression, or kindness. It is worth mentioning that simple production meant only for travel can be ignored, as those can easily create infinite loops and obscure decision making process. If those production are ignored we must assume that player is present to any location he have access to. The construction of the gameplay sequence ends when it is impossible to find any more matching productions, or the one that are available are used repeatedly.

The process allows us to generate the set of the possible story paths (excluding detected loops). As a result, we can find:

- the average number of players actions needed to reach the conclusion of the story,
- situations where player cannot reach the conclusion of the story (story loops, story dead ends
- missing productions,
- characters crucial to the story arc,
- unused characters and items.

2.3 Godot as Tool for Graph Visualization

In this research we have decided to use Godot Engine [13], a free and open-source game engine. It comes with tools that allow for easy graph building, storing said graphs as JSON format and what is the most important, making seamless animations based on selected path found within the graph. Figure 4 illustrate how a graph can be represented in Godot Engine application.

Graph represents a situation within a story, where each vertex corresponds to a graphic asset that is later used to generate animation.

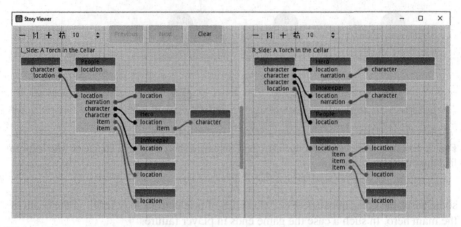

Fig. 4. Graph visualization using Godot Engine, where each block represents a vertex of a graph. Vertices relate to bidirectional color-coded edges: yellow edge represent relation between locations, black represent presence of a character in the location, magenta represents items and blue represents narration information. (Color figure online)

3 Graph Representation

In Godot Engine each object is represented by a node in hierarchical order. Such hierarchy can be saved as text scene file. This functionality allows for easy saving and loading of production. Although the scene file format is readable for human, we have decided that making productions outside of Godot Engine is more desirable, as we want to separate building story elements from the tool used for graph processing and visualization. Reason for this is that Godot engine is complex tool and a story writer might find it difficult to use it.

3.1 Graph Textual Representation

For text representation of a graphs, we decided to use JSON format as it is readable and easy to use.

Following is example of single production:

```
{
"Title": "Dragon fight - dragon defeat",
"L_Side":{
    "Vertex":{
        "Locations":{ "Dragon's lair":"" },
        "Characters":{ "Knight":"aggressive", "Dragon":"" },
        "Narration":"",
        "Items":{ "Sword":"" }
    },
    "Edges":{
        "Knight":"Dragon's lair", "Dragon":"Dragon's lair", "Sword":"Knight"
    }
},
"R_Side":{
    "Vertex":{
        "Locations":{ "Dragon's lair":"" },
        "Characters":{ "Knight":"", "Dragon":"defeated" },
        "Narration":{ "Dragon is defeated":"" },
        "Items":{ "Sword":"", "Dragon tooth":"" }
    },
    "Edges":{
        "Knight":"Dragon's lair", "Dragon":"Dragon's lair",
        "Dragon tooth":"Dragon's lair",  "Sword":"Knight",
        "Dragon is defeated":"Dragon"
    }
}
}
```

In the example above a production is presented where a simple situation takes place. Situation is located in Dragon's lair where a dragon resides. A knight arrives to the location and fight takes place, resulting in dragon's defeat. The production here is divided into left side and right side, by looking at the change in the graph we see that the dragon gains attribute "defeated" and loses a tooth, dragon's lair gains a tooth and narration is added.

3.2 From Graph to Animation

At first, we start with a set of possible productions, and a path to go through these productions to reach certain conclusion. We call it a list of productions. Each of the productions is a separate JSON file that looks like the example shown earlier. Next, we parse the file and load those productions into Godot Engine as dictionary data structure [14]. Here we can visualize each production as a graph shown on Fig. 4. Such representation is not visually helpful, but it allows for graph editing if needed. In Godot Engine we have art asset corresponding to every vertex from the production. e.g. (Fig. 5):

```
"Items": { "Sword":"Enchanted", "Shield":"" }
```

Every item (sword, coin, etc.) must have a corresponding graphical representation. Same goes for location, character, etc. The graph itself does not represent specific relations between objects, e.g. we do not know where exactly in the cellar is the bottle, but the information that the bottle is in the cellar exist. That way the animation components can assume location of objects.

While processing the production from left to right side, if the character changes location, we can animate the character moving from location to location, same goes from changing the ownership of the objects, conflict, dialogs, and so on.

Fig. 5. Example graphic assets connected to the graph nodes: sword, shield.

There is one restriction though. It is necessary to predefine spatial relations between the locations, as the transitions from location to location is not known from the production. E.g. Hero travels from one town to another, or hero moves form one side of the road to another. This layout of the locations needs to be defined outside of the production.

4 Conclusion and Future Work

Research so far has shown promise as the tool allows for fast visualization of stories, testing plot points, and can serve for emergent story telling. It is possible to look through several plot paths or if needed all of them. We find it interesting how story writing might be divided between multiple writers, and the emergent stories can be surprising.

Future work will focus on animation aspect, and how to use Godot graph tool to swiftly create animation components that are context aware. E.g. it would be impractical for writers to include in production information about exact positions of specific objects yet loading a production in Godot and seeing it as animated sequence allows for easy enhancement of animated sequences, with additional positional, or timing details. Furthermore, it is necessary to research methods of detecting story loopholes, or possible infinite story loops that are typical annoyance in videogame story design.

References

1. Sanchez, D., Florez, H.: Improving game modeling for the quoridor game state using graph databases. In: Rocha, Á., Guarda, T. (eds.) ICITS 2018. AISC, vol. 721, pp. 333–342. Springer, Cham (2018). https://doi.org/10.1007/978-3-319-73450-7_32
2. Konert, J., Wendel, V., Göbel, S., Steinmetz, R.: Towards an analysis of cooperative learning-behaviour in social dilemma games. In: Proceedings of the European Conference on Games-based Learning, 2011 January, pp. 329–332 (2011)
3. Putzke, J., Fischbach, K., Schoder, D.: Power structure and the evolution of social networks in massively multiplayer online games. In: 18th European Conference on Information Systems, ECIS 2010, 13 p. (2010)
4. Sato, M., Anada, K., Tsutsumi, M.: Formulations of patterns by a graph model for the game of Go. J. Comput. Methods Sci. Eng. **17**(S1), S111–S121 (2017)
5. Ślusarczyk, G.: Graph-based representation of design properties in creating building floor-plans. Comput. Aided Des. **95**, 24–39 (2018)
6. Strug, B., Paszyńska, A., Paszyński, M., Grabska, E.: Using a graph grammar system in the finite element method. Int. J. Appl. Math. Comput. Sci. **23**(4), 839–853 (2013)

7. Chang, Y.-S., Chen, M.Y.-C., Chuang, M.-J., Chou, C.-H.: Improving creative self-efficacy and performance through computer-aided design application. Thinking Skills Creativity **31**, 103–111 (2019)
8. Grabska-Gradzińska, I., et al.: Graph-based data structures of computer games. In: Annual International Conference on Computer Games, Multimedia & Allied Technology, pp. 88–96 (2013)
9. Grabska-Gradzińska, I., et al.: Towards a graph-based model of computer games. In: Das, V.V., Ezendu, A. (eds.) Advances in Information Technologies and Communication 2012: Proceedings of Joint International Conferences on ICT, CIT, PECS and EMIE - 2012. Computer Science Series, ISSN 2213-2805; 3. Amsterdam, ACEEE, pp. 34–39 (2012)
10. Grabska-Gradzińska, I.: How to predict behavior at risk: educational game story analysis using layered graphs and eyetracking system. In: Ślusarczyk, G., Strug, B., de Wilde, P. (eds.) Proceedings of the 23rd International Workshop on Intelligent Computing in Engineering: EG-ICE 2016: 29 June–1 July Kraków, Poland. Kraków: EG-ICE 2016 Organizing Committee, pp. 75–84 (2016)
11. Papadimitriou, C.H., Yannakakis, M.: Shortest paths without a map. Theoret. Comput. Sci. **84**(1), 127–150 (1991)
12. Rozenberg G.: Handbook of Graph Grammars and Computing by Graph Transformation, vol. 1–3. World Scientific (1997–99)
13. Linietsky, J., Manzur, A., et al.: Godot Engine Homepage. https://godotengine.org/. Accessed 23 Dec 2019
14. Manzur, A., Marques, G.: Godot Engine Game Development in 24 Hours, Sams Teach Yourself: The Official Guide to Godot 3.0 (2018)

Cascade PID Controller Optimization
Using Bison Algorithm

Anezka Kazikova[1]([⊠])[ID], Krystian Łapa[2][ID], Michal Pluhacek[1][ID],
and Roman Senkerik[1][ID]

[1] Department of Informatics and Artificial Intelligence,
Tomas Bata University, Zlin, Czech Republic
kazikova@utb.cz

[2] Department of Computational Intelligence, Czestochowa University of Technology,
Czestochowa, Poland
krystian.lapa@pcz.pl

Abstract. Meta-heuristic algorithms are reliable tools for modern optimization. Yet their amount is so immense that it is hard to pick just one to solve a specific problem. Therefore many researchers hold on known, approved algorithms. But is it always beneficial? In this paper, we use the meta-heuristics for the design of cascade PID controllers and compare the performance of the newly developed Bison Algorithm with well-known algorithms like the Differential Evolution, the Genetics Algorithm, the Particle Swarm Optimization, and the Cuckoo Search. Also, in the proposed approach, the controller parameters were encoded to increase the chance of reducing the controller structure, and thus facilitate the automatic selection of its configuration. The simulations were performed for three different control problems and checked whether the use of cascade structures could bring significant benefits in comparison to the use of classic PID controllers.

Keywords: PID optimization · cascade PID controllers ·
Meta-heuristics

1   Introduction

The goal of a typical control system is to achieve the set state of a specific element of the controlled object. Such an element can be, e.g., the speed of a motor or the position of some mass. The difference between the current and the set state is called an offset. The control system should efficiently decrease the offset while also taking into account various other control criteria [1]. This is achieved by properly affecting the object by basing it on the control signal. The most commonly used in practice PID controllers [2] generate a control signal by amplifying the offset signal and its integral and derivative. To ensure efficient operation of the PID controller, three gain factors should be selected (proportional, integral, and differentiating). Therefore, the problem of optimizing three

© Springer Nature Switzerland AG 2020
L. Rutkowski et al. (Eds.): ICAISC 2020, LNAI 12415, pp. 406–416, 2020.
https://doi.org/10.1007/978-3-030-61401-0_38

parameters arises, which is unfortunately often dealt with by a trial and error method, or the parameters are selected based on expert knowledge.

Control systems are constantly evolving, and new solutions in this field are emerging. Starting from FOPID controllers [3], through cascade PID controllers [4], and ending with controllers based on artificial intelligence (e.g. fuzzy systems [5], neural networks [6]) or hybrid solutions [7]. Along with their complexity and the increased number of parameters that need to be optimized, their control capabilities also increase. The cascade or fuzzy-based controllers mentioned above can already be based on a larger number of signals (not only offset), but they also allow to eliminate control symmetry and other defects appearing in standard PID controllers [8]. However, a larger number of signals means that an expert often selects the controller structure a priori.

The development of control systems increased the computational complexity and the difficulty of optimizing their parameters. Population-based meta-heuristic algorithms (PBA) seem to be suitable methods for such optimization. Their idea is based on processing a population of individuals, each representing one solution of the addressed problem, similarly as it would be dealt with in the real world. The gain of meta-heuristics lies in an accessible and quick solution, improving in the process: beneficially for ever-changing, complex systems.

Meta-heuristics usually root in mimicking bio-inspired phenomena: how did nature manage the optimization. Simulations of various principles from genetics, the theory of evolution, or movement patterns of a variety of animal species, created a significant number of optimization methods like the Differential Evolution [9], the Genetic Algorithm [10], the Particle Swarm Optimization [11], the Grey Wolf Optimizer [12], or the Cuckoo Search [13]. And since the source of inspiration is unlimited, the number of bio-inspired algorithms rises as well [14].

The continuous development of population-based algorithms makes it difficult to select one to solve a specific problem. Moreover, according to the theory of No Free Lunch in optimization, there is no single optimal method to solve all problems [15]. As a result, in many new papers, the old, well-known, and proven population algorithms such as GA, DE, PSO, and CS are being used (or their modifications) [16,17]. However, the increase in complexity of the solved problems causes new population algorithms to find their place (see, e.g., [14,18]). New algorithms are using a variety of different mechanisms to overcome the optimization problems [19], such as population division into subgroups with different behaviour [20], dynamic adaptation of parameters [21,22], population restart [23], or boosting the exploration of the feasible solution area [24].

In this paper, the idea of a cascade PID controller with a dynamic structure is proposed. This approach frees the user from the need to design the exact controller structure. To cope with that, a Bison Algorithm (BA [24]) is used to optimize the controller parameters. The idea of this paper is also to check whether a new algorithm, such as BA, allows one to get better results compared to classic population-based algorithms. The results were verified on three control problems.

The structure of the paper is as follows: in Sect. 2 a proposed method is described, in Sect. 3 the simulations are described and summarized, and in Sect. 4 the conclusions are drawn.

2   Methods

This section describes the proposed controller structures, the method for their evaluation, and finally, the Bison Algorithm, which was used to optimize them.

2.1   Proposed Controller Structures

The output for typical parallel form of PID controller is calculated as follows:

$$u(t) = K_p \cdot e(t) + K_i \cdot \int_0^t e(t)\, dt + K_d \cdot \frac{de(t)}{dt}, \tag{1}$$

where $u(t)$ is control signal, $e(t)$ is offset and K_p, K_i, K_d are proportional, integral and derivative gains. If the gain value is equal to zero, corresponding element of controller can be treated as reduced, which as a result allows to obtain the P, I, D, PI, PD or ID controllers. In the case of population-based algorithms, parameter values usually take random real values during initialization, so the chance that a given controller element will be initialized as a reduced one is virtually none. That is why, in this paper we propose an approach that will increase the chance of creating a population of controller solutions in which some elements are reduced at the very beginning:

$$u(t) = r(K_p) \cdot e(t) + r(K_i) \cdot \int_0^t e(t)\, dt + r(K_d) \cdot \frac{de(t)}{dt}, \tag{2}$$

where $r(K)$ is defined as follows:

$$r(K) = \begin{cases} 0 & \text{for} \quad K < K^- + \alpha \cdot (K^+ - K^-) \\ \frac{(K - K^- - \alpha \cdot (K^+ - K^-))}{(K^+ - K^-)} & \text{for} \quad \text{else} \end{cases}, \tag{3}$$

where K^- and K^+ is minimum and maximum value that K can take, α stands for coefficient setting below which value K is treated as zero. It is worth noting that the Eq. (3) scales the parameter K accordingly so that the final value of it will be within the appropriate range.

Cascade PID controllers use multiple PID blocks connected in cascades. The structure of such controllers depends on the given simulation problem and the number of signals that can be used. In connection with the above, further examples of problems and structures proposed for them will be described further below. The proposed structures use PID blocks by the formula (2). This approach to dynamic structure selection of cascade PID controllers is new and does not require the use of additional binary parameters or hybrid algorithms, such as in paper [1].

Water Tank Test (WTT). In this problem the purpose of the controller is to maintain the desired water level h^* in the tank by changing the water inflow. The tank has: a surface area A, a controllable water inflow q_{in}, an external water inflow q_{ex}, an additional emergency water outflow q_{em} (e.g. when more water is needed in emergency situations) and s a water outflow q_{out}. The water level in the tank is determined as follows (see e.g. [25]):

$$\dot{h} = \frac{1}{A} \left(q_{in} + q_{ex} - q_{em} - s \cdot \sqrt{2gh} \right), \tag{4}$$

where $g = 9.81 \, \text{m/s}^2$ is the gravitational acceleration. The proposed controller structure for this problem is shown in Fig. 1.a).

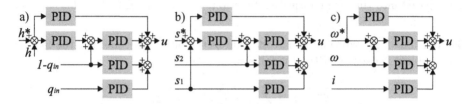

Fig. 1. Proposed cascade PID structures for control problems under consideration: a) WTT, b) MSD, c) DCM.

Mass Spring Damper (MSD). In this problem, the purpose of the controller is to maintain the desired position s^* of mass m_1 by managing the control force F. The mass is connected via spring to the mass m_2 and then by another spring to constant point y. The positions of masses are marked analogously as s_1 and s_2 and the stiffness constant k for both masses were assumed to be the same. The equations of such model are described as follows (see, e.g., [26]):

$$\begin{cases} s_1 = v_1 \cdot t + \frac{1}{2} a_1 \cdot t^2 \; v_1 = a_1 \cdot t \; a_1 = \frac{1}{m_1} \left(k \cdot (s_2 - s_1) - v_1 \cdot y \right) \\ s_2 = v_2 \cdot t + \frac{1}{2} a_2 \cdot t^2 \; v_2 = a_2 \cdot t \; a_2 = \frac{1}{m_2} \left(k \cdot (F - s_2) - v_2 \cdot y \right) \end{cases} . \tag{5}$$

The proposed controller structure for this problem is shown on Fig. 1.b).

DC Motor (DCM). In this problem the purpose of the controller is to maintain the desired motor speed ω^* by managing input voltage F. The motor has: the speed ω, moment of inertia of the rotor J, viscous friction constant b, motor torque $T = K_t \cdot i$ (where i is armature current and K_t is motor torque constant), electric inductance L, electric resistance R and counter-electromotive force $e = K_e \cdot \dot{\omega}$ (where K_e is electromotive force constant). The equations of such model are described as follows (see e.g. [27]):

$$\begin{cases} \dot{\omega} = \frac{1}{J} \left(K_t \cdot i - b \cdot \omega \right) \\ \dot{i} = \frac{1}{L} \left(-R \cdot i + V - K_e \cdot \omega \right) \end{cases} . \tag{6}$$

The proposed controller structure for this problem is shown on Fig. 1.c).

It should be noted that the proposed approach with the dynamic reduction of the structure will allow the reduction of entire blocks in cascade structures. Because of that, a simplified controller can be obtained, and the redundant controller's input signals will not be used. Therefore, a similar approach can be used for developing structures for other simulation problems, and the optimization algorithm should itself correct the structure and select signals that bring the most benefits in the control process.

2.2   Fitness Function

To evaluate the controller, four control criteria were used, and then they were aggregated into the single-objective function, which is described in this section.

Error. The first criterion counts the sum of the offsets in time. For the first of the problem it can be written as follows:

$$error = \frac{1}{J} \sum_{j=1}^{J} |h^*(t_j) - h(t_j)|, \tag{7}$$

where t_j stands for discrete-time point $(j = 1, ..., J)$, J stands for time sample. For the rest of the simulation problems, it can be defined analogously.

Overshoot. The second criterion is an overshoot, i.e. exceeding the desired water level for WTT problem (for the rest of simulation problems it can be calculated analogously):

$$over = \max_{j=1,...,J} \{h(t_j) - h^*(t_j)\}. \tag{8}$$

Oscillations. The third criterion is occurrence of oscillations calculated as the sum of changes in controller output $u(t_k)$:

$$oscs = \frac{1}{J-1} \sum_{j=2}^{J} |u(t_j) - u(t_{j-1})|. \tag{9}$$

Suit. The last criterion's purpose is to check matching the signal to the desired one. In control systems, a steady offset error may appear (an error that persists in steady-state [28]). Checking if the signal is close to the given one can eliminate such cases, and this can be calculated as follows for the WTT problem:

$$suit = \frac{1}{K} \sum_{k=1}^{K} \begin{cases} 0 \text{ for } |h^*(t_k) - h(t_k)| < \beta \\ 1 \text{ for } \qquad else \end{cases}, \tag{10}$$

where β is an acceptable offset of the signal. For the rest of the simulation problems, this criterion can be defined analogously.

Fitness. In this paper the four presented above criteria are aggregated into single-objective function, which should be minimized and it is defined as follows:

$$fitness = error \cdot w_e + over \cdot w_v + oscs \cdot w_o + suit \cdot w_s, \qquad (11)$$

where **w** stands for weights of components that might differ for each simulation problem. It is worth noting that the above function does not take into account the complexity of the controller structure. Thanks to this, the optimization of parameters will not strive to obtain the simplest structure but to obtain the structure best suited for the given problem. If one wants to achieve simpler structures, one should include an additional criterion to assess the complexity of the structure.

2.3 Bison Algorithm Description

The Bison Algorithm is a recent swarm algorithm inspired by the behavior of bison herds [24]. When bison are in danger, they form a circle with the strongest on the outline, trying to protect the weak ones inside. The algorithm simulates this movement by shifting the individuals closer to the center of several fittest solutions. Since bison are also persistent and remarkable runners, the algorithm devotes a small set of solutions to explore the search space; dividing the population into two groups: the swarming and the running group.

The main loop of the algorithm starts by computing the target of the swarming movement, and the swarming group moves in a direction towards the target, if it improves their quality. The running group shifts in the run direction vector, which is slightly altered after each iteration. If a runner comes upon a promising solution, better than at least one of the swarming ones, the newly discovered solution is copied to the swarming group, and it becomes the target of the next movement; otherwise, the target is computed from several fittest solutions.

Algorithm 1. Bison Algorithm Pseudocode

1. generate the swarming group randomly
   generate the running group around the best bison
   generate the $run\ direction = random(\frac{ub-lb}{45}, \frac{ub-lb}{15})_{dim}$
2. for every migration round m do
3.   determine the swarming target:
4.   if $f(runner_{(m-1)}) < f(swarmer_{(m-1)})$ then
5. $center = runner_{(m-1)}$
6.   else
7.   compute the center of the strongest solutions:
           $weight = (1, 2, 3, ..., s)$
           $center = \sum_{i=1}^{s} \frac{weight_i \cdot x_i}{\sum_{j=1}^{s} weight_j}$
8.   for every bison in the swarming group do
9.   compute new position candidate x_{new}:
           $x_{new} = x_{old} + (center - x_{old}) \cdot random(0, overstep)_{dim}$
10.   if $f(x_{new}) < f(x_{old})$ then move to the x_{new}

11.   end for
12.   adjust the run direction vector
           $run\ direction\ =\ run\ direction\ \cdot\ random(0.9,\ 1.1)_{dim}$
13.   for every bison in the running group do
14.   move: $x_{new}\ =\ x_{old}\ +\ run\ direction$
15.   end for
16.   check boundaries
17.   if $f(x_{runner})\ <\ f(x_{swarmer})$
18.   then copy x_{runner} to the swarming group
19.   sort the swarming group by $f(x)$ values
20. end for

Where:

- *run direction* is the run direction vector,
- *ub* and *lb* are the upper and lower boundaries of the search space,
- x_{new} and x_{old} represent the current and the previous solutions respectively,
- and *dim* is a dimension,
- *s* is the elite group size parameter defining the number of the fittest solutions for center computation,
- *overstep* parameter defines the maximum length of the swarming movement,
- and *swarm group size* parameter sets number of bison performing the swarming movement.

3   Simulations

In the simulations, the same assumptions were made for all algorithms: number of evaluations: 25000, number of individuals in the population: 50, simulation repetitions: 100, algorithm parameters were selected following the suggestions from the literature (see e.g. [9–11, 13, 24]).

The following parameters were set: for WTT: $h^* = 1\,\mathrm{m}$, $A = 4.0\,\mathrm{m}^2$, $q_{out} = s \cdot \sqrt{2gh}$, $s = 0.05\,\mathrm{m}^2$, simulation time $T = 100\,\mathrm{s}$, time step $dt = 0.1\,\mathrm{s}$, $w_e = 10$, $w_v = 0.01$, $w_o = 1.0$, $w_s = 0.1$, q_{ex} and q_{em} are shown in Fig.2.a)., for MSD: $m_1 = m_2 = 0.2\,\mathrm{kg}$, $k = 10$, $y = 0.5\,\mathrm{m}$, simulation time $T = 10\,\mathrm{s}$, time step $dt = 0.001\,\mathrm{s}$, $w_e = 1$, $w_v = 0.01$, $w_o = 0.5$, $w_s = 0.1$, s^* is shown in Fig. 2.b). for DCM: $J = 0.01$ kg· $\mathrm{m}^2/\mathrm{s}^2$, $b = 0.1$ Nms, $K_t = 0.01$ Nm/Amp, $L = 0.5\,\mathrm{H}$, $R = 1.0$ ohm, $K_e = 0.01\,\mathrm{Nm/Amp}$, simulation time $T = 8\,\mathrm{s}$, time step $dt = 0.005\,\mathrm{s}$, $w_e = 1$, $w_v = 0.01$, $w_o c = 0.1$, $w_s = 0.1$ and ω^* is shown in Fig. 2.c).

3.1   Simulation Results

Detailed simulation results are shown in Table 1, while examples of the operation of the obtained control systems are shown in Fig. 3.

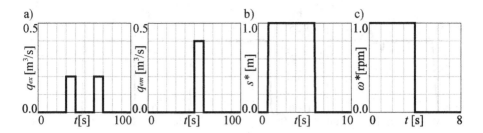

Fig. 2. Signals that vary in time for: a) WTT, b) MSD, c) DCM.

Table 1. Simulation results. Top results are marked in bold (results not worse by 5% from the best-found value in each row were considered as the top ones), and the worst results are underlined (results worse twice then the best-found value in each row were considered as the worst). Simulation time was averaged for all considered problems.

	Problem	Structure	GA	DE	PSO	CS	BA
Average simulation results	WTT	PID (2)	**0.6754**	0.6628	0.7002	**0.6674**	**0.6679**
	WTT	Cascade PID (2)	1.0282	0.8297	1.0791	0.7917	**0.7122**
	MSD	PID (2)	0.2222	**0.1580**	<u>0.4694</u>	**0.1635**	**0.1608**
	MSD	Cascade PID (2)	<u>0.2281</u>	**0.0372**	<u>1.8853</u>	**0.0445**	**0.0445**
	DCM	PID (2)	**0.0245**	<u>0.0633</u>	**0.0246**	**0.0245**	**0.0245**
	DCM	Cascade PID (2)	<u>0.0929</u>	**0.0249**	<u>0.1173</u>	**0.0206**	**0.0208**
	Times in top		2	3	1	4	5
	Times in unnaceptable		2	1	3	0	0
Best simulation results	WTT	PID (2)	**0.6572**	**0.6418**	**0.6414**	**0.6402**	**0.6351**
	WTT	Cascade PID (2)	0.7607	**0.6609**	**0.6576**	0.6921	**0.6488**
	MSD	PID (2)	**0.1189**	**0.1189**	**0.1189**	0.1220	**0.1189**
	MSD	Cascade PID (2)	**0.0348**	**0.0333**	0.0365	0.0366	**0.0341**
	DCM	PID (2)	**0.0245**	<u>0.0633</u>	**0.0245**	**0.0245**	**0.0245**
	DCM	Cascade PID (2)	**0.0205**	**0.0203**	**0.0205**	**0.0205**	**0.0205**
	Times in top		5	5	5	4	6
	Times in unnaceptable		0	1	0	0	0
	Average time (s)		190	193	333	328	242

3.2 Simulation Conclusions

The use of cascade PID controllers has brought a significant improvement in control for MSD and DCM problems (see Table 1). Moreover, depending on the problem, optimization of the structure automatically discards redundant elements (see Fig. 3). Optimization algorithms have allowed to find good parameters at which the states of the object tend to quickly settle in the control process without the phenomenon of overshooting and other disturbances (see Fig. 3), even for the WTT problem with two external signals changing in time (see Fig. 2.a). The Bison Algorithm performed well compared to the other meta-heuristics and obtained top results for most of the considered problems.

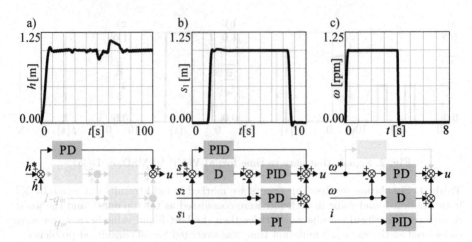

Fig. 3. Examples of the operation of the obtained control systems for: a) WTT, b) MSD, c) DCM. Reduced structure elements have been grayed out.

4   Conclusion

In this paper, we used several meta-heuristic algorithms to design PID controllers, focusing on the potential benefits of cascade layout over the classic one. We concluded that cascade PID controllers might be beneficial and that an increased number of dimensions does not harm the performance of the population-based algorithms.

On several problems of our experiment, the recent Bison Algorithm was able to outperform the Differential Evolution. The results brought us to consider the contribution of using novel meta-heuristics over the well-established and most-used optimization algorithms. Therefore, the future direction of our research should focus on more applications of metaheuristics, the novel ones included.

Acknowledgement. This work was supported by the Internal Grant Agency of Tomas Bata University under the Projects no. IGA/CebiaTech/2020/001. This work is also based upon support by COST (European Cooperation in Science & Technology) under Action CA15140, Improving Applicability of Nature-Inspired Optimisation by Joining Theory and Practice (ImAppNIO). The work was further supported by resources of A.I.Lab at the Faculty of Applied Informatics, Tomas Bata University in Zlin (ailab.fai.utb.cz).

References

1. Łapa, K., Cpałka, K., Przybył, A.: Genetic programming algorithm for designing of control systems. Inf. Technol. Control **47**(5), 668–683 (2018)
2. Alia, M.A., Younes, T.M., Al Subah, S.: A design of a PID self-tuning controller using LabVIEW. J. Softw. Eng. Appl. **4**(03), 161 (2011)

3. Zeng, G.Q., Chen, J., Dai, Y.X., Li, L.M., Zheng, C.W., Chen, M.R.: Design of fractional order PID controller for automatic regulator voltage system based on multi-objective extremal optimization. Neurocomputing **160**, 173–184 (2015)

4. Dash, P., Saikia, L.C., Sinha, N.: Automatic generation control of multi area thermal system using Bat algorithm optimized PD-PID cascade controller. Int. J. Electr. Power Energy Syst. **68**, 364–372 (2015)

5. Ferdaus, M.M., Anavatti, S.G., Garratt, M.A., Pratama, M.: Development of c-means clustering based adaptive fuzzy controller for a flapping wing micro air vehicle. J. Artif. Intell. Soft Comput. Res. **9**(2), 99–109 (2019)

6. He, W., Chen, Y., Yin, Z.: Adaptive neural network control of an uncertain robot with full-state constraints. IEEE Trans. Cybern. **46**(3), 620–629 (2015)

7. Lapa, K., Cpałka, K.: Flexible fuzzy PID controller (FFPIDC) and a nature-inspired method for its construction. IEEE Trans. Ind. Inf. **14**(3), 1078–1088 (2017)

8. Ang, K.H., Chong, G., Li, Y.: PID control system analysis, design, and technology. IEEE Trans. Control Syst. Technol. **13**(4), 559–576 (2005)

9. Back, T.: Evolutionary Algorithms in Theory and Practice: Evolution Strategies, Evolutionary Programming, Genetic Algorithms. Oxford University Press, Oxford (1996)

10. Goldberg, D.E., Holland, J.E.: Genetic algorithms and machine learning. Mach. Learn. **3**(2), 95–99 (1988)

11. Kennedy, J.: Particle swarm optimization. In: Encyclopedia of Machine Learning, pp. 760–766. Springer, Heidelberg (2011). https://doi.org/10.1007/978-0-387-30164-8_630

12. Mirjalili, S., Mirjalili, S.M., Lewis, A.: Grey wolf optimizer. Adv. Eng. Softw. **69**, 46–61 (2014)

13. Yang, X.-S., Deb, S.: Cuckoo search via Levy flights. In: Proceedings Of World Congress on Nature Biologically Inspired Computing (NaBIC 2009), India, December 2009, pp. 210–214. IEEE Publications (2009)

14. Gogna, A., Tayal, A.: Metaheuristics: review and application. J. Exp. Theor. Artif. Intell. **25**(4), 503–526 (2013)

15. Yang, X.S.: Free lunch or no free lunch: that is not just a question? Int. J. Artif. Intell. Tools **21**(3), 1240010 (2012). https://doi.org/10.1142/S0218213012400106

16. Yang, X.-S., Deb, S.: Engineering optimisation by Cuckoo search. Int. J. Math. Model. Numer. Optim. **1**(4), 330–343 (2010)

17. Rahmat-Samii, Y.: Genetic algorithm (GA) and particle swarm optimization (PSO) in engineering electromagnetics. In: 17th International Conference on Applied Electromagnetics and Communications, 2003. ICECom 2003, pp. 1–5. IEEE (2003)

18. Miguel, L.F.F., Miguel, L.F.F.: Assessment of modern metaheuristic algorithms-HS, ABC and FA-in shape and size optimisation of structures with different types of constraints. Int. J. Metaheuristics **2**(3), 256–293 (2013)

19. Xiong, N., Molina, D., Ortiz, M.L., Herrera, F.: A walk into metaheuristics for engineering optimization: principles, methods and recent trends. Int. J. Comput. Intell. Syst. **8**(4), 606–636 (2015)

20. Kadavy, T., Pluhacek, M., Viktorin, A., Senkerik, R.: Multi-swarm optimization algorithm based on firefly and particle swarm optimization techniques. In: Rutkowski, L., Scherer, R., Korytkowski, M., Pedrycz, W., Tadeusiewicz, R., Zurada, J.M. (eds.) ICAISC 2018. LNCS (LNAI), vol. 10841, pp. 405–416. Springer, Cham (2018). https://doi.org/10.1007/978-3-319-91253-0_38

21. Caraveo, C., Valdez, F., Castillo, O.: A new meta-heuristics of optimization with dynamic adaptation of parameters using type-2 fuzzy logic for trajectory control of a mobile robot. Algorithms **10**(3), 85 (2017)
22. Ochoa, P., Castillo, O., Soria, J.: Fuzzy differential evolution method with dynamic parameter adaptation using type-2 fuzzy logic. In: 2016 IEEE 8th International Conference on Intelligent Systems (IS), pp. 113–118. IEEE (2016)
23. Kadavy, T., Pluhacek, M., Viktorin, A., Senkerik, R.: Partial population restart of firefly algorithm using complex network analysis. In: 2017 IEEE Symposium Series on Computational Intelligence (SSCI), pp. 1–7. IEEE (2017)
24. Kazikova, A., Pluhacek, M., Kadavy, T., Senkerik, R.: Introducing the run support strategy for the bison algorithm. In: Zelinka, I., Brandstetter, P., Trong Dao, T., Hoang Duy, V., Kim, S.B. (eds.) AETA 2018. LNEE, vol. 554, pp. 272–282. Springer, Cham (2020). https://doi.org/10.1007/978-3-030-14907-9_27
25. Sabri, L.A., Al-mshat, H.A.: Implementation of fuzzy and PID controller to water level system using labview. Int. J. Comput. Appl. **116**(11), 6–10 (2015)
26. Lapa, K., Szczypta, J., Venkatesan, R.: Aspects of structure and parameters selection of control systems using selected multi-population algorithms. In: Rutkowski, L., Korytkowski, M., Scherer, R., Tadeusiewicz, R., Zadeh, L.A., Zurada, J.M. (eds.) ICAISC 2015. LNCS (LNAI), vol. 9120, pp. 247–260. Springer, Cham (2015). https://doi.org/10.1007/978-3-319-19369-4_23
27. Cheon, K., Kim, J., Hamadache, M., Lee, D.: On replacing PID controller with deep learning controller for DC motor system. J. Autom. Control Eng. **3**(6), 452–456 (2015)
28. Rajamani, M.R., Rawlings, J.B., Qin, S.J.: Achieving state estimation equivalence for misassigned disturbances in offset-free model predictive control. AIChE J. **55**(2), 396–407 (2009)

Optimization of the Values of Classifiers Parameters – Is it Still Worthwhile to Deal with it?

Daniel Kostrzewa$^{(\boxtimes)}$ ⓘ, Konrad Karczewski, and Robert Brzeski ⓘ

Department of Applied Informatics, Silesian University of Technology,
Gliwice, Poland
{daniel.kostrzewa,robert.brzeski}@polsl.pl

Abstract. This paper presents a comparison of the use of several selected optimization algorithms. They were applied to determine the parameters of classifiers. The value of these parameters should have a significant impact on the quality of the classification, and their determination is not a trivial process. This article checks how selected optimization algorithms deal with the task of determining the values of classifier parameters. Four algorithms were selected: particle swarm optimization, simulated annealing, cuckoo optimization algorithm, and lion optimization algorithm. The process of parameter determination was carried out using the five selected classifiers on several selected sets of data.

Keywords: Particle swarm optimization · Simulated annealing · Cuckoo optimization algorithm · Lion optimization algorithm · Classification · Data analysis · Accuracy · Weka · UCI Machine Learning Repository

1 Introduction

The quality of data classification depends on many factors. It may be influenced by the data set, as the quality of the collected data may vary. In the set of collected attributes, there may be ones that do not carry information about the assignment of the data vector to the appropriate class or the value of this information is small. In this way, these types of attributes only bring unnecessary noise. Attributes can include outliers, values that, for some reason, deviate from typical, correct, positively affecting the classification process. The quality of the classification may also depend on the used classifiers. There is no one universal classifier that would give the best results for all classification cases. Depending on many factors (e.g., size of the data set, number of data vectors, number of attributes in the vector, number of classes, nature of data, occurring noise),

This work was supported by Statutory Research funds of Department of Applied Informatics, Silesian University of Technology, Gliwice, Poland (02/100/BKM20/0006 - DK, 02/100/BK_20/0003 - RB).

L. Rutkowski et al. (Eds.): ICAISC 2020, LNAI 12415, pp. 417–428, 2020.
https://doi.org/10.1007/978-3-030-61401-0_39

as well as factors whose nature is unknown, different classifiers give the best results. Classification quality may also be influenced by the parameters settings of the used classifiers. In its simplest form, the default parameters can be used. An attempt may also be made to match these parameters for a given data set for the specificity of the classification task. Typically, the proper selection of classifier parameters improves the quality of the classification. However, this is a tedious and time-consuming task. That is why the idea came to automate this process using optimization algorithms. Of course, such an algorithm must be adapted to a given classifier, because each classifier has its parameters that can be set (there are also classifiers without any parameters). Such work of using the optimization algorithms has been done, and its results are presented in this article.

When using optimization algorithms, not only the quality of classification obtained in the next stage is important, but also the length of the optimization process itself. This length of time not supposed to be too long in the context of the task being carried out.

Many optimization algorithms can be used to search for beneficial parameter sets. They search a given space of solutions in order to find a satisfactory result, within an acceptable time, the solution that is most beneficial for a given problem.

The primary purpose of this work is, therefore, to implement, test, and compare four selected, known in scientific literature algorithms (two classic and two newer, evolutionary) that will optimize the parameters of the classifiers.

1.1 Related Work

In the field of computer science and mathematics, the optimization problem is defined as the task of finding the best solution from a set of all solutions called the solution space. Optimization algorithms [8, 12, 16, 17, 31] have been used and developed for several dozen years. These algorithms are an iterative procedure (usually) that aims to find the optimal solution. In practice, in most cases, it is only the pursuit of an optimal solution, i.e., an acceptable solution obtained in the available, reasonable time. Due to this time limit, this is typically not the best global solution.

There are some publications in the scope of determining the classifier parameters, optimization of parameters, automatic determination of values. In [33], the possibility of determining the best set of parameters for Weka classifiers for a given data set is presented. This is done using Bayesian optimization methods in the Auto-Weka 2 overlay. However, no experiments have been presented there. In [5] for three machine learning algorithms (support vector machine, random forest, and rotation forest), the impact of learning parameters was examined, and guidelines for setting these values were given. In [4], performance tests for nine classifiers implemented in the Weka Framework were presented, and the effect of set parameters on the accuracy was compared. In [32], a set of classifiers has been tested for the performance of defect prediction models with automated parameter optimization. In [20, 34] is indicated that in random forest and naive Bayes, the default parameters are not optimal.

In the current research, it was decided to test four selected optimization algorithms. Two of them are the classic ones: particle swarm optimization (PSO) [21, 29, 37] and simulated annealing (SA) [19, 22, 36]. The other two are newer algorithms, inspired by nature [11, 14, 15]: cuckoo optimization algorithm (COA) [18, 28, 41] and lion optimization algorithm (LOA) [40]. In the conducted research they were adapted to determine the classifier parameters [1, 7, 23].

The selection of optimization algorithms for both the classic and newer evolutionary ones is intentional. To some extent, there is a debate about the introduction of subsequent, usually more complex algorithms make sense [30]. The debate whether the classic algorithms are no longer good enough. Do evolutionary algorithms bring something new – better? Does the degree of complexity of newer algorithms hinder or even block their application to solving problems in real-world applications [10, 25]?

1.2 Contribution

The main contribution of this work is to compare the operation of optimization algorithms in the process of determining the parameters of classifiers. It is important here to check whether such optimization is possible within a given time. It is also essential to check whether the classification result improves with automatically determined parameter values for the used classifiers. If so, how much does this result improve?

The second element is to investigate if there is a difference between the optimization of classical and new evolutionary algorithms (COA, LOA). Checking if newer evolutionary algorithms are able to improve the result compared to existing ones. It is important to verify whether there are differences when optimizing parameters for various classifiers. It is also crucial to examine whether there are differences in the quality of the classification, depending on the data set used.

The next element is the implementation of these optimization algorithms for the process of determining classifier parameters. In this way, it will be checked and shown whether such optimization of classifier parameters makes sense at all, does it work and what results it gives.

1.3 Paper Structure

The second section focuses on presenting four implemented optimization algorithms. Section three contains a description of the executed research. Here, the information on the research methodology and data sets used for the experiment can be found. Section four presents and discusses the obtained results. Also included here is a ranking of optimization algorithms in terms of the accuracy of searching the solution space. The last fifth section consists of a summary of the work done and several ideas that may form further development of research in this area.

2   Optimization Algorithms

Typically, an optimization algorithm is an iterative procedure. In the current research, it was decided to implement four methods (two traditional classical and two new evolutionary ones) to compare the effectiveness of their operation.

Classic algorithms have been implemented and presented by their inventors many years ago. The first is particle swarm optimization – PSO [21, 29]. It is based on the population of particles, a stochastic algorithm that was inspired by the social behavior of biological organisms (e.g.., flocks of birds, schools of fish), simulating the intelligence of the swarm based on mutual interactions between individuals. The second is simulated annealing – SA [19, 22, 36]. It is a probabilistic technique used to search for the approximate global optimum of a given function. The name and inspiration of this solution come from metallurgy, where the annealing process determines the heating and controlled cooling of a particular metal.

To compare the results achieved by the mentioned traditional algorithms, two new evolutionary algorithms were selected, focusing on the simulation of the particular group's way of life of animals, such as the cuckoo optimization algorithm (COA) and the lion optimization algorithm (LOA). They have been proposed and implemented over the last few years. In general, these solutions are much more complex than traditional optimization systems.

Evolutionary algorithms are specific simulations with the following advantages:

- Traditional optimization methods are not immune to dynamic changes in the environment and require a full restart to provide a solution. The opposite is evolutionary computing, which can be used to adapt solutions to changing circumstances.
- They can be applied to almost all optimization problems.
- Evolutionary algorithms can be combined with other optimization techniques.

Cuckoo optimization algorithm, COA [18, 28, 41], is an evolutionary algorithm inspired by the life of the bird species, called the cuckoo, in which their unique lifestyle and the way they lay eggs, play a significant role. The second evolutionary algorithm that has been implemented for this work is the lion optimization algorithm, LOA [40]. It is an evolutionary algorithm based on the behavior and social organization of lions. All four algorithms have been properly adapted and implemented to determine parameters for selected classifiers.

3   Experiments

A custom test environment has been created to conduct relevant experiments. This environment uses the free Weka library [38] version 3.8, which provides machine learning set of algorithms [3, 9, 24, 26] for data mining. In the study was decided to carry out tests on a set of five classifiers [38, 39]. Selected classifiers are:

- J48 – C4.5 algorithm based on decision trees.
- JRip – an algorithm that uses a rules-based machine learning method.
- Multi-layer perceptron (MLP) – uses a backpropagation algorithm to teach neural network the object recognition.
- Random tree (RT) – an algorithm consisting of constructing a decision tree adopting K randomly selected attributes for each node.
- Simple logistic (SL) – a classifier building linear logistic regression models.

Classification quality can be examined and compared in many ways [2, 6, 13, 27]. The choice of the appropriate method usually depends on the purpose of the classification. In current research was utilized one of the most commonly used and thus the easiest for possible comparisons – the accuracy parameter.

Each of selected classifiers has parameters that can be set, and that affects the quality of the classification. A range of valid values has been set for each of these parameters (values that fall outside the range are not taken into account during optimization). The selection of acceptable limits was carried out using the experimental method. It was noticed that the parameter from a specific value did not affect the classification, or at least this effect is insignificant. For this reason, appropriate ranges of values, have been carefully selected in such a range, that has a tremendous impact on the effectiveness and the process of predicting decision classes.

Having previously prepared all the optimization algorithms, the experiments began. For this purpose, four different data sets were used (Table 1) [35].

During the selection of these data sets, the desire to test various collections of information was guided. The result was the selection of five sets that differ from each other in terms of the number of attributes and their types (numerical and categorical), the number of objects described, and the number of classes.

Table 1. Comparison of the structures of used data sets.

Name of the data set	No. of objects	No. of attributes	No. of classes
Iris	150	4	3
Glass Identification	214	9	6
Optical Recognition of Handwritten Digits	5620	64	10
White Wine Quality	4897	11	7

All used data come from the UCI Machine Learning Repository website. Table 1 lists the characteristics (number of classes, attributes, objects) of data sets that were used for the experiments. Each of these sets was randomly divided into two subsets in an 80%–20% ratio, taking into account the distribution of the number of labels in the set. The bigger part was used to optimize. During this process, it was divided ten times by cross-validation into a training and validation set. By using these sets, the classifier was taught and then tested to determine the best set of parameters. The test set (20% of the whole set) was used after the optimization was completed to determine the final accuracy of the classifier. In this step, the most favorable set of parameters was used. This set was found by the optimization procedure.

To avoid falsifying results by getting the optimization algorithm stuck at the local extreme, it was decided to optimize the parameters of the classifier five times independently. That is, each optimization algorithm was run five times for each data set. The condition for the operation of the optimization algorithms was their execution time. Additional experiments have shown that for the test conditions (PC with Intel Core i7 with 32 GB RAM), 3 s is enough. This is the optimization time without classification.

In this way, a series of experiments were carried out, and the average results (arithmetic averages of five optimizations for a given data set) and their analysis are presented in Sect. 4.

4   Obtained Results

This sections present the results of the classification, carried out with five classifiers, which were optimized by four optimization algorithms. The quality of the classification was measured by the accuracy parameter, and its percentage value is given.

4.1   Results for Individual Data Sets

In order to be able to compare the results obtained, each algorithm has been assigned an appropriate number of points according to the following description: 4 points is the best result – the highest value of the accuracy parameter, 3 points – the result is higher than the difference of the highest result and the standard deviation, 2 points – the result, lower than the difference of the highest result and the standard deviation, which is not the lowest result, 1 point – the result, lower than the difference of the highest result and the standard deviation, being the lowest result.

Table 2. Classification results of the Iris data set.

	PSO	SA	COA	LOA	avg
J48	96.7	96.7	96.7	96.7	96.7
JRip	98.7	98.7	96.7	97.3	97.8
MLP	94.7	80.0	100.0	95.3	92.5
RT	97.3	96.7	98.7	89.3	95.5
SL	100.0	100.0	100.0	100.0	100.0
avg	97.5	94.4	98.4	95.7	96.5
sd	1.78				
p	3	1	4	2	

where: avg – average, sd – standard deviation, p – number of points.

The first set (Table 2) refers to the results obtained for the Iris data set. As can be seen, the effectiveness of the classification has proven to be very high. The standard deviation of 1.78 was calculated for this data set. Subtracting this value from the highest average accuracy of the solution space, it can be assumed that the PSO and COA managed the task at almost the same high level. Other algorithms, whose results are below the limit set by the standard deviation, performed the task slightly worse.

Table 3. Classification results of the Glass Identification data set.

	PSO	SA	COA	LOA	avg
J48	70.7	67.4	67.4	71.2	69.2
JRip	64.7	66.4	70.3	67.3	67.2
MLP	67.4	58.1	70.1	57.2	63.2
RT	74.0	67.1	54.0	65.2	65.1
SL	46.5	44.9	42.4	45.4	44.8
avg	64.7	60.8	60.8	61.3	61.9
sd	1.86				
p	4	1	1	2	

Table 3 shows the results obtained for the Glass data set. The obtained results of accuracy are much worse, mainly due to the nature of the data (quite a small number of objects concerning the number of classes). Nevertheless, in the vast majority of cases, the accuracy of at least 60% was reached. This set of data was best handled by the PSO algorithm, the rest was much worse (in relation to the standard deviation).

Table 4. Classification results of the Optical Recognition of Handwritten Digits data set.

	PSO	SA	COA	LOA	avg
J48	89.3	90.5	90.5	89.6	90.0
JRip	88.4	88.4	89.7	88.9	88.9
MLP	97.7	97.1	92.0	97.7	96.2
RT	73.5	69.8	62.0	67.3	68.1
SL	96.3	96.2	96.3	96.1	96.2
avg	89.0	88.4	86.1	87.9	87.9
sd	1.26				
p	4	3	1	3	

Table 4 summarizes the results of the experiments for the Optical Recognition of Handwritten Digits (Optical abbreviated) data set. The differences in the outcomes of the optimization algorithms are much smaller than for the Iris and Glass sets. This is evidenced by the lower value of standard deviation and by the fact that two algorithms (LOA and SA) were in the range that allowed to award 3 points.

Table 5. Classification results of the White Wine Quality data set.

	PSO	SA	COA	LOA	avg
J48	56.6	59.2	59.2	58.8	58.5
JRip	54.1	53.5	52.1	53.3	53.3
MLP	47.0	50.4	46.5	50.5	48.6
RT	47.0	50.4	50.6	49.7	49.4
SL	48.2	44.1	38.8	43.7	43.7
avg	50.6	51.5	49.4	51.2	50.7
sd	0.92				
p	3	4	1	3	

Table 5 presents analogous results for the White Wine Quality collection. The SA algorithm managed best to optimize the classifiers for this set of data, and the LOA and PSO are slightly worse.

After the evaluation of the tasks completed by all the optimization algorithms, the points scored by them were counted. The summary results are presented in Table 6. According to the points awarded to the algorithms, the PSO algorithm proved to be the best. The second and third place were taken by LOA and SA, respectively. The COA algorithm was the worst.

Table 6. Summary of points achieved by all optimization algorithms.

	PSO	SA	COA	LOA
Total points	14	9	7	10

Table 7. Obtained results for the applied optimization algorithms.

	PSO	SA	COA	LOA	avg
Iris	97.5	94.4	98.4	95.7	96.5
Glass	64.7	60.8	60.8	61.3	61.9
Optical	89.0	88.4	86.1	87.9	87.9
Wine	50.6	51.5	49.4	51.2	50.7
avg	75.4	73.8	73.7	74.0	74.2

The averaged results for individual algorithms and data sets are presented in Table 7. It can be noted that the differences between the performance of algorithms are not significant, and they confirm the values of point rankings from Table 6. However, the averages do not correspond to the differences of points achieved by the algorithms.

4.2 Comparison of the Effectiveness of Searching the Solution Space

The critical comparison to be made is whether the optimization performed by different algorithms improves the classification results against the classification using the default values of the classifiers' parameters. For this purpose, Table 8 collects the accuracy values for each classifier using the default parameters.

Table 8. Obtained results for default parameters – without optimization process.

	Iris	Glass	Optical	Wine	avg
J48	90.0	76.7	85.8	56.4	77.2
JRip	83.3	60.5	86.9	51.9	70.7
MLP	93.3	72.1	96.5	54.8	79.2
RT	93.3	67.4	79.9	59.0	74.9
SL	93.3	62.8	95.3	53.3	76.2
avg	90.7	67.9	88.9	55.1	75.6

Table 9. Classification results obtained for the used classifiers.

	Iris	Glass	Optical	Wine	avg	Not opt	%
J48	96.7	69.2	90.0	58.5	78.6	77.2	1.8
JRip	97.8	67.2	88.9	53.3	76.8	70.7	8.7
MLP	92.5	63.2	96.2	48.6	75.1	79.2	−5.1
RT	95.5	65.1	68.1	49.4	69.5	74.9	−7.2
SL	100.0	44.8	96.2	43.7	71.2	76.2	−6.6

where: Not opt. – average results for default parameters – without optimization process, % – percentage improvement (or deterioration) in results.

Table 9 presents a summary of average accuracy obtained for particular optimization algorithms and classifiers together with accuracy values for classifiers without parameter optimization. In only two out of five cases, a slight average improvement in classification quality was achieved.

However, it is worthwhile to compare the data presented in Tables 8 and 9. In ten out of twenty cases (number of classifiers times number of datasets), optimization has led to a better quality of classification.

5   Conclusions

The main objective of the research was to compare optimization algorithms solving the problem of selecting parameters of classifiers.

The first conclusion is that classical optimization algorithms allow achieving similar or even slightly better results than newer evolutionary ones. This is due to the simplicity of these methods and, consequently, to the possibility of performing much more iterations at the same time than advanced optimization methods.

However, the most important conclusion that can be drawn from our work is that before attempting to select the values of the parameters of the classifiers, it is necessary to consider the specific goal that one wants to achieve. A very short optimization time (without taking into account the classification carried out during the optimization process) was intended to ensure the sensibility of the whole optimization task, i.e., checking whether in a short time it is possible to achieve much better results than using the default values. Unfortunately, it is not so easy. It is evident that the parameters of the classifier affect the quality of the classification, but the determination of the best (or at least very good) set is not so easy and depends on many factors (e.g., the data set on which the classification is carried out).

Our intention is not to prove that optimizing the parameters of classifiers does not make sense, or that it is not worthwhile to invest time in this task. If one's goal is, for some reason, to pursuit the improvement of classification quality by a small percentage, then it is feasible. However, it will probably require a lot of time and determination.

References

1. Adam, A., Shapiai, M.I., Tumari, M., Zaidi, M., Mohamad, M.S., Mubin, M.: Feature selection and classifier parameters estimation for EEG signals peak detection using particle swarm optimization. Sci. World J. **2014**, Article ID 973063 (2014)
2. Agrawal, R., Imielinski, T., Swami, A.: Database mining: a performance perspective. IEEE Trans. Knowl. Data Eng. **5**(6), 914–925 (1993)
3. Alpaydin, E.: Introduction to Machine Learning. MIT Press, Cambridge (2020)
4. Amancio, D.R., et al.: A systematic comparison of supervised classifiers. PloS One **9**(4), e94137 (2014)
5. Bagnall, A., Cawley, G.C.: On the use of default parameter settings in the empirical evaluation of classification algorithms. arXiv preprint arXiv:1703.06777 (2017)
6. Ben-David, A.: Comparison of classification accuracy using Cohen's weighted kappa. Expert Syst. Appl. **34**(2), 825–832 (2008)
7. Bergstra, J.S., Bardenet, R., Bengio, Y., Kégl, B.: Algorithms for hyper-parameter optimization. In: Advances in Neural Information Processing Systems, pp. 2546–2554 (2011)
8. Binitha, S., Sathya, S.S., et al.: A survey of bio inspired optimization algorithms. Int. J. Soft Comput. Eng. **2**(2), 137–151 (2012)
9. Bishop, C.M.: Pattern Recognition and Machine Learning. Springer, New York (2006)

10. Bonyadi, M.R., Michalewicz, Z., Barone, L.: The travelling thief problem: the first step in the transition from theoretical problems to realistic problems. In: 2013 IEEE Congress on Evolutionary Computation, pp. 1037–1044. IEEE (2013)

11. Chakraborty, A., Kar, A.K.: Swarm intelligence: a review of algorithms. In: Patnaik, S., Yang, X.-S., Nakamatsu, K. (eds.) Nature-Inspired Computing and Optimization. MOST, vol. 10, pp. 475–494. Springer, Cham (2017). https://doi.org/10.1007/978-3-319-50920-4_19

12. Civicioglu, P., Besdok, E.: A conceptual comparison of the cuckoo-search, particle swarm optimization, differential evolution and artificial bee colony algorithms. Artif. Intell. Rev. **39**(4), 315–346 (2013). https://doi.org/10.1007/s10462-011-9276-0

13. Costa, E., Lorena, A., Carvalho, A., Freitas, A.: A review of performance evaluation measures for hierarchical classifiers. In: Evaluation Methods for Machine Learning II: Papers from the AAAI 2007 Workshop, pp. 1–6 (2007)

14. Darwish, A.: Bio-inspired computing: algorithms review, deep analysis, and the scope of applications. Future Comput. Inform. J. **3**(2), 231–246 (2018)

15. Dhal, K.G., Ray, S., Das, A., Das, S.: A survey on nature-inspired optimization algorithms and their application in image enhancement domain. Arch. Comput. Methods Eng. **26**(5), 1607–1638 (2019). https://doi.org/10.1007/s11831-018-9289-9

16. Elbeltagi, E., Hegazy, T., Grierson, D.: Comparison among five evolutionary-based optimization algorithms. Adv. Eng. Inform. **19**(1), 43–53 (2005)

17. Fister Jr, I., Yang, X.S., Fister, I., Brest, J., Fister, D.: A brief review of nature-inspired algorithms for optimization. arXiv preprint arXiv:1307.4186 (2013)

18. Gandomi, A.H., Yang, X.S., Alavi, A.H.: Cuckoo search algorithm: a metaheuristic approach to solve structural optimization problems. Eng. Comput. **29**(1), 17–35 (2013). https://doi.org/10.1007/s00366-011-0241-y

19. Goffe, W.L., Ferrier, G.D., Rogers, J.: Global optimization of statistical functions with simulated annealing. J. Econom. **60**(1–2), 65–99 (1994)

20. Jiang, Y., Cukic, B., Menzies, T.: Can data transformation help in the detection of fault-prone modules? In: Proceedings of the 2008 Workshop on Defects in Large Software Systems, pp. 16–20 (2008)

21. Kennedy, J., Eberhart, R.: Particle swarm optimization. In: Proceedings of ICNN 1995-International Conference on Neural Networks, vol. 4, pp. 1942–1948. IEEE (1995)

22. Kirkpatrick, S., Gelatt, C.D., Vecchi, M.P.: Optimization by simulated annealing. Science **220**(4598), 671–680 (1983)

23. Kostrzewa, D., Brzeski, R.: Adjusting parameters of the classifiers in multiclass classification. In: Kozielski, S., Mrozek, D., Kasprowski, P., Małysiak-Mrozek, B., Kostrzewa, D. (eds.) BDAS 2017. CCIS, vol. 716, pp. 89–101. Springer, Cham (2017). https://doi.org/10.1007/978-3-319-58274-0_8

24. Marsland, S.: Machine Learning: An Algorithmic Perspective. CRC Press, Boca Raton (2015)

25. Michalewicz, Z.: Ubiquity symposium: evolutionary computation and the processes of life: the emperor is naked: evolutionary algorithms for real-world applications. Ubiquity **2012**, 1–13 (2012)

26. Mitchell, T.M., et al.: Machine Learning. MacGraw-Hill Companies, Boston (1997)

27. Powers, D.M.: Evaluation: from precision, recall and F-measure to ROC, informedness, markedness and correlation. J. Mach. Learn. Technol. **2**, 37–63 (2011)

28. Rajabioun, R.: Cuckoo optimization algorithm. Appl. Soft Comput. **11**(8), 5508–5518 (2011)

29. Sammut, C., Webb, G.I. (eds.): Encyclopedia of Machine Learning and Data Mining. Springer, Boston, MA (2017). https://doi.org/10.1007/978-1-4899-7687-1
30. Sörensen, K.: Metaheuristics–the metaphor exposed. Int. Trans. Oper. Res. **22**(1), 3–18 (2015)
31. Spall, J.C.: Introduction to Stochastic Search and Optimization: Estimation, Simulation, and Control, vol. 65. Wiley, Hoboken (2005)
32. Tantithamthavorn, C., McIntosh, S., Hassan, A.E., Matsumoto, K.: Automated parameter optimization of classification techniques for defect prediction models. In: Proceedings of the 38th International Conference on Software Engineering, pp. 321–332 (2016)
33. Thornton, C., Hutter, F., Hoos, H.H., Leyton-Brown, K.: Auto-WEKA: automated selection and hyper-parameter optimization of classification algorithms. CoRR, abs/1208.3719 (2012)
34. Tosun, A., Bener, A.: Reducing false alarms in software defect prediction by decision threshold optimization. In: 2009 3rd International Symposium on Empirical Software Engineering and Measurement, pp. 477–480. IEEE (2009)
35. UCI Machine Learning Repository: University of California, School of Information and Computer Science. http://archive.ics.uci.edu/ml/datasets/. Accessed 1 Oct 2019
36. Van Laarhoven, P.J., Aarts, E.H.: Simulated annealing. In: Simulated Annealing: Theory and Applications, vol. 37, pp. 7–15. Springer, Dordrecht (1987). https://doi.org/10.1007/978-94-015-7744-1_2
37. Wang, D., Tan, D., Liu, L.: Particle swarm optimization algorithm: an overview. Soft. Comput. **22**(2), 387–408 (2018). https://doi.org/10.1007/s00500-016-2474-6
38. Weka 3: http://www.cs.waikato.ac.nz/~ml/weka/. Accessed 1 Oct 2019
39. Wu, X., et al.: Top 10 algorithms in data mining. Knowl. Inf. Syst. **14**(1), 1–37 (2008). https://doi.org/10.1007/s10115-007-0114-2
40. Yazdani, M., Jolai, F.: Lion optimization algorithm (LOA): a nature-inspired metaheuristic algorithm. J. Comput. Des. Eng. **3**(1), 24–36 (2016)
41. Zheng, H., Zhou, Y.: A novel cuckoo search optimization algorithm based on Gauss distribution. J. Comput. Inf. Syst. **8**(10), 4193–4200 (2012)

A Population-Based Method
with Selection of a Search Operator

Krystian Łapa[1]([⊠])[ID], Krzysztof Cpałka[1][ID], Tacjana Niksa-Rynkiewicz[2][ID],
and Lipo Wang[3][ID]

[1] Department of Computational Intelligence, Czestochowa University of Technology,
Czestochowa, Poland
{krystian.lapa,krzysztof.cpalka}@pcz.pl
[2] Department of Marine Mechatronics, Gdańsk University of Technology, Gdańsk,
Poland
tacniksa@pg.edu.pl
[3] Nanyang Technological University, Singapore, Singapore
elpwang@ntu.edu.sg

Abstract. This paper presents a method based on a population in which
the parameters of individuals can be processed by operators from various population-based algorithms. The mechanism of selecting operators
is based on the introduction of an additional binary parameters vector
located in each individual, on the basis of which it is decided which
operators are to be used to modify individuals' parameters. Thus, in
the proposed approach, many operators can be used simultaneously for
this purpose. As part of the paper various methods of initializing binary
parameters, various population sizes, and their impact on the operation
of the algorithm were tested. The simulation was carried out on a well-
known set of benchmark functions.

Keywords: Population-based algorithms · Meta-heuristics · Search
operator · Evolutionary algorithms

1 Introduction

In population-based algorithms a single solution is represented by parameters
encoded within one individual [41]. A population of individuals is iteratively
processed in order to improve the solution found. The quality of the solution is
determined for each individual by a fitness function appropriate for the given
simulation problem. Due to the fact that population-based algorithms are not
directly related to the problem under consideration, they can be used to solve any
problems in which the solution is determined by the set of parameters sought.
This allows the use of such meta-heuristic algorithms [17] to solve many types
of problems - from finding the minima of benchmark functions, through optimization of control system parameters (e.g. PID [38]), optimization of parameters of computational intelligence systems (e.g. fuzzy systems [25,35,36], neural

© Springer Nature Switzerland AG 2020
L. Rutkowski et al. (Eds.): ICAISC 2020, LNAI 12415, pp. 429–444, 2020.
https://doi.org/10.1007/978-3-030-61401-0_40

networks [7,13,14,19–22,24,28], intelligent biometric systems [45–48], intelligent modeling systems [3], etc.), to optimization of many other processes [2,18,23,40]. It is worth emphasizing computational intelligence systems that are developing at an enormous pace and still allow for further improvement of performance and optimization of operation time (see e.g. [5,6]).

A multitude of applications, parallel development of other methods of artificial intelligence and an increase in computational possibilities stimulate a continuous development of population-based algorithms (see e.g. [9,29,31–33,37]). However, the development of population-based algorithms has fallen victim to the universality of these methods. Currently, hundreds of population-based algorithms and their variants are being developed. This makes it rather troublesome to choose the best algorithm for a given problem [1]. It is also difficult to compare these algorithms and to find specific paths for their further development. According to [10] a possible path for a future development of such algorithms may consist in their unification, ensembles, and use of various techniques within them.

In this paper, a further development of the unification approach [26] is proposed, in which each individual has a set of additional parameters that determine which operators should be used to change its base parameters. The encoded base parameters are sought within the ranges of values specified by the problem-called search space. Depending on the extent to which operators can change the parameters of an individual, they can be qualified as exploration operators (large parameter changes) or exploitation operators (small parameter changes). In the literature operators (or approaches) that pass smoothly from exploration to exploitation can also be found (see e.g. [12]). The proposed approach assumes a possibility of using operators from any algorithms, and in addition, the proposed method of selecting operators allows an automatic use of those that prove most successful in improving individuals. As part of this paper, the effect of population initialization and population size on the algorithm's operation was compared. The proposed method was tested on a set of well-known benchmark functions [27].

The structure of the paper is as follows: Sect. 2 presents a review of operators from different population algorithms, Sect. 3 describes the proposed solution, Sect. 4 discusses the results of the simulation, and finally Sect. 5 presents the conclusions.

2   Background

Basic operators for modifying individual's parameters include crossover and mutation operators. In the case of the problems considered in this paper, in which the parameters are represented by real values, the arithmetic crossover can be used:

$$\begin{cases} \mathbf{x}_{c1} := \alpha \cdot \mathbf{x}_{p1} + (1 - \alpha) \cdot \mathbf{x}_{p2} \\ \mathbf{x}_{c2} := \alpha \cdot \mathbf{x}_{p2} + (1 - \alpha) \cdot \mathbf{x}_{p1}, \end{cases} \tag{1}$$

where $\mathbf{x}$ stands for parameters vector ($\{p1, p2\}$ indexes stand for parent individuals, $\{c1, c2\}$ indexes stand for new individuals), α stands for a random number from range $\langle 0; 1 \rangle$. The solution causes that the new individual's parameters have values between the parameters drawn from the selected parents. Therefore, depending on where the solutions are located in the search space, the operator can be considered as an exploration or an exploitation operator. This operator is often used because potentially good new solutions can be found between the parents selected by an appropriate method (e.g. the roulette wheel [34]). However, using this operator might result in a disadvantageous fast convergence of the algorithm. To maintain some randomness, the mutation operator can be used:

$$\mathbf{x} := \mathbf{x} + (\alpha - 0.5) * m_{range}, \tag{2}$$

where m_{range} is the mutation range [34]. Such an operator can be qualified to the exploitation group because it searches the space around a given solution. Of course, the task of the algorithm is also to determine when (or with what probability) which operator should be used and how to change its parameters. The right selection of operators will allow one to maintain an appropriate compromise and transition between exploration and exploration of the search space [4], and thus better optimization results.

The introduction of the PSO [16] algorithm also had a significant impact on the development of population-based algorithms. This algorithm proposes the following mechanism to modify individual's parameters:

$$\begin{cases} \mathbf{v}_i := \omega \cdot \mathbf{v}_i + \varphi^b \cdot \alpha_i^b \cdot \left(\mathbf{x}_i^b - \mathbf{x}_i \right) + \varphi^g \cdot \alpha_i^g \cdot \left(\mathbf{x}^g - \mathbf{x}_i \right) \\ \mathbf{x}_i := \mathbf{x}_i + \mathbf{v}_i, \end{cases} \tag{3}$$

where i stands for the individual's index, $\mathbf{x}^b$ stands for the best parameters found for each individual, $\mathbf{x}^g$ stands for the best global parameters, $\{\varphi^b, \varphi^g\}$ stand for the algorithm parameters [16], ω stands for inertia weight, $\mathbf{v}$ stands for individual velocity, i.e. the main element distinguishing this algorithm. Calculation of the velocity (3) consists of three parts: (a) using the previous value, (b) the difference between best individual's parameters and individual's current parameters (exploitation), and (c) the best global parameters and current parameters (exploration) - therefore, several different patterns of behavior can be distinguished within the scope of such an operation.

A noteworthy algorithm is also the DE [30], in which individual's parameters are modified as follows:

$$\mathbf{x}_i := \begin{cases} \mathbf{x}_{p1} + F \cdot (\mathbf{x}_{p2} - \mathbf{x}_{p3}) \text{ for } \alpha < CR \text{ or } i = R \\ \mathbf{x}_i \text{ otherwise,} \end{cases} \tag{4}$$

where F and CR are algorithm parameters [30], R is a randomly selected index (due to this, at least one child parameter will be modified, which prevents a premature algorithm convergence).

The development of population-based algorithms has brought about many different solutions, similar in some respects, and different in others. The operators of the BAT algorithm [43] are worth mentioning here in their relation to exploration:

$$\begin{cases} f_i := f_{\min} + (f_{\max} - f_{\min}) \cdot \alpha \\ \mathbf{v}_i := \mathbf{v}_i + (\mathbf{x}_i - \mathbf{x}^g) \cdot f_i \\ \mathbf{x}_i := \mathbf{x}_i + \mathbf{v}_i, \end{cases} \tag{5}$$

where f_i are bats' frequencies [43], and exploitation

$$\mathbf{x}_i := \mathbf{x}_i + \cdot \bar{A}_t, \tag{6}$$

where ϵ is a random number from range $\langle -1; 1 \rangle$, $\bar{A}_t$ is an average loudness for all bats for iteration t of algorithm [43]. What distinguishes the BAT algorithm is the introduction of individual parameters (loudness and pulse rate) changed depending on the situation in the population and the iteration of the algorithm. Other interesting operators can be found in:

- the CS algorithm [42], in which the worst individuals are replaced with new ones,
- the ABC [15], where the population is divided into different types of individuals,
- the FFA [44], where the individual is subject to modification only if the parent has a better value of the fitness function,
- the GWO [12], where individuals are directed towards not one but the three best individuals and the balance between exploration and exploitation is changed in time,
- the BTO [8] algorithm, where information from previous iterations of the algorithm is used,
- the FWA [39], where the number of descendants and the range of parameter modification depend on the individual's fitness function value.

A large number of population-based algorithms with different operators also causes hybrid solutions combining the operation of several algorithms (see e.g. [11]). Of course, operation of population algorithms depends not only on the operation of parameter modification operators, but also on the specific fundamentals of a given algorithm. Each algorithm can be distinguished by the strategy of parent selection, strategies for replacing individuals in the population, division of the population, selection of parameter values, etc. All these elements should be selected so that the algorithm properly explores the search space and at the same time does not get stuck too quickly in the local optimum. This paper will present a unified method in which operators from any algorithms can be used and the algorithm behavior can be adapted to the simulation problem.

Algorithm 1 Proposed method

1: set the number of individuals (POP) and that of fitness function calls (NFC)
2: calculate iterations (ITER): ITER = NFC/POP
3: initialize the POP - parameters $\mathbf{x}$ and $\mathbf{v}$ randomly, parameters $\mathbf{b}$ according to the
   initialization method, parameters $\mathbf{x}^b := \mathbf{x}$ (see parameters individual's, Fig. 1)
4: evaluate the POP and initialize $\mathbf{x}^g$ to $\mathbf{x}$ parameters of the best individual (see (3))
5: **for** $i := 1$ **to** ITER **do**
6:     **for** $ch := 1$ **to** POP **do**
7:         select ch-th individual from the POP for modification
8:         modify individual's parameters $\mathbf{v}$, $\mathbf{x}$, and $\mathbf{x}^b$ according to Fig. 1
9:         modify individual's parameters $\mathbf{b}$ using mutation and crossover (Section 3)
10:         narrow individual's parameters $\mathbf{x}$ to the search space and repair $\mathbf{b}$ using (7)
11:         evaluate the individual using a fitness function
12:     **end for**
13:     update $\mathbf{x}^g$ to parameters $\mathbf{x}$ of the best individual
14: **end for**
15: present the best found parameters coded in $\mathbf{x}^g$

---

3   Proposed Method

This paper presents a method based on the approach described in [26]. Its idea
is based on extending the set of individuals' parameters with additional binary
vector $\mathbf{b}$, according to which operators are selected to modify the individual.
When the parameter value is equal to 1, the operator associated with it is used
to modify the parameters of the individual. This approach does not limit the
number of the operators used simultaneously. When looking at it from a different
perspective, this method can be treated as a method with one super-operator
built of many sub-operators (similarly, the PSO can be seen in the same way).
The processing of real value parameters of the proposed algorithm is based on
the velocity transmission mechanism as used in the PSO. The algorithm idea is
shown in detail in Fig. 1 and in Algorithm 1.

This article assumes the use of a set containing operators. These operators
are used to modify real value parameters, and thus affect the parameter vectors

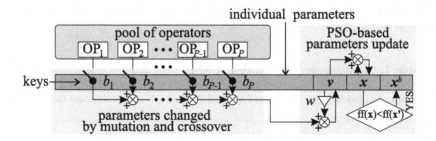

Fig. 1. The idea of processing parameters. If the b_p parameter is equal to 1, then the
operator OP_p is treated as active and affects the modification of the $\mathbf{v}$ vector.

x and **v** (see Fig. 1). The additional vector itself is of a binary type, which needs to have additional mechanisms introduced for its modification. To this end, a binary mutation was used with the probability of a single parameter mutation p_m, uniform crossover with the probability of p_c, and a parent selected from the population by the roulette wheel method. The use of crossover in this way allows the propagation of operators that have improved individuals in the whole population. The use of mutation means that the algorithm can change its approach during operation and start using new operators.

Real parameters of the individuals are usually initialized randomly. Binary parameters can also be initialized in the same way. This paper uses different approaches to initializing the binary parameters **b** to examine their impact on learning. This - in the context of operator selection - has not been discussed in the literature so far.

The idea of the first initialization (INIT1) is to "activate" only one operator during the initialization:

$$b_{i,p} = \begin{cases} 1 \text{ for } p = R \\ 0 \text{ otherwise,} \end{cases} \tag{7}$$

where $p = 1, 2, ..., P$ stands for the index of an operator, P is the number of operators (see Fig. 1), R is a random number from set $\{1, 2, ..., P\}$. It is worth adding that the mechanism specified by formula (7) was also used as a repair mechanism applied when the number of active operators is equal to 0 ($\sum_{p=1}^{P} b_{i,p} = 0$).

The second initialization approach (INIT2) uses a mechanism with a likelihood of operator activation along with another mechanism ensuring that at least one operator will be active. In the second approach to initialization (INIT2) the number of active operators must be greater or equal to 1. Those operators for which the random number in the $[0, 1]$ range is greater than the probability of activating p_a are activated:

$$b_{i,p} = \begin{cases} 1 \text{ for } p = R \text{ or } \alpha < p_a \\ 0 \text{ otherwise,} \end{cases} \tag{8}$$

where p_a is activation probability. Increasing the number of simultaneously active operators during the initialization can have a completely different impact on the algorithm.

Finally, the third initialization (INIT3) has all operators active during the initialization: $b_{i,p} = 1$.

Table 1. Obtaining the same number of NFCs with different population sizes.

Number of individuals (POP)	Number of iterations (ITER)	Number of fitness function calls (NFC)
50	1000	50000
100	500	50000
200	250	50000

4   Simulations

The simulations were conducted for 10 benchmarks from the CEC13 set [27] (C01-C10) with dimension $D = 50$. For each simulation case 200 repetitions were performed and the results were averaged and normalized for each benchmark function. The following parameters were adopted as part of the simulation: $p_m = p_c = 5\%$, $P = 16$, $p_a = 50\%$. The parameters of the operators used were selected in accordance with the suggestions provided, among others, in [26]. The used operators are described in Sect. 2 and shown in Figs. 2 and 3.

In the simulation were used sixteen operators (see Fig. 3) whose conceptual bases are described in Sect. 2. The method of their implementation is analogous to the one presented in [26].

Population size is key to population-based algorithms. In various papers and algorithms, this value is different, starting from a small number of individuals (e.g. 20) and ending with a larger number of individuals (e.g. 500). To correctly compare cases with different numbers of individuals, a similar computational complexity within each of the cases should be provided. One of the key elements in terms of complexity is the number of calls of the fitness function (NFC). It is important that it should be identical for each case, so for algorithms with more individuals, fewer iterations should be performed. In this paper, all the simulation variants were tested in accordance with the guidelines for providing the same number of NFCs as shown in Table 1.

4.1   Simulation Results

The detailed results for each benchmark function are presented in Table 2 and summarized in Table 4. The impact of the initialization method and population size on the obtained results is presented in Table 3 and in Fig. 2 while a comparison of the results with those obtained with the other methods in Table 5. The use of individual operators for various benchmark functions is shown in Fig. 3.

4.2   Simulation Conclusions

Analyzing the results from Tables 2 and 4, it can be seen that for different problems better results can be obtained by different approaches, which is consistent with the No Free Lunch theorem for optimization. In the case of NFC = 50000, the best results were given by the INIT1 initialization variant and a population with the size of 100. In the case of using a larger number of NFC, a greater number of individuals managed to obtain a better result, mainly as a result of obtaining a higher population diversity a greater possible population diversity (see Table 4).

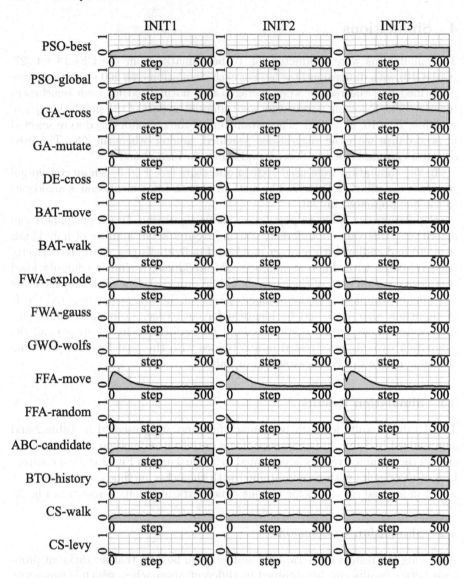

Fig. 2. Comparison of initialization methods for the C06 benchmark POP = 100 and ITER = 500. The vertical axis stands for the average percentage usage of the operator relative to a single individual. The operator's details can be found in e.g. [26].

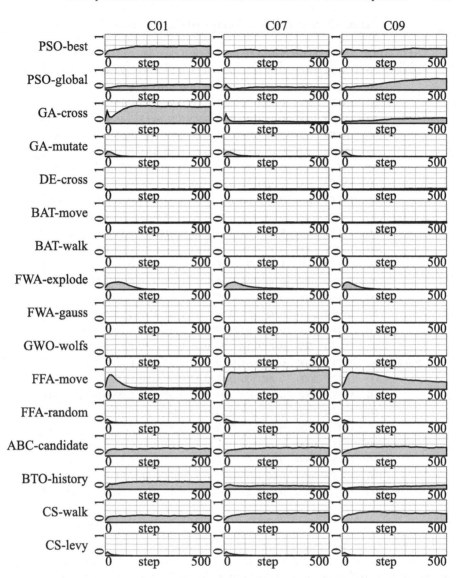

Fig. 3. Comparison of the operators used for different benchmarks for the INIT1, POP = 100, ITER = 500. The vertical axis stands for the average percentage usage of the operator relative to a single individual. The operator's details can be found in e.g. [26].

Table 2. Averaged and normalized simulation results.

NFC	POP	INIT	ITER	C01	C02	C03	C04	C05	C06	C07	C08	C09	C10
50000	50	INIT1	1000	0.01	0.45	0.51	0.71	0.19	1.00	0.74	0.88	0.92	0.16
	100	INIT1	500	0.00	0.56	0.41	0.79	0.17	0.47	0.34	0.91	0.42	0.16
	200	INIT1	250	0.02	0.74	0.61	0.70	0.58	0.55	0.14	1.00	0.08	0.73
	50	INIT2	1000	0.01	0.65	0.84	0.92	0.15	0.85	0.86	0.87	0.95	0.23
	100	INIT2	500	0.01	0.68	0.71	0.88	0.52	0.73	0.51	0.86	0.49	0.28
	200	INIT2	250	0.15	0.87	0.87	0.86	0.30	0.51	0.23	0.86	0.18	1.00
	50	INIT3	1000	0.12	0.71	0.70	0.96	0.15	0.84	1.00	0.83	1.00	0.28
	100	INIT3	500	0.02	0.77	0.86	0.97	0.58	0.66	0.57	0.73	0.52	0.39
	200	INIT3	250	0.04	1.00	1.00	1.00	1.00	0.70	0.35	0.81	0.18	0.86
100000	50	INIT1	2000	0.00	0.17	0.32	0.22	0.00	0.68	0.55	0.61	0.70	0.03
	100	INIT1	1000	0.00	0.13	0.18	0.27	0.11	0.61	0.25	0.65	0.35	0.03
	200	INIT1	500	0.00	0.18	0.10	0.31	0.01	0.31	0.07	0.73	0.09	0.04
	50	INIT2	2000	1.00	0.23	0.46	0.28	0.00	0.69	0.76	0.51	0.88	0.06
	100	INIT2	1000	0.00	0.23	0.34	0.32	0.00	0.58	0.49	0.50	0.47	0.03
	200	INIT2	500	0.00	0.23	0.22	0.39	0.01	0.27	0.14	0.54	0.10	0.05
	50	INIT3	2000	0.00	0.27	0.49	0.34	0.00	0.90	0.95	0.56	0.90	0.48
	100	INIT3	1000	0.00	0.22	0.30	0.36	0.03	0.61	0.50	0.41	0.42	0.03
	200	INIT3	500	0.00	0.32	0.25	0.41	0.03	0.26	0.23	0.46	0.15	0.06
200000	50	INIT1	4000	0.00	0.01	0.09	0.00	0.00	0.26	0.58	0.38	0.53	0.01
	100	INIT1	2000	0.00	0.00	0.06	0.02	0.00	0.29	0.20	0.34	0.27	0.00
	200	INIT1	1000	0.00	0.00	0.00	0.03	0.00	0.08	0.00	0.25	0.00	0.00
	50	INIT2	4000	0.00	0.04	0.23	0.02	0.00	0.23	0.76	0.22	0.75	0.00
	100	INIT2	2000	0.00	0.05	0.12	0.01	0.00	0.48	0.53	0.17	0.38	0.00
	200	INIT2	1000	0.00	0.04	0.07	0.07	0.00	0.00	0.14	0.08	0.10	0.00
	50	INIT3	4000	0.00	0.07	0.23	0.04	0.00	0.64	0.84	0.18	0.67	0.01
	100	INIT3	2000	0.00	0.05	0.14	0.04	0.00	0.35	0.51	0.10	0.37	0.04
	200	INIT3	1000	0.00	0.07	0.09	0.08	0.00	0.22	0.20	0.00	0.11	0.00

In addition, as the population size increased, the average number of active operators decreased (see Table 3). Despite the fact that the number of active operators was different at the beginning for different initialization methods (see Fig. 2), it was on a relatively similar level in the algorithm (see Fig. 2 and Table 3). Nonetheless, the best results were obtained with the INIT1 initialization (see Table 2). In addition, depending on the simulation problem, the algorithm chose different operators (see Fig. 3). Therefore, it can be concluded that the algorithm automatically adjusts the optimal operators to both the problem and algorithm step. An increase in the number of active operators during initialization only causes deterioration of the algorithm's operation.

Table 3. Comparison of the impact of the initialization method and population size on the results obtained. The best values are in bold. AVG stands for averaged normalized value from C01–C10 benchmarks and OPER stands for averaged number of activate operators used for single individual.

NFC	POP	AVG	OPER	INIT	AVG	OPER
50000	50	0.62	2.51	INIT1	**0.50**	**2.43**
	100	**0.53**	2.45	INIT2	0.60	2.46
	200	0.60	**2.40**	INIT3	0.65	2.47
100000	50	0.44	2.52	INIT1	**0.26**	**2.43**
	100	0.28	2.43	INIT2	0.33	2.45
	200	**0.20**	**2.38**	INIT3	0.33	2.45
200000	50	0.23	2.49	INIT1	**0.11**	**2.42**
	100	0.15	2.43	INIT2	0.15	2.42
	200	**0.05**	**2.35**	INIT3	0.17	2.42
AVG	50	0.43	2.51	INIT1	**0.29**	**2.43**
	100	0.32	2.43	INIT2	0.36	2.44
	200	**0.28**	**2.37**	INIT3	0.38	2.45

Table 4. Summary and details of the results presented in Table 2. PLC stands for the algorithm position according to the AVG, PNFC stands for the algorithm position relative to the same NFC value, TT1 stands for the number of times the best position was obtained relative to the NFC value, TT3 stands for the number of times the top three positions were obtained relative to the NFC value, and APLC stands for the average place relative to the NFC value.

NFC	POP	INIT	ITER	AVG	PLC	PNFC	TT1	TT3	APLC	OPER
50000	50	INIT1	1000	0.56	21	3	1	5	4.30	2.50
	100	INIT1	500	0.42	17	1	4	8	2.70	2.42
	200	INIT1	250	0.52	20	2	3	5	4.50	2.37
	50	INIT2	1000	0.63	25	7	1	4	5.20	2.51
	100	INIT2	500	0.57	22	4	0	0	4.80	2.46
	200	INIT2	250	0.58	23	5	0	3	5.40	2.41
	50	INIT3	1000	0.66	26	8	0	2	5.90	2.52
	100	INIT3	500	0.61	24	6	1	1	5.70	2.46
	200	INIT3	250	0.69	27	9	0	2	6.50	2.41

(continued)

Table 4. (*continued*)

NFC	POP	INIT	ITER	AVG	PLC	PNFC	TT1	TT3	APLC	OPER
100000	50	INIT1	2000	0.33	16	7	1	4	4.90	2.50
	100	INIT1	1000	0.26	12	4	2	5	3.90	2.41
	200	INIT1	500	0.18	7	1	4	6	3.40	2.36
	50	INIT2	2000	0.49	19	9	0	1	6.60	2.53
	100	INIT2	1000	0.30	15	6	0	3	4.50	2.43
	200	INIT2	500	0.20	9	2	0	4	4.40	2.38
	50	INIT3	2000	0.49	18	8	1	1	7.20	2.53
	100	INIT3	1000	0.29	14	5	1	1	5.40	2.43
	200	INIT3	500	0.22	10	3	1	5	4.70	2.39
200000	50	INIT1	4000	0.19	8	7	1	2	5.60	2.48
	100	INIT1	2000	0.12	4	4	1	6	3.60	2.42
	200	INIT1	1000	0.04	1	1	5	8	2.30	2.35
	50	INIT2	4000	0.22	11	8	0	1	6.20	2.50
	100	INIT2	2000	0.17	6	6	0	1	5.60	2.43
	200	INIT2	1000	0.05	2	2	1	6	3.70	2.35
	50	INIT3	4000	0.27	13	9	0	0	7.60	2.49
	100	INIT3	2000	0.16	5	5	0	2	5.60	2.44
	200	INIT3	1000	0.08	3	3	2	4	4.80	2.35

Table 5. Comparison of obtained averaged and normalized results with the other results from the literature. The best value is in bold.

ALGORITHM	C01	C02	C03	C04	C05	C06	C07	C08	C09	C10	AVG
Proposed & INIT1	0.00	0.00	0.00	0.04	0.00	0.00	0.01	0.10	0.04	0.00	**0.019**
Proposed & INIT2	0.00	0.00	0.01	0.05	0.00	0.00	0.02	0.07	0.04	0.00	0.020
Proposed & INIT3	0.00	0.01	0.01	0.06	0.00	0.00	0.02	0.00	0.05	0.00	0.015
DE	0.02	0.24	0.08	0.45	0.01	0.05	0.08	0.51	0.06	0.13	0.162
GA	0.22	0.96	0.14	1.00	0.00	0.11	0.09	1.00	0.24	0.12	0.389
GWO	0.36	0.21	0.25	0.25	0.49	0.31	0.09	0.10	0.35	0.59	0.301
FWA	1.00	1.00	1.00	0.54	1.00	1.00	1.00	0.16	1.00	1.00	0.871
PSO	0.54	0.46	0.31	0.33	0.34	0.51	0.21	0.73	0.40	0.73	0.454
BAT	0.53	0.27	0.24	0.20	0.30	0.39	0.06	0.23	0.21	0.57	0.300
CS	0.10	0.20	0.04	0.11	0.06	0.07	0.02	0.13	0.20	0.16	0.109
FFA	0.03	0.09	0.02	0.00	0.02	0.02	0.03	0.15	0.29	0.04	0.069

Increasing the number of iterations to 2000 or 4000 (see Table 2) allowed for a further improvement of the results (see Table 3). This means that even with such a large number of iterations, the algorithm continued to improve individuals and the population did not stagnate. In addition, the algorithm allowed to obtain the best results in comparison with the other population algorithms from which the operators were selected (see Table 5).

5 Conclusions

In this paper, an algorithm with a pool of operators for modifying individuals' parameters was presented. The use of operators was based on the values of the additional binary vector. This approach allowed not only to adapt the algorithm to a given simulation problem but also to obtain very good results compared to classic population-based algorithms. In addition, different initialization variants and population sizes show that the algorithm works best when only one operator is active during initialization and the size of the population is large. Further research will be directed, among others, to the development of the algorithm and its application in other simulation problems.

Acknowledgment. This paper was financed under the program of the Minister of Science and Higher Education under the name 'Regional Initiative of Excellence' in the years 2019–2022, project number 020/RID/2018/19 with the amount of financing PLN 12 000 000.

References

1. Adam, S.P., Alexandropoulos, S.-A.N., Pardalos, P.M., Vrahatis, M.N.: No free lunch theorem: a review. In: Demetriou, I.C., Pardalos, P.M. (eds.) Approximation and Optimization. SOIA, vol. 145, pp. 57–82. Springer, Cham (2019). https://doi.org/10.1007/978-3-030-12767-1_5

2. Bałanda, M., Pełka, R., Fitta, M., Laskowski, L., Laskowska, M.: Relaxation and magnetocaloric effect in the Mn 12 molecular nanomagnet incorporated into mesoporous silica: a comparative study. RSC Adv. **6**(54), 49179–49186 (2016)

3. Bartczuk, L., Przybył, A., Cpałka, K.: A new approach to nonlinear modelling of dynamic systems based on fuzzy rules. Int. J. Appl. Math. Comput. Sci. (AMCS) **263**, 603–621 (2016)

4. Besbes, O., Gur, Y., Zeevi, A.: Optimal exploration-exploitation in a multi-armed bandit problem with non-stationary rewards. Stoch. Syst. **9**(4), 319–337 (2019)

5. Bilski, J., Kowalczyk, B., Żurada, J.M.: Application of the givens rotations in the neural network learning algorithm. In: Rutkowski, L., Korytkowski, M., Scherer, R., Tadeusiewicz, R., Zadeh, L.A., Zurada, J.M. (eds.) ICAISC 2016. LNCS (LNAI), vol. 9692, pp. 46–56. Springer, Cham (2016). https://doi.org/10.1007/978-3-319-39378-0_5

6. Bilski, J., Smolag, J., Żurada, J.M.: Parallel approach to the Levenberg-Marquardt learning algorithm for feedforward neural networks. In: Rutkowski, L., Korytkowski, M., Scherer, R., Tadeusiewicz, R., Zadeh, L.A., Zurada, J.M. (eds.) ICAISC 2015. LNCS (LNAI), vol. 9119, pp. 3–14. Springer, Cham (2015). https://doi.org/10.1007/978-3-319-19324-3_1

7. Cao, Y., Samidurai, R., Sriraman, R.: Stability and dissipativity analysis for neutral type stochastic Markovian jump static neural networks with time delays. J. Artif. Intell. Soft Comput. Res. **9**(3), 189–204 (2019)

8. Civicioglu, P.: Backtracking search optimization algorithm for numerical optimization problems. Appl. Math. Comput. **219**(15), 8121–8144 (2013)
9. Dawar, D., Ludwig, S.A.: Effect of strategy adaptation on differential evolution in presence and absence of parameter adaptation: an investigation. J. Artif. Intell. Soft Comput. Res. **8**(3), 211–235 (2018)
10. Del Ser, J., et al.: Bio-inspired computation: where we stand and what's next. Swarm Evol. Comput. **48**, 220–250 (2019)
11. Dziwiński, P., Bartczuk, Ł., Paszkowski, J.: A new auto adaptive fuzzy hybrid particle swarm optimization and genetic algorithm. J. Artif. Intell. Soft Comput. Res. **10**(2), 95–111 (2020)
12. Faris, H., Aljarah, I., Al-Betar, M.A., Mirjalili, S.: Grey wolf optimizer: a review of recent variants and applications. Neural Comput. Appl. **30**(2), 413–435 (2018). https://doi.org/10.1007/s00521-017-3272-5
13. Javaid, M., Abbas, M., Liu, J.B., Teh, W.C., Cao, J.: Topological properties of four-layered neural networks. J. Artif. Intell. Soft Comput. Res. **9**(2), 111–122 (2019)
14. Kamimura, R.: Supposed maximum mutual information for improving generalization and interpretation of multi-layered neural networks. J. Artif. Intell. Soft Comput. Res. **9**(2), 123–147 (2019)
15. Karaboga, D., Basturk, B.: A powerful and efficient algorithm for numerical function optimization: artificial bee colony (ABC) algorithm. J. Global Optim. **39**(3), 459–471 (2007). https://doi.org/10.1007/s10898-007-9149-x
16. Kennedy, J., Eberhart, R., Particle swarm optimization. In: Proceedings of ICNN 1995-International Conference on Neural Networks (IEEE), vol. 4, pp. 1942–1948 (1995)
17. Korytkowski, M., Senkerik, R., Scherer, M.M., Angryk, R.A., Kordos, M., Siwocha, A.: Efficient image retrieval by fuzzy rules from boosting and metaheuristic. J. Artif. Intell. Soft Comput. Res. **10**(1), 57–69 (2020)
18. Krell, E., Sheta, A., Balasubramanian, A.P.R., King, S.A.: Collision-free autonomous robot navigation in unknown environments utilizing PSO for path planning. J. Artif. Intell. Soft Comput. Res. **9**(4), 267–282 (2019)
19. Laskowski, Ł.: Hybrid-maximum neural network for depth analysis from stereo-image. In: Rutkowski, L., Scherer, R., Tadeusiewicz, R., Zadeh, L.A., Zurada, J.M. (eds.) ICAISC 2010. LNCS (LNAI), vol. 6114, pp. 47–55. Springer, Heidelberg (2010). https://doi.org/10.1007/978-3-642-13232-2_7
20. Laskowski, Ł.: Objects auto-selection from stereo-images realised by self-correcting neural network. In: Rutkowski, L., Korytkowski, M., Scherer, R., Tadeusiewicz, R., Zadeh, L.A., Zurada, J.M. (eds.) ICAISC 2012. LNCS (LNAI), vol. 7267, pp. 119–125. Springer, Heidelberg (2012). https://doi.org/10.1007/978-3-642-29347-4_14
21. Laskowski, Ł., Laskowska, M., Jelonkiewicz, J., Boullanger, A.: Spin-glass implementation of a hopfield neural structure. In: Rutkowski, L., Korytkowski, M., Scherer, R., Tadeusiewicz, R., Zadeh, L.A., Zurada, J.M. (eds.) ICAISC 2014. LNCS (LNAI), vol. 8467, pp. 89–96. Springer, Cham (2014). https://doi.org/10.1007/978-3-319-07173-2_9
22. Laskowski, Ł., Laskowska, M., Jelonkiewicz, J., Boullanger, A.: Molecular approach to hopfield neural network. In: Rutkowski, L., Korytkowski, M., Scherer, R., Tadeusiewicz, R., Zadeh, L.A., Zurada, J.M. (eds.) ICAISC 2015. LNCS (LNAI), vol. 9119, pp. 72–78. Springer, Cham (2015). https://doi.org/10.1007/978-3-319-19324-3_7
23. Laskowska, M., et al.: Functionalized mesoporous silica thin films as a tunable nonlinear optical material. Nanoscale **33**, 12110–12123 (2017)

24. Ludwig, S.A.: Applying a neural network ensemble to intrusion detection. J. Artif. Intell. Soft Comput. Res. **9**(3), 177–188 (2019)
25. Łapa, K., Cpałka, K., Wang, L.: New method for design of fuzzy systems for nonlinear modelling using different criteria of interpretability. In: Rutkowski, L., Korytkowski, M., Scherer, R., Tadeusiewicz, R., Zadeh, L.A., Zurada, J.M. (eds.) ICAISC 2014. LNCS (LNAI), vol. 8467, pp. 217–232. Springer, Cham (2014). https://doi.org/10.1007/978-3-319-07173-2_20
26. Łapa, K., Cpałka, K., Wang, L.: A method for nonlinear fuzzy modelling using population based algorithm with flexibly selectable operators. In: Rutkowski, L., Korytkowski, M., Scherer, R., Tadeusiewicz, R., Zadeh, L.A., Zurada, J.M. (eds.) ICAISC 2017. LNCS (LNAI), vol. 10245, pp. 263–278. Springer, Cham (2017). https://doi.org/10.1007/978-3-319-59063-9_24
27. Liang, J.J., Qu, B.Y., Suganthan, P.N., Hernández-Díaz, A.G.: Problem definitions and evaluation criteria for the CEC 2013 special session on real-parameter optimization. Technical report, Computational Intelligence Laboratory, Zhengzhou University, Zhengzhou, China and Nanyang Technological University, Singapore, **201212**(34), pp. 281–295 (2013)
28. Nobukawa, S., Nishimura, H., Yamanishi, T.: Pattern classification by spiking neural networks combining self-organized and reward-related spike-timing-dependent plasticity. J. Artif. Intell. Soft Comput. Res. **9**(4), 283–291 (2019)
29. Ono, K., Hanada, Y., Kumano, M., Kimura, M.: Enhancing Island model genetic programming by controlling frequent trees. J. Artif. Intell. Soft Comput. Res. **9**(1), 51–65 (2019)
30. Price, K.V.: Differential evolution. In: Dubitzky, W., Wolkenhauer, O., Cho, K.H., Yokota, H. (eds.) Handbook of Optimization, pp. 187–214. Springer, New York (2013). https://doi.org/10.1007/978-1-4419-9863-7_419
31. Rafajłowicz, W.: A hybrid differential evolution-gradient optimization method. In: Rutkowski, L., Korytkowski, M., Scherer, R., Tadeusiewicz, R., Zadeh, L.A., Zurada, J.M. (eds.) ICAISC 2015. LNCS (LNAI), vol. 9119, pp. 379–388. Springer, Cham (2015). https://doi.org/10.1007/978-3-319-19324-3_35
32. Rafajłowicz, W.: Cosmic rays inspired mutation in genetic algorithms. In: Rutkowski, L., Korytkowski, M., Scherer, R., Tadeusiewicz, R., Zadeh, L.A., Zurada, J.M. (eds.) ICAISC 2017. LNCS (LNAI), vol. 10245, pp. 418–426. Springer, Cham (2017). https://doi.org/10.1007/978-3-319-59063-9_37
33. Rafajłowicz, E., Rafajłowicz, W.: Fletcher's filter methodology as a soft selector in evolutionary algorithms for constrained optimization. In: Rutkowski, L., Korytkowski, M., Scherer, R., Tadeusiewicz, R., Zadeh, L.A., Zurada, J.M. (eds.) EC/SIDE -2012. LNCS, vol. 7269, pp. 333–341. Springer, Heidelberg (2012). https://doi.org/10.1007/978-3-642-29353-5_39
34. Rutkowski, L.: Computational Intelligence: Methods and Techniques. Springer, Heidelberg (2008). https://doi.org/10.1007/978-3-540-76288-1
35. Rutkowski, T., Romanowski, J., Woldan, P., Staszewski, P., Nielek, R., Rutkowski, L.: A content-based recommendation system using neuro-fuzzy approach. In: Proceedings of the 2018 IEEE International Conference on Fuzzy Systems (FUZZ-IEEE), Rio de Janeiro, pp. 1–8 (2018)
36. Rutkowski, T., Łapa, K., Jaworski, M., Nielek, R., Rutkowska, D.: On explainable flexible fuzzy recommender and its performance evaluation using the akaike information criterion. In: Gedeon, T., Wong, K.W., Lee, M. (eds.) ICONIP 2019. CCIS, vol. 1142, pp. 717–724. Springer, Cham (2019). https://doi.org/10.1007/978-3-030-36808-1_78

37. Sadiqbatcha, S., Jafarzadeh, S., Ampatzidis, Y.: Particle swarm optimization for solving a class of type-1 and type-2 fuzzy nonlinear equations. J. Artif. Intell. Soft Comput. Res. 8(2), 103–110 (2018)
38. Szczypta, J., Przybył, A., Cpałka, K.: Some aspects of evolutionary designing optimal controllers. In: Rutkowski, L., Korytkowski, M., Scherer, R., Tadeusiewicz, R., Zadeh, L.A., Zurada, J.M. (eds.) ICAISC 2013. LNCS (LNAI), vol. 7895, pp. 91–100. Springer, Heidelberg (2013). https://doi.org/10.1007/978-3-642-38610-7_9
39. Tan, Y., Zhu, Y.: Fireworks algorithm for optimization. In: Tan, Y., Shi, Y., Tan, K.C. (eds.) ICSI 2010. LNCS, vol. 6145, pp. 355–364. Springer, Heidelberg (2010). https://doi.org/10.1007/978-3-642-13495-1_44
40. Tambouratzis, G.: Using particle swarm optimization to accurately identify syntactic phrases in free text. J. Artif. Intell. Soft Comput. Res. 8(1), 63–77 (2018)
41. Tambouratzis, G., Vassiliou, M.: Swarm algorithms for NLP-the case of limited training data. J. Artif. Intell. Soft Comput. Res. 9(3), 219–234 (2019)
42. Yang, X.S., Deb, S., Cuckoo search via Lévy flights. In: 2009 World Congress on Nature & Biologically Inspired Computing (NaBIC, IEEE), pp. 210–214 (2009)
43. Yang, X.S., Bat algorithm: literature review and applications. arXiv preprint arXiv:1308.3900 (2013)
44. Younes, M., Khodja, F., Kherfane, R.L.: Multi-objective economic emission dispatch solution using hybrid FFA (firefly algorithm) and considering wind power penetration. Energy 67, 595–606 (2014)
45. Zalasiński, M., Cpałka, K.: Novel algorithm for the on-line signature verification using selected discretization points groups. In: Rutkowski, L., Korytkowski, M., Scherer, R., Tadeusiewicz, R., Zadeh, L.A., Zurada, J.M. (eds.) ICAISC 2013. LNCS (LNAI), vol. 7894, pp. 493–502. Springer, Heidelberg (2013). https://doi.org/10.1007/978-3-642-38658-9_44
46. Zalasiński, M., Cpałka, K.: New algorithm for on-line signature verification using characteristic hybrid partitions. In: Wilimowska, Z., Borzemski, L., Grzech, A., Świątek, J. (eds.) Information Systems Architecture and Technology: Proceedings of 36th International Conference on Information Systems Architecture and Technology – ISAT 2015 – Part IV. AISC, vol. 432, pp. 147–157. Springer, Cham (2016). https://doi.org/10.1007/978-3-319-28567-2_13
47. Zalasiński, M., Cpałka, K., Hayashi, Y.: New fast algorithm for the dynamic signature verification using global features values. In: Rutkowski, L., Korytkowski, M., Scherer, R., Tadeusiewicz, R., Zadeh, L.A., Zurada, J.M. (eds.) ICAISC 2015. LNCS (LNAI), vol. 9120, pp. 175–188. Springer, Cham (2015). https://doi.org/10.1007/978-3-319-19369-4_17
48. Zalasiński, M., Cpałka, K., Rakus-Andersson, E.: An idea of the dynamic signature verification based on a hybrid approach. In: Rutkowski, L., Korytkowski, M., Scherer, R., Tadeusiewicz, R., Zadeh, L.A., Zurada, J.M. (eds.) ICAISC 2016. LNCS (LNAI), vol. 9693, pp. 232–246. Springer, Cham (2016). https://doi.org/10.1007/978-3-319-39384-1_21

A Markov Process Approach
to Redundancy in Genetic Algorithms

Wojciech Rafajłowicz[✉]

Department of Computer Engineering,
Wroclaw University of Science and Technology, Wroclaw, Poland
`wojciech.rafajlowicz@pwr.edu.pl`

Abstract. We propose and investigate two Markov chain models in order to provide recommendations on the selection of genotype redundant encoding schemes in genetic algorithms (GA). It was deduced from these Markov chains why classic encoding methods lead to a insufficiently broad search of GA's. Then, modifications, concerning additional redundancy in genotype encoding algorithms, are proposed and investigated regarding its influence on mutations and recombinations. Finally, the results of extensive simulation studies are reported that indicate classes of goal functions for which these modifications provide better search results and/or smaller variances of them.

Keywords: Genetic algorithms · Redundancy · Markov processes

1 Introduction

The simplicity of a simulated, genetic evolution as an optimization method holds researchers' attention and is the subject of current investigations [11,12,14,17, 23,23,24]. Even though it consists of a small number of easy steps, this methods have proved useful in many different fields.

The representation of a decision variable in most optimization problems is generally very simplistic. It consists of a simple, binary representation of each dimension by the finite number of bits in the genotype. Of course, when representation of non-numeric data is required e.g. in the traveling salesman problem (TSP), other methods like permutation encoding are required. A good survey of encoding problems is presented in [16].

Biological genomes work in a more complicated manner. It is more of a quaternary notation. It is a well-known fact that four DNA nucleotides form A-T (adenine – thymine) and G-C (cytosine – guanine) pairs. These base pairs not only allow DNA replication but also allow for a certain redundancy in the genome sequence.

Some work into investigating redundancy was carried out by implementing dominance/recessiveness mechanism in biological genotype, see [4,5,7]. A broad survey of further development can be found in [2].

© Springer Nature Switzerland AG 2020
L. Rutkowski et al. (Eds.): ICAISC 2020, LNAI 12415, pp. 445–453, 2020.
https://doi.org/10.1007/978-3-030-61401-0_41

In the case of TSP redundancy (many genotypes encoding a single route) is considered as problem and methods of avoiding it are presented in [18]. On the other hand in paper [19] trivial voting is shown to provide improvement over simple genetic mapping. A more general, experimental analysis was carried out in [22].

In previous papers regarding redundancy, simple methods of mutation were used. A simple mutation is realized as the probability of changing each bit in a simulated genotype. This method is based on DNA replication errors. But these are not the only cause of mutagenesis. Other factors like radiation, can cause much larger changes due to an error-prone DNA autorepair mechanism. We can simulate this by a mechanism proposed in the next section.

Markov models were previously used in modeling behavior of genetic algorithms in the context of a general framework like [9] or investigating possibilities of parallelization [6]. A very similar method to that presented in this paper was used in [13]. Markov models were also used to investigate separated parts of a genetic algorithm (GA) like the selection process in [3], but our goals are different than in the latter paper. Those methods must not be confused with using Markov models as models of some processes and genetic algorithms as an optimization method.

A typical genetic algorithm, in each epoch, selects a group of better performing solutions. Each pair of these is recombined (crossed over) and the resulting new solutions are mutated. This process is repeated until a new population has been achieved of the desired size.

In this paper we will concentrate on genotype encoding. The outline is as follows. In Sect. 2 a redundant, triple-voting encoding is proposed and its behavior during mutation is investigated. In Sect. 3 only recombination-related behaviors are studied. Additionally, numerical simulations in Sect. 4 show how mutation and recombination behave together.

2   Proposed Redundant Genotype Encoding

Even though a redundant, triple-voting scheme for genotype encoding is named trivial in many papers, a multitude of possible configurations can be proposed. The simplest scheme for triple voting is shown in Fig. 1. This method is very robust, and calculations had shown that it is nearly impossible to have phenotype

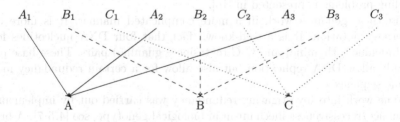

Fig. 1. Redundancy with redundant bits distributed.

change even in case of a large mutation. If we consider a genotype to be a random string of bits with equal probability between **0** and **1** (a coin toss is a typical example) then a simple analysis reveals that the probability of A being **1** is still $\frac{1}{2}$. What is of interest for us here is the probability that a single mutation in a redundant genotype would change the outcome, i.e. the result of voting.

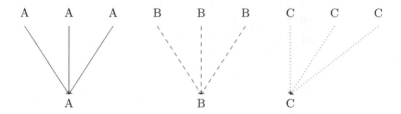

Fig. 2. Redundancy with redundant bits clustered.

We investigate how a triple-redundant bit (so three bits in a genotype) change during mutations in order to compare redundant and non-redundant encoding. Let us denote a probability of any single genotype bit mutation by p. Then we must also assume that all bit's mutations are independent. Finally, we consider triple bits forming a resulting bit. From a mutation point of view, we can clearly see that whichever of the previously proposed layouts is used, the result would be the same.

Since we assumed that mutations are independent then the probability that the n bits would be mutated in a triple is

$$p^n \cdot (1 - p)^{3-n}. \tag{1}$$

We can describe this in the form of a stochastic process with A_1^i, A_2^i, A_3^i being possible states of the three bits at time i. Then $A^i = [A_1^i, A_2^i, A_3^i]$ is triple $A^i = [A_1, A_2, A_3]$ is a process state at time i. We can calculate the probability of changing state at time $i + 1$ to any given state. We must also note that there is no memory in that process – future behavior of a system depends only on current state A^i and not the previous ones $A^{i-1}, ... A^0$. So this process has a Markov property and it can be described using a method devised for Markov processes.

In order to formulate a process's transition matrix, we must label states. The simplest solution is to use a natural binary code so a state number (starting from 0) would be our triple in the binary representation. Our three bits $[A_1^i, A_2^i, A_3^i]$ code a single number.

Table 1 shows the number of required bit changes to change the state. The probabilities of changing states can be calculated using Eq. (1). Probabilities of transition between states form an 8×8 matrix hereafter denoted by P. It can be easily shown that the resulting matrix is a doubly stochastic matrix e.a. both columns and rows sum up to probability 1. Additionally, all states are reachable

Table 1. Number of mutations required to change the state.

	000	001	010	011	100	101	110	111
000	0	1	1	2	1	2	2	3
001	1	0	2	1	2	1	3	2
010	1	2	0	1	2	3	1	2
011	2	1	1	0	3	2	2	1
100	1	2	2	3	0	1	1	2
101	2	1	3	2	1	0	2	1
110	2	3	1	2	1	2	0	1
111	3	2	2	1	2	1	1	0

so the transition can occur (possibly with a different probability) from any state to any other state.

What interests us the most is the distribution of the resulting states. Especially a question one has to ask: is any one of them dominant. The solution is given by a stationary distribution of the Markov process with P as the transition matrix. Conditions for the existence of a stationary distribution of such processes can be found in [1]. In order to calculate this distribution, further denoted by π, we must calculate

$$P\pi = \pi. \tag{2}$$

So vector π is an eigenvector of matrix P associated with eigenvalue 1. It is obvious that vector π can be multiplied by scalar constant.

After calculating we have $\pi = [\frac{1}{8}, \frac{1}{8}, \frac{1}{8}, \frac{1}{8}, \frac{1}{8}, \frac{1}{8}, \frac{1}{8}, \frac{1}{8}]$. From this we can arrive at some conclusions for the mutation process.

- After a large (theoretically infinite) number of mutations, the proportion of each state in a population is the same in the genotype. Since half of the states translate to 1 and other half to 0 (see Fig. 1 and 2) we do not have any skewness.
- A genotype has the number of zeros and ones close to each other. It is very difficult for a genotype to achieve a different distribution (for example a larger number of 0). It is true also for a traditional genotype. This is why much more complicated genotype-phenotype mappings are proposed.
- For 75% of the population one mutation is enough to change state from 0 to 1 or vice versa. This part of the population behaves like a standard, non-redundant genotype.

3   Recombination

In the previous section, the distribution of redundant bits was irrelevant. It becomes a factor when investigating the recombination of two genotypes. Again, only one triple-redundant bit is considered. This means that we compare triple-redundant encoding with single-bit encoding only. We construct a different Markov chain in this section.

Let us investigate the more obvious solution from Fig. 1. A simple crossing can have one of the following possibilities:

- The crossing point would lay inside any of three redundant genotypes. Only this one would be crossed, the other two will not change.
- The crossing point would be between genotypes – even less change.

These facts suggest (as will subsequent simulations show) that this form of redundancy is highly robust to any change. It might be a good feature for living organism DNA but not in genetic optimization.

The other proposed form (see Fig. 2) is much more interesting.

$$
\begin{array}{cccc}
 & A & B & C \\
\times & \times & \times & \times \\
 & X & Y & Z
\end{array}
$$

Fig. 3. Possible crossing points ABC with XYZ.

Inside our redundant triple, a recombination can occur at points marked by a cross in Fig. 3. In normal recombination, these points are equally probable.

In order to investigate properties of this crossing let us consider two triples (as in Fig. 3) jointly denoted $ABCXYZ$ of bits up to a total of six. Let us for example consider $\frac{101}{011}$. As a result we can have $\frac{101}{011}$, $\frac{111}{001}$, $\frac{011}{101}$ and $\frac{011}{101}$ with equal probability. We also see that two different points lead to the same resulting state. This reasoning can be done for all possible combinations of bits up to a total of 64. Thus the transition matrix will be 64×64. It is inconvenient to write it down as in the previous situation. We can plot it instead due to the exact numbers in it. In Fig. 4 a darker color corresponds to a higher probability of transition.

Clearly, we can see that most combinations of bits have a high probability of staying in the current state – crossing leads to a lack of change.

For a recombination transition matrix more then one stationary distribution exists. Overall there are 18 of these. We use the same technique to visualize them as a transition matrix.

In Fig. 5 we can clearly see that a triple would have a tendency to spread evenly with each one keeping just a few accessible states. Only the marginal of these (all zeros and all ones) stay in their state wherever crossing occurs. This, in conjunction with the previous section regarding mutation, allows us to conclude that redundancy reduces the probability of change – a genotype is more robust. This feature in nature is helpful – most mutations are not positive. In optimization, we want more change. Again there is no simple way to change the total number of 0 or 1 in recombination. In Fig. 4 the lower left and upper right corners are empty.

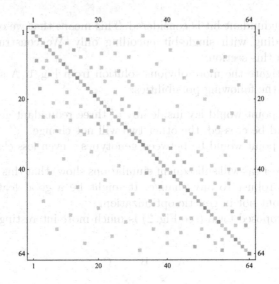

Fig. 4. The transition matrix for redundant crossing.

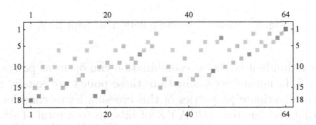

Fig. 5. All of the stationary distributions for a transition matrix in recombination. Each possible distribution (number on the vertical axis) is depicted as a horizontal line where one square depicting probability for each state (subsequent number in the horizontal axis).

4   Numerical Results

The corollaries justified in Sects. 2 and 3 lead to the following conclusion: we can expect that behavior of the redundant coding scheme would be similar to that of a traditional genotype with a smaller crossing probability. The forgotten fact in that reasoning is the effect of additional robustness on evolution of the system.

The comparison between different methods is usually done by standard test functions known as benchmarks. Generally, these test functions can be found in research papers like [10] or [15] and we shall use the well-known names of the test functions. Typical benchmark problems require us to find the minimum of the specified function. Additionally, most versions of genetic algorithm can work only for $f \geq 0$ and look for the maximum of the function.

A well known solution to this problem is to find $C \geq f(x)$, $x \in X$ and find the maximum of

$$g(x) = C - f(x) \tag{3}$$

The results of simulations that are presented below come from test runs, data averaged over 50 trial runs with a 300 bit genotype, 10 dimensions, 150 elements in population and 50 iterations. We must remember that the final results and their accuracy are not under investigation here. We want to compare two genotype encodings, not assess the effectiveness of the genetic algorithm.

The results for a traditional genotype are shown in Table 2.

Table 2. Results for traditional genotype encoding.

Pcross	Ackley		Ball		Rastrigin		Rosenbrock		Schwefel	
	f	3σ	f	3σ	f	3σ	f	3σ	f	3σ
0.01	83.42	3.34	48.9	1.38	9922	35	9906	92.6	8829	710
0.02	83.53	3.29	48.9	1.15	9921	36.4	9904	97.3	8818	908
0.05	83.35	3.06	48.9	1.30	9923	37.9	9886	143.3	8822	779
0.1	83.43	2.98	48.9	1.12	9921	33.2	9890	108.7	8809	731
0.15	83.25	3.06	48.9	1.07	9919	25.7	9905	104.1	8851	745
0.2	83.05	2.83	48.9	1.41	9921	31.5	9907	95.4	8846	810

In case of a redundant genotype, the results are shown in Table 3.

We can compare results between these two representations. It is clearly visible that for a simple sphere (ball) and Ackley function the results are almost identical with slightly smaller variance between trial runs. In the case of the Rosenbrock function, results for the redundant genotype are slightly worse, with larger variance. This atypical behavior can be attributed to a very narrow valley of multidimensional test function. In case of the Rastrigin function the redundant results are better (9929 maximum value versus 9923) with 30% smaller

Table 3. Results for benchmark functions in case of redundant encoding for different crossing probabilities.

Pcross	Ackley		Ball		Rastrigin		Rosenbrock		Schwefel	
	f	3σ	f	3σ	f	3σ	f	3σ	f	3σ
0.01	83.9	3.37	48.6	1.33	9927	29.7	9900	94.4	8664	779
0.02	83.7	2.64	48.6	1.09	9884	88.5	8510	573	9926	27.3
0.05	83.89	2.71	48.2	1.22	9929	26.18	9843	129	8323	580
0.1	83.77	2.29	48.1	1.42	9927	20	9827	146	8219	494
0.15	83.89	3.09	48	1.51	9929	23.3	9822	151	8158	438.
0.2	83.8	2.12	48.1	1.53	9926	24.63	9809	163	8125	481

variance. Direct comparison can be seen in Fig. 6 In case of another multimodal function – Schwefel function results aren't surprising. Maximum function values are smaller as is the variance of the result.

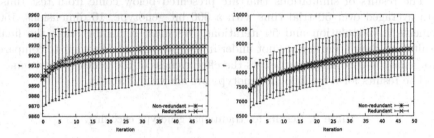

Fig. 6. Comparison between redundant and non-redundant genotype for commonly used $p = 0.15$ in case of the Rastrigin function and Schwefel function.

5   Conclusion

In the paper, theoretical results regarding redundant genotypes were provided representing mutation and recombination as Markov processes in order to investigate the algorithm properties. As a result, we concluded that redundant notation will lower mutation and recombination rates but increase the robustness of population elements.

We should take into account that both operators were investigated separately. In most cases absorbing states of crossover can be left by mutation and unreachable can be entered in the same way.

In the experimental part, it was shown that these conclusions were not contradicted by trial runs. An insight into types of benchmark functions had shown when such behavior can give a positive increase of the efficiency of genetic algorithms.

This approach can be modified into use in swarm algorithms like in [20,21] or in differential evolution [8].

References

1. Allen, L.J.S.: An Introduction to Stochastic Processes with Applications to Biology. CRC Press, Boca Raton (2010)
2. Bhasin, H., Mehta, S.: On the applicability of diploid genetic algorithms. AI Soc. **31**(2), 265–274 (2016)
3. Chakraborty, U.K., Deb, K., Chakraborty, M.: Analysis of selection algorithms: a Markov chain approach. Evol. Comput. **4**(2), 133–167 (1996)
4. Chiam, S.C., Goh, C.K., Tan, K.C.: Issues of binary representation in evolutionary algorithms. In: 2006 IEEE Conference on Cybernetics and Intelligent Systems. IEEE (2006)

5. Chiam, S.C., et al.: Improving locality in binary representation via redundancy. IEEE Trans. Syst. Man Cybern. Part B Cybern. **38**(3), 808–825 (2008)
6. Cantú-Paz, E.: Markov chain models of parallel genetic algorithms. IEEE Trans. Evol. Comput. **4**(3), 216–226 (2000)
7. Collingwood, E., Corne, D., Ross, P.: Useful diversity via multiploidy. In: Proceedings of IEEE International Conference on Evolutionary Computation 1996. IEEE (1996)
8. Dawar, D., Ludwig, S.A.: Effect of strategy adaptation on differential evolution in presence and absence of parameter adaptation: an investigation. J. Artif. Intell. Soft Comput. Res. **8**(3), 211–235 (2018)
9. Davis, T.E., Principe, J.C.: A Markov chain framework for the simple genetic algorithm. Evol. Comput. **1**(3), 269–288 (1993)
10. Eiben, A.E., Bäck, T.: Empirical investigation of multi-parent recombination operators in evolution strategies. Evol. Comput. **5**(3), 347–365 (1997)
11. Leon, M., Xiong, N.: ADAPTING DIFFERENTIAL evolution algorithms for continuous optimization via greedy adjustment of control parameters. J. Artif. Intell. Soft Comput. Res. **6**(2), 103–118 (2016)
12. Mizera, M., Nowotarski, P., Byrski, A., Kisiel-Dorohinicki, M.: Fine tuning of agent-based evolutionary computing. J. Artif. Intell. Soft Comput. Res. **9**(2), 81–97 (2019)
13. Nix, A.E., Vose, M.D.: Modeling genetic algorithms with Markov chains. Ann. Math. Artif. Intell. **5**(1), 79–88 (1992)
14. Ono, K., Hanada, Y., Kumano, M., Kimura, M.: Enhancing Island model genetic programming by controlling frequent trees. J. Artif. Intell. Soft Comput. Res. **9**(1), 51–65 (2019)
15. Ortiz-Boyer, D., Hervás-Martínez, C., García-Pedrajas, N.: CIXL2: a crossover operator for evolutionary algorithms based on population features. J. Artif. Intell. Res. (JAIR) **24**, 1–48 (2005)
16. Ronald, S.: Robust encodings in genetic algorithms: a survey of encoding issues. IEEE International Conference on Evolutionary Computation 1997. IEEE (1997)
17. Rotar, C., Iantovics, L.: Directed evolution - a new metaheuristc for optimization. J. Artif. Intell. Soft Comput. Res. **7**(3), 183–200 (2017)
18. Simon, S., Asenstorfer, J., Millist, V.: Representational redundancy in evolutionary algorithms. In: IEEE International Conference on Evolutionary Computation 1995, vol. 2. IEEE (1995)
19. Shackleton, M., Shipma, R., Ebner, M.: An investigation of rredundant genotype-phenotype mappings and their role in evolutionary search. In: Proceedings of the 2000 Congress on Evolutionary Computation 2000, vol. 1. IEEE (2000)
20. Tambouratzis, G.: Using particle swarm optimization to accurately identify syntactic phrases in free text. J. Artif. Intell. Soft Comput. Res. **8**(1), 63–77 (2018)
21. Tambouratzis, G., Vassiliou, M.: Swarm algorithms for NLP - the case of limited training data. J. Artif. Intell. Soft Comput. Res. **9**(3), 219–234 (2019)
22. Weicker, K., Weicker, N.: Burden and benefits of redundancy. Found. Genet. Algorithms **6**, 313–333 (2001)
23. Yang, C., Moi, S., Lin, Y., Chuang, L.: Genetic algorithm combined with a local search method for identifying susceptibility genes. J. Artif. Intell. Soft Comput. Res. **6**(3), 203–212 (2016)
24. Yin, Z., O'Sullivan, C., Brabazon, A.: An analysis of the performance of genetic programming for realised volatility forecasting. J. Artif. Intell. Soft Comput. Res. **6**(3), 155–172 (2016)

Fuzzy Control of Exploration and Exploitation Trade-Off with On-Line Convergence Rate Estimation in Evolutionary Algorithms

Adam Slowik[✉]

Department of Electronics and Computer Science, Koszalin University of Technology,
Sniadeckich 2 Street, 75-453 Koszalin, Poland
aslowik@ie.tu.koszalin.pl

Abstract. In this paper, the fuzzy control of exploration and exploitation trade-off with on-line convergence rate estimation in evolutionary algorithms is presented. We introduce to the proposed algorithm three fuzzy systems (Mamdani type-1). These fuzzy systems are responsible for controlling the parameters of an evolutionary algorithm, such as selection pressure, crossover probability and mutation probability. While creating the fuzzy rules in the proposed fuzzy systems, we assumed that, at the start, the algorithm should possess maximal exploration property (low selection pressure, high mutation probability, and high crossover probability), while at the end, the algorithm should possesses maximal exploitation property (high selection pressure, low mutation probability, and low crossover probability). Also, in the paper we propose a method for estimating the algorithm convergence rate value. The proposed approach is verified using test functions chosen from literature. The results obtained using the proposed method are compared with the results obtained using evolutionary algorithms with a different selection operator, and standard values for crossover and mutation probability.

1 Introduction

In evolutionary algorithms the trade-off between exploration and exploitation is very important [1]. This problem has been of interest to researchers for decades and is still worth exploring by scientists [2]. The balance between exploration and exploitation of the solutions search space can be controlled using such factors as selection pressure, probability of mutation, and probability of crossover [3]. We know that if we change the value of selection pressure, then the balance between exploration and exploitation of solutions space will also change [4]. When the selection pressure is low, the solutions space is "widely" searched (the algorithm possesses higher exploration properties). However, when selection pressure is high, the solutions space is "locally" searched by the algorithm (the algorithm possesses higher exploitation properties). In literature, we can

© Springer Nature Switzerland AG 2020
L. Rutkowski et al. (Eds.): ICAISC 2020, LNAI 12415, pp. 454–463, 2020.
https://doi.org/10.1007/978-3-030-61401-0_42

find papers where the selection pressure was controlled in order to obtain a suitable balance between exploration and exploitation properties in evolutionary algorithm. In the paper [5], the method for steering the selection pressure in each iteration of evolutionary algorithm is presented. In [6], the author proposes an extension of the method presented in [5]. The proposed extension involves adding the fuzzy system for the automatic control of the value of the α parameter, which is responsible for the value of the selection pressure in the method presented in [5]. If crossover and mutation probabilities are properly selected, the higher value corresponds to a more global search of solutions in the search space (the algorithm possesses a higher property for the exploration of solutions space). If the values of crossover and mutation probabilities are lower, then the solutions space is searched in a more locally manner (the algorithm possesses a higher property for the exploitation of solutions space). In literature, we can find papers where the values of crossover and mutation probabilities are controlled in evolutionary algorithms. In the paper [12], the value of mutation probability is controlled by chromosome similarity. In [13], the authors propose dynamic changes of mutation probability based on population stability. Lin et al. [14] present generic scheme for adapting crossover and mutation probabilities. The crossover and mutation rates are adapted in response to the evaluation results of the respective offspring in the next generation. The paper [15] presents the crossover probability selection technique based on population diversity. The fuzzy logic controller is used for the proper selection of the crossover operator and its probability. Khmeleva et al. [16] propose a fuzzy logic controlled genetic algorithm. Based on such parameters as fitness diversity in population, chromosome diversity, and the number of iterations with unchanged fitness, the new values of crossover and mutation rates are computed using the fuzzy logic controller [17,18]. In this paper, an extension of the method described in [6] is presented. This extension involves the application of additional fuzzy systems to control the mutation and crossover probabilities. Due to additional fuzzy controllers, the three factors, including selection pressure, probability of mutation, and probability of crossover, are simultaneously used for steering the balance between the exploration and exploitation of solutions space in the proposed method. Additionally, we also propose a simple metric to quickly estimate the normalized value of the convergence rate of the evolutionary algorithm. The proposed approaches were tested using test functions chosen from literature (CEC benchmarks [7,8]). The results obtained using the proposed approaches were compared with the results obtained using evolutionary algorithms with different selection schemes and standard values of mutation probability and crossover probability.

The method presented in this paper is known as F^3MIX (Three Fuzzy Mix Method). The presentation of the paper is as follows: in Sect. 2 we present the F^3MIX method, in Sect. 3 we present the estimation of the convergence rate, in Sect. 4 we present the assumed test functions, in Sect. 5 we present some experimental results, and finally in Sect. 6 we present the conclusions.

2   F^{3}MIX Method

The F^{3}MIX method is an extension of the FMIX method [6] with elitist strategy, and it operates as follows. In the F^{3}MIX method there are three fuzzy systems (OR - Min, AND - Max, Mamdani type-1 with defuzzification as the center of gravity method). First for selection pressure control, second for mutation probability control, and third for crossover probability control. Each of these systems possesses two inputs and one output. The inputs are the same for all systems. The first input is a GP (Generation Percentage) and is computed as follows:

$$GP = \frac{T}{T_{max}} \tag{1}$$

where: T is a current number of iteration, T_{max} is an assumed maximal number of iterations.

The second input is an NPD (Normalized Population Diversity) and is computed as follows:

$$NPD = \frac{PD - PD_{min}}{PD_{max} - PD_{min} + \epsilon} \tag{2}$$

where: NPD is a normalized value of population diversity, PD_{min} is a minimal value of population diversity (we have assumed that the PD_{min} is equal to 0; it is in the case when all individuals in populations are the same), PD_{max} is a maximal value of population diversity obtained until now, ϵ is a small positive number (we assume ϵ equal to 10^{-6}), PD is a current population diversity and is computed as follows:

$$PD = \sum_{p=1}^{P} \sum_{r=1}^{R} (x_{p,r} - c_p)^2 \tag{3}$$

where: $x_{p,r}$ is a value of p-th decision variable in the r-th individual, P is a number of variables in the optimized function, R is a number of individuals in population, c_p is a mean value of the p-th decision variable. The c_p is computed as follows:

$$c_p = \frac{\sum_{r=1}^{R} x_{p,r}}{R} \tag{4}$$

The linguistic variable GP and NPD possesses five linguistic values: Low (L), Low Medium (LM), Medium (M), High Medium (HM), and High (H). The shape of the fuzzy terms for these variables is shown in Fig. 1a.

2.1   Fuzzy Control of Selection Pressure

This fuzzy system possesses one output, which is represented by the linguistic variable α. The $\alpha \in [-1; 1]$ is a parameter, which is responsible for the selection

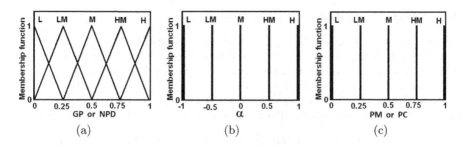

Fig. 1. Graphical representation of fuzzy sets, which represent: the input linguistic values GP or NPD (a), the output linguistic value α (b), the output linguistic values PM or PC (c)

pressure in mix selection [5]. Using the value of α parameter, the values of relative fitness for all individuals in the population are calculated as follows:

◇ for the best individual (if $\alpha \geq 0$)

$$rfn_{max} = rf_{max} + \alpha \cdot (1 - rf_{max}) \tag{5}$$

◇ for others individuals (if $\alpha \geq 0$)

$$rfn = rf \cdot (1 - \alpha) \tag{6}$$

◇ for all individuals (if $\alpha < 0$)

$$rfn = rf + \alpha \cdot \left(rf - \frac{1}{R}\right) \tag{7}$$

where: rfn_{max} is a new relative fitness of the best individual, rf_{max} is an old relative fitness of the best individual, rfn is a new relative fitness of the chosen individual, rf is an old relative fitness of the chosen individual, α is a value of the scaling factor $\alpha \in [-1; 1]$, R is a number of individuals in the population.

The linguistic variable α possesses five linguistic values: Low (L), Low Medium (LM), Medium (M), High Medium (HM), and High (H). The shape of the fuzzy terms for this variable is shown in Fig. 1b. The knowledge database for α control (KB_α) consists of 25 fuzzy rules, which are as follows:

$$KB_\alpha = \left\{ \begin{array}{l} (^L_L L)_1, (^L_{LM} L)_2, (^L_M LM)_3, (^L_{HM} M)_4, (^L_H M)_5, \\ (^{LM}_L L)_6, (^{LM}_{LM} LM)_7, (^{LM}_M M)_8, (^{LM}_{HM} M)_9, (^{LM}_H M)_{10}, \\ (^M_L LM)_{11}, (^M_{LM} M)_{12}, (^M_M M)_{13}, (^M_{HM} M)_{14}, (^M_H HM)_{15}, \\ (^{HM}_L M)_{16}, (^{HM}_{LM} M)_{17}, (^{HM}_M M)_{18}, (^{HM}_{HM} HM)_{19}, (^{HM}_H H)_{20}, \\ (^H_L M)_{21}, (^H_{LM} M)_{22}, (^H_M HM)_{23}, (^H_{HM} H)_{24}, (^H_H H)_{25} \end{array} \right\} \tag{8}$$

For example, the first rule $(^L_L L)_1$ from the KB_α can be decoded as $Rule_1$: If (GP is L) and (NPD is L) Then α is L.

2.2 Fuzzy Control of Mutation Probability

This fuzzy system possesses one output, which is represented by the linguistic variable PM. The $PM \in [0; 1]$ is a parameter, which is responsible for the mutation probability in the evolutionary algorithm. The linguistic variable PM possesses five linguistic values: Low (L), Low Medium (LM), Medium (M), High Medium (HM), and High (H). The shape of the fuzzy terms for this variable is shown in Fig. 1c. The knowledge database for PM control (KB_{PM}) consists of 25 fuzzy rules, which are as follows:

$$
KB_{PM} = \left\{
\begin{array}{l}
(^L_L H)_1, (^L_{LM} H)_2, (^L_M HM)_3, (^L_{HM} M)_4, (^L_H M)_5, \\
(^{LM}_L H)_6, (^{LM}_{LM} HM)_7, (^{LM}_M M)_8, (^{LM}_{HM} M)_9, (^{LM}_H M)_{10}, \\
(^M_L HM)_{11}, (^M_{LM} M)_{12}, (^M_M M)_{13}, (^M_{HM} M)_{14}, (^M_H LM)_{15}, \\
(^{HM}_L M)_{16}, (^{HM}_{LM} M)_{17}, (^{HM}_M M)_{18}, (^{HM}_{HM} LM)_{19}, (^{HM}_H L)_{20}, \\
(^H_L M)_{21}, (^H_{LM} M)_{22}, (^H_M LM)_{23}, (^H_{HM} L)_{24}, (^H_H L)_{25}
\end{array}
\right\} \tag{9}
$$

For example, the second rule $(^L_{LM} H)_2$ from the KB_{PM} can be decoded as $Rule_2$: If (GP is L) and (NPD is LM) Then PM is H.

2.3 Fuzzy Control of Crossover Probability

This fuzzy system possesses one output, which is represented by the linguistic variable PC. The $PC \in [0; 1]$ is a parameter, which is responsible for the crossover probability in the evolutionary algorithm. The linguistic variable PC possesses five linguistic values: Low (L), Low Medium (LM), Medium (M), High Medium (HM), and High (H). The shape of the fuzzy terms for this variable is shown in Fig. 1c. The knowledge database for PC control (KB_{PC}) consists of 25 fuzzy rules, which are as follows:

$$
KB_{PC} = \left\{
\begin{array}{l}
(^L_L H)_1, (^L_{LM} H)_2, (^L_M HM)_3, (^L_{HM} HM)_4, (^L_H M)_5, \\
(^{LM}_L H)_6, (^{LM}_{LM} HM)_7, (^{LM}_M HM)_8, (^{LM}_{HM} M)_9, (^{LM}_H LM)_{10}, \\
(^M_L HM)_{11}, (^M_{LM} HM)_{12}, (^M_M M)_{13}, (^M_{HM} LM)_{14}, (^M_H LM)_{15}, \\
(^{HM}_L HM)_{16}, (^{HM}_{LM} M)_{17}, (^{HM}_M LM)_{18}, (^{HM}_{HM} LM)_{19}, (^{HM}_H L)_{20}, \\
(^H_L M)_{21}, (^H_{LM} LM)_{22}, (^H_M LM)_{23}, (^H_{HM} L)_{24}, (^H_H L)_{25}
\end{array}
\right\} \tag{10}
$$

For example, the third rule $(^L_M HM)_3$ from the KB_{PC} can be decoded as $Rule_3$: If (GP is L) and (NPD is M) Then PC is HM.

3 Estimation of Convergence Rate

The idea for estimating the convergence rate is based on a window with equal size W (we assume $W = 100$), in which the average values of objective function for successive iterations are stored. Based on the data from the window, we approximate this data (using the least-squares method) to the linear function. The maximum absolute value of the directional coefficient obtained until now is stored in a_{max} variable. In each iteration, the normalized value of convergence rate NCR is computed as follows:

$$
NCR = \frac{a_{max} - |a|}{a_{max}} \tag{11}
$$

where: $|a|$ is an absolute value of the directional coefficient obtained in the current algorithm iteration. The value of NCR is from the range $[0; 1]$. The NCR value is higher when the algorithm is more converged into the prescribed value.

4   Assumed Test Functions

The 15 test functions were chosen from literature [7,8] to verify the proposed method. The symbols for individual test functions are as follows: GM is a global minimal value, n is a number of decision variables. The presented functions are currently widely used as benchmarks for quality testing of evolutionary methods (CEC 2005 and 2014 benchmarks [7,8]). The properties of individual test functions are written in brackets after the test function name. The symbols in brackets have the following meaning: U – unimodal function, M – multimodal function, S – separable function, N – non-separable function. In all test functions the evolutionary algorithm tends to minimize their values.

◇ De Jong function F1: (U, S)
$\sum_{i=1}^{n} x_i^2$; $-100 \leq x_i \leq 100$; GM $= 0$ in $(x_1, x_2, ..., x_{50}) = (0, 0, ..., 0)$; $n = 50$

◇ Ackley function F2: (M, N)
$20 - 20 \cdot \exp\left(-0.2 \cdot \sqrt{\frac{1}{n} \cdot \sum_{i=1}^{n} x_i^2}\right) + \exp(1) - \exp\left(\frac{1}{n} \cdot \sum_{i=1}^{n} \cos\left(2 \cdot \pi \cdot x_i\right)\right)$;
$-100 \leq x_i \leq 100$; GM $= 0$ in $(x_1, x_2, ..., x_{50}) = (0, 0, ..., 0)$; $n = 50$

◇ Griewank function F3: (M, N)
$\frac{1}{4000} \cdot \sum_{i=1}^{n} x_i^2 - \prod_{i=1}^{n} \cos\left(\frac{x_i}{\sqrt{i}}\right) + 1$
$-600 \leq x_i \leq 600$; GM $= 0$ in $(x_1, x_2, ..., x_{50}) = (0, 0, ..., 0)$; $n = 50$

◇ Rastrigin function F4: (M, S)
$10 \cdot n + \sum_{i=1}^{n} \left(x_i^2 - 10 \cdot \cos\left(2 \cdot \pi \cdot x_i\right)\right)$
$-500 \leq x_i \leq 500$; GM $= 0$ in $(x_1, x_2, ..., x_{50}) = (0, 0, ..., 0)$; $n = 50$

◇ Schwefel function F5: (M, S)
$418.9828872724339 \cdot n - \sum_{i=1}^{n} \left(x_i \cdot \sin\left(\sqrt{|x_i|}\right)\right)$
$-500 \leq x_i \leq 500$; GM $= 0$ in $(x_1, x_2, ..., x_{20}) = (420.96874636, ..., 420.96874636)$; $n = 20$

◇ HappyCat function F6: (M, N)
$|\sum_{i=1}^{n} x_i^2 - n|^{0.25} + \frac{\left(0.5 \cdot \sum_{i=1}^{n} x_i^2 + \sum_{i=1}^{n} x_i\right)}{n} + 0.5$
$-100 \leq x_i \leq 100$; GM $= 0$ in $(x_1, x_2, ..., x_{50}) = (-1, -1, ..., -1)$; $n = 50$

◇ Non-Continuous Rastrigin function F7: (M, S)
$\sum_{i=1}^{n} \left(y^2 - 10 \cdot \cos\left(2 \cdot \pi \cdot y_i\right) + 10\right)$; $y_i = \begin{cases} x_i, & \text{when } |x_i| < 0.5 \\ round\left(2 \cdot x_i\right)/2, & \text{when } |x_i| \geq 0.5 \end{cases}$
$-500 \leq x_i \leq 500$; GM $= 0$ in $(x_1, x_2, ..., x_{50}) = (0, 0, ..., 0)$; $n = 50$

◇ Non-Continuous Expanded Schaffer function F8: (M, S)
$F\left(y_1, y_2\right) + F\left(y_2, y_3\right) + ... + F\left(y_{n-1}, y_n\right) + F\left(y_n, y_1\right)$; $F\left(x, y\right) = 0.5 + \frac{\left(sin^2\left(\sqrt{x^2+y^2}\right) - 0.5\right)}{\left(1 + 0.001 \cdot \left(x^2 + y^2\right)\right)^2}$
$y_i = \begin{cases} x_i, & \text{when } |x_i| < 0.5 \\ round\left(2 \cdot x_i\right)/2, & \text{when } |x_i| \geq 0.5 \end{cases}$
$-500 \leq x_i \leq 500$; GM $= 0$ in $(x_1, x_2, ..., x_{50}) = (0, 0, ..., 0)$; $n = 50$

◇ Rotated Expanded Schaffer function F9: (M, N)
$F\left(x_1, x_2\right) + F\left(x_2, x_3\right) + ... + F\left(x_{n-1}, x_n\right) + F\left(x_n, x_1\right)$; $F\left(x, y\right) = 0.5 + \frac{\left(sin^2\left(\sqrt{x^2+y^2}\right) - 0.5\right)}{\left(1 + 0.001 \cdot \left(x^2 + y^2\right)\right)^2}$ $-500 \leq x_i \leq 500$; GM $= 0$ in $(x_1, x_2, ..., x_{50}) = (0, 0, ..., 0)$; $n = 50$

◇ HGBat function F10: (M, N)
$|\left(\sum_{i=1}^{n} x_i^2\right)^2 - \left(\sum_{i=1}^{n} x_i\right)^2 |^{0.5} + \frac{\left(0.5 \sum_{i=1}^{n} x_i^2 + \sum_{i=1}^{n} x_i\right)}{n} + 0.5$
$-100 \leq x_i \leq 100$; GM $= 0$ in $(x_1, x_2, ..., x_{50}) = (0, 0, ..., 0)$; $n = 50$

◇ Bohachevsky function F11: (U, N)
$\sum_{i=1}^{n-1} \left(x_i^2 + 2 \cdot x_{i+1}^2 - 0.3 \cdot \cos\left(3 \cdot \pi \cdot x_i\right) - 0.4 \cdot \cos\left(4 \cdot \pi \cdot x_{i+1}\right) + 0.7\right)$

$-15 \leq x_i \leq 15$; GM $= 0$ in $(x_1, x_2, ..., x_{50}) = (0, 0, ..., 0)$; $n = 50$
◇ Rosenbrock function F12: (M, N)
$$\sum_{i=1}^{n-1} \left(100 \cdot \left(x_i^2 - x_{i+1} \right)^2 + (x_i - 1)^2 \right)$$
$-5 \leq x_i \leq 5$; GM $= 0$ in $(x_1, x_2, ..., x_{50}) = (0, 0, ..., 0)$; $n = 50$
◇ Scaled Rastrigin function F13: (M, S)
$$10 \cdot n + \sum_{i=1}^{n} \left(\left(10^{\frac{i-1}{n-1}} \cdot x_i \right)^2 - 10 \cdot \cos \left(2 \cdot \pi \cdot 10^{\frac{i-1}{n-1}} \cdot x_i \right) \right)$$
$-5 \leq x_i \leq 5$; GM $= 0$ in $(x_1, x_2, ..., x_{50}) = (0, 0, ..., 0)$; $n = 50$
◇ Skew Rastrigin function F14: (M, S)
$$10 \cdot n + \sum_{i=1}^{n} \left(y_i^2 - 10 \cdot \cos \left(2 \cdot \pi \cdot y_i \right) \right) ; y_i = \begin{cases} 10 \cdot x_i, & when \ x_i > 0 \\ x_i, & otherwise \end{cases}$$
$-5 \leq x_i \leq 5$; GM $= 0$ in $(x_1, x_2, ..., x_{50}) = (0, 0, ..., 0)$; $n = 50$
◇ Schaffer function F15: (M, N)
$$\sum_{i=1}^{n-1} \left(x_i^2 + x_{i+1}^2 \right)^{0.25} \cdot \left[sin^2 \left(50 \cdot \left(x_i^2 + x_{i+1}^2 \right)^{0.1} \right) + 1 \right]$$
$-100 \leq x_i \leq 100$; GM $= 0$ in $(x_1, x_2, ..., x_{50}) = (0, 0, ..., 0)$; $n = 50$

5   Experimental Verification of Proposed Method

In order to verify the proposed method, we have run the evolutionary algorithms with different selection operators and standard values of crossover ($pc = 0.7$) and mutation probability ($pm = 0.05$). The number of individuals in the population was equal to $R = 50$, the maximal number of iterations was equal to $T_{max} = 5000$. Detailed information on the test functions and their dimensionality are presented in Sect. 4. In each evolutionary algorithm we have used a simple one-point crossover operator, and a simple mutation operator. Also, the elitist strategy was added to each selection scheme, in addition to roulette selection, truncation selection, deterministic selection, and tournament selection. In F^3MIX, the selection pressure (α), crossover probability ($pc_{F^3MIX} = pc \cdot PC$) and mutation probability ($pm_{F^3MIX} = pm \cdot PM$) were steered using fuzzy controllers presented in Sect. 2. In each evolutionary algorithm the computations were repeated 20-fold. The results obtained using the different methods are presented in Table 1. The symbols in Table 1 have the following meaning: MET - name of the method, F^{3}MIX - proposed approach, FMIX - fuzzy mix method [6], MIX - mix method [5], TRU - truncation method (truncation parameter equal to 50%) [10], DET - deterministic method [10], TOU - tournament method (tournament group size equal to 2) [10], FAN - fan selection method ($\alpha = 0.3$) [9], and ROU - roulette method [11].

From Table 1, it can be seen that in all cases the results obtained using the F^{3}MIX method are better than the results obtained using other methods.

In the second experiment, we have verified the normalized convergence rate factor (NCR). Therefore, we have added NCR to the F^{3}MIX method. The algorithm was stopped when $NCR \geq 0.99999$. All other parameters were the same as in the previous experiment. Table 2 presents the obtained results. The symbols in Table 2 have the following meaning: FValue - average value of objective function, Iterations - average value of iteration number when algorithm was stopped, t-Test - the value of t-Student statistical test parameter.

Table 1. Average values of the best results obtained after 20-fold repetition of each evolutionary algorithm method

SM	F1	F2	F3	F4	F5
F^3MIX	16.7773 ± 17.797	2.3493 ± 1.2204	0.6385 ± 0.326	681.4066 ± 812.1737	460.6846 ± 194.7384
FMIX	65.2623 ± 56.5552	4.4414 ± 2.2967	1.2337 ± 0.6069	1249.7 ± 1157.4	552.3314 ± 137.8336
MIX	61.8323 ± 71.352	3.5843 ± 2.1212	1.5642 ± 0.5309	1903 ± 2168	508.2093 ± 219.0428
TRU	8097 ± 2787	18.4355 ± 1.2685	51.9699 ± 29.8268	186920 ± 77694	1882.2 ± 343.2477
DET	9245.9 ± 4835.7	14.5738 ± 3.4021	107.3421 ± 37.4514	292790 ± 113950	3288.4 ± 425.6226
TOU	10115 ± 3866	19.3819 ± 1.0032	93.2434 ± 41.662	202600 ± 109000	2864.2 ± 282.246
FAN	70.4246 ± 71.2435	3.3742 ± 1.8999	1.3795 ± 0.9747	1678.8 ± 2181.7	516.9648 ± 190.6491
ELI	82.1431 ± 67.03	3.8939 ± 1.9651	1.5843 ± 1.1491	1133.9 ± 1629.9	526.4237 ± 155.8615
ROU	36861 ± 15805	20.4693 ± 0.6017	248.0006 ± 116.9837	992280 ± 482460	6808 ± 506.0358
SM	F6	F7	F8	F9	F10
F^3MIX	2.0011 ± 0.5451	544.0813 ± 427.8529	0.9513 ± 0.2411	0.9719 ± 0.1823	24.6117 ± 41.2322
FMIX	2.72072 ± 1.2329	3376.5 ± 3204	1.1206 ± 0.2706	1.0884 ± 0.3065	88.7926 ± 101.9288
MIX	3.1116 ± 1.7969	2238.2 ± 2628.2	1.1889 ± 0.212	1.2186 ± 0.2388	55.3167 ± 60.914
TRU	72.0508 ± 27.4309	145810 ± 70747	4.6637 ± 1.2426	4.9229 ± 1.4854	8181.8 ± 2754.5
DET	139.992 ± 55.6182	301060 ± 97866	4.8846 ± 1.6071	4.8252 ± 1.8046	10829 ± 5224.7
TOU	119.767 ± 43.9095	253010 ± 105730	5.005 ± 1.4742	5.3754 ± 1.5298	13651 ± 5192.5
FAN	2.9657 ± 1.6341	1326.1 ± 1613.7	1.1924 ± 0.2069	1.1118 ± 0.1623	60.7545 ± 50.3972
ELI	3.6131 ± 1.7836	1824.2 ± 2134.4	1.2111 ± 0.2025	1.2007 ± 0.1566	64.2427 ± 90.4285
ROU	386.548 ± 169.1069	759930 ± 370540	8.6807 ± 3.2439	9.3188 ± 2.1602	36285 ± 16836
SM	F11	F12	F13	F14	F15
F^3MIX	3.1409 ± 2.9004	56.9849 ± 12.2234	18.5455 ± 9.4953	3.3776 ± 2.5743	4.8145 ± 1.3329
FMIX	5.7846 ± 6.1126	100.309 ± 105.5075	21.4613 ± 10.6666	8.2686 ± 4.6462	7.5413 ± 2.5465
MIX	4.6241 ± 4.0483	89.5501 ± 49.2131	22.0877 ± 14.0088	6.9439 ± 3.1945	6.3077 ± 2.4308
TRU	517.304 ± 264.4996	18302 ± 8105.8	340.1653 ± 192.7479	337.3495 ± 202.5355	77.3238 ± 25.4218
DET	713.85 ± 324.995	26323 ± 17251	668.568 ± 276.5714	555.1926 ± 406.1911	99.1753 ± 30.2918
TOU	661.954 ± 365.4663	26846 ± 16827	573.7617 ± 346.706	458.1841 ± 243.54	92.7077 ± 29.6855
FAN	6.7288 ± 5.6557	102.7021 ± 74.7475	21.1455 ± 13.5555	7.8736 ± 3.2528	6.7999 ± 2.0958
ELI	3.7176 ± 2.7833	76.1004 ± 20.461	28.0938 ± 13.7904	6.0908 ± 3.3366	7.8294 ± 2.4509
ROU	2817.8 ± 1271.6	108600 ± 55758	3812.8 ± 914.5228	3279.5 ± 1499.8	201.0052 ± 75.2914

Table 2. Average values obtained after 20-fold repetition of the F^3MIX method with the NCR method

SM	F1	F2	F3	F4	F5
FValue	39.6214 ± 110.3638	1.8961 ± 1.1989	0.9389 ± 0.4611	731.1567 ± 810.7331	517.9896 ± 283.0632
Iterations	4855.2 ± 1054.5	5059.1 ± 147.6167	4569.9 ± 1144.9	4912.8 ± 541.0468	4697.1 ± 1010.3
|t-Test|	0.890737	1.15472	2.318765	0.18897	0.72701
SM	F6	F7	F8	F9	F10
FValue	2.0978 ± 1.0135	835.3141 ± 1117.6	0.8887 ± 0.2902	0.9478 ± 0.2345	29.9115 ± 48.1643
Iterations	4905.6 ± 650.9043	4908.4 ± 481.1554	5012.9 ± 347.4143	4876.3 ± 956.8856	4663.7 ± 856.7629
|t-Test|	0.366275	1.060797	0.72324	0.35367	0.364359
SM	F11	F12	F13	F14	F15
FValue	1.6693 ± 0.8322	61.5596 ± 13.6481	22.2729 ± 23.2672	4.7903 ± 4.0407	4.4752 ± 1.761
Iterations	5032.3 ± 267.9607	4426.6 ± 1430.4	4437.3 ± 1402.2	4499.4 ± 1336.6	4545.1 ± 878.8811
|t-Test|	2.12583	1.088367	0.646529	1.285272	0.66966

From Table 2, it can be seen that in most cases the algorithm was stopped before reaching the maximal number of iterations (when NCR value was higher than 0.99999). The statistical importance of the results obtained using the F^3MIX (with NCR - see Table 2) and F^3MIX method (see Table 1) were checked. Based on the t-Test values (see Table 2), we can see that the hypotheses on the equality of average values is true with a trust level of 98% (the t-Test values must be lower than 2.4286). Therefore, we can say that the results obtained using F^3MIX and F^3MIX (with NCR) are the same from the statistical point of view (despite the different number of iterations).

6   Conclusions

As we can see from Table 1, in all cases the results (average values) obtained using the proposed approach are better or comparable to the results obtained using other methods. The lowest values of standard deviation can be observed for the functions F6, F8, F9, and F12. The highest values of standard deviation can be observed for functions F4, and F10. After introducing the normalized convergence rate into the evolutionary algorithm, we can see that the algorithm can be stopped before reaching the maximum number of iterations. Moreover, the results obtained using F^3MIX without normalized convergence rate and F^3MIX with normalized convergence rate are the same from the statistical point of view with a trust level of 98%. In five cases the average function values obtained using F^3MIX with NCR are lower than the average function values obtained using F^3MIX without NCR. In our future research, we plan to conduct a much deeper exploration into the problem of estimating the convergence rate in an evolutionary algorithm.

Acknowledgment. This work was supported by Polish National Science Center (NCN) under a research grant 2018/02/X/ST6/02475.

References

1. Liu, S., Mernik, M., Bryant, B.R.: Entropy-driven parameter control for evolutionary algorithms. Informatica **31**, 41–57 (2007)
2. Hussain, A., Muhammad, Y.S.: Trade-off between exploration and exploitation with genetic algorithm using a novel selection operator. Complex Intell. Syst. **6**(1), 1–14 (2019). https://doi.org/10.1007/s40747-019-0102-7
3. Xie, H., Zhang, M., Andreae, P.: An analysis of constructive crossover and selection pressure in genetic algorithm. In: Proceedings of Genetic and Evolutionary Computation Conference, pp. 1739–1746 (2007)
4. Back, T.: Selective pressure in evolutionary algorithms: a characterization of selection mechanisms. In: Proceedings of 1st IEEE Conference on Evolutionary Computing, pp. 57–62 (1994)

5. Słowik, A.: Steering of balance between exploration and exploitation properties of evolutionary algorithms - mix selection. In: Rutkowski, L., Scherer, R.,
   Tadeusiewicz, R., Zadeh, L.A., Zurada, J.M. (eds.) ICAISC 2010. LNCS (LNAI),
   vol. 6114, pp. 213–220. Springer, Heidelberg (2010). https://doi.org/10.1007/978-
   3-642-13232-2_26
6. Słowik, A.: Fuzzy control of trade-off between exploration and exploitation properties of evolutionary algorithms. In: Corchado, E., Kurzyński, M., Woźniak, M.
   (eds.) HAIS 2011. LNCS (LNAI), vol. 6678, pp. 59–66. Springer, Heidelberg (2011).
   https://doi.org/10.1007/978-3-642-21219-2_9
7. Suganthan, P.N., et al.: Problem definitions and evaluation criteria for the CEC
   2005 special session on real-parameter optimization. Technical report, Nanyang
   Technological University, Singapore, Report number 2005005, May 2005
8. Liang, J.J., Qu, B.Y., Suganthan, P.N.: Problem definitions and evaluation criteria
   for the CEC 2014 special session and competition on single objective real-parameter
   numerical optimization. Technical report 201311, Computational intelligence laboratory, Zhengzhou University, Zhengzhou, China and Technical report, Nanyang
   Technological University, Singapore, December 2013
9. Słowik, A., Białko, M.: Modified version of roulette selection for evolution algorithms – the fan selection. In: Rutkowski, L., Siekmann, J.H., Tadeusiewicz, R.,
   Zadeh, L.A. (eds.) ICAISC 2004. LNCS (LNAI), vol. 3070, pp. 474–479. Springer,
   Heidelberg (2004). https://doi.org/10.1007/978-3-540-24844-6_70
10. Michalewicz, Z.: Genetic Algorithms + Data Structures = Evolution Programs.
    Springer, Berlin (1996). https://doi.org/10.1007/978-3-662-03315-9
11. Goldberg, D.E.: Genetic Algorithms in Search, Optimization, and Machine Learn-
    ing. Addison-Wesley Publishing Company Inc., New York (1989)
12. Smullen, D., Gillett, J., Heron, J., Rahnamayan, S.: Genetic algorithm with self-
    adaptive mutation controlled by chromosome similarity. In: IEEE Congress on
    Evolutionary Computation (CEC), Beijing, pp. 504–511 (2014)
13. Xu, J., Pei, L., Zhu, R.: Application of a genetic algorithm with random crossover
    and dynamic mutation on the travelling salesman problem. In: 8th International
    Congress of Information and Communication Technology, ICICT 2018, Procedia
    Computer Science, vol. 131, pp. 937–945 (2018)
14. Lin, W., Lee, W., Hong, T.: Adapting crossover and mutation rates in genetic
    algorithms. J. Inf. Sci. Eng. 19(5), 889–903 (2003)
15. Varnamkhasti, M.J., Lee, L.S., Bakar, M.R., Leong, W.J.: A genetic algorithm with
    fuzzy crossover operator and probability. Adv. Oper. Res. 2012 (2012). Article ID
    956498, 16 pages
16. Khmeleva, E., Hopgood, A.A., Tipi, L., Shahidan, M.: Fuzzy-logic controlled
    genetic algorithm for the rail-freight crew-scheduling problem. KI - Künstliche
    Intelligenz 32(1), 61–75 (2017). https://doi.org/10.1007/s13218-017-0516-6
17. Lapa, K., Cpalka, K.: Flexible fuzzy PID controller (FFPIDC) and a nature-
    inspired method for its construction. IEEE Trans. Industr. Inf. 14(3), 1078–1088
    (2018)
18. Cpałka, K.: Design of Interpretable Fuzzy Systems. SCI, vol. 684. Springer, Cham
    (2017). https://doi.org/10.1007/978-3-319-52881-6

An Improved Local Search Genetic Algorithm with Multi-crossover for Job Shop Scheduling Problem

Monique Simplicio Viana[1]([✉]) [iD], Orides Morandin Junior[1] [iD],
and Rodrigo Colnago Contreras[2] [iD]

[1] Federal University of São Carlos, São Carlos, Brazil
{monique.viana,orides}@ufscar.br
[2] University of São Paulo, São Carlos, Brazil
contreras@usp.br

Abstract. Recent works are using meta-heuristics to address the problem class known in the literature as Job Shop Scheduling Problem (JSSP) because of its complexity, since it consists of combinatorial problems and belongs to the set of NP-Hard computational problems. In this type of problem, one of the most discussed goals is to minimize the makespan, which is the maximum production time of a series of jobs. A widely used meta-heuristic in JSSP is the Genetic Algorithm (GA) due to its good performance in scheduling problems. However, for problems with high complexity, some form of hybridization in GA may be required to improve search space performance, for example, by including specialized local search techniques. It is proposed in this work the use of specialized and improved local search operators in the meta-heuristic GA with multi-crossover strategies in order to minimize makespan in JSSP: The Multi-Crossover Local Search Genetic Algorithm (mXLSGA). Specifically, all operators of the proposed algorithm have local search functionality beyond their original inspirations and characteristics. The developed method has been evaluated on 58 instances from well-established benchmarks. Experimental results have proven that mXLSGA is competitive and versatile compared to the state-of-the-art methods.

Keywords: Genetic Algorithm · Local search · Multi-crossover · Job Shop Scheduling Problem · Combinatorial optimization

1 Introduction

Scheduling problems have been extensively researched in recent years because it is a high complexity combinatorial optimization problem and it is classified as NP-Hard. Among the machine scheduling problems, there are several variations, such as Job Shop Scheduling Problem (JSSP), Flexible Job Shop Scheduling Problem (FJSSP), Flow Shop Scheduling Problems, etc. In this paper, we will discuss the JSSP variant.

© Springer Nature Switzerland AG 2020
L. Rutkowski et al. (Eds.): ICAISC 2020, LNAI 12415, pp. 464–479, 2020.
https://doi.org/10.1007/978-3-030-61401-0_43

In recent years, several meta-heuristic approaches have been proposed to treat the JSSP, such as Greedy Randomized Adaptive Search Procedure (GRASP) [8], Local Search Genetic Algorithm (LSGA) [22], Parallel Agent-based Genetic Algorithm (PaGA) [6], Agent-based Local Search Genetic Algorithm (aLSGA) [5], Golden Ball Algorithm (GB) [24], Initial Population Based Genetic Algorithm (IPB-GA) [17], Memetic Algorithm (MA) [19], Improved Biogeography-Based Optimization (IBBO) [23], Grey Wolf Optimization (GWO) [15], Hybrid Grey Wolf Optimization (HGWO) [14], Memetic Chicken Swarm Optimization (MeCSO) [25], Genetic Algorithm with a critical-path-guided Giffler and Thompson crossover operator (GA-CPG-GT) [18] and Discrete Wolf Pack Algorithm (DWPA) [26].

Most state-of-the-art studies on JSSP have validated the methods proposed in traditional benchmark sets in the literature, such as Fisher and Thompson [11], Lawrence [20], Applegate and Cook [4] and Adams, Balas and Zawack [1], and considered the minimization of makespan as a performance criterion for the evaluation of possible solutions of a JSSP.

We observe from the literature review that JSSP is a relevant academic topic and it has attracted the attention of many researchers because it has a combinatorial behavior and it is classified as NP-Hard, which makes it very difficult to solve by exact approaches, which encourages treatment by alternative methods such as meta-heuristics.

Several approaches of the meta-heuristic GA have been successfully performed on many combinatorial optimization problems, such as machine scheduling problems, for example, JSSP. However, for problems with greater complexity, GA needs to engage with particular problem methods to make the approach effective. Hybridization is a satisfactory and widely used way to improve the performance of GA. Local search techniques are very common forms of hybridization which have been used in several studies to improve GA performance, such as in [5,10,21,22].

In this paper, a new GA approach with improved local search techniques (mXLSGA) is proposed to minimize the makespan in JSSP. Three local search operators are proposed, one of which is embedded in a multi-crossover operator; one as a mutation operator; and another of massive behavior. Such procedures are enhancements based on [27] and [5] methods.

The sections of this article are organized as follows. Section 2 describes the formulation of JSSP. Section 3 presents the details of the proposed mXLSGA method. In Sect. 4, the results are presented and compared with the works of the state-of-the-art. Section 5 presents the conclusion and future works.

2   Formulation of Job Shop Scheduling Problem

JSSP is a combinatorial optimization problem belonging to the NP-Hard class of computational problems, which means it is a problem whose processing time is non-polynomial. Specifically, a JSSP can be defined as being a set of N jobs to be processed into a set of M machines. In JSSP, each job must be processed by all

M machines and each job has a sequence of operations with M distinct elements belonging to the set of all possible operations. The sequences of operations are usually different for each job. The scheduling problem of JSSP-type production is finding a job sequence for each machine to optimize a specific performance criterion, which is usually makespan. Some restrictions must be followed in this problem [28]:

- Each job can be processed on a single machine at a time;
- Each machine can process only one job at a time;
- Operations are considered non-preemptive, i.e., cannot be interrupted,
- Configuration times are included in processing times and are independent of sequencing decisions.

In this work, makespan is adopted as a measure of performance, which is considered to be the total time required to complete the production of a series of jobs. The makespan performance measurement formulation is generally used in JSSP approaches as an objective function that guides algorithms using meta-heuristics to search for appropriate solutions.

Mathematically, suppose the following specifications of JSSP:

- $J = \{J_1, J_2, ..., J_N\}$ as the set of jobs;
- $M = \{m_1, m_2, ..., m_M\}$ as the set of machines;
- $O = (O_1, O_2, ..., O_{N \cdot M})$ is the sequence that defines the priority with which each job has its processing started on each of the machines of its respective script,
- $T_i(O)$ representing the time the job J_i takes to be processed by all machines in its script, and thus it is considered finished according to the sequence of operations defined in O.

Then, according to [9], the JSSP makespan (MKS) measure represented can be defined as the value presented in Eq. (1).

$$MKS = \max_i T_i(O), \qquad (1)$$

which is a measure given according to the order of operations defined in O, since the time that each job takes to be considered finished is given according to the processing order defined in the schedule.

3   Multi-crossover Local Search Genetic Algorithm for JSSP

In this section, we will discuss fundamental concepts to the execution of the proposed algorithm and we will also specify the improved methods defined in this work for better efficiency. In short, our contributions are comprised in the following topics:

- An improved crossover operator based on the version of [27], including a multi-crossover strategy with the goal of increasing the search capability of the method by using a framework based on a set of crossover functions.
- An improved local search technique in union with a generalized version of the mutation operator proposed in [5], including a variable parameterization.
- An improved version of the elite local search operator of [5], expanding the search space by utilizing a set of mutation functions.

3.1 Genetic Representation

Except for the presence of specific operators of each work, the basic structure of a GA continues to be formed by the repetition loop that involves two main operators: crossover operator and mutation operator. This structure is preserved in the vast majority of state-of-the-art techniques. The codification used to represent a possible solution (chromosome) of the problem can be done in many different ways, as highlighted in [16].

In this paper, a codification equivalent to one of the most common representations of the literature is used, which is known as "coding by operation order", first presented in [7]. Since, in this representation, the solution space of a JSSP of N jobs and M machines is formed by chromosomes $c \in \mathbb{N}^{N \cdot M}$, such that exactly M coordinates of c are equal to i (representing the job index i), for every $i \in \{1, 2, ..., N\}$.

Figure 1 shows some examples of chromosomes (c_1, c_2 and c_3) that obey such formulation in a JSSP with 2 jobs ($N = 2$) and 3 machines ($M = 3$). As the formulation requires, index job 1 and index job 2 appear exactly 3 times, since 3 is the number of machines in the problem.

$$c_1 = (1, 1, 2, 1, 2, 2) \qquad c_2 = (2, 2, 2, 1, 1, 1) \qquad c_3 = (1, 2, 1, 2, 1, 2)$$

Fig. 1. Examples of chromosomes in representation by operation order.

This codification determines that the priority of each operation on machine allocation. As an example, let $c = (1, 2, 1, 1, 2, 2)$ be a chromosome in a 2×3 dimension JSSP. In this case, the order established by c defines that the following actions must be performed sequentially and it should only be initiated if it can be performed in parallel with the previous action or if the previous action has already been completed:

- 1st) Job 1 must be processed by the 1st machine of its script.
- 2nd) Job 2 must be processed by the 1st machine of its script.
- 3rd) Job 1 must be processed by the 2nd machine of its script.
- 4th) Job 1 must be processed by the 3rd machine of its script.
- 5th) Job 2 must be processed by the 2nd machine of its script.
- 6th) Job 2 must be processed by the 3rd machine of its script.

Thus, one way to generate initial population in this type of configuration is to create a group of chromosomes equal to $(1, ..., 1, 2, ..., 2, ..., N, ..., N)$, in which each of the N jobs of a JSSP appears in exactly M positions, and then randomly rearrange all coordinates of each chromosome.

3.2   Fitness Function

The objective function, or fitness function, of the optimization problem discussed here can be modeled according to the function F, defined in Eq. (2) given below:

$$F : \mathbb{O} \longrightarrow \mathbb{R}$$
$$O \longmapsto F(O) := \max_i T_i(O), \tag{2}$$

where $\mathbb{O}$ is the set of all possible sequences for the defined JSSP. That is, if $O \in \mathbb{O}$, then O is a sequence of operations that defines the start processing priority for N jobs on M machines. In other words, $\mathbb{O}$ is the feasible set of solutions in which our method must perform its search.

The lower the makespan value of a schedule, the less time must be taken to finish a given set of jobs. Thus, the algorithm should look for configuration options for a schedule in order to minimize the time spent to complete the jobs processing on the set of machines that configure the JSSP.

3.3   Selection Mechanism

Selection strategies are used so that we can choose individuals to reproduce and to create new populations in evolutionary algorithms. In this paper, individuals should be selected to participate in the crossover process with probability equivalent to their fitness value, which is known as roulette wheel selection [12]. The selection approach for generating a new population used in the proposed algorithm was the roulette wheel selection with retaining model, in which the probability of an individual being selected is proportional to its fitness value and, certainly, the best individual in the current population is transferred to the new population.

3.4   Proposed Multi-crossover Operator

Crossover Functions. The proposed crossover operator consists of using more than one crossover function in search area adaptation [27] strategies. Thus, our proposal is in the form of a framework that considers a set of n_X crossover functions to combine chromosomes. Thus, we define this set to be $\mathcal{F}_X$, presented in Eq. 3.

$$\mathcal{F}_X = \{f_{X,1}, f_{X,2}, ..., f_{X,n_X}\}. \tag{3}$$

Let us consider in this paper, without loss of generality, that each function $f_X \in \mathcal{F}_X$ is a function that combines two parent chromosomes from the feasible set resulting in only one child chromosome. That is, each function of $\mathcal{F}_X$ takes the form of $f_X : \mathbb{O} \times \mathbb{O} \to \mathbb{O}$.

In this work, we will focus on two main crossover functions [3,13] for conducting our assessments and evaluations: Partially Mapped Crossover (PMX) and Order-based Crossover (OX2). These functions are two of the most widely used crossover functions in the specialized literature on JSSP solution by genetic algorithm. In this way, $\mathcal{F}_X = \{\text{PMX}, \text{OX2}\}$ for our experiments, however, the same conclusions of our method can be obtained with any set $\mathcal{F}_X$.

OX2 (Fig. 2 - right) doesn't require any correction or projection steps as its feasibility is guaranteed by construction. This is because the technique only matches the order in which jobs appear in parents. In detail, initially, a random number of genes are fixed. An offspring inherits in its coordinates the exact position these genes assume in one parent and completes the remaining positions with the other parent's unfixed genes.

PMX (Fig. 2 - left) combines two chromosomes from two previously randomly defined cutoff points. To generate the child chromosomes, the strategy is to mix the genes internal to the cutoffs in one parent with the genes external to the cutoffs in another parent. This procedure can generate infeasible solutions, which are usually corrected in JSSP applications by projecting the individuals generated into feasible space with respect to the Hamming distance [5].

An example of OX2 and PMX application is presented in Fig. 2.

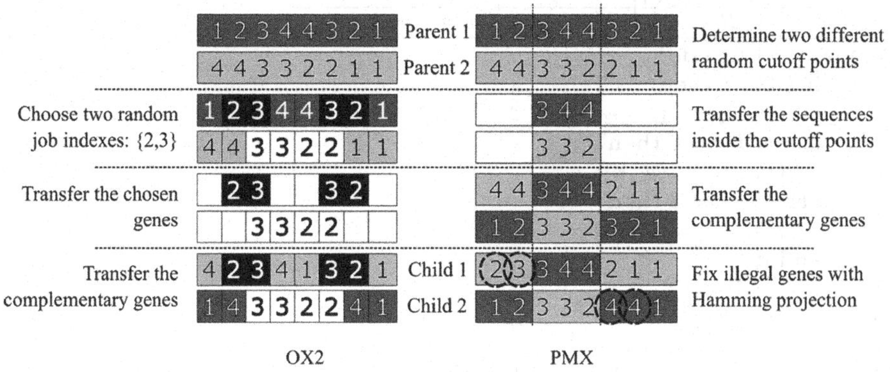

Fig. 2. Comparison between the steps of the OX2, on the left, and PMX, on the right, crossover techniques.

Multi-crossover Operator. As a crossover operator, a more embracing and rigorous version of the crossover operator of [27] is proposed. We suppose that the use of distinct crossover techniques increases the power of local exploitation since they define different strategies to combine the same individuals and thus it allows the investigation of different search areas. Thus, the crossover operator works from three randomly selected individuals in the population and occasionally different crossover techniques defined by $\mathcal{F}_X$ is applied in all possible pairs of these three chromosomes until three offsprings are found that surpass their respective parents or until each pair has performed R_c crossovers. Detailed operator schematics are presented in Algorithm 1.

Thus, in all possible pairs of three individuals randomly taken in the population, a set of distinct crossover functions are eventually performed until a solution is generated that has a fitness value better than a parent's fitness value or until the algorithm performs R_c crossover.

The search criteria of this operator is far stricter than the search criteria of the operators of [27], since the operators of these authors perform crossover until a solution is found whose fitness value is better than the worst fitness value presented in the entire population, and the fitness value of parents is not necessarily important for the procedure. Therefore, the proposed operator should be able to find good solutions more easily than the crossover operator of [27], since it performs a more careful and strict search. Furthermore, the use of different crossover techniques increases the search on feasible space, since the

---

Algorithm 1. Proposed multi-crossover operator.

Input:	(p_1, p_2, p_3)	3 randomly selected individuals
	F	Fitness function
	$\{f_{X,1}, ..., f_{X,n_X}\}$	Set of crossover functions
	R_c	Max crossovers for each pair

1: **for** $k := 1$ to 3 **do**
2:     **if** $k == 1$ **then**
3:         $(P_1, P_2) := (p_1, p_2)$
4:     **else if** $k == 2$ **then**
5:         $(P_1, P_2) := (p_1, p_3)$
6:     **else if** $k == 3$ **then**
7:         $(P_1, P_2) := (p_2, p_3)$
8:     **end if**
9:     $F_{P_1} := F(P_1)$
10:     $F_{P_2} := F(P_2)$
11:     **for** $i := 1$ to R_c **do**
12:         $f_X := \text{rand\_set}(\{f_{X,1}, ..., f_{X,n_X}\})$ ▷ rand_set(Y) returns some element in Y
13:         $\hat{c}_i := f_X(P_1, P_2)$
14:         $F_i := F(\hat{c}_i)$
15:         **if** $F_i < F_{P_1}$ or $F_i < F_{P_2}$ **then**
16:             break
17:         **end if**
18:     **end for**
19:     $i^* := \arg \min_i \{F_i\}$
20:     $c_k := \hat{c}_{i^*}$
21: **end for**

Output: (c_1, c_2, c_3) | Generated individuals

solutions must be generated by distinct crossover methodologies and, therefore, the search area can be explored by distinct strategies.

3.5 Proposed Mutation Operator

Mutation Functions. Similar to the crossover operator, the proposed mutation operator works according to a set of n_{mut} mutation functions in a framework. That is, in the mutation process performed in the proposed method, a chromosome may be mutated with a mutation specified by one of the functions of set $\mathcal{F}_{mut}$, defined in Eq. 4.

$$\mathcal{F}_{mut} = \{f_{mut,1}, f_{mut,2}, ..., f_{mut,n_{mut}}\}, \tag{4}$$

where each function $f_{mut} \in \mathcal{F}_{mut}$ is a mutation function that operates with respect to two coordinates i and j of a chromosome, making these functions of the form presented in Eq. (5).

$$f_{mut} : \mathbb{O} \times \{1, 2, ..., N \cdot M\}^2 \longrightarrow \mathbb{O} \\ (c, (i, j)) \longmapsto f_{mut}(c, (i, j)) \,. \tag{5}$$

In our work, we focus on the three most commonly used mutation functions in JSSP: Swap, Inverse and Insert [2], respectively represented by the functions f_{swap}, $f_{inverse}$ and f_{insert}. Thus, all tests performed on our evaluations are made according to $\mathcal{F}_{mut} = \{f_{swap}, f_{inverse}, f_{insert}\}$, the same considerations are made generally. In Fig. 3, the comparative operation of the considered mutation functions is presented.

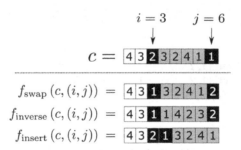

Fig. 3. Scheme of mutation functions.

Local Search Mutation Operator. As mutation operator it is proposed to generalize local search operator of [5] as a variation of [27] mutation operator. Thus, for each individual generated in the crossover operator, one mutation function of $\mathcal{F}_{mut}$ is chosen randomly and applied successively R_m times in randomly chosen coordinates of the chromosome keeping the beneficial modifications and proceeding with the mutation method from them, giving rise to a mutant population with the same number of individuals as the child population. However, in order to maintain the traditional characteristics of the mutation operator, which is to cause chromosome disturbance regardless of the presence of process improvement or worsening, the option of a simple mutation was added in a percentage of individuals. Therefore, only a percentage ϵ_{LS} of the population of children is mutated in a local search form, and a percentage $1 - \epsilon_{LS}$ is given a simple mutation. The scheme is presented in Algorithm 2.

Algorithm 2. Proposed mutation operator.

Input:	P_{child}	Set of individuals generated in Algorithm 1
	F	Fitness function
	$\mathcal{F}_{mut}$	Set of mutation functions
	ϵ_{LS}	Usage of local search strategy (in %)
	R_m	Max mutations for each pair
	$N \times M$	JSSP dimension

1: $f_{mut} := \text{rand\_set}(\{f_{mut,1}, f_{mut,2}, ..., f_{mut,n_{mut}}\})$
2: $P_{mut} := \{\}$
3: **for** $c \in P_{child}$ **do**
4:     **if** $\text{rand}([0,1]) \leq \epsilon_{LS}$ **then**
5:         $F_c := F(c)$
6:         **for** $i := 1$ to R_m **do**
7:             $r_1 := \text{rand\_set}(\{1, 2, ..., N \cdot M\})$
8:             $r_2 := \text{rand\_set}(\{1, 2, ..., r_1 - 1, r_1 + 1, ..., N \cdot M\})$
9:             $\hat{c} := f_{mut}(c, (r_1, r_2))$
10:            $F_{\hat{c}} := F(\hat{c})$
11:            **if** $F_{\hat{c}} \leq F_c$ **then**
12:                $c := \hat{c}$
13:                $F_c := F_{\hat{c}}$
14:            **end if**
15:        **end for**
16:    **else**
17:        $r_1 := \text{rand\_set}(\{1, 2, ..., N \cdot M\})$
18:        $r_2 := \text{rand\_set}(\{1, 2, ..., r_1 - 1, r_1 + 1, ..., N \cdot M\})$
19:        $c := f_{mut}(c, (r_1, r_2))$
20:    **end if**
21:    $P_{mut} := P_{mut} \cup \{c\}$
22: **end for**

Output: P_{mut} | Population of mutated individuals

3.6 Proposed Massive Local Search Operator

In this work, we propose as massive local search operator an improvement of the elite local search proposed in [5]. A massive local search operator has as its primary objective to evaluate which disturbances made with respect to some mutation function improve an individual's fitness. The main purpose of this procedure is to perform thorough searches in regions close to known good solutions, as such solutions have been determined to be better than their respective parents and likely to enhance the solutions of previous generations. This procedure is performed taking into consideration all possible combinations within the coordinates of a good individual. In [5], this procedure is performed only with the mutation function f_{swap} on the best individual in the population. In this paper, we propose that this procedure occurs using different possible functions in a given set of mutation functions, that is, it is proposed to randomly take a perturbation function within a set of mutation functions before each massive local search. In other words, it is intended to perform massive local searches by possibly using the same set of mutation functions $\mathcal{F}_{\text{mut}}$, presented in Eq. (4), and specified for our experiments as $\{f_{\text{swap}}, f_{\text{inverse}}, f_{\text{insert}}\}$. In this case, the algorithm not only performs the successive substitution of operations in a given solution, but occasionally, the technique performs successive insertions and inversions, increasing the diversification of the massive local search performed. Suppose that, over the generations, using a set of mutation functions instead of just one function can improve operator searchability. Besides, it is proposed that this massive local search be performed on the two best individuals who are distinct in the population, as this procedure may help to avoid stagnation in local optimum and promoting the permanence of two different good genetic heritages. Thus, the massive local search operator proposed is coded in Algorithm 3.

Algorithm 3. Proposed massive local search operator.

Input:	$\{c_{\text{best},1}, c_{\text{best},2}\}$	Two best different individuals
	F	Fitness function
	$\mathcal{F}_{\text{mut}}$	Set of mutation functions
	$N \times M$	JSSP dimension

1: $f_{\text{mut}} := \text{rand\_set}(\{f_{\text{mut},1}, f_{\text{mut},2}, ..., f_{\text{mut},n_{\text{mut}}}\})$
2: **for** $k := 1$ to 2 **do**
3:     $F_k := F(c_{\text{best},k})$
4:     **for** $i := 1$ to $N \cdot M$ **do**
5:         **for** $j := 1$ to $N \cdot M$ **do**
6:             $\hat{c}_{\text{best},k} := f_{\text{mut}}(c_{\text{best},k}, (i,j))$
7:             $\hat{F}_k := F(\hat{c}_{\text{best},k})$
8:             **if** $\hat{F}_k \leq F_k$ **then**
9:                 $c_{\text{best},k} := \hat{c}_{\text{best},k}$
10:                $F_k := \hat{F}_k$
11:            **end if**
12:        **end for**
13:    **end for**
14: **end for**

Output:	$\{\hat{c}_{\text{best},1}, \hat{c}_{\text{best},2}\}$	Improved individuals

3.7   Scheme of Use for Proposed Operators: Algorithm Structure

The use of all operators together follows a methodology similar to that used by [5], which consists of performing crossover, followed by performing a local search on all generated offsprings and ending with the massive local search around of the two best different individuals. The other operators of initial population generation and new population generation comprise respectively the beginning and the end of the proposed method. Figure 4 shows the flowchart containing all steps of the proposed mXLSGA, which is the proposed meta-heuristic for application in JSSP instances.

4   Implementation and Experimental Results

4.1   Experimental Environment

To evaluate the proposed approach, experiments were performed in 58 JSSP instance scenarios, 3 FT instances [11], 40 LA instances [20], 10 ORB instances [4] and 5 ABZ instances [1]. The results obtained in the execution of the tests were compared with papers from the specific literature. The articles determined for each comparison were selected because they are relevant works in the literature, which deal with the JSSP with the same specific instances and, when existing, papers published in the last three years were adopted. The papers selected for comparison of results were as follows: GA-CPG-GT [18], DWPA [26], GWO [15], HGWO [14], MA [19], IPB-GA [17] and aLSGA [5]. The proposed algorithm was coded using Matlab software and the tests were performed on a computer with 2.4 GHz Intel(R) Core i7 CPU and 16 GB of RAM. In most of the comparative works, the authors do not mention the processing time of their techniques, since this measure varies from computer to computer and is relative to the author's language and programming skills. We proceed in the same way.

4.2   Default Parameters

The configuration of parameters for the mXLSGA was established through tests and also taking into consideration, when possible, a closer parameterization of the works that were used for comparison. In this way, the parameters were defined as follows: Population size = 100; Maximum number of generations = 100; Crossover probability = 0.95; Mutation probability = 1; Percentage of child individuals to get local search mutation $\epsilon_{LS} = 0.95$; Maximum number of crossover $R_c = 10$ and Total number of mutations $R_m = 2 \cdot N \cdot M$. In addition, the sets $\mathcal{F}_X$ and $\mathcal{F}_{mut}$ are respectively defined in Sects. 3.4 and 3.5. The proposed mXLSGA method was executed 10 times for each JSSP instance and the best value obtained was used for comparison with other papers.

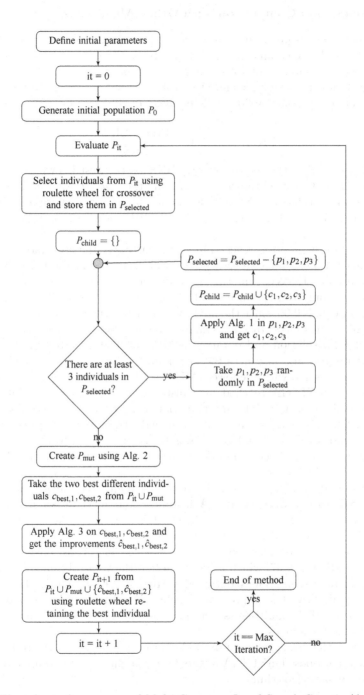

Fig. 4. Flow chart of our proposed Multi-Crossover Local Search Genetic Algorithm.

4.3   Results and Comparison with Other Algorithms

Table 1 shows the results derived from the LA [20], FT [11], ORB [4] and ABZ [1] instance tests. The columns indicate, respectively, the instance that was tested, the instance size (number of Jobs × number of Machines), the optimal solution of each instance, the results achieved by each method (best solution found and error percentage (Equation (6)), and the mean of the error for each benchmark (MErr).

$$\text{Error}(\%) = 100 \times \frac{\text{Best} - \text{BKS}}{\text{BKS}}, \tag{6}$$

where "Error (%)" is the relative error, "BKS" is the best known Solution and "Best" is the best value obtained by executing the algorithm for each instance.

As shown in Table 1, mXLSGA found the best known solution in 100% of FT instances, 70% of LA instances, 30% of ORB instances, and 40% of ABZ instances.

The mXLSGA proposal reached in 28 LA instances the best known solution and obtained a mean relative error (MErr) of 0.61. The method that achieved a lower error was HGWO, but this work did not test in all LA instances, and if we compare only the instances that HGWO was tested, ILSGA would have gotten MErr equals 0.00, since the mXLSGA achieved the best known solution in the first 20 LA instances. In FT instances, the mXLSGA reached in 3 instances the best known solution and obtained a MErr of 0.00. In ORB instances, the mXLSGA reached in 3 instances the best known solution and obtained a MErr 0.54, it is the method with the lowest MErr of all compared algorithms. In ABZ instances, the mXLSGA reached in 2 instances the best known solution and obtained a MErr of 4.46. The method that achieved a minor error was GA-CPG-GT, but this work did not test in all ABZ instances, and if we compare only the instances that GA-CPG-GT was tested, mXLSGA would have gotten 0.00 relative mean error, i.e., the mXLSGA achieved the best known solution in the first 2 ORB instances.

In particular, our method surpassed the technique on which it was based, which in this case is aLSGA. In LA instances, our method got 6 BKS more than aLSGA. The aLSGA obtained in the LA instances a MErr of 0.80 and mXLSGA obtained a MErr of 0.61, but aLSGA was tested only in the first 35 LA instances, if we consider the MErr only for the 35 LA instances, mXLSGA would get a MErr of 0.37, which is less than half the value obtained by aLSGA. For ORB instances, mXLSGA obtained a MErr less than one third of the one obtained by aLSGA. The improvement achieved by mXLSGA is certainly due to the insertion of the multi-crossover operator and the enhancements employed in local search techniques.

Analyzing the data presented in Table 1, we can see that in the tested JSSP instances, the proposed mXLSGA results better or equal to the compared results of state-of-the-art algorithms.

Table 1. Comparison of computational results between mXLSGA and other algorithms. The symbol "-" means "no evaluated in that instance".

Instance	Size	BKS	mXLSGA Best	Error (%)	GA-CPG-GT Best	Error (%)	DWPA Best	Error (%)	GWO Best	Error (%)	HGWO Best	Error (%)	MA Best	Error (%)	IPB-GA Best	Error (%)	aLSGA Best	Error (%)
LA01	10×5	666	666	0.00	666	0.00	666	0.00	666	0.00	666	0.00	666	0.00	666	0.00	666	0.00
LA02	10×5	655	655	0.00	655	0.00	655	0.00	655	0.00	655	0.00	655	0.00	655	0.00	655	0.00
LA03	10×5	597	597	0.00	597	0.00	614	2.84	597	0.00	597	0.00	597	0.00	599	0.33	606	1.50
LA04	10×5	590	590	0.00	590	0.00	598	1.35	590	0.00	590	0.00	590	0.00	590	0.00	593	0.50
LA05	10×5	593	593	0.00	593	0.00	593	0.00	593	0.00	593	0.00	593	0.00	593	0.00	593	0.00
LA06	15×5	926	926	0.00	926	0.00	926	0.00	926	0.00	926	0.00	926	0.00	926	0.00	926	0.00
LA07	15×5	890	890	0.00	890	0.00	890	0.00	890	0.00	890	0.00	890	0.00	890	0.00	890	0.00
LA08	15×5	863	863	0.00	863	0.00	863	0.00	863	0.00	863	0.00	863	0.00	863	0.00	863	0.00
LA09	15×5	951	951	0.00	951	0.00	951	0.00	951	0.00	951	0.00	951	0.00	951	0.00	951	0.00
LA10	15×5	958	958	0.00	958	0.00	958	0.00	958	0.00	958	0.00	958	0.00	958	0.00	958	0.00
LA11	20×5	1222	1222	0.00	1222	0.00	1222	0.00	1222	0.00	1222	0.00	1222	0.00	1222	0.00	1222	0.00
LA12	20×5	1039	1039	0.00	1039	0.00	1039	0.00	1039	0.00	1039	0.00	1039	0.00	1039	0.00	1039	0.00
LA13	20×5	1150	1150	0.00	1150	0.00	1150	0.00	1150	0.00	1150	0.00	1150	0.00	1150	0.00	1150	0.00
LA14	20×5	1292	1292	0.00	1292	0.00	1292	0.00	1292	0.00	1292	0.00	1292	0.00	1292	0.00	1292	0.00
LA15	20×5	1207	1207	0.00	1207	0.00	1273	5.46	1207	0.00	1207	0.00	1207	0.00	1207	0.00	1207	0.00
LA16	10×10	945	945	0.00	946	0.10	993	5.07	956	1.16	959	1.48	946	0.10	946	0.10	946	0.10
LA17	10×10	784	784	0.00	784	0.00	793	1.14	790	0.76	784	0.00	784	0.00	784	0.00	784	0.00
LA18	10×10	848	848	0.00	848	0.00	861	1.53	859	1.29	857	1.06	858	1.17	853	0.58	848	0.00
LA19	10×10	842	842	0.00	842	0.00	888	5.46	845	0.35	845	0.35	-	-	866	2.85	852	1.18
LA20	10×10	902	902	0.00	907	0.55	934	3.54	937	3.88	946	4.87	-	-	913	1.21	907	0.55
LA21	15×10	1046	1059	1.24	1090	4.20	1105	5.64	1090	4.20	-	-	1081	3.34	1081	3.34	1068	2.10
LA22	15×10	927	935	0.86	954	2.91	989	6.68	970	4.63	-	-	954	2.91	970	4.63	956	3.12
LA23	15×10	1032	1032	0.00	1032	0.00	1051	1.84	1032	0.00	-	-	1032	0.00	1032	0.00	1032	0.00
LA24	15×10	935	946	1.17	974	4.17	988	5.66	982	5.02	-	-	976	4.38	1002	7.16	966	3.31
LA25	15×10	977	986	0.92	999	2.25	1039	6.34	1008	3.17	-	-	999	2.25	1023	4.70	1002	2.55
LA26	20×10	1218	1218	0.00	1237	1.55	1303	6.97	1239	1.72	-	-	-	-	1273	4.51	1223	0.41
LA27	20×10	1235	1269	2.75	1313	6.31	1346	8.98	1290	4.45	-	-	-	-	1317	6.63	1281	3.72
LA28	20×10	1216	1239	1.89	1280	5.26	1291	6.16	1263	3.86	-	-	-	-	1288	5.92	1245	2.38
LA29	20×10	1152	1201	4.25	1247	8.24	1275	10.67	1244	7.98	-	-	-	-	1233	7.03	1230	6.77
LA30	20×10	1355	1355	0.00	1367	0.88	1389	2.50	1355	0.00	-	-	-	-	1377	1.62	1355	0.00
LA31	30×10	1784	1784	0.00	1784	0.00	1784	0.00	1784	0.00	-	-	1784	0.00	1784	0.00	1784	0.00
LA32	30×10	1850	1850	0.00	1850	0.00	1850	0.00	1850	0.00	-	-	1868	0.97	1851	0.05	1850	0.00
LA33	30×10	1719	1719	0.00	1719	0.00	1719	0.00	1719	0.00	-	-	-	-	1719	0.00	1719	0.00
LA34	30×10	1721	1721	0.00	1725	0.23	1788	3.89	1721	0.00	-	-	-	-	1749	1.62	1721	0.00
LA35	30×10	1888	1888	0.00	1888	0.00	1947	3.125	1888	0.00	-	-	1901	0.68	1888	0.00	1888	0.00
LA36	15×15	1268	1295	2.12	1308	3.15	1388	9.46	1311	3.39	-	-	-	-	1334	5.20	-	-
LA37	15×15	1397	1415	1.28	1489	6.58	1486	6.37	-	-	-	-	-	-	1467	5.01	-	-
LA38	15×15	1196	1246	4.18	1275	6.60	1339	11.95	-	-	-	-	1258	5.18	1278	6.85	-	-
LA39	15×15	1233	1258	2.02	1290	4.62	1334	8.19	-	-	-	-	-	-	1296	5.10	-	-
LA40	15×15	1222	1243	1.71	1252	2.45	1347	10.22	-	-	-	-	-	-	1284	5.07	-	-
MErr (LA)				**0.61**		**1.50**		**3.52**		**1.27**		**0.38**		**0.77**		**1.99**		**0.80**
FT06	6×6	55	55	0.00	55	0.00	-	-	55	0.00	55	0.00	55	0.00	55	0.00	55	0.00
FT10	10×10	930	930	0.00	935	0.53	-	-	940	1.07	951	2.25	937	0.75	960	3.22	930	0.00
FT20	20×5	1165	1165	0.00	1180	1.28	-	-	1178	1.11	1178	1.11	1182	1.45	1192	2.31	1165	0.00
MErr (FT)				**0.00**		**0.60**		**-**		**0.73**		**1.12**		**0.73**		**1.84**		**0.00**
ORB01	10×10	1059	1068	0.84	1084	2.36	-	-	-	-	-	-	-	-	1099	3.77	1092	3.11
ORB02	10×10	888	889	0.11	890	0.22	-	-	-	-	-	-	-	-	906	2.02	894	0.67
ORB03	10×10	1005	1023	1.79	1037	3.18	-	-	-	-	-	-	-	-	1056	5.07	1029	2.38
ORB04	10×10	1005	1005	0.00	1028	2.28	-	-	-	-	-	-	-	-	1032	2.68	1016	1.09
ORB05	10×10	887	889	0.22	894	0.78	-	-	-	-	-	-	-	-	909	2.48	901	1.57
ORB06	10×10	1010	1019	0.89	1035	2.47	-	-	-	-	-	-	-	-	1038	2.77	1028	1.78
ORB07	10×10	397	397	0.00	404	1.76	-	-	-	-	-	-	-	-	411	3.52	405	2.01
ORB08	10×10	899	907	0.88	937	4.22	-	-	-	-	-	-	-	-	917	2.00	914	1.66
ORB09	10×10	934	940	0.64	943	0.96	-	-	-	-	-	-	-	-	-	-	943	0.96
ORB10	10×10	944	944	0.00	967	2.43	-	-	-	-	-	-	-	-	-	-	944	0.00
MErr (ORB)				**0.54**		**2.07**		**-**		**-**		**-**		**-**		**3.04**		**1.69**
ABZ05	10×10	1234	1234	0.00	1238	0.32	-	-	-	-	-	-	-	-	1241	0.56	-	-
ABZ06	10×10	943	943	0.00	947	0.42	-	-	-	-	-	-	-	-	964	2.22	-	-
ABZ07	20×15	656	695	5.94	-	-	-	-	-	-	-	-	-	-	719	9.60	-	-
ABZ08	20×15	665	713	10.03	-	-	-	-	-	-	-	-	-	-	738	13.88	-	-
ABZ09	20×15	679	721	6.34	-	-	-	-	-	-	-	-	-	-	742	9.43	-	-
MErr (ABZ)				**4.46**		**0.37**		**-**		**-**		**-**		**-**		**7.14**		**-**

5 Conclusion

The objective of this work was to develop an approach to makespan reduction in job shop scheduling instances. The proposed technique for achieving the goal was a GA with improved local search techniques and a multi-crossover operator. To evaluate the proposed approach, experiments were conducted in 58 JSSP instances of varying complexity. The instances used were FT [11], LA [20], ORB

[4] and ABZ [1]. The results obtained were compared with other approaches in related works: GA-CPG-GT [18], DWPA [26], GWO [15], HGWO [14], MA [19]), IPB-GA [17] and aLSGA [5].

By analyzing the results obtained we can observe that the proposed method achieves competitive results in JSSP instances and it's able to find good makespan results. The mXLSGA obtained competitive MErr with respect to the results achieved by the compared algorithms in the LA, ORB and ABZ instances. In the FT instance mXLSGA got 0.00% error and tied with the aLSGA algorithm. Through the analysis of the results we can see that mXLSGA is a competitive and versatile method that achieves good results in instances of varying complexity.

In future works, we will study the feasibility of the method in similar combinatorial optimization problems, such as flexible job shop scheduling problems, flow shop scheduling, etc. Also, further performance measurement parameters may be included for algorithm evaluation.

Acknowledgements. This study was financed in part by the Coordenação de Aperfeiçoamento de Pessoal de Nível Superior - Brasil (CAPES) - Finance Code 001.

References

1. Adams, J., Balas, E., Zawack, D.: The shifting bottleneck procedure for job shop scheduling. Manag. Sci. **34**(3), 391–401 (1988)
2. Amjad, M.K., et al.: Recent research trends in genetic algorithm based flexible job shop scheduling problems. Math. Probl. Eng. **2018** (2018)
3. Anand, E., Panneerselvam, R.: A study of crossover operators for genetic algorithm and proposal of a new crossover operator to solve open shop scheduling problem. Am. J. Ind. Bus. Manag. **6**(06), 774 (2016)
4. Applegate, D., Cook, W.: A computational study of the job-shop scheduling problem. ORSA J. Comput. **3**(2), 149–156 (1991)
5. Asadzadeh, L.: A local search genetic algorithm for the job shop scheduling problem with intelligent agents. Comput. Ind. Eng. **85**, 376–383 (2015)
6. Asadzadeh, L., Zamanifar, K.: An agent-based parallel approach for the job shop scheduling problem with genetic algorithms. Math. Comput. Modell. **52**(11–12), 1957–1965 (2010)
7. Bierwirth, C., Mattfeld, D.C., Kopfer, H.: On permutation representations for scheduling problems. In: Voigt, H.-M., Ebeling, W., Rechenberg, I., Schwefel, H.-P. (eds.) PPSN 1996. LNCS, vol. 1141, pp. 310–318. Springer, Heidelberg (1996). https://doi.org/10.1007/3-540-61723-X_995
8. Binato, S., Hery, W.J., Loewenstern, D.M., Resende, M.G.C.: A grasp for job shop scheduling. In: Ribeiro, C.C., Hansen, P. (eds.) Essays and Surveys in Metaheuristics. ORCS, vol. 15, pp. 59–79. Springer, Boston (2002). https://doi.org/10.1007/978-1-4615-1507-4_3
9. Chaudhry, I.A., Khan, A.A.: A research survey: review of flexible job shop scheduling techniques. Int. Trans. Oper. Res. **23**(3), 551–591 (2016)
10. Essafi, I., Mati, Y., Dauzère-Pérès, S.: A genetic local search algorithm for minimizing total weighted tardiness in the job-shop scheduling problem. Comput. Oper. Res. **35**(8), 2599–2616 (2008)

11. Fisher, C., Thompson, G.: Probabilistic learning combinations of local job-shop scheduling rules. In: Industrial scheduling, pp. 225–251 (1963)
12. Goldberg, D.E., Holland, J.H.: Genetic algorithms and machine learning. Mach. Learn. **3**(2), 95–99 (1988)
13. Goldberg, D.E., Lingle, R., et al.: Alleles, loci, and the traveling salesman problem. In: Proceedings of an International Conference on Genetic Algorithms and their Applications, vol. 154, pp. 154–159. Lawrence Erlbaum, Hillsdale (1985)
14. Jiang, T.: A hybrid grey wolf optimization for job shop scheduling problem. Int. J. Comput. Intell. Appl. **17**(03), 1850016 (2018)
15. Jiang, T., Zhang, C.: Application of grey wolf optimization for solving combinatorial problems: job shop and flexible job shop scheduling cases. IEEE Access **6**, 26231–26240 (2018)
16. Jorapur, V., Puranik, V., Deshpande, A., Sharma, M.: Comparative study of different representations in genetic algorithms for job shop scheduling problem. J. Softw. Eng. Appl. **7**(07), 571 (2014)
17. Jorapur, V.S., Puranik, V.S., Deshpande, A.S., Sharma, M.: A promising initial population based genetic algorithm for job shop scheduling problem. J. Softw. Eng. Appl. **9**(05), 208 (2016)
18. Kurdi, M.: An effective genetic algorithm with a critical-path-guided Giffler and Thompson crossover operator for job shop scheduling problem. Int. J. Intell. Syst. Appl. Eng. **7**(1), 13–18 (2019)
19. Lamos-Díaz, H., Aguilar-Imitola, K., Pérez-Díaz, Y.T., Galván-Núñez, S.: A memetic algorithm for minimizing the makespan in the job shop scheduling problem. Revista Facultad de Ingeniería **26**(44), 113–123 (2017)
20. Lawrence, S.: Resource constrained project scheduling: an experimental investigation of heuristic scheduling techniques (supplement). Carnegie-Mellon University, Graduate School of Industrial Administration (1984)
21. Meeran, S., Morshed, M.: A hybrid genetic tabu search algorithm for solving job shop scheduling problems: a case study. J. Intell. Manuf. **23**(4), 1063–1078 (2012)
22. Ombuki, B.M., Ventresca, M.: Local search genetic algorithms for the job shop scheduling problem. Appl. Intell. **21**(1), 99–109 (2004)
23. Piroozfard, H., Wong, K.Y., Asl, A.D.: An improved biogeography-based optimization for achieving optimal job shop scheduling solutions. Procedia Comput. Sci. **115**, 30–38 (2017)
24. Sayoti, F., Riffi, M.E., Labani, H.: Optimization of makespan in job shop scheduling problem by golden ball algorithm. Indonesian J. Electr. Eng. Comput. Sci. **4**(3), 542–547 (2016)
25. Semlali, S.C.B., Riffi, M.E., Chebihi, F.: Memetic chicken swarm algorithm for job shop scheduling problem. Int. J. Electr. Comput. Eng. **9**(3), 2075 (2019)
26. Wang, F., Tian, Y., Wang, X.: A discrete wolf pack algorithm for job shop scheduling problem. In: 2019 5th International Conference on Control, Automation and Robotics (ICCAR), pp. 581–585. IEEE (2019)
27. Watanabe, M., Ida, K., Gen, M.: A genetic algorithm with modified crossover operator and search area adaptation for the job-shop scheduling problem. Comput. Ind. Eng. **48**(4), 743–752 (2005)
28. Xhafa, F., Abraham, A.: Metaheuristics for Scheduling in Industrial and Manufacturing Applications, vol. 128. Springer, Heidelberg (2008). https://doi.org/10.1007/978-3-540-78985-7

Signature Partitioning Using Selected Population-Based Algorithms

Marcin Zalasiński[1]([✉]) [iD], Krzysztof Cpałka[1] [iD], Tacjana Niksa-Rynkiewicz[2] [iD], and Yoichi Hayashi[3] [iD]

[1] Department of Computational Intelligence, Czestochowa University of Technology, Częstochowa, Poland
{marcin.zalasinski,krzysztof.cpalka}@pcz.pl
[2] Department of Marine Mechatronics, Gdask University of Technology, Gdańsk, Poland
tacniksa@pg.edu.pl
[3] Department of Computer Science, Meiji University, Tokyo, Japan
hayashiy@cs.meiji.ac.jp

Abstract. Dynamic signature is a biometric attribute which is commonly used for identity verification. Artificial intelligence methods, especially population-based algorithms (PBAs), can be very useful in the dynamic signature verification process. They are able to, among others, support selection of the most characteristic descriptors of the signature or perform signature partitioning. In this paper, we focus on creating the most characteristic signature partitions using different PBAs and comparing their effectiveness. The simulations whose results are presented in this paper were performed using the BioSecure DS2 database distributed by the BioSecure Association.

Keywords: Dynamic signature verification · Population-based algorithms · Fuzzy systems · Biometrics

1 Introduction

The signature is a biometric attribute used in behavioral biometrics for identity verification [16,43]. It is also used as a commonly socially acceptable form of authorization. The dynamic signature (DS) is described by signals changing over time and contains information about the dynamics of a signing process. This type of signature is acquired using a digital input device, e.g. a graphic tablet or smartphone.

Artificial intelligence methods, especially population-based algorithms (PBAs) [5,18,25,26,28,30,37], fuzzy systems (FSs) [9,22,27,29,31–33,35,36], and their combinations [2,19,37], are very effective tools supporting identity verification using the DS [38–42]. It has been proved, among others, in our previous paper [41], in which a new method for horizontal partitioning of the dynamic signature has been presented. In this paper, we focus on signature partitioning

© Springer Nature Switzerland AG 2020
L. Rutkowski et al. (Eds.): ICAISC 2020, LNAI 12415, pp. 480–488, 2020.
https://doi.org/10.1007/978-3-030-61401-0_44

with the use of different PBAs, comparing effectiveness of the proposed method to other ones and comparing PBAs' effectiveness. After the partitioning process, characteristic descriptors of the signature are created in the partitions. Their suitability for the dynamic signature verification is evaluated using an authorial fuzzy one-class classifier [7]. It does not require forged signatures samples at the training phase, like e.g. other popular classifiers based on SVM or neural networks [3,11,14,15,17,21,34].

This paper is organized into four sections. Section 2 presents the idea of the population-based approach for horizontal signature partitioning. Section 3 discusses the simulation results while Sect. 4 presents the conclusions.

2   Population-Based Approach for Horizontal Signature Partitioning

Partitioning of the dynamic signature is one of the methods used for creating characteristic descriptors of the signature which are used in the identity verification process. Horizontal partitioning is implemented on the basis of the values of signals describing dynamics of the signature. Descriptors created in partitions extracted in this process contain information about similarity of the signature trajectories in the regions associated with high and low values of signals describing the dynamics of the signing process. In this paper, we assume that horizontal partitions are determined using PBAs. PBAs are heuristic methods which process a population of solutions in order to effectively search space of considerations. A single solution in the population is called an individual or a chromosome (in the genetic algorithm). It is evaluated by the fitness function (FF) of the form suited to the considered problem. The value of the FF is determined for each individual in the population and it determines its chances of survival. Details of the proposed method are presented in this section.

A partitioning algorithm is performed using J reference signatures of user i. They should be pre-processed using commonly known methods [8] to, among others, match their lengths. Next, we use a PBA to select division points $div_i^{\{s\}}$ used for creating the partitions where s is a signal used for determining a partition. In our method each individual $\mathbf{X}_{i,ch}$ from the population encodes two division points determined for user i:

$$\begin{aligned}
\mathbf{X}_{i,ch} &= \left\{ div_i^{\{v\}}, div_i^{\{z\}} \right\} \\
&= \left\{ X_{1,ch}, X_{2,ch} \right\},
\end{aligned} \tag{1}$$

where v is a velocity signal of the signature and z is a pressure signal of the signature.

The algorithm uses a specially designed fitness function (FF) to evaluate individuals in the population. The value of the FF results from the values of descriptors created in the partitions determined using division points encoded in the individuals and the ratio between the number of the discretization points in the signature partitions. In order to determine the value of the FF the following steps have to be performed:

Step 1. Calculation of the values of ratio $Rp_{i,j}^{\{s\}}$ between the number of the discretization points in the signature partitions associated with the same signal s:

$$Rp_{i,j}^{\{s\}} = \begin{cases} 1 - \dfrac{Kc_{i,1}^{\{s\}}}{Kc_{i,0}^{\{s\}}} \text{ for } Kc_{i,0}^{\{s\}} \geq Kc_{i,1}^{\{s\}} \\ 1 - \dfrac{Kc_{i,0}^{\{s\}}}{Kc_{i,1}^{\{s\}}} \text{ otherwise,} \end{cases} \tag{2}$$

where i is the index of the user, j is the index of the reference signature, s is the signal of the signature used for creating the partition, p is the index of the partition, $Kc_{i,p}^{\{s\}}$ is the number of discretization points in partition p of user i created on the basis of signal s.

Step 2. Normalization of the descriptors' values representing similarity of the training signatures to the template. This process is performed by membership function $\mu\left(d_{i,j,p}^{\{s,a\}}\right)$ defined as follows:

$$\mu\left(d_{i,j,p}^{\{s,a\}}\right) = \frac{1}{1 + \exp\left(5 - 2 \cdot d_{i,j,p}^{\{s,a\}}\right)}, \tag{3}$$

where $d_{i,j,p}^{\{s,a\}}$ is the descriptor of signature j of user i calculated using trajectory a (x or y) in partition p determined using signal s.

Step 3. Averaging the parameters values. The values computed in the previous steps are averaged in the context of each reference signature j of the user. It is performed as follows:

$$\begin{cases} avgD_{i,j} = \dfrac{\left(\mu\left(d_{i,j,0}^{\{v,x\}}\right) + \mu\left(d_{i,j,1}^{\{v,x\}}\right) + \ldots \atop \ldots + \mu\left(d_{i,j,0}^{\{z,y\}}\right) + \mu\left(d_{i,j,1}^{\{z,y\}}\right)\right)}{4 \cdot p} \\ avgR_{i,j} = \frac{1}{2} \cdot \left(Rp_{i,j}^{\{v\}} + Rp_{i,j}^{\{z\}}\right), \end{cases} \tag{4}$$

where $avgD_{i,j}$ is the average value of descriptors in the context of signature j of user i and $avgR_{i,j}$ is the average value of parameters $Rp_{i,j}^{\{s\}}$ in the context of signature j of user i.

Step 4. Calculation of the value of the FF. It is performed using weighted algebraic triangular norm $T^* \{\cdot\}$ [4]:

$$\begin{aligned} F\left(\mathbf{X}_{i,ch}\right) &= \\ &= T^* \begin{Bmatrix} avgD_{i,1}, \ldots, avgD_{i,J}, \\ avgR_{i,1}, \ldots, avgR_{i,J}; \\ wD_{i,1}, \ldots, wD_{i,J}, \\ wR_{i,1}, \ldots, wR_{i,J} \end{Bmatrix} \\ &= \begin{pmatrix} (1 - wD_{i,1} \cdot (1 - avgD_{i,1})) \cdot \ldots \\ \cdot (1 - wR_{i,J} \cdot (1 - avgR_{i,J})) \end{pmatrix}, \end{aligned} \tag{5}$$

where t-norm $T^* \{\cdot\}$ is a generalization of the usual two-valued logical conjunction (studied in the classical logic), $wD_{i,j} \in [0,1]$ and $wR_{i,j} \in [0,1]$ are the weights of importance of arguments $avgD_{i,j}$ and $avgR_{i,j}$.

The purpose of the PBA for creating vertical partitions is a maximization of the FF in form (5). Values of division points $div_i^{\{v\}}$ and $div_i^{\{z\}}$ of the best chromosome in the population are used for creating the partitions. The horizontal partitions indicated by the elements of vector $\mathbf{p}_i^{\{s\}} = \left[p_{i,k=1}^{\{s\}}, p_{i,k=2}^{\{s\}}, \ldots, p_{i,k=K_i}^{\{s\}} \right]$ are determined as follows:

$$p_{i,k}^{\{s\}} = \begin{cases} 1 \text{ for } s_{i,j=jBase,k} < div_i^{\{s\}} \\ 2 \text{ for } s_{i,j=jBase,k} \geq div_i^{\{s\}}, \end{cases} \tag{6}$$

where k is the index of the signal sample, K_i is the number of signal samples, $jBase$ is the index of the base signature which is the training signature most similar to the others. This step is performed only in the learning phase for the reference signatures.

Next, templates of the signature are created. They are averaged fragments of the reference signatures represented by the shape trajectories. They are indicated by the elements of vector $\mathbf{tc}_{i,p}^{\{s,a\}} = \left[tc_{i,p,k=1}^{\{s,a\}}, \ldots, tc_{i,p,k=Kc_{i,p}^{\{s\}}}^{\{s,a\}} \right]$ determined as follows:

$$tc_{i,p,k}^{\{s,a\}} = \frac{1}{J} \sum_{j=1}^{J} a_{i,j,p,k}^{\{s\}}, \tag{7}$$

where $\mathbf{a}_{i,j,p}^{\{s\}} = \left[a_{i,j,p,k=1}^{\{s\}}, \ldots, a_{i,j,p,k=Kc_{i,p}^{\{s\}}}^{\{s\}} \right]$ is a trajectory (x or y) of reference signature j of user i created on the basis of signal s, which belongs to partition p. This step is performed only in the learning phase.

Next, descriptors $d_{i,p}^{\{s,a\}}$ of signature j are created in the following way:

$$d_{i,j,p}^{\{s,a\}} = \sqrt{\sum_{k=1}^{Kc_{i,p}^{\{s\}}} \left(tc_{i,p,k}^{\{s,a\}} - a_{i,j,p,k}^{\{s\}} \right)^2}. \tag{8}$$

This step is also performed in the test phase for a test signature.

Finally, the classification of the signature is performed. This process is implemented using the flexible fuzzy one-class classifier proposed in our previous works. A detailed description of the classifier can be found, among others, in [7].

3   Simulations

The simulations were performed using the BioSecure dynamic signature database DS2 [10]. It contains signatures of 210 users. The signatures were acquired in two sessions using a digitizing tablet, each of them containing 15 genuine signatures and 10 skilled forgeries per person. In the training phase, we used 5 randomly selected genuine signatures of each signer. In the test phase, we used 10 genuine signatures and 10 so-called skilled forgeries [13] of each signer. In the simulations we used 4 selected PBAs: the differential evolution algorithm (DE, [24]), the imperialist competitive algorithm (ICA, [1]), the golden ball algorithm (GB, [23]), and the grey wolf optimizer algorithm (GWO, [20]). The assumptions about these algorithms can be summarized as follows:

- the number of individuals in the population: 100,
- the method of selecting individuals in the DE and GB (also the selection method of players that face each other to score a goal): the roulette wheel method,
- parameter CR in the DE: 0.5, parameter F in the DE: 0.75,
- number of empires in the ICA: 10, parameter ϵ in the ICA: 0.1, parameter β in the ICA: 2.0, parameter γ in the ICA: 0.15,
- the number of goal chances in the GB: 20, the number of teams in the GB: 10, and the number of matches in the league competition in the GB: number of teams·number of teams (each team plays with each other).

The conclusions from the simulations can be summarized as follows:

- The accuracy of the method proposed in this paper is relatively high in comparison to the methods of the other authors collected in paper [12] and the method using a traditional way of creating horizontal partitions, proposed in [6] (see Table 1).

Table 1. Comparison of the accuracy of the method using the on-line signature partitioning with the PBA to the other methods for the DS verification using the BioSecure database. The best results are given in bold.

Id.	Method	Average FAR	Average FRR	Average error
1	Different methods presented in [12]	–	–	3.48%-30.13%
2	Method using horizontal partitioning presented in [6]	2.94%	4.45%	3.70%
3	Our method using DE	2.92%	3.24%	3.08%
4	Our method using ICA	2.94%	3.34%	3.14%
5	Our method using GB	2.96%	3.36%	3.16%
6	Our method using GWO	**2.86%**	**2.98%**	**2.92%**

– The accuracy of the proposed method is relatively high regardless of the type of the used PBA. It is especially important in the context of comparison with our previous method which uses partitions determined without the support from PBAs. It confirms the correctness of the adopted assumptions and it means that the population-based approach can be used to create signature partitions which are better suited to the individual dynamics of signing.
– The GWO algorithm was the best in the context of creating horizontal partitions in comparison to the DE, ICA, and GB algorithms.

4   Conclusions

In this paper, we present a method for on-line signature verification based on population-based horizontal partitioning by different PBAs. The purpose of the paper was to assess how the use of different population-based algorithms (PBAs) affects the effectiveness of the dynamic signature verification using horizontal partitioning. The conducted simulations have proved that the use of different PBAs can help create partitions which are better suited to the individual user, which improves the effectiveness of the identity verification process. Moreover, the best PBA from the tested algorithms has been the GWO algorithm.

In the future, we are planning to test different PBAs in the context of other types of signature partitioning.

Acknowledgment. This paper was financed under the program of the Minister of Science and Higher Education under the name 'Regional Initiative of Excellence' in the years 2019–2022, project number 020/RID/2018/19 with the amount of financing PLN 12 000 000.

References

1. Atashpaz-Gargari, E., Lucas, C.: Imperialist competitive algorithm: an algorithm for optimization inspired by imperialistic competition. In: Proceedings of the IEEE Congress on Evolutionary Computation, vol. 7, pp. 4661–4666 (2007)
2. Bartczuk, Ł., Przybył, A., Cpałka, K.: A new approach to nonlinear modelling of dynamic systems based on fuzzy rules. Int. J. Appl. Math. Comput. Sci. (AMCS) **263**, 603–621 (2016)
3. Cao, Y., Samidurai, R., Sriraman, R.: Stability and dissipativity analysis for neutral type stochastic Markovian jump static neural networks with time delays. J. Artif. Intell. Soft Comput. Res. **9**(3), 189–204 (2019)
4. Cpałka, K.: Design of Interpretable Fuzzy Systems. SCI, vol. 684. Springer, Cham (2017). https://doi.org/10.1007/978-3-319-52881-6
5. Dziwiński, P., Bartczuk, Ł., Paszkowski, J.: A new auto adaptive fuzzy hybrid particle swarm optimization and genetic algorithm. J. Artif. Intell. Soft Comput. Res. **10**(2), 95–111 (2020)
6. Cpałka, K., Zalasiński, M., Rutkowski, L.: A new algorithm for identity verification based on the analysis of a handwritten dynamic signature. Appl. Soft Comput. **43**, 47–56 (2016)

7. Cpałka, K., Zalasiński, M., Rutkowski, L.: New method for the on-line signature verification based on horizontal partitioning. Pattern Recogn. **47**, 2652–2661 (2014)
8. Fierrez, J., Ortega-Garcia, J., Ramos, D., Gonzalez-Rodriguez, J.: HMM-based on-line signature verification: feature extraction and signature modeling. Pattern Recogn. Lett. **28**, 2325–2334 (2007)
9. Grycuk, R., Gabryel, M., Nowicki, R., Scherer, R.: Content-based image retrieval optimization by differential evolution, Proceedings of the IEEE Congress on Evolutionary Computation (CEC), vol. 1, pp. 86–93 (2016)
10. Homepage of Association BioSecure. http://biosecure.it-sudparis.eu. Accessed 13 Nov 2019
11. Duda, P., Jaworski, M., Cader, A., Wang, L.: On training deep neural networks using a streaming approach. J. Artif. Intell. Soft Comput. Res. **10**(1), 15–26 (2020)
12. Houmani, N., et al.: BioSecure signature evaluation campaign (BSEC'2009): evaluating online signature algorithms depending on the quality of signatures. Pattern Recogn. **45**, 993–1003 (2012)
13. Jain, A.K., Ross, A.: Introduction to biometrics. In: Jain, A.K., Flynn, P., Ross, A.A. (eds.) Handbook of Biometrics. Springer, Berlin-Heidelberg (2008). https://doi.org/10.1007/0-306-47044-6_1
14. Javaid, M., Abbas, M., Liu, J.B., Teh, W.C., Cao, J.: Topological properties of four-layered neural networks. J. Artif. Intell. Soft Comput. Res. **9**(2), 111–122 (2019)
15. Kamimura, R.: Supposed maximum mutual information for improving generalization and interpretation of multi-layered neural networks. J. Artif. Intell. Soft Comput. Res. **9**(2), 123–147 (2019)
16. Linden, J., Marquis, R., Bozza, S., Taroni, F.: Dynamic signatures: a review of dynamic feature variation and forensic methodology. Forensic Sci. Int. **291**, 216–229 (2018)
17. Ludwig, S.A.: Applying a neural network ensemble to intrusion detection. J. Artif. Intell. Soft Comput. Res. **9**(3), 177–188 (2019)
18. Łapa, K.: Meta-optimization of multi-objective population-based algorithms using multi-objective performance metrics. Inf. Sci. **489**, 193–204 (2019)
19. Łapa, K., Cpałka, K., Wang, L.: New method for design of fuzzy systems for nonlinear modelling using different criteria of interpretability. In: Rutkowski, L., Korytkowski, M., Scherer, R., Tadeusiewicz, R., Zadeh, L.A., Zurada, J.M. (eds.) ICAISC 2014. LNCS (LNAI), vol. 8467, pp. 217–232. Springer, Cham (2014). https://doi.org/10.1007/978-3-319-07173-2_20
20. Mirjalili, S., Mirjalili, S.M., Lewis, A.: Grey wolf optimizer. Adv. Eng. Softw. **69**, 46–61 (2014)
21. Nobukawa, S., Nishimura, H., Yamanishi, T.: Pattern classification by spiking neural networks combining self-organized and reward-related spike-timing-dependent plasticity. J. Artif. Intell. Soft Comput. Res. **9**(4), 283–291 (2019)
22. Nowicki, R., Scherer, R., Rutkowski, L., A hierarchical neuro-fuzzy system based on S-implications. In: Proceedings of the International Joint Conference on Neural Networks, vol. 1, pp. 321–325 (2003)
23. Osaba, E., Diaz, F., Onieva, E.: Golden ball: a novel meta-heuristic to solve combinatorial optimization problems based on soccer concepts. Appl. Intell. **41**(1), 145–166 (2014). https://doi.org/10.1007/s10489-013-0512-y
24. Price, K.V., Storn, R.M., Lampinen, J.A.: Differential Evolution: A Practical Approach to Global Optimization. NCS. Springer, Heidelberg (2005). https://doi.org/10.1007/3-540-31306-0

25. Rafajłowicz, W.: A hybrid differential evolution-gradient optimization method. In: Rutkowski, L., Korytkowski, M., Scherer, R., Tadeusiewicz, R., Zadeh, L.A., Zurada, J.M. (eds.) ICAISC 2015. LNCS (LNAI), vol. 9119, pp. 379–388. Springer, Cham (2015). https://doi.org/10.1007/978-3-319-19324-3_35
26. Rafajłowicz, W.: Cosmic rays inspired mutation in genetic algorithms. In: Rutkowski, L., Korytkowski, M., Scherer, R., Tadeusiewicz, R., Zadeh, L.A., Zurada, J.M. (eds.) ICAISC 2017. LNCS (LNAI), vol. 10245, pp. 418–426. Springer, Cham (2017). https://doi.org/10.1007/978-3-319-59063-9_37
27. Rafajłowicz, W., Domski, W., Jabłoński, A., Ratajczak, A., Tarnawski, W., Zajda, Z.: Fuzzy reasoning in control and diagnostics of a turbine engine – a case study. In: Rutkowski, L., Scherer, R., Korytkowski, M., Pedrycz, W., Tadeusiewicz, R., Zurada, J.M. (eds.) ICAISC 2019. LNCS (LNAI), vol. 11508, pp. 335–345. Springer, Cham (2019). https://doi.org/10.1007/978-3-030-20912-4_32
28. Rafajłowicz, E., Rafajłowicz, W.: Fletcher's filter methodology as a soft selector in evolutionary algorithms for constrained optimization. In: Rutkowski, L., Korytkowski, M., Scherer, R., Tadeusiewicz, R., Zadeh, L.A., Zurada, J.M. (eds.) EC/SIDE -2012. LNCS, vol. 7269, pp. 333–341. Springer, Heidelberg (2012). https://doi.org/10.1007/978-3-642-29353-5_39
29. Rafajłowicz, W., Rafajłowicz, E.: A rule-based method of spike detection and suppression and its application in a control system for additive manufacturing. Appl. Stoch. Models Bus. Ind. **34**, 645–658 (2018)
30. Riid, A., Preden, J.S.: Design of fuzzy rule-based classifiers through granulation and consolidation. J. Artif. Intell. Soft Comput. Res. **7**, 137–147 (2017)
31. Rutkowski T., Romanowski, J., Woldan, P., Staszewski, P., Nielek, R., Rutkowski, L.: A content-based recommendation system using neuro-fuzzy approach. In: Proceedings of the 2018 IEEE International Conference on Fuzzy Systems (FUZZ-IEEE), Rio de Janeiro, pp. 1–8 (2018)
32. Rutkowski, T., Łapa, K., Jaworski, M., Nielek, R., Rutkowska, D.: On explainable flexible fuzzy recommender and its performance evaluation using the Akaike information criterion. In: Gedeon, T., Wong, K.W., Lee, M. (eds.) ICONIP 2019. CCIS, vol. 1142, pp. 717–724. Springer, Cham (2019). https://doi.org/10.1007/978-3-030-36808-1_78
33. Sadiqbatcha, S., Jafarzadeh, S., Ampatzidis, Y.: Particle swarm optimization for solving a class of type-1 And type-2 fuzzy nonlinear equations. J. Artif. Intell. Soft Comput. Res. **8**, 103–110 (2018)
34. Shewalkar, A., Nyavanandi, D., Ludwig, S.A.: Performance evaluation of deep neural networks applied to speech recognition: RNN, LSTM and GRU. J. Artif. Intell. Soft Comput. Res. **9**, 235–245 (2019)
35. Scherer, R.: An ensemble of logical-type neuro-fuzzy systems. Expert Syst. Appl. **38**(10), 13115–13120 (2011)
36. Scherer, R.: Designing boosting ensemble of relational fuzzy systems. Int. J. Neural Syst. **20**(5), 381–388 (2010)
37. Szczypta, J., Przybył, A., Cpałka, K.: Some aspects of evolutionary designing optimal controllers. In: Rutkowski, L., Korytkowski, M., Scherer, R., Tadeusiewicz, R., Zadeh, L.A., Zurada, J.M. (eds.) ICAISC 2013. LNCS (LNAI), vol. 7895, pp. 91–100. Springer, Heidelberg (2013). https://doi.org/10.1007/978-3-642-38610-7_9
38. Zalasiński, M., Cpałka, K.: Novel algorithm for the on-line signature verification using selected discretization points groups. In: Rutkowski, L., Korytkowski, M., Scherer, R., Tadeusiewicz, R., Zadeh, L.A., Zurada, J.M. (eds.) ICAISC 2013. LNCS (LNAI), vol. 7894, pp. 493–502. Springer, Heidelberg (2013). https://doi.org/10.1007/978-3-642-38658-9_44

39. Zalasiński, M., Cpałka, K.: New algorithm for on-line signature verification using characteristic hybrid partitions. In: Wilimowska, Z., Borzemski, L., Grzech, A., Świątek, J. (eds.) Information Systems Architecture and Technology: Proceedings of 36th International Conference on Information Systems Architecture and Technology – ISAT 2015 – Part IV. AISC, vol. 432, pp. 147–157. Springer, Cham (2016). https://doi.org/10.1007/978-3-319-28567-2_13

40. Zalasiński, M., Cpałka, K., Hayashi, Y.: New fast algorithm for the dynamic signature verification using global features values. In: Rutkowski, L., Korytkowski, M., Scherer, R., Tadeusiewicz, R., Zadeh, L.A., Zurada, J.M. (eds.) ICAISC 2015. LNCS (LNAI), vol. 9120, pp. 175–188. Springer, Cham (2015). https://doi.org/10.1007/978-3-319-19369-4_17

41. Zalasiński, M., Cpałka, K., Łapa, K., Przybyszewski, K., Yen, G.G.: On-line signature partitioning using a population based algorithm. J. Artif. Intell. Soft Comput. Res. **10**, 5–13 (2020)

42. Zalasiński, M., Cpałka, K., Rakus-Andersson, E.: An idea of the dynamic signature verification based on a hybrid approach. In: Rutkowski, L., Korytkowski, M., Scherer, R., Tadeusiewicz, R., Zadeh, L.A., Zurada, J.M. (eds.) ICAISC 2016. LNCS (LNAI), vol. 9693, pp. 232–246. Springer, Cham (2016). https://doi.org/10.1007/978-3-319-39384-1_21

43. Zois, E.N., Alexandridis, A., Economou, G.: Writer independent offline signature verification based on a symmetric pixel relations and unrelated training-testing data sets. Expert Syst. Appl. **125**, 14–32 (2019)

Pattern Classification

Breast Cancer Classification from Histopathological Images Using Transfer Learning and Deep Neural Networks

Abdulrahman Aloyayri[1,2]([⊠]) [iD] and Adam Krzyżak[1]

[1] Department of Computer Science and Software Engineering, Concordia University,
Montreal H3G 1M8, Canada
a_aloyay@encs.concordia.ca, adam.krzyzak@concordia.ca
[2] Faculty of Computer Science Department, Saudi Electronic University, Riyadh, Saudi Arabia
a.aloyayri@seu.edu.sa

Abstract. Early diagnosis of breast cancer is the most reliable and practical approach to mitigate cancer. Computer-aided detection or computer-aided diagnosis is one of the software technologies designed to assist doctors in detecting or diagnosing cancer and to reduce mortality using medical image analysis. Recently, Convolution Neural Networks became very popular in medical image analysis helping to process vast amount of data to detect and classify cancer in a fast and efficient manner. In this paper, we implemented deep neural networks ResNet18, InceptionV3 and ShuffleNet for binary classification of breast cancer in histopathological images. We have used networks pre-trained by the transfer learning on the ImageNet database and with fine-tuned output layers trained on histopathological images from the public dataset BreakHis. The highest average accuracy achieved for binary classification of benign or malignant cases was 98.73% for ResNet18, followed by 97.65% for ShuffleNet and 97.44% for Inception-V3Net.

Keywords: Histopathological images · Breast cancer · Deep convolutional neural networks · Transfer learning · Binary classification

1 Introduction

Cancer is one of the most common causes of death worldwide. According to the World Health Organization (WHO), cancer is the second leading cause of death globally, and in 2018 it caused approximately 9.6 million fatalities worldwide. Breast cancer is a widespread disease that many women are facing in their life; however, breast cancer can also appear in men. According to the Breast Cancer Institute, breast cancer is one of the deadliest diseases that afflict women in the world. Early diagnosis is the most dependable and reliable method for successfully managing cancer. In contrast, postponement of diagnosis may result in cancer spreading throughout the body and may be difficult to treat and control. Furthermore, late diagnosis leads to reduced odds at successful treatment. There are many early diagnosis approaches for breast cancer. They include self-examination at home, breast screening or visiting a doctor. These methods reduce the rate of mortality

© Springer Nature Switzerland AG 2020
L. Rutkowski et al. (Eds.): ICAISC 2020, LNAI 12415, pp. 491–502, 2020.
https://doi.org/10.1007/978-3-030-61401-0_45

and boost a chance for successful treatment. The most popular breast imaging diagnostic tools are breast ultrasound, magnetic resonance imaging (MRI), computed tomography (CT), thermography, mammography, cytopathological and histopathological imaging. The most commonly used early breast cancer detection modalities are ultrasound and mammography. Computer-aided detection (CAD) software or computer-aided diagnosis of cancer is software technology aimed at assisting doctors in detecting or diagnosing cancer and at reducing mortality by automatically processing medical imaging data. CAD is software for classification and grading of breast images to benign and malignant classes or stages. Recent years witness the explosive growth of artificial intelligence (AI) and its applications. Among the most successful areas of AI is machine learning (ML) including deep learning (DL). One of the most spectacular successes DL was obtained by the convolutional neural network (CNN) capable of automatically extracting features from images and classifying them with stunning accuracy [1, 2]. CNN is an effective technique to find patterns in data to recognize objects in different applications of computer vision and to extract features automatically to classify images (see Fig. 1). CNNs used in the medical field to classify cancer efficiently requires many training images. Standard CNNs contain many hidden layers that can be trained to extract features automatically. They contain convolution layers and pooling layers. The convolution layer uses a set of moving convolutional windows that convolve with the input image and extract features in the process. The pooling layer decreases the spatial size of the convolutional layer. There are two types of pooling layers: max pooling and average pooling. Max pooling yields the max value of the pooling window; the average pooling returns the average value from the pooling window. After learning features from layers, CNN performs classification using a fully connected output layer. There are many pre-trained deep neural networks such as AlexNet, GoogLeNet, Inception-V3Net, ResNet50, VGGNet19 and ShuffleNet which can be used to extract features automatically from natural images and to classify images using transfer learning.

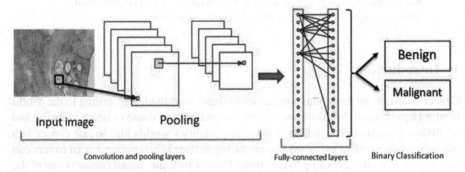

Fig. 1. Convolutional neural network workflow.

2   Related Works

This section focuses on the literature survey relevant to the main topic of this paper, i.e. classification of medical images. We briefly review breast cancer classification with different types of images and datasets. Many techniques have been published and improved to detect and classify breast cancer using deep neural networks with different architectures. The difficult task of medical image analysis and classification is to classify histopathological images based on the structure of the cells and complex morphology and texture. Many modern methods have been proposed to resolve the challenging issue of image classification such as deep learning models and pre-trained deep neural networks. Traditional image classification approaches used standard features such as colour, texture, and standard classifiers such as support vector machines, random forests. In [3] the authors proposed two systems for the detection of melanoma in dermoscopy images using texture and colour features. The first system used in their implementation involves the following three steps to classify skin lesions: automatic segmentation, color and texture features extraction and training of a classifier to perform binary classification, whereas the second system uses local features and the bag-of-features classifier. Paper [4] is concerned with the detection of granularity in dermoscopy images of skin lesions, which allows discriminating melanoma from non-malignant skin lesions using colour and texture features. Paper [5] discusses MRI brain image classification based on the weighted-type fractional Fourier transform to extract spectra from each image-based on the support vector machine. Deep learning has been used in many domains and achieved high performance in applications such as natural language processing, speech recognition and computer vision. Convolutional Neural Network (CNN) is an algorithmic technique for deep learning classification that learns from images, sounds, text and videos. CNNs have obtained extraordinary performance in different subjects of computer vision, such as image classification, image segmentation and face recognition. Paper [6] states that Convolutional Networks (ConvNets) is a biologically inspired flexible architecture that can learn invariant features. The authors demonstrated how deep learning can learn and extract features automatically. Furthermore, they pointed out that ConvNets have several stage architectures, and each layer has input and output called feature maps, which represents extracted features. Convolutional layers, pooling layers and fully connected layers are the main three types of layers in ConvNets architecture. The serious problem facing deep learning is that many data are unlabeled. Also, they observed that unsupervised learning with sparse predictive decomposition [7], and ConvNets require a large number of data for training. In [8] the authors proposed a new system based on local binary patterns histograms on histopathology images that is aware of the heterogeneity of local texture patterns through heterogeneity-based weighting. They used homogeneity and the second moment (variance) of local neighbourhoods based on heterogeneity information to better capture information in histopathology images. They experimented with three datasets: KimiaPath24 dataset, IDC datasets and BreakHis datasets. They achieved the best performance on the KimiaPath24 dataset. In papers [9] and [10] the Authors used pre-trained DenseNet and in [11] they adopted VGG19 as the base model and inserted the attention modules at different positions. Paper [12] discusses breast cancer histopathological image classification using convolutional neural networks with a small SE-ResNet module. The objective of [13] was to compare two deep networks, namely VGG16 and ResNet50 in cancer detection. The effect of layer-wise fine-tuning in the magnification-dependent classification of breast cancer histopathological images was discussed in [14]. A common problem with medical data is the imbalance problem (unequal number of samples from different categories), which makes training of CNN a challenging task. The authors of [14] used pre-trained AlexNet CNN and evaluated their system on BreakHis public dataset. The BreakHis is an imbalanced dataset. The imbalance creates inevitable problems. The use of transfer learning mitigates the issue of data inadequacy and it results in faster training than when the whole network is learned from scratch.

3   Methodology

In this section, we present the main contributions and describe the proposed method used in the task of the binary classification of breast cancer from histopathological images. There have been numerous studies on applications of deep learning to classification of breast cancer from histopathological images. In this paper, we use a publicly available database called BreakHis [15]. When building our framework we used the following steps:

1. Build our dataset from BreakHis
2. Data preprocessing
3. Data augmentation on the training set
4. Model training
5. Classification and model evaluation.

First, to obtain the database and to have access to the microscopic biopsy images, one must request and fill the form online from the Laboratory of Vision, Robotics, and Imaging of the Federal University of Parana, Brazil [2]. For each input image, we used some pre-processing techniques to improve its quality. The next section explains in detail pre-processing used in the implementation. After pre-processing, we used an image-based approach to randomly divide the dataset at proportion 70–30 into training set and test set. Next, we applied data augmentation to increase the size of the training dataset. Augmentation involved image operations such as resizing, rotation and reflection. After training the parameters of the network on the train set evaluate its performance on the test set using metrics such as classification accuracy and confusion matrices. The results of the experimental study are presented in the next sub-section.

3.1   Dataset Description

In this paper, we use the Breast Cancer Histopathological Image Classification (BreakHis) Database from the Laboratory of Vision Robotics and Imaging at the Federal University of Parana, Brazil [2]. The dataset BreakHis is divided into two main groups: benign tumours and malignant tumours with different magnification factors (40X, 100X, 200X, 400X). The images in the dataset are RGB images of resolution 700X × 460 pixels in 3-channels. There are 2,480 benign samples and 5,429 malignant samples from 82 patients. Additionally, benign images represent four classes: Adenosis (A), Fibroadenoma (F), Phyllodes Tumor (PT) and Tubular Adenoma (TA). Malignant images represent four classes: Ductal Carcinoma (DC), Lobular Carcinoma (LC), Mucinous Carcinoma (MC) and Papillary Carcinoma (PC). The following table (Table 1) describes the distribution of images in the BreakHis dataset according to cancer sub-types.

Table 1. The distribution of images from the BreakHis dataset by cancer categories

Types	Sub-types	40X	100X	200X	400X	Total
Benign	A	114	113	111	106	**444**
	F	253	260	264	237	**1014**
	PT	109	121	108	115	**453**
	TA	149	150	140	130	**569**
Malignant	DC	864	903	896	788	**3451**
	LC	156	170	163	137	**626**
	MC	205	222	196	169	**792**
	PC	145	142	135	138	**560**
Total		**1995**	**2081**	**2013**	**1820**	**7909**

The following figure (Fig. 2) shows samples of cancer at different magnifications: the malignant cases in the first row and benign cases in the second row.

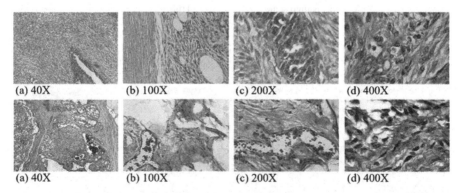

(a) 40X (b) 100X (c) 200X (d) 400X

(a) 40X (b) 100X (c) 200X (d) 400X

Fig. 2. Slides of benign and malignant breast cancer under different magnifications.

3.2 Data Pre-processing

Before using the data, we size-normalized it to make it consistent with the requirements of different networks. Resizing of input images was accomplished via data rescaling and cropping to ensure that image sizes fit each pre-trained deep neural network. The networks used in this paper are pre-trained deep neural network ResNet18, ShuffleNet and Inception-V3Net, and they all require different input image sizes. Specifically, Inception-V3Net uses 299 × 299 images, ResNet18 and ShuffleNet use 224 × 224 images.

3.3 Data Augmentation

CNN requires a considerable amount of data for learning its parameters. A standard technique for expanding the training data set is augmentation [16]. Augmentation helps in improving system performance, reduces the chance of overfitting and mitigates data imbalance. There are many techniques for data augmentation. They include random reflection, rotations and horizontal or vertical translations. We applied data augmentation only to the training set, and the test set has not been augmented. The transformations used in augmentation of our training set are presented in Table 2 below and examples of data augmentation using rotations by 90° and 180° and by flipping are shown in Fig. 3.

Table 2. Transformations used in data augmentation

Parameters	Value
Range of rotation	90°, 180°
Random reflection	True
Range of horizontal shear	True
Range of vertical shear	True
Range scale	True

Original Image   Rotation and Reflection Images

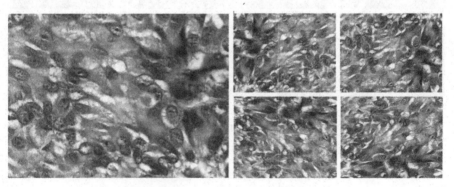

Fig. 3. Illustration of data augmentation.

3.4   Transfer Learning

Considering the complexity of medical imaging and in particular of histopathological images, transfer learning helps to boost performance classification. Transfer learning is a method that can be applied in learning of deep neural networks. It allows knowledge gained in solving one type of problem to be transferred to solving related problems. Typically, the first layers of deep nets are trained on large datasets of images, e.g., on ImageNet, which contains about 14 million images from 20,000 categories and then the last layers of the nets are trained on the specific problem at hand, e.g., on breast cancer classification and grading problem. Fine-tuning of the deep net in combination with transfer learning allows for much faster and more efficient learning than training all network weights (often millions of them), starting with randomly initialized weights. The final three output layers of our classifier are as follows: fully connected layer, SoftMax layer and output classification layer. The final layers are trained on the BreakHis dataset of histopathological images. In other words, we extract all layers from the pre-trained network except for the last three layers. The fully connected output layer has the number of outputs consistent with the number of classes in the dataset. Furthermore, we increase the value of the Weight Learn Rate Factor (WLRF) and the Bias Learn Rate Factor (BLRF) to boost the learning rate of the output layers weights.

3.5   Training Methodology

After implementing transfer learning in the pre-trained network and setting both values for WLRF and BLRF to 20, training of the network requires adjusting sizes of input images depending on the network used. The Adaptive Moment Estimation algorithm (Adam [17]) was used in network optimization and values of important parameters are listed in Table 3 below.

Table 3.   Properties of training methodology.

Property	Value
Initial learning rate	1e−4 (0.0001)
Learn rate schedule	Piecewise
Squared gradient decay factor	0.99
Epoch	15
Mini batch size	128

3.6   Dataset Experimental Protocol

There are two possible ways for using data for training and testing of the classifier: one is the image-based approach, and the other is a patient-based approach. Different studies implemented the dataset in terms of the image-based approach, see, e.g., [14, 18, 19]; in contrast, paper [10] implemented in their experiment the patient-based approach. In this paper, we used the image-based approach with 5-fold cross-validation and divided the dataset by randomly selecting 70% of the data for the training set and 30% for the testing set. We implemented data augmentation on the training set to balance the classes and to avoid overfitting. Furthermore, we implemented dropout in each pre-trained neural network to prevent it from overfitting. The optimizer algorithm is Adaptive Moment Estimation (Adam), and we set the learning rate to 0.0001, decay factor to 0.99, and the batch size to 128. We measured the performance of our neural network classifiers using standard metrics such as classification accuracy, precision, sensitivity, specificity, and F_1 score.

4   Experimental Results

In this section we will present the results of our experiments with three deep neural networks pre-trained by transfer learning that were applied to breast cancer classification using histopathological images. The system is trained and tested on image data from the publicly available BreakHis dataset of 7909 real samples (images) from 82 patients, divided into two subsets of 2,480 benign samples and 5,429 malignant samples. We present classification results for ResNet18, ShuffleNet and Inception-V3Net deep neural network classifiers tested on images from BreakHis with different magnification factors of 40x, 100x, 200x, 400x and compare their performance in the table below (Table 4).

Table 4. Comparison of deep neural networks performance for different magnifying factors

Neural network	Magnifying factors	Accuracy	Precision	Sensitivity	Specificity	F1 score
ResNet18	40x	99.49%	99.21%	99.77%	99.21%	99.49%
	100x	98.11%	97.69%	98.56%	97.67%	98.12%
	200x	98.91%	99.19%	98.62%	99.20%	98.91%
	400x	98.42%	97.27%	99.64%	97.21%	98.44%
Overall average		**98.73%**	**98.34%**	**99.15%**	**98.32%**	**98.74%**
ShuffleNet	40x	98.76%	99.21%	98.31%	99.21%	98.76%
	100x	97.55%	97.65%	97.43%	97.67%	97.54%
	200x	96.90%	96.37%	97.48%	96.33%	96.92%
	400x	97.39%	96.10%	98.78%	95.99%	97.42%
Overall average		97.65%	97.33%	98.00%	97.30%	97.66%
Inception-V3Net	40x	97.77%	96.65%	98.97%	96.57%	97.80%
	100x	97.72%	97.57%	97.89%	97.56%	97.73%
	200x	97.30%	97.14%	97.48%	97.13%	97.31%
	400x	96.96%	96.07%	97.93%	95.99%	96.99%
Overall average		97.44%	96.86%	98.07%	96.81%	97.46%

According to our experiments in Table 4 above, the best performance accuracy, precision, sensitivity, specificity, and F_1 score have been achieved by ResNet18 for different magnifying factors (40x, 100x, 200x, 400x). It was followed by ShuffleNet and Inception-V3Net (Fig. 4).

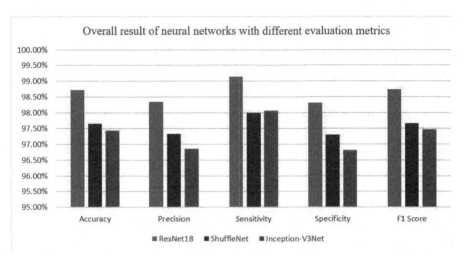

Fig. 4. Comparison of performances of three deep neural networks.

4.1 Comparison with the State-of-the-Art Approaches

In this sub-section, we compare the performance of our deep neural networks with the state-of-the-art techniques applied in the literature to classification of histopathological images from the BreakHis dataset. Several studies, see [20–22], applied deep learning models to diagnostics of breast cancer using histopathological images from the same dataset. All of the studies used different pre-trained deep neural networks. We applied three pre-trained (by transfer learning) neural networks ResNet18, ShuffleNet and Inception-V3Net in image-based binary classification (benign or malignant). ResNet18 achieved the best results for different magnifying factors except for study [23], where Inception with ResNet-V2 with data augmentation was used. However, our ResNet18 did better when they did not use data augmentation. When other studies used Inception-V3Net neural network from our study, our network obtained higher accuracy (Table 5).

Paper [18] adapted the VGG16 pre-trained neural network as the base model for hashing. The authors presented a densely connected multi-magnification framework to generate the discriminative binary codes by exploiting the histopathological images with multiple magnification factors. In paper [23] they implemented InceptionV3 and Inception_ResNetV2 networks, however our ResNet18 performed best. Furthermore, when [18] used Inception_ResNetV2 network with up to 7 times increased dataset sizes by augmenting the original dataset by the left and right rotations, they achieved the best image-based performance in binary classification.

Table 5. Comparison of accuracies of our neural nets with the State-of-the-Art approaches

Study	Year	Neural network	40x	100x	200x	400x	Overall average accuracy
[22]	2019	IRRCNN	97.95%	97.57%	97.32%	97.36%	97.7%
[18]	2019	VGG16	95.62%	95.03%	97.04%	96.31%	96.00%
[19]	2019	Inception-V2Net	91.05%	88.93%	88.76%	87.42%	89.04%
[19]	2019	ResNet50	94.01%	93.34%	95.04%	94.96%	94.33%
[20]	2019	Inception-V3Net	95.7%	95.7%	95.7%	95.7%	95.7%
[22]	2019	ResNet-50	91.2%	91.7%	92.6%	88.9%	91.1%
[23]	2019	Inception-V3Net	96.84%	96.76%	96.49%	94.71%	96.2%
[23]	2019	InceptionResNetV2	97.9%	96.88%	96.98%	96.98%	97.18%
[23]	2019	IRV2 with Aug.	99.79%	99.37%	99.43%	99.1%	99.42%
This paper	2020	ResNet18	99.49%	98.11%	98.91%	98.42%	98.73%
This paper	2020	ShuffleNet	98.76%	97.55%	96.90%	97.39%	97.65%
This paper	2020	Inception-V3Net	97.77%	97.72%	97.30%	96.96%	97.44%

5 Conclusions

In this paper, we compared three pre-trained deep convolutional networks in the task of image-based breast cancer classification using histopathological images. We applied the following pre-trained deep convolutional neural networks: ResNet18, Inception-V3Net and ShuffleNet to automatically extract features and classify breast cancer to benign and malignant classes. We used publicly available database BreakHis consisting of 7,909 histopathological images from 82 patients with different magnifying factors of 40x, 100x, 200x, 400x. We applied data augmentation for boosting the size of the training set and for balancing the classes and transfer learning. We applied several performance evaluation metrics such as accuracy, precision, sensitivity (recall), specificity and F_1 score for each magnifying factor. ResNet18 achieved the best overall average accuracy of 98.73% followed by ShuffleNet 97.65% and Inception-V3Net 97.44%, i.e., our ResNet18 had an excellent overall performance. In future work, we plan to investigate the performance of our deep nets and related models in the patient-based classification of breast cancer using histopathological images.

References

1. Mckinney, S.M., et al.: International evaluation of an AI system for breast cancer screening. Nature **577**(7788), 89–94 (2020)

2. Spanhol, F.A., Oliveira, L.S., Petitjean, C., Heutte, L.: Breast cancer histopathological image classification using convolutional neural networks. In: Proceedings of 2016 International Joint Conference on Neural Networks (IJCNN), pp. 2560–2567 (2016)

3. Barata, C., Ruela, M., Francisco, M., Mendonca, T., Marques, J.S.: Two systems for the detection of melanomas in dermoscopy images using texture and color features. IEEE Syst. J. **8**(3), 965–979 (2014)

4. Stoecker, W.V., et al.: Detection of granularity in dermoscopy images of malignant melanoma using color and texture features. Comput. Med. Imaging Graph. **35**(2), 144–147 (2011)

5. Zhang, Y.-D., Chen, S., Wang, S.-H., Yang, J.-F., Phillips, P.: Magnetic resonance brain image classification based on weighted-type fractional Fourier transform and nonparallel support vector machine. Int. J. Imaging Syst. Technol. **25**(4), 317–327 (2015)

6. LeCun, Y., Kavukcuoglu, K., Farabet, C.: Convolutional networks and applications in vision. In: Proceedings of 2010 IEEE International Symposium on Circuits and Systems, Paris, pp. 253–256 (2010)

7. Kavukcuoglu, K., Ranzato, M., LeCun, Y.: Fast inference in sparse coding algorithms with applications to object recognition, arXiv preprint arXiv:1010.3467 (2008)

8. Erfankhah, H., Yazdi, M., Babaie, M., Tizhoosh, H.R.: Heterogeneity-aware local binary patterns for retrieval of histopathology images. IEEE Access **7**, 18354–18367 (2019)

9. Nawaz, M., Sewissy, A.A., Soliman, T.H.A.: Multi-class breast cancer classification using deep learning convolutional neural network. Int. J. Adv. Comput. Sci. Appl. (IJACSA) **9**(6), 316–322 (2018)

10. Gupta, V., Bhavsar, A.: Sequential modeling of deep features for breast cancer histopathological image classification. In: Proceedings of 2018 IEEE/CVF Conference on Computer Vision and Pattern Recognition Workshops (CVPRW), pp. 23335–23357 (2018)

11. Wu, P., Qu, H., Yi, J., Huang, Q., Chen, C., Metaxas, D.: Deep attentive feature learning for histopathology image classification. In: Proceedings of IEEE 16th International Symposium on Biomedical Imaging (ISBI 2019), pp. 1865–1868 (2019)

12. Jiang, Y., Chen, L., Zhang, H., Xiao, X.: Breast cancer histopathological image classification using convolutional neural networks with small SE-ResNet module. PLOS One **14**(3), e0214587 (2019)

13. Ismail, N.S., Sovuthy, C.: Breast cancer detection based on deep learning technique. In: Proceedings of 2019 International UNIMAS STEM 12th Engineering Conference (EnCon), pp. 89–92 (2019)

14. Sharma, S., Mehra, R.: Effect of layer-wise fine-tuning in magnification-dependent classification of breast cancer histopathological image. Vis. Comput. **36**(9), 1755–1769 (2019). https://doi.org/10.1007/s00371-019-01768-6

15. Spanhol, F.A., Oliveira, L.S., Petitjean, C., Heutte, L.: A dataset for breast cancer histopathological image classification. IEEE Trans. Biomed. Eng. **63**(7), 1455–1462 (2016)

16. Kassani, S.H., Kassani, P.H.: A comparative study of deep learning architectures on melanoma detection. Tissue Cell **58**, 76–83 (2019)

17. Kingma, D.P., Lei Ba, J.: Adam: a method for stochastic optimization. In: Proceedings of 2015 International Conference on Learning Representations (ICLR), arXiv:1412.6980 (2015)

18. Gu, Y., Yang, J.: Densely-connected multi-magnification hashing for histopathological image retrieval. IEEE J. Biomed. Health Inform. **23**(4), 1683–1691 (2019)

19. Sabari, D.N., Saravanan, R., Anbazhagan, J., Koduganty, P.: Comparison of deep feature classification and fine tuning for breast cancer histopathology image classification. In: Communications in Computer and Information Science Recent Trends in Image Processing and Pattern Recognition, pp. 58–68 (2019)

20. Xiang, Z., Ting, Z., Weiyan, F., Cong, L.: Breast cancer diagnosis from histopathological image based on deep learning. In: Proceedings of 2019 Chinese Control and Decision Conference (CCDC), pp. 4616–4619 (2019)

21. Zhang, X., et al.: Classifying breast cancer histopathological images using a robust artificial neural network architecture. In: Rojas, I., Valenzuela, O., Rojas, F., Ortuño, F. (eds.) IWBBIO 2019. LNCS, vol. 11465, pp. 204–215. Springer, Cham (2019). https://doi.org/10.1007/978-3-030-17938-0_19

22. Alom, M.Z., Yakopcic, C., Nasrin, M.S., Taha, T.M., Asari, V.K.: Breast cancer classification from histopathological images with inception recurrent residual convolutional neural network. J. Digit. Imaging 32(4), 605–617 (2019)

23. Xie, J., Liu, R., Luttrell, J., Zhang, C.: Deep learning based analysis of histopathological images of breast cancer. Front. Genetics 10, 1–19. (2019)

Visualization of Membership Distribution in Strings Using Heat Maps

Łukasz Culer$^{(\boxtimes)}$ and Olgierd Unold$^{(\boxtimes)}$

Department of Computer Engineering,
Wrocław University of Science and Technology, Wrocław, Poland
{lukasz.culer,olgierd.unold}@pwr.edu.pl

Abstract. Grammar inference methods allow us to create grammars and automata based on provided data. Those automata can be utilized as classifiers for yet unknown strings. Fuzzy sets theory allowed the implementation of a gradual level of strings' membership and made effective error handling feasible and automata classifiers more applicable in real-life tasks. In this paper, we reversed the currently existing approach - instead of focusing on the whole string membership, we made an approach to determine membership distribution throughout string letters and visualize it using a heat map.

Keywords: Formal languages · Grammar inference · Fuzzy logic · Heat map

1 Introduction

Grammar inference is a study area that describes creation of grammars or automata based on provided data. It covers many diverse approaches [5]. There is a major distinctions between methods based on mathematically proved procedure using specific constraints (formal methods) and those which define heuristics aiming to create a fitting grammar (empirical methods).

Managing errors was a topic of numerous papers especially in the context of formal languages. The first attempt was made in [1]. The authors were trying to create automata based on provided strings. In the second part of the experiment they provided strings that contained errors (misplaced letters). They noticed, that algorithm produces many more states than for errorless strings while creating exact representation. Minimalization of incorrectly classified strings with a given confidence level as a learning target provided promising results. This idea was utilized and extended in numerous approaches like [12] or [15]. In [14] strings with incorrectly set labels were analyzed.

Fuzzy logic defined within the Fuzzy set theory was introduced in [17]. It is one of many-valued logics. In contradiction to standard Boolean logic which allows only crisp, two states of logic value (0 and 1) fuzzy logic allows assigning a real number from a closed interval of 0 and 1. What is more, operators that are counterparts for Boolean logic ones were also defined. Fuzzy truth values are

© Springer Nature Switzerland AG 2020
L. Rutkowski et al. (Eds.): ICAISC 2020, LNAI 12415, pp. 503–513, 2020.
https://doi.org/10.1007/978-3-030-61401-0_47

also known as membership values as they can be utilized as a fitting measure and constitute a mean to represent vagueness and uncertainty.

The fuzzy variant of formal languages was introduced for the first time in [7]. It implemented fuzziness as a membership value of grammar rule which informs about the uncertainty of being a part of the grammar. Superiority of classification performance over crisp grammars has been proven in numerous papers [8,9,16]. Fuzzy grammars were also utilized as an method to handle errors in the input data [2].

Heat maps are a popular method of data visualization where one dimension is expressed by color. Two different colors are assigned to two edge values that have to be displayed. Colors from gradient created from the former two colors are assigned to values that correspond to them in a defined way (linear progress in value usually denotes a linear move in gradient). Traditionally, low values of the expressed attribute are represented by colors associated with low temperature (purple, blue) whereas high values with ones associated with high temperature (orange, yellow). Heat maps are the primary way of representation in Kohonen's Self Organizing Maps which are employed e.g. in bioinformatics [18]. One of the most widespread application is for different environmental maps, starting from the weather visualization (temperature, atmospheric pressure) to terrain height [10].

The most popular way of visualization within formal languages are different kinds of derivation trees which describe the syntactic structure of a string created on a basis of the defined grammar. The other ones are Sequence Logos [13] which are used in bioinformatics and present a sequence conservation in protein sequences or DNA/RNA.

Typically, fuzzy logic is applied to grammar inference systems to provide additional data for classification. This additional data are represented by rules labeled with memberships. String classification produce its membership value based on those rules. String membership value has a similar meaning to the one applied to rules - it describes the uncertainty of string being part of the language due to grammar imperfectness and errors in strings. String membership can be then defuzzified (employing various techniques) to obtain a crisp classification label if necessary. It is worth noting that the string is still described with a single value.

There are many other weighted alternatives for fuzzy grammars such as stochastic grammars. For the needs of our research, we selected fuzzy grammars as a target of our grammar inference algorithms. They were selected due to their flexibility (there is no need to sum probabilities to 1) and better-suited weight meaning (the grade of being a part of grammar rather than the probability of selection given rule variant) compared to their stochastic counterparts. A comprehensive comparison between fuzzy and probabilistic theory was described in [6].

Our research was motivated by the need for a more detailed analysis of classified strings by context-free grammars. Our work suggests that there is a possibility of reverse membership propagation (from the root of a parse tree instead of propagation to the root). This propagation results in string terminals labeled by a membership value. Obtained value can reflect the certainty of given terminal correctness.

In this paper, we present a method of obtaining membership values for any string terminals based on fuzzy grammar that generates it. Obtained data are then visualized using a heat map. Colors assigned to each terminal allow identifying areas with low membership easily.

Firstly, we introduce the basic notations (Sect. 2) with the procedure of obtaining string membership based on a given grammar. The following chapter will cover the attempt to assign membership for each strings' terminal (Sect. 3) which will be visualized using a heat map (Sect. 4). We will provide the example in Sect. 5. Finally, we will make conclusions based on obtained results (Sect. 6).

2 Preliminaries

Notations introduction will start with basic context-free grammar definitions which were originally defined in [7]. In this paper we will represent grammar as quadruple $G = (V_N, V_T, P, S)$ where terminals set are denoted as V_T and non-terminals set as V_N. It is worth noting that $V_T \cap V_N = \emptyset$. Elements of V_T compose strings. The set of finite strings created using terminals is denoted as V_T^* whereas its single element as x. P is the notion for the rule (production) set and S is highlighted non-terminal (therefore $S \in V_N$) known as a start symbol.

As it was previously mentioned the membership value of any string x in language L can be denoted as $\mu_L(x)$. Membership value takes a real number from a closed interval of 0 and 1. Based on that we can define a fuzzy language as a fuzzy set in V_T^* so it can be also expressed as a set of pairs:

$$L = \{x, \mu_L(x)\}, x \in V_T^* \tag{1}$$

As V_N, V_T and S are defined in the same way for both crisp and fuzzy grammar, P have a different form for fuzzy grammars. As they are also fuzzified we define them as rewriting rules with assigned membership value:

$$\mu(\alpha \to \beta) = \rho, \rho \in (0, 1] \tag{2}$$

It can be also expressed in a more concise form of $\alpha \xrightarrow{\rho} \beta$. For context-free grammar $\alpha \in V_N$ and $\beta \in (V_N \cup V_T)^*$.

Based on previously introduced basic information we can define how strings are derivable from others. One string is directly derivable from another with the application of the specific rewriting rule $\alpha \to \beta$ if this transformation can be expressed as:

$$\gamma\alpha\delta \xrightarrow{\rho} \gamma\beta\delta \tag{3}$$

where $\gamma, \delta \in (V_N \cup V_T)^*$. In that case we can say that $\gamma\beta\delta$ is directly derivable from $\gamma\alpha\delta$.

For strings that require the application of multiple rewriting rules a derivation chain can be defined as below:

$$\alpha_1 \xrightarrow{\rho_2} \alpha_2 \cdots \alpha_{m-1} \xrightarrow{\rho_m} \alpha_m \qquad (4)$$

Equation 4 is understood as a derivation chain from α_1 to α_m.

We define that the language $L(G)$ is generated by the grammar G. Any string of terminals x belongs to the language $L(G)$ if and only if at least one derivation chain from highlighted symbol S to the given string x exist. x is in $L(G)$ with a membership grade given by the formula 5:

$$\mu_{L(G)}(x) = S_{norm}(T_{norm}(\mu(S \to \alpha_1), \\ \mu(\alpha_1 \to \alpha_2), \cdots, \mu(\alpha_m \to x))) \qquad (5)$$

where S_{norm} and T_{norm} can be selected accordingly to the given problem. In Eq. 5 S_{norm} is taken over all possible derivation chains from S to x. It is worth noting that this approach is valid for any subchain.

3   Membership Distribution in the String

3.1   Language Example

To demonstrate the concepts described in this section we introduce the example of language and grammar generating it with managing possible errors. The example was formerly described in [2].

Firstly, we will present the crisp language of given attributes. Let L_0 be the language over alphabet $\Sigma = a, b$ in which strings contain an equal number of a and b:

$$L_0 = \{w | w \in \{a, b\}^+, \#_a(w) = \#_b(w)\}, \qquad (6)$$

where $\#_\sigma(w)$ is the number of σ terminals that are in the string w. It is worth noting that all words in L_0 are even. In the next step the language L_0 will be fuzzified and potential errors that could occur in strings will be handled. The type of handled error is a random replacement of one terminal with another which makes numbers of terminal a and b unequal. However, the length of the example still should be even. Errors decrease membership value of string with error but not at the same level - replacements by a symbol are considered more crucial. Lets define fuzzy language L_1 over Σ where μ_{L_1} is defined in a given way:

$$\mu_{L_1}(w) = \begin{cases} 1 \Leftrightarrow \#_a(w) = \#_b(w) \wedge w \neq \lambda \\ 0.9 \Leftrightarrow \#_b(w) \geqslant \#_a(w) + 2 \wedge |w| \bmod 2 = 0 \\ 0.1 \Leftrightarrow \#_a(w) \geqslant \#_b(w) + 2 \wedge |w| \bmod 2 = 0 \\ 0 \Leftrightarrow w = \lambda \vee |w| \bmod 2 = 1 \end{cases} \qquad (7)$$

where $|w|$ is the length of a string w and λ is an empty string.

Language L_1 is generated by the grammar $G_{L_1} = (V_N^{L_1}, V_T^{L_1}, P^{L_1}, S)$, where $V_N^{L_1} = \{S, A, B\}$, $V_T^{L_1} = \{a, b\}$ and $P = \{S \xrightarrow{1} AB, S \xrightarrow{1} BA, A \xrightarrow{1} SA, A \xrightarrow{1} AS, B \xrightarrow{1} SB, B \xrightarrow{1} BS, S \xrightarrow{0.1} AA, S \xrightarrow{0.9} BB, A \xrightarrow{1} a, B \xrightarrow{1} b\}$.

It is worth noting that rules $S \rightarrow AA$ and $S \rightarrow BB$ are responsible for parsing erroneous examples with a lowered membership.

3.2   Analysis

As a next step we will analyze derivation trees of examples instead of derivation chains. It is easy to notice that, like chains, many derivation trees may exist due to syntactic ambiguity. The set of multiple derivation trees is also known as a parse forest [3]. Trees visualize way of derivation and show which non-terminal was replaced with which non-terminals or terminals on a given stage.

We will analyze derivation trees with graph theory formalism [4]. Directed graphs with weights denoted as G_ω will be considered. They are represented by a triplet (V, A, δ) where V is a node set and A is edge set that contains ordered pairs of vertices. (a, b) represents edge from node a to node b. δ is function $A \rightarrow \mathbb{R}$ that for every edge $e \in A, \delta(e)$ returns weight of this edge. The special cases of weighted graphs are fuzzy graphs where weights are understood as edges' membership values and express their uncertainty [11].

Therefore, we will represent non-terminals and terminals as nodes (terminals as special ones - leaves) with directed, weighted edges connecting them. The edges will be constructed on the base of rewriting rules linking non-terminals with their non-terminal and terminal replacements. The weight of the edge corresponds to the membership value of the origin rule.

We present an example of the derivation of string $bbaa$ in Fig. 1. The string was derived using the grammar defined in the previous section.

Two of four possible derivation trees were presented. We can note that the path between the start non-terminal and each terminal in the string can be created. As a path we understand a chain of connected nodes:

$$p = x_1, x_2, \cdots, x_{n-1}, x_n \qquad (8)$$

Due to the syntactic ambiguity and the existence of various derivation trees we have to consider multiple paths connecting every non-terminal and terminal. All possible paths linking a and b can be expressed as in Eq. 9:

$$P^{a,b} = \{P_1^{a,b}, P_2^{a,b}, \cdots, P_{n-1}^{a,b}, P_n^{a,b}\} \qquad (9)$$

We can notice that edges in the path are created with the use of different rules. Those rules could have various membership values that express our uncertainty about associated edges. Based on that we can calculate membership value for a given path:

$$\mu(p) = t_{norm}(\mu(x_1, x_2), \cdots, \mu(x_{n-1}, x_n)) \qquad (10)$$

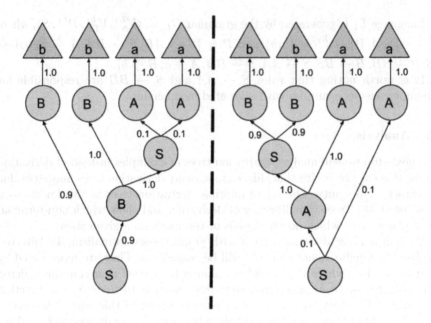

Fig. 1. The example of two derivation trees for string *bbaa*

Considered paths end with specific terminals at a specific position in the string. Therefore, those paths memberships can be also considered as those terminals at the given position membership grade.

However, as we previously mentioned, there may exist many paths with various membership values that end in a given terminal. Hence, there is a need to determine a way to obtain an output value from many path membership values. In [11] the strength (membership) of connectedness between two nodes is defined as the maximum strength (membership) of all paths between them. However, obtaining maximum value ignores the occurrence of paths with lower membership values. To take them into account the resultant of all path memberships will be their average value:

$$\mu(P^{a,b}) = \frac{\sum_{j=1}^{n} \mu(P_j^{a,b})}{n} \tag{11}$$

Consequently, our certainty about a given terminal will be a combination of memberships determined with Eq. 11.

Finally, a membership grade of the terminal at the given position in the string w denoted as w_i can be expressed as a combination of all possible path memberships from the start non-terminal to the given terminal:

$$\mu(w_i) = \mu(P^{S,w_i}) = \frac{\sum_{j=1}^{n} \mu(P_j^{S,w_i})}{n} \tag{12}$$

4   Heat Map Visualization

The method which we described in the previous section produces a string which terminals are annotated with membership value. The most straightforward way to present obtained data will be a table with two rows. One will contain consequent terminals and the second one membership values that correspond to them as in the Table 1. However, it appears to be difficult to analyze and compare because it needs conscious decoding of numbers that are placed above terminals.

Table 1. The example of the labeled string

1.00	1.00	0.92	0.65	0.74	0.89	1.00
a	b	b	a	c	b	c

The representation described above contains three dimensions. The first one is the position in the string which is represented by the order of terminals. The second one is the of terminal that is expressed by a proper letter. Membership value as third dimension is placed above the terminal as a number. Two first dimensions are represented in a way that is familiar to people - a string of letters. The third one can be easily clarified by expressing it as terminals' colors.

In Sect. 1 we introduced general properties of heat maps. To apply them, edge values and colors have to be selected first. Color picked for the lowest value is red since it should represent the biggest uncertainty. We select the green color for the least ambiguous terminals due to its association with correctness. The selection of edge values is clear due to the properties of the membership grade which could have an assigned value from a closed interval from 0 to 1.

The next issue is mapping from a membership value to a color. Colors are expressed in the RGB color model where constituents are represented by 8-bit values (therefore, by integer numbers from range 0 to 255):

$$C = (C_R, C_G, C_B) \tag{13}$$

where C is a color represented by the triplet. C_R, C_G and C_B correspond to red, green and blue constituents consecutively. As we previously mentioned, for membership value 0.0 obtained color is red ($C_R = 255$ and $C_G = C_B = 0$) and for 1.0 green ($C_G = 255$ and $C_R = C_B = 0$). For other membership grades red and green constituents change evenly. Consequently, color for terminal w_i can be determined using formula 14.

$$C_{w_i} = (255 - \lfloor \mu(w_i) \cdot 255 \rfloor, \lfloor \mu(w_i) \cdot 255 \rfloor \cdot 255, 0) \tag{14}$$

The last step is a color adjustment to increase contrast. Classic histogram equalization used traditionally to increase contrast does not fit well for this application. Small fluctuations around full membership were stretched to become fully red and give a false impression of having 0.0 membership value. Instead, colors are stretched only in the direction of the full membership and spread evenly inside boundaries to expand existing clusters. We execute this operation before obtaining colors because it is easier to perform it with membership values. Firstly, a set of unique membership values M_u is created based on values linked with terminals in string w. Then a minimum (M_u^{min}) value above them is found. (M_u^{min}) is a constant for a linear transformation function. We determine a slope value using formula $\frac{1-M_u^{min}}{|M_u|-1}$. Finally, membership values inside M_u are sorted in ascending order and transformed in a given manner:

$$\underset{i\in 1..|M_u|}{\forall} M_n^i = M_u^{min} + (i-1)\frac{1-M_u^{min}}{|M_u|-1} \tag{15}$$

where M_n is a corresponding set of new membership values that are spread evenly.

We present the example of visualization created using the described procedure in Fig. 2.

aabbbbbbbaa

Fig. 2. The example of a created heat map

5   Application

5.1   Source of Data

In this section we will present examples of the application with the use of language described previously [2] in Sect. 3.1. We manually created strings that were parsed with the defined grammar. Then terminals within string were labeled with memberships and visualized with a heat map. Strings were created in a way to expose the behavior and attributes of grammar, language and heat map generation procedure.

5.2   Examples

We present examples of generated heat maps as a list of figures below (Fig. 3, Fig. 4, Fig. 5, Fig. 6 and Fig. 7). Each example is labeled with a short description.

abab

Fig. 3. The heat map for the string *abab* - the most straightforward, correct string.

bbaa

Fig. 4. The heat map for the string *bbaa* - string with clustered terminals, however still correct.

babbab

Fig. 5. The heat map for the string *babbab* - palindromic string with an uneven number of each type of terminals.

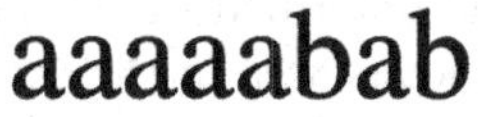

aaaaabab

Fig. 6. The heat map for the string *aaaaabab* - *abab* string with additional four *a* terminals on the left side.

abbbbbbbbba

Fig. 7. The heat map for the string *abbbbbbbbba*- *abba* string with additional eight *b*'s in the center.

5.3   Results Analysis

Firstly, it is easy to note that example *abab* is marked with green color, as expected, since it is a fully correct string. However, correct string *bbaa* contains more shades of green what suggests decreased membership value. The analysis of parse trees found out that some derivation trees utilized also rules $S \rightarrow AA$ or $S \rightarrow BB$ created for handling errors. Both rules have different membership values, therefore multiple overlapping derivation trees created more shades. It can be considered as imperfect error handling rules, however, they were meant only for the classification process and utilized its properties. One of them is a fact that trees with lower membership values would be rejected (hence those containing error handling rules were not needed). This was also the reason for stretching possible colors in the direction of the full membership as it was meant to be a counterbalance for dimming proper parse trees by invalid ones. Further research is needed for this kind of situation.

Strings *babbab* and *abbbbbbbbba* are characterized by two pairs of different terminals on edges and multiplied terminal string in the center aiming to simulate errors in this area. According to the intuition the lowest membership value is located in the center of the string. What is interesting it changes gradually. What needs to be noted is the fact that in example *abbbbbbbbba* proper pairs of *ab* or *ba* are not necessarily created with *b* terminals nearest to *a* terminals. Proper pairs could wrap multiplying pairs *bb*. Further analysis of all derivation trees showed that their number with *bb* pairs increases when they are located closer to the center what explains given forms of heat maps. For example *babbab* this works similarly.

Another interesting issue is local increases of membership which occur in *babbab* string. However, they are far more visible in the example of *aaaaabab*. We defined it as *abab* string with four *a* terminals on the left. We see that first, third and fifth *a* terminals have higher membership value than others. It is caused by the property of grammar that errors are simulated by a terminal exchange in a pair from a different terminal to the same. Therefore, proper pair *ab* has to wrap even number of *a* terminals. It is easy to see that *a* in *ab* pairs that fulfill this condition overlap with *a* terminals with higher membership value. The described phenomenon overlaps with one described in the previous paragraph; If we get closer to the center of the erroneous area in the string then the membership will be lower due to a higher density of derivation trees containing low-membership rules.

6   Conclusions

As it was proved, in the previous chapter the analysis of heat maps can aid research with new insights that provides more knowledge about how created grammars work. It also gives a tool which can point out more delicate and interesting areas of string to focus on. Those areas could be significantly useful in the context of analyzing biological data like DNA or protein strings. Potential progress would be crucial for Amyloids in particular.

Future work will cover the area of combination results from different derivation trees. It is crucial to distinguish more clearly what is the reason of lower membership values which can be an evidence of an error occurrence or a side effect of grammar imperfection.

Acknowledgements. The research was supported by the National Science Centre Poland (NCN), project registration no. 2016/21/B/ST6/02158.

References

1. Angluin, D., Laird, P.: Learning from noisy examples. Mach. Learn. **2**(4), 343–370 (1988). https://doi.org/10.1023/A:1022873112823
2. Asveld, P.R.: Fuzzy context-free languages–part 1: generalized fuzzy context-free grammars. Theor. Comput. Sci. **347**(1), 167–190 (2005). https://doi.org/10.1016/j.tcs.2005.06.012. http://www.sciencedirect.com/science/article/pii/S0304397505003592
3. Billot, S., Lang, B.: The structure of shared forests in ambiguous parsing. In: Proceedings of the 27th Annual Meeting on Association for Computational Linguistics, pp. 143–151. Association for Computational Linguistics (1989)
4. Diestel, R.: Graph Theory. Graduate Texts in Mathematics, 3rd edn., vol. 173 (2005)
5. de la Higuera, C.: Grammatical Inference: Learning Automata and Grammars. Cambridge University Press, New York (2010)

6. Kosko, B.: Fuzziness vs. probability. Int. J. Gen. Syst. **17**(2–3), 211–240 (1990)
7. Lee, E.T., Zadeh, L.A.: Note on fuzzy languages. In: Fuzzy Sets, Fuzzy Logic, and Fuzzy Systems: Selected Papers by Lotfi A Zadeh, pp. 69–82. World Scientific (1996)
8. Min, W., Zhi-wen, M.: An evolution strategy for the induction of fuzzy finite-state automata. J. Math. Stat. **2**(2), 386–390 (2006)
9. Molina-Lozano, H., Vallejo-Clemente, E.E., Morett-Sanchez, J.E.: DNA sequence analysis using fuzzy grammars. In: 2008 IEEE International Conference on Fuzzy Systems (IEEE World Congress on Computational Intelligence), pp. 1915–1921. IEEE (2008)
10. Moumtzidou, A., Vrochidis, S., Chatzilari, E., Kompatsiaris, I.: Discovery of environmental resources based on heatmap recognition. In: 2013 IEEE International Conference on Image Processing, pp. 1486–1490. IEEE (2013)
11. Pal, A.: Introduction to fuzzy graph theory. Int. J. Appl. Fuzzy Sets Artif. Intell. (IJAFSAI) **6**(1), 101–112 (2016)
12. Ron, D., Rubinfeld, R.: Learning fallible deterministic finite automata. Mach. Learn. **18**(2), 149–185 (1995).https://doi.org/10.1023/A:1022899313248
13. Schneider, T.D., Stephens, R.M.: Sequence logos: a new way to display consensus sequences. Nucleic Acids Res. **18**, 6097–6100 (1990)
14. Sebban, M., Janodet, J.C.: On state merging in grammatical inference: a statistical approach for dealing with noisy data, vol. 2, pp. 688–695, January 2003
15. Taubenfeld, G.: On learning from queries and counterexamples in the presence of noise (2017)
16. Unold, O.: Fuzzy grammar-based prediction of amyloidogenic regions. In: Heinz, J., Higuera, C., Oates, T. (eds.) Proceedings of the Eleventh International Conference on Grammatical Inference. Proceedings of Machine Learning Research, vol. 21, pp. 210–219. PMLR, University of Maryland, College Park, 05–08 September 2012
17. Zadeh, L.: Fuzzy sets. Inf. Control **8**(3), 338–353 (1965)
18. Zhang, L., Zhang, A., Ramanathan, M.: VizStruct: exploratory visualization for gene expression profiling. Bioinformatics **20**(1), 85–92 (2004)

Random Projection in the Presence of Concept Drift in Supervised Environments

Moritz Heusinger[1($\boxtimes$)] and Frank-Michael Schleif[2]

[1] Department of Computer Science,
University of Applied Sciences Würzburg-Schweinfurt,
Sanderheinrichsleitenweg 20, Würzburg, Germany
`moritz.heusinger@fhws.de`
[2] School of Computer Science, University of Birmingham,
Edgbaston, Birmingham B15 2TT, UK
`frank-michael.schleif@fhws.de`

Abstract. In static environments Random Projection (RP) is a popular and efficient technique to preprocess high-dimensional data and to reduce its dimensionality. While RP has been widely used and evaluated in stationary data analysis scenarios, non-stationary environments are not well analyzed. In this paper we provide an evaluation of RP on streaming data including a concept of altering dimensions. We discuss why RP can be used in this scenario and how it can handle stream specific situations like *concept drift*. We also provide experiments with RP on streaming data, using state-of-the-art streaming classifiers like *Adaptive Hoeffding Tree* and concept drift detectors on streams containing altering dimensions.

1 Introduction

A common problem in data analysis tasks, like classification is the high dimensionality of the data. This can lead to the phenomenon, that the distance to the nearest data point is very close to the distance to the farthest data point. Given the data is intrinsically low dimensional, the dimensionality can be reduced.

To address this problem, there exist different projection and embedding methods. The most common projection technique is the Principal Component Analysis (PCA).Furthermore, embedding techniques like Locally Linear Embedding, ISOMAP, Multidimensional Scaling and t-distributed Stochastic Neighbour Embedding (t-SNE) are widely used [22].

These methods have one problem in common. They are often working on high-dimensional but not very high-dimensional data, e.g. thousands of input dimensions. In [17] it is recommended to preprocess very high-dimensional data to a dimensionality of 30 via PCA before applying t-SNE. However, PCA is costly taking $\mathcal{O}(d^2 n + d^3)$, where n is the number of samples and d the number of features [24]. Hence, less expensive dimensionality reduction techniques are

© Springer Nature Switzerland AG 2020
L. Rutkowski et al. (Eds.): ICAISC 2020, LNAI 12415, pp. 514–524, 2020.
https://doi.org/10.1007/978-3-030-61401-0_48

desirable. This points to Random Projection (RP), which is a dimensionality reduction method to reduce the dimensionality of data from very high to high, e.g. from 10,000 to 1,000 dimensions [1]. The guarantees given by Random Projection are based on the Johnson Lindenstrauss (JL) lemma [12], which is also used to determine a suitable number of dimensions where the projection does not make an error greater than ϵ. While JL lemma guarantees that *distances* are preserved with good probability by a random projection, a proof for similarities by mean of a dot–product was provided in [13].

In this paper we discuss the introduced distortion of RP in streaming environments and evaluate it on data streams containing concept drift (CD). We also introduce a concept addressing the altering of dimensions in non-stationary data. Finally, we take a look at the performance of CD *detectors* on projected data streams.

2   Related Work

In stationary environments as well as in streaming data, dimensionality reduction is a topic of interest. On one hand to enable the visualization of data, but on the other hand to reduce complexity of algorithms. Especially in streaming environments this is important because of the limited amount of time to predict the label y for an incoming data point x [5].

Some dimensionality reduction algorithms have been adapted to work with streaming data. In [10] an online PCA for evolving data streams has been published, which only keeps track of a subspace of small dimensions that capture most of the variance in the data.

Furthermore, there are existing stream manifold learning algorithms. In [23] error metrics for learning manifolds on streaming data are provided. The idea is to learn the manifold only on a fraction of the stream, until the embedding is stable and then do the embedding by a nearest neighbour approach. The authors used this concept to propose a stream ISOMAP algorithm. Random Projection has already been applied in the fields of non-stationary data. A stream clustering algorithm called streamingRPHas, which uses RP and locality-sensitivity hashing and achieves beneficial results was published in [6]. Another work uses a Hoeffding Tree Ensemble to classify streaming data, but instead of working on high dimensions, it works on a lower dimensional space, the dimensionality reduction is done by RP [20]. Both approaches use RP in streaming context without taking the effect of CD on RP into account, which is a major challenge in supervised streaming analysis. It was also not analyzed or proven for non-stationary environments w.r.t. Johnson-Lindenstrauss lemma.

So far a study of CD detectors and altering dimensions on projections obtained by RP is missing. Hence, we try to fill this gap with this work.

3 Preliminaries

3.1 Random Projection

First, we review some material about the JL lemma and particularities of RP for stationary data. We consider a data set $\mathbf{X}$ with datapoints $\mathbf{x} \in \mathbb{R}^d$ in a d-dimensional space. The data are subject to a random projection to obtain a lower dimensional representation of the data. In RP the d-dimensional input data is projected on a k-dimensional ($k \ll d$) subspace using a random matrix $\mathbf{R} \in \mathbb{R}^{k \times d}$.

The distortion introduced by RP π is asserted by the fact that π defines an ϵ-embedding with high probability defined by:

$$(1 - \epsilon)\|\mathbf{u} - \mathbf{v}\|^2 < \|\pi(\mathbf{u}) - \pi(\mathbf{v})\|^2 < (1 + \epsilon)\|\mathbf{u} - \mathbf{v}\|^2 \tag{1}$$

where $\mathbf{u}$ and $\mathbf{v}$ are any rows taken from data with n samples and d dimensions and π is a projection by a random Gaussian $\mathcal{N}(0, 1)$ matrix $\mathbf{R}$ [7] or a sparse Achlioptas matrix [2].

To determine a minimum number of dimensions in the projected space, the lemma is given by:

$$k >= \frac{4 \log n}{(\epsilon^2/2 - \epsilon^3/3)} \tag{2}$$

where the error made by the projection is less than ϵ [2]. There exist different approaches for generating a sparse random projection matrix $\mathbf{R}$. One approach creates $\mathbf{R}$ by drawing samples from $\mathcal{N}(0, 1)$ and is called Gaussian RP. The other approaches create $\mathbf{R}$ with entries $r_{i,j}$ where i denotes the i-th row and j the j-th column of $\mathbf{R}$, mainly differing in the density:

$$r_{i,j} = \sqrt{s} \begin{cases} -1 & \text{with probability } \frac{1}{2s} \\ 0 & \text{with probability } 1 - \frac{1}{s} \\ +1 & \text{with probability } \frac{1}{2s} \end{cases} \tag{3}$$

In [1] it is recommended to generate the density as shown in Eq. (3) with $s = 3$ to get better results than by Gaussian RP. In [15] it is recommended to use $s = \sqrt{d}$ instead of $s = 3$ because this speeds up the computation of the projection in comparison to the previous approach by having a more sparse matrix $\mathbf{R}$. The first method is often referred to as sparse RP while the latter is called very sparse RP.

3.2 Stream Analysis

Many preprocessing algorithms can not be applied to streaming data, because there are some particularities [3] when analyzing data in non-stationary environments:

- process an instance at a time t and inspect it (at most) once
- use a limited amount of time to process each instance
- use a limited amount of memory
- be ready to give an answer (prediction, clustering, patterns) at any time
- adapt to temporal changes

Some algorithms have been adapted to work with streaming data with a comprehensive review given in [3]. Often, restrictions of these adapted algorithms are stronger than restrictions of corresponding offline versions. E.g. statistics cannot be calculated over the whole data set $\mathbf{X} = \{\mathbf{x}_1, \mathbf{x}_2, ..., \mathbf{x}_t\}$, because the data become available once at a time. Thus, whenever a data point $\mathbf{x}_t$ arrives at time step t at the model h, the model takes this data point into account by learning an adapted model $h_t = train(h_{t-1}, \mathbf{s}_t)$, where $\mathbf{s}_t$ is the tuple consisting of $\mathbf{x}_t$ and its corresponding label y_t. Thus, when applying RP we will project one data point $\mathbf{x}_t$ at time t by our initially created projection matrix $\mathbf{R}$ to provide the projected data set to an online learning algorithm.

Another problem in non-stationary environments is CD which means that joint distributions of a set of samples $\mathbf{X}$ and corresponding labels $\mathbf{y}$ changes between two timesteps:

$$\exists \mathbf{X} : p(\mathbf{X}, \mathbf{y})_t \neq p(\mathbf{X}, \mathbf{y})_{t-1} \tag{4}$$

Note, that we can rewrite Eq. (4) to

$$\exists \mathbf{X} : p(\mathbf{X})_t p(\mathbf{y} \mid \mathbf{X})_t \neq p(\mathbf{X})_{t-1} p(\mathbf{y} \mid \mathbf{X})_{t-1} \tag{5}$$

If there is only a change in the prior distribution $p(\mathbf{X})$ then it is called virtual drift. There are five types of drift categorized by the change over time. Figure 1

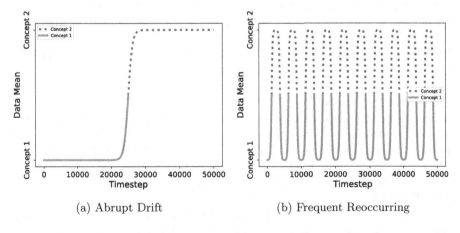

(a) Abrupt Drift   (b) Frequent Reoccurring

Fig. 1. Different types of drifts, one per subfigure and illustrated as data mean. The different styles mark the dominate concept at given time step. The vertical axis shows the data mean and the transition from one to another concept. Given the time axis the speed of the transition is given. The figures are inspired by [8].

shows the two drift types used in this paper. For a comprehensive study of various CD types see [8] and [21]. For this case online classification algorithms use statistical tests to detect CD between two distributions. These tests are adapted and used as so-called CD detectors (CDD) (e.g. Adaptive Windowing [4] and Kolmogorov-Smirnov Windowing [21]) by testing Eq. (5).

4   Random Projection in Non-stationary Environments

4.1   Matrix Creation and Projection

Assume we have a stream with a fixed number of dimensions, which will not change over time, we can generate the projection matrix similar as in the offline setting. Depending on a fast projection in non-stationary settings, RP-VS [15] seems to be most suitable. The matrix creation of $\mathbf{R}$ and projection of $\mathbf{X}$ is of order $\mathcal{O}(dkn)$, however if $\mathbf{X}$ is sparse, we only need $\mathcal{O}(ckn)$ with $\mathbf{X}$ having c non-zero elements per column.

After the matrix creation of $\mathbf{R}$ is done at the beginning of a stream in $\mathcal{O}(ck)$, we can project single datapoints $\mathbf{x} \in \mathbf{X}$ one after each other, performing $\mathbf{R} \times \mathbf{x}$. Note, that in so far considered stream scenarios d does not change over time. Thus, $\mathbf{R}$ does not need to be updated during the stream.

4.2   Distortion

As shown in Eq. (2), a suitable number of k dimensions making an error less than ϵ can be calculated when n is known. Furthermore, there exist bounds which do not rely on n, but need other statistics over the data which are not known prior in streaming settings [14]. Hence, we will focus on JL lemma.

In streaming contexts n is unknown and potential infinite. However, stream classifiers store a fixed number of samples, in a window $\mathbf{W}$ [5,16] or prototypes θ which represent statistics of the data [11]. We have to keep in mind, that the goal of RP is to preserve the distances in our data. A window-based stream classifier only calculates distances between stored samples in $\mathbf{W}$ and newly arriving datapoints. The window-size or number of prototypes is known prior to deploying a classifier. Hence, calculation of k by Eq. (2) is possible.

For clarification, we assume a window $\mathbf{W}$ of size $w = 1,000$ which is a common window size [5]. Preserving distances between this window and a batch of 10 datapoints arriving at a time t leads us to $n = 1010$. Now, we calculate k from Eq. (2) by filling in our n and a suitable ϵ. Setting $\epsilon = 0.2$ leads us to $k >= 1596$. Note, that the window has to be filled at the beginning of a stream, thus $|\mathbf{W}| < w$.

$$k_w \geq k_n \geq \frac{4 \log w}{(\epsilon^2/2 - \epsilon^3/3)} \tag{6}$$

However, this is not a problem, because JL lemma still holds as shown in Eq. (6) due to the fact, that $\forall n < w \in \mathbb{Z}^+ \ k_n \leq k_w$, where n represents the size of our partially filled window, and w is the maximum window size.

4.3   Concept Drift

As stated in Sect. 3.2, CD is a key challenge in streaming environments. Modern CDDs detect changes in the distribution by performing statistical tests [4,21]. These tests are performed on every single dimension of the data. Hence, on d dimensional data, KSWIN performs d Kolmogorow-Smirnow tests at every t. A solution to address the slow performance is to perform the statistical test on a performance indicator of a classifier, e.g. accuracy. However, this has the disadvantage that CD can only be detected after the change in the distribution leading to statistical relevant misclassifications. Hence, monitoring a performance indicator is a suboptimal heuristic. In summary it might be desirable to work with not too high dimensional data, to be fast enough to address the other particularities of streaming data, especially time constraints. Thus, RP seems to be a suitable tool, which can reduce detection time of CDDs by allowing to perform the tests only k times. To be reliable the CDD has to detect drifts which exist in d dimensions in a k dimensional space obtained by RP. We experimentally validate this in Sect. 5.

4.4   Altering Dimensions

We want to consider the case, that a feature of a data stream will be removed or a new feature is added, e.g. because a sensor gets replaced with another sensor or the user of the model decides to take more or less dimensions into account. RP and the underlying classifier needs to handle this change. Assume d as number of dimensions, then the described scenario happens when $d_{t-1} \neq d_t$ at a given timestep t. Hence, the random matrix $\mathbf{R}$ needs to be adapted.

Here we assume a sparse matrix generated by Eq. (3) with $s = \sqrt{k}$. When a dimension is removed in the high dimensional space, we remove the corresponding column of $\mathbf{R}$. Thus, removing a dimension $\mathbf{X}_{:,j}$, where : denotes all rows and j the j-th column of $\mathbf{X}$, leading to a new random matrix $\mathbf{R}_t = \mathbf{R}_{t-1} \setminus \mathbf{R}_{:,j}$. A classifier would still receive k dimensions and does not have to handle altering dimensions in forms of features. However, due to the possible change in one of the k dimensions it introduces CD which can be handled by a CDD in advance. It is also possible, that a new feature gets added during the stream, thus we assume that this feature is appended to $\mathbf{X}$. Assuming $\mathbf{X}_{old}$ has a column length of j, the newly added dimension will be in $\mathbf{X}_{:,j+1}$. Thus, we also need a new column in $\mathbf{R}$, which should be generated by Eq. (3) and $s = \sqrt{d}$. The possible introduced CD should be handled in the same fashion as described for removing dimensions. Furthermore, only d changes, thus number of rows k of $\mathbf{R}$ remain static because they can be addressed by our proposed fixed length window. In summary RP allows the conversion of altering number of dimensions into CD, which can be handled by CDDs instead of training a new classifier.

5   Experiments

In this section we provide experiments[1] on the topics of Sect. 4.

In our first experiment, we analyze performance and runtime of stream classifiers by using common stream generators [8] and real high dimensional data. We are using Reuters dataset[2] which includes 4,773 features and project it to k_W dimensions. As stream generators we use SEA and LED, for details we refer to [8]. These generators are low dimensional, thus we enrich every sample with meaningful dimensions to get up to 10,000 features. Furthermore, we evaluate the performance of the classifiers on high dimensional space compared to low k_W dimensional space, obtained by RP. As projection method, RP-VS is used. As benchmark classifiers we use Adaptive Robust Soft Learning Vector Quantization (ARSLVQ) [11], Adaptive Random Forest (ARF) [9] and Hoeffding Adaptive Tree (HAT) [5] as state-of-the-art streaming classifiers.

Table 1. Comparison of projected concept drift streams w.r.t. accuracy.

Algorithm Dataspace	ARF Original	ARF Projected	RSLVQ$_{ADA}$ Original	RSLVQ$_{ADA}$ Projected	HAT Original	HAT Projected
SEA$_G$	99.50 ± 0.50	99.64 ± 0.38	98.95 ± 1.70	96.75 ± 2.77	77.54 ± 0.59	48.25 ± 7.87
SEA$_A$	99.46 ± 0.41	99.77 ± 0.14	99.14 ± 1.39	98.47 ± 1.56	75.39 ± 0.21	61.97 ± 1.97
LED$_G$	99.99 ± 0.00	99.99 ± 0.00	100.00 ± 0.00	100.00 ± 0.00	99.93 ± 0.00	99.91 ± 0.02
LED$_A$	100.00 ± 0.00	99.99 ± 0.00	100.00 ± 0.00	100.00 ± 0.00	99.91 ± 0.02	99.94 ± 0.02
Reuters	98.74 ± 0.10	96.19 ± 0.53	99.64 ± 0.00	99.47 ± 0.00	oom	85.03 ± 0.00

Table 1 contains comparison of achieved accuracy scores by the different classifiers in the original and projected space. In most cases, performance remains approximately equal. HAT shows significant decrease on SEA streams in the projected space. On Reuters data HAT ran out of memory (oom) in high dimensional space in our test setup. However, in projected space it achieves acceptable results. Table 2 shows corresponding runtime in seconds. We can see, that tremendous

Table 2. Comparison of projected concept drift streams w.r.t. runtime in seconds.

Algorithm Dataspace	ARF Original	ARF Projected	RSLVQ$_{ADA}$ Original	RSLVQ$_{ADA}$ Projected	HAT Original	HAT Projected
SEA$_G$	9591 ± 1007	3547 ± 139	1291 ± 0	1265 ± 1	13271 ± 322	2403 ± 31
SEA$_A$	10055 ± 925	3567 ± 75	1269 ± 1	1260 ± 1	14439 ± 109	2461 ± 16
LED$_G$	6890 ± 726	2660 ± 211	1247 ± 0	871 ± 1	47645 ± 2889	5511 ± 637
LED$_A$	6986 ± 708	2656 ± 217	1229 ± 1	860 ± 0	48448 ± 2275	5668 ± 571
Reuters	225.25 ± 3.07	165.2 ± 4.16	3.68 ± 0.01	2.74 ± 0.01	oom	76.47 ± 0.13

---

[1] All experiments are implemented in Python supported by the scikit-multiflow framework [18].

[2] https://github.com/ChristophRaab/stvm, we are using 'org vs people'.

runtime improvements can be achieved by working on a lower dimensional space. $RSLVQ_{ADA}$ saves up to 30% on LED generators. Improvements for more complex classifiers like ARF and HAT are more advanced by saving up to ~90%. Such time savings can make a crucial difference in a reliable stream classification scenario, as time is one of the critical challenges. According to performance decrease of HAT on SEA, it has to be evaluated if a potential trade-off between accuracy and runtime is desirable depending on the scenario. However, in our experiments this only happened with one classifier on one specific stream.

In the next step, we evaluate the performance of classifiers on stream generators, containing altering dimensions. By projecting the 10,000 dimensional space to k_W dimensions, the classifiers are trained on the projected space again. However, we remove 1,000 samples from the high dimensional space at iteration 7,500 and restore them at iteration 22,500 having a total of 30,000 iterations. This represents a scenario where sensor A is replaced by a different sensor B, while later on A is used again. As shown in Sect. 4.4 this should introduce abrupt CD in the projected space at given timesteps. Hence, we are using ARF and OzaBagging (OB) [19] in combination with Adaptive Windowing (Adwin) as active CDD.

Table 3. Accuracy of classifiers on streams containing altering dimensions. Learning and predicting is done on projected data obtained by RP.

Algorithm d	ARF_{Adwin} Static	ARF_{Adwin} Altering	OB_{Adwin} Static	OB_{Adwin} Altering
SEA	99.49 ± 0.10	99.28 ± 0.04	96.91 ± 0.09	96.99 ± 0.04
LED	99.84 ± 0.16	99.05 ± 0.12	90.19 ± 3.93	87.39 ± 3.48

Table 3 shows, that there is no relevant difference between SEA with and without altering dimensions. On LED we see a slight decrease in accuracy, especially by OB_{Adwin}. However, the used classifiers can handle this scenario obtaining a desirable accuracy. Given the alternative of learning a new classifier from scratch whenever altering dimensions come up, our suggested scenario is superior, because classifiers are still pretrained.

In the last experiment we are using a CDD to compare if a CDD is able to detect the same drifts in low as in high dimensions. As an example detector we are using the Kolmogorov-Smirnov Windowing (KSWIN) [21] algorithm. As stream SEA generator in a reoccurring CD setting is used, where the first drift starts at iteration 2,000, has width of 1,000 and pause of 1,000. Due to the high dimensionality of the data which is still given after dimensionality reduction, we are setting the confidence of KSWIN to 0.00001 as a rule of thumb. A total of 20,000 samples are used and thus 9 drifts occur in the data. We stick to our example of Sect. 4.2 projecting 10,000 to $k_W = 1594$ dimensions.

As shown in Fig. 2, which shows 2,000 iterations of the 20,000 iterations of this study, drifts are much more often detected than they were introduced, no matter if we have high dimensional data or projected data. This is due to the fact that KSWIN suffers from the curse of dimensionality too and has much more *false positives* when data is high dimensional [21]. However, the projection leads to less *false positives* while still detecting the introduced drifts. Overall, the detected drifts in high dimensions are 267 and only 100 in projected space, which is a decrease of more than 50% on *false positives*. Thus, RP is able to reduce the *false positive* detection rate while still detecting the introduced drifts. Furthermore, statistical tests only need to be performed k instead d times.

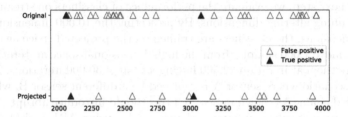

Fig. 2. Detected drifts in high dimensions compared to low dimensions on 2,000 datapoints of SEA stream.

6   Conclusion

In summary our experiments have shown, that using RP in non-stationary environments can save lots of time on some classifiers. While the RSLVQ$_{ADA}$ shows a moderate improvement, the effect is strong in case of other state-of-the art methods like ARF and HAT. Our results show, that applying RP in majority has no negative impact w.r.t. accuracy on CD streams. Thus, the usage of RP on streaming data leads to enormous runtime savings and the error is bounded on window- and prototype-based classifiers. Also we have introduced the concept of altering dimensions in non-stationary environments and how this scenario can be efficiently handled by adaptive stream classifiers. Our results have shown, that handling altering dimensions with RP and CDD classifiers only lead to a slight decrease in accuracy. Furthermore, we have experimentally shown, that detecting CDs in projected spaces obtained by RP leads to less *false positive* detections and saves runtime.

Acknowledgement. We are thankful for support in the FuE program Informations- und Kommunikationstechnik of the StMWi, project *OBerA*, grant number IUK-1709-0011// IUK530/010.

References

1. Achlioptas, D.: Database-friendly random projections. In: Proceedings of the Twentieth ACM SIGMOD-SIGACT-SIGART Symposium on Principles of Database Systems, pp. 274–281. ACM (2001)

2. Achlioptas, D.: Database-friendly random projections: Johnson-Lindenstrauss with binary coins. J. Comput. Syst. Sci. **66**, 671–687 (2003)
3. Aggarwal, C.C.: A survey of stream classification algorithms. In: Data Classification: Algorithms and Applications (2014)
4. Bifet, A., Gavaldà, R.: Learning from time-changing data with adaptive windowing. In: Proceedings of the Seventh SIAM International Conference on Data Mining, Minneapolis, Minnesota, USA, 26–28 April 2007, pp. 443–448 (2007)
5. Bifet, A., Gavaldà, R.: Adaptive learning from evolving data streams. In: Adams, N.M., Robardet, C., Siebes, A., Boulicaut, J.-F. (eds.) IDA 2009. LNCS, vol. 5772, pp. 249–260. Springer, Heidelberg (2009). https://doi.org/10.1007/978-3-642-03915-7_22
6. Carraher, L.A., Wilsey, P.A., Moitra, A., Dey, S.: Random projection clustering on streaming data. In: 2016 IEEE 16th ICDMW, pp. 708–715 (2016)
7. Dasgupta, S., Gupta, A.: An elementary proof of a theorem of Johnson and Lindenstrauss. Random Struct. Algorithms **22**, 60–65 (2003)
8. Gama, J., Zliobaite, I., Bifet, A., Pechenizkiy, M., Bouchachia, A.: A survey on concept drift adaptation. ACM Comput. Surv. **46**(4), 1–37 (2014)
9. Gomes, H.M., et al.: Adaptive random forests for evolving data stream classification. Mach. Learn. **106**(9), 1469–1495 (2017). https://doi.org/10.1007/s10994-017-5642-8
10. Grabowska, M., Kotłowski, W.: Online principal component analysis for evolving data streams. In: Czachórski, T., Gelenbe, E., Grochla, K., Lent, R. (eds.) ISCIS 2018. CCIS, vol. 935, pp. 130–137. Springer, Cham (2018). https://doi.org/10.1007/978-3-030-00840-6_15
11. Heusinger, M., Raab, C., Schleif, F.-M.: Passive concept drift handling via momentum based robust soft learning vector quantization. In: Vellido, A., Gibert, K., Angulo, C., Martín Guerrero, J.D. (eds.) WSOM 2019. AISC, vol. 976, pp. 200–209. Springer, Cham (2020). https://doi.org/10.1007/978-3-030-19642-4_20
12. Johnson, W.B., Lindenstrauss, J.: Extensions of Lipschitz mappings into a Hilbert space. Contemp. Math. **26**, 189–206 (1984)
13. Kaban, A.: Improved bounds on the dot product under random projection and random sign projection. In: Proceedings of the 21th ACM SIGKDD. KDD 2015, pp. 487–496. ACM, New York (2015)
14. Klartag, B., Mendelson, S.: Empirical processes and random projections. J. Funct. Anal. **225**(1), 229–245 (2005)
15. Li, P., Hastie, T.J., Church, K.W.: Very sparse random projections. In: Proceedings of the 12th ACM SIGKDD, pp. 287–296. ACM (2006)
16. Losing, V., Hammer, B., Wersing, H.: KNN classifier with self adjusting memory for heterogeneous concept drift. In: Proceedings of the - IEEE, ICDM, pp. 291–300 (2017)
17. van der Maaten, L., Hinton, G.: Visualizing data using t-SNE. J. Mach. Learn. Res. **9**, 2579–2605 (2008)
18. Montiel, J., Read, J., Bifet, A., Abdessalem, T.: Scikit-multiflow: a multi-output streaming framework. J. Mach. Learn. Res. **19**(72), 1–5 (2018)
19. Oza, N.C.: Online bagging and boosting. In: 2005 IEEE International Conference on Systems, Man and Cybernetics, vol. 3, pp. 2340–2345 (2005)
20. Pham, X.C., Dang, M.T., Dinh, S.V., Hoang, S., Nguyen, T.T., Liew, A.W.: Learning from data stream based on random projection and Hoeffding tree classifier. In: DICTA 2017, pp. 1–8 (2017)

21. Raab, C., Heusinger, M., Schleif, F.M.: Reactive soft prototype computing for frequent reoccurring concept drift. In: Proceedings of the 27. ESANN, pp. 437–442 (2019)
22. Sacha, D., et al.: Visual interaction with dimensionality reduction: a structured literature analysis. IEEE Trans. Vis. Comput. Graph. **23**(1), 241–250 (2017)
23. Schoeneman, F., Mahapatra, S., Chandola, V., Napp, N., Zola, J.: Error metrics for learning reliable manifolds from streaming data. In: Proceedings of the 2017 SIAM International Conference on Data Mining, pp. 750–758. SIAM (2017)
24. Wold, S., Esbensen, K., Geladi, P.: Principal component analysis. Chemometr. Intell. Lab. Syst. **2**, 37–52 (1987)

Brazilian Lyrics-Based Music Genre Classification Using a BLSTM Network

Raul de Araújo Lima$^{(\boxtimes)}$ ⓘ, Rômulo César Costa de Sousa$^{(\boxtimes)}$ ⓘ,
Hélio Lopes$^{(\boxtimes)}$ ⓘ, and Simone Diniz Junqueira Barbosa$^{(\boxtimes)}$ ⓘ

PUC-Rio, Rio de Janeiro 22430-060, Brazil
{rlima,rsousa,lopes,simone}@inf.puc-rio.br
http://www.inf.puc-rio.br/

Abstract. Organize songs, albums, and artists in groups with shared similarity could be done with the help of genre labels. In this paper, we present a novel approach for automatic classifying musical genre in Brazilian music using only the song lyrics. This kind of classification remains a challenge in the field of Natural Language Processing. We construct a dataset of $138,368$ Brazilian song lyrics distributed in 14 genres. We apply SVM, Random Forest and a Bidirectional Long Short-Term Memory (BLSTM) network combined with different word embeddings techniques to address this classification task. Our experiments show that the BLSTM method outperforms the other models with an F1-score average of 0.48. Some genres like *gospel*, *funk-carioca* and *sertanejo*, which obtained 0.89, 0.70 and 0.69 of F1-score, respectively, can be defined as the most distinct and easy to classify in the Brazilian musical genres context.

Keywords: Music genre classification · Natural language processing · Neural networks

1 Introduction

Music is part of the day-to-day life of a huge number of people, and many works try to understand the best way to classify, recommend, and identify similarities between songs. Among the tasks that involve music classification, genre classification has been studied widely in recent years [12] since musical genres are the main top-level descriptors used by music dealers and librarians to organize their music collections [9].

Automatic music genre classification based only on the lyrics is considered a challenging task in the field of Natural Language Processing (NLP). Music genres remain a poorly defined concept, and boundaries between genres still remain fuzzy, which makes the automatic classification problem a nontrivial task [9].

Traditional approaches in text classification have applied algorithms such as Support Vector Machine (SVM) and Naïve Bayes, combined with handcraft

© Springer Nature Switzerland AG 2020
L. Rutkowski et al. (Eds.): ICAISC 2020, LNAI 12415, pp. 525–534, 2020.
https://doi.org/10.1007/978-3-030-61401-0_49

features (POS and chunk tags) and word count-based representations, like bag-of-words. More recently, the usage of Deep Learning methods such as Recurrent Neural Networks (RNNs) and Convolutional Neural Networks (CNNs) has produced great results in text classification tasks.

Some works like [4,5,7] focus on classification of mood or sentiment of music based on its lyrics or audio content. Other works, like [9], and [10], on the other hand, try to automatically classify the music genre; and the work [1] tries to classify, besides the music genre, the best and the worst songs, and determine the approximate publication time of a song.

In this work, we collected a set of about 130 thousand Brazilian songs distributed in 14 genres. We use a Bidirectional Long Short-Term Memory (BLSTM) network to make a lyrics-based music genre classification. We did not apply an elaborate set of handcraft textual features, instead, we represent the lyrics songs with a pre-trained word embeddings model, obtaining an F1 average score of 0.48. Our experiments and results show some real aspects that exist among the Brazilian music genres and also show the usefulness of the dataset we have built for future works.

This paper is organized as follows. In the next section, we cite and comment on some related works. Section 3 describes our experiments from data collection to the proposed model, presenting some important concepts. Our experimental results are presented in Sect. 4, and Sect. 5 presents our concluding remarks and future work.

2   Related Works

Several works have been carried out to add textual information to genre and mood classification. Fell and Sporleder [1] used several handcraft features, such as vocabulary, style, semantics, orientation towards the world, and song structure to obtain performance gains on three different classification tasks: detecting genre, distinguishing the best and the worst songs, and determining the approximate publication time of a song. The experiments in genre classification focused on eight genres: Blues, Rap, Metal, Folk, R&B, Reggae, Country, and Religious. Only lyrics in English were included and they used an SVM with the default settings for the classification.

Ying et al. [12] used Part-of-Speech (POS) features extracted from lyrics and combined them with three different machine learning techniques – k-Nearest-Neighbor, Naïve Bayes, and Support Vector Machines – to classify a collection of 600 English songs by the genre and mood.

Zaanen and Kanters [11] used the term frequency and inverse document frequency statistical metrics as features to solve music mood classification, obtaining an accuracy of more than 70%.

In recent years, deep learning techniques have also been applied to music genre classification. This kind of approach typically does not rely on handcraft features or external data. In [10], the authors used a hierarchical attention network to perform the task in a large dataset of nearly half a million song lyrics, obtaining an accuracy of more than 45%. Some papers such as [6] used word embedding techniques to represent words from the lyrics and then classify them by the genre using a 3-layer Deep Learning model.

3   Methods

In this chapter we present all the major steps we have taken, from obtaining the dataset to the proposed approach to address the automatic music genre classification problem.

3.1   Data Acquisition

In order to obtain a large number of Brazilian music lyrics, we created a crawler to navigate into the *Vagalume*[1] website, extracting, for each musical genre, all the songs by all the listed authors. The implementation of a crawler was necessary because, although the *Vagalume* site provides an API, it is only for consultation and does not allow obtaining large amounts of data. The crawler was implemented using Scrapy[2], an open-source and collaborative Python library to extract data from websites.

From the Vagalume's music web page, we collect the song title and lyrics, and the artist name. The genre was collected from the page of styles[3], which lists all the musical genres and, for each one, all the artists. We selected only 14 genres that we consider as representative Brazilian music, shown in Table 1. Figure 1 presents an example of the Vagalume's music Web page with the song *"Como é grande o meu amor por você"*[4], of the Brazilian singer Roberto Carlos. Green

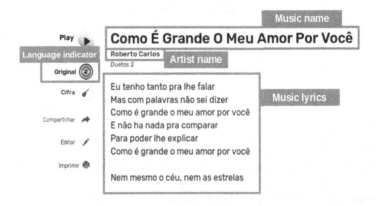

Fig. 1. An example of a Vagalume's song web page. (Color figure online)

---

[1] https://www.vagalume.com.br/.

[2] https://scrapy.org/.

[3] https://www.vagalume.com.br/browse/style/.

[4] https://www.vagalume.com.br/roberto-carlos/como-e-grande-o-meu-amor-por-voce-letras.html.

boxes indicate information about music that can be extracted directly from the web page. From this information, the language in which the lyrics are available can be obtained by looking at the icon indicating the flag of Brazil preceded by the *"Original"* word.

After extracting data, we obtained a set of 138, 368 songs distributed across 14 genres. Table 1 presents the number of songs and artists by genre. In order to use the data to learn how to automatically classify genre, we split the dataset into tree partitions: training (96, 857 samples), validation (27, 673 samples), and test (13, 838 samples). The total dataset and splits are available for download[5].

Table 1. The number of songs and artists by genre

Genre	#songs	#artists
Gospel	33, 344	800
Sertanejo	27, 417	543
MPB	16, 785	282
Forró	11, 861	191
Pagode	8, 199	174
Rock	8, 188	396
Samba	6, 221	111
Pop	4, 629	338
Axé	4, 592	63
Funk-carioca	4, 557	279
Infantil	4, 550	70
Velha-guarda	3, 179	24
Bossa-nova	3, 105	38
Jovem-guarda	1, 741	18

3.2   Word Embeddings

Word embeddings is a technique to represent words as real vectors, so that these vectors maintain some semantic aspects of the real words. Basically, vectors are computed by calculating probabilities of the context of words, with the intuition that semantically similar words have similar contexts, and must therefore have similar vectors.

Word2Vec[6], by Mikolov *et al.* [8], is one of the first and most widely used algorithms to make word embeddings. It has two architectures to compute word

---

[5] https://drive.google.com/open?id=1b681ChByK737CpASYImFB4GfuqPdrvBN.
[6] https://code.google.com/archive/p/word2vec/.

vectors: Continuous Bag-Of-Words (CBOW) and Skip-gram. CBOW gets a context as input and predicts the current word, while Skip-gram gets the current word as input and predicts its context.

In this work, we use the Python Word2Vec implementation provided by the Gensim[7] library. The Portuguese pre-trained word embeddings created by [2] and available for download[8] was used to represent words as vectors. We only used models of dimension 300 and, for Word2Vec, Wang2Vec, and FastText, skip-gram architectured models.

3.3 Bidirectional Long Short-Term Memory

Long Short-Term Memory (LSTM) is a specification of Recurrent Neural Network (RNN) that was proposed by Hochreiter and Schmidhuber [3]. This kind of network is widely used to solve classification of sequential data and is designed to capture time dynamics through graph cycles. Figure 2 presents an LSTM unity, which receives an input from the previous unit, processes it, and passes it to the next unit.

The following equations are used to update C_t and h_t values.

$$f_t = \sigma(W_f h_{t-1} + U_f x_t + b_f)$$

$$i_t = \sigma(W_i h_{t-1} + U_i x_t + b_i)$$

$$\widetilde{C}_t = tanh(W_C h_{t-1} + U_C x_t + b_C)$$

$$C_t = f_t \times C_{t-1} + i_t \times \widetilde{C}_t$$

$$o_t = \sigma(W_o h_{t-1} + U_o x_t + b_o)$$

$$h_t = o_t \times tanh(C_t)$$

where W_f, W_i, W_C, W_o are the weight matrices for h_{t-1} input; U_f, U_i, U_C, U_o are the weight matrices for x_t input; and b_f, b_i, b_C, b_o are the bias vectors.

Basically, a Bidirectional LSTM network consists of using two LSTM networks: a forward LSTM and a backward LSTM. The intuition behind it is that, in some types of problems, past and future information captured by forward and backward LSTM layers are useful to predict the current data.

3.4 Proposed Approach

Our proposed approach consists of three main steps. Firstly, we concatenate the title of the song with its lyrics, put all words in lower case and then we clean up the text by removing line breaks, multiple spaces, and some punctuation (,!.?). Secondly, we represent the text as a vector provided by a pre-trained word embeddings model. For classical learning algorithms like SVM and Random Forest, we generate, for each song, a vectorial representation by calculating the

---

[7] https://radimrehurek.com/gensim/index.html.
[8] http://nilc.icmc.usp.br/embeddings.

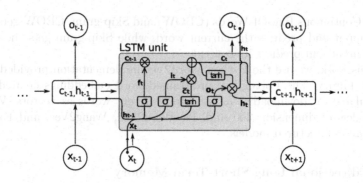

Fig. 2. The Long Short-Term Memory unit.

average of the vectors of each word in the song lyrics that can be can be expressed by the equation below:

$$vector(L) = \frac{1}{n} \sum_{w \in L} vector(w)$$

where L is the song lyrics, w is a word in L, and n is the number of words in L. If a word does not have a vector representation in the word embeddings model, it is not considered in the equation. For the BLSTM algorithm, the representation was made in the format of a matrix, as shown in Fig. 3, where each line is a vector representation of a word in the lyrics. In the third step, we use as features the generated representation for the genre classification tasks using SVM, Random Forests, and BLSTM.

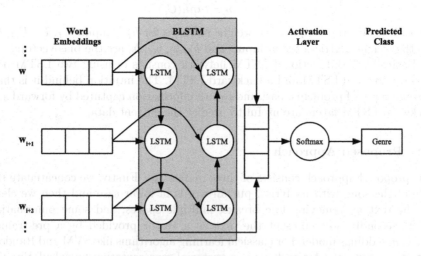

Fig. 3. Our BLSTM model architecture

4 Experimental Results

In this section, we describe our experiments. We used the Linear SVM and Random Forest Scikit-learn[9] implementations and Keras[10] on top of TensorFlow[11] for the BLSTM implementation. In this study, we did not focus on finding the best combination of parameters for the algorithms, so that for SVM we used the default parameters, and for Random Forest we used a number of 100 trees. Our BLSTM model was trained using 4 epochs, with Adam optimizer, and 256 as the size of the hidden layer.

As we can see in Table 2, our BLSTM approach outperforms the other models with an F1-score average of 0.48. In addition, we can note that the use of Wang2Vec pre-trained word embeddings made it possible to obtain better F1-score results in BLSTM, which is not necessarily noticed in other cases, since for SVM and Random Forest, Glove and FastText, respectively, were the techniques that obtained better F1-scores.

Table 2. Classification results for each classifier and word embeddings model combination

System	Model	Precision	Recall	F1-score
SVM	Word2Vec	0.290	0.143	0.120
	Wang2Vec	0.297	0.144	0.121
	FastText	0.278	0.144	0.120
	Glove	0.296	0.144	**0.124**
Random forest	Word2Vec	0.388	0.197	0.212
	Wang2Vec	0.386	0.197	0.207
	FastText	0.404	0.203	**0.215**
	Glove	0.394	0.199	0.210
BLSTM	Word2Vec	0.492	0.454	0.465
	Wang2Vec	**0.515**	**0.460**	**0.477**
	FastText	0.417	0.350	0.360
	Glove	0.492	0.460	0.470

Table 3 shows the BLSTM classification results for each genre. We can see that the genres *gospel*, *funk-carioca* and *sertanejo* have a greater distinction in relation to the other genres, since they were better classified by the model. In particular, *funk-carioca* obtained a good classification result although it did not have a large number of collected song lyrics.

In gospel song lyrics, we can identify some typical words, such as *"Deus"* (God), *"Senhor"* (Lord), and *"Jesus"* (Jesus); in *funk-carioca*, songs have the

---

[9] https://scikit-learn.org/.

[10] https://keras.io/.

[11] https://www.tensorflow.org/.

words *"bonde"* (tram), *"chão"* (floor) and *"baile"* (dance ball), all used as slang; in *sertanejo*, some of the most common words are *"amor"* (love), *"coração"* (heart) and *"saudade"* (longing). The occurrence of these typical words could contribute to the higher performance of F1-scores in these genres.

Table 3. Detailed result of BLSTM

Genre	F1-score
Gospel	0.89
Funk-carioca	0.70
Sertanejo	0.69
Forró	0.53
Axé	0.49
MPB	0.49
Pagode	0.48
Infantil	0.47
Rock	0.46
Velha-guarda	0.38
Samba	0.35
Bossa-nova	0.31
Pop	0.26
Jovem-guarda	0.19
Average	*0.481*

The *bossa-nova* and *jovem-guarda* genres, which have few instances in the dataset, are among the most difficult ones to classify using the model. The *pop* genre, by contrast, has a small distribution between the number of songs and the number of artists, and could not be well classified by our model. This may indicate that our model was unable to identify a pattern due to the low number of songs per artist, or that the song lyrics of this genre cover several subjects that are confused with other genres.

Figure 4 shows the confusion matrix of the results produced by our BLSTM model. We can notice that many instances of class *forró* are often confused with class *sertanejo*. Indeed, these two genres are very close. Both *Forró* and *sertanejo* have as theme the cultural and daily aspects of the Northeast region of Brazil. Instances of class *infantil* are often confused with class *gospel*: in *infantil* we have music for children for both entertainment and education. In some of the songs, songwriters try to address religious education, which could explain the confusion between those genres. The *MPB* (Brazilian Popular Music) genre was the most confused of all, which may indicate that song lyrics of this genre cover a wide range of subjects that intersect with other genres.

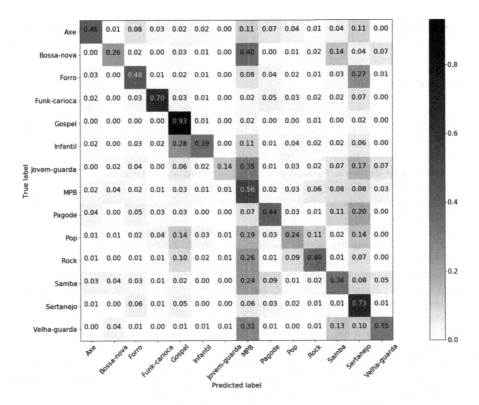

Fig. 4. Normalized confusion matrix

5   Conclusion and Future Works

In this work we constructed a dataset of 138, 368 Brazilian song lyrics distributed in 14 genres. We applied SVM, Random Forest, and a Bidirectional Long Short-Term Memory (BLSTM) network combined with different word embeddings techniques to address the automatic genre classification task based only on the song lyrics. We compared the results between the different combinations of classifiers and word embedding techniques, concluding that our BLSTM combined with the Wang2Vec pre-trained model obtained the best F1-score classification result. Beside the dataset construction and the comparison of tools, this work also evidences the lack of an absolute superiority between the different techniques of word embeddings, since their use and efficiency in this specific task showed to be very closely related to the classification technique.

As future work, it is possible to explore the dataset to identify genre or artist similarities, generating visualizations that may or may not confirm aspects preconceived by the consumers of Brazilian music. It is also possible to perform classification tasks by artists of a specific genre.

Acknowledgments. Simone Barbosa thanks CAPES and CNPq (process #311316/2018-2). Hélio Lopes thanks CAPES and CNPq (process #313654/2017-4).

References

1. Fell, M., Sporleder, C.: Lyrics-based analysis and classification of music. In: Proceedings of COLING 2014, the 25th International Conference on Computational Linguistics: Technical Papers, pp. 620–631 (2014)
2. Hartmann, N., Fonseca, E., Shulby, C., Treviso, M., Rodrigues, J., Aluisio, S.: Portuguese word embeddings: evaluating on word analogies and natural language tasks (2017). arXiv preprint arXiv:1708.06025
3. Hochreiter, S., Schmidhuber, J.: Long short-term memory. Neural Comput. **9**(8), 1735–1780 (1997)
4. Hu, X., Downie, J.S.: When lyrics outperform audio for music mood classification: a feature analysis. In: ISMIR, pp. 619–624 (2010)
5. Hu, Y., Chen, X., Yang, D.: Lyric-based song emotion detection with affective lexicon and fuzzy clustering method. In: ISMIR, pp. 123–128 (2009)
6. Kumar, A., Rajpal, A., Rathore, D.: Genre classification using word embeddings and deep learning. In: 2018 International Conference on Advances in Computing, Communications and Informatics (ICACCI), pp. 2142–2146. IEEE (2018)
7. Laurier, C., Grivolla, J., Herrera, P.: Multimodal music mood classification using audio and lyrics. In: 2008 Seventh International Conference on Machine Learning and Applications, pp. 688–693. IEEE (2008)
8. Mikolov, T., Sutskever, I., Chen, K., Corrado, G.S., Dean, J.: Distributed representations of words and phrases and their compositionality. In: Advances in Neural Information Processing Systems, pp. 3111–3119 (2013)
9. Scaringella, N., Zoia, G., Mlynek, D.: Automatic genre classification of music content: a survey. IEEE Signal Process. Mag. **23**(2), 133–141 (2006)
10. Tsaptsinos, A.: Lyrics-based music genre classification using a hierarchical attention network (2017). arXiv preprint arXiv:1707.04678
11. Van Zaanen, M., Kanters, P.: Automatic mood classification using tf* idf based on lyrics. In: ISMIR, pp. 75–80 (2010)
12. Ying, T.C., Doraisamy, S., Abdullah, L.N.: Genre and mood classification using lyric features. In: 2012 International Conference on Information Retrieval & Knowledge Management, pp. 260–263. IEEE (2012)

Machine Learning for Web Intrusion Detection: A Comparative Analysis of Feature Selection Methods mRMR and PFI

Thiago José Lucas[1], Carlos Alexandre Carvalho Tojeiro[2],
Rafael Gonçalves Pires[1], Kelton Augusto Pontara da Costa[1(✉)],
and João Paulo Papa[1]

[1] Department of Computing, São Paulo State University, Bauru, Brazil
{thiago.j.lucas,kelton.costa,joao.papa}@unesp.br, rafapires@gmail.com
[2] College of Technology, Ourinhos, São Paulo, Brazil
carlos.tojeiro@fatecourinhos.edu.br

Abstract. Select from the best features in a complex dataset that is a critical task for machine learning algorithms. This work presents a comparative analysis between two resource selection techniques: Minimum Redundancy Maximum Relevance (mRMR) and Permutation Feature Important (PFI). The application of PFI to the dataset in issue is unusual. The dataset used in the experiments is HTTP CSIC 2010, which shows great results with the mRMR observed in a related work [22]. Our PFI tests resulted in a selection of features best suited for machine learning methods and the best results for an accuracy of 97% with logistic regression and Bayes Point Machine, 98% with Support Vector Machine, and 99.9% using an artificial neural network.

Keywords: Intrusion detection · Machine learning · Feature selection

1 Introduction

Identifying web attacks is a complex task in the face of a variety of present warnings and zero-day threats that come up all the time. To create more efficient intrusion detection systems, the use of machine learning techniques reaches out as a choice to traditional security system implementation methods [6].

According to Symantec's Internet Security Report [23], there was a 56% increase in the number of web attacks seen in 2018 when compared to the previous year. An Open Web Application Security Project (OWASP) [15], a community that receives data for secure web application improvement, saves a detailed report that documents a variety of recent attacks they use as users of the web. Because of the complexity of packages and the different anatomy of attacks, Web attack-focused data sets have a large number of resources, or they often become

© Springer Nature Switzerland AG 2020
L. Rutkowski et al. (Eds.): ICAISC 2020, LNAI 12415, pp. 535–546, 2020.
https://doi.org/10.1007/978-3-030-61401-0_50

slow sorting and results negatively influenced by irrelevant resources. In building predictive models, one of the most critical issues is finding the most relevant features for the model used. There are several ways to measure [5] resources.

This study compares mRMRM and PFI resource selection methods focused on web attacks. The dataset used in the experiment was HTTP CSIC 2010, and the tests were run on the Microsoft Azure Machine Learning Studio (MAMLS) platform, which is a Machine Learning experiment execution platform in the [7] edition.

A relevant contribution regarding this work is the first application of PFI as a resource selection technique in the HTTP CSIC 2010 dataset. As of this writing, no works have been found in the literature involving the PFI and the dataset, as mentioned above.

This work is organized as follows: Sect. 2 provides a literature review divided into Subsects. 2.1 where an anatomy of the HTTP CSIC 2010 dataset; Sect. 2.2 with a brief survey of recent work used by an HTTP CSIC 2010 dataset; Sect. 2.3 with the first resource selection method (mRMR); Subsect. 2.4, which addresses the second resource selection method (PFI). In Sect. 3 is documented a list of materials and methods used in the experiments, followed by Sect. 4 presents the results of the experiments and a comparative analysis between the results achieved with mRMR and PFI; Sect. 5 includes the test conclusions as well as some suggestions for future research that can be explored.

2   Literature Review

This section defines the anatomy of the dataset used in experiments, as well as recent resource collection work using the same database. Also reviewed are the methods compared in work: mRMR and PFI.

2.1   HTTP CSIC 2010 Dataset

The HTTP CSIC 2010 dataset contain data from automated intrusion tests on a e-Commerce website and can be used to security tests of general web servers [8]. It has been developed by "Information Security Institute" of CSIC (Spanish Research National Council).

The dataset used in the tests for this work has also been successfully applied for web intrusion detection in several circumstances, as can be seen in [1,2,9,11, 14,17,22,24–26] and [27].

According to the authors, web traffics usually has its own sensitive data, which makes it difficult for web-focused datasets to focus on attacks. By this, it was therefore defined to generate our traffic, simulating unauthorized access in different forms of attacks. As a result, the data in the dataset is not sensitive but describes the most nearby possible real kind of attacks. The dataset contains 36,000 legitimate and 25,000 abnormal HTTP connections, and it is relevant to note that one connection can generate multiple packets, which makes the dataset size larger than the number of rows. The dataset has several attacks, such as:

- SQL injection [29]: the attacker additions, through HTTP strings, features of SQL rules so that the target performs the sent code;
- Buffer overflow [20]: identified as one of the attacks with the most significant damage potential. Attacker increases memory size limit on variables to gain access to sensitive storage areas;
- Information gathering - [16] described as a critical Social Engineering process, the attacker seeks sensitive information from organizations or people available on the Internet;
- Files disclosure - consists of illegal disclosure of files usually confidential;
- CRLF injection [13]: a method in which the attacker can insert HTML data into HTTP packets in browser-server communication;
- XSS [21]: cross-site scripting attack, it is the most commonly employed web attack technique. It consists in the execution of arbitrary code by the attacker, including data through HTTP packets on web servers.

The dataset anatomy consists of an array of 223,585 rows, which are the packages and 18 columns, which are the features. Given the complexity of the matrix, it was necessary to implement proper feature selection techniques to reduce the dataset dimensionality. In their entirety, follow the features available in Table 1:

Table 1. Dataset description features label

Feature Label (FL)	Description Feature (DF)
index(IN)	Value that relates multiple packets to a single connection
method(MT)	HTTP encapsulation method, which can be "GET", "POST" or "PUT"
URL	Full address including protocol, host and requested resource
protocol	Specification of the OSI reference model, the application layer protocol
userAgent	Identification of the application on the host that originated the packages
pragma	HTTP header parameter that controls cache usage
cacheControl	The corresponding parameter to pragma
accept	Types of formats allowed by the customer in response to your request
acceptEncoding	Encoding type accepted in responses
acceptCharset	Text encoding type accepted in answers
acceptLanguage	type of language accepted in answers
host(HO)	Specifies the destination socket through the string host + port
connection	Connection condition - open/close

(*continued*)

Table 1. (continued)

Feature Label (FL)	Description Feature (DF)
contentLength(CL)	Defines the total packet size
contentType(CT)	Specifies the package content type
cookie(CO)	Details about the connection among packet cookies
payload(PL)	Package contents to be processed by the application
label	The label is given to the package, which can be either "norm" or "anom"

2.2   Recent Work on HTTP CSIC 2010 Dataset

An work that can be observed in [22] used mRMR as a feature selection method in the dataset allowed great results.

The authors provided Accuracy, Precision, Recall, and F1-Score results, which made possible a complete comparison with experiments using PFI. An accuracy of 93.6% was obtained using a combination of the machine learning algorithms C45, CART, Random Tree, and Random Forest [14].

A detection method using J48 obtained an accuracy of 95.9% and was superior to other methods compared by authors such as Adaboost and Naive Bayes [12]. Using Random Forest compared to K-means, it was possible to obtain an accuracy of 90% with the first classifier [10].

2.3   mRMR - Minimum Redundancy Maximum Relevance

The only approach in the literature applying the mRMR feature selection method to the dataset purpose of this work can be found in [22]. Still [4], describe that although the most commonly used methods in MAMLS are Filter-based and Fisher discriminant analysis, both did not provide satisfactory results for the HTTP CSIC 2010 database. Due to this case, the authors applied mRMR and later use the features chosen by the method in the construction of several classifiers.

The mean idea of mRMR is to observe in the examined dataset which features are most relevant and which are redundant in a choice process. The final aim is to generate a data subset containing a reduced number of features that can represent the dataset as a whole from a reduced number of data representations (columns) [18,19]. Therefore the algorithm consists in maximizing relevance Eq. 1 and reducing redundancy Eq. 2:

$$\frac{1}{|S|^2} \sum_{i,j \in S} I(i,j) \tag{1}$$

$$\frac{1}{|S|} \sum_{i \in S} I(h,i) \tag{2}$$

The Eq. 1 assumes that $|S|$ is the dataset feature set, $I(i,j)$ the entropy between i and j considering two compared features. Equation 2 considers h as the target class label, which in the case of the HTTP CSIC 2010 dataset can be "norm" or "anom".

Later employing mRMR to the analyzed dataset, it concluded that the most relevant features are: cookie, payload, URL, contentLength, contentType, host, and method.

To perform feature selection with mRMR [22] implemented in Python via the Recursive Feature Elimination (RFE) class present in the Scikit learn library.

2.4 Permutation Feature Importance (PFI)

The importance of the permutation feature starts from a data fit estimate, where it is possible to filter the most important classes of the *dataset* and discard those that have a lower association with the result, generating significant improvement in the predictive model [3]. The PFI function available from MAMLS was inspired by the randomization technique used in Random Forests to work as a model-independent resource classifier that is compatible with regression models.

To [5], the idea of PFI is to look for relevant scores for each of the dataset features. Measurements are classified by calculating the sensitivity of a model to random permutations of resource values, a kind of review that looks for the class that combines a relevant contribution to predictive performance, pointing out how much a chosen score metric can deviate after the exchange the values of this feature.

The importance of permutation is that if a feature is not useful for predicting a result, changing or exchanging its values will not result in a significant reduction in model performance. After a model is trained, PFI creates a random permutation of a feature, randomly changes column values, and examines the performance of the input model in the modified dataset by iterating for each of the classes, returning the feature list. Most important, according to the ones that reached the most important scores. This is chosen as performance decreases after randomly changing class values, and when metrics use measures such as Accuracy, Precision, Coefficient of Determination.

The PFI rating is defined as $Pb - Ps$, where Pb is the base performance metric score, and Ps is the metric performance score after the shuffle, which is independent of the metric chosen in the module, a higher value implies a more relevant feature. If the evaluation metric used is an error metric, the score will be set to $-(Pb - Ps)$. Thus, whatever metric you choose in the module, the result with the highest score determines that it is the essential resource [5].

3   Methodology

In this section, we describe the relation of materials and methods used along with the development of this paper. Figure 1 shows the process flow so that PFI could extract the best features:

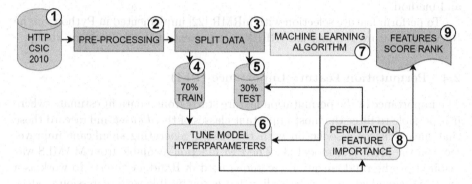

Fig. 1. Systematic process flow in MAMLS for PFI application.

The process can be explained as follows:

1. Dataset used in the experiment cited HTTP CSIC 2010;
2. Data preprocessing. The strings were converted to integer values, and consequently, all values were normalized in the range $(0, ..., 1)$;
3. Arbitrary data distribution considering using a 70% sample for training and 30% for testing;
4. Training random sample corresponding to 70% of the dataset;
5. Random sampling of tests corresponding to 30% of the dataset;
6. Tuning function that allows obtaining, based on accuracy tests, the best hyperparameters for each "dataset x machine learning algorithm" [28] relation. The best hyperparameters are chosen by inputting training data (4), the selected machine learning algorithm (7), and standard output is processed by testing samples (5) and the PFI function (8). The list of the best hyperparameters can be seen in Table 3;
7. For each machine learning algorithm adopted, the process repeats itself entirely. In the tests, the process was repeated eight times due to the selected machine learning algorithms. More details on the chosen algorithms can be seen in Sect. 4;
8. PFI application to obtain the best features. More information about the feature selection method can be seen in Subsect. 2.4;

9. Final output of the process, where a ranking containing scores for all features can be observed. In the experiments were used only features whose score was more significant than zero. The ratio of scores for each machine learning algorithm can be seen in Table 2.

4   Results and Discussion

In order to compare the effectiveness of mRMR with PFI, all binary classifiers that have a role in MAMLS have been implemented the Logistic Regression (LR), Decision Forest (DF), Decision Jungle (DJ), Boosted Decision Trees (BDT), Support-Vector Machine (SVM), Bayes Point Machine (BPM), Averaged Perceptron (AP) and Neural Network (NN).

In each case, the best hyperparameters were found using the "Tune-model Hyperparameters" function related to the PFI feature selection method that allows extracting the best performance from each classifier.

The PFI was applied individually for each Machine Learning algorithm among the eight analyzed. Each application resulted in a ranking of the relevance of features for the classification method analyzed. The Table 2 lists the scores of the method and feature relation.

After generating the data subsets based on Table 2 scores, Machine Learning algorithms were applied to observe performance against the mRMR experiment performed on [22]. To make the present experiment reproducible, Table 3 documents the relationship of hyperparameters for each classifier using PFI.

Any parameters not displayed in Table 3 have been set to their default values on the MAMLS platform.

Table 2. PFI features score per ML Algorithm (in %)

Dataset feature	LR	DF	DJ	BDT	SVM	BPM	AP	NN
index	0.5	0.5	15	40	34	0.01	34	39
method	0.3	–	0.1	0.1	0.3	0.001	0.5	0.3
url	1.2	6	2	0.1	2	–	3	1.2
host	0.4	–	0.2	–	0.4	0.001	0.3	0.3
contentLength	8	1	8	–	1	0.2	2	0.06
contentType	22	–	–	22	10	–	21	23
cookie	7	–	0.7	7	20	31	16	12
payload	5	2	4	5	11	12	12	8

Table 3. Relationship of hyperparameters to the adopted classification models

Model	Hyperparameter	Best value
LR	Optimization tolerance	0.000004
	L1 Weight	0.014528
	L2 Weight	0.023673
	Memory size	25
DF	Maximum depth of the DT/Number of DT	14
	Minimum number of samples per leaf node	2
	Number of random splits per node	945
DJ	Number of optimization steps per decision DAG layer	7130
	Maximum width of the decision DAGs	71
	Maximum depth of the decision DAGs	92
	Number of decision DAGs	10
BDT	Number of leaves	36
	Minimum leaf instances	7
	Learning rate	0.333128
	Number of trees	182
SVM	Number of iterations	92
	Lambda	0.000013
AP	Learning rate	0.87
	Maximum number of iterations	9
NN	Learning rate	0.030998
	Number of iterations	139

To measure the efficiency of the classification algorithms, the values resulting from Eqs. 3, 4, 5 and 6 were used. It has been considered that True positives (TP) classifications are anomalous events labeled as anomalous (correctly), True negatives (TN) are normal events labeled as normal (correctly), False positives (FP) are normal events labeled as anomalous (wrongly), and False negatives (FN) correspond to anomalous events predicted as normal (wrongly).

$$\text{Accuracy} = \frac{TP + TN}{TP + TN + FP + FN} \tag{3}$$

$$\text{Precision} = \frac{TP}{TP + FP} \tag{4}$$

$$\text{Recall} = \frac{TP}{TP + FN} \tag{5}$$

$$\text{F1-Score} = 2\frac{\text{Precision} \times \text{Recall}}{\text{Precision} + \text{Recall}} \tag{6}$$

The Table 4 lists the results obtained from the experiments with PFI and their comparisons with the values obtained with mRMR [22].

Table 4. Final results - PFI vs mRMR per Classifier (in %)

Algorithm	Accuracy		Precision		Recall		F1-Score	
SVM	0.95	**0.98**	0.94	**0.97**	0.92	**0.97**	0.93	**0.97**
BPM	0.90	**0.97**	0.89	**0.98**	0.87	**0.94**	0.88	**0.96**
AP	0.83	**0.96**	0.8	**0.96**	0.79	**0.95**	0.78	**0.95**
NN	0.84	**0.99**	0.83	**0.99**	0.82	**0.98**	0.79	**0.99**
DF	0.66	**0.77**	0.68	**0.90**	**0.69**	0.56	0.64	**0.69**
DJ	0.62	**0.70**	0.63	**0.88**	**0.60**	0.43	**0.62**	0.57
BDT	0.64	**0.88**	0.65	**0.94**	0.68	**0.78**	0.65	**0.85**
LR	**0.97**	0.97	0.92	**0.97**	0.95	**0.96**	0.96	**0.97**
	mRMR	PFI	mRMR	PFI	mRMR	PFI	mRMR	PFI

In Fig. 2, it is possible to observe the comparison of accuracy measurements for each classifier, to make the superiority of PFI over mRMR clearer.

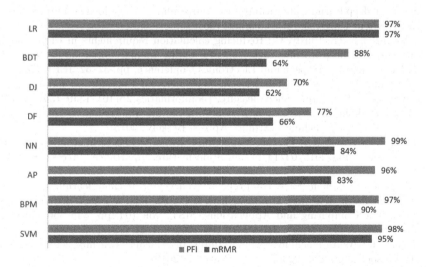

Fig. 2. Comparison of accuracy values between PFI and MRMR.

5   Conclusion and Future Work

The experiments performed in this paper document the superiority of the PFI feature selection method compared to mRMR in the context of web intrusion detection. The results show a significant improvement in all classification models except Logistic Regression, where the results are the same in both cases. The fact that the PFI method chooses the best features for each classifier individually may be the reason for its better results compared to the mRMR method, which makes a generic feature selection, regardless of the classification model to be used. It is noteworthy that the work focusing on the comparison between the presented methods is unprecedented, as well as the application of the PFI to the dataset of this research. Future research aims to investigate whether the results for PFI in relation to mRMR are also superior in other datasets in other contexts, that is, in detecting attacks of other natures.

Acknowledgments. The authors are grateful to FAPESP grants #2017/22905-6, #2013/07375-0, #2014/12236-1, and #2019/07665-4, as well as CNPq grants #429003/2018-8, #307066/2017-7, and #427968/2018-6.

References

1. Alrawashdeh, K.: Toward a hardware-assisted online intrusion detection system based on deep learning algorithms for resource-limited embedded systems. Doctoral dissertation, University of Cincinnati (2018)
2. Alrawashdeh, K., Purdy, C.: Reducing calculation requirements in FPGA implementation of deep learning algorithms for online anomaly intrusion detection. In: IEEE National Aerospace and Electronics Conference, pp. 57–62. IEEE (2017)
3. Altmann, A., Tolosi, L., Sander, O., Lengauer, T.: Permutation importance: a corrected feature importance measure. Bioinformatics **26**(10), 1340–1347 (2010)
4. Barga, R., Fontama, V., Tok, W.H., Cabrera-Cordon, L.: Predictive Analytics with Microsoft Azure Machine Learning. Apress, Berkely (2015)
5. Bleik, S.: Permutation Feature Importance. https://blogs.technet.microsoft.com/machinelearning/2015/04/14/permutation-feature-importance. Accessed 3 Dec 2019
6. Chapaneri, R., Shah, S.: A comprehensive survey of machine learning-based network intrusion detection. In: Satapathy, S.C., Bhateja, V., Das, S. (eds.) Smart Intelligent Computing and Applications. SIST, vol. 104, pp. 345–356. Springer, Singapore (2019). https://doi.org/10.1007/978-981-13-1921-1_35
7. Etaati, L.: Azure machine learning studio. In: Machine Learning with Microsoft Technologies, pp. 201–223. Apress, Berkeley (2019)
8. Giménez, C.T., Villegas, A.P., Marañón, G.Á.: HTTP data set CSIC 2010. Information Security Institute of CSIC, Spanish Research National Council (2010)
9. Go, W., Lee, D.: Toward trustworthy deep learning in security. In: Proceedings of the 2018 ACM SIGSAC Conference on Computer and Communications Security, pp. 2219–2221. ACM (2018)
10. Han, E.: Analyzing and classifying web application attacks. Int. J. Adv. Electron. Comput. Sci. **2**(4) (2015)

11. Kaur, S., Singh, M.G.: Network Security Model for Attack Signature Generation, Tracking and Analysis. Doctoral dissertation (2015)
12. Kozik, R., Choraś, M., Renk, R., Hołubowicz, W.: A proposal of algorithm for web applications cyber attack detection. In: Saeed, K., Snášel, V. (eds.) CISIM 2014. LNCS, vol. 8838, pp. 680–687. Springer, Heidelberg (2014). https://doi.org/10.1007/978-3-662-45237-0_61
13. Maini, R., Bvducoep, P., Pandey, R., Kumar, R., Gupta, R.: Automated web vulnerability scanner. Int. J. Eng. Appl. Sci. Technol. **4**(1), 132–136 (2019). ISSN 2455-2143
14. Nguyen, H.T., Torrano-Gimenez, C., Alvarez, G., Petrović, S., Franke, K.: Application of the generic feature selection measure in detection of web attacks. In: Herrero, Á., Corchado, E. (eds.) CISIS 2011. LNCS, vol. 6694, pp. 25–32. Springer, Heidelberg (2011). https://doi.org/10.1007/978-3-642-21323-6_4
15. Owasp Foundation: OWASP Top 10 Application Security Risks 2017. https://www.owasp.org/index.php/Top_10-2017_Top_10. Accessed 1 Dec 2019
16. Parthy, P.P., Rajendran, G.: Identification and prevention of social engineering attacks on an enterprise. In: 2019 International Carnahan Conference on Security Technology (ICCST), pp. 1–5. IEEE (2019)
17. Perez-Villegas, A., Torrano-Gimenez, C., Alvarez, G.: Applying Markov chains to web intrusion detection. In: Proceedings of Reunión Espanola sobre Criptología y Seguridad de la Información (RECSI 2010), pp. 361–366 (2010)
18. Radovic, M., Ghalwash, M., Filipovic, N., Obradovic, Z.: Minimum redundancy maximum relevance feature selection approach for temporal gene expression data. BMC Bioinformatics **18**(1), 9 (2017)
19. Masud Rana, Md., Ahmed, K.: Feature selection and biomedical signal classification using minimum redundancy maximum relevance and artificial neural network. In: Uddin, M.S., Bansal, J.C. (eds.) Proceedings of International Joint Conference on Computational Intelligence. AIS, pp. 207–214. Springer, Singapore (2020). https://doi.org/10.1007/978-981-13-7564-4_18
20. Ren, J., Zheng, Z., Liu, Q., Wei, Z., Yan, H.: A buffer overflow prediction approach based on software metrics and machine learning. Secur. Commun. Netw. (2019)
21. Rodríguez, G.E., Torres, J.G., Flores, P., Benavides, D.E.: Cross-site scripting (XSS) attacks and mitigation: a survey. Comput. Netw. **1666**, 106960 (2019)
22. Smitha, R., Hareesha, K.S., Kundapur, P.P.: A machine learning approach for web intrusion detection: MAMLS perspective. In: Wang, J., Reddy, G.R.M., Prasad, V.K., Reddy, V.S. (eds.) Soft Computing and Signal Processing. AISC, vol. 900, pp. 119–133. Springer, Singapore (2019). https://doi.org/10.1007/978-981-13-3600-3_12
23. Symantec Internet Security Threat Report. https://www.symantec.com/content/dam/symantec/docs/reports/istr-24-2019-en.pdf. Accessed 30 Nov 2019
24. Torrano-Giménez, C., Perez-Villegas, A., Alvarez, G.: An anomaly-based approach for intrusion detection in web traffic (2010)
25. Torrano-Gimenez, C., Perez-Villegas, A., Alvarez, G.: A self-learning anomaly-based web application firewall. In: Herrero, Á., Gastaldo, P., Zunino, R., Corchado, E. (eds.) Computational Intelligence in Security for Information Systems. Advances in Intelligent and Soft Computing, vol. 63, pp. 85–92. Springer, Heidelberg (2009). https://doi.org/10.1007/978-3-642-04091-7_11
26. Torrano-Gimenez, C., Péerez-Villegas, A., Álvarez, G., Fernández-Medina, E., Malek, M., Hernando, J.: An anomaly-based web application firewall. In: SECRYPT, pp. 23–28 (2009)

27. Torrano-Gimenez, C., Nguyen, H.T., Alvarez, G., Petrovic, S., Franke, K.: Applying feature selection to payload-based web application firewalls. In: International Workshop on Security and Communication Networks, pp. 75–81. IEEE (2011)
28. Wang, B., Gong, N.Z.: Stealing hyperparameters in machine learning. In: 2018 IEEE Symposium on Security and Privacy (SP), pp. 36–52. IEEE (2018)
29. Zhang, H., Zhao, B., Yuan, H., Zhao, J., Yan, X., Li, F.: SQL injection detection based on deep belief network. In: Proceedings of the 3rd International Conference on Computer Science and Application Engineering, p. 20. ACM (2019)

A Mathematical Model for Optimum Error-Reject Trade-Off for Learning of Secure Classification Models in the Presence of Label Noise During Training

Seyedfakhredin Musavishavazi, Mehrdad Mohannazadeh Bakhtiari,
and Thomas Villmann$^{(\boxtimes)}$

Saxony Institute for Computational Intelligence and Machine Learning (SICIM),
University of Applied Sciences, Mittweida, Germany
villmann@hs-mittweida.de

Abstract. In the present contribution we investigate the mathematical model of the trade-off between optimum classification and reject option. The model provides a threshold value in dependence of classification, rejection and error costs. The model is extended to the case that the training data are affected by label noise. We consider the respective mathematical model and show that the optimum threshold value does not depend on the presence/absence of label noise. We explain how this knowledge could be used for probabilistic classifiers in machine learning.

1 Introduction

Automatic classification constitutes a crucial part in many technical systems based on machine learning. The evaluation of the classification model usually is done evaluating regarding quantities like accuracy, F-measure, ROC-curve etc. for training and test data [1,2]. However, generally it is not possible to achieve perfect accuracy in real applications due to noise and errors/outliers in the data. One possibility to deal with those difficulties is to think about reject options [3]. The respective probabilistic model dates back to C.K. CHOW [4], where the mathematical theory is based on a Bayesian approach. CHOW'S model provides the mathematical analysis for optimum reject thresholds investigating the trade-off between error and reject based on related classification costs [5]. Several approaches exist to integrate these concepts into classification learning algorithms [6–9].

Differently from the data noise one can consider label noise in training data, i.e. the labeling might be incorrect with a given probability which should be reflected in training [10,11]. Yet, the mathematical analysis of this situation taking CHOW'S perspective is not done so far. In this paper we develop the respective mathematical model.

All authors contributed equally.

L. Rutkowski et al. (Eds.): ICAISC 2020, LNAI 12415, pp. 547–554, 2020.
https://doi.org/10.1007/978-3-030-61401-0_51

The remainder of the paper is as follows: We start with an introduction of the original trade-off model for reject options based on a Bayesian approach and cost for misclassifications, correct classifications and rejects, which was developed under the assumption of non-probabilistic crisp label assignments. This approach is afterwards reconsidered accepting label noise. Finally, we sketch how to integrate this approach in probabilistic machine learning classifiers.

2   Chow's Model of Error-Reject-Trade-off for Classification

We suppose data $\mathbf{x} \in X \subseteq \mathbb{R}^n$ which have to be classified into classes $C = \{1, \ldots, N_C\}$. We consider the conditional probabilities $P(\mathbf{x}|i)$ that a data point $\mathbf{x}$ is observed under the assumption of class $i \in C$. Accordingly, a data point should be assigned to class k if both

$$p_k \cdot P(\mathbf{x}|k) \geq p_i \cdot P(\mathbf{x}|i)$$

using the *a-posteriori class probabilities* $p(i|\mathbf{x}) = \frac{p_i \cdot P(\mathbf{x}|i)}{P(\mathbf{x})}$ and

$$p_k \cdot P(\mathbf{x}|k) \geq (1-t) \cdot \sum_{i=1}^{N_C} p_i \cdot P(\mathbf{x}|i)$$

are valid where $\mathbf{p} = (p_1, \ldots, p_c)$ is *the prior* class distribution with class priors p_i and $t \in [0,1]$ is the threshold value for classification reject. Here $P(\mathbf{x}) = \sum_i p_i \cdot P(\mathbf{x}|i)$ is the absolute data probability. Then a data point is rejected whenever

$$P^{\max}(\mathbf{x}) = \max_i (p_i \cdot P(\mathbf{x}|i)) < (1-t) \cdot P(\mathbf{x})$$

holds. We define the trigger function

$$\theta(t, P(\mathbf{x})) = P^{\max}(\mathbf{x}) + t - 1 \tag{1}$$

which allows to introduce the reject threshold dependent error rate

$$E(t) = \int_X \sum_{i=1}^{N_C} \sum_{\substack{j=1 \\ j \neq i}}^{N_C} H(\theta(t, P(\mathbf{x}))) \cdot p_i \cdot P(\mathbf{x}|i) \, d\mathbf{x}$$

where $H(\bullet)$ is the *Heaviside function* detecting here the events that a data point has to be classified. Analogously,

$$R(t) = \int_X H(1 - \theta(t, P(\mathbf{x}))) \cdot P(\mathbf{x}) \, d\mathbf{x}$$

is the threshold dependent rejection rate also denoted as the *expected rejection risk* for threshold t. The correct classification rate is $C(t) = 1 - E(t) - R(t)$ whereas the acceptance probability (rate) is $A(t) = C(t) + E(t)$. If we take

$$m(\mathbf{x}) = \frac{P^{\max}(\mathbf{x})}{P(\mathbf{x})}$$

as the maximum of all a-posteriori class probabilities $p(i|\mathbf{x})$, the pattern $\mathbf{x}$ is rejected whenever

$$m(\mathbf{x}) < 1 - t \qquad (2)$$

holds [4]. Using the trigger function (1) we can partition the data space X into the subsets, *acceptance area* $X_A = \{\mathbf{x} \in X | \theta(t, P(\mathbf{x})) > 0\}$ and *rejection area* $X_R = \{\mathbf{x} \in X | \theta(t, P(\mathbf{x})) \leq 0\}$ with

$$C(t) = \int_{X_A} m(\mathbf{x}) \cdot P(\mathbf{x})\, d\mathbf{x} \text{ and } E(t) = \int_{X_A} (1 - m(\mathbf{x})) \cdot P(\mathbf{x})\, d\mathbf{x}$$

are valid. Further the error rate is bounded by $E(t) \leq t \cdot A(t) \leq t$.

If costs are assigned to each classification decision as well as to the reject decision, an optimum threshold value can be adjusted. In particular, let c_c and c_e be the cost for correct and incorrect classification, respectively, whereas c_r is the cost for a reject usually being in the relation $c_e > c_r > c_c$. Then the optimum reject threshold is obtained as

$$t = \frac{c_r - c_c}{c_e - c_c} \qquad (3)$$

to minimize the overall risk [4].

3 Classification of Data by a Classifier in the Presence of Label Noise for Training

3.1 Formal Description of Label Noise in Training Data and the Predictive Model

Let $T = \{(\mathbf{x}, \mathbf{y}(\mathbf{x})) \in X \times [0,1]^{N_C} | X \subseteq \mathbb{R}^n\}$ be a *training set* with N_C as the number of classes $C = \{1, \ldots, N_C\}$ as before. The class assignments $y_j(\mathbf{x}) = \{0,1\}$ together with $\sum_{j=1}^{N_C} y_j(\mathbf{x}) = 1$ would determine a crisp labeling. We can interpret the assignments as the conditional probabilities $y_j(\mathbf{x}) = p(j|\mathbf{x})$. Thus the presence of label noise can be taken as a relaxed condition $y_j(\mathbf{x}) \in [0,1]$ assuming that $m(\mathbf{x}) = 1 - \varepsilon$ with $0 < \varepsilon \ll 1$, i.e. we assume a dominance of the probability for the true class $c^*(\mathbf{x}) \in C$ whereas the remaining probability is distributed over all other classes. Hence, taking into account the reject condition (inequality) (2) we can conclude that a rejection has to be applied if $\varepsilon > t$ is valid for a known label noise level ε. Generally, we suppose $t \geq 1 - \frac{1}{N_C}$.

Let $\mathscr{C}_W$ be a classifier model depending on the parameter set W delivering the class conditional probabilities $p_W(j|\mathbf{x})$ with $\sum_{j=1}^{N_C} p_W(j|\mathbf{x}) = 1$ such that $\mathbf{p}_W(\mathbf{x}) = (p_W(1|\mathbf{x}), \ldots, p_W(N_C|\mathbf{x}))$ is the *predicted* conditional class probability vector for a given data $\mathbf{x}$.

A usual approach to compare the model outcome with the target of the training set is the application of divergences. The Kullback-Leibler divergence

$$D_{KL}(\mathbf{y}(\mathbf{x}) || \mathbf{p}_W(\mathbf{x})) = \sum_{j=1}^{c} y_j(\mathbf{x}) \cdot \log\left(\frac{y_j(\mathbf{x})}{p_W(j|\mathbf{x})}\right)$$

is the most common one [12]. However, other choices like Rényi-divergences or other more general divergences are applicable [13–15].

In the next step we introduce a *class-wise decision rule* by

$$d_j(\mathbf{x}_i) = \frac{y_j(\mathbf{x}) \cdot \log\left(\frac{y_j(\mathbf{x})}{p_W(j|\mathbf{x})}\right)}{D_{KL}(\mathbf{y}(\mathbf{x})\|\mathbf{p}_W(\mathbf{x}))} \in [0,1]$$

which, in fact, can be seen as a *class density function* because $\sum_{j=1}^{N_C} d_j(\mathbf{x}) = 1$. The higher the value $d_j(\mathbf{x})$ the more likely is the class j for the given data $\mathbf{x}$. Thus, we define the model based *prediction*

$$\phi_W(\mathbf{x}) = c \in C \text{ if } d_c(\mathbf{x}) \geq d_j(\mathbf{x}); \quad \forall j \in C$$

such that for the Kronecker symbol $\delta_{\phi_W(\mathbf{x})}^{c^*(\mathbf{x})} = 1$ is valid for a correct classification and $\delta_{\phi_W(\mathbf{x})}^{c^*(\mathbf{x})} = 0$ otherwise.

Corresponding to the results in Sect. 2 we consider the classification options

- *correct classification:* $\theta(t, P_W(\mathbf{x})) > 0$ and $\delta_{\phi_W(\mathbf{x})}^{c^*(\mathbf{x})} = 1$
- *incorrect classification:* $\theta(t, P_W(\mathbf{x})) > 0$ and $\delta_{\phi_W(\mathbf{x})}^{c^*(\mathbf{x})} = 0$
- *reject:* $\theta(t, P_W(\mathbf{x})) \leq 0$

Thus the model based probability of correct classification becomes

$$C_W(t, \mathbf{x}) = \sum_{j=1}^{c} H(\theta(t, P_W(\mathbf{x}))) \cdot \delta_{\phi_W}^{c^*} \cdot P_W(j, \mathbf{x}) \tag{4}$$

with $P_W(j, \mathbf{x}) = p_j \cdot p_W(j|\mathbf{x})$ and whereas the probability of incorrect classification is

$$E_W(t, \mathbf{x}_i) = \sum_{j=1}^{c} H(\theta(t, P_W(\mathbf{x}))) \cdot \left(1 - \delta_{\phi_W}^{c^*}\right) \cdot P_W(j, \mathbf{x}) \tag{5}$$

and the rejection probability is given as

$$R_W(t, \mathbf{x}_i) = \sum_{j=1}^{c} H(-\theta(t, P_W(\mathbf{x}))) \cdot P_W(j, \mathbf{x}). \tag{6}$$

This leads to $C(t, \mathbf{x}) + E(t, \mathbf{x}) + R(t, \mathbf{x}) = p(\mathbf{x})$ and integration with respect to $\mathbf{x}$ yields the quantities $C(t)$, $E(t)$ and $R(t)$ as introduced in Sect. 2 whereas the overall classification costs are given as

$$Cost(t, W) = c_c \int_{\mathbf{x}} C_W(t, \mathbf{x}) \, d\mathbf{x} + c_e \int_{\mathbf{x}} E_W(t, \mathbf{x}) \, d\mathbf{x} + c_r \int_{\mathbf{x}} R_W(t, \mathbf{x}) \, d\mathbf{x}$$

taking the costs c_c, c_e and c_r as before. Obviously, the poor use of the Kronecker quantity $\delta_{\phi_W(\mathbf{x})}^{c^*(\mathbf{x})}$ neglects the label noise. This deficiency will be remedied in the next section.

3.2 Optimum Model Configuration in the Presence of Label Noise for Training Data

To take into account the label noise we consider $\omega_j(\mathbf{x})$ as a cost of classification of an observed data $\mathbf{x}$ with the dominant class $c^*(\mathbf{x})$ into the j-th class assuming $\sum_{j=1,j\neq c^*}^{N_C} \omega_j(\mathbf{x}) = c_e$. Further we take $\omega_{c^*}(\mathbf{x}) = c_c$ and $\boldsymbol{\omega}(\mathbf{x}) = (\omega_1(\mathbf{x}),\ldots,\omega_{N_C}(\mathbf{x}))^T$. Hence, we get $\sum_{j=1}^{N_C} \omega_j(\mathbf{x}) = c_c + c_e$.

This setting does not influence the calculation of the quantities $c_c \cdot C_W(t,\mathbf{x})$ and $c_r \cdot R_W(t,\mathbf{x})$ according to (4) and (6), respectively. However, the error cost $c_e \cdot E_W(t,\mathbf{x})$ is now recalculated as

$$E_W^*(t,\mathbf{x},\boldsymbol{\omega}(\mathbf{x})) = \sum_{j=1}^{c} \sum_{\substack{i=1 \\ j\neq i}}^{c} H(\theta(t,P_W(\mathbf{x}))) \cdot \left(1 - \delta_{\phi w}^{c^*}\right) \cdot \omega_i(\mathbf{x}) \cdot P_W(j,\mathbf{x}) \quad (7)$$

taking the probabilistic label noise into account. Thus we get the new overall classification costs

$$Cost^*(t,W) = c_c \int_{\mathbf{x}} C_W(t,\mathbf{x})\,d\mathbf{x} + \int_{\mathbf{x}} E_W^*(t,\mathbf{x},\boldsymbol{\omega}(\mathbf{x}))\,d\mathbf{x} + c_r \int_{\mathbf{x}} R_W(t,\mathbf{x})\,d\mathbf{x}$$

under the assumption of label noise. We denote by

$$\varrho_r(P_{W^*}) = \int_{\mathbf{x}} R_{W^*}(t,\mathbf{x})\,d\mathbf{x}$$

the optimum model rejection rate, which is in fact independent from the label noise. This can be seen mathematically analyzing the optimum acceptance rate

$$\varrho_A(P_{W^*}) = 1 - \varrho_r(P_{W^*})$$

delivered by a optimal parameter set W^*. For this purpose we consider

$$\hat{\varrho}_A(P_W) = c_c \cdot \int_{\mathbf{x}} C_W(t,\mathbf{x})\,d\mathbf{x} + \int_{\mathbf{x}} E_W^*(t,\mathbf{x},\boldsymbol{\omega}(\mathbf{x}))\,d\mathbf{x}$$

$$= c_c \cdot \int_{\mathbf{x}} \sum_{j=1}^{c} H(\theta(t,P_W(\mathbf{x}))) \cdot \delta_{\phi w}^{c^*} \cdot P_W(j,\mathbf{x})\,d\mathbf{x}$$

$$+ \int_{\mathbf{x}} \sum_{j=1}^{c} \sum_{\substack{i=1 \\ j\neq i}}^{c} H(\theta(t,P_W(\mathbf{x}))) \cdot \left(1 - \delta_{\phi w}^{c^*}\right) \cdot \omega_i(\mathbf{x}) \cdot P_W(j,\mathbf{x})\,d\mathbf{x}$$

$$= \int_{\mathbf{x}\in X_A} \sum_{j=1}^{c} H(\theta(t,P_W(\mathbf{x}))) \cdot \delta_{\phi w}^{c^*} \cdot \omega_j(\mathbf{x}) \cdot P_W(j,\mathbf{x})\,d\mathbf{x}$$

$$+ \int_{\mathbf{x}\in X_A} \sum_{j=1}^{c} \sum_{\substack{i=1 \\ j\neq i}}^{c} H(\theta(t,P_W(\mathbf{x}))) \cdot \left(1 - \delta_{\phi w}^{c^*}\right) \cdot \omega_i(\mathbf{x}) \cdot P_W(j,\mathbf{x})\,d\mathbf{x}$$

$$= \int_{\mathbf{x}\in X_A} \sum_{j=1}^{c} H(\theta(t,P_W(\mathbf{x}))) \cdot P_W(j,\mathbf{x})$$

$$\cdot \left[\delta_{\phi W}^{c^*} \cdot \omega_j(\mathbf{x}) + \sum_{\substack{i=1 \\ j \neq i}}^{c} \left(1 - \delta_{\phi W}^{c^*} \right) \cdot \omega_i(\mathbf{x}) \right] d\mathbf{x}$$

$$= \int_{\mathbf{x} \in X_A} \sum_{j=1}^{c} H\left(\theta\left(t, P_W(\mathbf{x}) \right) \right) \cdot P_W(j, \mathbf{x})$$

$$\cdot \left[c_c + c_e \right] d\mathbf{x}$$

$$= \left[c_c + c_e \right] \cdot \int_{\mathbf{x} \in X_A} \sum_{j=1}^{c} H\left(\theta\left(t, P_W(\mathbf{x}) \right) \right) \cdot P_W(j, \mathbf{x}) \, d\mathbf{x}$$

where we assumed correct classification costs c_c equal for all classes.[1] Hence, the optimum reject threshold (3) of the model without label noise remains valid also in the presence of label noise.

4 Integration in Probabilistic Machine Learning Classifiers

So far we did not specified the probabilistic model $P_W(\mathbf{x})$ depending on the parameter set W. However, it is obvious that we could take an arbitrary probabilistic machine learning model, e.g. a deep network with softmax output [16]. Although those networks frequently provide superior performance, their disadvantage is the lack of interpretability [17]. Although many attempts are made to explain deep models, the inherent requirement of interpretability should be determining the network design [18,19].

Prototype based models in machine learning rely on the vector quantization principle which obviously realizes interpretability [20]. For classification learning the respective family of learning vector quantizers (LVQ) is well-known for robust and powerful classification performance [21–23]. These models distribute prototype vectors $\mathbf{w}_k$ in the data space to detect the underlying data density. In case of classification learning each prototype is assigned to a class, i.e. the prototype is assigned with a class label $c(\mathbf{w}_k) \in C$. Thus, the set $W = \{\mathbf{w}_k\}_{k=1}^{M}$ plays the role of adjustable parameters which can be optimized by stochastic gradient descent learning [24]. Respective probabilistic LVQ models are the Robust Soft LVQ (RSLVQ, [25]) or the Probabilistic LVQ (PLVQ, [26]). Recently, a generalized probabilistic LVQ model was introduced where the prototypes are assumed to be more general so-called components, which form the parameter set W [27]. The underlying probabilistic models is inspired by cognitive-psychological models [28]. Also these networks are trained by stochastic gradient descent learning and deliver finally a probabilistic model $P_W(\mathbf{x})$.

5 Conclusion

In this contribution we provide a mathematical analysis of the optimum classification reject trade-off in the presence of label noise. We show that the resulting

---

[1] The generalization to class-wise correct classification costs is obvious.

optimum threshold value remains unchanged compared to the model without noise. We briefly outline, how this approach could be integrated into probabilistic machine learning classifiers like probabilistic learning vector quantizers. Future work should extend the model to so-called possibilistic classifiers which relax the requirement that the delivered class probabilities sum up to one. This is of particular interest for medical diagnostic support systems, because patient may suffer from several diseases which would correspond to high probabilities.

Acknowledgement. M. Mohannazadeh Bakhtiari is supported by a PhD-grant of the European Social Fund (ESF). S. Musavishavazi is supported by an ESF-project-grant supporting local cooperations between industry and universities for innovative research developments.

References

1. Fawcett, T.: An introduction to ROC analysis. Pattern Recogn. Lett. **27**, 861–874 (2006)
2. Pastor-Pellicer, J., Zamora-Martínez, F., España-Boquera, S., Castro-Bleda, M.J.: F-measure as the error function to train neural networks. In: Rojas, I., Joya, G., Gabestany, J. (eds.) IWANN 2013. LNCS, vol. 7902, pp. 376–384. Springer, Heidelberg (2013). https://doi.org/10.1007/978-3-642-38679-4_37
3. Herbei, R., Wegkamp, M.H.: Classification with reject option. Can. J. Stat. **34**(4), 709–721 (2006)
4. Chow, C.K.: On optimum recognition error and reject tradeoff. IEEE Trans. Inf. Theory **16**(1), 41–46 (1970)
5. Hansen, L.K., Liisberg, C., Salamon, P.: The error-reject tradeoff. Open. Syst. Inf. Dyn. **4**, 159–184 (1997)
6. Pillai, I., Fumera, G., Roli, F.: Multi-label classification with a reject option. Pattern Recogn. **46**, 2256–2266 (2013)
7. Bartlett, P.L., Wegkamp, M.H.: Classification with a reject option using a hinge loss. J. Mach. Learn. Res. **9**, 1823–1840 (2008)
8. Yuan, M., Wegkamp, M.H.: Classification methods with reject option based on convex risk minimization. J. Mach. Learn. Res. **11**, 111–130 (2010)
9. Villmann, T., et al.: Self-adjusting reject options in prototype based classification. In: Merényi, E., Mendenhall, M.J., O'Driscoll, P. (eds.) Advances in Self-Organizing Maps and Learning Vector Quantization. AISC, vol. 428, pp. 269–279. Springer, Cham (2016). https://doi.org/10.1007/978-3-319-28518-4_24
10. Frénay, B., Verleysen, M.: Classification in the presence of label noise: a survey. IEEE Trans. Neural Netw. Learn. Syst. **25**(5), 845–869 (2014)
11. Villmann, A., Kaden, M., Saralajew, S., Hermann, W., Biehl, M., Villmann, T.: Reliable patient classification in case of uncertain class labels using a cross-entropy approach. In: Verleysen, M. (ed.) Proceedings of the 26th European Symposium on Artificial Neural Networks, Computational Intelligence and Machine Learning (ESANN 2018), Bruges, Belgium, pp.153–158. i6doc.com, Louvain-La-Neuve (2018)
12. Kullback, S., Leibler, R.A.: On information and sufficiency. Ann. Math. Stat. **22**, 79–86 (1951)

13. Rényi, A.: On measures of entropy and information. In: Proceedings of the Fourth Berkeley Symposium on Mathematical Statistics and Probability, Berkeley. University of California Press (1961)

14. Cichocki, A., Amari, S.-I.: Families of alpha- beta- and gamma- divergences: flexible and robust measures of similarities. Entropy **12**, 1532–1568 (2010)

15. Villmann, T., Cichocki, A., Principe, J.: Information theory related learning. In: Verleysen, M. (ed.) Proceedings of European Symposium on Artificial Neural Networks (ESANN 2011), pp. 1–10. i6doc.com, Louvain-La-Neuve (2011)

16. Goodfellow, I., Bengio, Y., Courville, A.: Deep Learning. MIT Press, Cambridge (2016)

17. Zeng, J., Ustun, B., Rudin, C.: Interpretable classification models for recidivism prediction. J. R. Stat. Soc. Ser. A. **180**, 1–34 (2017)

18. Rudin, C.: Stop explaining black box machine learning models for high stakes decisions and use interpretable models instead. Nat. Mach. Intell. **1**(5), 206–215 (2019)

19. Villmann, T., Saralajew, S., Villmann, A., Kaden, M.: Learning vector quantization methods for interpretable classification learning and multilayer networks. In: Sabourin, C., Merelo, J.J., Barranco, A.L., Madani, K., Warwick, K. (eds.) Proceedings of the 10th International Joint Conference on Computational Intelligence (IJCCI), Sevilla, pp. 15–21. SCITEPRESS - Science and Technology Publications, Lda, Lissabon (2018). ISBN 978-989-758-327-8

20. Biehl, M., Hammer, B., Villmann, T.: Prototype-based models in machine learning. Wiley Interdiscip. Rev. Cogn. Sci. **2**, 92–111 (2016)

21. Kaden, M., Lange, M., Nebel, D., Riedel, M., Geweniger, T., Villmann, T.: Aspects in classification learning - review of recent developments in Learning Vector Quantization. Found. Comput. Decis. Sci. **39**(2), 79–105 (2014)

22. Kohonen, T.: Self-Organizing Maps. SSINF, vol. 30. Springer, Heidelberg (1995). https://doi.org/10.1007/978-3-642-97610-0

23. Villmann, T., Bohnsack, A., Kaden, M.: Can learning vector quantization be an alternative to SVM and deep learning? J. Artif. Intell. Soft Comput. Res. **7**(1), 65–81 (2017)

24. Sato, A., Yamada, K.: Generalized learning vector quantization. In: Touretzky, D.S., Mozer, M.C., Hasselmo, M.E. (eds.) Advances in Neural Information Processing Systems 8. Proceedings of the 1995 Conference, pp. 423–429. MIT Press, Cambridge (1996)

25. Seo, S., Obermayer, K.: Soft learning vector quantization. Neural Comput. **15**, 1589–1604 (2003)

26. Villmann, A., Kaden, M., Saralajew, S., Villmann, T.: Probabilistic learning vector quantization with cross-entropy for probabilistic class assignments in classification learning. In: Rutkowski, L., Scherer, R., Korytkowski, M., Pedrycz, W., Tadeusiewicz, R., Zurada, J.M. (eds.) ICAISC 2018. LNCS (LNAI), vol. 10841, pp. 724–735. Springer, Cham (2018). https://doi.org/10.1007/978-3-319-91253-0_67

27. Saralajew, S., Holdijk, L., Rees, M., Asan, E., Villmann, T.: Classification-by-components: probabilistic modeling of reasoning over a set of components. In: Proceedings of the 31st Conference on Neural Information Processing Systems (NeurIPS 2019), pp. 2788–2799. MIT Press (2019)

28. Biederman, I.: Recognition-by-components: a theory of human image understanding. Psychol. Rev. **94**(2), 115–147 (1987)

Grid-Based Approach to Determining Parameters of the DBSCAN Algorithm

Artur Starczewski[1]([⊠]) and Andrzej Cader[2,3]

[1] Institute of Computational Intelligence, Częstochowa University of Technology,
Al. Armii Krajowej 36, 42-200 Częstochowa, Poland
`artur.starczewski@iisi.pcz.pl`
[2] Information Technology Institute, University of Social Sciences,
90-113 Łódź, Poland
`acader@san.edu.pl`
[3] Clark University, Worcester, MA 01610, USA

Abstract. Clustering is a very important technique used in many fields in order to deal with large datasets. In clustering algorithms, one of the most popular approaches is based on an analysis of clusters density. Density-based algorithms include different methods but the Density-Based Spatial Clustering of Applications with Noise (DBSCAN) is one of the most cited in the scientific literature. This algorithm can identify clusters of arbitrary shapes and sizes that occur in a dataset. Thus, the DBSCAN is very widely applied in various applications and has many modifications. However, there is a key issue of the right choice of its two input parameters, i.e the neighborhood radius (*eps*) and the *MinPts*. In this paper, a new method for determining the neighborhood radius (*eps*) and the *MinPts* is proposed. This method is based on finding a proper grid of cells for a dataset. Next, the grid is used to calculate the right values of these two parameters. Experimental results have been obtained for several different datasets and they confirm a very good performance of the newly proposed method.

Keywords: Clustering algorithms · Data mining · DBSCAN

1 Introduction

Clustering algorithms discover naturally occurring structures in datasets. Nowadays, extensive collections of data pose a great challenge for clustering algorithms. So, many researchers create different new clustering algorithms or modify existing approaches [5,6,11,19,21]. It is worth noting that data clustering is applied in various areas, e.g. biology, spatial data analysis, or business. The key issue is the right choice of input parameters because the same algorithm can produce different results depending on applied parameters. This problem can be resolved by using different cluster validity indices, e.g., [10,26,29,30]. Generally, clustering algorithms can be divided into four categories: partitioning,

© Springer Nature Switzerland AG 2020
L. Rutkowski et al. (Eds.): ICAISC 2020, LNAI 12415, pp. 555–565, 2020.
https://doi.org/10.1007/978-3-030-61401-0_52

hierarchical, grid-based, and density-based clustering. Well-known partitioning algorithms include the K-means or Partitioning Around Medoids (PAM) [3,32]. The next clustering category called hierarchical is based on an agglomerative or divisive approach, e.g. the Single-linkage, Complete-linkage, Average-linkage, or Divisive ANAlysis Clustering (DIANA) [17,23]. On the other hand, the grid-based approach creates a grid of cells for a dataset, e.g. the Statistical Information Grid-based (STING) or Wavelet-based Clustering (WaveCluster) methods [18,28,31]. The last category can be represented by the Density-Based Spatial Clustering of Application with Noise (DBSCAN) algorithm [9] which has many modifications [7,12,13,15,27]. This algorithm can discover clusters of an arbitrary shape and size but requires two input parameters, i.e. the *eps* and the *MinPts*. The determination of these parameters is very important for the DBSCAN algorithm to work properly. It is important to note that clustering methods can be used during the process of designing various neural networks [1,2], fuzzy, and rule systems [4,8,14,16,20,22,24,25].

In this paper, a new approach to determining the *eps* and *MinPts* parameters is proposed. It is based on the creation of a proper grid of cells and the grid is used to define the values of the two parameters. This paper is organized as follows: Sect. 2 presents a description of the *DBSCAN* clustering algorithm. In Sect. 3 the new method for determining the parameters is outlined, while Sect. 4 illustrates the experimental results on datasets. Finally, Sect. 5 presents the conclusions.

2   The DBSCAN Algorithm

The concept of the *DBSCAN* algorithm is presented in this section. As mentioned above, this algorithm is very popular, because it can find clusters of arbitrary shapes and requires only two input parameters, i.e. the *eps* and the *MinPts*. The *eps* is usually determined by the user and it has a large influence on the creation of clusters. The next parameter, i.e. the *MinPts* is the minimal number of neighboring points belonging to the so-called *core point*. Let us denote a dataset by X, where point $p \in X$. The following definitions (see [9]) will be helpful in understanding how the DBSCAN algorithm works.

Definition 1: The *eps-neighborhood* of point $p \in X$ is called $N_{eps}(p)$ and is defined as follows: $N_{eps}(p) = \{q \in X | dist(p,q) \leq eps\}$, where $dist(p,q)$ is a distance function between p and q.

Definition 2: p is called the *core* if the number of points belonging to $N_{eps}(p)$ is greater or equal to the *MinPts*.

Definition 3: Point q is *directly density-reachable* from point p (for the given *eps* and the *MinPts*) if p is the *core point* and q belongs to $N_{eps}(p)$.

Definition 4: if point q is *directly density-reachable* from point p and the number of points belonging to $N_{eps}(q)$ is smaller than the *MinPts*, q is called a *border point*.

Definition 5: Point q is a *noise* if it is neither a *core point* nor a *border point*.

Definition 6: Point q is *density-reachable* from point p (for the given *eps* and the *MinPts*) if there is a chain of points $q_1, q_2, ..., q_n$ and $q_1 = p$, $q_n = q$, so that q_{i+1} is *directly density-reachable* from q_i

Definition 7: Point q is *density-connected* to point p (for the given *eps* and the *MinPts*) if there is point o such that q and p are *density-reachable* from point o.

Definition 8: Cluster C (for the given *eps* and the *MinPts*) is a non-empty subset of X and the following conditions are satisfied: first, $\forall p, q$: if $p \in C$ and q is *density-reachable* from p, then $q \in C$, next $\forall p, q \in C$: p is *density-connected* to q.

The DBSCAN algorithm creates clusters according to the following: at first, point p is selected randomly if $|N_{eps}(p)| \geq MinPts$, than point p will be the *core point* and a new cluster will be created. Next, the new cluster is expanded by the points which are *density-reachable* from p. This process is repeated until no cluster is found. On the other hand, if $|N_{eps}(p)| < MinPts$, then point p will be a *noise*, but this point can be included in another cluster if it is *density-reachable* from some *core point*.

3   Grid-Based Approach to Determining the Eps and MinPts Parameters

The right choice of the *eps* and *MinPts* parameters is a fundamental issue for the high performance of the DBSCAN algorithm. The proposed method is based on a uniform grid of cells which is created for a dataset. In order to provide a clearer explanation of this new approach, an example of a 2-dimensional dataset is generated. Figure 1 shows this dataset consisting of 1200 elements located in four clusters, i.e. 200, 250, 300 and 450 elements per cluster, respectively. Next, for this dataset an example grid of cells can be created, e.g. consisting of 100 cells (10 x 10). Figure 2 shows this uniform grid of cells. It can be noted that the

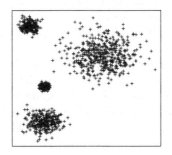

Fig. 1. An example of a 2-dimensional dataset consisting of four clusters.

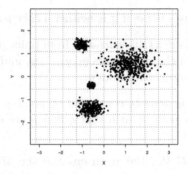

Fig. 2. Uniform grid consisting of 100 cells (10 x 10) for the example dataset.

proper grid can be used to define the value of the *eps* parameter, but the key issue is an appropriate choice of the size of the grid, which has a big influence on the value of the parameter. In this new method, a way of solving this problem is proposed and it consists of a few steps. First, several grids of cells are created, where the size of rows and columns of grids change in a wide range, i.e. from 2 to 90 (2 x 2 and 90 x 90 cells). So, the number of cells is changed from 4 to 8100. Such a number of cells gives precise information about the properties of a dataset. Let us denote the size of a grid by G_{size}. For all the created grids, three ranges can be defined as in the following:

$$
\begin{aligned}
range1 \quad for \quad 2 \le \ G_{size} \ \le \ 30 \\
range2 \quad for \quad 30 < \ G_{size} \ \le \ 60 \\
range3 \quad for \quad 60 < \ G_{size} \ \le \ 90
\end{aligned}
\tag{1}
$$

It is worth noting that the second parameter of the DBSCAN algorithm, i.e. the *MinPts* is also very important and it affects a number of so-called noise data. Generally, the choice of this parameter is often realized individually depending on a dataset, but very often the *MinPts* equals 4, 5, or 6. Such values of this parameter ensure a good compromise between the size of clusters and an amount of noise data in most cases. So, in this new approach, the values of the *MinPts* are selected from 4 to 6. As mentioned above, the sizes of the grids range from 2 to 90. Next, in all the created grids are found cells which include only 4 elements. Then, the grid which includes a maximum number of cells with four elements is found and the size of the grid is noted by G_{max4}. Furthermore, the grids which include a maximum number of cells with 5 and 6 elements are also found and the sizes of grids are noted by G_{max5} and G_{max6}. In the next step, the $dist_4$, $dist_5$ and $dist_6$ parameters are determined for the G_{max4}, G_{max5} and G_{max6} grid sizes, respectively. The values of these parameters are maximum distances between the elements of the cells which include 4, 5, and 6 elements, respectively. Next, if condition ($G_{max4} > G_{max5} > G_{max6}$) is fulfilled, the value of the *eps* is defined as follows:

$$eps = \begin{cases} a * dist_4 & for \quad G_{max4} \in range1 \\ b * dist_5 & for \quad G_{max4} \in range2 \\ c * dist_6 & for \quad G_{max4} \in range3 \end{cases} \quad (2)$$

where factors a, b and c are experimentally determined and their values are 1, 1.2 and 1.5, respectively. On the other hand, the $MinPts$ is expressed as follows:

$$MinPts = \begin{cases} 4 & for \quad G_{max4} \in range1 \\ 5 & for \quad G_{max4} \in range2 \\ 6 & for \quad G_{max4} \in range3 \end{cases} \quad (3)$$

Sometimes, for different datasets condition $(G_{max4} > G_{max5} > G_{max6})$ may not be fulfilled. This means that the clusters have a different density because when the $MinPts$ increases and the clusters have a similar density, the maximum number of cells should be decreased. In these cases, when the condition is not fulfilled the values of the a, b, and c factors should be increased so that they equal 2. In Table 1 are presented the values of G_{max4}, G_{max5} and G_{max6} calculated for the example dataset. It can be observed that for the $MinPts$ equal to 5, the size of the grid is larger than the size for the $MinPts$ equal to 4. So, clusters are of different density in the dataset (see Fig. 1). Condition $(G_{max4} > G_{max5} > G_{max6})$ is not fulfilled and the b parameter is increased (equals 2). Moreover, when the $MinPts$ is equal to 4, G_{max4} is 52 and is included in $range2$. Thus, $eps = b * dist_5$ (see Eq. 2) and the values of the eps and $MinPts$ parameters are 0.20 and 5, respectively. Such values of input parameters are used in the $DBSCAN$ algorithm.

Table 1. Values of G_{max4}, G_{max5} and G_{max6} for the example dataset

Maximum number of cells	Values of the $MinPts$	Number of cells
$G_{max4} = 52$ $(52 \times 52 - 2704$ cells$)$	4	33
$G_{max5} = 62$ $(62 \times 62 - 3844$ cells$)$	5	24
$G_{max6} = 48$ $(48 \times 48 - 864$ cells$)$	6	17

Figure 3 shows the results of the $DBSCAN$ clustering algorithm for the example dataset. In the next section, the results of the experimental tests are presented to confirm the effectiveness of the new approach.

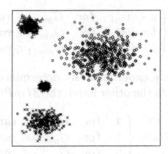

Fig. 3. Results of the *DBSCAN* clustering algorithm for the example dataset.

4   Experimental Results

In this section, several experiments have been conducted on 2-dimensional artificial datasets. In these experiments, the *DBSCAN* algorithm is used to cluster the data. As mentioned above, the *eps* and *MinPts* parameters play a very important role in creating correct clusters by this clustering algorithm. So, they are defined based on the new method described in Sect. 3 and the calculated values of these parameters are presented in Table 3. Moreover, the evaluation of the accuracy of the DBSCAN algorithm is conducted by a visual inspection. It is worth noting that the artificial datasets include clusters of various shapes and sizes. On the other hand, for clustering multidimensional datasets, determining the input parameters of the DBSCAN algorithm is very difficult.

Table 2. A detailed description of the artificial datasets

Datasets	No. of elements	Clusters
Data 1	700	2
Data 2	700	3
Data 3	3000	3
Data 4	1000	3
Data 5	900	4
Data 6	500	4
Data 7	500	4
Data 8	1800	5
Data 9	700	6

Table 3. The *eps* and *MinPts* values used by the DBSCAN algorithm

Datasets	eps	MinPts
Data 1	0.36	5
Data 2	0.22	4
Data 3	0.16	6
Data 4	0.20	5
Data 5	0.34	6
Data 6	0.33	5
Data 7	0.20	5
Data 8	0.23	5
Data 9	0.21	5

4.1 Datasets

In the conducted experiments nine 2-dimensional datasets are used. Most of them come from the R package. The artificial data are called *Data* 1, *Data* 2, *Data* 3, *Data* 4, *Data* 5, *Data* 6, *Data* 7, *Data* 8 and *Data* 9, respectively. They consist of a various number of clusters, i.e. 2, 3, 4, 5, and 6 clusters. The scatter plot of these data is presented in Fig. 4. As it can be observed on the plot, the clusters are located in different areas and some of the clusters are very close to each other and the others are quite far apart. For instance, *Data* 1 is a so-called spirals problem, where the points are on two entangled spirals, in *Data* 5 the elements create a Gaussian, square, triangle and wave shapes and *Data* 6 consists of 2 Gaussian eyes, a trapezoid nose and a parabola mouth (with a vertical Gaussian one). Moreover, the sizes of the clusters are different and they contain a various number of elements. In Table 2 is shown a description of these datasets.

4.2 Experiments

The experimental analysis is designed to evaluate the performance of the new method to specify the *eps* and *MinPts* parameters. As mentioned above, these parameters are very important for the *DBSCAN* algorithm to work correctly. In standard approaches, they are determined by a visual inspection of the sorted values of a function which computes a distance between each element of a dataset and its k-th nearest neighbor. The new approach described in Sect. 3 is based on finding a proper grid of cells and it makes it possible to determine these two input parameters. In these experiments, the nine 2-dimensional datasets used are called *Data* 1, *Data* 2, *Data* 3, *Data* 4, *Data* 5, *Data* 6, *Data* 7, *Data* 8 and *Data* 9 datasets. It is worth noting that the value of the *MinPts* parameter is also chosen when the size of the grid changes from 2 to 90 (2 x 2 and 90 x 90 cells). Then, when these parameters are specified by the new method, the *DBSCAN* algorithm can be used to cluster these datasets. Figure 5 shows the results of

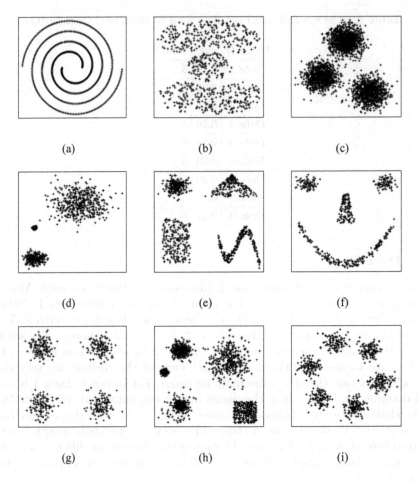

Fig. 4. Examples of 2-dimensional artificial datasets: (a) *Data* 1, (b) *Data* 2, (c) *Data* 3, (d) *Data* 4, (e) *Data* 5, (f) *Data* 6, (g) *Data* 7, (h) *Data* 8 and (i) *Data* 9.

the *DBSCAN* algorithm, where each cluster is marked with different signs. The data elements classified as the *noise* are marked with a circle. Thus, despite the fact that the differences in the distances and the shapes between clusters are significant, all the datasets are clustered correctly by the *DBSCAN*. Moreover, a number of the data elements classified as noise in all the datasets is relatively insignificant.

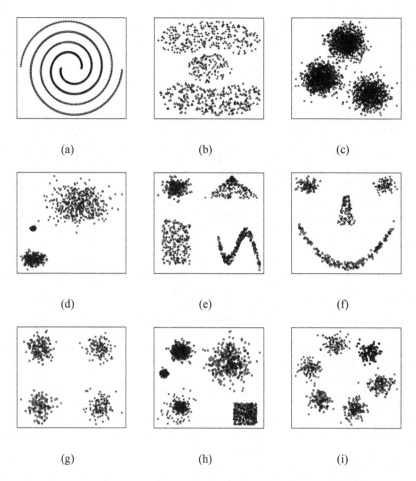

Fig. 5. Results of the *DBSCAN* clustering algorithm for 2-dimensional datasets: (a) *Data* 1, (b) *Data* 2, (c) *Data* 3, (d) *Data* 4, (e) *Data* 5, (f) *Data* 6, (g) *Data* 7, (h) *Data* 8 and (i) *Data* 9

5   Conclusions

In this paper, a new approach is proposed to calculate the *eps* and *MinPts* parameters of the DBSCAN algorithm. It is based on finding the right grid of cells, which is selected from many other grids. As mentioned above, the sizes of the grids change from 2 to 90. It is worth noting that the determination of the *MinPts* parameter is also difficult and it is often chosen empirically depending on datasets being investigated. In this new method, the values of the *MinPts* parameter are selected from 4 to 6. Generally, the right grid of cells makes it possible to correctly calculate these two input parameters. In the conducted experiments, several 2-dimensional datasets were used, where a number of clusters, sizes, and shapes were very different. All the presented results confirm the high efficiency of the newly proposed approach.

References

1. Bilski, J., Smolag, J., Żurada, J.M.: Parallel approach to the Levenberg-Marquardt learning algorithm for feedforward neural networks. In: Rutkowski, L., Korytkowski, M., Scherer, R., Tadeusiewicz, R., Zadeh, L.A., Zurada, J.M. (eds.) ICAISC 2015. LNCS (LNAI), vol. 9119, pp. 3–14. Springer, Cham (2015). https://doi.org/10.1007/978-3-319-19324-3_1

2. Bilski, J., Wilamowski, B.M.: Parallel Levenberg-Marquardt algorithm without error backpropagation. In: Rutkowski, L., Korytkowski, M., Scherer, R., Tadeusiewicz, R., Zadeh, L.A., Zurada, J.M. (eds.) ICAISC 2017. LNCS (LNAI), vol. 10245, pp. 25–39. Springer, Cham (2017). https://doi.org/10.1007/978-3-319-59063-9_3

3. Bradley, P., Fayyad, U.: Refining initial points for k-means clustering. In: Proceedings of the Fifteenth International Conference on Knowledge Discovery and Data Mining, pp. 9–15. AAAI Press, New York (1998)

4. Bologna, G., Hayashi, Y.: Characterization of symbolic rules embedded in deep DIMLP networks: a challenge to transparency of deep learning. J. Artif. Intell. Soft Comput. Res. 7(4), 265–286 (2017)

5. Chen, X., Liu, W., Qui, H., Lai, J.: APSCAN: a parameter free algorithm for clustering. Pattern Recogn. Lett. 32, 973–986 (2011)

6. Chen, J.: Hybrid clustering algorithm based on PSO with the multidimensional asynchronism and stochastic disturbance method. J. Theor. Appl. Inform. Technol. 46, 343–440 (2012)

7. Chen, Y., Tang, S., Bouguila, N., Wang, C., Du, J., Li, H.: A fast clustering algorithm based on pruning unnecessary distance computations in DBSCAN for high-dimensional data. Pattern Recogn. 83, 375–387 (2018)

8. D'Aniello, G., Gaeta, M., Loia, F., Reformat, M., Toti, D.: An environment for collective perception based on fuzzy and semantic approaches. J. Artif. Intell. Soft Comput. Res. 8(3), 191–210 (2018)

9. Ester, M., Kriegel, H.P., Sander, J., Xu, X.: A density-based algorithm for discovering clusters in large spatial databases with noise. In: Proceeding of 2nd International Conference on Knowledge Discovery and Data Mining, pp. 226–231 (1996)

10. Fränti, P., Rezaei, M., Zhao, Q.: Centroid index: cluster level similarity measure. Pattern Recogn. 47(9), 3034–3045 (2014)

11. Hruschka, E.R., de Castro, L.N., Campello, R.J.: Evolutionary algorithms for clustering gene-expression data. In: Data Mining, Fourth IEEE International Conference on Data Mining (ICDM 2004), pp. 403–406. IEEE (2004)

12. Karami, A., Johansson, R.: Choosing DBSCAN parameters automatically using differential evolution. Int. J. Comput. Appl. 91, 1–11 (2014)

13. Lai, W., Zhou, M., Hu, F., Bian, K., Song, Q.: A new DBSCAN parameters determination method based on improved MVO. IEEE Access 7, 104085–104095 (2019)

14. Liu, H., Gegov, A., Cocea, M.: Rule based networks: an efficient and interpretable representation of computational models. J. Artif. Intell. Soft Comput. Res. 7(2), 111–123 (2017)

15. Luchi, D., Rodrigues, A.L., Varejao, F.M.: Sampling approaches for applying DBSCAN to large datasets. Pattern Recogn. Lett. 117, 90–96 (2019)

16. Ferdaus, M.M., Anavatti, S.G., Matthew, A., Pratama, G., Pratama, M.: Development of C-means clustering based adaptive fuzzy controller for a flapping wing micro air vehicle. J. Artif. Intell. Soft Comput. Res. **9**(2), 99–109 (2019). https://doi.org/10.2478/jaiscr-2018-0027

17. Murtagh, F.: A survey of recent advances in hierarchical clustering algorithms. Comput. J. **26**(4), 354–359 (1983)

18. Patrikainen, A., Meila, M.: Comparing subspace clusterings. IEEE Trans. Knowl. Data Eng. **18**(7), 902–916 (2006)

19. Pei, Z., Hua, X., Han, J.: The clustering algorithm based on particle swarm optimization algorithm. In: Proceedings of the 2008 International Conference on Intelligent Computation Technology and Automation, Washington, USA, vol. 1, pp. 148–151 (2008)

20. Prasad, M., Liu, Y.-T., Li, D.-L., Lin, C.-T., Shah, R.R., Kaiwartya, O.P.: A new mechanism for data visualization with TSK-type preprocessed collaborative fuzzy rule based system. J. Artif. Intell. Soft Comput. Res. **7**(1), 33–46 (2017)

21. Rastin, P., Matei, B., Cabanes, G., Grozavu, N., Bennani, Y.: Impact of learners' quality and diversity in collaborative clustering. J. Artif. Intell. Soft Comput. Res. **9**(2), 149–165 (2019). https://doi.org/10.2478/jaiscr-2018-0030

22. Riid, A., Preden, J.-S.: Design of fuzzy rule-based classifiers through granulation and consolidation. J. Artif. Intell. Soft Comput. Res. **7**(2), 137–147 (2017)

23. Rohlf, F.: Single-link clustering algorithms. In: Krishnaiah, P.R., Kanal, L.N., (eds.) Handbook of Statistics, vol. 2, pp. 267–284 (1982)

24. Rutkowski, T., Łapa, K., Nielek, R.: On explainable fuzzy recommenders and their performance evaluation. Int. J. Appl. Math. Comput. Sci. **29**(3), 595–610 (2019). https://doi.org/10.2478/amcs-2019-0044

25. Rutkowski, T., Łapa, K., Jaworski, M., Nielek, R., Rutkowska, D.: On explainable flexible fuzzy recommender and its performance evaluation using the akaike information criterion. In: Gedeon, T., Wong, K.W., Lee, M. (eds.) ICONIP 2019. CCIS, vol. 1142, pp. 717–724. Springer, Cham (2019). https://doi.org/10.1007/978-3-030-36808-1_78

26. Sameh, A.S., Asoke, K.N.: Development of assessment criteria for clustering algorithms. Pattern Anal. Appl. **12**(1), 79–98 (2009)

27. Shah G.H.: An improved DBSCAN, a density based clustering algorithm with parameter selection for high dimensional data sets. In: Nirma University International Engineering (NUiCONE), pp. 1–6 (2012)

28. Sheikholeslam, G., Chatterjee, S., Zhang, A.: WaveCluster: a wavelet-based clustering approach for spatial data in very large databases. Int. J. Very Large Data Bases **8**(3–4), 289–304 (2000)

29. Shieh, H.-L.: Robust validity index for a modified subtractive clustering algorithm. Appl. Soft Comput. **22**, 47–59 (2014)

30. Starczewski, A.: A new validity index for crisp clusters. Pattern Anal. Appl. **20**(3), 687–700 (2017)

31. Wang, W., Yang, J., Muntz, R.: STING: a statistical information grid approach to spatial data mining. In: Proceedings of the 23rd International Conference on Very Large Data Bases. (VLDB 1997), pp. 186–195 (1997)

32. Zalik, K.R.: An efficient k-means clustering algorithm. Pattern Recogn. Lett. **29**(9), 1385–1391 (2008)

Particle Classification Based on Movement Behavior in IPSO Stochastic Model

Krzysztof Wójcik[(✉)] [iD], Tomasz Kulpa [iD], and Krzysztof Trojanowski [iD]

Cardinal Stefan Wyszyński University in Warsaw, Warsaw, Poland
{krzysztof.wojcik,tomasz.kulpa,k.trojanowski}@uksw.edu.pl

Abstract. In Particle Swarm Optimization, the behavior of particles depends on the parameters of movement formulas. In our research, we identify types of particles based on their movement trajectories. Then, we propose new rules of particle classification based on the two attributes of the measure representing the minimum number of steps necessary for the expected particle location to obtain its stable state. The new classification clarifies the division into types of particles based on the observation of different shapes of their movement trajectories.

Keywords: PSO with inertia weight · Particle convergence expected time · Particle movement trajectories.

1 Introduction

Particle Swarm Optimization (PSO) is a modern heuristic optimization technique, where a population of moving objects explores a search domain to find the most valuable point in this space. Objects, called particles, undergo Newtonian mechanics rules: they are defined by location, velocity, and inertia. Particles cooperate by sharing information about already found good points in the space, and they are attracted to these points. PSO represents a heuristic approach because the strength of attraction is not deterministic but controlled by factors randomized in every step. Therefore, trajectories of particles may be slightly different even if the particles have identical configurations, that is, the same location, attractors, and values of movement parameters.

Among numerous variants of PSO, we selected PSO with inertia weight (IPSO) for the analysis. To better understand, predict, and control particle movement, stochastic models of a particle are subject to the analysis performed under modeling assumptions. In this research, we study movement trajectories of the expected value of particle location in the stochastic model. We observe types of trajectories and propose new rules of particle classification based on their movement trajectories and two attributes of a particle convergence expected time under stagnation assumption. The particle convergence expected time is the minimal number of steps necessary for the expected particle location to obtain its stable state. The swarm becomes stagnant when no particles can find a better position anymore, which means that the attractors remain unchanged over time.

The text consists of 6 sections. Section 2 presents a brief review of selected areas of PSO theoretical analysis concerning order-1 stability, the stochastic model in the PSO

L. Rutkowski et al. (Eds.): ICAISC 2020, LNAI 12415, pp. 566–575, 2020.
https://doi.org/10.1007/978-3-030-61401-0_53

method with inertia weight (IPSO), and particle behavior. In Sect. 3, we distinguish several types of behavior of particle expected location with respect to chosen initial parameters. In Sect. 4, a measure of particle convergence is recalled, and two related attributes are derived. In Sect. 5 these attributes are used to propose a classification of particle movement trajectories. Section 6 summarizes the presented research.

2   Related Work

Particles are the primary elements of a swarm, each representing a certain proposition of a solution, intending to find an optimal solution. Their movement can be generally described by the equation

$$x_i(t + 1) = x_i(t) + v_i(t + 1), \tag{1}$$

where x_i is the location of the particle, and v_i—velocity of the particle.

2.1   Particle Swarm Optimization with Inertia Weight (IPSO)

In the IPSO method movement of particles is described by the set of equalities

$$\begin{cases} \mathbf{v}_{t+1} = w \cdot \mathbf{v}_t + \varphi_{t,1} \otimes (\mathbf{y}_t - \mathbf{x}_t) + \varphi_{t,2} \otimes (\mathbf{y}_t^* - \mathbf{x}_t) \\ \mathbf{x}_{t+1} = \mathbf{x}_t + \mathbf{v}_{t+1}, \end{cases} \tag{2}$$

where $\mathbf{v}_t$ is a vector of particle velocities, $\mathbf{x}_t$ is a vector of particle locations, $\mathbf{y}_t$ is the best location that the particle has found so far, $\mathbf{y}_t^*$-the best location found by particles overall, w is an inertia weight, $\varphi_{t,1}$ and $\varphi_{t,2}$ are random variables, $\otimes$ is a Hadamard product. Furthermore, we assume $\varphi_{t,1} = R_{t,1}c_1$, $\varphi_{t,2} = R_{t,2}c_2$, where c_1, c_2 are acceleration coefficients, $R_{t,1}$ and $R_{t,2}$ are vectors of numbers generated from a uniform distribution over an interval of $[0, 1]$.

2.2   IPSO Stochastic Model

Let's assume stagnation in IPSO method [2]: $\mathbf{y}_t = \mathbf{y}$, $\mathbf{y}_t^* = \mathbf{y}^*$ for sufficiently large t. In this case the velocity equation is as follows:

$$\mathbf{v}_{t+1} = w \cdot \mathbf{v}_t + \varphi_{t,1} \otimes (\mathbf{y} - \mathbf{x}_t) + \varphi_{t,2} \otimes (\mathbf{y}^* - \mathbf{x}_t). \tag{3}$$

Substituting $\mathbf{v}_{t+1} = \mathbf{x}_{t+1} - \mathbf{x}_t$ and limiting to a single dimension allows us to rewrite the equation as:

$$x_{t+1} = (1 + w - \varphi_{t,1} - \varphi_{t,2})x_t - wx_{t-1} + \varphi_{t,1}y + \varphi_{t,2}y^*. \tag{4}$$

In [1], it is shown that the equilibrium point for a particle is a weighed average of y, y^* and is equal to $\frac{\varphi_1 y + \varphi_2 y^*}{\varphi_{t,1} + \varphi_{t,2}}$. Still, without loss of generality, we can assume $y = y^*$ and reformulate (4) as

$$x_{t+1} = (1 + w - \phi_t)x_t - wx_{t-1} + \phi_t y, \tag{5}$$

where $\phi_t = \varphi_{t,1} + \varphi_{t,2}$. From now on we will relate to (5) as the **stochastic model** where x_t is a random variable representing particle location in time t.

2.3 Order-1 Analysis in IPSO Stochastic Model

In 2009, Poli [4] used the expected value of particle locations and presented a stability definition

$$\lim_{t \to \infty} E[\mathbf{x}_t] = \mathbf{y}, \tag{6}$$

which he named order-1 stability, or first-order stability. He also proposed the following stability area for IPSO stochastic model:

$$0 < E[\phi_t] < 2(1 + w), \quad -1 < w < 1, \tag{7}$$

2.4 Particle Movement Trajectories in the PSO Method

One of the first observations of convergent particle movement trajectories can be found in [2] and [3] by Ozcan and Mohan. In the latter paper, the authors noticed a surprising behavior of a particle "jumping" from one sinusoidal to another. In 2003, Trelea [5] identified three elementary types of particle movement behavior in the deterministic model of PSO: (1) harmonic oscillatory convergence, (2) non-oscillatory convergence, (3) zigzagging, and presented the areas of their occurrence.

3 Types of Particle Movement Trajectories

In earlier publications, the authors study the particle trajectories for the deterministic model of PSO. However, one can take advantage of the fact that there exists an analogy between the deterministic and the order-1 stochastic model and study the expected value of particle location trajectories. When the expected value operator is applied to both sides of (5), the movement equation takes the form

$$e_{t+1} = (1 + w - f)e_t - we_{t-1} + fy, \tag{8}$$

where $e_t = E[x_t]$ and $f = E[\phi_t]$. Through empirical observations of the parameter space where the IPSO method is order-1 stable ($-1 < w < 1, 0 < f < 2(w + 1)$) we distinguished four basic convergent particle behavior types: (1) non-oscillatory (Fig. 1a), (2) harmonic-oscillatory (Fig. 1b) (3) "double helix" (Fig. 1d), (4) zigzagging (Fig. 1c), (5) mixed (Fig. 1e).

From empirical observations of particle movement for different parameter configurations we can notice the following regularities:

1. for lower values of $|w|$ the trajectory is more difficult to observe due to the particle converging quickly,
2. increasing the value of $|w|$ results in more distinctive trajectory of the particle due to the particle memorizing its previous step which acts as an attractor for the particle in the next step,
3. observed trajectories of the particle movement have a clearly defined shape (oscillatory harmonic, non-oscillatory, "double helix" –type and zigzagging) for extreme values of f (extreme in terms of convergence area defined by the set of inequalities (7)). For the intermediate values of f an evolution from one type to the other can be observed.

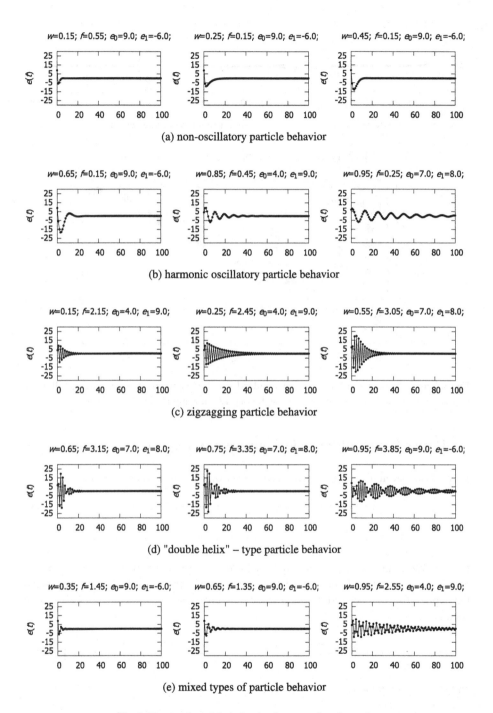

(a) non-oscillatory particle behavior

(b) harmonic oscillatory particle behavior

(c) zigzagging particle behavior

(d) "double helix" – type particle behavior

(e) mixed types of particle behavior

Fig. 1. Types of particle behavior for $w > 0$ and $y = 0$

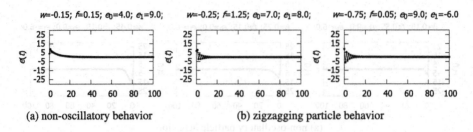

(a) non-oscillatory behavior   (b) zigzagging particle behavior

Fig. 2. Types of particle behavior for $w < 0$ and $y = 0$

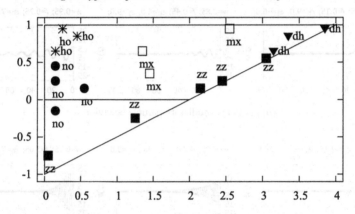

Fig. 3. Selected configurations (f, w) in the order-1 stability parameter domain with the following types: no–non-oscillatory, ho–harmonic oscillatory, zz–zigzagging, dh–double helix, mx–mixed

4 Upper Bound of Particle Convergence Expected Time

In [6], for a given $\delta > 0$, *particle convergence expected time (pcet)* is defined as:

$$pcet(\delta) = min\{s \mid e_t < \delta \text{ for all } t \geq s\}. \tag{9}$$

Briefly, the particle convergence expected time *pcet* is the minimal number of steps necessary for the expected particle location to be sufficiently close to zero assuming, that configuration parameters belong to the order-1 region and the attractor coordinate equals zero. Also in [6], the upper bound for *pcet* was introduced, namely *pcetub* and the explicit formula derived. For real value of γ given by $\gamma = \sqrt{(1 + w - f)^2 - 4w}$ it is equal to:

$$pcetub(\delta) = max\left(\frac{\ln \delta - \ln(2|k_2||\lambda_1 - 1|)}{\ln|\lambda_1|}, \frac{\ln \delta - \ln(2|k_3||\lambda_2 - 1|)}{\ln|\lambda_2|}, 1\right) \tag{10}$$

and for imaginary value of γ it is equal to:

$$pcetub(\delta) = max\left(\frac{\ln \delta - \ln(|\lambda_1 - 1|(|k_2| + |k_3|))}{\ln|\lambda_1|}, 1\right) \tag{11}$$

where λ_1 and λ_2 are:

$$\lambda_1 = \frac{1 + w - f + \gamma}{2} \text{ and } \lambda_2 = \frac{1 + w - f - \gamma}{2}$$

and k_1, k_2 and k_3 are given by

$$k_1 = y, \text{ and } k_2 = \frac{\lambda_2(e_0 - e_1) - e_1 + e_2}{\gamma(\lambda_1 - 1)}, \text{ and } k_3 = \frac{\lambda_1(e_1 - e_0) + e_1 - e_2}{\gamma(\lambda_2 - 1)},$$

where $e_2 = (1 + w - f)e_1 - we_0 + fy$.

Figure 4 depicts example graphs of $pcetub(e_0, e_1)$ for selected configurations (f, w) and $\delta = 0.0001$.

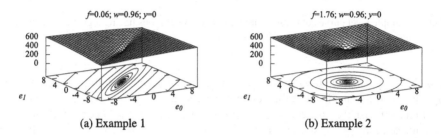

(a) Example 1   (b) Example 2

Fig. 4. Example graphs of $pcetub(e_0, e_1)$ for selected configurations (f, w) and $\delta = 0.0001$

One can observe that for the selected configurations (f, w) graphs of $pcetub(e_0, e_1)$ printed in Fig. 4 have regular shape of a funnel. We assumed that the attractor y^* is in the origin of Euclidean space; hence, this is also the point of the minimum value of the shape. When the first and the second location of a particle is the same as its attractor, the particle has already obtained its equilibrium state. It does not move anymore, and its convergence time equals zero.

For the fixed values of f and w, the contours of $pcetub(e_0, e_1)$ printed on the plane E_0, E_1 resemble ellipses. Figure 5 depicts example level curves, which represent particle configurations sets having a given constant value of $pcetub$. An ellipse can be characterized by two parameters: an angle coefficient for the major axis and its eccentricity, that is, a ratio between the minor and the major radius. For the simplicity of calculations, we approximate an angle coefficient for the major axis by the slope of the linear regression line a (see Fig. 5). The outcome of the division of two values: a distance from the origin of Euclidean space to the nearest point in an example level curve and a distance to the farthest point in the same level curve approximates eccentricity $\varepsilon(f, w)$. Pictures of the two characteristics: $a(f, w)$ and $\varepsilon(f, w)$ are presented in Figs. 6a and 6b and described below.

Figure 6a shows the mean values of the slope of the linear regression line a of contours of $pcetub(e_0, e_1)$ obtained from a series of 50 independent evaluations. The means are generated for a grid of configurations (f, w) starting from $[f = 0.04, w = -0.97]$

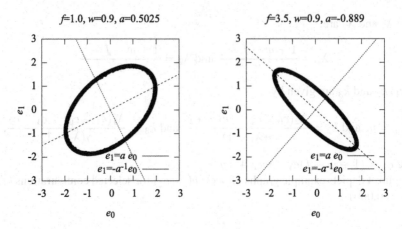

Fig. 5. Example level curves obtained from particle configurations having a given constant value of $pcetub$ and their respective linear regression lines: $e_1 = ae_0$

and changing with step 0.05 in both directions (which gave 80×40 points). The configurations from outside the stable region have assigned a constant value of minus one.

Figure 6b visualize the eccentricity $\varepsilon(f, w)$. This figure is also generated for a grid of configurations (f, w) starting from $[f = 0.04, w = -0.97]$ and changing with step 0.05 in both directions and shows means obtained from a series of 50 independent evaluation. As in Fig. 6a, $\varepsilon(f, w)$, for the configurations from outside the stable region we have assigned a constant value, however, in this case, they are set to 0.00001.

5   Classification

In Sect. 3, we showed the dependencies between two values f and w and the trajectory of particle movement. In Sect. 4, we analyzed the convergence time to equilibrium, and we introduced attributes a, ε, which characterize the measure $pcetub$ for given values of f and w. In this section, we present how these attributes are used to classify particle movement in accordance with the regularities observed in Sect. 3.

5.1   Correlation Between a, ε and Particle Trajectories

Through observations of the evolution of particle behavior together with incremental values of f, we can notice that when ε is relatively close to zero, then the shape of trajectory is easily identifiable, regardless of the type of the shape. In turn, when ε is large, the behavior of the particle consists of several types mixed.

Moreover, in regions of small ε, we can distinguish between the different types of trajectories by manipulating the values of a, respectively, when it is large-negative, small-negative, small-positive, and large-positive.

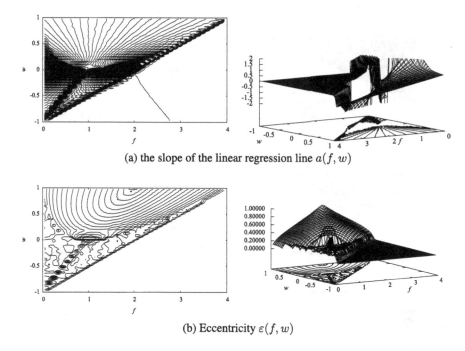

(a) the slope of the linear regression line $a(f, w)$

(b) Eccentricity $\varepsilon(f, w)$

Fig. 6. A graphical visualization of the slope of the linear regression line a of contours of $pcetub(e_0, e_1)$ and the eccentricity (ε) of contours of $pcetub(e_0, e_1)$

5.2 Classification of Particles

Considering the threshold values from the previous subsection, we obtain areas in which the following trajectories are identified: "double helix" -type, zig-zagging, harmonic oscillatory, non-oscillatory and an area of mixed types. Formally, classification conditions use thresholds $T1_{\text{ang}}, T2_{\text{ang}}, T_{\text{ecc}}$:

$$\text{class } A: \; \varepsilon < T_{\text{ecc}} \text{ and } a\,\text{sgn}\,w > T2_{\text{ang}} \tag{12}$$

$$\text{class } B: \; \varepsilon > T_{\text{ecc}} \tag{13}$$

$$\text{class } C: \; \varepsilon < T_{\text{ecc}} \text{ and } a\,\text{sgn}\,w < T1_{\text{ang}} \tag{14}$$

$$\text{class } D: \; \varepsilon < T_{\text{ecc}} \text{ and } 0 < a\,\text{sgn}\,w < T2_{\text{ang}} \tag{15}$$

$$\text{class } E: \; \varepsilon < T_{\text{ecc}} \text{ and } 0 > a\,\text{sgn}\,w > T1_{\text{ang}} \tag{16}$$

where $\text{sgn}\,w = 1$ for $w \geq 0$ and $\text{sgn}\,w = -1$ for $w < 0$. Due to the non-continuous behavior of the parameter a along the w = 0 line shown in Fig. 6a, we employ the sgn function in classification conditions.

The adoption of the threshold mentioned above, values results in the division of parameter domain w, f into areas depicted in Fig. 7 with the following indication: (1) non-oscillatory slowly converging—type A, (2) harmonic oscillatory—type E, (3) double helix—type D, (4) zigzagging—type C, (5) mixed—type B.

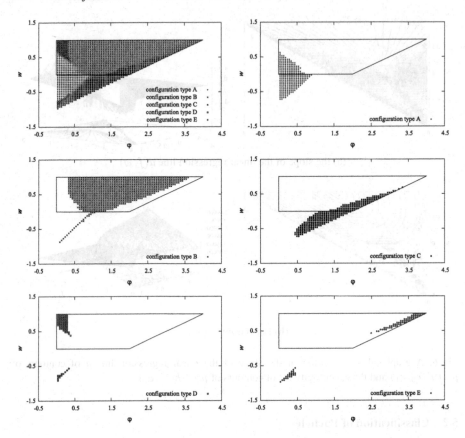

Fig. 7. Five types of particles: classification based on the attributes $a(f, w)$ and $\varepsilon(f, w)$ and thresholds $T1_{\text{ang}} = -1.3$, $T2_{\text{ang}} = 1.3$ and $T_{\text{ecc}} = 0.3$

5.3   Discussion

In [5], the author distinguishes between six different types of particle behavior, while we propose five types. In our research, we do not differentiate between slow and fast convergence for the oscillatory type, as well as the asymmetric and symmetric variants for the zigzagging type. Furthermore, our proposition includes the "mixed" type, which is not recognized in [5].

The obtained areas in the parameter space f, w, are similar to those outlined in [5]. The ridge present in Fig. 6b is equivalent to the straight line identifying the change of sign for the real part of the eigenvalues, which marks the behavior change of the particle from oscillatory to zigzagging.

Finally, it has to be stressed that the borders dividing the particle behavior types in Fig. 7 in reality are fuzzy, and their purpose is to mark the transition areas between the types.

6   Conclusions

In this paper, we propose a classification of particles in the view of the correlation between movement trajectories and the attributes related to the measure *pcetub*. The classification is based on three threshold values $T1_{\mathrm{ang}}$, $T2_{\mathrm{ang}}$ and T_{ecc}. We identify four basic types of particle behavior, together with a complimentary mixed type. The types are compliant with the results obtained in the literature; however, there are several differences that were discussed in Sect. 5.3.

The main novelty of research conducted in this paper lies in outlining a clear connection between particle behavior and a measure characterizing convergence time. The new classification based on *pcetub* clarifies the division into types of particles based on the observation of different shapes of trajectories.

References

1. van den Bergh, F., Engelbrecht, A.P.: A study of particle swarm optimization particle trajectories. Inform. Sci. **176**(8), 937–971 (2006). https://doi.org/10.1016/j.ins.2005.02.003
2. Ozcan, E., Mohan, C.K.: Analysis of a simple particle swarm optimization system. In: Intelligent Engineering Systems Through Artificial Neural Networks, Proceedings of the 1998 Artificial Neural Networks in Engineering Conference. (ANNIE 1998), vol. 8, pp. 253–258. ASME Press, St. Louis (1998)
3. Ozcan, E., Mohan, C.K.: Particle swarm optimization: surfing the waves. In: Proceedings of the 1999 Congress on Evolutionary Computation. (CEC 1999), vol. 3, p. 1944 (1999)
4. Poli, R.: Mean and variance of the sampling distribution of particle swarm optimizers during stagnation. IEEE Trans. Evol. Comput. **13**(4), 712–721 (2009). https://doi.org/10.1109/TEVC.2008.2011744
5. Trelea, I.C.: The particle swarm optimization algorithm: convergence analysis and parameter selection. Inform. Process. Lett. **85**(6), 317–325 (2003). https://doi.org/10.1016/S0020-0190(02)00447-7
6. Trojanowski, K., Kulpa, T.: Particle convergence expected time in the PSO model with inertia weight. In: Proceedings of the 8th International Joint Conference on Computational Intelligence. (IJCCI 2016), 9–11 November 2016, ECTA, Porto, Portugal, vol. 1, pp. 69–77. SciTePress (2016). https://doi.org/10.5220/0006048700690077

Combination of Active and Random Labeling Strategy in the Non-stationary Data Stream Classification

Paweł Zyblewski[ID], Paweł Ksieniewicz[ID], and Michał Woźniak[✉][ID]

Department of Systems and Computer Networks, Wrocław University of Science and Technology, Wybrzeże Wyspiańskiego 27, 50-370 Wrocław, Poland
{pawel.zyblewski,pawel.ksieniewicz,michal.wozniak}@pwr.edu.pl

Abstract. A significant problem when building classifiers based on data stream is information about the correct label. Most algorithms assume access to this information without any restrictions. Unfortunately, this is not possible in practice because the objects can come very quickly and labeling all of them is impossible, or we have to pay for providing the correct label (e.g., to human expert). Hence, methods based on partially labeled data, including methods based on an active learning approach, are becoming increasingly popular, i.e., when the learning algorithm itself decides which of the objects are interesting to improve the quality of the predictive model effectively. In this paper, we propose a new method of active learning of data stream classifier. Its quality has been compared with benchmark solutions based on a large number of test streams, and the results obtained prove the usefulness of the proposed method, especially in the case of a low budget dedicated to the labeling of incoming objects.

Keywords: Data stream classification · Active learning · Concept drift

1 Introduction

The design of classifiers for streaming data is the subject of intensive research because, currently, for most decision tasks, data is arriving continuously [4]. During the construction of such a type of system, we must take into account several vital issues, such as limited both memory and computing resources, which means that not all incoming data can be memorized and that each object can be analyzed at most once [3]. Another difficulty encountered in the construction of stream data classifiers is the phenomenon called *concept drift*, which means that when we use and train the classification model, the probability characteristics of the classification model may change at the same time [5]. Therefore, the classifier dedicated to this type of task, in addition to taking into account the limitations of available computing and memory resources, must ensure a correct response to *concept drift*.

© Springer Nature Switzerland AG 2020
L. Rutkowski et al. (Eds.): ICAISC 2020, LNAI 12415, pp. 576–585, 2020.
https://doi.org/10.1007/978-3-030-61401-0_54

In this work, we will also deal with another critical problem encountered during streaming data analysis, namely access to the correct label for incoming objects. Many of the methods described in the literature ignore this topic, assuming that labels are always available. They ignore the fact that, on the one hand, even if we could label the incoming objects, they can come quickly enough that labeling all of them will be impossible, or they may come around the clock, which strongly hinders such labeling for logistical reasons. On the other hand, the cost of labeling should be also taken into consideration. Sometimes their cost is negligible, e.g., in the case of weather forecasting (we can get a label with a delay, but the cost is only related to the observation and imputing it into the system). However, for most cases, such as medical diagnostics, labels are the result of human experts' effort, so labeling involves the cost of their work. Given the above, the assumption that labels are for free is unrealistic and limits the possibility of using many methods in real decision problems [1].

In our work, we focus on minimizing the necessary cost of data labeling using the so-called *active learning* approach [11]. It concentrates on choosing only the so-called "interesting" objects for labeling. The use of *active learning* for streaming data processing has been noticed, among others [9,13], however it is still not widely used. Hence, it is worth noting the work of Bouguelia et al. [2], who proposed a new active learning query strategy based on instance weighting. Ksieniewicz et al. [7] used one of the active learning strategies-*query by example* based on the values of the support function to improve neural network's prediction. [6] proposed employing different active learning strategy (*query by committee*) to classify non-stationary data streams. It is also worth mentioning the work [12], where the authors used the strategy to build a classifiers ensemble employing both the active approach and random labeling. As mentioned above, we will deal with the construction of classifiers for stream data, while focusing on the methods of adapting individual models, and not as on most works on constructing classifier ensemble. We assume that the data stream will be analyzed in the so-called data chunk, i.e., specific batches of data.

In our previous works, we noticed that in the event of rapid changes, using labeling strategies only for data close to decision boundaries may not be enough to adapt the classifier to the new distribution sufficiently (especially in the case where the changes in the distributions are very significant). Therefore, we propose that the classifier should receive, in addition to selected labeled objects by the active learning strategy, a pool of randomly selected objects from each chunk.

In a nutshell, the main contributions are as follows:

- Proposition of the BALS (*Budget Labelling Active learning Strategy*) algorithm, which improves the classification model both based on randomly labeled examples and instanced labeled by a chosen active learning strategy.
- Exhaustive experimental evaluation of the proposed method compared with the random labeling and active learning strategy for the pool of data streams with different types of concept drift.

2   Methods

The research presented in this work is based on three approaches to classifiers' building on stream data with limited labeling. The first of them is, hereinafter referred to as the BLS, *Budget Labeling*, in which for each data chunk we adopt a fixed, same for each analyzed data subset, percentage of randomly selected samples for which actual labels are obtained. This approach is presented in Algorithm 1.

Algorithm 1. Pseudocode for BLS.

Input:
    Classifier (Ψ)
    Budget (b)
1: **while** *Stream* **do**
2:     $X, y \leftarrow$ GETCHUNK(*Stream*)   ▷ Get samples from incoming data chunk.
3:     $X_b, y_b \leftarrow$ CHOOSEBUDGET(b, X, y) ▷ Randomly select percentage of instances.
4:     $\Psi \leftarrow$ UPDATECLASSIFIER(Ψ, X_b, y_b)   ▷ Update the classifier using randomly
                                                                                                                    selected samples.
5: **end while**

The second approach is a simple *active learning* solution, further described by the ALS acronym and presented in Algorithm 2. In the case of this method, after incrementally training the model on the fully labeled first data chunk (steps $4-5$), the processing of each subsequent one begins with collecting the support of existing models (which forces the application of probabilistic classifiers) obtained for the current chunk. The objects are later sorted according to the distance from the decision boundary, which for a binary problem means an absolute difference from the value of .5. Real labels are obtained for objects for which the calculated absolute difference does not exceed the set threshold t (step 7).

The last analyzed solution showed in Algorithm 3, which is the main research contribution of this work, further described by the acronym BALS, combinines both above-mentioned approaches. It uses an active strategy, typical for ALS (steps $7-8$), but each performed active selection of objects is supplemented by a certain, predetermined random samples pool, like in BLS strategy (steps $9-10$).

3   Experimental Study

3.1   Objectives

The main purpose of experimental research is to evaluate the quality of the BALS method compared to the methods (BLS and ALS). We will be primarily interested in answering the question whether, using a small budget for data labeling, we can obtain a classifier that on the one hand will have a quality comparable to the learned classifier on all learning objects, and whether the response time to drift (restoration time) will be shorter, and the deterioration will be less than the reference methods.

Algorithm 2. Pseudocode for ALS.

Input:

 Classifier (Ψ)
 Threshold (t)
 $k \leftarrow -1$
1: **while** *Stream* **do**
2:     $k \leftarrow k + 1$
3:     $X, y \leftarrow \text{GETCHUNK}(Stream)$ ▷ Get samples from incoming data chunk.
4:     **if** $k == 0$ **then**
5:         $\Psi \leftarrow \text{UPDATECLASSIFIER}(\Psi, X, y)$ ▷ Update the classifier using the whole
                                                                      first data chunk.
6:     **else**
7:         $X_a, y_a \leftarrow \text{SELECTSAMPLES}(t, X, y)$ ▷ Select instances to update the
                                                                      classifier using *active learning*.
8:         $\Psi \leftarrow \text{UPDATECLASSIFIER}(\Psi, X_a, y_a)$ ▷ Update the classifier using selected
                                                                      instances.
9:     **end if**
10: **end while**

Algorithm 3. Pseudocode for BALS.

Input:

 Classifier (Ψ)
 Threshold (t)
 Budget (b)
 $k \leftarrow -1$
1: **while** *Stream* **do**
2:     $k \leftarrow k + 1$
3:     $X, y \leftarrow \text{GETCHUNK}(Stream)$ ▷ Get samples from incoming data chunk.
4:     **if** $k == 0$ **then**
5:         $\Psi \leftarrow \text{UPDATECLASSIFIER}(\Psi, X, y)$ ▷ Update the classifier using the whole
                                                                      first data chunk.
6:     **else**
7:         $X_a, y_a \leftarrow \text{SELECTSAMPLES}(t, X, y)$ ▷ Select instances to update the
                                                                      classifier using *active learning*.
8:         $\Psi \leftarrow \text{UPDATECLASSIFIER}(\Psi, X_a, y_a)$ ▷ Update the classifier using selected
                                                                      instances.
9:         $X_b, y_b \leftarrow \text{CHOOSEBUDGET}(b, X, y)$ ▷ Randomly select percentage of
                                                                      instances.
10:        $\Psi \leftarrow \text{UPDATECLASSIFIER}(\Psi, X_b, y_b)$ ▷ Update the classifier using randomly
                                                                      selected samples.
11:    **end if**
12: **end while**

3.2 Setup

The experimental evaluation was carried out by the implementation of the three considered methods consistent with the *scikit-learn* [10] API, according to the *Test-Then-Train* evaluation methodology using synthetic data streams obtained using generator implemented in the *stream-learn* module [8]. Source code for experiments as well as deyailed results are available on the public *GitHub* repository[1].

The base model for the tested methods was the incremental MLP probabilistic classifier with *ReLu* activation function, *Adam* solver and one hidden layer consisting of one hundred artificial neurons. When testing the BLS approach, the budget of 5, 10 and 20% was analyzed, a single threshold of absolute distance $t = .2$ from the decision boundary was used for the ALS method, and for the BALS method proposed in this paper the threshold of $t = .2$ was used with compensation in the form of budget usage on the same thresholds as in the BLS method.

The analysis was based on six types of synthetic streams, replicated 10 times for stability of the achieved results. Streams include three concept drift types (i.e. *sudden, gradual* and *incremental*) in combination with two approaches to repetitive concepts (*recurrent* and *non-recurrent* drift). Each data stream contains half a million instances (1000 data chunks, 500 instances each) and 9 concept drifts.

3.3 Results

The experimental studies carried out were divided into three sections. The first section, represented in Fig. 1, presents the runs for individual approaches to the construction of the MLP-based model for data containing *sudden* drifts. As we mention above the detailed results are available on the public *GitHub* repository.

As can be seen, the BLS approach for *non-recurring sudden* drifts is characterized by a constant learning curve that builds the model in a similar way for each of the following concepts. The learning curve achieved has lower dynamics than the full model (marked with dotted lines) and, in no case, achieves the maximum ability to generalize. The reduced learning dynamics is directly caused by the reduction in the number of learning objects. Interestingly, there are no significant differences in quality between the use of 5, 10 or 20% of objects.

For recurrent drifts, a slight change in the behavior of the BLS approach can be seen. Failure to achieve full discriminatory ability leads to the model retaining information from previous concepts, even after they have been changed. While in the case of the first drift, which introduces a new distribution of problem classes for the first and only time, the reduction of quality during a sudden change occurs in the same way as in the full model. In other situations, the quality decrease is less noticeable. However, it does not reduce significantly with subsequent repetitions of *recurrent* drifts, and each time relatively quickly, the other models achieve higher classification quality than BLS.

---

[1] https://github.com/w4k2/bals.

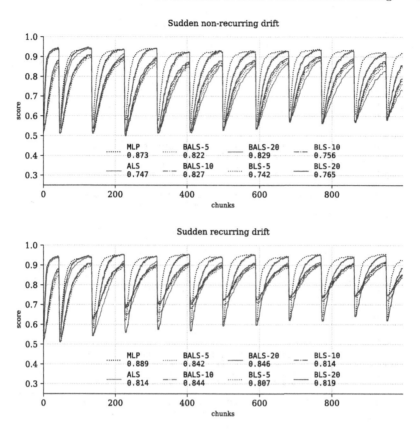

Fig. 1. Exemplary results for the stream affected by a sudden concept drift.

The most interesting in this case is the observation of the behavior of the ALS classification approach. While in the case of the first and second concept (regardless of concept repetition), its ability to achieve the full possible classification accuracy (relative to MLP trained on a fully labeled data chunk) can be seen, its progressive degeneration with subsequent drifts is equally visible. In the case of *non-recurring* drifts, with the occurrence of the third concept it equals BLS, degrading in accuracy over time. In the case of *recurrent* drifts, due to the previously described remembering of old concepts by BLS, this degeneration occurs even faster and already with the appearance of second drift, ALS turns out to be over-performed by the competitor based on a random budget.

Observation of the BALS method for the first two concepts is identical to the ALS approach, in both cases leading to the achievement of the generalization ability of the classifier built on fully labeled data. It is positively surprising, however, that the introduction of even a small percentage of random patterns sensitizes such a method to the degeneration of subsequent drifts typical for BLS. The difference between the two standard approaches (BLS and ALS) and the combined approach is not just a simple improvement in classification accuracy.

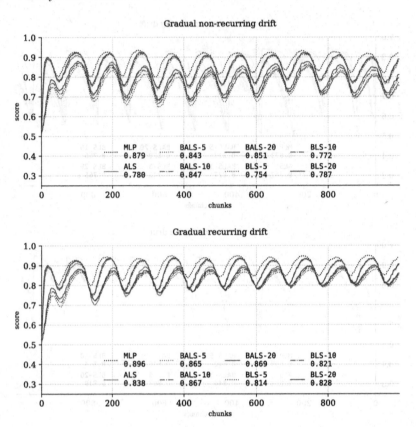

Fig. 2. Exemplary results for the stream affected by a gradual concept drift.

It can be seen here that the introduction of randomly selected patterns allows the BALS method to achieve the full possible classification accuracy each time (although also sometimes with decreasing dynamics).

The proportional to learning time degeneration of the BLS approach is probably due to the growing certainty of the predictions made, in the case of analysis of the supports achieved, which means their strong polarization, and thus a gradual, rapid reduction of the number of objects located near the decision boundary. This means that the solution based on support thresholding – over time – assigns fewer and fewer objects as potentially useful in labeling. The phenomenon of this polarization is reduced by introducing seemingly different patterns for the built recognition model, modifying the statistical distribution of obtained support, which is a direct result from the new concept *signaling itself* for a need for increased learning rate.

Interestingly, the percentage of random patterns added to the active labeling model does not seem to have a significant impact on the classification accuracy or the learning curve dynamics. Even a small number of such objects (5%) causes BALS to cease exhibiting the degenerative tendencies of the pure ALS model.

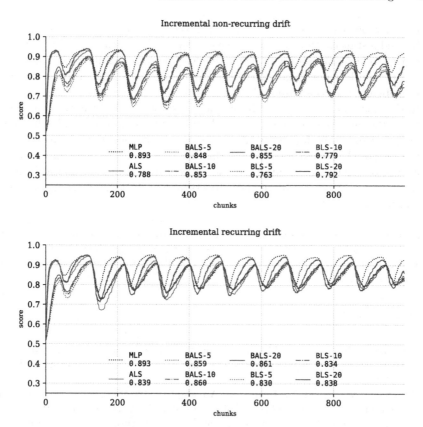

Fig. 3. Exemplary results for the stream affected by an incremental concept drift.

Observations made for *sudden* drifts, including both approaches to drift recurrence, can be directly transferred to those for *gradual* (Fig. 2) and *incremental* drift (Fig. 3). The dynamics of the concept changes themselves do not seem to have a major impact on the relationships between the analyzed algorithms, so the conclusions made for *sudden* drift can be simply generalized for all problems considered in the research.

4   Conclusions

The paper presents a modification of the active learning method dedicated to non-stationary data stream classifiers. The proposed algorithm, in addition to the pool of objects selected for labeling (according to the rule that objects close to decision boundaries have a large impact on model modification), also received a small number of randomly selected objects from among the other instances belonging to an analyzed data chunk. This approach caused the classifier to stabilize faster after the *concept drift* than BLS or ALS. Also, the deterioration of BALS quality is lower than the reference algorithms. It is also worth noting that:

- the BALS outperforms ALS algorithm due to the use of an additional fraction of labeled instances. However, its size was very small compared to the fraction of objects selected according to the active learning rule. Additionally, increasing its number does not significantly improve the quality of the proposed method.
- It is obvious that the proposed model obtained slightly worse results compared to the classifier based on a fully labeled learning set, but the time needed to reach the same performance is very short. The results presented in this paper are promising, therefore, they encourage us to continue our work on employing the proposed method for another classification model as classifier ensemble as well to use the information on the *concept drift* rapidness to establish the proportion between the number of objects labeled by active learning algorithm and by random choosing.

Acknowledgements. This work was supported by the Polish National Science Centre under the grant No. 2017/27/B/ST6/01325 as well as by the statutory funds of the Department of Systems and Computer Networks, Wroclaw University of Science and Technology.

References

1. Abdallah, Z.S., Gaber, M.M., Srinivasan, B., Krishnaswamy, S.: Adaptive mobile activity recognition system with evolving data streams. Neurocomputing **150**, 304–317 (2015)
2. Bouguelia, M., Belaïd, Y., Belaïd, A.: An adaptive streaming active learning strategy based on instance weighting. Pattern Recogn. Lett. **70**, 38–44 (2016)
3. Cano, A., Zafra, A., Ventura, S.: A parallel genetic programming algorithm for classification. In: Corchado, E., Kurzyński, M., Woźniak, M. (eds.) HAIS 2011. LNCS (LNAI), vol. 6678, pp. 172–181. Springer, Heidelberg (2011). https://doi.org/10.1007/978-3-642-21219-2_23
4. Gaber, M.M.: Advances in data stream mining. Wiley Interdisc. Rev. Data Min. Knowl. Discovery **2**(1), 79–85 (2012)
5. Krawczyk, B., Minku, L.L., Gama, J., Stefanowski, J., Woźniak, M.: Ensemble learning for data stream analysis: a survey. Inform. Fusion **37**(Supplement C), 132–156 (2017)
6. Krawczyk, B., Pfahringer, B., Wozniak, M.: Combining active learning with concept drift detection for data stream mining. In: Abe, N., et al. (eds.) IEEE International Conference on Big Data, Big Data 2018, 10–13 December 2018, Seattle, WA, USA, pp. 2239–2244. IEEE (2018). https://doi.org/10.1109/BigData.2018.8622549
7. Ksieniewicz, P., Woźniak, M., Cyganek, B., Kasprzak, A., Walkowiak, K.: Data stream classification using active learned neural networks. Neurocomputing **353**, 74–82 (2019). https://doi.org/10.1016/j.neucom.2018.05.130, http://www.sciencedirect.com/science/article/pii/S0925231219303248, Recent Advancements in Hybrid Artificial Intelligence Systems
8. Ksieniewicz, P., Zyblewski, P.: Stream-learn-open-source python library for difficult data stream batch analysis. arXiv preprint arXiv:2001.11077 (2020)
9. Kurlej, B., Woźniak, M.: Active learning approach to concept drift problem. Logic J. IGPL **20**(3), 550–559 (2012)

10. Pedregosa, F., et al.: Scikit-learn: machine learning in Python. J. Mach. Learn. Res. **12**, 2825–2830 (2011)
11. Settles, B.: Active Learning. Morgan and Claypool Publishers, San Rafael (2012)
12. Shan, J., Zhang, H., Liu, W., Liu, Q.: Online active learning ensemble framework for drifted data streams. IEEE Trans. Neural Netw. Learn. Syst. **30**(2), 486–498 (2019). https://doi.org/10.1109/TNNLS.2018.2844332
13. Zliobaite, I., Bifet, A., Pfahringer, B., Holmes, G.: Active learning with drifting streaming data. IEEE Trans. Neural Netw. Learn. Syst. **25**(1), 27–39 (2014)

Bioinformatics, Biometrics and Medical Applications

The Utilization of Different Classifiers to Perform Drug Repositioning in Inclusion Body Myositis Supports the Concept of Biological Invariance

Óscar Álvarez-Machancoses[1] , Enrique deAndrés-Galiana[1,2] ,
Juan Luis Fernández-Martínez[1(✉)] , and Andrzej Kloczkowski[3,4(✉)]

[1] Group of Inverse Problems, Optimization and Machine Learning. Department of Mathematics, University of Oviedo C. Federico García Lorca, 18, 33007 Oviedo, Spain
jlfm@uniovi.es
[2] Department of Computer Science, University of Oviedo C. Federico García Lorca, 18, 33007 Oviedo, Spain
[3] Battelle Center for Mathematical Medicine, Nationwide Children's Hospital, Columbus, OH, USA
andrzej.kloczkowski@nationwidechildrens.org
[4] Department of Pediatrics, The Ohio State University, Columbus, OH, USA

Abstract. In this research work, we introduce several novel methods to identify the defective pathways in highly uncertain phenotype prediction problems. More specifically, we applied these methodologies for phenotype prediction associated with drug repositioning for rare diseases such as the Inclusion Body Myositis and obtained a better understanding of the disease mechanism. The novelty of our research is based on the fact that the classifiers utilized to build the genetic signatures were based on completely different approaches, namely; gene Fisher ratios, generation of random genetic networks or genetic network likelihoods to sample and relate the altered genes to possible drugs via the connectivity maps. This scheme provides a more effective drug design/repositioning since it helps to understand the disease mechanisms and to establish an optimum mechanism of action of the designed drugs. By comparing the different classifiers, we conclude that the Fisher's ratio, Holdout and Random Forest samplers are the most effective, since they provide similar insights into the genetic mechanisms of the disease and bear low computational costs. Furthermore, our work supports the concept of Biological Invariance, assuming that the results of the analysis of the altered pathways should be independent of the sampling method utilized for the assessment of the inference. However, the effectiveness of the candidate drugs and the gene targets predicted by our approach should be pre-clinically studied and clinically tested.

Keywords: Biological Invariance · Machine learning · Inclusion body myositis · Drug repositioning · Phenotype prediction

© Springer Nature Switzerland AG 2020
L. Rutkowski et al. (Eds.): ICAISC 2020, LNAI 12415, pp. 589–598, 2020.
https://doi.org/10.1007/978-3-030-61401-0_55

1 Introduction

1.1 The Inclusion Body Myositis

Inclusion Body Myositis (IBM) is one of the most common inflammatory muscular diseases, characterized by a progressive weakening of muscular tissues in elder adults [1]. As IBM progresses, it leads to a severe disability. IBM is considered a rare disease with a low prevalence rate and with still unknown causes of the disease [2]. Currently, two key hypotheses about the nature of the disease coexist: the first one suggests an inflammation immune reaction produced by a virus infection [3] while the second hypothesis proposes a degenerative disorder nature of the IBM linked with aging of muscle fibers and abnormal accumulation of pathogenic proteins in myofibrils [4]. The currently conducted major clinical trials of IBM are focused on the following drugs:

1. **Arimoclomol**: this drug targets the adequate folding of proteins clearing the abnormal clumps within the muscle [5].
2. **Pioglitazone**: also utilized in diabetes, is used to target the function of defective mitochondria in order to increase muscular strength [6].
3. **Rapamycin**: this drug is involved in regulating cell growth and metabolism and has an immuno-suppressive effect [7].
4. **Follistatin**: the main mechanism of this drug is myostatin blockade, a protein in charge of inhibiting muscle growth [8].

1.2 On the Drug Discovery Problem

Drug discovery is the process in which potential chemical compounds with a set of desired properties for therapeutic purposes are being identified. This process is highly capital intensive, with an estimated average cost of 2.8 billion dollars for a new drug [9]. Despite this enormous effort, the majority of newly tested drugs fail in the Phase-II of clinical trials, which consists on appraising candidate drugs' efficacy and their safety for patient populations [10]. Therefore, novel robust AI techniques are immediately needed to help solving this issue and to assist in the optimal decision-making processes, based on the full understanding of Mechanisms of Action (MoA) of newly proposed drugs and on the prediction of their potential toxicities [11]. This is considered an open problem in pharmacogenomics and pharmacokinetics and forms the forefront of pharmaceutical industry research. Additionally, a new approach focusing on Precision Medicine is needed, which aims to tailor the medical treatment to individuals. Precision medicine should evolve towards the design of efficient drugs and optimization of their dosage and delivery depending on individual genetic and epigenetic factors. To advance Precision Medicine, both genomic kits for molecular diagnostics and computational algorithms to make optimal decisions are extremely needed [12].

Drug repositioning, often called drug repurposing involves the investigation of existing FDA approved drugs for new therapeutic purposes. This approach removes the problem of potential toxicity of newly proposed drugs, speeds up, and lowers costs of the drug discovery problem. Generally speaking, most common sources that might originate a disease include: transcriptional defects in the mRNA, inherited genomic defects, mutations caused by viruses or bacteria, and epigenetic alterations of the DNA. Many times, these causes are unclear, therefore, a robust sampling of the altered pathways is required in order to design/repurpose drugs that target these pathways in order to reestablish homeostasis.

Since these problems are highly complex and there are no commonly available models, computational and machine learning methods can be used to identify the causes (altered pathways) and their effects (diseases). From the mathematical point of view these are inverse problems related to the phenotype prediction that consist of identifying the genes that cause the disease expression [13].

1.3 On the Phenotype Prediction Problem

In phenotype prediction problems, it is possible to define the uncertainty space relative to the classifier $L^*(g)$, $M_{tol} = \{g : O(g) < E_{tol}\}$. This uncertainty space consists of the sets of highly predictive genetic networks; composed of the sets of genes g that classify the samples with a prediction error $O(g)$ lower than E_{tol}. These networks are placed in different flat curvilinear valleys of the cost function topography, $O(g)$ [14, 15]. Due to this complexity and the undetermined character of these problems, the uncertainty space has a very high dimension and, as a consequence, the characterization of the genetic pathways is ambiguous, because of the existence of many equivalent genetic networks that could predict the phenotype with similar accuracy [13, 16]. Artificial Intelligence methods are capable of performing these tasks by sampling the altered pathways and utilizing the outcome to propose newly repurposed drugs [17].

Different sampling techniques have been already introduced and applied to the analysis of genetic pathways [18, 19]. These techniques were inspired by Bayesian analysis, which could be used to sample the conditional probability distribution function of the genetic signatures related to the phenotype prediction problem, $P(g/c^{obs})$, according to Bayes' rule:

$$P\left(g/c^{obs}\right) \sim P(g)P\left(c^{obs}/g\right) \tag{1}$$

In the above expression (g) is the prior distribution used to sample the genetic signatures and $P(c^{obs}/g)$ is the likelihood of the genetic signature g, that depends on the its predictive accuracy $O(g)$. Here $P(g/c^{obs})$ is called the posterior distribution of g with respect to the observed class c^{obs}. Nevertheless, the aim here is not find the posterior probability distribution, but sampling the genetic networks that are involved in the disease development.

To tackle the phenotype prediction problem, different classifiers such as Nearest-Neighbor approaches [20, 21], Extreme Learning Machines [22] or Random Forests [23] could be utilized. In this paper, we present a set of new classifiers that could be applied to robustly sample the altered genetic pathways before performing optimal selection of compounds via repositioning of already approved drugs by using the Connectivity Map (CMap) [24]. The CMap methodology allows to rank the drugs that act on the altered genes to achieve homeostasis. Most of these drugs are already approved by FDA. This analysis helps with orientation of clinical trials to avoid target-centric approaches that have no connection with the genomics of the disease.

2   Materials and Methods

2.1   Datasets

To analyze the altered pathways involved in IBM, we have utilized a dataset which contains 22283 genetic probes and 34 samples, divided into 11 healthy controls and 23 IBM patients [25, 26]. In addition, this dataset contains also 6 patients with polymyositis (PM). This experiment has a highly undetermined character due to the fact that the number of genetic probes (22283) is much larger than the number of samples (34). This is a common difficulty in the phenotype prediction causing a high ambiguity in the phenotype determination, and affecting the final results, if the modeling approach doesn't address properly this problem.

2.2   Methodology

Fisher's Ratio Sampler

The Fisher's ratio sampler considers the discriminatory power of the deferentially expressed genes according to the Fisher's ratio to induce the prior sampling distri-bution. Genes are first ranked according to their Fisher's ratio. After finding the most discriminatory genes, the algorithm finds the small-scale signatures that better discrim-inate between classes through a recursive feature elimination, estimating the predictive accuracy through leave-one-out cross-validation (LOOCV) and a k-NN classifier. The idea is to find the minimum number of header genes that provide the highest predic-tive accuracy. Besides, different genetic networks with a similar predictive accuracy exist. Finally, a Random sampling utilizing a prior sampling probability proportional to the genetic network's Fisher's ratio is applied. In this sense, we are prioritizing the discriminatory power of genes according to the Fisher's ratio.

$$FR_i = \frac{(\mu_{i1} - \mu_{i2})^2}{\sigma_{i1}^2 + \sigma_{i2}^2} \tag{2}$$

where μ_{ij} is a measure of the center of mass of the probability distribution of the gene i in class j, and σ_{ij} is a measure of its dispersion within this class. Discriminatory genes correspond to higher Fisher's ratios since they have a low intra-class dispersion and high inter-class distance between the centers of gene distribution. Therefore, once the network is randomly built a LOOCV predictive accuracy is determined and a posterior analysis serves to identify the defective pathways according to the most frequently sampled genes [14].

Holdout Sampler

The Holdout sampler is based on bootstrapping techniques. The algorithm generates a space of different random 75/25 data bags (or holdouts), so that, the 75% of data is used for training and the remaining 25% for blind validation. For each Holdout, the genes are ranked according to their discriminatory power associated with their Fisher's ratio and those with the highest predictive performance are considered in the blind validation set, with a given tolerance:

$$M_{tol} = \left\{ \mathbf{g} : \frac{\|\mathbf{L}^*(\mathbf{g}) - \mathbf{c}^{obs}\|_2}{\|\mathbf{c}^{obs}\|_2} < tol \right\} \tag{3}$$

As a final step, we perform a posterior analysis in order to find the minimum size genetic signatures with a validation predictive accuracy higher than 90% [18]. All these genetic signatures are related to the IBM phenotype.

Random Forest Sampler

Random Forests (RF) are random decision trees for classification via ensemble learning. RF have been used for phenotype prediction and uncertainty analysis [27]. Important genetic networks are identified by constructing bootstrap samples of data using the 75/25 ratio, as in the Holdout sampler. After performing the training, the estimation of the classification error is obtained. The classification error is calculated at each branch of the decision tree to get an unbiased estimate of the classification error for the i-th tree. An overall out-of-bag (OOB) error rate is given when the specified numbers of trees are dded to the forest. The OOB error rate obtained for each pathway is used to rank pathways. The smaller the OOB error rate, the better its ability to classify the phenotypes of interest.

2.3   Drug Repositioning

The final step consists of gathering the information on the altered pathways for IBM from each classifier in order to perform drug repositioning. We have utilized the Connectivity Map (CMAP) web application to identify the potential biological relationships between the altered pathways and FDA approved drugs [24]. The Connectivity Map is a highly popular bioinformatics tool developed at the Broad Institute that has been extensively utilized to study drug repositioning and prediction of possible side-effects. To repurpose drugs, we look in CMAP for drugs tested in different cell lines at different doses that are able to reestablish the homeostasis, i.e. the genes overexpressed in the disease are down-regulated and the expression of underexpressed genes is increased. This is carried out by formulating an outlier sum for each potential drug in the CMAP database in order to model an overall disease-drug connectivity provided the altered genes in a disease:

$$OS_i = \sum_{g=1}^{N} z_{g,i}^{min} l_z \left(z_{g,i}^{min} \geq z_\alpha \right) + z_{g,i}^{max} l_z \left(z_{g,i}^{max} \geq z_\alpha \right) \tag{4}$$

Here $z_{g,i}^{min}$ and $z_{g,i}^{max}$ are the z-scores derived from the p-values of the minimum and maximum statistics of a given drug in the CMAP, which suggest that a given drug is capable to upregulate or downregulate the phenotypic expression of the altered genes in a disease. Here z_α refers to the z-score associated with the α significance level, (we used the default value $\alpha = 0.05$) and l_z is the indicator function which takes the value 1 when the input is true or 0, otherwise. A potential drug is identified via the Kolmogorov-Smirnov test to calculate the similarity of a drug perturbed expression profile to the gene expression profile, calculated according to the outlier sum, OS_i. Since the algorithm used to query drugs is deterministic, the list of predicted drugs will always be the same as long as the list of over- and underexpressed genes is the same. This feature highlights the importance of having a robust computational method to perform analysis of altered pathways [28].

3 Results and Discussion

In Table 1, we present the list of the 10 most frequently sampled genes by each sampler. The human leukocyte antigen (HLA) genes belonging to the Major Histocompatibility Complex (MCH) Class I are the most important ones as they appear to be sampled by the three samplers. Actin genes and calcium binding protein genes appear to be sampled by the three algorithms, in addition to genes related to immunodeficiency and interferon regulatory genes.

Table 1. List of most-frequently sampled overexpressed genes by each algorithm.

Fisher's ratio sampler	Holdout sampler	Random forest sampler
SP100	S100A4	HLA-B
HLA-DPA1	EEF1A1	HLA-A
IGK/IGKC	HLA-C	HLA-C
S100A13	HLA-B	NDUFS7
NES	FTL	HLA-G
CD74	EEF1A1	TMEM140
ANXA2	HLA-A	TMSB10
HLA-F	HLA-G	ACTG1
B3GALT4	TMEM140	S100A6
UCP2	PSME2	MLLT11

It is also worth remarking that these genes appear to be related in other disease phenotypes, such as Muscular Dystrophy or Becher Muscular Dystrophy. It is of utmost importance to better understand other phenotypic expressions associated with these genes, since drugs utilized in other diseases could potentially treat IBM. As shown in Table 2, the main and common pathways involved in IBM are:

1. Immune Response Role of DAP12 receptors in NK cells (actin, HLA and Immunoglobulin Kappa genes).
2. Immune response IFN alpha/beta signaling pathways (HLA genes).
3. Interferon Gamma Signaling (HLA genes).
4. Antigen Presentation-Folding, Antigen Processing and Presentation and Assembly and Peptide-Loading of MHC Class I.
5. Allograft Rejection Pathway.

Table 2. List of the pathways associated to the sampled genes by each algorithm.

Fisher's ratio sampler	Holdout sampler	Random forest sampler
Immune response NFAT in immune response (14.31)	Antigen processing-cross presentation (23.79)	Antigen presentation-folding, Assembly and peptide-loading of MHC class I (31.29)
Allograft rejection (12.48)	Antigen presentation-folding, assembly and peptide loading of class I MHC (23.45)	Immune response role of DAP12 receptors in NK Cells (25.89)
Immune response Lectin induced Complement pathway (11.60)	Allograft rejection (19.65)	Immune response IFN Alpha/beta signaling pathway (24.26)
G-protein signaling N-RAS regulation pathway (11.50)	Immune response IFN Alpha/Beta signaling pathway (17.87)	Allograft rejection (23.85)
MHC class II antigen presentation (9.96)	Interferon gamma signaling (14.45)	Interferon gamma signaling (22.29)

Based on these results, our study indicates a set of pathways that are widely accepted to play a crucial role in inflammatory myopathies, such as the Major Histocompatibility Complex (MHC) class I molecules and transcription factors involved in MHC class I regulation. We show the relevance of the immune response and the importance of some genes involved in protein degradation in inflammatory myopathies. Consequently, the outcomes could be generalized to other inflammatory myopathies.

Table 3 shows the list of repositioned drugs indicated by CMAP which have been tested mainly in three cell lines: (1) HL60, Human Leukemia Cell Line, (2) MCF7, Human Breast Adenocarcinoma Cell Line and (3) PC3, Human Prostate Cancer Cell Line. As a consequence, repurposed drugs should undergo clinical trials in order to finally demonstrate their effectiveness. Among the current clinical trials, we could find Arimoclomol, a drug that was discovered as a candidate to treat insulin resistance and diabetic complications such as retinopathy, neuropathy and nephropathy [29]. Arimoclomol is believed to function by stimulating a normal cellular protein repair pathway through the activation of molecular chaperones. Damaged proteins, forming aggregates, are thought to play a major role in many diseases. In this sense, repurposed drugs such as Resveratrol or LY-294002, which targets PI3Ks, become the target of many pharmacological treatments, both in clinical trials and in clinical practice. PI3Ks play an important role in glucose regulation and tumor expression. Similarly, to Arimoclomol, Pioglitazone is utilized to target the function of defective mitochondria in order to increase muscular strength, although it was originally developed to treat diabetes.

Other drugs under clinical trials focused on treating IBM are Rapamycin, an immunosuppressive drug such as the repurposed drugs Genistein and Cyclosporine, or even

Table 3. List of potential drugs found through CMAP database and their MoA.

Drug	Mechanism of action
Estradiol (HL60)	A naturally occurring hormone that circulates endogenously within the human body. It mediates its effects across the body through potent agonism of the Estrogen Receptor (ER), which is located in various tissues including in the breasts, uterus, ovaries, skin, prostate, bone, fat, and brain
LY-294002 (MCF7)	A morpholine-containing chemical compound that is a potent inhibitor of numerous proteins, and a strong inhibitor of phosphoinositide 3-kinases (PI3Ks)
Monensin (MCF7)	A polyether antibiotic isolated from *Streptomyces cinnamonensis*. In laboratory research, monensin is used extensively to block Golgi transport
Genistein (MCF7)	Genistein is a soy-derived isoflavone and phytoestrogen with antineoplastic activity. Genistein exhibits antioxidant, antiangiogenic, and immunosuppressive activities
Thalidomide (PC3)	A medication used to treat a number of cancers including multiple myeloma, graft-versus-host disease, and a number of skin conditions including complications of leprosy. It is suggested that it inhibits the process of angiogenesis, its inhibition of cereblon, a ubiquitin ligase, and its ability to generate reactive oxygen species which in turn kills cells
Cyclosporine (MCF7)	An immunosuppressant medication and natural product. It is used to treat rheumatoid arthritis, psoriasis, Crohn's disease, nephrotic syndrome, and in organ transplants to prevent rejection
Resveratrol (MCF7)	It is thought to act like antioxidants, protecting the body against damage that can put one at higher risk for things like cancer and heart disease. It has gained a lot of attention for its reported anti-aging and disease-fighting powers

Thalidomide, which stimulates some of the immune system cells to attack myeloma cells [30]. In addition to this, two troublesome medicaments were suggested: Estradiol and Thalidomide. It is generally found that myositis disorders have a higher incidence in women than men, causing highly symptomatic and inflammatory cutaneous and prox-imal muscle disease. Estradiol-induced down regulation of estrogen has been found to be effective in the treatment of skin myositis [31].

The repurposed drugs indicated by CMAP belong to several categories, such as muscle relaxants, anti-inflammatory agents or antioxidants. The suggested repurposed drugs agree with the list of drugs that undergo current clinical trials.

4 Conclusions

In this paper, we presented several simple, effective methodologies to sample the altered pathways in the phenotype prediction problem applied to drug repositioning for IBM. The advantage of the samplers presented in this paper is their robustness, since all samplers detect similar altered pathways, supporting the idea of Biological Invariance. The proposed methodology helps to generate new therapeutic targets and to reposition already known drugs for preclinical studies and clinical trials, speeding up the discovery of new therapies. We demonstrated that a proper understanding of the altered pathways is very important in drug repositioning. The current target-centric approach which does not address optimal Mechanisms of Action problem has been considered as the main reason responsible for the high attrition rate and very low productivity in the development of new drugs. This paradigm should be abolished and novel robust methods to sample the altered pathways and to properly address the high intrinsic degree of uncertainty of the problem are needed. The knowledge provided by the robust sampling of the altered pathways is useful to design target-centric approaches based on gene analytics. We have shown the importance of compounds acting on antiviral agents and on the interferon pathways; results that support the current clinical trials of new IBM drugs. In addition, the proposed approach can be applied to other rare and non-rare (common) diseases.

Acknowledgments. We acknowledge financial support from NSF grant DBI 1661391, and NIH grant R01 GM127701.

References

1. Dalakas, M.C.: Polymyositis, dermatomyositis, and inclusion-body myositis. New Engl. J. Med. **325**(21), 1487–1498 (1991)
2. Griggs, R.C., et al.: Inclusion body myositis and myopathies. Ann. Neurol. Official J. Am. Neurol. Assoc. Child Neurol. Soc. **38**(5), 705–713 (1995)
3. Ghannam, K., et al.: Upregulation of immunoproteasome subunits in myositis indicates active inflammation with involvement of antigen presenting cells, CD8 T-cells and IFNγ. PLoS One **9**(8), e104048 (2014)
4. Rose, M.R.: 188th ENMC international workshop: inclusion body myositis, 2–4 December 2011, Naarden the Netherlands. Neuromusc. Disord. **23**(12), 1044–1055 (2013)
5. Machado, P., et al.: Lb0002 safety and tolerability of arimoclomol in patients with sporadic inclusion body myositis: a randomized, double-blind, placebo controlled, phase IIa proof-of-concept trial. Ann. Rheum. Dis. **72**(Suppl 3), A164–A164 (2013)
6. Gualano, B., et al.: Resistance training with vascular occlusion in inclusion body myositis: a case study. Med. Sci. Sports Exerc. **42**(2), 250–254 (2010)
7. Prevel, N., Allenbach, Y., Klatzmann, D., Salomon, B., Benveniste, O.: Beneficial role of rapamycin in experimental autoimmune myositis. PLoS One **8**(11), e74450 (2013)
8. Mendell, J.R., et al.: Follistatin gene therapy for sporadic inclusion body myositis improves functional outcomes. Mol. Ther. **25**(4), 870–879 (2017)
9. DiMasi, J.A., Grabowski, H.G., Hansen, R.W.: Innovation in the pharmaceutical industry: new estimates of R&D costs. J. Health Econ. **47**, 20–33 (2016)
10. Cook, D., et al.: Lessons learned from the fate of AstraZeneca's drug pipeline: a five-dimensional framework. Nature Rev. Drug Discov. **13**(6), 419 (2014)
11. Scannell, J.W., Blanckley, A., Boldon, H., Warrington, B.: Diagnosing the decline in pharmaceutical R&D efficiency. Nature Rev. Drug Discov. **11**(3), 191 (2012)
12. Álvarez-Machancoses, Ó., Fernández-Martínez, J.L.: Using artificial intelligence methods to speed up drug discovery. Expert Opin. Drug Discov. **14**(8), 769–777 (2019)

13. de Andrés-Galiana, E.J., Fernández-Martínez, J.L., Sonis, S.T.: Design of biomedical robots for phenotype prediction problems. J. Comput. Biol. **23**(8), 678–692 (2016)
14. Cernea, A., et al.: Sampling defective pathways in phenotype prediction problems via the Fisher's ratio sampler. In: Rojas, I., Ortuño, F. (eds.) IWBBIO 2018. LNCS, vol. 10814, pp. 15–23. Springer, Cham (2018). https://doi.org/10.1007/978-3-319-78759-6_2
15. Fernández-Martínez, J.L., Fernández-Muñoz, Z., Tompkins, M.J.: On the topography of the cost functional in linear and nonlinear inverse problems. Geophysics **77**(1), W1–W15 (2012)
16. Fernández-Martínez, J.L., Fernández-Muñoz, Z., Pallero, J.L.G., Pedruelo-González, L.M.: From Bayes to Tarantola: new insights to understand uncertainty in inverse problems. J. Appl. Geophys. **98**, 62–72 (2013)
17. de Andrés-Galiana, E.J., Fernández-Martínez, J.L., Sonis, S.T.: Sensitivity analysis of gene ranking methods in phenotype prediction. J. Biomed. Inform. **64**, 255–264 (2016)
18. Fernández-Martínez, J.L., et al.: Sampling defective pathways in phenotype prediction problems via the holdout sampler. In: Rojas, I., Ortuño, F. (eds.) IWBBIO 2018. LNCS, vol. 10814, pp. 24–32. Springer, Cham (2018). https://doi.org/10.1007/978-3-319-78759-6_3
19. Cernea, A., et al.: Comparison of different sampling algorithms for phenotype prediction. In: Rojas, I., Ortuño, F. (eds.) IWBBIO 2018. LNCS, vol. 10814, pp. 33–45. Springer, Cham (2018). https://doi.org/10.1007/978-3-319-78759-6_4
20. Saligan, L.N., Fernández-Martínez, J.L., de Andrés-Galiana, E.J., Sonis, S.: Supervised classification by filter methods and recursive feature elimination predicts risk of radiotherapy-related fatigue in patients with prostate cancer. Cancer Inform. **13**, CIN-S19745 (2014)
21. Altman, N.S.: An introduction to kernel and nearest-neighbor nonparametric regression. Am. Stat. **46**(3), 175–185 (1992)
22. Huang, G.-B., Zhu, Q.-Y., Siew, C.-K.: Extreme learning machine: theory and applications. Neurocomputing **70**(1–3), 489–501 (2006)
23. Breiman, L.: Random forests. Mach. Learn. **45**(1), 5–32 (2001)
24. Lamb, J.: The connectivity map: a new tool for biomedical research. Nat. Rev. Cancer **7**(1), 54 (2007)
25. Greenberg, S.A.: Molecular profiles of inflammatory myopathies. Neurology **59**(8), 1170–1182 (2002)
26. Greenberg, S.A.: Proposed immunologic models of the inflammatory myopathies and potential therapeutic implications. Neurology **69**(21), 2008–2019 (2007)
27. Pang, H., et al.: Pathway analysis using random forests classification and regression. Bioinformatics **22**(16), 2028–2036 (2006)
28. Fernández-Martínez, J.L., Álvarez, Ó., de Andrés-Galiana, E.J., de la Viña, J.F.S., Huergo, L.: Robust sampling of altered pathways for drug repositioning reveals promising novel therapeutics for inclusion body myositis. J Rare Dis. Res. Treat **4**(2), 7–15 (2019)
29. Kürthy, M., et al.: Effect of BRX-220 against peripheral neuropathy and insulin resistance in diabetic rat models. Ann. New York Acad. Sci. **967**(1), 482–489 (2002)
30. McBride, W.G.: Thalidomide and congenital abnormalities. Lancet **278**(7216), 1358 (1961). https://doi.org/10.1016/s0140-6736(61)90927-8
31. Sereda, D., Werth, V.P.: Improvement in dermatomyositis rash associated with the use of antiestrogen medication. Arch. Dermatol. **142**(1), 70–72 (2006)

Predicting Coronary Artery Calcium Score from Retinal Fundus Photographs Using Convolutional Neural Networks

Sooah Cho[1], Su Jeong Song[2], Joonseok Lee[1], JiEun Song[1], Min Soo Kim[1], Minyoung Lee[1], and JoonHo Lee[1(✉)]

[1] Samsung SDS, Seoul, Korea
{sooah.cho,joonholee}@samsung.com
[2] Department of Ophthalmology, Samsung Hospital, Seoul, Korea

Abstract. Coronary Artery Calcium Score (CACS) is a prognostic indicator for coronary atherosclerosis that can cause a stroke or heart attack. Cardiac computed tomography (CT) is widely used to calculate CACS. For asymptomatic patients, however, a CT-based screening tes is not recommended due to an unnecessary exposure to radiation and high cost. In this paper, we propose a deep learning approach to predict CACS from retinal fundus photographs. Our approach is non-invasive and can observe blood vessels without any side effects. Contrasted to other approaches, we can predict CACS directly using only retinal fundus photographs without the electronic health record (EHR) data. To overcome data deficiency, we train deep convolutional neural nets (CNNs) with retinal fundus images for predicting auxiliary EHR data related to CACS. In addition, we employ a task-specific augmentation method that resolves flare phenomenon typically occurred in a retinal fundus image. Our empirical results indicate that the use of auxiliary EHR data improves the CACS prediction performance by 4.2%, and flare augmentation by 2.4% on area under the ROC curve (AUC). Applying both methods results in an overall 6.2% improvement. In the light of feature extraction and inference uncertainty, our deep learning models can predict CACS using only retinal fundus images and identify individuals with a cardiovascular disease.

Keywords: Coronary Artery Calcium Score · Retinal fundus photographs · Deep learning

1 Introduction

Cardiovascular disease is a major cause of death according to the World Health Organization [23]. Coronary atherosclerosis can cause oxygen deprivation in cardiac muscles and blockage of blood flow in cerebral vessels that lead to heart

---

S. Cho–First author

© Springer Nature Switzerland AG 2020
L. Rutkowski et al. (Eds.): ICAISC 2020, LNAI 12415, pp. 599–612, 2020.
https://doi.org/10.1007/978-3-030-61401-0_56

attacks and strokes. An established clinical marker for atherosclerosis is Coronary Artery Calcium Score (CACS) [18]. CACS is a reliable risk estimator of myocardial infarction, coronary death, and all-cause mortality [2]. CACS also gives one of the most useful cardiovascular disease risk stratification refiners [11] and has a strong association with major cardiovascular outcomes in an asymptomatic person [9].

CACS enables a non-invasive diagnosis to coronary atherosclerosis, but cardiac computed tomography (CT) is typically required to assess CACS, causing an inevitable exposure to radiation [9]. Therefore, despite its importance for cardiovascular disease risk stratification, American College of Cardiology/American Heart Association (ACC/AHA) recommends not use cardiac CT-based CACS for asymptomatic patients in avoiding cancer risks from radiation exposure [5]. (Cost would be another factor.) For such reasons, it is difficult to assess CACS for asymptomatic patients in an early stage. We expect that CACS prediction from retinal fundus photographs can help find early asymptomatic patients.

Deep learning has been successfully applied in medical analytics, thanks to large medical data archives consisting of retinal fundus, MRI, and CT images that help train models to predict medical conditions and diagnoses. For example, the performance of convolutional neural nets (CNNs) for predicting eye diseases from retinal fundus photographs [6,10,14] is comparable to that by a human medical expert. Nikolas et al. propose predicting CACS from chest CT images using deep learning method [13]. Yet, there is no CACS prediction based on non-CT images such as retinal fundus image. Retinal fundus photographs are appropriate to detect blood vessel changes caused by coronary atherosclerosis since they provide a non-invasive way to observe abundant blood vessels on retinal fundus. Predicting CACS from retinal fundus images seems reasonable because CACS is associated with retinopathy [22]. Also, it is shown that retinal vessel atherosclerosis is strongly correlated with atherosclerotic changes in coronary arteries [20].

In this paper, we present a deep learning approach for CACS prediction that uses only retinal fundus images. Although retinal funduscopy is not a traditional means to assess CACS, deep learning makes it possible to predict CACS by data-driven, visual examination of extracted deep features. We propose practical methods to improve the CACS prediction performance when having small data. The proposed methods are explained in Sect. 4, and experimental results are discussed in Sect. 5.

2   Related Work

Gulshan et al. [10] suggests a diabetic retinopathy prediction model based on Inception-v3 [19] and shows the area under the receiver operating characteristic curve (AUC) of 0.991 for EyePACS-1 dataset and 0.990 for Messidor-2 dataset [10]. Burlina et al. [6] proposes age-related macular degeneration grading classification method based on AlexNet [12] that achieves an AUC between 0.94 and 0.96. Poplin et al. [16] can predict the major adverse cardiovascular events from retinal fundus photographs and actual cardiovascular risk factors. They have achieved an AUC of 0.73, which is comparable to European Systemic Coronary Risk Evaluation calculator (SCORE).

There are CNN-based CACS prediction methods using CT images. Lessmann et al. [13] propose a CNN architecture to detect coronary artery calcification region from chest CT that achieves a performance comparable to trained radiologists. Santini et al. [18] suggest coronary artery calcification region segmentation by classifying small patches. They have shown the Pearson correlation coefficient of 0.983, which is equivalent to manual segmentation performed by a human expert.

Alluri et al. [2] have presented the history, limitations, and improvement of CACS detection technology. Greenland et al. [9] review the effects of CACS on clinical decision making and cost-effectiveness in preventive cardiology. The US Preventive Service Task Force have found out that the use of CACS makes a small improvement in discriminating cardiovascular risks [7].

The relationship between retinal vessels and cardiovascular diseases (or cardiovascular risk factors) has been studied. McClintic et al. [15] survey the relationship between retinal microvascular abnormalities and coronary heart disease. Tabatabaee et al. [20] have discovered a strong correlation between retinal atherosclerosis and coronary artery atherosclerotic changes. Wang et al. [21] have shown that retinal vessel diameter predicts cardiovascular disease risk and stroke-related mortality in middle-aged patients. Encouragingly, we have identified our CNN models support these findings by acquiring Grad-CAM images [24], which will be explained in detail in Sect. 5.

3 Clinical Background

Traditional CACS analysis is based on four risk levels [9]. The risk level of a patient is 'very low' when CACS is measured 0, 'low' between 1 and 100, 'intermediate' between 101 and 400, and 'high' for 401 and above [9]. Simpler CACS categories of 'zero' or 'non-zero' are more useful in a clinical treatment such as the preventive statin and/or aspirin and the selection of cholesterol and blood pressure therapeutic targets [9]. For example, a moderate patient with the cardiovascular disease risk of 7.5–20% should be prescribed to a statin drug only if CACS is nonzero.

We consider the CACS prediction a binary classification problem (i.e., with zero and nonzero classes). There is a high likelihood that a proper treatment will not be available in early stages of calcification because it is asymptomatic when CACS is small (<100). Thus, the prediction of nonzero CACS is important to detect an early stage of calcification in progress without CT screening.

4 Approach

4.1 Data Augmentation

We apply image augmentation techniques, flip, rotate, affine transform, blurring, and noise injection to train our CACS prediction model. We use 3×3

and 7×7 kernels to blur the images. We add Gaussian and salt-and-pepper noises randomly. In particular, retinal fundus photographs have a distinctive quality degradation known as flare phenomenon, which is caused by external light sources. Figure 1 shows retinal fundus photographs with flare phenomenon.

Fig. 1. Flare phenomenon in retinal fundus photo images

We try to solve the flare phenomenon problem with our flare augmentation method illustrated in Fig. 2. Four linear flare masks (in left, right, up, and down directions) and a circular flare mask are applied to the original image. The intuition behind our masking is to focus on removing part of information of the images regardless of the color since a color of flare has no information to train. Such augmentation has an advantage of improving the learning accuracy of degraded retinal fundus photos.

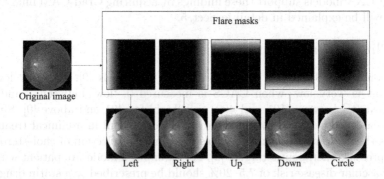

Fig. 2. Proposed flare augmentation method to improve CACS prediction

4.2   Utilizing Auxiliary Information from EHR Data

Insufficient training examples are the most difficult problem for deep learning in general. Our case here is similar as we cannot locate large enough retinal fundus image datasets to train our CACS prediction model. Also, cardiac CT scans that can acquire CACS is not used for screening, but only for patients suspected of heart disease. Other EHR data matched with retinal fundus photographs, however, are relatively abundant as shown in Fig. 3.

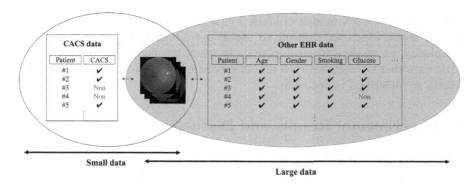

Fig. 3. Comparison of CACS data and other EHR data matched with retinal fundus photographs

We propose a method to improve the CACS prediction accuracy by utilizing auxiliary information from electronic health record (EHR), namely EHR data fusion. Since some EHR data can be acquired by regular checkups or blood test, our method has an advantage of improving prediction performance even if it is difficult to obtain additional CACS matching retinal fundus photographs. Figure 4 shows how to improve the CACS prediction performance by EHR data Fusion. The CACS inference pipeline consists of two stages. Stage 1 is further divided into block 1 for predicting CACS and block 2 for predicting EHR data with retinal fundus photographs. Stage 2 performs the final CACS prediction via logistic regression based on results from the stage 1 inference. The feature of the proposed method is to use EHR values predicted by CNNs instead of using the original EHR data for training the logistic regression model. Overall, our method allows us to predict CACS from fundus images alone, i.e., without any additional EHR data at inference time.

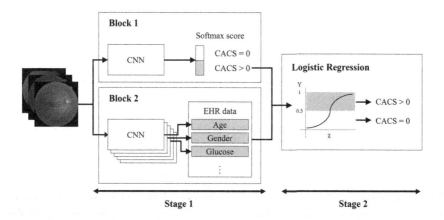

Fig. 4. EHR data fusion to improve CACS prediction

We train the CNN models of block 2 using only numerical EHR data except clinical notes, which are difficult to use as a training label. To reduce model complexity, we apply statistical analysis to select key factors from quantitative EHR data that are significant to CACS prediction. The analysis procedure and results are described in Sect. 5.3.

5   Experimental Results and Discussion

5.1   Data and Modeling

Dataset. Our experiment adheres to the tenets of the Declaration of Helsinki, and the empirical protocol is reviewed and approved by the institutional review board of the hospital. The requirement for written informed consent is waived because of the retrospective and anonymized retinal images. Among 28,824 subjects who participated in the comprehensive medical checkups including CACS measurement between January 2010 and December 2017, 2,696 participants are randomly sampled for our dataset. Fundus photographs are taken with various manufacturers' nonmydriatic fundus camera.

CACS is measured by multi-detector CT (MDCT). All CT scans are acquired by a Lightspeed VCT XTe-64 slice MDCT scanner (GE Healthcare, Tokyo, Japan) with a standardized scanning protocol, using 40 mm × 2.5 mm section collimation, 400 ms rotation time, 120 kV tube voltage, and 124 mAs (310 mA by 0.4 s) tube current under ECG-gated dose modulation. Quantitative CACS is calculated according to the method described by Agatston et al. [1].

We perform our experiment using 5,344 retinal fundus photographs acquired from 2,696 patients, which are sampled by the procedure described above. Every image is annotated with CACS value acquired from cardiac CTs as well as twenty-two types of EHR data acquired from various clinical screening such as blood test. We then divide these images into three sets as Stage 1 training, Stage 2 training, and testing. The number of images in each set is shown in Table 1.

Table 1. Experimental dataset constituents

	Stage 1 training set	Stage 2 training set	Test set	Total
Patients	1,510	608	578	2,696
Photographs	2,992	1,209	1,143	5,344

Baseline Model. We train ImageNet-pretrained Resnet50 using the Stage 1 training set and take it as our baseline. Since there is no previously published work that can predict CACS from retinal fundus photographs, we use this baseline for our evaluation.

5.2 Selecting Key Factors with Statistical Analysis

Rather than using well-known key factors, we select the key factors for our CACS prediction by statistical analysis, a traditional means to choose significant features for a supervised machine learning problem. This is because there can be factors other than well-known key factors that have not studied sufficiently, and our CACS prediction problem is previously unstudied. We apply an ensemble feature selection method that improves robustness by excluding irrelevant features [17] from many-variate EHR data. Our EHR data contain 22 factors, and we assume a linear relationship between each factor and CACS to simplify our analysis for feature selection. The overall procedure is described in Fig. 5.

We apply four linear statistical models, namely ordinary least squares (OLS), stepwise selection (SS), LASSO regression (LR), recursive feature elimination (RFE). We include one nonlinear model, random forest (RF), to handle any nonlinearity present. The final key factors are selected by counting the number of occurrences of each feature over all lists and ranking them according to their occurrences [4] since each statistical model has different criteria such as p-value and feature importance.

We evaluate the significance of each factor by following criteria. The significant factors are selected based on p-value which is less than 0.05 based on 90% confidence interval in OLS. And, SS select factors by repeating forward selection and backward elimination based on p-value. In case of LR, factors are selected based on their coefficient value after the model tuning with appropriate regularization coefficients. Also, factors are selected after removing other factors that have the lower coefficients from logistic regression fit with 4-fold cross validation in RFE. And finally, factors that have high importance are considered as significant factors in RF. After the statistical analysis, we find six key factors: age, pulse wave velocity (PWV) of right side, glucose, total cholesterol, smoking and gender. The analysis results are shown in Table 2.

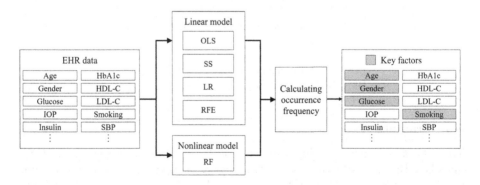

Fig. 5. Key factor selection procedure through statistical analysis on EHR data

Table 2. Statistical key factor analysis

Factor	Used statistical methods				
	OLS	SS	LR	RF	RFE
Age	O	O	O	O	O
PWV(left)		O	O	O	
PWV(right)		O	O	O	O
IOP(left)					
IOP(right)		O			
Glucose		O	O		O
Total cholesterol		O	O		O
HbA1c			O		
SBP					
DBP	O		O		
Smoking	O	O	O		
Gender	O	O	O		O
Blood urea nitrogen					
Creatinine					
Uric acid					
Triglycerides				O	
HDL-C				O	
LDL-C				O	
Insulin			O		
Height					O
Weight					O
BMI		O	O		

*PWV: pulse wave velocity; IOP: intraocular pressure;
SBP: systolic blood pressure; DBP: diastolic blood pressure;
HDL-C: high-density lipoprotein cholesterol;
LDL-C: low-density lipoprotein cholesterol;
BMI: body mass index

5.3 Training

Training of our model is illustrated in Fig. 6. At Stage 1, we train the CNN models of Block 1 using the Stage 1 training set as inputs and the corresponding CACS values as labels. The CNN models of Block 2 are also trained using the same Stage 1 training data but with the key factors as labels. We preprocess every image with flare augmentation. For Stage 2, we train the logistic regression model with the inference results from CNNs in Blocks 1 and 2, using the Stage 2 training set. The logistic regression model can also be trained with the real

EHR data. However, we intend to construct a robust model regardless of the difference between the meta information inferred from the retinal fundus images and real EHR data. The performance of key factor predictions by the Block 2 CNNs is summarized in Table 3.

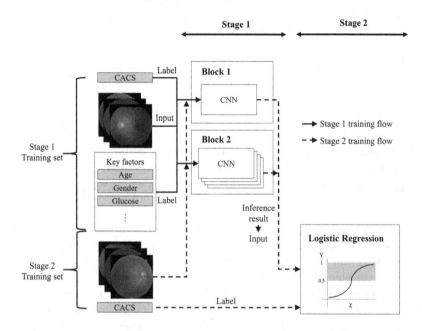

Fig. 6. An overview of training Stages 1 and 2 for our CACS prediction

5.4 Experimental Result and Analysis

CACS Prediction. Our CACS prediction is a binary classification task, thus we evaluate the performance using the AUC metric. We also evaluate the performance of our models by bootstrapping 90% of the test set for 100 times, providing a 95% confidence interval. The AUC results are presented in Table 4.

Table 3. Prediction performance of CNNs in Block 2

Factor	Metric	Value (95% CI)
Gender	AUC	0.874 (0.849–0.898)
Smoking	F1-Score	0.430 (0.399–0.457)
Age (year)	MAE	3.514 (3.365–3.667)
Glucose (mg/dl)		10.454 (9.846–11.256)
Total Cholesterol (mg/dl)		29.327 (28.148–30.767)
PWV (m/s)		0.143 (0.135–0.152)

In case of using only flare augmentation, the performance is improved by 2.4% compared to the baseline. When EHR data fusion is applied without key factor selection, there is no performance improvement because marginal EHR factors are used to train Block 2 CNN models. In case of using only EHR data fusion with key factor selection, the performance is improved by 4.2%. When we use augmentation and EHR data fusion with key feature selection together, the AUC is improved by 6.2%, which makes our best-case performance.

Table 4. CACS prediction results of test set

Method	AUC (95% CI)	Improvement
Baseline	0.713 (0.676-0.749)	–
Flare augmentation	0.730 (0.694–0.765)	2.4%
EHR data fusion w/o key feature selection	0.713 (0.686–0.747)	0%
EHR data fusion w/key feature selection	0.743 (0.717–0.767)	4.2%
Proposed method	**0.757 (0.733–0.785)**	**6.2%**

CACS Matched Dataset Expansion Effect. In addition, we run another test to observe the performance change as the number of images with CACS label increases. We train the CACS prediction CNN model using Stage 1 training set and Stage 2 training set as depicted in Fig. 7. As described in Table 5, the baseline AUC is 0.746 as the dataset expands, and the performance increases to an AUC of 0.787 when flare augmentation is used. The baseline performance improves to 4.6% on the dataset expansion. With data augmentation (image flip, rotation etc.), the performance can be improved to 5.5%. Since the Stage 2 training set is used to train Stage 1 CNN models, we cannot observe the performance improvement by EHR data fusion.

Table 5. Additional test results with increased dataset

Method	AUC (95% CI)	Improvement
Baseline w/expanded dataset	0.746 (0.716–0.777)	–
Flare Augmentation	0.787 (0.753–0.816)	5.5%

Interpretability. We analyze whether or not CACS can be predicted with retinal images as posed in Sect. 3. We apply the Grad-CAM method [24] to the baseline CNN model to investigate which part of the input image is primarily used for prediction. As shown in Fig. 8 (b), when CACS is predicted from the input image (a), CACS is predicted mainly from retinal vessels. This is consistent with the statistical study that the cardiovascular risk factor is significant with retinal vessels, as mentioned earlier. Qualitatively speaking, our CNN models can extract the features necessary for CACS prediction.

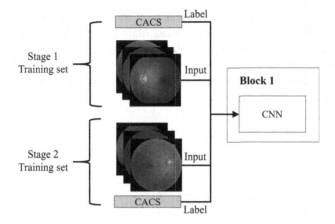

Fig. 7. Training procedure for observing performance change by increased dataset

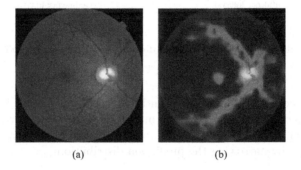

(a)   (b)

Fig. 8. Interpretability result: (a) an example of retinal fundus photograph and (b) class activation map using Grad-CAM to proposed CNN model

Uncertainty. In addition to the classification accuracy, we have investigated the uncertainty of our model output. By uncertainty, we do not mean the softmax values [8], but a method of analyzing the degree of assurance that the model provides based on the probability intervals. We observe performances of baseline and our method in terms of sensitivity, outliers, and error changes according to confidence intervals. To obtain the distribution of CACS inference softmax values, we generate five additional CACS prediction CNN models with different initial random seed variables. By doing so, five softmax values per one image can be generated, and the distribution of the CACS prediction is obtained using the softmax values of the nonzero class. Since it is important to find patients with nonzero CACS, we observe how the uncertainty changes based on the confidence interval when the recall of the CACS zero class is fixed to a specific value.

Figure 9 shows the sensitivity variation of (a) the baseline model and (b) our model according to the confidence interval. 0% means the result of average softmax values without the confidence interval and indicates all test data are used for inference. As the confidence interval level increases, the number of outliers also increase. In this case, sensitivity is calculated based on the inference results excluding outliers as a reject option. In conclusion, our method can infer more data compared to the baseline even when the confidence interval increases. In case of 99% confidence interval level, our model can predict more than 200 images while maintaining sensitivity.

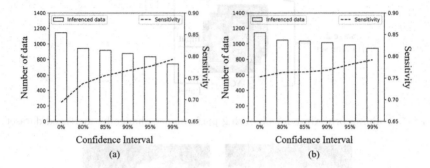

Fig. 9. Sensitivity variation of inference data from (a) baseline model and (b) our model according to confidence interval

Figure 10 shows the proportion of outlier and error of (a) the baseline model and (b) our model, respectively. Our model shows a lower percentage of the outlier decision than the baseline. Therefore, our model successfully decreases the uncertainty by narrowing the prediction distribution.

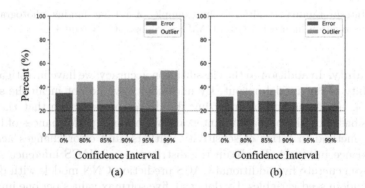

Fig. 10. Outliers vs. errors ratio of (a) baseline model and (b) our model

6   Conclusion

In this paper, we have proposed a new approach to predict CACS by integrating different modalities. Our approach has an advantage of using only retinal fundus photographs at inference time and can be used for screening asymptomatic cardiovascular disease patients from retinal fundus examination without any radiation exposure. Since we have small CACS data matched with retinal fundus photographs, we have focused on improving the CACS prediction performance under a limited environment.

Our future work includes predicting CACS with massive additional data. Such addition will help us extend our current binary CACS prediction model to multi-class prediction or regression models. There is an opinion that similar results can be achieved by classifying predicted EHR features. Perhaps, a similar performance can be achieved by the CNN that predicts the EHR features only. This can be meaningful if predicted EHR data are more influential than predicted CACS, so we plan to study this case. These further studies will likely have a clinical significance as each clinical treatment is different depending on how CACS are categorized (value-wise) [3]. We expect that these studies will make our algorithms more robust and strengthen the clinical significance of retinal fundus images as a cardiovascular disease indicator.

Acknowledgement. We thank Youngjune Gwon (Vice President, Samsung SDS) for improving the manuscript.

References

1. Agatston, A.S., Janowitz, W.R., Hildner, F.J., Zusmer, N.R., Viamonte, M., Detrano, R.: Quantification of coronary artery calcium using ultrafast computed tomography. J. Am. Coll. Cardiol. **15**(4), 827–832 (1990)
2. Alluri, K., Joshi, P.H., Henry, T.S., Blumenthal, R.S., Nasir, K., Blaha, M.J.: Scoring of coronary artery calcium scans: history, assumptions, current limitations, and future directions. Atherosclerosis **239**(1), 109–117 (2015)
3. Blaha, M.J.: Personalizing treatment: between primary and secondary prevention. Am. J. Cardiol. **118**(6), 4A–12A (2016)
4. Brahim, A.B., Limam, M.: Ensemble feature selection for high dimensional data: a new method and a comparative study. Adv. Data Anal. Classif. **12**(4), 937–952 (2018)
5. Budoff, M.J., et al.: Assessment of coronary artery disease by cardiac computed tomography: a scientific statement from the american heart association committee on cardiovascular imaging and intervention, council on cardiovascular radiology and intervention, and committee on cardiac imaging, council on clinical cardiology. Circulation **114**(16), 1761–1791 (2006)
6. Burlina, P.M., Joshi, N., Pekala, M., Pacheco, K.D., Freund, D.E., Bressler, N.M.: Automated grading of age-related macular degeneration from color fundus images using deep convolutional neural networks. JAMA Ophthalmol. **135**(11), 1170–1176 (2017)
7. Curry, S.J., et al.: Risk assessment for cardiovascular disease with nontraditional risk factors: us preventive services task force recommendation statement. JAMA **320**(3), 272–280 (2018)
8. Gal, Y.: Uncertainty in deep learning. Ph.D. thesis, University of Cambridge (2016)
9. Greenland, P., Blaha, M.J., Budoff, M.J., Erbel, R., Watson, K.E.: Coronary calcium score and cardiovascular risk. J. Am. Coll. Cardiol. **72**(4), 434–447 (2018)

10. Gulshan, V., et al.: Development and validation of a deep learning algorithm for detection of diabetic retinopathy in retinal fundus photographs. JAMA **316**(22), 2402–2410 (2016)
11. Jellinger, P.S., et al.: American association of clinical endocrinologists and American college of endocrinology guidelines for management of dyslipidemia and prevention of cardiovascular disease. Endocr. Pract. **23**(s2), 1–87 (2017)
12. Krizhevsky, A., Sutskever, I., Hinton, G.E.: ImageNet classification with deep convolutional neural networks. In: Advances in Neural Information Processing Systems, pp. 1097–1105 (2012)
13. Lessmann, N., et al.: Automatic calcium scoring in low-dose chest CT using deep neural networks with dilated convolutions. IEEE Trans. Med. Imaging **37**(2), 615–625 (2017)
14. Li, Z., He, Y., Keel, S., Meng, W., Chang, R.T., He, M.: Efficacy of a deep learning system for detecting glaucomatous optic neuropathy based on color fundus photographs. Ophthalmology **125**(8), 1199–1206 (2018)
15. McClintic, B.R., McClintic, J.I., Bisognano, J.D., Block, R.C.: The relationship between retinal microvascular abnormalities and coronary heart disease: a review. Am. J. Med. **123**(4), 374 e1–374 e7 (2010)
16. Poplin, R., et al.: Prediction of cardiovascular risk factors from retinal fundus photographs via deep learning. Nature Biomed. Eng. **2**(3), 158 (2018)
17. Saeys, Y., Abeel, T., Van de Peer, Y.: Robust feature selection using ensemble feature selection techniques. In: Daelemans, W., Goethals, B., Morik, K. (eds.) ECML PKDD 2008. LNCS (LNAI), vol. 5212, pp. 313–325. Springer, Heidelberg (2008). https://doi.org/10.1007/978-3-540-87481-2_21
18. Santini, G., et al.: An automatic deep learning approach for coronary artery calcium segmentation. EMBEC/NBC -2017. IP, vol. 65, pp. 374–377. Springer, Singapore (2018). https://doi.org/10.1007/978-981-10-5122-7_94
19. Szegedy, C., Vanhoucke, V., Ioffe, S., Shlens, J., Wojna, Z.: Rethinking the inception architecture for computer vision. In: Proceedings of the IEEE Conference on Computer Vision and Pattern Recognition, pp. 2818–2826 (2016)
20. Tabatabaee, A., Asharin, M., Dehghan, M., Pourbehi, M., Nasiri-Ahmadabadi, M., Assadi, M.: Retinal vessel abnormalities predict coronary artery diseases. Perfusion **28**(3), 232–237 (2013)
21. Wang, J.J., et al.: Retinal vessel diameter and cardiovascular mortality: pooled data analysis from two older populations. Eur. Heart J. **28**(16), 1984–1992 (2007)
22. Wong, T.Y., et al.: Relation of retinopathy to coronary artery calcification: the multi-ethnic study of atherosclerosis. Am. J. Epidemiol. **167**(1), 51–58 (2007)
23. World Health Organisation: Fact sheet cardiovascular diseases (CVDS) (2017)
24. Xu, K., et al.: Show, attend and tell: neural image caption generation with visual attention. In: International Conference on Machine Learning, pp. 2048–2057 (2015)

Mesh Geometric Parameters
for Modeling Signal Transmission
in the Presynaptic Bouton

Maciej Gierdziewicz[✉][iD]

Chair of Applied Computer Science, Faculty of Automation, Electrical Engineering,
Computer Science and Biomedical Engineering, AGH University of Science
and Technology, Al. Mickiewicza 30, 30-059 Cracow, Poland
gierdzma@agh.edu.pl

Abstract. In this paper the generation of a geometrical model for simulation of the transport process inside the bouton of the biological neuron is considered. The transport is modeled in three-dimensional space by using nonlinear diffusion-like partial differential equation. The geometry of the bouton is modeled in two ways. One of them is the geosphere and the other one is the globe. The quality of the mesh elements is examined.

Keywords: Presynaptic bouton · Three-dimensional mesh
generation · Mesh quality measures

1 Introduction

Dynamical processes such as the neurotransmitter (NT) flow, that take place inside the neural cell [6], are modeled by using partial differential equations (PDE) [1] - the tool that has been used in this context for decade. To solve the equation of this type analytically, numerical methods usually have to be applied [1]. In order to perform the calculations accurately, the appropriately designed mesh of the analyzed object should be created. In biology, the boundary conditions are generated by the modeled biological structure and its substructures, for instance the cell and its organelles. Furthermore, the specifics of numerics in Finite Elements Method (FEM), that is commonly used for numerical solution of PDE with complex boundary conditions, forces the use of a high quality mesh [3]. First of all, mesh cells should be regular: for the two-dimensional case each cell should be, optimally, an equilateral triangle, and in the three-dimensional case - a regular tetrahedron. Generally, it is impossible because of the geometric properties of the modeled object. Moreover, three-dimensional space cannot be covered with regular tetrahedra. In reality, the elements of a tetrahedral mesh are of different sizes and shapes. Usually, the tetrahedra in some regions where the different parts of the model meet are, of necessity, smaller and they are often of worse quality.

The work has been accomplished with the use of PL-Grid computing infrastructure.

L. Rutkowski et al. (Eds.): ICAISC 2020, LNAI 12415, pp. 613–625, 2020.
https://doi.org/10.1007/978-3-030-61401-0_57

In this paper the problem of creation of a good quality 3-dimensional mesh for numerical simulation of processes in the presynaptic bouton is studied. Two geometrical three-dimensional models of the bouton are considered. They are compared by using various measures of the mesh quality, one of them having been introduced by the author.

2   The Model of a Presynaptic Bouton

The model of NT synthesis, transport and release is nonlinear, diffusive-like - see the paper [1]. In order to set up a model of presynaptic bouton, the appropriate three-dimensional mesh had to be created. It should be stressed that mesh generation is a non-trivial task, especially in the case when the geometry of the modeled object is complex [4,7]. In general, the researcher can be faced with the following problems.

1. **Optimal density of the mesh.** The properties of the tetrahedral mesh of any 3D object must agree with the intended utilization of the model. In general, the more dense the mesh, the more tetrahedra are defined and the smaller average tetrahedron size is. On the other hand, the larger the number of elements of the mesh, the longer time it takes to execute every simulation step since the main program loop is supposed to iterate on all the tetrahedra. Therefore the chosen resolution of the net is a compromise between those requirements.

2. **Geometric parameters of the tetrahedra.** The quality of the three-dimensional tetrahedral mesh is assessed on the basis of the quality of its elements (tetrahedra). The process of mesh evaluation usually consists of two steps. First, the appropriate measure of a single tetrahedron should be defined. Then, the set of the values of that parameter calculated for all the elements is created. The final result would be optimal if all the tetrahedra were regular, which is impossible. So, it has to be close to optimal: either all or nearly all the elements, depending on the desired application, should not differ too much from the regular ones [4].

   Many quantities may be used to describe a tetrahedron. We discuss some of them in the following simplified case. Let all vertices of the tetrahedron be fixed except one vertex v, and let $q(v)$ be the quality measure of the tetrahedron. It is postulated [4], among others, that $q(v)$ should have the following properties:

   (a) For incorrect (degenerate) elements $q(v) = 0$;
   (b) The measure is scale-invariant i.e. the quality values of two elements of different sizes but of the same shape are equal;
   (c) The measure is normalized to limit its maximum value to 1;
   (d) For nearly all degenerate elements, the gradient of $q(v)$ (with respect to v) is nonzero;
   (e) Unless v coincides with another vertex, $q(v)$ is a smooth function of v coordinates.

The parameters were tested in the following way. The base of the tetrahedron was assumed to be an equilateral triangle of edge length a, lying on the xy plane. Although such a choice limits the diversity of analyzed tetrahedra, it proved sufficient to grasp the differences among mesh quality measures. The coordinates (x, y, z) of the vertices denoted by, let us say, K, L and M were $(-a/2, -a\sqrt{3}/6, 0)$, $(a/2, -a\sqrt{3}/6, 0)$ and $(0, a\sqrt{3}/3, 0)$. The fourth vertex of the tetrahedron, let us say, N, had variable coordinates (x_t, y_t, z_t). It was assumed that $z_t > 0$. The idea was to depict the quality of the tetrahedron obtained in this way as the function of (x_t, y_t, z_t). In order to achieve this, the halfspace $z > 0$ had to be stratified in some way.

The most natural approach seemed to choose some discrete set of points, and to arrange them according to the distance from the center of the basis. The points were located on the hemisphere and were selected as the half of the points of the geosphere model. The number of points was equal to 3904. The calculations of the quality of the tetrahedron were performed for hemispheres with various values of the radius r. The special values of r were: (a) the value $a\sqrt{2/3} \approx 0.81650a$ when the hemisphere contains the point $N = (x_t, y_t, z_t) = (0, 0, \sqrt{2/3}a)$ for which the tetrahedron $KLMN$ is regular, (b) the value $a\sqrt{3}/3 \approx 0.57735a$ for which the hemisphere contains the vertices of the basis. The results presented in Fig. 1.

The hemispheres in five rows of this figure are of the same size: the radius is always 1.6 though, in fact, it is variable. To facilitate comparing, the color scale in all graphs is always the same: from 0.0 (blue) to 1.0 (red).

The parameters considered below are as follows: let S be the total surface, and V - the volume, of the tetrahedron. Then the first of the defined parameters is $SV = \sqrt{S}/\sqrt[3]{V}$, ranging from $SV_{min} = \sqrt[4]{3}\sqrt[6]{72} \approx 2.68433$ (for a regular tetrahedron) to infinity. Transforming the range $(SV_{min}; \infty]$ to $(0; 1]$ gives $Q_1 = SV_{min}/SV$. This is a slightly modified formula taken from [4] where, in its original shape, it was $Q_{1s} = \sqrt[4]{3^7}V/\sqrt[4]{(S_1^2 + S_2^2 + S_3^2 + S_4^2)^3}$. It should be mentioned that Q_1 is easier to compute than Q_{1s}. The calculations, after obtaining S and V, involve only finding two roots, simple sum and division. Moreover, both the denominator and the numerator at the right hand side have linear dimension regardless of the dimension of the space. Consequently, the proposed formula may be used in 4D (for a polychoron) or, in general, in n-dimensional space, also when $n > 4$. The plots of quality measure Q_1, given in Fig. 1 (first row), show that it is, in general, more liberal that the other measures: the red areas are larger than in the next rows. The second one is the value mentioned in [4]. This is the ratio of the longest edge and the radius of the inscribed sphere: $ER = l_{max}/r_{ins}$, which ranges from $ER_{min} = 2\sqrt{6} \approx 4.89898$, for a regular tetrahedron, to infinity. After the standardization put forward in [4] the following formula is obtained: $Q_2 = ER_{min}/ER$, giving the values plotted in the second row of Fig. 1. The third one is the value

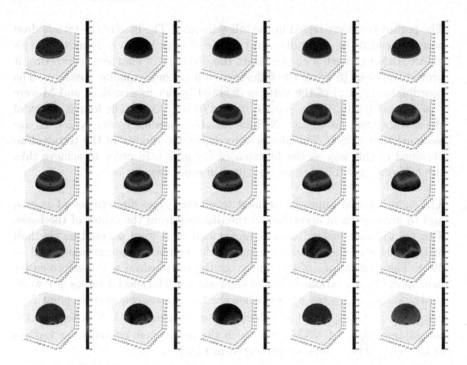

Fig. 1. Quality measures, in rows (Q_1, Q_2, Q_3, Q_4, Q_5), of a tetrahedron with three fixed vertices as a function of 4th vertex coordinates. The ratio of hemisphere radius to tetrahedron base edge length varies for columns, increasing from left to right and is equal to 1/8, 1/2, 1, 5 and 10 (from left to right) (Color figure online)

applied in the TetGen program [5] i.e. the longest edge divided by the smallest height (EH) $EH = l_{max}/h_{min}$, with the range similar as in the previous example i.e. from $EH_{min} = \sqrt{3/2} \approx 1.22474$ to infinity, following the same rule as before: "the larger the value, the worse the tetrahedron". Again, the parameter $Q_3 = EH_{min}/EH$ is the standardized version of EH_{min} and is presented in the third row od Fig. 1. It is visible that the parameters Q_2 and Q_3 are more restrictive than Q_1; they punish irregular tetrahedra for which the projection of the fourth vertex onto the base plane defined by first three vertices lies far from the middle of the base. The red areas in the plots are much smaller than in the first plot. The last two parameters have been introduced in this paper for comparison. They are named $MAXS$ and $MINS$, and they have been computed as the ratios of the largest (S_{max}) or the smallest (S_{min}) face measure, respectively, to the total surface (S) of the tetrahedron. These both measures detect symmetry of the tetrahedron. This symmetry is a crucial feature of a regular tetrahedron and, on the other hand, it is not detected by any of the previous measures. This property of Q_4 and Q_5 manifests by symmetric distribution of colors in Fig. 1 in last two rows. The formula for the first of those two parameters is $MAXS = S_{max}/S$, and its value ranges from 0.25 to 0.5 i.e. $MAXS \in [0.25; 0.5)$. The quality measure $Q_4 = 4(0.5 - MAXS)$ has the theoretical range from 0 to 1. The distribution of Q_4 is shown in Fig. 1 in the fourth row. The formula for the second parameter is $MINS = S_{min}/S$, and its value ranges from 0 to 0.25 i.e. $MINS \in (0; 0.25]$. The quality measure $Q_5 = 4MINS$ ranges from 0 to 1.

Each of the aforementioned non-standardized quantities (SV, ER, EH, MAXS and MINS) is positive and dimensionless, and its best value indicates that the tetrahedron is regular. All the measures, except MINS, reach their minimal values for the regular tetrahedron, and converge to infinity (with the exception of MAXS, which converges to 0.5) when the shape of the tetrahedron becomes more irregular. The MINS value behaves differently: the closer to zero, the worse the tetrahedron which in this case resembles a needle. On the other hand, the maximum value 0.25 is attained for a regular tetrahedron. Moreover, the value near 0.25 of both the MAXS and the MINS does not necessarily mean that the tetrahedron is regular - it may be a sliver-type. For example, a tetrahedron with vertices $(-100, 0, 0)$, $(100, 0, 0)$, $(0, -100, 0.01)$ and $(0, 100, 0.01)$ has $MINS = MAXS = 0.25$ (all faces have equal areas) but it is very flat, far from being regular. Other irregular tetrahedron with the vertices at $(-0.01, 0, 0)$, $(0.01, 0, 0)$, $(0, -0.01, 100)$ and $(0, 0.01, 100)$ is a wedge-type and also has $MINS = MAXS = 0.25$.

The numerical approximation of a gradient of a given function depends strongly on the largest angle (planar angle for a triangle and spherical or dihedral angle for a tetrahedron) [4]. Thus, the condition number of the stiffness matrix should be kept to a minimum. Theoretically, to solve a partial differential equation numerically, the above mentioned quality measures Q_1–Q_5 should be as close to the ideal ones as possible for each of the mesh elements. However, not all deviations from the ideal have strong negative influence on the calculations with FEM. Moreover, it turns out that tetrahedrons with faces far from optimal are still of a quality good enough to be used for numerical analysis of the model [4].

3. **Boundary conditions that have to be satisfied by the mesh.** If the structure to model is complex and it contains many substructures with their own surfaces which consist of triangles of very different size and quality then the generated mesh must take into account these substructures and the joints between them, which further impairs the mesh generation.

The 3D mesh should be of a good quality not only in its 3D aspect but also in its 2D aspect as well. This concerns the quality of the surface of the mesh and, especially, the parts belonging to distinct areas. The quality of a 2D (triangular) mesh of the surface of the bouton which topologically remains similar to the 3D ball is assessed analogically to the quality of the 3D net. The quality measures that correspond to the ones defined for the spatial meshes are as follows: the perimeter divided by the square root of the surface (PS2), the longest edge divided by the radius of the inscribed sphere (in that case the 2D sphere is a circle) (ER2), the longest edge divided by the smallest height (EH2) or the function of the ratio of the largest and smallest edge length, respectively, to the total perimeter of the triangle (MAXE and

MINE). Similar as in the 3D case, the best (the smallest) attainable values of the above measures (except MINE) are: $PS2_{min} = 2 \times 27^{1/4} \approx 4.55901$, $ER2_{min} = 2 \times 3^{1/2} \approx 3.4641$, $EH2_{min} = 2/[3^{1/2}] \approx 1.1547$, $MAXE_{min} = 1/3 \approx 0.3333$, and the largest MINE is $MINE_{max} = 1/3 \approx 0.3333$. For the first three measures the upper bound is infinity whereas for the fourth one (MAXE) it is equal to 0.5, and the lower bound for the last parameter (MINE) is 0.

4. **The mesh inconsistency.** One of the possible inconsistencies of the mesh results from the fact that its boundary is not a closed surface. The program creating tetrahedral mesh is trying to create tetrahedra outside the bouton. Such a problem is sometimes termed as *leaking* and results from the errors in creating the mesh, namely, the points which should be the common vertices of the adjacent tetrahedra, become separate vertices, thus creating the gap between the walls (Fig. 2, left). Note that the size of the gap is about one tenth or less of the 2D mesh element (triangle) size. The way to cope with that problem is called *welding* and may be usually described as joining together two adjacent, sometimes very close nodes.

Another example of leaking, "double edge", is presented in Fig. 2 (middle). In this case, it was impossible to depict the cleft and the edges in one picture since the size of the cleft is less than one thousandth of the edge length. Also, for two pairs of points the distance is so small that they cannot be drawn separately.

Intersection is in a way opposite to leakage, though they often appear simultaneously. The edge of one tetrahedron is intersecting with the face of another one and, as a result, some subset of the 3D mesh volume is defined twice (see Fig. 2, right). Note that the two separate vertices which should be joined to form one common vertex are very close to each other. Again, the distance between them is actually several orders of magnitude smaller than the lengths of the edges themselves.

5. **Measures of the mesh quality.** The measures of the mesh quality can by either the extreme values of the quality parameters or other characteristics of the distribution of a parameter e.g. the maximum value of SV, ER, EH, or MINS, or minimum value of MAXS. These quantities, that are sometimes used to describe the mesh, and also the distributions themselves, are presented as tables and histograms.

3   Simplified Geometrical Models of the Bouton

The geometry of the bouton was modeled in two various ways, using basically two different objects - the geosphere and the ball (globe). Note that the geosphere surface consists only of triangles, nearly equally-shaped and nearly equilateral, whereas the globe surface contains two types of polygons: 1) equal isosceles (but not necessarily equilateral) triangles; and 2) trapezoids. The two above models are known to differ in some aspects, two of which are most commonly mentioned. First, with the globe mesh it is easier to create shapes with edges along meridians and circles of latitude. Secondly, with the geosphere mesh it is easier to make a relatively smooth surface with a smaller number of mesh elements.

3.1 The Geosphere as the Simplest Geometric Model of the Sphere

The geosphere, a commonly available wireframe structure which is utilized e.g. as a 2D mesh of the surface of a sphere, is a model made up of almost equilateral triangles. The calculations reveal that for a standard geosphere 2D mesh the characteristics may exceed the ideal values by 1.3% to 25.5%. Thus, the geosphere is a good reference point to compare the mesh parameters and the quality of 3D meshes. The analyzed model of the geosphere surface comprised 15680 triangular faces and 7482 vertices. The quality measures for the geosphere model with comparison to their ideal values are presented in the upper part of Table 1.

Other important measure of the triangle quality was its minimal and maximal angle. For the considered mesh this value fell between the values of 48.53° and 71.98°. The auxiliary measure of the quality of the triangles making up the surface was the triangle area. It ranged from $S_{min} = 0.001903\,\mu m^2$ to $S_{max} = 0.002051\,\mu m^2$. Therefore, the ratio S_{max}/S_{min} was 107.8%. The surface mesh was then submitted as the input data to the TetGen program which produced the tetrahedral mesh of the sphere. The input parameters for the TetGen program were as follows. The maximal "aspect ratio" i.e. the maximal value of EH was 7.7, the minimal dihedral angle DA was 19° and the maximal tetrahedron volume VT was $0.0002\,\mu m^3$. In the resulting 3D mesh, the number of nodes was 121358, the number of boundary faces was 63196, and the number of tetrahedra was 644999. The parameters of the sphere were as in the lower part of Table 1. The distributions of all the quality measures of the geosphere tetrahedral mesh are in the left column of Fig. 3. These parameters are the reference point for the next calculations.

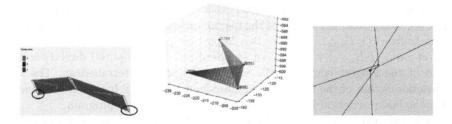

Fig. 2. Mesh inconsistencies. The example of "leakage" (left): two overlapping parts create a gap that can be seen in the bottom left and bottom right parts of the figure; The example of a "double edge" (middle): Tick mark labels of the axes are expressed in nanometers and placed every 2 nm. The size of the cleft between the blue face and the red face is about 10^{-3} nm and therefore it is not visible; The example of "intersecting" (right): Two separate vertices extremely close to each other, visible in the center. The distance between them is approximately 10^{-3} nm. These two vertices should be joined to form a single one.

Table 1. Mesh quality of the geosphere surface model.

Name	Definition	Ideal	Min	Max	Max/ideal
GEOSPHERE SURFACE MODEL					
$PS2$	$P/\sqrt{S}$	$2\sqrt[4]{27} \approx 4.55901$	4.55903	4.6104	1.011
$ER2$	E_{max}/R	$2\sqrt{3} \approx 3.4641$	3.4684	3.9245	1.133
$EH2$	E_{max}/H_{min}	$2/\sqrt{3} \approx 1.1547$	1.1575	1.4527	1.258
$MAXE$	E_{max}/P	$1/3 \approx 0.3333$	0.3337	0.3702	1.111
$MINE$	E_{min}/P	$1/3 \approx 0.3333$	0.2913	0.3325	1.144[a]
GEOSPHERE 3D MODEL					
SV	$\sqrt{S}/\sqrt[3]{V}$	$\sqrt[4]{3}\sqrt[6]{72} \approx 2.6843$	2.6844	4.7147	1.756
ER	E_{max}/R	$2\sqrt{6} \approx 4.8989$	4.9301	37.4427	7.643
EH	E_{max}/H_{min}	$\sqrt{3}/\sqrt{2} \approx 1.2247$	1.2398	14.628	11.944
$MAXS$	S_{max}/S	$1/4 = 0.2500$	0.2503	0.4434	1.774
$MINS$	S_{min}/S	$1/4 = 0.2500$	0.0639	0.2498	3.912[a]

[a]This value is calculated differently - as ideal/min.

3.2 The Ball (Globe) as the Simplest Geometric Model of the Presynaptic Bouton

The globe is a sphere divided into spherical polygons by meridians and circles of latitude. A typical globe is a depiction of the Earth's surface. For example, one may draw a globe with 24 meridians and 13 circles of altitude - or rather 11, if we exclude poles as degenerate circles. The simplest object used for modeling a presynaptic bouton consisted of two such globes placed concentrically, with neurotransmitter release area at the bottom of the outer globe and with the supply zone boundary inside the inner globe.

The program which has been used to generate a three-dimensional mesh of the globe has a set of input parameters that have to be defined. One limitation that is strictly observed is that of the maximum volume of a single mesh element (tetrahedron) (VT_{max}). Another two important parameters are the maximum aspect ratio (EH_{max}) which is not standardized but computed directly as the ratio of the longest edge and the shortest height of a tetrahedron. The last restriction is that of the minimum dihedral angle (DA_{min}). It should be stressed that the last restriction is the most strictly observed in the program.

The 2-dimensional mesh is generated in such a way that each spherical polygon is replaced by a flat polygon with vertices at the same points. The quality of the globe mesh was tested in the following subspace of the above parameters: $EH_{max} \in [4.0; 10.0]$, $VT_{max} \in [0.0006; 4.0]$ and $DA_{min} \in [10°; 19°]$. The best quality was achieved when the imposed restrictions were: $EH_{max} = 10.0$, $DA_{min} = 13°$ and $VT_{max} = 0.0012$.

The corresponding histograms for the globe quality measures are shown in the right column of Fig. 3.

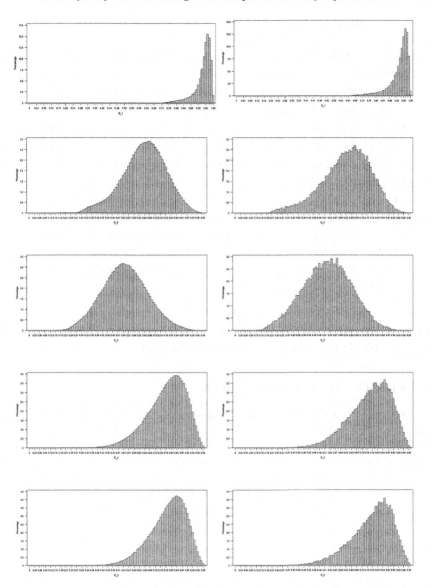

Fig. 3. Distributions of standardized parameters of the tetrahedral meshes: geosphere (left column) and globe (right column). First row: distribution of the standardized mesh quality measure SV; Next rows: standardized distributions of the parameters ER, EH, $MAXS$ and $MINS$.

The next step was, as it has been done previously, to generate the optimized mesh. Its quality was checked for different values of input TetGen parameters. Those parameters after preliminary tests were set to $EH_{max} \in [70; 100]$,

Table 2. Mesh quality of the globe model of the bouton.

Name	Definition	Ideal	Min	Max	Max/ideal
GLOBE SURFACE MODEL					
PS2	$P/\sqrt{S}$	$2\sqrt[4]{27} \approx 4.55901$	4, 55910	6.3549	1.394
ER2	E_{max}/R	$2\sqrt{3} \approx 3.4641$	3.4792	9.6114	2.775
EH2	E_{max}/H_{min}	$2/\sqrt{3} \approx 1.1547$	1.1647	4.5749	3.962
MAXE	E_{max}/P	$1/3 \approx 0.3333$	0.3348	0.4575	1.429
MINE	E_{min}/P	$1/3 \approx 0.3333$	0.1617	0.3325	2.061[a]
GLOBE 3D MODEL					
SV	$\sqrt{S}/\sqrt[3]{V}$	$\sqrt[4]{3}\sqrt[6]{72} \approx 2,68433$	2.68503	4.23589	1.578
ER	E_{max}/R	$2\sqrt{6} \approx 4.89898$	4.97976	28.12424	5.741
EH	E_{max}/H_{min}	$\sqrt{3}/\sqrt{2} \approx 1.22474$	1.26564	11.40720	9.314
MAXS	S_{max}/S	$1/4 = 0.25$	0.25037	0.44492	1.780
MINS	S_{min}/S	$1/4 = 0.25$	0.06135	0.24977	4.075[a]

[a]This value is calculated differently - as ideal/min.

$DA_{min} \in [1°; 20°]$, $VT_{max} = 1000\,\mu m^3$. The best quality was achieved for $EH_{max} = 100; DA_{min} = 2°; VT_{max} = 1000$ (Table 2).

3.3 First Comparison of the Models

The statistical parameters of the 3D meshes of the models described in this paper are presented in Table 3. The minimal values of the parameters were not included in the table because they did not convey much information of the quality of the mesh since their values were always close to the ideal ones; the

Table 3. Mesh quality measures of the bouton models.

Name	Definition	Ideal	Mean	SD	Median	P90	P99	Max
GEOSPHERE								
SV	$\sqrt{S}/\sqrt[3]{V}$	$\sqrt[4]{3}\sqrt[6]{72} \approx 2.68433$	2.84749	0.15648	2.79918	3.03451	3.46124	4.71468
ER	E_{max}/R	$2\sqrt{6} \approx 4.89898$	7.78874	1.82397	7.38168	9.92162	14.42310	37.44269
EH	E_{max}/H_{min}	$\sqrt{3}/\sqrt{2} \approx 1.22474$	2.38374	0.66151	2.24651	3.20865	4.62071	14.62800
MAXS	S_{max}/S	$1/4 = 0.25$	0.30413	0.02705	0.30016	0.34145	0.37957	0.44339
MINS	S_{min}/S	$1/4 = 0.25$	0.19808	0.02518	0.20173	0.16303[a]	0.15112[a]	0.06385[a]
GLOBE								
SV	$\sqrt{S}/\sqrt[3]{V}$	$\sqrt[4]{3}\sqrt[6]{72} \approx 2.68433$	2.88477	0.20380	2.81796	3.11881	3.74693	4.23589
ER	E_{max}/R	$2\sqrt{6} \approx 4.89898$	8.20721	2.40916	7.56507	10.90243	18.32399	28.12424
EH	E_{max}/H_{min}	$\sqrt{3}/\sqrt{2} \approx 1.22474$	2.54553	0.85918	2.32799	3.59229	5.75653	11.40720
MAXS	S_{max}/S	$1/4 = 0.25$	0.30769	0.02907	0.30364	0.34783	0.38617	0.44492
MINS	S_{min}/S	$1/4 = 0.25$	0.19443	0.02878	0.19953	0.15380[a]	0.13958[a]	0.06135[a]

[a]In this row the values P90, P99, max are replaced with P10, P5, min, respectively.

relative differences never exceeded 1.23% which confirmed that the best elements of the mesh were always of a very good quality.

Inspection of the results in Table 3 reveals that for the simplified bouton models (the geosphere model and the globe model) the mean and the median lay relatively close to the ideal value and all these three values were within the range of one standard deviation of the corresponding parameter.

3.4   Further Optimizations Involving Modifications of the Surface and Improvement of Dihedral Angles

Mesh Quality. The results did not look satisfactory, so additional modifications and closer inspection of the results seemed unavoidable. The former was performed by using the Stellar program [2]. The latter was done by comparing the simulation results for the worst mesh with those for the best one.

The advantage of Stellar over other existing software is that it contains transformations like inserting new vertices, deleting vertices, removing one of the endpoints of an edge resulting in edge contraction, smoothing or removing boundary or near-boundary vertices of the mesh, boundary edge removal, multi-face removal and, above all, compound operations made up of all the above transformations.

Since the modifications done by the Stellar software focus mainly on improving the distribution of dihedral angles of mesh tetrahedra, which the software author considers crucial for performing numeric calculations (see [2] and the relevant references therein), the Table 4 summarizes the results of improving. The extreme values of the parameters SV, ER, EH, MAXS and MINS after improving the mesh are given in Table 5.

Table 4. Mesh quality improvement with Stellar software for the bouton models

Improv. stage	Number of nodes	Number of faces	Number of tetrahedra	Ideal DA	Min DA	Max DA	Improv. (min)	Improv. (max)
GEOSPHERE								
before	121358	63196	644999	70.53°	5.83°	164.92	–	–
after	125915	64062	472414	70.53°	37.50	140.41	6.43	1.17
GLOBE								
before	7567	6354	39853	70.53°	7.90°	162.18°	–	–
after	8850	5096	26283	70.53°	37.44°	139.46°	4.74	1.16

Table 5. Mesh quality measures of the bouton models after improvement.

Name	Definition	Ideal	Mean	SD	Median	P90	P99	Max
GEOSPHERE								
SV	$\sqrt{S}/\sqrt[3]{V}$	$\sqrt[4]{3}\sqrt[6]{72} \approx 2.68433$	2.80129	0.06310	2.79255	2.88640	2.97954	3.33775
ER	E_{max}/R	$2\sqrt{6} \approx 4.89898$	7.47835	1.29978	7.26340	9.07162	11.85719	24.99427
EH	E_{max}/H_{min}	$\sqrt{3}/\sqrt{2} \approx 1.22474$	2.31219	0.54216	2.21765	2.98423	4.11482	9.75960
MAXS	S_{max}/S	$1/4 = 0.25$	0.30716	0.02864	0.30297	0.34659	0.38850	0.43438
MINS	S_{min}/S	$1/4 = 0.25$	0.19643	0.02555	0.19967	0.16305[a]	0.14975[a]	0.04684[a]
GLOBE								
SV	$\sqrt{S}/\sqrt[3]{V}$	$\sqrt[4]{3}\sqrt[6]{72} \approx 2.68433$	2.81312	0.06964	2.80272	2.90532	3.01900	3.21246
ER	E_{max}/R	$2\sqrt{6} \approx 4.89898$	7.76157	1.49536	7.47481	9.66496	12.82559	19.98282
EH	E_{max}/H_{min}	$\sqrt{3}/\sqrt{2} \approx 1.22474$	2.46626	0.66469	2.33056	3.31735	4.71825	7.41859
MAXS	S_{max}/S	$1/4 = 0.25$	0.31461	0.03285	0.30945	0.36080	0.40590	0.43614
MINS	S_{min}/S	$1/4 = 0.25$	0.18995	0.02885	0.19390	0.15030[a]	0.13593[a]	0.06181[a]

[a]In this row the values P90, P99, max are replaced with P10, P5, min, respectively.

4 Concluding Remarks

The obtained results lead to the conclusions that there exists no universal measure of the element quality. In particular, the SV quality measure is the least sensitive to the distortion of the quality measures of a mesh element (of a tetrahedron), discussed in this paper. It reacts only to very flat or needle-shaped elements i.e. when one of the faces is extremely large or extremely small. The ER measure is more sensitive for distorted elements, but not necessarily for symmetric slivers or for needle-shaped tetrahedra. The EH measure is more sensitive for slivers and needles and it is also a little more sensitive for short edges. The MX coefficient is sensitive to the presence of one or three short edges. It tolerates symmetric needles and, to less extent, symmetric wedges. The quantity MN is also sensitive to short edges, especially in needles. It tolerates slivers. The SV parameter is the only of the discussed ones that has the property of improving in concert with the quality of dihedral angles of tetrahedra. The best results may be obtained by using several quality measures simultaneously.

References

1. Bielecki, A., Kalita, P., Lewandowski, M., Skomorowski, M.: Compartment model of neuropeptide synaptic transport with impulse control. Biol. Cybern. **99**, 443–458 (2008)
2. Klingner, B.: Tetrahedral mesh improvement. Ph.D. thesis, University of California at Berkeley, Department of Electrical Engineering and Computer Sciences (2009)
3. Liu, T., Bai, S., Tu, B., Chen, M., Lu, B.: Membrane-channel protein system mesh construction for finite element simulations. Mol. Based Math. Biol. **3**, 128–139 (2015)
4. Shewchuk, J.R.: Delaunay refinement algorithms for triangular mesh generation. Comput. Geom. **22**, 21–74 (2002)

5. Si, H.: TetGen, a Delaunay-based quality tetrahedral mesh generator. ACM Trans. Math. Softw. **41**(2) (2015). Article 11
6. Tadeusiewicz, R.: New trends in neurocybernetics. Comput. Methods Mater. Sci. **10**, 1–7 (2010)
7. Zhou, Y., Zhang, C., Bo, P.: Efficient tetrahedral mesh generation based on sampling optimization. Comput. Animat. Virtual Worlds **26**(6), 577–588 (2015)

Instance Segmentation of Densely Packed Cells Using a Hybrid Model of U-Net and Mask R-CNN

Tomasz Konopczyński[1,4(✉)], Ron Heiman[1], Piotr Woźnicki[1,3], Paweł Gniewek[2], Marie-Cécilia Duvernoy[2], Oskar Hallatschek[2], and Jürgen Hesser[1]

[1] Department of Data Analysis and Modeling in Medicine,
Mannheim Institute for Intelligent Systems in Medicine, Medical Faculty Mannheim,
Heidelberg University, Heidelberg, Germany
konopczynski.tomasz@gmail.com

[2] Departments of Physics and Integrative Biology, University of California,
Berkeley, CA 94720, USA

[3] Faculty of Medicine, Medical University of Warsaw, Warsaw, Poland

[4] Tooploox Ltd., Wrocław, Poland

Abstract. In malignant tumors and microbial infections, cells are commonly growing under confinement due to rapid proliferation in limited space. Nonetheless, this effect is poorly documented despite influencing drug efficiency. Studying budding yeast grown in space-limited microenvironments is a great tool to investigate this effect, conditioned on a robust cell instance segmentation. Due to confinement, cells become densely packed, impairing traditional segmentation methods. To tackle that problem, we show the performance of Mask-RCNN based methods on our dataset of budding yeast populations in a space-limited environment. We compare a number of methods, which include the pure Mask R-CNN, the 1st and 2nd place solution of the 2018 Kaggle Data Science Bowl and a watershed ensemble variant of Mask R-CNN and U-Net. Additionally, we propose a Hybrid model that combines a semantic and an instance segmentation module in a sequential way. In the latter, the encoder-decoder architecture used for semantic segmentation produces a segmentation probability map, which is concatenated with the input image and then fed into the Mask R-CNN network in order to achieve the final instance segmentation result. Consequently, this model is able to efficiently share and reuse information at different levels between the two network modules. Our experiments demonstrate that the proposed model performs best and achieves a mean Average Precision (mAP) of 0.724 and a Dice coefficient of 0.9284 on our dataset.

Keywords: Cell segmentation · Instance segmentation · U-Net · Mask R-CNN

T. Konopczyński, R. Heiman and P. Woźnicki—Equal contribution.

L. Rutkowski et al. (Eds.): ICAISC 2020, LNAI 12415, pp. 626–635, 2020.
https://doi.org/10.1007/978-3-030-61401-0_58

1   Introduction

Cellular growth in confined environments leads to dense cellular populations and emergent mechanical forces between them. These forces lead to collective behaviors that may span a whole population [7,16–18]. While the former confers an enhanced resilience to classic anti-microbial and tumor targeting drugs [8,22], the latter has recently been recognized as being an underlying mechanism of wound healing [21], cancer metastasis [24] and embryonic development [17]. The background of heterogeneous mechanical stresses, responsible for these processes, remains elusive. Thus, experimental characterization of the dense geometry of compacted populations is of significant importance. Microfluidic experiments using model organisms, e.g. *Saccharomyces cerevisiae* (budding yeast), offer an in-vitro strategy to assess these questions [5]. Analysing such data, however, presents a challenge to traditional segmentation techniques as they are typically not very effective for microscopic dense cell populations. As a consequence, a large amount of high-throughput experimental data had to be manually processed which impaired the potential of working with big datasets. This issue has been limiting further progress.

Recently, deep learning techniques have become the dominating strategy for cell segmentation [2]. In this context, well-known architectures are the U-Net [20] for semantic segmentation and the Mask R-CNN [9] for instance segmentation. Most of the recent approaches to cell segmentation build upon them and add their own original architecture extensions and modifications. Chen *et al.* [3] use a U-Net with a bipartite graph instead of sole skip connections, Vuola *et al.* [25] describe an ensemble model of U-Net and Mask R-CNN in combination with a gradient boosting model and Liu *et al.* [15] apply Mask R-CNN with a conditional random field for post-processing. The advancement in biomedical image segmentation is further accelerated by many recent instance cell segmentation competitions, including the Kaggle Data Science Bowl 2018 (DSB2018), where highly sophisticated solutions were proposed.

In this paper we compare a number of existing methods for cell instance segmentation, including pure Mask R-CNN, the 1st and 2nd place solutions of the DSB2018 as well as an ensemble model of the U-Net and the Mask R-CNN with watershed-based merging. Moreover, we introduce a two-stage Hybrid model that combines U-Net and Mask R-CNN architectures. It utilizes the assets of both methods where the semantic context provided by the U-Net is included in order to improve the instance segmentation masks with Mask R-CNN.

All the models are trained and evaluated on a dataset of budding yeast populations in a space-limited environment. We show that the hybrid model yields the best segmentation results.

1.1   Related Work

The breakthrough in Deep Learning on the task of biomedical image segmentation was achieved by the U-Net architecture [20]. It is a fully-convolutional network (FCN) comprising an encoder and decoder part, with skip connections between them. The encoder part is a regular convolutional neural network for extracting image features. The decoder part tries to map the features to the space domain by gradually applying transposed convolutions. The output of the decoder yields a class-probability for each pixel which is the output segmentation map. The skip connections enable the network to calculate image features at different scales, similar to the FPN backbone in Mask R-CNN. Being a FCN, arbitrary input sizes can be used for the network. The vanilla U-Net contains a basic, five-stage CNN as the encoder. However, this can be exchanged by a deeper feature extraction network, as e.g. ResNet [10]. When the training data set is small, a pretrained encoder network can be employed with subsequent fine-tuning on the training data set. Popular datasets for pretraining are ImageNet [6] or COCO[14].

For instance segmentation, the Mask R-CNN [9] architecture has been shown to perform successfully on biomedical images [12,15,25]. Mask R-CNN extends the previously devised object detection and classification algorithm Faster R-CNN [19] by making it instance aware. It consists of a CNN backbone for feature extraction, typically a residual network [10] in conjunction with a feature pyramid network (FPN) [13]. It is followed by a region proposal network, an FCN which selects possible regions of interest and their coordinates. Next, a ROI-Align layer is applied to create a fixed size feature map for the network head. The ROI-Align layer replaces the ROI-Pooling from Faster R-CNN in order to give a more fine-grained alignment for segmentation without the use of quantization. The Mask R-CNN network has three outputs which are combined in the network head. The classification and the bounding box regression output are calculated by fully-connected layers and are used for object detection. Additionally, in order to get the segmentation results, the algorithm adds a fully-convolutional network on top of the ROI-Align layer. This mask branch works in parallel to the object detection branch. Thus, the loss function of the algorithm is $L_{total} = L_{cls} + L_{bbox} + L_{mask}$. When using a FPN in the backbone, the network head is inherently applied to multiple scales and is therefore leading to a more precise segmentation and detection result. In the standard version of Mask R-CNN 5 different feature map scales are used. The interested reader is referred to [9] for further information.

The Kaggle Data Science Bowl 2018 focused on cells' nuclei instance segmentation and therefore, it had some topical relation to our dataset. Thus, we applied the 1st and 2nd place solutions from this competition to our dataset as well. We wanted to check whether these approaches were applicable in an out-of-the-box manner on a similar but still different dataset. The 1st place solution (K1) [23] develops very deep U-shaped encoder-decoder architectures, including deep residual and densely connected nets, such as ResNet101, ResNet152, DenseNet169 and Inception-v4. Their networks effectively use a second channel with nuclei contours to predict semantic mask and borders between the nuclei. In order to better generalize from little training data, the solution performs heavy, data specific augmentation, among others channel shuffling, blurring and

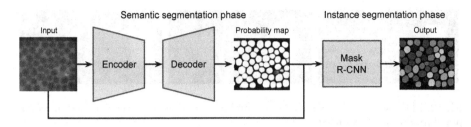

Fig. 1. Our proposed model: the first stage is an encoder-decoder U-Net architecture. The predicted probability map by the semantic segmentation phase is fed, together with the original image, into the second stage module - Mask R-CNN.

multiple geometric transformations. For post-processing, a gradient boosting algorithm is applied on morphological features of each cell candidate.

The 2nd place solution (K2) [11] makes use of the standard Mask R-CNN backbone. In order to make the network instance-aware, eight more outputs describing the relative positions of each pixel within every instance are added.

Another way to improve the score is to use an ensemble of U-Net and Mask R-CNN. A straightforward technique to merge predictions from the instance and semantic segmentation models is the watershed transform, an example of such a method is presented in [1].

2   Methods

Our proposed hybrid model consists of two stages and is depicted in Fig. 1. The first stage is a deeply-supervised encoder-decoder U-Net network with skip-connections and auxiliary outputs. Its purpose is to generate probabilistic segmentation maps, which, combined with the original image, form the input for the second stage. The U-Net is further extended by using pre-computed weight maps, which emphasize cell borders of the target image. We modify the cross-entropy loss function explicitly by adding a weight map W_i for cell borders to put more emphasis on them. The weight maps are calculated for each pixel using a distance transform. We finally apply the weighted sum of such a pixel weighted cross-entropy and Dice as a loss function for the network output and the auxiliary outputs:

$$\mathcal{L}_1 = -\frac{1}{N}\sum_{i=1}^{N}\left[\sum_k \left[(1+w_{ik})^{\lambda}\cdot y_{ik}\cdot\log\hat{y}_{ik}\right] + \alpha\frac{2\cdot\left|Y_i\odot\hat{Y}_i\right|}{|Y_i|+\left|\hat{Y}_i\right|}\right], \quad (1)$$

where $\hat{Y}_i$ and Y_i indicate the predicted and ground truth mask, respectively, on one image. w_{ik}, y_{ik} and $\hat{y}_{ik}$ denote k-th element of W_i, Y_i and $\hat{Y}_i$, respectively. λ is a weight map factor, α a scalar weight factor, N is the batch size and $\odot$ the Hadamard product.

Fig. 2. Fluorescence images for three exemplary experiments of the confined microbial population from the dataset.

The second stage comprises a Mask R-CNN network. Our Mask R-CNN implementation uses the ResNet101 [10] and an FPN [13] as a backbone. Standard outputs of Mask R-CNN are combined in the network head. The parallel output branches enable the model to jointly predict the detection bounding box and the segmentation mask for every cell in the image. We use a multi-task loss on each sampled region of interest (ROI), as described in [9]. It is defined as:

$$\mathcal{L}_2 = \alpha\mathcal{L}_{cls} + \beta\mathcal{L}_{bbox} + \gamma\mathcal{L}_{mask} \tag{2}$$

where $\mathcal{L}_{cls}$ is a log loss over both classes, $\mathcal{L}_{bbox}$ is the robust L_1 loss function (smooth L_1), $\mathcal{L}_{mask}$ is the average binary cross-entropy loss and α, β, γ are scalars that control the strength of the corresponding term.

In total, the U-Net and the Mask R-CNN architectures are concatenated in a way that takes advantage of additional high-level semantic context to generate instance-aware masks. We hypothesize that the additional information from the U-Net helps to guide the optimization of the second stage network and allows for the modelling of more complex inter-pixel dependencies.

3   Experiments

3.1   Dataset

The dataset features images from multiple experiments on budding yeast populations in space-limited environments. *Saccharomyces cerevisiae* S288C was grown at 30 °C in polydimethylsiloxane microfluidic chambers of sizes 60 μm × 20 μm × 10 μm or 55 μm × 30 μm × 10 μm. Complete Supplement Medium (CSM) supplemented with 2% dextrose was supplied through narrow nutrient channels (as described in [4]). A fluorescent dye (Alexa Fluor 488 dextran 3 kW at concentration 0.1 mg/mL) was added to the culture medium in order to visualize the space between cells. The chambers were imaged using an inverted microscope (Nikon Eclipse TI) with a 40x/N.A. 1.30 objective via epifluorescence using a filter set for GFP. The image resolution is 7 pixels for 1 μm.   A total of 235 images were used for this study –192 for training and 43 for testing. The test set contains 5,688 cells in total. Example images from the dataset and corresponding ground truth segmentation masks are shown in Figs. 2 and 4.

Table 1. Results on the test set. We provide results for the mean average precision (mAP) score, the Adjusted Rand Index (ARI), the Dice coefficient and the Jaccard index. The mAP thresholds range from 0.5 to 0.95 with a step size of 0.05.

Model	mAP	ARI	Dice	Jaccard
1st place (ResNet152)	0.615	0.9522	0.9108	0.837
2nd place	0.654	0.9898	0.917	0.846
Mask R-CNN	0.713	0.9970	0.9255	0.861
Watershed ensemble	0.712	0.9971	0.9257	0.862
Hybrid model	**0.724**	**0.9972**	**0.9284**	**0.866**

3.2 Setup

We compare our hybrid model to four other algorithms described in Sect. 1 — Mask R-CNN, K1, K2 and the watershed ensemble method. We implement the watershed ensemble technique to merge the U-Net predictions with Mask R-CNN. Then the asphericity is calculated for every new region, which is not included in the Mask R-CNN output, and the region is added if it fulfills the desired morphological criteria. This results in adding a few extra cells found by the U-Net to the Mask R-CNN output. We base our U-Net[1] and Mask R-CNN[2] implementations on publicly available code and customize the model as described in Sect. 2. For the pure Mask R-CNN variant, we employ the same implementation as above and for K1 and K2 we apply the author's implementations [11,23]. We use the default hyperparameter search space proposed by the authors and chose the best performing set for the baseline.

3.3 Training Details

The training of the hybrid model was done in the following way: First, only the semantic segmentation module was trained alone to learn the pixel-wise probability map. It was trained for 300 epochs with a learning rate of 0.0002 decreasing by half every 100 epochs. Next, the weights of the semantic segmentation module were frozen and the instance segmentation module was trained by using both the output from the semantic segmentation part and the original input image. The instance segmentation module was trained for 100 epochs with a learning rate of 0.0001 and for 50 epochs with a learning rate reduced to 0.00001. We use pre-training on the COCO dataset [14] for both stages of the model. Other pre-training options, as e.g. on the DSB2018 dataset, have been tried as well but they have not improved the results. We employed standard data augmentation techniques, including vertical and horizontal flips, random crops and random scaling in the range [0.9, 1.1].

---

[1] https://github.com/Confusezius/unet-lits-2d-pipeline.
[2] https://github.com/matterport/Mask_RCNN.

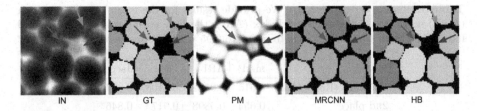

Fig. 3. An example on a ROI from the test set. The input image (IN) is concatenated with a probability prediction map (PM) for the second stage of the network. The red arrow indicates a cell that was missed and the blue arrow points to a wrongly detected cell by the pure Mask-RCNN (MRCNN). The Hybrid model (HB) correctly assigns both regions. The probability mask of the U-Net generates a hint for the second module but the final decision for segmentation is made by the Mask R-CNN. This proceeding avoids misclassifications. According to the ground truth (GT) both models miss the cell indicated by the green arrow. (Color figure online)

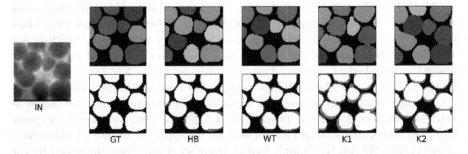

Fig. 4. Comparison of the segmentation results for different methods. We compare our Hybrid model (HB) with Watershed ensemble (WT), 1st place Kaggle (K1) and 2nd place Kaggle (K2). Top: Instance segmentation predictions with different random colors assigned for the cells. Bottom: Semantic segmentation predictions with false positive pixels marked in orange and false negative ones in purple. (Color figure online)

4   Results and Discussion

We compare all the models described in the previous sections by means of mAP, Adjusted Rand Index (ARI), Dice and Jaccard Index. The Hybrid model achieves the best scores in terms of all the compared metrics (see Table 1). We report a mAP of 0.724, Dice score of 0.9284 and an ARI of 0.9972 on the test set. The ARI is calculated on the true positive regions only, so it reflects the accurate separation between neighbouring cells. The higher mAP of the Hybrid model indicates superior instance segmentation outcomes across a variety of intersection over union (IoU) thresholds. It should be noted that simpler approaches like the pure Mask R-CNN and the watershed ensemble also produce pretty good results. K1 and K2, which do not feature a full Mask R-CNN network, get the lowest scores. While it is true that these models have employed multiple techniques for better generalization across different types of data, we assume that our compact

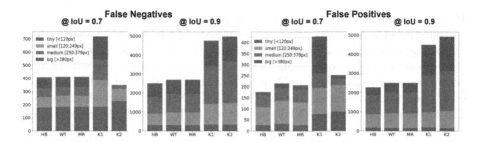

Fig. 5. Number of misclassified cells for different cell sizes and at two IoU thresholds: 0.7 and 0.9 for false Negatives and false Positives. Compared methods: Hybrid model (HB), Watershed ensemble (WT), Mask R-CNN (MR), 1st place Kaggle (K1), 2nd place Kaggle (K2). At IoU = 0.9 our model is clearly more precise than the others and produces fewer errors of both types.

and space-limited settings differ significantly from the data used in DSB2018 and therefore, a simple transfer of their methods is not sufficient to achieve top scores. Additionally, it also emphasizes the strength of the Mask R-CNN architecture on our dataset. Figure 4 presents a qualitative comparison between the predicted segmentation masks.

We also show the number of misclassified cells for different cell sizes at two IoU thresholds (Fig. 5). All the algorithms struggle equally with detecting tiny cells. However, for larger cell sizes the difference between the methods becomes more apparent. At IoU = 0.7, for false negatives, the Hybrid model performs similarly to the watershed ensemble and worse than K2. However, for false positives, it is the superior method. At IoU = 0.9, for both false negatives and false positives, the Hybrid model performs best. As K2 achieves the best score for IoU = 0.7 for false negatives, but the worst at IoU = 0.9, we conclude that K2 is good at detecting cells but it lacks the precise cell border segmentation. These conclusions are consistent with what we observe in Fig. 4, namely that the segmentation masks are more precise for the Hybrid model. Furthermore, this reassures our assumption that due to the hints by the first-stage U-Net, fewer regions are wrongly detected as cells.

Figure 3 gives another example for this behaviour. With the help of the probability mask generated by the semantic segmentation, the Hybrid model can correctly find cells, which were mistakenly assigned either as false positives or as false negatives by the pure Mask R-CNN method.

5 Conclusions

In this paper, we compare a number of methods for instance segmentation on our dataset of densely packed budding yeast cells. These form a model population for other eukaryotic cells, e.g. tumor cells, and are therefore of high clinical relevance. We present a Hybrid model combining U-Net and Mask R-CNN architectures and compare it with other well-known algorithms. It is shown that the

Hybrid model gives more accurate segmentation results (best scores for mAP and Dice) and avoids wrongly detected regions. Thus, regarding our dataset, exploiting the features of both U-Net and Mask R-CNN in the described manner provides an advantage over using the algorithms separately, even with distinct post-processing steps, or ensembling them with the watershed technique. However, simpler approaches like the pure Mask R-CNN and the watershed ensemble also produce good results. We believe that our findings about the Hybrid model could be generalized to other datasets from the medical field displaying a various range of cell densities. Therefore, we encourage researchers to apply our approach in order to verify this hypothesis.

References

1. Barnes, R., Lehman, C., Mulla, D.: Priority-flood: an optimal depression-filling and watershed-labeling algorithm for digital elevation models. Comput. Geosci. **62**, 117–127 (2014)
2. Caicedo, J.C., et al.: Evaluation of deep learning strategies for nucleus segmentation in fluorescence images. BioRxiv (2019)
3. Chen, J., Banerjee, S., Grama, A., Scheirer, W.J., Chen, D.Z.: Neuron segmentation using deep complete bipartite networks. In: Descoteaux, M., Maier-Hein, L., Franz, A., Jannin, P., Collins, D.L., Duchesne, S. (eds.) MICCAI 2017. LNCS, vol. 10434, pp. 21–29. Springer, Cham (2017). https://doi.org/10.1007/978-3-319-66185-8_3
4. Delarue, M., et al.: Self-driven jamming in growing microbial populations. Nat. Phys. **12**(8), 762–766 (2016)
5. Delarue, M., et al.: SCWiSh network is essential for survival under mechanical pressure. Proc. Natl. Acad. Sci. **114**(51), 13465–13470 (2017). https://doi.org/10.1073/pnas.1711204114
6. Deng, J., Dong, W., Socher, R., Li, L.J., Li, K., Fei-Fei, L.: ImageNet: a large-scale hierarchical image database. In: 2009 IEEE Conference on Computer Vision and Pattern Recognition, pp. 248–255. IEEE (2009)
7. Gniewek, P., Schreck, C.F., Hallatschek, O.: Jamming by growth. arXiv e-prints arXiv:1810.01999, October 2018
8. Hall-Stoodley, L., Costerton, J.W., Stoodley, P.: Bacterial biofilms: from the natural environment to infectious diseases. Nat. Rev. Microbiol. **2**(2), 95–108 (2004)
9. He, K., Gkioxari, G., Dollár, P., Girshick, R.: Mask R-CNN. In: ICCV (2017)
10. He, K., Zhang, X., Ren, S., Sun, J.: Deep residual learning for image recognition. In: Proceedings of the IEEE Conference on Computer Vision and Pattern Recognition, pp. 770–778 (2016)
11. Jacobkie: DSB 2018 Jacobkie 2nd place solution. https://github.com/jacobkie/2018DSB/
12. Johnson, J.W.: Adapting mask-RCNN for automatic nucleus segmentation. arXiv preprint arXiv:1805.00500 (2018)
13. Lin, T.Y., Dollár, P., Girshick, R., He, K., Hariharan, B., Belongie, S.: Feature pyramid networks for object detection. In: Proceedings of the IEEE Conference on Computer Vision and Pattern Recognition, pp. 2117–2125 (2017)
14. Lin, T.-Y., et al.: Microsoft COCO: common objects in context. In: Fleet, D., Pajdla, T., Schiele, B., Tuytelaars, T. (eds.) ECCV 2014. LNCS, vol. 8693, pp. 740–755. Springer, Cham (2014). https://doi.org/10.1007/978-3-319-10602-1_48

15. Liu, Y., Zhang, P., Song, Q., Li, A., Zhang, P., Gui, Z.: Automatic segmentation of cervical nuclei based on deep learning and a conditional random field. IEEE Access **6**, 53709–53721 (2018)
16. Montel, F., et al.: Stress clamp experiments on multicellular tumor spheroids. Phys. Rev. Lett. **107**, 188102 (2011)
17. Park, J.A., Atia, L., Mitchel, J.A., Fredberg, J.J., Butler, J.P.: Collective migration and cell jamming in asthma, cancer and development. J. Cell Sci. **129**(18), 3375–3383 (2016)
18. Park, J.A., Kim, J.H., Bi, D., et al.: Unjamming and cell shape in the asthmatic airway epithelium. Nat. Mater. **14**, 1040–1048 (2015)
19. Ren, S., He, K., Girshick, R., Sun, J.: Faster R-CNN: towards real-time object detection with region proposal networks. In: Advances in Neural Information Processing Systems, pp. 91–99 (2015)
20. Ronneberger, O., Fischer, P., Brox, T.: U-Net: convolutional networks for biomedical image segmentation. In: Navab, N., Hornegger, J., Wells, W.M., Frangi, A.F. (eds.) MICCAI 2015. LNCS, vol. 9351, pp. 234–241. Springer, Cham (2015). https://doi.org/10.1007/978-3-319-24574-4_28
21. Sadati, M., Qazvini, N.T., Krishnan, R., Park, C.Y., Fredberg, J.J.: Collective migration and cell jamming. Differentiation **86**(3), 121–125 (2013). Mechanotransduction
22. Tannock, I.F., Lee, C.M., Tunggal, J.K., Cowan, D.S.M., Egorin, M.J.: Limited penetration of anticancer drugs through tumor tissue. Clin. Cancer Res. **8**(3), 878–884 (2002)
23. Topcoders2018: DSB 2018 [ods.ai] topcoders 1st place solution. https://github.com/selimsef/dsb2018_topcoders/
24. Tse, J.M., et al.: Mechanical compression drives cancer cells toward invasive phenotype. Proc. Natl. Acad. Sci. **109**(3), 911–916 (2012). https://doi.org/10.1073/pnas.1118910109. https://www.pnas.org/content/109/3/911
25. Vuola, A.O., Akram, S.U., Kannala, J.: Mask-RCNN and U-net ensembled for nuclei segmentation. arXiv preprint arXiv:1901.10170 (2019)

Blue-White Veil Classification in Dermoscopy Images of the Skin Lesions Using Convolutional Neural Networks

Piotr Milczarski[1]([⊠]) [iD] and Łukasz Wąs[2] [iD]

[1] Faculty of Physics and Applied Informatics, Department of Computer Science,
University of Lodz, Pomorska Str. 149/153, 90-226 Lodz, Poland
piotr.milczarski@uni.lodz.pl
[2] Institute of Mechatronics and Information Systems, Lodz University of Technology,
Stefanowskiego Str. 18/22, Lodz, Poland
lukasz.was@p.lodz.pl

Abstract. In the dermatology, Three-Point Checklist of Dermatology is defined and it is proved to be a sufficient screening method in the skin lesions assessments during the checking by dermatology expert. In the method there is a criterion of blue-whitish veil appearance within the lesion defined and it can be classified using a binary classifier. In the paper, we show the results of CNN application to the problem of the assessment of whether the blue-white veil is present or absent within the lesion using the pre-trained VGG19 CNN network, trained and tested on the prepared images taken from the PH2 dataset.

Keywords: CNN · Dermoscopy · Skin lesion asymmetry · Pre-trained convolutional neural networks · VGG19

1 Introduction

In the dermatology, the Three-Point Checklist of Dermatology (3PCLD) [1, 2] is defined and it is proved to be a sufficient screening method in the skin lesions assessments during the checking by dermatology expert. In the method there are criteria of asymmetry in shape, hue and structure distribution within the lesion defined and it can have value either 0, 1 or 2, presence or absence of the pigmented network and blue-white veil [1–3]. The Seven-Point Checklist (7PCL) [4, 5] is the other screening method for the lesions' assessment. That method takes into account pigment network and blue-white veil as the assessment factors, but also streaks pigmentation, regression structures, dots and globules and vascular structures [3–6]. The next example of the screening method is ABCD rule [7–9], which also defines the symmetry/asymmetry of the lesion.

In the paper, we show the results of CNN application to the problem of the blue-white veil within the skin lesion in the dermoscopic images. We build the neural network with the help of the available pre-trained VGG19 convolutional neural network [10]. From the available networks e.g. AlexNet, GoogleNet and Inception-ResNet-v2, the VGG19 requires medium computational power and provides satisfactory results even

L. Rutkowski et al. (Eds.): ICAISC 2020, LNAI 12415, pp. 636–645, 2020.
https://doi.org/10.1007/978-3-030-61401-0_59

with relatively small but well described the PH2 dataset [11]. We compare the best results achieved by the mentioned pre-trained network. The results varies from 91 to more than 99%.

The effective knowledge acquisition schemes are necessary for constructing large systems supporting the dermatological diagnosis [9, 12–15]. In three checklist of dermoscopy suspicious lesion equals at least two points [1–3] out of three. Melanoma is a life-threatening disease that is completely cured if removed in the early stages [13]. This statement is also confirmed by the statistics shown by the European Cancer Information System [16] and American Cancer Society [17]. Therefore, the removal of all lesions that clinically might be suspicious for melanoma is warranted while minimizing the excision of benign lesions. In order to spread the use of dermoscopy approach with pigmented skin lesions (PSL) various attempts have been made in the last years by developing more or less simplified methods of dermoscopic diagnosis.

The three or seven criteria were important in distinguishing malignant from pigmented skin lesions [5]. These three criteria are asymmetry atypical pigment network and blue-white structures (a combination of earlier categories of blue-whitish veil and regression structures) a preliminary calculations showed that presences of any of two of these criteria indicates a high likelihood of melanoma.

The paper is organized as follows. In Sect. 1 we introduced checklist of dermoscopy. In Sect. 2 we present and discuss methods of used datasets to acquire dermoscopy lesion information Blue-whitish veil clinical description and used methods of verification are thoroughly described. The Blue-whitish veil dermatological search methods are discussed in Sect. 3. Research and discussion of the results are presented in Sect. 4. The final results are given in the following section. Finally, Sect. 6 presents the conclusions.

2 Datasets Used in Dermoscopy

Dermoscopy is a non-invasive skin imaging technique, which permits visualization of features of pigmented melanocytic neoplasms that are not discernable by examination with the naked eye. We conduct our research on a certain type of data sets which contains clinical description of skin lesion. The PH2 dataset [11] consists of dermoscopic images which are described as follows. The dermoscopic images were obtained at the Dermatology Service of Hospital Pedro Hispano (Matosinhos, Portugal) under the same conditions through Tuebinger Mole Analyzer system using a magnification of 20 times. They are 8-bit RGB color images with a resolution of 768×560 pixels.

This image database contains a total of 200 dermoscopic images of melanocytic lesions, including 80 common nevi, 80 atypical nevi, and 40 melanomas. The PH2 database includes medical annotation of all the images namely medical segmentation of the lesion, clinical and histological diagnosis and the assessment of several dermoscopic criteria (colors; pigment network; dots/globules; streaks; regression areas; blue-whitish veil) [4, 11, 18].

The ISIC Archive contains the largest publicly available collection of quality controlled dermoscopic images of skin lesions [19]. Presently, the ISIC Archive contains over 24,000 dermoscopic images, which were collected from leading clinical centers internationally and acquired from a variety of devices within each center.

The overarching goal of the ISIC Melanoma Project is to support efforts to reduce melanoma-related deaths and unnecessary biopsies by improving the accuracy and efficiency of melanoma early detection. To this end the ISIC is developing proposed digital imaging standards and creating a public archive of clinical and dermoscopic images of skin lesions.

Dermatologists who specialize in skin cancer routinely employ total body photography and dermoscopy as diagnostic tools for the detection and diagnosis of melanomas [20]. Total body photography permits the early detection of changing lesions and avoidance of biopsy of stable lesions. Dermoscopes, simple handheld devices that eliminate surface glare and magnify structures invisible to the "naked eye", significantly improve the distinction of melanomas from other skin lesions. When used by skin cancer specialists, total body photography and dermoscopy make it possible to detect melanoma very early in its evolution, while decreasing the number of unnecessary biopsies and improving recognition of atypical lesions. In clinical trials, training in dermoscopy or sequential imaging led to improvements in early detection of melanoma for both non-specialist dermatologists and primary care physicians. Specialized systems for image acquisition, storage, and retrieval have been developed for physicians to facilitate total body photography assisted follow up and digital dermoscopic monitoring.

The dataset contains a representative mix of images of both malignant and benign skin lesions. Before release, the challenge dataset was randomly partitioned into both a training and test sets, with about 900 images in the training set and about 350 images in the test set.

- Segmentation: Lesions have been segmented against background normal skin and miscellaneous structures by expert dermatologists.
- Dermoscopic Features: Lesions have been locally annotated for clinical dermoscopic features by expert dermatologists.
- Disease State: The gold standard for the diagnosis of skin lesions is pathology. Images in the ISIC archive have been derived from centers with expert pathology that can be deemed the gold standard. Benign lesions included in the archive without the benefit of pathology diagnosis are reviewed by multiple experts and only included in the event of unanimous clinical diagnosis.

The DermCS dataset consists of dermoscopic images which are described as follows. The DermCS is a database for evaluating computerized image-based prediction of the seven-point skin lesion malignancy checklist. The dataset includes over 2000 clinical and dermoscopy color images, along with corresponding structured metadata tailored for training and evaluating computer-aided diagnosis (CAD) systems.

Among those who work with and analyze these collections of clinical dataset images are those who work with it as a state of the art methodology using seven point checklist of dermoscopy [5].

3 Blue-Whitish Veil Clinical Description and Methods Used in the Veil Verification

3.1 Three-Point Checklist of Dermatology [1, 2]

In 2003, during the Virtual Consensus Net Meeting on Dermoscopy (CNMD) a simple algorithm, called Three-Point Checklist of Dermatology (3PCLD), was established to distinguish malignant from benign pigmented skin lesions.

The 3PLCD algorithm relies on the following criteria:

1. Asymmetry in structure and/or in color in one or two axis of the lesion. The contour shape of the lesion does not impact on the symmetry.
2. Atypical network, defined as pigmented network with thickened lines and irregular distribution.
3. Blue-white structures, namely any white and/or blue color visible in the lesion, including blue-white veil, scar-like depigmentation, and regression structures such as peppering.

3.2 Seven-Point Checklist [5]

Odds ratios of each of the 7 criteria were calculated by multivariate analysis. seven-point score of 2 was given to the 3 criteria with odds ratios more than 5, and a score of 1 was given to the 4 criteria with odds ratios less than 5.

By the simple addition of the individual scores a minimum total score of 3 is required for the diagnosis of melanoma, whereas a total score of less than 3 is indicative of a non-melanoma. Seven-Point Checklist: definition and histopathologic correlates of the 7 melanoma-specific dermoscopic criteria:

1. Atypical pigment network
2. Blue-whitish veil
3. Atypical vascular pattern
4. Irregular streaks
5. Irregular pigmentation
6. Irregular dots/globules
7. Regression structures

The authors pay attention to one of the criteria which is blue-whitish veil that carries a large risk factor for melanoma its correct diagnosis reduces the risk of illness.

3.3 Blue-Whitish Veil Significance

Blue-whitish veil is a blue and focal structureless zone with an overlying white "ground-glass" haze. It occurs in raised/palpable areas of a lesion [1]. Histologically, it corresponds to heavily pigmented melanocytes and/or melanophages or melanin in the dermis (in melanocytic lesions), in combination with acanthosis and compact orthokeratosis [5].

Blue-whitish veil is associated with melanoma, but can also be seen in Spitz/Reed nevi and in non-melanocytic lesions such as SK, BCC and pyogenic granuloma [4].

In the latter years, a lot of analytical methods based on scored algorithms have been introduced both to simplify the dermoscopic learning and to improve the early melanoma detection. The seven-point checklist, published in 1998, represents one of the most and latest validated dermoscopic algorithms due to its high sensitivity and specificity, also when used by non-experts [4].

To validate this algorithm, a univariate statistical analysis was used to determine the differences between melanoma and nevi. A score of 2 points was assigned to the criteria with odds ratios >5, (major criteria), while a score of 1 point was assigned to the criteria with odds ratios <5 (minor criteria). A minimum total score of 3 allows identifying melanoma with a sensitivity of 95% and a specificity of 75%. In other words, at least two dermoscopic criteria (one major and one minor) must be present for a suspicious diagnosis. According to a revised, simplified seven-point checklist, the presence of at least one of the seven criteria should allow the diagnosis of melanoma with a sensitivity of 85–93% and a specificity between 45 and 48% [5].

In 2003 the various dermoscopic algorithms (classical pattern analysis, the ABCD rule, Menzies' method and the seven-point checklist) were re-evaluated and tested by non-experts [9]. In details, 16 physicians not familiar with dermoscopy examined images of 20 pigmented lesions using the different methods, before and after an Internet-based training course on dermoscopy. The results showed a significant improvement in the dermoscopic diagnosis of melanoma after the Web training for pattern analysis with the ABCD rule and Menzies' method, but not for the seven-point checklist, which allowed higher sensitivity even before the web course. For this reason, the seven-point checklist is considered among the algorithms with the best sensitivity for the non-expert investigators. Afterward, in the Consensus Net Meeting on Dermoscopy, the value of the seven-point checklist was definitively confirmed.

The main methods of recognition of blue-whitish veil are usually of dermoscopy combined with methods of regional analysis and color recognition and its certain combination (see Fig. 1). The steps of the blue-white veil detection procedure are demonstrated on the right image (Fig. 1b).

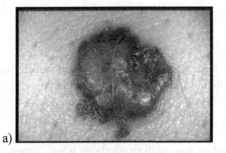
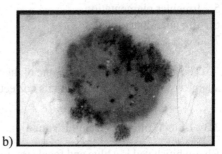

a)   b)

Fig. 1. Melanoma with blue-white veil [4]: a) clinical image; b) dermoscopy image. (Color figure online)

Practiced by experienced observers, this imaging modality offers higher diagnostic accuracy than observation without magnification [2–5]. Dermoscopy allows the identification of dozens of morphological features one of which is the blue-white veil (irregular, structureless areas of confluent blue pigmentation with an overlying white "ground-glass" film) [6]. This feature is one of the most significant dermoscopic indicators of invasive malignant melanoma, with a sensitivity of 51% and a specificity of 97% [7]. Figure 1 shows a melanoma with a blue-white veil.

4   The Dermatological Methods of the Blue-Whitish Veil Recognition

Dermatologists in their assessment of the lesions use the ABCD, 3PCLD and 7CPL that were introduced based on their experts' experience. In both scales one of the factor features is the asymmetry of the shape, hue and structures distributions. The asymmetry of the lesion has discrete values: 0 for symmetric in 2 perpendicular axes; 1 for symmetric in 1 axis and 0 for having no symmetry ones. PH2 is one of the reference dermoscopic datasets with the data validated by the dermatology experts.

The mechanism of transforming the disease image into a kind of diverse template of specific features is aimed at displaying some important from the experts (doctors) point of view features such as pathways in the lesion as well as preparing material for further extraction of the features.

An important feature in the segmentation of the specific features of the lesion is the ability to more accurately present specific elements of the lesion and bypass its correlation with the skin without lesion, which in the initial analysis may be a factor negating or reducing the accuracy of the initial opinion.

The correct selection of specific features, in particular blue veil and pigmented network, also has an impact on the analysis of the contours of specific disease fragments, which, in conjunction with the work on the modified algorithm of contour approximation, can give complementation effects and introduce a broader outline for the expert opinion.

We extract a specific number of features from patterns that are important information in the classification process. From the obtained set of features we can extract global and local features. The set of local features represents the color and texture (pattern). For each region, the features representing colors consist of the mean and variance of one channel in the RGB and HSV color space.

An important aspect is also the physical size of the lesion, or its fragment, on which further analysis will be carried out, which is why the authors, together with a domain expert, introduce the minimum physical size of a certain part of the image/skin lesion for which further activities regarding the analysis of the specific fragment pattern will be carried out. Currently, dermoscopes can determine the physical length and provide this information for further processing needs. So it is extremely important to perform properly the segmentation process which is based on seven- or three-point check list of dermatology [9].

The correct selection of specific features, in particular the blue veil and pigmented network, also has an impact on the analysis of specific disease fragments, which, in conjunction with the work on the process of extracting the multiple disease features, can give complementary effects and provide a broader outline for an expert opinion [13]. One of the research methodologies which is used to conduct proper segmentation process based on specific disease feature of skin lesion is the blue-white structured method of comparison.

In the research, we used the images that are stored in the accessible PH2 database with their reference data. It is used in the presented research as a testing set. Only 167 images out of 200 images have lesions borders limited to the image area but all images are used in the research [11].

5 Research and Discussion of the Results

In the research, we have used the VGG19 convolutional neural network [10] and the images derived from the PH2 dataset [11]. VGG-19 is a convolutional neural network that is 19 layers deep: 16 convolutional layers and 3 fully connected layers, that has the trainable weights.

In the first step, we have made the images smaller and cropped them so as to fit to the VGG19 pre-trained network. From the 768 × 568 images we achieved 224 × 224 images but the proportions of the lesions were not changed. We also did the best effort to be sure that the lesion is within the cropped square image. The problem of the PH2 dataset is that it has only 200 images altogether with 36 images containing blue-white veil. To expand the dataset and not to lose more data than it is needed in the first step, we have transformed the images using isometric transformations i.e. rotation by 90, 180, 270°, mirror symmetry by their horizontal and vertical axis. In that way we achieved 1200 images with 216 containing blue-whitish veil.

To estimate the classification of the VGG19 we have used two approaches on how to prepare the training and testing sets named BW1 and BW3 respectively. Set BW1 is divided as follows. 1000 images achieved by isometric transformations were used as a training set. The original images were used as the test set, so it gave us 200 images. Set BW3 is divided as follows. 27 random images and their isometric copies from the set are taken from the subset with absent blue-white veil, altogether 162 images. To the testing set we also added 6 random images and their corresponding isometric copies. We have 198 images in the testing set. The rest was used as the training set. We have 1002 images in the training set.

Table 1. A confusion matrix for the BW1, with accuracy 94.5%

BW value from PH2	Number of images with a given BW	A	P
A	164	158	6
P	36	5	31
Total	200		

The methods were tested in Matlab2019a working on the computer with Intel i7-6820 with 16 GB of RAM, nVidia GTX 1070 with 8 GB of GDRAM. In the research, we also used Deep Learning Toolbox v12.1, Statistics and Machine Learning Toolbox v 11.5 and Parallel Computing Toolbox v7.0. The mean time of the CNN network building varied from 4 to 5.5 min. The Matlab has been working using graphics acceleration. The exemplary confusion matrices for both sets are shown in Table 1 for BW1 and in Table 2 for the BW3 approaches.

Table 2. A confusion matrix for the BW3, with accuracy 90.9%

BW value from PH2	Number of images with a given BW	A	P
A	162	150	12
P	36	6	30
Total	200		

Table 3. The chosen confusion matrix factors with their average (AVG), variance (VAR), minimum (MIN) and maximum (MAX) values

CM factor		BW1	BW3
ACC[%]	AVG	96.4	90.5
	VAR	1.9	5.0
	Min	94.5	82.8
	Max	99.0	97.0
TPR[%]	AVG	92.8	96.7
	VAR	2.8	10.9
	Min	83.3	83.3
	Max	100	100
FPR[%]	AVG	2.8	10.9
	VAR	2.1	5.8
	Min	0.6	3.7
	Max	6.1	21.0
F1	AVG	0.90	0.79
	VAR	0.05	0.09
	Min	0.85	0.68
	Max	0.97	0.92
MCC	AVG	0.88	0.76
	VAR	0.06	0.10
	Min	0.82	0.64
	Max	0.97	0.91

While training we have used a model having 4 epochs and 400 iterations. In the BW1 case the average accuracy was $96.4 \pm 1.9\%$. In the BW3 case the average accuracy was $90.5 \pm 5.0\%$.

The chosen factors derived from the confusion matrix are presented in Table 3. We can see that opposite to the accuracy the true positive rate (TPR) is higher in the BW3 approach. This shows that sensitivity of the method is high.

The false positive rate (FPR) for the BW1 is lower than for BW3 but the value 10.9 $\pm 5.5[\%]$ is satisfactory. The calculated F1 score and Matthews correlation coefficient (MCC) also show values closer to value 1. Therefore, the VGG19 pre-trained convolutional neural network shows very good results that can be used in the evaluation of the Three-Point Checklist of Dermatology and Seven-Point Checklist of Dermatology.

6   Conclusions

The correct selection of specific features, in particular the blue-whitish veil and pigmented network, has an impact on the analysis of specific disease fragments. The process can give complementary effects and provide a broader outline for expert opinion in conjunction with the work on the process of extracting the multiple disease features. One of the research methodologies which is used to conduct proper features segmentation based on specific disease feature of skin lesion is the Three-Point Checklist of Dermatology (3PCLD) as in Seven-Point Checklist (7PCL).

In the research, we have used the VGG19 [10] pre-trained CNN network and PH2 dermoscopic image dataset [11]. The results achieved are quite promising. The average accuracy was above 90%. The networks usually quite well classified the images of the lesions. The images with present blue-white veil were rarely underestimated. In the 5 rounds the type II error was around 7.2% in the BW1 case and 3.3% in BW3 one.

References

1. Soyer, H.P., Argenziano, G., Zalaudek, I., et al.: Three-point checklist of dermoscopy. A new screening method for early detection of melanoma. Dermatology **208**(1), 27–31 (2004)
2. Argenziano, G., Soyer, H.P., et al.: Dermoscopy of pigmented skin lesions: results of a consensus meeting via the internet. J. Am. Acad. Dermatol. **48**(9), 679–693 (2003)
3. Milczarski, P.: Symmetry of Hue distribution in the images. In: Rutkowski, L., Scherer, R., Korytkowski, M., Pedrycz, W., Tadeusiewicz, R., Zurada, J.M. (eds.) ICAISC 2018. LNCS (LNAI), vol. 10842, pp. 48–61. Springer, Cham (2018). https://doi.org/10.1007/978-3-319-91262-2_5
4. Kawahara, J., Daneshvar, S., Argenziano, G., Hamarneh, G.: Seven-point checklist and skin lesion classification using multitask multimodal neural nets. IEEE J. Biomed. Health Inform. **23**(2), 538–546 (2019)
5. Argenziano, G., Fabbrocini, G., et al.: Epiluminescence microscopy for the diagnosis of doubtful melanocytic skin lesions. Comparison of the ABCD rule of dermatoscopy and a new 7-point checklist based on pattern analysis. Arch. Dermatol. **134**, 1563–1570 (1998)
6. Carrera, C., Marchetti, M.A., Dusza, S.W., Argenziano, G., et al.: Validity and reliability of dermoscopic criteria used to differentiate nevi from melanoma: a web-based international dermoscopy society study. JAMA Dermatol. **152**(7), 798–806 (2016)

7. Nachbar, F., Stolz, W., Merkle, T., et al.: The ABCD rule of dermatoscopy. High prospective value in the diagnosis of doubtful melanocytic skin lesions. J. Am. Acad. Dermatol. **30**(4), 551–559 (1994)
8. Milczarski, P., Stawska, Z., Maslanka, P.: Skin lesions dermatological shape asymmetry measures. In: Proceedings of the IEEE 9th International Conference on Intelligent Data Acquisition and Advanced Computing Systems: Technology and Applications, IDAACS, pp. 1056–1062 (2017)
9. Menzies, S.W., Zalaudek, I.: Why perform dermoscopy? The evidence for its role in the routine management of pigmented skin lesions. Arch. Dermatol. **142**, 1211–1222 (2006)
10. Simonyan, K., Zisserman, A.: Very deep convolutional networks for large-scale image recognition. In: Conference Track Proceedings of 3rd International Conference on Learning Representations (ICRL), San Diego, USA, (2015)
11. Mendoncca, T., Ferreira, P.M., Marques, J.S., Marcal, A.R.S., Rozeira, J.: PH2 – a dermoscopic image database for research and benchmarking. In: 35th Annual International Conference of the IEEE Engineering in Medicine and Biology Society (EMBC), Osaka, pp. 5437–5440 (2013)
12. Was, L., Milczarski, P., Stawska, Z., Wiak, S., Maslanka, P., Kot, M.: Verification of results in the acquiring knowledge process based on ibl methodology. In: Rutkowski, L., Scherer, R., Korytkowski, M., Pedrycz, W., Tadeusiewicz, R., Zurada, J.M. (eds.) ICAISC 2018. LNCS (LNAI), vol. 10841, pp. 750–760. Springer, Cham (2018). https://doi.org/10.1007/978-3-319-91253-0_69
13. Celebi, M.E., Kingravi, H.A., Uddin, B.: A methodological approach to the classification of dermoscopy images. Comput. Med. Imaging Graph. **31**(6), 362–373 (2007)
14. Was, L.: Analysis of skin diseases using segmentation and color hue in reference to melanocytic lesions. In: Rutkowski, L., Korytkowski, M., Scherer, R., Tadeusiewicz, R., Zadeh, L.A., Zurada, Jacek M. (eds.) ICAISC 2017. LNCS (LNAI), vol. 10245, pp. 677–689. Springer, Cham (2017)
15. Milczarski, P., Stawska, Z., Was, L., Wiak, S., Kot, M.: New dermatological asymmetry measure of skin lesions. Int. J. Neural Netw. Adv. Appl. **4**, 32–38 (2017)
16. European Cancer Information System (ECIS). https://ecis.jrc.ec.europa.eu. Accessed 21 Feb 2020
17. ACS – American Cancer Society. https://www.cancer.org/research/cancer-facts-statistics.html. Accessed 21 Feb 2020
18. Milczarski, P., Stawska, Z.: Classification of Skin Lesions Shape Asymmetry Using Machine Learning Methods. In: Barolli, L., Amato, F., Moscato, F., Enokido, T., Takizawa, M. (eds.) WAINA 2020. AISC, vol. 1150, pp. 1274–1286. Springer, Cham (2020). https://doi.org/10.1007/978-3-030-44038-1_116
19. The International Skin Imaging Collaboration: Melanoma Project. http://isdis.net/isic-project/. Accessed 21 Mar 2020
20. Argenziano, G., Soyer, H.P., De Giorgi, V., et al.: Interactive Atlas of Dermoscopy. EDRA Medical Publishing and New Media, Milan (2002)

Automatic Generation of Parallel Cache-Efficient Code Implementing Zuker's RNA Folding

Marek Palkowski[✉], Wlodzimierz Bielecki, and Mateusz Gruzewski

Faculty of Computer Science and Information Systems, West Pomeranian University of Technology in Szczecin, Zolnierska 49, 71210 Szczecin, Poland
{mpalkowski,wbielecki}@wi.zut.edu.pl
http://www.wi.zut.edu.pl

Abstract. We propose a technique to automatically generate parallel cache-efficient code for computational biology tasks. The approach is dedicated to dynamic programming problems. As an example, we consider RNA folding code based on Zuker's approach. First, the algorithm searches all reading array accesses whose index order is different from the order of loop nest indexes. Such accesses imply column-order data scanning that is not cache-efficient for C++ programs. To improve data locality, the order of array indexes is changed so that row-order data scanning takes place. Then, the algorithm rewrites cells of original arrays to transposed arrays after each writing. So, mirror transposed arrays are formed at each step of Zuker's algorithm that preserves the validity of that algorithm. Modified serial code with data movement reduction is generated by a pre-processing tool. Then, such a code is transformed by the TRACO compiler into cache-efficient parallel code. For this purpose, TRACO applies the Integer Set Library to extract statement instance schedules. Output code is multi-threaded with OpenMP pragmas. The results of an experimental study carried out on a modern Intel i7 processor with 12 threads for various RNA sequence lengths confirm the efficiency of the proposed approach.

Keywords: Computational biology · The Zuker algorithm · RNA folding · Transpose · Loop skewing

1 Introduction

Automatic optimization of bioinformatic programs by means of optimizing compilers is a current challenging task. Non-serial polyadic dynamic programming (NPDP) cores of RNA folding or DNA sequences alignment expose irregular dependence patterns that prevents automatic generation of effective parallel code. For example, the state-of-the-art PluTo compiler [2] based on the affine transformation framework is unable to tile all loops in the loop nest for Nussinov's and Zuker's approaches [6,7]. It also cannot parallelize John McCaskill's

© Springer Nature Switzerland AG 2020
L. Rutkowski et al. (Eds.): ICAISC 2020, LNAI 12415, pp. 646–654, 2020.
https://doi.org/10.1007/978-3-030-61401-0_60

algorithm [3] or generate parallel code for Smith-Waterman DNA sequences alignment for three input sequences [8]. Fortunately, those codes can be optimized within the polyhedral model without finding affine transformations [7].

The authors of PluTo, Bondhugula and et al. presented dynamic parallel tiling for the Zuker's optimal RNA secondary structure prediction [6]. 3-d iterative tiling is based on dynamic scheduling and reduction chains. Operations along each chain can be reordered in order to eliminate cycles in an inter-tile dependence graph. Their approach involves a dynamic scheduling of tiles, rather than the generation of a static schedule and corresponding static code.

Wonnacott et al. introduced 3-d tiling of "mostly-tileable" loop nests of RNA secondary-structure prediction code in paper [10]. But, the paper does not consider any parallel code, tiling is represented with serial code.

Li and et al. proposed a manual solution (*transpose* method) for Nussinov's RNA folding algorithm. Using lower and unused part of Nussinov's array, they changed column reading to more efficient row reading. Diagonal scanning exposes parallelism in output code. The experimental study was presented on CPUs and GPUs architectures. Zhao et al. improved the *transpose* method and demonstrated its application for generation of high performance and energy-efficient codes. However, authors do not present any multi-threaded implementation [11].

The *Transpose* algorithm has some limitations. First, Li and co-authors did not present any way to automatically generate code, a manual effort is needed to generate code. Second, the authors presented code for only Nussinov's recurrence and then discuss the usability of the approach for more complex RNA folding like Zuker's recurrence, where the upper triangles of arrays are only used. Finally, extracting parallelism is possible if only diagonal scanning can be applied. To extract parallelism, the user must find a schedule for each statement in a program loop nest. The method has to be manually performed with a need for code validity checking for each NPDP bioinformatics algorithm.

In this paper, we present an algorithm to automatically generate program loop nests, which implements array transposition and element row reading order. First, the algorithm envisages changing source code by means of a pre-processing tool. Next, a modified loop nest is parallelized by the TRACO compiler [1], which applies the ISL scheduler [9]. Code generation is realized without any developers' effort. We study the efficiency of generated code on modern Intel I7 cores for Zuker's RNA folding and compare it with that of codes generated with other closely related techniques. We discuss the applicability of the algorithm to other computation biology tasks and outline future work in the conclusion.

2   Automatic Array Transpose and Scheduling

To provide an automatic transposition of arrays and code generation, we propose the algorithm presented below.

Algorithm 1. Automatic array transposition algorithm

1: **Input**: Set of statements of the input loop nest, S; set of two-dimensional arrays referred in the loop nest, V.
2: **Output**: Set of modified statements S, set of transposed arrays V', and modified code.
3: **procedure** AUTO-TRANSPOSE(S, V)
4:    **for each** s in S **do**
5:        Calculate vector of surrounding loop indexes $I(s)$ for statement s
6:        Calculate set $A(s, v \in V)$ including all reading accesses to arrays included in set V
7:        **for each** a in $A(s, v)$ **do**
8:            For each array access a, calculate vector ad so that each its element is the position number of the index expression of the corresponding element of vector I.
9:            **if** e **then**lements of ad are **not**lexicographically sorted
10:                Swap elements of access a
11:                Prepare transposed array v and replace this array for a
12:                Add array v to V'
13:            **end if**
14:        **end for**
15:    **end for**
16:    **for each** v in V' **do**
17:        ForEach s in S
18:        **if** s writes the value of cell to v **then**
19:            Rewrite this value to the transposed array of v after the s execution of s.
20:        **end if**
21:    **end for**
22: **end procedure**

The algorithm is limited to two-dimensional arrays and array index expressions must contain only one loop index variable like for the code implementing Zuker's algorithm[1].

First, we find all statements and arrays in the input loop nest. For each statement, we prepare a vector of surrounding loop indexes I. Then, we calculate all reading array accesses and present them with a vector ad of length 2. We replace index expressions in ad with the numbers of positions of loop indexes in vector I. Column-reading takes place when elements of vector ad do not lexicographically sorted.

In such a case, we form transposed arrays to achieve row-reading and initialize these arrays with values of original ones.

---

[1] An expression of the form $i+k$ prevents applying the presented algorithm, however, it is still an affine form and we plan developing an algorithm extension adapted to an arbitrary affine expression in our future work.

A program implementation of the presented algorithm transforms source code into a new serial cache-efficient program. Then, transformed code is redirected to the TRACO compiler to extract parallelism and generate target parallel code.

TRACO is an automatic source-to-source optimizing compiler implemented mainly by means of the ISL library.

ISL allows us to extract legal statement instance schedules, which enable for program parallelization so that all available dependences in the original program are respected. ISL returns schedules in the form of relations which map each statement instance to a multidimensional time. Then applying extracted schedules, wave-fronting is used to generate parallel code. More details about the ISL scheduler are presented in the ISL manual [9].

3   Optimizing Zuker's RNA Folding Code

The well-known Zuker algorithm is widely used for free energy minimization of RNA folding. The approach uses a "nearest neighbor" and thermodynamic parameters to predict the most stable secondary structure for a single RNA sequence by computing its minimal free energy. The algorithm time complexity is $\mathcal{O}(N^4)$, and its memory complexity is $\mathcal{O}(N^2)$, where N is the length of the sequence. The time complexity can be reduced to $\mathcal{O}(N^3)$ by limiting the length of the interior loop.

The algorithm is executed in two steps for a given single RNA sequence as input. First, it calculates the minimal free energy of an RNA sequence. Second, it performs a trace-back to recover a secondary structure with base pairs. The first step of computing energy matrices is crucial to improve the performance because it consumes more than 99% of total execution time.

The main recursion of Zuker's algorithm for all i, j with $1 \le i < j \le N$ is the following.

$$W(i,j)) = \begin{cases} W(i+1,j) & (1) \\ W(i,j-1) & (2) \\ V(i,j) & (3) \\ \min_{i<k<j} \{W(i,k) + W(k+1,j)\} & (4) \end{cases}$$

Below, we present the computation of V.

$$V(i,j)) = \begin{cases} eH(i,j) & (5) \\ V(i+1,j-1) + eS(i,j) & (6) \\ \min_{\substack{i \le i' \le j' \le j \\ 2 < i'-i+j-j' < d}} \{V(i',j') + eL(i,j,i',j')\} & (7) \\ \min_{i<k<j-1} \{W(i+1,k) + W(k+1,j-1)\} & (8) \end{cases}$$

where eH (hairpin loop), eS (stacking) and eL (internal loop) are the structure elements of energy contributions in the Zuker algorithm.

Listing 1 shows the affine loop nest for finding the minimums of the V and W energy matrices. Statements $s1$, $s2$, $s3$ are based on Expressions 3, 8, and 4, respectively. Statement $s4$ includes Expressions 5, 6, and 7. Statement $s5$ meets Expression 1 and 2.

Listing 1. Zuker's recurrence loop nest

```
for (i = N−1; i >= 0; i−−){
 for (j = i+1; j < N; j++) {
  for (k = i+1; k < j; k++){
   for (m=k+1; m <j; m++){
    if(k−i + j − m > 2 && k−i + j − m < 30)
     V[i][j] = MIN(V[k][m] + EL(i,j,k,m), V[i][j]);     // s1
   }
   W[i][j] = MIN ( MIN(W[i][k], W[k+1][j]), W[i][j]);     // s2
   if(k < j−1)
    V[i][j] = MIN(W[i+1][k] + W[k+1][j−1], V[i][j]);     //s3
  }
  V[i][j] = MIN( MIN (V[i+1][j−1] + ES(i,j), EH(i,j), V[i][j]);
                                                          // s4
  W[i][j] = MIN( MIN ( MIN ( W[i+1][j], W[i][j−1]), V[i][j]), W[i][j]);
                                                          // s5
 }
}
```

We apply the presented algorithm to Zuker's RNA folding code to get the following results.

Input: S = {s1, s2, s3,s4, s5}, V = {V, W, ES, EH}.

We calculate I and A.
I(s1) = i,j,k,m : [1,2,3,4], I(s2) = I(s3) = I(s4) = I(s5) = i,j,k : [1,2,3]

A = {**s1** => V:k,m; V:i,j; **s2**=>W:i,k; W:k+1,j; W:i,j;
s3 => W:i+1,k; W: k+1,j-1; V: i,j; **s4** => V:i+1,j-1, ES: i,j; EH: i,j; V: i,j
s5 => W:i+1,j; W:i,j-1; V:i,j; W: i,j; }.

Within set A, we found two vectors with lexicographically unsorted elements:
s2 => W:**k+1(3)**, **j(2)** → [3,2],
s3 => W:**k+1(3)**, **j-1(2)** → [2,3].

Addressing according to those vectors is not cache-efficient, i.e., it is a column-reading for those statements. So, we replace those array accesses with WT:j,k+1 and WT:j-1,k+1, respectively.

Next, we calculate V'={W} and prepare a transposed copy of W, WT. Statements $s2$ and $s5$ write the value of cell [i,j] to array W. We rewrite the value of this cell to WT, i.e. WT[j][i] = W[i][j], with the swapped indexes ($s2a$ and $s5a$) to maintain the current content of W in transposed matrix WT.

The modified code with the marked changes is presented below.

Listing 2. Zuker's recurrence loop nest

```
for (i = N−1; i >= 0; i−−){
 for (j = i+1; j < N; j++) {
  for (k = i+1; k < j; k++){
   for (m = k+1; m <j; m++){
    if(k−i + j − m > 2 && k−i + j − m < 30)
```

```
      V[i][j] = MIN(V[k][m] + EL(i,j,k,m), V[i][j]);     // s1
    }
    W[i][j] = MIN ( MIN(W[i][k], WT[j][k+1]), W[i][j]);    // s2
    WT[j][i] = W[i][j];                                      // s2a
    if (k < j-1)
       V[i][j] = MIN(W[i+1][k] + WT[j-1][k+1] , V[i][j]);   //s3
    }
    V[i][j] = MIN(MIN (V[i+1][j-1] + ES(i,j), EH(i,j), V[i][j]);
                                                              // s4
    W[i][j] = MIN(MIN (MIN (W[i+1][j], W[i][j-1]), V[i][j]), W[i][j]);
                                                              // s5
    WT[j][i] = W[i][j];                                      // s5a
  }
}
```

For the original loop nest, ISL returns the following schedules for each statement.

$s1[i,j,k,m] \rightarrow [-i+j,k,3+m] : i >= 0 \wedge j < N \wedge k > i \wedge m > k \wedge -29-i+j+k \le m \le -3-i+j+k \wedge m < j$

$s2[i,j,k] \rightarrow [-i+j,0,k] : i \ge 0 \wedge 2+i \le j < N \wedge i < k < j$

$s3[i,j,k] \rightarrow [-i+j,k,-i+j+k] : i >= 0 \wedge j < N \wedge i < k <= -2+j$

$s4[i,j] \rightarrow [-i+j,j] : 0 \le i \le -2+N \wedge i < j < N$

$s5[i,j] \rightarrow [-i+j,j] : 0 \le i \le -2+N \wedge i < j < N$

The first element of the output tuple of each relation above is the following $-i+j$. It corresponds to the well-known skewing transformation and it is de-facto diagonal scanning proposed by Li and co-authors in paper [4].

Then, we apply the ISL scheduler for the transformed code with transposed matrices and obtain the following dependence relations.

$s1[i,j,k,m] \rightarrow [-i+j,-j+k,3+m] : i \ge 0 \wedge j < N \wedge k > i \wedge m > k \wedge -29 - i+j+k \le m \le -3-i+j+k \wedge m < j$

$s2[i,j,k] \rightarrow [-i+j,0,k] : i \ge 0 \wedge 2+i \le j < N \wedge i < k < j$

$s2a[i,j,k] \rightarrow [-i+j,0,k] : i \ge 0 \wedge 2+i \le j < N generating \wedge i < k < j$

$s3[i,j,k] \rightarrow [-i+j,-j+k,-i+j+k] : i \ge 0 \wedge j < N \wedge i < k \le -2+j$

$s4[i,j] \rightarrow [-i+j,0] : 0 \le i \le -2+N \wedge i < j < N$

$s5[i,j] \rightarrow [-i+j,0] : 0 \le i \le -2+N \wedge i < j < N$

$s5a[i,j] \rightarrow [-i+j,0] : 0 \le i \le -2+N \wedge i < j < N$

By means of the comparison of the obtained sets of dependence relations, we conclude that the differences are the following: for the transformed code, instances of *s1* and *s3* are mapped to $[-i + j, j-k,...]$ instead of $[-i+j, k, ...]$, *s4* and *s5* are mapped to $[-i+j,0]$ instead of $[-i+j,j]$, *s2* has the same schedule, and *s2a*, *s5a* have the same schedule as *s2* and *s5*, respectively. We observe similar schedules calculated by ISL for original and cache-efficient codes.

The last step is automatic parallel code generation on the basis of the obtained ISL schedules. The target code is presented in Listing 3.

Listing 3. Target code generated by TRACO

```
for( c0 = 1; c0 < 2 * N - 2; c0 += 1)
#pragma omp parallel for
 for( c1 = c0/2 + 1; c1 <= min(N - 1, c0); c1 += 1) {
   register int t = N+c0-2*c1;
   register int r = N-c1-1;
   for( c4 = -c0 + c1; c4 < -1; c4 += 1) {
    for( c12 = max(t-c1+c4-28, t+c4+1); c12 < min(t, t-c1+c4-1); c12++)
     V[r][t] = MIN(V[(t+c4)][c12] + EL(r, t, t+c4, c12), V[r][t]);
     V[r][t] = MIN(W[t+1][t+c4] + W[t-1][t+c4)+1], V[r][t]);
    }
    for( c10 = N - c1; c10 < t; c10 += 1) {
     W[r][t] = MIN ( MIN(W[r][c10], W[t][c10+1]), W[r][t]);
     WT[t][r] = W[r][t];
    }
    V[r][t] = MIN(MIN (V[r+1][t-1] + ES(r,t), EH(r,t)), V[r][t]);
    W[r][t] = MIN( MIN(MIN ( W[r+1][t], W[r][t-1]), V[r][t]), W[r][t]);
    WT[t][r] = W[r][t];
 }
```

Table 1. Time of code execution (in seconds) and code speed-up

N	Original	Transpose & Skewing		Speed-up
	1 Thread	1 Thread	12 Threads	S = Original/TS(12)
1000	21.16	1.13	0.24	88.17
1500	102.06	3.52	0.64	159.47
2000	317.87	7.67	1.51	210.51
2500	773.00	14.46	2.87	269.34
3000	1595.98	24.11	5.16	309.11
3500	2946.11	37.31	7.75	380.13
4000	4923.23	54.99	11.83	416.15
4500	7819.65	76.66	16.61	470.74
5000	11474.01	104.37	21.4	536.17
6000	–	177.46	40.9	–
7000	–	279.18	60.18	–
8000	–	413.80	89.23	–
9000	–	581.35	126.45	–
10000	–	793.88	182.05	–

4   Experimental Study

We examined code performance on an Intel i7-8700 processor (3.2 GHz, 4.6 GHz in turbo, 6 cores, 12 threads, 12 MB Cache), 16 GB RAM and Ubuntu 18.4. Codes were compiled using the GCC version 7.3.0 with the O3 option.

The transpose algorithm implementation is available at the website https:// github.com/lshadown/dynamic-transposer. The TRACO compiler with sources and examples is accessible at the page traco.sourceforge.net.

Table 1 shows time and speed-up for various sequence lengths, N, from 1000 to 10000. We present time for the original code and the code generated by the presented approach (columns *Transpose & Skewing*) in serial and parallel flavours. The last column presents speed-up calculated as a ratio of original program time and transformed code time for 12 threads. It is worth nothing that achieved speed-up is super-linear, i.e., the value of speed-up is greater than the number of thread used (12). Such an achievement is possible due to significant increasing code locality by means of matrix transposition.

We did not measure original code execution time for the longest sequences because it takes more than three hours on the computer applied, whereas optimized code for sequences with ten thousand of nucleotides is computed in a few minutes.

Table 2 presents the execution time of the code generated by the presented approach and that of the related code of the Vienna RNA package [5] (2.4.11 version). Vienna is the well-known state-of-the-art bioinformatics package including Zuker's algorithm implementation for RNA folding with energy minimization. The code generated by the proposed approach computes sequences up to 5000 nucleotides in shorter or comparable time than that for Vienna code. The Viena RNA package is more efficient for longer sequences. However, it is worth nothing that our code is generated automatically without any boosting and can be adapted to other DP algorithms without any manual effort.

Summing up, we may conclude that the discussed results of the experimental study show that the presented approach can be successfully applied in practical solutions.

Table 2. Execution time (in seconds) of the Zuker RNA folding codes and the Vienna RNA package for 12 threads and different lengths of RNA strands. mRNAs acquired from the NCBI database.

Sequence	Length	Transpose & Skewing	ViennaRNA
MAPK1, trans. var. 1	5916	32.39	31.99
MAPK1, trans. var. 1	1514	0.67	1.25
MAP2K5, trans. var 2	2355	2.51	3.47
MAP2K7, trans. var. 1	3515	8.18	9.02
MAP2K6, trans. var. 2	13577	385.60	277.43
MAP3K2	10870	210.83	150.49
MAP4K3, trans. var 1	4335	13.20	15.13
MAP4K4, trans. var. 4	7183	61.10	51.44

5 Conclusion

In this paper, we presented an approach to automatic generation of optimized code for dynamic programming tasks. As an example, we chose Zuker's RNA folding algorithm. Original serial code is a fourfold-nested loop nest, which exposes irregular dependences. We improved its locality by means of an algorithm, which automatically extracts arrays to be transposed and then forms them and uses in a modified code. The approach was implemented in the C language and first generates the serial cache-efficient code of Zuker's algorithm. Then, that code is transformed by means of the TRACO optimizing compiler into parallel code preventing high locality of source code. TRACO uses the ISL library to find statement instance schedules to be applied to generate parallel code. For the discussed code, schedules extracted imply the usage for parallelization the skewing technique. Under experiments carried out on Intel i7 for twelve threads, we have observed the target code acceleration equal up to several hundred times.

In future work, we plan to extend the approach to three and more dimensional arrays with arbitrary affine expressions representing array indexes. We are going also to examine the performance of the approach for other computational biology tasks.

References

1. Bielecki, W., Palkowski, M.: A parallelizing and optimizing compiler - TRACO (2013). http://traco.sourceforge.net
2. Bondhugula, U., Hartono, A., Ramanujam, J., Sadayappan, P.: A practical automatic polyhedral parallelizer and locality optimizer. SIGPLAN Not. **43**(6), 101–113 (2008). http://pluto-compiler.sourceforge.net
3. Ganzha, M., Maciaszek, L.A., Paprzycki, M. (eds.): Proceedings of the 2019 Federated Conference on Computer Science and Information Systems, FedCSIS 2019, Leipzig, Germany, 1–4 September 2019, Annals of Computer Science and Information Systems, vol. 18 (2019). https://doi.org/10.15439/978-83-952357-8-8
4. Li, J., Ranka, S., Sahni, S.: Multicore and GPU algorithms for Nussinov RNA folding. BMC Bioinform. **15**(8), S1 (2014). https://doi.org/10.1186/1471-2105-15-S8-S1
5. Lorenz, R., et al.: Viennarna package 2.0. Algorithms Mol. Biol. **6**(1), 26 (2011)
6. Mullapudi, R.T., Bondhugula, U.: Tiling for dynamic scheduling. In: Rajopadhye, S., Verdoolaege, S. (eds.) Proceedings of the 4th International Workshop on Polyhedral Compilation Techniques, Vienna, Austria, January 2014
7. Palkowski, M., Bielecki, W.: Parallel tiled Nussinov RNA folding loop nest generated using both dependence graph transitive closure and loop skewing. BMC Bioinform. **18**(1), 290 (2017)
8. Palkowski, M., Bielecki, W.: Parallel tiled codes implementing the Smith-Waterman alignment algorithm for two and three sequences. J. Comput. Biol. **25**(10), 1106–1119 (2018). https://doi.org/10.1089/cmb.2018.0006
9. Verdoolaege, S.: Integer set library - manual. Tech. rep. www.kotnet.org/skimo//isl/manual.pdf (2011)
10. Wonnacott, D., Jin, T., Lake, A.: Automatic tiling of mostly-tileable loop nests. In: IMPACT 2015: 5th International Workshop on Polyhedral Compilation Techniques, Amsterdam, The Netherlands (2015)
11. Zhao, C., Sahni, S.: Cache and energy efficient algorithms for Nussinov's RNA folding. BMC Bioinform. **18**(15), 518 (2017)

Artificial Intelligence in Modeling and Simulation

Semantic Classifier Approach to Document Classification

Piotr Borkowski[(✉)] [iD], Krzysztof Ciesielski, and Mieczysław A. Kłopotek [iD]

Institute of Computer Science, Polish Academy of Sciences,
ul. Jana Kazimierza 5, Warszawa, Poland
{piotrb,kciesiel,klopotek}@ipipan.waw.pl
https://ipipan.waw.pl/

Abstract. We propose a new document classification method, bridging discrepancies (so-called semantic gap) between the training set and the application sets of textual data. We demonstrate its superiority over classical text classification approaches, including traditional classifier ensembles. The method consists of combining a document categorization technique with a single classifier or a classifier ensemble.

Keywords: Semantic gap · Semantic similarity · Document categorization · Document classification · Classifier ensembles

1 Introduction

The text document classification methods have been derived predominantly from corresponding data mining techniques that were designed to handle long input data records, like Naive Bayes, Wide-Margin Winnow and L-LDA. These methods are quite successful both in data mining and in text mining, though one important drawback occurs related to text mining. While in data mining the meaning and the value range of individual attributes of an object are relatively well defined, it is not the case in text mining anymore. The same content may be expressed in different ways, using different words (via synonyms, list of hyponyms) while the same word can express different things in different contexts. This would not be a big obstacle if not the fact that traditional techniques would require significantly larger bodies of training data, which makes an unbalanced sample much more likely. Not only because of the size of the data sample but also the heterogeneity of the data sources that need to be combined. It is even worse when the trained classifiers need to be applied to unseen data from a dataset that touches the same topic from the human point of view but is written in a completely different style from the computer point of view. This gives rise to the so-called *semantic gap*, that is when the training and application data sets are semantically similar, their syntactical and bag-of-words view differ. In such a case understanding the semantics of documents would be needed, which is unavailable for traditional data mining techniques.

In this paper, we propose two new document classification methods: SemCla (*Semantic Classifier*) and SemCom (*Committee with Semantic Categorizer*), bridging the semantic gap between the training set and the application sets of textual data. The

ⓒ Springer Nature Switzerland AG 2020
L. Rutkowski et al. (Eds.): ICAISC 2020, LNAI 12415, pp. 657–667, 2020.
https://doi.org/10.1007/978-3-030-61401-0_61

methods consist of combining an unsupervised *document categorization technique* with a single classifier or a classifier ensemble. Via this component, the traditional notion of document similarity (based on angles between vectors in term space) is amended to include the concept of *semantic similarity*. The notion of semantic similarity as used in this paper was described in [3,5]. Both methods introduced in the paper are based on our SemCat (Semantic Categorizer) algorithm, which has also been introduced in [3,5].

In Sect. 2 we define the problem of document categorization and semantic classification and recall the work done on the subject by other researchers. In Sect. 3 we describe one of the categorization methodologies, SemCat, in more detail. Subsequently, we show in Sect. 4, how the SemCat can be used in the classical task of classification.

In Sect. 5 we explain the setup of experiments we performed to show the usefulness of SemCla and SemCom algorithms in classification tasks. In subsequent Sect. 6 showing the results of these experiments, we demonstrate the superiority of the semantic classification methods (SemCom and SemCla) over classical text classification approaches, including traditional classifier ensembles for text classification tasks (Sect. 6.1) as well as in cases when the so-called semantic gap occurs (Sect. 6.2).

Section 7 summarizes achieved results and outlines future research directions.

1.1 Our Contribution

Our contribution in this paper consists in:

- constructing a new supervised classifier (SemCla) based on unsupervised semantic document categorizator (SemCat),
- demonstrating the feasibility of the new classifier for bridging the semantic gap between test and training set of data,
- designing a heterogeneous committee (SemCom) that combines classical classifiers and the semantic classifier.

The novelty of the proposed algorithms encompasses the following aspects:

- SemCat algorithm does not require a specially prepared training set. If the right taxonomy is available, SemCat can be used for different languages and domains. Because of using taxonomy it can be quickly updated to have a version that is based on the most current concepts (e.g. new concepts in the structure like Wikipedia are being added on a regular basis).
- SemCat works well for a demanding Polish language. The projection algorithm enables to obtain the results of categorization for any subset of taxonomy. In this way, one can create a classifier that returns results for a given set of documents. This way of constructing new classifiers is fast and there is no need to construct relevant learning sets.
- SemCla is based on SemCat algorithm, hence it helps to overcome the problem of the semantic gap because it is based on document semantics.
- SemCla works differently from the "bag of words" approach, which is why it complements classical methods well in standard applications. This means that it can be used in conjunction with these methods to improve the classification capability of their committee.

2   Previous Work

The task of *categorization* is to assign one or more labels (categories) to a document, or a group of documents (cluster labeling). It finds multiple practical applications, especially for assisting in text retrieval tasks: in web page classification, e-mail and memo organization, expanding queries with new terms, expanding/improving ontologies, etc. (We are aware that terms "classification" and "categorization" are not very precise and are often confused [6]. An alternative word for "categorization" could be "labeling".)

The categorization task can be viewed formally as a special case of classification [16,17], but with a couple of differences. (1) The number of categories significantly exceeds the number of classes in a typical classification task. (2) Categories may be flat and disjoint, but they may form a tree or even a hierarchy (acyclic graph). (3) More than one category may be assigned to a single document. Therefore typical classification methods do not fit well to the task of categorization. Diverse methods have been proposed to attack the problem of categorization. Some of them are based on clustering. The most popular representatives of this brand of approaches are Nonnegative Matrix Factorization (NMF), Latent Semantic Analysis (LSA), Probabilistic LSA (PLSA), and Finite Mixture of Multidimensional Bernoulli Distributions described in [18]. Other map the document contents to semantic resources, in particular to Wikipedia ($\mathfrak{W}$). This approach was exploited in *Wikipedia Miner Project* developed at the University of Waikato in Hamilton, New Zealand [8,10,11]. It uses $\mathfrak{W}$ topics as categories. The basic idea was key phrase indexing. For terms from $\mathfrak{W}$ their "keyphraseness" [9] that is share of occurrences in $\mathfrak{W}$ links is computed. The terms are searched in a document to be categorized. Terms with multiple meanings are disambiguated (via a trained classifier) by choosing the meaning most close to the document topic. For training purposes, documents annotated with keyphrases are assigned categories. Then a classifier is trained.

In this paper, we exploit the unsupervised categorization method, SemCat, introduced in [3,5]. Unlike Wikipedia Miner, no classifiers are used, so no training corpora are needed. It is not based on $\mathfrak{W}$ links. Instead the category graph of $\mathfrak{W}$ is exploited. A novelty is also the usage of more challenging Polish language [20]. Furthermore, we develop a classification method SemCla suitable to apply for data with the semantic gap.

The problem of the "semantic gap" is understood in literature in many ways. We focus on the aspect encountered in text retrieval where data come for different domains. The next paragraphs give a brief overview of the approaches that have been proposed.

The article [15] shows a review of the *cross-domain text categorization* problem. Unlike the classical case, the training and the test data originates from different distributions or domains. This is very common in practical tasks because we often do not have a suitable data set of labeled documents. Often we have a topically related corpus, but presenting the same (or semantically similar) information in a different way, e.g. using different vocabulary. Many algorithms have been developed or adapted for cross-domain text classification, there are conventional algorithms: Rocchio's Algorithm, Decision Trees like: CART, ID3, C4.5; Naive Bayes classifier, KNN, Support Vector Machines (SVM); and some novel cross-domain classification algorithms: Expectation-Maximization Algorithm, CFC Algorithm, Probabilistic Latent Semantic

Analysis (PLSA), Latent Dirichlet Allocation (LDA), Co-cluster based Classification Algorithm [19].

Paper [12] gives a general overview of the problem of the semantic gap in information retrieval. Authors focus on two separate tasks: text and multimedia mining/image retrieval. The semantic gap in text retrieval is defined as the usage of different words (synonyms, hypernyms, hyponyms) to describe the same object. In the part about text retrieval authors concentrate on reorganizing search results by using the post-retrieval clustering system. They work on search results ("snippets") and enhance them by adding so called *topics*. The topic is a set of words (they have similar meaning) that was as an outcome of PLSA or LDA on some external data collection. After adding a topic to the snippet they carry out clustering or labeling. In [13] authors propose a way to improve categorization by adding semantic knowledge from Wikitology (knowledge repository based on 𝔚). They used various text representation and text enrichment techniques and used SVM to learn a model of classification. In [4] PLSA related ideas are used for document modeling via combining semantic resources and statistically extracted topics. Another approach to categorization, on which we base our research, is described in [3,5]. We recall it in more detail in the next section.

3   Taxonomy-Based Semantic Categorization Method SemCat

The taxonomy-based categorization method SemCat was described in detail in [3,5]. Below we present only its brief summary.

3.1   Outline of the Algorithm

A taxonomy of categories (a directed acyclic graph with one root category) like Wikipedia (𝔚) category graph or *Medical Subject Headings* (MeSH) ontology[1] is assumed. The taxonomy has to be connected to a set of concepts as follows: every concept is linked to one or more categories. Every category and concept is tagged with a string label. Strings connected with categories are used as an outcome for the user. And those attached to concepts are used for mapping a text of a document into the set of concepts.

For the experimental design, we used 𝔚 category graph with the concept set of 𝔚 pages. Tags for 𝔚 categories were their original string names. The set of string tags connected with a single 𝔚 page consists of the lemmatized page name and all names of disambiguation pages that link to that page. To categorize a document, we remove stop words and very rare/frequent words, lemmatize, find phrases and calculate normalized *tfidf* weights for terms and phrases. Calculation of a standard *term frequency inverse document frequency* is based on word frequencies from the collection of all 𝔚 pages. Then we map document terms and phrases into a set of concepts. In the case of homonyms, we disambiguate the concept assignment: we select the concept that is the nearest by similarity measure defined by Eqs. (1) and (2) (see Sect. 3.2) to the set of concepts that was mapped in an unambiguous way.

When every term in the document is assigned to a proper concept (𝔚 page), then all concepts are mapped to 𝔚 categories. In this way, usually one term maps to more

---

[1] https://www.nlm.nih.gov/mesh/.

than one category. We transfer the weight associated with that term proportionally to all its categories. The sum of weights assigned to the categories equals to the sum of *tfidf* for terms. The outcome of that procedure is a ranked list of categories with weights. In the last step we can transform the weighted ranking and/or choose top-N categories out of it.

3.2 Similarity Measures

The semantic similarity measures used below have been introduced in [3,5]. Let us only recall the formulas.

For a category k let $IC(k) = 1 - log(1 + s_k)/log(1 + N)$, where s_k is the number of taxonomy concepts in the category k and all its subcategories, and N is the total number of taxonomy concepts.

For two given categories k_1 and k_2 let $MSCAIC(k_1, k_2) = \max\{IC(k) : k \in CA(k_1, k_2)\}$ where $CA(k_1, k_2)$ is the set of super-categories for both categories k_1 and k_2. Then define $MSCA(k_1, k_2) = \{k : IC(k) = MSCAIC(k_1, k_2)\}$. Define Lin and Pirro-Seco similarity:

$$sim_{\text{Lin}}(k_1, k_2) = \frac{2 \cdot MSCAIC(k_1, k_2)}{IC(k_1) + IC(k_2)} \tag{1}$$

$$sim_{\text{PirroSeco}}(k_1, k_2) = \frac{1}{3}\left(3 \cdot MSCAIC(k_1, k_2) - IC(k_1) - IC(k_2) + 2\right) \tag{2}$$

The similarity between pages p_i and p_j is computed by aggregation of similarity between each pair of categories (k_i, k_j) so that p_i belongs to the category k_i and p_j to k_j:

$$sim_{\text{PAGE}}(p_i, p_j) = max\{sim_{\text{CAT}}(k_i, k_j) : p_i \in k_i \wedge p_j \in k_j\} \tag{3}$$

4 Application to Classification Task

To demonstrate the value of semantic information for classification purposes, we exploited SemCat as an ingredient (to a classifier ensemble) in the classical classification algorithms and their committees, SemCom, as well as a stand-alone classifier SemCla.

In this section, we introduce SemCla and SemCom. The Reader is warmly recommended to refer to literature on commonly known classification algorithms we used in our experiments, that is Naive Bayes [1], Wide-Margin Winnow [2,7], Labeled LDA (L-LDA) [14], as well as the committees of classifiers (bagging type ensembles) built upon Naive Bayes classifier and Wide-Margin Winnow.

4.1 Semantic Classification

Below we present a description of a new *semantic classifier* that we call SemCla. It is based on a category representation of a document produced by SemCat (see Sect. 3.1), which is used in combination with semantic measures (see Sect. 3.2).

Outline of the Algorithm. Recall that SemCat uses words and phrases from the document to produce a list of categories with weights. This representation of a document can be considered as a vector of weights for all $\mathfrak{W}$ categories. Therefore we call it a *vector of categories*. We use it to calculate cosine product. We found out that the algorithm performs better when for each category from the vector of categories we add a super-category of it (according to $\mathfrak{W}$ hierarchy) with weight equal the initial weight multiplied by a constant α (we used the value $\alpha = 0.33$). Thus we obtain the *extended category vector*. The semantic classification is performed in the way described below.

1. documents from training and test sets are categorized to obtain category vectors that represent their content,
2. category vectors for all documents are changed into extended category vectors (for constant α),
3. we classify a new document (represented by its extended category vector) by finding the nearest group (in the sense of the cosine product) in the training set.

4.2 Ensemble of Classifiers

The experimental setting was also based on the ensemble of classifiers. For each document, the classification process is carried out by every classifier in the ensemble (it may also be a classifier of the same type, but trained on a different learning sample). Then the results of all classifiers are aggregated as the final ensemble classifier. In the existing implementation this can be done in three ways: (a) each classifier has one vote – category with the highest number of votes is selected; (b) votes counting additionally takes into account the weights of classification results (this option requires that all classifiers are of the same type); (c) ranks of the elements returned by the classifier are aggregated instead of raw votes or weights. In the case when two (or more) categories received the same number of votes, the result is selected at random from among the winning categories. The SemCom classifier is constructed as an ensemble of one SemCat and a number of classical classifiers.

5   Experimental Setup

5.1   Performed Experiments

We performed two types of experiments. The first experiment aimed at demonstrating that forming a semantic classifier from a semantic categorizer improves the classification correctness in *classic classification task* (Table 1). The second experiment was designed to show that a semantic categorizer is capable of *bridging the semantic gap* between the training data and the test data (Table 2).

5.2   Benchmark Data Sets

For the experimental purpose, we used two different benchmark data sets. We needed different datasets because of the distinct nature of the investigated problems.

Benchmark Used for Classification Comparison – DMOZ Dataset

The benchmark data set was based on Polish subdirectory of DMOZ taxonomy (Open Directory Project) http://dmoztools.net/. It contains 1121 text files of Polish web pages just with HTML tags removed. Selected documents belong to 15 directories that map into $\mathfrak{W}$ categories. They are astronomy, biology, economics, philosophy, physics, graphics, history, linguistics, mathematics, education, politics, law, religious studies, sociology, technology. None of these categories is a subcategory of another one in the $\mathfrak{W}$ taxonomy. We omitted a few cases of multi-labeled documents.

Benchmark Containing Data with Semantic Gap

The second benchmark was made of documents downloaded from the various news page. It consists of training and evaluation part, they come from various domains. We used separate collections to achieve different wordings in each of them. The training set consists of news from the popular science portal kopalniawiedzy.pl merged with documents from one directory from forsal.pl (the domain about finance and economy). In this way, a collection of documents belonging to 7 classes was created, their labels are given in bold. Below we show a more detailed description of the training set.

- documents from kopalniawiedzy.pl: **astronomy-physics** $N = 311$; **humanities** $N = 244$; **life science** $N = 3222$; **medicine** $N = 3037$; **psychology** $N = 1758$; **technology** $N = 6145$;
- documents from forsal.pl from the directory *Giełda* (Stock exchange): **business** $N = 1986$.

For evaluation we downloaded directories from www.rynekzdrowia.pl (containing medical news – labeled as **medicine**) and merged it with economical documents from www.forsal.pl and www.bankier.pl (market, finances, business – labeled as **business**). The following datasets were used for evaluation:

- directories from www.rynekzdrowia.pl: Ginekologia (Gynecology): **medicine** $N = 1034$; Kardiologia (Cardiology): **medicine** $N = 239$; Onkologia (Oncology): **medicine** $N = 1195$,
- directories from www.forsal.pl: Waluty (Currencies): **business** $N = 2161$; Finanse (Finances): **business** $N = 1991$,
- documents from www.bankier.pl: **business** $N = 978$.

5.3   Efficiency Measures

To assess the efficiency of the studied algorithms we use two different measures. The first one is commonly used standard *accuracy* measure: $acc_{0-1}(x,y) = \mathbf{1}_x(y)$, the second one is modified accuracy based on similarity measure Lin (Eq. (1) in Sect. 3.2). The difference is in using Lin measure (based on $\mathfrak{W}$ taxonomy) instead of indicator function: $acc_{Lin}(x,y) = sim_{Lin}(x,y)$. The motivation for using the latter measure is that standard accuracy does not take into account the dependence between categories. In case when we make a wrong prediction we would like to know how much the predicted category is different from the real one.

5.4 Classical Classification Task

The first part of the experimental work concerned the comparison of various methods of text classification. We proceeded on documents from DMOZ corpus with a fixed set of labels described in Sect. 5.2. Documents were divided into separate groups based on their text length measured by the number of characters (C): *short* ($1000 \leq C < 2000$), *medium* ($2000 \leq C < 10,000$), *long* ($10,000 \leq C$). Files shorter than 1000 characters were not processed. The results for various classification methods are presented in Table 1. They were divided by a file size and efficiency measure. Methods based on the categorization algorithm return a list of weighted $\mathfrak{W}$ categories. Therefore we transformed the outcome categories into the target set of 15 categories and took only one category with the highest weight. Categorization was based on a selection of 10 words (only nouns)/phrases with the highest *tfidf* from the document. The experiments were performed for different values of parameters, but other settings gave worse results. All of these methods took only nouns from the document.

We present results for individual classifiers followed by those of an ensemble of classifiers (heterogeneous committees).

5.5 Classification for Data with the Semantic Gap

The second experiment focuses on the problem of the semantic gap which is observed in the classification of data from different domains. For such data often two documents express the same concepts, but as they use different wording (because of existing of synonyms, hypernyms, hyponyms), the conventional classification/clustering algorithms, based on standard bag-of-words approach, do not work well. Such classifiers often do not recognize different linguistic representations for test and training set. Some works relating to the problem were presented in Sect. 2. Our approach thoroughly presented above, is different from them. There are other linguistic phenomena such as ellipsis, paraphrase, and others. We focus on synonyms, hypernyms, hyponyms because of $\mathfrak{W}$ structure on which our algorithm is based. We deal with hyper-/hyponyms relation because of $\mathfrak{W}$ category graph structure we operate on. This graph is built on these kinds of relations. With synonym relation, we cope during the phase of mapping words/phrases from the text into $\mathfrak{W}$ pages. The string set attached to a single $\mathfrak{W}$ page contains the page title and all its synonyms. They are extracted from all names of disambiguation pages that point to this particular page. In Table 2 we present SemCla, ensembles and the heterogeneous committee with semantic classifier.

6 Results

6.1 Classical Task

As can be seen in Table 1, SemCla performs not worse than the baseline algorithms even though the "training" consists only in storing the group/class representative, hence it is quick. Though a committee of traditional classifiers can outperform SemCla, a committee engaging a SemCla yields the best results (see the last two lines).

Table 1. The average values and standard deviations (given in brackets) of accuracy measure: Lin and standard accuracy for DMOZ dataset. The training set was sampled from Wikipedia.

	acc_{Lin}				acc_{0-1}			
	short	medium	long	all	short	medium	long	all
SemCat	0,496	0,598	0,681	0,58	0,423	0,535	0,602	0,513
(1 run)	(0,465)	(0,459)	(0,426)	(0,46)	(0,495)	(0,499)	(0,492)	(0,5)
Various classifiers – means of 25 runs								
W-M Winnow	0,565	0,68	0,752	0,654	0,5	0,624	0,699	0,599
	(0,025)	(0,028)	(0,034)	(0,023)	(0,025)	(0,03)	(0,035)	(0,024)
Bayes	0,459	0,548	0,679	0,533	0,373	0,473	0,605	0,458
	(0,03)	(0,024)	(0,026)	(0,023)	(0,045)	(0,034)	(0,032)	(0,033)
L-LDA	0,475	0,573	0,707	0,562	0,424	0,524	0,673	0,515
	(0,029)	(0,023)	(0,026)	(0,021)	(0,034)	(0,025)	(0,026)	(0,022)
SemCla	0,559	0,616	0,719	0,61	0,499	0,559	0,68	0,552
	(0,015)	(0,014)	(0,014)	(0,012)	(0,018)	(0,013)	(0,017)	(0,011)
25 × (B,W)	0,599	0,707	0,79	0,69	0,529	0,662	0,742	0,638
	(0,453)	(0,427)	(0,377)	(0,432)	(0,5)	(0,473)	(0,439)	(0,481)
25 × (B,W,SCla)	**0,626**	**0,73**	**0,824**	**0,715**	**0,588**	**0,691**	**0,797**	**0,677**
	(0,461)	(0,417)	(0,363)	(0,427)	(0,493)	(0,463)	(0,404)	(0,468)

It is also worth stressing the fact that however SemCla (contrary to SemCat) is supervised, it can also be used in the unsupervised version. For such a setting, instead of using unobservable document labels as training classes , one can use document clusters, where clustering is also based on the semantic categorization (SemCat algorithm) and applies semantic similarity measures defined in Sect. 3.2. We are going to investigate this direction more deeply in the future, since it has a big advantage in cases where document labels are unavailable and training set cannot be created (e.g. collections of web pages).

6.2 Semantic Gap

It can be seen in Table 2 (Columns 1–3) that the usage of terms alone gives poor results when the semantic gap occurs. This means actually that our SemCla algorithm uses a much deeper insight into the document content than just a category label assignment.

Further, committees of traditional classifiers (Column 5) improve over single classifiers but committees engaging the semantic classifier (Column 6) or consisting of multiple semantic classifiers alone (Column 4) lead to much better results (a bag of categories instead of a bag of words).

Table 2. The average values and standard deviations (given in brackets) of accuracy measure for data with a semantic gap. Columns 1–3 are the average of 25 repetitions for the studied sets. Columns 4–6 are the result of a single classification by various classifier committees.

	Means of 25 runs			Committees		
	B	W	SemCla	25 × SemCla	25 × (B,W)	25 × (B,W,SemCla)
Bankier (Business Biznes)	0,701	0,611	0,841	0,847	0,715	0,801
	(0,04)	(0,051)	(0,012)	(0,36)	(0,452)	(0,4)
Forsal (Currencies)	0,987	0,924	0,994	0,995	0,99	0,998
	(0,006)	(0,032)	(0,001)	(0,073)	(0,098)	(0,046)
Forsal (Finances)	0,959	0,925	0,983	0,982	0,963	0,982
	(0,012)	(0,022)	(0,003)	(0,133)	(0,189)	(0,133)
Gynecology	0,617	0,581	0,801	0,813	0,723	0,809
	(0,082)	(0,108)	(0,049)	(0,39)	(0,448)	(0,394)
Cardiology	0,916	0,891	0,942	0,938	0,951	0,969
	(0,025)	(0,046)	(0,009)	(0,241)	(0,217)	(0,174)
Oncology	0,84	0,856	0,883	0,884	0,894	0,935
	(0,026)	(0,04)	(0,016)	(0,32)	(0,308)	(0,247)

7 Conclusions

In this paper, we demonstrated the value of the semantic approach to the task of document classification. In particular, we show here that an unsupervised approach to the classification is possible when using the semantic approach. This may be considered as an interesting result by itself. Acknowledgedly, the semantic classifier we introduce does not perform as well as ensembles of traditional classifiers but apparently, an inclusion of a semantic categorizer into such an ensemble is capable of significant improvement of its performance in classic classification tasks.

However, the semantic classifier turns out to be superior to classical approaches to classification in case of the semantic gap between the training data and the data for which the classifier is to be applied. This fact opens up new horizons for application of machine learning methods in the classification of documents in cases e.g. of mergers between various corporations where the local culture leads usually to the development of specific languages different between the firms.

References

1. Aas, K., Eikvil, L.: Text categorisation: a survey. Report No. 941, June 1999
2. Bekkerman, R.: Automatic categorization of email into folders: benchmark experiments on enron and SRI corpora. Tech. rep, UMass CIIR (2004)
3. Borkowski, P.: Methods of semantic categorization in the task of text document analysis. Ph.D. thesis, Institute of Computer Science of Polish Academy of Sciences, Warsaw (2019) (in Polish)

4. Chemudugunta, C., Holloway, A., Smyth, P., Steyvers, M.: Modeling documents by combining semantic concepts with unsupervised statistical learning. In: Sheth, A., et al. (eds.) ISWC 2008. LNCS, vol. 5318, pp. 229–244. Springer, Heidelberg (2008). https://doi.org/10.1007/978-3-540-88564-1_15

5. Ciesielski, K., Borkowski, P., Kłopotek, M.A., Trojanowski, K., Wysocki, K.: Wikipedia-based document categorization. In: Bouvry, P., Kłopotek, M.A., Leprévost, F., Marciniak, M., Mykowiecka, A., Rybiński, H. (eds.) SIIS 2011. LNCS, vol. 7053, pp. 265–278. Springer, Heidelberg (2012). https://doi.org/10.1007/978-3-642-25261-7_21

6. Jacob, E.: Classification and categorization: a difference that makes a difference. Libr. Trends **52**, 515–540 (2004)

7. Littlestone, N.: Learning quickly when irrelevant attributes abound: a new linear-threshold algorithm. Mach. Learn. **2**, 285–318 (1988)

8. Medelyan, O., Witten, I.H., Milne, D.: Topic indexing with wikipedia. In: Proceedings of the First AAAI Workshop on Wikipedia and Artificial Intelligence (WIKIAI 2008) (2008)

9. Mihalcea, R., Csomai, A.: Wikify!: linking documents to encyclopedic knowledge. In: Proceedings of CIKM 2007, Lisbon, Portugal, pp. 233–242. ACM (2007)

10. Milne, D., Witten, I.H.: An open-source toolkit for mining wikipedia. Artif. Intell. **194**, 222–239 (2013)

11. Milne, D.N., Witten, I.H.: Learning to link with wikipedia. In: Proceedings of CIKM 2008, pp. 509–518. ACM (2008)

12. Nguyen, C.T.: Bridging semantic gaps in information retrieval: context-based approaches. In: ACM VLDB 2010 (2010)

13. Rafi, M., Hassan, S., Shaikh, M.S.: Content-based text categorization using wikitology. CoRR abs/1208.3623 (2012)

14. Ramage, D., Hall, D., Nallapati, R., Manning, C.D.: Labeled LDA: a supervised topic model for credit attribution in multi-labeled corpora. In: Proceedings of the 2009 Conference on EMNLP: Volume 1, EMNLP 2009, pp. 248–256. Association for Computational Linguistics (2009)

15. Ramakrishna Murty, M., Murthy, J., Prasad Reddy, P., Satapathy, S.: A survey of cross-domain text categorization techniques. In: RAIT 2012, pp. 499–504. IEEE (2012)

16. Sebastiani, F.: Machine learning in automated text categorization. ACM Comp. Surv. **34**(1), 1–47 (2002)

17. Sebastiani, F.: Text categorization. In: Text Mining and its Applications to Intelligence, CRM and Knowledge Management, pp. 109–129. WIT Press (2005)

18. Seppänen, J.K., Bingham, E., Mannila, H.: A simple algorithm for topic identification in 0–1 data. In: Lavrač, N., Gamberger, D., Todorovski, L., Blockeel, H. (eds.) PKDD 2003. LNCS (LNAI), vol. 2838, pp. 423–434. Springer, Heidelberg (2003). https://doi.org/10.1007/978-3-540-39804-2_38

19. Wang, P., Domeniconi, C., Hu, J.: Using wikipedia for co-clustering based cross-domain text classification. In: ICDM 2008, pp. 1085–1090. IEEE (2008)

20. Wróblewska, A., Sydow, M.: DEBORA: dependency-based method for extracting entity-relationship triples from open-domain texts in Polish. In: Chen, L., Felfernig, A., Liu, J., Raś, Z.W. (eds.) ISMIS 2012. LNCS (LNAI), vol. 7661, pp. 155–161. Springer, Heidelberg (2012). https://doi.org/10.1007/978-3-642-34624-8_19

A Parallel and Distributed Topological Approach to 3D IC Optimal Layout Design

Katarzyna Grzesiak-Kopeć[(✉)] [iD] and Maciej Ogorzałek [iD]

Department of Information Technologies, Jagiellonian University in Kraków, Kraków, Poland
katarzyna.grzesiak-kopec@uj.edu.pl

Abstract. The task of 3D ICs layout design involves the assembly of millions of components taking into account many different requirements and constraints such as topological, wiring or manufacturability ones. It is a NP-hard problem that requires new non-deterministic and heuristic algorithms. Considering the time complexity, the commonly applied Fiduccia-Mattheyses partitioning algorithm is superior to any other local search method. Nevertheless, it can often miss to reach a quasi-optimal solution in 3D spaces. The presented approach uses an original 3D layout graph partitioning heuristics implemented with use of the extremal optimization method. The goal is to minimize the total wire-length in the chip. In order to improve the time complexity a parallel and distributed Java implementation is applied. Inside one Java Virtual Machine separate optimization algorithms are executed by independent threads. The work may also be shared among different machines by means of The Java Remote Method Invocation system.

Keywords: 3D floorplanning · Extremal optimization · Layout hypergraph · Partitioning

1 Introduction

Optimal layout design is one of the main engineering design tasks. The search space is composed of: (1) design components and their topological connections and (2) design objectives and constraints. Usually, this space is too large to perform an effective deterministic search procedure and some heuristic algorithms are applied to obtain a globally near-optimal solution. In the year 2017, the transistor count (a number of transistors on an integrated circuit (IC)) exceeded 19 billions! [19]. Hence, the physical arrangement of chip components comprises a myriad of conditions.

3D ICs design definitely improves circuit blocks packing density and dramatically decreases the total interconnect wire length. Along with the interconnect wire length reduction the power consumption is decreased as well. The third dimension allows heterogeneous technology integration such as digital and analog. Different components can be manufactured separately according to their technology and then stack together on a single chip. And last but not least, 3D design not only gives a smaller footprint but the total volume minimization, which is very suitable for commonly used mobile devices [6]. There are two major groups of 3D integration technologies: integration using

© Springer Nature Switzerland AG 2020
L. Rutkowski et al. (Eds.): ICAISC 2020, LNAI 12415, pp. 668–678, 2020.
https://doi.org/10.1007/978-3-030-61401-0_62

chip stacking and Through Silicon Vias (TSVs), and native 3D integration. The latter approach is still in its infancy. Despite the abundance of electronic design automation tools for 2D integration, there is still a great need for the specific 3D tools, methods and flows to support the growth of the 3D IC market. Most available software packages are extensions of those used for planar (2D) design [5].

The proposed native 3D layout design approach introduces three separate design representation layers, namely the semantic layer, the presentation layer and the optimization control one. Possible solutions are generated with use of a simple shape grammar supervised by an intelligent derivation controller. The shape grammar is defined by the designer, who also provides a specific design knowledge in a form of predicates. The predicates are fed into the generation and optimization procedures. The total wire-length of a generated result may be further optimized adopting a knowledge intensive 3D ICs layout hypergraph representation described in [9], together with the elaborated neighborhood optimization heuristics presented in [10].

This article mainly deals with the total wire-length minimization. The main novel contribution is the *volume optimization* procedure for eliminating gaps/empty spaces in the generated 3D structure. The 3-step intelligent wire-length optimization approach is illustrated by the example of application to the MCNC benchmark circuits (MCNC) [18] using a parallel and distributed Java implementation. First, the knowledge intensive 3D ICs layout hypergraph representation together with the elaborated neighborhood optimization heuristics are introduced. Then, the wire-length extremal optimization is described. After that, the procedure of the volume optimization together with the parallel and distributed implementation are explained. Finally, the proposed wire-length optimization heuristics is applied to the MCNC set of benchmark circuits and the experimental results are reported.

2 Related Work

The today's 3D ICs technology still has various limitations such as a layer-like structure, where a number of device layers is restricted and the inter-layer height is fixed. Still, a quasi-3D placement problem is much more complex than a true-2D one. Generally, the placement problem is known to be NP-hard [15]. Adding an extra dimension to the solution space definitely increases the difficulty of the circuit design task in many aspects. When taking into account a placement problem with n components and k layers, a 2D solution may be divided into $n^{(k-1)}/(k-1)!$ different k-layer 3D floorplans [16]. Common techniques for global placements are: partitioning-based algorithms, analytic techniques and stochastic algorithms [13, 14]. Recursive partitioning are constructive techniques with average CPU requirements and versatility. The netlist and the layout are recursively divided into smaller sets/problems according to a cut-based cost function until the parts are small enough to be solved optimally. Analytic techniques, such as quadratic placement and force-directed placement, are constructive ones with relatively low CPU requirements and average versatility. They use an objective quadratic or otherwise non-convex function, that can be minimized/maximized via mathematical analysis. Stochastic algorithms introduce a random factor into the cost function optimization procedure. The best known stochastic placement algorithm is simulated annealing (SA). SA is an iterative approach with high CPU requirements where not much memory but a long execution time is needed to reach the desired solution. A generated initial placement is perturbed until the annealing process reaches an equilibrium state or the algorithm stops after a prescribed number of iterations.

Today's global placement algorithms model wire length with mathematical functions and use numerical methods to optimize them [14]. The components actual dimensions are initially ignored in order to find a seed placement. After that, they are gradually introduced into the optimization procedure to prevent unbalanced densities and routing congestion. The most popular approaches are based on analytic techniques and nonlinear optimization.

3   Intelligent Wire-Length Optimization

Aside from 3D technological hurdles, the interconnect wire-length minimization is one of the crucial circuit design requirements. We propose a 3-step optimization approach (see Fig. 1) where the only input of the task is a netlist given in a YAL file format. A netlist description defines the connectivity of an electronic circuit together with the parameters (like dimensions and pins) of the devices. In the first step, a YAL file is parsed into a layout hypergraph, which is a knowledge intensive representation of a netlist structure and its components [9]. In the second step, a topological partitioning procedure using the extremal optimization is applied to the layout hypergraph in order to find a special arrangement of components. Finally, in the third step, a parallel distributed volume optimization is performed by squeezing the intermediate layout solution. The relative positions of the components are preserved while the gaps and empty spaces are removed.

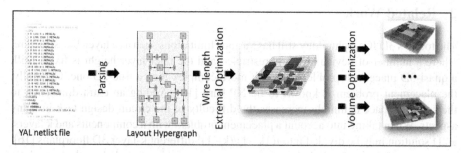

Fig. 1. The 3-step intelligent wire-length optimization approach.

3.1   Transforming Netlist into a Layout Hypergraph

In electronic design, a netlist is a text description of the electronic circuit connectivity. It consists of several related lists: a list of terminals (pins), a list of instances (components) and a list of signals connected to terminals (connections). It may also contain some attribute information. The connectivity information from a netlist may be formally represented in the form of a graph with appropriate semantic mappings. Graphs are data structures especially useful to represent different relational issues in a variety of systems (such as electric circuits, traffic, chemical processes or social networks). In the basic definition a graph depict only binary relations but its generalization, called a hypergraph, effectively abolish this limitation.

3.2 Wire-Length Extremal Optimization

In the context of IC design, a hypergraph representation is applied to solve the wire-length minimization task. The commonly implemented recursive partitioning algorithm splits netlists into parts, just like in the case of 2D floorplans, using only a single dimension [1]. Unfortunately, the approach with a dimension limiting to the k-way partitioning often fails to find a near optimal solution in 3D. Hence, the 3D topological partitioning of the layout hypergraph has been proposed [10]. Instead of striving for the minimal and balanced cut of the graph, a topology-oriented neighborhood grouping is performed. Bearing in mind the grid-like chip topology, the diamond-shaped von Neumann neighborhood is considered. The Manhattan distance is used to measure the distance between two cells in the IC grid. The shorter adjacent component wire connections are achieved, the better total wire-length solution is obtained. Adopting the building block hypothesis, where the optimal global solution is the sum of the optimal local neighborhoods, entails the selection of the Extremal Optimization (EO) implementation [2]. The search space is limited by a predefined maximal chip volume. Neglecting original dimensions, the chip components are placed in this cuboid in such a way that each cell is either occupied by a component or empty. Empty cells that are not located in the boundary of the chip are not welcome and, if possible, should be eliminated from the final solution. Components designate the solution features and they are evaluated on the basis of the range of their neighborhoods (for details see [11]).

3.3 Volume Optimization

The τ-EO optimal topological partitioning of the layout hypergraphs generates solutions in a predefined 3D grid cuboid and neglects the actual dimensions of the modules. In such an approach some cells in the grid usually remain empty (see Fig. 2). In most cases it is possible to eliminate at least some of these gaps without violating the optimal spatial arrangement of components. In other words, the relative arrangement of components is preserved.

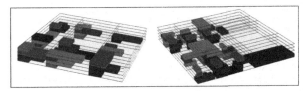

Fig. 2. The τ-EO example results for the MCNC benchmark.

3.3.1 Squeezing

The elaborated step-by-step squeezing procedure moves the chip components towards a predefined rallying point P along either the X or the Y axis. The *Single Component Move Algorithm* proceeds in the following way. If a component cannot be moved in a selected direction it is added to *immobileComponentsX* or *immobileComponentsY*, respectively. A component that is immobile in both directions is blocked and removed from *possibleMovesQueue*. A rallying point P is selected arbitrary by the designer. It can be a center of the chip or one of the corners of the chip bounding box, or a center of mass of the chip or any other point in 3D. A current move of a component is selected randomly from a queue of possible moves (*possibleMovesQueue*). If a new component position is not closer to P it will be rejected. Otherwise, it is verified whether a new position collides with other components. When the currently sliding component collides with any component that is blocked (immobile), its moves in the selected direction are also blocked. Summing up, a component is translated if and only if it is approaching the point P and no collision with other components is recognized. The algorithm pseudocode is presented in Fig. 3.

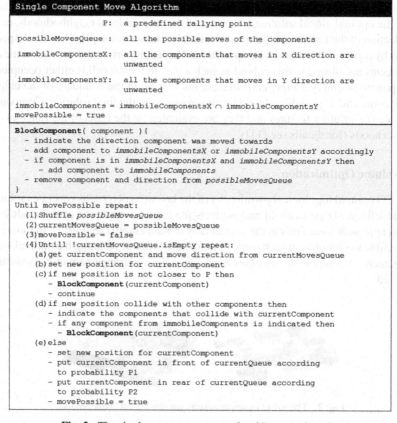

Fig. 3. The single component move algorithm pseudocode.

Let us consider the squeezing example in Fig. 4. A rallying point P is a left-bottom-front corner of the chip bounding box. The first step (see Fig. 4.1) presents some intermediate situation where three components have already been recognized as blocked (*immobileComponents*). In the following steps, only moves towards the point P along the X axis are considered. Unfortunately, the *currentComponent* selected in the next step (the blue one) (see Fig. 4.2) cannot be moved in the preferred direction due to the collision with another component (green). Since the colliding green component is still marked as mobile, the action is just neglected at this moment and may be reconsidered in the future. In Fig. 4.3 the move of the *currentComponent* (green) is admissible and performed. After that, the green component cannot be translated any further and if it is selected in any of the following steps it will be blocked and marked as *immobileComponent*. In Fig. 4.4, the blue component is selected once again and moved towards P as close as it is possible – till it collides with the orange one. In the last two situations (see Fig. 4.5–6), the orange component and the blue one, respectively, are moved to their final locations.

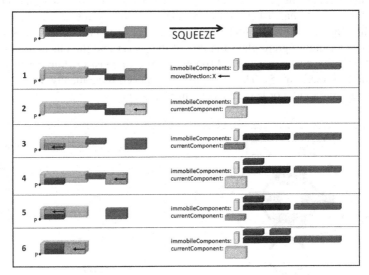

Fig. 4. The example arrangement of components before and after the squeezing; (1)–(6) selected intermediate steps. (Color figure online)

It is also possible to move at the same time a whole bundle of components. Such a move is allowed if: (1) all the components in a bundle can move in the same direction and the move place them closer to P, (2) no collision occurs. Applying a bundle approach to the example in Fig. 4, the whole squeezing could be performed in two steps instead of five. In the first move, a bundle of three components (orange, green and blue) would be translated towards P along the X axis and the orange component would reach its final position. In the second move, a bundle of two last components (green and blue) would be translated to its terminal location.

3.3.2 Parallel and Distributed Computations

Taking into account the grid-like structure of the plausible results, the number of possible moves in each step is upper bounded by the number of components multiplied by 2 (the X and the Y direction). The final result is dependent on the actual sequence of moves because they are strongly correlated with each other. Hence, the randomize selection of the next action has been introduced and the *possibleMovesQueue* is shuffled before the current move selection. Furthermore, in order to maximize the number of analyzed available solutions, parallel and distributed computations have been applied.

Distributed computations are shared among autonomous computers that communicate with each other in order to achieve a common goal. The computers are independent which means that they do not physically share processors or memory. They communicate and coordinate their work using messages passed over a network. They may play different roles and be organized in different ways. There are two predominant architectures: client-server and peer-to-peer architecture [3].

The volume optimization application is written in Java. Multiple optimization procedures are executed in parallel either by independent threads inside one Java Virtual Machine or are shared between many machines by means of The Java Remote Method Invocation system. In the latter case, the client-server architecture is adopted. One instance of the program plays the role of the server and the others are run in the client mode. The server generates and spools optimization tasks, while the clients fetch and do the jobs (see Fig. 5). The client list is managed dynamically and at any time machines are able to join or leave the computing system.

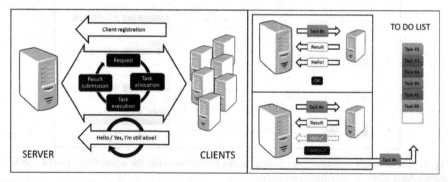

Fig. 5. The parallel and distributed calculation scheme of the squeezing and the fault tolerant task realization scheme.

The proposed system architecture is fault tolerant. All the tasks are unified and kept in a single queue. Each type of the task is elaborated by a dedicated plugin that is matched by the object type. The server distributes the tasks among clients and waits for "hello" messages which confirm that the clients are still working. If no "hello" is received from a client for a specified period of time, the client timeout is recorded and its unfinished task is going back to the queue.

The squeezed τ-EO results for the MCNC benchmark are presented in Fig. 6. The cell sizes are no longer adjusted to the maximal component dimensions. Many unwanted empty spaces are successfully removed while preserving the relative spatial relations of components.

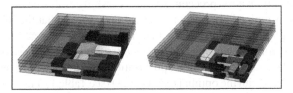

Fig. 6. The squeezed τ-EO results for the MCNC benchmark.

4 Experimental Results

The MCNC benchmark netlists (MCNC) [18] are one of the most frequently used for floorplanning and placement problems. Five block packing instances are given in a YAL file format. Their characteristics are listed in Table 1, where the columns denote: the file name (YAL datafile), the number of components (Blocks), the number of nets (Nets), the minimal, the maximal and the average number of interconnected components respectively (Neighbors no/min/max/avg). As stated before, by *neighbors* we denote components that comprise a single net. Each component may be a part of many different nets.

Table 1. Characteristics of the MCNC benchmark instances. Optimal wire-lengths for *apte*, *xerox*, and *hp* for the original die size (after [7]). Wire-length for *ami33* and *ami49* after [8]. Values are given in μm.

YAL datafile	Blocks	Nets	Neighbors no			Original size	Wire-length *optimal
			Min	Max	Avg		
apte.yal	9	97	8	8	8	10 500 × 10 500	513 061*
xerox.yal	10	203	9	9	9	5 831 × 6 412	370 993*
hp.yal	11	83	5	10	7	4 928 × 4 200	153 328*
ami33.yal	33	123	32	32	32	2 058 × 1 463	58 627
ami49.yal	49	408	2	35	18	7 672 × 7 840	640 509

In [8] the optimal wire-length in 2D for the three smallest MCNC instances (*apte*, *xerox* and *hp*) was calculated. It also was stated, that computing wire-length optimal packings for the two remaining instances (*ami33* and *ami49*) is still far beyond the realms of possibility. The basic half-perimeter model (HPWL) for a wire-length calculation was applied, where the wire-length of a net is a half of the perimeter of the bounding rectangle that encloses all the pins of the net. It is one of the most widely used approximation schemes. In such a way calculated optimal results together with the results reported in [8] for *ami33* and *ami49* are given in Table 1.

The extremal optimization procedure was successfully evaluated in [11] and different approaches were examined [12]. The numerical data proved that the initial component layout basically does not matter for the final result as was expected for a fine defined extremal optimization task. In this article, the total wire-length approximation results, calculated after the squeezing volume optimization, are presented. In order to compare the proposed solution with the optimal results in 2D (see Table 1), the HPWL wire-length model approximation was applied. The third dimension was introduced into a formula as the height of the bounding cube of the components which belong to a net. Thus, the wire-length $w(n)$ of a net n is calculated as follows:

$$w(n) = max_{c',c'' \in n} \left| c'_x - c''_x \right| + max_{c',c'' \in n} \left| c'_y - c''_y \right| + max_{c',c'' \in n} \left| c'_z - c''_z \right| \quad (1)$$

where c' and c'' are components that belong to a network n and c_x, c_y, c_z denote *(x, y, z)* position of a component c, respectively.

Although many floorplanning approaches are applied to the MCNC set of benchmarks there are only a few that contain comparable wire-lengths in 2D, like [8, 17]. It is caused by the fact that the authors do not use the original die sizes (Table 1) but modify them by scaling, rotating or splitting block modules in order to reduce whitespaces [20, 21]. In this way, the chip components are changed and an essentially different layout task is solved. Still, it was reported in [4], that depending on the number of chip layers, the average 28% to 51% reduction in the total wire-length may be achieved in 3D. Our results presented in Table 2 confirm this premise. Apart from the *ami49* instance, the total wire-length was reduced by 21–73% compared to the best results in 2D [8]. Only in the case of *ami49* circuit, the total wire-length is by 10% longer. Yet, it is by 34% better that the 2D result presented in [17].

Table 2. The wire-lengths results in μm for the MCNC benchmark instances.

Article	apte	Xerox	hp	ami33	ami49
This (3D)	137 325	290 183	105 848	42 183	704 135
(Funke et al 2016) [8] (2D)	513 061	370 993	153 328	58 627	640 509
(Liu and Nannarelli 2008) [17] (2D)	614 602	404 278	253 366	96 205	1 070 010
(Nain and Chrzanowska-Jeske 2011) [20] (3D)	–	–	–	22 500	446 800
(Xie and Zhao 2015) [21] (3D)	–	297 440	124 819	27 911	547 491

In [21] various perturbations that change the original modules are allowed to handle 3D floorplans, namely rotation and resize. Even though, our results for *xerox* and *hp* are a bit better. However, when bigger benchmarks are considered (*ami33* and *ami49*) our wire-length are by 33% and 22% longer. Taking into account 3D solutions for *ami33* and a*mi49* in [20] where some modules are split and their parts are assigned to different device layers, our results are by 47% and 37% worst.

At the first glance, the proposed approach seems to be inferior to others when applied to bigger benchmarks. However, it must be stressed out that changing the original modules changes the whole layout task. Hence, the achieved solutions are incomparable. Our approach is general and does not use any specific knowledge about circuit building blocks except of the netlist. It does not modify the building blocks structure. Considering the generated four-layer 3D floorplan of *ami49* (Fig. 7), some may criticize it for too many gaps (white spaces) comparing to the floorplans presented in [20]. Therefore, one may assume that when perturbations of original modules are allowed the total wire-length, which is satisfactory right now, will even improve.

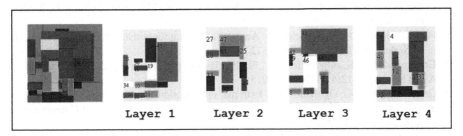

Fig. 7. The 3D floorplan of *ami49*.

5 Conclusions

This article presents an original and general 3-step intelligent approach to the total wire-length minimization in the integrated circuits design. In the first step, a netlist YAL file is parsed into the elaborated layout hypergraph representation. After that, a topological partitioning with a use of the extremal optimization is applied to optimize the relative positions of the components in the chip. And finally, a parallel distributed volume optimization is performed. The squeezing procedure is executed in order to minimize the total wire-length of the final solution.

There is no a priori knowledge needed to solve the floorplan puzzle. Only the original block modules sizes and the netlist connectivity information are considered. That is why, the reported numerical results for both the chip volume size and the total wire-length are very promising and encourage to continue this research. In the future work, the knowledge about the circuit building blocks may be incorporated to allow components perturbations. Furthermore, the exact pin points positions used in the wire-length calculation formula would give precise instead of the rough results.

References

1. Ababei, C., et al.: Placement and routing in 3D integrated circuits. IEEE Des. Test **22**(6), 520–531 (2005)

2. Boettcher, S.: Extremal optimization: heuristics via coevolutionary avalanches. Comput. Sci. Eng. **2**(6), 75–82 (2000)
3. Coulouris, G., Dollimore, J., Kindberg, T., Blair, G.: Distributed Systems: Concepts and Design (5th Edition). Addison-Wesley, Boston (2011). ISBN 0-132-14301-1
4. Das, S., Chandrakasan, A., Reif, R.: Three-dimensional integrated circuits: performance, design methodology, and CAD tools. In: Proceedings of the IEEE Computer Society Annual Symposium on VLSI (2004)
5. De Micheli, G., Pavlidis, V., Atienza, V., Leblebici, Y.: Design methods and tools for 3D integration. In: Symposium on VLSI Tech Digest of Technical Papers, pp. 182–183 (2011)
6. Dong, X., Xie, Y.: System-level cost analysis and design exploration for three-dimensional integrated circuits (3D ICs). In: Proceedings of the 2009 Asia and South Pacific Design Automation Conference (ASP-DAC 2009). IEEE Press, Piscataway (2009)
7. Funke, J., Hougardy, S., Schneider, J.: Wirelength optimal rectangle packings. In: Proceedings of the Fourth International Workshop on Bin Packing and Placement Constraints, Nantes, France (2012)
8. Funke, J., Hougardy, S., Schneider, J.: An exact algorithm for wirelength optimal placements in VLSI design. VLSI J. **52**, 355–366 (2016)
9. Grzesiak-Kopeć, K., Ogorzałek, M.: 3D ICs layout hypergraph representation. Comput.-Aided Des. Appl. **12**(4), 425–430 (2015)
10. Grzesiak-Kopeć, K., Ogorzałek, M.: Extremal optimization approach to 3D design of inte-grated circuits layouts. In: The 7th International Conference on Advanced Computational Intelligence (ICACI) (2015b)
11. Grzesiak-Kopeć, K., Oramus, P., Ogorzałek, M.: Using shape grammars and extremal optimization in 3D IC layout design. Microelectron. Eng. **148**, 80–84 (2015)
12. Grzesiak-Kopeć, K., Oramus, P., Ogorzałek, M.: Hypergraphs and extremal optimization in 3D integrated circuit design automation. Adv. Eng. Inform. **33**, 491–501 (2017)
13. Hentschke, R.F.: Algorithms for wire length improvement of VLSI circuits with concern to critical paths. Ph.D thesis, Porto Alegre: PPGC da UFRGS (2007)
14. Kahng, A.B., Lienig, J., Markov, I.L., Hu, J.: VLSI Physical Design: From Graph Partitioning to Timing Closure. Springer, Netherlands (2011)
15. Lengauer, T.: Combinatorial Algorithms for Integrated Circuit Layout. Wiley, Hoboken (1990)
16. Li, Z., et al.: Hierarchical 3-D floorplanning algorithm for wirelength optimization. IEEE Trans. Circ. Syst. I: Regul. Papers **53**(12), 2637–2646 (2006)
17. Liu, W., Nannarelli, A.: Net balanced floorplanning based on elastic energy model. In: NORCHIP, pp. 258–263 (2008)
18. MCNC: The MCNC set of benchmark circuits. http://lyle.smu.edu/~manikas/Benchmarks/MCNC_Benchmark_Netlists.html. Accessed 9 June 2015
19. Mujtaba, H.: Hardware report: AMD naples high-performance server chips pack 32 cores, 64 threads – based on Zen with 8-channel memory, 128 PCIe lanes, launch in Q2 (2017). https://wccftech.com/amd-naples-server-chip-32-core-64-thread-preview. Accessed 10 March 2018
20. Nain, R.-K., Chrzanowska-Jeske, M.: Fast placement-aware 3-D floorplanning using vertical constraints on sequence pairs. IEEE Trans. Very Large Scale Integr. (VLSI) Syst. **19**(9), 1667–1680 (2011)
21. Xie, Y., Zhao, J.: Die-stacking Architecture, Die-stacking Architecture 1. Morgan and Claypool, San Rafael (2015)

From Victim to Survivor: A Multilayered Adaptive Mental Network Model of a Bully Victim

Fakhra Jabeen[✉], Charlotte Gerritsen, and Jan Treur

Vrije Universiteit, 1081 HV Amsterdam, The Netherlands
fakhraikram@yahoo.com, {cs.gerritsen,j.treur}@vu.nl

Abstract. Peer victimization is usually addressed with hazardous short and long term effects. Social surroundings and cyber technology act as a fertile ground for perpetrators to target victims. Fragile and lonely people are often targeted by aggressors or bullies who may make them feel like a 'loser'. This results in their withdrawal from society and can result in suicidal or revenge thoughts. In this paper, we present a complex multi-layered adaptive mental network model based on cognitive and psychological literature. The network model is simulated for three type of victims: a) passive, b) assertive and c) ambivert using case studies. It can be used as a basis in classification and to provide support of the victims.

Keywords: Bully-Victim · Victim of aggressor · Multilayered adaptive mental network

1 Introduction

"Bullying is pushing someone around and making them feel like a failure . . . if you are blackmailing or threatening them, that is bullying. . . . If it is playful teasing, no, but if you are hurting someone's feelings, yes." [1]

Cyber-technology expands bullying into the technological realm, where perpetrators use smart devices to target and cause an intentional harm to their victims. Most victims experience distress, along with frustration, anger, and sadness due to threat to their self-image. This can have long-lasting effect over the health and esteem of a person, and may even result in school violence or suicide [2, 3].

Bullying-victims are usually neurotic or submissive by nature [4], which makes them the targets and lead them to withdraw and avoid bullies. They are usually not extrovert, as they are not much social or outgoing, and due to their shy and isolated nature recurrence of aggression is almost inevitable [4]. If victims are ambivert by nature (i.e. neither introverted nor extroverted) and they give their bully a 'stop' signal, it will not only help them to stop bullying [4] but also not to become aggressors. Different studies conducted in psychology and social science focused on behavioral traits of a victim [5, 6]. A study conducted in the domain of network modeling showed the mental processes of a

© Springer Nature Switzerland AG 2020
L. Rutkowski et al. (Eds.): ICAISC 2020, LNAI 12415, pp. 679–689, 2020.
https://doi.org/10.1007/978-3-030-61401-0_63

victim that focuses on a fight or a flight reaction of a victim. However, in that reference, internalizing mechanisms or learning from experience and the personality of a victim was not considered [7].

This paper presents a biologically inspired complex multi-layered adaptive mental network addressing the personality of a victim, using first-order network layer for how learning impacts his or her internalizing behavior, and a second-order network layer affecting the learning rate and persistence of the learning. Section 2 explains the related work; while Sect. 3 presents the multilayered adaptive network model; Sect. 4 presents the simulation scenarios, and; Sect. 5 discusses the network model in comparison to available data; and Sect. 6 concludes the paper.

2   Related Work

Related work for a victim of an aggressor is presented in three streams: the cognitive literature, the behavioral literature, and by exploring the advancements in artificial intelligence in victim modeling and detection. There is vast literature available, which discusses the mental organization of a victim [6] and how his nature helps him to choose the right strategy to react to his aggressors [4].

While discussing the neurological or cognitive aspect, victims are identified by low self-esteem, making them susceptible to the bullies. Their cognitive attributions internalize bullying message as a threatening message (e.g., "people hate me"), which makes them feel threat and insecure. It leads to anxiety, which raises the cortisol levels in adults [6] and victim may get thoughts of taking revenge or committing suicide. Brain parts like the hippocampus (long-term/short-term memory), the amygdala (e.g., with the feeling of threat/anxiety) play the role for memory emotions and the motivations. These motivations along with the prefrontal cortex (PFC) involves in forming strategies to react to bullying. PFC is responsible to choose his own actions, with a complete ownership and learn to make long-term solutions/decisions.

An extravert person is not often bullied, so a victim is usually identified by his passive and submissive nature [8]. They appear lonely, shy and may show internalizing social difficulties like socially withdrawn [6]. They are lonely and afraid to tell anyone, because of lack of satisfaction and trust [9]. They have complaints of anxiety, anger or stress as few signs of high neuroticism [10] and usually do not retaliate bully. They experience low academic functioning and usually alienated as 'losers' [4, 6]. An ambivert victim react assertively for self-defense (e.g. an aggressive/assertive response depending on the context), whenever needed [6]. As this angry behavior of a victim is usually the result of threatened egotism, experienced by the victim [5], so his reaction may not only raise his self-confidence but also leave a positive message to bystanders(or other victims) to stand by him [6].

Machine learning techniques were also applied to detect cyberbullying traces, however, most of them relate by the bully perspective [11, 12], therefore support cant be aimed if a person reports him as a victim. Similarly, a temporal-causal study of a victim discussed flight and fight reaction of a victim [7]. However, there is no model designed, which explains the personality of a victim making him the target and his possible reactions.

3   A Multilayered Adaptive Mental Network Model of a Victim

This section presents a multilayered mental network model for a victim of an aggressor using a three layered reified architecture based on [13, 14], and the literature mentioned above. In this architecture, each layer signifies a specific role of the model. For example, Layer I indicates the base-model, while layer II and III represent the adaptive nature of the model, by plasticity and meta-plasticity respectively. The model is presented in Fig. 1, and the information of each layer is depicted in Table 1 and Table 2.

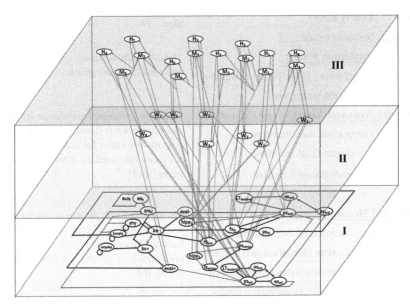

Fig. 1. Multi-layered reified network architecture for a victim. (Color figure online)

Layer I for the base network

The base layer (Layer I) contains the conceptual representation of the base model, based on the real-world scenarios by *states* and *connections*. A *connection* is a causal relationship between two states. For example, consider a causal relationship between states X and Y: $X \rightarrow Y$. All states along with X incoming to Y, have an influence over Y with a certain *speed*. Its *activation level* is the *aggregated impact* of all incoming states and varies by *connection weights* and *activations* of the incoming states. The *aggregated impact* is computed through different *combination functions* [15]:

Connection Weight $\omega_{X,Y}$ indicates how strong state X influences state Y. The magnitude ranges between 0 and 1. A suppression effect on Y is categorized by a negative connection.

Speed Factor η_Y indicates how fast state Y can change its value (range: 0–1) due to a causal impact.

Table 1. Categorical explanation of states of the base model (Layer I).

Categories		References
Stimulus States:		*Stimulus is sensed and leads to representation:* [15]
es_b	Input from aggressor/bully	
srs_b	Sensory representation state of victim	
Person's Nature States:		*children who are socially isolated and exhibit other internalizing problems become increasingly victimized over time...* [4]
Shy	Shy nature	
Lonely	Lonely nature	
outgoing	Sociable nature	
Cognitive Attribution States:		*"Children are anxious, self-doubting, and tend to submit quickly"* [4]
bs_i	Belief state i =+/- (positive/negative)	
$eval_i$	Evaluation state i =+/-	
Avoidance (avd) and Assertive (ast) States:		*"the idea of internal simulation is that in a certain context (..goals and attitudes) preparation states for actions ...in turn activate other sensory representation states"* [15]
ps_i	Preparation state i=avd/ast	
$LT_{Goal(i)}$	Long-term Goal i=avd/ast	
os_i	Ownership state i=avd/ast	
es_i	Execution state i=avd/ast	
Feeling and Memory States:		*it is assumed that the preparation for the response is also affected by the level of feeling ... integration of emotion in preparation of actions (pg 239: Treur, 2016),* [6]
ps_i	Preparation state i=th (threat)/stress	
fs_i	Feeling state i=th/stress /anxiety(anx)	
$hipp_1$	Hippocampus: Brain region for avd	
$hipp_2$	Hippocampus: Brain region for ast	

Combination Function $c_Y(..)$ is chosen to compute the causal (aggregated) impact of all incoming states ($X_i : i = 1$ to N) for state Y. Certain standard combination functions are already defined, and can be used to compute aggregated impact of Y.

Layer I consist of 24 states, which presents a scenario of how a victim reacts when his self-image is in danger. Bullying (es_b) act as input to the model. It activates sensory representation state of the victim (srs_b). His personality plays an important role in deciding how to react to an aggressor/bully. A passive person (shy; lonely), internalizes (eval-) the stimulus (for example: "people don't like me") and avoids bully. However, an assertive victim will communicate his concerns to control the bullying environment. In Fig. 1 negative belief (bs-) internalize (eval-), along with the elevation of the feelings of threat (fs_{th}) and anxiety (fs_{anx}). They aggregate to prepare for avoidance behavior (ps_{avd}). Anxiety or threat usually arise due to past memories ($hipp_1$). He regulates (os_{avd}) himself by avoidance (es_{avd}), as a long term solution (LT_{Goal}). However, avoidance behavior results in social isolation ($ps_{th} \rightarrow$ lonely).

For an ambivert person, first he tries to act in passive manner, but feeling of threat stresses him ($ps_{stress}: fs_{th} \rightarrow ps_{stress}$) and he learns not to react passively (ps_{avd}), so he gets

Table 2. Explanation of States in Layer II and III.

States per Layer			References
Layer II (Plasticity /Hebbian learning for Omega states):			*First-order adaptation layer for plasticity by Hebbian learning* [15, 16]
W_1:	$W_{ps_{avd}, hipp_1}$	for $ps_{avd} \to hipp_1$	
W_2:	$W_{hipp_1, fs_{th}}$	for $hipp1 \to fs_{th}$	
W_3:	$W_{hipp_1, fs_{anx}}$	for $hipp1 \to fs_{anx}$	
W_4:	$W_{fs_{th}, ps_{stress}}$	for $fs_{th} \to ps_{stress}$	
W_5:	$W_{hipp_2, ps_{avd}}$	for $ps_{stress} \to hipp_2$	
W_6:	$W_{hipp_2, fs_{stress}}$	for $hipp_2 \to fs_{stress}$	
W_7:	$W_{fs_{stress}, ps_{ast}}$	for $fs_{stress} \to ps_{ast}$	
W_8:	$W_{eval+, ps_{ast}}$	for $eval+ \to ps_{ast}$	
Layer III (Meta-Plasticity/Learning rate and persistence):			*Second-order adaptation layer for meta-plasticity to control the Hebbian learning* [16]
M_i:	Persistence for $i = W_j$: $j = 1,...,8$		
H_i:	Learning rate for $i = W_j$: $j = 1,...,8$		

assertive (ps_{ast}). It is already activated if he or she is assertive by nature. Here his stress (ps_{stress}) activates learning and based on past experiences ($hipp_2$), his stress (fs_{stress}) is increased. As a result, he chooses assertive reaction as a regulation strategy, knowing (os_{ast}) his long-term goals (LT_{Goals}). This strategy helps him decrease shyness and his loneliness. Here black horizontal connections indicate a positive incoming connections to a state. The adaptive connections are represented by green horizontal connections, while purple horizontal connections indicate suppression of a state from an incoming connection.

Layer II for First-Order Network Adaptation
This layer has eight states based on adaption (Hebbian Learning), indicated by omega states W_i (where $i = 1$ to $8 \Leftrightarrow$ eight green colored connections at Layer I (Table 2)). The involved states act as presynaptic and postsynaptic states for a specific connection. For example, consider state W_1 (also denoted by $W_{ps_{avd}, hipp_1}$), which is responsible for connection $ps_{avd} \to hipp_1$, ps_{avd} and $hipp_1$ act as presynaptic and post-synaptic states for learning. For more details about the Hebbian learning principle in network-oriented modeling, see [14, 15].

Layer III for Second-Order Network Adaptation
Layer III adds an abstraction level to learning behavior of states at layer II. Here, 16 meta-plasticity related states: M_i and H_i are presented. The former indicates persistence, while the latter specify the learning rate for $i = W_1$ to W_8 states in Layer II. For example, M_1 (also denoted as $M W_{ps_{avd}, hipp_1}$), controls the persistence of $W_1/W_{ps_{avd}, hipp_1} W_{ps_{avd}, hipp_1}$

at Layer II, with the incoming connections (blue) from the states ps_{avd} and $hipp_1$ respectively, and along with H_1 it suppresses W_1 (red connection from M_1 to W_1 state).

For the computation of impacts of states, we used three type of combination functions (Fig. 1) which are:

a) For 9 states (es_b; outgoing; bs−; bs+; eval+; $LT_{Goal(avd)}$; $LT_{Goal(ast)}$; os_{avd}; os_{ast}), we used the Euclidian function, with order $n>0$ and scaling factor λ as the sum of connection weights of a particular state:

$$\mathbf{eucl}_{n,\lambda}(V_1, \ldots, V_k) = \sqrt[n]{(V_1^n + \ldots + V_k^n)/\lambda}$$

b) For 31 states ($srs_{s,b}$; shy; lonely; eval−; $hipp_1$; $hipp_2$; fs_{th}; fs_{anx}; fs_{stress}; ps_{avd}; ps_{ast}; ps_{th}; ps_{stress}; es_{avd}; es_{ast}; H_i; M_i $i = 1$–8), **alogistic** function (positive steepness σ and threshold $\tau <1$) was used:

$$\mathbf{alogistic}_{\sigma,\tau}(V_1, \ldots, V_k) = [(1/(1 + e^{-\sigma(V_1+ \cdots +V_k -\tau)})) - 1/(1 + e^{\sigma\tau})](1 + e^{-\sigma\tau})$$

where each V_i is the single impact computed by the product of weight and state value: $\omega_{X,Y} X(t)$.

c) Lastly, for the 8 adaptation states (W_1; W_2; W_3; W_4; W_5; W_6; W_7; and W_8) we used Hebbian learning principle defined by the following combination function:

$$\mathbf{hebb}_{\mu}(V_1, V_2, W) = V_1 V_2(1 - W) + \mu W$$

Mathematically, a reified-architecture based model is represented as [14]:

1. At every time point t, the activation level of state Y at time t is represented by $Y(t)$, with the values between [0,1].
2. Single impact of state X on state Y at time t is represented by $\mathbf{impact}_{X,Y}(t) = \omega_{X,Y} X(t)$; where $\omega_{X,Y}$ is the weight of connection $X \to Y$.
3. Special states are used to model network adaptation based on the notion of reification network architecture. For example, $\mathbf{W}_{X,Y}$ represents an adaptive connection weight $\omega_{X,Y}(t)$ for the connection $X \to Y$, while $\mathbf{H}_Y$ represents an adaptive speed factor $\eta_Y(t)$ of state Y. Similarly, $\mathbf{C}_{i,Y}$ and $\mathbf{P}_{i,j,Y}$ represent adaptive combination functions $c_Y(..., t)$ over time and its parameters respectively. Combination functions are built as a weighted average from a number of basic combination functions $bcf_i(..)$, which take parameters $P_{i,j,Y}$ and values V_i as arguments. The universal combination function $c^*_Y(..)$ for any state Y is defined as:

$$\mathbf{c}^*_Y(S, C_1, \ldots, C_m, P_{1,1}, P_{2,1}, \ldots, P_{1,m}, P_{2,m}, V_1, \ldots, V_k, W_1, \ldots, W_k, W)$$
$$= W + S[C_1\mathrm{bcf}_1(P_{1,1}, P_{2,1}, W_1V_1, \ldots, W_kV_k) + \ldots$$
$$+ C_m\mathrm{bcf}_m(P_{1,m}, P_{2,m}, W_1V_1, \ldots, W_kV_k)]/(C_1 + \ldots + C_m) - W]$$

where at time t:

- variable S is used for the speed factor reification $\mathbf{H}_Y(t)$
- variable C_i for the combination function weight reification $\mathbf{C}_{i, Y}(t)$
- variable $P_{i, j}$ for the combination function parameter reification $\mathbf{P}_{i, j, Y}(t)$
- variable V_i for the state value $X_i(t)$ of base state X_i
- variable W_i for the connection weight reification $\mathbf{W}_{Xi, Y}(t)$
- variable W for the state value $Y(t)$ of base state Y.

4. Based on the above universal combination function, the effect on any state Y after time Δt is computed by the following *universal difference equation* as:

$$Y(t + \Delta t) = Y(t) + [\mathbf{c} *_Y (\mathbf{H}_Y(t), \mathbf{C}_{1,Y}(t), \ldots, \mathbf{C}_{m,Y}(t), \mathbf{P}_{1,1}(t), \mathbf{P}_{2,1}(t), \ldots,$$
$$\mathbf{P}_{1,m}(t), \mathbf{P}_{2,m}(t), X_1(t), \ldots, X_k(t), \mathbf{W}_{X_1,Y}(t), \ldots, \mathbf{W}_{X_k,Y}(t), Y(t)) - Y(t)]\Delta t$$

which also can be written as a *universal differential equation*:

$$\mathbf{d}Y(t)/\mathbf{d}t = \mathbf{c} *_Y (\mathbf{H}_Y(t), \mathbf{C}_{1,Y}(t), \ldots, \mathbf{C}_{m,Y}(t), \mathbf{P}_{1,1}(t), \mathbf{P}_{2,1}(t), \ldots, \mathbf{P}_{1,m}(t),$$
$$\mathbf{P}_{2,m}(t), X_1(t), \ldots, X_k(t), \mathbf{W}_{X_1,Y}(t), \ldots, \mathbf{W}_{X_k,Y}(t), Y(t)) - Y(t)$$

We simulated our model using a dedicated Reified Network Engine [16], by providing input of the characteristics of the network model represented by role matrices. A role matrix is a compact specification with the concept of the role played by each state with a specified type of information. Detailed information for our model can be found online [13, 17].

4 Example Scenarios

Reaction of a victim of an aggressor depends mostly on the personality of a victim a) Passive, or b) Assertive, or c) Ambivert. In this section, we present the simulation scenarios of three strategies by victim based upon his nature:

4.1 An Avoidance Strategy (Passive Reaction)

To understand this strategy, let's consider a social environment, in which there is a peer who is being victimized by calling bad names. His reaction can be like "They called me bad names, and I didn't know what else to do than walk away from them". Or "I started to go together with Sara and Joy after a month in the new class. However, after some weeks they began to run away from me during breaks, laughing and whispering and hiding different places (pause). That is why I am alone." [18]. These type of reactions are common in victims, due to their passive nature.

While looking into the simulation results in Fig. 2, when es_b is 1 and shy and lonely is also active, then srs_b is activated along with bs− (magenta), his internalization (eval-) gets active at $t = 10$. bs− makes the feelings of threat (fs_{th}) and anxiety active (purple-bold) and causes an avoidance reaction (ps_{avd}; es_{avd}) to elevate along with regulation states ($LT_{Goal(avd)}$; os_{avd}). Feeling of threat fs_{th} (pink-bold) increases and makes him stressed (blue curve: ps_{stress}) at $t = 200$, however, as his anxiety becomes much higher, so he choose avoidance strategy (e.g. upping the privacy on social media)

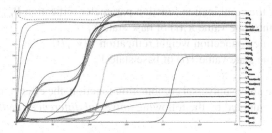

Fig. 2. The victim chooses an avoidance strategy but feels stressed. (Color figure online)

Looking into the plots of Layer II and III (Fig. 3), learning behavior can be seen for M_i, H_i and W_i where $i = 1$ (pink), 2 (purple), 3 (brown), and 4 (green). W_5 (red) arises, however it doesn't play its role except the victim has stress (ps_{stress}). Rest of omega states don't show any dynamics for $i = 6$ to 8. Therefore, learning rates (H_i) and persistence (M_i) are constant, and the corresponding W_i are zero. For example, H_8 and M_8 are constant, thus $W_8/W_{eval+, ps_{ast}}$ remains zero showing that there is no learning overtime. It would not be wrong to say that all omega states associated to assertive behavior will stay low along with constant M and H, as the person is not assertive by nature.

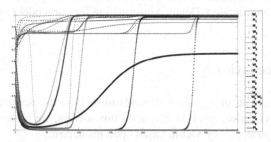

Fig. 3. Plots of Layer II and III. No learning except for the states W_1 to W_4 (shown by asterisk). (Color figure online)

4.2 An Assertive Strategy (Assertive Reaction)

Although this is a rare case but, to understand this strategy, consider the scenario when a new boy enters in a social circle, where all peers are not well-aware of his nature and if they try to piss him off. He gives them a 'Stop' signal, without hurting own esteem.

Considering the simulation in Fig. 4a, an assertive victim has his positive belief (bs+) as high, which activates the states related to the assertive behavior (ps_{ast}; es_{ast}; $LT_{Goal(ast)}$; os_{ast}), making the avoidance strategy related states (yellow-dotted) low (=0). Here eval+(orange) is followed by bs+ at time point $t = 10$. Then ps_{ast} (blue) is activated along with well-aware long-term goals with $LT_{Goal(ast)}$ (orange) and os_{ast} (purple), and es_{ast} (yellow)

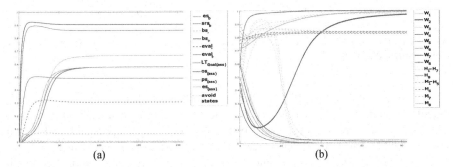

(a)   (b)

Fig. 4. a) An outgoing reaction towards a bully. b) plots of Layer II and III. Learning is only observed in assertive behavior (i =8: bold). (Color figure online)

Plots of Layer II and III (Fig. 4b), shows that only $W_8/W_{eval+, psast}$ has learning (time point t >25). All M_i and H_i ($i = 1$ to 7) stays constant, i.e. between 0.8 to 0.9, thus no learning is observed for W_i. However, H_8 (red), M_8 (mustard) and W_8 (blue) show the learning dynamics. So the avoidance behavior is not observed while being assertive.

4.3   Change of Strategy (Ambivert Reaction)

An example scenario can be a peer, who is not very outgoing by nature except his social circle. When targeted, he initially tries to avoid the bully by ignoring his dirty talk, or avoiding to confront him. However, when this doesn't stop him, and he feel threatened he talks to his elders and then the situation gets better. It is an expected reaction and by this, his self-confidence is raised, and shyness is reduced. As a result, bullying is stopped and self-worth is maintained.

While looking into the simulation explained in Fig. 5, we can see an ambivert victim who, tries to avoid bully first. In this case, all states related to the avoidance behavior get activated during time point $t = 0$–50. However, as the time passes, threat to his ego (fs_{th}: purple) causes stress (ps_{stress}:yellow).This leads to change his strategy, so he switches from avoidance to an assertive reaction at $t = 50$–120. Assertiveness (shaded region with ps_{ast}; $LT_{Goal(ast)}$; os_{ast}; es_{ast}) gets high and suppress the avoidance related states (ps_{avd}; $LT_{Goal(avd)}$; os_{avd}; es_{avd}), along with the avoidance related feelings (fs_{th}; fs_{anx}). Eventually, his ego/self-confidence (black dotted: bs+) gets higher, and shyness (golden dotted) or loneliness (dark green dotted) are lowered (0 and 0.9 respectively). Assertive reaction gets low $t = 250$, as bully is handled. Here, it is to be noted, that in contrast with shyness (shy), loneliness doesn't drop to 0 (0.85 at $t = 310$). The reason is the dynamics of his nature, that is he gets assertive only when needed.

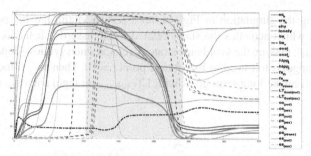

Fig. 5. Victim chooses avoidance strategy first and then an assertive strategy (shaded region). (Color figure online)

Plots of Layer II and III (Fig. 6), show that all W states learned over the time. But around time point $t = 110$, state W_8 (yellow) learns even faster and reach its maximum value. As a result, this causes the rest of the W states to get suppressed, and then it remains equilibrium showing that he learned how to react in an assertive manner.

In each of the simulation experiments (Fig. 2 to Fig. 5) presented in this section, it is shown that each pattern is reaching an equilibrium as each state doesn't show further dynamics.

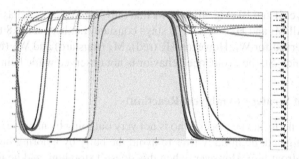

Fig. 6. Plots of Layer II and III. Learning of all states (W_1 to W_8) over time (Color figure online)

5   Conclusion

A biologically inspired multilayered adaptive network model of a victim of an aggressor, is presented based on cognitive, psychological and social literature, using a multilayered reified architecture. Hebbian learning effects are also observed. If a person is shy and lonely, loneliness increases over the time by his avoidance reaction. Also, it shows that threat to ego, increases the stress over the time, to make the victim assertive. In future, we aim to study the model with respect to related data, and to devise support strategies and therapies to the victim.

References

1. Espelage, D.L., Asidao, C.S.: Conversations with middle school students about bullying and victimization. J. Emotional Abuse **2**, 49–62 (2001)
2. Jabeen, F.: How happy you are: a computational study of social impact on self-esteem. In: Staab, S., Koltsova, O., Ignatov, D.I. (eds.) SocInfo 2018. LNCS, vol. 11186, pp. 108–117. Springer, Cham (2018). https://doi.org/10.1007/978-3-030-01159-8_10
3. Schenk, A.M., Fremouw, W.J.: Prevalence, psychological impact, and coping of cyberbully victims among college students. J. Sch. Violence **11**, 21–37 (2012)
4. Juvonen, J., Graham, S. (eds.): Peer harassment in school: the plight of the vulnerable and victimized. Guilford Press, New York (2001)
5. Resseguier, B., Léger, P.-M., Sénécal, S., Bastarache-Roberge, M.-C., Courtemanche, F.: The influence of personality on users' emotional reactions. In: Nah, F.F.-H.F.-H., Tan, C.-H. (eds.) HCIBGO 2016. LNCS, vol. 9752, pp. 91–98. Springer, Cham (2016). https://doi.org/10.1007/978-3-319-39399-5_9
6. Smokowski, P.R., Evans, C.B.R.: Bullying and Victimization Across the Lifespan: Playground Politics and Power. Springer International Publishing, Cham (2019)
7. Hirzalla, N.A., Maaiveld, T.M., Jabeen, F.: Fight or flight: a temporal-causal analysis of the behavior of a bully-victim. In: Nguyen, N.T., Chbeir, R., Exposito, E., Aniorté, P., Trawiński, B. (eds.) ICCCI 2019. LNCS (LNAI), vol. 11683, pp. 154–166. Springer, Cham (2019). https://doi.org/10.1007/978-3-030-28377-3_13
8. Huang, K.: Viewing the anti-social personality transformation of school bullying victims from the perspective of experimental analysis. Psychol. Behav. Sci. **8**, 55 (2019)
9. Chou, W.-J., Liu, T.-L., Yang, P., Yen, C.-F., Hu, H.-F.: Bullying victimization and perpetration and their correlates in adolescents clinically diagnosed with ADHD. J Atten. Disord. **22**, 25–34 (2018)
10. Suls, J., Martin, R.: The daily life of the garden-variety neurotic: reactivity, stressor exposure, mood spillover, and maladaptive coping. J. Pers. **73**, 1485–1510 (2005)
11. Sedano, C.R., Ursini, E.L., Martins, P.S.: A bullying-severity identifier framework based on machine learning and fuzzy logic. In: Rutkowski, L., Korytkowski, M., Scherer, R., Tadeusiewicz, R., Zadeh, L.A., Zurada, J.M. (eds.) ICAISC 2017. LNCS (LNAI), vol. 10245, pp. 315–324. Springer, Cham (2017). https://doi.org/10.1007/978-3-319-59063-9_28
12. Xu, J.-M., Jun, K.-S., Zhu, X., Bellmore, A.: Learning from bullying traces in social media. In: Proceedings of the 2012 Conference of the North American Chapter of the Association for Computational Linguistics: Human Language Technologies, pp. 656–666. Association for Computational Linguistics, Stroudsburg (2012)
13. Treur, J.: Modeling higher order adaptivity of a network by multilevel network reification. Netw. Sci. **8**(S1), S110–S144 (2020). https://doi.org/10.1017/nws.2019.56
14. Treur, J.: Multilevel network reification: representing higher order adaptivity in a network. In: Aiello, L.M., Cherifi, C., Cherifi, H., Lambiotte, R., Lió, P., Rocha, Luis M. (eds.) COMPLEX NETWORKS 2018. SCI, vol. 812, pp. 635–651. Springer, Cham (2019). https://doi.org/10.1007/978-3-030-05411-3_51
15. Treur, J.: Network-Oriented Modeling. Springer International Publishing, Cham (2016)
16. Treur, Jan: Network-Oriented Modeling for Adaptive Networks: Designing Higher-Order Adaptive Biological, Mental and Social Network Models. SSDC, vol. 251. Springer, Cham (2020). https://doi.org/10.1007/978-3-030-31445-3
17. Victim Specifications (2019). https://github.com/MsFakhra/Bully-Victim-Specifications
18. Lund, I., Ertesvåg, S., Roland, E.: Listening to shy voices: shy adolescents' experiences with being bullied at school. J. Child Adolesc. Trauma **3**(3), 205–223 (2010)

Faster Convention Emergence by Avoiding Local Conventions in Reinforcement Social Learning

Muzi Liu[1](✉), Ho-fung Leung[1], and Jianye Hao[2]

[1] The Chinese University of Hong Kong, Hong Kong, China
liumuzi@link.cuhk.edu.hk, lhf@cuhk.edu.hk
[2] Tianjin University, Tianjin, China
jianye.hao@tju.edu.cn

Abstract. In this paper, we propose a refinement of multiple-R [1], which is a reinforcement-learning based mechanism to create a social convention from a significantly large convention space for multi-agent systems. We focus on the language coordination problem, where agents develop a lexicon convention from scratch. As a lexicon is a set of mappings of concepts and words, the convention space is exponential to the number of concepts and words. We find that multiple-R suffers from local conventions, and refine it to the independent-R mechanism, which excludes neighbors' rewards from the value update function, and thus avoids local conventions. We also explore how local conventions influence the dynamics of convention emergence. Extensive simulations verify that independent-R outperforms the state-of-the-art approaches, in the sense that a more widely adopted convention emerges in less time.

Keywords: Artificial intelligence in modeling and simulation · Multi-agent systems

1 Introduction

Coordination among autonomous agents is essential for cooperative goal achievement in open multi-agent systems (MAS), as incompatible actions usually incur resource cost to the participating agents [2]. In the process of cooperative goal achievement, the conformity to a convention helps to simplify agents' decision-making process and hence improve the efficiency of agent societies [3]. Since a centralized entity that directly enforces a convention requires the imposition of global rules, a convention that emerges in a decentralized manner is more feasible for coordination in MASs [3,4].

The study of social convention emergence explores how agents involved in repeated coordination games can reach consensus through local interactions [4]. Some researchers focus on characterizing the dynamics of convention emergence process. Airiau and Sen [5] explore the emergence of convention through social

© Springer Nature Switzerland AG 2020
L. Rutkowski et al. (Eds.): ICAISC 2020, LNAI 12415, pp. 690–701, 2020.
https://doi.org/10.1007/978-3-030-61401-0_64

learning [6], and study the effect of network characteristics on the emergence speed. They observe and explain the formation of stable local conventions, which hinders global convention emergence. Similar phenomena are also investigated in [7], where stable local conventions are stated to benefit coordination. Other works concentrate more on developing efficient mechanisms of convention emergence. Most of the approaches are spreading-based, but some researchers also branch out to reinforcement learning-based (RL-based) approaches.

Challenges appear along with the increase of convention space, including issues related to convention quality and emergence efficiency [1,8]. One particular research problem that captures the challenge of convention space explosion is the *language coordination problem* [9], which is an imitation of how human develop languages from scratch. Recently, RL-based approaches for lexicon coordination problem have been proposed by Wang et al. [1]. Inspired by the classic Q-learning algorithm and its variants [10], they propose two efficient mechanisms, multiple-Q and multiple-R (MR), that ensure high-quality final conventions.

In this work, we modify MR through understanding and characterizing the dynamics of the convention emergence process. Our refined RL-based strategy, independent-R (IR), overcomes the limitations caused by local conventions. Simulations show that IR outperforms the state-of-the-art approaches, in the sense that a more widely adopted convention emerges in a shorter time.

2   Related Work

The studies about social conventions in multi-agent systems have long been attracting researchers. Since Shoham and Tennenholts addresses the question about the efficiency of convention evolution led by local decisions of agents in multi-agent systems [11], many researchers have studied and proposed possible strategies to shrink the time of convention stabilization [1,4,6,8,9,11–13].

Some works [1,8,12,13] propose mechanisms designed for a particular challenging problem in large and open MASs, the *language coordination problem*. The problem was originated from Luc Steels' model [9], where a group of distributed agents develops a vocabulary to name themselves and to identify each other using spatial relations. SRA [13] and FGJ [12] are two spreading-based mechanisms for the problem. SRA makes use of a sophisticated agent architecture design to create high-quality conventions. On the other hand, FGJ introduces a set of influencer agents equipped with high-quality lexicons, so that the agent population is guided towards the adoption of high-quality conventions. While the above two methods are both set in static networks, Hasan et al. extend SRA by leveraging a topology-aware utility computation mechanism and equipping agents with the ability of reorganizing their neighborhood [8].

In addition to spreading, some RL-based approaches have been proposed recently [1], and remarkably accelerate convention emergence in large convention space. However, as the learning mechanisms take advantage of neighbors' learned information, they suffer from the emergence of local conventions, which slows down the emergence of a global convention.

3   Language Coordination Game

We consider a situation where a language emerges among a population of agents in a bottom-up manner. A language is simplified to a lexicon, which is a set of mappings from words to concepts. Every agent has a lexicon. Interactions occur between a pair of agents. Through the interactions, agents accumulate their knowledge of others' lexicons and adjust their own lexicons accordingly. They try to align with others by learning from experience. Therefore, after repeated interactions, lexicons in the whole population tend to converge. Ideally, every agent will eventually have the same lexicon, which we consider as a convention.

To formally define language coordination game, we introduce three components as follows: (a) language coordination problem, (b) interaction model, and (c) convention emergence problem.

3.1   Language Coordination Problem

To describe the situation where agents develop a language in a decentralized fashion, we first model a language as a *lexicon*. A lexicon contains a set of *words* (W) and a set of *concepts* (C), where each word is mapped to a concept. In a lexicon, it is possible that one concept is mapped to multiple words (*synonymy*), or multiple concepts are mapped to a single word (*homonymy*). We consider a lexicon with one-to-one mappings has the highest quality. Initially, each agent has a lexicon, where each word is arbitrarily mapped to a concept. Through repeated interactions, agents learn to adjust their lexicons so that they can succeed in more interactions.

Interactions, which can be either successful or failed, are modeled as two-player $|W|$-action coordination games. For each interaction, there are two agents that participate in it. The two participating agents are called *speaker* and *hearer*, whose lexicons are $L_{speaker}$ and L_{hearer} respectively. The speaker and the hearer interact under a certain concept, which is selected before the interaction. The concept selection may follow certain frequency distribution, which represents the appearing frequency of each concept. Suppose the selected concept is c. During an interaction, the speaker sends a word $w_{speaker}$ to the hearer, where concept-word mapping $(c, w_{speaker}) \in L_{speaker}$. Upon receiving $w_{speaker}$, the hearer also finds a word w_{hearer}, where $(c, w_{hearer}) \in L_{hearer}$. If $w_{speaker} = w_{hearer}$, the interaction succeeds; otherwise the interaction fails. In a successful interaction, the hearer receives a positive reward; in a failed interaction, the hearer receives a negative reward.

3.2   Interaction Model

We consider a population of N agents, where all the agents are connected following a static network topology. In each interaction, an agent randomly selects a neighbor to interact with. The interaction model of the multi-agent system is represented by an undirected graph, $G = (V, E)$, where G is the network structure, V is the set of nodes ($|V| = N$), E is the set of edges. If $v_i, v_j \in V$ and

$(v_i, v_j) \in E$, then v_i, v_j are *neighbors*. $N(i)$ is the *neighborhood* of node i, where $N(i) = \{v_j | (v_i, v_j) \in E\}$. A *path* between v_i, v_j is a sequence of edges connecting a sequence of nodes which begins with v_i and ends with v_j. The *distance* between two nodes is the shortest path between them. Three representative networks are considered: random, small-world [14], and scale-free network [15].

3.3 Convention Emergence Problem

We model the language coordination problem as a convention emergence problem. A desirable convention is a one-to-one lexicon adopted by all agents in the network. As every lexicon can become the convention, the convention space contains all possible lexicons, the size of which is $|W|^{|C|}$. The convention space is large even for a moderate number of words and concepts. Thus, following [1], we decouple a lexicon into concept-word mappings. Hence each lexicon can be defined as a Markov strategy, and the dynamics of interactions in each episode can be modeled as a two-player Markov Game $\langle S, \{A_i\}_{i \in V}, \{R_i\}_{i \in V}, T \rangle$, where

- S is the set of states, which corresponds to the concepts.
- V is the set of all agents.
- $\{A_i\}_{i \in V}$ is the collection of action sets. $\forall i \in V$, A_i contains all the words.
- $\{R_i\}_{i \in V}$ is the set of payoff functions. $R_i : S \times A_i \times A_j \rightarrow R$, where agent i and j are the interacting agents. R_i satisfies the Gaussian distribution.
- T is the state transit function: $S \times A_i \times A_j \rightarrow Prob(S)$, where agent i and j are the interacting agents. T models concept usage frequencies.

Algorithm 1. Convention emergence framework

1:	**for** each episode **do**	7:	actionSelection()
2:	**for** each agent **do**	8:	policyUpdate()
3:	lexiconInitialization()	9:	lexiconUpdate()
4:	**while** transition $< \lambda$ **do**	10:	**end while**
5:	conceptTransition()	11:	**end for**
6:	neighborSelection()	12:	**end for**

---

4 A Convention Emergence Framework

4.1 Overall Algorithm

Algorithm 1 describes the overall framework of repeated language coordination games. Initially, each agent has an initial lexicon, in which words are randomly mapped to each concept. To develop a convention, agents discard old lexicons (line 3) and construct new lexicons in each episode. The constructed lexicons are in fact composed by the concept-word mappings that are selected in interactions of current episode. To construct a lexicon, in each episode, each agent initiates interactions for λ times as a hearer (line 4). Each interaction focuses on one concept, which is determined by a concept transition function (line 5).

During an interaction (line 6 to line 9), the hearer randomly selects a neighbor as the speaker (line 6). Based on its policy, the hearer selects a word as its action for the focused concept (line 7); the speaker also selects a word as the speaker's action. If both of the hearer and the speaker select the same word, the interaction is successful. In the case of successful interaction, the hearer receives a positive reward; otherwise, the hearer receives a negative reward. According to the reward it receives, the hearer updates its policy (line 8) to get higher rewards in future interactions. The word selected by the hearer will be mapped to the concept of this interaction, and the mapping becomes a part of the hearer's lexicon (line 9). The details of policy update will be introduced in Sect. 4.3.

The mappings from the selected words to the focused concepts in all λ interactions of the current episode compose the hearer's new lexicon. A lexicon convention emerges when all agents in the network has the same lexicon.

4.2 Convention Establishment

To establish a convention in an agent society, there are mainly two types of approaches. One is spreading-based approach, where agents spread conventions through information transfer. A typical transfer strategy is copy-transfer: an agent simply replicates its neighbors' lexicons. Another class of techniques is reinforcement learning, where agents learn conventions by repeatedly interacting with other agents. Up to now, the most efficient method to establish conventions is a RL-based approach, which is called multiple-R (MR) [1]. However, instead of learning from interactions, the MR mechanism mainly uses neighbors' learning results to guide an agent's own policy. The interference from neighbors largely affects agents' policies, and thus they always align with neighbors instead of the whole network. In this situation, local conventions are likely to emerge and hinder the emergence of a global convention.

Grounded on the above analysis, we propose independent-R learning strategy, which is a RL-based strategy basing on the up-to-date MR strategy [1]. The main improvement is that we avoid the interference from neighbors, and thus prevents the emergence of local conventions.

4.3 Independent-R Learning Strategy

Value Function Update. The following strategy corresponds to the policy update in the independent-R mechanism (line 8 in Algorithm 1).

In an interaction focused on concept s, assume the hearer agent i takes word a as action, and receives a reward $r(s, a)$. $r(s, a)$ is positive if the interaction succeeds, or negative otherwise. The hearer takes average of the rewards it has received for (s, a) in recent n episodes and updates $R_i(s, a)$ accordingly. Let

$n_i(s, a)$ be the number of interactions in recent n episodes, where the interaction is under concept s and agent i selects word a. Initially, $R_i(s, a)$ is 0. Formally:

$$R_i(s, a) \leftarrow R_i(s, a) + \frac{r(s, a) - R_i(s, a)}{n_i(s, a)}. \tag{1}$$

Then, agent i updates its Q-table:

$$Q_i(s, a) \leftarrow Q_i(s, a) + \alpha(R_i(s, a) - Q_i(s, a)), \tag{2}$$

where α is the learning rate. $Q_i(s, a)$ may fluctuate a lot if α is too large.

Action Selection. In the agent interaction, the pair of participating agents will select actions following certain action selection strategy (line 7 in Algorithm 1). We adopt the action selection design in [1] as follows.

For an interaction of concept s, let RA_i be the set of words that has been mapped to the concepts in set $S\backslash\{s\}$ in current episode. To determine the word a_i for this interaction, agent i uses ε-greedy strategy to choose the word with the highest utility from set $A_i\backslash RA_i$, which is the set of words that are not mapped to any concept yet in current episode:

$$a_i \leftarrow \begin{cases} argmax_{a\notin RA_i} Q_i(s, a) & \text{with probability } 1 - \varepsilon \\ \text{a random word} \in A_i\backslash RA_i & \text{with probability } \varepsilon \end{cases} \tag{3}$$

If there are multiple actions with maximum utilities, agent will randomly select one from these actions.

4.4 Comparison with Multiple-R

Independent-R (IR) only uses an agent's own rewards to update its strategy, while MR uses a weighted average of neighbors' rewards. In MR, agent i updates its recent average rewards $R_i(s, a)$ as same as (1). However, in addition to $R_i(s, a)$, agent i also computes the weighted average of neighbors' rewards:

$$\overline{r} = \sum_{j\in N(i)\cup\{i\}} f(i, j)R_j(s, a), \tag{4}$$

where $f(i, j) = \frac{degree(j)}{\sum_{k\in N(i)\cup\{i\}} degree(k)}$. Then, agent i updates its Q-value $Q_i'(s, a)$:

$$Q_i'(s, a) \leftarrow Q_i'(s, a) + \alpha(\overline{r} - Q_i'(s, a)). \tag{5}$$

We note that the information of neighbors' degree takes effect implicitly when agents interact, hence it is not used in the value update function (2) of IR. For each interaction, the speaker is randomly selected by the hearer from its neighborhood. Thus, agents who have larger degree will be selected by more hearers and participate in more interactions. Through repeated interactions, lexicons adopted by high degree agents naturally have more influence.

We also note that taking others' rewards into account reduces the effects of the agents' own rewards, especially the reward received from the most recent interactions. When an agent i is updating $Q_i'(s, a)$, the reward $r(s, a)$ it just received will first be divided by $n_i(s, a)$ to compute $R_i(s, a)$ as (1), and then the average reward $R_i(s, a)$ is further multiplied by a fraction $f(i, j)$ in (4). Thus neighbors' rewards and the agent i's own past rewards together play a big part in Q-values, suppressing the influence of immediate reward $r(s, a)$.

5　Experiments and Results Analysis

We conduct experiments on several typical networks, including random, scale-free, and small-world networks. The performance of IR is compared with the state-of-the-art approaches including multiple-R with teacher-student mechanism (MR+TS) [1], TA [8], FGJ [12], and SRA [13].

We define dominant lexicon convention as the one shared by the most agents. Based on previous works, the metrics used for comparison are as follows:

- **Efficiency**: Efficiency measures how fast a network converges into a dominant lexicon convention. The criterion used for measurement are followings:
  - **Average Communicative Efficacy (ACE)**: The proportion of successful interactions in total. It measures the level of coordination.
  - **Proportion of Agent Compliant with Convention (ACC)**: The proportion of agents adopting dominant lexicon.
- **Effectiveness**: A mechanism is effective if it is able to converge into a widely adopted lexicon convention within a reasonable amount of time. It is reflected by reaching high ACC in a reasonable number of episodes.

5.1　Simulation Setup

We conduct experiments on three network topologies: random, scale-free, and small-world, where scale-free and small-world networks are generated by Barabasi-Albert model [15] and Watts and Strogatz small-world model [14] respectively. The random networks are generated by randomly connecting two nodes continuously from a uniform spanning tree of the complete graph. Each network consists of $1,000$ agents and $20,000$ edges, so that the average degree is 20. Following [1,8], both the number of concepts and words are 10, thus the size of convention space is 10^{10}. For each agent, the concept transition number λ is 20. The learning rate α is 0.02. We adopt the random frequency distribution as the concept usage frequency. Specifically, the 20 concept transitions are divided into two sections, and each concept is selected exactly once in each section. Thus, the sequence of concept transitions in a section is a random permutation of the concept set. In this way, each agent initiates equal number of interactions in each episode for each concept. Each realization executes for $60,000$ episodes and all the presented results are the averages over 50 realizations of each network.

5.2   Simulation Results

The results of simulation for small-world networks are shown in Fig. 1. Similar results also apply to random and scale-free networks. The figure presents how the proportion of agent compliant with convention (ACC) and average communication efficacy (ACE) evolves over time. We add the performances of other approaches in small-world networks in Fig. 1 for comparisons. The results of other approaches are provided in [1]. The results support that IR is the most effective and efficient approach compared with state-of-the-art approaches.

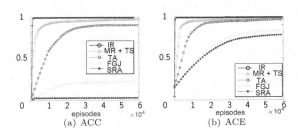

(a) ACC   (b) ACE

Fig. 1. ACC and ACE figure for small-world network

For effectiveness, the figure shows that when convention stabilizes, the ACC of IR is the highest, which is over 0.99. It suggests that the dominant lexicon is adopted by almost every agent in IR. As the dominant lexicon convention is widely accepted, IR is the most effective approach over the existing approaches.

For efficiency, from Fig. 1a, we can observe that IR is the most efficient method, since it needs much less number of episodes to reach the same ACC as other approaches. For example, TA approach requires almost 30,000 episodes, and MR+TS requires almost 10,000 episodes for ACC to reach 0.9, while IR only needs hundreds of episodes. The performances of FGJ and SRA are even worse, as their ACC cannot reach 0.9 in given 60,000 episodes.

The ACE figure also shows a similar pattern. For example, when ACE is 0.9, the fastest approach MR+TS takes 12,968 time-steps for random network, while IR requires only 524 time-steps. As expected, ACE grows rapidly along with ACC, since the higher rate of successful interactions is a result of higher proportion of agents adopting a same lexicon.

In conclusion, the simulation results show that IR is more efficient and more effective than state-of-the-art approaches, in the way that it requires less time steps to have more agents adopting the dominant lexicon convention.

6   The Emergence of Local Conventions

From the experimental results, we observe that IR outperforms other approaches significantly, as it is more efficient and more effective. However, there is only a slight difference between MR and IR, namely the Q-value update function.

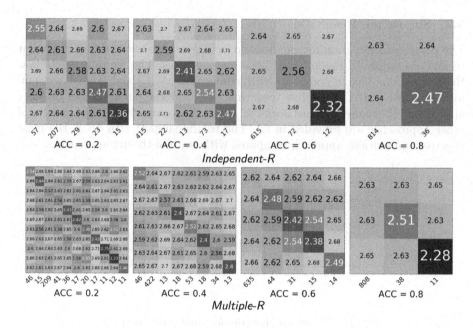

(a) Large amount of groups with small sizes

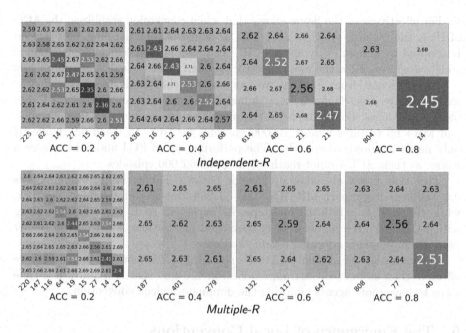

(b) Small amount of groups with large sizes

Fig. 2. Group distance figure. Each block represents a group distance. The two coordinates are the two measured groups. Group sizes are labeled on x-axis. The upper row is the group distances in IR and the lower row is in MR when ACC = 0.2, 0.4, 0.6, 0.8 in the same network. Only the groups having more than 10 agents are recorded.

The reason why IR outperforms MR is that local conventions may appear in MR, and hinder the emergence of global convention. It is mentioned in [1] that the ACE of MR is high even when the ACC is low, which means a lot of interactions succeed even though there exist no dominant lexicons. It supports our finding that local conventions emerge in the network, and thus most of the interactions happen between agents who are in the same group, leading to high proportion of successful interactions even when there is no dominant lexicon.

6.1 Local Conventions Emergence

To verify the emergence of local conventions in MR, we present simulation results to confirm the existence of local conventions in MR mechanism.

To describe local conventions, we use *group* to refer to the set of agents that adopt a same lexicon, and *group distance* to measure the distance between pairs of groups. Specifically, for a lexicon p, let $G_p = (V_p, E_p)$ be a subgraph of $G = (V, E)$, where V_p is the set of agents that adopt lexicon p, and E_p is the set of edges $(v_i, v_j) \in E$, where $v_i, v_j \in V_p$. Let $d(v_i, v_j)$ be the distance between nodes v_i and v_j. Then the group distance between G_p and G_q is defined by $D(G_p, G_q) = \frac{\sum_{v_i \in V_p, v_j \in V_q} d(v_i, v_j)}{|V_i| \times |V_j|}$.

The group distance between a group and itself reflects how closely the agents inside the group are connected. If $D(G_p, G_p)$ is significantly smaller than $D(G_p, G_{p\prime})$ for all other $p\prime$, it indicates that p is a local convention among G_p. A small group distance between G_p and itself indicates that most of the agents inside G_p are neighbors with one another. Thus agents inside G_p will mostly interact with agents inside G_p. As they all adopt lexicon p, these interactions always succeed. By repeated interactions, their lexicons are confirmed by each other. In this way, the local convention is reinforced inside such a group.

From Fig. 1 we can observe that ACC increases monotonically during convention emergence, and converges to 1 with the number of episodes increasing. We record the group distances when ACC reaches 0.2, 0.4, 0.6, 0.8 in MR and IR. Only the groups having more than 10 agents are recorded.

Figure 2 shows how the group distances evolve in two typical simulations. Figure 2a shows the situation where there are a lot of small groups; and Fig. 2b shows the situation where there are few groups with significant sizes.

There are two rows of graphs shown in Fig. 2a and Fig. 2b. The upper rows show the data collected using IR approach, while the lower rows show the data collected using MR in the same network. In each row, there are four graphs. From the left to right, the four graphs show the data corresponding to the episode when $ACC = 0.2, 0.4, 0.6, 0.8$ respectively. In each graph, there are small blocks with numbers labeling on. The number and color of a block at coordinate (g_1, g_2) show the group distance $D(g_1, g_2)$. The exact size of each group is labeled on the x coordinate. For a group g, if the color of the block (g, g) is apparently darker from the blocks in the same row, then $D(g, g)$ is significantly smaller than $D(g, g')$ for all g', and the lexicon of group g is more likely a local convention.

In Fig. 2a, we can observe that compared to graphs of IR, there are more blocks in the graphs of MR, which means there are more groups in MR. Also, the diagonal lines on graphs of MR are clearer than those of IR, indicating that groups in MR are more closely connected than in IR. These closely connected groups in MR shows that local conventions appear in these groups as we expect.

Figure 2b shows the situation where there are several groups with significant size. For example, when ACC = 0.4, there are only one group of size 400 and several small groups smaller than 70 in IR; while in MR, there are two groups of size around 200 and one group of size 400. These large groups persist and compete with each other during the whole process of convention emergence.

From simulations and the above analysis, we conclude that compared to MR, agents equipped with IR produce less local convention groups with smaller sizes, and thus speed up the emergence of global convention.

6.2   Analysis of Multiple-R Approach

As we mentioned before, the only difference between MR and IR is that MR collects rewards from neighbors to update Q-values while IR does not. Nonetheless, local conventions appear and hinder the emergence of global convention in MR more frequently than in IR. It is reasonable to infer that collecting neighbors' rewards increases the emergence of local conventions in MR.

In MR, for an agent i, as the value update function (5) includes the average rewards $\bar{r}$ of i's neighbors, and the rewards of high degree neighbors are largely weighted by $f(i, j)$ in (4), agents always quickly align with high degree neighbors. Also, it is highly likely that other agents in i's neighborhood $N(i)$ are connected to the same high degree node and adopt the same lexicon as well. Thus agent i and its neighbors always receive positive rewards from their interactions, and the lexicon they adopt is reinforced. Therefore, it is difficult for lexicons outside of i's neighborhood to affect agent i after the local convention is formed. The quick adoption to lexicons of the high degree agents and the ineffectiveness of distant lexicons lead to a large amount of local conventions in the network.

In addition, it is harder and slower for a global convention to supersede local conventions in MR. To supersede a local convention group, the boundary agents of the group need to adopt the global convention first, so that they can influence their neighbors inside the group by interactions. However, as the immediate rewards from agent interactions only takes a small part in $\bar{r}$, the influence of agent interactions is overwhelmed by high degree neighbors in (4). The boundary agents will hardly switch to a new lexicon, since they are affected more by their high degree neighbors inside the group. Thus the local conventions are difficult to assimilate, which significantly slow down the emergence of a global convention.

7   Conclusion and Future Work

In this work, we propose a new RL-based approach, independent-R, basing on the previous multiple-R mechanism, which avoids local conventions and thus accelerates global convention emergence. We find that using neighbors' average rewards to adjust an agent's own rewards causes the emergence of local conventions, which largely hinder the global convention emergence. We value the information obtained from interactions by an agent itself, instead of the information given by neighbors, so that local conventions are less likely to appear. Extensive simulations indicate that IR outperforms the state-of-the-art approaches, in the sense that a more widely adopted convention emerges in a shorter time.

As future work, one of the worthwhile directions is to capture the influential factors for the formation of local conventions in large convention space, or to explore possible mechanisms to utilize local conventions.

References

1. Wang, Y., Lu, W., Hao, J., Wei, J., Leung, H.-F.: Efficient convention emergence through decoupled reinforcement social learning with teacher-student mechanism. In: Proceedings of 17th International Conference on Autonomous Agents and MultiAgent Systems (2018)
2. Marchant, J.M., Griffiths, N., Leeke, M.: Manipulating conventions in a particle-based topology. In: Coordination, Organizations, Institutions and Norms in Agent Systems Workshop: A workshop of the 12th International Conference on Autonomous Agents and Multiagent Systems: AAMAS2015 (2015)
3. Sen, O., Sen, S.: Effects of social network topology and options on norm emergence. In: Padget, J., et al. (eds.) Coordination, Organizations, Institutions and Norms in Agent Systems V (2010)
4. Mihaylov, M., Tuyls, K., Nowé, A.: A decentralized approach for convention emergence in multi-agent systems. Auton. Agent. Multi-Agent Syst. **28**, 479–779 (2014)
5. Airiau, S., Sen, S., Villatoro, D.: Emergence of conventions through sociallearning. Auton. Agent. Multi-Agent Syst. **28**, 779–804 (2014)
6. Sen, S., Airiau, S.: Emergence of norms through social learning. In: Proceedings of 20th International Joint Conference on Artifical Intelligence (2007)
7. Hu, S., Fung Leung, H.: Achieving coordination in multi-agent systems by stable local conventions under community networks. In: Proceedings of 26th International Joint Conference on Artificial Intelligence (2017)
8. Hasan, M.R., Raja, A., Bazzan, A.: Fast convention formation in dynamic networks using topological knowledge. In: Proceedings of 29th AAAI Conference on Artificial Intelligence (2015)
9. Steels, L.: A self-organizing spatial vocabulary. Artif. Life **2**, 319–332 (1995)
10. Hasselt, H.V.: Double q-learning. In: Advances in Neural Information Processing Systems 23. Curran Associates Inc. (2010)
11. Shoham, Y., Tennenholts, M.: Emergent conventions in multi-agent systems: initial experimental results and observations (preliminary report). In: Proceedings of Knowledge Representation and Reasoning (1992)
12. Franks, H., Griffiths, N., Jhumka, A.: Manipulating convention emergence using influencer agents. Auton. Agent. Multi-Agent Syst. **26**(3), 315–353 (2013)
13. Salazar, N., Rodrigues Aguilar, J.A., Arcos, J.L.: Robust coordination in large convention spaces. AI Commun. **23**(4), 357–372 (2010)
14. Watts, D.J., Strogatz, S.H.: Collective dynamics of 'small-world' networks. Nature **393**, 440–442 (1998)
15. Barabasi, A.-L., Albert, R.: Emergence of scaling in random networks. Science **286**, 509–512 (1999)

Empirical Mode Decomposition Based Data Augmentation for Time Series Prediction Using NARX Network

Olusola Oluwakemi Abayomi-Alli[1] , Tatjana Sidekerskienė[2] ,
Robertas Damaševičius[1] , Jakub Siłka[3], and Dawid Połap[3(✉)]

[1] Department of Software Engineering, Kaunas University of Technology, Kaunas, Lithuania
{olusola.abayomi-alli,robertas.damasevicius}@ktu.lt
[2] Department of Applied Mathematics, Kaunas University of Technology, Kaunas, Lithuania
tatjana.sidekerskiene@ktu.lt
[3] Faculty of Applied Mathematics, Silesian University of Technology, Gliwice, Poland
kubasilka@gmail.com, dawid.polap@polsl.pl

Abstract. Neural networks (NNs) have recently achieved significant performance gains for time series forecasting. However, they require large amounts of data to train. Data augmentation techniques have been suggested to improve the network training performance. Here, we adopt Empirical Mode Decomposition (EMD) as a data augmentation technique. The intrinsic mode functions (IMFs) produced by EMD are recombined with different weights to obtain surrogate data series, which are used to train a neural network for forecasting. We use M4 time series dataset and a custom nonlinear auto-regressive network with exogenous inputs (NARX) for the validation of the proposed method. The experimental results show an improvement in forecasting accuracy over a baseline method when using EMD based data augmentation.

Keywords: Data augmentation · Empirical Mode Decomposition · Surrogate data · Time series forecasting · NARX network

1 Introduction

The forecasting of time-series addresses the problem of predicting the future values of data sequence based on their values from the past. Recently, deep neural networks (DNNs) have demonstrated significant performance gains for time series forecasting [1] and classification [2]. However, DNNs usually require many data for training, which may not always be available. The latter problem is sometimes referred to small data challenge [3]. Data augmentation is applied for generating supplemental data to enhance training of machine learning systems, e.g., for image classification [4] or speech recognition [5]. Authors in [6] defined data augmentation as deformations of training data instances without modifying the semantic characteristics of the data. Such modifications or perturbations are appended to the training dataset aiming to account for unseen data. Although such approach is commonly used in image processing where image transforms

© Springer Nature Switzerland AG 2020
L. Rutkowski et al. (Eds.): ICAISC 2020, LNAI 12415, pp. 702–711, 2020.
https://doi.org/10.1007/978-3-030-61401-0_65

such as scaling and rotation maintain the semantics of the original image, for one-dimensional data series it has not been widely applied.

Previous study from Guennec et al. [7], suggested the use of window slicing for data augmentation. Window slicing extracts time series slices and performs classification at the slice level. At training, each slice has a class assigned the same class and a classifier is trained to recognize slices from a time series. Um et al. [8] described several data augmentation techniques, some of which also are usable for time series augmentation. These include: time-warping, when data is compressed or extended by changing the sample time interval; scaling, when the data magnitude in a window is scaled; magnitude-warping, when the data window is convolved with a smooth curve; and jittering is adding some noise. Bergmeir et al. [9] apply an STL decomposition on the seasonal series or a loess decomposition to obtain the residuals. Then the residuals are bootstrapped with moving average to generate new series. There are also several bootstrapping approaches used some of which include tapered block bootstrap [10] and dependent wild bootstrap [11]. Surrogate series can be created using models that recreate the spectral characteristics [12] or statistical features of real data [13]. Then surrogate data can be employed to augment the true data for identifying patterns that were not represented in the original data [14], or for improving forecasting results [15]. Surrogate data can be created using statistical models, which generate data randomly subject to constraints of a model, or by assigning random phases and computing the inverse Fourier transform of the signal's periodogram [16]. Another approach is to decompose time series into its constituents [17, 18] and then reassemble these series using different weights. Other method is associative memory [21, 22], which together with deep neural networks and spiking neural networks find many applications in signal processing.

We propose a method for surrogate data generation using Intrinsic Mode Functions (IMF) obtained through Empirical Mode Decomposition (EMD) [19]. We validate our approach on the custom neural network designed for time series forecasting tasks.

2 Methods

2.1 Empirical Mode Decomposition

The principal concept of (Empirical Mode Decomposition) EMD is to split the original time series into a set of smooth curves, named intrinsic mode functions (IMF). The IMFs are almost orthogonal functions, which have a varying frequency and amplitude. An IMF has to satisfy these requirements: the count of zero-crossings and extrema can not differ more than by one. The means of the local minima envelope and the local maxima envelope are zero. The iterative algorithm that derives an IMF is called the sifting process. It is described in Fig. 1 and by these steps:

1. Find all the local extrema of $x(t)$. Interpolate between the maxima of $x(t)$ and fit a cubic spline to get the top envelope max $e(t)$. Interpolate between the minima of $x(t)$ and fit a cubic spline to get the bottom envelope min $e(t)$.
2. Calculate the mean value of the bottom and top envelopes:

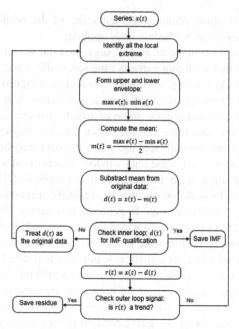

Fig. 1. Algorithm of Empirical Mode Decomposition (EMD)

$$m(t) = \frac{(\max e(t) - \min e(t))}{2}. \tag{1}$$

3. Extract the difference $d(t) = x(t) - m(t)$.
4. Check if $d(t)$ is an IMF. If true, output it as the next IMF and replace $x(t)$ with the residue $r(t) = x(t) - d(t)$; if false, replace $x(t)$ with $d(t)$.
5. Iterate steps 1–3 until the residue becomes a monotonous.

2.2 Surrogate Series Generation

Surrogate data are usually created using well-defined models that recreate the semantical or morphological features of the original data. Here for the generation of surrogate time series we propose using the IMF obtained by applying EMD. As a result of EMD, the original series $x(t)$ can be reconstructed as follows:

$$x(t) = \sum_i IMF_i(t) + r(t), \tag{2}$$

here r is the residue error, which is usually negligible.

Using matrices, the decomposition process can be specified using identity matrix I as

$$X = I \cdot IMF + r(t) \tag{3}$$

The surrogate series are produced as a randomly weighted summation of IMFs:

$$\tilde{X} = n\frac{R}{\sum R} \cdot IMF + r(t) \tag{4}$$

here $\tilde{X}$ is the surrogate, R is a vector of random values drawn from [0,1] with uniform distribution, and n is the count of IMFs.

To apply the method, we construct a model of forecasting (see Fig. 2). There $X(t)$ is original data. After EMD, we get n intrinsic mode functions (IMF_i). The first IMF captures the highest frequency component and can be removed from further use, if the input is noisy. The remaining IMFs are multiplied by a random matrix R and summed. The surrogate series are used as input for neural network (NN) training.

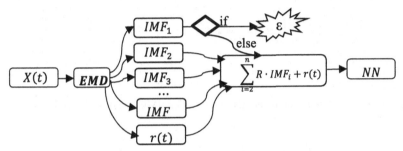

Fig. 2. Schema of the surrogate time series generation model. EMD – Empirical Mode Decomposition. IMF – Intrinsic Mode Function. NN – Neural Network.

The generation of surrogate series is illustrated by an example in Fig. 3. It shows the original time series, its decomposition into IMFs, and 20 sample surrogate series generated by a sum of randomly weighted IMFs (the residual is not weighted).

2.3 Neural Network Design

NARX is a dynamic recurrent neural network (RNN) with feedback connections. In the NARX, the subsequent value of the output $y(k)$ is regressed on the preceding values of the output and input series. The NARX model is realized using a feed-forward NN to approximate the function f (see Fig. 4). The NARX is defined as:

$$y(k) = f\left(y(k-1), y(k-2), \ldots, y(k-n_y), u(k-1), u(k-2), \ldots, u(k-n_u)\right) \tag{5}$$

The input vector is described in Eq. (6):

$$u(k) = (u_1(k), \ldots u_K(k))', d(k) = (d_1(k), \ldots d_L(k))', k = 1..M \tag{6}$$

here $u(n)$ is the input, $d(n)$ is the output, k is the sequence number, K and L is the number of perceptrons in the input and output layer, respectively.

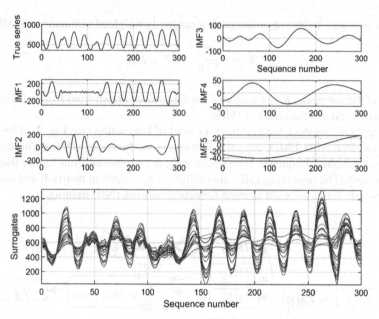

Fig. 3. Illustration of surrogate series generation. IMF – Intrinsic Mode Function.

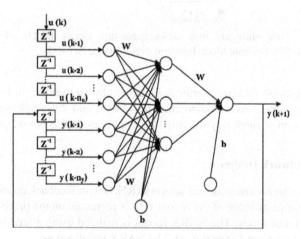

Fig. 4. Architecture of NARX neural network

The training of NARX is implemented using back-propagation (BP) training (Levenberg-Marquardt optimization is used) in three steps as explained below.

1. Calculation of the status of the activation functions $x(k)$ of each neuron starting from $u(k)$, $x(k-1)$ and $y(k-1)$ or the activation of the output layer if it is fed into a specific neuron;

2. Calculation of the backpropagation error of each neuron starting from $k = N..1$, $x(k)$ and $y(k)$ using Eqs. (7–10).

$$\delta_j(N) = \big(d_j(N) - y_j(N)\big)\,(\partial f(u))/\partial u|_{u=z_j(T)} \tag{7}$$

$$\delta_i(N) = \left[\sum\nolimits_{j=1}^{L} \delta_j(N)w_{ji}^{out}\right](\partial f(u))/\partial u|_{u=z_i(k)} \tag{8}$$

$$\delta_j(k) = [\big(d_j(k) - y_j(k)\big)\sum\nolimits_{i=1}^{N}\delta_i(k+1)w_{ji}^{back}](\partial f(u))/\partial u|_{u=z_j(k)} \tag{9}$$

$$\delta_i(k) = \left[\sum\nolimits_{i=1}^{N}\delta_i(k+1)w_{ji} + \sum\nolimits_{j=1}^{L}\delta_j(k)w_{ji}^{out}\right](\partial f(u))/\partial u|_{u=z_i(k)} \tag{10}$$

here $\delta_j(N)$ is the BP error of the output neuron, $\delta_i(N)$ is the BP error of the neuron in the hidden layer with activation $x_i(N)$, $\delta_j(k)$ and $\delta_i(k)$ are the BP errors of the output neuron and the one located in the hidden layer in the preceding series instance k, and $z_i(k)$ is the potential of each neuron. After finding the BP error, the weights of neurons are calculated using Eqs. (11–14):

$$w_{ij} = w_{ij} + \gamma\sum\nolimits_{k=1}^{N}\delta_i(k)x_j(k-1) \tag{11}$$

$$w_{ij}^{in} = w_{ij}^{in} + \gamma\sum\nolimits_{k=1}^{N}\delta_i(k)u_j(k) \tag{12}$$

$$w_{ij}^{out} = w_{ij}^{out}\gamma\begin{cases}\sum_{k=1}^{N}\delta_i(k)u_j(k) \text{ if } j \text{ is an output neuron}\\ \sum_{k=1}^{N}\delta_i(k)x_j(k) \text{ if } j \text{ is a hidden neuron}\end{cases} \tag{13}$$

$$w_{ij}^{back} = w_{ij}^{back} + \alpha\sum\nolimits_{k=1}^{N}\delta_i(k)y_j(k-1) \tag{14}$$

where w_{ij} is the weight of the hidden neuron, w_{ij}^{in}, w_{ij}^{out} and w_{ij}^{back} are the input, output and feedback weights, α is a coefficient used for optimization of the error.

To demonstrate that the use of surrogate series for training does not depend upon the configuration of NARX, we considered different NN configurations (Fig. 5):

- One hidden layer with 8 neurons (NN Configuration 1)
- Two hidden layers with 5 hidden neurons each (NN Configuration 2)

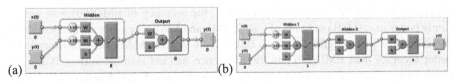

Fig. 5. The NARX configurations considered in experiments: Configuration 1 (a) and Configuration 2 (b)

3 Experiments and Results

3.1 Dataset

We use the M4 dataset [20], which has 100,000 series of hourly, daily, weekly, monthly, quarterly, and yearly data. We used only the hourly subset of the dataset, which has 414 time series, with the minimum number of observations of 700.

3.2 Performance Evaluation and Statistical Analysis

We predict the 1-step ahead value of time series and assess our model accuracy using MAE (Mean Absolute Error), MAPE (Mean Absolute Percentage Error), Mean directional accuracy (SignAcc), MSE (Mean Squared Error), MSPE (Mean Squared Prediction Error), Pearson correlation (CR), RMSE (Root Mean Square Error), and RMSPE (Root Mean Square Percentage Error) metrics. Here MSE is the error between true output and predicted value. Pearson correlation assesses the direction and strength of the linear regression among two variables. Mean directional accuracy compares the forecasted direction of (upward or downward) to the true direction. MSPE is the expected value of the squared difference between the predicted and true values. MAE is an average distance between true and predicted observations. MAPE is a relative accuracy expressed in terms of percentage. RMSE is the quadratic root of differences between true and predicted values. For checking the statistical significance of the results have we used the Wilcoxon signed rank-sum test. This test is used when the normality of the data cannot be assumed and there are two independent samples. Here, the null hypothesis is that a randomly accuracy from one of the techniques will be better than a randomly selected accuracy from another technique.

3.3 Results

We considered 20 (EMD(20)) and 50 (EMD(50)) surrogate series generated. The comparison of time series prediction (414 hourly series from M4 dataset) results in terms of eight accuracy metrics discussed in Subsect. 3.2 are presented in Fig. 6 (for NN Configuration 1) and Fig. 7 (for NN Configuration 2).

We also have evaluated the performance of network training in terms of for how many time series the accuracy metric value has been improved in comparison with the results of the baseline NARX network. These results are presented in Fig. 8.

The results of statistical analysis using the Wilcoxon signed rank-sum test show that for both NN configurations, EMD(20) and EMD(50) produced significantly better ($p < 0.001$) accuracy (all metrics) results than the baseline network. When comparing EMD(20) and EMD(50), for Configuration 1, the accuracy of EMD(50) was significantly better ($p < 0.001$) in terms of CR, RMSE, and MAE. For other accuracy metrics, the difference was insignificant ($p > 0.05$). Note that for MAE, EMD(20) produced better accuracy than EMD(50), but the difference was not significant ($p > 0.05$). For Configuration 2, the accuracy of EMD(20) was significantly better than that of EMD(50) ($p < 0.001$) in terms of CR, RMSE, MAE and MSE. For other metrics, the difference was insignificant ($p > 0.05$). Such results may imply overfitting, which means that the

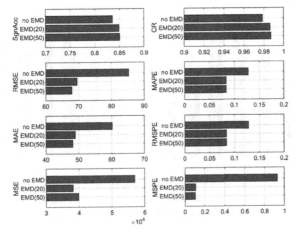

Fig. 6. Comparison of accuracy for Configuration 1: NARX trained using original time series (baseline) vs NARX trained using surrogate series generated using the EMD-based approach. no EMD – baseline, surrogate series are not used. EMD(20) – 20 surrogate series used for training. EMD(50) – 50 surrogate series used for training.

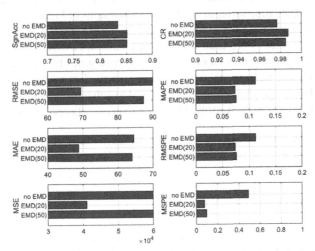

Fig. 7. Comparison of accuracy for Configuration 2: NARX trained using original time series (baseline) vs NARX trained using surrogate series generated using the EMD-based approach. no EMD – baseline, surrogate series are not used. EMD(20) – 20 surrogate series used for training. EMD(50) – 50 surrogate series used for training.

number of surrogate time series used for training should be chosen carefully, as it may not necessarily produce better results. However, for both network configurations, the EMD(50) allowed to achieve improved accuracy metric values on a larger number of time series than EMD (20) ($p < 0.01$).

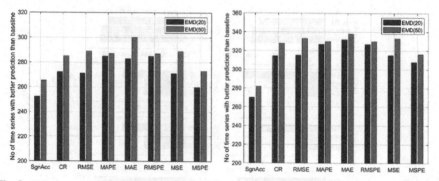

Fig. 8. Number of time series with higher accuracy achieved when using EMD based surrogate series for NARX training (left: Configuration 1, right: Configuration 2). EMD(20) - 20 surrogate series used for training. EMD(50) - 50 surrogate series used for training.

4 Conclusions

For deep learning, data augmentation is an essential method for getting the best results. In this study, we implemented data augmentation method for time series forecasting and constructed surrogate time series using linear combinations of Intrinsic Mode Functions (IMF) obtained from Empirical Mode Decomposition (EMD).

The surrogate series were used for training a custom NARX neural network. The results on the M4 dataset show an improvement in time series forecasting results.

Future work will address the application of various data augmentation method in other areas, where augmentation has been proved to enhance the performance, such as in image segmentation, speech recognition or human activity recognition.

Acknowledgments. Authors acknowledge contribution to this project of the Program "Best of the Best 4.0" from the Polish Ministry of Science and Higher Education No. MNiSW/2020/43/DIR/NN4.

References

1. Capizzi, G., Napoli, C., Bonanno, F.: Innovative second-generation wavelets construction with recurrent neural networks for solar radiation forecasting. IEEE Trans. Neural Netw. Learn. Syst. **23**(11), 1805–1815 (2012)
2. Zębik, M., Korytkowski, M., Angryk, R., Scherer, R.: Convolutional neural networks for time series classification. In: Rutkowski, L., Korytkowski, M., Scherer, R., Tadeusiewicz, R., Zadeh, Lotfi A., Zurada, Jacek M. (eds.) ICAISC 2017. LNCS (LNAI), vol. 10246, pp. 635–642. Springer, Cham (2017). https://doi.org/10.1007/978-3-319-59060-8_57
3. Qi, G.-J., Luo, J.: Small data challenges in big data era: a survey of recent progress on unsupervised and semi-supervised methods. CoRR abs/1903.11260 (2019)
4. Mikołajczyk, A., Grochowski, M.: Data augmentation for improving deep learning in image classification problem. In: Interdisciplinary PhD Workshop, pp. 117–122. (2018)
5. Park, D.S., et al.: Specaugment: a simple data augmentation method for automatic speech recognition. arXiv preprint arXiv:1904.08779 (2019)

6. Eyobu, S.O., Han, D.S.: Feature representation and data augmentation for human activity classification based on wearable IMU sensor data using a deep LSTM neural network. Sensors **18**(9), 2892 (2018)

7. le Guennec, A., Malinowski, S., Tavenard, R.: Data augmentation for time series classification using convolutional neural networks. In: Proceedings of the ECML/PKDD Workshop on Advanced Analytics and Learning on Temporal Data, Porto, Portugal (2016)

8. Um, T.T., et al.: Data augmentation of wearable sensor data for parkinson's disease monitoring using convolutional neural networks. In: 19th ACM International Conference on Multimodal Interaction; Glasgow, UK, 13–17 November (2017)

9. Bergmeir, C., Hyndman, R.J., Benítez, J.M.: Bagging exponential smoothing methods using STL decomposition and Box-Cox transformation. Int. J. Forecast. **32**(2), 303–312 (2016)

10. Paparoditis, E., Politis, D.: Tapered block bootstrap. Biometrika **88**(4), 1105–1119 (2001)

11. Shao, X.: The dependent wild bootstrap. J. Am. Stat. Assoc. **105**(489), 218–235 (2010)

12. Maiwald, T., Mammen, E., Nandi, S., Timmer, J.: Surrogate data - a qualitative and quantitative analysis. In: Dahlhaus, R., et al. (eds.) Mathematical Methods in Signal Processing and Digital Image Analysis. Understanding Complex Systems. Springer, Heidelberg (2008). https://doi.org/10.1007/978-3-540-75632-3_2

13. Prichard, D., Theiler, J.: Generating surrogate data for time series with several simultaneously measured variables. Phys. Rev. Lett. **73**(7), 951–954 (1994)

14. Kaefer, P.E., Ishola, B.I., Corliss, G.F., Brown, R.H.: Using surrogate data to mitigate the risks of natural gas forecasting on unusual days. In: 35th International Symposium on Forecasting (2015)

15. Duncan, G.T., Gorr, W.L., Szczypula, J.: Forecasting analogous time series. In: Principles of Forecasting: A Handbook for Researchers and Practitioners, pp. 195–213 (2001)

16. Schreiber, T., Schmitz, A.: Surrogate time series. Physica D **142**, 346–382 (1999)

17. Sidekerskienė, T., Woźniak, M., Damaševičius, R.: Nonnegative matrix factorization based decomposition for time series modelling. In: Saeed, K., Homenda, W., Chaki, R. (eds.) CISIM 2017. LNCS, vol. 10244, pp. 604–613. Springer, Cham (2017). https://doi.org/10.1007/978-3-319-59105-6_52

18. Sidekerskiene, T., Damasevicius, R., Wozniak, M.: Zerocross density decomposition: a novel signal decomposition method. In: Dzemyda, G., et al. (eds.) Data Science: New Issues, Challenges and Applications. Studies Comp. Intelligence, vol. 869 (2020)

19. Huang, N.E., et al.: The empirical mode decomposition and the Hilbert spectrum for nonlinear and non-stationary time series analysis. In: Proceedings of the Royal Society of London. Series A: Mathematical, Physical and Engineering Sciences, vol. 454(1971), pp. 903–995 (1998)

20. Makridakis, S., Spiliotis, E., Assimakopoulos, V.: The M4 Competition: 100,000 time series and 61 forecasting methods. Int. J. Forecast. **36**(1), 54–74 (2020)

21. Horzyk, A., Starzyk, J.A.: Associative data model in search for nearest neighbors and similar patterns. In: 2019 IEEE Symposium Series on Computational Intelligence (SSCI), pp. 933–940. IEEE, December 2019

22. Shewalkar, A., Nyavanandi, D., Ludwig, S.A.: Performance evaluation of deep neural networks applied to speech recognition: RNN, LSTM and GRU. J. Artif. Intell. Soft Comput. Res. **9**(4), 235–245 (2019)

23. Nobukawa, S., Nishimura, H., Yamanishi, T.: Pattern classification by spiking neural networks combining self-organized and reward-related spike-timing-dependent plasticity. J. Artif. Intell. Soft Comput. Res. **9**(4), 283–291 (2019)

Ensemble Forecasting of Monthly Electricity Demand Using Pattern Similarity-Based Methods

Paweł Pełka[✉] and Grzegorz Dudek

Electrical Engineering Faculty, Częstochowa University of Technology, Częstochowa,
Poland
{p.pelka,dudek}@el.pcz.czest.pl

Abstract. This work presents ensemble forecasting of monthly electricity demand using pattern similarity-based forecasting methods (PSFMs). PSFMs applied in this study include k-nearest neighbor model, fuzzy neighborhood model, kernel regression model, and general regression neural network. An integral part of PSFMs is a time series representation using patterns of time series sequences. Pattern representation ensures the input and output data unification through filtering a trend and equalizing variance. Two types of ensembles are created: heterogeneous and homogeneous. The former consists of different type base models, while the latter consists of a single-type base model. Five strategies are used for controlling a diversity of members in a homogeneous approach. The diversity is generated using different subsets of training data, different subsets of features, randomly disrupted input and output variables, and randomly disrupted model parameters. An empirical illustration applies the ensemble models as well as individual PSFMs for comparison to the monthly electricity demand forecasting for 35 European countries.

Keywords: Medium-term load forecasting · Multi-model ensemble forecasting · Single-model ensemble forecasting · Patter-based forecasting

1 Introduction

Load or electricity demand forecasting is an essential tool for power system operation and planning. Mid-term electrical load forecasting (MTLF) involves forecasting the daily peak load for future months as well as monthly electricity demand. MTLF is necessary for maintenance scheduling, fuel reserve planning, hydro-thermal coordination, electrical energy import/export planning, and security assessment. Deregulated power systems need MTLF to be able to negotiate forward contracts. Therefore, the forecast accuracy translates directly into financial performance for energy market participants.

Methods of MTLF can be divided into a conditional modeling approach and an autonomous modeling approach [1]. The former focuses on economic analysis and long-term planning of energy policy and uses input variables describing

L. Rutkowski et al. (Eds.): ICAISC 2020, LNAI 12415, pp. 712–723, 2020.
https://doi.org/10.1007/978-3-030-61401-0_66

socio-economic conditions, population migrations, and power system and network infrastructure. The latter uses input variables including only historical loads or, additionally, weather factors [2,3].

For MTLF the classical statistical/econometrics tools are used as well as machine learning tools [4]. The former include ARIMA, exponential smoothing (EST) and linear regression [5]. Problems with adaptability and nonlinear modeling of the statistical methods have increased researchers' interest in machine learning and AI tools [6]. The most popular representatives of these tools are neural networks (NNs) which have very attractive features such as learning capabilities, universal approximation property, nonlinear modeling, and massive parallelism [7]. Among the other machine learning models for MTLF, the following can be mentioned: long short-term memory [8], weighted evolving fuzzy NNs [2], support vector machine [9], and pattern similarity-based models [10].

In recent years ensemble learning has been widely used in machine learning. Ensemble learning systems are composed of many base models. Each of them provides an estimate of a target function. These estimates are combined in some fashion to produce a common response, hopefully improving accuracy and stability compared to a single learner. The base models can be of the same type (single-model or homogeneous ensemble) or of different types (multi-model or heterogeneous ensemble). The key issue in ensemble learning is ensuring diversity of learners [11]. A good tradeoff between performance and diversity underlies the success of ensemble learning. The source of diversity in the heterogeneous case is a different nature of the base learners. Some experimental results show that heterogeneous ensembles can improve accuracy compared to homogenous ones [12]. This is because the error terms of models of different types are less correlated than the errors of models of the same type. Generating diverse learners which give uncorrelated errors in a homogeneous ensemble is a challenging problem. Diversity can be achieved through several strategies. One of the most popular is learning on different subsets of the training set or different subsets of features. Other common approaches include using different values of hyperparameters and parameters of learners. In the field of forecasting, it was shown that ensembling of the forecasts enhances the robustness of the model, mitigating the model and parameter uncertainty [13].

In this work we build heterogeneous and homogeneous ensembles for MTLF using pattern similarity-based forecasting models (PSFMs) [10] as base learners. PBSMs turned out to be very effective models (accurate and simple) for both mid and short-term load forecasting [14,15]. In this study, we investigate what profit we will achieve from an ensembling of the forecasts generated by PBFMs. For heterogeneous ensemble, we employ k-nearest neighbor model, fuzzy neighborhood model, kernel regression model, and general regression neural network. For homogeneous ensemble, we employ a fuzzy neighborhood model and generate its diversity using five strategies.

The remainder of this paper is structured as follows. In Sect. 2, we present pattern representation of time series, a framework of the pattern similarity-based forecasting, and PSFMs. In Sect. 3, we describe heterogeneous and homogeneous ensemble forecasting using PSFMs. Sect. 4 shows the setup of the empirical experiments and the results. Finally, Sect. 5 presents our conclusion.

2   Pattern Similarity-Based Forecasting

2.1   Pattern Representation of Time Series

Monthly electricity demand time series express a trend, yearly cycles, and random component. To deal with seasonal cycles and trends in our earlier work, we proposed similarity-based models operating on patterns of the time series sequences [10], [14]. The patterns filter out the trend and those seasonal cycles longer than the basic one and even out variance. They also ensure the unification of input and output variables. Consequently, pattern representation simplifies the forecasting problem and allows us to use models based on pattern similarity.

Input pattern $\mathbf{x}_i = [x_{i,1}x_{i,2}...x_{i,n}]^T$ is a vector of predictors representing a sequence $X_i = \{E_{i-n+1}, E_{i-n+2}, ..., E_i\}$ of n successive time series elements E_i (monthly electricity demands) preceding a forecasted period. In this study we use the following definition of x-pattern components:

$$x_{i,t} = \frac{E_{i-n+t} - \overline{E}_i}{D_i} \tag{1}$$

where $t = 1, 2, ..., n$, $\overline{E}_i$ is a mean of sequence X_i, and $D_i = \sqrt{\sum_{j=1}^{n}(E_{i-n+j} - \overline{E}_i)^2}$ is a measure of its dispersion.

The x-pattern defined using (1) is a normalized vector composed of the elements of sequence X_i. Note that the original time series sequences X_i having different mean and dispersion are unified, i.e. they are represented by x-patterns which all have zero mean, the same variance and also unity length.

Output pattern $\mathbf{y}_i = [y_{i,1}y_{i,2}...y_{i,m}]^T$ represents a forecasted sequence of length $m = 12$: $Y_i = \{E_{i+1}, E_{i+2}, ..., E_{i+m}\}$. The output pattern is defined similarly to the input one:

$$y_{i,t} = \frac{E_{i+t} - \overline{E}_i^*}{D_i^*} \tag{2}$$

where $t = 1, 2, ..., m$, and $\overline{E}_i^*$ and D_i^* are coding variables described below.

Two variants of the output patterns are considered. In the first one, denoted as V1, the coding variables, $\overline{E}_i^*$ and D_i^*, are the mean and dispersion, respectively, of the forecasted sequence Y_i. But in this case, when the forecasted sequence Y_i of the monthly electricity demands is calculated from the forecasted y-pattern, $\widehat{\mathbf{y}}_i$, using transformed Eq. (2):

$$\widehat{E}_{i+t} = \widehat{y}_{i,t}D_i^* + \overline{E}_i^*, \quad t = 1, 2, ..., m \tag{3}$$

the coding variables are not known, because they are the mean and dispersion of future sequence Y_i, which has just been forecasted. In this case, the coding variables are predicted from their historical values. In the experimental part of the work, the coding variables are predicted using ARIMA and ETS.

To avoid forecasting the coding variables we use another approach. Instead of using the mean and dispersion of the forecasted sequence Y_i as coding variables, we introduce in (2) and (3) as coding variables the mean and dispersion of sequence X_i, i.e. $\overline{E}_i^* = \overline{E}_i$, $D_i^* = D_i$. When the PSFM generates the forecasted y-pattern, the forecast of the monthly demands are calculated from (3) using known coding variables for the historical sequence X_i. This variant of the y-pattern definition is denoted as V2.

2.2   Forecasting Models

Pattern similarity-based forecasting procedure can be summarized in the following steps [10]:

1. Mapping the original time series sequences into x- and y-patterns.
2. Selection of the training x-patterns similar to the query pattern $\mathbf{x}$.
3. Aggregation of the y-patterns paired with the similar x-patterns to obtain the forecasted pattern $\widehat{\mathbf{y}}$.
4. Decoding pattern $\widehat{\mathbf{y}}$ to get the forecasted time series sequence $\widehat{Y}$.

In step 3, y-patterns are aggregated using weights which are dependent on the similarity between a query pattern $\mathbf{x}$ and the training x-patterns. The regression model mapping x-patterns into y-patterns is of the form:

$$m(\mathbf{x}) = \sum_{i=1}^{N} w(\mathbf{x}, \mathbf{x}_i)\mathbf{y}_i \tag{4}$$

where $\sum_{i=1}^{N} w(\mathbf{x}, \mathbf{x}_i) = 1$, $w(.,.)$ is a weighting function.

Model (4) is nonlinear if $w(.,.)$ maps $\mathbf{x}$ nonlinearly. Different definitions of $w(.,.)$ are presented below where the PSFMs are specified.

k-Nearest Neighbor Model estimates $m(.)$ as the weighted average of the y-patterns in a varying neighborhood of query pattern $\mathbf{x}$ (this model is denoted as k-NNw). The neighborhood is defined as a set of k nearest neighbors of $\mathbf{x}$ in the training set Φ. The regression function is as follows:

$$m(\mathbf{x}) = \sum_{i \in \Omega_k(\mathbf{x})} w(\mathbf{x}, \mathbf{x}_i)\mathbf{y}_i \tag{5}$$

where $\Omega_k(\mathbf{x})$ is a set of indices of k nearest neighbors of $\mathbf{x}$ in Φ and the weighting function is of the form [15]:

$$w(\mathbf{x}, \mathbf{x}_i) = \frac{v(\mathbf{x}, \mathbf{x}_i)}{\sum\limits_{j \in \Omega_k(\mathbf{x})} v(\mathbf{x}, \mathbf{x}_j)} \tag{6}$$

$$v(\mathbf{x}, \mathbf{x}_i) = \rho\left(\frac{1 - d(\mathbf{x}, \mathbf{x}_i)/d(\mathbf{x}, \mathbf{x}^k)}{1 + \gamma d(\mathbf{x}, \mathbf{x}_i)/d(\mathbf{x}, \mathbf{x}^k)} - 1\right) + 1 \tag{7}$$

where $\mathbf{x}^k$ is the k-th nearest neighbor of $\mathbf{x}$ in Φ, $d(\mathbf{x}, \mathbf{x}_i)$ is a Euclidean distance between $\mathbf{x}$ and its i-th nearest neighbor, $\rho \in [0, 1]$ is a parameter deciding about the differentiation of weights, and $\gamma \geq -1$ is a parameter deciding about a convexity of the weighting function.

Fuzzy Neighborhood Model. (FNM) takes into account all training patterns when constructing the regression surface [16]. In this case, all training patterns belong to the query pattern neighborhood, with a different membership degree. The membership function is dependent on the distance between the query pattern $\mathbf{x}$ and the training pattern $\mathbf{x}_i$ as follows:

$$\mu(\mathbf{x}, \mathbf{x}_i) = \exp\left(-\left(\frac{d(\mathbf{x}, \mathbf{x}_i)}{\sigma}\right)^\alpha\right) \tag{8}$$

where σ and α are parameters deciding about the membership function shape.

The weighting function in FNM is as follows:

$$w(\mathbf{x}, \mathbf{x}_i) = \frac{\mu(\mathbf{x}, \mathbf{x}_i)}{\sum\limits_{j=1}^{N} \mu(\mathbf{x}, \mathbf{x}_j)} \tag{9}$$

Membership function (8) is a Gaussian-type function. The model parameters, σ and α, shape the membership function and thus control the properties of the estimator.

Nadaraya-Watson Estimator. (N-WE) estimates regression function $m(.)$ as a locally weighted average, using in (4) a kernel K_h as a weighting function:

$$w(\mathbf{x}, \mathbf{x}_i) = \frac{K_h(\mathbf{x} - \mathbf{x}_i)}{\sum\limits_{j=1}^{N} K_h(\mathbf{x} - \mathbf{x}_j)} \tag{10}$$

When the input variable is multidimensional, the kernel has a product form. In such a case, for a normal kernel, which is often used in practice, the weighting function is defined as [15], [14]:

$$w(\mathbf{x}, \mathbf{x}_i) = \frac{\exp\left(-\sum\limits_{t=1}^{n} \frac{(x_t - x_{i,t})^2}{2h_t^2}\right)}{\sum\limits_{j=1}^{N} \exp\left(-\sum\limits_{t=1}^{n} \frac{(x_t - x_{j,t})^2}{2h_t^2}\right)} \tag{11}$$

where h_t is a bandwidth for the t-th dimension.

The bandwidths decide about the bias-variance tradeoff of the estimator.

General Regression Neural Network Model. (GRNN) is composed of four layers: input, pattern (radial basis layer), summation and output layer [17]. The pattern layer transforms inputs nonlinearly using Gaussian activation functions of the form:

$$G(\mathbf{x}, \mathbf{x}_i) = \exp\left(-\frac{\|\mathbf{x} - \mathbf{x}_i)\|^2}{\sigma_i^2}\right) \tag{12}$$

where $\|.\|$ is a Euclidean norm and σ_i is a bandwidth for the i-th pattern.

The Gaussian functions are centered at different training patterns $\mathbf{x}_i$. The neuron output expresses a similarity between the query pattern and the i-th training pattern. This output is treated as the weight of the i-th y-pattern. So the pattern layer maps the n-dimensional input space into N-dimensional space of similarity, where N is a number of training patterns. The weighting function implemented in GRNN is defined as:

$$w(\mathbf{x}, \mathbf{x}_i) = \frac{G(\mathbf{x}, \mathbf{x}_i)}{\sum\limits_{j=1}^{N} G(\mathbf{x}, \mathbf{x}_j)} \tag{13}$$

The performance of PSFMs is related to the weighting function parameters governing the smoothness of the regression function (4). For wider weighting function the model tends to increase bias and decrease variance. Thus, too wide weighting function leads to oversmoothing, while too narrow weighting function leads to undersmoothing. The PSFM parameters should be adjusted to the target function.

3   Ensemble Forecasting Using PSFMs

Two approaches for ensemble forecasting are used: heterogeneous and homogeneous. The former consists of different base models, while the latter consists of a single-type base model. In the heterogeneous approach, we use the PSFMs described above as base models. A diversity of learners, which is the key property that governs an ensemble performance, in this case, results from different types of learners.

To control the diversity in the homogeneous approach we use the following strategies [18]:

1. Learning on different subsets of the training data. For each ensemble member a random training sample without replacement of size $N' < N$ is selected from the training set Φ.
2. Learning on different subsets of features. For each ensemble member the features are randomly sampled without replacement. The sample size is $n' < n$. In this case, the optimal model parameters may need correction for ensemble members due to a reduction in Euclidean distance between x-patterns in n'-dimensional space relative to n-dimensional space.

3. Random disturbance of the model parameters. For FNM the initial value of width σ is randomly perturbed for k-th member by a Gaussian noise: $\sigma_k = \sigma \cdot \xi_k$, where $\xi_k \sim N(0, \sigma_s)$.
4. Random disturbance of x-patterns. The components of x-patterns are perturbed for k-th member by a Gaussian noise: $x_{i,t}^k = x_{i,t} \cdot \xi_{i,t}^k$, where $\xi_{i,t}^k \sim N(0, \sigma_x)$.
5. Random disturbance of y-patterns. The components of y-patterns are perturbed for k-th member by a Gaussian noise: $y_{i,t}^k = y_{i,t} \cdot \xi_{i,t}^k$, where $\xi_{i,t}^k \sim N(0, \sigma_y)$.

Standard deviations of the noise signals, $\sigma_s, \sigma_x, \sigma_y$, control the noise level and are selected for each forecasting task as well as N' and n'.

The first strategy controlling diversity is similar to bagging [19], where the predictors are built on bootstrapped versions of the original data. In bagging, unlike our approach, the sample size is $N' = N$ and the random sample is drawn with replacement. The second strategy is inspired by the random subspace method [20] which is successfully used to construct random forests, very effective tree-based classification and regression models. Note that the diversity of learners has various sources. They include data uncertainty (learning on different subsets of the training set, learning on different features of x-patterns, learning on disturbed input and output variables) and parameter uncertainty.

The forecasts of y-patterns generated by K base models, $\widehat{\mathbf{y}}_k$, are aggregated using simple averaging to obtain an ensemble forecast:

$$\widehat{\mathbf{y}} = \frac{1}{K} \sum_{k=1}^{K} \widehat{\mathbf{y}}_k \tag{14}$$

In this study we use the mean for aggregation, but also other functions, such as median, mode, or trimmed mean could be used. As shown in [21] a simple average of forecasts often outperforms forecasts from single models and a more complicated weighting scheme does not always perform better than a simple average.

When the y-pattern is determined from (14), the forecasted monthly demands $\widehat{\mathbf{E}}$ are calculated from (3) using coding variables which are determined from history or predicted, depending on the model variant, V1 or V2.

4   Simulation Study

In this section, we apply the proposed ensemble forecasting models to mid-term load forecasting using real-world data: monthly electricity demand time series for 35 European countries. The data are taken from the publicly available ENTSO-E repository (www.entsoe.eu). The time series differ in levels, trends, variations and yearly shapes. They differ also in a length, i.e. they cover: 24 years for 11 countries, 17 years for 6 countries, 12 years for 4 countries, 8 years for 2 countries, and 5 years for 12 countries. The models forecast for the twelve months of 2014 (last year of data) using data from the previous period for training.

We built four heterogeneous ensembles:

Ensemble1 composed of PSFMs described in Sect. 3, i.e. k-NNw, FNM, N-WE
and GRNN, which are trained on the y-patterns defined with the coding
variables determined from the historical sequence X_i (y-pattern definition
V2).

Ensemble2 composed of PSFMs which are trained on the y-patterns defined
with the coding variables predicted for the forecasted sequence Y_i using
ARIMA (y-pattern definition V1). The base models, in this case, are denoted
as k-NNw+ARIMA, FNM+ARIMA, N-WE+ARIMA and GRNN+ARIMA.

Ensemble3 composed of PSFMs which are trained on the y-patterns defined in
the same way as for Ensemble2, but the coding variables are predicted using
ETS. The base models, in this case, are denoted as k-NNw+ETS, FNM+ETS,
N-WE+ETS and GRNN+ETS.

Ensemble4 composed of all variants of PSFM models mentioned above for
Ensemble1, Ensemble2 and Ensemble3, i.e. twelve models.

For prediction the coding variables we used the ARIMA and ETS implementations in R statistical software environment: functions `auto.arima` and
`ets` from the `forecast` package. These functions implement automatic ARIMA
and ETS modeling, respectively, and identify optimal models estimating their
parameters using Akaike information criterion (AICc) [22].

The optimal values of hyperparameters for each PSFM were selected individually for each of 35 time series in the grid search procedure using cross-validation.
These hyperparameters include: length of the x-patterns n, number of nearest
neighbors k in k-NNw (linear weighting function was assumed with $\rho = 1$ and
$\gamma = 0$), width parameter σ in FNM (we assumed $\alpha = 2$), bandwidth parameters
h_t in N-WE, and bandwidth σ in GRNN.

The forecasting errors on the test sets (mean absolute percentage error,
MAPE) for each model and each country are shown in Fig. 1 and their averaged
values are shown in Table 1. In Table 1 also median of the absolute percentage
error (APE), interquartile ranges of APE and root mean square error (RMSE)
averaged over all countries are shown. The forecasting accuracy depends heavily
on the variant of the coding variables determination. The most accurate variant on average is V1+ETS and the least accurate is variant V2 where coding
variables are determined from history.

Figure 2 shows the ranking of the models based on MAPE. The rank is calculated as the average rank of the model in the rankings performed individually
for each country. As you can see from this figure, the Ensemble4 and Ensemble3
models were the most accurate for the largest number of countries. Model N-
WE took the third position. Note that ensemble combining the group of PSFMs
(V1+ARIMA, V1+ETS or V2) occupies a higher position in the ranking than
individual members of this group. The exception is N-WE which achieves better
results than Ensemble1. A similar conclusion can be drawn from the ranking
based on RMSE.

The homogeneous ensembles were built using FNM in variant V2 as a base
model. Five strategies of diversity generation described in Sect. 3 were applied.

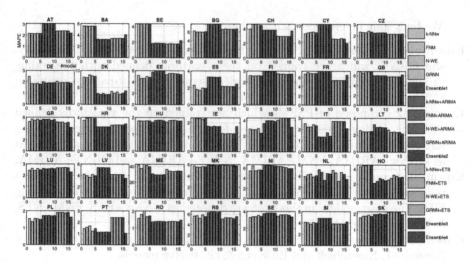

Fig. 1. MAPE for each country.

Table 1. Results for base models and heterogeneous ensembles.

Model	Median APE	$MAPE$	IQR	$RMSE$
k-NNw	2.89	4.99	4.06	368.79
FNM	2.88	4.88	4.43	354.33
N-WE	2.84	5.00	4.14	352.01
GRNN	2.87	5.01	4.30	350.61
Ensemble1	2.88	4.90	4.13	351.89
k-NNw+ARIMA	2.89	4.65	4.02	346.58
FNM+ARIMA	2.87	4.61	3.83	341.41
N-WE+ARIMA	2.85	4.59	3.74	340.26
GRNN+ARIMA	2.81	4.60	3.77	345.46
Ensemble2	2.90	4.60	3.84	342.43
k-NNw+ETS	2.71	4.47	3.43	327.94
FNM+ETS	2.64	4.40	3.34	321.98
N-WE+ETS	2.68	4.37	3.20	320.51
GRNN+ETS	2.64	4.38	3.35	324.91
Ensemble3	2.64	4.38	3.40	322.80
Ensemble4	2.70	4.31	3.49	327.61

Ensembles constructed in this way are denoted as FNMe1, FNMe2, ...FNMe5. In the FNMe2 case, where the diversity is obtained by selection n' x-pattern components, the optimal width parameter σ (selected for a single FNM) is corrected for ensemble members by the factor $(n'/n)^{0.5}$. This is due to a reduction

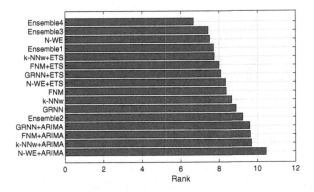

Fig. 2. Ranking of the models.

in Euclidean distance between x-patterns in n'-dimensional space relative to the original n-dimensional space.

The forecasts were generated independently by each of $K = 100$ ensemble members. Then the forecasts were combined using (14). The following parameters of the ensembles were selected on the training set using a grid search:

- size of the random sample of training patterns in FNMe1: $N' = 0.85N$,
- size of the random sample of features in FNMe2: $n' = 0.925n$,
- standard deviation of the disruption of width parameter σ in FNMe3: $\sigma_s = 0.475$,
- standard deviation of the disruption of x-patterns in FNMe4: $\sigma_x = 0.4$,
- standard deviation of the disruption of y-patterns in FNMe5: $\sigma_y = 0.65$.

Table 2 shows the results for FNM ensembles. It can be seen from this table that the errors for different sources of diversity are similar. It is hard to indicate the best strategy for member diversification. When comparing results for FNM ensembles and single base model FNM (see Table 1), we can see a slightly lower MAPE for ensembles with the exception of FNMe5 where MAPE is the same as for FNM. But RMSE is higher for ensemble versions of FNM than for single FNM.

Figure 3 shows the ranking of the FNM ensembles based on MAPE. The ensembles FNMe1-FNMe4 are more accurate then FNM for most countries.

Table 2. Results for FNM homogeneous ensembles.

Model	Median APE	MAPE	IQR	RMSE
FNMe1	2.88	4.84	4.18	370.52
FNMe2	2.85	4.84	4.06	366.35
FNMe3	2.80	4.83	4.23	371.94
FNMe4	2.90	4.86	4.10	373.73
FNMe5	2.97	4.88	4.18	375.84

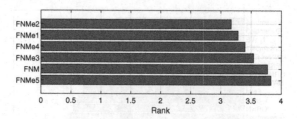

Fig. 3. Ranking of the FNM homogeneous ensembles.

Ensemble FNMe5 turned out to be less accurate than FNM. A similar conclusion can be drawn from the ranking based on RMSE.

5   Conclusion

Ensemble forecasting is widely used for improving the forecast accuracy over the individual models. In this work, we investigate single-model and multi-model ensembles based on pattern-similarity forecasting models for mid-term electricity demand forecasting. The key issue in ensemble learning is ensuring the diversity of learners. The advantage of heterogeneous ensembles is that the errors of the base models are to be weakly correlated because of the different nature of the models. But in our case the PSFMs are similar in nature, so we can expect error correlation. The results of simulations do not show a spectacular improvement in accuracy for homogeneous ensemble comparing to its members. However, the ranking shown in Fig. 2 generally confirms better results for ensembles than for their members.

In homogeneous ensembles, we can control a diversity level of members. We propose five strategies for this including strategies manipulating training data and model parameters. Among them, strategies based on learning on different subsets of training data and different subsets of features turned out to be most effective.

References

1. Ghiassi, M., Zimbra, D.K., Saidane, H.: Medium term system load forecasting with a dynamic artificial neural network model. Electri. Power Syst. Res. **76**, 302–316 (2006)
2. Pei-Chann, C., Chin-Yuan, F., Jyun-Jie, L.: Monthly electricity demand forecasting based on a weighted evolving fuzzy neural network approach. Electr. Power Energy Syst. **33**, 17–27 (2011)
3. Pełka, P., Dudek, G.: Pattern-based forecasting monthly electricity demand using multilayer perceptron. In: Rutkowski, L., Scherer, R., Korytkowski, M., Pedrycz, W., Tadeusiewicz, R., Zurada, J.M. (eds.) ICAISC 2019. LNCS (LNAI), vol. 11508, pp. 663–672. Springer, Cham (2019). https://doi.org/10.1007/978-3-030-20912-4_60

4. Suganthi, L., Samuel, A.A.: Energy models for demand forecasting - a review. Renew. Sust. Energy Rev. **16**(2), 1223–1240 (2002)
5. Barakat, E.H.: Modeling of nonstationary time-series data. Part II. Dynamic periodic trends. Electr. Power Energy Syst. **23**, 63–68 (2001)
6. González-Romera, E., Jaramillo-Morán, M.A., Carmona-Fernández, D.: Monthly electric energy demand forecasting with neural networks and Fourier series. Energy Convers. Manage. **49**, 3135–3142 (2008)
7. Chen, J.F., Lo, S.K., Do, Q.H.: Forecasting monthly electricity demands: an application of neural networks trained by heuristic algorithms. Information **8**(1), 31 (2017)
8. Bedi, J., Toshniwal, D.: Empirical mode decomposition based deep learning for electricity demand forecasting. IEEE Access **6**, 49144–49156 (2018)
9. Zhao, W., Wang, F., Niu, D.: The application of support vector machine in load forecasting. J. Comput. **7**(7), 1615–1622 (2012)
10. Dudek, G.: Pattern similarity-based methods for short-term load forecasting - Part 1: principles. Appl. Soft Comput. **37**, 277–287 (2015)
11. Brown, G., Wyatt, J.L., Tino, P.: Managing diversity in regression ensembles. J. Mach. Learn. Res. **6**, 1621–1650 (2005)
12. Wichard, J., Merkwirth, C., Ogorzałek, M.: Building ensembles with heterogeneous models. In: Course of the International School on Neural Nets (2003)
13. Petropoulos, F., Hyndman, R.J., Bergmeir, C.: Exploring the sources of uncertainty: why does bagging for time series forecasting work? Eur. J. Oper. Res. **268**(2), 545–554 (2018)
14. Dudek, G., Pełka, P.: Medium-term electric energy demand forecasting using Nadaraya-Watson estimator. In: Proceedings of IEEE 18th International Conference Electric Power Engineering EPE 2017, pp. 1–6 (2017)
15. Dudek, G.: Pattern similarity-based methods for short-term load forecasting - part 2: models. Appl. Soft Comput. **36**, 422–441 (2015)
16. Pełka, P., Dudek, G.: Prediction of monthly electric energy consumption using pattern-based fuzzy nearest neighbour regression. In. Proceedings of Conference Computational Methods in Engineering Science CMES 2017, ITM Web Conference, vol. 15, pp. 1–5 (2017)
17. Pełka, P., Dudek, G.: Medium-term electric energy demand forecasting using generalized regression neural network. In: Świątek, J., Borzemski, L., Wilimowska, Z. (eds.) ISAT 2018. AISC, vol. 853, pp. 218–227. Springer, Cham (2019). https://doi.org/10.1007/978-3-319-99996-8_20
18. Dudek, G.: Ensembles of general regression neural networks for short-term electricity demand forecasting. In: Proceedings of IEEE 18th International Conference Electric Power Engineering EPE 2017, pp. 1–5 (2017)
19. Breiman, L.: Bagging predictors. Mach. Learn. **24**(2), 123–140 (1996)
20. Ho, T.K.: The random subspace method for constructing decision forests. IEEE Trans. Pattern Anal. Mach. Intell. **20**(8), 832–844 (1998)
21. Chan, F., Pauwels, L.L.: Some theoretical results on forecast combinations. Int. J. Forecast. **34**(1), 64–74 (2018)
22. Hyndman, R.J., Athanasopoulos, G.: Forecasting: Principles and Practice. 2nd edn. OTexts, Melbourne, Australia (2018). OTexts.com/fpp2. Accessed 4 Oct 2019

Author Index

Abayomi-Alli, Olusola Oluwakemi   I-702, II-39

Abel, Mara   II-117

Alberti, Michele   II-505

Almeida, Matheus Santos   II-265, II-400

Alojzy Kłopotek, Mieczysław   II-130

Aloyayri, Abdulrahman   I-491

Álvarez-Machancoses, Óscar   I-589

Ananthakumar, Usha   II-31

Angelov, Plamen   I-124

Banach, Michał   I-3

Barbosa, Simone Diniz Junqueira   I-525

Bartczuk, Łukasz   I-315

Beckedahl, Derrick   II-277

Benato, Barbara Caroline   I-242

Bi, Ruixuan   II-466

Bielecki, Wlodzimierz   I-646

Bilski, Jarosław   I-15, I-27

Bobek, Szymon   II-290

Borkowski, Piotr   I-657

Boshchenko, Alina   I-203

Britto, André   II-265, II-400

Brzeski, Robert   I-417

Bugatti, Pedro Henrique   I-50, II-59

Bujok, Petr   I-363

Bukowski, Leszek   II-435

Cader, Andrzej   I-555

Cao, Jinde   II-466

Carbonera, Joel Luís   II-117

Castro, Leandro Nunes de   II-165

Cho, Sooah   I-599

Chu, Yue   II-466

Ciecierski, Konrad A.   I-39

Ciesielski, Krzysztof   I-657

Contreras, Rodrigo Colnago   I-464

Costa, Kelton   II-19

Cpałka, Krzysztof   I-429, I-480

Cruz, Luigi Freitas   I-50, II-59

Culer, Łukasz   I-503

Czerski, Dariusz   II-130

da Costa, Kelton Augusto Pontara   I-535

Dadas, Sławomir   II-301

Damaševičius, Robertas   I-702, II-39

de Andrés-Galiana, Enrique   I-589

de Araújo Lima, Raul   I-525

de Castro, Leandro N.   II-176

de Gusmão, Rene Pereira   II-400

de Sousa Silva, Mardlla   II-59

de Sousa, Rômulo César Costa   I-525

Deac-Petruşel, Mara Renata   II-140

Diep, Quoc Bao   I-376, II-445

Dioşan, Laura   II-210

Drozda, Pawel   II-435

Duda, Piotr   II-315, II-455

Dudek, Grzegorz   I-60, I-712

Duvernoy, Marie-Cécilia   I-626

Dymova, Ludmila   I-305

Dziwiński, Piotr   I-315

Emmendorfer, Leonardo Ramos   I-387

Estivill-Castro, Vladimir   II-152

Falcão, Alexandre Xavier   I-242

Fernández-Martínez, Juan Luis   I-589

Filippov, Aleksey   I-326

Frączek, Ewa   I-71

Freire, Mauricio Noris   II-165

Fröhlich, Piotr   I-77

Gabryel, Marcin   II-325

Gadri, Said   I-90

Gałkowski, Tomasz   II-3

Gelenbe, Erol   I-77

Gerritsen, Charlotte   I-679

Gierdziewicz, Maciej   I-613

Gilmore, Eugene   II-152

Glushchenko, Anton I.   I-103

Gniewek, Paweł   I-626

Goetzen, Piotr   I-315

González, Sahudy Montenegro   II-231

Gorse, Denise   I-170

Grabska, Ewa   I-397

Grabska-Gradzińska, Iwona   I-397

Grochowski, Michał   I-134
Gruzewski, Mateusz   I-646
Grycuk, Rafał   II-19
Gryz, Jarek   II-481
Grzesiak-Kopeć, Katarzyna   I-668
Guo, Jianhua   II-466
Gurjar, Shailendra   II-31

Hallatschek, Oskar   I-626
Hao, Jianye   I-690
Hayashi, Yoichi   I-480, II-455
He, Xuanlin   I-114
Heiman, Ron   I-626
Hennebold, Christoph   II-243
Henzel, Joanna   II-336
Hesser, Jürgen   I-626
Heusinger, Moritz   I-514
Hexel, René   II-152
Hłobaż, Artur   II-369
Huang, Wei   II-466

Idźkowski, Bartosz   I-71
Ingold, Rolf   II-505

Jabeen, Fakhra   I-679
Jaworski, Maciej   I-124, II-85
Jemioło, Paweł   II-357
Jobczyk, Krystian   II-346
Junior, Joel J. S.   II-176
Junior, Orides Morandin   I-464

Kadavy, Tomas   II-423
Kamola, Mariusz   I-39
Karczewski, Konrad   I-417
Karczmarek, Paweł   II-188
Kasabov, Nikola   I-114
Kazikova, Anezka   I-406
Kęsik, Karolina   II-95
Khachumov, Mikhail   II-492
Kiersztyn, Adam   II-188
Kim, Min Soo   I-599
Klawikowska, Zuzanna   I-134
Kloczkowski, Andrzej   I-589
Kłopotek, Mieczysław A.   I-657, II-199
Kłopotek, Robert A.   II-199
Kluska, Jacek   I-280
Kluza, Krzysztof   II-357

Kojecký, Lumír   I-147
Koller, Thomas   II-505
Konopczyński, Tomasz   I-626
Korytkowski, Marcin   II-380
Kosiński, Piotr   II-369
Kostrzewa, Daniel   I-417
Kowalczyk, Bartosz   I-15
Krzyżak, Adam   I-491, II-3
Ksieniewicz, Paweł   I-576
Kulpa, Tomasz   I-566
Kumova, Bora I.   II-243
Kurach, Damian   I-338
Kusy, Maciej   I-280
Kwolek, Bogdan   I-180

Łapa, Krystian   I-406, I-429
Lastochkin, Konstantin A.   I-103
Lee, JoonHo   I-599
Lee, Joonseok   I-599
Lee, Minyoung   I-599
Leung, Ho-fung   I-690
Ligęza, Antoni   II-346, II-357
Lim, Ye-Sheen   I-170
Limboi, Sergiu   II-210
Liu, Muzi   I-690
Lopatin, Vladyslav   I-180
Lopes, Hélio   I-525
Łoziński, Paweł   II-130
Lucas, Thiago José   I-535

Maślanka, Paweł   II-369
Mazurko, Anton   II-220
Mikołajczyk, Agnieszka   I-134
Milczarski, Piotr   I-636, II-369
Milkowska, Kamila   II-380
Modrzejewski, Mateusz   I-193
Mohannazadeh Bakhtiari, Mehrdad   I-547
Musavishavazi, Seyedfakhredin   I-547

Nalepa, Grzegorz J.   II-290
Napoli, Christian   II-103
Neruda, Roman   I-261
Neuhold, Erich   I-90
Nielek, Radosław   II-412
Niklaus, Joel   II-505
Niksa-Rynkiewicz, Tacjana   I-429, I-480
Nogueira, Rodrigo Ramos   II-231

Nowak, Jakub   II-380
Nowak, Leszek   I-397

Ogorzałek, Maciej   I-668
Okulska, Inez   II-388
Oliveira, Joel A.   II-400

Palkowski, Marek   I-646
Papa, João Paulo   I-231, I-242, I-535
Passos, Leandro A.   I-231, I-242
Pawara, Pornntiwa   I-203
Pedrycz, Witold   II-188
Pełka, Paweł   I-712
Pereira, Clayton   I-231
Perełkiewicz, Michał   II-301
Petrov, Vladislav A.   I-103
Pillay, Nelishia   II-277
Pires, Rafael Gonçalves   I-535
Pluhacek, Michal   I-406, II-423
Połap, Dawid   I-702, II-49, II-95
Poświata, Rafał   II-301
Procházka, Štěpán   I-261
Przybyszewski, Krzysztof   II-325
Puchalski, Bartosz   I-215

Rafajłowicz, Ewaryst   II-71
Rafajłowicz, Wojciech   I-445, II-71
Rakus-Andersson, Elisabeth   I-338
Ribeiro, Luiz Carlos Felix   I-231, I-242
Roder, Mateus   I-231, I-242
Rokita, Przemysław   I-193
Romanov, Anton   I-326
Rubach, Paweł   II-253
Rutkowska, Danuta   I-338, II-412
Rutkowski, Leszek   I-124, II-85, II-412
Rutkowski, Tomasz   II-412
Rutkowski, Tomasz A.   I-215

Saito, Priscila Tiemi Maeda   I-50, II-59
Sakata, Tiemi C.   II-231
Saller, Dirk   II-243
Santos, Reneilson Y. C.   II-400
Scherer, Magdalena   II-380
Scherer, Rafał   II-19, II-435
Schleif, Frank-Michael   I-514
Schomaker, Lambert R. B.   I-203
Senkerik, Roman   I-406, II-423, II-445
Sevastjanov, Pavel   I-351
Shandiz, Amin Honarmandi   I-159

Sidekerskienė, Tatjana   I-702
Sikora, Marek   II-336
Siłka, Jakub   I-702
Singh, Divyanshu   I-252
Skoczeń, Magda   II-71
Skubalska-Rafajłowicz, Ewa   I-3
Slowik, Adam   I-454
Smoląg, Jacek   I-27
Song, JiEun   I-599
Song, Su Jeong   I-599
Srivastava, Gautam   II-49
Starczewski, Artur   I-555
Starczewski, Janusz T.   II-103
Starosta, Bartłomiej   II-130
Staszewski, Paweł   II-85
Stawska, Zofia   II-369
Stolze, Markus   II-505
Susan, Seba   I-252
Świątek, Jerzy   I-292
Sydow, Marcin   II-130
Szachewicz, Jakub   I-193
Szelążek, Maciej   II-290
Szupiluk, Ryszard   II-253

Talun, Arkadiusz   II-380, II-435
Tao, Dacheng   II-85
Tojeiro, Carlos Alexandre Carvalho   I-535
Tóth, László   I-159
Tragarz, Magdalena M.   II-290
Treur, Jan   I-679, II-518
Tripathi, Mayank   I-252
Trojanowski, Krzysztof   I-566
Truong, Thanh Cong   I-376, II-445

Ullah, Nimat   II-518
Unold, Olgierd   I-503

Viana, Monique Simplicio   I-464
Vidnerová, Petra   I-261
Viktorin, Adam   II-423
Vilasbôas, Fabricio G.   II-176
Villmann, Thomas   I-547

Walkowiak, Tomasz   II-220
Wang, Lipo   I-429, II-315
Wąs, Łukasz   I-636
Wieczorek, Michał   II-39
Wiering, Marco A.   I-203
Winnicka, Alicja   II-95
Wiśniewski, Piotr   II-357

Wójcik, Krzysztof   I-566
Woldan, Piotr   II-455
Woźniak, Marcin   II-39, II-49, II-95
Woźniak, Michał   I-576
Woźnicki, Piotr   I-626
Wróbel, Michał   II-103
Wrosz, Izajasz   I-271

Yang, Jie   I-114
Yang, Ran   II-466
Yarushkina, Nadezhda   I-326

Zabinski, Tomasz   I-280
Zajdel, Roman   I-280
Zalasiński, Marcin   I-480
Zamorski, Maciej   I-292
Zelinka, Ivan   I-147, I-376, II-423, II-445
Zhao, Xuan   II-466
Zięba, Maciej   I-292
Zieliński, Bartosz   II-369
Znamirowski, Maciej   II-357
Żurada, Jacek M.   I-15
Zyblewski, Paweł   I-576

Printed in the United States
By Bookmasters